P9-DNB-326

Building:
3000 Years of Design Engineering and Construction

Bill Addis

Building: 3000 Years of Design Engineering and Construction

Bill Addis

acknowledgements

My interest in the history of building engineering goes back over thirty years during which time I have been a member of the History Study Group of the Institution of Structural Engineers in London. I am indebted to all the members of this group for helping me develop my understanding of engineering history. I give special mention to the late Frank Newby, James Sutherland, Lawrance Hurst, Mike Bussell, Mike Chrimes, Malcolm Tucker, Robert Thorne, Alec Skempton, Rowland Mainstone, Loren Butt, Julia Elton, and Derek Sugden.

Among many others who share my interest in engineering history, and who have helped me in providing information and images for my book, I would like to mention Werner Lorenz, Santiago Huerta, Ed Diestelkamp, Mark Wilson Jones, James Campbell, and Hentie Louw.

I am especially grateful to Mike Bussell who has regularly given me the benefit of his encyclopedic knowledge the last two hundred years of construction history. He also diligently read and improved a large part of the manuscript and made many helpful suggests regarding bibliographic matters.

Likewise I am greatly indebted to Mike Chrimes, the librarian at the Institution of Civil Engineers in London who gave me access to the originals of a great many of the illustrations used in the book and whose staff were regularly of great help in finding reference material. Mike also read much of the manuscript and made many suggestions for its improvement as well as helping me track down much obscure material.

I am grateful to Norman Smith, who helped me improve the sections on Roman and mediaeval times, and to Janet Delaine who helped me avoid make many errors concerning Roman engineering and history.

This book would have been impossible without the enthusiasm and commitment of the editorial and research staff at Phaidon Press. I am grateful to Julia Rydholm and Holly LaDue for their tireless search for images and, especially, to Megan McFarland who did everything an author could wish for in organizing the whole project, being incredibly patient with me during the slow progress that characterizes a part-time author, and generally making the book as good as it is.

Last, but not least, I thank Oscar, Orlando and Tess, my family who have been so patient, and tolerated my preoccupation with the book over the last few years, with special thanks to Tess who also helped track down numerous books and illustrations.

Bill Addis

Phaidon Press Limited
Regent's Wharf
All Saints Street
London N1 9PA

Phaidon Press, Inc.
180 Varick Street
New York, NY 10014

www.phaidon.com

First published 2007
Reprinted in 2008

ISBN 978 0 7148 4146 5

A CIP catalogue record for this book is available from the British Library.

Designed by mgmt. design
Printed in China

introduction

This book traces the origins of the knowledge and design skills that engineers use today when designing buildings. For convenience, I group these together under the term "building engineering," although, unlike the word "architecture," building engineering does not imply a single professional discipline. No English-speaking engineers call themselves building engineers; they call themselves structural engineers, building services engineers, acoustic engineers, and so on, according to their specialist discipline.

The essence of building engineering design is the ability to plan, before the start of construction, how a building is to be built. This requires, in turn, an understanding of how the completed building will work—how it will convey gravity, wind, or earthquake loads down to the foundations; how it must be heated, ventilated, and lit to create a comfortable internal environment how sounds will be reflected and absorbed in order to create an appropriate room acoustic, and so on.

As this process involves trying to predict the future, perhaps the most important of the engineer's skills is to generate sufficient confidence that a proposed design for a building will, indeed, perform as intended. This would be quite easy if the proposed building were identical to one already constructed. However, unlike automobiles rolling off a production line, most buildings, especially large ones, are unique in many respects. One strand of the history of building engineering then, is to trace how engineers have generated that necessary confidence before construction commences. Today, engineers usually generate the confidence to build using computers to generate mathematical models of the engineering behavior of the various aspects of a building's performance. These models effectively encapsulate the knowledge and experience of how buildings and materials behave, built up by engineers over many hundreds of years. In the past, engineers had to rely on their own experience, on the engineering and scientific knowledge that could be written down in books, and on the results of experiments either at full size or on scale models.

Another important skill engineers need when planning the construction of a building is the ability to communicate a proposed design, not only to secure the all-important approval of the developer or client, but also to provide instructions to the many hundreds of people involved in constructing the design precisely as the engineer has conceived it, in order for it to work. While the use of drawings and scale models for this purpose goes back to ancient Egypt, it was only in the Renaissance that techniques were developed for representing complex three-dimensional shapes on paper, and the method of orthographic projection that we use today was devised only in the late eighteenth century.

Throughout history, building designers have often surpassed the requirement for functionality, designing structures also intended to be impressive. Whether the client was a Roman emperor currying the favor of the citizens of Rome, or religious leaders seeking to impress the gods, or a nobleman or businessman seeking to demonstrate his enormous wealth, the consequence was the same—buildings that were bigger and better than their predecessors. Building engineers have thus constantly been required to innovate. However, innovation is a risky business. The first person to build a masonry vault or dome spanning 20 meters was venturing into the unknown; the second person to do so was not. Another of the engineer's skills, then, is managing the risk that is constantly present when doing something for the first time. Yet this raises a problem for engineers: How can they generate necessary confidence without giving away the very nature of the innovation?

This dilemma was well understood by the Italian Renaissance engineer and building designer Filippo Brunelleschi. A competition was held in 1420 to find someone to construct a masonry dome for the cathedral in Florence, one that needed to be larger than any constructed since the Pantheon in Rome in the first century A.D. The Renaissance historian Vasari recounts how Brunelleschi proposed a method for building the dome without needing a massive structure inside the cathedral to support its centering. This utterly unprecedented idea was received with scepticism, incredulity, and even hostility. More than once the panel of judges demanded to know how Brunelleschi would accomplish the task, but he refused to tell, arguing that doing so would enable anyone else to use his idea. Finally, to convey the point he was making, he requested that an egg be brought to the room. He threw down a challenge to those who had entered the competition: whoever could stand the egg on its end on a flat piece of marble should build the cupola. All tried and failed. Then Brunelleschi tapped the egg lightly on the marble to flatten one end, and stood it up with ease. The others complained that they could have done the same if they had realized that they were allowed to. Brunelleschi replied simply that they would also have been able to build the dome using his method if he had shown them his plans. He got the job.

In this book I concentrate on how the engineering aspects of buildings have been designed, and I deal mainly with large buildings, since they have always presented the greatest engineering challenges. This strand of building history has been dealt with less thoroughly than the history of architecture, and has also been overlooked in many excellent books on the history of civil engineering. Wherever possible, I have discussed the design methods and procedures used by building designers. These are, to the design engineer, what theories and hypotheses are to the research scientist. While the history and philosophy of science is a well-established academic discipline, the development of design rules and procedures has attracted relatively little attention by authors, despite the fact that they form the core of the engineer's work.

Although I do not deal comprehensively with the development of building materials, construction methods, or engineering science, I touch on all these themes when necessary to trace the development of building engineering design. These subjects are well covered by many books, and I have included the best of these in the bibliography. Similarly, I have ventured into the histories of other branches of engineering where they have clearly influenced developments in building engineering.

The development of building engineering, like other branches of technology, has tended to take place in those countries that have been most prosperous at different times during the last three thousand years. Since I deal with the origins of modern building engineering design, which, in turn, are based mainly on the science and technology of Europe, there is little discussion of the science and technology of other cultures, such as China, India, and the Arabic cultures of the Middle East.

The focus of this volume begins in the Eastern Mediterranean, in ancient Egypt and Greece, and then moves to the Roman empire. From the late medieval period to the mid-nineteenth century, developments are concentrated in France, Germany, Italy, and England. Our modern approach to engineering, based on scientific understanding, began in these countries in the early seventeenth century and had reached maturity by around 1850.

Beginning in the mid-nineteenth century, many Europeans took their building engineering expertise across the Atlantic, and were able to benefit from the commercial prosperity that flourished in the United States and led to the growth of high-rise building. The extreme climate in many parts of the U.S. also encouraged American engineers to master the indoor climate of buildings. Since the early twentieth century, building engineering in Europe and America has developed hand in hand as improved transportation and communications have overcome natural barriers. If the two cultures are to be differentiated, European building engineers have tended to innovate as a process of exploration, almost for its own sake, while American engineers have innovated in order to bring commercial benefits. In recent decades, engineers in Japan and elsewhere in the Far East have been particularly successful in rigorously developing many ideas originating in Western countries. These cultural characteristics do mean that even in the twentieth century, a disproportionate number of major innovations in building engineering have originated in Europe, while they have been developed with considerable commercial success mainly outside Europe.

Since earliest times, engineering has developed according to which of two political and economic climates has been dominant—war and peace. Until the eighteenth century, the word "engineer" referred to a military engineer whose work included not only making weapons, but also designing and constructing earthworks, fortifications, and military buildings, as well as providing supplies of water and even changing the courses of rivers. For much of their time engineers were engaged in military projects; during times of peace, however, they often turned their skills to civic or religious projects. For the many civic buildings in ancient Rome we should be thankful for the Pax Romana—the two or three centuries during which the Roman empire was relatively stable. The cathedral in Florence, whose dome was designed by Brunelleschi, is one of many buildings in Renaissance Italy whose construction was interrupted for several years while walls and fortifications were rebuilt to defend the city from increasing threats from neighboring states. Most of the designers of ancient temples, medieval cathedrals, and Renaissance palaces learned their skills and earned their main incomes designing and constructing fortifications or weapons of war. The Roman engineer Vitruvius and the Renaissance engineers San Gallo the Younger and Leonardo da Vinci are prominent examples.

In talking about engineering over many centuries and in many lands, there are inevitably difficulties with terminology. It is an anachronism to use the words "engineer" and "architect" about anyone active before about 1450. Our modern idea of the engineer was covered by many words in Greek and Latin. The ancient Greek word *architekton* does not mean "architect" as we use the word today; rather, it would be better translated as "master builder" or even "construction manager." My use of the word "building designer" to minimize confusion is, of course, also anachronistic, and does not mean there was such a profession; nevertheless, it does convey the sense I intend.

The subject of dates besets any writer on history. I have used various standard works such as Sir Banister Fletcher's *A History of Architecture,* and specialist authors on different periods. But experts are wont to disagree, and no building can be given a single date, since its design can precede its completion by anything from one to one hundred years. I hope I have avoided simple mistakes, but most buildings have complex origins and scholars are forever rewriting history. The question of authorship of buildings and ideas is similarly subjective. The names of certain individuals often become prominent, but sometimes for curious reasons. Big ideas in science, such as force and temperature, were developed by many people over many decades or longer. Likewise, all large buildings involve teams of people, many of whom help develop the building as finally completed. Establishing precise authorship is virtually impossible, even today. I have tried to focus more on what was achieved than on who achieved it.

In my wanderings around engineering history, I have never ceased to be amazed by two frequent discoveries: how skillful and ingenious our ancestors were, and the early existence of examples of what I, and many others, have believed to be recent or new ideas. My aim, then, is to celebrate the achievements of many remarkable men (sadly, women have featured little in engineering history until the late twentieth century) and to share the wonder, amazement, and humility I have felt while learning about the history of building engineering.

Bill Addis

chapter 1

Building and Engineering in Ancient Times 1000 B.C. to A.D. 500

People and Events

Materials and Technology

From c. 1500 B.C. Large stone columns and beams in temples and palaces

From c. 1500 B.C. Large, hollow bronze castings in China

From c. 1400 B.C. Earliest known brick arch in a building, Ur, Mesopotamia (0.8m span)

From c. 1200 B.C. The Iron Age

Knowledge and Learning

Design Methods

From c. 1000 B.C. Geometric design procedures for buildings

Design Tools: Drawing and Calculation

From 1000 B.C. or earlier Plans, elevations, and physical scale models in Egypt, Greece, and Rome

From 1000 B.C. or earlier Use of the abacus in China, India, the Middle East, and countries bordering the Mediterranean

From c. 1000 B.C. Geometric calculation using rule and compass

Buildings

c. 1780 B.C. Building laws in the Code of King Hammurabi of Babylon

c. 1600 B.C. Palace of King Minos, Knossos, Crete

c. 1300 B.C. Temple of Amun, Karnak, Egypt

1700 1600 1500 1400 1300 1200 1100 1000 900 80

c. 720–320 B.C. Hellenic Greece

c. 725–700 B.C. Homer's *Illiad*

c. 640–546 B.C. Thales (geometrician)

c. 582–507 B.C. Pythagoras (geometrician and scientist)

c. 320 to c. 100 B.C. Hellenistic Greece

fl. 300 B.C. Euclid (geometrician)

c. 287–212 B.C. Archimedes (engineer and physicist)

c. 280–220 B.C. Philon of Byzantium (engineer)

c. 285–222 B.C. Ctesibius of Alexandria (engineer)

c. 429–347 B.C. Plato (philosopher)

c. 428–c. 347 B.C. Archytas (author of first mechanics textbook)

c. 80–c. 25 B.C. Vitruvius (engineer)

27 B.C. Augustus becomes Roman emperor

c. A.D. 10–75 Heron of Alexandria (engineer)

A.D. 79 Vesuvius erupts, burying Herculaneum and Pompeii

c. A.D. 55–c. 130 Apollodorus of Damascus (engineer)

A.D. 395 Roman Empire splits into West and East

A.D. 410 Imperial Rome falls to invaders

c. 720 B.C. Earliest known brick barrel vault, Assyria

From c. 500 B.C. (Stone) beams that reflect bending moments

c. 150 B.C.–A.D. 50 Masonry arch aqueducts for Rome's water supply

From c. 100 B.C. Timber roof trusses

From c. 100 B.C. Masonry arches in buildings

From c. 100 B.C. Masonry domes

From c. 100 B.C. Glazed windows

From c. 80 B.C. Central heating through ductwork (hypocaust system)

From c. 50 B.C. Widespread use of hydraulic cement and wrought iron in buildings

c. A.D. 70 Double glazing in baths at Herculaneum

c. A.D. 80 Earliest known use of greenhouse effect to heat buildings

From c. 600 B.C. Books on mathematics and science

From c. 400 B.C. Books on mechanics and engineering

c. 500 B.C. Science of acoustics first developed by Pythagoras

290 B.C. "Museum" (university) of Alexandria, Egypt, founded by Ptolemy Soter

c. 230 B.C.–A.D. 646 Engineering school at Alexandria, Egypt, founded by Ctesibius

c. 25 B.C. Vitruvius, *De Architectura* (book on construction and military engineering)

From c. 450 B.C. Numerical design procedures for weapons and buildings

500 B.C. or earlier Numerical calculations using fractions

c. 700 B.C. The Heraion, Olympia, Greece (first major Doric temple)

c. 600–270 B.C. The Seven Wonders of the World (excluding the Pyramids)

c. 450–438 B.C. The Parthenon, Athens, Greece

c. 200 B.C. *Insulae* (Roman apartment buildings)

c. A.D. 72–80 Flavian Amphitheater or Colosseum, Rome, Italy

c. A.D. 104–109 Baths of Trajan, Rome

c. A.D. 112–13 Trajan's Column, Rome

c. A.D. 118–26 Pantheon, Rome

c. A.D. 126–c.127 Baths of Hadrian, North Africa

A.D. 211–16 Baths of Caracalla, Rome

c. A.D. 298–306 Baths of Diocletian, Rome

A.D. 308–25 Basilica of Maxentius/Constantine, Rome

700 | 600 | 500 | 400 | 300 | 200 | 100 BC | 0 | 100 AD | 200 | 300 | 400 | 500

Building and Engineering in Ancient Times 1000 B.C. to A.D. 500

Building and Engineering Before Hellenic Greece

It is appropriate to begin using the word "engineering" in association with building design and construction from the time when people started to use large stones in preference to timber, mud bricks, or small stones that could be lifted by one or two people. Lifting and maneuvering large stones into position required great skill. It has been a frequent topic of speculation how men in ancient Egypt quarried and manipulated some 2.3 million stones weighing about 2.5 tons[1] each to build the Great Pyramid of Cheops (Khufu) at Giza in around 2500 B.C. This was achieved without having to lift the stones off the ground; the forces needed to move them were reduced to a human scale by sliding the stones, using ramps and a variety of wedges and levers. At about the same time in England, stones weighing 20 tons or so were raised to a height of about 6 meters to construct
1 Stonehenge. In about 1500 B.C. Egyptian engineers quarried, moved, and raised into position three stone obelisks, each weighing about 450 tons. The subsequent removal of one of them (known as the Vatican Obelisk) from Egypt, its reerection in Rome, and its subsequent relocation were equally impressive feats of engineering (see chapter 3, pp. 159–63).

As important as the mechanical expertise needed to erect structures made of large stones were the many measuring and surveying skills required to produce stones of the right shape and to set out the orientation and a plan on the ground, probably in relation to the sun and astronomical constellations. In the case of the pyramids, the designers also had to plan the shape and location of the many rooms and tunnels inside, and to construct them required great skill in the use of geometry and surveying techniques in three dimensions. It must also have required considerable planning and management ability to organize, direct, and motivate some one hundred thousand workers over a period of twenty years or so. Such expertise enabled ancient engineers to plan—or, in modern language, to design—their large projects before construction commenced. The history of building engineering, then, is the story of how engineers have planned or designed their buildings, and the increasing accuracy with which they have learned to predict the future.

The earliest clear evidence we have of the use of mathematics, engineering science, and formal, sequential procedures in design is from about 450 B.C., in lands of the eastern Mediterranean under the influence of Greek civilization. Both mathematics and the art of designing large buildings and cities were introduced into Europe from India and the Middle East. Indeed, perhaps the earliest written evidence relating to the art of building can be found in the legal code established in Babylon c. 1780
B.C. by its first ruler, Hammurabi (reigned 1792–1750 3
B.C.). The Code of Hammurabi, which governed all aspects of society, included specific building laws that

1

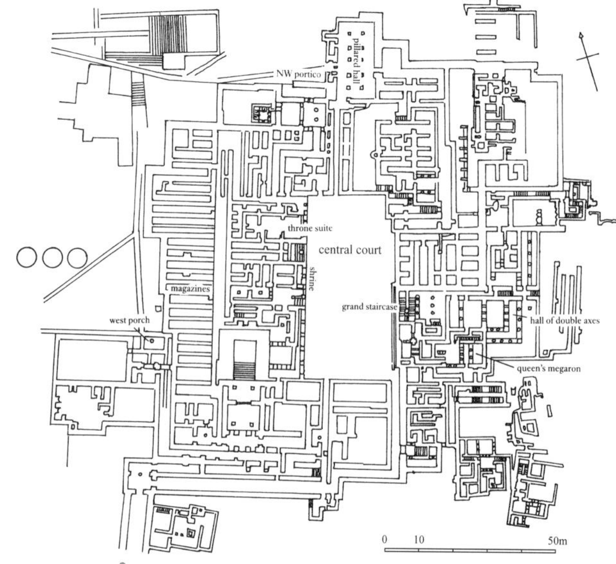

2

Col. XXXV.

COLUMN XXXVI.

If a builder build a house for a man and complete it, (that man) shall give him two shekels per SAR of house as his wage.

If a builder build a house for a man and do not make his construction firm and the house which he has built collapse and cause the death of the owner of the house, that builder shall be put to death.

If it cause death of a son of the owner of the house, they shall put to death the son of that builder.

If it cause death of a slave of the owner of the house, he shall give to the owner of the house a slave of equal value.

If it destroy property, he shall restore whatever it destroyed, and because he did not make the house which he built firm and it collapsed, he shall rebuild the house which collapsed from his own property (at his own expense).

If a builder build a house for a man and do not make its construction meet the requirements and a wall fall in, that builder shall strengthen that wall at his own expense.

3

4

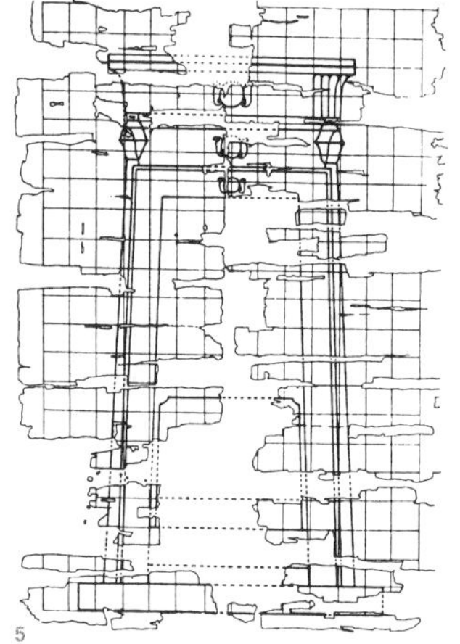

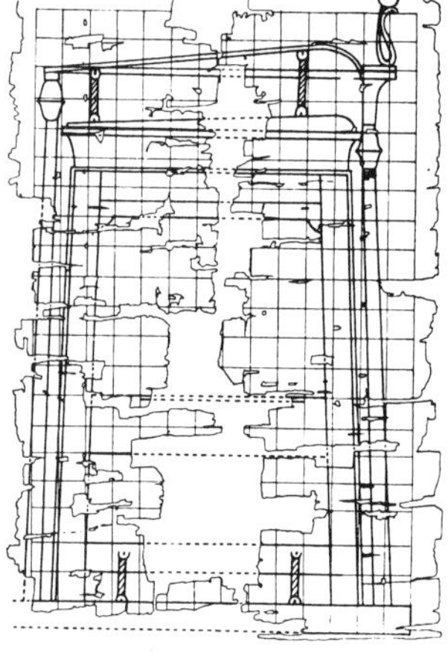

5

convey both the idea of professional responsibility and the fact that such work required specialized skills.

Some of the best-preserved remains from this era are on the Mediterranean island of Crete, where the Minoan people flourished, especially between about 1800 and
2 1600 B.C. The royal palace of Minos, constructed at Knossos, was not especially impressive for its scale, but represented the very latest in building comfort for the royal family. Good daylight was provided throughout the interior by means of light wells; water was piped to the palace, and sanitary arrangements included a device for flushing the toilet.

By around 1500 B.C. temples and palaces commissioned for rulers of the many Egyptian dynasties had more or less reached the limit of what was technically possible using the stone columns and beams that were routinely employed in building large, single-story colonnades and halls. Among the most impressive of these early build-
4 ings is the Great Temple of Amun at Karnak, constructed in many phases by successive kings from about 1550 B.C. onward. The hypostyle hall covered an area about 100 meters by 50 meters—approximately the size of a soccer field or a large medieval cathedral. The roof was made from huge planks of stone resting on stone beams, supported, in turn, on 134 columns. The 12 columns of the central colonnade are about 22 meters tall, about 3.5 meters in diameter, and measure about 7.2 meters between centers; the remaining 122 columns are each about 13 meters high and nearly 3 meters in diameter. The colonnade is lit by clerestory windows about 5 meters high, and the rest of the hall is lit naturally through inclined slots in the stone-plank ceiling.

From around this time we have an early example of an
5 Egyptian drawing on papyrus depicting a building, though whether this was a design yet to be constructed or a record of something already built, we do not know.

Designing and constructing a monument such as the Temple of Amun required an approach to building that differed markedly from what worked for small-scale domestic structures. In earlier times most buildings would have been made of mud or mud bricks and timber, and roofed in thatch. The scale was human—seldom more than 3 or 4 meters high—and constructed of materials and components that could be easily handled by a few carpenters and relatively unskilled laborers. Materials would be quite cheap, and even labor, the main cost, was likely to be paid for with little more than food.

A temple, by contrast, had to be large, to house the statue of a god, and to involve spans larger than needed for domestic structures. Its form needed to be different to achieve its special function, and might have been chosen to echo other temples in distant cities. A degree of permanence was expected, calling for the use of stone and, to cover the roofs, perhaps the new fired-clay tiles introduced around 1800–1700 B.C. Not only were more costs involved, but nontraditional building skills and construction methods as well. A temple 8 or 10 meters high required huge quantities of stone which might have had to be brought from some distance, needed to be ordered far ahead of time, and required the work of many people. The person given responsibility for carrying out such a vast project needed approval for his proposals and was expected to show his client at least one sketch or a small model. He probably also had to estimate how long it would take to build, and give some indication of how much the materials would cost. The workforce had to be organized and given precise instructions about the numbers and sizes of stones required. Different teams of workers also needed to know how their separate contributions would fit together to make the whole. And discussions had to be conducted using mutually understood concepts and rational argument. In essence, we have a process little different from that undertaken today on every large building project.

In general, it was during the thousand years between about 1500 and 500 B.C. that the Egyptians and the ancient Greeks of the Hellenic period developed the skill we now know as "design" in the building process. It was

1 Stonehenge, Wiltshire, England, c. 2000 B.C. Engraving by William Stukeley, 1720s. 2 Palace of King Minos, Knossos, Crete, c. 1600 B.C. Plan. 3 Laws for builders in the Code of Hammurabi, c. 1780 B.C. Engraved in cuneiform script on stele, with English translation at right. 4 Temple of Amun at Karnak, c. 1300 B.C. Entrance to hypostyle hall. Photograph by Gustave Le Gray, 1867. 5 Side and front elevations of an Egyptian shrine, drawn on papyrus, c. 1400 B.C.

born out of the need to plan and construct large and increasingly sophisticated buildings and was made possible by the economic prosperity, cultural richness, and intellectual skills that were evolving so rapidly during the same period. We can only pick up the story when written evidence appears, from around 500 B.C., with the emergence of the Greek culture that dominated the many peoples linked by the Mediterranean sea.

Engineering and Building in Ancient Greece

The city-states in the eastern Mediterranean were beginning to prosper from around the eighth century B.C. Through trade and war the Greeks had established a cultural heritage that transcended geographic and even linguistic boundaries. This was the Hellenic period, when Homer (c. 750–700 B.C.) was writing what became a common history, uniting many previously disparate communities. As the Greeks' sense of identity and pride grew, so too did their desire to establish impressive and long-lasting manifestations of their culture. They began building on a scale far greater—both in size and quantity— than in previous times. And, as with many peoples since, they wanted to ensure that their buildings would reflect their cultural identity and differentiate them from earlier and neighboring peoples from whom they had learned so much. They were also determined to ensure that construction was undertaken responsibly.

City-states flourished throughout modern mainland Greece, Turkey, and southern Italy, as well as on the islands of the eastern Mediterranean, and they began to assert and display their prosperity in the form of public buildings such as markets, temples, theaters, and other places of assembly. Unlike the few enormous buildings constructed under Egyptian royal patronage, these public structures represented the creation of a more democratic built environment, replicated many times in many places. While the Greeks had learned how to design large buildings from the Egyptians, they formalized design procedures, devising many ingenious solutions to improve both the building processes and the quality of the finished buildings. For example, it was common practice by the fifth century B.C. for each stone drum of a column to be located by a hardwood peg in the center and to bear on the drum below only on a circumferential annulus that
6 was ground precisely flat to ensure the column's stability. Although this method was more economical and practical than trying to ensure bearing over the whole area, it would still have required many hours of patient labor for each drum.

At roof level, the stone blocks forming the frieze and architrave were linked one to another by means of H-
shaped iron clamps. This idea had been used by the 8
Egyptians, and many variations had been tried using clamps of copper and bronze as well as iron. According to the Roman naturalist Pliny the Elder (c. 23–79 A.D.), the stone beams, spanning over 8 meters between columns and weighing nearly 20 tons, were raised into position using ramps of earth.

Early masonry building relied on long beams of stone to span two columns. The Latin word for beam, *trabs*, gives us the phrase "trabeated architecture." Crucial questions for the building designer at the time would have been: How far can a stone beam span? For a certain span, how deep and broad should the beam be? Is a rectangle the most efficient cross section? Should a beam have a constant cross section along its length? These questions were not answered in scientific and mathematical terms until Galileo published *Discourses on the Two New Sciences* in 1638, and they were explored by many scientists thereafter. This does not mean, however, that Greek engineers could not know some of the answers. Any child knows how to break a stick by bending it, and that a thin strip of wood bends more easily than a thicker one. From these and related observations it is not a huge step to realize that making a beam thicker in the center would be an effective way to strengthen it. Alternatively, making a beam thinner at its ends would be an intelligent way of making it lighter without losing much of its structural capacity. While we seldom see evidence of this type of thinking in buildings, for reasons discussed below, ancient craftsmen and engineers well understood these matters. The sophisticated design of Greek weapons such as *ballistae* (mounted crossbows) is evidence enough of their engineering understanding and technical skill.

Although such structural sophistication is seldom found in Greek buildings, there are sufficient examples to indicate that some building engineers had a good understanding of bending. For example, as stone is much weaker in tension than in compression, the most efficient

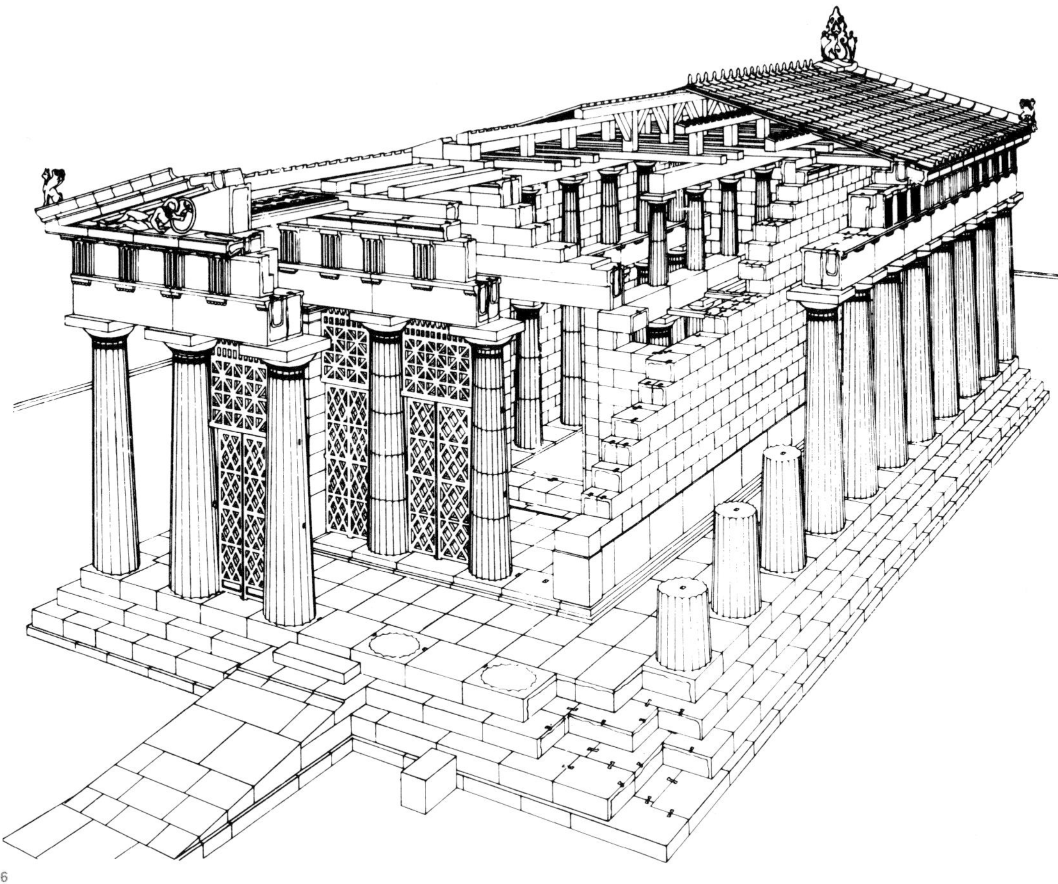

6

cross section for a beam has more material where it carries tension than where it suffers tension. In a beam spanning two columns or across a window or door opening, this would be the lower part of the beam. And this is just what we find in the remains of a number of stone
9 beams dating from the sixth to the fourth centuries B.C.

One remarkable beam, from the island of Samothrace in the north Aegean, 6 meters long and dating from the fourth century B.C., demonstrates an understanding of both the most effective cross section and the benefits of
making the beam deepest at midspan. Its elevation cor- 10
responds approximately to what we would now call the bending moment diagram, which indicates the resistance to bending that a beam must develop in order to carry its own weight and the superimposed loads.

If such understanding did exist, then why was it not more widely employed? The answer is probably an economic one. Timber and stone were the main structural materials, and both of these are manufactured into useful building components by cutting them down to size, from a tree

6 Temple of Aphaia, Aegina, Greece, c. 500 B.C. Cutaway isometric drawing showing construction.

and large rock, respectively. While it was possible to continue working the materials to achieve the most efficient, lightest possible structural form, there soon came a point when the added cost of further work was not repaid by benefits in structural performance; for many purposes a uniform beam with a rectangular section was adequate. Generally speaking, the size and weight of pieces of stone would be reduced to what could be conveniently transported to a site and erected in position. Usually it would be unwise on safety grounds to try to achieve the least-weight solution, since this would increase the risk of failure, and the design of structures is principally about keeping risk to an acceptable level. The exception is when the very lightest structure is needed to achieve the greatest span—as in the case of the beam from Samothrace. This fundamental truth still applies to much stone and timber used in building today. It was only with the introduction of cast iron in the late eighteenth century that economy of material weight became the dominant influence on sizing structural members; unlike a timber or stone beam, the cost of a cast iron beam increases directly in proportion to the weight of iron it contains.

Because timber perishes, there is very little evidence of how the roof structures of Greek temples were formed. In the main they consisted of sloping rafters supported at either end. This technique uses timber in bending, for which it is well suited, as it has a high tensile strength. However, since it is not very stiff, it is prone to large deflection under load, so the spans need to be kept quite short—up to 6 or 7 meters. For longer spans, the rafters would have needed support at midspan to avoid large deflections from the heavy clay-tile roof covering. There is no evidence in early Greek times of roof trusses of the type that became common during the medieval period.

The success of these various developments in masonry construction can best be judged by the very best of what was constructed during the Hellenic and Hellenistic eras. During the third and second centuries B.C., a number of writers drew up lists of what they considered to be man's greatest achievements. By about 100 B.C. a consensus had been reached on what constituted the Seven Wonders of the Ancient World; it is noteworthy that six of the seven were the work of the finest building and civil engineers of their day. The oldest was the Great Pyramid of Cheops, which, at about 150 meters high, remained the tallest structure in the world until the cathedral spires of the fourteenth century, and is the only one of the Seven Wonders that survives today. The next oldest were the Hanging Gardens of Babylon, built alongside the Euphrates River and dating from around 600 B.C. Though the size, location, and age of the legendary gardens are still a matter of debate, many descriptions make it clear that they were truly remarkable. ("Hanging" was the word used to describe many lofty structures, including, for instance, the massive masonry dome at Hagia Sophia in Constantinople, built A.D. 532–37.) The water needed for the gardens' continuous irrigation had to be raised about 50 meters from the river below using man-powered machines, and channels built from mud were made waterproof using either lead sheet or asphalt. The Greek writer Strabo (c. 63 B.C.–A.D. 21) described the gardens in the first century B.C., already some five hundred years after they are believed to have been constructed, so it is likely they were no longer fully operational and may even have already been in ruins:

> *It consists of arched vaults, which are situated, one after the another, on checkered, cube-like foundations. The checkered foundations, which are hollowed out, are covered so deep with earth that they admit of the largest of trees, having been constructed of baked brick and asphalt ... The ascent to the uppermost terrace-roofs is made by a stairway; and alongside these stairs there were screws, through which the water was continually conducted up into the garden from the Euphrates by those appointed for the purpose.*[2]

Another of the Seven Wonders was the Temple of Artemis 7 at Ephesus, completed around 300 B.C. The first shrine to the goddess Artemis had been built at Ephesus around 550 B.C. and was reputed to contain a sacred stone (a meteorite) that had "fallen from Jupiter" — the ancient Greek equivalent of "fallen from Heaven." The temple

7 Second Temple of Artemis at Ephesus, completed c. 350 B.C. on the site of an earlier shrine dating to c. 550 B.C. Digital reconstruction. 8 Top: Iron I- and Z- clamps used to bind adjacent stones in Greek and Roman temple construction; Bottom: Stone drums of a column with a central peg of iron or hardwood. 9 Sections of shaped stone beams in Greek buildings. 10 Sections of a stone beam used to support a marble coffered ceiling, from Samothrace, late fourth century B.C.

7

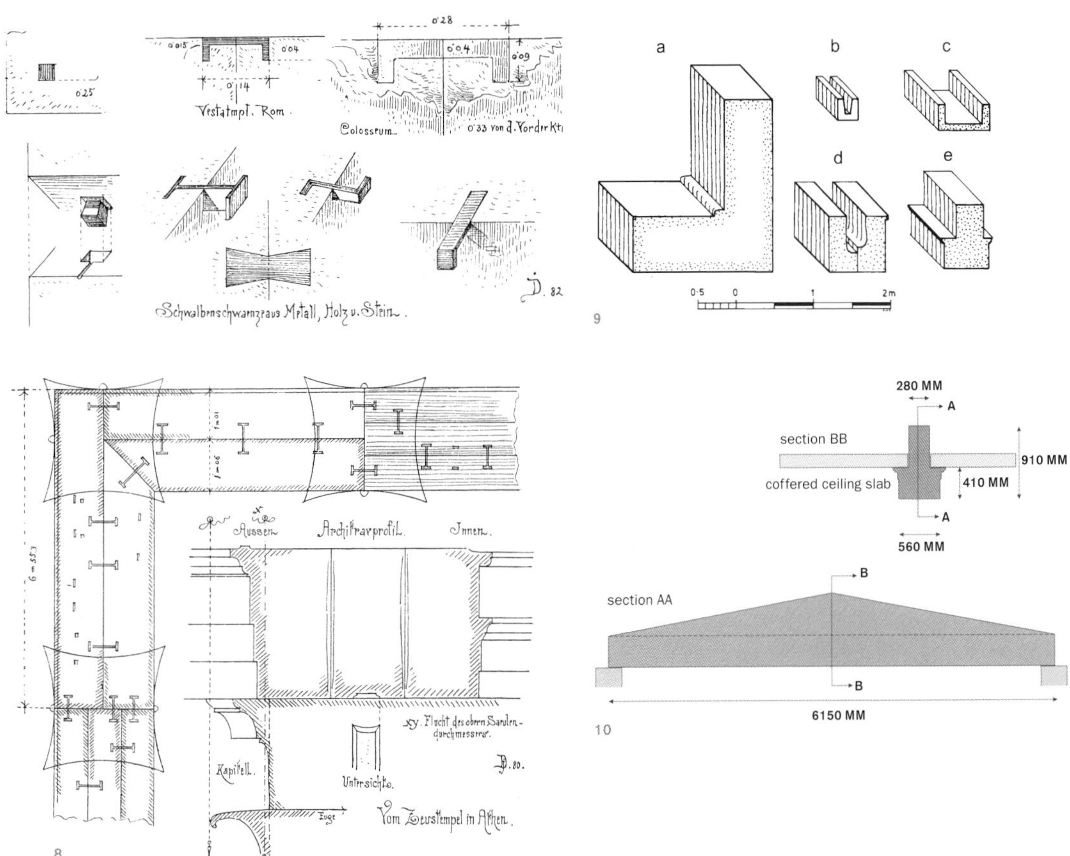
Vestatmpl. Rom.
Colosseum
Schwalbenschwanz aus Metall, Holz u. Stein.
a
b
c
d
e
Aussen
Architravprofil.
Innen.
Kapitell.
Untersicht.
Vom Zeustempel in Athen.
280 MM
A
section BB
910 MM
coffered ceiling slab
410 MM
560 MM
B
section AA
6150 MM

9

8

10

had columns about 18 meters tall, and it probably occupied an area similar to the one rebuilt in the 350s B.C. on the same site after the earlier building was destroyed by fire. The rebuilt temple had more than 120 columns 19 meters high; the structure was about 129 meters long by 68 meters wide. This enclosed a volume more than seven times greater than that of the Parthenon in Athens (447–438 B.C.), which measured 66 meters by 32 meters, with columns about 10 meters high. The temple survived for more than seven hundred years, until it was demolished and the stone used to construct a Christian church. In a book written around 230 B.C. describing the Seven Wonders of the World, the author expresses his particular admiration for the Temple at Ephesus:

> *I have seen the walls and Hanging Gardens of ancient Babylon, the statue of Zeus at Olympia, the Colossus of Rhodes, the great Pyramids and the tomb of Mausolus. But when I saw the temple at Ephesus rising to the clouds, all these other wonders were put in the shade.*[3]

The Colossus of Rhodes, a statue completed in around 280 B.C., celebrated the city's victory over the besieging troops of Demetrios, one of Alexander the Great's generals. Rhodes had sided with another of Alexander's former generals, Ptolemy Soter, who later became ruler of Egypt in Alexandria as Ptolemy I (c. 367–283 B.C.). The statue was located at the entrance to the natural harbor of the city of Rhodes, the capital of the island of the same name, which lies some 30 kilometers off the southwestern coast of modern Turkey. It was some 35 meters high, standing on a plinth about 16 meters high. The figure was posed in a traditional Greek manner: naked, wearing a spiked crown, shading its eyes from the rising sun with its right hand, with a cloak draped over its left arm. Philon of Byzantium (see p. 26) writes of the Colossus that it consisted of a core of two or three stone columns rising up to the level of the head, and linked by architraves or stone beams, probably at more than one level. From the columns was constructed an armature of wrought iron bars that reached outward to where the surface of the figure would be hung. To these iron bars were riveted bronze plates that had been cast, hammered into shape, and polished to create the shining outer surface of the statue. Much of the metal for the statue was said to have been recycled from the many war machines left behind when Demetrios was defeated and fled the island. The Colossus was destroyed by an earthquake in the year 224 B.C., and many of its pieces lay where they fell until Arabs conquered Rhodes in A.D. 656.

One of the longest surviving of the Seven Wonders of the Ancient World was the lighthouse built on the island of
Pharos, marking the entrance to the harbor of the new 11
city of Alexandria in Northern Egypt. Alexander the Great had founded the city in 332 B.C. but died in 323 B.C. before much had been completed, and work was continued by his successor as ruler of Egypt, Ptolemy Soter. Two deep-water harbors were constructed at the western extremity of the Nile delta, one for the Nile River traffic, the other for Mediterranean Sea trade. Ptolemy commissioned the building of the lighthouse in 290 B.C. to serve both as a guide for navigators and as an icon for the new and prospering city. It was completed in 270 B.C. in the reign of Ptolemy Soter's son, Ptolemy II. The lighthouse was constructed of dressed stone, with lead sheet to improve the bearing between layers, and consisted of three parts. A number of estimates put the lighthouse at some 300 cubits (about 120 meters) high. The bottom section was a hollow square building, about 32 meters square and 65 meters high, inside which were about fifty rooms and a ramp to allow the delivery of construction materials via horse-drawn carts. Set on this base was an octagonal tower about 32 meters high and 12 meters in diameter. Above this was a nearly cylindrical tower, tapering from perhaps 6 to 4 meters in diameter, and about 20 meters high, with a staircase leading to the cupola where the beacon burned and the lighthouse keepers lived and stored the fuel for the fire. It was said that the light, by night, or the smoke, by day, from the lighthouse was visible at a distance of 60 kilometers.

The designer of the lighthouse, Sostrates of Knidos, achieved immortality through a neat bit of subterfuge. After Ptolemy II refused his request to have his name carved into the base of the structure, he defied the ruler by having the following inscription incised into the masonry: "Sostrates son of Dexiphanes of Knidos on behalf of all mariners to the savior gods." This was covered with a layer of plaster into which Ptolemy's name was carved. Over time, however, the plaster broke away, revealing Sostrates' inscription.

The lighthouse was a great tourist attraction; food was

sold at the observation platform at the top of the first level, and visitors could climb up for an even better view from the pinnacle of the eight-sided tower. It was reported as still intact and operating as a lighthouse in 1115, although it had already suffered some damage from earthquakes. Like many ancient structures in the eastern Mediterranean, its fate was finally sealed by the movements of Earth. After major damage in one earthquake in 1303, the lighthouse was destroyed by another in 1326.

Construction had, then as now, its impact on the environment; in ancient Greece both serious economic consequences and examples of ingenious design helped mitigate these effects. As the city-states of the Greek world grew and built more and more, so the availability of natural resources was stretched. Wood was needed in large quantities for making both ships and buildings, and especially for making charcoal needed to smelt mineral ores. Enormous quantities of metals were being produced—tin, lead, copper, bronze, and, especially, iron—and each ton of metal needed many tons of charcoal for its production.

By the fifth century B.C. many parts of Greece had been virtually stripped of trees. The philosopher Plato found the hills of his native Attica "like the bones of a corpse, denuded of its once-living flesh."[4] As fuel shortages grew, local government was forced to legislate; at one time Athens banned the use of olive wood for making charcoal and prohibited the export of any timber to neighboring regions. On the island of Cos, wood for domestic heating and cooking was taxed to control its use, while on Delos, which had no local sources, the sale of charcoal was taken into state hands to prevent racketeering. The serious shortage of timber must also have contributed to the growing use of masonry in building construction.

Apart from the use of timber in buildings and ships and for smelting, wood was also essential for domestic life, being the only fuel available for cooking and heating homes through cold winters. A creative response to fuel shortages was to reduce the need for heating by devising more sophisticated buildings. Designers learned how to harness and take advantage of the sun's energy by using it to heat the building fabric by day and release this energy during the cooler evenings. Shading devices such as porticoes allowed the low, winter sun to penetrate deep into a building while also providing shade from the higher, summer sun. Interior rooms were also kept cool with small, north-facing windows to minimize the heating effects of direct sunlight while providing some ventilation. With no glass for this purpose available at this time, windows had shutters to keep out the cold of winter.

The growing town of Olynthus in northern Greece provides
an example of such solar-conscious design. When new 12, 13
housing was needed in the fifth century B.C. for about 2,500 people, a substantial development was planned on a site north of the existing town as carefully as any similar development today. The streets ran east to west to ensure that the apartments faced south, and apartments were of two types according to whether they were on the north or south side of a street. Each was designed with rooms facing south onto a courtyard to ensure maximum benefit from the winter sun.

Many other Greek towns are testimony to this planning, and Priene, in modern Turkey, is one of the most spectacular. As the old town became ever more plagued by flooding and its unhealthy consequences, it was decided in about 350 B.C. to relocate the entire community of about four thousand people to a better site on the side of a hill. This wholesale move allowed planners to map out every detail of their new town, including a good supply of water and drainage. The orientation of buildings and streets took into account not only the direction of the sun to bring the benefits of solar gain, but also the direction of prevailing winds. Cold winds came from the north, and the northern walls of houses were built thicker to achieve better insulation.

Several philosophers and scientists, including Socrates, Plato, and Aeschylus, all drew attention in their writings to these and other sensible ways of designing towns and buildings as illustrations of the scientific principles they were developing to explain how the world worked. Aristotle (384–322 B.C.) observed in one of his books that a "rational approach" to town planning and building design was "the modern fashion" of his day.[5] The key word here is "rational," for it highlights what we might identify as the Greek philosopher's main contribution to engineering: the formalization of logic and its use to

11

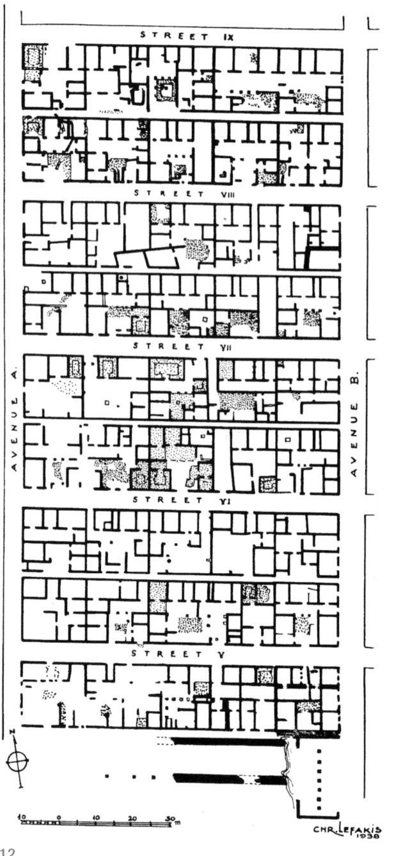

12

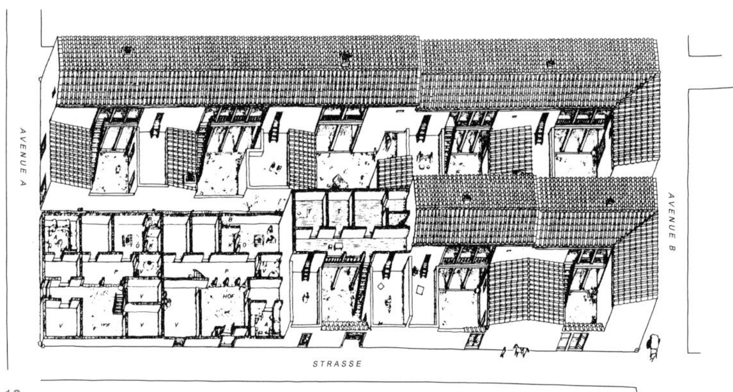

13

11 Lighthouse at Pharos, Alexandria, 270 B.C. Designer: Sostrates of Knidos. Reconstruction drawing. 12 Town plan of Olynthus, northern Greece, fifth century B.C. 13 Block of houses in Olynthus. Reconstruction drawing.

convince people of certain points of view by means of logical argument.

Mathematics, Science, and Engineering in Classical Times

It is hardly an exaggeration to say that Greek philosophers established the very way that people in Western cultures think about the world. They devised methodical approaches to describing the world—music, astronomy, botany, zoology, and so on. They sought to give structure and order to their ideas, to establish patterns, relationships, and hierarchies. Taxonomy was king or, rather, queen, because above all, the aim of these philosophical minds was to connect ideas using the invisible thread called logic.

One of the most potent tools the Greeks developed and exploited was geometry. They defined two types, one based on objects in a real world and the other on ideas in an abstract world. They learned to distinguish a square or circular stone, whose shape can be checked by measurement, from an abstract square or circle, whose dimensions and many geometric properties can be known without resorting to verification. Mathematicians from Thales (c. 636–c. 546 B.C.) and Pythagoras (c. 582–507 B.C.) to Euclid (fl. 300 B.C.) used geometry as a vehicle for the highest of the Greek arts: logic and rhetoric. Using abstract lines in the mind—perhaps sketched on paper for those unable to imagine clearly—it was possible to argue with total certainty that, for instance, a certain line was twice the length of another.

In an uncertain and unpredictable world, the ability to prove something beyond doubt provided philosophers with a key to unlocking the mysteries of the universe. Geometry was a manifestation of the rules according to which the world was constructed. This was the premise that underlay the remarkable work of Pythagoras and his followers, who strove to explain the world in terms of geometry and simple proportions. His archetypal example was music and the science of harmonics. The various consonant musical intervals—the octave, fifth, fourth, and so on—corresponded to simple subdivisions (2:1, 3:2, 4:3) of the length of a vibrating string. Similarly, the universe was conceived as a series of (perfect) concentric spheres whose radii were in simple ratios that corresponded to musical intervals. Indeed, the science of harmonics served the Greeks almost as well as modern physics and chemistry serve us today in helping to explain why the universe is how it is. The power of harmonics as a key to understanding the world can be judged by its survival as one of the core subjects taught at centers of learning until the seventeenth century. Johannes Kepler, Galileo, René Descartes, and even Isaac Newton moved easily and often consequentially from mathematics to astronomy, harmonics, statics, and optics in their studies of planetary motions.

Greek philosophers, mathematicians, and physicists developed the science of mechanics and used the same logical rigor developed in geometry to explain and prove the idea of mechanical advantage underlying the key devices that enabled man to multiply the power of his own limited strength: the lever, the wedge, the screw, and the pulley. This approach to explaining the physical world was first recorded in writing around 400 B.C. by Archytas (c. 428–c. 347 B.C.) of Tarentum (a town in southern Italy), who is sometimes called the father of mathematical mechanics. Archytas came from the Pythagorean school of physics and mathematics, and his books *On Pipes* and *On Mechanics* are the earliest on these subjects that have survived. The work on mechanics set the pattern that was followed and developed by nearly every writer on mathematics and physics during the classical era, right up to Anthemius and Eutocius in the sixth century A.D. Among Archytas's many other works on mathematical topics is *On Harmony*, which described the science based on musical theory and geometry that was as important for him in explaining how the world worked as was mechanics. Aristotle wrote of his admiration for a certain mechanical toy Archytas made for amusing young children. Archytas also made a model bird, somehow powered by compressed air, that flew a distance of some 200 meters, and he wrote a remarkable account of an imaginary journey around the world in a hermetically sealed sphere.

While many of the early philosophers, mathematicians, and scientists in ancient Greece may have worked for intellectual reward, most of their efforts were linked closely to more worldly matters—specifically, the art of war. This embraced surveying, measurement, and the design and making of ships, fortifications, and weapons such as catapults and ballistae. These philosophers

GEOMETRY: PROOFS AND AXIOMS

The formal basis of geometry is a small number of axioms. All truths or theorems in geometry are generated from these axioms by application of various rules of inference and previously proven theorems.

GIVEN:
Quadrilateral **ABCD**

REQUIRED:
To construct a triangle equal in area to quad **ABCD**

CONSTRUCTION:
Join **AC**; through **D** draw **DE** parallel to **AC** meeting **BC** produced in **E**. Required triangle is **ΔABE**

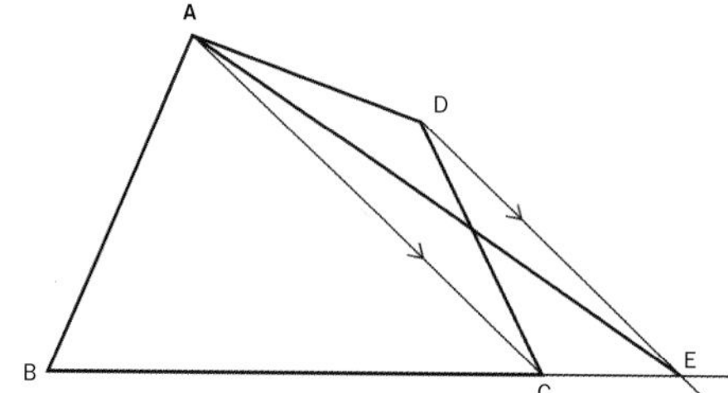

PROOF:

Area of quad **ABCD** = **ΔABC** + **ΔACD** in area

ΔACD = **ΔACE** in area (On same base **AC** between same parallels **AC** and **DE**)

∴ **ABCD** = **ΔABC** + **ΔACE** in area

Area of **ΔABE** = **ΔABC** + **ΔACE** in area

∴ **ABCD** = area of **ΔABE**

Quod erat demonstrandum (QED)

and scientists also undertook research to establish, for example, how to improve the throwing power of weapons and the speed and effectiveness of ships. There seem to have been two formal means of acquiring engineering knowledge that could be applied to military uses, over and above the craft skills of building and manufacturing. Military skills were taught at military colleges, while a more general and scientific education, including the study of academic subjects such as mechanics, geometry, and astronomy, was offered at one of the schools where the great academics of the day taught. It is likely that many establishments served both purposes. Unfortunately, surprisingly little information has come down to us about these schools. Plato (429–347 B.C.) set up his academy in Athens in 387 B.C. with both educational and political aims in mind, and various philosophers, lawyers, astronomers, and mathematicians were associated with the school. It is not known if there were curricula or even formal lectures at this time, but when Aristotle studied there twenty years later, we know he was taught rhetoric and politics. Aristotle soon joined the teaching staff and is known to have taught rhetoric and dialectic. The academy survived in various forms until A.D. 529.

Aristotle left Plato's academy after twenty years and was soon given support by Alexander the Great to found a rival institution, the Lyceum, in Athens in 335 B.C. It offered formal lectures in a wide range of subjects, many of which were given by Aristotle himself—logic, physics, astronomy, meteorology, zoology, metaphysics, theology, psychology, politics, economics, ethics, rhetoric, and poetics. One of Aristotle's most far-reaching achievements was to set the theoretical sciences on a logical footing, based, like geometry, on a series of axioms. His work preceded Euclid's formal axiomatic structure for geometry by some thirty or forty years.

In 290 B.C. Ptolemy Soter (Ptolemy I) founded the museum at Alexandria with the declared purpose of collecting all written works of authority, of promoting the study of literature and art, and of stimulating and assisting experimental and mathematical scientific investigation and research.

The word "museum" meant a shrine to the Muses, but it would be more appropriate today to call it a university. It drew some inspiration from the broad curriculum of the Lyceum and became the most successful of all the ancient schools, the model upon which all modern academic and learning institutions were based. During the following nine hundred years it attracted scholars and pupils from throughout the Western and Eastern Roman Empire. An important part of the museum complex was the famous library of Alexandria, which is believed to have contained nearly three-quarters of a million books at its peak.

The list of names linked to the University of Alexandria as teacher or student is impressive, including, among others, the geometrician Euclid and the engineers Archimedes, Ctesibius, Philon, and Heron of Alexandria. To indicate the high level that Greek and Roman engineering reached, it is worth considering the careers, achievements, and writings of the most eminent of these men.

Engineers in Hellenistic Greece

Archimedes of Syracuse, in Sicily (c. 287–212 B.C.), probably studied at the University of Alexandria, and soon became widely known for devising two of the most lasting machines known to mankind: Archimedes' screw, still used today to raise water, and the compound pulley. The Roman historian Plutarch, writing in about A.D. 100, describes a dramatic experiment that the king of Syracuse, Hieron, set up for Archimedes to demonstrate his compound pulley. In a letter to King Hieron, Archimedes claimed that, given sufficient force, any given weight might be moved with his pulley system.

> *Hieron was struck with amazement at this, and asked Archimedes to carry out an actual experiment to demonstrate a great weight being moved by a small engine. A cargo ship in the king's arsenal was selected, which would require great labor and many men to draw out of the dock; it was loaded with many passengers and a full freight, and Hieron sat down to watch. With hardly any effort, Archimedes pulled the rope in the compound pulley and drew the ship in a straight line, as smoothly and evenly as if she had been in the sea.*[6]

Archimedes' engineering skills drew him into serving the king as a military engineer, and his reputation became legendary, both in his own land and among those of its enemies. Most successful and famous among his achievements were the machines he devised for the defense of his hometown, Syracuse, when it was attacked by the Romans in the siege of 212 B.C. As Plutarch wrote:

> *When Archimedes began to ply his engines, and shot against the land forces of the assailants all sorts of missiles and immense masses of stones, which came down with incredible din and sped; nothing whatever could ward off their weight, but they knocked down in heaps those who stood in their way, and threw their ranks into confusion. At the same time huge beams were suddenly projected over the ships from the walls, which sank some of them with great weights plunging down form on high; others were seized at the prow by iron claws, or beaks like the beaks of cranes, drawn straight up into the air, and then plunged stern foremost into the depths, or were turned round and round by means of enginery within the city, and dashed upon the steel cliffs that jutted out beneath the wall of the city, with great destruction of the fighting men on board, who perished in the wrecks. Frequently, too, a ship would be lifted out of the water into mid-air, whirled hither and thither as it hung there, a dreadful spectacle, until its crew had been thrown out and hurled in all directs, when it would fall empty upon the walls or slip away from the clutch that had held it.*[7]

Archimedes was nevertheless a rather reluctant engineer. He developed the war engines only at the request of his friend the king of Syracuse and wrote nothing on his military expertise. Plutarch nicely conveys Archimedes' ambivalent attitude:

> *Archimedes possessed such a lofty spirit, so profound a soul, and such a wealth of scientific theory, that although his inventions had won for him a name and fame for superhuman sagacity, he would not consent to leave behind him any treatise on this subject, but regarding the work of an engineer and every art that ministers to the needs of life as ignoble and vulgar, he devoted his earnest efforts only to those studies the subtlety and charm of which are not affected by the claims of necessity. These studies, he thought, are not to be compared with any others; in them the subject matter vies with the demonstration, the former [subject matter] supplying grandeur and beauty, the latter [demonstration] precision and surpassing power.*[8]

It is, of course, this aspect of Archimedes' great talents that has established his reputation today as the greatest of all the ancient physicists and mathematicians. He is now universally known for his famous principle: that the upthrust on an immersed body is equal to the weight of the displaced liquid. He is also now credited with having developed an early ancestor of calculus, his method of exhaustion, a process of integration that enabled him to calculate the area of irregular shapes. However, Archimedes' works on mathematics and physics were virtually unknown during his lifetime and long thereafter. They became widely known only after they were edited and published by the Greek scientist Eutocius of Ascalon (c. A.D. 480–540) some seven hundred years later.

Ctesibius of Alexandria (c. 285–222 B.C.) was an Egyptian military engineer whose reputation was second only to that of Archimedes. He wrote two books on the mechanics and engines of war, both now lost: *Memorandum on Mechanics* and *Belopoietica*. He devised numerous catapults, including one that used springs made of bronze, whose advantage over springs made from organic materials (ropes and animal sinews) was that their performance was unaffected by moisture. His work on the compressibility and elasticity of air was also important, and has earned him the title "father of pneumatics." He devised the suction pump that is still used today to raise water, and many machines powered by water or pneumatics, some of which incorporated mechanical gears. Among these was a hydraulic hoist capable of raising large weights, and his famous water clock.

Perhaps Ctesibius's greatest achievement in the development of engineering of all kinds, however, was that he is believed to have been the founder and the first principal of the School of Engineering in Alexandria. Founded in c. 230 B.C. and closely linked to the museum of Alexandria, its purpose was to educate and train mechanical and military engineers. If Ptolemy Soter's "museum" should today be called a university, Ctesibius' school should be called an "école polytechnique," to use the phrase coined for the new engineering school set up in eighteenth-century France, and dedicated to bridging the gap between theory and practice (see chapter 6, p. 302).

Philon of Byzantium (c. 280–220 B.C.) was probably a military engineer, though none of his practical exploits are recorded. He is known to us mainly for his treatise on warfare and the art of siege. Philon augmented whatever he already knew about military engineering with information he gathered from those who had firsthand experience. He visited the great arsenals at Rhodes and Alexandria to talk to the engineers about the latest military strategies and the design and construction of the latest weapons. At Alexandria, for instance, he encountered Ctesibius, who had recently developed his new bronze-spring catapult. Philon's treatise was written in nine books:[9]

1. *Introduction*
2. *On the Lever*
3. *On the Building of Seaports*
4. *On Catapults*
5. *On Pneumatics*
6. *On Automatic Theaters*
7. *On the Building of Fortresses*
8. *On Besieging and Defending Towns*
9. *On Stratagems*

Sadly, only four of these books have survived complete (Books 4, 5, 7, and 8). His Book 8 offers advice on various ways of defending town walls from both land and sea attack. To capture a town through a siege, Philon first advises that it is important to make proper use of machines such as catapults and other war engines. But, as he goes on, it is equally important to try to starve the inhabitants of the town, to bribe suitable people for assistance, to poison the townspeople, and to use cryptography to pass secret messages. He also stresses the importance of a good doctor, and argues that those who have been injured in battle so badly that they cannot work again should be awarded pensions, while the wives of those killed should be provided for.

His book on catapults (Book 4) is the most important for the history of engineering design. While it is one of the first substantial works on mechanics, it is not that of an academic mathematician. It provides the scientific basis that underlies the working of various war engines and machines and, most significantly, records the design procedures used by Greek military engineers to determine the key dimensions of weapons such as the catapult and ballista. Although Philon was reporting the current military engineering design methods, they were, of course, simply the latest of a long tradition. Given their sophistication, it is not unreasonable to suppose they were the most up-to-date versions of similar methods dating back at least a hundred years.

Philon tells us that the Greeks designed stone-throwing ballistae and arrow-throwing catapults using formulas that related every dimension of the finished machine back to a single base unit: the "module." In the case of the Greek ballista called the *palintone*, the module was the diameter of the stone to be thrown. The design formula had been determined from experience and experiment, which had established that, in order to achieve a certain range, the diameter (D) of the torsion springs varies in proportion to the cube root of the mass (M) of the stone missile, i.e., $D = 1.1\sqrt[3]{(100\ M)}$. The design method Philon describes goes on to give the dimensions of more than a dozen key components of the palintone, all based on multiples of the fundamental module, the diameter of the springs, D. In 250 B.C. this calculation would pose a challenge to the designer of a catapult—how to find the cube root of a number—and one of Philon's contributions to mathematical knowledge was to devise a geometric solution to this calculation problem. In fact, much of the time, the answer would no doubt have been obtained from tables that gave the precalculated answers for a selection of common sizes of catapult. The use of this cubic relationship is remarkably mature for its time and was not surpassed in sophistication for more than fifteen hundred years. This type of design procedure was very similar to ones used by building designers from this era, as recorded later by Vitruvius (see below).

Engineering and Building in Roman Times

There was no clear or sudden transition from Greek to Roman engineering. Rome had been a town, or rather a state, growing in importance since the Roman Republic was founded in 509 B.C. Its engineering skills and achievements had developed alongside those of other city-states around the Mediterranean. The classical architecture of Athens had already influenced Rome by the fifth century B.C., when the Temples of Saturn (498 B.C.) and Castor and Pollux (484 B.C.) were constructed, and these buildings, much rebuilt, still had a prominent place in the Roman Forum of A.D. 200 (their ruins survive today). As with all ancient cities, later developments in Rome overlay earlier ones, and were all influenced by practices and events in the places with which they traded. Both the Roman empire and the city of Rome had grown in prosperity during the first century B.C., and there had been a huge campaign of building roads, water supplies, and fortifications throughout the empire. Things took a dramatic turn in 45 B.C. when Julius Caesar (100–44 B.C.) became elected as the first (and last) Dictator Perpetuus; a year later, he was assassinated. In 27 B.C., after a decade and a half of shared and disputed leadership, the Roman Senate conferred on Caesar's great-nephew and adopted son Octavian (63 B.C.–A.D. 14), who was already a consul of the city, the titles Augustus ("the exalted") and Princeps ("leading citzen"). The senate swore an oath of allegiance to him as Imperator and now, with sole control of the Roman army, he became the effective leader of the entire Roman empire. Like other leaders before and since, Augustus established and stamped his authority by means of building—building on an unprecedented scale. Before examining some of these masterpieces, however, this discussion will focus on more everyday aspects of building and engineering.

One of the most important means by which the Romans maintained the high level of engineering technology achieved by the Greeks was through the educational infrastructure that had been developed, notably at the university and engineering school at Alexandria. This remained the foremost learning establishment throughout the entire duration of the Roman Republic and Roman empire. Here engineering was taught based on the books of the great Greek writers and, presumably, many Roman ones whose works and even names are lost to us. Virtually the sole surviving engineering books from this period are those written by Heron of Alexandria (c. A.D. 10–75), who was probably the most prolific technical and scientific writer of his day.[10] Nothing is known of his early life, but it is likely that he trained as an engineer, and he became well known as a lecturer at the university and engineering school at Alexandria. He clearly had considerable ability in the practical as well as the mathematical and scientific aspects of mechanics. His textbooks and lecture notes comprised both original work as well as commentaries on, and reworkings of, the classic themes established before him by Euclid, Archimedes, and others. Among a long list of works attributed to Heron, the following are widely acknowledged to be his:

Mechanica (in three books)

Metrica, devoted to methods of measurement

Zygia, or *On Balancing* (lost), mentioned by the Greek mathematician Pappus of Alexandria (c. A.D. 290–350)

On the Dioptra, which deals with theodolites and surveying

Commentary on Euclid's Elements

Belopoeica, which describes how to construct engines of war and covers ground similar to that in works by Philon and Vitruvius

Camarica, or *On Vaultings* (lost), mentioned by Eutocius of Ascalon

The Pneumatica (in two books), a study of mechanical devices worked by air, steam, or water pressure

The Automaton Theater, describing a puppet theater worked by strings, pulleys, drums, and weights

Water Clocks (in four books)

Catoprica, dealing with light, vision, and mirrors

A lost work on how to use an astrolabe mentioned in the tenth century.

Mechanica, Heron's treatises on mechanics for engineers, mainly follow the ideas of Archimedes, covering the theoretical concepts and principles underlying various machines and giving practical examples of their use. Book 1 examines how to construct three-dimensional shapes in a given proportion to a given shape. It also examines the theory of motion and certain problems in statics, including the theory of the balance. In Book 2 Heron discusses the lifting of heavy objects with a lever, a pulley, a wedge, or a screw. There is a discussion on centers of gravity of plane figures. Book 3 examines various methods of moving and transporting objects by such means as cranes and sleighs, and also looks at wine presses as one application of the screw to obtain mechanical advantage. Of interest to the history of building engineering is a single, tantalizing reference, by the sixth-century mathematician and technical writer Eutocius of Ascalon, to a lost book on vaulting written by Heron. The mathematician Pappus of Alexandria described Heron's approach:

> *The engineers* [mechanikoi] *of Heron's school say that engineering can be divided into a theoretical and a practical part; the theoretical part is composed of geometry, arithmetic, astronomy and physics; the practical part comprises making things from metals, building, carpentry, painting and anything involving skill with the hands.*[11]

Marcus Vitruvius Pollio

Only one book on building design and construction survives from Greek and Roman times: *De Architectura* (*On Architecture*), by Vitruvius (active 46–30 B.C.), published in Rome about 25 B.C. Although written in Roman times, the content of his book belongs culturally to both Greece and Rome. It is clear from the acknowledgments in his text that many authors had written on the same subjects during the previous few centuries, and Vitruvius admits to having drawn heavily on them. Thus, when Vitruvius writes about how to design a temple, it is not clear how old this guidance is. In the present context, this does not really matter. From the evidence of the many buildings that survive from ancient Greece it would seem likely that much of his design guidance could date from three or four centuries earlier—say 400 B.C. This is especially true of his descriptions of the Doric and Ionic methods of designing temples. On some subjects, such as acoustics, Vitruvius imported wholesale into his book Greek ideas and words from many centuries earlier. On other subjects, including materials and the design and construction of weapons, Vitruvius is writing from his own experience, and so his guidance can be assumed to be that current in around 50 B.C.

Vitruvius was an engineer who worked during the first century B.C., first in the service of both Julius Caesar and Augustus. He trained and began his career as a military engineer, building and repairing ballistae and *scorpiones* (catapults). Later in life his engineering and project management skills led to his being appointed to take charge of various civil engineering projects (probably water supply), and he likely played a significant (though unknown) role in the rebuilding of Rome, the city Augustus would later boast that he "found built of brick and left built of marble."[12] We know of only one project with which his name can be linked: the large basilica at Fano, a town in central Italy on the Adriatic Sea.

Vitruvius wrote his book late in life—probably in retirement, if the life of construction engineers and project managers was as hectic then as it is today—and dedicated it to Augustus, who had been his main patron. Remarkably, his book has been known, almost continuously, for more than two thousand years. Many manuscript copies survived into the fifteenth century, and in 1486 the first printed edition was published. All these copies must have

DE ARCHITECTURA BY VITRUVIUS (C. 25 B.C.)

The work is divided into ten books, of which the last, on military engineering, Vitruvius's original profession, is the largest. The contents of each is as follows:

1. THE EDUCATION OF THE ENGINEER AND BUILDING DESIGNER; THE SCOPE OF ENGINEERING; PLANNING OF CITIES
2. MATERIALS FOR CONSTRUCTION OF BUILDINGS
3. THE DESIGN AND CONSTRUCTION OF TEMPLES
4. THE ARCHITECTURE AND STYLES OF TEMPLES
5. THE DESIGN AND CONSTRUCTION OF PUBLIC BUILDINGS
6. THE DESIGN AND CONSTRUCTION OF PRIVATE HOUSES
7. MATERIALS FOR THE FINISHING OF BUILDINGS
8. FINDING AND PROVIDING WATER FOR CITIES
9. ASTRONOMY, SUNDIALS, AND WATER CLOCKS
10. MECHANICAL ENGINEERING–MACHINES FOR LIFTING WEIGHTS AND RAISING WATER; WATERWHEELS AND MILLS; WEAPONS, INCLUDING CATAPULTS AND BALLISTAE, AND SIEGE MACHINES.

He alternates throughout between design and construction—how to determine the sizes, relative disposition, and orientation of components, and how to select and use suitable materials. He stresses particularly the importance of economy—the proper management of materials and the construction site, as well as using common sense to reduce costs, for instance, by avoiding materials that are not available locally, and those that are difficult to work with and use. He also counsels care in matching the cost of the work to the size of the client's purse, and the need to provide the client with a building fit for the purpose intended.

Vitruvius distinguishes three branches of engineering (architectura): building engineering, the making of timepieces, and the fabrication of machines, both construction plant and large weapons of warfare. He sees these three arts united in their reliance upon three skills: working with materials to make things, being able to measure and survey, and being able to calculate using geometry and arithmetic.

BUILDING ENGINEERING

FORTIFIED TOWNS AND PUBLIC WORKS

DEFENSE: Town walls, towers, gates, and permanent devices for resisting hostile attack

RELIGIOUS USE: Temples and other momuments to immortal gods

UTILITARIAN PURPOSES: Harbors, public meeting places such as markets, theaters, baths, colonnades, promenades

WORK FOR PRIVATE INDIVIDUALS (HOUSES)

TIMEPIECES

SUNDIALS AND WATER CLOCKS

MECHANICAL ENGINEERING

CONSTRUCTION PLANTS AND EQUIPMENT

CRANES, HOISTS, HODOMETER

WEAPONS

BALLISTAE, SCORPIONES, TORTOISES

remained a mystery for readers in northern Europe, however, for they contained no illustrations of the buildings Vitruvius described.

Translations of Vitruvius first became available in French in 1673 and in English in 1692; as might be expected, these and subsequent renditions tend to reflect the background and attitudes of the translator as well as those of Vitruvius. This is perhaps most noticeable in the use of the words "architect" and "architecture" to describe Vitruvius and the content of his book. A Greek architekton was literally a controller and organizer of the workforce—perhaps a project manager in today's language. The Greek word *architektura* embraced what today would be called both engineering and architecture, and Vitruvius used the word *architecti* as a transliteration from Greek, since there was no suitable Latin word. The difficulties Vitruvius had in translating Greek ideas into Latin have been compounded by translators of Vitruvius's Latin text into modern European languages; many misunderstandings about construction technology have been introduced by translators ignorant of the subject. The following translation of Vitruvius's opening lines of Book I, Chapter I perhaps respects his own attitudes as an engineer rather better than most modern versions:

> *Architektura [engineering and architecture] is a body of knowledge comprising many disciplines and sciences which can also be applied in other arts. Finished works are born of skill in manufacture and design. Manufacturing skill comes from the constant study of craftsmanship and the working of materials to create whatever the desired result. Designing is the ability to convey the scheme for the finished object to others and to provide a rational explanation for the scheme using engineering knowledge and scientific principles.*[13]

The original Latin lines are as follows:

> *Architecti est scientia pluribus disciplinis et variis eruditionibus ornata quae ab ceteris artibus perficiuntur. Opera ea nascitur ex fabrica et ratiocinatione. Fabrica est continuata ac trita usus meditatio, quae manibus perficitur e materia cuiuscumque generis opus est ad propositum deformationis. Ratiocinatio autem est, quae res fabricatas sollertiae ac rationis proportione demonstrare atque explicare potest.*[14]

Vitruvius on Greek Design Procedures

From Vitruvius's detailed description of the design procedures for Doric and Ionic temples we learn three things about the planning and construction of buildings in ancient Greece: first, that the Greeks had developed sequential processes for designing buildings; second, that such undertakings relied upon drawing and geometry; and third, that these methods somehow embodied the means for giving the designer confidence that a resulting building would stand and would work in other ways as intended.

Doric and Ionic designs for temples were both established around 600 B.C.—Doric on the Greek mainland and in southern Italy and Sicily; Ionic in Asia Minor and the Mediterranean islands. They differed not only in appearance but also in the way they were constructed.

The Doric designs, as repeated by Vitruvius from Greek 14
sources, were elegantly simple in conception. They required the selection of a single, fundamental module, equal to one-half the diameter of a column, "and this module once fixed, all the parts of the work are adjusted by means of calculations based upon it."[15] As in other sections of *De Architectura*, where he describes ancient Greek practices, Vitruvius uses the Greek word *embates* for module, as there was no current Latin word. Thus, according to the particular set and sequence of calculations used, a design procedure for the various dimensions of an entire building could be established, allowing the architect a certain freedom to select particular multiples and ratios to suit the structure's purposes. This is precisely the same method that 15
had been developed by the designers of catapults and ballistae, and, given that military technology has always been in advance of nonmilitary technology, we can assume that the use of the module was developed first for building weapons.

Ionic designs were more complex and sophisticated than Doric ones. They did not relate every building element to a single module, but rather formed a sequence of derivations, so that the dimensions of each element were figured successively from a preceding one, usually that which came immediately before it. The ratios between successive parts were also more complex than in the Doric style, and the ratios between widely separated parts were very hard to calculate. This design plan allowed much more scope for experimentation and variation.

Following a design procedure of the type Vitruvius gives for Doric and Ionic temples involved both simple arithmetic calculations and geometrical constructions done with ruler and compass. This made it possible to generate, before construction began, the dimensions of the entire building and its components, which could then be communicated to the workforce. When we look at things this way, we can see that a design procedure and a sketch of a building are much more than a set of instructions to construction workers. In today's language they are a mathematical model of the building—an abstract representation of the structure that allows one to experiment, to try out ideas without actually executing them. Such tools allow one to predict the consequences of design decisions and to explore the possible occurrence of problems further along in the design process, and so avoid them. This was the true legacy of Greek engineers as developed from the sixth century B.C. The codifiction of design procedures also served as a convenient means of storing the knowledge gained from past projects, enabling others to access this information and disseminate it throughout the land. A design procedure could travel in the head of just one person. Indeed, it was the possibility of many different people being able to design similar buildings that led to the very idea of a more or less uniform style; otherwise, structures that might appear in neighborhoods or provinces were likely to reflect local aesthetic preferences and differing levels of skill in design and construction.

A successful, established design procedure would clearly engender confidence in its users. There was, however, something more fundamental at work. In ancient Greece, geometry was far more than simply a branch of mathematics, as we might now describe it. In the way we now use physics, chemistry, and other sciences, Greek geometricians effectively invented the ideas of proof and logic. Using merely geometry and simple arithmetic rules, they elucidated the fundamental laws that explained how the world worked. The Greek study of harmonics had identified the many and complex ratios between lengths of strings that create musical notes, in harmony or in dissonance. Such ratios, too, could surely find a rational place in building design. Mechanics, as well, was already well developed in explaining, for instance, levers and pulleys, and this lent further weight and confidence to the geometric and arithmetic methods used in design procedures. It is impossible to say precisely how such attempts at explaining the world using harmonics, geometry, and mechanics helped building designers; we have no written records and few well-preserved buildings to offer any definitive proof. The main point is that geometry and mechanics were not only abstract sciences, but practical arts. By using geometry and mechanics one could achieve reliable and, most importantly, predictable results.

But what, the twenty-first-century mind might ask, does this have to do with engineering? Surely these Greek design procedures are purely geometric or "architectural." Where is the analysis of loads and deflections and stresses that structural engineers now undertake? In one sense, the question is merely anachronistic; the modern mathematical concepts of load and stress simply did not yet exist. In another sense, the question seeks evidence about how the Greeks took account of the strengths of the materials they used and how they related these to the sizes of various building elements. The answer has to be that the early design rules and procedures, such as those passed on to us by Vitruvius, embodied all the many influences on the final form of a building element—its visual appearance, structural duty, material properties, method of construction, and so on. The design procedures that appear to us to be "merely" geometric were also founded upon much practical knowledge that all experienced engineers knew: the largest size of stone component that could be lifted by different means, the distance that could be spanned by a beam made from different types of stone, the area of roof that a timber rafter could support. It is a mistake to presume that the lack of modern engineering science means Greek engineers were ignorant of how structures worked. Rather, the means had not yet developed for storing such knowledge in written or diagrammatic form, and thus conveying it from one person to another. More than 1,500 years would pass before these means were developed.

Vitruvius on Environmental Design

Vitruvius recommends orienting a house to obtain the greatest benefit from solar heating, and adds further advice on how different room layouts, house styles, and

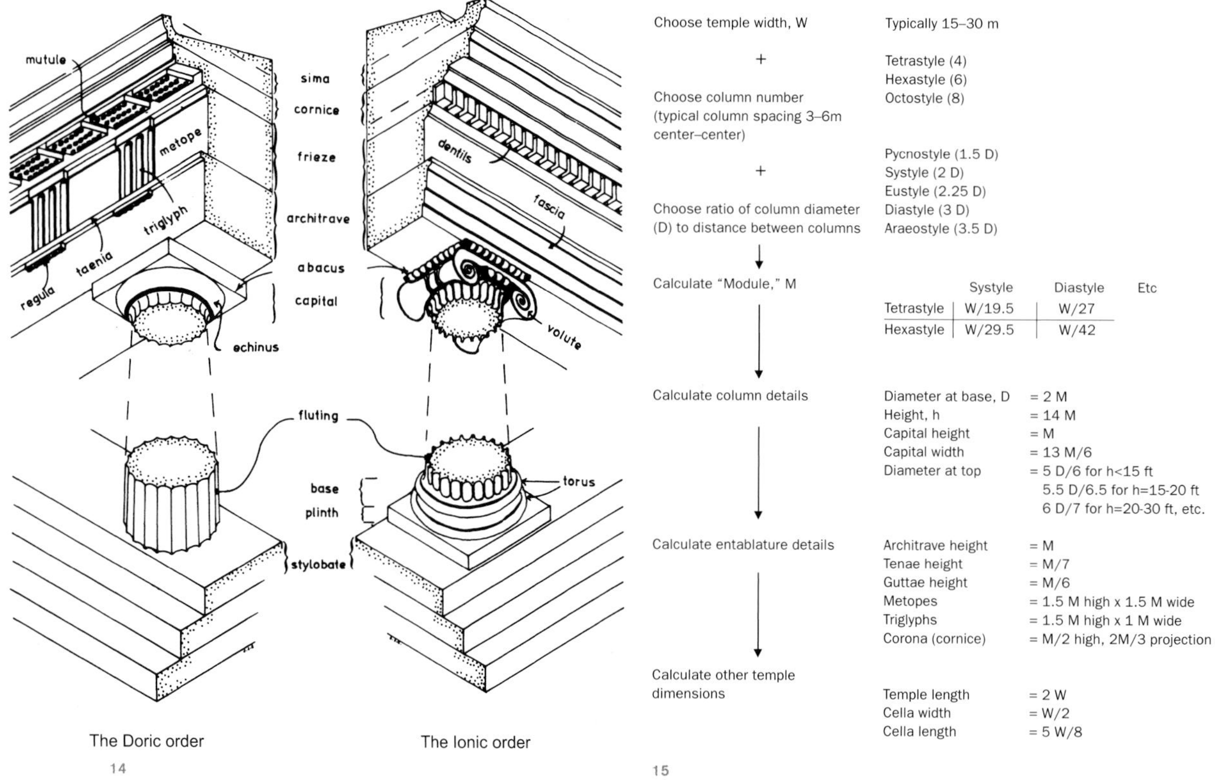

design details are best suited to various locations in the Roman empire, depending on temperature, rainfall, humidity, prevailing winds, and latitude. He also advises, in his usual rational way, on the locations of towns in relation to the sea, rivers, marshes that emit unhealthy vapors, and so on. Temples should preferably face toward the west so that those approaching the altar with offerings or sacrifices are facing the sunrise. If this is not possible, the orientation should ensure that the god housed in the temple's sanctuary has the widest possible view of the city, and vice versa. Temples alongside rivers or roads should face them to enable passersby to view the gods in their sanctuaries and pay their devotions face to face.

Vitruvius devotes a whole chapter to the orientation of streets in relation to the winds—four of them, according to some, but eight according to "more careful investigators"[16]—and gives careful instructions on how to find the directions of these winds precisely, using the shadow of a gnomon (as in a sundial). In one town on the island of Lesbos, for example, people apparently fell ill when the wind was from the south, were set coughing when it came from the northwest, and, although they recovered when it came from the north, were unable to stand around in the streets because of the severe cold. A more general piece of advice was that most winds could bring disease, and so houses should be sealed as well as possible to keep them out.

14 Elements of the Doric and Ionic orders. 15 Flowchart showing design procedure for a temple in the Doric style, c. 600–400 B.C., based on a description by Vitruvius, c. 25 B.C.

No less important to public health was a supply of potable water; Vitruvius devotes one whole book of his ten to this matter. He deems rainwater to be preferable to groundwater because, he says, it has been produced by heat—the evaporation of water to form clouds. Many houses used their roofs to harvest rainwater and store it for domestic use. Vitruvius talks of the varying purity of ground water, river water, and springs, advising that, generally, the clearer and less aromatic the water, the more wholesome it is; boiling water improves its quality. He also discusses the various salts that spring water may contain, many of them curative. Some springs, however, had to be used with care. In one ancient spring, the water was excellent for bathing but, if drunk, would cause one's teeth to fall out the same day. On the delicate subject of toilets and the destiny of foul water, Vitruvius is silent—uncharacteristically, especially as he probably worked for some time as a water engineer in Rome.

Vitruvius on Acoustics and Theater Design

If the Greek approach to public health was still rather primitive, the same cannot be said of their skill with acoustics, especially in theaters. As with other building types, Vitruvius advises on their location—away from winds from "marshy districts and other unwholesome quarters,"[17] wise counsel for an open-air theater—and their orientation. He also addresses key geometric issues such as plan, section, sight lines, numbers and locations of entrances and exits, and their general construction. Good air circulation is needed to prevent the audience from becoming uncomfortable.

Finally, and most extensively, Vitruvius also goes into great and highly theoretical detail on the subject of acoustics. This was not his own work. He was largely repeating what he must have found in various Greek treatises on acoustics, which in turn probably date back to Pythagoras, who first developed the subject around 530 B.C. Vitruvius deals with acoustics from several points of view. He introduces harmonics—"an obscure and difficult branch of musical science, especially for those who do not know Greek"[18]—and acknowledges the writings of the fourth-century B.C. philospher and musical theorist Aristoxenus. Harmonics explains the pitch of notes and the intervals between them in the Greek musical scale, as well as why some combinations of notes are concordant and others discordant.

Concerning the choice of location for a new theater, Vitruvius tells his reader that the acoustics of the site should be taken into account. The site must not have an echo, or give rise to strong sound reflections that would interfere with the sound reaching the listener directly and thus impair intelligibility. Vitruvius then discusses sound in the auditorium—in particular, the need for sound of different frequencies to travel from the stage to the ears of every member of the audience by a direct route, in the manner of waves created by a pebble thrown into water. This logically leads to both raked seating and a semicircular plan. He advises against vertical reflective surfaces that will prevent sound from reaching the upper tiers of seats, since this particularly impairs the intelligibility of word endings, which, in Greek and Latin, are vital to comprehension. Such reflected waves, he says, can also interfere with the direct waves and distort sounds for the listener. These explanations differ remarkably little from basic acoustical principles today.

Vitruvius also discusses the use of sounding vessels, (now known as Helmholtz resonators, after the nineteenth-century German physicist who explained how they function), which reinforce certain frequencies of the human voice and can increase intelligibility. These open-ended vessels were made of bronze and tuned to six notes of the chromatic scale. Two sets of six were arranged beneath a tier of seats symmetrically on either side of the center line of the theater. For a particularly large theater, two additional sets of vessels would be installed in higher rows, each a few semitones lower in pitch—a total of thirty-six different notes. Vitruvius admits that he knows of no theaters built in Rome with sounding vessels. This is because "the many theaters that are constructed in Rome every year contain a good deal of wood, which does not lead to the same problems with reflections as stone."[19] Also, he says, the timber panels themselves can resonate in a manner similar to the air in a sounding vessel, and so improve intelligibility. As to the effectiveness of sounding vessels, they have not been demonstrated to improve intelligibility, and that is probably why they were not used in Rome. Whether the Roman theaters were as good as the Greek 16
ones, we do not know, but there is no doubt that both were designed with a great understanding of acoustics and expertise in using this knowledge to achieve demonstrably better results.

One final recommendation from Vitruvius on acoustics was for a senate house. The height of a senate house should be half the width of the building, he says, and *coronae*, or cornices, made of woodwork or stucco, should be fixed halfway up the inside faces of the walls around the entire room. Without these, he says, the voices of men engaged in discourse would be lost in the high roof. Coronae enable the sound of the voices to be "detained before rising," and so more intelligible to the ear.[20]

The Legacy of Roman Engineering

Perhaps the most remarkable thing about building engineering and construction methods used in Greek and early Roman times is that they were much the same as those used for the next two thousand years. This is not to denigrate later generations; rather, it is to acknowledge the remarkable progress that had already been made by about 100 B.C. There are many amazing things about construction technology in these times, but among the most astonishing to us today are these:

- *precision in measuring and surveying skills*
- *manufacture of artificial construction materials (brick, concrete, and iron) in enormous quantities*
- *discovery of hydraulic cement (see Appendix D)*
- *use of the arch and barrel vault*
- *use of timber framing for bridges and centering for arches, vaults, and domes*
- *use of design procedures and plans, elevations, and perspective drawings as a normal part of the building designer's work*
- *ability to manipulate stones of huge size and weight, and lift them to great heights*
- *skill in managing the logistics needed to marshal vast supplies of materials*
- *training and organizing large numbers of workers.*

Roman engineers had learned and developed these skills mainly in the construction of roads and bridges for both military and commercial purposes, building fortifications, and devising means to supply water to serve the needs of the growing cities. Their achievements in these fields were accelerated and made cheaper through the exploitation of two particular technical developments: the arch, and the use of concrete. The Romans invented neither of these technologies—both go back to the beginning of civilization—but they certainly exploited them more effectively than anyone else.

The arch and its extrusion, the barrel vault, allowed relatively small and manageable stones or bricks to make structures of large span—both for bridges and aqueducts and, later, for roofs and as universal substructures in buildings. This was in great contrast to the huge stones needed to make a Greek temple. The savings in time and cost must have been huge. Because they work in compression, arches can be made of stone of nearly any quality, unlike the beams in trabeated construction, which had to be of the very highest quality. Stones suitable for arches could be found nearly anywhere rather than transported from particular quarries; they could be carried easily on small carts, and, where no stones were available, clay bricks could be substituted. For use in buildings, where a high-quality surface finish would often be required, stones or bricks of poor or variable quality would be covered with stucco or plaster and painted. The Romans also discovered the economic benefits of using mortar in their masonry construction; it meant that only the exposed or visible surface of a stone or brick structure needed be finished to a high specification. The other faces could be roughly finished, since any unevenness would be filled by the mortar. Taking this idea to its extreme, the Romans developed the technique of placing bricks or stone on the inner face of the timber formwork and filling the void with concrete. When the formwork was removed the effect was a concrete wall faced with brick or stone. Different arrangements and patterns of the brick were given different names. *Opus reticulatum*, for example, was made using bricks or stones in the form of a square-based pyramid, and laid to form a diamond pattern on the exposed face of the wall. When low-quality brick or stone was used, the surface could be made to look nearly perfect by rendering with a coat of stucco or plaster.

Brick arches and vaults reduced construction times and costs substantially, compared to traditional masonry construction. The widespread use of concrete probably led to an even greater reduction. (For details of concrete and its manufacture, see Appendix 3.) The raw materials were widely available throughout the empire and could be transported loose or in containers of any size; water would be available at or near the construction site. Quick lime, used to make the lime mortar, had to be conveyed from the local lime kiln, but the fine, sandy aggregate was widely available, and coarse aggregate could be found in

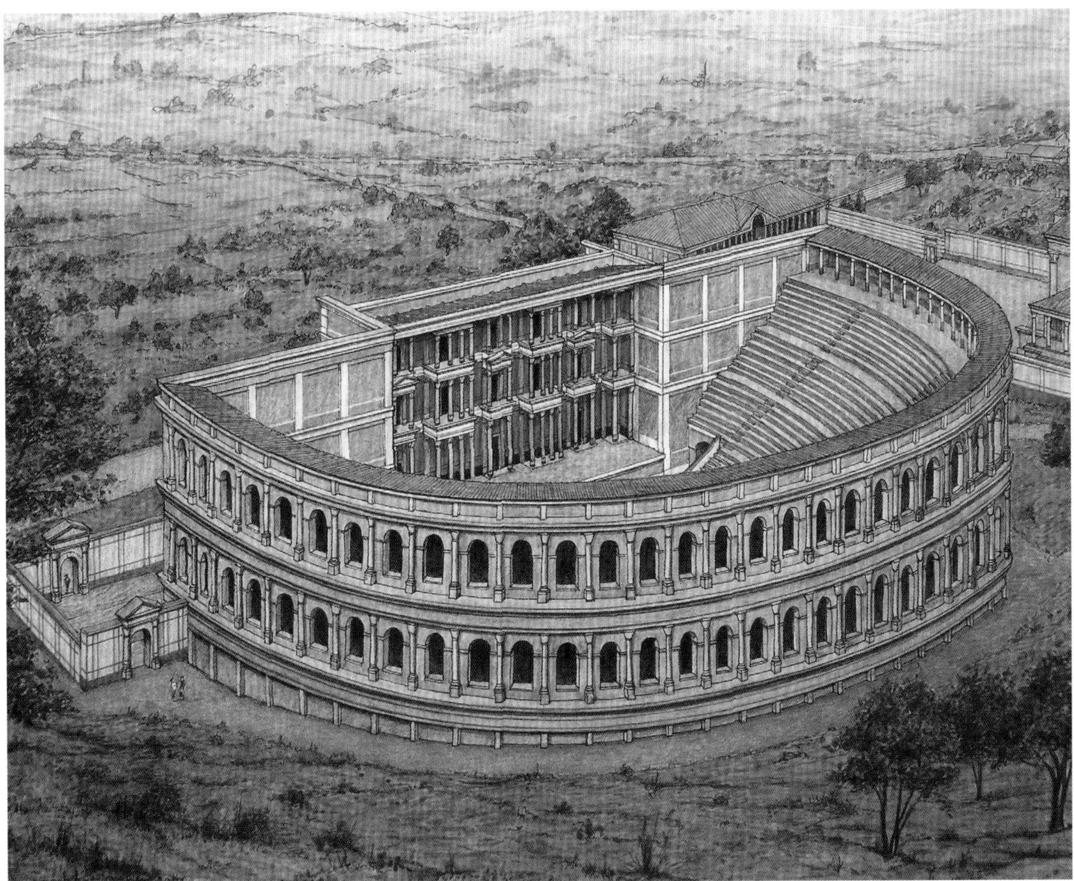

16

16 Roman theater, Triers, Germany, c. A.D. 200. Reconstruction drawing. 17 (Overleaf) Roman aqueducts as painted by Zeno Diemer, 1914. Aqua Marcia (shown under repair at right) was completed c. 145 B.C.; Aquae Tepula and Julia were added in 127 B.C. and 33 B.C. Aqua Anio Novus, built on top of Aqua Claudia (at left), was completed in A.D. 52.

local quarries or made by crushing larger rocks and stones of any quality. Concrete could be formed into any shape possible using timber formwork, and was ideally suited to being made and placed by large numbers of relatively unskilled workers or troops. The timber formwork was often probably the scarcest resource, though with care, it could be used many times.

Famously, of course, the Romans are credited with discovering and exploiting hydraulic cement, which completes the chemical process of curing in the presence of excess water—in other words, it will harden under water. Though found in many places around the foot of Mount Vesuvius, it was the town of Puteoli (modern Pozzuoli) that gave its name to the crucial ingredient, pulvis Puteolanus (modern pozzolana). In fact, the Romans were not the first to have discovered that adding certain minerals to lime mortar would create this property. Among other materials that produce the same effect is what Vitruvius refers to as *carbuncular* stone, produced when certain stones were heated in fires. Whatever its origins, however, hydraulic cement revolutionized the use of concrete from about 150 B.C. in making such structures as waterproof aqueducts, marine harbors, and concrete foundations in wet ground.

The first masonry arch bridge in Rome, the Pons Aemilius, was built between 179–142 B.C.; two more were constructed around 62 and 46 B.C. However, the most impressive structures were erected to supply water
17 to Rome: aqueducts. One of these, forming part of the Aqua Claudia, completed under Claudius (ruled A.D. 41–54), carried water to the city on an arched structure some 13 kilometers long, and much of it is still standing. The Roman aqueduct in Segovia in Spain, completed c. A.D. 109, remained in use into the twentieth century.

Roman timber engineering represented a marked improvement over the use of timber in ancient Greece. We do not know when the use of timber in structural frames with mortised joints was developed. Such construction must have been employed in making siege towers and temporary structures—for instance, to provide support and access when large ships were being built. The most direct evidence we have for timber frame construction are the many masonry arches that were being built from the second century B.C. Every arch and vault the Romans erected would have required a substantial timber structure to support the considerable weight of the stones, brick, or concrete until the span was complete. Details of these structures must remain a matter of speculation, since they were temporary. Some of these must have spanned more than 20 meters. We do know that the timber bridge erected over the River Danube by the engineer Apollodorus for the emperor Trajan (ruled A.D. 98–117)
had twenty-one spans each of between 35 and 40 me- 18
ters. From this evidence alone it is reasonable to assume that, by the second century A.D., Roman engineers had carpentry skills that could at least match those of the medieval cathedral builders. A timber roof truss spanning 20 19
meters would thus have been within their capability, although no direct evidence of one has survived.

By this time both iron and bronze were also abundant, though their use in buildings was limited. Iron was used for cramps to locate stones in masonry structures and sometimes embedded in concrete, though not as reinforcement in the sense we mean today. Bronze was sometimes used for more than decorative purposes. Three bronze columns about 7 meters tall, and the capital of a fourth column, have survived from Roman times
in the Basilica di San Giovanni in Laterano in Rome. The 20
church dates from the early fourth century but was much altered in the Middle Ages and Renaissance. Legend has it that the bronze was taken from the prows of ships captured from Mark Antony (c. 82–30 B.C.) in Egypt.

Vitruvius was active as an engineer in the few decades before Augustus transformed Rome through his patronage of the construction industry. By way of introducing this remarkable era, it is thus fitting to look at the one building we know for certain was designed and built by
Vitruvius, the new basilica at Fano in eastern Italy just 21, 23
south of Rimini. Though now lost, it represented the culmination of 500 or 600 years of continuous development of building and engineering techniques throughout Italy, Greece, and farther afield, and was typical of many civic buildings of pre-imperial Italy. It consisted of a courtyard formed on three sides by two-story buildings, with a larger, full-height assembly room and colonnade forming the fourth side. The courtyard was covered by a pitched roof spanning some 18.5 meters in width and 37 meters in length. The tiled roof was supported by timber beams about 600 millimeters square,

18

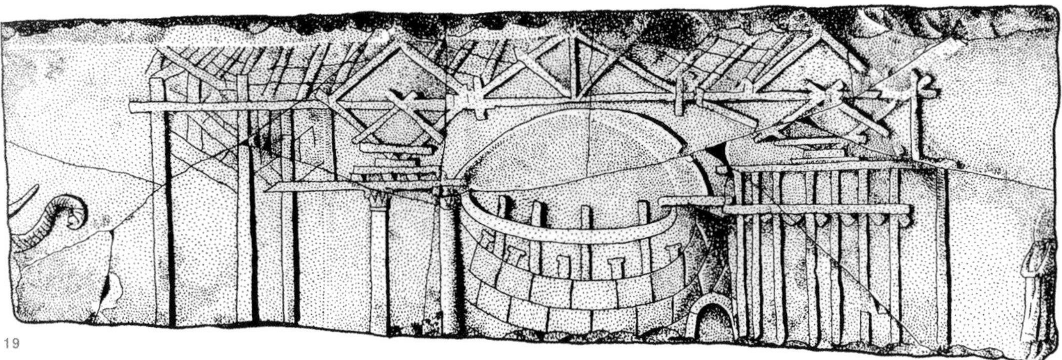

19

18 Trajan's bridge across the Danube, modern Romania, c. A.D. 100. Designer: Apollodorus of Damascus. Shown on relief from Trajan's Column, Rome, A.D. 113. 19 Relief showing timber roof structure and temporary works in Rome.

supported, in turn, on stone columns 1.5 meters in diameter and 15 meters tall.

While unremarkable in the history of building, it is just this that makes Vitruvius's basilica noteworthy. Here is an ordinary structure carried out in a small town on the Adriatic coast that nevertheless required considerable construction skills: the largest timbers were about 20 meters long and would have weighed 4 or 5 tons, and the drums making up the main columns must have weighed nearly 20 tons each. Lifting and maneuvering such heavy objects into position without power from steam or electricity was no mean feat, and would be a great challenge for engineers even today, yet such skills were clearly
22 widespread in the early Roman empire. This building and countless others like it are testimony to the Romans' ability to marshal rather modest techniques to produce structures of great variety and quality, and with a healthy concern for the prudent use of resources, too. In a manner not unfamiliar to us today in the guise of "value engineering," Vitruvius observed that he managed, at Fano, to avoid various awkward construction tasks by omitting an ornamental entablature as well as a second tier of columns and a line of screens, and hence was able to reduce the overall cost of the building.

While Vitruvius's basilica does not survive, there are plenty of contemporary remains that confirm Roman towns of this period to be remarkably sophisticated—notably the port of Ostia, near Rome, and the towns of Herculaneum and Pompeii, which were mummified in A.D.
25 79 following the eruption of Mount Vesuvius. A Roman provincial town was a fine and proud place. Many roads were paved, and there was a civic water supply and some drainage. As well as a variety of private housing, there might have been a dozen or more prominent public buildings, including many temples, a basilica, the forum, a public market, several baths and theaters, and an amphitheater, all enclosed by a town wall.

Roman Apartment Buildings: *Insulae*

In the larger cities of Italy the Romans erected apartment buildings called *insulae* (islands). These buildings typically occupied an entire block between parallel
24, 26 streets, had retail outlets at ground level, and facades, often with balconies, that overlooked the street, much as we do today. Typically they might be about 50 by 30 meters, though much larger and smaller examples are known. The ground plan of each story was very similar, and the building was covered by a single roof. They were usually four or five stories high, though some must have been higher, for Augustus imposed a height limit of 70 Roman feet—seven or maybe eight stories. Such buildings date back to at least the third century B.C.—we have written evidence from that time of a cow that found its way up to the third story of a Roman insula. Also, they were not only built in Italy; when the Romans sacked Carthage in 146 B.C., they found six-story buildings there. A group of apartments, or *cenaculae*, were accessed from a common stair that opened onto the street. Insulae often had a supply of water for drinking, washing, and flushing the latrines that were connected to the sewer system. This water was available only at ground-floor level because the lead pipes that distributed the water from the aqueducts were unable to sustain the high water pressure that would be needed to pipe the water to upper floors. Since the first century B.C. insulae usually had kitchens, though cooked food was readily available at the many restaurants and *tabernae*, the Roman equivalent of fast-food outlets. By the first century A.D., many new insulae—for instance several at Pompeii and Herculaneum and one at Ostia, the Mediterranean port that served Rome—had latrines on the first floor connected directly to the sewer.

The insulae effectively turned the private house inside out. Unlike the classic Vitruvian house, or domus, which looked inward onto a central atrium, the facade of an insula was open and public, and the inhabitants looked out on the city. Within some insulae a courtyard provided light to the windows of rooms away from the street facade. The most sought-after apartments were on the ground and first floors, not only because they provided a view over the street, but because they were easiest to escape from in the event of a fire.

However, the new street-facing facades brought their problems, most noticeably noise, even though, by the second century, glazed windows had largely replaced windows with only curtains or shutters. In Book 12 of his collection of epigrams the satirist Martial (c. A.D. 40–c. 104) tells his readers it is the noise of the city that so regularly drives him to stay in his rather squalid villa in the countryside. In his third-floor apartment in an insula

20

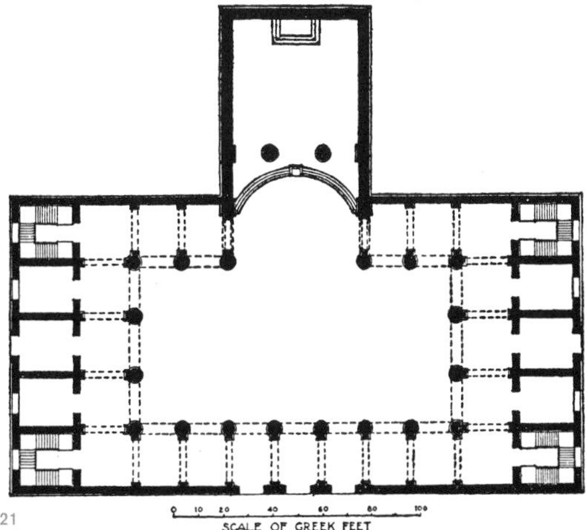

21

22

23

20 Basilica di San Giovanni in Laterano, Rome, originally dedicated in 324 on the site of a Roman palace. Redesigned by Francesco Borromini, 1646–50. Three of the bronze columns date from c. A.D. 100. 21 Basilica, Fano, Italy, c. 30 B.C. Floor plan. 22 Relief on the sarcophagus of the Haterii family tomb, Rome, c. A.D. 100, showing Roman crane powered by five men in the treadwheel. 23 Basilica at Fano. Architect and engineer: Vitruvius. Interior.

24

25

26

24 Casa di Diana, a typical Roman apartment block, or *insula*, Ostia, Italy, first century B.C. Reconstruction model.
25 Roman timber-frame construction, Pompeii, Italy, first century A.D. 26 Wall-painting showing builders at work, from the tomb of Trebius Justus, Rome, early fourth century A.D.

on the Quirinal hill in Rome there was constant disturbance. Before dawn he was awakened by the noise of the bakers, and morning brought the noise of the schoolteachers. All day there was the constant hammering of the coppersmiths and the gold beaters, and the jingling coins of the moneychangers. There were the cries of beggars and shopkeepers, the singing and dancing of worshippers involved in religious rites. Evening brought the noise of clashing cooking pots and drunken sailors. On top of this there was the rumble of cartwheels, the shouts of carters, and the screeching of ungreased axles, not only during the day but throughout the night. So great had been the traffic congestion in the narrow streets of Rome a century earlier that Julius Caesar had decreed that most wheeled vehicles could be moved only at night.

Fire was a constant threat to buildings, despite the fact that walls were made with incombustible materials—mud brick in low-rise buildings and fired brick and concrete for taller buildings. Many small buildings had a timber frame infilled with masonry and timber floor beams and floor boards, and most buildings had timber roof structures supporting the roof tiles. The situation was aggravated by the persistent use of wattle and daub for walls and partitions—a type of construction that Vitruvius wished had never been invented—and, of course, Rome's narrow streets. Vitruvius recommended the use of larch, especially for the boarding used to make the eaves of insulae, to prevent fire from spreading to adjacent buildings, for this wood, he claimed, did not catch fire from flames or from burning coals. After the conflagration that engulfed the greater part of Rome in A.D. 64 , the emperor Nero (A.D. 37–68) required that streets be widened, that the height of insulae be limited to 60 feet or six stories to ensure easier escape from fires, and that commercial premises operating fires, such as bakers and metalworkers, be separated from adjacent residential buildings by double walls and an air gap. He required that fireproof construction be employed and that balconies be constructed to allow easier escape from fires. He also invested in improvements to the city water supply so that water was more easily available to extinguish fires.

The insulae were usually privately owned. A developer would secure permission to build, and then construction probably proceeded to complete the first premises as soon as possible to generate income and begin to repay the loan that would have been necessary to finance the project. As with all construction driven by commercial pressures, the desire to build quickly led to inferior quality and jerry-building. Although many insulae were constructed of good-quality concrete and fired brick, this was not always so. While buildings of more than two stories had to be made with fired brick or concrete with brick facing, it was a common practice among contractors to use large amounts of rubble within walls and correspondingly less concrete. While these walls were prone to cracking, collapses were not common. It was probably in the construction of these private-sector insulae that the commercial benefits of concrete were most successfully realized—concrete walls with a thin facing of brick could be built much more rapidly than with ashlar or high-quality fired bricks.

At least one property developer devised an ingenious, if not ruthless, way of making his fortune by exploiting the vulnerability of many buildings to fire at a time when Rome had no organized firefighters. The general and politician Marcus Licinius Crassus (c. 115–53 B.C.) owned a group of trained firefighter slaves. When a building caught fire he would rush to the place and try to buy it from the desperate owner, often negotiating a good price in the panic. As soon as the owner had sold him the building his firefighters would get to work. Usually the building could be saved, and, after some repair and renovation, Crassus was able to rent it out or sell it at a profit. This technique proved very successful, for he became the richest man and most powerful landowner of his time. Despite the these various dangers, by A.D. 300, the majority of the Roman population lived in insulae—there were more than 45,000 of them, while there were fewer than 2,000 single-family houses.

Roman Heating and Environmental Design

Roman building engineers and contractors were well able to deal with most of the issues we now describe as "building comfort"—the engineering of the internal environment. Both ordinary and larger buildings made intelligent use of daylight and shade and were appropriately ventilated. Rainwater was usually collected from the roofs, which sloped inward to the central open atrium, where the fire for cooking was located; it was the blackening of the walls and roof from this fire that originally gave the atrium its name, from *ater*, the Latin word for black.

By Vitruvius's time it was already common for larger houses to have central heating where winters were harsh, both in Italy and beyond as the Romans moved north in their colonization of Europe. The Roman
27 hypocaust heated buildings by means of hot air fed into a plenum beneath the stone floors at ground-floor level and then carried upward through many clay ducts embedded in the ground-floor walls to warm them. In some two-story buildings the warm air was conveyed further upward through ducts in the first-floor rooms and vented to atmosphere at roof level, in order to generate the necessary pressure difference to drive the air through the ducts. The hypocaust is said to have been invented and widely marketed from around 80 B.C. by the entrepreneur Sergius Orata, who used the system to warm the water of fish-rearing ponds. He was reputed to have made his fortune installing the furnace-driven heating system in public baths and private palaces. Although the use of hypocausts for public baths (*thermae*) spread quickly, it was only from the third century A.D. that they were installed in the houses of the well-off, especially in the northern, colder parts of the empire.

However, the hypocaust needed fuel, and the only fuel in Italy was wood. A large hypocaust might need 120 kilograms of wood per hour—about a ton per day. The Roman historian Livy (59 B.C.–A.D. 17) commented around 350 B.C. that the hills near Rome were as thickly forested as Germany. By Vitruvius's time, much of Italy had lost its woods and, although there was some coppicing of trees for fuel, timber for all purposes was being imported from hundreds of miles away. Around the same time the geographer Strabo (c. 63 B.C.–c. A.D. 21) reported that the inhabitants of the island of Elba had to shut their iron mines for lack of fuel, and the naturalist Pliny the Elder attributed the decline of the metal industries in Campania in southern Italy to the same cause.

The shortage and expense of fuel forced the Romans, just as it is forcing us today, to seek more effective ways of using the sun's energy. Vitruvius advocates the Greek practice of shutting in the north sides of houses and opening the south sides to the warm sun. He advises those building houses in more temperate climates to locate their dining rooms to face the setting sun to get its benefits during the evening meal. From the first century A.D., Roman builders began putting glass or thin sheets of mica or selenite in the windows of the more expensive houses; the statesman and philosopher Seneca (3 B.C.–A.D. 65) mentions in a letter written toward the end of his life that translucent windows had been invented within his own lifetime. Not only did the translucent panes let light in, they also trapped the sun's heat, since the panes allowed high-frequency light radiation to enter but prevented the low-frequency thermal radiation from escaping by the window—the very same principles used today. Pliny the Younger (c. 61–113) refers to one of his favorite rooms as a *heliocaminus*—a sun oven. The baths at Hadrian's villa at Tivoli (built 120–125) had one such room, and there was another, including under-floor heating, at the public baths built around 150 in Ostia. All of these would have had windows glazed with either glass or mica. Roman gardeners at this time were using the same idea when they covered their exotic plants with glazed cold frames in winter, and wealthy Romans grew exotic plants in small greenhouses; the satirist Martial complained that his rooms were so cold that he would be better off being treated as well as his patron's plants.

The "*Grands Projets*" of Imperial Rome

The formation of the Roman empire in 27 B.C. marked the beginning of the most extraordinary period of Roman engineering and building construction. Its success was born out of the very political system itself: absolute authority combined with the need to disguise and somehow justify itself as the consequence of popular feelings. Rome's many generations of dictators and political leaders, but especially the emperors from Augustus on, felt almost obliged to invest huge amounts of money in public works—government buildings, temples, city infrastructure, places of leisure and entertainment, and, not least, monuments celebrating the empire's greatness. For neither the first nor the last time in history, the construction industry was crucial to the fulfillment of politicians' dreams. The boom in construction was, to a large extent, a direct consequence of the *Pax Romana*, the name given to the two centuries of relative peace in Europe, beginning when Augustus came to power. The construction of civic buildings and city infrastructure was the best way of maintaining the skills of military

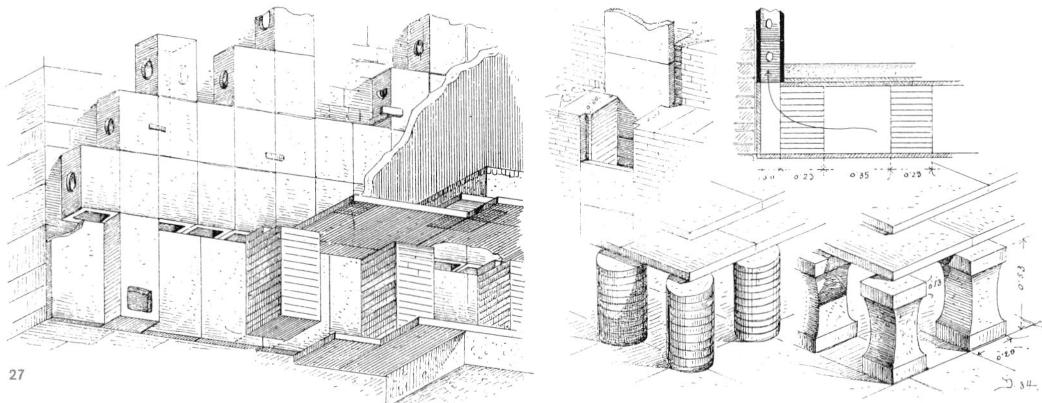

engineers while they were not required for the construction of fortifications and siege weapons.

The Roman emperors' aspirations could be realized only because of the extraordinary development of engineering skills that had occurred during the previous few centuries. Within just two or three hundred years the Greeks had learned to design and construct huge buildings such as the Parthenon. By 50 B.C. the Romans were constructing large buildings as a matter of course in their growing empire. The next 250 years saw what must be the most remarkable period of construction and building engineering in history—even more remarkable than in the twentieth century, perhaps, since it was achieved without the help of science that makes it so much easier to model our buildings and predict their behavior, and without electric motors and diesel or gasoline engines that allow us to move and raise materials with such ease. By the first century A.D. the construction boom had grown to include the full range of public and private buildings and most of the civil engineering infrastructure we know today. The scale of these buildings and other works was simply enormous. Apart from a number of notable but extremely rare exceptions, building on this scale was never achieved again using timber and masonry or concrete. It was only with the use of iron and steel in the mid-nineteenth century that many Roman achievements were surpassed.

Progress in engineering, as in mathematics and science, is cumulative. However, such progress evolves in different ways, according to each discipline's nature. Mathematics and science are characterized by being knowledge of a type that can be written down and, hence, taught, learned, and easily passed on and further developed from generation to generation. From the time of the earliest writings on engineering in ancient Greece, it was recognized that engineering differs from science in that it consists of two types of knowledge: a theoretical or scientific side that can be written down, and a practical side that can be learned only by doing. Engineering knowledge can grow and progress only if there is continuity in both of its component sides. At the height of the Roman Empire, engineering education flourished at the main "polytechnic" or engineering school of the empire at Alexandria, and in the many local schools at which the thousands of military engineers needed by the Roman armies were

27 Cutaway drawing of a typical Roman hypocaust, showing under-floor structure and furnace, hollow ducts in walls, and exhaust at roof level.

trained. Here the geometry and mechanics developed by the great Greek mathematicians, scientists, and engineers were taught. Geometry enabled engineers to visualize and communicate shapes in both two and three dimensions, and gave them the means to set out the form of a small component or a large building in order to guide the craftsmen or constructors. The mechanics of the four fundamental means of gaining mechanical advantage were taught, just as they were still (or, rather, again) being taught in the nineteenth century: the lever, the wedge, the pulley, and the screw. Indeed, the ability to design and build weapons and buildings, based upon a theoretical understanding of mechanics and practical understanding of materials and forces, differed little between Roman times and the early eighteenth century.

When Augustus began his reign he needed to make an immediate and dramatic statement of his grand intentions to the people of Rome and farther afield, and he set about rebuilding the capital city. During his rule of forty-five years he transformed it, giving him every justification for the boast he made later in life that he found Rome built of brick and left it built of marble. Yet there was still plenty to do after Augustus died in A.D. 14. Even today, the map of Rome bears witness to successive emperors' efforts to leave their mark on the city, much as the presidents of France did in the twentieth century with their "*grands projets*," such as the Centre Pompidou.

Brutal editing is needed to make a small selection of projects illustrate the remarkable legacy of the emperors, and to concentrate on Rome is to ignore other excellent Roman building projects in France, Spain, England, and elsewhere. Yet the examples included here show Roman building design and engineering at their very best.

The Flavian Amphitheater, or Colosseum (c. 72–80)

The earliest known permanent amphitheater in Italy was completed in about 80 B.C. at Pompeii, where seating for 20,000 was provided in a building that measured 133 by 102 meters. Rome's first amphitheater dates from Julius Caesar's time, when a modestly sized temporary timber structure had been built. This probably consisted of little more than tiered rows of seating arranged around an arena. The first permanent amphitheater in Rome was constructed during the time of Augustus, but probably burned down in the fire of A.D. 64.

By A.D. 72 the political climate was again right for a major public work to be constructed, and the new emperor, Vespasian (ruled A.D. 69–79), the first of the Flavian dynasty, seized the opportunity and commissioned a new amplitheater to stage regular free entertainments for the public. These included the famous gladiatorial contests (though, contrary to the Hollywood image of Rome, only occasionally did they result in human death). The arena was also used to put lions, tigers, elephants, and other exotic animals on show, and they were often set to fight each other to the death, or slaughtered in huge numbers by gladiators. On one occasion soon after its opening, it was said that the arena was flooded to allow the staging of a mock naval battle.

The amphitheater was constructed on the site of what had been an ornamental pond in the garden of former emperor Nero's palace. The Flavian amphitheater's modern name—the Colosseum, first recorded in the eleventh century—is believed to have originated from its proximity to the huge statue, or colossus, that Nero had commissioned depicting himself as a sun god and erected at the entrance to his palace, the Domus Aurea. At about 35 meters tall (including its plinth), this statue was similar in size to the more famous one at the mouth of the harbor of Rhodes that had been built some 300 years earlier. Nero's colossus consisted of a metal structural frame (probably made of bronze) supporting a cladding of gilded bronze plate. When Vespasian came to power, he had the original head remodeled to remove the likeness of Nero, and about fifty years later, the emperor Hadrian had the statue moved—reputedly using twenty-four elephants to do so—a few tens of meters nearer to the amphitheater to make room for the building of a new temple to Venus and Roma.

The Flavian amphitheater was the largest ever built and 28
took about a decade to construct. It was completed

28 Flavian Amphitheater, or Colosseum, c. 72–80. Shown in a reconstruction model of ancient Rome. 29 Fresco from Pompeii showing a velarium shading some of the seating in the amphitheater, first century A.D. 30 Flavian Amphitheater, or Colosseum. Cross section and cutaway isometric drawing.

28

29

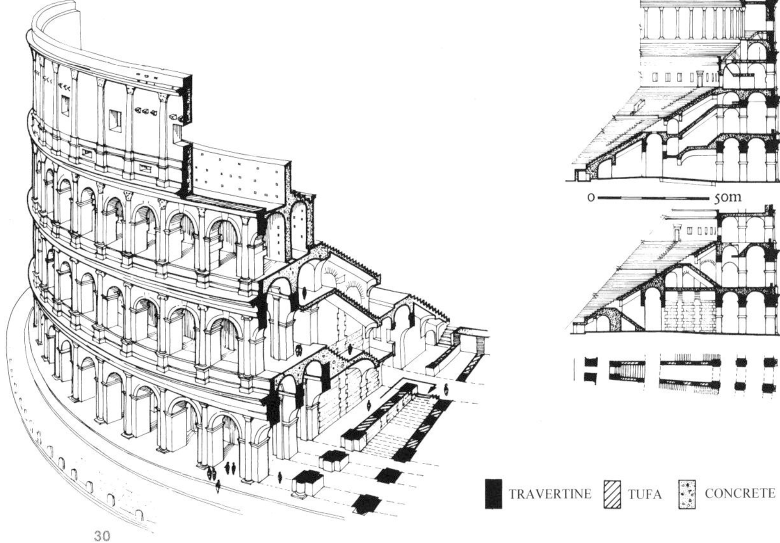

30

during the reign of Vespasian's son Titus (ruled 79–81) and dedicated in A.D. 80. The building was seriously damaged by fire following lightning strikes in A.D. 217 that destroyed all the timber structures, including the floor. The building was restored to its former glory by the emperor Alexander Severus (ruled 222–35).

In some ways the engineering of the Colosseum is unremarkable, though its complex three-dimensional geometry must have been very difficult to set out. The structure is a series of eighty radial barrel vaults that were raked and tapered in a manner that was already in common use, and no large spans were involved. The former pond of Nero's palace garden was filled and a huge foundation of concrete and stone was laid. Upon this was constructed the tiered seating, made largely of concrete faced with brick or travertine, and stones of the light-
30 weight rock called tufa. The outer two rings of the building were constructed largely of solid travertine, strikingly white and glistening in its appearance. The floor of the elliptical arena, about 86 by 54 meters, was of timber, covered with sand, supported on a labyrinth of concrete walls and vaults. During the life of the building, various improvements were made to the under-floor machinery, sometimes on three levels, that incorporated cages for wild animals, rooms for humans, and corridors and mechanical lifts to conduct them up to the floor of the arena itself.

What makes everything about the building remarkable, however, is its astonishing size. In plan it is an ellipse, 188 by 156 meters on a northwest–southwest major axis, covering an area of some 6 acres (2.4 hectares). More than 100,000 cubic meters of travertine marble had to be delivered to the site, accomplished by using an army of ox-drawn carts. The Colosseum towered to a height of 48 meters—equivalent to the height of a modern sixteen-story office building. While estimates of its seating capacity vary, a figure of about 50,000 seems to be a conservative one.

The structure that supports the raked seating is a series of arches and vaults springing from walls or piers, and is more void than solid. Not only did this represent a huge saving on building costs, but the honeycomb of spaces it formed provided all the access and circulation routes to convey the 50,000 or more spectators to and from their seats. The foundations were of concrete, while the piers and arcades of the lower two levels were made with blocks of travertine. Many of these blocks were originally linked by wrought iron cramps which have been long since removed and recycled, leaving the many holes we see today. Over 300 tons of iron were needed for this purpose alone. Partition walls in the lower two levels were made of lightweight tufa. Most of the vaults on all levels, and the entire structure of the upper two levels, were constructed of mass concrete; only the walls were faced with brick.

A certain mystery still surrounds what was the most audacious structural engineering challenge: the canvas canopy, or *velarium*, which could be deployed for special occasions to shade a part of the seating. We know that sailors from the nearby port of Ostia used the velarium at the Colosseum, but the precise mechanics have not yet been satisfactorily explained or recreated, and most attempts are highly fanciful. It is unlikely that it covered all the seating, or that it was suspended from radial ropes hanging from the top of wood masts. Any sailor would know that this would break the masts. More likely, only a few hundred seats were shaded by draping sail material over parallel ropes, as suggested in a painting found in
the ruins of Pompeii that shows such a canopy on its am- 29
phitheater. The Colosseum remained in use for more than four hundred years, although the sophisticated machinery for handling the animals probably fell into disrepair quite regularly. After many renovations by various emperors, the Colosseum witnessed its last spectacle in 523. The building was finally abandoned after suffering severe damage in a number of earthquakes; it was subsequently used as a fortress in medieval times and, during the Renaissance, refurbished to stage bullfights. However, it often served as a convenient source of building materials. Given the architectural demands of the Renaissance and the Vatican, it is only thanks to the resistance of Roman concrete to the elements and the recycling industry that we still have this and so many other remnants of ancient Rome.

Apollodorus and the *Grands Projets* of Emperors Trajan and Hadrian

By the time Trajan came to power, in A.D. 98, the Roman empire had grown almost to its greatest extent, and the tradition of "*grands projets*" was firmly established.

Trajan had the good fortune to have, in his chief architect, Apollodorus (c. 55–c. 130), one of the most talented structural engineers of all time. Apollodorus is believed to have come from Damascus (in today's Syria), near the eastern edge of the Roman Empire. After a career as a military engineer he was eventually appointed chief public works engineer (*praefectus fabrum*) to two of the greatest Roman emperors, Trajan (ruled 98–117) and Hadrian (ruled 117–138). Like Vitruvius, he wrote about military machines and siege engines, but his writings do not survive and we know little of his life save the remarkable works he engineered. As with Rubens and Shakespeare, there have been suggestions that he could not have done all the work attributed to him, that there may have been two or more individuals with the same name and, indeed, that he was responsible for many other works that he did not, in fact, have a hand in. As in a modern firm of structural engineers, Apollodorus as the principal no doubt played a part in many designs that were actually largely undertaken by members of his staff, and he surely collaborated with other designers who concentrated more on the works' appearance than on their manner of construction. The following list of major projects linked to his name is widely agreed upon and is truly impressive. Like most imperial works (mainly Trajan), many are known by the name of the emperor who commissioned them.

- *Trajan's Forum (c.98–112), incorporating various buildings*
- *Trajan's Basilica (c. 98) in the Forum*
- *The Baths of Trajan (c. 104–109)*
- *Trajan's market buildings (c. 98–112), incorporating flying buttresses, built at the northern side of Trajan's Forum*
- *A concert hall (unidentified)*
- *Trajan's bridge over the River Danube in modern Romania (c. 105–106). This was a series of twenty-one timber truss arches, each spanning 35 to 40 meters between masonry piers about 40 meters high, forming a bridge with a total length of about a kilometer. It is depicted on Trajan's column.*
- *Trajan's Column (c. 112–13), built at the western end of Trajan's Forum*
- *The Pantheon (c. 118–26)*
- *The Temple of Venus and Rome (c. 121–135), consisting of two huge concrete barrel vaults spanning 20 meters*

Trajan's Forum and Market (c. 98–112)

In the year he came to power Trajan began the first of his *grands projets* with plans for a massive new forum in the center of Rome incorporating a library, basilica, and other buildings around a large square, with a public market to the northeast. The market is remarkable 31
for Apollodorus's use of flying buttresses to carry the outward thrust of the six large concrete vaults to shear walls, which then carry the forces down to the 33
foundations.

Trajan's Column (c. 112–13)

Trajan's Column was erected during his lifetime to celebrate his many achievements. Apart from the carved re- 32
lief that narrates these achievements, the column is remarkable for its construction, especially the feat of lifting the nineteen cylindrical stone drums, each about 3.7 34
meters in diameter and weighing some 20 tons. The topmost stone, weighing 55 tons, had to be lifted to a height of 37 meters before being moved sideways to sit atop the other stone drums. All this was undertaken within 6 meters of the adjacent buildings, and we can only wonder at how this was done using seven or eight cranes with a capacity of 8 tons.

The Baths of Trajan (c. 104–09)

Of all Trajan's *grands projets*, perhaps the most spectacular was the public baths complex, equivalent to a huge modern spa, which was of a size and luxury that would have been the envy of the world. In an era when few people had the facilities or the space to bathe at home, public baths (*balnea*) had long been a normal part of city life. At this time, Rome is believed to have had several hundred public baths, a number that had grown to more than 800 by the fourth century, but these were small, functional buildings. The idea of building baths, or *thermae*, on a grander scale began with the emperor Agrippa around 20 B.C. His baths, built within a stone's throw of the first Pantheon building that he had commissioned, were initially for his own use. He donated them to the city, and their great success with the public inspired several future emperors to use similar means of gaining popularity. Nero's baths were dedicated in A.D. 62, and the emperor Titus built his baths, as he had the Colosseum, on part of the site occupied by Nero's palace, in A.D. 79–81. However, it was Trajan who turned *thermae* into true palaces for the people on

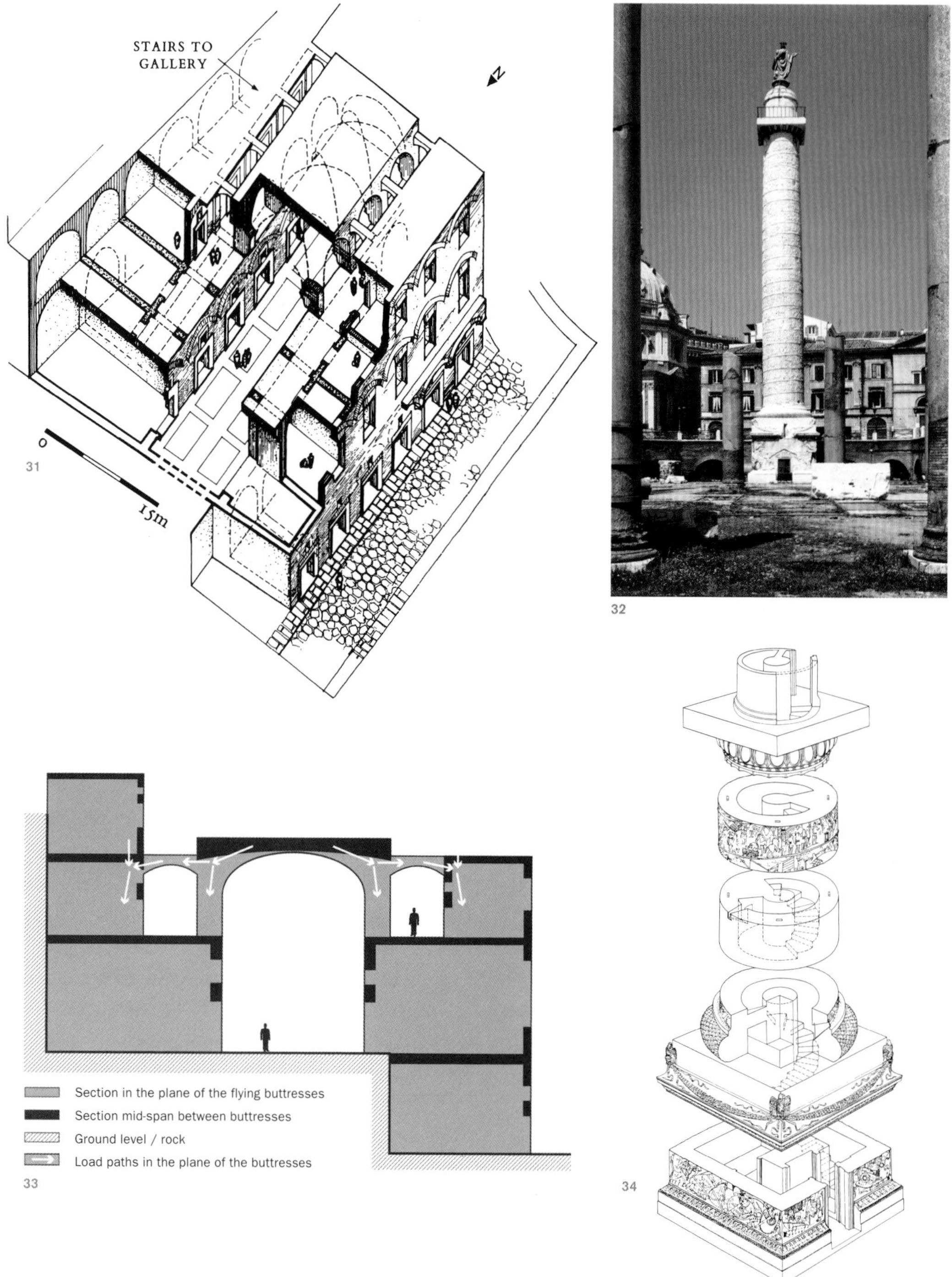

31 Trajan's Market, Rome, c. 98–112. Structural design: Apollodorus of Damascus. Cutaway isometric. 32 Trajan's Column, Rome, c. 112–13. Designer and engineer: Apollodorus of Damascus. 33 Trajan's Market. Diagram showing flying buttresses conducting vault thrusts to shear walls and down to the foundations. 34 Trajan's Column. Isometric drawing of construction. Each stone drum contains one half-circle of the staircase and was cut before being lifted into place.

a scale that would match even the largest of our leisure centers of today.

The design and execution of the baths were the work of Trajan's chief engineer, Apollodorus. He brought to the occasion a number of ideas that had been used on a smaller scale and was able to take advantage of imperial patronage to execute a masterpiece on an imperial scale. The rectangular site extends over about 10 hectares, and the main building itself was about 175 by 135 meters. Trajan's Baths were truly enormous, with seating for some 1,500 bathers and a total capacity of perhaps twice this number in addition to the large num-
35 bers of staff on duty. At the heart of the complex are the four main spaces: the *caldarium*, *tepidarium*, and *frigidarium* (respectively, hot, warm, and cool rooms and
36 baths), and the *natatio*, an open-air swimming pool. On either side of these main areas were various smaller rooms for massage, exercise, and relaxation. With a clear span of 23 meters, the frigidarium was wider than any subsequent cathedral nave—most Gothic cathedral naves span about 12 meters—and at 32 meters high it would be exceeded in height only by the cathedral at Beauvais. Its size would be matched only by the cathedral at Florence, whose nave spans about 20 meters and rises to more than 40 meters. Less is known about the details of the Baths of Trajan than those of Hadrian, built to Apollodorus's designs at the end of his life in Leptis Magna in North Africa. Their general layout and the appearance of the frigidarium were similar, though a little smaller.

The huge rectangular frigidarium was formed by three rectangular structural bays, as we now call them. Each bay was a concrete groined vault 18.5 meters long, 23 meters wide, and about 32 meters high, formed by the intersection of two barrel vaults at right angles. This idea had been used many times before on a smaller scale—indeed, it was a standard way of roofing over a square room. At the Baths of Trajan, however, not only did the vaults span a huge distance, they were very much higher than any previous groined vault, and great care was needed to carry the lateral thrusts down to the foundations. This was achieved by using large side vaults to carry the thrust in the curved plane of the vault by working in shear, in just the way that a shear wall is today used to carry wind loads down to a building's foundations. These shear, or buttress, vaults are a remarkable feat of engineering no less ingenious than the flying buttress developed a thousand years later, and demonstrate the great skill the designers had developed in visualizing forces in not only two dimensions but in three. One of the most interesting features of the vaults is that they are rectangular in plan, and this led to a rare and significant deviation from the Roman habit of using only semicircular vaults in their buildings. If two arches rise to the same height at the center of the vault yet have different spans, only two alternatives are possible: one of the vaults must be either elliptical in section, or must be slightly pointed in the manner of many Gothic vaults.

In this large room within a Roman pleasure palace we have the prototype of the Christian church architecture that dominated Europe for the eighteen hundred years following Trajan's reign. It established the practical upper limit to height and width that is possible without the substantial use of iron or steel. It established the means for concentrating the loads of a roof predominantly into four columns on a square or rectangular grid, allowing access from all four directions. It established the idea of the structural bay that would give architects unprecedented flexibility in their building forms, since it could be repeated as often as needed, in two directions if necessary.

The Pantheon (c. 118–26)

Conceived only forty years after the Colosseum was
opened, the Pantheon represents a major step forward in 38
structural engineering, and Apollodorus almost certainly played a major role in its design. It was commissioned by the emperor Hadrian to replace an earlier building on the site that had burned down. This, in turn, had replaced the original Pantheon founded by the consul Marcus Agrippa in about 25 B.C., which had also burned down, in A.D. 80. It was perhaps the fate of the timber roofs of the earlier buildings that prompted the search for a fireproof solution and the subsequent creation of the largest single span built before the nineteenth century. The dome of the Pantheon spans about 44 meters and its height is about the same. Even Brunelleschi's dome for Florence Cathedral (1434) and the dome of Saint Peter's in Rome (1590) spanned a meter or so less. The Pantheon shows the hand of Apollodorus at work with its use of shear vaults and the very boldness of its size.

The dome of the Pantheon is built mainly of concrete, but this word masks many engineering subtleties. Concrete domes were not new. The first ones known are two 6-meter semidomes in Pompeii that were built more than 200 years earlier. Nero's palace, the Domus Aurea, had an octagonal dome spanning some 14 meters. All these were made from the usual Roman concrete mix—alternate layers of cement paste and broken brick, not the semihomogeneous material we use today. But the Pantheon dome is three times the diameter of the one in the Domus Aurea.

Whether they learned from previously built domes or from large concrete arches and vaults, the dome's engineers knew that such a structure pushes outward at its springing and that, as with an arch, the abutments need to resist the overturning moment by being thick at their base. This outward thrusting of a series of segments of the dome also causes the circumference to tend to lengthen near the springing. In a masonry dome the individual bricks or voussoirs open up, while in a dome made from a homogeneous material, tension stresses, called hoop stresses by analogy with the metal hoops used in wooden barrels, are able to develop. The magnitude of these hoop stresses depends on the total weight of material above, and can be reduced by making the dome as light as possible.

In the Pantheon the weight of the dome is reduced in sev-
41 eral ways. First of all, the concrete uses progressively less dense *caementae*, or aggregate, as we would call it, as it rises up the building. In the foundations the aggregate consists of travertine chippings, the waste product from dressing large travertine blocks used in parts of the building. In the first level of the Pantheon the aggregate consists of alternate layers of travertine and tufa. In the second story the aggregate is alternate layers of tufa and tile fragments, while the upper story and lower part of the dome has an aggregate made mainly of broken bricks. The next, thin band of the dome has an aggregate consisting of alternate layers of broken brick and tufa, while the aggregate in the remainder of the dome is alternate layers of lightweight tufa and pumice.

In addition to reducing the density of the concrete used, the full cross section of the dome reduces progressively from the springing toward the crown, and the center of the dome is missing entirely to form an oculus. Finally, the lower parts of the dome are lightened by perhaps a further 10 percent by being deeply coffered on the inside.

The concrete was laid on formwork in horizontal layers. At some point, depending on the stiffness of the formwork, the rate at which the concrete hardened, and when the formwork was removed, the concrete would begin working as a true dome, developing radial compressive stresses and corresponding circumferential stresses that would have been in tension near the springing. Although good-quality concrete probably would have been strong enough in tension to withstand these hoop stresses, the concrete in the Pantheon dome has cracked along radial lines near the springing. However, such cracking occurs only once in the structure's history and does not threaten the overall stability of the dome, since each pair of opposite segments is stable in itself. The cracks have been well repaired on the inside for aesthetic reasons, and on the outside to prevent water ingress. More serious would have been bending of the thin dome due to an excessive ratio of load to thickness, but the large thickness of the dome near its springing has prevented this from occurring.

The walls have their own structural story to tell. They are, in fact, far from being solid. Apart from the large niches at ground level and smaller ones higher up, they contain voids and a corridor entirely hidden from view. Thus, the 39
walls consist of much less material than if they had been solid, ranging from perhaps 35 percent solid at the attic level to about 50 percent at ground level. Clearly this saved on building materials, and at ground level especially, the niches had the important function of housing statues believed to represent the seven planetary deities to whom the building was dedicated. However, one has to marvel at the structural efficiency of this design, too. By keeping the full depth of the wall, its stability against overturning due to horizontal forces is maintained while economizing on material. And having the denser and

35 Baths of Trajan, Rome, c. 104–109. Designer and engineer: Apollodorus of Damascus. Reconstruction drawing.
36 Baths of Trajan. Plan. 37 Pantheon, Rome, c. 118–26. Drawing showing relieving arches and vaults serving as shear vaults within the walls. 38 Pantheon.

35

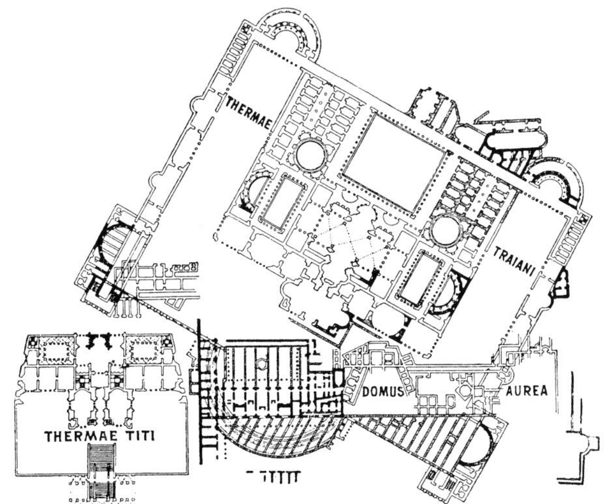

36

37

38

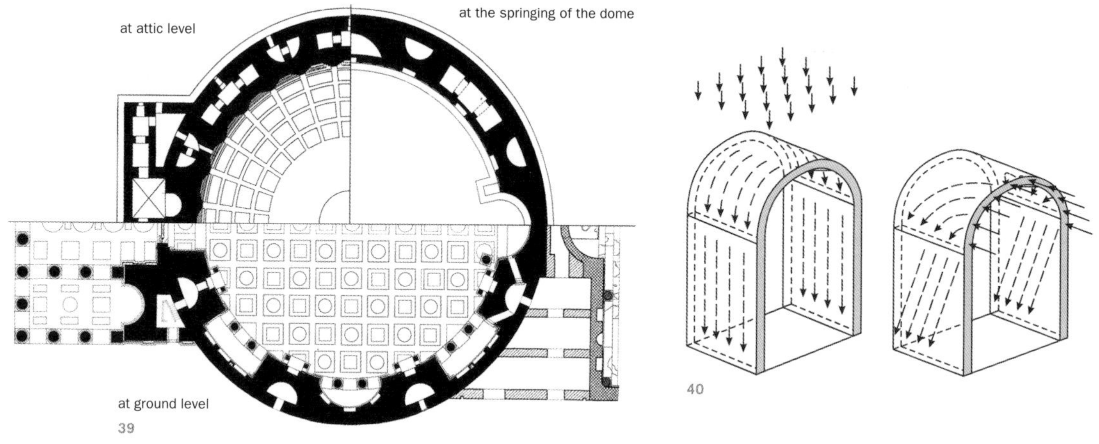
at attic level
at the springing of the dome
at ground level

39

40

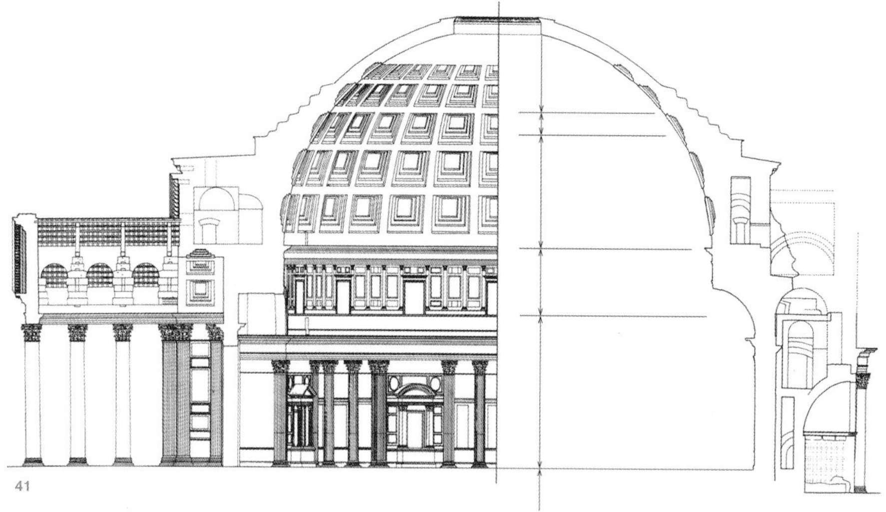

41

42

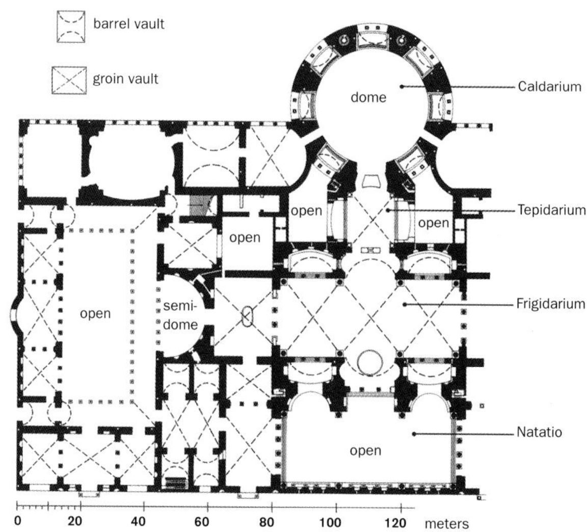
barrel vault
groin vault
dome
Caldarium
open
open
open
Tepidarium
open
semi-dome
Frigidarium
Natatio
open
0
20
40
60
80
100
120
meters

43

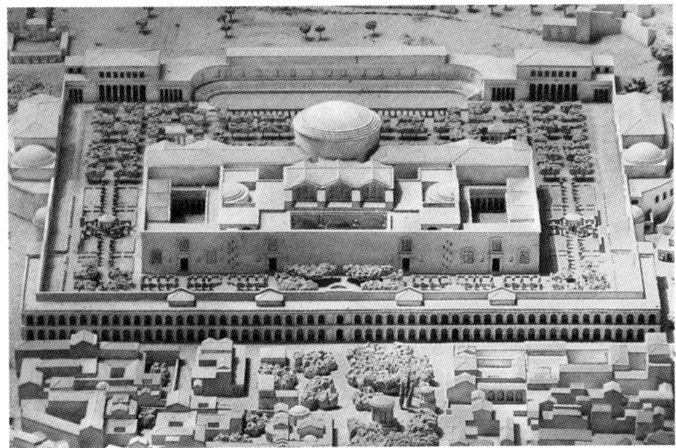

44

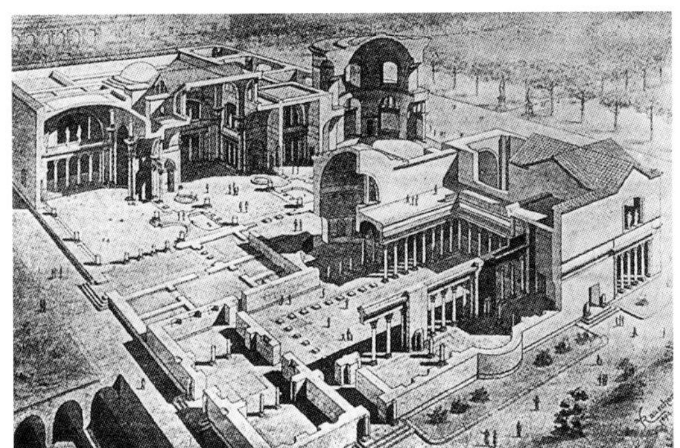

45

heavier parts of the wall at the top serves well to deflect the load path more quickly toward the vertical, just in the way that the pinnacles atop a Gothic buttress achieve the same result.

However, the most remarkable structural device of all in the Pantheon is nearly hidden from view. Above the entrance and each of the seven niches at ground level are two arches, or rather, short barrel vaults, one above the
37, 40 other, stretching the full 6-meter depth of the wall. These serve two purposes. First, they act as "relieving" arches or vaults, collecting the gravity loads from above and directing them into the load-bearing walls that act as columns at ground level. This device was often used in Roman brick structures, though seldom on such a large scale. However, the vaults have an equally important role in working as shear or buttress structures to carry the horizontal thrust from the dome in the same way they are used to carry the outward thrust of the groined vaults at Trajan's baths. Their use at the Pantheon points to the hand of Apollodorus and represents a subtle improvement in the way they are ingeniously integrated into the wall of the building. Similar shear vaults would be exploited in an even more breathtaking way more than 400 years later in the church of Hagia Sophia in Byzantium.

The Baths of Caracalla (211–16)

The baths of Emperor Caracalla (ruled 211–17), built just 42, 43,
a few hundred meters from the Baths of Trajan, were 44, 45
even more extensive and offered even more facilities than the latter. Although these baths were built some hundred years after those devised by Apollodorus, they were a very close copy. And, because a considerable proportion of the buildings remain today, they have proved a fruitful object of study that has given us a good understanding of how they were built. Apart from the three main heated rooms of the *thermae*, the whole complex had nearly fifty smaller rooms with places for changing, ball games and other sports, gymnastics, masseurs and hairdressers, lectures, meetings, libraries, and shops. Another distinguishing feature of Caracalla's baths was the huge caldarium, which was circular in plan and covered by a concrete dome; it was a near replica of the Pantheon, with a slightly smaller span (35 meters) but the same height (43 meters). In the walls of this caldarium, as at the Pantheon, shear vaults and shear walls are

39 Pantheon, Rome, c. 118–26. Plan showing arrangement of voids in the structure at different heights. 40 Baths of Trajan, Rome, c. 104–109. Designer and engineer: Appolodorus of Damascus. Diagrams showing vertical and horizontal loads on shear vaults. 41 Pantheon. Cross section showing construction features and use of concrete: density decreases with height. 42 Baths of Caracalla, Rome, 211–16. Reconstruction view of the frigidarium. 43 Baths of Caracalla. Plan. 44 Baths of Caracalla. Reconstruction model. 45 Baths of Caracalla. Reconstruction drawing, cutaway perspective.

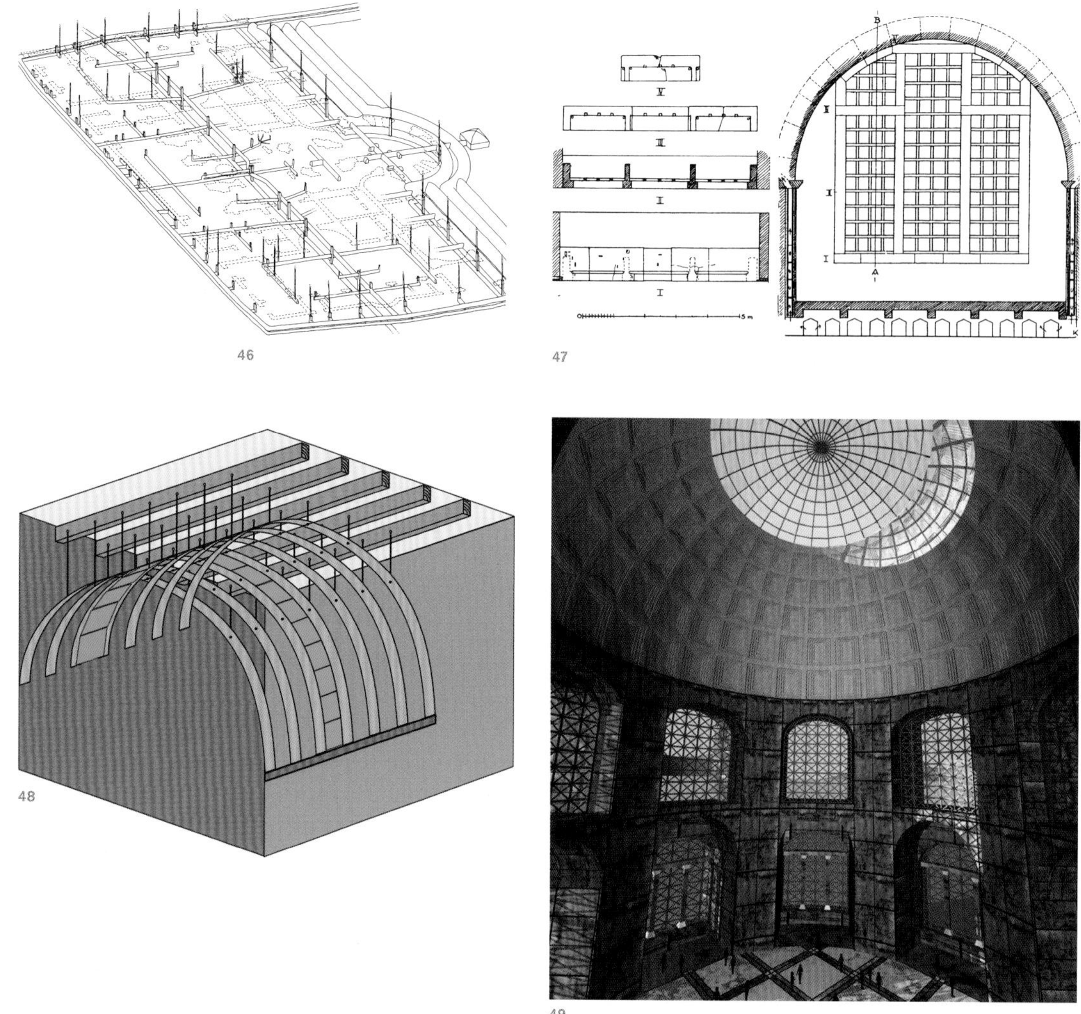

46 Baths of Caracalla, Rome, 211–16. Diagram of rainwater down-pipes and drains. 47 Baths of Faustina at Miletos, modern Turkey, second century A.D. Reconstruction drawing of glazed window. 48 Diagram of Roman iron-framework ceiling vaults in hot bath rooms, as described by Vitruvius, c. 25 B.C. 49 Baths of Caracalla. Reconstruction drawing of the *cella solearis*, showing a hypothetical glazed central portion of the dome.

used to carry the lateral thrusts of the dome down to the foundations.

While the huge bath buildings were remarkable for their structural engineering, they were, of course, made possible only by the development of a highly sophisticated heating system that could supply enormous quantities of hot water and air; the air temperature in a *laconicum*, or sweating room, the Roman ancestor of our sauna, was in excess of 100 degrees centigrade. This was made possible by huge wood-burning boilers and the hypocaust. The heart of the hypocaust was the *praefurnium*, or furnace, which was fueled by wood and ran almost constantly; a large system would take two or three days to heat up to the required temperature. The hot gases heated water in three bronze cauldrons to different degrees, with the hotter boilers being filled with preheated water from the next cooler one. The water in the boilers was then distributed to the appropriate pools in the baths. The heat was also used to warm the many rooms, both by heating the fabric of the building and by introducing heated air into the rooms through ducts. Matching the supply of hot water was an equally sophisticated system of drainage for both used bathwa-
46 ter and rainwater.

Vitruvius offered some guidance on constructing baths more than a century before Trajan's were being planned. He recommended that the building should be oriented with the hotter rooms on southwest side, to benefit most from the sun's afternoon heat—and all three of Rome's imperial baths are indeed so laid out. In Book V, chapter 10 of *De Architectura*, Vituvius then goes on to describe how to build the furnaces and the raised, or "suspended," floors of the hypocaust, called *suspensurae*:

> *The suspended floors of the hot baths are to be constructed as follows. First the surface of the ground is paved with tiles of a foot and a half inclining towards the furnace, so that if a ball be thrown into it, it will roll back to the mouth of the furnace; thus the hot gases from the furnace will better spread out under the floor. Upon this floor, pillars of eight-inch bricks are built at such a distance from each other, that tiles of two feet may span between them. The pillars should be two feet high, and be capped with clay mixed with hair, on which are placed the two foot tiles which support the floor.* [21]

Thus, most of the heat to the baths came from the underground furnace through the floor, as in a natural hot spring. Hot gases were also passed through an arrangement of tubular clay ducts embedded in the walls to provide additional heating. (This feature had been introduced into the hypocaust system from the early first century A.D.)

Vitruvius says that vaulted ceilings in baths would function best if made of masonry. However, he goes on to describe how they should be built if they are of "framework" 48
construction with tiles on the underside:

> *Let iron bars or arcs be made and hang them from the [timber] framework or by means of iron hooks set as close together as possible, and let these bars be placed at such distances that each pair of them may support and carry an unflanged tile. Thus the entire vaulting will be completed supported on iron. These vaults should have their joints on their upper side daubed with clay mixed with hair and the under side, facing the floor, should be plastered first with crushed tile mixed with lime and then covered with polished stucco in relief or smooth. Vaults in hot bath rooms will be more serviceable if they are doubled; for then the moisture from the heat will not be able to spoil the timber of the framework and will be able to circulate between the two vaults.* [22]

Finally, Vitruvius discusses the construction of a laconicum, or sauna. Such a room, he says, should adjoin the tepidarium to benefit from the adjacent heat. It should be circular to ensure that it is heated evenly, and its height from the floor to the foot of the dome should be equal to its diameter. An aperture should be left in the center of the dome and covered by a bronze disk hanging from chains, thus allowing the temperature of the sauna to be regulated by raising or lowering the disk.

Roman baths depended for their heating not only on the hypocaust but also on large glazed windows to retain the hot air in the rooms and achieve some solar gain, as well as provide some natural light. Glass had 47
become a significant architectural component around 100 B.C. By the second century A.D. panes of glass could be made in sizes up to 1.5 meters by 0.5 to 0.75 meters that were supported by stone mullions and held in place by iron bars, much as they are in medieval cathedrals. The largest of these windows at Caracalla's

50

51

baths must have been some 8 meters wide and 18 meters high. At a public bath in Herculaneum there is evidence that double glazing was used, both to improve insulation and reduce the condensation that would rot their timber window frames.

An intriguing mystery surrounds a room in Caracalla's baths, rooms known as the *cella solearis*, or caldarium, as we now call it. A near contemporary account singles out this room for special comment. It reports that "lattices of either bronze or copper were placed over [the room] and support the entire vault" and that "the span is so great that experienced engineers say it could not have been done."[23] Archaeologists still do not agree about how the cella solearis was roofed over. It was circular, about 43 meters to the inside of the domed roof, and 35 meters in diameter—around three quarters the span of the Pantheon. The cella solearis was heated by the hypocaust beneath to a temperature of perhaps around 45 degrees Celsius. It was on the south side of the building and had five glazed upper windows, each around 12 meters high by 8 meters wide, above lower ones about 10 meters high. To maintain the high temperature the roof must have been a closed dome, not with an open oculus at its center like the Pantheon. These large windows would have helped warm the room by solar gain, like the heliocaminus mentioned above. However, even with the light provided by these windows, a closed dome would have made it relatively dark inside. This scenario suggests a highly plausible solution to the mystery of the "lattices of either bronze or copper." It would have been entirely possible to have constructed a glazed, domed roof with metal ribs, similar in conception to the glass houses of early-nineteenth century Europe, spanning an

50 Baths of Diocletian, Rome, c. 298–306. Painting by Edmond-Jean-Baptiste Paulin, 1880. 51 Basilica of Maxentius (Basilica of Constantine), Rome, 308–25. Artist's rendering.

enlarged oculus in the concrete dome. The ribs might have been of bronze or of iron clad in bronze or copper
49 sheet, and would certainly have been spectacular enough to attract the adulation of visitors.

Later Roman Vaulted Structures

Apollodorus's giant vaults and, indeed, the layout of the whole *thermae* were a precedent used on many occasions. Some seventy years after Caracalla's baths, the emperor Diocletian (ruled 284–305) commissioned the
50 largest of all the *thermae*, which provided seating for around 3,000 bathers and catered to perhaps 5,000 users in total.

Remarkably, the frigidarium of these baths has survived into the twenty-first century and is in daily use, converted, with characteristic genius, by Michelangelo in 1563 into the church of Santa Maria degli Angeli. In doing this he exploited the bidirectional nature of the vaulted form by making the three transverse bays of the Roman building into the longitudinal nave of his church. Some 200 years later, the axis of the space was again rotated when the original three bays were transformed into a transept as the church was enlarged to its present form by the construction of a new nave.

The final example of Apollodorus's three-bay structural form was its use in around A.D. 310 in the basilica of em-
51 peror Maxentius (reigned 306–12), which was completed and modified by emperor Constantine during his reign (312–37). This was the largest version of the vaulted structural form, with three bays each 23 meters long, 36 meters high, and spanning a massive 25 meters. With the aisles on either side of the main room, the entire building covered an area of about 80 meters by 60 meters, interrupted at ground level by only four columns.

Greek and Roman building engineers surely achieved as much as it was possible to do without the use of modern engineering science. They did this by applying what we could call qualitative science, consisting of rational arguments based on experience, enabling them to think beyond what had been previously achieved, and arrive at a solution. It was augmented by experiments in the sense that new ideas were tried and successes incorporated into mainstream building. As would arise again, especially in the eighteenth century, Greek and Roman engineers and scientists devised ways of encapsulating some of their experience and understanding in books and in educational curricula. This they accomplished most notably at the university and polytechnic school of Alexandria, a model that was taken up (on a smaller scale) in Constantinople and probably in other cities, too.

Greatest progress was made in structural engineering using masonry (including concrete), partly because the stability of masonry construction is independent of scale. If a model brick vault measuring a meter wide stands, then so, too, will a geometrically similar vault twenty times larger—a phenomenon that would benefit the engineers of medieval and later cathedrals. In other words, models would have been, and doubtless were, effective as part of the design process. This is not true of structures that involve the bending of structural elements. The design methods used for some stone-throwing weapons in the fifth century B.C. indicate that ancient engineers knew that not all phenomena vary in linear relationship. This understanding would not be recognized (in print) again until the early seventeenth century in the writings of Galileo.

chapter 2

The Medieval Era 500–1400

People and Events

c. 474–c. 534 Anthemius of Tralles

c. 500–c. 550 Isidorus of Miletus

800 Charlemagne crowned first Holy Roman Emperor

Materials and Technology

From c. 500 Wrought iron used in tied masonry arches

c. 600 Windmill developed in Persia

From c. 800 Use of crank in Europe

c. 800 Wrought iron tie used in masonry dome

Knowledge and Learning

646 University, engineering school, and library of Alexandria destroyed

From c. 700 Translation of Greek mathematics and science into Arabic

Design Methods

Design Tools: Drawing and Calculation

876 First confirmed use of decimal zero, India

Buildings

c. 490–549 Sant' Apollinare Nuovo, Ravenna, Italy

532–37 Saint Sophia, Constantinople (now Istanbul, Turkey)

c. 526–47 San Vitale, Ravenna, Italy

c. 670 Great Mosque, Qairawan, Tunisia

c. 786–805 Palatine Chapel, Aachen, Germany

c. 819–26 Unexecuted plan for monastery, Saint Gall, Switzerland

500 600 700 800 900

1095–99 First Crusade

1147–1254 Six later crusades

1086 *Domesday Book* of William the Conqueror

c. 1175–c. 1240 Villard de Honnecourt

c. 1300–60 Heinrich Parler

c. 1175–1253 Robert Grosseteste

c. 1214–94 Roger Bacon

c. 1330–60 Peter Parler

c. 1230–1309 James of St. George

1335–1405 William Wynford

c. 1325–1400 Henry Yevele

1347–52 Black Death sweeps Europe

1347–52 Giovanni da Fontana

c. 1000 First use of magnetic compass

From 1250–1300 Gunpowder and cannon, first developed in China, arrive in Europe

c. 1100 Papermaking by Moors

From c. 1250 Widespread use of masonry for civic and domestic buildings

From 1180s Windmills in Europe

From c. 1300 Assaying becomes quantitative and more reliable

c. 1320s–c. 1450s Evolution of cannon from bronze and wrought iron to cast iron

From c. 1050 Import into Northern Europe of Arabic mathematics, science, and (later) fortification technology

c. 1120 Translation of Euclid from Arabic into Latin

From c. 1125 Books on practical and theoretical geometry

From c. 1200 Natural philosophy (science) in universities of Paris and Oxford

c. 1220 Jordanus Nemorarius, *De Ponderibus* (early treatise on statics)

c. 1400 First European manuals on military engineering

1391–1402 Expertises on design of Milan Cathedral (Duomo), Milan, Italy

From c. 1200 Cathedral plans and elevations devised by "rotating the square"

1390s Brick and plaster scale model (1:8) made for design of San Petronio, Bologna, Italy

976 First use of Hindu-Arabic numerals in Europe (Spain)

From c. 1200 Medieval mason's square

c. 1200 Algebra introduced into Europe

c. 1250 Hindu-Arabic numerals spread to parts of southern Europe

c. 1300 First use of a graph to display data

From 1325 Documented evidence of tracing floors in many cathedrals

1050s–1250s Principal Italian, French, and English masonry castles

1386–present Milan Cathedral (Duomo), Milan, Italy

c. 1050–1350s Principal European cathedrals

1390–1437 San Petronio, Bologna, Italy

c. 1120–1215 Sainte Marie-Madeleine at Vézelay, France

1093–1133 Durham Cathedral, Durham, England

1163–1250 Cathedral of Notre Dame, Paris, France

1194–1221 Chartres Cathedral, Chartres, France

c. 1088–1130 Monastery at Cluny, France

1153–1265 Baptistery, Pisa, Italy

c. 1150–1250 Krak des Chevaliers, Syria

1283–89 Harlech Castle, Wales

1000 **1100** **1200** **1300** **1400**

The Medieval Era 500–1400

East Meets West

By A.D. 300 the western, European half of the Roman empire was already beginning its long and slow decline; the task of defending a huge perimeter frontier against attack from neighboring countries, especially along the northern edge from the Rhine River to the Caspian Sea, was finally proving too onerous. During the third century, Alexandria, in Egypt, and Antioch, in Asia Minor, had established themselves as commercial cities to rival Rome. To these two metropolises the emperor Constantine (ruled 306–37) added Byzantium, which he developed to become the new capital of the Eastern Empire, renaming it Constantinople in 330. Gradually, more trade bypassed Rome altogether, and both it and many other European cities started a slow decline. Even Rome's food supplies dwindled as the eastern cities bought up the stores of cheap grain from Egypt that had sustained much of Italy. By 395, when the Roman empire was formally divided into the Western and Eastern empires, Rome was already suffering commercial collapse and widespread poverty. The once-famous road and water infrastructures in the cities of the Western empire were falling into disrepair. Even in Rome the aqueducts soon failed to provide the city with all the water it needed, and the enterprises and buildings that depended on this water could no longer function.

These commercial and economic events were accompanied by the growth of Christianity, especially in the Eastern Empire. Emperor Constantine was the first to be baptized, and a church to Saint Sophia was first dedicated in Constantinople in 360. It was damaged by riots and fire in 404, and rededicated after reconstruction in 415. Emperor Justinian came to power in 527; shortly afterward, in 532, riots again broke out in Constantinople and the second church was destroyed by fire. Justinian seized the opportunity to assert his authority by commissioning a new church on an unprecedented scale. It would draw upon a great many architectural and building traditions as well as the great structural engineering achievements of the past. In fact it came to represent the culmination and, indeed, the conclusion of a thousand years of building innovation in both the Western Empire and the Middle East, which probably had a stronger cultural influence on the region around Byzantium than did Rome.

We know about the construction projects in Justinian's reign from the account written around 560 by his official historian, Procopius. The book, *De Aedificiis* (On Buildings), is a catalog of literally thousands of construction projects that were being undertaken in his name, most of which were the building or rebuilding of fortifications around the huge perimeter of the empire. In the tradition of the great emperors of the early Roman era, beginning with Augustus, Justinian sought to establish his authority and reputation through construction. Because he was the leader of a now-Christian empire, many of the projects were churches, and Procopius's book opens with a lengthy eulogy to the greatest of all the works built under Justinian's patronage, the Church of Saint Sophia, or Hagia Sophia (532–37).

The Church of Saint Sophia, Constantinople (532–37) Though lacking in the sorts of technical details we would like to read, Procopius's own words nevertheless convey his amazement at the vastness of the engineers' achievements:

The church has become a spectacle of great beauty, stupendous to those who see it and altogether incredible to those who hear of it, for it soars to a height to match the sky ... and looks down on the remainder of the city.... It subtly combines its mass with the harmony of its proportions, having neither any excess nor any deficiency ... it is considerably more noble than those which are huge beyond measure, and it abounds in sunlight and reflection of the sun's rays from the marble. Indeed, you might say that the space is not illuminated by the sun from outside, but that the radiance is generated within, so great is the abundance of light that bathes this shrine all round.

The inner form of the church has been wrought in the following fashion. A construction of masonry rises from the ground, not in a straight line, but so as to describe a semicircular shape in plan (which is called a half-cylinder by specialists), and this towers to a precipitous height. The extremity of this structure terminates in the fourth part of a sphere, and above it another crescent-shaped form is lifted up by the adjoining parts of the building, wonderful in its beauty yet altogether terrifying by the apparent precariousness of its composition. For it seems somehow to float in the air with no apparent means of support, soaring aloft to the peril of those beneath it, yet actually it is built with quite extraordinary firmness and security. On either side of this, columns are placed on the ground, in a half-circle on plan, as if making way for one another in a dance, and above them rises a crescent-shaped form, apparently suspended....

Emperor Justinian and the engineers Anthemius and Isidore used a great many devices to provide stability to the church, suspended, as it is, in mid-air. Most of these are beyond my comprehension and I find it impossible to express them in words; one device only I shall describe here in order to demonstrate the strength of the whole world. It is as follows. The piers which I have just mentioned are not built like ordinary masonry, but in this fashion. Courses of stone have been laid in a four-square shape; they are hard by nature, but worked smooth, and those of them that were intended to form the lateral projections of the piers have been cut at an angle, while the ones that were assigned an intermediary position have been made rectangular. These were joined together not with lime, which they call "asbestos" [unable to be slaked], nor with asphalt, the pride of Semiramis in Babylon, nor with any other similar substance, but with lead poured into the interstices, which has penetrated into all the intervening spaces and having hardened in the joints, binds the stones together. [1]

The Church of Saint Sophia was designed in 532–33 after the previous church had been destroyed by fire in 532. Construction began in 535 and was substantially complete by 537. In scale, Saint Sophia is similar to, though 52
a little larger than, the Baths of Trajan and the Pantheon. Like the baths, the principal volume of the church is composed of three parts, or bays, as we would now call them; but unlike the baths, the basic structural system is the dome, or semidome, rather than the barrel vault. The central area is square in plan and covered by a brick dome spanning some 30 meters, springing from four huge arches that also serve as short shear or buttress vaults. 53, 54
The thrust of the dome is carried in the longitudinal direction by two semidomes, which serve as huge buttresses and distribute the outward thrust to a variety of smaller domes, cross vaults, arches, and columns at lower levels, and from there to the foundations. The height of the central dome is about 55 meters above the floor, which is rather higher than that of the Pantheon (44 meters) and the Basilica of Maxentius (about 36 meters). At about 76 meters, the total length of the main, column-free space is a little larger than the basilica (about 70 meters).

The designers and engineers for the Church of Saint Sophia were Anthemius of Tralles (c. 474–c. 534) and the younger Isidorus of Miletus (c. 500–c. 550), both of whom were engineer–mathematicians in the mold of Archimedes and Heron. Anthemius' work *Peri Paradoxon Mechanematon* (On Paradoxical Mechanisms) includes a surviving fragment on burning mirrors which discusses in detail conic sections and their properties. He was also credited with having repaired some large damaged flood defenses. Isidorus studied engineering at the polytechnic school in Alexandria, which was still the foremost engineering school in the world some seven hundred years after its founding. As Procopius tells us:

The emperor, disregarding all considerations of expense, hastened to begin construction and raised craftsmen from the whole world. It was Anthemius of Tralles, the most learned man in the discipline called engineering

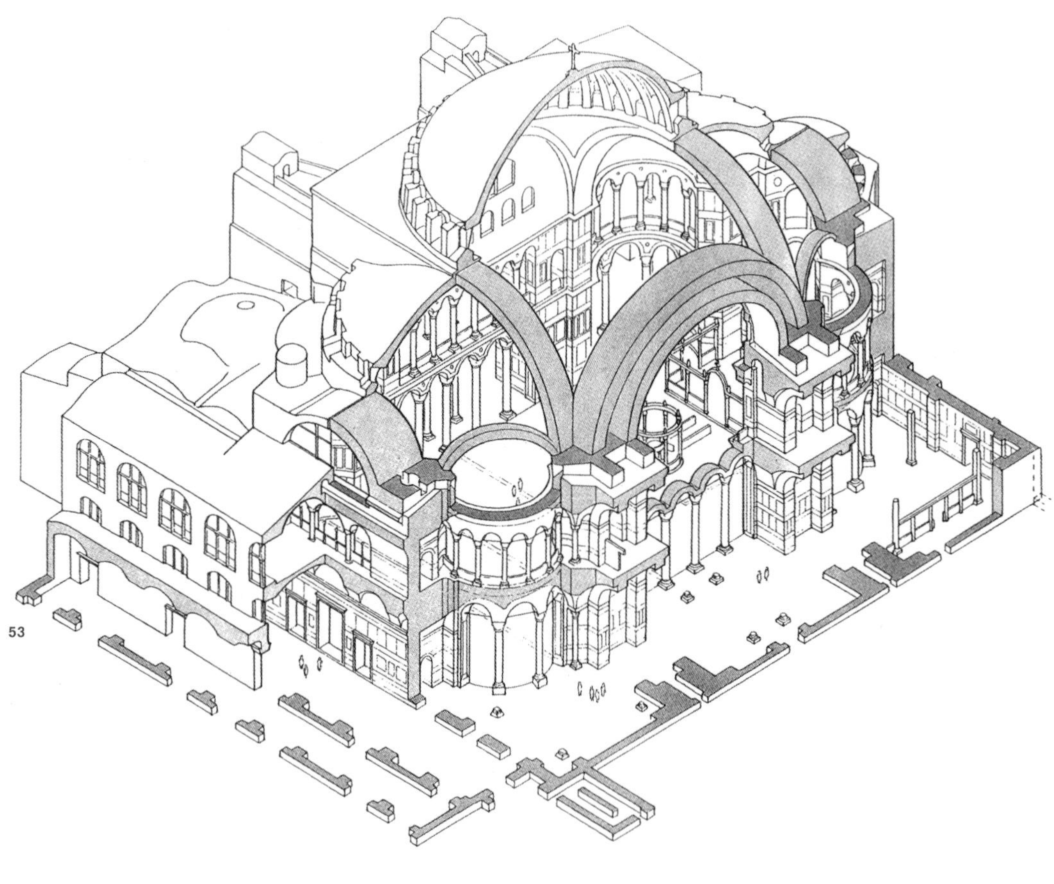
53

54

55

52 (previous page) Saint Sophia, Constantinople (now Istanbul), 532–37. Designers and engineers: Anthemius of Tralles and Isidorus of Miletus. Interior, after 1849 restoration. 53 Saint Sophia. Cutaway isometric drawing. 54 Saint Sophia. Cutaway isometric drawing. 55 Saint Sophia. Detail of iron tie on interior columns. Iron ties were widely used to carry outward thrusts of arches, especially during construction.

> [mechanike logiotatos], *not only of all his contemporaries, but also as compared to those who had lived long before him, that ministered to the emperor's zeal by regulating the work of the builders and preparing in advance designs of what was going to be built. He had as partner another engineer* [mechanopoios] *called Isidorus, a native of Miletus, who was intelligent in all respects and worthy to serve the Emperor Justinian.*[2]

The fundamental difference between Saint Sophia and its Roman antecedents is that it is constructed entirely in masonry rather than concrete. Stone blocks were used for the main load-bearing piers and various smaller columns and arches, and brick for the main arches, vaults, and domes, and for the many load-bearing and partition walls. Lime mortar was used for the brickwork, and, crucially, there is no evidence of classic Roman concrete construction—either mass concrete, or brick facing with concrete infill, or hydraulic cement using pozzolana. A considerable amount of iron was used, both in the form of cramps to secure adjacent large stones and as ties, up to 40 by 50 millimeters in cross section and 3.7 meters long, linking the tops of columns at the point from which various small arches spring. The function of these ties is not entirely clear, since the arches are always well buttressed by neighboring arches or substantial walls. Like similar ties in the jack arches of late eighteenth-century mills and warehouses, they may well have been used mainly during construction and to provide stability as the lime mortar hardened.

The present central dome is not all original, and it is indicative of the inherent stability of masonry domes that it was possible for parts of it to be repaired and reconstructed. Some five months after an earthquake in December 557, part of the original dome—the eastern semidome and the main eastern arch—collapsed. On this occasion the entire dome was rebuilt and the opportunity taken to increase the rise of the central dome from the original 8 meters to nearly 15 meters. This reduced the outward thrust and would have helped allay fears that the shallowness of the original dome had led to some alarming movements of the structure, and perhaps contributing to the collapse after the earthquake. In 989 the western half of the building collapsed after an earthquake and was rebuilt. In 1346 the eastern end collapsed a second time and was again rebuilt.

The Decline of the Roman Empire

The economic decline in the Western empire during the fourth century was followed, inexorably, by the demise of the Eastern empire during the late sixth and early seventh centuries. This occurred despite the efforts of Emperor Justinian to revitalize the Eastern empire in the manner successfully used by Augustus: a comprehensive military and civil construction campaign. Justinian had paid for the reconstruction and improvement of fortifications along the extensive borders of the empire, funding the refurbishment of old civic buildings and churches and the construction of many new ones. He had also deployed newly trained and well-equipped armies to strategic points around the huge perimeter of the empire.

What had worked for Augustus five centuries earlier, however, did not work for Justinian. Times were different. The border was longer and more distant from the empire's hub, and people were less prepared to pay taxes to the central administration. In the intervening half millennium the neighboring countries had not been stagnant; their armies were now often better trained and equipped than the Roman armies, which had not developed their military technologies and strategies to meet the new threats. And finally there were the taxes: An army and its fortifications needed to be paid for. The huge tax burden levied by the imperial center was very unpopular at the perimeter, especially since the numbers and locations of troops were not sufficiently flexible and were increasingly inadequate to meet the growing variety and number of incursions from outside.

Gradually more and more of the farmers who owned the titles to their own plots of land under Roman law decided it would be of greater and more immediate benefit to give their land rights and a proportion of their harvests to a local landowner in return for the protection of locally organized troops and the town fortifications and protection from the emperor's tax collectors. As Christianity spread, the church, too, became involved in this voluntary process of virtual enslavement of the population to the local barons in the system we know as feudalism.

The period of European history that followed the fall of the Roman empire serves to show how intimately linked the construction industry was, and still is, with economic prosperity, a functioning system of government, and, in

56

57

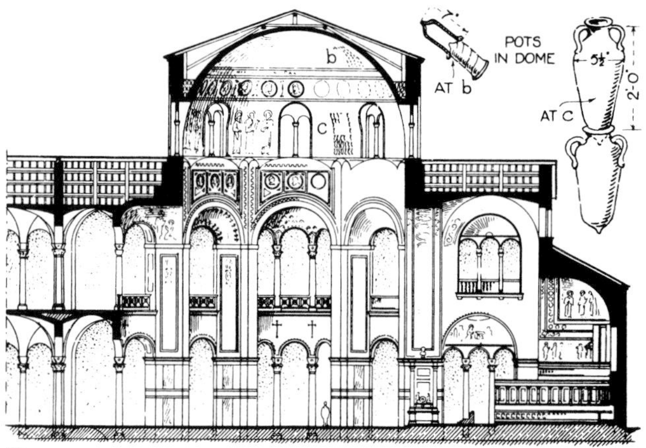

58

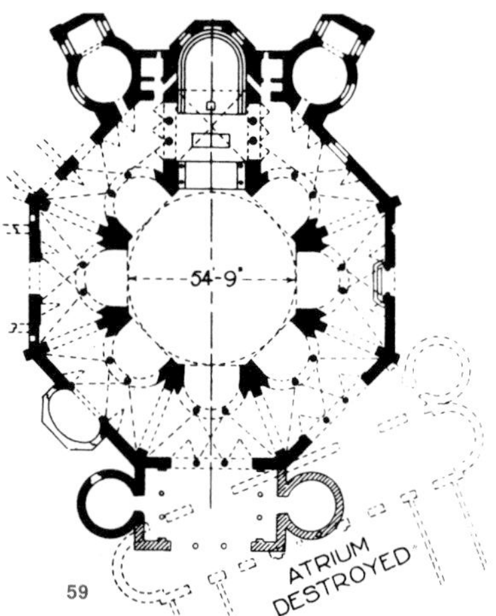

59

56 Sant' Apollinare Nuovo, Ravenna, c. 490–549. 57 San Vitale, Ravenna, c. 526–47. 58 San Vitale. Section and detail of hollow clay amphora used to reduce the weight of the dome. 59 San Vitale. Plan of dome.

particular, a reliable source of taxation. The Greek and Roman empires had invented and developed the very idea of the city and the construction industry that was needed to create it. The survival of the city depended upon a whole series of infrastructures apart from the construction industry: trade, transport, mass housing, the supply of water and food, and some degree of sanitation. These infrastructures required a skilled engineering sector to provide ships, vehicles, bridges, buildings, aqueducts, drainage, and so on. No less important was the need for highly skilled military engineers to defend the cities' rulers and leaders, their infrastructures, and perhaps their inhabitants.

With the demise of international trade routes and a centralized government able to raise sufficient income from taxes to pay for defense and the maintenance of the infrastructures, the great cities and their way of life crumbled, both metaphorically and literally. Within a remarkably short time, cities all over the former empire fell prey to the armies of neighboring peoples. The invading armies, such as the Huns and Goths in the Western empire in the fifth century, Persians in Alexandria (616), and Arabs in southern Spain (711), looted and destroyed many of the large buildings by way of imposing their own cultures. Other buildings were adapted to the needs of the invading culture and others simply fell into disuse and decayed, often providing a useful source of recycled construction materials.

As the Western Roman empire declined, so invasions from the East brought building ideas from the Byzantine empire and farther afield. The Western Christian church architecture that would develop during the early Middle Ages incorporated and blended Roman building forms such as the basilica with ideas from the Middle East, especially the central-plan church. In the early sixth century the city of Ravenna in northern Italy was occupied by the Ostrogoths, who came from the eastern Balkans adjacent to the Black Sea. Two buildings constructed in Ravenna at the same time illustrate the meeting of East and West. The Basilica of Sant' Apollinare Nuovo, in
56 Roman style, was begun in 490 and completed in 549. The Church of San Vitale (c. 526–47) is built on a char-
57, 58 acteristic Byzantine central plan.The dome at San Vitale, spanning 16.7 meters, is formed using the Roman technique for making lightweight domes with hollow clay vessels in preference to bricks or concrete. In the lower 59
part of the dome the vessels are *amphorae* (wine bottles) about 600 millimeters tall and 150 millimeters in diameter, while toward the crown smaller, cuplike pots about 170 millimeters long and 60 millimeters in diameter are used.

As the Roman empire was invaded from adjacent territories, so new ideas of building began to penetrate the Roman way of thinking, especially from the Islamic world. From the seventh century, Muslim builders brought from northern Africa to southern Spain their characteristic arches supported on slender columns—an altogether more delicate type of structure than the Romans had developed. The sense of poise and balance they achieved is often breathtaking, and it is easy to see why they inspired the designers of the later Christian cathedrals
in the medieval era. 60, 61

The first successful defense against invasions from beyond the borders of the former Roman empire was in 732 at Tours, in France, when the Frankish leader Charles Martel defeated an Arab army and gave his name to what became the Carolingian dynasty. Martel's grandson, Charlemagne (c. 742–814), was crowned as the first Holy Roman Emperor in Saint Peter's Basilica in Rome on Christmas Day, 800. Despite his religious title, he was primarily a military leader and succeeded in reestablishing Christianity in Western Europe by brutal means. However, Charlemagne also embraced the idea of monasticism as a means for stabilizing the new Holy Roman Empire, and this led to a substantial wave of new building construction, some of the finest examples of which, fortunately, survive. The Palatine Chapel in Aachen, Germany, built between about 786 and 805, illustrates that the best designers were still able to construct remarkable buildings. 62

The Oratory of Theodulph in Germigny-des-Prés, France, completed about 806, is an altogether more restrained building with its simple and stark masonry structure. It illustrates the essence of the emerging Romanesque style
that was linked to the growing monastic movement. 63

From this same period there survives the earliest example of a drawing of a medieval building. The plan for a new monastery at Saint Gall in Switzerland (c. 819–26) shows

60

61

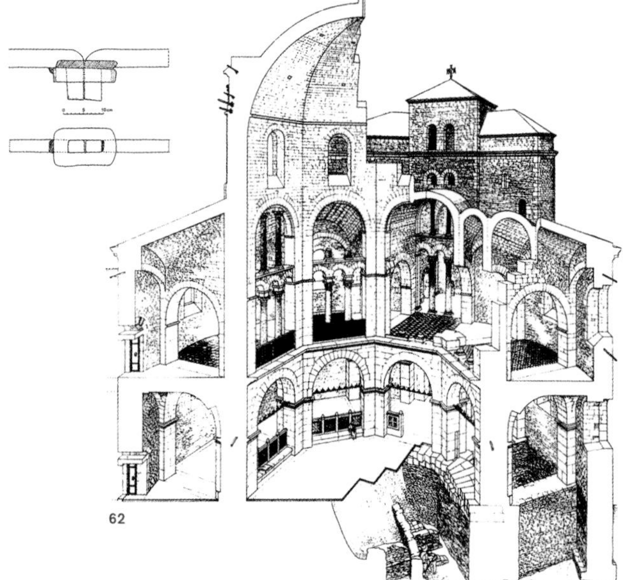

62

63

60 The Great Mosque, Qairawan, Tunisia, c. 670. Interior with columns stabilized by iron ties. 61 The Great Mosque, Cordoba, Spain, c. 786. Vaulted roof of the Capilla de Villaviciosa, with pronounced ribs. 62 Palatine Chapel, Aachen, Germany, c. 786–805. Cutaway isometric and detail of iron tie used to carry outward thrust of the dome. 63 Oratory of Theodulph, Germigny-des-Prés, France, c. 806.

what is virtually a small town, laid out as a grid like the
64 Roman insulae, with a huge chapel at its center. From an engineering history point of view, the key feature of this plan is that it was not executed. It was a drawing whose purpose was to convey the designers' intentions.

Technological Revolutions in the Middle Ages

During the early medieval era in Europe, up to about A.D. 1100, a great deal of construction was undertaken. While there is evidence of a gradual progression of architectural styles, however, there seems to have been little innovation in engineering—a fact perhaps due to two factors. First, much of the great legacy left by the Roman building engineers survived, and served as evidence of what was possible to achieve. On the other hand, there was less money available to the small states into which the empire had fragmented, and less motivation to make the grand gestures that characterized imperial rule. The earliest signs of what became a widespread growth of building began in France in the eleventh century on two fronts: the construction of fortifications and fortified houses in masonry, and an increase in church building. These developments had their roots in various agricultural and technological changes during the previous centuries that had helped the earlier medieval rural communities prosper and grow.

The period we call "medieval" was effectively the period during which the technologies necessary to create cities were rediscovered and developed. About seven hundred years elapsed between the demise of the Roman empire and the reinvention of the city in a new form. The pace of change and progress was slow for two main reasons. First, both the feudal barons and the towns were fiercely independent, competitive, and highly suspicious of sharing anything with their neighbors. Nations, such as they existed at all, were formed from fragile and capricious alliances that often broke down and reformed in new patterns. This environment resembled that of the early Greek city-states, and differed utterly from the common purpose that existed during the Roman period, when the latest military and civil technologies spread quickly throughout the empire. To a large extent, the very concept of an empire meant a whole series of shared ideas and technologies. Without huge cities and international trade, the need for massive civil and building engineering projects evaporated.

Second, by A.D. 700 there had been a near total collapse of the systems by which engineering knowledge was generated, practiced, learned, taught, and preserved for future generations. Like all imperial societies, the Romans guarded their strategic knowledge by keeping it within the army and its related infrastructure. They did not set about teaching the residents of occupied territories the engineering knowledge and skill that was crucial to making weapons, for example. The practical understanding needed to interpret and use such knowledge was lost as the army withdrew, and, finally, as the people who had that knowledge died without the opportunity to pass it on to the following generation. There were, of course, many Greek and Roman engineering textbooks, but most were lost or destroyed by those who were not able to make use of them and hence did not understand their value. Even the texts that did survive recorded only certain aspects of engineering knowledge: that which could be written down (illustrations were very rare and none has survived). During the early medieval period the incentives and mechanisms for maintaining, disseminating, and developing the ancient technologies were largely absent.

This is not to say, however, that basic building and related technologies disappeared altogether. Most of them survived in pockets all over the former Roman empire—the manufacture of iron and glass and the use of hydraulic cement,[3] or constructing a vault or even a hypocaust. The building needs of communities were scaled down to match local wealth and the skills of the local construction industries. There was also a huge building stock surviving in the former empire's major towns, and, with modest repair and maintenance, this continued to be used through the medieval period, especially where the climate was forgiving.

In the absence of a major imperial driving force, it is hardly surprising that no significant engineering developments can be said to have occurred in the European building industry during the centuries following Rome's decline. However, the lack of such an influence provided the stimulus for a very different type of progress: the development of local self-sufficiency and prosperity. The situation in early medieval France, Germany, and England must have been similar to that experienced by former iron curtain countries after the disintegration of

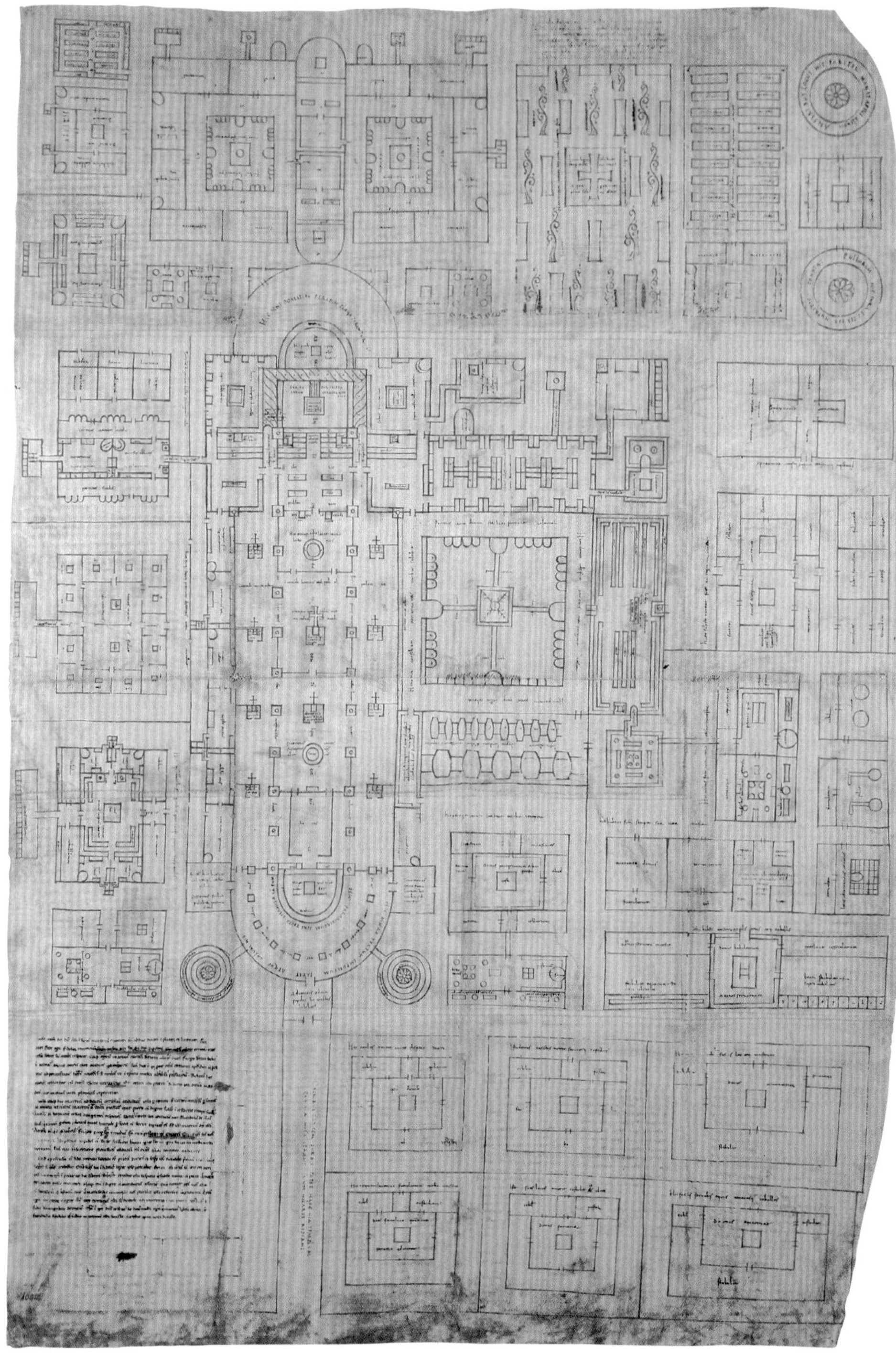

64

64 New monastery, Saint Gall, Switzerland. Unexecuted plan, c. 819–26.

the U.S.S.R. in the 1990s and the disappearance of central control from Moscow.

The first requirement of self-sufficiency and prosperity was food, and the eighth and ninth centuries saw some major developments in agriculture. Some were technological—the efficiency of the plow was improved, and a new harness for horses was devised that did not press on the animals' windpipe, enabling them to pull with greater force. Together these developments halved the time needed to till a field. No less significant was the innovation in northern Europe of the three-field system of crop rotation, first recorded in 763. This was more suited to the northern climate than the former two-field system used in the Mediterranean region, which had been imposed by the invading Romans. The result was an immediate increase in crop yield of about 30 percent, rising to about 50 percent by the twelfth century as more and more efficient systems were discovered through constant experimentation with different plowing, planting, and harvesting regimes.

Major agricultural progress was followed by advances in what we now call mechanical engineering, especially the development of the waterwheel as a source of power. From today's viewpoint, the list of mechanical technologies that the Romans did or did not devise is full of surprises. For example, they used gear wheels to convey power from one shaft to a parallel one, and also from one shaft to another at right angles. However, they knew of no means of converting the rotary motion of a waterwheel to the reciprocating motion needed to drive a saw back and forth, or vice versa. The crank, which appears so obvious a device to us, was unknown in Europe until around 800 A.D. Surprisingly, perhaps the humblest of all machines that use the crank, the carpenter's brace and bit, was not invented until around 1420, in Holland.

With the exception of the waterwheel, the Romans did not devise any machine operated by a power other than that generated by man or animal. The windmill was unknown, and even the waterwheel was used for a single purpose: to turn millstones to grind corn. As usual, what the Romans did they did on a big scale. For example, in about A.D. 310 they built a large flour mill at Barbegal, in southern France, near Arles, driven by water fed from local streams by a purpose-built aqueduct. This facility consisted of two flights (parallel rows) of eight waterwheels each, which drove a total of thirty-two mills capable of grinding twenty-eight tons of grain in a twenty-four-hour period. Such examples were rare, and the knowledge and understanding of waterwheel and mill technology essentially belonged to the occupying Roman army and generally remained in its hands. Such expertise served the needs of garrisons and the local administration, and disappeared when the occupying power withdrew.

The use of waterwheels during early medieval times began slowly, but eventually spread from town to town throughout Europe over the next three hundred years. This time, however, the mechanical understanding of waterwheel technology resided in the local community at a grassroots level, so to speak, and included the full infrastructure needed to ensure its survival and growth: local iron production wherever possible, the skills to provide a constant flow of water, millwrights to maintain and repair the machinery, and the apprentice system to train the next generation. In the mid-tenth century we find the first reliable evidence for waterwheels used to power processes other than milling flour: a fulling mill. A 65
century later a waterwheel was being used to blow air into a furnace to melt iron. Both were also remarkable in that they used a crank mechanism to the convert the rotary motion of the wheel to reciprocating motion. The Domesday Book of 1086, a survey commanded by William the Conqueror, records that England had 5,624 mills in some 3,000 communities; the numbers would have been at least as high in continental European countries. The eleventh century also saw the first use of a tide mill that used the ebb and flow of the tide to drive the waterwheel, evidence of the ingenuity of those who happened not to live near a suitable river. One was built at the entrance to the port of Dover, in England, soon after 1066.

During the next hundred years machines driven by water or wind power were developed to perform more and more of the labor previously done by human power—fulling, tanning, laundering, sawing, and crushing anything from rocks to olives. Machines were devised to operate bellows for furnaces and hammers for forges, grindstones for sharpening tools and polishing, mills for grinding pigments for cloth dyes and devices for pulping wood or cloth for paper and processing mash for beer. The

65

harnessing of water and wind power during the twelfth and thirteenth centuries was an industrial revolution at least as significant as the more famous one in the eighteenth century. With each new machine, people began to notice that some were more effective than others in using the water or wind power; these were the seeds of the concepts that would, in the eighteenth century, become known as "energy" and "efficiency." The idea of storing energy also seems to have been born in the mid-thirteenth century. By raising a large weight, the potential energy thereby stored could be released and used by attaching a rope and enabling it to drive a machine, such as a clock, as it slowly fell. The trebuchet (an engine for hurling heavy missiles) relied on the same principle in a simpler form. At around the same time we find the first use of a spring, in the form of a bent sapling, being used in conjunction with a treadle, to drive a lathe. Metal springs were used in locks in the mid-thirteenth century, and to drive a clock mechanism in around 1430.

Transport also underwent a number of revolutions in the medieval period. Through the ninth and tenth centuries, the spread of the stirrup and the growing use of iron shoes enabled horses to carry their riders faster and farther. From earliest times, all freight wagons had been two-wheeled, to enable them to negotiate corners and the vagaries of rugged roads. The ninth century saw the first use of the pivoted front axle, which made four-wheeled wagons a practical proposition. The new harness developed for plowing also allowed several pairs of horses to work as teams, and the development of simple braking mechanisms enabled a single man to control

65 Villard de Honnecourt, sketch of water-powered sawmill, c. 1230.

even large wagons carrying heavy loads. Nevertheless, despite these technical developments, various circumstances—their cost, their limited benefits compared to two-wheeled wagons, and the dearth of good roads—delayed the widespread use of large four-wheeled wagons until the twelfth or thirteenth century.

Taken together, the improvements in the effectiveness of the horse-drawn plow and the range of applications of water power, the use of a new source of power (wind), and the means of storing energy for potential future use were evidence of a new attitude toward the world. Medieval Europe was discovering, or rediscovering, the deliberate act of achieving technical progress using the process we now call scientific or experimental method—that is, imagining something that did not exist and undertaking practical experiments to try to achieve it. The thirteenth-century English philosophers Robert Grosseteste and Roger Bacon, and like-minded thinkers, were the first to articulate the process and record it in a way that could be learned by others—a fundamental characteristic of modern science and engineering.

These technical developments gradually had their effect on the patterns of settlement in northern Europe. Like droplets of water condensing out of saturated air, people began living together in larger and larger groups. They did this both because it was possible—using horses meant they could live farther from the fields they tended—and because there were economic benefits in doing so: A blacksmith or miller could do better when serving the needs of many hundreds of people. Increasingly efficient agriculture generated food surpluses that could be traded or sold in markets and, as land transport improved, even exported to neighboring towns far from the sea or navigable rivers.

As populations began to coalesce to form villages and towns, so their future prosperity became dependent upon these towns and the benefits they brought. The church played an important part in shaping and maintaining these new urban communities, and the construction of a church was an effective, almost essential part of this process. The local landowners and barons played an equally important role, for their wealth, too, came to depend on the success of towns as the catalyst for the trade in surplus agricultural production. This prosperity fueled the manufacturing of goods, both those needed to promote further economic growth and those needed to soak up the escalating accumulation of wealth that the landowners and the church were amassing.

Thus, by the twelfth century, towns had become essential to the European economy, and the more prosperous of them aspired to the status of a city. This meant constructing larger churches and civic buildings, centers of learning that would later become universities, infrastructure such as water supply, some drainage, roads and bridges, and, of course, fortifications to defend these fruits of newfound wealth. Leading the field in this commercial race were the city-states of northern Italy, closely followed by the prosperous towns of German-speaking countries and France.

The Rediscovery of Greek Scholarship

The final ingredient that fueled the twelfth-century revolution in building engineering was the rediscovery of the idea of scholarship. In the ninth century the established orthodoxy was Christian scholarship, which prospered throughout the medieval period within the monasteries. Progress was slow; indeed, progress was not the goal of monastic learning. Intellects of the tenth century relied largely on the writings of only a few great philosophers from many centuries before—especially Augustine (354–430) and Boethius (480–524), Bishop Isidore of Seville (c. 560–636), and the Venerable Bede (673–735). The principal aim of these scholars was to develop Christian thought, and this constantly and inevitably led them back to the Bible. Their work consisted of two main activities: exegesis, explaining events and phenomena by reference back to biblical texts; and hermeneutics, or seeking ever more subtle, and sometimes curious, interpretations of the text of the Bible. Not surprisingly, there is little in the Bible that addresses what we now call natural philosophy or science, and even less that would be of use to someone designing or constructing buildings.

Nevertheless, both Augustine and Boethius did address building design, albeit only briefly. Like the Greek philosophers before them they sought to explain the universe in terms of geometry, number, and harmony, addressing every field of what we now call natural science: optics, acoustics, astronomy, music, mechanics, botany.

Augustine and Boethius learned much of this directly from Greek sources. By the ninth and tenth centuries, however, the Greek sources and detailed explanations of these ideas had been lost, and reading Augustine and Boethius without their Greek antecedents must have been like reading the text of a book about an artist without any of the illustrations.

Augustine and Boethius augmented their explanations of the world with what they saw as manifestations of the same principles they found in the Bible. Augustine, for instance, used the biblical passage *"Omnia in mensura et numero et pondere disposuisti"* ("Thou hast ordered all things in measure, and number, and weight") (Wis. 11:21), together with the philosophy of Pythagoras and Plato to formulate his interpretation of the Christian universe, its creation and its order. Concerning the design of buildings, he drew attention to the details, including dimensions, of several significant structures in the Bible: the Ark of Noah, Moses' Tabernacle, Solomon's Temple, and the Celestial Temple revealed to Ezekiel in a vision. Much later a well-known fourteenth-century Masonic poem even claimed that Solomon actually "taught" architecture in a manner "but little different from that used today,"[4] and that this science was directly transmitted to France. The writings of Augustine and Boethius dominated the early Middle Ages, and the cosmic applicability of the laws of harmony features boldly in writings about both music and building throughout the medieval period.

While such guidance was probably of limited practical use to a builder of earthly structures, there is little doubt that Augustine and Boethius's purpose in frequently addressing these matters in their writings was to give man confidence in himself, both in a general way and when faced with particular choices and decisions. As we see throughout the development of building design, this reflects the building designer's predicament—the need for some sort of explanation and knowledge of successful precedent to serve as a basis for an engineer's confidence to build, especially when attempting something for the first time.

During the eleventh century this firmly established body of Christian scholarship in northern Europe was abruptly shaken by an entirely new source of ideas and learning: the contents of libraries in Moorish-occupied Spain. The prophet Muhammad had united the Arab countries of the Middle East, and, upon his death in 632, the main goal of Islam had become to spread his influence both into the future and geographically beyond his homeland. Within just two years of his death, land armies were dispatched westward and overran the Middle East, Egypt (including Alexandria, the jewel in the Eastern Roman empire), and the entire Mediterranean border of Africa. When they reached Spain in about 700, they found the Christian Visigoth kingdom that had been established after the Romans had left some 250 years earlier. While the Arabs suppressed Christianity and its scholarship, they brought their own learning and what they had absorbed from Greek and Roman culture. Most importantly, they brought into Spain Arabic translations and some originals of a large number of works by the great Greek and Roman philosophers, mathematicians, and scientists.

As the Christian forces in northern Spain eventually retaliated and pushed south during the eleventh century, the contents of the great libraries in Moorish Spain were gradually discovered, the prize trophy being Toledo in 1085. News of these works spread to northern Europe in the eleventh century, and several scholars made visits and learned Arabic in order to study them. One was Adelard of Bath (c. 1080–1160), who was studying with the scholar Thierry of Chartres (c. 1100–1155). Adelard visited Dominicus Gundissalinus, the archdeacon of Segovia and a scholar of the Arabic translations of the Greek philosophers. There he came across a copy of Euclid's *Elements of Geometry* in Arabic, which he translated into Latin for the first time. When he brought this and other works back to his fellow scholars at Chartres in the mid-1120s (some say a few years later), it had a profound effect on the nature of their learning and was soon far from being strictly religious. Thierry's *Heptateuchon*, describing the curriculum for the seven liberal arts, included geometry and arithmetic and recommended further reading on surveying, measurement, practical astronomy, and medicine. It was even claimed by some that, under Thierry's influence, the school of Chartres attempted to transform theology into geometry.

Geometry had, of course, survived as a practical art throughout the Middle Ages, but the rediscovery of Euclid did lead to a great improvement in the level of geometrical knowledge that could be learned. This made it possible to draw building designs more accurately, and was of great practical use in the construction process, both in setting out the building and in checking the finished parts and their relative dispositions for accuracy. Such an improvement alone would have enabled builders to contemplate larger and taller buildings. However, it was in its capacity to help provide some sort of explanation and justification of designs and design decisions that geometry probably had a more profound effect. Euclid introduced into the medieval consciousness a crucial new ingredient: the notion of a proof using the logic of geometry. Medieval scholars created, quite literally, a new type of geometry—*geometria theorica*. This provided the perfect tool for the scholars at Chartres to argue their views more logically and with greater conviction and, hence, to justify decisions made. Like the Greek scholars a thousand years earlier, they sought ways of applying the new tool in every possible way and context. A similar phenomenon would occur some six hundred years later with the invention of calculus, when scientists and mathematicians searched for every possible application of this new mathematical device (see chapter 4, p. 222).

Theoretical and Practical Geometry

The first medieval scholar to distinguish between "*geometria theorica et practica*" was Hugh of Saint Victor (1096–1141), sometime between about 1125 and 1141. Following the precedent of Plato and Aristotle, he argued that geometry, like branches of philosophy, should be divided into *theorica* and *practica*. He argued the distinction between practical skills of geometry and the theoretical (contemplative) skills that were contained in Euclid. Hugh put geometry as a theoretical tool to good use in practical ways—for instance, in helping to explain and justify information given in the Scriptures. He calculated that the reported size of Noah's Ark (40,000 inches long) would indeed have been large enough to accommodate all the animals of the world and their food. A pupil of Hugh's, a Scottish monk named Richard of Saint Victor (d. 1173), used geometry to interpret several architectural exemplars mentioned in the Bible and even argued that the Celestial Temple described in Ezekiel must have resembled a late Romanesque cathedral.

There soon followed many more geometry textbooks—eleven are known to have existed between 1125 and 1280, and over seventy copies of two of them survive today. Some were purely practical, with guidance on all manner of calculations as well as geometry, including commercial arithmetic and the proportions of constituents needed to make different alloys for coins. Others dealt with geometry more philosophically and discussed the purpose of the different branches of geometry. One anonymous work from the mid-twelfth century distinguished the two branches of geometry as follows:

> *There are two parts of geometry, the theoretical and the practical. The theoretical is that which contemplates proportions, quantities and their measures by the speculation of the mind alone. The practical is when we measure the unknown quantity of some thing by the experience of the senses."*[5]

Another, written around 1140 by Domenicus Gundissalinus, gave a more detailed distinction clearly defining not only the theoretical and practical aspects of geometry but also their respective "purposes" and "duties":

	GEOMETRIA THEORICA	GEOMETRIA PRACTICA
FINIS *(purpose)*	*to teach something*	*to do something*
OFFICIUM *(duty)*	*to give reasons and dispel doubt*	*to give measurements or limits which the work should not surpass*[6]

Here we see a description of geometry in the twelfth century as a body of knowledge that was serving a function for cathedral designers very similar to the role of mechanics and statics in engineering today. It was used in teaching, and not only provided certain quantitative results but also had a certain capacity to explain things, and hence to provide reasons and justification for decisions and choices. In a phrase that appears to anticipate modern limit state design in structural engineering by some 800 years, twelfth-century geometry was also used to set "limits which the work should not surpass" (see chapter 8, p. 470).

As well as a practical tool, geometry was an intellectual device that enabled people, literally, to think new types of thought, to articulate abstract ideas that were previously unimaginable, to embody the rigor of logic in their discussions and arguments. Following the philosophical separation of theory and practice in geometry, it became a common theme in many geometry treatises to discuss the interdependence of theory and practice, anticipating many similar discussions about engineering during the nineteenth and twentieth centuries.

The Scientific Revolution of the Thirteenth Century

Until the twelfth century the study of science had largely consisted of studying the works of earlier scholars, writing mainly commentaries on their predecessors' explanations, and seeking ways of trying to reconcile ideas about the natural world with those contained in the Bible. There was seldom any attempt to bring new data or observations into the argument. The result, it has to be said, was often obscure, revisiting the same themes again and again, bringing to mind the legendary medieval debate about how many angels could fit onto the head of a pin.

The new scholarship that grew from the rediscovery of the works of the great Greek philosophers, mathematicians, and scientists led to what can only be called a major scientific revolution. The principal result was to introduce into the debating arena a secular system of logic and rhetoric. In geometry there was the unprecedented opportunity to make links between an abstract world of the intellect and the real world of measurable dimensions and angles. It is perhaps no great surprise that the main focus of the scientists' attention was optics—the behavior of light rays, the phenomena of reflection and refraction, how lenses and prisms worked, and, above all, explaining the shape and colors of the rainbow and the formation of sun dogs (parhelia) and halos around the sun and moon.

The list of European scholars studying scientific topics in the thirteenth and fourteenth centuries is a surprisingly long one, running to several hundred. One of the most important was Robert Grosseteste (c. 1175–1253), who developed an approach to scientific knowledge that was fundamentally different from the classical approach based solely on observation and contemplation. Grosseteste was the foremost intellect of his day in mathematics and natural science, especially optics, and was arguably the father of the scientific revolution in the Middle Ages that brought the most significant progress in scientific thinking since Aristotle. Born of humble parents at Stradbroke in Suffolk, England, he was educated, perhaps first in Paris and then at Oxford in theology and the natural sciences. He became a distinguished lecturer and the first rector of the school the Franciscans established in Oxford around 1224. Between 1214 and 1231 Grosseteste held in succession the archdeaconries of Chester, Northampton, and Leicester and, in 1235, accepted the bishopric of Lincoln, in whose diocese Oxford lay. He saw geometry at the heart of any attempt to understand the world: "Without geometry it is impossible to understand nature, since all forms of natural bodies are in essence geometrical and can be reduced to lines, angles and regular figures."[7]

Grosseteste was the first to develop what we now call the hypothetico-deductive method in science, in which a hypothesis is made and tested by examining its logical consequences. Put simply, it led to an entirely new way of creating knowledge and, in turn, soon led to the search for and discovery of new types of knowledge.

One of these new avenues of inquiry was what is known today as statics, and the earliest name associated with this was Jordanus Nemorarius (c. 1180–c. 1237). He came from Germany, but very little is known of his life save that he lectured on mathematics at the University of Paris. His influence, though, was considerable. He was the first scholar since Greek times to consider statics, and the first to represent a force graphically as a line with length and direction, and he used this approach to consider the equilibrium of a bent lever. He developed the Aristotelian mechanics of the pulley by dealing with the forces acting on a body on an inclined plane. This may not seem a huge step to us, but the monumental leap was transferring the idea of a force into two dimensions; previously the only force considered had been gravity. It was then a relatively small jump to seeing forces as amenable to treatment using the powerful and well-established tool of geometry. Like many scholars, Jordanus put his intellect to work on military engineering. He analyzed the mechanics of the trebuchet by considering the potential of the counterweight to deliver useful energy (as we would call it) as it fell, concluding that it was the vertical fall that was important, not the route, inclined or curved, by which it fell. In this and discussions of the lever, he was using what we would now call the principle of virtual work—a major step forward from Aristotle's principle of virtual velocities. His books became widely known and respected throughout the world of scholars. His most famous work, *De Ponderibus* (On Weight) (c. 1220), was quoted by many later scientists and mathematicians over the next two centuries.

Perhaps the best known and most influential of the medieval philosophers was Roger Bacon (c. 1214–94). He studied geometry, arithmetic, music, and astronomy as a young man first at Oxford and then at the University of Paris from 1234, where he was awarded his degree in theology around 1241. Simultaneously he pursued a serious interest in alchemy, on which he wrote one of his many books. But he had little respect for the scholars teaching science in Paris, because they clearly were not basing their ideas on observations of the real world. He reserved praise for just one man, Peter of Maricourt (c. 1210–c. 1270), who, by experiment, developed various metallic alloys for use in armor and was probably the same "Petrus" who first studied magnetism in an experimental manner. Bacon's reputation as a lecturer spread both in Paris and, from 1247, in Oxford, where he came under the influence of Robert Grosseteste's ideas on science, which he took up and developed with enthusiasm. Perhaps due to ill health, but also because his ideas were increasingly seen as threatening to the established orthodoxy, Bacon finally left Oxford in 1257 and entered the Order of Friars Minor, continuing his interest in the sciences despite the disapproval of his superiors.

In 1266 Bacon wrote to Pope Clement IV, composing what looks remarkably similar to an application for a research grant that a mathematician or scientist might make today. His proposal was for an encyclopedia of all the sciences, to be worked on by a team of collaborators and coordinated by a body in the church. His principal aim was to show the pope that sciences had a rightful role in the university curriculum. The pope, misunderstanding the letter as a statement that the encyclopedia already existed, asked to see the work, which Bacon then set about writing, eventually resulting in three volumes. He later embarked on even bolder projects—*General Principles of Natural Philosophy* and *General Principles of Mathematics*—though neither of these was completed. Around 1278 Bacon was put in prison by his fellow Franciscans, charged with introducing "suspected novelties" into his teaching. Nevertheless, he did not refrain from putting forward his views, and they were as aggressively stated in his last writings in 1293 as at any time in his life.

Bacon clearly had a remarkable imagination and proposed numerous ideas of what man might achieve through a scientific understanding of the world. His experimental interest in alchemy included the discovery of an explosive mixture containing saltpeter (potassium nitrate), similar to what we might now call gunpowder. His most important scientific work was on the use of geometry in studying and explaining optical phenomena demonstrated with lenses and mirrors. Among his notes on optics, he wrote, "Mathematics is the door and the key to the sciences," and he famously proposed the idea of the telescope, a challenge that the Oxford scientist Leonard Digges and his son Thomas would meet nearly three hundred years later. As Bacon relates in his *Opus Majus* (Great Work):

> *For we can so shape transparent bodies [lenses], and arrange them in such a way with respect to our sight and objects of vision, that the rays will be refracted and bent in any direction we desire, and under any angle we wish, we may see the object near or at a distance. . . . So we might also cause the Sun, Moon and stars in appearance to descend here below . . .*[8]

Bacon's influence on the development of science was considerable. His writings provide an insight into the developing medieval mind that was also creating the great cathedrals of the period. In many ways the cathedrals were the product of just the same experimental approach that Bacon was describing.

Between the eleventh and thirteenth centuries the medieval mind created and began to demonstrate that the understanding generated by scholarship could be directed to useful purpose—an idea far in advance of Greek science. The following extraordinary passage from Bacon's writings (c. 1260) shows the degree to which man's entire relationship with his world had changed and his imagination awakened and stimulated. Thoughts such as these had, quite literally, been inconceivable a century or two earlier.

> *Machines may be made by which the largest ships, with only one man steering them, will be moved faster than if they were filled with rowers; wagons may be built which will move with incredible speed and without the aid of beasts; flying machines can be constructed in which a man . . . may beat the air with wings like a bird . . . ; machines will make it possible to go to the bottom of seas and rivers.*[9]

The medieval era was a period of constant and profound technological and scientific development; the zeitgeist touched every aspect of human activity. By the end of this era, especially the two centuries from about 1100 to 1300, we find major changes in every corner of life. This was the time that musical notation was being developed, which not only made music available to posterity, but also provided the opportunity to experiment and create entirely new musical forms. The unique identities of modern European languages were being established, and they were being used for the first time in place of Latin as a means of conveying complex ideas in both fact and fiction. Painters and sculptors were beginning to portray secular subjects. The first cathedral schools were being founded, some of which became our first universities—Padua, Paris, Oxford, Cambridge, Durham, and others. Finally, we must remember that all these cultural, scholarly, mechanical, and religious changes were taking place in a lively political and military climate. The Norman invasion of England in 1066 was just one of several in Western Europe during the eleventh century that was followed by the need to consolidate and establish identities for the newly occupied territories.

The Construction Boom in Late Medieval Europe

By the eleventh century the growing number of prosperous landowners and towns in central Europe led to what can only be called a construction boom. Their substantial assets needed defending. Vernacular buildings and fortifications consisting of earthworks and simple timber structures were no longer adequate. Masonry construction, and its careful design to suit its purpose (to resist ever more ingenious siege equipment and military tactics) was the answer. The benefits of better-fortified houses and castles were soon apparent, and the idea spread quickly in France and parts of what are now central and southern Germany, Switzerland, and northern Italy. Of course, the improvement of defenses triggered an arms race, which, for neither the first nor the last time in history, served as a powerful stimulus and source of funds for both the construction and mechanical engineering industries.

As well as building castles and fortifications to defend strategic positions, many entire towns were protected by large walls with turrets. The most spectacular of these to remain, albeit restored with a certain romantic touch by Eugène Emmanuel Viollet-le-Duc (1814–79) in the nineteenth century, is the town of Carcassonne in southwestern France, a truly remarkable sight to behold. The new 66
wave of castle building was taken across the English Channel with the Norman conquest of England. King William (William the Conqueror) began constructing his first castles just two years after the invasion, and other
rich and powerful families soon followed his lead. The 67, 68
erection of these castles, especially in France and England, represented a building boom on a large scale. During the period from about 1050 to 1250, more than a thousand castles were constructed or reconstructed in France, and about fifteen hundred in England and Wales, where, in the year 1200 alone, there are records of three hundred and fifty under construction.

The skills needed to undertake this work were generally not new, but they were now required on a massive scale. The eleventh century saw the creation of a much-enlarged workforce of trained construction engineers and craftsmen. Some would have become specialists in techniques appropriate to military construction, such as the design of walls that would afford protection from missiles and keep out attackers while allowing defenders to shoot their assailants. Other workers, however—the masons, carpenters, glazers, and metalworkers—would have been able to switch freely between military and civil building work. Or rather, they would be available as long as their skills were not required by a monarch or duke with urgent military needs. Such men had considerable power and authority in these matters; the workforce needed for the construction of Chester Castle in northwestern England in the early thirteenth century, for example, was conscripted by the king from more than twenty counties as far away as Dorset, Kent, and Norfolk. The story all over Europe was very similar.

Developments in Europe accelerated after the First Crusade (1095–99), when returning soldiers brought expertise from the Middle East. The First Crusade had been initiated by the pope in response to a plea from the emperor of the eastern Roman empire in Constantinople to expel Muslim occupiers of Jerusalem, and it was followed

66 Carcassonne, France. Medieval fortified city restored by Eugène Viollet-le-Duc in the mid-nineteenth century.

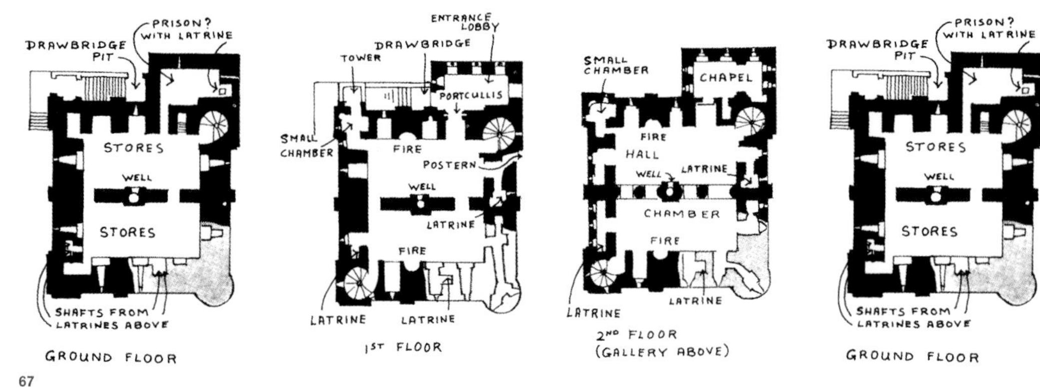

67

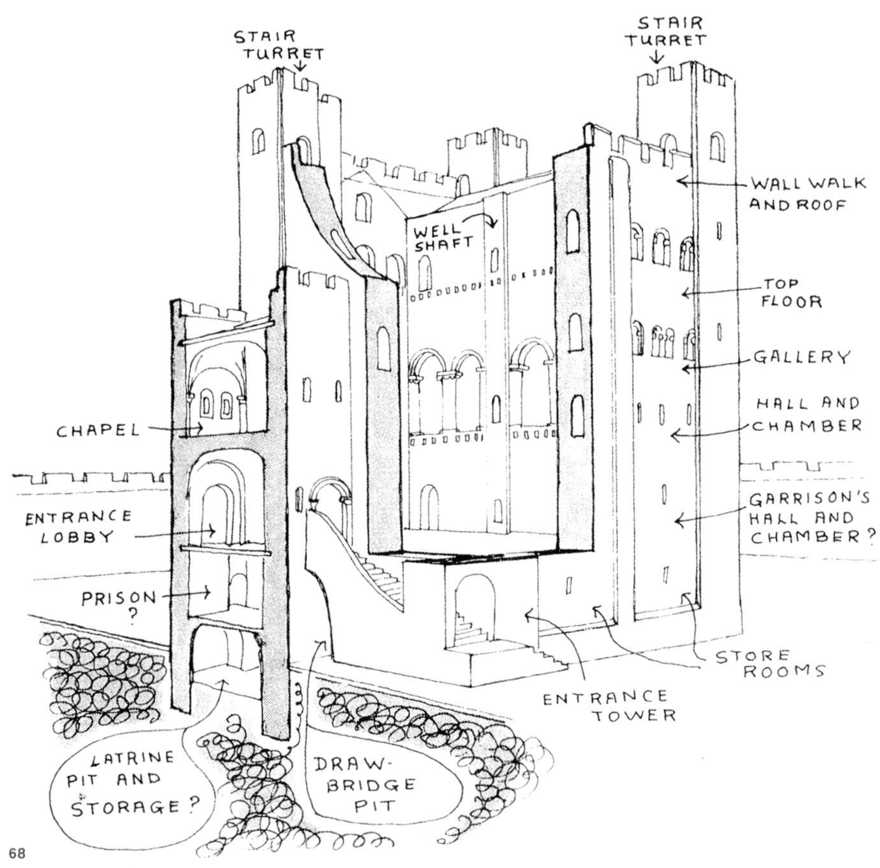

68

67 Rochester Castle, Kent, 1127–c. 1200. Floor plans. 68 Rochester Castle. The keep (the most fortified part of a medieval castle). 69 Master builder receiving instructions from the king, reputedly James of St. George and King Edward I, c. 1280. 70 Harlech Castle, Harlech, Wales, 1283–89. Designer and engineer: James of St. George. Reconstruction.

69

70

by six more campaigns between 1147 and 1254. The Crusaders quickly learned the effectiveness of the masonry curtain wall as a means for defending a central citadel. As they captured territory for the pope, the Crusaders also gained practical experience as they constructed and reconstructed fortifications for their own use by employing local engineers and builders. When they returned to Europe, the Crusaders brought back to Italy and France not only descriptions of Middle Eastern building methods and designs for fortifications but also local builders and military engineers, probably as prisoners. The art of constructing masonry fortifications spread quickly through Europe. One of the first of the new designs of castle was built at Gaillard in Normandy for King Richard I (the Lionheart), who had led the Third Crusade (1189–92) alongside the German Emperor Frederick I and French King Philip Augustus.

In Britain, castle design reached its peak in the thirteenth century with the work of master builder James of St.
69 George (c. 1230–1309) for England's King Edward I. James was born in the independent state of Savoy, which occupied parts of present-day France, Italy, and Switzerland. There, with his father, he had designed and built a number of new forts, using the ideas about masonry fortification that the Crusaders had encountered in their campaigns in the Middle East. Particularly ingenious was the idea of building rooms with cross walls around the inside of the main wall. These served both to buttress the wall from inside and provide a continuous 'wall walk' to enable the defenders easy access to any part of the circumference. It was from one of these castles—Saint Georges d'Espéranche in Savoy, built for Edward's cousin—that Master James took his full name. Working as master mason, engineer, and project manager, James was directly responsible for at least twelve of the seventeen castles in Wales that Edward commanded to be built, rebuilt, or strengthened. His first project, the rebuilding of Rhuddlan Castle, was begun in 1277, and his last, the castle at Beaumaris, begun in 1295, would have been his masterpiece had he lived to complete it.

These forts and castles were stunning examples of logical engineering thought, as carefully designed to serve their purpose as a complex machine. Beyond each point where an attacking force might gain entry was yet another barrier, and at these places the attackers were delayed in the open, where they were easy targets for the bowmen and stone-throwers on the high walls above. To undertake his work for Edward, James brought several colleagues he had worked with in Savoy. These included the experienced military engineer or *ingeniator*, Master Bertrand de Saltu, and three master masons, Master Manasser from the Champagne region of France, John Francis from Savoy, who was probably the builder of the castle of Brignon in canton Valais in Switzerland, and

Albert de Menz, probably also from Savoy. James also brought Stephen the Painter, who had already served Edward in redecorating Westminster Hall in London prior to his coronation in 1272.

The most spectacular of James' finished works was the castle at Harlech, in Wales (1283–89), where he developed the walls within walls idea to its most sophisticated
70 form. Between the outer wall and the main wall of the castle was a flat, exposed "outer ward," everywhere overlooked from above. Should attackers manage to penetrate the main wall into the courtyard or "inner ward," the defenders could retreat to the safety of the rooms high above the fortified gatehouse.

The tasks of managing the construction workforce and extracting payment from the client were probably as challenging for James as they are today. While constructing Beaumaris, James wrote to the king's exchequer:

> *In case you should wonder where so much money could go in a week, we would have you know that we have needed and shall continue to need—400 masons, both cutters and layers, together with 2,000 less skilled workmen, 100 carts, 60 wagons and 30 boats bringing stone and sea coal; 200 quarrymen; 30 smiths; and carpenters for putting in the joists and floor boards and other necessary jobs. All this takes no account of the garrison mentioned above, nor of the purchase of material, of which there will have to be a great quantity. . . . The men's pay has been and still is very much in arrears, and we are having the greatest difficulty in keeping them because they simply have nothing to live on.*
>
> *P.S. And, Sirs, for God's sake be quick with the money for the works, as much as ever our lord the king wills; otherwise everything done up till now which have been to no avail.*[10]

In the story of building engineering, however, the nonmilitary role of the castle is perhaps more significant than its military function. Throughout Europe the castles of the medieval period became increasingly opulent residences for barons, dukes, and monarchs, as well as their families and many members of their court, not least because building a house of masonry served to demonstrate the owner's wealth. Toward the end of this era, in some castles of the fourteenth and fifteenth centuries, the military function of castles receded as the need for defense waned. The earlier pattern of a wall surrounding several buildings was superseded by a much-thickened wall integrating rooms, surrounding a courtyard.

The development of the castle or fortified house represents a significant step forward from the early medieval period, toward the idea of a building as a means of providing its occupants with comfort. Until this time most windows were not glazed. The etymology of the word window, "wind eye," reveals that its original function had little to do with lighting. A wooden flap or door could be opened or closed to regulate ventilation and heat loss. We see in these more domestic buildings of the fourteenth century the use of construction techniques that had previously been used in fortifications and churches: masonry walls, and larger rooms and roof spans. To lighten the larger rooms and gloomy interiors, windows increasingly were glazed, although the glass panes were often translucent rather than transparent, and sometimes colored. We also see the improved provision of building services: heating and running water. Masonry allowed the construction of chimneys and fireplaces in the colder parts of central Europe, not only in a kitchen, separated from the main living rooms, but also in the living rooms themselves. By the end of the medieval period masonry construction was being widely used for many buildings, both civic and residential, in the prosperous towns of Germany, France, and central Europe. In England such buildings were generally erected using timber-frame construction for another two hundred years, with masonry construction used only for fortifications, churches, and houses for the rich and powerful.

The Design and Construction of Cathedrals

One result of the proliferation of castles and fortifications was the creation of a well-trained workforce, in addition to improved skills in designing large buildings and organizing their construction. Religious leaders benefited from these advancements when seeking the means to establish Christianity more firmly throughout Europe. Small churches were built in nearly every town and village, and existing churches were enlarged or rebuilt to create what we now know as cathedrals. In France, during the three centuries from about 1050, some eighty cathedrals, five hundred large churches, and several tens of thousands of parish churches were built. In England and Wales more than thirty cathedrals and many thousands of churches were constructed during the same period.

By the eleventh century the largest religious buildings had become rather cumbersome. Though magnificent in their way, the columns of Durham Cathedral (1093–1133) in northern England, for example, were bulky in proportion to the rest of the building, and the relatively small and few windows lent a rather somber air to the in-
71 terior. From about this time we begin to notice the seeds of change. Medieval Christianity was now firmly established throughout much of Europe, and the new orthodoxy was beginning to find that the old buildings did not meet its changing needs and aspirations. New exigencies led to new ways of building. At Durham Cathedral we find the horizontal thrusts of the vaults carried out above covered aisles by means of what later would be called flying buttresses, though here they are hidden in the interior of
72 the building. In the priory church at Vézelay, France, constructed in the early twelfth century, the columns are smaller than at Durham and the interior lighting much improved by increasing the size of the windows and using
73 light-colored stone. These and a host of other new ideas about building developed and spread quickly from the late eleventh century, and the medieval cathedral was born: the culmination of parallel developments in scholarship, philosophy, science, architecture, and building engineering. The results were astonishing. The vaulted roof,
74, 75, the flying buttresses, and the huge windows of nearly any
76, 77 medieval cathedral are awe-inspiring. These are at once buildings of exceptional beauty and technical sophistication that need no expert knowledge to appreciate.

Cathedrals have been a focus of attention by engineering historians for a number of reasons. First, they have survived in large numbers in nearly every country in Western Europe, largely unaltered and serving almost their original purpose. The longevity of the church establishment has also ensured that we have many more records of the building activities that were undertaken. Second, their purpose was more architecturally symbolic than it was functional, and generally they were much larger than even the largest castle. No matter how impressive the engineering of medieval castles, the cathedrals clearly represent a more advanced stage in the development of structural engineering and the use of daylight to illuminate a building interior. The third and most significant difference between the cathedrals and castles was the nature of the environment in which they were conceived. Their origin lay in religious scholarship and, increasingly during the eleventh and twelfth centuries, secular scholarship.

The builders of cathedrals shared construction technologies and skills with builders of castles and military fortifications, both at the craft level and among those who identified themselves, in today's terminology, as building designers and project managers. The same people would work on both types of projects as the opportunity arose. Such large projects generally did not have a single design and construction team, as a modern building does. Also, very few cathedrals were built on "greenfield" sites. There was usually an existing building from Norman or earlier times that was either removed or heavily altered. A cathedral was, therefore, often built in an organic process rather than to a single plan, with major additions and developments spanning the careers of many dozens of designers, craftsmen, and construction managers.

We know far more about the design and construction of medieval cathedrals than about buildings from Roman times. First of all, we have direct evidence: the buildings themselves. Many documents relating directly to the designs of cathedrals have survived, including sketchbooks of details and plans. Many substantial working drawings survive, some of them as parts of building contracts. We also know the names of many hundreds of the individuals who were involved with their design and construction. Unfortunately, we have no explicit design procedures dating from the early days of cathedral design, and only a few from later. This is hardly surprising, considering the secrecy surrounding the skills of tradesmen such as the masons; it was forbidden to divulge any information outside the masons' lodge, either to other masons or non-masons. One of the most valuable documents that survives is a sketchbook belonging to one Villard de Honnecourt (c. 1175–c. 1240), a mason who worked on a number of cathedrals in France. Sixty-six pages of his parchment book remain extant (from the probable ninety-six-page original), giving a visual record of some of the projects he was involved in, annotated in French, and much more besides. The 256 surviving sketches include 94 human and sculptural representations, 43 animal figures, 44 building plans and elevations, 13 machines and

72 73 74 75 76 77

71 (opposite page) Durham Cathedral, Durham, England, 1093–1133. Nave. 72 Durham Cathedral. Internal flying buttresses. 73 Sainte Marie-Madeleine, Vézelay, France, c. 1120–1215. Nave. 74 Chartres Cathedral, Chartres, France, 1194–1221. 75 Saint Étienne de Bourges, Bourges, France, 1195–1270. 76 Sainte-Chapelle, Paris, 1246–48. 77 Aachen Cathedral, Germany, choir, c. 1355–1414. Windows (restored mid-twentieth century).

78

79

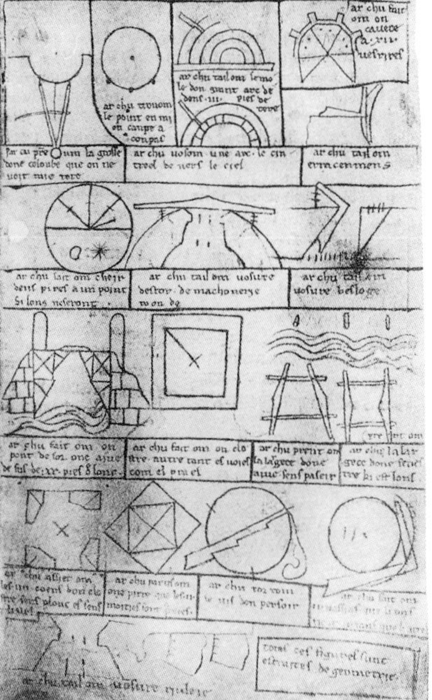

80

78 Villard de Honnecourt, drawing of flying buttresses at Notre Dame, Reims, France, c. 1230. 79 Villard de Honnecourt, plan for a church (above), and plan for Saint Étienne, Meaux, France (below), c. 1230. 80 Villard de Honnecourt, sketch of various geometric techniques, including the use of the medieval mason's square, c. 1230.

gadgets, including a reciprocating saw powered by a waterwheel, and many drawings of geometric constructions. Villard visited Laon Cathedral in northern France (he wrote: "Nowhere have I seen a tower as fine as that at
78 Laon"[11]) and the cathedrals at both Reims and Chartres. He also visited Hungary, calling at Lausanne in Switzerland on his return journey, a voyage of more than 3500 kilometers that took at least four months. Some sketches show inaccurate representations of details, suggesting he made them from drawings of schemes that were superseded by, or perhaps copied from, his col-
79 leagues' similar sketchbooks.

Among the many details of the mason's tools drawn by Villard and depicted in many other contemporary illustrations, one is worth particular mention: the L-shaped me-
80 dieval mason's square. It was made of metal, and the outer right angle of the square and the inner right angle were not parallel, but rotated by about 9°. While the purpose of this square is not fully understood today, it would have enabled its user to create a portion of a circular arc, perhaps for the stone voussoirs of an arch—one-tenth of a right angle if the angle was, indeed, 9°. It probably had various lines marked along the length of its arms and would have served to calculate and set out a variety of angles. As well as being clearly an icon of the mason's art, it was also an instrument akin to the engineer's slide rule or calculator in modern times.

Designing Cathedrals

Designing a cathedral was not as difficult as it might sound. Most importantly, the twelfth-century masons already knew that structures on that scale could be built; many large buildings had been erected before the late medieval period, especially in France and Italy. Masons who had visited Italy also knew what the Romans had built. Trajan's surviving work alone would have given a good idea of some practical upper limits. And in the surviving baths of Diocletian they had the basic model for the vaulted bay that could be repeated at liberty in both directions. In fact, the cathedrals of the twelfth and thirteenth centuries were rather smaller than the Roman baths. Also, the medieval masons were using dressed stone rather than concrete, and building in masonry is remarkably forgiving. One need only ensure that the masonry everywhere carries only compressive forces, and that nowhere does it carry bending moments, for this would cause the joints between stones to open up. Since the compressive stresses in the stone, even at the foot of a 150-meter steeple, are very small compared to the strength of the material (less than about 10 percent), the strength of the masonry is virtually irrelevant to the success of the structure as a whole. And, as long as the individual voussoirs bear well upon each other, the success of an arch is not highly dependent on the geometry of its curves.

In many ways, of course, cathedrals were designed—that is to say, plans and elevations laid out, and the relative sizes of individual components defined—much as buildings had been for more than two thousand years. Masons and carpenters knew the limitations of their materials, and much of their experience could be codified and passed on to others as design rules or design procedures. Also, masonry is quite tolerant of variations, such as the shape of an arch, due to the whim of either an abbot or his mason. Both models and drawings were used 81
at least as early as 1200 to convey the design of a proposed abbey or cathedral to the building client, and, no doubt, to the team of builders responsible for its detail design and construction. Although most models and drawings have been lost, some fine examples have been preserved. Among the many drawings that have survived
in the archive of Strasbourg Cathedral are images of 82
works that were executed, as well as various plans for unexecuted projects. The parchment surface often reveals changes to the proposed scheme, reflecting, no doubt, the patron's changing preferences.

During this late medieval period we have evidence that designers were coming to see design as something more than merely following empirical rules. The science of geometry played an important role in helping to generate the confidence needed to experiment with new ideas.

It would be wrong, however, to conclude that geometry was somehow an engenderer of medieval cathedral designs. Rather, it was one of the many means by which people were able to realize an idea having as much to do with religious, cultural, and scholarly aspirations as with building construction or church architecture. It is worth recalling the scientific revolution that was underway, and the use to which geometry was being put in other disciplines. Robert Grosseteste, for example, was not only a philosopher and scholar; shortly after becoming bishop of Lincoln, he was involved with work on the cathedral there at a very practical level, as the building client, while the nave and the chapter house were being designed and constructed.

Like the Greeks before them, medieval man believed in the absolute truths of number and geometry and used these to explain the world. Numbers could generate various ratios, squares, multiples, series, and so on; in geometry there were circles, triangles, squares, spheres, cubes, and the many properties associated with these shapes. We know that cathedral designers devised many complex procedures to create an enormous range of plans and elevations. These were based mainly on two fundamental geometric techniques, or subroutines, in the language of modern computing: combining various circular arcs, and "rotating the square." This latter procedure involves creating a square with an area half that of another by joining the centers of each of the four sides. This idea was not new; indeed, it is to be found in Vitruvius's introduction to Book IX of his *De Architectura*, devoted to geometry and astronomy. We also see evidence of this and similar geometric constructions in early Islamic art, for example, in the eighth-century ribbed vault at Córdoba Cathedral in southern Spain. Vitruvius illustrates the method, which he attributes to Plato, using the hypothetical problem of doubling the area of a "field" just 10 feet square. In Villard's drawing of Laon Cathedral the plan of the tower is based on a number of rotated
83, 85 squares. A reconstruction of the likely sequence of design steps used at the cathedral in Bern, Switzerland, has shown a correspondence with the entire actual floor
84 plan to within 60 millimeters.

At the very end of the Middle Ages, in 1486, we find the first written evidence of a medieval design procedure. In that year a booklet was published by the retired master mason Mathes Roriczer of Regensburg, Germany (c. 1440–c. 1495), explaining the method for designing a pinnacle and a finial. The Roriczer family provided four men in three successive generations of master masons who held the post of Dombaumeister (cathedral master builder) in Regensburg, so Mathes's pedigree was strong. The booklet runs to a dozen pages and takes the reader step-by-step through the sequence of operations
87 needed to create the full design for a finial. Roriczer also published a short guide to geometry in German, which included his design procedure for pinnacles.

A similar booklet appeared a year or so later, written by Hanns Schmuttermayer of Nürnberg (c. 1450–c. 1520), a goldsmith (ornaments at this time often contained elements from cathedral design). Schmuttermayer composed the book "for the instruction of our fellowmen and all masters and journeymen who use this high and liberal art of geometry."[12] The differences in the detail between Roriczer and Schmuttermayer's design procedures for pinnacles suggest they came independently from a common source, which both authors indicate had been in use for over a hundred years and originated in Prague. While it is disappointing that our only record of design procedures from this time is for such minor, almost trivial components of a cathedral, it does show us an actual example of their use of the rotating square and, in Schmuttermayer's approach, the methodical setting out of the various dimensions that his technique generates—a set of preferred dimensions, so to speak, each $\sqrt{2}$
(about 1.4) times larger or smaller than the next. 86

It is clear that devising new ways of designing cathedrals during the twelfth and thirteenth centuries was due not only to technological developments in the conventional sense, as no new materials or structural devices were invented; rather, old ones were used in new ways and new combinations. In parallel with the growing skills in masonry, carpentry, and construction techniques, cathedral architects had to come up with novel ways of arranging building plans, and the disposition of their many parts, before beginning construction, following a path similar to that blazed by ancient building designers. The ever-increasing size of their undertakings required medieval designers to formulate new ways to experiment with, develop, and communicate a design to the patron, both to raise the necessary confidence in the scheme and to secure permission to build, and then to convey specifications to contractors and materials suppliers. This new methodology was an intellectual development in the minds of both the designers and the builders.

Constructing Cathedrals

Illustrations of cathedrals under construction adorn many medieval manuscripts, and show us the plant and
equipment the builders used. 88, 89, 93

81

82

While some materials used in medieval cathedrals and Roman buildings are similar, there are also differences, and often in the ways they were employed. Perhaps most strikingly, medieval builders worked with stone cut to moderate, manageable sizes rather than the huge blocks the Romans used. The most common Roman materials, fired brick and mass concrete, are entirely absent in medieval buildings. Cathedral roofs were covered with lead sheet rather than the baked clay tiles used in Roman times. Roof trusses were made of timber and rigid mortise-and-tenon joints fixed with wooden pegs. While this type of truss was more sophisticated than a roof using propped rafters and beams, such as Vitruvius would have used for his basilica at Fano, the medieval methods of joining large timbers would have been familiar to the Roman engineers who made timber structures to serve as centering for their enormous masonry arches and concrete vaults.

As in many of the larger Roman buildings, wrought iron was widely used in cathedrals, especially for tying together large blocks of stone. However, the iron was more often used with greater precision where tension forces needed to be carried—for example, as ties

81 Saint Maclou, Rouen, France, 1434–1521. Model of wood and papier maché. Height exceeds 1 meter. 82 Drawing from the Strasbourg Cathedral archives for an unexecuted scheme for a church facade from the 1250s.

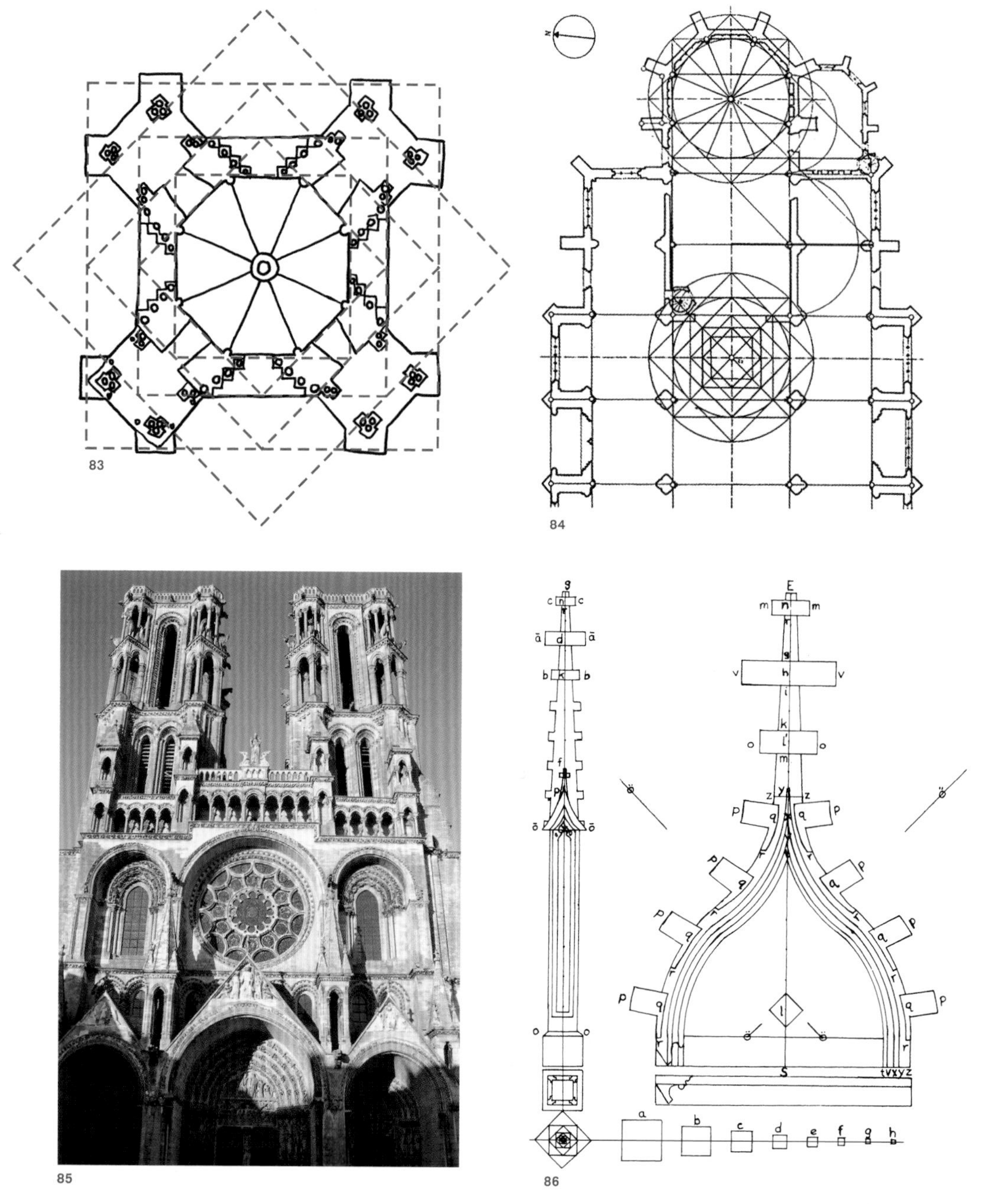

83 Villard de Honnecourt, plan of the tower of Laon Cathedral, overlaid with the grid of rotated squares used to generate the plan, c. 1230. 84 Bern Cathedral, Bern, Switzerland, c. 1418. Plan overlaid with grid of rotated squares. 85 Laon Cathedral, Laon, France, c. 1160–1215. 86 Hanns Schmuttermayer, design procedure for a gablet, c. 1488. 87 Mathes Roriczer, steps from the design procedure for a pinnacle, 1486.

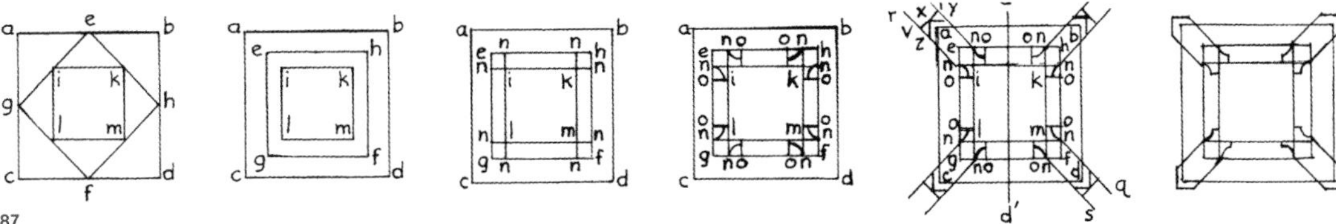

87

between the tops of walls or columns from which arches sprang, a technique already in use at Hagia Sophia in the mid-sixth century and in many later Islamic buildings. The earliest known use of a tied arch in a medieval cathedral was at Soissons, France, around 1170. At Sainte-Chapelle in Paris (1246–48), which served originally as King Louis IX's own chapel, an elaborate series of iron ties restrained not only the main arches but the
90, 91 ribs of the apse as well.

Perhaps the most dramatic use of iron was for the mullions and frames in the many large windows in cathedrals. In this case the flat iron bars were used to resist
92 the loads on windows caused by wind loads. Finally, there was glass, used in later Roman times but not on the scale or with the architectural skill found in medieval stained glass windows.

Without a doubt the most remarkable feature of medieval cathedrals is their structure—the means devised for carrying gravity and wind loads to the foundations. The remarkable new building forms were made possible by four principal structural innovations: the quadripartite, ribbed vault, the buttress, the flying buttress, and the masterful use of the weight of the masonry to increase the stability of these unprecedentedly tall buildings. The characteristic form and appearance of a medieval cathedral is the direct consequence
94, 95, of these four innovations being used in combination.
96, 97 Rather than carrying the forces of gravity and wind to the ground through massive walls and piers, as the Romans did, the stone vaults and ribs concentrate these forces into thin structural elements and finally slender columns of relatively small cross-section to create a stone skeleton of great delicacy. The balancing of this complex flow of forces in three dimensions required great skill.

Large churches of the Romanesque period resisted horizontal wind loads by virtue of the sheer mass and the wide base of the columns and walls. A thick wall or column such as those at Durham Cathedral can carry the inclined loads due to wind or the outward thrust of an arch or vault entirely within its width. The stability against overturning is due mainly to the width of the base, just as a person can better resist a sideways push with legs astride than with legs together. Such large walls and columns occupy a significant portion of the floor area of the building and require a large quantity of masonry as well.

The medieval designers elected to use the pointed arch in preference to the Roman semicircular arch. This brought several advantages. Pointed arches, for a given span, exert a lower outward thrust. Also, for a given span, the rise of the arch can be adjusted to a range of different heights simply by varying the radius of curvature of the two arms of the arch. This was far more flexible than the Roman arch, whose height is fixed by the span. The Roman barrel vault was also replaced by a series of discrete structural bays, rectangular in plan, formed by quadripartite vaults (intersecting pointed vaults). The use of ribs in a quadripartite vault, infilled with the masonry shell of the vault itself, shows a clear separation of primary and secondary structural functions.

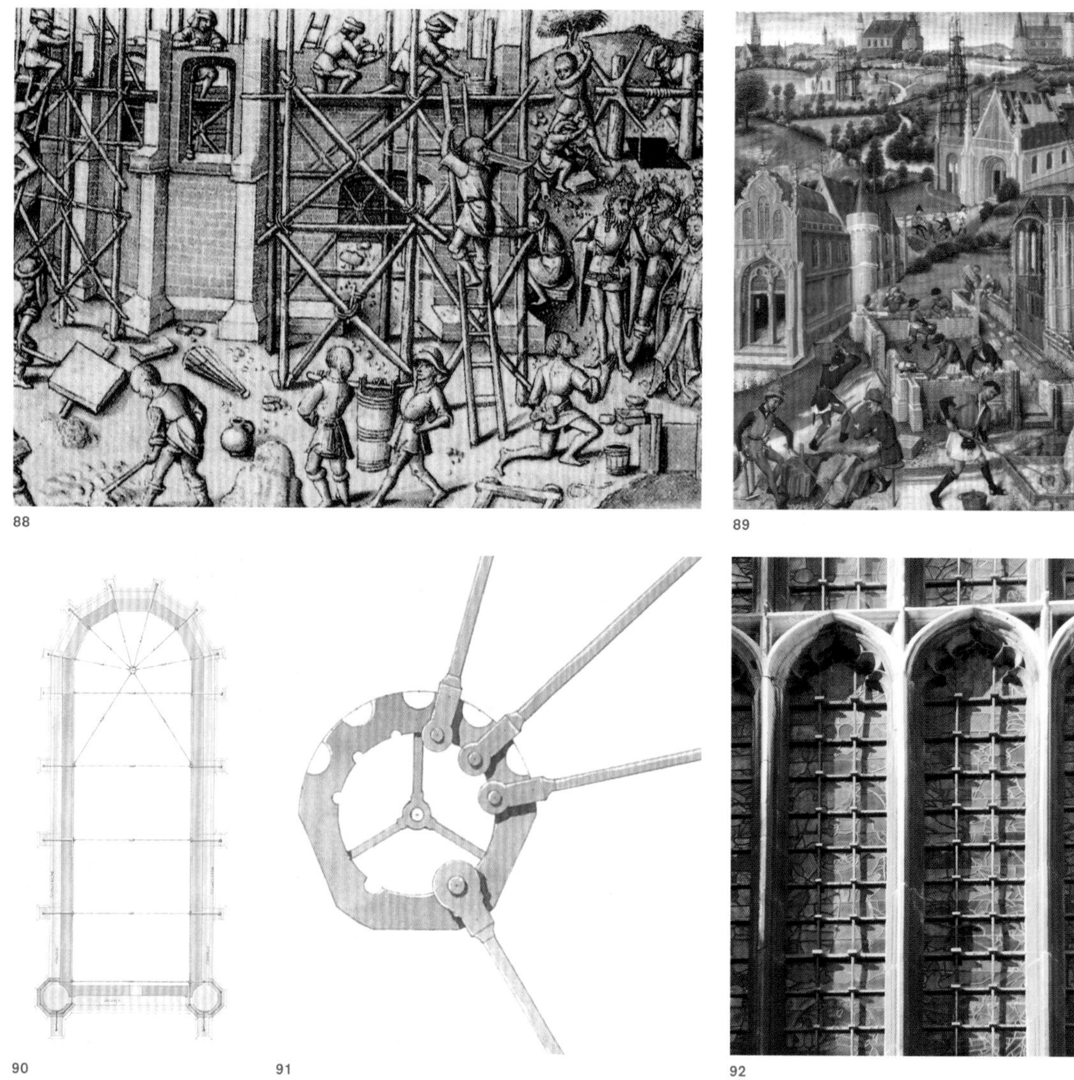

88

89

90

91

92

88 Fifteenth-century illustration of scaffolding being used in cathedral construction. 89 Fifteenth-century illustration showing church construction. 90 Sainte-Chapelle, Paris, 1246–48. Drawing of iron ties used to carry the thrust of arches. These were determined to be unnecessary and removed during restoration in the nineteenth century. 91 Sainte-Chapelle. Detail of the iron connector for ties in the apse. 92 Chapel at King's College, Cambridge, 1446–1547. Detail of iron mullions. 93 Modern representation of cathedral construction.

Philippe FIX

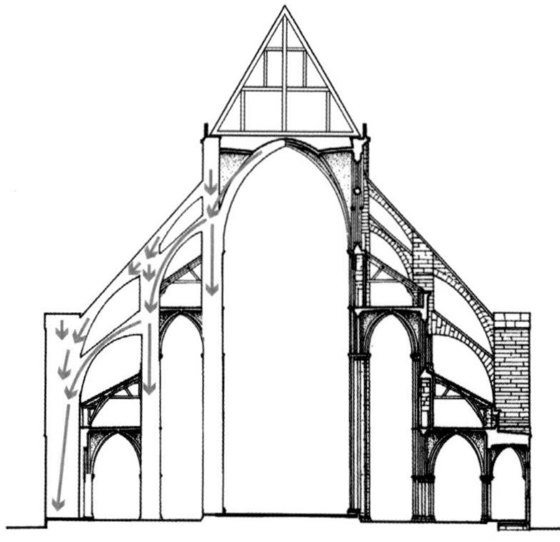

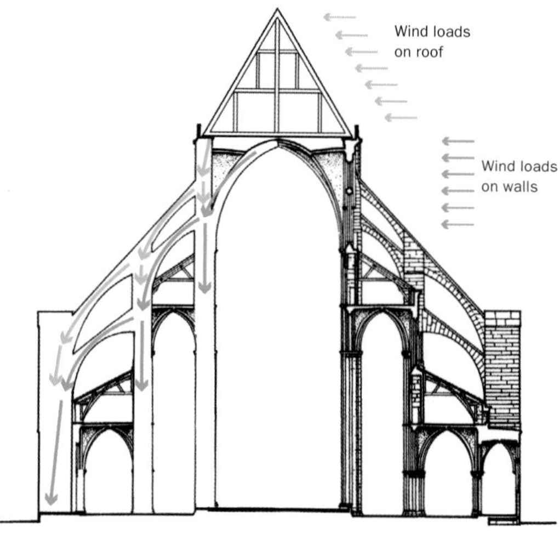

94 Load paths of thrusts from main vault and buttresses, due to gravity.

Load paths of forces due to wind

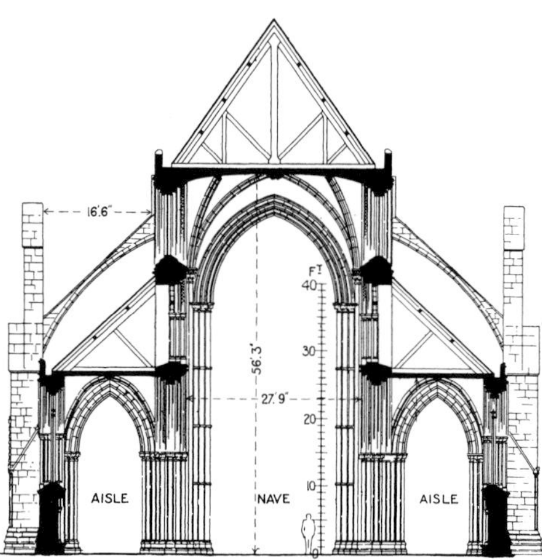

95

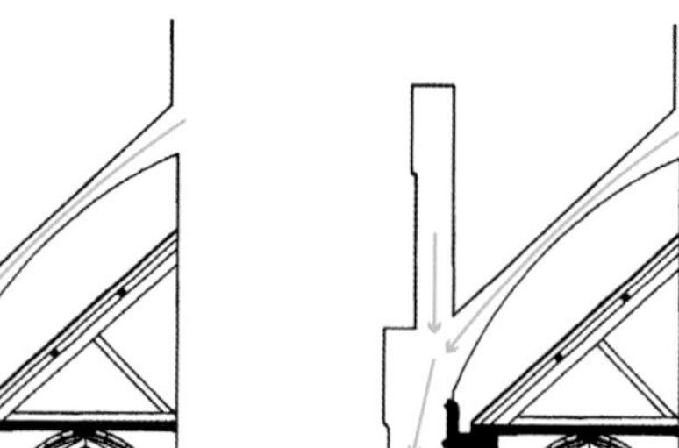

(a) Force in flying buttress sheers the top of the main buttress

(b) Weight of pinnacle applies compressive prestress and prevents shear failure of buttress

96

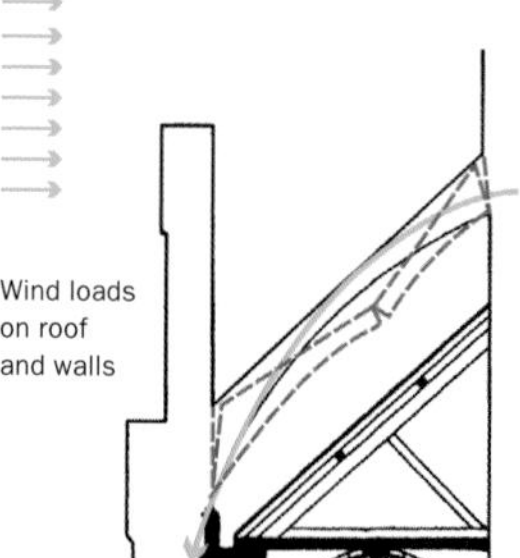

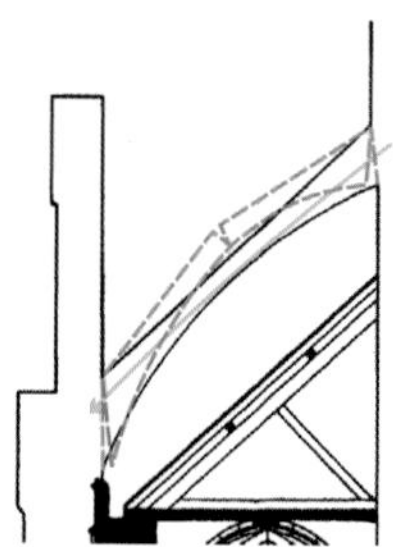

(a) Wind from left
Load path touches upper face of buttress; would collapse downwards

(b) Wind from right
Load path touches lower face of buttress; would collapse upwards

97

A masonry barrel vault exerts downward and outward thrust along the whole of the length of its support walls. In the ribbed vault, most of all forces are concentrated in the ribs, and can thus be conveyed directly to the tops of columns. At this point, the vertical component of the loads can be carried vertically down a column. Concentrating the horizontal loads at high level into a number of discrete locations makes it possible to convey them to the foundations using a series of buttresses. This means the wall in between buttresses serves no structural purpose and can be replaced by windows. Alternatively, the horizontal loads can be conveyed further outward, still at high level, so that the space beneath can be used. Since the intermediate walls or columns now have to carry only vertical loads, they can be very slender indeed. Having been carried over one or two bays beneath, the loads can then be conveyed via a buttress to the foundations.

The loads on heavy masonry buildings can usually be considered as constant. Actually, this means that the variation of loads caused by winds is small in proportion to the weight of the structure. In a flying buttress this is not the case. The only purpose of the upper tier of flying buttresses in a cathedral is to carry wind loads, and their size and weight need be only the minimum necessary to perform this function. One of the most remarkable achievements of the medieval engineers is how close they managed to approach the minimum cross section needed for a flying buttress.

The final structural innovation found in medieval cathedrals is the deliberate use of weight to improve stability. This technique was used in an obvious way at roof level, where large stone pinnacles sit atop columns or buttresses above the level of the rest of the structure. Their purpose is twofold. First, they help prevent overturning, just as it is more difficult to overturn a stool with someone sitting on it than one that is vacant. Second, they help prevent the loads in a flying buttress from pushing the upper stones of a buttress sideways.

Dead weight is also employed to achieve the necessary stability in the large windows of medieval cathedrals, such as those in the end walls of the nave. The wind load 98, 99
on these windows can be huge—perhaps 80 or 90 tons—and is conveyed to the building foundations by stone mullions just a few tens of centimeters thick. In the case of England's Gloucester Cathedral, for example, the mullions span some 22 meters and are made of individual stones no more than about 2 meters long. These re- 100
markable structures work because the mullions function as a vertical, flat arch, spanning between the top and bottom of the window. This is achieved by using the weight of masonry above the window to ensure that the mullions are highly loaded in compression. This slender column of stones can thus resist horizontal wind loads by the same means that allows someone to pick up a line of a dozen wooden blocks by pushing them tightly together from either end. The axial loads in the mullions of a large window might be 10 tons and, in the radial spokes of a large rose window, maybe 7 tons.

These four structural innovations produced what was effectively a "stone skeleton," permitting not only large enclosed volumes interrupted only by lightweight columns, but also the enormous windows. These windows were extraordinary for the wonderful interior illumination they provided, increasing the area of fenestration from typically 30 or 40 percent to around 80 percent of the area of the walls. The large, colorful windows quickly transcended the functions of illumination and draft prevention, and were soon serving as the medieval equivalent of an Omnimax cinema screen, enabling the clergy to deliver powerful messages to churchgoers.

Considering the structural innovation involved in the stone skeleton, it is remarkable how few major failures there seem to have been. This is even more remarkable since most structural failures in cathedrals were due to the movement or differential settlement of the foundations. Such movement could compromise the stability of an entire wall or cathedral tower or, at least, cause it to

94 Diagram illustrating the path of gravity loads (left) and wind loads (right) through vaults and flying buttresses.
95 Lichfield Cathedral, Lichfield, England, 1195–c. 1330. Section showing flying buttresses; these span 5.3 meters and are the most slender of all flying buttresses. 96 Lichfield Cathedral. Section of buttresses showing the prestressing function of a stone pinnacle to prevent shear failure. 97 Lichfield Cathedral. Section of flying buttress showing line of thrust and collapse mechanism for different wind loads.

tilt slightly and open up alarming cracks between parts of the building. The causes of such problems were not fully understood until the 1920s, when the modern science of soil mechanics was developed.

The small number of structural collapses is partly due to the fact that many of the structural techniques were but minor modifications to established practice. However, it is very likely that structural models of innovative vaults and buttresses were built—it would have been foolish for a man to try something so new and on such a large scale without somehow trying to ensure that it would work. Fortuitously, the way that masonry structures work as structures is largely independent of scale (see chapter 1, p. 52). We know of one model that, whether constructed as a test of the structural viability of the design or not, would certainly have served this purpose. The designer of the church of San Petronio in Bologna (1390–1437), Antonio di Vicenzo, visited both the Florence and Milan cathedrals while they were under construction. On his return to Bologna he commissioned a model of his proposed design, made of brick and plaster, at about one-eighth scale. It was around 19 meters long and 6 meters high, and large enough for a person to walk inside. The model would have been assumed to demonstrate that the proposed church would be stable, just as it gave a reliable idea of what the future church would look like, inside and out. And the fact that the church was built and was, indeed, stable would have shown that such an assumption had been justified.

It would be wrong to assume that there was just one way of building the new stone skeleton, and we see far more variety of structural detail in cathedrals than in earlier buildings. For example, the roughly contemporary flying buttresses at the cathedrals of Chartres, Le Mans, and Notre Dame in Paris, while all serving the same function,
101 vary a great deal in their structure.

Another structural innovation was the masonry cone within the hemispherical dome of the Baptistery adjacent
102, 103 to the cathedral in Pisa, Italy (1153–1265). This reduces the outward thrust of a full hemispherical dome and was known to Christopher Wren, who would use a similar device at Saint Paul's Cathedral in London in the late seventeenth century (see chapter 4, pp. 198–208).

As experience and expertise grew in handling the loads in masonry vaults, so it was found that the vaults would also work and convey their loads to the tops of columns without the need for large ribs. The fan vault, with no diagonal ribs at all, was a uniquely English development, and was effectively a shell of masonry. In the case of King's College Chapel, Cambridge (1446–1547), where the fan vaults were completed in 1515, this shell spans more than 12 meters, with a vault varying in thickness
from about 150 millimeters down to as little as 50 millimeters. 106
At the vault of the Lady Chapel of Henry VII in Westminster Abbey, London (1503–12), the builders used great skill to create the illusion that some of the masonry of the vault is carrying tension forces. 104, 105

Although constructing an entire cathedral might span the careers of several designers, we are aware of the names of some individuals who stand out from the rest, particularly when they had royal connections. Two such examples are the near contemporaries and friends Henry Yevele, associated mainly with the nave of Canterbury Cathedral, and William Wynford, who remodeled Winchester Cathedral.

Henry Yevele (c. 1325–1400) was born in Yeaveley near Ashbourne in Derbyshire, and his earliest training as a mason was in the English Midlands. He was apprenticed under the king's master mason, William of Ramsey, and worked at Uttoxeter Church and later on the presbytery of Lichfield Cathedral, the spire of Ashbourne Church, and Tutbury Abbey Church. He was only about thirty when he was appointed as a mason to Edward, Prince of Wales, and from 1360 to the end of his life he held the position of "Devisor of Masonry" to King Richard II. Yevele was responsible for the design, construction (as a building contractor), or repair of many royal works, including Westminster Hall, Durham Cathedral, Rochester Castle, and, most famously, the nave of Canterbury Cathedral. 107

98 Gloucester Cathedral, Gloucester, England, c. 1100. Window in the east wall of the choir, measuring 21.8 m x 11.5 m.
99 Cathedral of Notre Dame, Paris, 1163–1250. Rose window with slender stone mullions. 100 Diagram showing how the mullions of a large window work as a vertical flat arch.

98

99

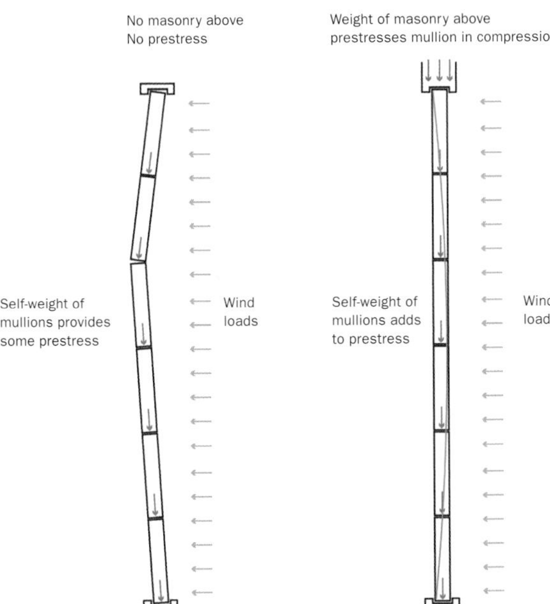
No masonry above
No prestress
Weight of masonry above
prestresses mullion in compression
Self-weight of
mullions provides
some prestress
Wind
loads
Self-weight of
mullions adds
to prestress
Wind
loads

100

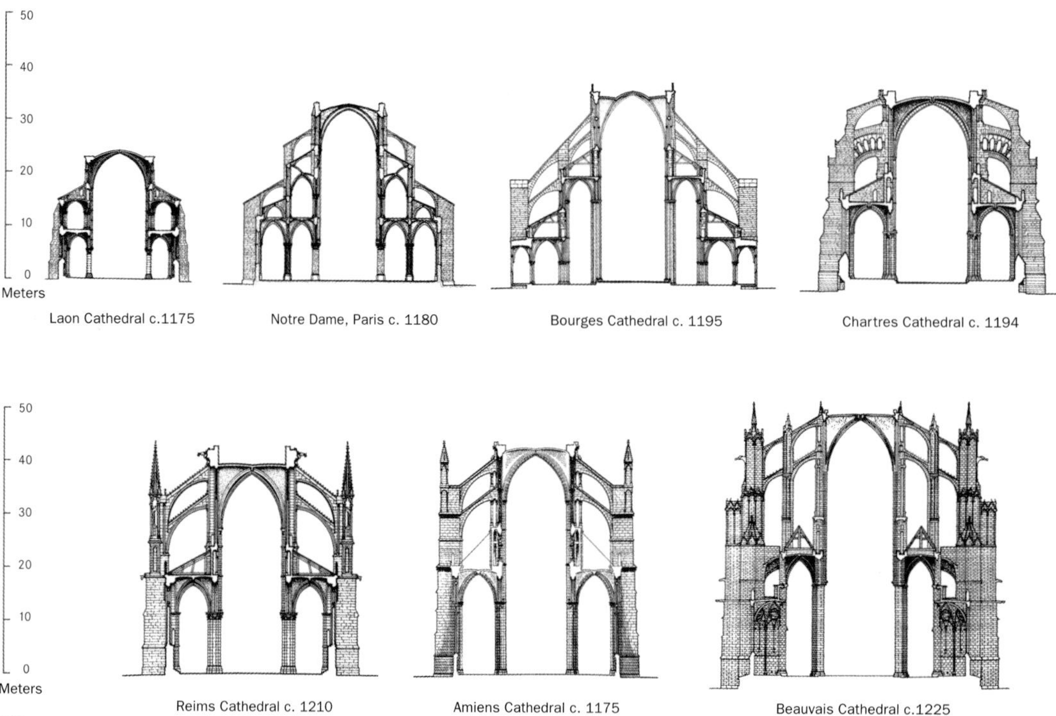

Laon Cathedral c.1175 | Notre Dame, Paris c. 1180 | Bourges Cathedral c. 1195 | Chartres Cathedral c. 1194

Reims Cathedral c. 1210 | Amiens Cathedral c. 1175 | Beauvais Cathedral c.1225

101

William Wynford (c. 1335–1405) was a mason who worked on the Great Gate and the royal lodgings at Windsor Castle in his early career. While at Windsor he met William of Wykeham, the clerk of the works, who would later become the bishop of Winchester. Through this connection, Wynford was appointed William of Wykeham's master mason, undertaking the design of many building projects with him and supervising their construction. At Winchester, Wynford devised a scheme whereby the Norman piers of the eleventh-century cathedral were ingeniously altered to the soaring perpendicu-
109. 110 lar-style profiles of the day. This was achieved first by
actually cutting down the stones of the Norman columns in situ and then building the columns up again with new stone. Working bay by bay along the building from west to east, the elevations were altered from the original three stories of the previous structure to two stories by knocking out the heads of the Norman main arcade and resetting the arches at a higher level. Finally, the entire nave was revaulted. Apart from his work at Winchester Cathedral, Wynford was involved in projects at Wells Cathedral, Winchester College, and New College, Oxford. He also worked on the castles at Donnington and Bodiam, as well as on his patron's castle residence at Highclere, all in southern England.

As design and building skills developed in the late medieval period, individuals learned to exploit masonry arch and vault construction in increasingly playful ways. We find a hint of humor in one of Villard de Honnecourt's sketches, where he shows a flat arch spanning an intermediate column, which is therefore redundant and could be removed without causing the
arch to collapse. While the fan vault was developed in 108
England, reducing the emphasis given to ribs, elsewhere
in Europe many designers accentuated the ribs, some- 111
times to an outrageous degree. In south Germany the Parler family of master masons, especially Heinrich

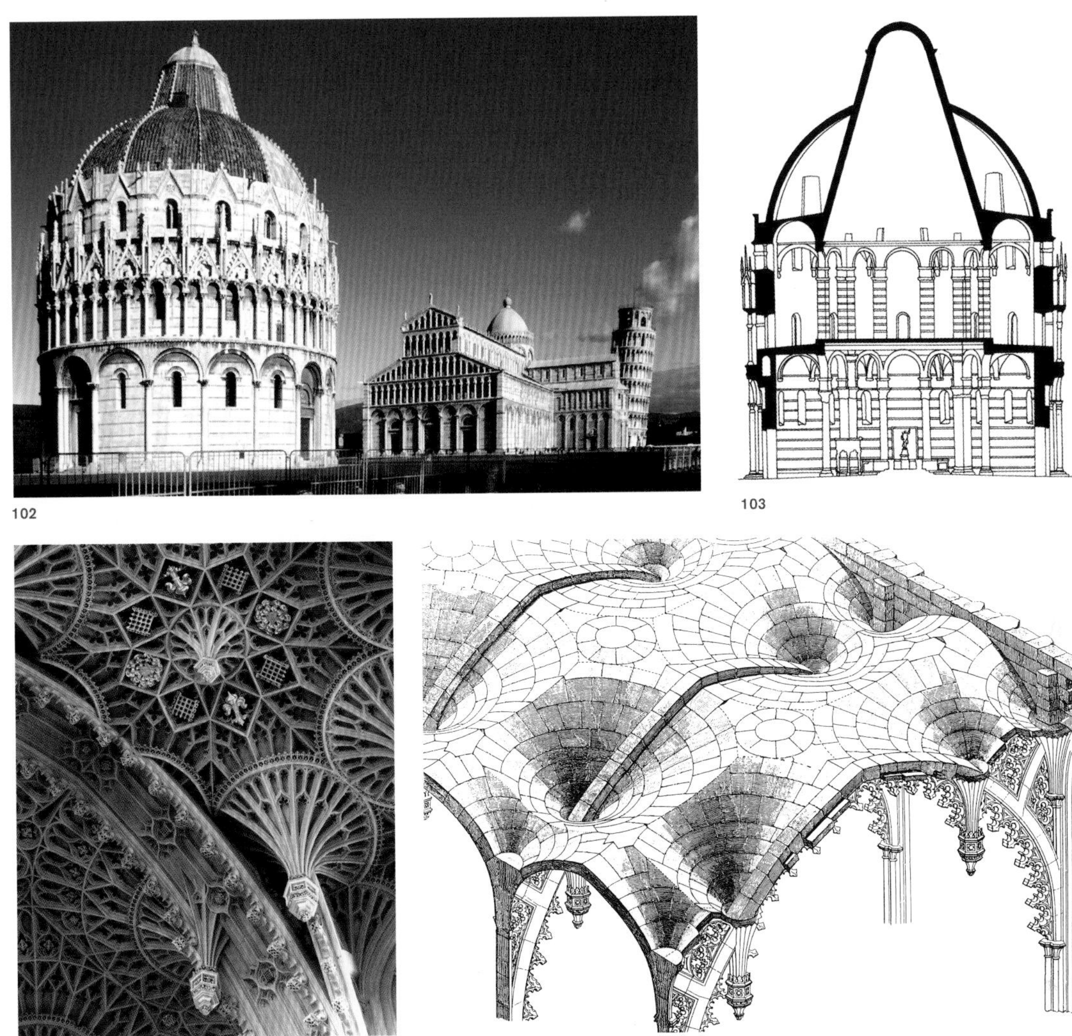

102

103

104

105

101 Comparative sections of French medieval cathedrals c. 1170–c. 1230. 102 The Baptistery, Pisa, 1153–1265. 103 The Baptistery. Section illustrating conical part of the dome that probably inspired Christopher Wren to use the same device at Saint Paul's Cathedral, London (1675–1710). 104 Lady Chapel of Henry VII, Westminster Abbey, London, 1503–12. Fan-vaulted roof. 105 Lady Chapel of Henry VII. Drawing of construction of the vault, shown from above.

107

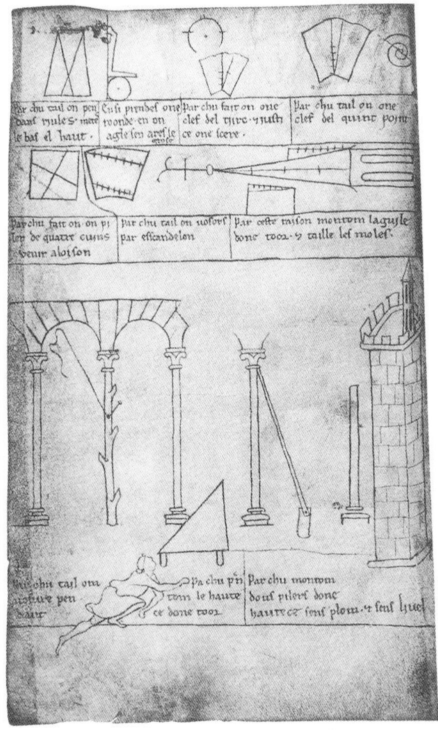

108

(c.1300–c.1360) and his son Peter (1330–99), were especially well-known for their ornate ribbed vaults. Peter was enticed to work in Prague, where he designed and built his most famous work, the Cathedral of St.
112 Vitus (1344–1929). Peter showed off his mastery in its elegantly vaulted nave, as well as in a delicate canopy of free-standing arch ribs. At the Saint Marien Church in Pirna, near Dresden in Germany, built in the 1520s, the unknown master mason went a step further even than Parler. As two ribs of his vault—nicknamed the Wild Man and Wild Woman—rise upward, they break free from the
114 wall to find their own independent paths to the ceiling. Although often dismissed as merely decorative, such tricks display a virtuoso understanding of statical equilibrium and the potential of masonry construction.

A series of episodes known as the Milan Expertises that took place in Italy between 1391 and 1402 provide a unique and remarkable insight into the way that fourteenth-century engineers approached the design of cathedrals, specifically the cathedral of Milan, known as the Duomo (1386–present).[13] The several Expertises were what we might now call official inquiries to decide how best to proceed with the construction of the new cathedral. A number of experts were invited from throughout Europe to offer their views, and the entire proceedings were recorded. They give us some intriguing hints of the current thoughts (but, sadly, very few hard facts) about how the structure of cathedrals worked. The main conclusion to be drawn from the written record of the Expertises is that there were as many viewpoints as

106 (opposite page) Chapel of King's College, Cambridge, 1446–1547. Fan vaults (completed 1515). 107 Canterbury Cathedral, Canterbury, England, 1070–1498. Nave (1377–1405). 108 Villard de Honnecourt, sketch of a flat arch, c. 1230.

109

110

there were people involved, none of whom found it easy to describe either the structure or their thought process in objective terms.

Begun in 1386, the cathedral in Milan was a massive building campaign by the duke of Lombardy to assert his authority and political influence over the territories newly annexed to his own territories. The cathedral was to be large, but not especially adventurous in structural engineering terms. Because of a lack of indigenous expertise, it borrowed heavily from cathedral designs in France and Germany, though it was felt that the construction could be undertaken by local builders and engineers. Within three years of the foundations' being started, however, the initial self-confidence had waned, and it was reluctantly agreed that direct help from the north would be required. Nicolas de Bonaventure, a Frenchman, was appointed as principal engineer. He immediately found fault with the foundations that had been sunk; those beneath the more heavily loaded columns at the crossing of nave and transept were no larger than those intended for less heavily loaded columns. Although suitable modifications were undertaken during the following year, it seems that Nicolas may have made other proposals concerning the proportions of the unbuilt upper parts of the building that would have transformed it into a scheme altogether too foreign for the Milanese, and he was fired. A German designer, Annas de Firimburg, was appointed, and he proposed a different scheme, but he, too, was fired. An envoy was sent to Cologne to find a replacement, but without success; then an attractive offer was made to Ulrich von Ensingen, the

109 Winchester Cathedral, Winchester, England, begun 1079. Drawing showing the nave before (right) and after (left) substantial alteration by William Wynford in the 1380s. 110 Winchester Cathedral. Nave.

111 Hieronymites Monastery, Belém, Portugal, 1502–52. 112 Cathedral of St. Vitus, Prague, 1344–1929. Master mason: Peter Parler. Rib-vaulted portico over the Golden Door. 113 Cathedral of Milan (Duomo), Milan, 1389–present. Flying buttresses. 114 Saint Marien Church, Pirna, Germany, 1520s. Free-flying ribs known as the Wild Man and Wild Woman.

chief engineer at Ulm Cathedral, but he turned it down. Finally, Heinrich Parler from Schwäbische Gmünd, in Germany, probably a cousin of Peter, was appointed at the end of 1391, by which time the foundations were already complete and the first piers and buttresses had been started. Heinrich was asked to inspect the proposed designs and the completed work, and to report as to how the project should be continued. A panel of foreign and Italian experts was gathered in May 1392 to consider Heinrich's findings and answers to eleven questions or *dubia* (doubts).

Heinrich's report was not favorable. He questioned the soundness of the completed foundation work, and judged several features of the design proposed for the structure above ground to be unsatisfactory. The issue of greatest significance was how high the nave and four side aisles should be and how their heights should be related to the ground plan, in particular whether they should be based on a square grid (*ad quadratum*) or a series of triangles (*ad triangulum*). The first scheme for the cathedral, probably by Nicolas de Bonaventure, the French engineer, had been based on an arbitrary vertical
115 grid of 10 *braccia* (1 milanese *braccio* = approx. 0.6 meters) rising from the existing foundations spaced at 14 braccia intervals. In 1391 this had been replaced by one based almost exactly on equilateral triangles with a vertical grid of 14 braccia (rounded up from the exact figure of approx. 13.86) Despite these earlier schemes, and the Italians' lack of experience with buildings of similar size, the Italians argued that the heights of the aisles could be chosen without precise regard or logical relation to the geometry of the plan or to the size of the foundations. Both Heinrich and the German representatives of the panel of experts said their long-established experience was that the section of the building had to take into account the foundations already constructed, and that the heights should be decided using a single, simple scheme based either on a square or triangular grid. Heinrich proposed a scheme based on a square, which would have resulted in the cathedral being taller than the two earlier schemes. Interestingly, Heinrich concluded that the main constraint on these heights was not structural, but, rather, to ensure adequate daylighting of the interior of the building: The nave would need to exceed the height of the adjacent aisle sufficiently to incorporate clerestory windows of sufficient size.

Unfortunately, the protocol for the panel of engineers summoned to assess Heinrich's report and to recommend how to continue was based on one-man-one-vote. While democratic, this took no account of the experience of the many members of the panel. Generally speaking, the views of the experienced engineers from Germany and France were overturned in favor of the majority of those of the Italian members. None of Heinrich's recommendations was accepted, and he was dismissed. The section finally adopted for the cathedral was a curious compromise based partly on the equilateral triangle scheme, with a vertical grid of 14 braccia, and partly on a 12-braccia grid. Heinrich also addressed a question of structural interest. He was asked whether transverse walls would be necessary in the side chapels of the aisles, and he concluded that they were not, because the additional strength they would provide was not required. Such walls serve as internal shear walls or buttresses to carry the outward thrust from the nave vaults to the
round. North of the Alps this was achieved using flying 113
buttresses, but the Italians did not like these. Their concern about the outward thrust was probably assuaged when the cathedral was finally built much lower than originally planned. Filippo Brunelleschi was one of several later engineers who used internal transverse walls to avoid the need for flying buttresses.

Construction proceeded for an additional two years without further guidance from abroad until, yet again, there was indecision as to how best to continue. In 1394 Ulrich von Ensingen, from Ulm, was finally persuaded to give his advice to the building committee, but like Heinrich before him, he failed to persuade the members to agree with his ideas and he left again after just six months. Nevertheless, the columns and walls continued to rise until, in April 1399, key decisions about the vaults could be put off no longer. Help from the north was summoned yet again and three French engineers arrived to advise, though only one, Jean Mignot, remained to see the task through.

Mignot, like his several predecessors, made no less than fifty-four criticisms based mainly on the fact that the design did not follow the rules he knew and, therefore, was in error and unacceptable. He put forward his criticisms forcefully and repetitively, which annoyed the Milanese, and they simply rejected nearly half of his points, arguing

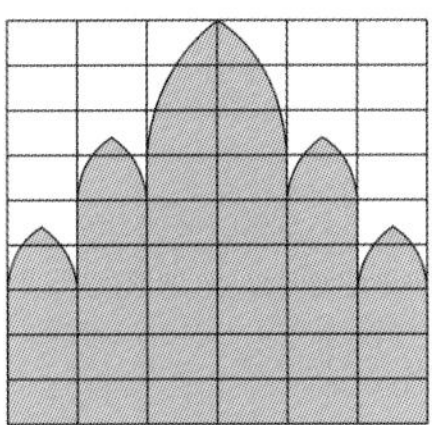
(A) 1390: di Vicenzo
6 bays wide, each 16 *braccia*
vertical unit 10 *braccia*
115

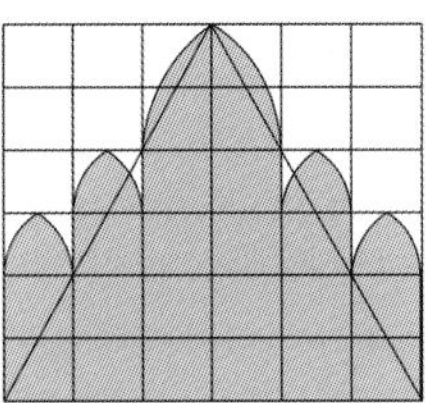
(B) 1391: Stomaico
each vertical unit 14 *braccia*
almost equilateral triangles

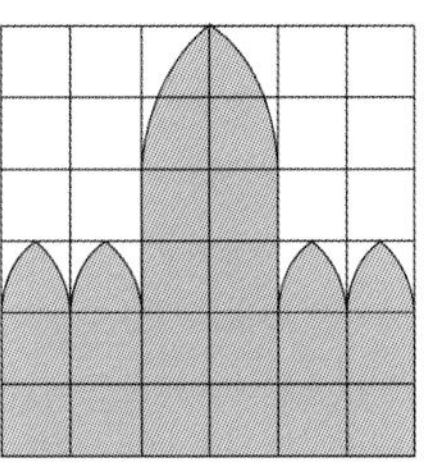
(C) 1392: probably Heinrich Parler
each vertical unit 16 *braccia*
square grid

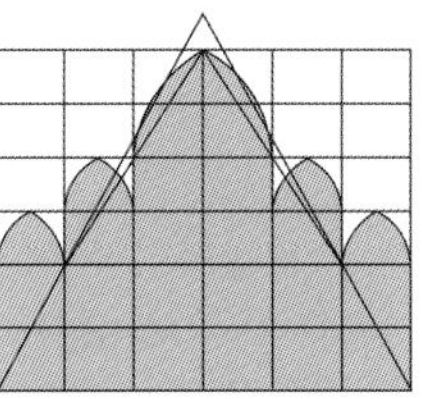
(D) 1392: hybrid scheme
2 vertical units of 14 *braccia*;
remaining units of 12 *braccia*
(Pythagorean 3:4:5 triangle)

that the building would never be finished if they addressed all of them. Of those remaining, one criticism was of great importance and related to the piers and buttresses. Finding the masonry blocks in some piers arranged too loosely, Mignot recommended they be locked together using iron cramps embedded in lead. He also recommended introducing iron ties between the heads of columns that supported a number of pointed arches. To this suggestion the building committee responded with outrage: they determined "to have pointed arches made according to the type suggested by many other good and expert engineers, who say concerning this that pointed arches do not exert a thrust on the buttresses, and . . . conclude that all the buttresses are strong and adequate to carry an even greater weight wherefore it is not required to make additional buttresses in any part of the church."[14]

Mignot's response was one of disbelief, and he called the supposed experts "ignoramuses." To reinforce his point Mignot put forward a number of arguments based on the science of geometry, to which the Italians replied, "the theory of geometry plays no part in the matter because theory is one thing and practice another" (*scientia est unum et ars est aliud*). Mignot then replied that "practice is nothing without theory" (*ars sine scientia nihil est*), to which the Italians responded by saying they had Aristotle's theories of statics and dynamics on their side and thus the cathedral was in order in every respect. In fact, the Italians' appeal to Aristotle was a bluff, for he had said nothing about the forces in vaults. The appeal was a desperate effort to save face, as was their deliberate misquotation of Mignot ("theory is nothing without practice") as support for their position. The transcribed minutes of these meetings attest to their lively and contentious nature.

In this and other parts of the proceedings of the Expertise there is clearly no objective rationale by which one opinion could be demonstrated to have more weight than another. Even though the French and German design methods for cathedrals were backed up by over two hundred years of experience, there seemed to be no way to convince the Milanese to accept them. In fact, within a year, most of Mignot's significant criticisms had been accepted, though by that time the first of the vaults had been partially constructed according to the original designs and demands to reconstruct them led to a further venting of passions. Finally, in October 1401, Mignot too was dismissed and the remaining construction seems to have progressed with no further help from north of the Alps. In conclusion, it is worth noting that the Milan cathedral is standing today, so the decisions reached around 1400, however arbitrary, have proven adequate.

115 Cathedral of Milan (Duomo). Diagram of proposed elevations, c. 1390, based on different sized modules.

A further point of interest in this story of the Milan cathedral is the degree to which buildings are embedded in national cultures, in part because they cannot be moved, but also because the ideas physically underlying their design, and the materials and crafts skills needed for their construction, could not easily be imported or exported. Such ideas were, and are, embedded in a society's way of thinking and its cultural infrastructure. While the French, English, and German cathedral designers and builders of the twelfth and thirteenth centuries shared enough of a common attitude to develop their buildings in similar ways, the Milanese of the 1390s were not yet ready to accept the engineering ideas from another culture. Curiously, it was another Italian city, Padua, that offered a rare example of a building design being imported from one culture to another. In around 1300 an Italian traveller to the Orient, an Augustinian friar named Giovanni, brought back plans and drawings of all the buildings he had seen, among which was the drawing of a roof of a great palace he had seen in India. So impressed were the people of Padua that they commissioned a copy to cover their own great civic hall. The roof, which still stands, is a timber barrel vault 75 meters long, spanning nearly 26 meters, with iron ties to carry the outward thrust of the vault.

There was, of course, more to monasteries and cathedrals than their structure. They were large enough to require that water, waste, and drainage be dealt with in an organized way. At roof level, flying buttresses took rainwater over the side aisles, and the ubiquitous gargoyle projected it away from the building facade. This was both to protect the stone beneath from wear and staining and to keep the water away from the windows, which would have also been vulnerable to damage from water. At the monastery of Christ Church in Canterbury, England, we find a very early and rare plan of the water supply and
116 drainage for the buildings.

The thermal performance of large abbeys and cathedrals is well known: in hot weather they are wonderfully cool and in very cold weather they can be comparatively warm. However, it would be misleading to suggest that this was the result of good environmental engineering design. This performance is characteristic of all masonry buildings and is a direct consequence of the thermal mass and inertia of the masonry. Nevertheless, we find evidence of careful engineering of the internal environment in many cathedrals in sunny climates, where the very small window area and the use of colored glass reduce the heating effect of direct sunlight. In northern Europe during much of the year, cathedrals are simply cold; large, single-glazed windows that let light in also let heat out. Such was the scale of the task of heating an entire cathedral that it was not really attempted until the nineteenth century, and even today it is both difficult and costly. What little heating existed was confined to the monks' accommodation quarters.

Likewise, for the legendary acoustic qualities of abbeys and cathedrals, we are rather more indebted to the skill of composers and musicians than to the buildings themselves or their designers. These large stone chambers have a long reverberation time because sound waves are reflected off their surfaces many, many times with little loss of intensity. This means that musical rhythms have to be slow to be intelligible, and that percussive instruments must not be used so as to avoid the inevitable machine-gun effect of any echo. The acoustics of the space favors those instruments with a gradual attack to each note, and that sustain their notes: the organ, flute, violin, and, of course, the human voice. For speech, however, the long reverberation time is a disaster. As the distance between speaker and listener increases, so the sound reaching the ear directly is increasingly swamped by the reflections arriving by longer, indirect paths. This ensures that words are generally unintelligible at any distance greater than a few meters, yet the phenomenon has an interesting architectural effect. Since the longer wavelengths of lower notes are more effectively reflected, people talking in cathedrals are naturally and unconsciously inclined to whisper (irrespective of any reverence for the religious nature of the buildings they may feel) because whispering removes the lower frequencies of the human voice. While this is a remarkable and rare example of a building's influence over the behavior of its users, it can hardly be attributed to the designers; it is an inevitable

116 Monastery of Christ Church, Canterbury, England. Original plan of water supply and drainage, 1150s. 117 Fountains Abbey, Ripon, England, c. 1150–c. 1250.

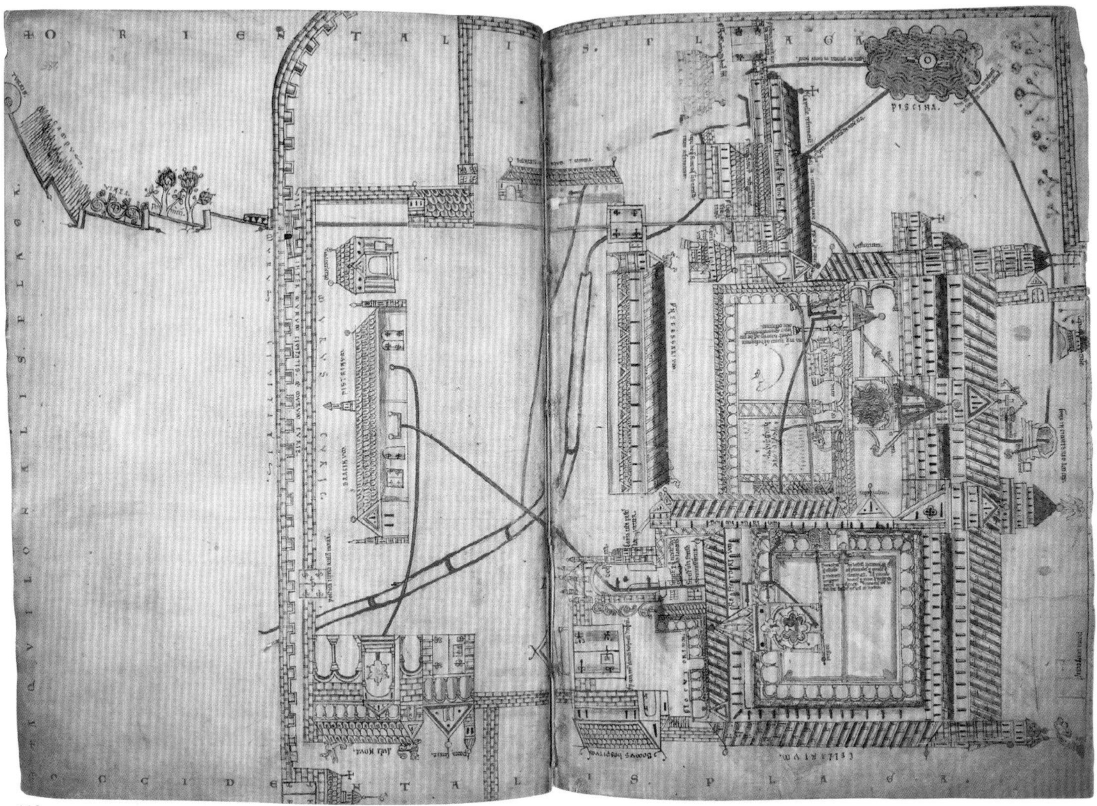

116

117

consequence of the size of the buildings and the materials used to construct them.

The End of an Era

By the end of the thirteenth century the art of masonry construction had largely surpassed that of the Roman empire of the second and third centuries A.D. For sheer opulence, however, even the largest cities in medieval Europe, especially north of the Alps, were still no match for Imperial Rome. The main reason for this was that the wealth of medieval Europe was concentrated largely in the Christian church, with its many branches competing with one another to win the souls of men and women and, no less important, the fortunes of rich families.

By the fourteenth century, the monasteries of France and England (especially England) had amassed huge wealth from two sources. The Cistercian monks at Fountains
117 Abbey in Yorkshire, England, for example, funded the entire construction of their new abbey during the twelfth and thirteenth centuries by selling to rich patrons the salvation of their souls in the afterlife through continued prayer—a medieval version of life insurance, so to speak. Once established, the monastery acquired huge areas of farmland which yielded a large income from both rent and selling agricultural produce. These lands also provided mineral resources, and the monks established what was, for the time, a relatively large industrial complex manufacturing cloth and many goods made of timber and iron which were sold throughout the region. Such autonomy, wealth, and power could not be tolerated by the monarchy for long and finally, in the 1530s, King Henry VIII ordered the suppression and destruction of British monasteries. A similar fate befell monasteries throughout Europe as the established church of Rome gradually removed them as a threat to its own authority.

The medieval building boom in Northern Europe, consisting mainly of castles and religious buildings, would soon be over, and the considerable wealth needed to fund any building boom would next be generated in northern Italy. Already in the thirteenth century, the ports of Genoa and Venice were encouraging the growth of international trade by sea, especially to the Middle East and beyond. It was not long before such trade had generated sufficient capital for bankers to want to fund manufacturing industries as a way of earning large returns on their investments. This wealth would be generated by the family dynasties that controlled the cities of northern Italy, and the intense rivalry between these families and cities would be good news for the building industry as they strove to surpass the opulence of their competitors.

chapter 3
The Renaissance
1400–1630

People and Events

1366–c. 1405 Konrad Kyeser

1377–1446 Filippo Brunelleschi

1404–72 Leon Battista Alberti

c. 1440–c. 1495 Mathes Roriczer

1439–1502 Francesco di Giorgio di Martini

c. 1450–c. 1520 Hanns Schmuttermayer

1452–1519 Leonardo da Vinci

c. 1460–c. 1520 Lorenz Lechler

Materials and Technology

1400–1500 Widespread mechanization using water power

From 1450s Printing using movable metal type

Knowledge and Learning

1405 Konrad Kyeser, *Bellifortis* (early military engineering manual)

c. 1480 Francesco di Giorgio, treatise on military and civil building

c. 1480–1510 Leonardo's drawings of structural behavior

1485 Alberti, *De re Aedificatoria* (book on building design and construction)

Design Methods

From 1486 First printed design manuals for cathedrals (Roriczer, Schmuttermayer)

Design Tools: Drawing and Calculation

From 1470s Drawing used as a design method (Di Giorgio and Leonardo)

Buildings

1420–36 Dome of Santa Maria del Fiore (Florence Cathedral), Florence, Italy

From 1434 Santo Spirito, Florence, Italy

c. 1480–1550 Renaissance fortifications by Sangallo family

1400 1410 1420 1430 1440 1450 1460 1470 1480 1490

c. 1500–77 Rodrigo Gil de Hontañon

1519 Charles V appointed Holy Roman Emperor

1543–1607 Domenico Fontana

1548–1620 Simon Stevin

1553–1617 Bernardino Baldi

1602 Dutch East India Company established

From 1550s Forced ventilation of deep mines in Germany

From c. 1600 Manufacture of machinery with interchangeable parts (Italy)

From 1550s Illustrated books on mechanics and manufacturing

1560s–1650s First scientific societies, established in Italy

1530–80 Illustrated books on architecture (Palladio et al.)

c. 1580s–1590s Baldi's notes on structural mechanics

c. 1500 Leonardo uses models of water channels for canal/river design

1500 Surviving wooden models of cathedrals

c. 1516 Lorenz Lechler, booklet on design procedures for vaults

c. 1565 Rodrigo Gil, manuscript on design procedures for arches and abutments

1586 Fontana uses models to plan moving Vatican Obelisk

c. 1500 Use of perspective drawings

c. 1550 Hindu-Arabic numerals in use throughout Europe

From 1550s Tables of squares, square roots, and trig functions published

c. 1610 Logarithms devised by John Napier

From 1580s Decimal fractions and notation developed

1580s Representation of forces by lines to enable calculation (parallelogram of forces)

From c. 1600 Stereotomy developed (drawings for stonecutting)

1620s–1630s First straight and circular slide rules

From c. 1530s Large civic buildings in Protestant countries

1530s Destruction of British monasteries

1540–80 Many villas by Palladio

c. 1540–1590 Dome of Saint Peter's Basilica, Rome, Italy

1559–84 Monastery of El Escorial, Madrid, Spain

1580–84 Teatro Olimpico, Vicenza, Italy

1591–1597 Hardwick Hall, Derbyshire, England

1618–19 Teatro Farnese, Parma, Italy

1510 1520 1530 1540 1550 1560 1570 1580 1590 1600 1610 1620 1630

The Renaissance 1400–1630

Engineering in the Renaissance

The idea of the Renaissance as the rediscovery or rebirth of the scholarly, literary, and artistic values and aspirations of classical Greece and Rome is a romantic picture that glosses over some down-to-earth realities. The luxury that indeed accompanied the widespread patronage of the arts in Italy was the outcome of a potent and highly successful interaction of international trade, technological progress, industrial manufacturing, commercial innovation, and, most significantly, the new European arms race that followed the arrival of gunpowder from China.

The technical developments in all branches of the engineering and manufacturing industries during the fourteenth and fifteenth centuries were astonishing. In 1300, machines powered by wind or water, and even the crank, were still considered novelties. By 1500, machinery for every possible process was ubiquitous in much of continental Europe, especially the German-speaking countries and northern Italy. The pulping of rags to make paper was among the first processes to be mechanized, and various types of printing machinery were developed in the mid-fifteenth century. Despite the inventiveness and growing prosperity of the German-speaking nations, it was in the cities and city-states of northern Italy that economic prosperity combined with a cultural revolution led to the various events we know as the Renaissance.

As would occur some three centuries later in England, northern Italy would generate its great prosperity through the mechanization of the spinning and weaving industries. Northern Italy had long been the main port of entry into Europe for silk from the Far East. Initially the silk had been imported already woven as cloth. In the fourteenth century, however, the Italians developed their own weaving machinery and began importing silk as thread. Spinning machinery followed, meaning that silk 118, 119 could be imported from the East in raw form. Finally, silkworms were successfully bred in Italy. Thus, the local production of raw silk, and its weaving into fine cloth, soon turned northern Italy from an importer of cloth and clothes to an exporter. Keeping the spinning and weaving machinery running created a large demand for bobbins and other wooden parts that were subject to wear, resulting in the development of a local domestic manufacturing industry. The parts were all produced to standard sizes in hundreds of workshops, and delivered to the mills. This was probably the first time in history that standardized and, hence, interchangeable components were used in the manufacture of machines. This forerunner of mass production was more flexible than the traditional practice of building an entire machine from a set of unique components; the spare part had been born. The idea of assembling artifacts from sets of identical, interchangeable parts was reinvented by a French gunsmith in the 1780s and later used with great success by the British navy in 1805 for manufacturing pulleys and blocks in Portsmouth.

The many technological advances that occurred during this time were not achieved without substantial investment of money, and Italy's preeminence can be partly

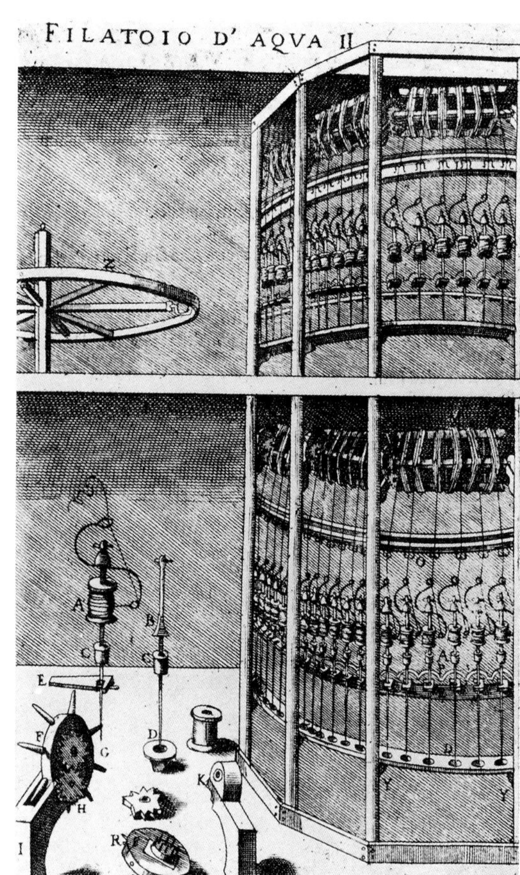

118

119

118 Vittorio Zonca, illustration of Italian spinning machinery, from *Novo Teatro di Machine et Edificii*, 1607. An early example of the manufacture of interchangeable parts. 119 Vittorio Zonca, illustration of water powered mill, from *Novo Teatro di Machine et Edificii*, 1607. As more and more processes were mechanized and powered by water, so buildings had to be designed to meet their needs. The textile industry led the way.

attributed to the financial infrastructure that developed there. The growth of commerce and trade in northern Italy during the fifteenth century generated a huge surplus of capital that enabled entrepreneurs both to invest directly in improvements in manufacturing and to establish banks that could fund even larger undertakings, such as the building of canals, in return for shares in the rewards of such projects. During the fifteenth and sixteenth centuries Venice, Milan, Bologna, Genoa, Florence, and many smaller towns vied with each other using building projects as one means of showing off the fruits of their commercial and industrial skills and demonstrating their civic pride.

Integral to the economic and industrial prosperity in northern Italy during the late fourteenth century was the development of a studio system of workshops that would have a strong influence on the practice of engineering and building design. This system involved a combination of some scholarly learning with an apprenticeship in practical skills, such as painting, sculpting in stone, and metalworking in bronze, gold, and iron. In many ways these studios resembled engineering workshops rather than our modern idea of an artist's studio. Paint had to be manufactured and stone had to be worked in the same way as on a building site, and the foundries producing huge bronze sculptures were little different from those making the latest cannon. The studios of such "artists," in the broadest sense of the word, became a fertile ground where a large range of skills were developed in harmony. Over the next two centuries these studios would produce several hundred men who excelled in several different fields: painting, sculpture, music, military and civil architecture, and literature, as well as mechanical, military, hydraulic, and civil engineering. It says something about our own times that modern historians of the Renaissance seldom portray the full breadth of activities of men such as Michelangelo, Donato Bramante, or Michele Sanmichele, whose work included many military and civil engineering projects in addition to their artistic work. In Renaissance Italy, many of the key individuals regularly switched between four related fields of activity: military engineering (weapons), military architecture (fortifications), civil engineering (earth and river works), and civil architecture (i.e., churches, palaces). Most such Renaissance artists were engaged in at least two of these fields, and many in all four. And many, of course, were also painters and sculptors. To a large extent, political events decided when people were engaged in civil or military work; when cities were at war or under threat, the civil work simply stopped.

Filippo Brunelleschi

One of the earliest products of the studio workshop system was Filippo Brunelleschi (1377–1446). From the engineering point of view, the dome, or cupola, of Cattedrale di Santa Maria del Fiore (the Florence 120
Cathedral), devised by Brunelleschi and constructed under his leadership, is the one building achievement of the Italian Renaissance that towered, quite literally, over all the others. This structure is the more remarkable for having been executed at the very beginning of the Renaissance, and is a tribute to the progress in building construction during the previous era.

Filippo Brunelleschi was born and grew up in the city of Florence, virtually in the shadow of the huge cathedral that was still under construction there. Like many of those who became engineers and architects at this time, he undertook what was effectively an engineering apprenticeship, in his case leading to the profession of goldsmith. This would have involved making complex clock mechanisms, as well as all the processes needed to cast bronze and gold, forge iron, and shape and join various metal components. He began his seven-year apprenticeship at the age of fifteen and afterward worked on various decorative sculptures, such as church altars. In 1401 he entered the competition to design and make decorated doors for the new baptistery in Florence. He narrowly failed to win but was nevertheless offered the opportunity to work under the guidance of the winner—the painter, sculptor, and goldsmith Lorenzo Ghiberti (c. 1378–1455). This did not suit Brunelleschi, who was becoming more ambitious. Determined to be supreme in another art rather than play second fiddle to Ghiberti, he left with his friend Donatello (c. 1386–1466), a sculptor, for Rome. During his six years there he was captivated by the buildings and ruins of the ancient city, which he studied in depth. There he learned the art of building and, according to legend, resolved to achieve two goals: to kindle the rebirth of great architecture to rival that of the Romans, and to provide the dome for the unfinished cathedral in his home town.

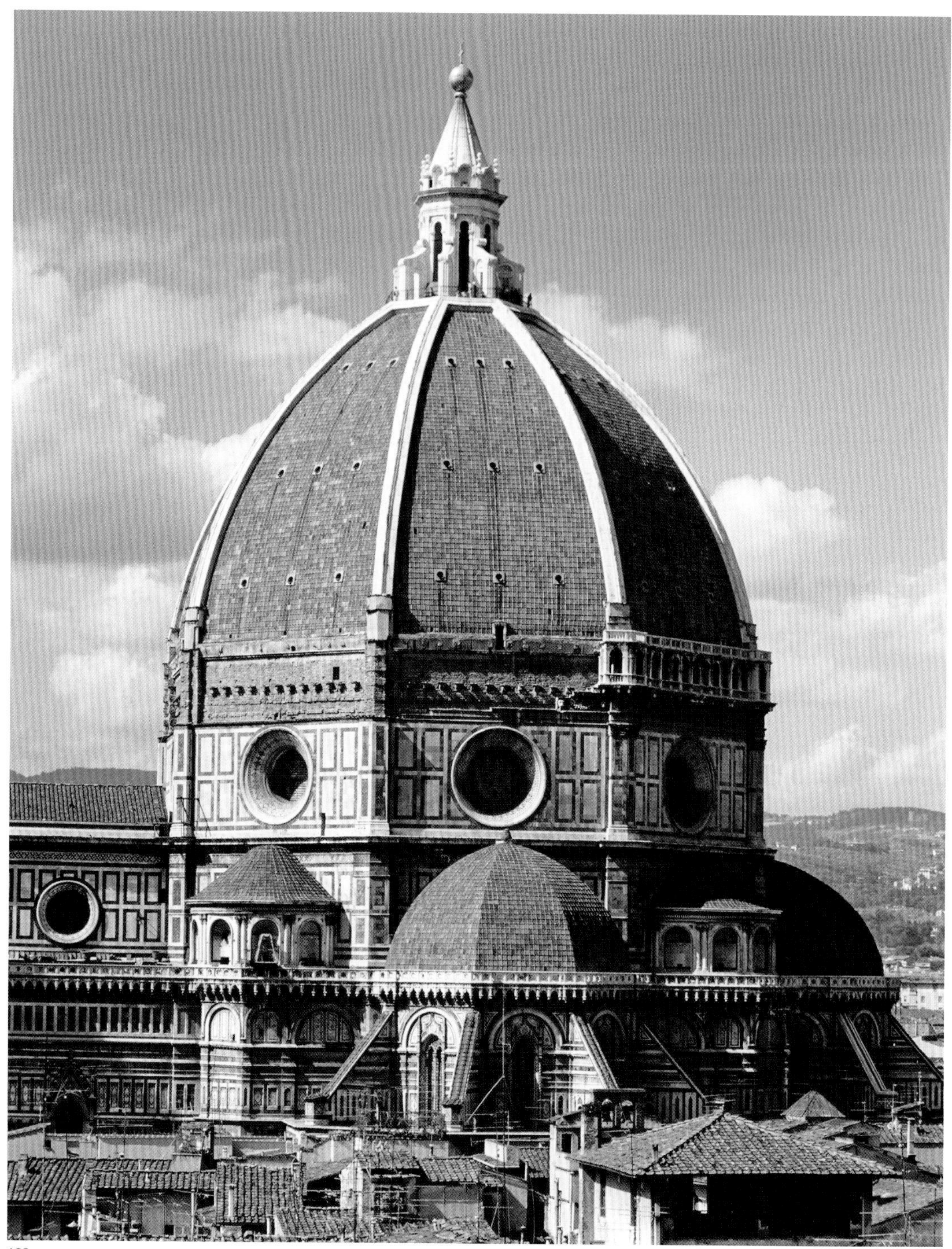

120

120 Santa Maria del Fiore, Florence, 1296–1436. Engineer of the dome: Filippo Brunelleschi, 1420–36. In scale the dome dwarfs the people visible on the viewing gallery in the lantern above the dome.

Brunelleschi worked as an engineer on a number of military and small civil projects before beginning his assignment on the dome at Florence in 1420, when he was then in his early forties. The cathedral's dome was substantially finished by 1436, though Brunelleschi died before the huge stone lantern was complete. During his time as engineer on the dome, he was also responsible for building fortifications in the Florence region, necessitating that his work on the dome take second place. In 1423 he was required to help fortify the town of Pistoia, and in the following year he began urgent work constructing a fortress at Malmantile, a town between Florence and Pisa. In 1430 his military expertise was again in demand to help with the battle against the neighboring town of Lucca. Today Brunelleschi is mainly remembered as the architect of three splendid churches in Florence—Santa Croce (completed 1442), San Lorenzo (begun 1419), and Santo Spirito (begun 1434)—designed in later life and now regarded as icons of the Italian Renaissance. Two of these were completed after his death using the excellent drawings and models, now lost, that Brunelleschi left to guide the builders.

The Florence Cathedral, or, familiarly, the Duomo, had been conceived as the crowning glory of Florence, one of the most prosperous cities in Europe, whose wealth had been generated by the textile industry. Using locally grown dyes and the best wool, imported from the Cotswolds, a range of hills in Gloucestershire, England, Florence made some of the finest fabrics in Europe.

A design had been adopted that would make Florence Cathedral one of the largest in the world. Work on the foundations began in 1296, with construction of the cathedral falling upon the shoulders of the *capomaestro*, whose responsibilities also included overseeing the building of fortifications in the Florentine region. Construction progressed slowly during the following century, when the workforce was needed for more urgent military building duties. One such "interruption" included the massive wall erected around Florence, around 7 meters high and 8 kilometers in circumference, which took some forty years to construct and was finally completed in the 1330s.

Those who chose the winning design for the new cathedral in 1295 were bold in their decision, for the position of the columns and walls demanded a large vault over the nave and an even larger span over the crossing. At the time, it was anticipated that a buttressed structure would be built in the Gothic style, and this was confirmed in 1366 when the then capomaestro, Giovanni di Lapo Ghini, was commissioned to produce a model of the entire building to indicate how it would be completed. By this time, however, fashions had changed and buttresses were thought to be an unwelcome reminder of Florence's traditional enemies to the north: France, Germany, and Milan.

An alternative plan was put forward by Neri di Fioravante, the leading building engineer in Florence at the time, who had constructed large vaults before and had recently completed the replacement for the Ponte Vecchio, which had been swept away in a flood. He believed a dome could be built to span the crossing, and that its outward thrust could be carried by means of internal "chains" of stone or wood rather than external buttresses. There were grave doubts about the possibility of such a solution, and no decision was made. Finally, in November 1367, the two designs were put to the citizens of Florence in a referendum; they chose the Neri proposal, largely, of course, for its appearance rather than its buildability.

Construction proceeded; the walls were raised to full height and vaults were built over the nave and aisles, leaving an octagonal void to be covered by a dome that would have to be larger than any span constructed since the Pantheon—a distance of some 42 meters between parallel sides. We do not know how the architects working on the project after 1367 expected the dome to be built, though they were at least aware that such a span was not unprecedented. Since that time a model, some 9 meters long and 5.5 meters high, had stood in the south aisle showing how the finished cathedral and dome would look. The key issue was how it might best be constructed and, no less important, by whom. In fact, the right man was needed: someone who had sufficient confidence in his own skill and understanding to know that he could take responsibility for the undertaking and, equally crucially, who was able to convince many dozens of skeptical people, both technical and nontechnical, that he was the one who could do it. He also had to achieve it for a price the client was prepared to pay.

Brunelleschi's solution did not appear overnight. He had known of the challenge since he was a small boy; everyone in Florence did. He was familiar with the great Imperial buildings by Apollodorus from the time he had spent in Rome. In 1407 those responsible for the construction of the cathedral called a conference, not very different from the Milan Expertises that had been called to discuss the construction of that city's cathedral a century earlier (see chapter 2, pp. 105–109). Brunelleschi was among the various master masons and builders who attended. Although no conclusions were reached as to how the dome should be built, Brunelleschi did suggest constructing an octagonal drum, about 10 meters tall with large circular holes, above the level of the vaults over the nave and transept. This, he argued correctly, would serve to direct the weight of the dome onto the eight massive piers that would support it. This proposal, however, also made the construction of the dome itself more difficult, since the drum was not well suited to carry any of the dome's outward thrust. A model of this scheme was made, and the drum was duly constructed from 1412 to 1414. Otherwise the conference bore no fruit, but it must have furnished Brunelleschi with a better understanding of current expertise in building domes, and undoubtedly left him more determined than ever to meet the challenge. In the next few years he became established as an engineer and architect of military buildings, while the Duomo's cupola no doubt continued to occupy his mind. By 1418 the cathedral wardens felt it was again time to address the question of how the dome should be built, and a second gathering of leading masons and engineers was organized, this time with experts summoned from France, Spain, Germany, and England, as well as Italy.

Brunelleschi was one of a handful to make serious proposals for the task. Another was Ghiberti, by now a well-established and highly respected artist, though with no experience of building, who submitted a small model made of bricks and timber centering that took just four days to assemble. The model Brunelleschi constructed was on a different scale altogether. It spanned 2 meters and was nearly 4 meters high; it used than five thousand bricks and fifty cartloads of lime for the mortar and took ninety days to complete. Most dramatically of all, he proposed that the dome could be built without the need for a massive structure rising from the cathedral floor to support the centering for the cupola; however, he refused to tell the officials how he would achieve it. This utterly unprecedented idea was received with skepticism, incredulity, and even hostility. More than once the panel of judges demanded to know, and he refused to elaborate. Finally, to make the point that it would be unwise for him to divulge his highly original idea, the biographer Giorgio Vasari tells us that Brunelleschi requested that an egg be brought to the room. He threw down the challenge that whoever could balance the egg on its end should build the cupola. All tried and failed. Then Brunelleschi tapped the egg lightly on the marble table to flatten one end, and stood it up with ease. The others complained that they could have done the same had they realized they were allowed to break the shell. Brunelleschi simply replied that they also would have known how to build the dome themselves had he showed them his plans. He got the job.

Brunelleschi was a canny operator when it came to protecting what we would now call his intellectual property rights. The panel's members were not sufficiently confident in him and his scheme to give him sole responsibility, so they awarded Ghiberti a joint role in the project. Brunelleschi strongly resented this, both because he knew Ghiberti was not capable of doing the work and because of the outcome of the earlier baptistery door competition. More than once during the initial stages of construction Brunelleschi made himself unavailable when especially difficult decisions were needed, saying that Ghiberti was equally responsible, only to be called in with greater urgency when Ghiberti was unable to solve the problems at hand. In 1425 Brunelleschi was finally given exclusive responsibility for the building of the dome.

Despite the large number of drawings Brunelleschi produced, both for the dome and at other times in his life, it is remarkable that none survive. Given his protective feelings about his ideas, it is not improbable that he himself ensured that they did not fall into the hands of others. Indeed, during the building of the dome, Brunelleschi became the first person to be granted a patent that protected an idea or design. Faced with huge transportation bills for carrying marble overland to Florence, he devised a boat that would bring the material by river at one-twelfth of the cost. This boat had a very shallow draft to overcome the Arno River's notorious lack of water. He was

121

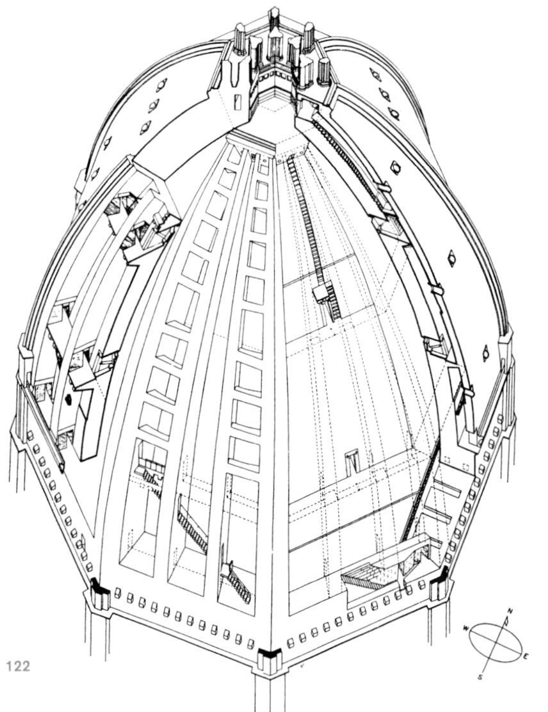

122

123

121 Santa Maria del Fiore, Florence, 1296–1436. Engineer of the dome: Filippo Brunelleschi, 1420–36. Cutaway isometric showing the double skin construction of the dome. 122 Santa Maria del Fiore. Cutaway isometric showing the positions of the stone and iron and timber "chains" carrying tensile forces in the dome. 123 Santa Maria del Fiore. Drawing of "herringbone" brickwork arches spanning between each major rib to allow the dome to be built without full centering.

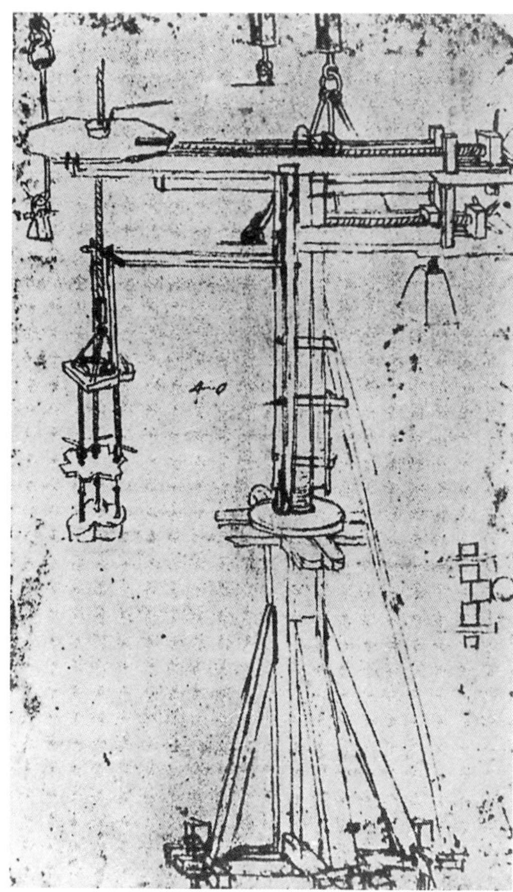

124

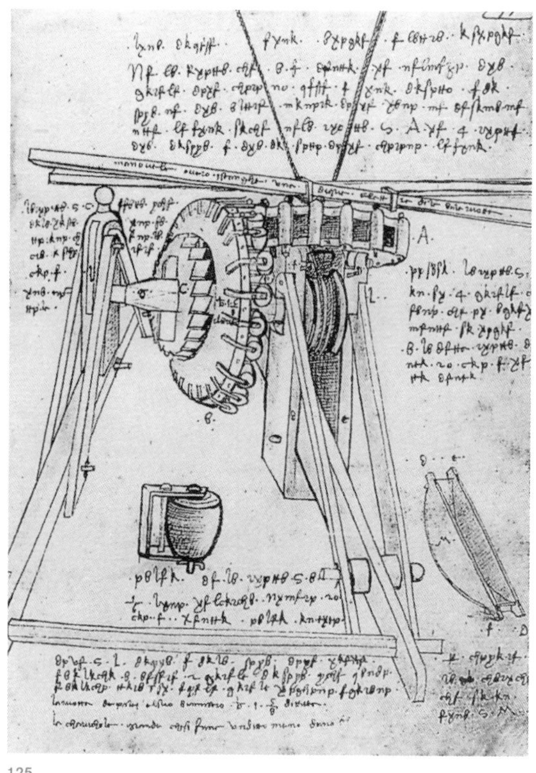

125

126

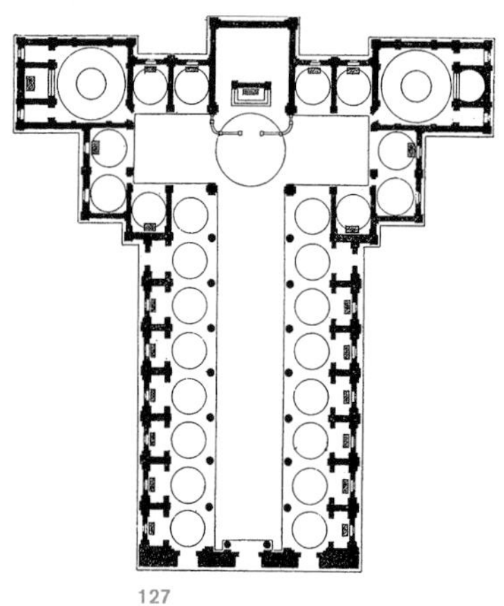

127

124 Leonardo da Vinci, drawing of Brunelleschi's 22-meter tall crane for lifting and maneuvering large stones, c.1475.
125 Buonaccorso Ghiberti, drawing of Brunelleschi's crane for lifting the lantern of the dome of Santa Maria del Fiore.
126 San Lorenzo, Florence, begun 1419. Architect: Filippo Brunelleschi. 127 San Lorenzo. Plan.

granted protection for three years, which was subsequently extended by a similar period, and was allowed to burn any boat made using similar principles. The only drawing of this device—possibly a barge that could rest on a wheeled carriage and be pulled by a rowboat in shallow waters—was made by Brunelleschi's Sienese friend, the military engineer known as Taccola (see p. 131), who included a rough sketch in one of his books. The boat, called *il badalone* ("the monster") by others, set off from Pisa in 1428 laden with 45 tons of marble. Unfortunately, it sank a few kilometers short of Florence, and Brunelleschi reverted to using conventional barges.

Brunelleschi's dome is a rich subject for study, with ever more innovation revealing itself. At the largest scale, it is ingenious for being a pair of thin shells linked by masonry ribs that is effectively 2 meters thick at the bottom, weighing about half as much as it would have if solid. The shell's stability and resistance to buckling were ensured by having the line of thrust remain within the thickness of the dome. Brunelleschi addressed the already well-understood tendency of domes to spread outward at their lowest points by incorporating two sys-
121, 122 tems for carrying the hoop tension forces. Three "chains" within the dome are formed by sandstone blocks linked by wrought iron cramps. A further chain of oak passes through the void between the two shells near the bottom of the dome, and can be seen by visitors ascending the stairway up to the lantern. Between each pair of ribs are several small arches in the horizontal plane, forming continuous circumferential rings. These carry wind loads to the principal ribs, and thus into the adjacent panels and downward to the main fabric of the building.

One of the most ingenious, and least visible, structural solutions that Brunelleschi devised was the means by which he avoided the need for substantial centering. For the lower portion of the dome, friction would be sufficient to hold the flat Roman bricks in place. Higher up, he knew that each ring of bricks would be stable when complete. The question was how to support all the other bricks until the last one was in place—similar to the need to support the stones of an arch until the last stone is in place. He solved the problem by building the straight sections of the dome's panels as flat arches between the main ribs. Each panel was divided into twelve voussoirs created by bricks, on edge, protruding from the two previous courses beneath. The angle subtended by each voussoir (360/(8 x 12) = nearly 4°) was just enough to enable the voussoirs to work as a "mini" flat arch composed of just three tapered flat bricks and spanning a total of about 1.4 meters. These could be 123
erected by two workmen with no need of centering at all. The visitor to the dome can see the edges of these bricks, which form what is usually referred to as a herringbone pattern—a term that implies more of a decorative function than the very basis by which one of the world's most remarkable structures was built.

Apart from these various structural engineering innovations, it was Brunelleschi's machinery that impressed many contemporaries. Leonardo da Vinci, who worked as an engineer on the last part of the dome—raising the golden sphere at the very top—used a crane, called a *castello*, that Brunelleschi invented, and sketched it in one of his notebooks. Ghiberti, as documented in 124
sketches left to us by his grandson, Buonaccorso, used another of Brunelleschi's cranes when constructing the 125
dome's lantern. Vasari, writing a century and a half later, refers to the architect "using counterweights and wheels for lifting [so that] he made it possible for a single ox to raise a load so heavy that previously it would hardly have been possible for six pairs of oxen to move it."[1] Vasari was also impressed by Brunelleschi's provision of a canteen serving food and wine to the workers at the level of the dome itself so they did not have to climb the 80 or 90 meters down to ground level and back up again at lunchtime.

None of Brunelleschi's other buildings presented challenges as great as the dome of the Florence Cathedral, though he often applied his ingenuity to them nevertheless. As a strong reaction to the extroverted structures of the medieval cathedrals, Brunelleschi, like many later designers, was keen to avoid buttresses, especially flying buttresses. Yet some structural device was needed to carry the horizontal thrusts of arches and vaults, as well as the wind loads, on a building and its roof.

At San Lorenzo in Florence, a church he began in 1419, 126
the same year his design for the dome was adopted, Brunelleschi used another ingenious structural device to achieve a building that, from outside, seems to have no

128

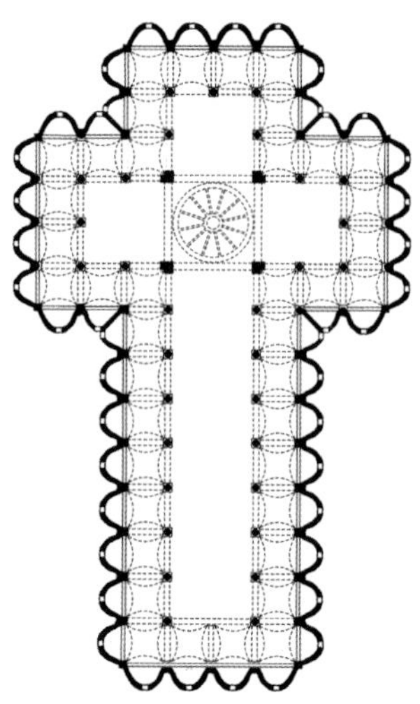

129

buttressing at all. In fact, he used internal buttresses, or shear walls, as we might now call them, that flank a
127 series of small alcoves or chapels.

At his much larger Santo Spirito church, begun in about 1434, Brunelleschi designed the external wall in the form
128, 129 of what is effectively a corrugated or folded plate. This achieves great structural depth using very little material, an idea used again in the twentieth century by such masters of building structure as Pier Luigi Nervi and Eladio Dieste (see chapter 9). The corrugations were filled in much later to create a plane facade.

Brunelleschi was the classic Renaissance man, skilled in numerous arts. During his apprenticeship as a goldsmith he learned firsthand how materials behave—how to make them, shape them, work them, join them, and decorate them. He learned the purposes to which they were best suited, and their limitations. He learned how the manufacturing of complex artifacts was organized. From direct observation he also learned how to analyze a manufactured object and determine how it was put together and how it worked. It was with this "engineer's eye" that he had studied the ancient buildings of Rome and, as Vasari writes, made many hundreds of sketches of them. Brunelleschi used drawing as a tool in his analytical process; it was a means to his understanding a particular engineering problem, and his gift for draftsmanship allowed him to exploit this talent more effectively than others. In combining his engineering understanding with his skill in representing his ideas on paper, Brunelleschi was virtually inventing the process we now call "engineering design"—a much more technical process than merely drawing on paper an object in the real world or the imagination. While Brunelleschi may not be the first person to have done this, he is the earliest we know to have used it so effectively. He studied in some depth many techniques of representing the three dimensional world on paper and, in around 1415, rediscovered the use of vanishing points for constructing accurate perspective

128 Santo Spirito, Florence, begun 1434. Architect: Filippo Brunelleschi. Drawing of exterior before the facade was made flat. 129 Santo Spirito. Plan.

drawings and representing distances accurately in the depth of a drawing. It is unfortunate that his sketchbooks have not survived, and we have only the notebooks of Leonardo to suggest what we might have found in those of Brunelleschi.

Leon Battista Alberti

Leon Battista Alberti (1404–72) was one of the most successful architects of the early Renaissance, but unlike Brunelleschi, he did not come from the workshop background and was not an engineer. Apart from the many palaces and churches he designed, he is best known for his book, *De re Aedificatoria* (On the Art of Building), which, like Vitruvius's book *De Architectura* nearly 1,500 years before, became a definitive reference work on building of the period. Alberti was born into a rich family in Genoa, excelled in his study of classics at the University of Padua, and began studying law at the University of Bologna. He abandoned these studies to capitalize on his social status and good education by writing a large number of books on a wide range of subjects, including agronomy, sculpture, the training of horses, geometry, and the topography of Rome. When he reached his mid-forties, he turned his interest to the fashionable subject of architecture. Although he completed the manuscript of *De re Aedificatoria* in around 1452, it was not published until 1485, thirteen years after his death, by his brother Bernardo, who took advantage of the growing market for works on building and architecture. Alberti's knowledge of these subjects was gained largely from the study of books, especially Vitruvius's, and from many visits to Rome. He also drew heavily on conversations with colleagues who had practical experience and firsthand knowledge about the art and science of building. By the mid-fifteenth century Vitruvius was well known through the many manuscript copies of *De Architectura* that were in circulation. No less than fifty-five of these survive to the present day, including twelve from the twelfth century alone and the remainder from the following two centuries up to 1486, when the first printed edition of Vitruvius's book appeared. Alberti's principal intention in writing his notes was to clarify Vitruvius, and provide a contemporary interpretation for those patrons wanting to commission buildings in the newly fashionable classical style. Perhaps the most notable features of his book are the constant reference he makes to classical precedent and the large numbers of classical writers he cites—often thirty or forty on a single page—with the purpose of justifying and lending credence to his own writing. This is undoubtedly a reflection of Alberti's scholarly approach and wide reading, which would have appealed to the sophisticated readers for whom he compiled *De re Aedificatoria*. It would also make the work attractive to the French and English intelligentsia who came to revere it so much in later centuries.

Alberti's manuscript, written in Latin, consists of vast miscellany in the form of unstructured text on all manner of topics concerning construction, building, and some civil engineering. This collection of notes was first given an orderly framework by the publisher of the 1512 Paris edition, who assembled them into 136 chapters grouped into ten books by way of emulating the organization of Vitruvius's book. Illustrations were added for the first time in the second edition of the Italian translation, published in 1550. It was first translated into English by Giacomo Leoni from the Italian edition in 1726 and is generally known through the third edition of this work, published in 1755 (still in print today, in facsimile form).

While the manuscript was clearly conceived with Vitruvius in mind, it differs considerably in the range of topics covered. It is more than twice the length of *De Architectura*, but gone are the chapters on military machines, astronomy, theaters, and the Greek science of acoustics. Apart from a few pages on where to site fortifications and how to make them suit their purpose, Alberti writes only of civil projects—all types of buildings, with a few sections on what we would now call civil engineering: bridges, drainage, canals, and docks. Like Vitruvius, he deals with the main building materials (with the exception of concrete) and the various structural elements—foundations, walls, floors, vaults, staircases, roofs, and so on. He was especially concerned to emphasize that the job of the building designer was to match the design to the needs of the client. Unlike later Renaissance authors, Alberti devotes relatively little space to classical styles, ornamentation, and building designs. The capitals and entablature of the four classical orders—Doric, Ionic, Corinthian and Composite—are covered in just two short chapters occupying just five pages of text.

Alberti's lack of practical experience and firsthand knowledge of construction was noted by several contemporaries. The architect and sculptor Filarete (Antonio Averlino, c. 1400–69) comments in his *Trattato di Architettura* (Treatise on Architecture) that Alberti, who wrote in Latin, was indeed a learned man; but, writing in the vernacular, Filarete proceeds to apologize ironically to his reader for covering down-to-earth technical details of building that Alberti did not discuss. Francesco di Giorgio Martini (1439–1502) (see pp. 133–36), who knew of Alberti's unillustrated manuscript, comments in the part of his own treatise devoted to architecture, *Trattato di Architettura Civile e Militare* (Treatise on Civil and Military Architecture), that it is essential for such a work to have illustrations, for otherwise the reader might interpret the text however he likes.

Writing in 1568, Vasari comments on the various errors Alberti made in his designs, which he attributes to the fact that Alberti concentrated rather more on writing than on his design work and that his practical experience lagged behind his theoretical knowledge. Vasari even suggested that the credit for his works should really be attributed to the men who actually carried them out, adding that "Alberti was extremely fortunate to have friends who understood him and who were able and willing to serve him, because architects cannot always stand over their work, and it is a great help if they can find someone to execute it faithfully and lovingly."[2]

Generally speaking, Alberti provides more technical detail than Vitruvius and occasionally ventures to give an engineering explanation. Most intriguing is his discussion of the arch:

> *There are different sorts of arches. The "entire" is the full half of a circle or that whose chord runs through the center of the circle. There is another which approaches more to the nature of a beam than of an arch, which we call the "imperfect" or "diminished" arch because it is not a complete semicircle, but a determinate part less, having its chord above the center and at some distance from it. There is also the composite arch, called by some the "angular" and by others an arch composed of two arches less than semicircles, and its chord has the two centers of two curved lines which mutually intersect each other [i.e., a pointed arch].*
>
> *That the entire arch is the strongest of all appears not only from experience but reason, for I do not see how it can possibly disunite of itself unless one wedge shoves out another, which they are so far from doing that they assist and support one another. And indeed, if they were to go about any such violence, they would be prevented by the very nature of ponderosity, by which they are pressed downward, either by the same superstructure or by that which is in the wedges themselves. This makes Varro say, that in arches the work on the right hand is kept up no less by that on the left than the work on the left is by that on the right. And if we look only into the thing itself, how is it possible for the middle wedge at the top, which is the keystone to the whole, to thrust out either of the two next side wedges, or how can that be driven out of its place by them? The next wedges in the turn of the arch, being justly counterpoised, will surely stand to their duty; and lastly, how can the two wedges under the two feet of the arch ever be moved while the upper ones stand firm?*
>
> *Therefore we have no need of a cord or bar in an entire arch, because it supports itself by its own strength. Whereas in diminished arches there is occasion either for an iron chain or bar or for an extension of wall on both sides that may have the effect of a bar to supply the want of strength that there is in the diminished arch, and make it equal to the entire.* [3]

In general terms Alberti is, of course, wrong in asserting that a semicircular arch exerts no side thrust. However, it must be remembered that Alberti was not a bridge builder. His direct experience of arches was mainly with small ones, for instance, above a window. Given a small lateral restraint, say from friction, and comparatively thick voussoirs, it is in fact possible to build a freestanding semicircular arch. We must also remember that Alberti was trying to express ideas for which there hardly yet existed a vocabulary, and clarity is further confused by Leoni's eighteenth-century translation. There is little doubt that Alberti understood how arches were built, as exemplified in the huge barrel vaults over the naves of his churches.

An example of a different but related problem is found in one of the illustrations included in Leoni's 1755 edition of Alberti. In the third book, Alberti correctly describes the use of inverted arches between the feet of brick piles to provide good foundations in soft ground, an idea used again by Robert Hooke in the 1670s (see chapter 4, p. 209). Leoni and his illustrator clearly did not understand how these arches worked, and showed them at floor level rather than the lowest point of the foundations.

On the strength of his knowledge of classical architecture, Alberti was able to secure architectural commissions from some of his influential friends and acquaintances. His first was to design a large town house for the wealthy Rucellai family in Florence in the mid-1440s. However, his design was for the facade only; the rest of the building was undertaken by others with more practical knowledge of construction. He designed a number of other facades for buildings being renovated in the classical style. Yet despite his design for the substantial San Andrea church in Mantua, which was built only after his death, his reputation thrived, and thrives today, on his book rather than on his talents as an architect. Nowhere does he address the key question that designers of large cathedrals faced, such as the thickness of walls or buttresses to support arches. He wrote mainly about building on a more modest scale that would have been well within the capability of the people he worked with. Also, being a professed architect and not an engineer, he perhaps felt that such a matter was not his concern.

From about the same period, north of the Alps, in southern Germany, there appeared the first example of a booklet devoted to the design of an entire cathedral. It was written by Lorenz Lechler (c. 1460–c. 1520), a German mason, as a series of "instructions" for his son, and dates from 1516. Lechler deals with many of the themes addressed by Villard de Honnecourt, Mathes Roriczer, and Hans Schmuttermayer, but goes further on matters relating to the larger picture. He recommends that the various dimensions of the plan and elevation should be simple multiples of the width of the choir—either 20 or 30 feet. For some parts he advocates using the familiar method of rotating the square. He recommends that the walls of the choir, carrying vertical loads only, be one-tenth of the span of the vault (2 feet for a 20-foot span, 3 feet for a 30-foot span), and adds that the wall thickness can be reduced by 3 inches if the stone is of good quality, or increased by 3 inches if the stone is of poor quality. A buttress for such a span, intended to carry the side thrust of the vault, needs to be a further two-tenths of the span in addition to the thickness of the wall, making a total of three-tenths of the span. On the subject of ribbed vaults, he says the depth of the ribs should be one third the wall thickness, and their width should be half their depth. Intermediate ribs have smaller dimensions reflecting, roughly, their structural duty. His procedures are very similar to the sequential use of a modular dimension described by Vitruvius for Doric temples. Lechler knew how cathedrals were built and what worked. He also knew that variations were possible; his "rules" were to be taken as guidance only, and he advises on the importance of using engineering judgment when applying such design rules:

> *Give to this writing [the handbook] careful attention, just as I have written it for you. However, it is not written in such a way that you should follow it in all things. For whatever seems to you that it can be better, then it is better, according to your own good thinking.*[4]

Although Lechler's rules do finally answer some of the questions about how medieval cathedrals were designed, there were so many successful exemplars at the time that such guidelines would have been little more than *aides-mémoires*. Certainly there is no hint that they allow the designer to experiment and push the limits of what was possible. Yet this is just what was happening in Italy at that very time.

Military Technology and Engineering

As the prosperity of cities grew, so they became more attractive prizes to fight for toward the end of the Middle Ages. New ways were sought to breach the ever more impregnable castles and city walls that had been developed from the eleventh through the thirteenth centuries. Trebuchets could launch heavy missiles (including the rotting carcass of a cow as an early form of biological warfare) over lofty fortifications from a range greater than that of the defenders' arrows, battering walls until they crumbled. However, they were very large machines, and difficult to move. Cannon that propelled their missiles using gunpowder made their initial appearances throughout Europe in the 1320s. The first ones were very small—perhaps only 10 or 20 kilograms in weight—and were correspondingly very mobile. Indeed, in those early days, their effect on enemies was probably as much psychological as it was physical. By the fifteenth century, however, cannon weighing a few hundred kilograms were able to fire missiles several hundred meters. Almost at a stroke, the art of warfare changed.

The cannon that led to this new type of warfare were made possible by the tremendous advances in the manufacture of metal artifacts in the fourteenth century,

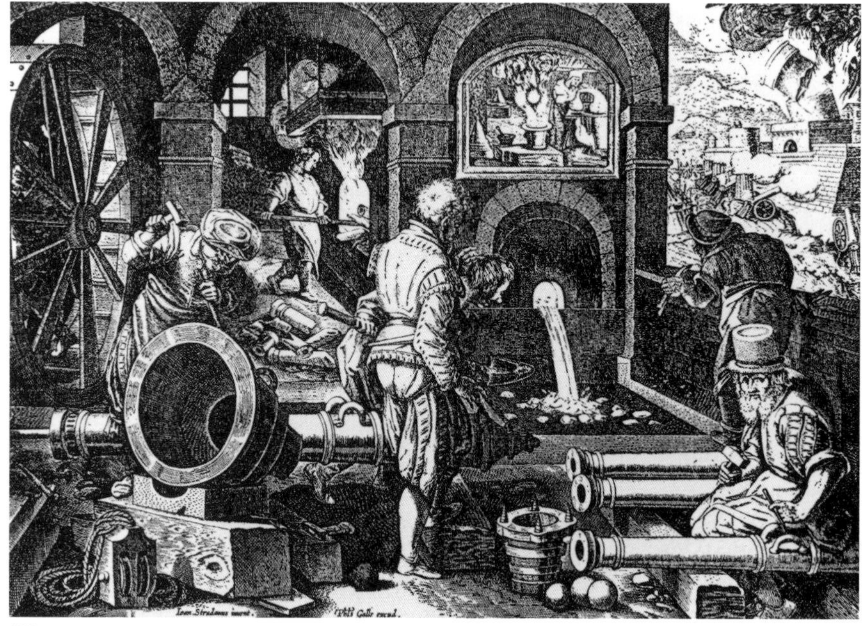

130

131

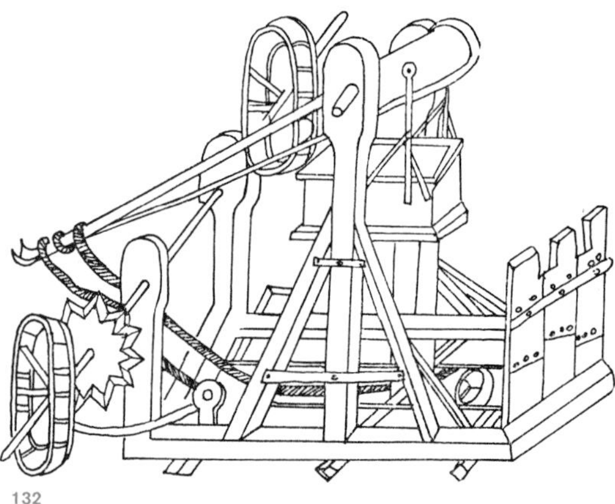

132

130 A sixteenth-century bronze cannon foundry. 131 Leonardo da Vinci, drawing of a cannon foundry, c. 1485.
132 Konrad Kyeser, illustration of a trebuchet, from *Bellifortis*, c. 1405.

especially in Germany. These included developments in the mining industry, furnace technology, the alchemy and metallurgy of creating alloys, and, most importantly, the art of assaying—the means by which the chemical composition of an alloy could be ascertained—which was vital to ensuring the desired alloy had been made. The properties of metal alloys could now be predicted with a much greater degree of confidence, and the risk of inferior quality thereby reduced. The early cannon were mostly made of forged copper alloys (bronze) or wrought iron. Large cast bronze cannon were being produced in the mid-fourteenth century, and cast iron, which required a higher furnace temperature, began to
131 replace bronze in the mid-fifteenth century. Although
cast iron soon became the cheaper alternative, it was the inferior choice; having a low strength in tension, more material was needed to resist the bursting forces of the explosion, so cast iron cannon were heavier and less maneuverable. Furthermore, its brittleness made cast iron particularly prone to catastrophic fracture, since the tiniest flaw in the casting could be the starting point for a crack that could spread with lightning speed if the stresses in the material were too high. Many were the deaths that resulted from such accidents. Nevertheless, the reliability of castings improved, and the quantity of material that could be melted in the fur-
130 naces increased. By the sixteenth century, cannon 2
meters long and weighing half a ton or so were being made in large numbers throughout Europe. At this time, the barrel of bronze or iron would be cast solid, and the bore fashioned using a machine with steel cutters set in a bronze mounting. The use of a clay core to make hollow castings would not be developed until the mid-seventeenth century. This technology would find its way into nonmilitary applications in the form of cast iron columns in buildings only in the 1780s.

The first engineering manuals appeared in manuscript form early in the Renaissance era, around 1400, and were much copied and widely circulated. They consisted of technical descriptions and sketches of military engines, weapons, wheeled vehicles, and various types of machines for lifting or moving heavy loads. Despite their technical content, however, it is unlikely that such manuals would have divulged secrets of much use to an enemy; the engineers' essential skills and experience could not be conveyed on the page. They more likely served as propaganda to deter enemies and to reinforce a country's or a ruler's reputation. Among the earliest of these was *Bellifortis* (Strong in War), written by the German military engineer Konrad Kyeser (1366–c. 1405) between 1402 and 1405. The largest of many surviving copies of his manuscript has 180 pages containing sketches and
descriptions of weapons, siege engines, and mobile, 132
floating, and folding bridges. But Kyeser goes beyond purely military equipment; he includes fixed bridges, water- and hand-powered mills, a wind-powered lifting machine and other lifting devices, diving suits and helmets, and manufacturing machines, with a whole chapter devoted to the uses of fire in kitchens and furnaces for heat- 133
ing water in bathing establishments. Kyeser does not, however, seem to have been interested in fortifications; the many castles he illustrates are for the purposes of demonstrating how the various siege engines work. His manuscript was circulated widely throughout the German-speaking world, and copies were still being made more than a century after its first appearance.

The Italians soon followed the early German examples. Brunelleschi sketched some of the machines he devised and used, and the scholar and scientist Giovanni da Fontana (c. 1393–c. 1455) was the first to compile an entire manuscript of drawings of machines, *Bellicorum Instrumentorum Liber* (Book of War Instruments) (c. 1420), which was annotated by text in cipher. The first Italian military engineer to record the latest mechanical and military technologies in the manner established by Kyeser was Mariano di Iacopo (1382–c. 1458), known as Il Taccola (the jackdaw, or crow). His books *De Ingeneis* (On Engines) (1430s) and *De Machinis* (On Machines) (1449) cover the same wide range as Kyeser and seem to draw on his and the works of others for their content. Although Taccola was clearly not a great innovator—his designs for various machines, weapons, and fortifications were already well known—the books spread his reputation far and wide, and he came to be known as the Sienese Archimedes. In fact, this appellation would have applied more suitably to Francesco di Giorgio Martini, one of Taccola's pupils, who was arguably the technical equal of Leonardo and compiled a treatise on military and civil architecture around 1480. Leonardo's manuscripts, which draw heavily on those of Francesco and other authors, date from the late 1480s to about 1510.

The first printed book on military engineering was *De re Militari* (On the Military Arts) by Roberto Valturio (1413–83), published in 1472. This was soon followed by others, among which were the first devoted solely to building design and construction: Alberti's *De re Aedifictoria*, and the small booklets by Roriczer and Schmuttermayer (see chapter 2). By the late sixteenth century there were many wonderfully illustrated books displaying the mechanical devices and manufacturing skills of the day. The best known of these encyclopedic books are *De re Metallica* (On the Nature of Metals) (Basel, 1556), by Agricola (Georg Bauer); *Le Diverse et Artificiose Machine* (Various and Ingenious Machines) (Paris, 1588), by Agostino Ramelli; *Machinae Novae* (New Machines) (Venice, 1595), by Faustus Verantius; and *Novo Teatro di Machine et Edificii* (New Theater of Machines and Buildings) (Padua, 1607), by Vittorio Zonca.

134, 135 The collective impression created by these manuscripts
136, 137 and books is one of consummate and comprehensive mastery of mechanical and hydraulic engineering. While these many technologies, especially those linked with the iron industry, were developed mainly to serve military purposes, they soon became available for civil applications in manufacturing and building.

The Profession of Military Engineer and Architect

The profession of architect, in the sense that we now understand it, was undoubtedly created in Italy during the Renaissance. However, architects at the time can be divided into two fundamentally different types. The smaller group consisted of those who received a classical education, including architectural history, and who worked mainly on civil projects. They practiced architecture with only limited firsthand experience of construction; Alberti and Sebastiano Serlio (1475–1554) are perhaps the best examples. The second, much larger group trained in the craft trades—Brunelleschi and Ghiberti as goldsmiths, Michelangelo as a sculptor and painter, Andrea Palladio as a mason; Franceso di Giorgio, the various members of the Sangallo family, Michele Sanmichele, and Donato Bramante also served apprenticeships in practical skills. These were generally the men who became military engineers and military architects, whose knowledge of building was gained mainly from designing and constructing fortifications. In midlife, Michelangelo also worked as a military architect, and for some years was responsible for the fortifications of Rome. A great many of these military engineers and architects turned their skills to nonmilitary building projects when the occasion arose, either when their military careers were over or when times were peaceful, and wealthy clients, including the church, placed commissions with them.

Francesco di Giorgio Martini was among the most prominent military engineers who excelled as well in military and, later, civil architecture. He was also a talented painter and sculptor. After a practical apprenticeship in the studios of one or more masters, he worked as a sculptor and on various building projects. His engineering talent was somehow noticed when he was in his twenties, for at the age of thirty, he was entrusted with maintaining the water supply, fountains, and aqueducts of Siena. In 1477 the city of Siena authorized him to move to Urbino to complete the design and supervise the construction of
the palace for Duke Federico da Montefeltro.This building 138
was among the most remarkable of its day, and is as imposing now as then. During the following twenty years at the Urbino court Francesco designed a number of palaces and churches, but these were few compared to the 130 or so fortresses he designed in the Montefeltro region, often with distinctive round towers to minimize the effect of 139
impact by cannonballs.

Francesco di Giorgio's engineering legacy has been passed down to us in his treatise *Trattato di Architettura Civile e Militare*, compiled around 1480 during his time at Urbino. Although it was not published in printed form until the nineteenth century, many manuscript copies were in circulation in his lifetime; Leonardo da Vinci, for example, who knew Francesco, owned a copy. The treatise has three distinct sections: on machines, on architecture, and on the art of fortification. The section on machines includes many original ideas, as well as some drawn from the works of Taccola and others: machines for lifting and
moving large weights, water-raising devices, mills, and 140, 141
various carriages with complex transmission systems; one is a hand-powered, four-wheel drive vehicle with independently steerable front and rear wheels. Leonardo

133 Konrad Kyeser, illustration of a heated bathhouse, from *Bellifortis*, c. 1405.

C
H
H
A
F
H
H
D
C
E
E
E
C
G
B

135

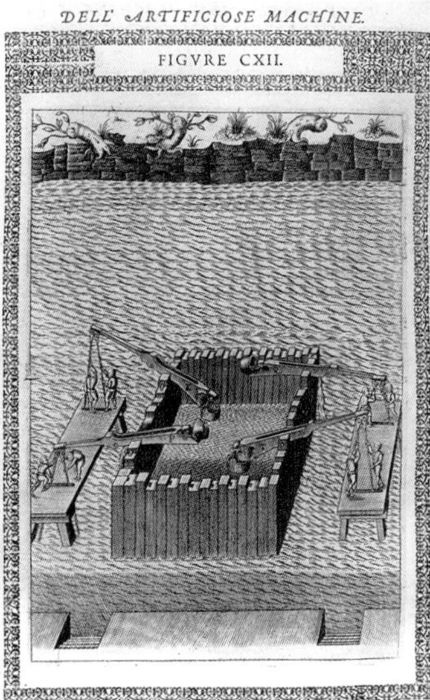

136

137

consulted this work in preparing many of his engineering illustrations; because of Leonardo's greater fame, his drawings are better known today than Francesco di Giorgio's, which do lack the skill of a great artist. In their technical detail and accuracy, however, Francesco's drawings are often superior to those of Leonardo.

The section on architecture covers content similar to that of Alberti in his *De re Aedificatoria* of some years earlier, since both took their inspiration from Vitruvius. For example, in choosing a site for a city, with regard to terrain, water, and wind, Francesco echoes Vitruvius in recommending the use of land on which sheep are seen to thrive. His treatment of private dwellings deals, of course, mainly with the luxurious palazzi that only the aristocracy and wealthy merchants might afford. After a short discussion of building materials he goes on to consider the best positions for staircases, chimneys, storerooms, and cellars. His rooms tend to follow Vitruvian precedent, and his gardens are symmetrical and highly geometric in the manner taken up by French landscape architects in the seventeenth and eighteenth centuries.

The section on the art of fortification is the most remarkable. It was the first significant European work on military architecture and was keenly studied at the time. The need for new fortifications resulted from an arms race stimulated by the increasing effectiveness of various military engines and, especially, the cannon. As it became more and more difficult, and indeed pointless, to defend a single building, the purpose of fortification turned to safeguarding a whole town by means of walls, ramparts, and ditches. This was especially important for the growing number of towns that flourished in areas without hills that provided natural sites for individual forts and castles. The focus of attack and defense became the people operating the artillery, rather than buildings themselves. The purpose of defensive fortification thus became focused on ensuring that the soldiers inside the city walls had a clear sight of every square meter of terrain outside

134 Agricola (Georg Bauer), illustration showing ventilation fans for mines, from *De re Metallica*, Basel, 1556.

135–137: Agostino Ramelli, illustrations from *Le Diverse et Artificiose Machine*, Paris, 1588. Left to right: A water-powered sawmill; a coffer dam under construction; and a water-powered pump.

those walls. It was also important for soldiers inside to be able to repel people attacking the walls themselves.

Francesco di Giorgio's fortifications were the product of a fertile imagination, and he took a highly analytical and technical approach to their design. He carefully thought through the logic of artillery sieges and made many brilliant technical innovations related to defense against cross fire, casemates (the vaulted chambers within ramparts from which to attack invaders), and the military use of tunneling. Most advanced, perhaps, was his conception of a total system of defense that allowed for rapid communication between nodal strongpoints; this led to 142 his trademark star-shaped plans with round towers at the projections. His ingenuity foreshadowed many developments in fortification that came to fruition throughout Europe during the following century. Francesco di Giorgio's treatise included plans and some perspective drawings of more than sixty citadels of many different forms, though he noted that their effectiveness depended more on the quality of their construction than on their shape. From the round towers, Francesco and later engineers pursued the idea of the bastion, which was to form the basis of all postmedieval fortifications, finally developed into its familiar pentagonal form by the Sangallo brothers (see below). Apart from their bastions, Francesco di Giorgio's fortresses were also characterized by their steep scarps and parapets protruding ominously from the tops of walls and towers.

In the same tradition as Francesco di Giorgio were the many members of the remarkable Sangallo family of engineers and architects. The founder of the family was Francesco Giamberti (1405–80), a wood-carver from Florence. His son Giuliano (1445–1516), later known as Giuliano da Sangallo, served an apprenticeship in a sculptor and mason's workshop. He worked as a mason on both fortifications and civil buildings and in 1483 was entrusted with renovating the fortifications at the harbor of Ostia, the port that served Rome. In the following years he worked on a number of projects for the Medici family, one of whose members, Lorenzo the Magnificent (1449–92), conferred on Giuliano the surname of "San Gallo," which he passed on to his descendants. Giuliano and his younger brother Antonio (1455–1534) worked on many fortifications both individually and together. After his brother's death, Antonio took over several of his commissions and demonstrated great talents as a military architect and engineer. He also worked under the guidance of Donato Bramante on the Church of the Madonna di San Biagio in Montepulciano (1518–37), and built a number of palaces. Antonio was later appointed by the Florentine government chief engineer of all works of fortification and, with Michelangelo, played a prominent role in building the city's defenses.

The nephew of Giuliano and Antonio was also called Antonio (1485–1546), and is now known as Antonio da Sangallo the Younger. He too was a builder, engineer, and architect, working first in Bramante's studio in Rome and later succeeding him in the building of St. Peter's. He enjoyed the favors of three successive Popes, Leo X (Giovanni de' Medici), Clement VII (Giulio de' Medici), and Paul III (Allesandro Farnese), and worked as designer and builder of several churches and palazzi, of which the most celebrated was the Palazzo Farnese in Rome. As a military architect and engineer he worked on the fortifications at Civitavecchia, Ancona, Florence, Parma, and Perugia, among many others. At least three other members of the family who also used the Sangallo appellation were military engineers and builders or architects.

Another Italian military engineer–architect who is nowadays better known for his painting and sculpture is Michelangelo Buonarotti (1475–1564). Michelangelo worked on the fortifications of Rome and, at the age of fifty-three, offered his services to Florence, where he was appointed governor and procurator general of the Florentine fortifications. In his capacity as a military engineer he was dispatched to inspect the defenses of Pisa, Livorno, and Ferrara, which were considered at the time to have the most advanced fortifications in Italy. He designed, coordinated, and directed the enormous Florentine defense effort, probably the largest construction project in the city since the erection of the city's medieval walls. In 1547, at the age of seventy-two, Michelangelo began his seventeen years' work completing the designs for Saint Peter's Basilica in Rome. He revised the several earlier designs and made the crucial decision to construct the huge dome with a double skin, similar to Brunelleschi's dome at Florence. Construction of the drum was under way when Michelangelo died, and the dome was completed, using the models, drawings, and instructions he left, by the engineer Domenico

138

139

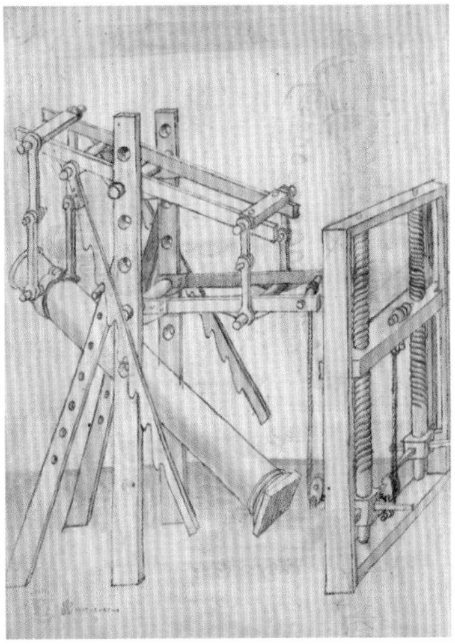

140

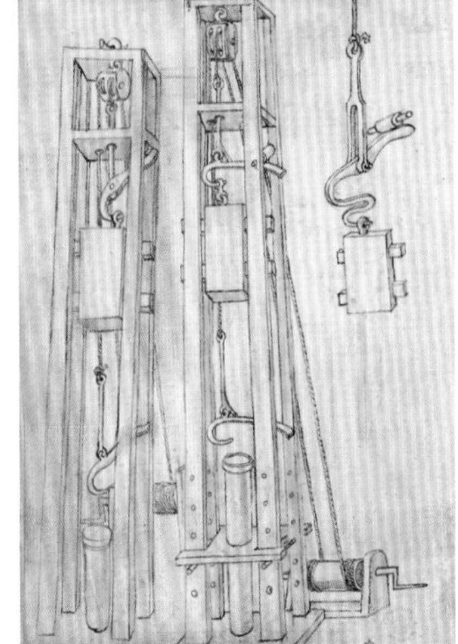

141

138 Palazzo Ducale, Urbino, c. 1444–82. Francesco di Giorgio took over as designer in 1477. 139 San Leo fortress, San Leo, Italy, 1480s. Designed and constructed by Francesco di Giorgio. 140 Francesco di Giorgio, illustration of a machine for raising columns. 141 Francesco di Giorgio, illustration of pile drivers.

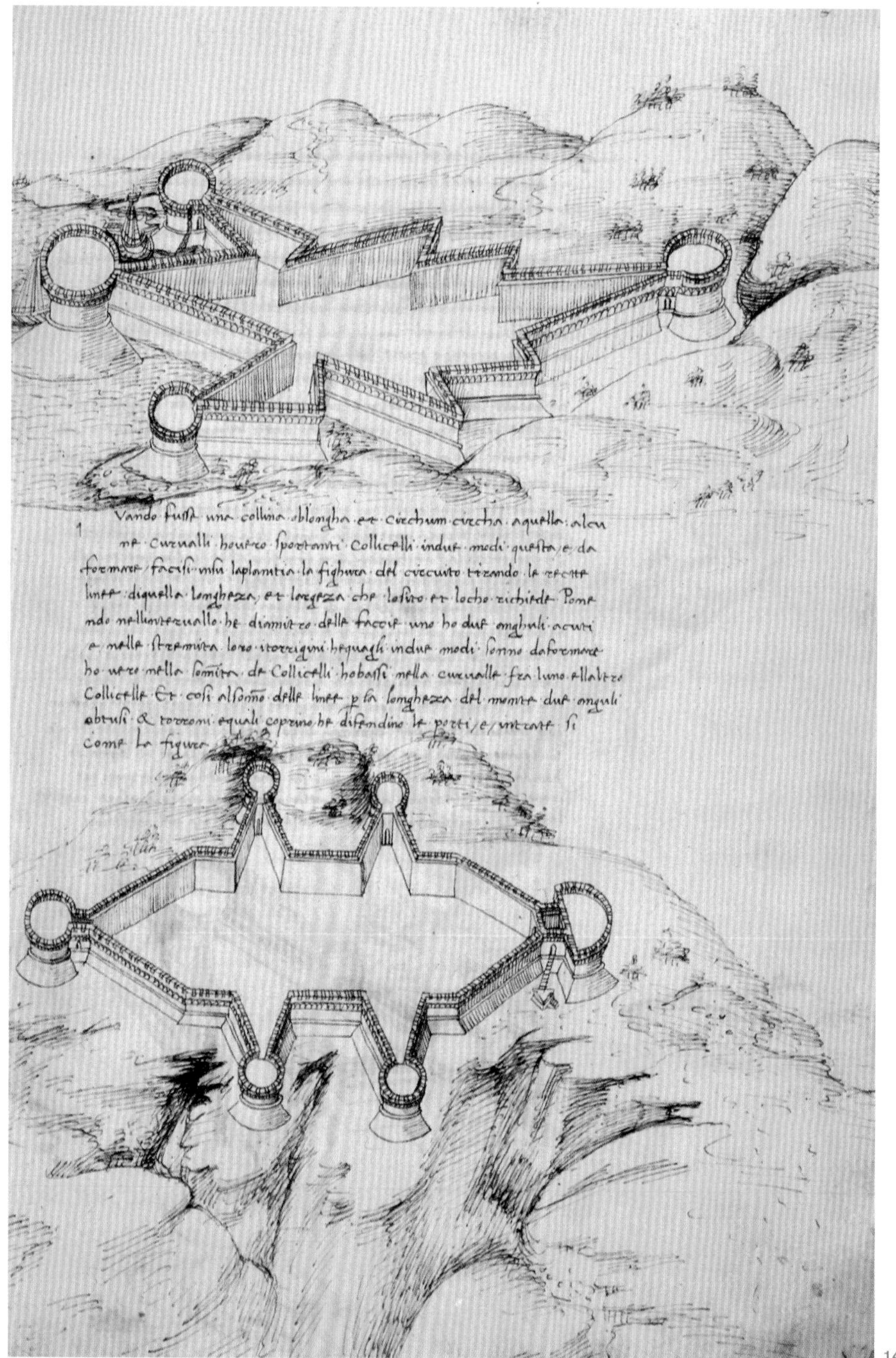

142

142 Francesco di Giorgio, plan of ramparts with bastions, from *Trattato di Architettura Civile e Militare*, c. 1482. 143 Santa Maria degli Angeli, Rome. Converted from the baths of the Emperor Diocletian (A.D. 300) by Michelangelo, c. 1561, and enlarged by Luigi Vanvitelli c. 1750. 144 Santa Maria degli Angeli. Plan of the Michelangelo and Vanvitelli churches superimposed on plan of the Roman baths.

143

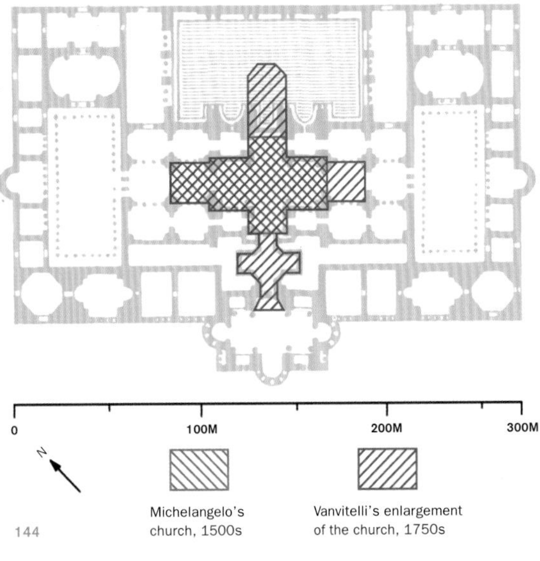

144

Fontana, (see pp. 159–63), and architect Giacomo della Porta (c. 1533–1602). This was the first building to be constructed in Rome on a scale to compete with and exceed the great building works of the second and third centuries. It marked a bold return to grandeur after the constant threat of attack and invasion, and various occupations and defeats by French armies that had plagued Italy during the fifteenth century, culminating in the ignominious sack of Rome and capture of the pope in 1527. In the last years of his life, Michelangelo also undertook
143 the enlarging of Santa Maria degli Angeli in Rome (c. 1561). The three bays of the nave of this church had formerly been the frigidarium of the Baths of Emperor Diocletian, dating from around A.D. 300. Michelangelo enlarged the church considerably by rotating the axis of the building, converting the original bays to the transept
144 and adding seven new bays to form a nave.

Leonardo da Vinci, Military and Civil Engineer

Of all the "universal men" of the Italian Renaissance, the most remarkable was Leonardo da Vinci (1452–1519). His interests covered virtually every branch of engineering and science, and his artistic talent was such that he merits a prominent place in history on this strength alone. Yet, except for the early period in his life, Leonardo's artistic endeavors were primarily a diversion from his principal occupation as a military, hydraulic, and civil engineer, to which he devoted his entire working life.

As a pupil Leonardo excelled at mathematics and served an apprenticeship in the studio of the Florentine goldsmith, sculptor, and artist Andrea del Verrocchio (1435–88). There, apart from developing his talent for painting, he also learned the art of casting huge statues in bronze. By the age of twenty-five he had his own studio in Florence and was broadening and deepening his knowledge of engineering by studying both the classical and medieval texts on theoretical mechanics, and the recent works of engineers such as Taccola, Francesco di Giorgio, Valturio, and others. When Leonardo realized he could improve upon many of these machines, he saw the opportunity for a new career. At the age of just twenty-eight, responding in a letter to a request from Lodovico Sforza (1451–1508), the regent (later duke) of Milan, to make a life-size bronze sculpture of a horse, Leonardo took the opportunity to describe the skills he believed made him well suited for a position as a military engineer. In this letter, he captured the scope and very essence of engineering in the late fifteenth century:

> *Having, My Most Illustrious Lord, seen and now sufficiently considered the proofs of those who consider themselves masters and designers of instruments of war and that the design and operation of said instruments is not different from those in common use, I will endeavour to make myself understood [by] making known my own secrets, and offering thereafter at your pleasure, and at the proper time, to put into effect all those things for which brevity are in part noted below - and many more, according to the exigencies of the different cases.*
>
> *I can construct bridges very light and strong, and capable of easy transportation. . . . I know how, in a place under siege, to remove water from the moats and make infinite bridges, trellis work, ladders and other instruments suitable to the said purpose. . . . I have the means of destroying every fortress or other fortification if it be not built of stone. . . . I have also means of making cannon easy and convenient to carry and with them throw out stones similar to a tempest and with the smoke from them cause great fear to the enemy. . . . If it should happen at sea, I have the means of constructing many instruments of offence and defence and vessels which will offer resistance to the attack of the largest cannon, powder and fumes. . . . I have means by tunnels and secret and tortuous passages, made without any noise, to reach a certain and designated point; even if it be necessary to pass under ditches or some river. . . . I will make covered wagons, secure and indestructible . . . which will break up the largest body of armed men. . . . Where cannon cannot be used I will contrive mangonels, dart throwers and machines for throwing fire . . . [and so on].* [5]

Leonardo went on to mention the services he could offer during peacetime as an architect, hydraulic engineer, sculptor, and painter, "which I can do as well as any other." He got the job. Leonardo served Sforza in Milan as a military engineer for nearly twenty years, until the duke fell from power in 1499. Leonardo then served as "engineer-general" to Cesare Borgia (1475/6–1507), who declared that "all engineers in all our domains shall confer with him and conform to his orders."[6] During this time Leonardo devised many horrific and gruesome weapons. On Borgia's fall from favor, Leonardo returned to Florence in 1506, where he worked as a consultant engineer, mainly on hydraulic engineering. His final years were spent France in the service of Francis I; during this time he undertook, among other things, experiments on the flow of water in canals. He died there at the age of sixty-seven.

Based on an understanding of practical engineering, Leonardo's career developed very much like that of a modern consulting engineer. His studies of mechanics enhanced his ability to think about engineering problems in the abstract, and his talent for drawing further enabled him to develop his engineering ideas. Indeed, such was his intellect and talent that he was able to master not only classical and medieval mechanics, but virtually the whole of science. The many thousands of notes he made effectively summarize scientific understanding in the late fifteenth century. In the field of physics, he addressed the same subjects that had been posed by Aristotle, revisited repeatedly in the medieval era, and that Galileo, Newton, and others would again address in later centuries. Although most of what Leonardo wrote was gleaned from others, he did propose some ideas that represented steps forward in scientific progress; for example, he suggested new theories for the propagation of light and sound, including the law of reflection. In mechanics, he mentioned the idea that a force is that which causes motion and acceleration. Nevertheless, Leonardo always had a practical outlook on his subjects; he was not a scholar, and scorned those who were—those who "go out puffed up and pompously dressed and decorated with the fruits not of their own labors but of those of others."[7]

What comes through in all of Leonardo's work is his practical and experimental approach to developing new knowledge. In this he followed the methodology that Robert Grosseteste and Roger Bacon had first conceived some two hundred years earlier. He articulated clearly a thoroughly modern attitude toward engineering, recognizing the importance of quantitative and scientific understanding: Among his axioms are the statements, "Let no man who is not a mathematician read the elements of my book," and "Practice must always be founded on sound theory." He also acknowledged the importance of gaining sufficient confidence in experience before relying upon it: "Before deducing a general rule from a specific case, try the experiment two or three times and observe if the experiments always give the same results."[8]

Leonardo applied this approach to several engineering disciplines. Through meticulous observation of bird flight, for example, he concluded that, for stable flight, the center of lift had to coincide with the center of gravity, and he used this knowledge to devise a number of flying machines. His main field of engineering research was hydraulics, especially as related to rivers and canals. He made many models to test and measure flow rates in open channels and over weirs, and he used particles of sawdust on the water's surface to make the flow lines visible. He also used models to investigate the causes of the scouring of river banks and river beds around the bases of bridge piers, and to study the effects of waves on embankments, all with the purpose of devising means for their reduction. He even looked for general relationships between variables, such as water depth and rate of flow from an orifice in a vessel; however, he fell short of the "correct" solution in this and other cases in assuming a linear relationship between variables rather than a quadratic or more complex relationship. Nevertheless, in taking this huge intellectual step, Leonardo transcended the accepted medieval belief that the world could be explained in purely geometric terms.

Unlike many of his contemporaries, Leonardo did not work as an architect. His notebooks contain a number of sketches of ramparts and a turreted square fort, but there is no indication that they were destined for a particular purpose. More likely they represent his "thinking on paper" at times when he was advising an architect or his patron on what to build. Likewise, he made a number of
145 sketches of alternative layouts for a cathedral similar in form to Saint Peter's in Rome. He even did a sketch
146 showing some ideas for solving Milan's traffic problems; he suggested to his patron that the city should be redeveloped, replacing the narrow medieval lanes with wide streets and separate ways for pedestrians and heavy vehicles. On another occasion he planned a proper sewage
147 system for the town of Urbino, with connections from each house leading into a main drain.

Nevertheless, Leonardo did not ignore the engineering of buildings. In a dozen or so sketches he reveals that he was exploring the very issues we would now call the science of the strength of materials and basic structural behavior, annotating many of these drawings with explanations of his experimental method. He was the first to leave us a record of thinking about materials and structures from an engineer's point of view, not only qualitatively, but also quantitatively. While the thirteenth-century scientist Jordanus had been the first, in his *De Ponderibus* of about 1220, to conceive of representing a force by a line on paper, Leonardo was the first to use this idea as a means for understanding how simple structures might actually work. The following note
describes an experiment he devised to measure the re- 150
lationship between the length and strength of a wire under tension—in other words, its tensile strength. As he wrote:

> *The object of this test is to find the load an iron wire can carry. Attach an iron wire 2 braccia long [about 1.2 meters] to something that will firmly support it, then attach a basket or any similar container to the wire and feed into the basket some fine sand through a small hole placed at the end of the hopper. A spring is fixed so that it will close the hole as soon as the wire breaks. The basket is not upset while falling, since it falls through a very short distance. The weight of sand and the location of the fracture are recorded. The test is repeated several times to check the results. Then a wire of half the previous length is tested and the additional weight it carries is recorded; then a wire of a quarter the length is tested, and so forth, noting each time the ultimate strength and the location of the fracture.*[9]

Scattered throughout Leonardo's manuscripts are many, often tiny sketches that indicate that he understood all the basic structural actions used in buildings. Each is drawn as a "thought experiment," as physicists call them today, indicating both deformations and the relative magnitude of loads, either as numbers or, more often, as weights drawn at different sizes. While many other engineers had probably been aware of these phenomena from ancient times, we are fortunate that Leonardo's sketches survive and show us directly what was going on in his mind.

Aristotle and other Greek scientists had understood the idea of statical equilibrium in a lever or a balance, but

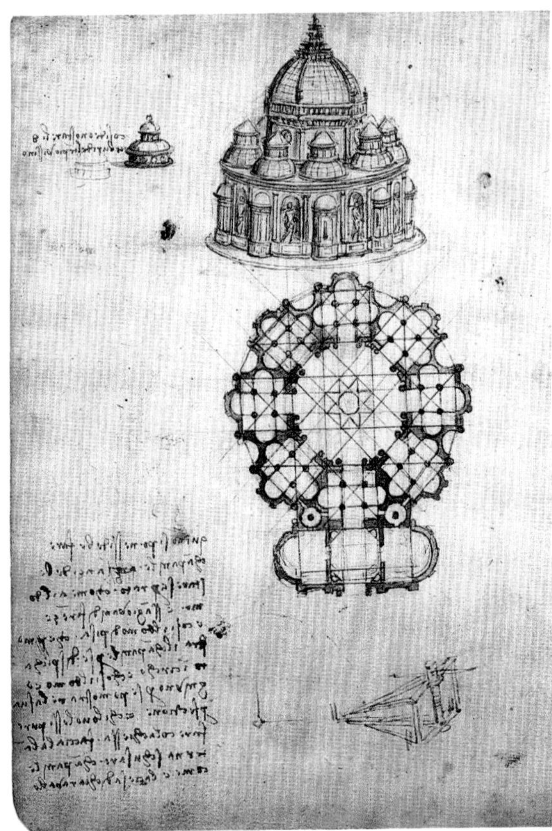

145

146

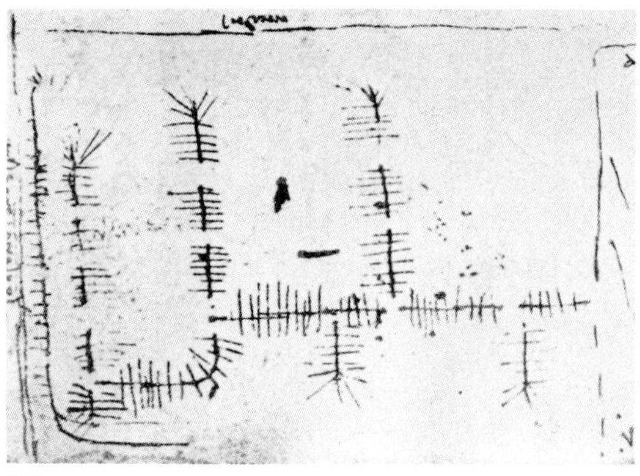

147

Leonardo was the first to express this idea graphically,
doing so with lines to represent the magnitude and direc-
151 tion of forces. Unlike his predecessors, he considered
nonvertical forces as well as the vertical force of gravity.
Leonardo used these ideas to imagine experiments illus-
152 trating the outward thrust of a simple roof structure and
148 of masonry arches of different heights. In another sketch
149 he illustrates different forces on the voussoirs of an arch,
though it is not clear which forces he thought they were.
He was aware of the influence of the thickness of a
153 voussoir arch on its stability, and used his feeling for
equilibrium to direct and balance the forces in a dome
154 and vaulted ceiling he proposed for Milan Cathedral.
155, 156 Leonardo included a number of sketches showing the
158 bending of beams, and how both deflection and strength
vary with a beam's dimensions. As with his tensile test,
the purpose of these experiments was to help answer another question Aristotle had posed: Why do long pieces of timber bend more easily than short ones, even when they are thicker? Leonardo was able to demonstrate that the flexibility of a beam depends, of course, on the relative proportions of thickness and length. He also considered
the internal forces that arise when a beam is bent. He il- 159
lustrated the different buckling strengths of columns of
various lengths and the bending of columns caused by ec- 157, 160
centric loads. Finally, he also illustrated the deformation
of a simple timber frame with rigid connections. 161

Leonardo's ideas and practice of engineering science were far ahead of his day. They were the results of what, to him, must have seemed the obvious way to go about things. Yet he did this outside the formal curricula of

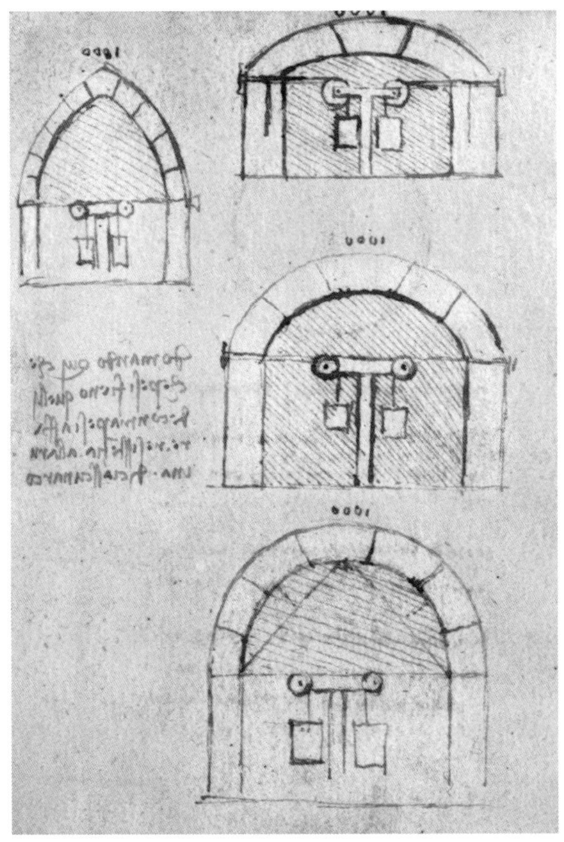

148

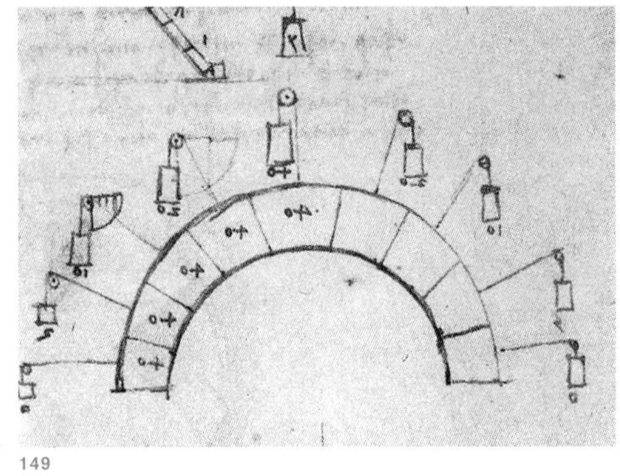

149

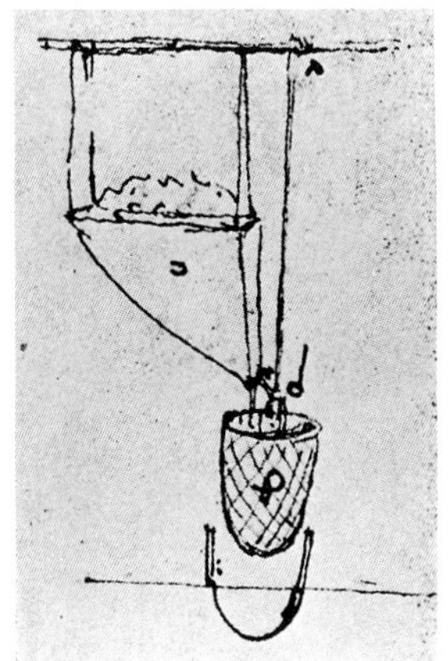

150

mathematics and science that were developing in some universities around Europe. He was solving practical problems, not trying to create a body of knowledge or an epistemology of engineering science. It is unfortunate for our understanding of medieval engineering that Leonardo did not compile the treatise on building that he proposed. Concerning the cracks that often appear in masonry structures, he indicates how important it is to establish the cause of the cracks before proposing the means of repairing or remedying them, likening this approach to that of a doctor who must diagnose an illness before proposing a treatment. He observed that horizontal and vertical cracks had different causes, as did cracks that were parallel and those that were wider at the top than at the bottom.

Like Brunelleschi before him, the young Leonardo possessed powers of observation and an ability to capture the world of three dimensions on paper. This ability developed alongside his mastery of the latest technologies

145 Leonardo da Vinci, cathedral designs. 146 Leonardo da Vinci, scheme for a city street on two levels, separating goods and delivery vehicles from pedestrians and light traffic. 147 Leonardo da Vinci, sketch of drainage system for the town of Urbino. 148 Leonardo da Vinci, diagram illustrating the outward thrust of arches. 149 Leonardo da Vinci, diagram illustrating the different forces carried by the voussoirs of a masonry arch. 150 Leonardo da Vinci, sketch of apparatus to test for variation of tensile strength with the length of a wire.

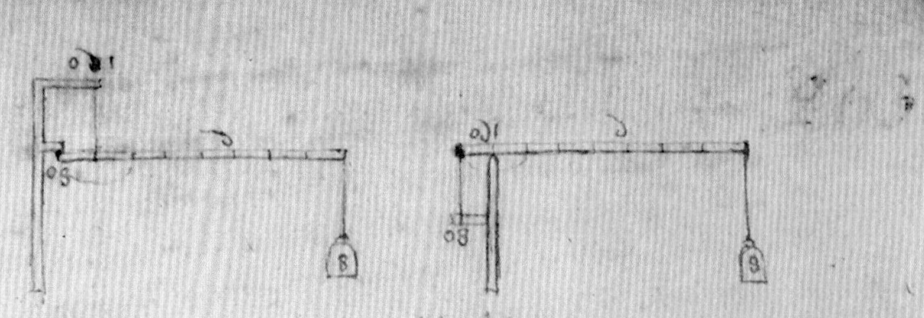

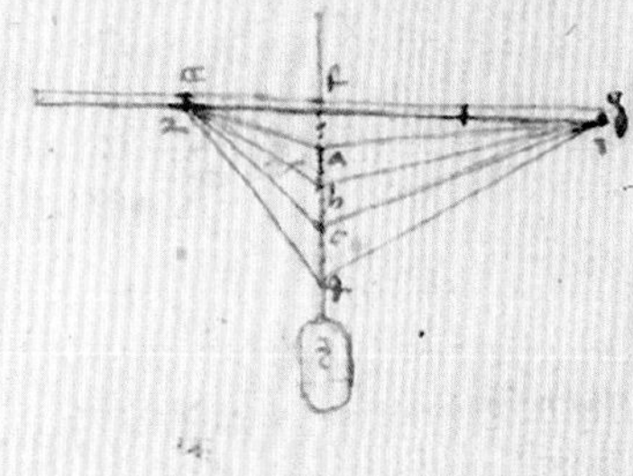

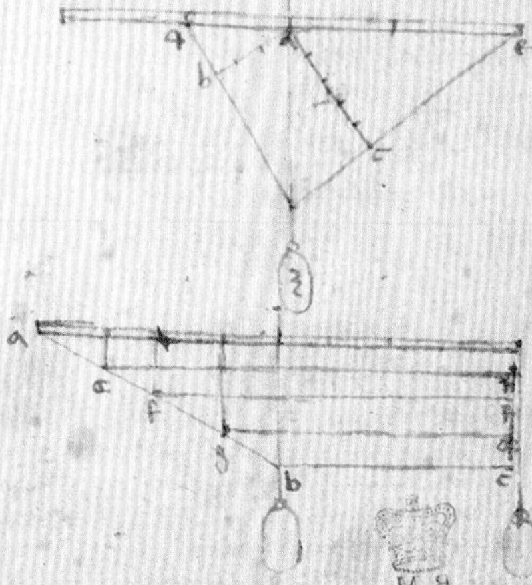

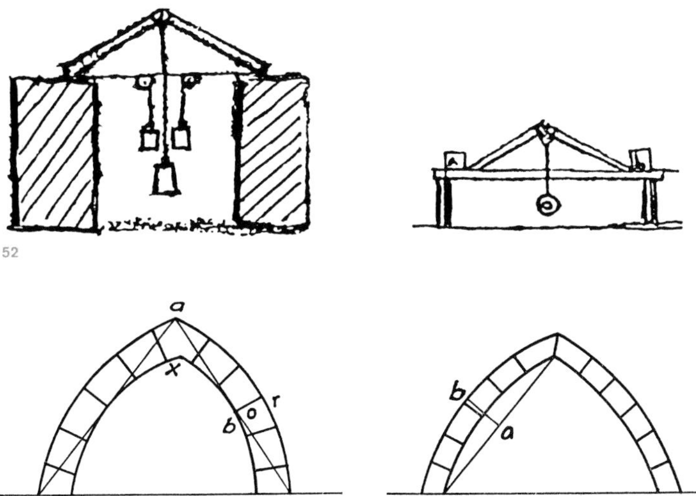

152

153

needed to make large bronze castings. What better preparation for becoming a design engineer? Unlike Brunelleschi, however, Leonardo left us a legacy of some 5,300 annotated drawings and designs (though many more sheets have been lost), giving us a unique insight into the skills of the first recognizable design engineer in the sense that we use that professional designation today. Leonardo's notebooks are a record of both his observations and his imagination; he jumped easily between the two, using sketches as an expression and extension of his thinking as he tested and developed engineering ideas on the page. They differ little from the sketchbook of an engineer, architect, or product designer today. Famously, of course, Leonardo's imagination was often in advance of fifteenth-century technology: his helicopter, for one, was not a practical proposition with regard to materials available during his lifetime. However, a replica of his glider design was made for a BBC television series in 2002, using materials that Leonardo could have used in the fifteenth century. It was successfully flown in England in 2003.[10]

Scholarship and Treatises on Architecture

The Italian Renaissance was, above all, the exploration and exploitation of the visual world. Beginning in the thirteenth century the use of representational illustrations in manuscripts had begun to increase. While some of these were representations of actual scenes from the real world (for example, completed buildings and buildings under construction), others existed only in the mind of the artist and were, effectively, building designs. Similarly, at this time, expressive paintings began to adorn the interiors of churches, with artists such as Giotto (1267–1337) showing how painting could capture and express emotion, space, and the imagination.

Engineers, especially Brunelleschi and Leonardo, integrated the process of drawing into the heart of the engineering design process. While painted and sculptural works of art remained physically integrated with churches, their influence was restricted to visitors and people who heard about the works through word of mouth. Paintings on canvas, however, could be

151 Leonardo da Vinci, graphical method for calculating forces in inclined strings supporting a weight. 152 Leonardo da Vinci, diagram illustrating lateral thrusts in a simple roof structure. 153 Leonardo da Vinci, diagram illustrating the equilibrium of masonry arches. (Overleaf) 154 Leonardo da Vinci, sketch of the structure for a masonry dome. Key points for the left half of the image are marked on the original manuscript by pin pricks, here overlaid with an orange line for visibility. 155 Leonardo da Vinci, page of sketches illustrating how the deflection of a beam varies with the point of application of the load, the load applied, and with its thickness and length.

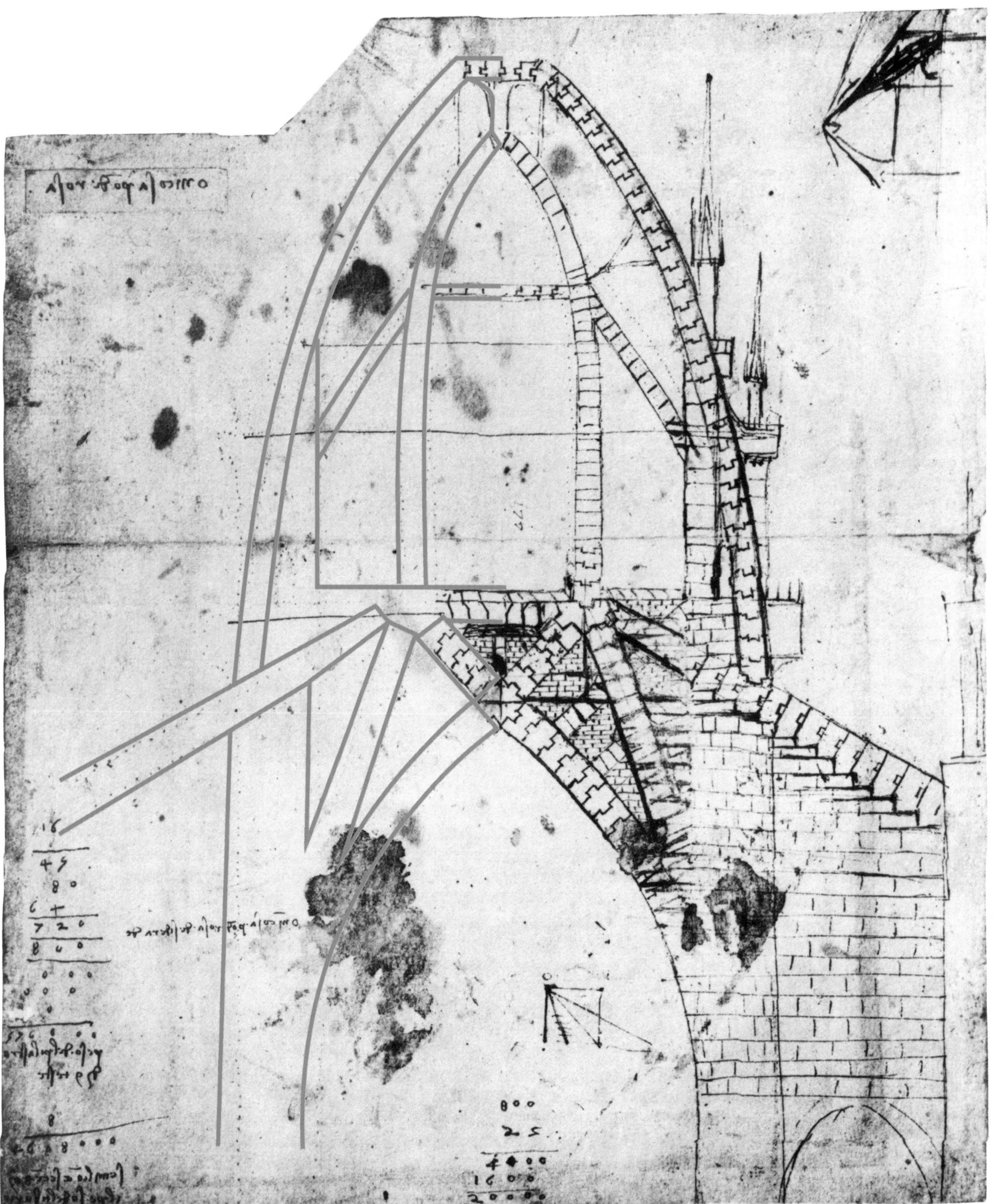

155

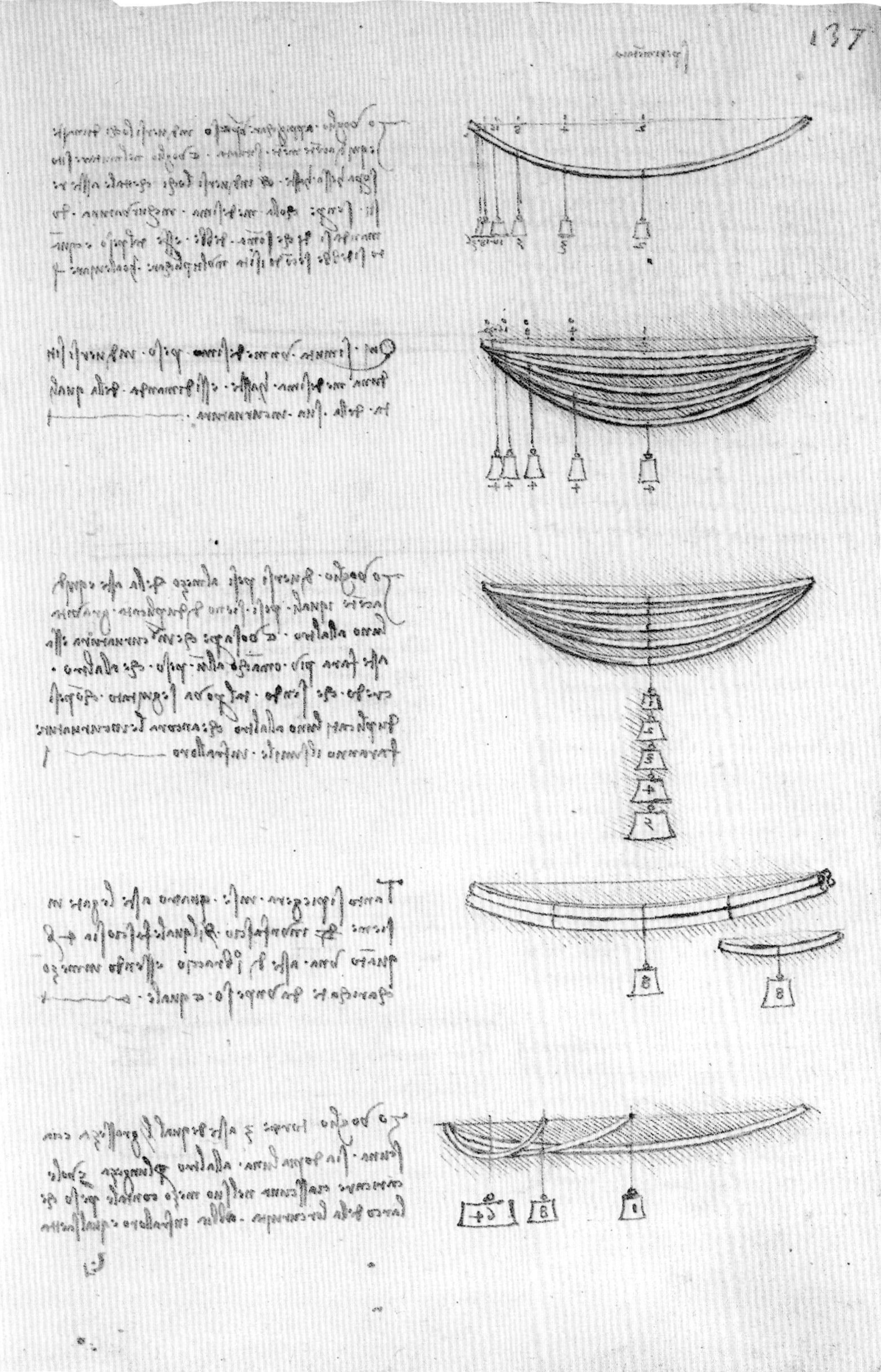

155

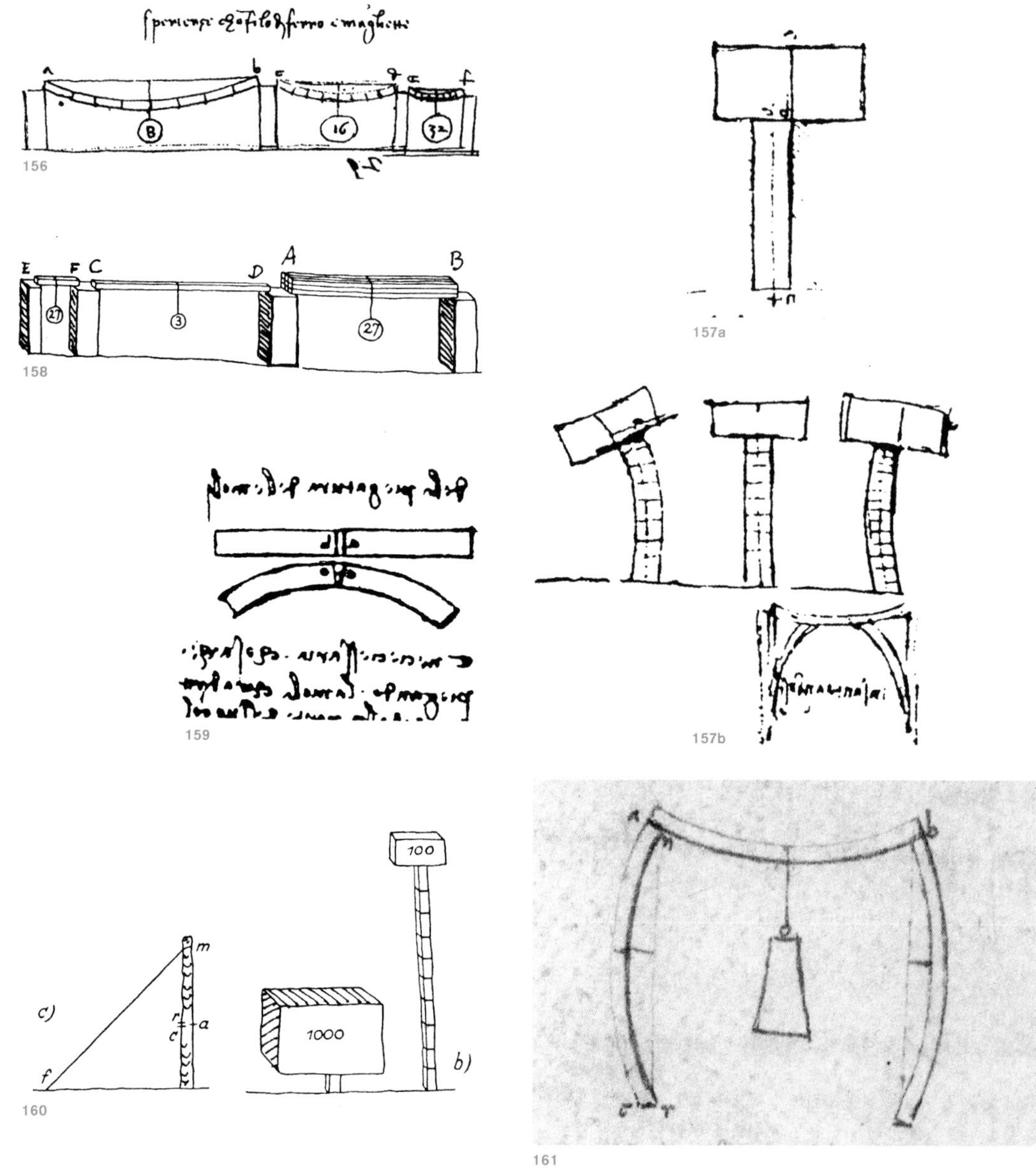

156 Leonardo da Vinci, sketch showing (incorrectly) the inverse linear relation between load and length of a beam; the relationship is actually the inverse of the cube of the length. 157 (a) and (b) Leonardo da Vinci, sketches showing bending in eccentrically loaded columns. 158 Leonardo da Vinci, sketch showing the linear variation of the strength of a beam with its length (actually the square of the length) and the number of similar beams (correct). 159 Leonardo da Vinci, sketch illustrating the extension in the upper face of a beam subject to bending, and compression in the lower face. 160 Leonardo da Vinci, diagram indicating (incorrectly) that the buckling strength of a column varies inversely with the length; in fact it varies inversely with the square of the length. 161 Leonardo da Vinci, sketch illustrating the bending of a portal frame.

transported far afield, and in this sense the Renaissance could be traded and exported. Illustrated manuscripts on military engineering were widely copied and circulated. But it was only in the sixteenth century when the mechanical means for reproducing images in print emerged that printed books began to embrace architecture and engineering. Ironically, it was in the same period that the two subjects began to be considered separate disciplines. The various books by Agostino Ramelli, Agricola, and others (see pp. 131–32) were devoted to machines, and featured buildings only as a context or backdrop. The illustrated, printed book played an essential role in the way architecture came to establish itself as an independent discipline; for this reason, perhaps, books devoted to architecture tended to underemphasize the role engineers and craftsmen played in the creation of buildings.

The many books that followed Alberti's were devoted to architecture and its classical roots; sections devoted to practical building construction and engineering diminished in size and importance. The first in this model were the books of Sebastiano Serlio, which came to be known collectively as his *Sette Libri dell'Architettura* (Seven Books of Architecture). Six were published in his lifetime, beginning with *Architettura Antica* (The Antiquities) in 1537 and *Ordini* (The Orders) in 1540. They were the first to capture and convey the essentially visual nature of architecture, and were lavishly illustrated with several hundred drawings. The illustrated book was highly successful at disseminating a knowledge of architecture—or rather, those aspects of architecture that can be captured in an illustrated book. The technical expertise needed to execute buildings could not yet be communicated in books; this still had to be learned on the construction site. In the hands of scholarly architects, the Renaissance classical style was thus largely a matter of appearances: facades and ornamental detailing.

The first significant book on the subject in French was written by Philibert de l'Orme (c. 1510–70), who was the son of a mason and became a successful architect, working for the royal family, among others, though very few of his buildings survive. His first book, *Nouvelles inventions pour bien bastir et a petits fraiz* (New Ways of Building Well and at Small Expense) (1561), focuses on practical building matters, including an idea he developed for constructing large arches from timber by pegging together many short planks—a process that resembles the laminated timber we know today (without the glue). This ingenious system became widely known through the book's 162, 163
publication and was used quite extensively, especially in 164, 165
France, into the nineteenth century. De l'Orme's later book, *Le Premier tome de l'architecture de Philibert de l'Orme* (The First Book of the Architecture of Philibert de l'Orme) (1567), was the first attempt in the French language to describe and define architecture. It combined a section giving practical guidance on how to construct various building elements, including vaults, with numerous illustrations of classical elements and details for their incorporation into architectural schemes.

Of all the books on building published during the Renaissance, *I Quattro Libri dell'Architettura* (The Four Books on Architecture) (1570), by Andrea Palladio (1508–80), was probably the most influential, partly because it followed Serlio's example in being well illustrated; about half of its two hundred or so pages are plans, sections, and elevations of both Palladio's own work and many of the great buildings of ancient Rome. These were immediately understandable to readers, and could effectively serve as a pattern book that others could copy. A second edition appeared in 1581, following Palladio's death, and another in 1601. Copies spread quickly throughout France, the Netherlands, and Germany, and translations into other languages soon followed. The English architect Inigo Jones had acquired a copy during his visit to Italy in 1614, and was almost solely responsible for introducing Palladio's designs into England. The first English translation, by Giacomo Leoni (who would also translate Alberti's *De re Aedificatoria*), appeared in 1715, and a second, by Isaac Ware, with much better reproductions of the illustrations, soon followed in 1738.

Palladio had trained in Vicenza as a stonemason and a sculptor and first encountered classical architecture when working for Count Giangiorgio Trissino, one of the city's leading intellectuals, who had designed his new loggia in the Roman style. Trissino recognized unfulfilled talents in the thirty-year-old mason and decided to house and educate him alongside the young aristocrats of the city, suggesting that he change his name from Andrea di Pietro della Gondola to the more classically respectable

Palladio. It was thus that he came to see Serlio's first book on the buildings of Rome. He visited Rome for the first time in 1541, when he was thirty-three, and was captivated. He would return several times, making dozens of sketches, which he used both in his own building designs and, later, to illustrate his Four Books.

Palladio's *Quattro Libri*—a single volume published in four sections, or books—demonstrates the final stage of separation between the role of architect and that of builder or engineer. There are but a few traces of interest in materials and construction methods, which he considered to be the responsibility of the builder. His useful advice is generally restricted to the building elements with which he was familiar as a mason. Book I begins with just a few paragraphs on each of the principal building materials and techniques: timber, stone, sand, lime mortar, metals, piles and foundations, and walls. After just eleven pages he has moved on to the five classical orders—Tuscan, Doric, Ionic, Corinthian and Composite—to which he devotes nine pages of text and twenty-one full-page lavish drawings. He then returns to building methods, dealing with vaults (in just ten lines), window and door openings, chimneys, stone staircases, and roofs. Book II is largely devoted to private houses and villas and features a great many of his own designs. Book III deals mainly with the layout of cities, with discussions of streets and piazzas, including several examples from ancient Rome, and a number of his own masonry bridges. Book IV is nearly as large as the first three combined and is dedicated almost exclusively to Roman temples.

Palladio was highly impressed by the great engineering achievements of the Romans—the large temples, the Pantheon, and the baths; he sketched an accurate reconstruction of the Baths of Emperor Caracalla. In his own work, however, unlike Brunelleschi and Alberti, Palladio did not push the limits of building engineering in terms of height or span or size or slenderness. His genius as an architect was to distill and capture the disposition of volumetric space, both solid and void, in classical Roman buildings, and reuse it on a more modest scale with appropriate classical detailing.

One of the few features of genuine engineering interest
166 are the stone staircases Palladio built and to which he devoted more space in his book than to any other building element. The steps of these so-called cantilever staircases appear to be supported at only one end, yet they are embedded in the walls to a depth of only a few centimeters—they clearly do not work as true cantilevers. In
fact, each step is supported partly by the step beneath 167
and partly by the wall, which prevents it from rotating about its long axis.This ingenious device was used widely in the following centuries, even in a reinforced-concrete version in the twentieth century.

The Italian Renaissance authors and de l'Orme were remarkably focused on classicism. They completely ignore not only the whole of French, English, and German cathedral building but even Italian masterpieces such as the cathedrals at Pisa, Milan, and Florence. As this denial of the late medieval masterpieces spread throughout Europe, it is no surprise to find such work being put down by use of the label "Gothic," after the name of one of the German peoples who were reputed to have destroyed the greatness of the Roman empire in the sixth century. Nor do we find in any of these books design rules for elements of their buildings. It was assumed that design details could be copied using the illustrations in the books as patterns for a certain style, or that the builders who carried out the works would know the appropriate materials and sizes.

The older blend of skills was still to be found away from the direct influence of the Italian Renaissance. In Spain, in about 1565, the Spanish cathedral designer Rodrigo Gil de Hontañón (c. 1500–77) was still concerned with collecting and rationalizing design rules. Although unpublished, his manuscript *Compendio de Arquitectura y Symetría de los Templos* (Compendium of Architecture and Symmetry of Churches) was felt to be useful enough to be copied and incorporated into another manuscript around 1680. It was finally published only in 1868, but by this time as a historical document rather than a useful design guide. Gil's guidance covers the plan and elevation of a cathedral, but is most interesting on arches and vaults. Of particular note in Gil's writings is the dissatisfaction he expresses about all the methods he has come across for sizing abutments. He strongly argues for design procedures based on reason, and his tone implies that Gil found the rules not convincing enough to provide him with the confidence he needed to use them in his own designs:

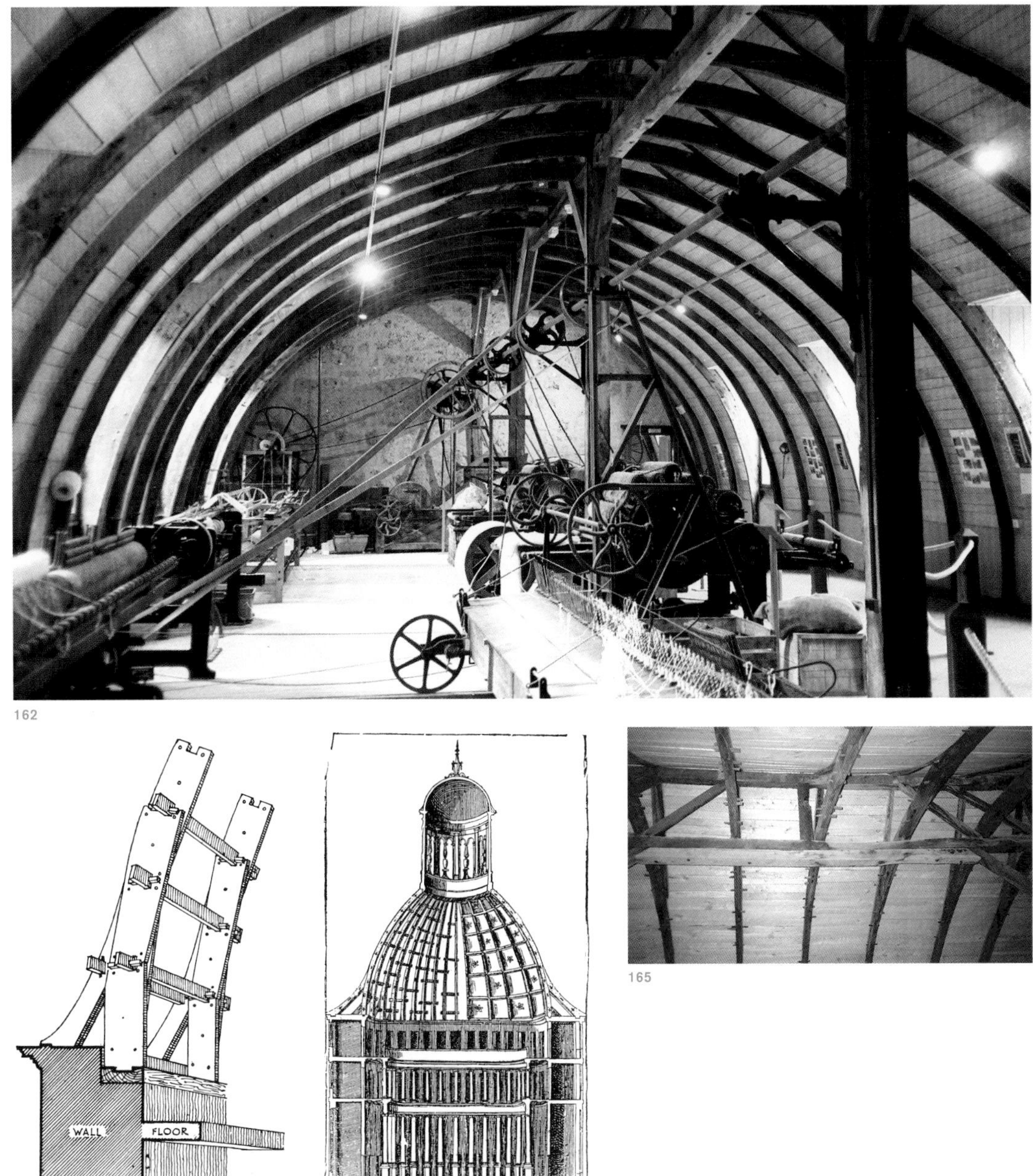

162 Roof of a factory in southern France, made using Philibert de l'Orme's system for making long timber ribs by pegging together multiple short planks, c. 1840. 163 Philibert de l'Orme, illustration of system for making long timber ribs, from *Nouvelles inventions pour bien bastir et a petits fraiz*, 1561. 164 Philibert de l'Orme, illustration of a dome made using his system. 165 Roof of factory in southern France, detail of timber rib.

166

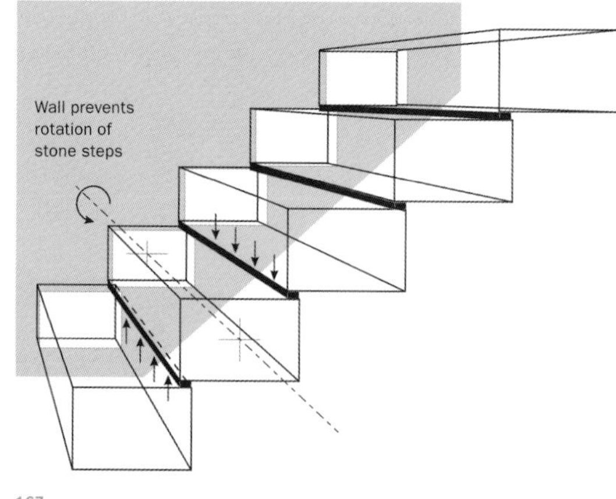

167

I have often tried to work out the size of abutment for any given size of arch and I have never found a rule that was adequate for me. I have inquired of other architects, both Spanish and foreign, and none seems to have managed to verify a rule other than by his own whim; and upon asking how we might know whether a certain abutment is enough, they reply that it was needed, but not for what reason. Some say a quarter [of the span] while others make certain geometrical constructions and dare to recommend them, believing them to be correct.[11]

Gil discusses seven design procedures for determining the dimensions of piers and buttresses in relation to walls or arches: four arithmetic formulae and three geometric methods. It is most likely that some of these were collected from other designers and that all of them represent a search for a method that generated plausible results, that correspond well with the dimensions of buttresses found to have been used successfully in churches, cathedrals, and other buildings. We might imagine someone with a list of measured dimensions, trying to work out an algorithm that could be used to generate them.

A modern structural engineer wants a column thickness to reflect the weight it has to support, which, in turn, might reflect the bay size—the area of floor or roof each column has to support. A modern engineer also seeks dimensional consistency, so that the formula yields a diameter in units of length. In Gil's arithmetic formulas we do not always find these conditions. A simple formula states that a buttress should be one quarter of the span (not too different from Lorenz Lechler's ratio of three-tenths), but another computes the diameter of a pier or column as:

$$Diameter = 0.5 \times \sqrt{(W + L + H)}$$

(Where W, L, and H are respectively the width or span of the vault, the length of the bay between adjacent piers, and the height of the piers on which the vault rests.)

While this formula does vary in the right direction (the larger the bay, the larger the column diameter), it does not yield a diameter in units of length, nor is there a clear logic as to why the height, length, and width should be added together. On the other hand, this and other formulae Gil discusses are the earliest that include a square or square root. He also knew that different methods yield different answers: for example, when discussing another arithmetic design procedure, he observed that "it is the most accurate [*cercano*, meaning close] and rational of all of the rules," even though he acknowledges that the result is different from the one Vitruvius recommends.[12]

166 Santa Maria della Carità, Venice, 1560–61, stone staircase. Architect: Andrea Palladio. 167 The mechanics of a so-called cantilever stone staircase. The wall prevents the individual treads from rotating, and each tread is supported by the one below.

168, 169 Gil presents two similar geometric methods for deriving both the thickness of the abutment required for a semicircular arch and the height of masonry such an arch could support. For an arch span of s, one gives an abutment thickness of 0.29s and a height of 1.04s; the other gives 0.32s and 1.45s. Another geometric design procedure—his most sophisticated—shows how the span of the arch, the thickness of the arch rib, and both the thickness and height of the abutment are all interrelated for both a semicircular and a pointed arch.

New Types of Buildings

As the affluence generated from international trade spread across Europe, the rich and the great celebrated and demonstrated their wealth in buildings that reflected both grandeur and technical sophistication. In France, for instance, many large châteaux were constructed from the early sixteenth century onward. The Château de
170 Chambord, in the Loire Valley (1519–47), was one of the first and the best, built mainly by craftsmen brought from
171 Italy; its large open staircases and exuberant chimneys show off the level of comfort afforded to the inhabitants. Nevertheless, it is likely that the systems for heating and ventilation by means of fires were, at this time, not yet very efficient. The first effective fireplace was said to have been that installed at the Louvre Palace in Paris in 1624 by the architect Louis Savot. He developed a fireplace in which air was drawn through passages under the hearth and behind the fire grate and discharged into the room through a grill in the mantel.

In Spain, one of the finest palaces of King Philip II was in-
172 corporated within the monastery of El Escorial, built near
173 Madrid between 1559 and 1584. A spectacular illustration captures the frenzy of the construction of this building, one of the largest and best Spanish examples of Renaissance architecture and engineering. Apart from its architectural merits, such as the very first grand staircase in a palace, the palace at El Escorial is notable as one of the first buildings constructed with stones cut to size and shape off-site. Progress had been extremely slow using the traditional method of building, in which irregular stones were only cut to size after the previous adjacent stones had been laid. It was decided to try speeding up the construction by using the newly developed art of stereotomy. This process involved carefully calculating the geometry of complex, non-uniform stones and making drawings of them so that masons could work on many stones simultaneously, and the stones could be placed in situ as soon as they were needed. This was a highly technical process requiring great mathematical skill and a degree of forward planning that was unusual at the time. Nevertheless, the investment in this new technique paid off and the speed of construction was increased considerably.

One particular feature of the building is of great engineering interest. The entrance to the monastery chapel is
roofed with a square masonry vault, 8 x 8 meters, which 174, 175
also forms part of the floor of the chapel above. The vault has both a flat extrados (upper surface) and a flat intrados (lower surface) and is a rare example of a two-way spanning version of a flat arch, like the one illustrated by Villard de Honnecourt (see chapter 2, p. 105).The vault itself is just 280mm thick for most of its span, and the stresses in the masonry are so high that the elastic deformation of the stone structure is actually noticeable. Someone walking on the vault can sense the elastic deflection, as if the floor were supported on timber beams.

During the sixteenth century in England, the traditional timber-framed manor houses began to give way to the larger-scale country houses made of stone, consciously constructed as state-of-the-art buildings to impress nobility and royalty. One of the finest of the sixteenth century
houses was Hardwick Hall in Derbyshire (1591–97), de- 176
signed by Robert Smythson (1536–1614), a mason turned surveyor and "architector," as he was described on a monument in the church where he was buried. It was commissioned by Elizabeth Talbot, Countess of Shrewsbury, to impress Queen Elizabeth I whenever she might be persuaded to visit (which, in fact, she never did). It included the latest fireplaces and chimneys to heat and ventilate every room and the most modern kitchen equipment available. Most spectacular are the enormous windows that allowed the owner and guests to survey the huge estate and its vistas. The effect was striking and well expressed in a contemporary rhyme whose origins have been lost: "Hardwick Hall, more glass than wall."

As well as spending their wealth on palatial residences, rich families also began to enhance their image by patronizing the performing arts. This was most prominent in Italy, where the first custom-designed theaters were built.

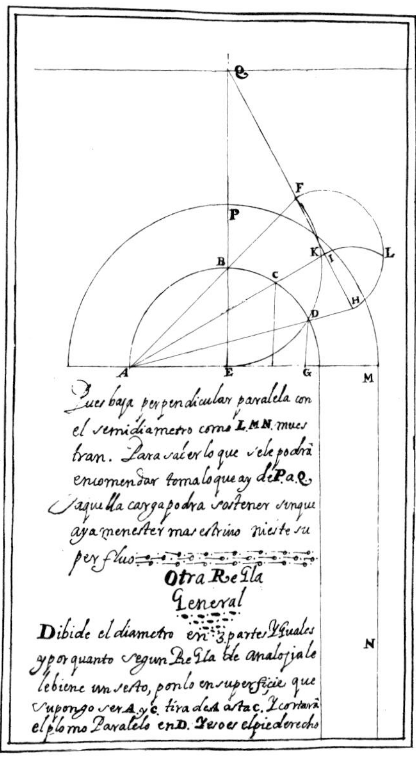

168

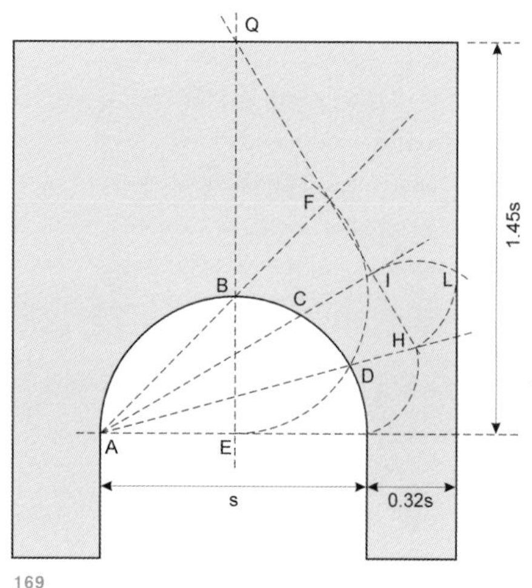

169

177 The earliest was Andrea Palladio's Teatro Olimpico, built in Vicenza between 1580 and 1584. This was a building type entirely without precedent, and squeezing it into a small site required a particularly ingenious design. While designed to resemble a Roman theater, it was much smaller, with seating for only around 600. As Palladio designed it, there was little provision for scenery or flats, though the stage area was later enlarged by providing three vistas, using false perspective to give the illusion of much greater depth.

The first theater to include comprehensive facilities for musicians, lighting effects, and stage machinery was the
178, 179 Teatro Farnese in Parma, Italy (1618–19). It was constructed in the enormous Great Hall of Arms on the first floor of the Villa Farnese, a room some 32 meters wide, 80 meters long and 23 meters high, whose roof was supported by one of the largest timber roof trusses of the day. The stage filled nearly half the space and the steeply-raked seating could accommodate an audience of 3500. As was usual in large rooms, the only acoustic treatment consisted in covering some parts of the stone walls with wooden panels. Unlike earlier theaters, however, whose ceilings usually consisted of stretched canvas sheets, the Teatro Farnese had a timber ceiling, which helped to reflect sounds from the stage in the direction of the seated audience. The theater was designed by Giovanni Battista Aleotti (1546–1636), a renowned military and hydraulic engineer who became the first Renaissance specialist in theater design. In 1589 he published the first translation from Greek of Heron of Alexandria's book *The Pneumatica* (see Chapter 1, p. 28), which described all manner of mechanical devices worked by air, steam, or water pressure.

Aleotti made the most of his interests and engineering experience by employing various types of machinery to create dramatic theatrical effects. These included translucent screens (flat wings or, simply, flats) that could be moved into position along grooves in the stage

170

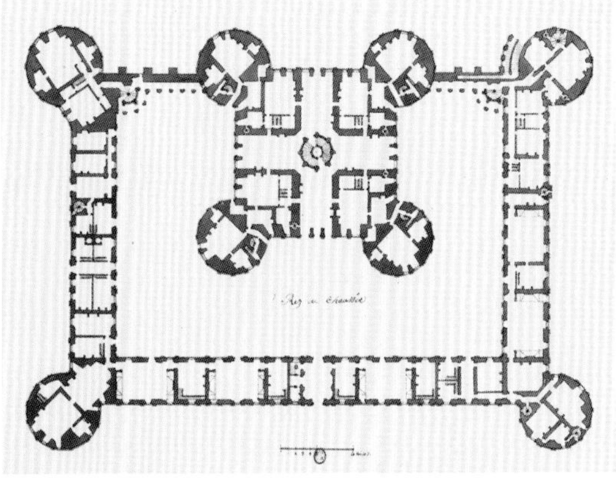
171

172

168 Rodrigo Gil de Hontañón, a design procedure for establishing the required thickness of abutment and height of superimposed masonry that a semicircular arch rib can carry, from *Compendio de Arquitectura y Symetriá de los Templos*, c. 1565. 169 Another of the design procedures described by Rodrigo Gil. 170 Château de Chambord, Chambord, France, 1519–47. Architect: Domenico da Cortona. 171 Château de Chambord. Plan. 172 Royal Monastery of San Lorenzo de El Escorial, Madrid, 1559–84. Architects: Juan Bautista de Toledo and Juan de Herrera.

173

173 Fabrico Castello, illustration of construction work on El Escorial, 1576. 174 Royal Monastery of San Lorenzo de El Escorial, Madrid, 1559–84. Architects: Juan Bautista de Toledo and Juan de Herrera. Photograph of flat vault spanning 8 meters. 175 El Escorial. Section of flat vault. 176 Hardwick Hall, Derbyshire, 1591–97. Architect: Robert Smythson.

174

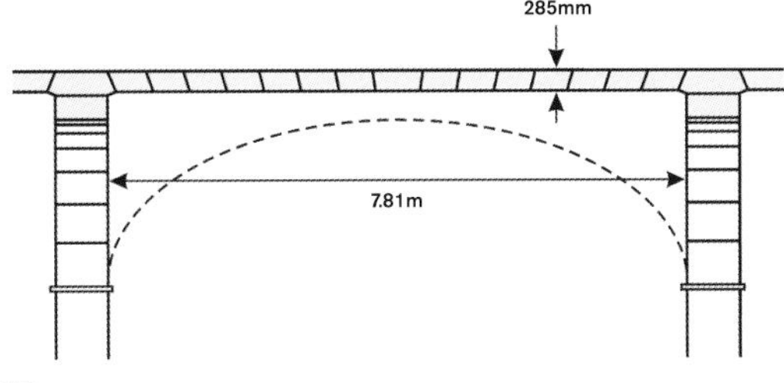

175

176

and lit from behind. On opening night the orchestra area, lined with lead to make it watertight, was intentionally flooded and several floating islands were brought in. Warriors and monsters fought on the islands, and the pageant ended with gods and goddesses flying (on ropes) back up to heaven.

Moving the many flats to effect a change of scene required a great many stagehands and precise coordination. To overcome these problems, the Teatro Farnese was one of the first theaters to be fitted with automated scene changing equipment, in the 1640s. In this system, devised by the set designer Giacomo Torelli (1608–78), the flats were mounted on poles that passed through slots in the stage on wheeled carriages, or "chariots," beneath. The carriages were connected by a series of ropes and pulleys to a single winch so that a dozen or so flats could be changed simultaneously by just one man, an effect so spectacular that it was often repeated during performances for no dramatic reason.

While creating spectacular effects clearly demanded considerable engineering skill, another feature of theaters was equally significant but less apparent—the congregation of large numbers of the public in a single building. This created two unprecedented engineering challenges: the ventilation of large public rooms, and the need to protect the public from the consequences of fires. These were first tackled in theaters in the mid-eighteenth century, for example by Jacques-Germain Soufflot (1713–80) (see chapter 5, pp. 254–55), and only fully resolved in the twentieth century. Learning how to design buildings that were safe and provided adequate air quality began on a smaller scale, however, with public buildings such as town halls. As well as meeting rooms and court rooms of various sizes, these usually contained a very large assembly room in which civic ceremonies and large public meetings could be held. In former times churches had often served this role, but as towns became more prosperous and states loosened their links to the established church, so dedicated

buildings were provided. This was most conspicuous in the Protestant countries of north Europe, where towns chose to invest their wealth in large civic buildings rather than in grander churches, as was the tendency in Roman
180 Catholic countries. The Old Civil Registry in Bruges
181 (1534–37), and the imposing town hall in Antwerp (1561–65), both in modern Belgium, were particularly fine examples. Such buildings are among the first that feature the exposed tops of ventilation ducts installed to exhaust foul air from the larger rooms. These ducts would become a feature of all public buildings during the seventeenth and eighteenth centuries, and they continued to be used through the late nineteenth century when mechanical ventilation was developed.

By the end of the Renaissance, then, spectacular buildings could be constructed without pushing at the boundaries of building engineering. As yet, science had made little impact on buildings. It was in other branches of engineering, especially with regard to the rapidly developing arts, and in response to civic, military, and shipbuilding needs, that the limits of technology and design methods were being expanded.

Civil Engineering and Shipbuilding

The growth of international trade placed increasing demands on both the ships that carried the goods and the ports, harbors, and waterways that served them. Carrying goods by sea along the northern coasts of continental Europe seemed to offer almost limitless commercial opportunities, which were exploited by Germany and Holland. In the Mediterranean, the ports of Venice and Genoa vied with each other to capture the lucrative trade into Europe from the East. This commercial maritime activity and the newly built navies in several European countries began to generate an increasing amount of civil engineering and construction work beginning in the fifteenth century. Throughout Europe, the greater size of the new ships and the increased trade required a huge construction program for new quays, harbors, and docks in every major port. The city of Amsterdam provides a good example. This had been a small settlement by a dam on the Amstel River in 1204. By 1500 it was one of the most prosperous cities in the world, with some forty thousand inhabitants—a thriving port with substantial fortifications and large numbers of masonry buildings erected on land reclaimed from the marshes. This reclamation experience had already established the Dutch as the world's leading civil engineers, and enabled them to develop the ports and towns of Rotterdam, Middleburg, and Antwerp in similar ways, and also to export their skills in hydraulic engineering throughout Europe.

The confidence gained in building harbors and draining marshlands led to bolder hydraulic engineering projects. From the late fifteenth century onward a number of rivers were canalized to improve their navigability, and the first man-made canals were cut to link major cities to the sea and to allow navigation from one river system into another. The many rivers and flat terrain of northern Italy proved ideal for transporting goods inland by water, and
many tens of miles of canals were constructed in the late 182
fifteenth century. Alberti describes a pound lock with two portcullis gates in *De re Aedificatoria*, and Leonardo drew a sketch of miter lock gates of a type that we use today, which he followed for the six locks he constructed for the main canal in the city of Milan, completed in 1497.

The benefits of canals were soon appreciated elsewhere in Europe, and in 1516 Leonardo da Vinci was consulted by Francis I, king of France, about the possibility of a *canal des deux mers*, a bold project to link the Atlantic Ocean and Mediterranean Sea that would only be undertaken and completed more than a century and a half later. By the middle of the sixteenth century canals were being constructed in other parts of Europe—in Holland, Brussels, Brandenburg in Germany, and at Exeter in England. All these early canals linked a river at one level to another river or the sea at a lower level, and this limited the situations in which they could be constructed. The versatility of the canal for transport was increased by harnessing a supply of water to feed a canal from a higher source that itself was not navigable—the so-called summit-feed canal. By this means canals could rise above their starting point, enabling boats to climb up over higher terrain. The first canal of this type was devised and constructed in France between 1604 and 1642 by Hugues Cosnier. It connected the river Loire at Briare to the river Loing at Montargis, providing a vital link to the river Seine and into Paris from central France and the Atlantic Ocean. Some 50 kilometers long, it rose nearly 40 meters through twelve locks to the summit before descending about 85 meters through twenty-eight locks to Montargis.

The land drainage and canal building undertaken in the fifteenth and sixteenth centuries marked the beginning of modern civil engineering and established Holland, Italy, and France as the world's leaders in the field. The methodical and scientific study of hydraulic engineering would develop in the early eighteenth century, independently of the work Leonardo had done, which was not known to engineers. In fact, civil engineering was not the only industry in which rational design methods using quantitative rules were being developed during the Renaissance. The other was the shipbuilding industry, and it is interesting that there is little evidence that either branch of engineering directly influenced the other.

In the fourteenth century, commercial vessels were still usually single-masted and quite small. As manufacturing and trade increased in the century, ship design developed rapidly, and independently, in the two main centers of economic activity in Europe, the ports of northern Italy and the northern coast of continental Europe. In the Mediterranean, especially Genoa and Venice, the gateway ports to Milan and central Europe, ships were of Roman carvel construction (with planks meeting flush at their edges) and a second mast was added, along with a central, submerged sternpost rudder. Along the northern coast of continental Europe, from Lübeck in the east to Antwerp, Amsterdam, Bruges, and, via river access, Cologne, Paris, and London, ships were clinker-built (with overlapping planks), but retained the steering oar for a full century after the time when the sternpost rudder was common in the Mediterranean. By the 1460s, however, the heavy clinker construction in the north had largely been replaced by carvel construction, and the addition of a third and even a fourth mast and sternpost rudder allowed ships to be built much larger while remaining controllable in high seas. The new maritime era had arrived. By the year 1500, ships of 600 tons were quite common, and many were even larger. In England Henry VII and VIII built up their famous navy between the 1480s and 1520s, and to do so they head-hunted the best ship designers and wrights from Spain, France, and especially from Genoa in Italy, often paying them at least a third more than their English counterparts. Henry VII's largest warship, the 1,000-ton *Regent*, built in 1489, was modeled on a French design and carried 151 cast iron and 29 bronze guns.

The new types of ships and their increasing size could not be conceived and achieved using traditional construction methods. Being of vast size, the design and manufacture of a ship more closely resembled that of a building than of small boats or machines. New designs and methods were gradually devised, and we find in the fifteenth century the very first signs of engineering science being used, albeit qualitatively—for example, to discuss, before construction began, the relative positions of both the center of gravity and the center of pressure, which are so vital to the stability of a ship. One of the earliest treatises in English on designing ships, compiled by Matthew 183 Baker (1530–1613), the master shipwright to Queen Elizabeth I and the Royal Navy, dates from the 1580s. He collected together the designs or "lines" of some thirty ships, seeking to demonstrate general design rules that captured the best precedent. This approach is very similar to that taken by Rodrigo Gil de Hontañón at about the same time concerning the design of cathedral buttresses (see pp. 150, 152). Baker also included his design for the *Revenge*, which Sir Francis Drake was to captain. Though not a large ship, it was much lighter than its contemporaries and much more maneuverable. Tantalizingly, Baker gave us no clue as to how he came up with this revolutionary scheme.

Calculations, Science, and Engineering

Toward the end of the sixteenth century, there was a growing interest in the use of mathematics in civil and building engineering, as there was in ship design. A striking example was the great lifting operation undertaken in 1586 by the Italian engineer Domenico Fontana (1543–1607) to move the Vatican Obelisk from its original location to one nearby, as part of the redevelopment around Saint Peter's Basilica.

The obelisk, like similar ones still to be seen in Paris and London, came from Egypt. It had been brought to the city on the orders of Emperor Caligula and erected around A.D. 41. It is 2.8 meters square at its thickest and a little over 25 meters long, and according to Fontana's calculations, weighed 963,537 and 35/48 Roman pounds (about 309 tons). This supposed accuracy of one-in-ten-million is indicative of his care if not his engineering common sense; but then, like many an engineering calculation, its purpose was to induce confidence in others as much as to establish precise quantities. In many

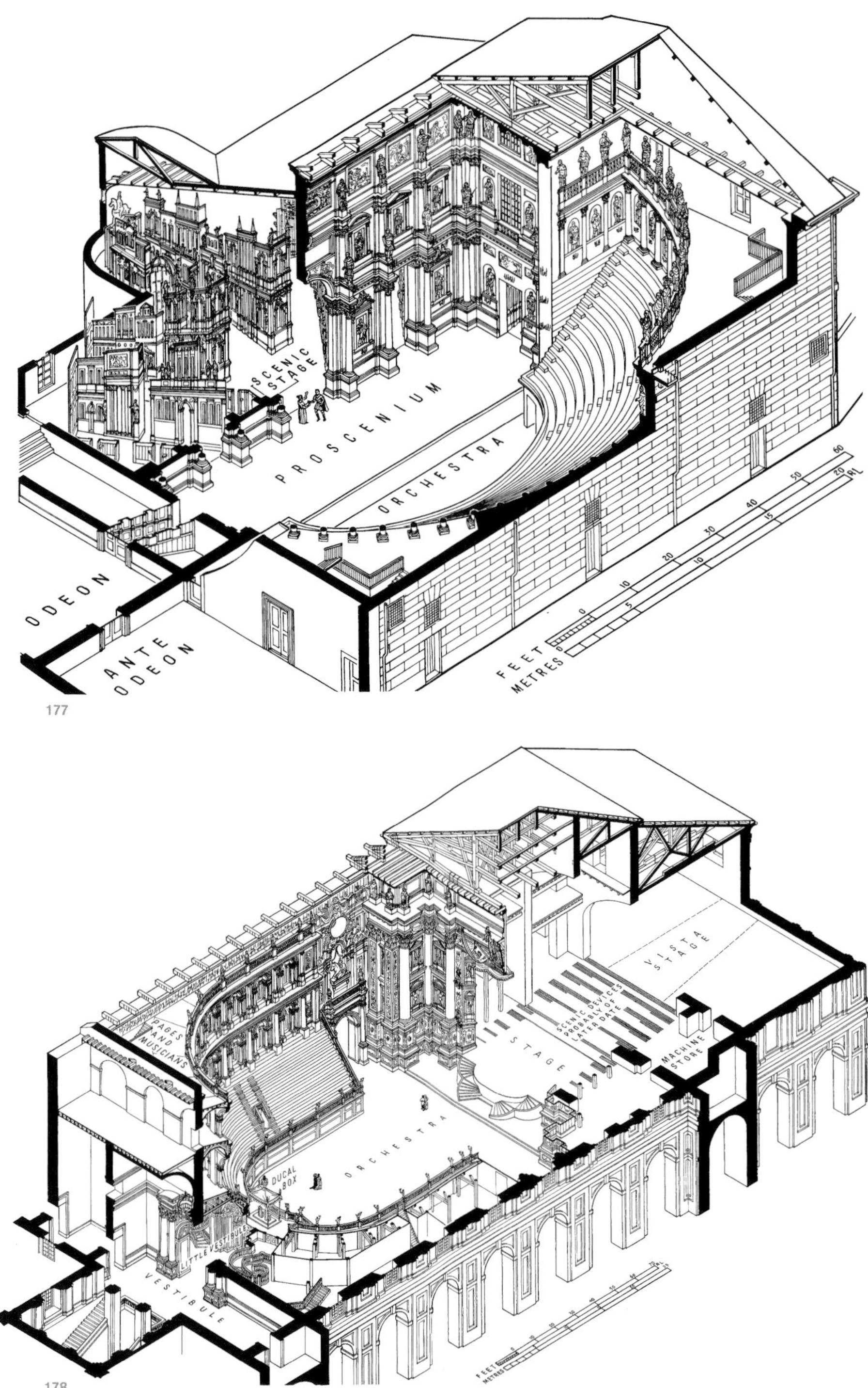

177 Teatro Olimpico, Vicenza, Italy, 1580–84. Architect: Andrea Palladio. Cutaway isometric. 178 Teatro Farnese, Parma, Italy, 1618–19. Architect: Giovanni Battista Aleotti. Cutaway isometric. 179 Teatro Farnese. Interior.

179

ways, of course, the engineering achievement of the ancient Romans who originally devised the means for transporting the obelisk from Egypt to Rome and erecting it there would have been even more remarkable than Fontana's work. The key to Fontana's story is that the public relations and printing industries had matured considerably in the intervening fifteen hundred years, and Fontana published a book in 1590 to celebrate completion of the event.

Domenico Fontana was one of the most talented building and civil engineers of his day. He had excelled in his mathematical studies and went to Rome at the age of twenty to work with his brother Giovanni, who was already engaged in building projects. In Rome Domenico's talent was recognized by Cardinal Montalto, who commissioned him to design and build a chapel and a small but lavish palace. When Montalto became Pope Sixtus V in 1585, he engaged Fontana not only to take charge of moving the obelisk but also to serve as the engineer responsible for completing the dome of Saint Peter's, which was still unfinished when Michelangelo died in 1564. Following the completion of these two projects Fontana designed the Vatican Library (1587–89) and the Lateran Palace (1586), among other buildings. He engineered a new water supply to Rome, the Aqua Felice, including an aqueduct and several fountains for its distribution. Fontana's patron Sixtus V died in 1590, and shortly thereafter his career took a sudden change. Clement VIII, who became Pope in 1592, was persuaded by Fontana's rivals and competitors to fire him, and that same year Fontana accepted an offer to become senior engineer and architect to the king in Naples. There, among other works, he devised and constructed a canal to prevent the flooding of low-lying ground, a new road along the coast, and a new royal palace. He also made major improvements to the port at Naples, though these works were not carried out until his death in 1607.

180

181

Fontana's work displays the regard for the "big picture" that characterizes the versatile engineer. He was as concerned with careful calculations of loads, quantities, manpower, and costs as with the impact of a large civil engineering scheme on the wider urban or rural landscape. He had the confidence to master complex technical issues while also taking responsibility for the organization of workers, the site, construction materials, and plant. We have no reason to believe, however, that he was unique in these respects. We know of his exploits mainly because of his prominent patronage. At this time, throughout Italy, much of France, and the German-speaking lands, there were many engineers with qualities similar to those of Fontana, though, as is generally the case today, their efforts are not preserved in detail for posterity.

By the early sixteenth century the obelisk was standing on the grounds of the Vatican, but the accumulation of a millennium and a half's rubbish and rubble had raised the surrounding ground level by several meters. For many decades there had been talk of moving the obelisk to a more suitable site. Finally, in 1585, the pope commanded that it be moved about 250 meters and erected at what would become the very center of the newly planned piazza in front of Saint Peter's Basilica. Proposals for how this could be done were sought from engineers in Rome, but none was felt to be sound. Further ideas were solicited through what was effectively an open competition, and more than five hundred proposals were received, mostly from the towns of northern Italy, but some from as far away as Greece and Rhodes. In his book *Della trasportatione dell'Obelisco Vaticano* (On the Transportation of the Vatican Obelisk) (1590), Fontana illustrated a number 184
of the methods being tested using models; his own model was some 2 meters tall and made of lead.

180 Old Civil Registry, Bruges, Belgium, 1534–37. 181 Town Hall, Antwerp, Belgium, 1561–65. Architect: Cornelis Floris de Vriendt.

To protect the fragile obelisk, Fontana strengthened it with large timbers bound with iron straps and rope. The iron alone weighed an additional 13 tons and the timbers and ropes a similar amount. The total weight to be lifted was 335 tons. To complement his careful calculations of the weight to be lifted, he determined the number of windlasses he would need, each driven by four horses, using various pulley blocks and rope 75 millimeters in diameter. He established by experiment that such a pulling arrangement would not break the rope, and so was sufficiently confident that the method was sound.

185 Fontana's organization of the process was impeccable. He required absolute obedience among the teams at each windlass and insisted upon total silence of the thousand or so workers and many more spectators, broken only by the sounds of a trumpet to begin driving the windlasses and of a bell to cease pulling. During the lifting processes, some of which lasted nearly twenty-four hours, he arranged for meals to be brought to the windlass teams and had a full supply of spare horses, men, ropes, blocks, and other materials should any replacements be needed. In modern language, he undertook a full risk assessment and anticipated every possible event or accident that might occur. He even ensured that those workers in danger from falling objects wore hard hats—actually, steel helmets. After about six months of design, site preparation, and construction of the lifting towers, raising the obelisk began on 28 April 1586. By 7
186 May it was ready to be lowered onto the carriage upon which it was to be moved to its new location.Over the summer the obelisk was dragged on its carriage along an earth-filled causeway some 8 meters high and more than 20 meters wide. Fontana was able to take advantage of the lower height of the new location, bringing the obelisk in at the right height to be rotated into position onto the 4-meter-tall pedestal with a minimum of lifting. The lifting gear used at the original location was dismantled and reerected in the final position, and the obelisk was ready for raising again onto its new pedestal on 10 September. The new foundation for the pedestal and obelisk had been prepared months earlier. A pit 14 meters square and 7 meters deep was dug and 6-meter oak piles were driven into the soft ground and capped with chestnut planks, which, Fontana explained, do not rot in wet ground. To provide a suitable bed for the masonry, a thick course of concrete was laid—concrete composed of broken brick, crushed stone, cement, and a number of medals commemorating the pope. Four bronze corner pieces were fitted to the base of the obelisk and metal shims inserted until it was absolutely vertical. The lifting towers were dismantled quickly and the obelisk was consecrated with a religious ceremony on 28 September, almost exactly a year after Fontana had been awarded the contract.

While Fontana's achievement was remarkable in itself, it was also symptomatic of widespread changes in engineering. The idea of using calculations to help predict the outcome of large-scale "experiments," such as moving an obelisk, building a ship, or constructing a building, was gaining acceptance. People were learning how to make use of the mathematical and scientific ideas that had been developed in ancient and medieval times. As often as not, it was engineers who forged these steps forward—engineers like the cathedral designers who learned how to use geometry to their advantage, and Fontana, who used simple statics to calculate the number of winches he would need.

The Flemish-born military and civil engineer Simon Stevin (1548–1620) was one of the first engineers of post-Roman times to straddle both worlds of his profession, the practical and the academic. Today he is sometimes credited as the father of statics. He was not, of course; he was just one of many who, since classical Greek times, made some progress toward discovering what we understand today by the term statics. Stevin was an outstanding engineer who built windmills, locks, and ports, and advised Prince Maurice of Nassau on constructing fortifications for Holland's war against Spain during this period. While employed by the Dutch army, Stevin devised a method of flooding the lowlands in the path of an invading army by opening selected sluices in dykes.

Stevin began formal studies in mathematics at the University of Leiden at age thirty-five and became familiar with Greek scientific authors as well as those from the Middle Ages. Later, while continuing his military career, he was appointed professor of mathematics at the University of The Hague. In 1604 he was appointed general quartermaster of the Dutch army and was chief inspector of flood defenses and hydraulic engineering.

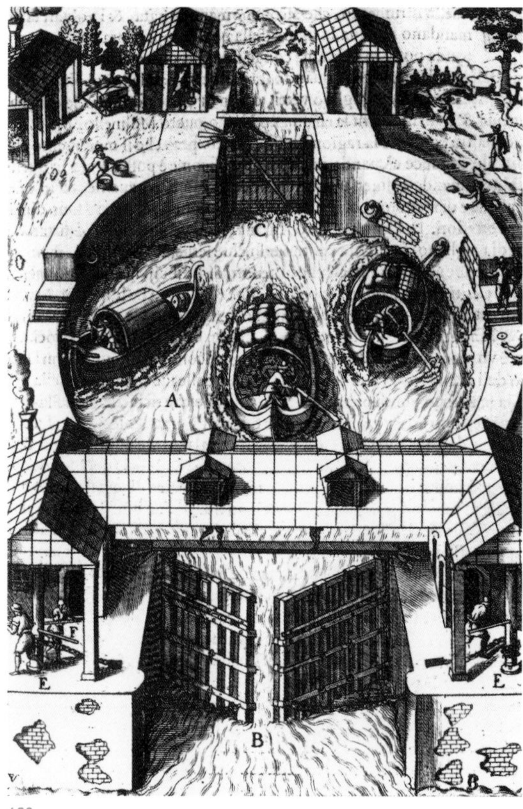

182

Stevin was constantly striving to make more effective, practical use of mathematics in his work as an engineer, whether it was arithmetic, mechanics, geodesy, astronomy, or accountancy. He published his work on hydrostatics and statics, *De Beghinselen der Weeghconst* (The Principles of Statics), in 1586. In this book Stevin does
187 indeed describe the representation of forces using geometry and shows what we now know as the parallelogram of forces. While of importance in the history of statics, however, Stevin's book did not lead to a breakthrough in how structures were designed; that would not come about until the nineteenth century. Other work by Stevin was of more immediate significance, however. For example, he—not Galileo—was the first person to demonstrate that stones of different weight fall with the same acceleration due to gravity. He also predicted that the universal introduction of decimal coinage, measures, and weights would be only a matter of time (though in Britain, the decimal system was not adopted until 1971). Of more practical use to all future engineers was Stevin's work on expressing numerical quantities using decimal fractions. Although he did not invent decimals (they had been used by the Arabs and the Chinese long before his time), he did help introduce their use in mathematics.

Unlike Stevin, the Italian mathematician Bernardino Baldi (1553–1617) was a leading scholar of his day. He worked under patronage of the duke of Urbino and was an abbot for more than twenty years. He had a knowledge of sixteen languages, translated several Greek works on mechanics, was a noted poet, and wrote perhaps one hundred books (most now lost). His key work on mechanics, *In Mechanica Aristotelis Problemata Exercitationes* (Discussions of Aristotle's Problems in Mechanics), was probably written in the 1580s and 1590s but published only posthumously, in 1621. Several decades before Galileo dealt with Aristotle's questions about the behavior of structures, Baldi wrote

183

182 Vittorio Zonca, illustration of canal lock with mitered gates, from *Novo Teatro di Machine et Edificii*, 1607.

183 Matthew Baker, ship designer at work with his assistant, from *Fragments of Ancient English Shipwrightry*, c. 1586.

184

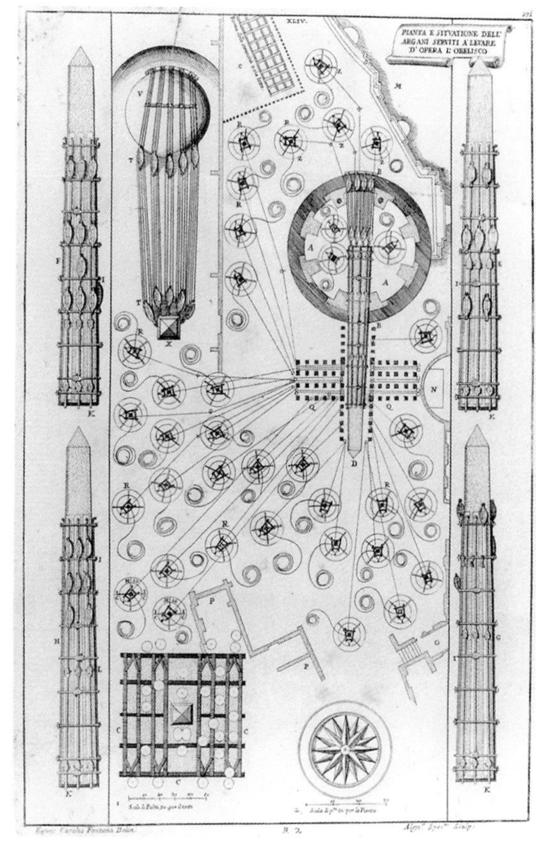

185

a commentary that went far beyond the original scope of these inquiries. Indeed, like Leonardo, he considered many of the structural issues that would concern engineering scientists during the following two centuries: how columns carry a load, the "solidity" of roof trusses and lintels, and, more generally, the distribution of weight over a surface and the mechanism by which a floor beam might collapse. He also considered the collapse of arches by the rotation of sections of the arch at hinges, an idea investigated experimentally by Augustin Danyzy (c. 1700–77) more than a century later. One of the most interesting aspects of Baldi's analysis, which is largely qualitative, is his explanation of why a thick arch is more stable than a thin one, since a thinner one 188
can collapse with only a small separation of the arch supports.

Even though Baldi was probably the first scholar to consider the behavior of structures in terms of statics and elasticity, his work seems not to have been widely known, at least by the many French engineering scientists who studied the subject in the eighteenth century. However, Baldi's oeuvre was probably familiar to Galileo, and we know that Christopher Wren owned a copy of his book *In Mechanica Aristotelis*, which Wren annotated meticulously.

184 Domenico Fontana, illustration of models of various proposal methods for moving the Vatican Obelisk, from *Trasportatione dell'Obelisco Vaticano*, 1590. 185 Domenico Fontana, plan of piazza showing the locations of horse-driven windlasses, from *Trasportatione dell'Obelisco Vaticano*, 1590.

Numeracy and the Art of Calculation

In the age of the electronic calculator and computer, it is easy to overlook the importance of being able to solve relatively simple math problems quickly and reliably without such devices. Consider, then, how tedious it was many centuries ago to perform calculations using Roman numerals; incorporating fractions of whole numbers was even more difficult. The solution taken by practical men was, of course, to avoid numerical calculations. This reason alone accounts for the huge popularity of applying geometric methods to designing buildings and performing related calculations, an approach that has been traditional from classical Greek times to the present day; then, as now, graphs and graphical methods are still used in most branches of engineering.

Our numerical system of ten digits, including the concept of zero, was developed in India, probably in the eighth century A.D., and was soon taken up by Arabic mathematicians. The earliest use of the Hindu-Arabic system of numbers in Europe dates from a manuscript written in Spain in 976. Despite its clear benefits, this new scheme was shunned for more than two centuries, even by learned men, who associated it with traders and heathens, not with mathematicians and scholarship. By the thirteenth century the Hindu-Arabic system had spread to parts of southern Europe, but it was only in the sixteenth century that it became universal and the familiar patterns of basic arithmetical calculations had been developed, after a great many experiments. By the early seventeenth century arithmetical calculations were being written in a form, and using most of the symbols, familiar to us today. Before these modern symbols were widely adopted, different mathematicians had used their own notation and each campaigned for its acceptance, rather in the way different computer software firms competed in the 1970s and 1980s to have their own operating systems and applications adopted, though without the commercial implications. For example, the symbols "+" and "-" were first used by Johannes Widman, a German mathematician, in 1489. The "=" sign first appeared in 1557. The method we now use for decimal notation for fractions is credited
189 to Simon Stevin, but many other mathematicians used similar devices in the late sixteenth century. It was the decimal point, first proposed by Christopher Clavius (1538–1612) and popularized by John Napier in his mathematical tables of logarithms, that was finally chosen as the most convenient, and survives today in two forms— 190, 192
as a full stop (.) in English-speaking countries and as a comma (,) in European countries. As late as 1630, the English mathematician William Oughtred (1574–1660), who was one of Christopher Wren's teachers at Oxford University, wrote a book describing the Hindu-Arabic numerical notation and advocating its use in preference to Roman numerals. He also promoted the use of decimal notation and the use of the symbol "x" to signify multiplication. Both the "_" sign for division and the "√" sign for square root first appeared in 1669. The Greek letter pi, "π," was not proposed as the ratio of the circumference to diameter of a circle until 1706.

In the world of building construction, the potential benefits of numeracy were beginning to be advocated in a few pocket books written by mathematicians. One of the first was a guide written in 1556 by Leonard Digges (c. 1520–c. 1559), the English mathematician, scientist and astronomer who also invented the theodolite and the telescope. He entitled his work *A Booke named Tectonicon, brieflie shewing the exact measuring, and speedie reckoning all manner of land, squares, timber, stone, steeples, pillers, globes, &c. Further, the perfect making and large use of the carpenter's ruler....* The little book of just fifty pages proved very popular, being the first of its kind written in English rather than the Latin used by authors of scholarly works on geometry. It was reprinted several times and formed the basis of *A geometrical practise, named Pantometria, divided into three books, Longimetra, Planimetra, and Stereometria . . .*, compiled and published posthumously under Leonard's name in 1571 by his son Thomas. Both books covered the basics of geometry needed for surveying and mensuration, and for marking up and setting out the carpentry and masonry elements of buildings. Apart from their use in the practical matters of construction, these and other early books on calculation using geometry were useful in helping craftsmen calculate prices, since these were often reckoned by the volume of cut stone or timber. Timber floorboards, for example, were reckoned in "board-feet," defined as:

> *One twelfth of {the length of timber (measured in feet) x the width (measured in inches)}*

This gave a measure of the volume of timber needed, assuming the boards were a standard one inch thick. In fact, it is unlikely that an experienced carpenter would

XLII
L' OBELISCO PIEGATO
MENTRE CALAVA
Eques Carolus Fontana Delin:
Alex.r Spec.ti Sculp.

186

have had much use for such a calculation; nor was it likely that carpenters would have bought the book. Rather, Digges was illustrating the wide range of potential uses for the relatively new art of numerical calculation. Of more immediate use was the mathematics of surveying and trigonometry that he described, which was especially useful to military engineers and in the art of gunnery. Digges was also known as a military architect and engineer, and wrote a book devoted entirely to gunnery, *An arithmeticall militarie treatise named Stratioticos*, published by his son Thomas in 1579 after his father's death, which became a classic reference work. Thomas Digges also became one of the country's leading astronomers and experts on navigation.

Following the widespread adoption of decimal notation in the late sixteenth century, the development of numerical methods was rapid. The Scottish mathematician John Napier (1550–1617) devised his so-called Napier's
191 bones to assist with arithmetic computations. These were not used by engineers directly, but rather by mathematicians in preparing tables of, for example, the square roots and cube roots of numbers, which engineers, ship designers, and scientists did employ.

Napier went on to devise his tables of "logarithms." These enabled the process of multiplication and division to be transformed into the simpler task of adding and subtracting two numbers. He first published these ideas, in Latin, in 1614, and in English translation two years later. His introduction conveys the sense of relief he (accurately) believed their use would bring:

> *Seeing there is nothing (right well-beloved Students of the Mathematics) that is so troublesome to mathematical practice, nor that doth more molest and hinder calculators, than the multiplications, divisions, square and cubical extractions of great numbers, which besides the tedious expense of time are for the most part subject to many slippery errors, I began therefore to consider in my mind by what certain and ready art I might remove those hindrances. And having thought upon many things to this purpose, I found at length some excellent brief rules to be treated of (perhaps) hereafter. But amongst all, none more profitable than this which together with the hard and tedious multiplications, divisions, and extractions of roots, doth also cast away from the work itself even the very numbers themselves that are to be multiplied, divided and resolved into roots, and putteth other numbers in their place which perform as much as they can do, only by addition and subtraction, division by two or division by three.*[13]

Naval architects were quick to realize the potential, in Napier's logarithms, of having a reliable method for calculating numbers quickly and accurately. When Matthew Baker's manual on ship design was published in a new edition in 1617, it was one of the first books to feature a section on the use of logarithms to facilitate design calculations. Logarithms and decimal notation made it much easier to determine the values of square roots and cube roots and the values of trigonometric functions (sine, cosine, and tangent). Many mathematicians carefully computed these values and published them as books of tables for use by navigators, surveyors, ship designers, and scientists. It would be many decades before such mathematical sophistication would be applied in civil engineering design, and it would not become common in building engineering until the early nineteenth century. But the precedent had been set and the trail blazed, and the uptake of mathematical methods in civil and building engineering would be all the quicker when it finally happened.

The slide rule, which would become the engineers' indispensable calculating tool from the early nineteenth century to the 1970s, was developed soon after the invention of logarithms. In 1624 the English mathematician
Edmund Gunter (1581–1626) made a ruler graduated 193
with a logarithmic scale. This was the same Gunter who devised the standard surveyor's chain, or "Gunter's chain," 66 feet long and composed of one hundred links, that was still in use in the second half of the twentieth century. The ruler, a "calculating line" or "Gunter," as it became known by seamen, was soon widely used by navigators to perform multiplication and division using dividers to add or subtract lengths taken from the scale.
William Oughtred had the idea in 1630 of placing two log- 194
arithmic scales next to each other and performing calculations by sliding one scale past the other. In his first

186 Domenico Fontana, illustration of the Vatican Obelisk being lifted from the carriage on which it was transported, from *Trasportatione dell'Obelisco Vaticano*, 1590.

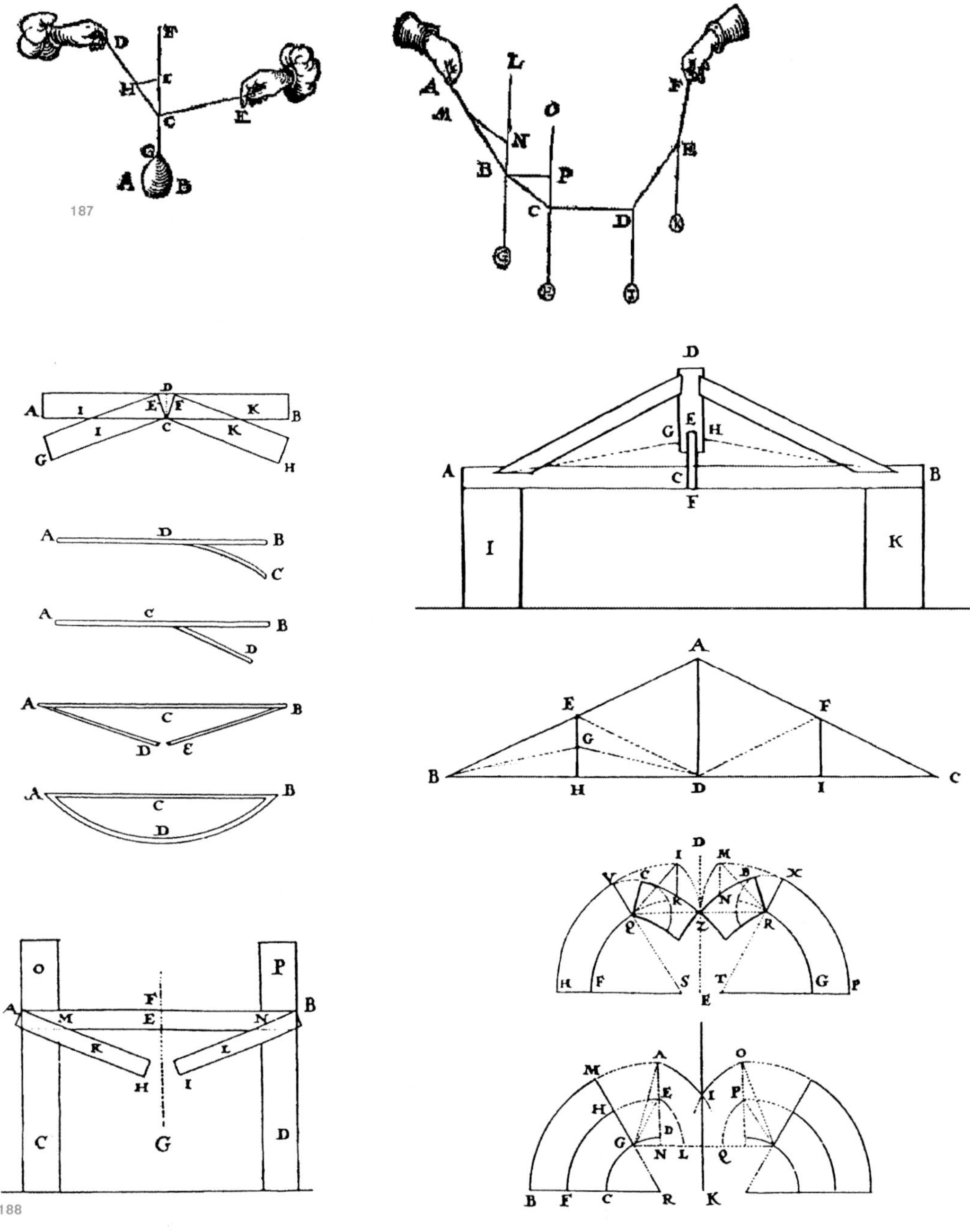

187 Simon Stevin, diagrams illustrating different sets of forces in equilibrium, and the representations of forces by lines of corresponding length and direction, from *De Beghinselen der Weeghconst*, 1586. 188 Bernardino Baldi, diagrams illustrating the bending and fracture of beams, forces in roof trusses, and the collapse mechanism of a masonry arch, from *In Mechanica Problematica Exercitationes*, 1621. 189 Simon Stevin, a page from *De Thiende*, 1585, showing a calculation written using Stevin's decimal notation. 190 Examples of decimal notation from the early sixteenth century (top) to the present (bottom). 191 "Napier's bones," a device designed by John Napier in 1617 to perform arithmetic calculations. 192 A mathematical equation written using Stevin's notation (right), and its modern equivalent (left).

16 S. STEVINS

III. VOORSTEL VANDE MENICHVVLDIGHINGHE.

Weſende ghegheven Thiendetal te Menichvuldighen, ende Thiendetal Menichvulder: haer Vytbreng te vinden.

TGHEGHEVEN. Het ſy Thiendetal te Menichvuldighen 32 ⓪ 5 ① 7 ②, ende het Thiendetal Menichvulder 89 ⓪ 4 ① 6 ②. TBEGHEERDE. Wy moeten haer Vytbreng vinden. WERCKING. Men ſal de gegevē getalē in oirden ſtellen als hier nevē, Menichvuldigende naer de gemeene maniere van Menichvuldighen met heele ghetalen aldus: Gheeft Vytbreng (door het 3ᵉ. Prob. onſer Fran. Arith.) 29137122: Nu om te weten wat dit ſijn, men ſal vergaderen beyde de laetſte gegeven teeckenen, welcker een is ②, ende het ander oock ②, maecken tſamen ④, waer uyt men beſluyten ſal, dat de laetſte cijffer des Vytbrengs is ④, welcke bekent weſende ſoo ſijn oock (om haer volghende oirden) openbaer alle dander, Inder voughen dat 2913⓪7①1②2③2④, ſijn het begheerde Vytbreng. BEWYS, Het ghegheven Thiendetal te menichvuldighen 32⓪5①7②, doet (als blijct

```
            ⓪①②
          3 2 5 7
          8 9 4 6
        1 9 5 4 2
      1 3 0 2 8
    2 9 3 1 3
  2 6 0 5 6
  2 9 1 3 7 1 2 2
          ⓪①②③④
```

189

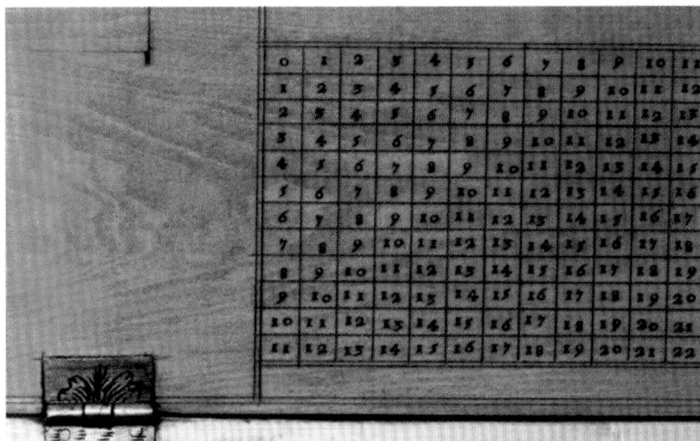

191

$2913\frac{7122}{10000}$	PRE STEVIN
2913|7122	RUDOLFF 1530 (number & remainder)
2913⓪7①1②2③2④	STEVIN 1585
2 9 1 3 7 1 2 2 ⓪①②③④	STEVIN 1585
⓪①②③④ 2 9 1 3 7 1 2 2	STEVIN 1585
(iv) 29137122	BEYER 1603
0 i ii iii iv 2913.7.1.2.2	BEYER 1603
$29137^{(1)}1^{(2)}2^{(3)}2^{(4)}$	NORTON 1608
/ // /// //// 2913,7 1 2 2	NAPIER 1617
$291\overset{\circ}{3}7122$	BÜRGI 1620
1. 2. 3. 4. 2913|7 1 2 2	JOHNSON 1623
$2913\,^{\underline{7122}}$	BRIGGS 1624
29137122④	KALCHEIM 1629
2913,7122	GIRARD 1629
$2913\lfloor\underline{7122}$	OUGHTRED 1631
2913.7122	WINGATE 1650
2913:7122	BALAM 1653
$2913.^{\underline{7122}}$	FOSTER 1659
(1) (2) (3) (4) 2913 7 1 2 2	OZANAM 1691
/ // /// //// 2913.7.1.2.2	JEAKE 1696
2913.7122	ENGLISH-SPEAKING COUNTRIES TODAY
2913,7122	CONTINENTAL EUROPE TODAY

190

TODAY	STEVIN 1585
$y = -\frac{111}{160}x + 45$	1 *Secund.*⊙ *Aequalem* $-\frac{111}{160}$ ⊙ + 45
$12y^4 + 23xy^2 + 10x^2$	12 *sec.*④ + 23① *M sec.*② + 10②

192

version the scales were circular; he made the more familiar linear device two years later. The name "slide rule" was first used in 1662, and both circular and linear types were in common use by navigators, ship designers, and scientists by the end of the seventeenth century. In the twentieth century, the slide rule was often referred to colloquially as a "guessing stick" or "slip stick." The speed and reliability of the slide rule is still praised by engineers older than about 55 who learned their engineering before the computer age. The Apollo 11 astronauts on the first manned trip to the moon in 1969, although equipped with computers, still took a slide rule.

By the end of the Renaissance period we can see evidence of all the key ingredients that later became what we call building engineering—formal methods of design relating to structural matters (as established by Lorenz Lechler and Rodrigo Gil de Hontañón), the use of drawings as a fundamental part of the process (Filippo Brunelleschi, Francesco di Giorgio, and Leonardo), the use of arithmetic to calculate quantities (Leonardo and Domenico Fontana), the development of numerical calculating devices (the slide rule), the use of a scientific approach to understand how engineering systems work, especially hydraulics and structures, and the use of this understanding to devise engineering solutions (Francesco di Giorgio, Leonardo, and Fontana).

While Italy led the world in engineering at this time and only a handful of key people have been identified, it would be wrong to assume that little or nothing was happening in France and the German-speaking countries, or that the named individuals were solely responsible for the new ideas. Much of the evidence we have is the result of historical accident—the survival of certain documents rather than others—and the inevitable bandwagon that accompanies the status of becoming a "famous" scientist or engineer. More significantly, we have records of only the literate and those inclined to write things down. Even today the written record of engineering is partial; very few engineers and project managers write anything of what they have done. In the sixteenth century there were many thousands of professional engineers, architects, and scientists throughout Europe. There were often good and frequent communications among these communities in different cities and lands. In northern Italy most such professionals knew one another; many were good friends. There were frequent opportunities for engineering ideas to be shared, discussed, and passed on. Although Francesco di Giorgio and Leonardo, for example, who knew each other well, left us with a wonderful record of Renaissance engineering, this represents the mere tip of an iceberg. In so many ways they were men of their time. They were not sole creators in the way that a novelist or composer is the sole author of his or her works. Many people were involved in all engineering projects, even Leonardo's experiments; many would have known and understood much of what Francesco and Leonardo knew, because these two men would have needed to tell them. Even though Brunelleschi was highly protective of his ideas, this was only until he had secured the contract for his dome. His ideas could be carried out only because he shared them with others, who, no doubt, communicated them to others. The contribution by those who have left written records is especially significant because they were devising methods of capturing some of their ideas and knowledge in forms that would enable other people to learn them without the medium of verbal transmission or hands-on experience. The history of building engineering is, to some extent, the story of collecting and conveying experience, and for nearly three thousand years there has been constant debate about what sort of engineering knowledge can be captured in this way—the relationship between what are often called "theory" and "practice."

LOGARITHMS

A calculation using logarithms is based on the algebraic property of indices that:

$$a^x \times a^y = a^{(x + y)}$$

The logarithm of a number is defined as the power to which a base number (such as 10) must be raised to give that number. Thus $\log_{10}(100) = \log_{10}(10^2) = 2$.

To multiply two numbers, their logarithms are found from tables and added together. The result is looked up in a table of "antilogarithms" to give the answer to the calculation. In the process of division, the logarithms are subtracted. Logarithms remained in daily use until the early 1970s, when electronic calculators were introduced.

PROBLEM

To calculate, to 4 significant figures, the density of a sample of stone weighing 2854 kg, whose volume, measured by immersion in water, is 1.275m^3.

DENSITY OF STONE

$$d = \text{weight} \div \text{volume}$$

$$d = (2854 \div 1.275)\ \text{kg/m}^3$$

$$\log(d) = \log(2854) - \log(1.275)$$

$$= \log(2.854) + \log(10^3) - \log(1.275)$$

NUMBER	LOG
2.854	0.4554
10^3	3.0000
sum	3.4554
1.275	0.1055
difference	3.3499

$$\log(d) = 0.3499$$

$$d = \text{antilog}(3) \times \text{antilog}\ (0.3499)$$

$$= 1000 \times 2.239$$

$$= 2239\ \text{kg/m}^3$$

THE SLIDE RULE

The two scales of a slide rule are logarithmic scales. The act of adding or subtracting lengths on these scales is, therefore, equivalent to multiplying and dividing, respectively. A calculation involving the numbers 1.3 and 5 shows that multiplying these figures gives the answer 6.5, and that 15 x 5 gives 65. The user of a slide rule had to remember carefully the position of the decimal point.

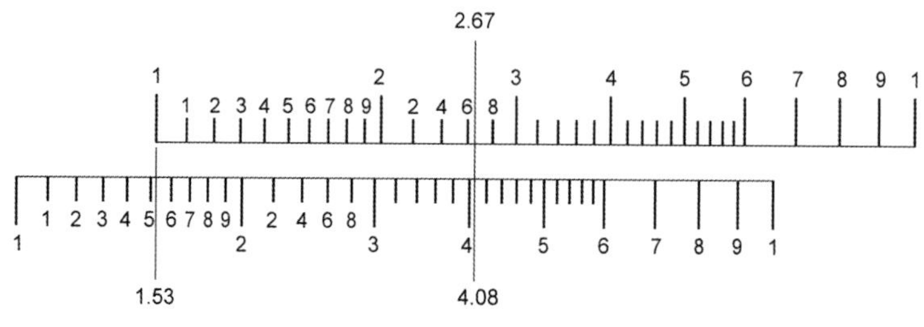

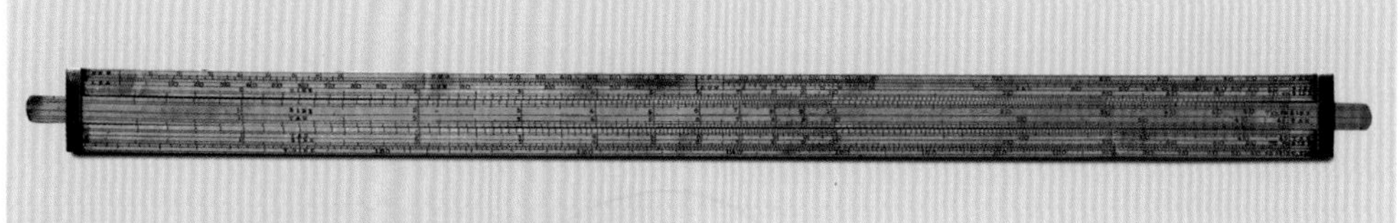

193

194

193 An early slide rule with logarithmic scales engraved on wood, 1630s. Like most slide rules made before 1850, it had no cursor. 194 Calculating device developed by William Oughtred, c. 1630, later refined to become the circular slide rule. Oughtred's book *The Circles of Proportion*, which described slide rules, was published in 1632.

chapter 4

Global Trading and the Age of Reason and Enlightenment

1630–1750

People and Events

1564–1642 Galileo Galilei

1618–86 François Blondel

1620–84 Edme Mariotte

1632–1723 Christopher Wren

1633–1707 Sébastien Le Prestre de Vauban

1635–1703 Robert Hooke

1642–48 English Civil War

1642–1727 Isaac Newton

1646–1716 Gottfried Leibniz

c. 1650–1780 Age of Reason and Enlightenment

1666 Great Fire of London

Materials and Technology

1600–1700 Widespread drainage and land reclamation in Europe

1666–81 Languedoc Canal, France, connecting Atlantic and Mediterranean

1670s Cast plate glass developed in France

Knowledge and Learning

1638 Galileo, *Dialogues Concerning Two New Sciences* (important Enlightenment treatise on science and materials)

1650s Early books with numerical design guidance for builders

1660 Royal Society, London, England, given formal status

1666 Académie des sciences, Paris, France, given formal status

1671 Académie royale d'architecture, Paris, France, founded

Design Methods

1660s Model tests to predict strength of beams (Mariotte and Hooke)

1670s Hanging chain model for dome of Saint Paul's Cathedral, London, England (Wren and Hooke)

Design Tools: Drawing and Calculation

c. 1630 Vernier scale devised for surveying instruments

c. 1630 Pantograph developed for copying drawings

1650 Graphical method of calculating timber quantities

Buildings

1650–75 Louvre Palace, Paris, France (under Louis XIV)

c. 1660–1710 Palace of Versailles, Versailles, France

1660s First ice houses built

1675–1711 Saint Paul's Cathedral, London, England

1630 1640 1650 1660 1670 168

1692–1761 Petrus van Musschenbroek

1693–1761 Bernard Forest de Bélidor

c. 1700–77 Augustin Danyzy

1707–83 Leonhard Euler

1707–88 Georges Leclerc, comte de Buffon

1713–80 Jacques-Germain Soufflot

1708 Steam powered pumping engine by Newcomen

1715 First reliable thermometer developed by Fahrenheit

1722 Réaumur's treatise on iron making

1707 School of Engineering, Prague, founded

1720s–1750s First scientific engineering textbooks

1729 Bélidor, *La Science des ingénieurs* (influential early engineering textbook)

1737–53 Bélidor, *L'Architecture hydraulique* (uses calculus)

1741 Royal Military Academy at Woolwich, England, founded

1747 École des ponts et chaussées founded in Paris, France

1748 École royale du génie de Mézières founded in France

1730s Model studies of masonry arch collapse (Augustin Danyzy)

c. 1740 Hanging chain and segment model for dome of Saint Peter's Basilica, Rome, Italy

1730s Geometrical approach to stereotomy by Frézier

1721 Lombe silk mill, Derby, England

1690 1700 1710 1720 1730 1740 1750

Global Trading and the Age of Reason and Enlightenment 1630–1750

Global Trading

Renaissance Italy had achieved remarkable excellence in virtually every sphere of human activity—literature, painting, sculpture, music, architecture, civil and military engineering, manufacturing, commerce, and banking. In doing so, however, it had become rather too preoccupied with itself. For the Italians, the world outside meant the sources of various essential and exotic materials such as copper, iron, tin, lead, silver, wool, cotton, silk, and spices. Given their location there was little the Italians could do to overcome this reliance on imported goods. The sole example of import substitution was a home-produced silk industry that gave Milan a monopoly in the manufacture of silk cloth, which it held until the early eighteenth century.

The primary role for Italy's military engineers was to protect the trade routes from the eastern and western Mediterranean and from north of the Alps that were key to its continuing prosperity. Italian fortifications lined the Adriatic and protected the strategically important islands of Malta, Crete, and Cyprus. As Italy's affluence and power grew, its European neighbors became increasingly envious and concerned, finally resorting to invasion as the best means of subduing the country's supremacy. By 1500 much of northern Italy was under the control of the German-speaking empire. By 1600 the French had taken control of the northwestern provinces, and most of central and southern Italy had come under Spanish influence. Venice alone retained its autonomy well into the eighteenth century.

While Italy had been increasingly preoccupied with self-preservation, enormous changes were taking place to the north, beyond the confines of the Mediterranean and the reaches of Italian influence. From the early thirteenth century, the countries bordering the north coast of continental Europe had been gradually creating their own trade routes. By 1500 as much trade was passing through the ports of France, the Netherlands, and Germany as through the ports of Italy. Italy's capacity to expand its trade was limited by the Muslim territories that ringed the entire eastern end of the Mediterranean, preventing direct access to the Indian subcontinent and more distant lands. Even more significant was the psychological limit to the Italians' world: the shores of the Mediterranean. Some men had dreams of venturing beyond these shores to seek direct routes to the East; but, while Christopher Columbus was a Genoese sailor, he raised the financing for his voyage to discover a trade route to the East Indies from the Spanish court. The Venetian Giovanni Caboto (John Cabot) secured funding for his exploration of the northern route across the Atlantic from England's King Henry VII. The lucrative

195

196

195 The expanding port of Amsterdam, from Olfert Dapper, *Historische beschrijving der stadt Amsterdam*, 1663.

196 Engraving of Dutch shipbuilding in the mid-eighteenth century, from P. Schenk, *Navigiorum Aedificio*, c. 1725.

trade routes around the southern tip of Africa to the East, and to Latin America, were developed in the sixteenth century by the Dutch, Spanish, Portuguese, and English, not the Italians.

By the middle of the sixteenth century Venetian ships had all but ceased sailing to the Netherlands, and by the end of the century Dutch and English vessels were entering the Mediterranean in growing numbers. By 1600 the seaborne trade in the English Channel exceeded that through Italian ports many times over, and this had direct consequences for the construction industries. As had happened during the thirteenth century, when sea trade in northern Europe had begun, the boom in commercial shipping in the seventeenth century generated a
195 need for better port facilities, both for the ships and for handling and storing the goods they carried. The changing patterns of sea trade were not only the result of commercial pressures. The shipbuilding industries of the North were developing, too, and prospering. By 1600
196 Dutch ships cost one third less than those made in Italy and their operating costs were lower by a similar amount. Although the Venetian fleet had maintained its size during the seventeenth century, by century's end more than half of its larger vessels were Dutch-built.

The growth of trade also had indirect consequences in northern Europe, for it led to increasing urbanization and larger towns. In 1500 Paris was the only city in northern Europe as large as Milan, Venice, and Naples; the Netherlands and Northern Italy were the most urbanized regions, with about one-tenth of their populations (four times the European average) living in towns. By 1600 European urbanization had reached 5 percent, with the Netherlands reaching three times this proportion. Amsterdam was nearly as large as Paris and was the fastest-growing town in Europe. The population of London had exploded on the back of increasing sea trade to become, with Naples and Constantinople, one of the three largest cities in Europe. By 1700 London was the first European city to reach a population of half a million.

Increasing trade and urbanization in northern Europe were accompanied by several important consequences. More food was needed, and literacy improved, accelerated by the growing success of printing. The rising number of people living in towns increased the demand for heating fuels, and coal began to replace wood as the fuel of choice. European coal production, centered mostly in England and Belgium, rose by a factor of three during the sixteenth century, and the annual consumption of coal in England alone—mainly for domestic heating in towns and cities—rose from 700,000 tons in 1600 to three million in 1715, representing more than four-fifths of European consumption. (Venice's decline can be seen in the fall of its exports of cloth to one-tenth over the same period.) The demand for urban heating created the need for cheaper coal, which was achieved through both greater productivity and reduced haulage costs. The steam engine was developed to extract water from mines so that they could be worked to greater depths; a steam engine built by Thomas Newcomen was first used in a Tyneside 197
colliery, in northern England, in 1708. It is no great surprise that the £250,000 investment needed to construct the first of the new wave of England's canals was provided by the duke of Bridgewater, the owner of coal mines that supplied Manchester and Liverpool. The first section of the Bridgewater Canal opened in 1761 and halved the cost of delivering the coal to Manchester, soon yielding its owner an annual income of some £80,000.

The use of iron in Europe grew steadily from about 125,000 tons a year in 1500 to more than 200,000 tons in 1715. The rapid rise in consumption in England, from 30,000 to 60,000 tons a year between 1715 and 1760, was stimulated mainly by the agricultural revolution and the need to manufacture agricultural implements required to produce food for the growing numbers of nonfarmers living in towns. The charcoal needed to make wrought iron was soon becoming scarce in England, leading to imports from Sweden for the best-quality iron, and Russia for the cheapest. The English iron industry received its badly needed salvation in the form of coal, of which there was a virtually limitless supply in England. Abraham Darby (1678–1717) began his search for a way to make iron with this fuel in around 1710, and soon had developed a method for using coke—coal that has had its volatile constituents removed by firing—to reduce the iron oxide ore to yield iron. (For more detail on the development of iron manufacture, see Appendix 2.) One of these volatile constituents, coal gas, would be used at the end of the eighteenth century to provide artificial light in buildings and later for public streetlighting.

197

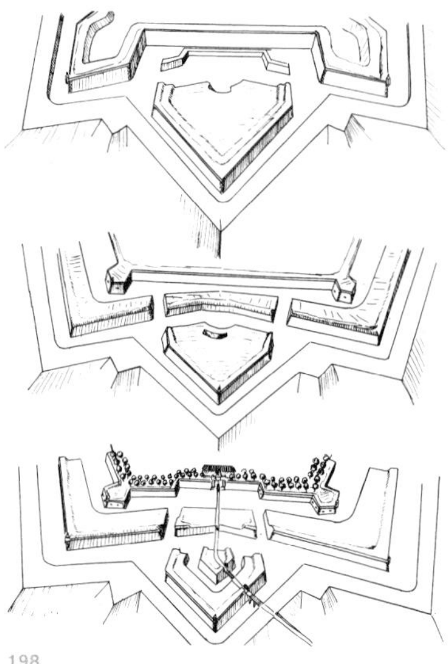

198

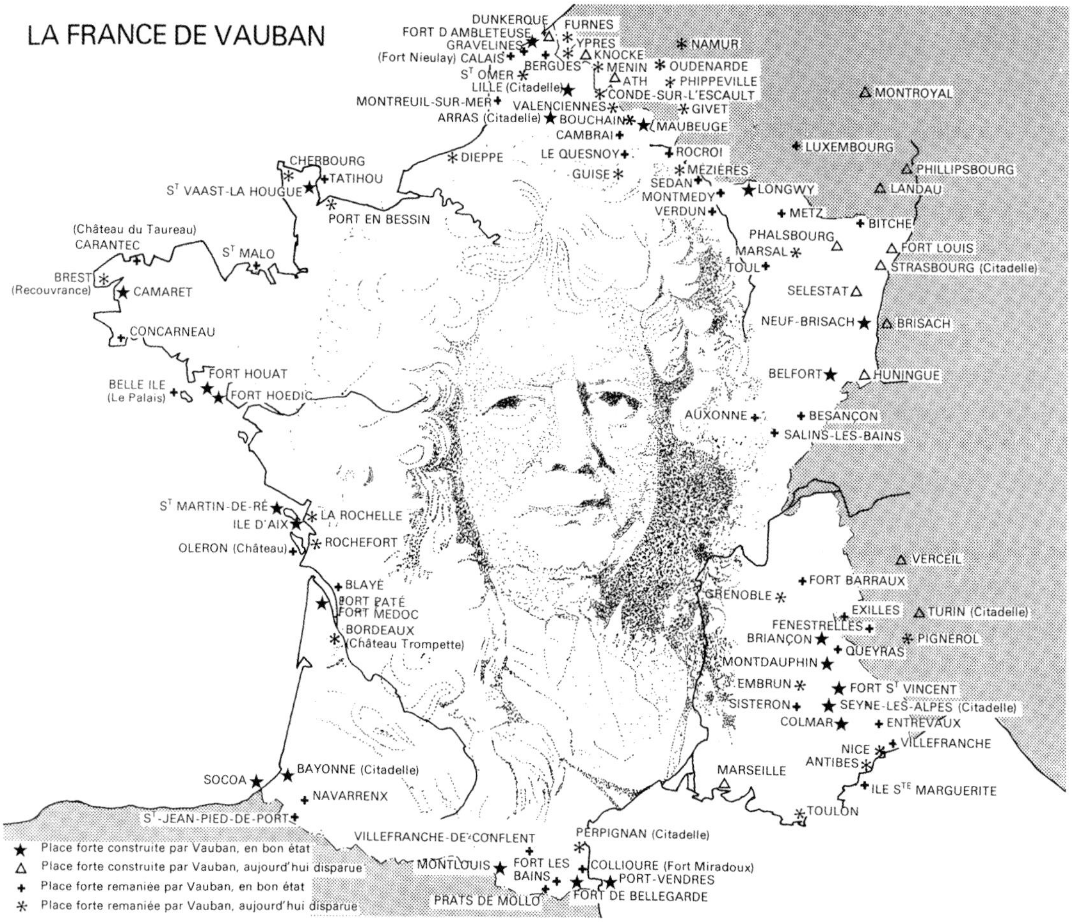

LA FRANCE DE VAUBAN

DUNKERQUE
FORT D AMBLETEUSE
GRAVELINES
(Fort Nieulay) CALAIS
FURNES
YPRES
KNOCKE
BERGUES
MENIN
NAMUR
OUDENARDE
S^T OMER
ATH
PHIPPEVILLE
LILLE (Citadelle)
CONDE-SUR-L'ESCAULT
MONTREUIL-SUR-MER
VALENCIENNES
GIVET
ARRAS (Citadelle)
BOUCHAIN
MAUBEUGE
CAMBRAI
MONTROYAL
DIEPPE
LE QUESNOY
ROCROI
LUXEMBOURG
CHERBOURG
TATIHOU
GUISE
MÉZIÈRES
PHILLIPSBOURG
S^T VAAST-LA HOUGUE
SEDAN
LONGWY
LANDAU
MONTMEDY
PORT EN BESSIN
VERDUN
METZ
BITCHE
(Château du Taureau)
CARANTEC
S^T MALO
PHALSBOURG
MARSAL
FORT LOUIS
TOUL
STRASBOURG (Citadelle)
BREST
(Recouvrance)
CAMARET
SELESTAT
CONCARNEAU
NEUF-BRISACH
BRISACH
FORT HOUAT
BELFORT
HUNINGUE
BELLE ILE
(Le Palais)
FORT HOEDIC
AUXONNE
BESANÇON
SALINS-LES-BAINS
S^T MARTIN-DE-RÉ
LA ROCHELLE
ILE D'AIX
OLERON (Château)
ROCHEFORT
VERCEIL
BLAYE
FORT BARRAUX
FORT PATÉ
FORT MEDOC
GRENOBLE
EXILLES
TURIN (Citadelle)
BORDEAUX
(Château Trompette)
FENESTRELLES
BRIANÇON
QUEYRAS
PIGNEROL
MONTDAUPHIN
EMBRUN
FORT S^T VINCENT
SISTERON
SEYNE-LES-ALPES (Citadelle)
COLMAR
ENTREVAUX
NICE
VILLEFRANCHE
ANTIBES
MARSEILLE
SOCOA
BAYONNE (Citadelle)
ILE S^TE MARGUERITE
NAVARRENX
TOULON
S^T-JEAN-PIED-DE-PORT
VILLEFRANCHE-DE-CONFLENT
PERPIGNAN (Citadelle)
MONTLOUIS
FORT LES BAINS
COLLIOURE (Fort Miradoux)
PORT-VENDRES
PRATS DE MOLLO
FORT DE BELLEGARDE

★ Place forte construite par Vauban, en bon état
△ Place forte construite par Vauban, aujourd'hui disparue
✚ Place forte remaniée par Vauban, en bon état
✳ Place forte remaniée par Vauban, aujourd'hui disparue

199

200

197 Atmospheric engine designed by Thomas Newcomen for the York Buildings Waterworks, London, c. 1730.   198 Three systems of fortification devised by Sébastien Le Prestre de Vauban in the seventeenth century.   199 Map of France showing locations of fortifications designed by Vauban.   200 Fortified town of Mont-Dauphin, France. Fortifications designed by Vauban, 1693.

Meanwhile, of course, as new cities and nations prospered, so their rulers strove to enhance their identities and their influence. As armaments became more and more powerful and towns flourished and grew, so too did their defenses need renewing, upgrading, or extending. Ships of war increased in size and potency, and new docks, shipyards, and harbors were needed to service the new and larger naval fleets. The skills of the great Italian engineers and military architects soon spread to France, Spain, and England, both through the movement of individuals—Leonardo da Vinci and Francesco di Giorgio were just two of many Italian military engineers who accepted the patronage of a foreign court—and the increasing number of books that came into circulation.

Of the countless European engineers who continued the work of their Italian predecessors, one stood out during the seventeenth century: the Frenchman Sébastien Le Prestre de Vauban (1633–1707), usually known simply
198 as Vauban. He developed to perfection the art of fortification through several stages, as military tactics and weapons, too, developed to outwit the new methods of defense. His designs were not formulaic; each scheme was devised precisely to meet the unique situation—the terrain, the existing fortifications, the types of armaments proposed for defense and those anticipated to be in enemy hands. His reputation was ubiquitous even during his lifetime; as a widely reproduced contemporary saying ran, "A town besieged by Vauban is a town lost; a town fortified by Vauban is impregnable." Vauban's name is associated with more than a hundred towns around the
199, 200 perimeter of France that survive in good condition today, including Belfort and Briançon in the east, and Mont-Louis and Bayonne in the southwest. It is testimony to his skills as a design engineer that most of these fortifications were constructed without his direct supervision and, in many cases, were erected after his death. While perhaps conceived as purely functional, his defense structures gave towns a characteristic and dramatic architectonic quality that they retain today.

Vauban was trained as a military engineer and was in military service his whole life; he undertook more than fifty military sieges and fought over a hundred campaigns. Nevertheless, his work often provided nonmilitary benefits to towns when, during peacetime, he was able to canalize rivers and create waterways for commercial enterprises. At the seaport city of Dunkerque, in northern France, his fortifications incorporated an entirely new harbor, jetties, storehouses, and workshops. He proposed creating a number of canals linking seaports to several inland towns of northern France and put forth the idea of a Rhine–Rhône canal through Alsace. He also spent a year or so supervising construction of the aqueduct he devised to carry the Languedoc Canal (Canal du Midi) (1666–81) over a river.

It was during the sixteenth and seventeenth centuries that civil engineers began to apply to nonmilitary projects the technical and project-management skills that military engineers had developed over the previous three centuries. This work was predominantly hydraulic engineering for such purposes as land drainage, flood prevention, building canals, and constructing bridges over rivers. The Dutch were masters of the art; their engineers had reclaimed huge areas of low-lying land from the sea. 201
Similar work was undertaken in East Anglia in England by migrant Dutch engineers such as Cornelius Vermuyden (1590–1677). The Languedoc Canal, which links the 202
Mediterranean to the Atlantic, was the first of several large canals to be constructed in France. Others followed in northern Europe and England as the economic benefits of cheap transport helped fuel the commercial and industrial trade that grew throughout the eighteenth century. Complementing the canals was a growing network of improved roads throughout Europe, built to a much higher quality than farmers' tracks, to carry horse-drawn coaches for people, goods, and, when necessary, troops. With canals and roads, of course, came the need for bridges, and the first concerted effort in northern 203
Europe to modernize the entire transportation infrastructure. The increasing demand for such works led in the eighteenth century to the new idea of civil engineering as a profession. This meant not only defining which specific types of projects civil engineers should address and solve but also establishing an institutional approach to the education and training that would be necessary to undertake such work. Engineering was starting to follow the precedent long established in the legal and medical professions.

Reason and Enlightenment

The two words used to describe this period of European history—Reason and Enlightenment—capture what we

201

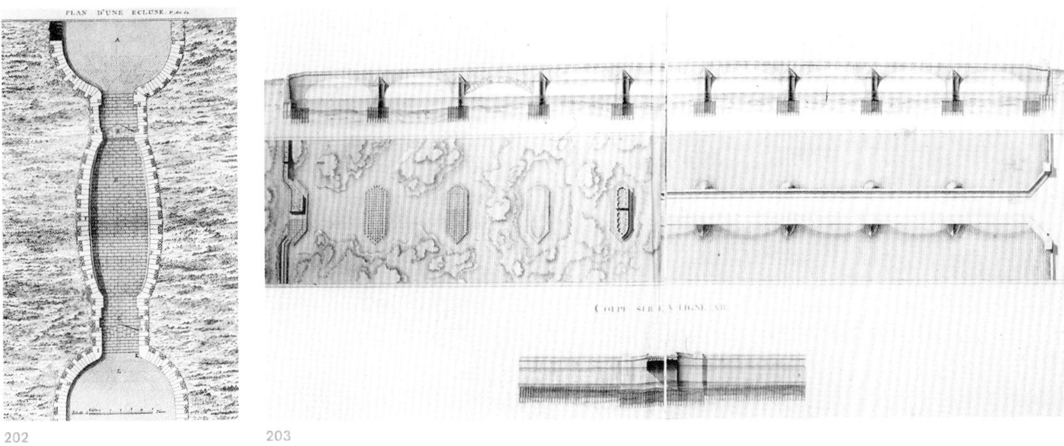

202 203

201 Seventeenth-century engraving of drainage/reclamation in The Netherlands. 202 Lock on the Languedoc Canal, France, 1666–81. From *Canaux de navigation, et spécialement du canal de Languedoc*, Paris, 1778. 203 Pont George V, bridge at Orléans, France, 1751–60. Engineer: Jean Hupeau. Plan and elevation.

204

205

204 (Previous pages) Margrave Opera House, Bayreuth, Germany, 1742–48. Architects: Giuseppe Galli-Bibiena and Joseph Saint-Pierre. 205 Santa Sindone Chapel, Turin, 1667–90. Architect: Guarino Guarini. Interior of the dome. 206 Hôtel-Dieu, Lyon, France, 1741–61. Architect: Jacques-Germain Soufflot. 207 Castle Howard, Yorkshire, England, 1699–1712. Architects: Sir John Vanbrugh and Nicholas Hawksmoor.

206

207

might today call the right- and left-brain aspects of human skill. On the one side there was the rational world of mathematics, philosophy, science, and rhetoric. On the other was what we call the world of the artist, encompassing literature, painting, music and architecture—although this kind of artist was very different from Brunelleschi, Francesco di Giorgio, Leonardo, and Michelangelo, who learned their trades as apprentices in dirty and noisy workshops and foundries. A list of just a few of the people from this age who have left their imprint on our Western culture reminds us of the richness and variety of creative talent.[1]

204, 205 The seventeenth and eighteenth centuries witnessed a
206, 207 remarkable blossoming of architectural styles and many individual architectural talents as more and more variations on the basic building types, facades, and layouts were devised. Hardly less amazing is that very few of the buildings of this time made new demands on engineers, so these years were primarily a period of consolidation of the basic skills of building engineering. The building engineers of the late medieval and Renaissance eras had matched and even surpassed the achievements of Apollodorus and other Roman engineers from a thousand and more years earlier. Progress in building engineering during the seventeenth and eighteenth centuries was, by comparison, much less spectacular. Rather than progressing dramatically, the engineering and craft skills that had been developed (mainly) in Renaissance Italy spread outward and more uniformly throughout Europe. For example, many "new" developments in seventeenth- and eighteenth-century England, such as the introduction of the triangulated timber roof truss, had been in use in France, Germany, and Spain for a century or more, and in Italy for even longer. Churches generally became more ornate rather than larger, palaces became ever more grand, and town houses grew in height to five or six stories. Since the birth of Protestantism after the Reformation in northern Europe in the mid-sixteenth century, surplus wealth was invested in civic buildings such as town halls and market buildings rather than in religious architecture. All this was achieved using the now-standard techniques of masonry construction for walls, columns, and domes, with timber floor beams and roof trusses. Timber frame construction was largely replaced by ashlar, for prestigious buildings, or by brickwork. As in earlier times, wrought iron bars were widely used to link large masonry blocks together, and iron tie rods were used to counter the outward thrust of arches, though this was increasingly considered visually unacceptable. Exemplars of every type of construction became widely known through books, and served as models to copy or imitate.

The idea of an Age of Reason evolved from a rather optimistic and naïve belief that the works of the Greek philosophers and their medieval and Renaissance interpreters would solve many, if not all, of the world's problems. This notion permeated society in the realms of

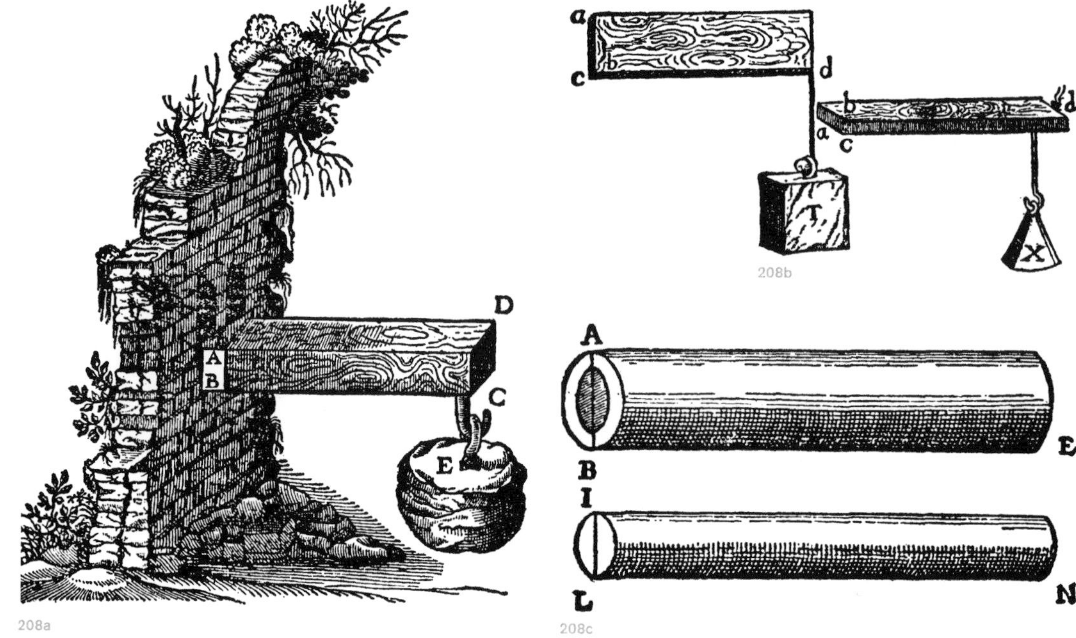

politics, science, art, and even religion. Thought and reason allowed human beings to wander in a universe unencumbered by the limitations of the real world and the people who inhabit it. As René Descartes and other philosophers taught, thought and reason are fundamental to our idea of ourselves and to building our self-confidence. The Greek philosophers had, quite literally, invented thinking: that is, the arts of reason and rhetoric.

Gradually, as the machine age evolved during the course of the medieval and Renaissance eras, man devised new ways of explaining the world about him in mechanical terms, without recourse to gods and mysterious interventions. The idea grew that the universe might be some sort of machine, and that its behavior might be similarly predictable. By the early seventeenth century, man realized that an intellectual understanding of the world might enable him to transform and improve things in that same world.

Before the Renaissance, engineers had approached their task mainly by observation and generalization—that is, empirically. They collected data about what worked and what didn't, and created formulas that summarized established practice. These design rules could be learned easily and provided a convenient means by which engineering knowledge could be stored and passed on to others, including younger generations. However, the use of such rules left little flexibility and excluded radical departures from precedent, as the Milan Expertises around 1400 showed (see chapter 2, pp. 105–09).

Toward the end of the Renaissance things were beginning to change. In the writings of Rodrigo Gil de Hontañón

208 Galileo Galilei, drawings illustrating variations in the strength of simple structures, from *Dialogues Concerning Two New Sciences*, 1638. (a) The load E and self weight of the beam BD cause fracture at AB. (b) The strength of a beam depends on its orientation when loaded, and varies as the depth. (c) The strength of solid and hollow rods made from the same amount of material increases with the overall diameter (an incorrect conclusion).

from around 1565, we sense his frustration at not finding a general rule that applied to the design of vaults and abutments (see chapter 3, pp. 150–53)—a frustration born of his belief that such a general rule might, or even must, exist, and his inability to find it. Matthew Baker, England's leading ship designer in the 1580s, also realized that following the designs of earlier ships would not provide guidelines that could generate a different and improved vessel. It was becoming clear to some engineers in all related disciplines that there were benefits to be gained by undertaking rational and careful experimentation—not only practical experiments, but also what physicists today call "thought experiments." Francesco di Giorgio set out the logical thinking that led him to new types of fortification and used drawings to depict weapons, machines, and buildings that had never been made or built before. Leonardo da Vinci used thousands of drawings to record not only his observations but also the results of the hundreds of "What if?" questions that went through his mind. He captured the answers that he imagined as sketches on the page, which threw up new questions and answers, and more sketches that effectively show how his mind was working its way through a problem toward a final solution. Leonardo went beyond thought experiments in hydraulic engineering and devised practical experiments to determine the flow of water in various channels. Bernardino Baldi undertook a thought experiment of his own concerning the mechanism by which a voussoir arch might collapse. These, and the unrecorded thoughts of many of Francesco di Giorgio, Leonardo, and Baldi's contemporaries, demonstrate the use of what we now call mathematical models of the real world, which involved geometry, hydrodynamics, and statics. In the case of the latter two disciplines, however, the mathematical concepts needed to represent the real world were generally still lacking.

The way forward was demonstrated by the science of astronomy. Greek and Arab astronomers had gathered huge quantities of data about the positions of the stars and planets, and devised mathematical models of the universe that allowed remarkably accurate predictions. This occurred despite the complex and irregular orbits that planets, appeared to follow and while it was assumed that the earth was the center of the universe. In the early sixteenth century, Nicolaus Copernicus (1473–1543) and Johannes Kepler (1571–1630) demonstrated that a much simpler mathematical model of the universe could be formulated if it were assumed that all the planets, including Earth, followed elliptical orbits around the sun. Nevertheless, they still did not understand why the orbits were ellipses, any more than the second-century astronomer Ptolemy (Claudius Ptolemaeus) could explain the irregular planetary orbits in his model of the universe. The idea that the planets might be constrained in their orbits by a force that could act over great distances and through space was proven only in the seventeenth century. Robert Hooke first propounded the theory in the mid-1660s, but neither his mathematical skills nor those of his good friend and fellow scientist Christopher Wren were up to demonstrating that this concept would indeed lead to the elliptical orbits Kepler had proposed. It was Isaac Newton who, in the mid-1680s, finally provided the mathematical proof.

The Strength of Materials

The success of these scientific achievements raised people's confidence that all subjects would benefit from such methodical study, both intellectual and practical. The study of the strength of materials was no exception. The physicist Galileo Galilei (1564–1642) provided some new and more useful answers to the questions that Aristotle and Archimedes had raised nearly two thousand years before about why things were as strong as they are, why sticks break at their midpoint when bent, and so on. Medieval philosophers and Renaissance mathematicians had considered these questions, too, but, lacking a mathematical representation of force, did not make much headway. Galileo was the first person to clearly distinguish between the strength of a material and that of an object made from that material—in other words, the difference between the properties of a material and of a structure—and hence paved the way for thinking in terms of stress (force per unit area) rather than force or strength. He used this approach to refute the opinion held by "many very intelligent people" (as Galileo called them) that the strength of a rope diminishes with its length. He drew a distinction between a weakness due to a smaller cross section and one due to an inferior quality of fiber. Thus he was able to argue that a longer rope was indeed likely to be weaker than a shorter one, but only because it was more apt to contain a manufacturing flaw or section of poor-quality material. The strength of the rope itself might vary, but not because of its length.

Galileo went on in his book *Dialogues Concerning Two New Sciences* of 1638 to address "the resistance which solid bodies offer to fracture by external forces." He wondered why it is that " . . . a rod of steel or of glass will sustain a longitudinal pull of a thousand pounds while a weight of fifty pounds would be quite sufficient to break it if the rod were fastened at right angles to a vertical wall."[2]

In other words, how can one relate the strength of a piece of material in the form of a cantilever to the strength of the same material in tension? In considering fracture, he assumed that a brittle material failed when the "absolute resistance to fracture" (tensile strength) was reached and the two parts of a cantilever subject to bending parted, appearing to rotate about a virtual ful-
208a crum at the lower surface of the beam. Throughout his
argument, however, Galileo considers only the relative strength of different beams; nowhere does he try to relate the strength of a beam to the absolute strength of the material of which the beam is made. Nevertheless, Galileo did deduce much that we still accept about the
208b fracture of a beam loaded in bending:

- *The strength of a heavy beam is proportional to the square of its length, and inversely to its breadth and the cube of its depth.*
- *It is easiest to break a beam in the center, where the bending moment is highest.*
- *The bending moment-diagram (not his words) for a cantilever is a straight line.*
- *It is essential to distinguish carefully between the contribution to bending made by an applied load and by the weight of the beam itself.*
- *A hollow tube is a stronger beam than a solid one made from the same amount of material. (He was wrong about the degree to which a hollow tube is stronger.)*

The main differences between his argument and those of today are:

- *He assumed that a round cantilever and a square one of equal area are equally strong; likewise, he was*
208c *wrong in his conclusion about solid and hollow rods.*
- *In both cases the strengths vary with shape or "second moment of area," not the depth or diameter (the idea of the second moment of area was developed first by Leonhard Euler around 1750; see p. 222).*
- *He placed the point of rotation of a beam at fracture at the lower face of the section.*

Although it is usual to say that Galileo was mistaken in this last conclusion, this is a little unfair. He was discussing fracture, not bending, and when a brittle material fractures it does so in tension as a crack propagates with explosive violence and speeds down through the section. The location of what we now call the neutral axis at the center of a rectangular section is a valid assumption only while the cantilever remains unbroken. If the cantilever breaks, its neutral axis effectively moves down as the fracture propagates, and does indeed end up at the bottom of the section.

Galileo's work was known to scientists and mathematicians throughout Europe, and, whereas in earlier times it might merely have provoked debate about its validity and hypothetical consequences, in these early days of the Age of Reason it stimulated different questions—for instance, did Galileo's argument enable someone to predict the strength of a real beam using a mathematical calculation? This query could be answered only by conducting experiments, which is just what two eminent scientists, the Frenchman Edme Mariotte (1620–84) and the Englishman Robert Hooke (1635–1703), undertook. Their work is of special interest not only for its scientific value but also for the manner in which it came about, as both men were involved in founding the two organizations that so well characterize the spirit of the Age of Reason: the Royal Society in London and the Académie des Sciences in Paris. These two bodies were the first to promote science as a highly respectable activity, which, through the research they encouraged in physics, chemistry, biology, and medicine in particular, would demonstrate during the next century the tangible benefits that such work could bring to the human race.

The first learned societies devoted to science, or the New Philosophy, as it was called, were formed in Italy to avoid the constraints imposed by the church, which effectively controlled what could be studied in universities. The Accademia dei Segreti (Academy of Nature's Secrets) was established in Naples in 1560, and the Accademia dei Lincei (Academy of Lynxes, named after an animal whose visual acuity was renowned), of which Galileo was a prominent member, was organized in

Rome in 1603 and lasted until 1630. The Accademia degli Investiganti (Academy of Investigators) was founded in 1650 in Naples, and the Accademia del Cimento (Academy of Experiment), which counted the mathematician and physicist Evangelista Torricelli (1608–47) among its members, was founded in Florence in 1657. Despite the valuable work such societies encouraged and the publication of many of their proceedings, all the early academies ceased their activities within a few decades, to be replaced by others founded by scientists with different interests in other cities. The Royal Society in London and Académie des Sciences in Paris were the first to outlive their founders and become national institutions that indeed survive to this day.

The origin of the Royal Society lies in a group of scientists who began meeting every two weeks in 1645 in both London and Oxford to discuss all manner of scientific and philosophical issues. Gresham College in London became their home after Christopher Wren was appointed professor of astronomy (the equivalent of modern physics) there in 1657. After the restoration to the throne of Charles II in May 1660, twelve members of this group decided that their nascent society ought to have a more formal status. On 28 November in that year, they agreed to found "a College for the Promoting of Physico-Mathematicall Experimentall Learning." Among the first of the organization's adherents were several scientists Wren had known at Oxford, including the chemist and physicist Robert Boyle (1627–91), mathematicians John Wallis and John Wilkins, and Robert Hooke. The group soon attracted the king's attention and was subsequently granted its official charter in 1662 as the Royal Society of London for the Promotion of Natural Knowledge. On Boyle's recommendation, Hooke was appointed its curator of experiments in the same year. Central to the ethos of the Royal Society were the experiments and demonstrations that Hooke and others after him conducted. These included experiments measuring the temperature and pressure of gases, demonstrations of various optical and mechanical devices, and even attempts at performing a blood transfusion on a live dog. The society soon began publishing books, including Hooke's *Micrographia* (1665), along with records of its meetings in the *Philosophical Transactions*, the oldest and longest-running scientific periodical still in publication. The Royal Society remains today the heart of the scientific research community in Britain, though its experimental work has long since passed into the university world.

The Académie des Sciences also began in the 1640s, with informal meetings whose attendees included René Descartes and Blaise Pascal; the group was given more formal status in 1666 at the instigation of the minister Jean-Baptiste Colbert (1619–83). The members met weekly in the king's new library in Paris—mathematicians on Wednesdays and scientists on Saturdays—where they repeated the classic experiments of physics and Mariotte undertook his research on the strength of materials and bending of beams. The group was given its royal charter in 1699, and its seventy members began meeting in the Louvre Palace itself. Like the Royal Society it began publishing scientific papers and mémoires, and regular reports of its meetings. It remains today a national voice for promoting scientific research in France. Scientific societies based on the earlier Italian, English, and French models were founded in the German states, Russia, Spain, and Scandinavia during the first half of the eighteenth century.

While today we associate the work of these learned academies with our most eminent and successful scientists, it was not always so. In terms of numbers the excellent were outnumbered by the mediocre, and for every Hooke or Mariotte there were many others who jumped on the research bandwagon, proposing all manner of improbable lines of research. Jonathan Swift (1667–1745) reminds us in his razor-sharp satires *A Tale of a Tub* (1704) and *Gulliver's Travels* (1726) that not all the investigations undertaken in the name of science were productive, and some verged on lunacy. On his voyage to Laputa, at the Academy of Lagado (i.e., the Royal Society), Gulliver encounters a man who has been working for eight years on devising a means of "extracting sunbeams out of cucumbers which were to be put into vials hermetically sealed, and let out to warm the air in raw inclement summers. He told [Gulliver] he did not doubt in eight years more, that he should be able to supply the Governor's gardens with sunshine at a reasonable rate . . . and entreated [Gulliver] to give him something as an encouragement to ingenuity, especially since this had been a very dear season for cucumbers."[3]

Robert Hooke was England's Leonardo. He was among the world's leading talents in designing and making scientific instruments and clocks, mechanical engineering, materials science, and structural mechanics, as well as astronomy, microscopy, chemistry, biology, physics, surveying, and architecture. From a poor family, Hooke gained a place at Christ Church College, Oxford, as a servitor—a student who earned his keep as the servant to another, wealthier student; he later became a chorister. While at Oxford he met Christopher Wren, Robert Boyle, and John Wilkins. Hooke first found an outlet for his remarkable inventiveness while working with Boyle, for whom he devised and made a vacuum pump for experiments with gases. By 1662 Hooke had developed the modern microscope, as well as the anchor escapement and balance-wheel escapement in his quest to invent a clock mechanism accurate enough to enable mariners to establish their longitude. This work on springs led him toward his famous law of elasticity, though at this time he was not willing to publish it for fear that others might learn to match the accuracy of his clock mechanisms. At the age of twenty-seven, Hooke was elected a fellow of the Royal Society, and in 1665 he was appointed professor of geometry (equivalent to modern physics) at Gresham College, as Christopher Wren had been.

Hooke undertook his first experimental work on the strength of materials and bending of beams between 1662 and 1664 at the Royal Society, where he and others carried out a large number of tests to establish the breaking strengths of wires in tension and beams in bending. To the modern eye these experiments seemed to involve a remarkable degree of randomness in the way materials, dimensions, and even temperature and air pressure were varied in the hope of discovering general or universal laws. Later work by Hooke concentrated first upon wood and metal and then upon "stones, baked earth, hair, horns, silk, bones, sinews, glass and the like" and led him to suggest his famous precept *ut tensio sic vis*—as the extension, so the force—applicable to "every springing body." This is now universally known as Hooke's Law, though Mariotte, too, had undertaken similar experiments and proposed the same principle under his own name. Hooke claimed to have first formulated his law in the 1650s during his work to perfect the spring balance wheel for clocks, but did not publish it until 1678 in De *Potentia Restitutiva* (Of Spring), doing so in anagram form—*ceiiinosssttuv (ut tensis sic vis)*—lest someone else steal the idea and benefit from using it.

Neither Hooke nor Mariotte performed their work in isolation from problems in the real world. Hooke was a very practical man, and applied his understanding to making many instruments and machines as well as to the design of buildings. Mariotte published his classic study of the bending of beams in a paper he wrote on the motion of fluids—a curious location explained by the fact that he had become interested in the strength of solids when commissioned to design the pipelines supplying water for the huge new fountains at the Palace of Versailles. The work of Hooke and Mariotte showed others how to tackle the problem of bending, and soon determining the theoretical strength and stiffness of beams occupied the attentions of the most eminent mathematicians and scientists of Europe. Some, including Antoine Parent (1666–1716), Charles Coulomb (1736–1806), and, later, Peter Barlow (1776–1862), Thomas Tredgold (1788–1829), and Jean-Marie-Constant Duhamel (1797–1872), focused on the strength of beams. Others, notably Jakob Bernoulli (1654–1705), Leonhard Euler (1707–83), Claude Louis Marie Henri Navier (1785–1836), and Barré de Saint-Venant (1797–1886) concerned themselves mainly with the bending behavior of beams before fracture—the stiffness or amount of deflection, the deflected shape of a beam, and also the vibration of rods and plates. It is interesting that during this period, attention swung between two vital structural issues. The strength of beams was the principal concern from, very roughly, 1638 to around 1730 and again from about 1775 to 1820, by which time the problem of fracture had at last been effectively solved; stiffness, on the other hand, was the main interest of engineering scientists from about 1730 to 1775 and again from the 1820s to the 1860s.

During the same period there was a parallel interest in the structural behavior of the arch. Rather than simply seeking evidence from completed buildings, scientists began looking at how arches actually worked and their behavior when they collapsed. The first successful application of statics to the arch was published in 1695 by the French academician Philippe de la Hire (or de Lahire; 1640–1718) in his book *Traité de mécanique*. The initial

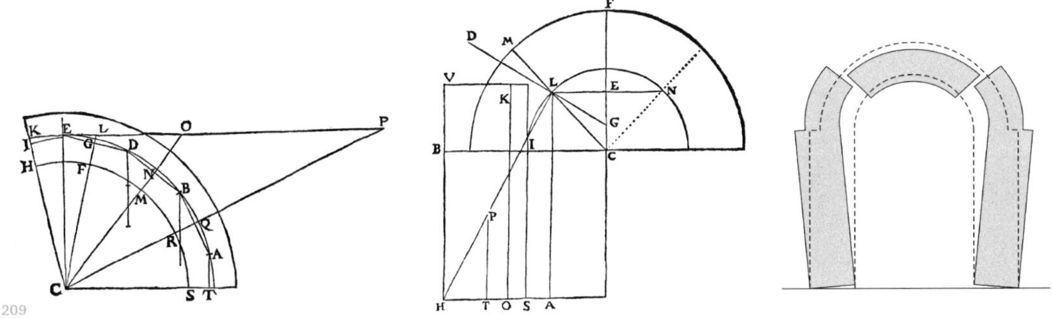

209

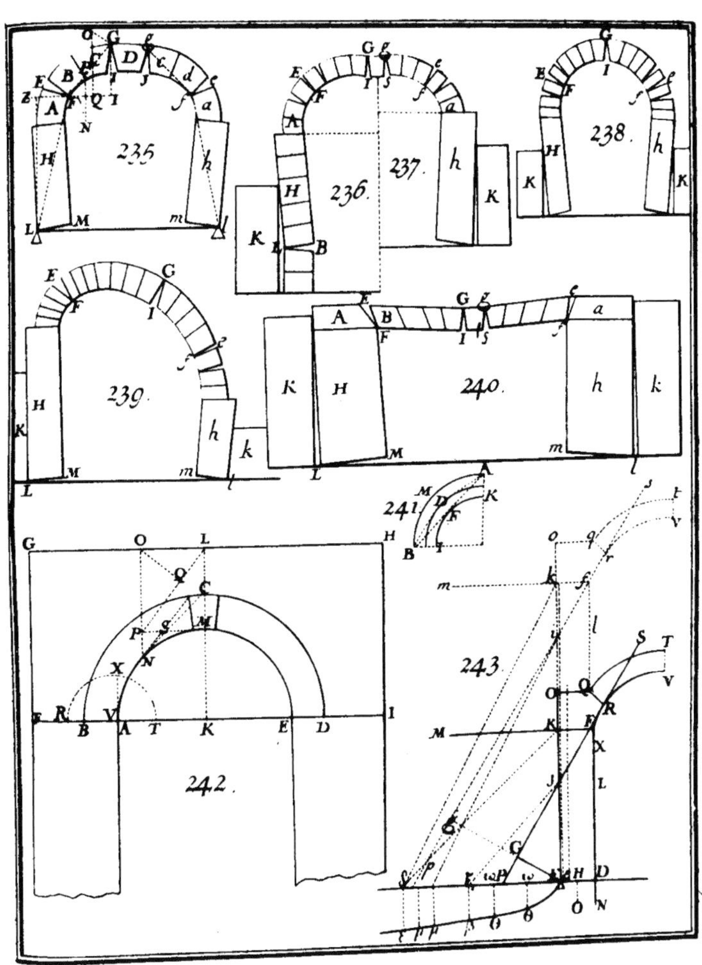

210

209 Philippe de Lahire, diagrams showing how the stability of a masonry arch and its manner of collapse are related to the weights of the voussoirs and the thickness of the arch ring, from papers published in 1695 and 1712. 210 Augustin Danyzy, results of tests done on plaster model arches, 1732.

211a

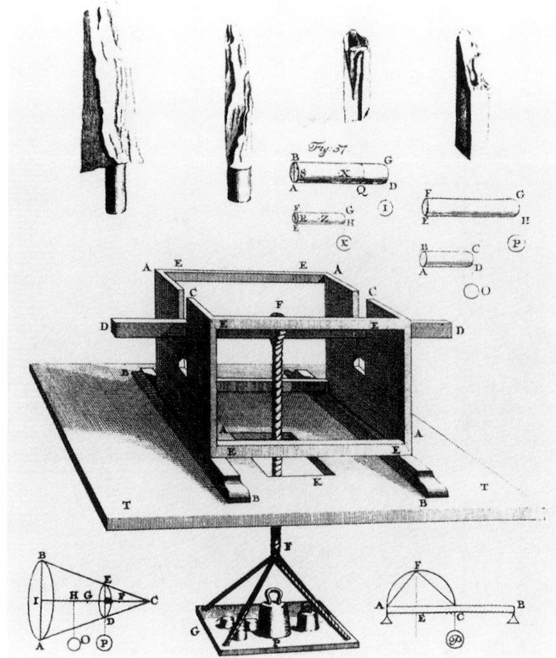

211b

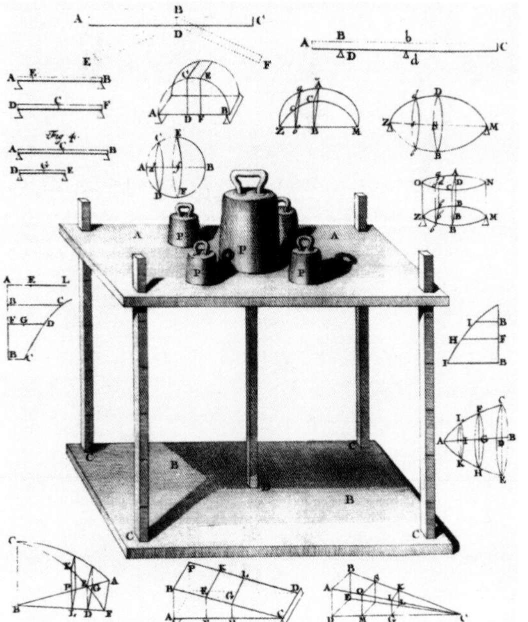

211c

212

question he considered was this: What weights must
209 the voussoirs of a semicircular arch have to ensure a structure's stability? To calculate the equilibrium conditions for the arch, he represented the forces by lines in a diagram that was related to the geometry of the arch itself. He thus used a geometric method to replace the combined action of forces along adjacent sides of a parallelogram by an equivalent third, single force along its diagonal, the method that would later be developed into the technique known as graphical statics. In a later work (1712), Lahire considered the long-studied problem of determining the size of abutment or wall needed to resist overturning by an arch above. Whereas Rodrigo Gil de Hontañón had tried to find design rules based on actual buildings, Lahire solved the problem in an abstract way using a mathematical model. His method was soon widely publicized, and his idea became firmly adopted when Bernard Forest de Bélidor included it in his book *La Science des ingénieurs* in 1729 (see pp. 212, 220–21, 223–24).

Following Baldi's insight that the collapse mechanism must always involve the rotation of voussoirs at a hinge, scientists had a line of experimentation to pursue. It was not long before people began proposing mathematical models of the behavior to try to explain it and even predict the outcome of tests on scale models. The French
210 scientist Augustin Danyzy (c. 1700–77) conducted a large number of tests on model arches with voussoirs made of plaster and reported his findings to the Société Royale des Sciences of Montpellier, in France, in 1732. These findings were published by his colleague Amédée Frézier in an appendix to his 1737 treatise on stereotomy (stonecutting), together with analytical methods for calculating the outward thrust of arches.

Engineers quickly came to realize that data being collected on the behavior of materials and structures in the name of scientific research would be of use to them. Soon many experiments were undertaken to establish the strength of materials—every type of timber used in construction, as well as iron made by different manufacturers, for example. Tests were performed on both small-scale (model) and full-size structural elements. Bélidor, for one, published the results of experiments he had conducted on the strength of small timber beams in *La Science des ingénieurs*. However, the most comprehensive and thorough tester of materials in the eighteenth century was without doubt Petrus van Musschenbroek (1692–1761), a professor of physics at the University of Utrecht and later at Leiden. Although the French physicist René-Antoine Ferchault de Réaumur (1683–1757) had performed mechanical tests on iron and steel in the 1720s during his research on converting wrought iron into steel, Musschenbroek was effectively the founder of
the art of materials testing. In his book *Physicae* 211
Experimentales et Geometricae of 1729 he presented results for more than twenty types of wood, as well as iron and other materials. He also determined the loads that caused slender struts to buckle, and established by experiment the formulas for calculating such behavior some three decades before Euler did so mathematically. Musschenbroek's work was widely known and used, especially in continental Europe, by engineers who wanted to justify the sizes of simple struts and tension elements such as wrought iron ties. They also used his data on the strength of materials, in conjunction with the current mathematical models for bending, to calculate beam strengths. For the design of beams, columns, and ties of normal size, it was, of course, unlikely that this scientific method of determining dimensions would have led to a savings of material or been "better" in any other way. The simple rules developed by builders over many centuries, such as defining the required depth of a beam as a certain fraction of its span, already yielded the most economical sizes.

Georges Louis Leclerc, comte de Buffon (1707–88), criticized the work of Musschenbroek and others with some justification when the results of their experiments were applied to large structures, because such scientific conclusions had been determined on the basis of very small test specimens that were just a few square centimeters in section and a few tens of centimeters long. Buffon and, later, at the École des ponts et chaussées (School of Bridges and Roads) in Paris, Emiland-Marie Gauthey,

211 Petrus van Musschenbroek, three apparatuses for measuring (a) the tensile strength of materials, (b) the deflection of beams in bending, and (c) the buckling strength of struts, all from *Physicae Experimentales et Geometricae*, 1729.
212 Pierre-Simon Girard, compression test rig for wooden struts, from *Traité analytique de la résistance des solides*, 1798.

212 Jacques-Elie Lamblardie, and Pierre-Simon Girard undertook tests of full-size structural members—wooden beams up to 9 meters long and struts up to 3 meters high, sometimes using loads of up to 10 tons and more.[4]

The numerous test results based on mathematical models that became available during the mid- to late eighteenth century enabled engineers to compare such hypothetical outcomes with the behavior of real structures. By this time many engineers had developed confidence in design techniques based on calculations rather than empirical data alone, although the range of structures to which they could apply such methods was still limited to beams, columns, struts, and ties.

Wren, Hooke, and Building Design

It might be thought that the scientific understanding developing throughout Europe during the Age of Reason soon would have led to changes in the way buildings were designed and constructed—perhaps through the agency of committees set up by governments, patrons, or scientific institutions. But in the seventeenth century there was no professional infrastructure—no committees reviewing design codes of practice, no technical press through which scientific developments were communicated to practicing engineers. In fact, the late seventeenth century did witness a new approach to designing and constructing buildings in Europe, but it was through the work of just two men—the eminent English scientists Christopher Wren (1632–1723) and Robert Hooke, together with, inadvertently, Thomas Farriner, the baker in whose premises the Great Fire of London began in 1666.

Both Wren and Hooke became building designers by accident when they rose to the challenge of restoring and rebuilding the heart of London after the terrible fire, but they became no ordinary designers of buildings. Neither Wren nor Hooke were masons-turned-architects, or military engineers-turned-architects, or gentlemen architects who had studied Alberti and the stylistic guides of Serlio and Palladio. They were the first building designers who had a good mathematical and scientific understanding of forces, which derived from their work at the Royal Society on gravitation and the orbits of planets as well as the experiments on bending and the strength of materials. Through their work on planetary motion under the action of forces in three-dimensional space, both men were familiar with using mathematical models to help comprehend phenomena at a scale that exceeded man's by many millions of times. Indeed, by comparison, even St. Paul's Cathedral was small and much more tangible. When faced with a problem, both Wren and Hooke would have approached its solution in a scientific manner as naturally as any engineer would today.

It was a full half century before other scientists in Europe were drawn into the world of building design and construction to study the stability of the dome at Saint Peter's Basilica in Rome (see pp. 226–32), and a more than a century before engineers designing ordinary buildings such as multistory factories began to use engineering science to help them improve their designs (see chapter 5). In bringing their understanding of science to the practical world of engineering and building design, Wren and Hooke also anticipated, by more than two centuries, the idea that underpins modern engineering education—namely, that you can derive an understanding of structures, without having been a builder yourself, by studying the mathematics and science of buildings.

Wren and Hooke established what was perhaps the first consulting design practice, embracing what we now call architecture and building engineering, though the modern distinction between these two disciplines would not have been familiar to them. Of the two principals, Wren was certainly the more proficient architect, while Hooke was the more skilled in practical engineering matters. As in all good partnerships, each stimulated and contributed to the work of the other.

Wren dominated the world of building in England during this period partly because he embodied the spirit of both Reason and Enlightenment in large and equal measures. He had studied at Wadham College, Oxford, and was appointed professor of astronomy at Gresham College, London, at the age of twenty-five. He moved back to Oxford in 1661 as the Savilian Professor of Astronomy, though he still worked fully as an architect and regularly attended meetings of the Royal Society in London and was its president from 1680 to 1682. Wren's work as an architect began with the chapel at Pembroke College, Cambridge, in 1663, but his reputation was famously boosted in the years following the Great Fire of London.

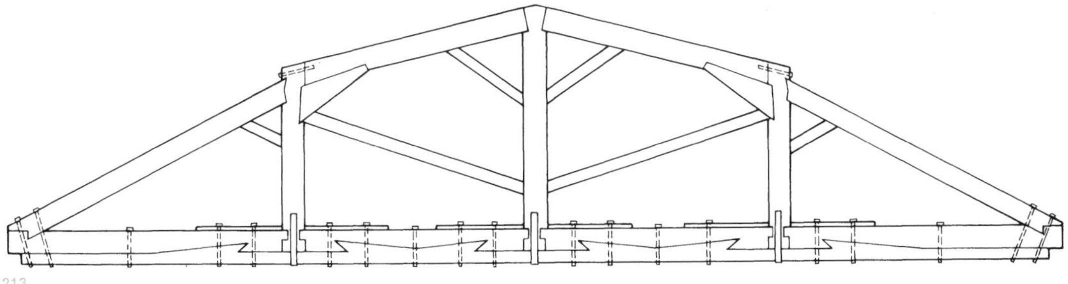

213

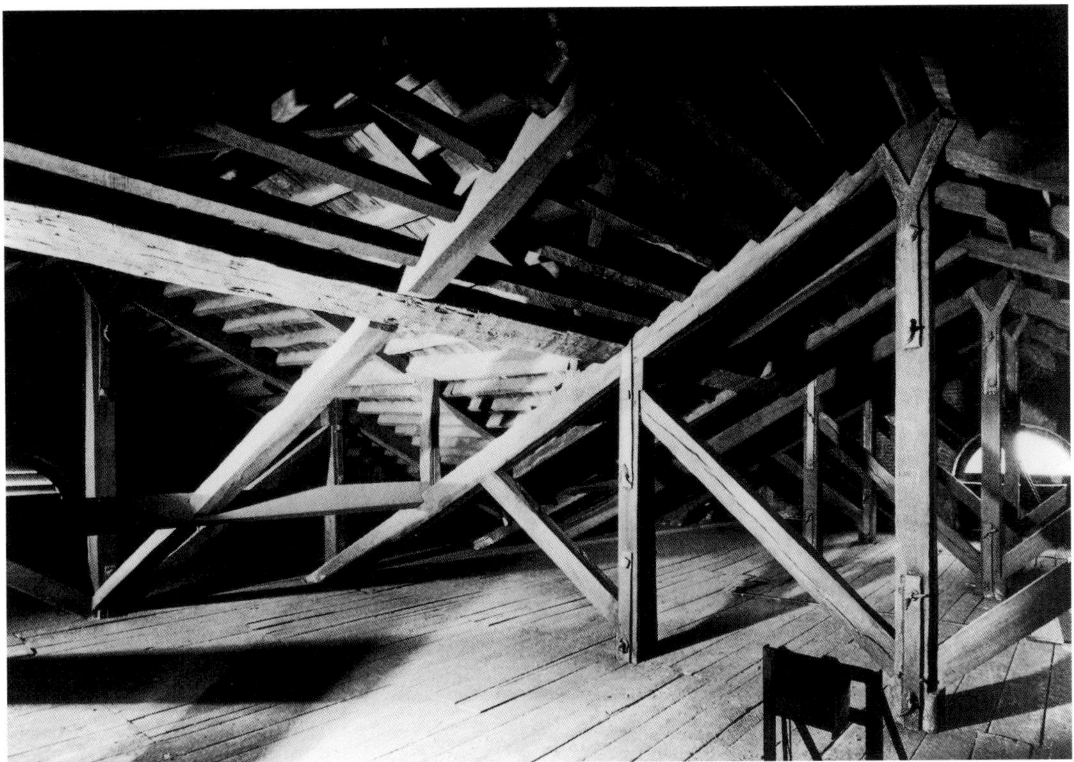

214

213 Sheldonian Theatre, Oxford, England, 1664–69. Architect and engineer: Sir Christopher Wren. Roof truss spanning 22 meters. 214 Trinity College Library, Cambridge, England, 1676–84. Architect and engineer: Sir Christopher Wren. Roof truss. By the mid-seventeenth century, iron ties and straps were increasingly used in large roof trusses to carry tensile forces. 215 (Overleaf) Trinity College Library. Interior.

The king appointed him as one of three surveyors to work alongside three others selected by the city of London, including Robert Hooke. Wren designed and supervised the construction of some fifty-three churches in the city; the largest and most famous is Saint Paul's Cathedral, which was finally completed in 1710. Wren was made surveyor general to the Crown in 1669, in which capacity he undertook a great many architectural and surveying commissions, including extensions to Hampton Court Palace and the Royal Hospital at Greenwich and an assessment of the structural stability of Salisbury Cathedral. This legacy established his renown as Britain's most talented and eminent architect until the twentieth century, though his abilities also included, in today's terminology, structural engineering and project management.

Wren was aware of the relatively few earlier works on statics, including those of Baldi, Stevin, and Galileo, and never ceased bringing his understanding of physics and mathematics into his thinking about building. He was the first engineer or architect to write about buildings in terms of forces and equilibrium, and in ways that are almost the same as we would today. His constant ingenuity derived largely from how he must have thought about a design challenge and the manner in which he set about devising his solutions. Toward the end of his life he prepared several (unfinished) papers on architecture and masonry construction, which were published only after his death, in *Parentalia: or Memoirs of the Family of the Wrens* (1750). In one of these it is clear that he was on the point of making the greatest leap of all in proposing to break with the traditions of Vitruvius, Alberti, and others who dealt only with proportions in architecture. Concerning how one should proportion an abutment to support an arch, Wren first echoes the words of Rodrigo Gil de Hontañón:

> *If the butment be more than enough, 'tis an idle expence of materials; if too little it will fail; and so for any vaulting; and yet no author hath given a true and universal rule for this, nor hath considered the various forms of arches.*[5]

He then goes on to point to the way forward clearly:

> *The design . . . must be regulated by the art of staticks, or invention of the centers of gravity, and the duly poising [of] all parts to equiponderate; without which, a fine design will fail and prove abortive. Hence I conclude, that all designs must, in the first place, be brought to this test, or rejected.*[6]

There is hardly a better example of his understanding of structures than in one of the first buildings he designed. The timber roof trusses of the Sheldonian Theatre in 213
Oxford (1664–69, now replaced) were of a unique form in Britain (it is likely that Wren took some inspiration from ideas brought back from Italy by his friend the architect Inigo Jones). The trusses were especially large for their time (22 meters); they rose less than half the height of similar roofs, and also had to support the considerable weight of books stored there by the Clarendon Press. The roof truss he used for the library of Trinity College, 214
Cambridge (1676–84), spanned 12 meters and was a more conventional design, but demonstrates his careful detailing and use of iron straps.

In an age when building was almost exclusively a world of brick, stone, and timber, Wren was not averse to experimenting with new materials. The tall railings erected around Saint Paul's in 1710 are reputedly the first architectural use of cast iron. And not only did he use chains of wrought iron in his dome, he also used straight wrought iron ties on a more modest scale to support the bookcases at Trinity College Library. These are anchored 215, 217
in the masonry walls and incline inward, hidden within the back-to-back bookcases to reduce the load they impose on the library floor at the first-story level. He used the same idea in repairs at the Bodleian Library in Oxford. At Hampton Court Palace, which Wren was commissioned to rebuild in 1685, his even bolder structural use of wrought iron was discovered recently when severe fire damage necessitated repairs. Within a partition wall, a hanger supports a floor beam directly from the 216
timber roof truss.

Wren was probably also the first designer of buildings to use iron columns. When expanding the capacity of the House of Commons in 1692, he introduced galleries. Because these were supported mainly by brackets, he was forced, on either side of the entry to the chamber, to use "two iron pillars and capitalls in iron of Tijou's work," as he described them in a memorandum.[7] The Frenchman Jean Tijou, Wren's master craftsman in 218
wrought iron, illustrated a solid iron column and its capital and base in his *A Newe Booke of Drawings*, published in 1693. Though no dimensions are given, the scale of the ornate wrought iron decoration of the capitals and their representation in a number of illustrations suggest

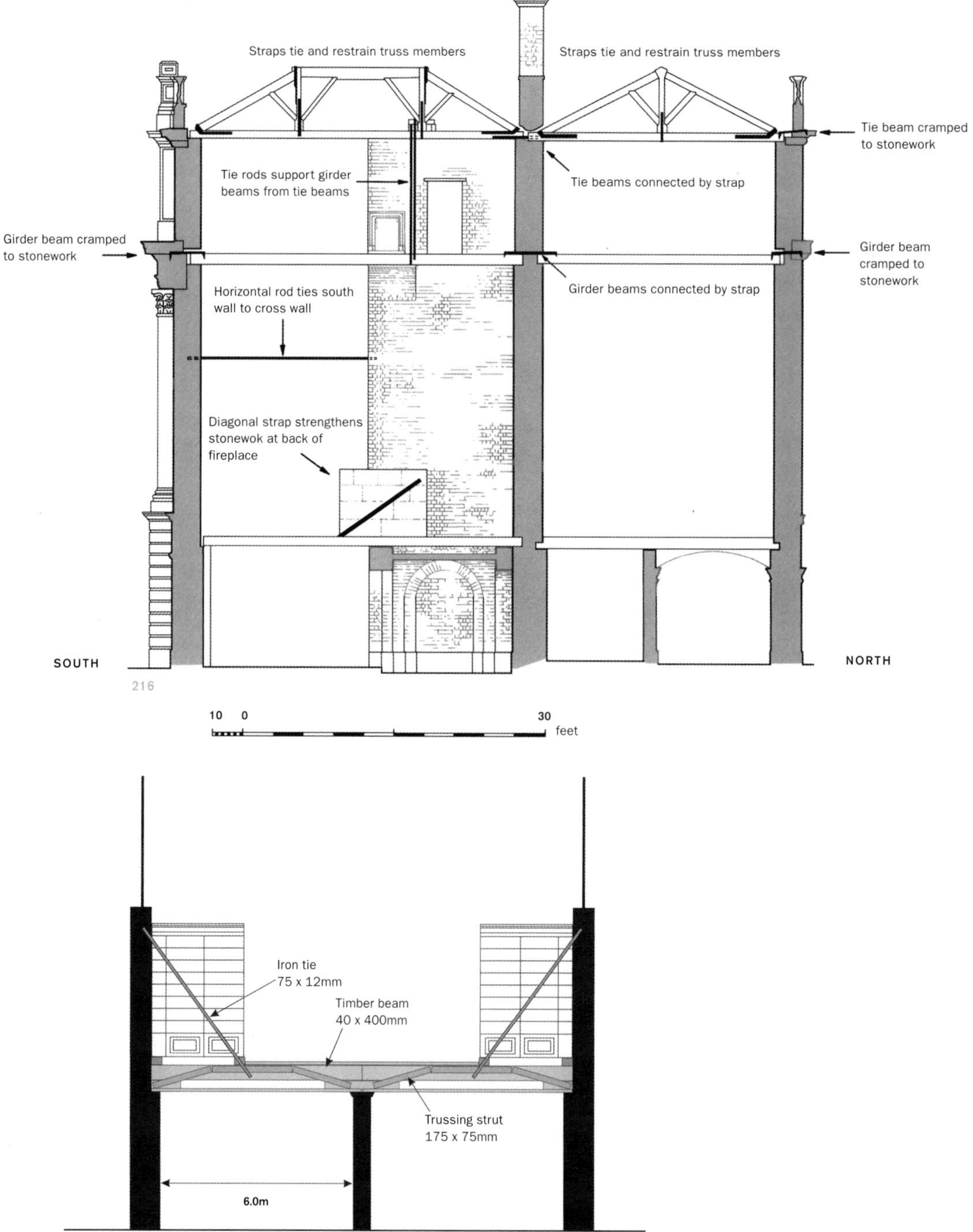

216 Hampton Court Palace, London, 1689–1702. Section of the south front extension showing Christopher Wren's use of iron ties. 217 Trinity College Library, Cambridge, England, 1676–84. Section showing Wren's use of iron ties. 218 Jean Tijou, drawing of a wrought iron column for the House of Commons, London,1693. 219 Collegiate chapel of St. Stephen (the debating chamber of the House of Commons), London, 1692 (enlarged 1707). 220 Collegiate Chapel of St. Stephen after fire in 1834, from Frederick Mackenzie, *The Architectural Antiquities of the Collegiate Chapel of St. Stephen, Westminster* (1844). The engraving shows the twisted remains of Tijou's wrought iron columns after the fire of 1834.

218

IEW of the HOUSE of COM
Arthur Onslow Esq. Speaker of the House of

219

220

221

222

221 Saint Paul's Cathedral, London, 1675–1710. Architect and engineer: Sir Christopher Wren. Free-standing walls hide Wren's flying buttresses from view. 222 Saint Paul's Cathedral. Two early sketches by Wren showing the line of thrust from the dome (not as built) following the form of an inverted catenary through the buttresses. 223 Saint Paul's Cathedral. Isometric drawing by R. B. Brook-Greaves and W. Godfrey Allen, 1923–28.

This drawing, which was commenced in October 1923 and carried out during the reparation of St. Paul's Cathedral, was completed in January 1928.
The inscriptions are the work of Percy Smith.
To WILLIAM DUNN, F.R.I.B.A.
who first suggested the idea of shewing the construction of St. Paul's Cathedral by Isometric Projection
– this drawing is inscribed by MERVYN EDMUND MACARTNEY, F.S.A. Surveyor to the Fabric –
Measured and drawn by R.B. BROOK-GREAVES in collaboration with W. GODFREY ALLEN
Valuable assistance has been rendered by Matthew Dawson F.R.I.B.A. & E.J. Bolwell
Published by the Architectural Press
Photo & Collo-type Donald Macbeth

that the columns were about 80 millimeters in diameter,
3.6 meters tall, and, more than likely given Tijou's trade,
made of wrought iron. The two prototypes used by Wren
219 in 1692 were copied when the galleries were widened in
1707 and additional iron columns were added to support
them. These, too, were most likely of wrought iron, although the new decorated capitals were wooden copies
of the Tijou originals, carved by Grinling Gibbons. A paint-
220 ing made in 1834 after a fire at the House of Commons
shows some of the columns as having "wilted," further
evidence that they were of wrought iron.

The most remarkable example of Wren's structural
engineering abilities is, of course, displayed in Saint
221 Paul's Cathedral. The building is a masterpiece of
three-dimensional structural engineering that demonstrates a remarkable sense of poise in how the weight
of the 1,000–ton stone lantern is conveyed down
through the dome, piers, arches, vaults, and walls to
the foundations. The building even incorporates flying
buttresses, though unlike in medieval cathedrals, they
are hidden from view, as they did not suit the Baroque
architectural style.

The "dome" of Wren's cathedral in fact is composed of
three elements. The main structural element is a cone
made of brick, which carries the weight of the lantern.
223 Inside this, and visible from the interior of the cathedral,
is a lightweight, hemispherical brick shell with an oculus,
on which are painted decorative frescoes. The hemispherical "dome" visible from outside is a lead-covered,
lightweight timber structure that is supported on the
brick cone. For the design of the cone Wren made use of
222 a new theorem of statics that his friend Robert Hooke
had established, making this the first time that a design
methodology based on statics was used for a major new
structure. This theorem stated that the best form of an
arch to span between two supports a given distance
apart, with a given rise, is that of an inverted hanging
chain, a curve known as a catenary. As Hooke expressed
it, *Ut continuum flexile, sic stabit contiguum rigidum
inversum* ("as hangs the flexible line, so but inverted
will stand the rigid arch"). As with his more famous law
of elasticity, Hooke published this in anagram form in
A description of helioscopes and some other instruments
(1676). Hooke wrote in his diary for 5 June 1675 that
Wren was making use of "my principle about arches" and
altered his model of the dome of Saint Paul's as a result.
The most efficient and economical shape for the brick
cone was calculated to be an elongated, gentle parabo- 224
loid. It is interesting, curious, and disappointing that
Hooke appears not to have made use of this elegant design procedure in any of his own building.

As had Brunelleschi and Michelangelo before him, Wren had to find a way of carrying the hoop stresses present in all domes that tend to cause them to burst outward near their base. Wren carried these forces in three wrought iron tension rings installed in the base of the cone.[8] These were made by Jean Tijou, the ironmaster who was working on the decorative wrought iron gates at Hampton Court Palace, another of Wren's current projects. By this means Wren was able to carry aloft the most massive of all stone lanterns using less material than similar domes. Furthermore, the dome seems to rest on a tall vertical drum, apparently in defiance of the outward thrust that domes exert. In its structural conception and lightness of the dome, Wren's achievement at Saint Paul's is unsurpassed. At 33 meters, the span of the dome over Saint Paul's was not the largest of its kind, but is undoubtedly one of the most ingenious and most economical of all the classical masonry domes in its use of material. At the Pantheon in Rome (span 43 meters) the span-to-thickness ratio is about 11; for Brunelleschi's dome at Florence (span 42 meters) it is about 21; at Saint Peter's, Rome (span 41.5 meters), it is around 30. The span-to-thickness ratio at Saint Paul's is about 37.

Although Robert Hooke is best known for his scientific work, he, like Wren, also became a successful designer of buildings and engineering structures. If Wren's move from academic, scientific life into architecture and building design had been rapid, Hooke's was virtually instantaneous. At the age of thirty-one, with no previous experience, and less than two weeks after the Great Fire had been extinguished on 6 September 1666, he submitted to the city his plan for its rebuilding. The city's aldermen approved of it and indeed, preferred it to that of the

224 Saint Paul's Cathedral, London, 1675–1711. Architect and engineer: Sir Christopher Wren. Section of the dome showing a modern superimposition of an inverted hanging chain, Wren's original iron chain, and the new chain inserted in the 1920s.

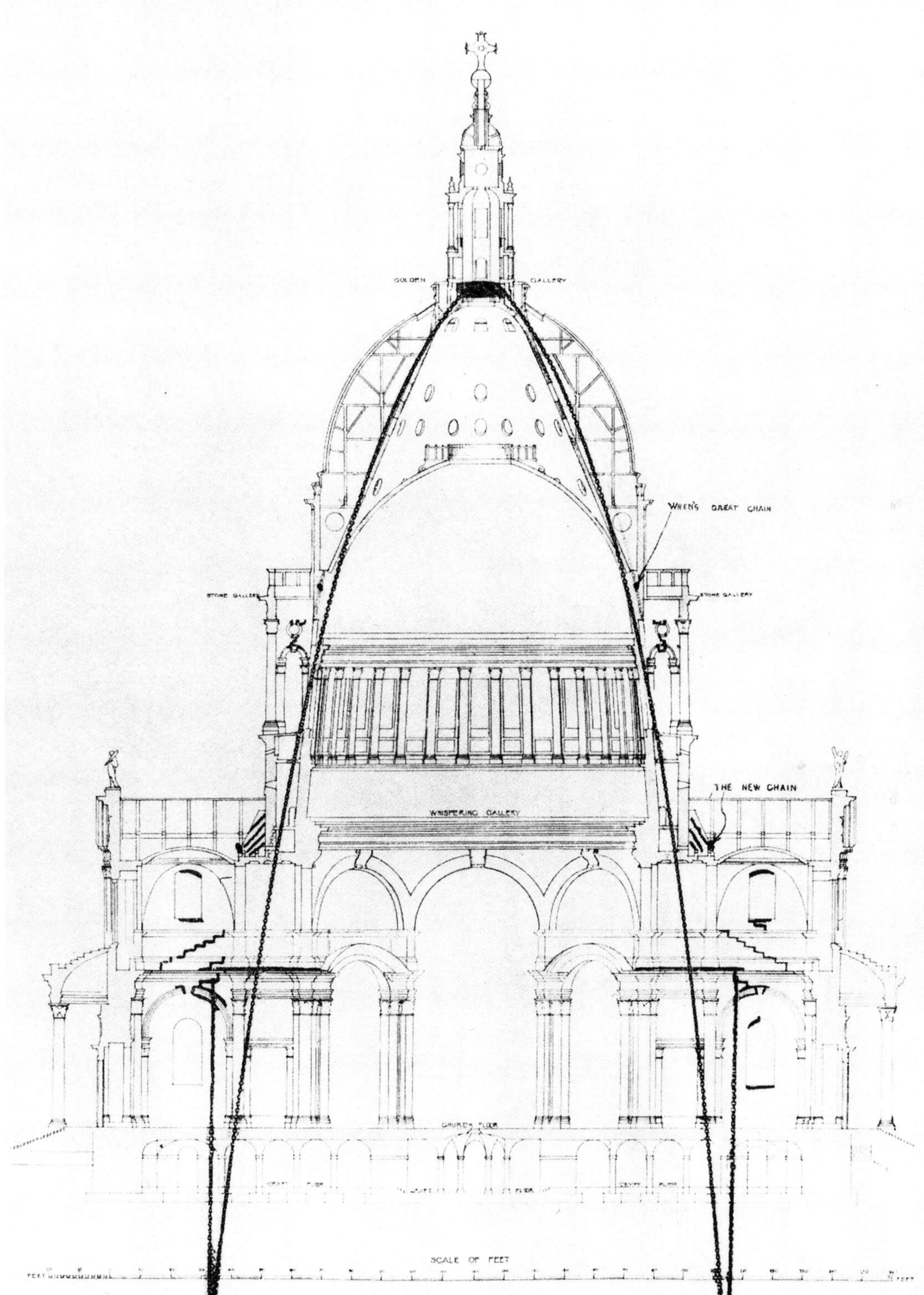
GOLDEN GALLERY
WREN'S GREAT CHAIN
STONE GALLERY
STONE GALLERY
THE NEW CHAIN
WHISPERING GALLERY
CHURCH FLOOR
SCALE OF FEET
FEET
CROSS SECTION THROUGH THE DOME SHOWING POSITION OF CRACKS AND DEPRESSIONS IN THE INTERIOR
N.B. The cracks and depressions are not shown to scale, but have been heavily marked to clearly indicate their positions.

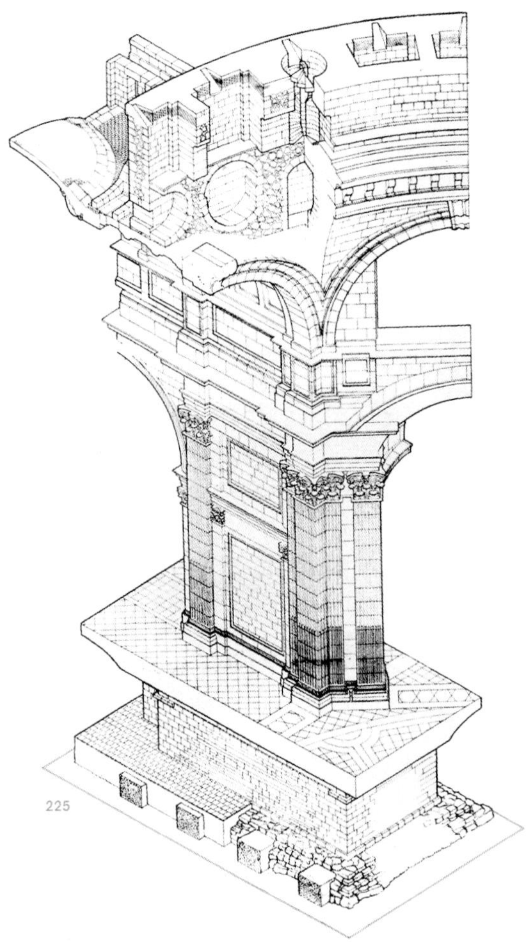

225

EXAMPLE 1
Start at A (= 12 inches)
Mark width of board = 14 inches (B1)
Join A to B1
Mark length of board = 9 feet (C1)
Draw C1 – D1 parallel to A – B1
Number of board feet (D1) 10 1/2

EXAMPLE 2
Likewise
Number of board feet (D2) = 11 1/3

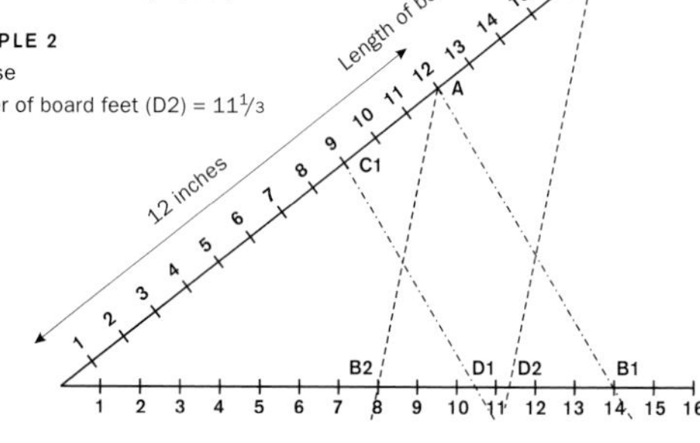

226

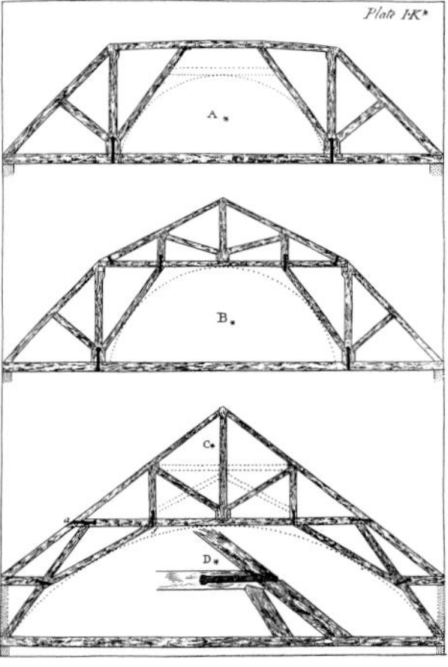

227

I COME now to fpeak of Girders, and firft for their Scantling. Take thefe Proportions,

If the Bearing be	Feet	The Girder muft be	Inches	Thick	Inches	Deep, and put Edge-ways.
	10		8		10	
	12		8 ½		10	
	14		9		10 ½	
	16		9 ½		10 ½	
	18		10		11	
	20		11		12	
	22		11 ½		13	
	24		12		14	

228

The Scantlings of Girders fhould be

	Feet.		Feet.		Inches.		
Lengths from	12	to	15	to be	10	by	8
	15		18		11		9
	18		21		12		10
	21		24		13		11
	24		27		14		12
	27		30		15		13

NOTE, That Girders fhould have at leaft 9 Inches Bearing in the Walls, and be bedded on Lintels, laid in Loam, with Arches turned over their Ends, that they may be renew'd at any Time without Damage to the Pier.

225 Saint Paul's Cathedral, London, 1675–1711. Architect and engineer: Sir Christopher Wren. Isometric view of a pier supporting the dome, showing the use of inverted arches to distribute the concentrated loads from the piers above to the vault spanning over the nave. 226 Diagram of Thomas Stirrup's graphical method for calculating the quantity of timber needed for a floor. 227 Francis Price, illustration of common roof trusses, from *A Treatise on Carpentry*, 1733. 228 Table of scantlings (timber dimensions) for floor construction, from the *Act for the Rebuilding of London*, 1668.

city surveyor, Peter Mills. On the strength of this plan Hooke was nominated as one of three surveyors put forward by the city to work alongside the three others put forward by the Crown, one of whom was Wren. At this time the term "architect" was not current, and the term "surveyor" described not only the carrying out of surveys of the damaged streets and properties, but also a variety of other tasks acting as the client's representative. These included negotiating contracts with landowners and contractors for the rebuilding, helping supervise much of this work on the city's behalf, and directing the builders and contractors in charge of houses, drainage, and other construction labor. This scope would have included what we now call designs for buildings, and so began Hooke's career as an architect. Within just a few years he was acting independently for private clients on a number of major buildings, notably the Royal College of Physicians, Warwick Lane, London (1672–78); Bethlehem (Bedlam) Hospital, London (1675–76); Montagu House, Bloomsbury, London (1675–79), which later became the first home of the British Museum; and Ragley Hall, Warwickshire (1679–83). He also designed the Monument to the Great Fire of London.

Hooke's early work after the fire included some major civil engineering projects, the largest of which was "planning" (that is, designing) and supervising construction of the 12-meter-wide canalized section of the river Fleet, which flowed south through London into the Thames River. He made a model of his and Wren's scheme for the wharves on each embankment, and oversaw the erection of the four competing 100-foot lengths of wharf that were built to compare the merits of the alternative designs; his and Wren's plan was chosen. There is circumstantial evidence that Hooke also designed and supervised construction of two or more masonry arch bridges over the Fleet Canal. All this work made Hooke a rich man. In the 1670s he was earning some £500 a year, a salary equivalent today to several hundred thousand pounds. During this phase of his career Hooke was constantly in discussion with Wren about his own work and his friend's, especially the London churches and, most importantly, the new Saint Paul's Cathedral. As work in the city petered out, Hooke continued as an architect on many private houses, a church in Buckinghamshire, and possibly at the dockyard in Plymouth. He was appointed surveyor to the dean and chapter of Westminster, a post he occupied from 1691 to 1697, while continuing, since the Great Fire, to hold his professorship at Gresham College.

Hooke's best-known contribution to building construction is probably his introduction of the counterbalanced sash window, as discussed later in this chapter. No less ingenious was his use of the inverted arch. Just as an arch can conduct loads around an opening such as a doorway, so when inverted can it spread the loads passing down two columns and distribute them over a large area beneath. This idea was not new, and the use of arches for building foundations in soft ground had been described in Alberti's *De re Aedificatoria*. Hooke used inverted arches in the foundations for Montagu House. As happened more than once, an idea probably first used by Hooke found its way into Wren's work, and he used the arches a year later in the foundations of Trinity College Library in Dublin. In his dome at Saint Paul's, Wren went on to use inverted arches in a particularly daring way, probably for 225
the first time in the structure of a building. At the base of the drum the loads are effectively carried in a series of brick columns on either side of staircases, and voids are introduced in the masonry to reduce the weight of the structure. Beneath the drum, the entire dome is supported on great masonry arches over the nave and transept; such arches, however, are not well suited to carrying point loads from columns. Wren used inverted arches as a transfer structure to spread and transform the concentrated loads from the columns into more uniformly distributed loads that are better suited to being carried by the arches.

Building and the Enlightenment

With regard to applying scientific understanding to the design and construction of buildings, Wren and Hooke were far ahead of their time. The path they blazed became overgrown through lack of use and would be rediscovered nearly half a century later by a different type of explorer, the civil engineers charged with building harbors, canalizing rivers to assist land drainage and navigation, and harnessing the power of water to drive mills. The benefits to be reaped from science would make their mark on buildings only in the last decade of the eighteenth century, a story explored in the next chapter. Yet even without the systematic use of scientific understanding, a number of important developments in building design would take place during the Enlightenment period.

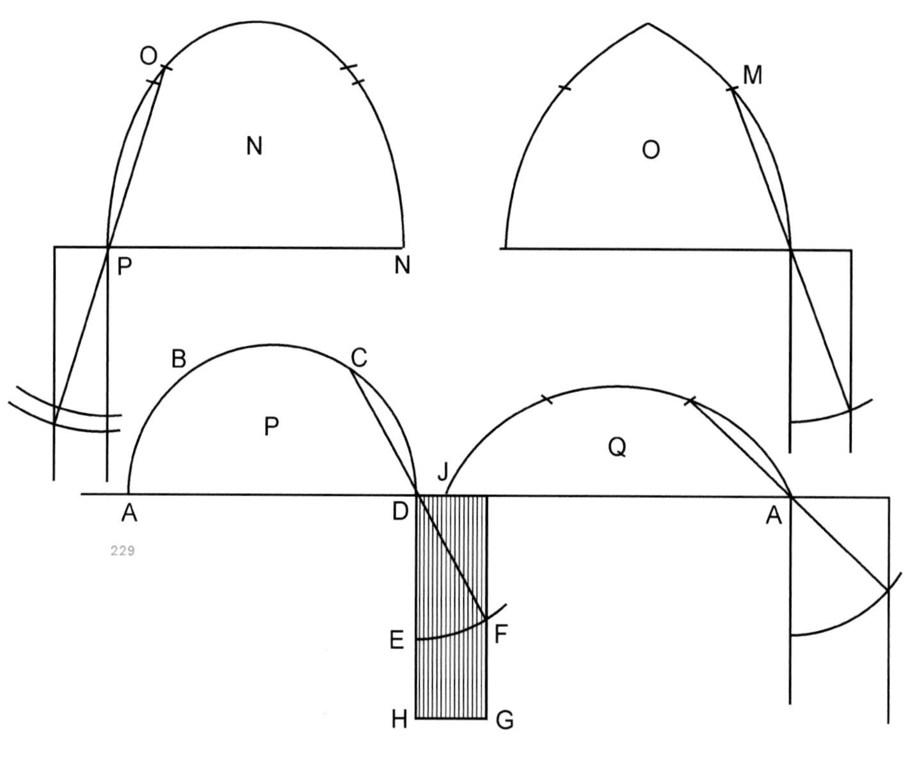

229

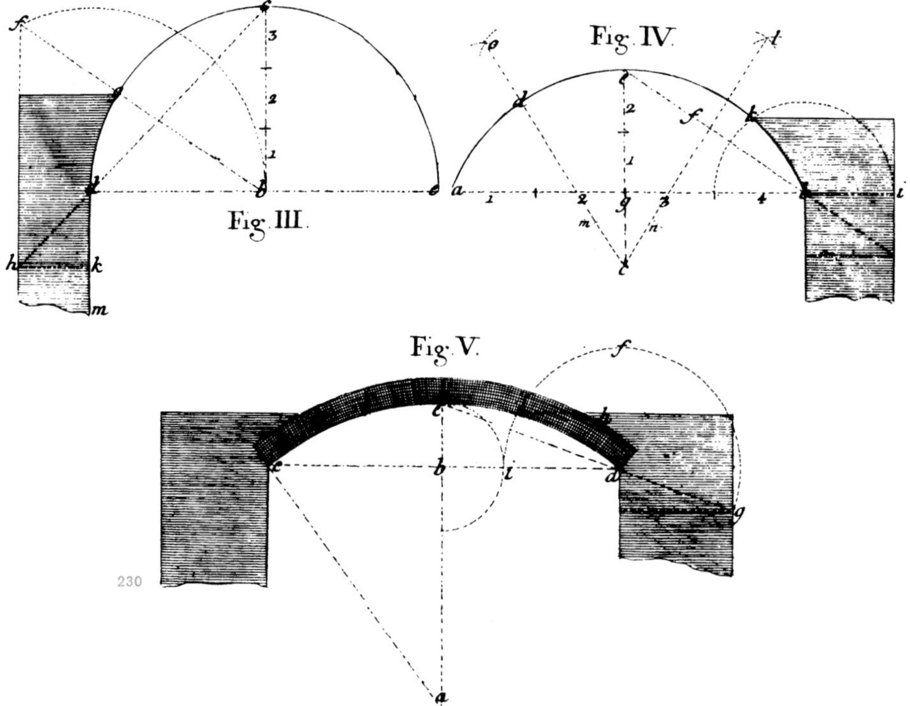

230

It was the prosperity of the age that enabled scientific and design talent to flourish, in terms of both patronage and the buildings and infrastructure of the city. Much of this opulence, of course, was designed to serve far more than merely functional needs. Cities and palaces became showpieces; their appearance became subject to fashion to an unprecedented degree; and, most importantly, their use was inseparably entwined with the new idea of leisure. Although the businessmen directly engaged with commerce and manufacturing probably had as little free time then as they do today, their families, those who invested in and profited from their businesses, and those who inherited this wealth had plenty of free time. They also wanted to live in better surroundings—larger, more stylish, and more comfortable town houses in urban settings and, of course, in country dwellings far from the increasingly dirty, squalid, and unhealthy cities.

Most building during this time was based on experience, common sense, and a growing number of technical innovations in both the building industry and in other industries. Nevertheless, the spirit of scientific study and the use of publication as a means to disseminate scientific ideas throughout the world did begin to affect the building designer. Various people began collecting technical information and guidance of use to designers and builders and publishing them in books or pamphlets.

Published Instruction on Building Design

Published throughout the sixteenth century and most of the seventeenth, the principal guidance on building construction and architecture was still provided by Alberti, Serlio, and Palladio, and derivative books based on these classics. As literacy and numeracy gradually began to reach down through the construction workforce, so building manuals or pocket books began to be printed. One of the earliest, published in 1556, had been the collection of useful calculations written by the astronomer Leonard Digges called *Tectonicon* (see chapter 3, p. 167). This publication was so popular that it was reprinted several times over the next century and a half, yet most craftsmen were unable to perform even simple computations. Well into the nineteenth century pocket books continued to show only tables of the results of calculations for commonly needed data rather than the mathematical methods used to generate them. After the invention of logarithms in the 1610s some carpenters' rulers were engraved with log scales that enabled them to perform multiplication using dividers to add the lengths on the scale. In 1651 the mathematician Thomas Stirrup wrote *The Artificer's Plain Scale: or the Carpenter's New Rule*,
which contained a simple geometric method for calculat- 226
ing board-feet that could be performed using only ruler and compass. Using the properties of similar triangles, it was an early ancestor of the nomogram, a graphical method for calculating the results of complex equations, that was developed in the late nineteenth century (see chapter 7, pp. 374–75).

These early design manuals did not usually include guidance on the sizes of timbers needed to make a floor or roof truss; however, an experienced carpenter would
know this. The first table of suitable dimensions for floor 228
girders and joists was published in 1668, not to serve as design guidance for builders but as a part of the building regulations that were established to set minimum sizes of timber elements in the new construction that followed the Great Fire of London in 1666. These served both to ensure a certain degree of safety in case of a fire, and to enable the authorities to condemn the work of the many disreputable builders who no doubt sought every way of exploiting the desperate need for new buildings by cutting construction costs.

During the eighteenth century, builders' manuals expanded their scope to encompass a wider range of practical information, such as tables of suitable dimensions for floor beams and roof trusses of different spans and, for the first time, drawings. Among the best known of
these in England were *A Treatise on Carpentry*, by Francis 227
Price (1733), *The Carpenter's Companion*, by James Smith (1733), *The Builder's Jewel*, by Batty Langley (1741), and *The Builder's Companion*, by William Pain (1758). They included tables of scantlings for floor

229 François Derand, design rule for sizing abutments for arches, from *L'Architecture des voûtes, ou l'art des traits et coupe des voûtes*, Paris, 1643. For any type of arch, N, O, P, or Q, a line from the third point (e.g., CD in arch P) is produced by an equal length (DF in arch P) to establish the width of the abutment (HG in arch P). 230 Caspar Walter, geometric design procedure for establishing abutment width and height, from *Brücken-Bau*, Augsburg, 1766.

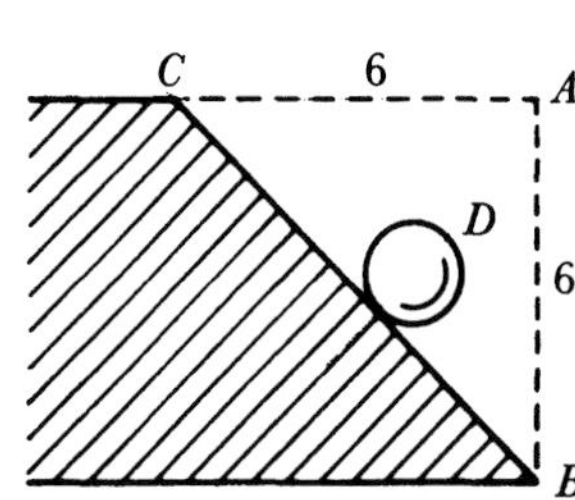

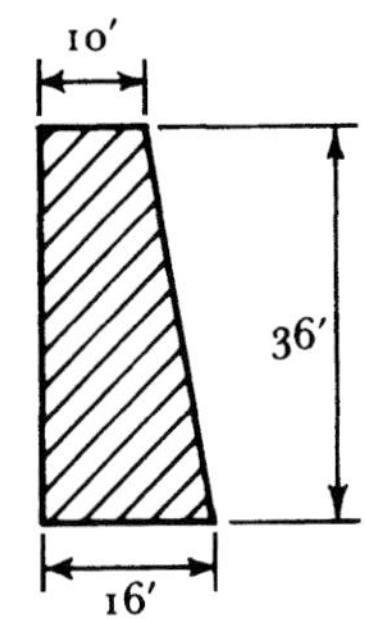

231

timbers in oak and fir for either "small" or "large" buildings—the only reference to the overall scale of buildings and the loads their floors might have to carry. They also showed illustrations of details of carpentry joints, and a selection of standard designs for roof trusses of different spans and trussed girders.

Many books at this time contained geometric methods for establishing the thickness of abutments for various types of arched vaults. The best known of these schemes involved creating three chords of equal length within the
229 curve of the arch, whether semicircular, pointed, or elliptical. Although this design method had already been in use for at least three hundred years, it was first published only in 1643, in *L'Architecture des voûtes* (The Architecture of Vaults) by the French scholar, Jesuit priest, and architect François Derand (1588–1644). The method subsequently became known as "Blondel's Rule" after it was also included in the massive *Cours d'architecture* (Course of Architecture) (1675–83) written by François Blondel (1618–86), the military engineer and architect to Louis XIV. Its simplicity and versatility led to its continued use until the late nineteenth century.

By the early eighteenth century a number of engineering scientists, including Lahire, Bélidor, and Pierre Couplet (c. 1680–1743), had successfully used statics to explain the thrust and stability of arches. Bélidor was rightly skeptical about the rationality of Blondel's Rule, since it took account of neither the thickness (and thus the weight) of the arch, nor the height of the abutment (and thus its stability against overturning). Nevertheless, he included it in his *Science des ingénieurs* of 1729 as a useful design method. Indeed, despite the increasing use of statics, Blondel's Rule and many other geometric design 230
procedures continued to be recommended throughout the eighteenth century.

Toward the end of the seventeenth century the first hint of change with regard to design rules that had been established up to then appeared; this new approach was based not on practical experience but on a mathematical model of the material, soil. The building manual
L'Architecture pratique (Practical Architecture) (1691) by 231
the architect Pierre Bullet (1639–1716) contained all the usual rules and quantities for masonry and timber elements of buildings, and included design rules for piled foundations. He advocated a trial pit to ascertain the types of soils into which the piles were to be driven and to detect any layers of different soil not visible at the surface. For marshy land he repeats the suggestion of a ratio of length-to-diameter of 12:1 that is found in design guides written by "good authors," though he considers this rule a bit conservative for long piles. He then turns to the subject of building ramparts and terrace walls, saying that it is necessary to know:

> *. . . how to give them an appropriate thickness in proportion to the height of soil they must retain . . . This rule has not yet been given by any writer on architecture, whether civil or military.*[9]

231 Pierre Bullet, diagrams explaining the angle of a slope formed by loose soil, and the size of retaining wall needed to support an embankment, from *L'Architecture pratique*, 1691.

Bullet then presents his derivation of a useful design rule, "based on the principles of mechanics." To create his mathematical model of the system, he likens the soil behind a retaining wall to a series of spheres which, if stacked in ideal fashion, would form a stable 60° pyramid. He then argues that, to prevent collapse of the retained soil, the retaining wall only has to hold back the 30° wedge of material between the pyramid and the face of the wall. For the sake of safety he argues it prudent to assume the angle of this wedge to be 45°. Bullet then asserts (incorrectly) that to prevent this wedge of soil from sliding down, the retaining wall will need to have the same weight as the wedge. Assuming the retaining wall is given a batter, or inclination, of 1 in 5, its dimensions can then be calculated. This is one of the very first examples of a scientifically based design rule for the building engineer.

The figure of 45° for the angle of failure of soil is repeated again and again in later works on earth pressure without further explanation, including Bélidor's *Science des ingénieurs*. It is interesting, and not uncommon in the history of design rules and codes, that another, somewhat later author, Couplet, "corrected" the implausible assumptions and faulty statics and proposed a more sophisticated ("better") design rule. Nevertheless, the examples he cited to illustrate the "improved" design method resulted in retaining wall dimensions little different from those derived using Bullet's rule.

Protection Against Fire in Britain

The history of regulations relating to fire hazard in England is typical of many countries. Even in the early seventeenth century, most dwellings in English towns and cities were still made mainly of timber, often with thatch roofs, and fire was a constant threat. Timber-frame buildings with wattle walls seldom had stone chimneys, and relied on vents in the roof or timber flues. In medieval times the outbreak of fires was accepted as largely inevitable, and public safety measures focused on extinguishing them and preventing their spread. Many towns imposed regulations: prohibiting thatch because it conveyed fire easily from one building to the next; requiring that party walls dividing two adjoining properties be of a minimum thickness and height; that streets have a minimum width of around 4 meters; and that balconies of houses on opposite sides of a street be no closer than about 3 meters. Larger houses were often required to have ladders available for firefighting and, in the summer months, to keep barrels of water by their doors. Each town had its firewatchers, and in dry months nightly curfews were often imposed. (Curfew derives from the French term *couvre-feu*, literally, "cover your fire.")

The benefits of using incombustible materials were well known and, indeed, had been required for new buildings by London's mayor since 1189. However, brick and stone were expensive; regulations were inadequately enforced and gradually lapsed, only to be revived with urgency after the next major fire in 1212, which killed more than three thousand people. Alehouses were singled out as particularly severe fire hazards, and were subsequently required to be built of stone. Bakeries and breweries were prohibited from using straw or reeds as fuel, all surplus timber had to be removed from their fabric, and walls had to be plastered and whitewashed; roofs could be covered with only tiles, shingles, or lead.

A number of tragic fires in the early 1600s again brought the issue of this hazard to the fore. Every large town was directed by the English government to take measures to avoid further disasters. Typical regulations included the prohibition of chimneys or flues built from timber. Other such rules called for a gap between brick chimneys and the timber structure of a house; floor beams of a size that could survive longer in a fire; and masonry walls that would be fully self-supporting without a window or door frames inserted in them. Between 1605 and 1661 in London alone, a dozen proclamations decreed that masonry be used in construction instead of timber. In 1656 the town of Winchester ordered its residents to replace all thatched roofs with tile or slate within one year; non-compliance would incur a fine of £10. After the Great Fire of London in 1666, which destroyed more than 13,000 houses, regulations were enforced more rigorously, not only in reconstructing the buildings ravaged by the fire, but throughout the land.

Firefighting equipment at this time, even in large cities, consisted of little more than buckets to carry water from streams or rivers. Mobile, hand-powered water pumps were developed in Germany in the late seventeenth century and exported to many countries, including Britain; in

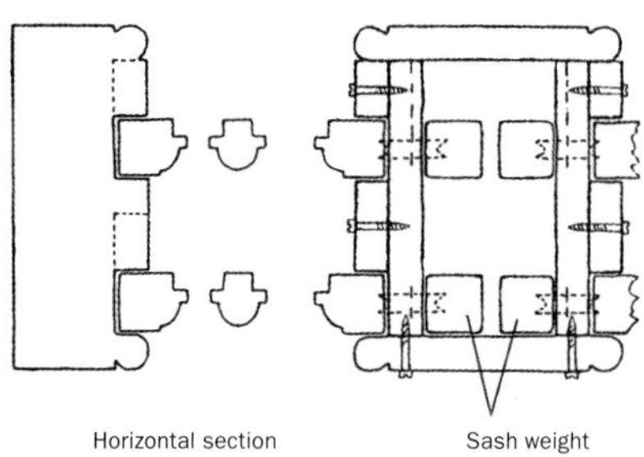

233

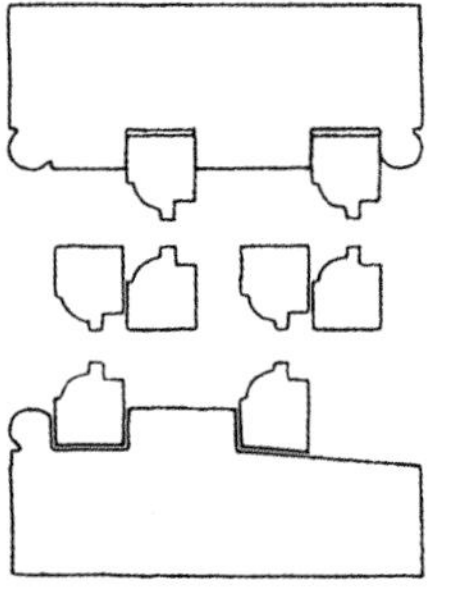

232

234

232 Sections of early sash windows, similar to those used at Montagu House and Hampton Court Palace, London, in the late seventeenth century. 233 Montagu House, London, 1675–79. Architect and engineer: Robert Hooke. 234 Hampton Court Palace, London, south front, c. 1695. Designer and engineer: Sir Christopher Wren.

the early eighteenth century these were increasingly equipped with flexible leather hoses, an idea brought from the Netherlands. The Great Fire was also a major stimulus for fire insurance, first offered in the following year by Nicholas Barbon (c. 1640–98), a doctor turned property developer who used the income from insurance premiums to pay a group of men to fight fires. By 1686 his firm insured 5,650 houses, with premiums for timber frame houses double those for brick. The number of insurance companies and their fire brigades grew quickly in the early eighteenth century. Each one had its own insignia of cast lead fixed to the wall of the houses covered by their insurance. Just as had been reported in ancient Rome, many were the instances of firefighters watching uninsured buildings burn until a premium was paid.

Ventilation, Daylight, Greenhouses, and Ice

Our modern attitudes toward fresh air and the recognition of its importance in creating a comfortable indoor climate were not widespread in the seventeenth century. Many felt that ventilation would allow foul air—of which there was plenty in the days before enclosed drains—to enter their homes from outside. People would shut all doors and windows tightly while burning fires and candles in the belief that the resulting fog was healthier—an attitude that indeed persists with some people to this day. Nevertheless, as scientists began investigating the nature of air, and proving that one of its constituents (oxygen) was both necessary for life and consumed when materials burned, so the benefits of ventilation began to be accepted.

Fires had been used for many centuries in the mining industry to ventilate the tunnels in underground mines. The rising hot air from a fire burning at the top of a mineshaft drew the stale and sometimes toxic air out of the mine, while fresh air was supplied through a pipe from the surface down to where the miners worked. In buildings, the wood or coal fires used for heating rooms and for cooking in the kitchen also provided the motive power to drive forced ventilation. Hot air rising up the chimney drew fresh air into the room beneath doors, and through ill-fitting windows and gaps between floorboards, thus replenishing oxygen for the fire and providing ventilation whether desired or not. The first treatise on how a domestic fire worked, including the role of the chimney in driving ventilation, was *La Méchanique du Feu* (The Mechanics of Fire) by Nicolas Gauger (c. 1680–1730), published in 1713. One of the earliest descriptions of a ventilation system installed specifically to remove "Air made foul by the Breath of so many People and the Steam of the Candles when used there" is found in the Course of Experimental Philosophy by the scientist John Theophilus Desaguliers (1683–1744), published in 1744. Around 1705 Christopher Wren installed four "ventilation pyramids" in the space above the House of Commons chamber to allow foul air to escape from vents in the ceiling, though they were not, apparently, very effective. In 1715 Desaguliers, a fellow of the Royal Society, was invited to "propose a method to evaporate the unhealthful breathing in the House of Commons"; during the course of this work he discovered Gauger's book, which he translated into English in 1715 as *Fires improv'd: Being a new method of building chimneys, so as to prevent their smoaking*. The rest of the story is best told in the words of Desaguliers himself:

> *At the corner of the House in the Cieling there is a Hole which was the Bottom of a truncated Pyramid going up six or eight Feet into the room over the House, set up by Sir Christopher Wren, to let the Air (made foul by the Breath of so many People, and the Steam of the Candles when used there) go out; but it so happen'd, that when the Tops of the Pyramids were open'd, the Air above being colder, and consequently denser, push'd down with Violence into the House, and became a Nuisance to people what sate under those Holes. I caus'd two Closets to be built at the End of the Room above the House of Commons between the two Pyramids above-mention'd; and leading a Trunk from those Pyramids to the square Cavities of Iron, that went round a Fire Grate fix'd in the Closets; as soon as a Fire was lighted in those Grates about Twelve o'Clock at noon, the Air came up from the House of Commons thro those heated Cavities into the Closets, and so went away up their Chimneys.*
>
> *Mrs Smith, the Housekeeper, who had Possession of the Rooms of the House of Commons, not liking to be disturb'd in her Use of those rooms, did what she could to defeat the Operation of these Machines; which she at last compass'd by not having the Fire lighted, 'till the House had sate some time, and was very hot: for then the Air in the Closets, that had not been heated, went down into the house to an Air rarer, and less resisting, whereby the House became hotter, instead of being cool'd. But when the Fire had been lighted before the meeting of the Members, the Air went up from the House into the Closets,*

> *and out of their Chimneys, and continued to do so the whole day, keeping the House very cool.*[10]

A much more visible series of developments in buildings during this period were the improvements in glass and windows, the introduction of which into even the poorest houses also helped prevent the spread of fire between adjacent buildings in densely packed town streets. Apart from providing better illumination, the windows in large buildings of the Enlightenment allowed people to look out onto their estates, if you had one, and on the world beyond. They reflected not only the wealth of the owners but also the developing boldness in the human psyche: This was the age of discovery—of the East Indies, America, circumnavigation, the first modern global empires, and even the heavens themselves. It was the popularity of windows among the wealthy that led the English government to levy a tax on both glass and domestic windows in 1696, principally to fund wars (mainly against the French). This tax grew steadily throughout the eighteenth century—between 1776 and 1808 alone the tax on a house with ten windows rose sevenfold—and was finally repealed only in 1851, the year the Crystal Palace was completed in London.

One improvement in windows was the development of flatter, more transparent glass that provided a better view. Another was the practice of increasing the amount of light that entered a window by using larger panes of glass and fewer and thinner glazing bars and mullions. A third was the development of the sash window, which allowed the window to serve as an effective means of controlling ventilation and which was far more attractive to the eye when open than a casement window.

232 The development and early use of the sash window is another interesting addendum to Hooke's work as an architect. It cannot be stated with certainty that he originated the idea of counterbalancing the weight of a vertical sliding window using lead weights and pulleys built into the casement. At the very least, however, he did play a significant part in its improvement and widespread adoption. As with so many things, he worked closely with Wren in this matter. Wren had seen counterweights fitted to existing sliding windows in the queen's apartment at Whitehall in 1669, and a couple of years later had specified the counterbalance to be built into the casement in some new windows in the same building. It would have been uncharacteristic of Wren to have devised such a mechanism, whereas Hooke possessed such talent in
abundance. While Hooke's Montagu House was being 233
built, he recorded in his diary of 1675 his instructions to the joiner installing sash windows how to prevent them from sticking. The early sash windows (c. 1672) were divided by a central mullion, and it was in Hooke's building for the Royal College of Physicians in London in 1673 that full-width sash windows were first used. These proportions were later used by Wren in several royal palaces 234
and set a pattern that lasted for the following two centuries in English architecture.

Providing this increased permeability of the facade, however, was in conflict with the other key functions of the building envelope: to keep unwanted noise out and to keep heat (usually) inside the building. In the seventeenth century, heat loss in houses of the rich who could afford large windows was solved by servants and coal rather than through engineering.

The conscious use of glass windows to moderate the internal environment of a building was developed in the horticultural world beginning in the mid-sixteenth century. One way the owner of a large country house could impress visitors was to grow the exotic fruits and other plants brought back from newly discovered and conquered lands—oranges, lemons, pineapples, countless decorative plants, as well as culinary and medicinal herbs. So were born the orangeries that were popular in palaces and large houses owned by the rich throughout Europe up to the end of the nineteenth century. The commercial opportunities of glass houses were soon recognized and exploited by the Dutch (especially in Leiden), who led the field in forcing commercial crops in the early 1600s. Already in the 1650s boilers were being used to generate steam that was fed directly into the air in greenhouses, both to raise the humidity and to provide some warmth. Much of our modern understanding of climates in greenhouses, and how they can be controlled, was known by 1700. By this date, for instance, greenhouses were being oriented and their glazing designed to ensure
maximum penetration by sunlight, and flue heating was 235, 236
provided in the winter months. The control of light, shade, 237
heat, ventilation, and humidity was done manually until the early 1800s.

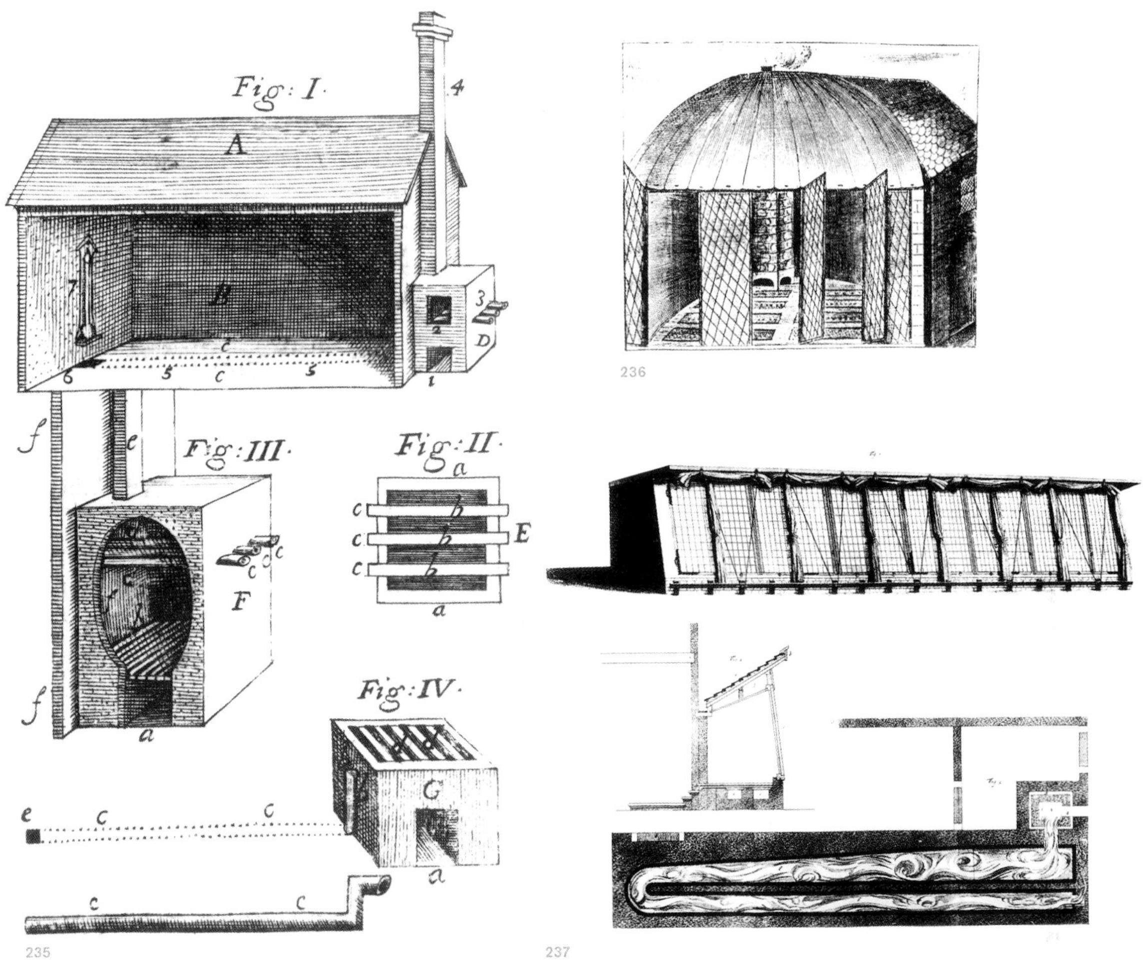

Maintaining a year-round supply of fresh produce on the large country estate was all the more difficult because of the lack of refrigeration in kitchens. The solution was the development of the icehouse, a purpose-built, well-insulated chamber that was filled with ice in the winter to provide a supply of this commodity for the kitchen, and even for making ice cream right through to the next winter. The earliest example known in Britain was built in 1660 for Charles II in Upper Saint James's Park in London, and it is likely that the idea was brought from France. Icehouses spread during the eighteenth and 238
nineteenth centuries with the growth of large country estates, and there are records of some still in use in the 1930s. It is estimated that around 2,500 were built in England alone, mainly between 1740 and 1875. A particularly fine and large example is the icehouse at Petworth House in southern England, constructed in 239, 240
1784; it has a diameter of 8 meters, and three chambers with a total capacity of about 210 cubic meters.

235 Scheme for a greenhouse heated by hot air, from John Evelyn, *Kalendarium Hortense*, London, 1691. 236 A German greenhouse, heated by a wood-burning, tile-covered stove, with full-height windows, from Heinrich Hesse, *Neue Garten-Lust*, 1696. 237 An early eighteenth-century Dutch forcing frame (small greenhouse) heated by hot gases in an underground flue.

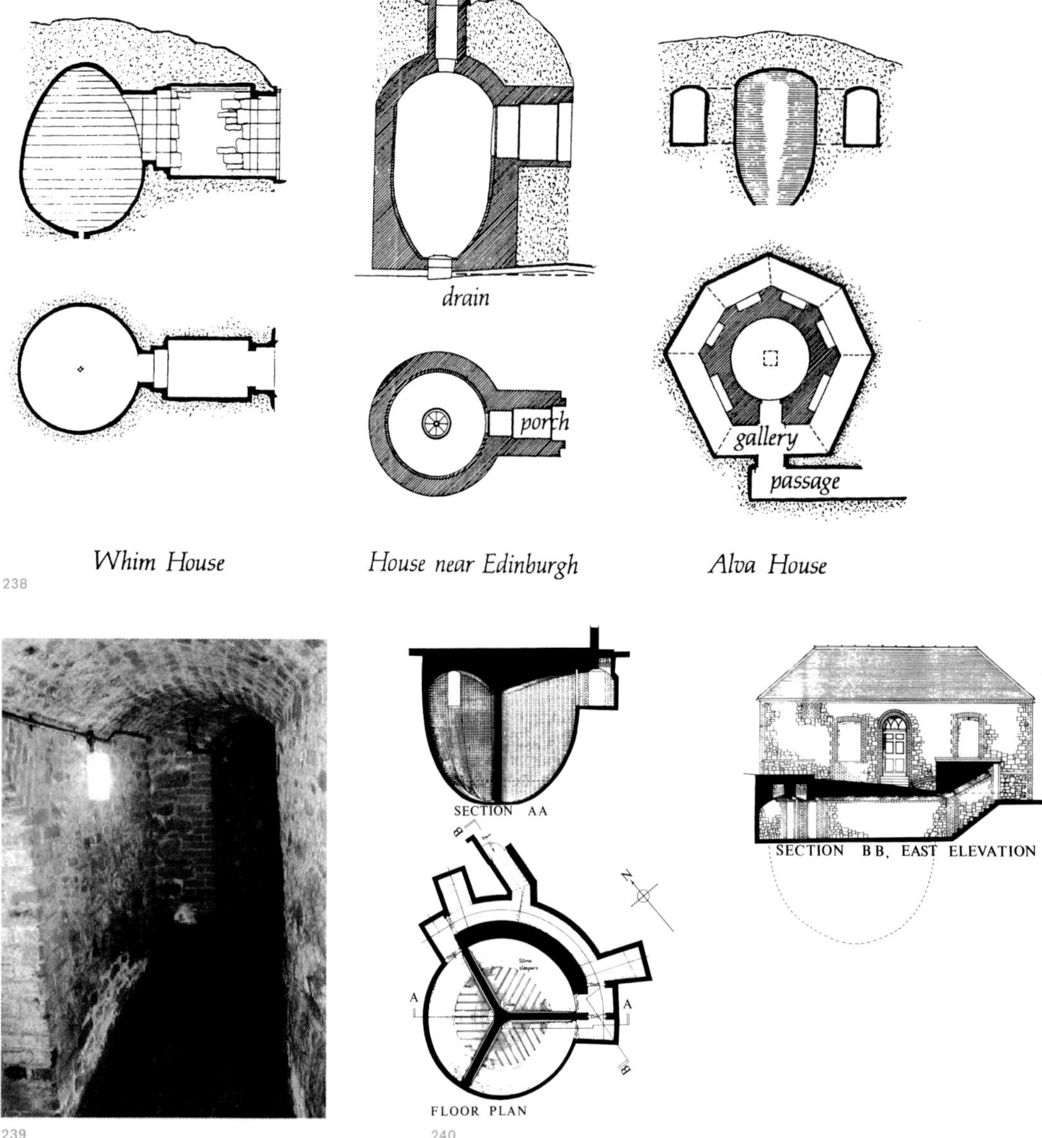

238 Three examples of icehouses built in Scotland in the eighteenth and nineteenth centuries. 239 Icehouse, Petworth, England, 1784. Corridor leading to the top of the ice chambers. 240 Icehouse, Petworth. Section, floor plan, and east elevation.

Although by 1797 the *Encyclopaedia Britannica* provided authoritative guidance on icehouse design, their construction varied considerably, and no standard seems to have emerged; it is easy to imagine the latest icehouse design being the subject of heated debate at dinner parties. Some icehouses were built at ground level , some half underground, and others fully underground. Some were square in plan, some circular, and others rectangular. Their sizes varied from a few cubic meters to over 200. Some were built of a single masonry skin, others of cavity wall construction with the void filled with charcoal, straw, or stones to improve insulation: one near Saint Austell in Cornwall had a cavity about 460 millimeters wide, with plugged holes to drain condensate from the void. Access into the icehouse was through one or more air or heat locks to prevent warm air from entering—one had five doors—and the corridor was sometimes doglegged to prevent direct light (and hence heat) from penetrating to the inside. Though it was generally recommended that the entrance be on the north side of the structure, many were built with access from the south. Trees and shrubs were usually planted to shade both the entrance and the icehouse itself.

A requirement of all icehouses was a drain from the lowest point for melt water; where the water table in the surrounding ground was high, this would limit the depth of the chamber. The drain was fitted with a U-bend to prevent vermin from entering, and the melt water could be pumped out to provide a source of chilled drinking water. Ventilation of the ice chamber was provided by a small pipe leading to the outside. The ice itself would usually rest on a wood grid at the bottom, with a lining of straw around the walls. Many chambers had a hole in the vaulted roof to allow ice to be loaded more easily. Icehouses were generally stocked with ice from nearby frozen lakes, but in mild winters such ice could be very thin and hence melt too quickly. On such occasions the ice might have to be brought from colder parts of the country such as East Anglia or the Lake District or, beginning in the middle of the nineteenth century, even imported from Scandinavia or North America. Although naturally formed ice was largely replaced by artificial ice toward the end of the nineteenth century, many ice houses continued in service into the twentieth century, when domestic refrigeration plants became available.

Science and Civil Engineering

Wren and Hooke were individuals of such exceptional talent that they were far ahead of their time. Teaching others how to undertake their approach would require the establishment of an entire educational infrastructure for engineering. This process would take over a century and came about not in the building industry, but to help meet the growing demands of major military and civil engineering projects—fortifications, ports and harbors, canals, and bridges. The result was the creation of a new profession, that of the civil engineer. It meant the formation of a community that shared certain skills and a common body of knowledge, as well as values and a code of working. Following the example of the older professions of medicine and law, civil engineering became defined by the body of knowledge that could be captured in books and by the formal means by which a person could train for and enter the profession.

The first engineering school of this era was founded in Prague, in what is today the Czech Republic, where a long tradition of technical education existed dating to 1344, when the Prague Public Engineering and Metallurgical School was founded. The new Estates School of Engineering was established in 1707 at the initiative of Josef Christian Willenberg, and was proclaimed as the first public engineering school in Central Europe. While under the leadership of its founder, the Estates School was directed toward military and fortification engineering, but its focus gradually turned toward civilian engineering under the management of its second professor, J. F. Sochor, who was also an outstanding artist, painter, and architect. This new direction continued after his death by F. A. Herget, a distinguished geodesic and hydraulic engineering specialist.

The first technical school in France devoted to military and civil engineering and building construction, L'Académie royale d'architecture, was founded in 1671 under the directorship of François Blondel, Louis XIV's military engineer and architect. The school's curriculum included applied mechanics, hydraulics, stereotomy, and other aspects of civil and military engineering. In 1675 the Corps des ingénieurs du génie militaire was formed, and several other schools of military engineering soon followed, including the École royale du génie de Mézières in 1748, where half the pupils' time was devoted to academic studies and half to practical work, and the École royale militaire, which opened in Paris in 1751. The first state school of navigation had opened in 1682, and in 1689 naval architects were accorded, by royal decree, the title of "Ingénieurs-constructeurs de la marine." The Corps des ponts et chaussées was formed in 1716 to supervise the construction of bridges and roads, which, of course, had both military and civil importance. The famous École des ponts et chaussées was opened in 1747.

Although these schools were formed to produce a well-educated and trained group of military men and civil servants, they also served to create an even more valuable and long-lasting asset: the body of written knowledge that came to be called civil engineering. As lecturers often do, many published what were effectively their lecture notes, producing the very first engineering textbooks. These were entirely different from the illustrated manuals of military hardware from the previous century, which served largely to demonstrate military superiority. Nor were they published with large book sales in mind; their main purpose was to define the curriculum of military engineering education and convey it to every military college in the land. But they also served to raise the status of the engineer by demonstrating the scope and depth of his skills, which usually would not have been apparent to those outside the profession. In addition, such books were a public demonstration of the academic activities of the eminent scientists and mathematicians who taught at the military schools. They reflected the culture of enlightenment and reason about them, a culture that was no better exemplified than in the great tradition of encyclopedias that flourished in the mid-eighteenth century, beginning with Ephraim Chambers's Cyclopaedia, published in London in 1728; this inspired and was soon surpassed by Denis Diderot's remarkable *Encyclopédie, ou Dictionnaire raisonné des sciences, des arts et des métiers* (Encyclopedia, or Classified Dictionary of Sciences, Arts, and Trades), which was published in thirty-five volumes over three decades beginning in 1751.

The most influential author of early engineering textbooks was Bernard Forest de Bélidor (1693–1761), "Commissaire Ordinaire de l'Artillerie, Professeur Royal des Mathématiques aux Écoles du même Corps, membre des Academies Royales des Sciences d'Angleterre et de Prusse, correspondant de celle de Paris," as he described himself on the title page of his first book, *La
Science des ingénieurs* (The Science of Engineers) 241
(1729). His second book, *L'Architecture hydraulique* 242
(Hydraulic Architecture), followed in four volumes between 1737 and 1753.[11] These two books set the standard for those that followed for over a century. Bélidor combined his work as a teacher of physics and mathematics at the artillery college, the École d'artillerie de la Fère-en-Tardenois at Aisne in France, with life as an active soldier—he went on to fight in several campaigns after his first two volumes had been published.

Bélidor's first book, whose full title is *La Science des ingénieurs—dans la conduite des travaux de fortification et d'architecture civile*, consists of six parts. The first deals with how to "use the principles of mechanics to establish the size of retaining walls in fortifications to ensure they are in equilibrium with the force of the earth they retain." His second part addresses the "mechanics of vaults to show how they thrust, and to determine the size of the abutments needed to carry them." The third part considers the properties of materials used in masonry construction, including their densities, and how they are made, transported, and employed on the construction site. As well as stone, brick, plaster, and lime, he discusses mortars and their ingredients, including lime, sand, and pozzolana. Part four deals with military and civil buildings; he first explains how to calculate the strength that different structural elements made from timber need to have in different parts of buildings, then addresses separately the strength of timber as a material and how to use its properties to establish the scantlings of timber components needed to perform their specific duties. He also considers the "good and bad qualities of iron." Part four continues with descriptions of how to construct a number of exemplar buildings. The fifth part deals with the decoration of buildings, in particular the five classical orders and how they should be used in combination. The sixth and final part explains how to design and plan the construction of fortifications and civil buildings, illustrated with several case studies.

Generally speaking, Bélidor's first book is rather in the mold of earlier such tomes. It treats mainly those issues that authors such as Alberti, Rodrigo Gil de Hontañón, Baldi, and Vauban had addressed in the past. It contains some information on mechanics and statics, but is far

from being a theoretical work in that it includes some very practical advice concerning materials and the con-
243 struction of buildings and fortifications. Design guidance is provided in the form of tables of key dimensions—for example, for retaining walls up to a height of 100 feet (30 meters).

The main difference between Bélidor's approach and that of earlier authors is the way he deals with components of any structure made from timber. Unlike typical eighteenth-century handbooks on carpentry, his does not simply give sizes for timber elements to suit different duties; he writes not as a builder or carpenter, but as an engineer. He considers the specific properties of the material—its strength per unit area, and weight per unit volume. Separately, he considers the size of the forces that a certain structural element needs to carry, forces that would be independent of the material used, whether different types of timber, or perhaps even iron. Bélidor also breaks new ground in describing carefully how to set about actually designing and planning a project, a subject addressed only rarely before and since his book.

Within a decade of *La Science des ingénieurs* Bélidor produced the first three hundred or so pages of his second book, *L'Architecture hydraulique*; the next installment was added about a decade later. Its scope, more focused than the first book, concentrates on hydraulic engineering, as the full title of the four-volume opus makes clear: *L'Architecture hydraulique, ou l'art de conduire, d'élever, et de ménager les eaux pour les différens* [sic] *besoins de la vie [et une] seconde partie, qui comprend l'art de diriger les eaux de la mer & des rivières à l'avantage de la défense des places, du commerce, & de l'agriculture*. In the way it treated the subject, however, *L'Architecture hydraulique* was radically different from all previous books on any aspect of engineering, and set the pattern for presenting engineering knowledge in the way that is familiar to us even today. *L'Architecture hydraulique* was also the first engineering book to make use of integral calculus to explain physical phenomena and, ultimately, to enable more sophisticated calculations.

The first chapter begins with three pages of definitions and axioms, followed by a complete treatise on mechanics, including how to calculate equilibrium conditions and the combined effect of several forces using the parallelogram of forces; principles of the five Aristotelian machines—that is, the lever, pulley, wedge, inclined plane, and screw; movement at constant speed and acceleration, both in free fall and down an inclined plane; the rolling of a wheel down a curved incline (which involved the use of integral calculus); and the oscillation of pendulums. This was compiled from the works of the leading mathematicians and scientists of the previous half century. The next chapter deals with friction and how to calculate its effect on machines and on the driving of piles. By this means an engineer could calculate the power—whether provided by horse or water—needed to drive machines of all types. Chapter 3 addresses the science of hydraulics, and the action of fluids on their containers and the surfaces upon which they impinge (such as the blades of a waterwheel). It looks at the discharge of water through orifices of different shapes, which Bélidor again uses integral calculus to analyze.

Bélidor wrote the two volumes of the second part of his book a decade or so later. Consisting of just over a hundred pages, they are devoted entirely to water-powered mills and machines—how to design and construct them, and how to calculate and improve their performance and efficiency.

L'Architecture hydraulique has two striking features. First is the entirely rational approach and rigorous methodology it employs, just like the work of Euclid and other Greek mathematicians and scientists. Each section is numbered—1492 in part 1 and 1200 in part 2—to allow easy reference and to emphasize the sense of structure to the knowledge edifice being built. Second, and what differentiates this publication from all its predecessors, is that Bélidor treats all his subjects in a quantitative manner wherever possible. It was also the first engineering book to include the use of calculus.

As engineering was integrated into the formal structure of military and civil engineering education in France, so too was the process of conveying engineering information by means of drawings. Very few engineers had the drawing skills that Brunelleschi and Leonardo used in developing their design ideas on paper. It was also important to distinguish two roles for drawing: one to help the engineer think in three dimensions and develop ideas, the other to convey the results of the design process to those who

CALCULUS

Calculus is the branch of mathematics by which different properties of mathematical models can be computated. Simple examples include calculating the slope and the positions of maxima and minima in two or three dimensions of any curved graph whose equation is known, and calculating the area enclosed by a curve or the volume enclosed by a surface whose equation is known. When the mathematical model or equation represents a physical phenomenon, such as the rate at which heat is transferred from a radiator to the air in a room or the stresses in a concrete shell, solutions to a differential equation (an equation using calculus) will yield, for example, the temperature of a room at a certain time, or the deflection of a concrete shell at a particular point.

The impact of calculus on mathematics, science, and engineering in the eighteenth century was at least as great as that of the computer in the twentieth century. The origins of calculus lie in ancient Greece, but its modern form and sophistication is due to Isaac Newton (1642–1727) and the philosopher and mathematician Gottfried Leibniz (1646–1716). The notation we use today was devised by Leibniz in the 1670s and first published in 1686.

Of particular note in the history of engineering are the specialists in applied mathematics who used calculus to create, for the first time, mathematical models of physical phenomena such as the movement of objects in gravitational fields, the bending of beams, the vibration of objects, the movement of fluids, the flow of heat through solids, and so on. Remarkably, the four men who contributed most in these early days were all from Basel, Switzerland. Jakob Bernoulli (1654–1705) and his younger brother Johann (1667–1748) were professors of mathematics at the university in that city, both of them concentrating mainly on mechanics. Jakob was the first to consider the deflection of elastic beams; until then, mathematicians had continued with Galileo's interest in the strength of beams rather than their stiffness. Jakob's son Daniel Bernoulli (1700–82) worked for much of his life as a professor of mathematics at Saint Petersburg Academy in St. Petersburg and is best remembered for his research on the movement and flow of fluids. Leonhard Euler (1707–83) was a pupil of Johann and was invited at the age of twenty to work with Daniel at Saint Petersburg Academy. He remained there for 20 years before moving to the Prussian Academy of Sciences in Berlin. In 1766, at age fifty-nine, Euler returned to Saint Petersburg, where he worked until his death.

Euler was incredibly prolific, writing 45 separate works and more than 700 papers. His name is well known to structural engineers as the man who devised the formula for calculating the load at which a column or strut will buckle in compression. Following Jakob Bernoulli's pioneering work on the elastic bending of beams, Euler made comprehensive analytical studies of the bending of beams and their deflected shape. He also introduced the concept of the "second moment of area" as the calculated property that expresses the stiffness of a beam section due to its cross-sectional shape (the I-value, in modern notation), rather than the material of which it is made. This was finally the quantitative analysis that resolved the observations made by Galileo about different cross sections.

Bélidor's four volumes of *L'Architecture hydraulique*, published from 1737 to 1753, were the first books written for practicing engineers that used calculus, especially in relation to mechanics and fluid dynamics, within just a few years of Daniel Bernoulli's original work.

241a

LA SCIENCE
DES
INGENIEURS
DANS LA CONDUITE DES TRAVAUX
DE FORTIFICATION
ET D'ARCHITECTURE CIVILE.
DÉDIÉ AU ROY.

Par M. BELIDOR, *Commiſſaire ordinaire de l'Artillerie, Profeſſeur Royal des Mathématiques aux Ecoles du même Corps, Membre des Académies Royales des Sciences d'Angleterre & de Pruſſe, Correſpondant de celle de Paris.*

A PARIS,

Chez CHARLES-ANTOINE JOMBERT, Libraire, rue Dauphine, à l'Image Notre-Dame.

M. DCC. XXXIX.

AVEC APPROBATION ET PRIVILEGE DU ROI.

241b

228 ARCHITECTURE HYDRAULIQUE, LIVRE I.

on aura après la réduction $\frac{b}{15h} \times \overline{6ann + 4ccq - 10anc}$, qui comprend la même choſe que la formule. (548)

Autre formule pour meſurer la même choſe lorſque le ſommet du triangle eſt en bas.

549. Quant au ſecond triangle CEA (fig. 72) nous ſervans des mêmes lettres, on aura AE (h), EC (b) :: AH ($h - x$), HG $= \frac{bh - bx}{h}$, qui étant multiplié par ydx, donne $\frac{bhydx - bxydx}{h}$; & tirant de l'équation à la parabole $x = \frac{yy}{p} - c$, & $dx = \frac{2ydy}{p}$ pour

FIG. 72. ſubſtituer les valeurs de x & de dx, on aura $\frac{2by^2dy}{p} - \frac{2by^4dy}{p^2h} + \frac{2bcy^2dy}{ph}$, dont l'intégral eſt $\frac{2by^3}{3p} + \frac{2bcy^3}{3ph} - \frac{2by^5}{5p^2h}$ pour l'expreſſion du ſolide : or ſi l'on ſubſtitue les valeurs d'y^3 & dy^5, on aura $\frac{2b}{3p} \times \overline{cp + px} \times \sqrt{cp + px} + \frac{2bc}{3ph} \times \overline{cp + px} \times \sqrt{cp + px} - \frac{2b}{5p^2h}$; & ſuppoſant $x = 0$, il reſte $\frac{2bc}{3} \times \sqrt{cp} + \frac{2bcc}{3h} \times \sqrt{cp} - \frac{2bcc}{5h} \times \sqrt{pc} = \frac{2bcq}{3} + \frac{2bccq}{3h} - \frac{2bccq}{5h}$, qui étant ajouté à la grandeur précedente avec des ſignes contraires, donne $\frac{2abhn}{3h} + \frac{2abcn}{3h} - \frac{2abnn}{5h} + \frac{2bccq}{5h} - \frac{2bchq}{3h} - \frac{2bchq}{3h}$ pour l'intégral complet, lorſque $x = h$, ou que $n = c + h$, ou $n = c + x$, parce qu'on a alors $cp + px = qq = pn$.

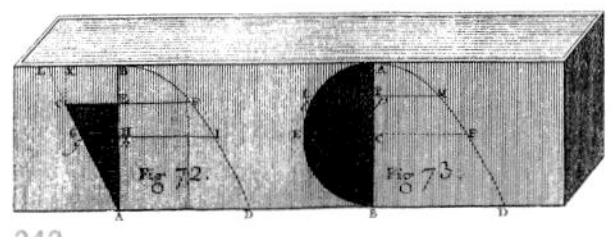

242

241 Bernard Forest de Bélidor, *La Science des ingénieurs*, Paris, 1729. Frontispiece (a) and title page (b). 242 Bernard Forest de Bélidor, *L'Architecture hydraulique*, 1737–53. Page showing the first appearance of calculus in an engineering textbook. The study concerns the flow of water over a weir.

Profil coupé sur le milieu
de la Courtine
Echelle du Plan
toises
Echelle du Profil
toises

243

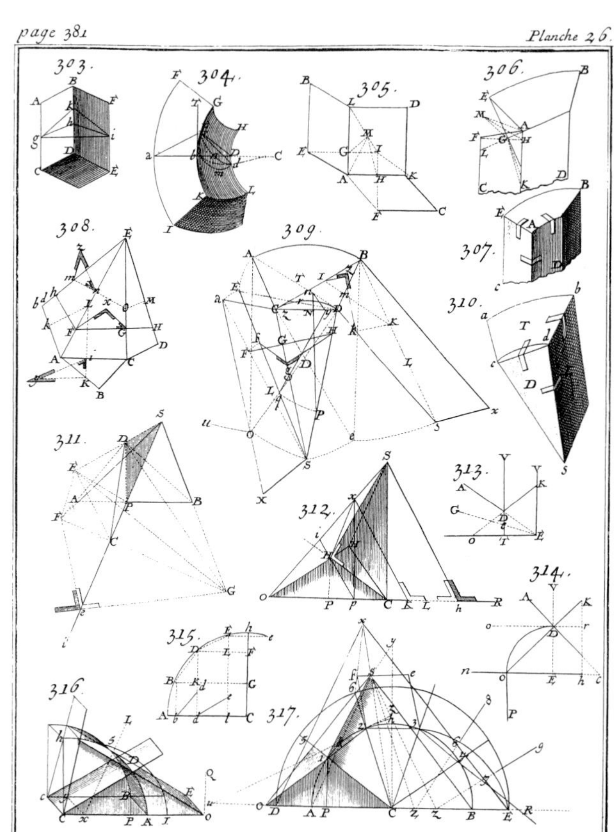
page 381
Planche 26.
303.
304.
305.
306.
307.
308.
309.
310.
311.
312.
313.
314.
315.
316.
317.

244

would have to carry it out. The latter required a more formal and rigorous approach than freehand sketches. The military colleges and the École des ponts et chaussées were instrumental in developing the methods by which such formal drawings should be produced, and drawing occupied a considerable part of the engineers' training. Many of the drawings conveyed not only the final appearance but also the construction methods to be used, and are now regarded as works of art in themselves.

At a more detailed level, there was the need to be able to construct both the final shape of masonry arches and vaults, and to create drawings of the individual stones that would be needed to build such a structure. Stonecutting, or *la coupe des pierres*, was not a trivial matter in complex three-dimensional vaulted structures; cutting stone to shape in the quarry could save valuable transport costs. The greatest benefit, though, was in speeding up the construction process. Without drawings, each new stone could be cut to shape accurately only after the previously laid stones were in place. With drawings of each stone, a great many could be cut to shape simultaneously before setting them all in place with great speed. The problem attracted the interests of many writers, but most famously Amédée Frézier (1682–1773), a French military engineer whose interest lay mainly in masonry construction. He developed a methodological approach to using drawing as a calculation tool in three dimensions. Others before him had conceived of the elevation (*orthographie*) and plan (*ichnographie*) of a building as a projection of an idealized view of the structure onto a flat (vertical or horizontal) plane. Frézier was the first, however, to envision them together in such a way that dimensions in one view could be linked geometrically to the other. His classic three-volume work on stonecut-
244 ting, *La Théorie et la pratique de la coupe des pierres et des bois pour la construction des voûtes et autres parties des bâtiments civils et militaires, ou traité de stéréotomie à l'usage de l'architecture* (Strasbourg and Paris, 1737–39), became a standard text at military engineering schools throughout France. He first addresses two- and three-dimensional geometry in the abstract, and deals with the geometrical constructions needed to generate the forms of oblique, double-curved, and helical 245
vaults, as well as the intersection of vaults. Finally, Frézier considers the shapes of individual stones needed to create such vaults. Bringing together in one place the effort of geometricians of the previous century or so who had solved many individual problems, especially those faced by the designers of ship hulls and sundials, Frézier elevated the subject to an all-embracing science capable of general application.

In these early days of science, we do not find the same degree of specialization that exists today. Apart from his mastery of geometry, Frézier possessed two other noteworthy talents. While pursuing his interest in botany in Chile, where he had been sent to spy on Spanish fortifications, he chanced upon the large Chilean beach strawberry, which he brought back and cultivated in France; it soon became the best and most fashionable strawberry in Europe. He also wrote the first major treatise on fireworks (1706), which remained the classic reference for planning public displays for more than half a century.

Science and Building Engineering

By the 1750s there was available to the building engineer a large amount of useful data on different materials of construction and structural elements. There was also a growing body of engineering science related to the structure of buildings. It would hardly be an exaggeration, however, to say that this engineering science and mathematics had not yet influenced the design and construction of buildings at all.

The list of scientific discoveries and the creation of mathematical models of so many aspects of our universe during the Age of Enlightenment and Reason is a long one. It was clear that the scientific methodology developed during the previous five or six centuries was at last taking man significantly beyond the understanding he had gained from Greek science and from the theological science that largely replaced it during the Middle Ages. Yet there was also a certain disappointment in the air. It became evident that few useful or practical benefits seemed to arise from merely understanding gravitation,

243 Bernard Forest de Bélidor, illustration showing designs for the curtain wall enclosing a fort, from *La Science des ingénieurs*, Paris, 1729. 244 Amédée Frézier, illustration of how three-dimensional stones can be drawn prior to cutting, from *La Théorie et la pratique de la coupe des pièrres*, Strasbourg and Paris, 1737–39.

the planetary orbits, the nature of light and the circulation of the blood, or knowing that oxygen existed and that hot substances cool at a predictable rate. Nevertheless, there was a feeling that such benefits should arise, and scientists and mathematicians continued their investigations with unfettered enthusiasm.

In addition to publishing their scientific papers, scientists and mathematicians during the early eighteenth century also embarked on publicizing their ideas for others to take up, especially those engaged in the "practical arts." Among the most significant such books in the field of structural mechanics were, for example, *Traité de mécanique* by Lahire (1695); *Nouvelle mécanique* by Pierre Varignon (1725); *Traité de la coupe des pierres* by Frézier (1737–39); and *The Principles of Mechanics* by William Emerson (1758). The subject of fluid mechanics yielded a similar list, including *Traité du mouvement des eaux* by Edme Mariotte (1686), Bélidor's books *La Science des ingénieurs* (1729) and *L'Architecture hydraulique*, and various treatises on geometrical subjects that advocated applications to many branches of practical arts, including the design of buildings and ships.

One problem with all these scientific studies was that they were dealing with practical arts that had been developing continuously for at least five hundred and sometimes a thousand years and that, by and large, had reached the limit of what was possible in their respective fields. Practical experimentation had established just about every feasible shape for arches and the realistic limits to their span. The same was true of timber floor beams and roof trusses, the sizes of waterwheels and gears for corn mills, and the shapes and sizes of ships and their various components.

A second obstacle was the means by which the scientists and mathematicians tried to convey their message. No builder or shipwright was going to be persuaded to change his working practices by words written by someone who had hardly set foot on a building site or in a shipyard. Nor, indeed, would even leading designers and builders have been familiar with the mathematical language of the scientists or the nature of the persuasive power that underlay its method. All the practical examples given in the books on mechanics mentioned above were perceived as much too simple and idealized to reflect actual materials and conditions in a real masonry arch, roof truss, or ship's mast.

The usefulness of these scientific manuals was further hindered by the natural tendency of scientists (even today) to make use of the latest fashionable techniques in the belief that this would lend their work greater credibility. Just as fuzzy logic was all the rage in the 1980s and chaos theory in the 1990s, so there is a hint of such a trend in the full title of Coulomb's classic work of 1773, *Essai sur une application des règles de maximis et minimis à quelques problèmes de statique, relatifs à l'architecture*.

Hence, although the scientists were right (we can say with hindsight) in believing that their approach would be fruitful, very few people, generally speaking, had any idea how it could be useful. From the mid-seventeenth century into the early nineteenth century practical and scientific approaches evolved, for the most part, along parallel but separate courses. Only by the 1850s were the two streams firmly linked and the beneficial results becoming clear for all to see.

Nevertheless, it eventually became clear that, in the right hands, science relating to engineering issues did have the potential to provide or improve understanding of something about a building or a ship, especially when it was a design challenge that lay outside common practice. This was what Wren faced at Saint Paul's. He was able to lift his confidence in his proposed scheme by making use of Hooke's hanging chain analogy to help devise an appropriate shape for the brick cone. However, Wren was one of the greatest scientists of the day. Hardly anyone else then alive would have been similarly persuaded by Hooke's insight; no one else would have understood why it could be used to define the shape of the cone. At that time, the intellectual leap was simply too great for other engineers and designers to make, given that there was no experience of a similar cone to rely upon.

It is perhaps no coincidence that another masonry dome provided the first opportunity to use scientific understanding derived from mathematical models to influence a construction project in a significant way. This was the

245

246 dome at Saint Peter's Basilica in Rome, designed by Michelangelo Buonarotti—then in his seventies—to complete the building designed by Donato Bramante and Antonio da Sangallo the Younger. Like Filippo Brunelleschi's dome, it was a double shell and was completed around 1590. To resist the dome's tendency to burst outward, three circumferential ties of wrought iron, each about 60 x 40 millimeters in section, were built in at different heights. By 1680, however, various cracks in the dome had been reported, which led to rumors that it was in danger. Further concerns arose after an earthquake in 1730; finally, in 1743, a detailed investigation of the dome was undertaken, and several measures proposed to remedy the problems. In addition to the radial or meridional cracks to which all masonry domes are prone, there were numerous horizontal, inclined, and vertical 248
cracks in many of the various supporting arches, piers, and walls. The main recommendation was the addition of three or four supplementary circumferential wrought iron hoops to restrain the outward bursting tendency of the hemispherical dome.

Fortunately for engineering history, the reigning pope, Benedict XIV, was a scholar with a keen interest in the developments in science and mathematics. He commissioned three of the leading mathematicians of the day, Thomas le Seur, François Jacquier, and Ruggiero Boscovich, to undertake a study of the problem and make their recommendations. It was published in 1743, and was an important milestone in structural history.

245 Hôtel de Ville, Arles, France, 1673. A stone vault spanning approximately 10 x 10 meters.

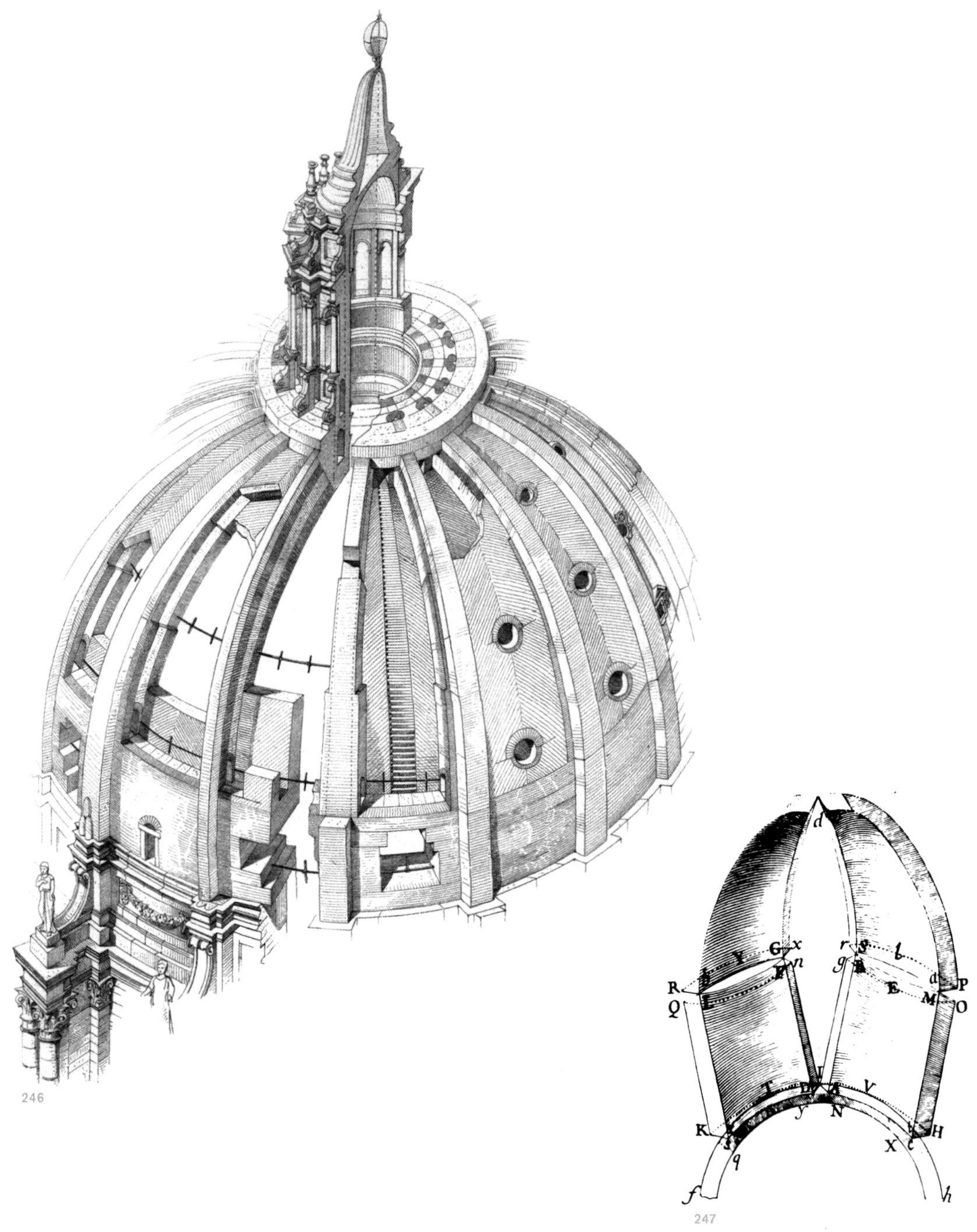

246 Saint Peter's Basilica, Rome, 1506–90. Dome designed by Michelangelo, built to a modified design by Giacomo della Porta. Cutaway isometric showing the position of the iron ties. 247 Saint Peter's Basilica. Illustration proposing the dome's possible mode of collapse, from Giovanni Poleni, *Memorie istoriche della gran cupola del Tempio Vaticano*, Padua, 1748. 248 Saint Peter's Basilica. Diagram of the dome showing cracks and the collapse mechanism thought responsible for them, from *Parere di tre mattematici sopra il danni, che si sono trovati nella cupola de S. Pietro*, Rome, 1743.

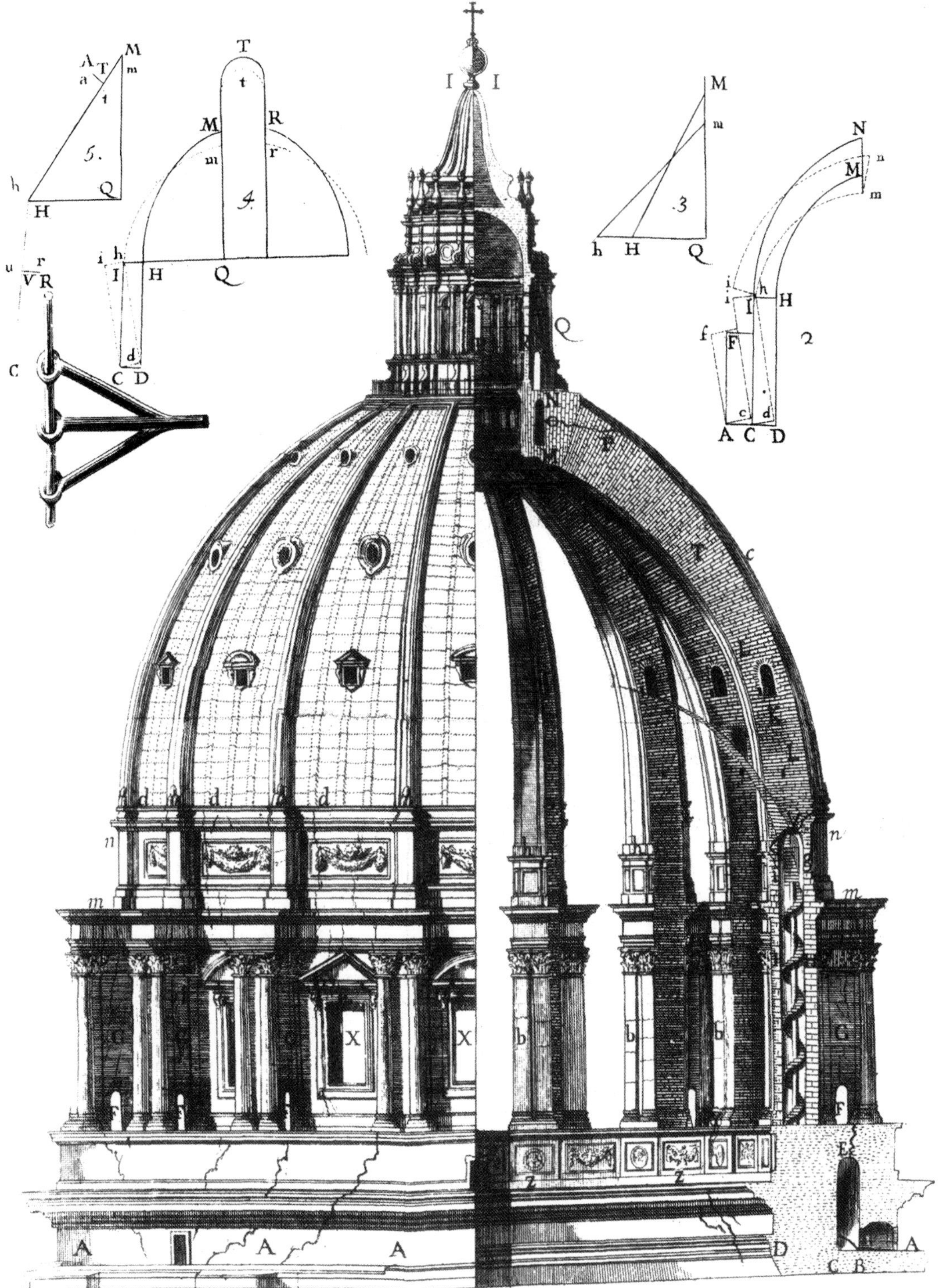

248

The authors devised mathematical models of the dome that they knew to be greatly simplified and idealized and, hence, inaccurate, but sufficiently dependable for their purposes. By calculating the weights of the materials in the dome, they created a mathematical model of the loads acting in the structure. They assumed that the original iron hoops would be loaded up to their yield strengths, and that the sections of the masonry dome remained intact. Thus they made mathematical models of the key materials in the dome, and another for the dome's structure. This treated the dome as a series of ten radial segments that remained intact, but could move relative to one another. Finally, they considered two different ways in which the supporting drum and the columns might behave—one assuming they remained united, the other assuming they could move independently.

The three mathematicians then "applied" the model loads to the model materials and structure, and calculated the outcome using the method nowadays called "virtual work" (a technique that has its origins in Aristotle).

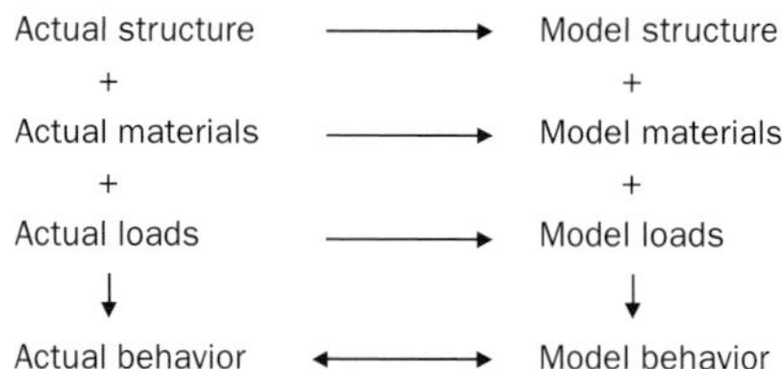

They used the outcome of this model behavior to predict the behavior of the actual structure, and compared their results with the cracks that had been observed. They concluded that, if the first of their assumptions about the drum and columns was valid, the dome was in no danger, even if the iron hoops were absent. However, if their second assumption was valid (that the columns could move independently of the drum), they demonstrated that the original iron hoops would be of insufficient strength and the dome would collapse. Overlooking the important fact that the dome had not collapsed, they went on to calculate the size and number of additional iron hoops that would be needed to prevent this imaginary event. While unrealistic, this conclusion was nevertheless a conservative and safe proposal.

Such an analytical procedure had never before been undertaken, and its novelty was its undoing. The calculations were ignored by the committee responsible for the fabric of the church. The committee's final recommendation was simply to continue to monitor the size of the cracks.

The pope was not satisfied and, as is often the case in such circumstances, he commissioned a second opinion, calling upon Giovanni Poleni (1685–1761), an academic from the University of Padua who was, successively, a professor of astronomy, physics, mathematics, and, finally, experimental philosophy. He also had experience as a consultant in his main area of expertise, hydraulics and hydraulic engineering. He was thus well qualified to take a fresh look at the work and recommendations of le Seur, Jacquier, and Boscovich.

Poleni criticized the model of the structure the mathematicians had used and the modes of collapse they had considered, on the grounds that they did not correspond to the behavior of the dome as indicated by the cracks.
He devised different mathematical models of both the 247
materials and the structure. He ignored the iron hoops and assumed that masonry, in general, had a large compressive strength and zero tensile strength—a fair assumption given that the joints between blocks did have zero tensile strength. He then divided the dome into fifty lunes (half orange slices) and considered the equilibrium of an opposing pair of lunes. He also observed that such an arch would be stable if the line of thrust lay entirely within the thickness of the masonry. Knowing Hooke's second law, defining the shape of a stable arch as the inversion of the corresponding hanging catenary, he made 250
a model using weights proportional to the distribution of weight in a pair of lunes and the weight of the lantern, and determined the shape of the line of thrust experimentally. By demonstrating that this shape did, indeed, lie within the masonry, he argued that each lune was stable and that, hence, an entire dome made up of fifty such

249 Saint Peter's Basilica. Section drawings showing Michelangelo's original scheme (left) and location of new iron ties proposed by Giovanni Poleni (right). 250 Giovanni Poleni, drawing of model used to establish the line of thrust in the dome of St. Peter's Basilica, from *Memorie istoriche della gran cupola del Tempio Vaticano*, Padua, 1748.

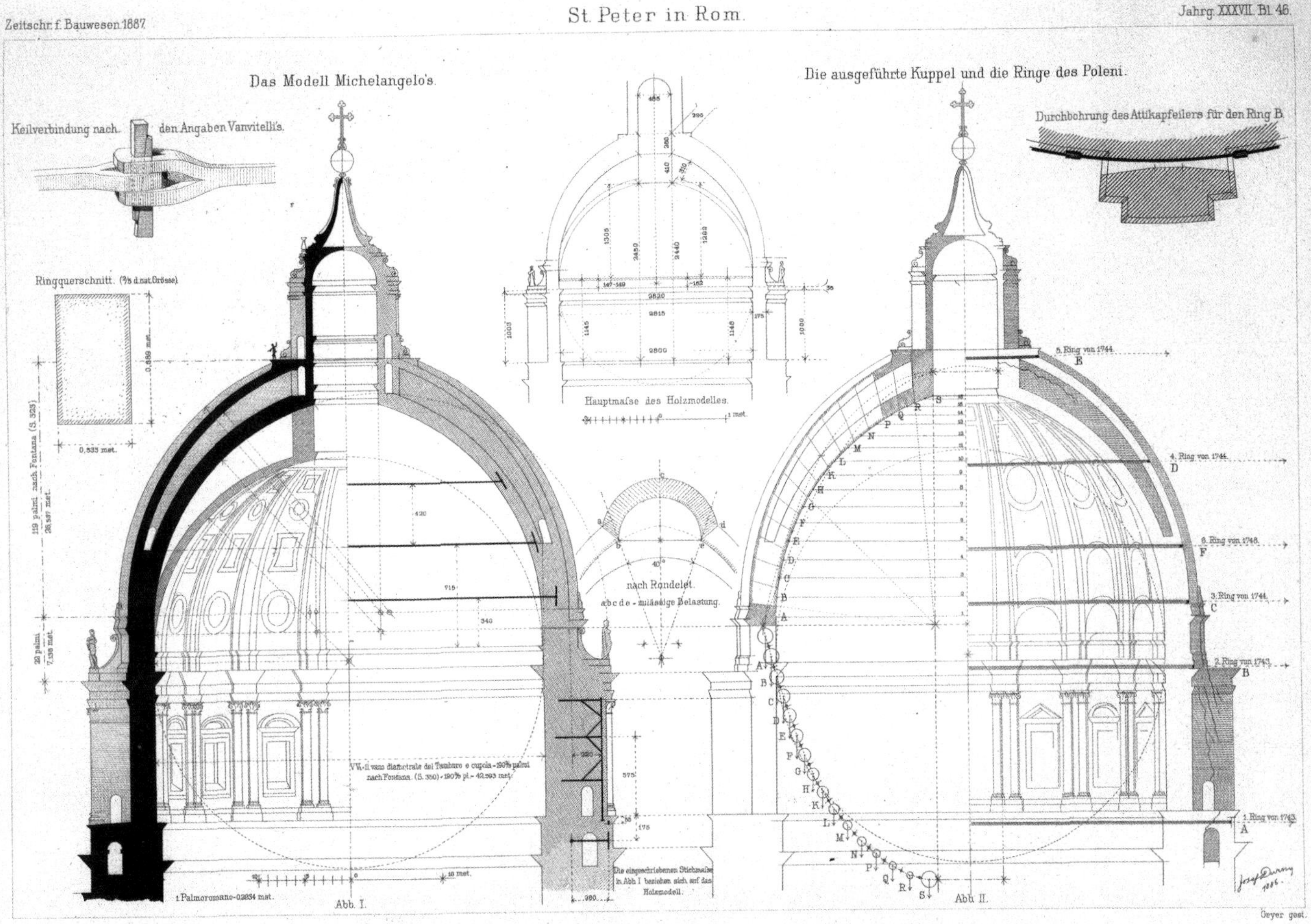

Zeitschr. f. Bauwesen 1887.
St. Peter in Rom.
Jahrg. XXXVII. Bl. 46.
Das Modell Michelangelo's.
Keilverbindung nach den Angaben Vanvitelli's.
Ringquerschnitt. (⅓ d. nat. Grösse).
0,333 met.
119 palmi nach Fontana (S. 323)
26,587 met.
22 palmi
7,136 met.
Hauptmaße des Holzmodelles.
1 met.
nach Rondelet.
abcde - mäßige Belastung.
Die ausgeführte Kuppel und die Ringe des Poleni.
Durchbohrung des Attikapfeilers für den Ring B.
5. Ring von 1744.
4. Ring von 1744.
6. Ring von 1748.
3. Ring von 1744.
2. Ring von 1743.
1. Ring von 1743.
VI. il vano diametrale del Tamburo e cupola = 190⅔ palmi nach Fontana. (S. 350) = 190⅔ pl. = 42,593 met.
1 Palmoromano = 0,2234 met.
10 met.
Die eingeschriebenen Stichmaße in Abb. I beziehen sich auf das Holzmodell.
Abb. I.
Abb. II.
Geyer gest.

249

TAVOLA. E.
FIG. XIV.
pag. 42.

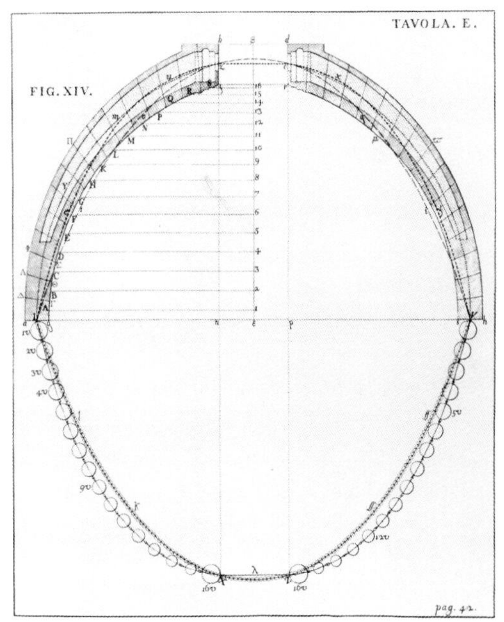

250

segments was also stable, even with the meridional cracks. This understanding of the structure anticipated by some two hundred years the limit state theorems that were developed in the 1950s.

Despite his conclusions, and probably as a compromise
that gave tacit acceptance of the work of his predeces-
249 sors, Poleni recommended adding four additional
wrought iron chains, a task that was carried out in 1744.
Each was made of between 16 and 38 links about 600
millimeters long and 90 x 55 millimeters in cross section.
An interesting footnote to this episode is that further remedial work in 1747 revealed that the middle of the original iron chains had, in fact, fractured. A fifth new iron ring
was added just below the point where the dome divides
into two shells.

By 1750 many leading civil engineers, especially in France, were using mathematical calculations based on engineering science in their work designing retaining walls, arch bridges, foundations, and projects involving the control of water flow. In all these fields it had been demonstrated that the use of such calculations could avoid failures and reduce quantities of materials needed for projects, and hence increase construction speeds. This was not yet the case in building engineering, but the success of the analysis of Saint Peter's dome demonstrated what the benefits could be. This would not be the last time that engineering science was applied to solve a problem with an existing building, or to understand the cause of a failure before it came to be used at the design stage of a project to ensure that the flaw would not arise in future. More generally, engineering science would come to be used in building design when it was seen how it could help avoid costly failures or reduce the quantities of materials needed in construction.

chapter 5

Engineering Becomes a Profession

1750–1800

People and Events

1708–1794 Jean-Rodolphe Perronet
1713–1780 Jacques-Germain Soufflot
1724–1792 John Smeaton
1726–1797 Jedediah Strutt
1728–1809 Matthew Boulton
1731–1800 Victor Louis
1732–1792 Richard Arkwright
1734–1829 Jean-Baptiste Rondelet
1736–1806 Charles Augustin Coulomb
1736–1819 James Watt
1746–1818 Gaspard Monge
1751–1822 Charles Bage
1753–1814 Benjamin Thompson (Count von Rumford)
1754–1839 William Murdock
1756–1827 Ernst Chladni
1756–1830 William Strutt
1757–1834 Thomas Telford
c. 1762–1839 George Saunders

Materials and Technology

From 1750s Evolution of ventilation systems in institutional buildings
From 1750s Development of fireproof construction in theaters
From 1750s Heating and ventilation in mills
1752 Cast iron columns and wrought iron beams used in Cistercian monastery at Alcobaça (near Lisbon), Portugal

Knowledge and Learning

1743 Stephen Hales, *A Description of Ventilators* (first book on ventilation)
1765–1813 Lunar Society, Birmingham, England

Design Methods

1750s Fire engineering approach to theater design, Lyon Theater, Lyon, France
1750s Smeaton's use of models to test watermills and windmills

Design Tools: Drawing and Calculation

From 1760s The *ingénieur artiste*—French combined design/construction drawings

Buildings

1754 Lyon Theater, Lyon, France
1756–59 Eddystone Lighthouse, near Plymouth, England
1757–90 The Panthéon (Church of Sainte Geneviève), Paris, France
1758–62 Naval Hospital at Stonehouse, Plymouth, England

1750 1755 1760 1765 1770

1776 U.S. Declaration of Independence

1788–1829 Thomas Tredgold

1789 French Revolution

1786 Papplewick Mill, Nottinghamshire, England, powered by rotary steam engine

1773 Hartley's fire plates patented

1779 Iron Bridge, Coalbrookdale, England, completed

From 1780s Development of fireproof construction in mills

From 1790s Cast iron beams and columns in mills and warehouses

1792 Development of gas lighting in buildings

1795–1805 Cast iron aqueducts by Telford

1771 Society of Civil Engineers founded in Britain

1771 John Aikin, *Thoughts on Hospitals* (early guide to hospital design)

1773 Charles Augustin Coulomb, *Essai . . . à quelques problèmes de statique, relatifs à l'architecture* (key paper on engineering)

1780s Several écoles d'arts et métiers founded in France

1790 George Saunders, *A Treatise on Theatres* (earliest design guide for theaters)

1794 École Polytechnique, Paris, France, founded

1795 Metric system of measurement

1797 First technical building periodical, Germany.

1799 Bauakademie, Berlin, Germany, founded

From 1780s Statics used in design of arch bridges

1790s Acoustics considered scientifically in theater design

1790s Earliest known design calculations for iron beams by Charles Bage

1775 First "Soho scales" (slide rules) manufactured by James Watt

1770s Orthographic (third angle) projection developed by Gaspard Monge

From 1770s Four-function mechanical calculators

1780 Press-copier patented by James Watt

1770 Cast iron columns used to support galleries in Saint Anne's Church, Liverpool, England

1771 Richard Arkwright's first mill in Cromford, England

1779–81 Wrought iron roof for the Louvre, Paris, France

1786–90 Théâtre Français, Paris, France

1792–93 Italian Works (silk mill), Derby, England

1794 Theatre Royal, Drury Lane, London, England

1794 Temple of the Muses bookstore, London, England

1796–97 Castle Foregate mill, Shrewsbury, England

1775 1780 1785 1790 1795 1800

Engineering Becomes a Profession 1750–1800

Civil Engineering in Britain

The civil engineering profession in Britain developed very differently from its counterpart in France. In Britain, there were formal systems for educating and training military engineers, but the state played no part in establishing similar systems for civil engineers until the late nineteenth century. There was also very little state patronage of civil engineering works; rare exceptions were the construction of roads in Scotland and the redevelopment and enlargement of the port of Dover on the English Channel. By contrast, the scope of the civil engineer's role in France was defined largely by the king and his government's plans for establishing the French nation. This meant a national infrastructure to ensure its defense, secure means of communication, and the safe conveyance of troops and goods within its boundaries. The model was largely that which had served Imperial Rome and the northern Italian states during the Renaissance. A French engineer of the eighteenth century, such as Charles Augustin Coulomb (see pp. 243–44), was a military engineer who would work on the construction of ports and harbors, a network of navigable rivers, canals, and roads, and fortifications. In turn, much of France's industry and manufacturing developed to service the creation of this national infrastructure.

The English navy's control of the seas at this time meant there was little threat to Britain of invasion, and its military construction was limited mainly to naval ports and harbors and the fortifications to defend them. Inland, the pressure to develop the infrastructure came from commerce and industry. Land drainage was undertaken to create agricultural land; roads, bridges, and waterways were financed by the tolls earned from conveying goods and people; the harnessing of water and steam power was driven by the needs of commercial manufacturing and providing water for the new industrial towns. The role of the eighteenth-century British engineer is ideally illustrated by John Smeaton (1724–92). Like many engineers of the day, he worked on land drainage, inland waterways, bridges, and harbors, as well as waterwheels, mills, pumps, and steam engines. Most famously he was responsible for the construction of the third Eddystone Lighthouse (1756–59), built on an isolated rock in the English Channel, 20 kilometers south of Plymouth.

Unlike typical engineers of his day, Smeaton did not serve an apprenticeship as a mason or millwright. As a child he learned to work with iron, making a lathe, among many other things. His father, however, was a lawyer, and because he considered manual labor a pursuit that was neither financially nor socially prudent, he sent his son to London at the age of eighteen to receive a legal education. Smeaton persisted for two years, but finally rebelled to follow his mechanical skills and his growing interest in science. He trained as a maker of scientific instruments, and set up in this business at the age of twenty-three. As his business thrived he began conducting experiments to

251

251 John Smeaton, illustration of model waterwheel, from *Philosphical Transactions of the Royal Society*, England, c. 1758. One of several models Smeaton used to establish the most effective type of waterwheel.

establish how much power could be harnessed from water and windmills. His scientific inquisitiveness and mechanical skills proved a potent combination, much as it had with Robert Hooke, and within a couple of years he was being consulted on engineering matters far distant from the world of scientific instruments. His increasing contact with the London scientific community and the esteem with which his scientific investigations were regarded led to his being elected a fellow of the Royal Society at the age of just twenty-nine.

By this time Smeaton had decided to pursue a career in engineering, and somehow got a commission to design a watermill. This was not, in itself, an unusual commission for an engineer, but in view of the fact that Smeaton was not a millwright, it was little short of astonishing. In the case of waterwheels, he used model tests to demonstrate that overshot wheels generated twice as much useful power as undershot wheels, and that undershot wheels were most efficient when the speed of the water was between two and two-and-a-half times the speed of the vanes of the wheel, not three times, as some emi-
251 nent scientists had asserted. He performed similar experiments to establish how the power output of a windmill varied on four key parameters: the area and
252 shape of sail, its angle to the wind, and the wind speed. In both sets of experiments Smeaton devised an ingenious way of eliminating the effects of friction in his models so that the results would be more reliable when scaled up to full size. Nevertheless, these were not the experiments of a physicist seeking to understand fluid mechanics; they were tests by a design engineer seeking ways of making machines that would serve their purpose more effectively.

In designing the new watermill Smeaton was able to apply general principles, based on science and tested using full-size and scale-model experiments, to an engineering problem in a field entirely unfamiliar to him. Approaching the project as an outsider and "from first principles," as we say today, he was able to challenge entrenched practices. He quickly saw the potential advantages of replacing with cast iron those timber components of machines that habitually wore out—gear teeth, driveshafts, and bearings. Though cast iron was more expensive and more difficult to work, such drawbacks were outweighed by the benefits of reduced maintenance and longer life.

Smeaton developed his knowledge of mechanical and civil engineering by every possible means. He was observant of engineering successes and failures, conducted his own experiments, studied the latest scientific papers, and read the latest and best books, including Dutch books on mills and French texts such as Bernard Forest de Bélidor's *Architecture hydraulique*. He also made a five-week tour of the Netherlands, studying that country's civil engineering works, including many of those described in the books he knew, and he visited Professor Petrus van Musschenbroek at Leiden University. It was on this visit that he encountered the hydraulic cements the Dutch used for their underwater structures. When Smeaton received the commission to design the new Eddystone Lighthouse, he undertook a series of experiments with different hydraulic setting agents—including Dutch tarras (trass) and pozzolana—to establish the best concrete mix. This fundamental work did much to establish concrete in England as the engineering material we know today, replacing the various and variable mixtures that had been available previously (see Appendix 3). Yet another object of Smeaton's inquiry, upon which he wrote one of his eighteen papers published by the Royal Society, was the nature of lightning and the damage it could do. The immediate consequence of this inquiry was that the Eddystone Lighthouse was one of the first buildings to be fitted with a lightning conductor. Smeaton provided a continuous electrical path by which electrons could flow from the sea up to the very top of the building and into the charged air above in order to discharge the clouds and prevent a lightning strike. By modern standards, the path was a tortuous one. To the rock on which the lighthouse stood was fixed an iron chain whose lower end was submerged in the sea at all times. A strip of lead connected this chain to the drainpipe of the kitchen sink, which was also made of lead. The sink was connected, in turn, to the copper flue pipe that rose from the kitchen up through the lantern to a copper ball at the highest point of the structure.

Smeaton was always keen to publish his work so that others might learn and benefit from his experience. He virtually gave up consulting work at age of fifty-nine "so that I may dedicate the Remains of my life... [to] publishing my Works that others of the Profession may be aided by my Experience."[1] His account of the design and construction of the lighthouse (1791) took him several years

to complete and is a classic of engineering literature. He describes the reasoning behind his thinking in developing every detail of the building. He paid particular attention to the pattern of stonecutting, by which he created what is virtually a three-dimensional jigsaw puzzle to en-
253, 254 sure that there was no chance that stones should be-
255 come dislodged.

In Britain, at least, Smeaton is generally regarded as the father of civil engineering, not so much for the works he undertook—though these were impressive enough—but rather for establishing the idea of civil engineering as a profession. The Eddystone Lighthouse made Smeaton's reputation, and soon he was receiving all manner of inquiries for engineering advice. This enviable situation enabled him to work as an independent consulting engineer for the rest of his life. He came to regard his position as similar to that of a lawyer or a doctor—someone who would be called upon for professional advice—rather than as a contractor who would undertake the physical work himself. As he said in a report in 1764:

> *I think it is necessary to give my opinion with that freedom that becomes me in a matter wherein I am consulted, and... where my opinion is desired in the way of my profession.*[2]

A little later he defined his idea of the consulting engineer:

> *I consider myself in no other light than as a private artist who works for hire for those who are pleased to employ me ... They who send for me to take my advice upon any scheme, I consider as my paymasters; from them I receive my propositions of what they are desirous of effecting.*[3]

When working on his book about Eddystone, he wrote to a friend, saying that he considered it:

> *... work that I expect will do more towards the forming of Civil Engineers in the future generation, than any thing that has yet appeared in favour of the profession; and indeed of much more real consequence to the public (if it is supposed that I am myself of any consequence) than any fresh examples I can now give in the executive part; the fundamental principles whereon I proceed.*[4]

Much that Smeaton accomplished is easily recognizable to the modern practitioner of the profession. As Bélidor pioneered in his great book, the translation of real engineering problems into simplified theoretical models was becoming a matter of course for the few engineers who were scientifically and mathematically educated. So, too, was the use of scale models to provide quantitative data for a full-size machine. The results were not very accurate or sophisticated by today's standards, and only very few engineering problems were susceptible to such treatment—the quantities of water flowing through pumps or waterwheels, and the quantities of mechanical work produced by waterwheels and windmills or needed to drive machines. Nevertheless, from Smeaton's calculations of the size or numbers of waterwheels needed to perform pumping duties, we can see that he had already established our modern approach to engineering design.

While Smeaton has become an engineering icon through his diaries and technical papers as well as many of his built works, many other engineers were treading similar paths. However, without the esprit de corps that French engineers enjoyed by virtue of their common training in military college, British engineers lacked a sense of community and identity. The emergence of an engineering community with shared interests and values was finally consolidated in 1771 with the formation of the Society of Civil Engineers. In true eighteenth-century style it was begun as a dining club with about twenty members, and, as such, still exists today. They met fortnightly to discuss professional matters and thus develop the sense of common purpose and what it meant to be an engineer that helped establish the profession we know today. A few years after Smeaton's death, the club was renamed the Smeatonian Society, often abbreviated to simply the Smeatonians.

Civil Engineering in France

In France the emphasis was on learning, and then, as now, the state took the initiative. The famous École des ponts et chaussées (School of Bridges and Roads) was opened in 1747. Naval colleges were founded in a number of the major ports, such as the one in Le Havre that opened in 1773, and the École des Mines (School of Mining) followed in 1783. The first of many Écoles d'arts et métiers (Schools of Arts and Crafts), which were rather less academic than the École des ponts et chaussées, though hardly less prestigious, opened in 1780. Other schools were opened to address the technical needs of craftsmen, too, for instance the École royale gratuite de

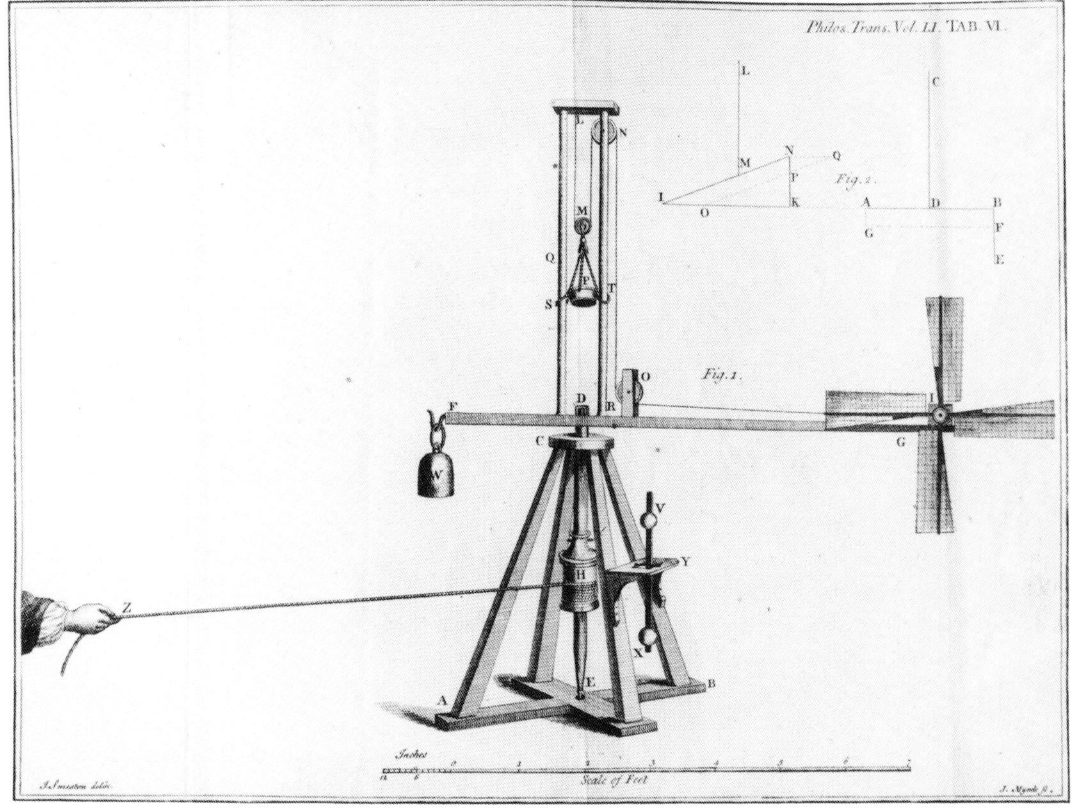

252

253

254

252 John Smeaton, illustration of windmill sail, from *Philosphical Transactions*, c. 1758. 253 Eddystone Lighthouse, 1756–59, originally located 20 km south of Plymouth, England. Engineer: John Smeaton. 254 Eddystone Lighthouse. Wooden model of individual interlocking stones forming the seventh layer. Site engineer: Josias Jessop. 255 (Overleaf) John Smeaton, engraving of Eddystone Lighthouse, from *A Narrative of the Building and a Description of the Construction of the Eddystone Lighthouse with Stone*, London, 1791.

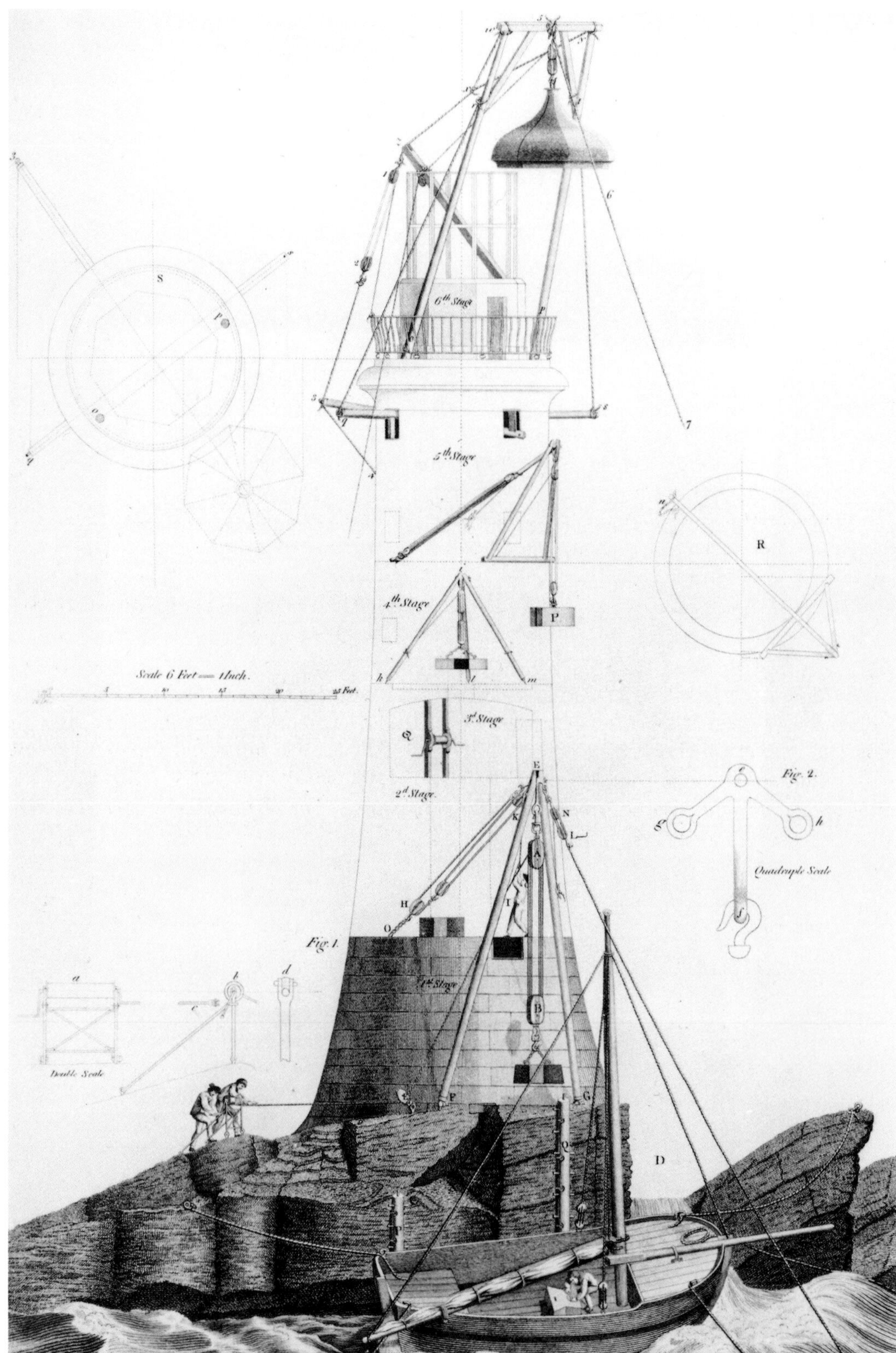
6th Stage
5th Stage
4th Stage
3d Stage
2d Stage
1st Stage
Scale 6 Feet = 1 Inch.
Fig. 1.
Fig. 2.
Quadruple Scale
Double Scale
S
R
P
D

255

dessin (the Royal Free School of Drawing), which was founded in 1766.

Under the directorship of the highway and bridge engineer Jean-Rodolphe Perronet (1708–94), the principal aim of the École des ponts et chaussées was to provide young engineers with a rational, analytical, and technical education. Perronet introduced a broad curriculum of mathematics and the physical sciences and used a number of competitions in different branches of the engineer's art —drawing, road design, bridges, river and maritime projects, architecture, and mapmaking—to test his students' intellectual skills in both deconstruction and construction. However, Perronet's radical scientific approach was not accepted calmly, since it was seen as a threat to the traditional French engineering concept of *solidité*, which had been the engineer's principal skill to deliver in his work. Solidité was more than a qualitative measure of strength and stability; it also embodied the appropriate balance between correct dimensions, good construction, and aesthetic appeal, and was seen rather as an unchanging quality. Perronet's mathematical and rational study of bridges and buildings, on the other hand, indicated that they might be constructed using less material, and this would mean changes in the way things were built. Debates about the relative merits of solidité and the scientific approach were overshadowed by the French Revolution of 1789. Once the government stabilized, however, the state finally accepted the benefits of the new ways of educating engineers. New schools were formed with the aim of polytechnic instruction—a multidisciplinary approach to the applied sciences and technical arts. The new École des ponts et chaussées had a broader mission than its predecessor. Courses were to be based on the very latest mathematics and physics and taught by the best possible academics. At first, however, it was not clear just how this tuition would actually work to the benefit the future engineer; as in much of French life following the Revolution, the idealism of theoretical study seemed to have only an indirect relevance to the real world.

Many of the great engineering scientists at this time were equally interested in mechanics, hydraulics, materials science, physics, and chemistry. Perhaps the best example of this kind of multitalented individual of the eighteenth century is Charles Augustin Coulomb (1736–1806). Although better known today by physicists and electrical engineers for the unit of electrical charge named after him, and for his work on electricity and magnetism, this work was done toward the end of his life after a full and successful career as a military engineer.

Coulomb attended school in Montpelier, in southern France, and in his late teens was introduced to the local Société royale des sciences, which held meetings to discuss scientific matters, undertook scientific research, and offered instruction in mathematics, anatomy, chemistry, botany, and physics. On the strength of a paper he presented on geometry, he was elected as a member at age twenty-one. During the following fifteen months he was employed by the society, attended its meetings regularly, and submitted other papers on mathematics and astronomy. He then decided on a military career and took a leave of absence to go to Paris to study for the entrance examination for the École du génie (School of Military Engineering) at Mézières, in northeastern France, which was then the best in the country. There Coulomb studied the standard engineering texts by Bélidor and Amédée Frézier, and designed and constructed many arches, bridges, and retaining walls as part of his practical training. He studied there for a year, graduating in 1761 at the age of twenty-five. After little more than two years, he was appointed to undertake the construction of new fortifications on the West Indies island of Martinique, where he worked for eight years with up to twelve hundred men in his charge. It was during this period that he began to develop his ideas about the science of engineering, drawing heavily on day-to-day observations of the large excavation and construction works he supervised.

On his return from Martinique in 1772, Coulomb managed to combine his military career with research and the publication of papers on a wide range of engineering subjects. Apart from his memoir on statics, discussed below, these works discussed topics ranging from the application of force to the possibility of aerial flight by man. On the strength of these essays, as well as a prize-winning paper on the design and construction of magnetic compasses, he was elected to the Académie des sciences in Paris in 1781. His interest in magnetism and electricity grew, and the seven papers he presented to the Académie between 1781 and 1795 provided the foundation for our modern understanding of electricity and magnetism. He even made a significant contribution to botany: when forced to live outside Paris to escape the turmoil that followed the French Revolution, he conducted experiments on poplar trees, establishing that sap flows in the trunk only through the central medullary canals. Despite this attention to other branches of science, he continued his work on engineering subjects of military importance, including a visit to the Royal Naval Hospital in Plymouth, England, to study its advanced ventilation design. During the 1780s and 1790s he wrote over three hundred papers or reports on machines, canals and navigation, structural engineering, public safety, health, and education.

Coulomb brought to engineering science the potent combination of practical engineering experience, theoretical and academic rigor, and a mastery of the role of experiments in developing and testing explanations of physical phenomena. His work in structural and civil engineering was driven mainly by the desire to design and build better fortifications and to find better solutions to the challenges that military engineers faced. In 1779 Coulomb took up the challenge set by the military academy at Rouen for its annual engineering prize to devise a means for removing a huge boulder that was submerged under the river Seine and interfered with navigation. In his paper he described a floating chamber that could be lowered over an obstacle; once lowered into position, workers could enter a sealed chamber through which a constant supply of fresh air would be pumped. Excavated materials would be removed through a series of air locks. Coulomb's calculations included the amount of air required by the workers involved, as well as the quantities of men and pumps needed to deliver the necessary number of air changes per hour. So well received were his proposals that they were published in the form of a book, *Recherches sur les moyens d'exécuter sous l'eau toutes sortes de travaux hydrauliques sans employer aucun épuisement* (Research on methods of performing all kinds of hydraulic work underwater without drainage) (1779), which became an engineering best-seller and was reprinted several times during the following fifty years.

Coulomb's primary contribution to building engineering was his *Essai sur une application des règles de maximis et minimis à quelques problèmes de statique, relatifs à l'architecture* (1773). Unlike the works of Bélidor and others, Coulomb's essay was written not as the basis for a course of lectures but as a scientific paper presented to the Académie des sciences in Paris. It is surely one of the most succinct and far-reaching works in the whole of engineering. In just forty pages (and two plates of illustrations) he deals with all the major issues facing the building engineer of the eighteenth century: the strength of columns, the thrust and stability of arches, the strength of beams, the strength of soils, and the thrust of soil on retaining walls. His treatment of columns, arches, and beams consists of a critical review and commentary on the then-current engineering science of these structural elements. His work on the behavior of soils and the thrust of soil on retaining walls, however, is almost entirely original, and he is rightly acclaimed as the father of soil mechanics. He proposed a new model for soil to account for its strength and its eventual failure in shear, by the formation of a slip plane. Coulomb's model of the material, unlike those of his predecessors, incorporated two independent mechanical properties for soil: its cohesion, or the degree to which the soil particles stick together; and its internal friction, or resistance to sliding, which depends on the force or pressure acting perpendicular to the plane of sliding. This relationship, which makes it possible to calculate the shear strength of soils, is still called "Coulomb's equation" and, with due account taken of the presence of groundwater (which Coulomb ignored) is still in regular use today.

It is regrettable that Coulomb did not fulfill one proposal he made to the Académie des sciences, which was to rewrite Bélidor's *Architecture hydraulique* and increase its scope to embrace the whole of civil and military engineering science.

Of the many significant contributions to engineering by the French military engineering corps, few would have such wide-reaching influence as the development of representing the three-dimensional world on paper. The French had already developed the art of representational drawing to a high degree, but such drawings did not provide the user with lengths or distances in the third dimension, out of the plane of the plan or section. In particular, these kinds of illustrations were of little use in setting out the complex forms of fortifications in an irregular, three-dimensional, hilly landscape—one of most important duties of the military engineer. Not only did the plan and section of the works have to be set out in rugged terrain; it was also essential to situate the whole so that the amounts of earth cut from one part of the site and used as fill in other areas were more or less balanced in order to reduce construction time and costs. Added to this was the equally complicated matter of "defiling" the fortification. This was the means by which the height of the fort and its individual parts were established in relation to the nearest high vantage points from which enemies could fire their guns. The whole process was extremely difficult to calculate using three-dimensional coordinate geometry, an approach that was highly prone to error and could take several weeks. Imagine the surprise of his commanding officer when the young Gaspard Monge (1746–1818) completed such a task in only few days. The commandant's first reaction was disbelief but, on checking the work, turned to wonder.

Monge had devised an entirely new approach to dealing with complex three-dimensional geometry in two-dimensional drawings: the technique that would become known as descriptive geometry or, in Britain, orthographic projection. In the English-speaking world, we know it today as third-angle projection. Its particular advantage was that, from any two views or sections of an object, any third view could be constructed by geometrical means, with complete accuracy. This was especially useful for establishing the true length of any line, which in most views would appear foreshortened. Using descriptive geometry, a drawing could always be created from a point of view perpendicular to any line, so that its length on the
256 drawing represented its true length. The technique could
also be used to locate, in three dimensions, the point at
which two lines intersect, or the line along which any two
257 planes or curved surfaces would intersect.

The importance of orthographic projection and its use in determining precise measurements in three dimensions was enhanced by an independent development in France: the establishment in 1795 of the universal metric system. Previously, each different region of Europe, and even individual cities, had its own standard measure of length. A drawing with dimensions notated in feet and inches from a town in Germany would not have been immediately useful in England, Italy, or France. This barrier disappeared in much of continental Europe when the meter was adopted as the general standard of measurement.

It was quickly recognized that descriptive geometry was an extremely powerful tool; however, its publication was prevented for nearly three decades on the grounds that it was a military secret. Monge first taught his method at the military school of Mézières, but during a short time as a government minister after the Revolution, Monge campaigned for a new type of engineering curriculum, a key part of which would be his descriptive geometry. As director of the École polytechnique, he delivered a course of lectures from 1794 to 1809 following a simple strategy: he would first teach his technique to a new generation of engineering teachers, who then took it into nearly every school in France. During the nineteenth century descriptive geometry spread, in slightly differing versions, throughout the world.

Iron and Fireproof Construction: The Early Use of Iron

Already by the middle of the eighteenth century it was becoming clear that the building industry could benefit from the many developments in mathematical and scientific thought that underpinned the Age of Reason. However, while construction materials and methods remained much as they had for many centuries, the new ways of thinking had little to teach the builder or building designer. This situation would change only when a new material was introduced into the building industry, one that did not have a long history of continuous development and improvement. That material was iron.

Iron, of course, was not a new material at all. Wrought iron, shaped by repeated heating and forging, was the material of the Iron Age; its strength and ductility made it suitable for all manner of tools, implements, and weapons. Cast iron, formed by pouring molten iron into a mold, required much higher furnace temperatures and was a more recent development. (The important differences between wrought and cast iron are discussed in detail in Appendix 2.) By around 1600 England had a near monopoly in making and exporting cast iron cannon as a cheaper alternative to those made of bronze. In 1620 Sweden joined this branch of the international arms race, and in 1697 there is mention of a French iron foundry casting a cannon weighing nearly a ton; the foundry had

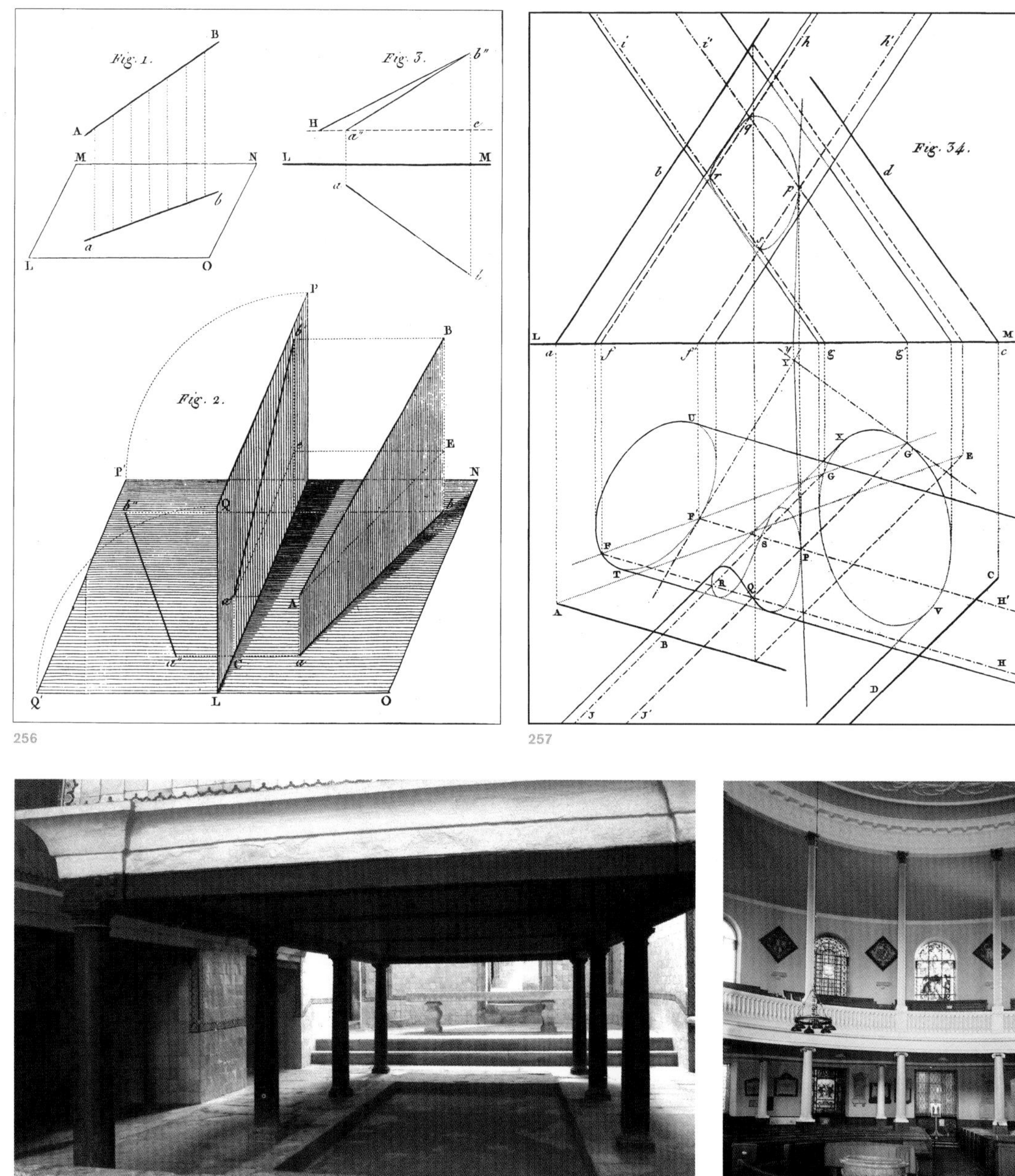

256 257 258 259

256 Gaspard Monge, plate illustrating method for projecting views of an object in space onto flat planes to generate true dimensions, from *Géometrie descriptive*, 1799. 257 Gaspard Monge, plate illustrating the application of his method of descriptive or projective geometry. 258 Cistercian Monastery at Alcobaça, near Lisbon, Portugal, 1752. Masonry hood over kitchen hearth. 259 Saint Chad's Church, Shrewsbury, England, 1790–92. Architect: George Steuart. Interior with cast iron columns supporting balcony and roof.

the facility to create larger castings by combining the output of four similar blast furnaces on the site. Thus, by 1750 or so, every naval shipyard and military arsenal in Europe would probably have had the capacity to cast iron objects of the size and weight of a column for use in a building, though at a cost much greater than the stone or timber equivalent. It is likely that this is the origin of the cast iron columns and wrought iron beams used in 1752 to support the huge hood over the hearth in the kitchen of the Cistercian monastery at Alcobaça, near Lisbon, in Portugal—the Cistercians were rich and their monastery was not far from the arsenal of the powerful Portuguese
258 navy. The brick hood, around 12 meters tall, is supported on eight wrought iron beams 2.75 meters long and 140mm deep that are, in turn, supported on eight cast iron columns, 1.8 meters tall and 180mm in diameter. These are the earliest known columns made from cast iron and beams made from wrought iron. The military arsenal in Saint Petersburg, Russia, was probably the origin of an entire house made of cast iron that the Italian adventurer and lover Giovanni Casanova mentions in his account of a visit to the city in the 1760s.

The next known use of cast iron columns was during 1770–72 to support the galleries in Saint Anne's Church in Liverpool, England. A short time later they were used near Ironbridge, the heart of the English iron industry. When the Bishop of Lichfield and Coventry consecrated the new All Saints Church at Wellington, some twelve miles east of Shrewsbury in Shropshire, in July 1790, he commented favorably on "the cast-iron Pillars by which the Galleries and Roof are supported, which…gave a superior Lightness to anything of the kind he had ever seen."[5] At Saint Chad's Church in Shrewsbury, completed in 1792, two tiers of cast iron
259 columns rise over 11 meters to the ceiling. Both All Saints and Saint Chad's churches were only a few miles from Coalbrookdale, the location of the largest ironworks in Britain, where the world's first iron bridge was erected in 1779. Cast iron made its first appearance in London at the Temple of the Muses bookshop in Finsbury Square, owned by James Lackington, which
260 opened in 1794. This structure, too, was praised especially for the large, open interior space made possible by using the thin columns. This early use of cast iron in England was driven mainly by the fact that such columns could be made more slender than masonry or timber alternatives. There is no suggestion that it was chosen for its fireproof qualities. It had been the same with the earliest use of wrought iron in buildings.

The French champion of neoclassical architecture, Jacques-Germain Soufflot (1713–80) revived Claude Perrault's technique of using wrought iron cramps in masonry construction in the early 1770s when he added a portico to the church of Sainte Geneviève in Paris, renamed the Panthéon after the French Revolution. Here he 261
extended the use of iron considerably, both in quantity and in technique. To help support the flat arch in the portico, for example, he used wrought iron in an approach that at least hints at the way steel is employed today in reinforced concrete, specifically to carry tension forces. 262, 264
The project engineer for this job, Jean-Baptiste Rondelet (1743–1829), would later illustrate this and other early remarkable uses of wrought iron in his encyclopedic book *Traité théorique et pratique de l'art de bâtir* (1802–17).

In 1776 Soufflot was invited to devise a means of housing the king's collection of paintings in the long gallery of the Louvre Palace, as well as a new entrance and stairway to provide access. To cover this staircase he proposed, in 1779, a roof with an external mansard profile and coved interior and a structure made entirely of wrought iron. The components, connections, and assem- 263
bly techniques were developed from those he had used previously at the Panthéon, and all the iron elements were of square or rectangular cross section. The roof spanned 16 meters and the iron frame supported a central glazed skylight spanning 5 meters that lit the stairwell beneath.

This roof, completed in 1781, a year after Soufflot's death, is the earliest known example of using wrought iron for a major structural element of a building. As with earlier uses of wrought iron by Soufflot and others, it was probably designed without any significant use of statics. However, it would have been well within the skills of both Soufflot and Rondelet to calculate a suitable cross sectional area of some of the iron members using their knowledge of timber roof structures and data about the strengths of iron and timber. To the modern eye there is no clear statical rationale for how the structure was thought to provide the required strength and stability. In particular, we see neither the triangulation now

260

expected in a truss, nor the clear intention that a structural element should work in compression, tension, or bending. The overall form of the roof was largely constrained by architectural requirements, while the size and arrangement of internal (invisible) structural members were influenced mainly by what it was possible to make in wrought iron and the practicalities of assembly. Large timber roofs and the timber structures built as temporary works for masonry vaults and centering for arch bridges would have served as reliable general precedents for the structural scheme. It is interesting, though, that the use of wrought iron for roof structures did not stimulate the development of more rational forms using statics, or a more economical use of the material. With royal patronage, economy was probably not a strong driving force.

Theaters and the Dawn of Fire Engineering

Theater, opera, and music came to form an especially prominent part of the life of leisure that characterized the Age of Enlightenment and was made possible by the period's newfound wealth and general prosperity. Examples of these ranged from royal patronage, such as Prince Esterházy of Hungary's support of the Austrian composer Franz Joseph Haydn, to the tens of thousands of amateur musicians playing in the drawing rooms or music rooms of newly built houses in both town and country. As the social value of music and theater grew, so the commercial potential of these arts was recognized, and beginning in the mid-seventeenth century public theaters and opera houses were built in most cities and in many smaller towns too.

Until this time, musical and theatrical performances had taken place in whatever large rooms were available, and generally these were far from satisfactory for performers and audience alike. When one Parisian theater troupe was seeking a new type of performance space in the 1540s, it had the idea of converting an existing indoor court from the game *jeu de paume* or "real [royal] tennis," as it was called in Britain. (The fashion for this sport waxed and waned, with a peak of about 1800 jeu de paume courts in Paris alone in the

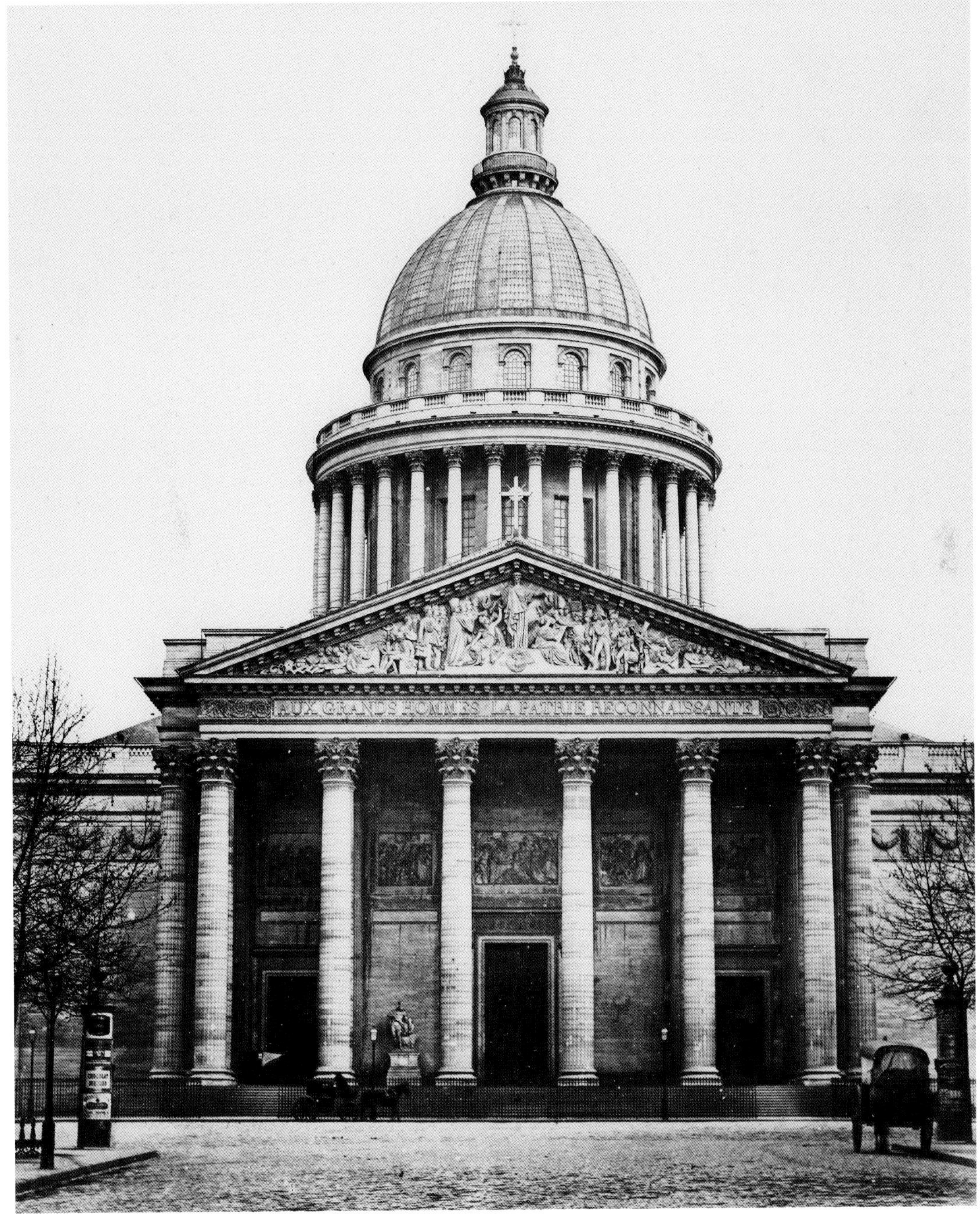

261

260 James Lackington's Temple of the Muses bookstore, Finsbury Square, London, England, 1794. Cast-iron columns support the upper floor. 261 The Panthéon (Church of Sainte Geneviève), Paris, 1757–90. Architect and engineer: Jacques-Germain Soufflot.

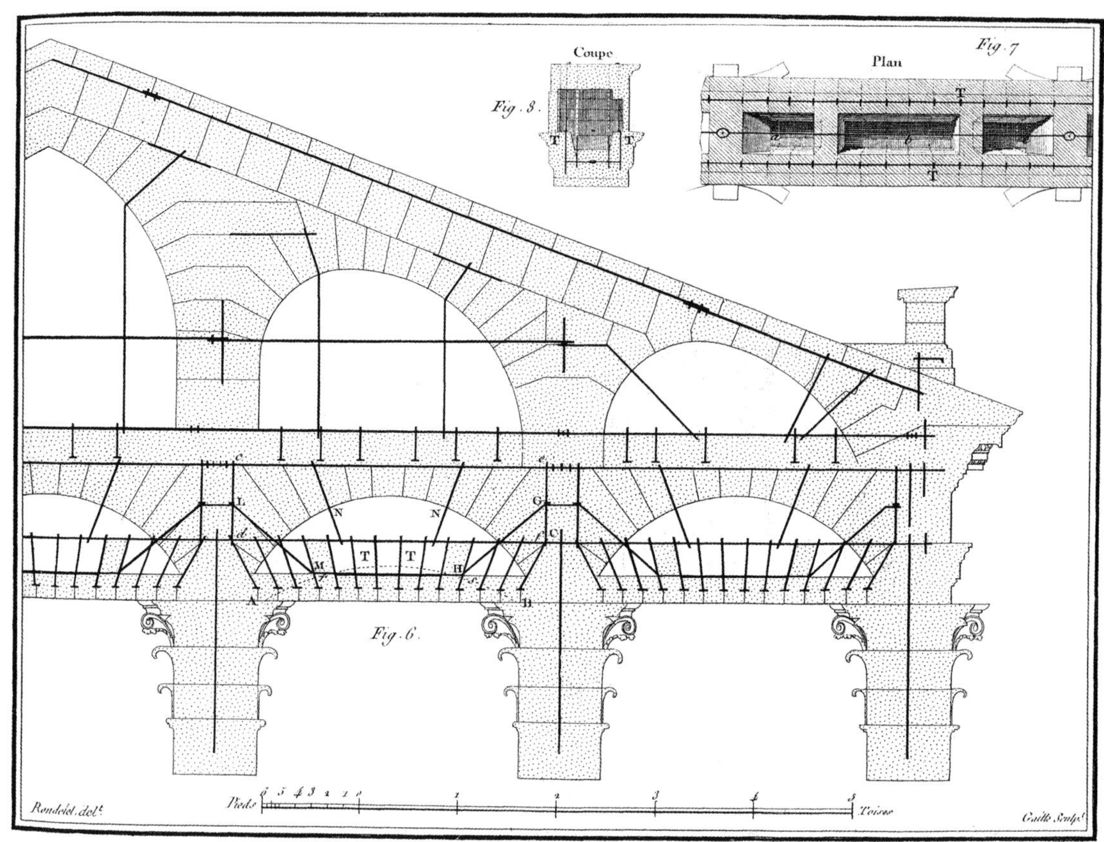

262

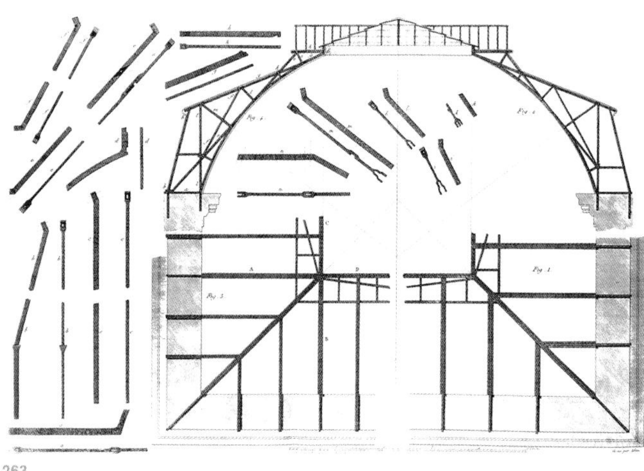

263

262 The Panthéon (Church of Sainte Geneviève). Section of portico showing wrought iron reinforcement. 263 Louvre Palace, Paris, roof, 1779–81. Designer: Jacques-Germain Soufflot. Site engineer: Jean-Baptiste Rondelet. Components and framework of the wrought iron structure. 264 (opposite page) The Panthéon (Church of Sainte Geneviève). Composite plan showing construction details at sixteen different levels of the dome.

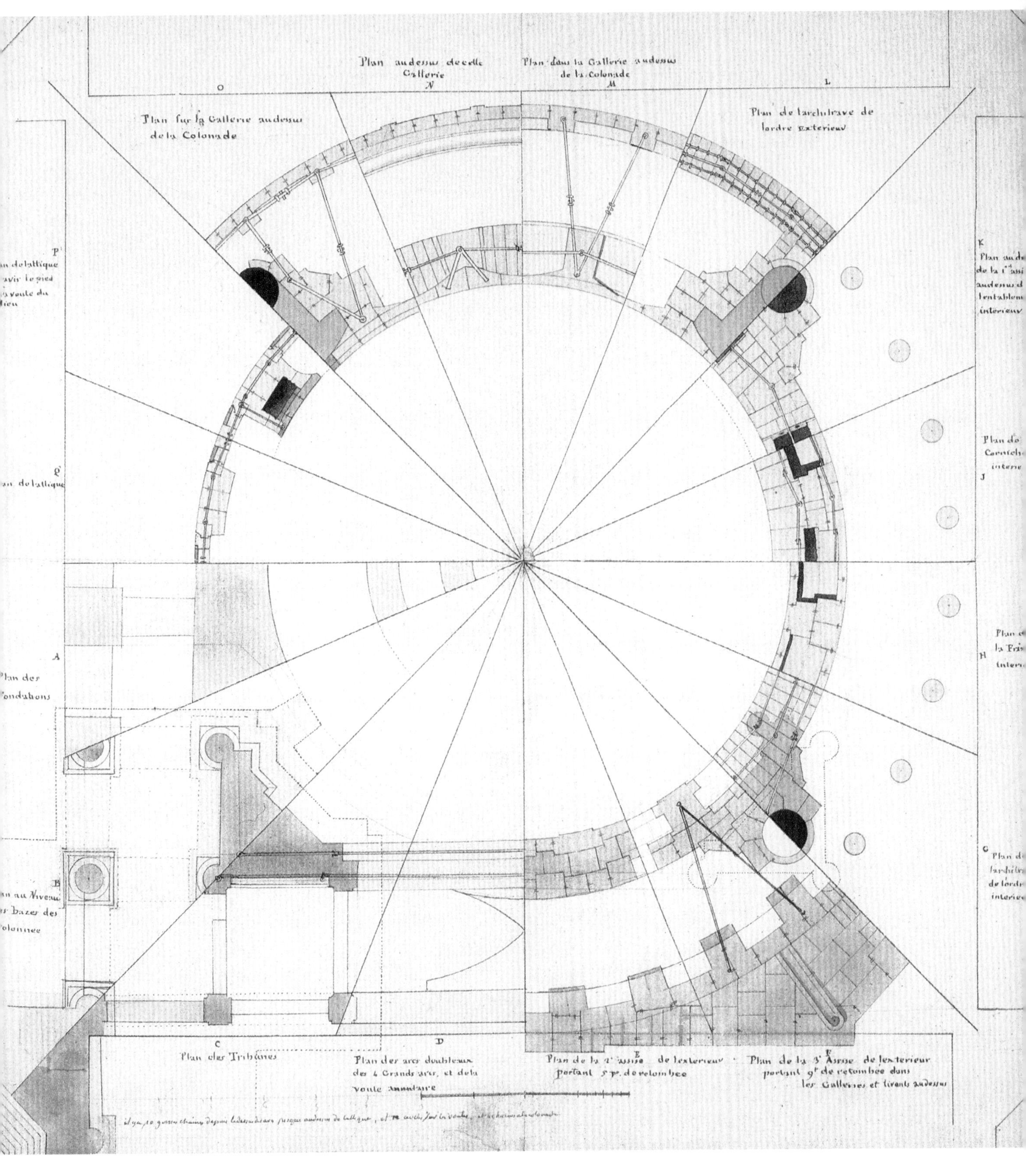
Plan audessus de cette Gallerie
N
Plan dans la Gallerie audessus de la Colonade
M
O
L
Plan sur la Gallerie audessus de la Colonade
Plan de larchitrave de lordre exterieur
Plan de la Frise interieur
Plan des Fondations
Plan des Tribunes
C
D
E
F
A
B
G
H
J
K
P
Q
Plan des arcs doubleaux des 4 Grands arcs, et de la voute annulaire
Plan de la 2e assise de lexterieur portant 5 p. de retombee
Plan de la 3e Assise de lexterieur portant 9 p. de retombée dans les Galleries et tirants audessus

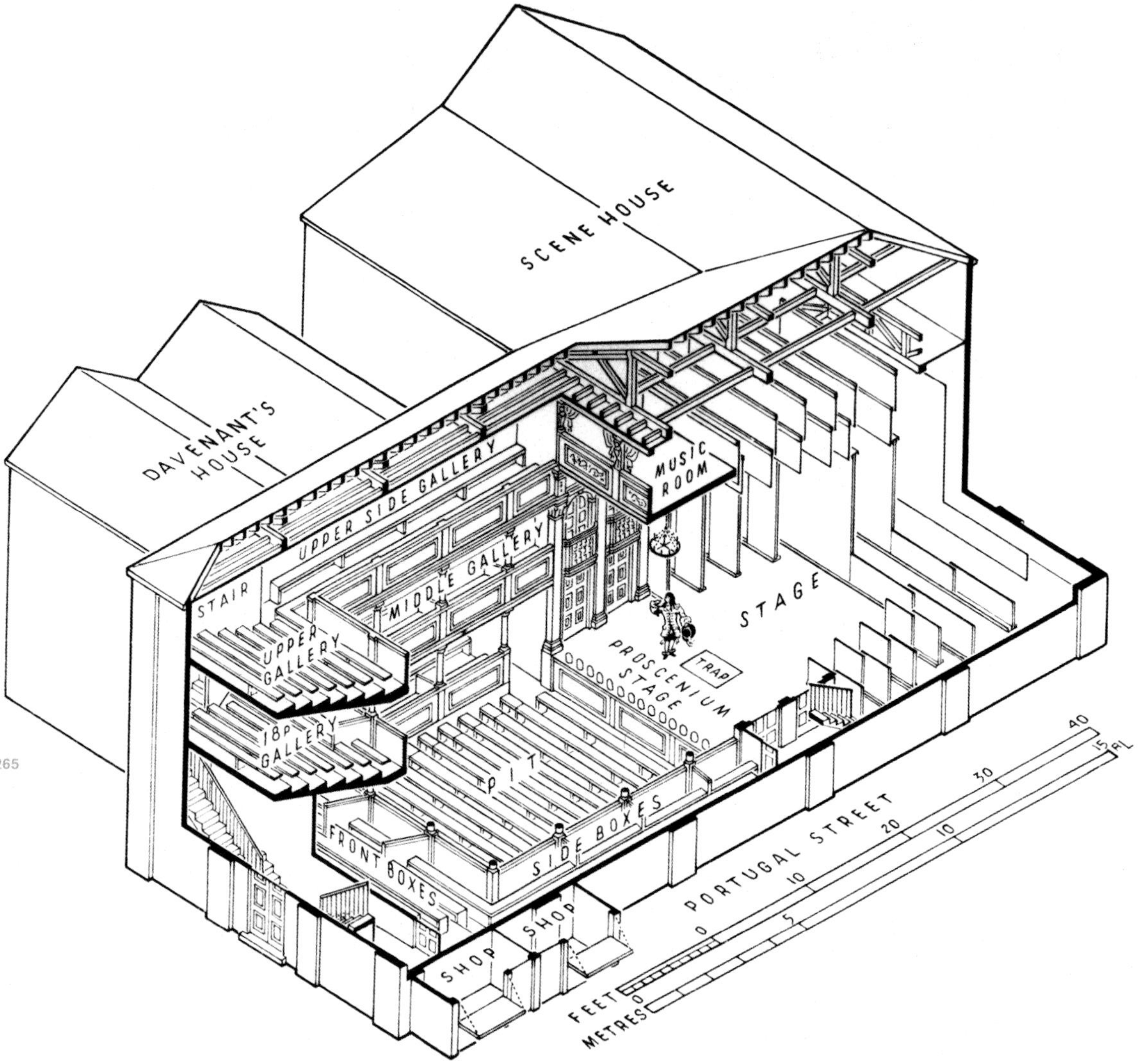

265

266

265 Lincoln's Inn Fields Theater, London, 1661. (Formerly a real tennis court.) Designer: Sir William Davenant. Cutaway section. 266 Royal tennis court at Hampton Court Palace, Surrey, England, 1626. Once converted into a theatrical performance space. 267 Lyon Theater, Lyon, France, 1754. Architect: Jacques-Germain Soufflot. Cutaway section.

267

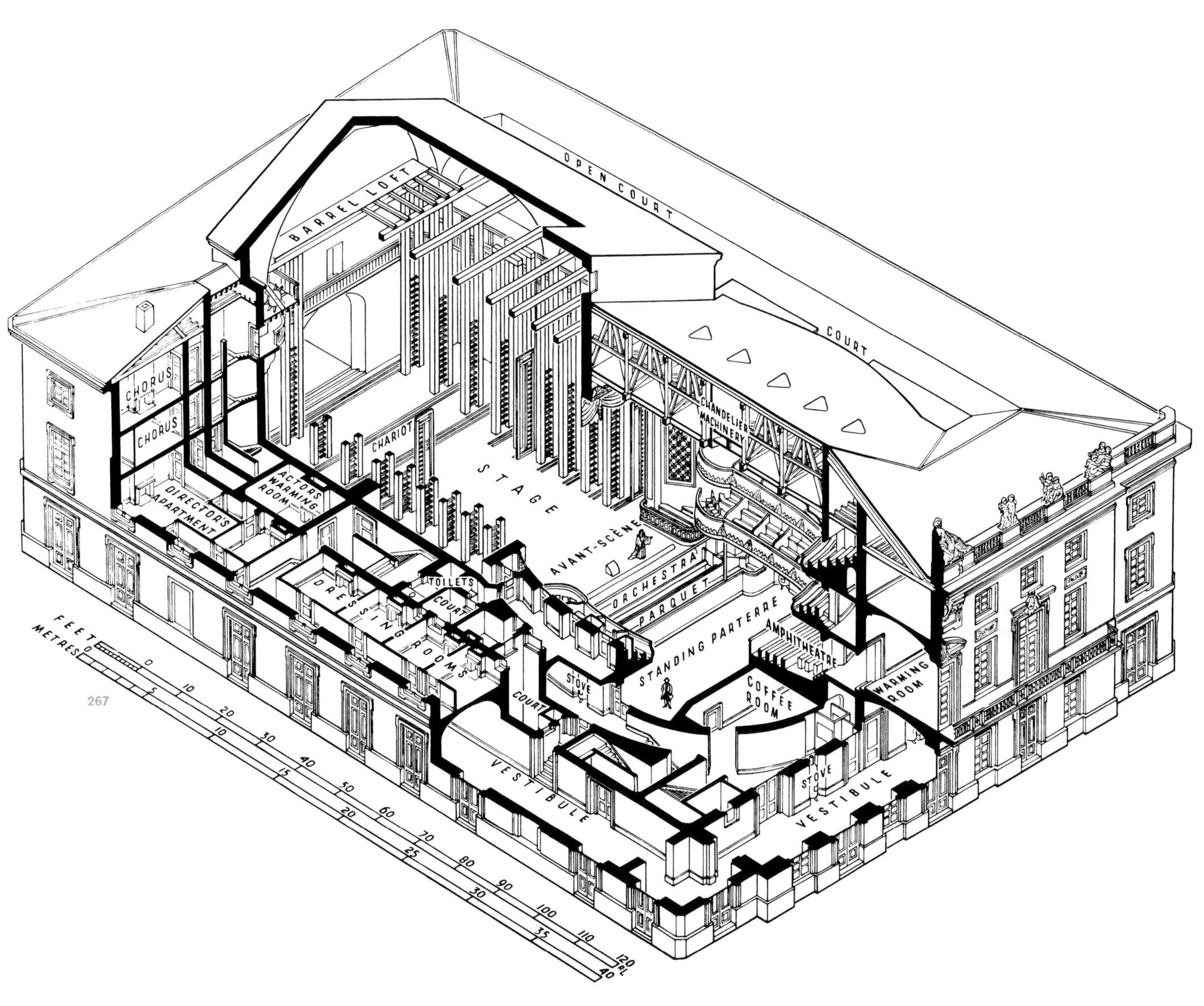

eighteenth century. It was not uncommon, therefore, for the owners of redundant courts to seek new uses for them.) In its new incarnation, this large performance space, about 33 meters long, 10 meters wide, and nearly as high, was fitted with three tiers of seating around the walls at one end, with a stage and room for the scenery and actors at the other. By the time the theater company had outgrown this space, and came to need a new and larger building, it had adapted its style of performance and acting so precisely to the space that they commissioned a new theater with precisely the same layout—and it became one of the first purpose-built theaters in Paris. In London, about a century later, another tennis court was adapted for theatrical use by Sir William Davenant, who had gained a monopoly on the presentation of all dramatic performance in the city after the restoration of the monarchy in 1660. By this time drama had moved on, and older theaters, like Shakespeare's Globe (built in 1598), could not provide the elaborate visual and mechanical effects that had become so popular in continental Europe. Sir William converted Lisle's Tennis Court, which adjoined his London home in Lincoln's Inn Fields, into a new theater capable of staging such performances by adding a large scenery house to service the stage. 265, 266

During the eighteenth century increasing numbers of theatrical productions called for spectacular stage effects involving rapid changes of scenery, coaches or chariots moving across the stage, or loud thunder claps. These required not only wider spans, but stronger roof structures to carry the stage machinery. Auditoriums were also growing larger, and roofs had to carry the weight of huge glass chandeliers. As well as these new structural requirements, there was also a growing demand for better protection from the consequences of disastrous fires, which were not uncommon. Not only were the scenery and the paint used for theatrical decoration highly flammable, so too were the seats and floor, and most of the structure of a theater was made of timber. Moreover, all of the lighting on stage and in the auditorium was provided by candles.

One of the first building designers to address the risk of fires in theaters in a comprehensive way was Soufflot, in the new theater in Lyon, in eastern France, completed in
267 1754. Most theater fires started on the stage, and Soufflot provided a series of protective measures enclosing this most vulnerable area. Running around the stage at high level was a stone gallery on which firefighting equipment was located; this consisted of two water reservoirs with several taps and a number of fire hoses made of leather. To prevent a fire spreading from the stage to the auditorium, the two areas were separated by full-height masonry walls on either side of the stage opening and by a wall that separated the two roof spaces. The stage and auditorium were themselves fully enclosed by masonry walls, with the minimum number of openings to reduce the risk of fire spreading outward from this inner core. This core was, in turn, flanked on either side by two open courts that would act as a firebreak in the event of a fire and protect the outer blocks of dressing and other rooms. Also, the theater was built on an island site, separated from adjacent buildings by streets that would serve as firebreaks. As much as possible of the balcony structure was made of masonry, and, finally, the stairwells were clad entirely in stone and roofed with stone vaulting to provide a safe means of evacuating the theater. Soufflot's approach follows precisely the approach that today is called "fire engineering" (see chapter 9).

The one feature of Soufflot's theater still vulnerable to fire was the structural timber used in the floors and roof. The second half of the eighteenth century saw various builders, architects, and engineers addressing this weakness by replacing structural timber with iron to create many versions of what came to be called "fireproof" construction methods. The earliest known use of iron in a floor structure was in 1782, when a Parisian architect known today only by the name of Ango was commissioned to build a mezzanine floor in a room of the house belonging to Charles-Joseph Panckoucke, who had recently been appointed supervising editor of the revision of the *Encyclopédie* compiled by French philosopher and critic Denis Diderot. Ango's floor consisted of three wrought iron girders, each 5.7 meters long with an overall depth of about 250mm and spaced 1.3 meters apart. Spanning these girders were iron bars placed 900mm apart. The entire iron frame, weighing over half a ton, was embedded in plaster of paris to form a slab measuring about 6.1 x 5.2 meters. 268

Whether this floor was constructed to reduce its thickness (compared to a timber floor), thus making the mezzanine possible, or whether it was intended as a fire-resistant structure, which it certainly was, we do not know. Ango's choice of client was a good one, for Panckoucke publicized the innovative construction in the *Encyclopédie méthodique* (Methodical Encyclopedia) (1782–1832), which he co-edited. This helped attract the attention of the Académie d'architecture, which sent someone to inspect the floor. The inspector reported in 1785, "we have found it very solid [... and] thus it is desirable that M. Ango's system should be practiced by all builders in order that many examples will come to confirm the favourable opinion we have given the experiment." Despite this endorsement and favorable publicity, however, Ango's system seems not to have been adopted by others to any marked degree.[6]

In 1785 another Parisian architect, Eustache Saint-Fart (1746–1822), who specialized in the design of hospitals, experimented with hollow, hexagonal clay pots to form flat vaults spanning wrought iron girders similar in form to those used by Ango. The Romans had used hollow clay 269
pots to build lightweight vaults but, in this case, it is clear that the primary aim of Saint-Fart's innovation was to create a fireproof construction system. It too was praised by the Académie d'architecture, and was used by many

builders, becoming known by the generic name *poteries et fer* (clay pots and iron).

By themselves, the successful demonstrations of fireproof construction by Soufflot, Ango, and Saint-Fart were not enough to bring about change in the building industry; however, fate was to lend a hand. On 8 June 1781 the Théâtre Français, home of the Comédie-Française in Paris, burned down in a terrible fire that claimed many victims. By chance the architect Victor Louis (1731–1800), recently acclaimed for his Bordeaux theater, had just been appointed to make improvements to the building. Work on a replacement theater was delayed, and when the project was resurrected in 1785, a new design, on a new site, was commissioned. Louis recognized the importance of removing flammable material from the fabric of the building and grasped the full significance of Soufflot's and Ango's use of iron and Saint-Fart's poteries et fer system. Timber floors were replaced by stone vaults and wooden stairs by stone flags; the tiered boxes were supported by wrought iron columns and rested on wrought iron brackets; the ceiling of the auditorium and various other parts of the building were made according to the poteries et fer technique. The theater was also the first building in which the roof truss was made entirely of wrought iron. Flat bars of this material were riveted to-
270, 271 gether to form trusses with a clear span of 28 meters.

The new theater opened in 1790, just a few months after the storming of the Bastille in Paris. So, despite the success of the Théâtre Français's fireproof construction and its widespread acclaim throughout Europe, political events stifled further development of the idea in France for more than two decades. Fireproof construction, including roof trusses of wrought iron, was used again in the 1820s, when several new theaters were built in Paris and in Saint Petersburg.

News of the structural use of iron in floors and roof structures traveled quickly across the Channel to England, where there was also a growing concern for how to prevent fires from spreading through buildings and between adjacent buildings. The Fires Prevention (Metropolis) Act of 1774 required that masonry party walls should have a certain minimum thickness (depending on the building's use), and that they should rise half a meter above the surface of the roof covering. When openings in party walls were necessary, they had to be fitted with a door of wrought iron at least 6mm thick. This legal requirement to use iron for fire protection purposes had just been preceded by the pioneering work of David Hartley (1732–1813), a member of Parliament, who had patented his "fireproof flooring" in 1773. This consisted of sheets of wrought iron, less than half a millimeter thick, that were nailed to the tops of timber joists beneath the floorboards. This solution also helped prevent 272
the spread of fire from one floor to another and blocked oxygen from reaching a fire, causing it to quickly extinguish itself. Similar results were achieved by filling the void between joists, up to the underside of the floorboards, with plaster ("pugging"), a solution that also improved sound insulation.

Hartley staged a dramatic public demonstration of his system's effectiveness to the mayor of London, among others, in a building constructed for the purpose on the edge of Putney Heath in that city. Parliament extended Hartley's patent in 1777 for a further thirty-one years, and the technique was widely used in domestic buildings in London. Yet despite this success, there was still skepticism. Following a number of terrible fires in the early 1790s, the Society of Architects decided to see whether "practicable and not expensive means might be devised which will confine a fire to one room in a house." Various systems were considered, including one rivaling Hartley's that was developed in the mid-1770s by Charles Stanhope, later Lord Mahon (1753–1816). This consisted of a lath-and-plaster sheet 50mm to 60mm thick fixed beneath the floorboards between the floor beams. The ceiling below was also of lath-and-plaster construction. A committee of the Society of Architects arranged a full-scale public fire test. Two new houses were constructed, one incorporating Hartley's fire plates, the other using Stanhope's system, and fires were set alight in the ground-floor rooms. Both systems performed well; so, too, did a section of exposed timbers that had been painted with a substance called "Wood's liquid." Though its constituents are no longer known, this paint was probably based on borax, alum, or ferrous sulphate, which earlier in the eighteenth century had all been used to provide stage scenery with some protection against fire.

News of the new Paris theater also reached the designers of the new Theatre Royal in Drury Lane, which opened in

1794. This was the first British theater to incorporate iron for its fire-resisting qualities in the form of wrought
273 iron columns supporting the boxes. The columns were much thinner than those made of timber, giving the audience much better views of the stage. When the theater was altered and improved in 1797, it was also equipped with the first iron safety curtain, which could be lowered in the event of a fire to separate the public auditorium from the stage and backstage areas. Following the example of Soufflot's theater in Lyon, its roof space was furnished with four cisterns holding water for use in case of fire. As a postscript to this episode, it should be noted that fireproof construction did not prevent all fires in theaters and was not adopted universally for over a century; tragedies resulting from theater fires remained common into the twentieth century. Nor were theaters the only buildings vulnerable to fire. It was as a direct consequence of a number of terrible fires in the cotton mills of England in the 1780s that the quest for fireproof construction was taken up as a matter of urgency in the 1790s. Just as the development of industrial manufacturing was an entirely British episode of history between about 1730 and 1820, so too were the building forms and construction methods that were devised to meet the new demands.

Silk, Cotton, and the First Mills

Improvements in window design, better means of controlling the internal environment, and the development of the icehouse all had been driven mainly by wealthy clients' twin demands for greater comfort and keeping up with the latest trends in living environments. Clothing fashions in the mid-eighteenth century were also the main stimulus for the development of an entirely new building type that would transform Britain and then the rest of the world during the following two centuries: mills—or, as they would later become known, manufactories, or simply factories.

In the late seventeenth century virtually all woven silk was imported into Britain from northern Italy, which produced the very best quality material. It was expensive and supplies were limited. Thomas Cotchett, a Derby lawyer, recognized the commercial opportunities and, in 1704, commissioned the mechanical engineer George Sorocold (1668–c. 1720) to build a water-powered mill on an island in the Derwent River in Derby, in the English Midlands. It was equipped with Dutch machinery, but this evidently did not perform well. In 1716 John Lombe, one of Cotchett's employees, became convinced that better machinery would solve the problems, and undertook a daring mission of industrial espionage. He went to Italy and got work in the Piedmontese factory that made the silk imported into the Derby area. There, so the story goes, he made careful drawings of the latest machines used for throwing the silk (twisting raw silk to make the fibers used in the weaving process) and smuggled them, at the risk of the death penalty, in bales of silk delivered to a merchant friend in England. Lombe left Italy in 1717, fleeing the Piedmont state's offer of a reward for his capture, with more drawings of machinery, accompanied by two Italian silk workers who would help him set up a new factory in England. The following year his brother Thomas was granted a patent for fourteen years for the silk-throwing machinery, and in 1721 the brothers commissioned a new mill building and waterwheel adjacent to Cotchett's.
There they installed new machinery made to the specifi- 274
cations of the Italian designs, and were soon running a thriving business in what became known as the Italian Works. This did not last long: the government of Piedmont was informed of the new silk mill by its ambassador in London, and in 1722 the export of raw silk to Britain was banned. John Lombe died that same year. Despite these setbacks, the Derby mill became a successful enterprise. When Thomas Lombe's patent expired in 1732, one of the Italian workers left Lombe's mill and established a rival mill in Stockport, near Manchester. Other silk mills were later established in Macclesfield (1743) and Congleton (1753).

The multistory building devised to house Lombe's new throwing machinery was the first of its kind, and the contrast with Cotchett's mill of just a few years earlier is 275
striking. While rather stark in its appearance, Lombe's mill is otherwise remarkably like the many thousands of similar buildings constructed in every industrial town in Britain during the following century and a half. The mechanization of various processes in the textile industry during the later eighteenth century was characterized by two developments. First, new types of machinery were either too large for the cottages where weaving and spinning had traditionally been done, or required more power to drive them than a person could manage. Second, increasing numbers of machines were concentrated

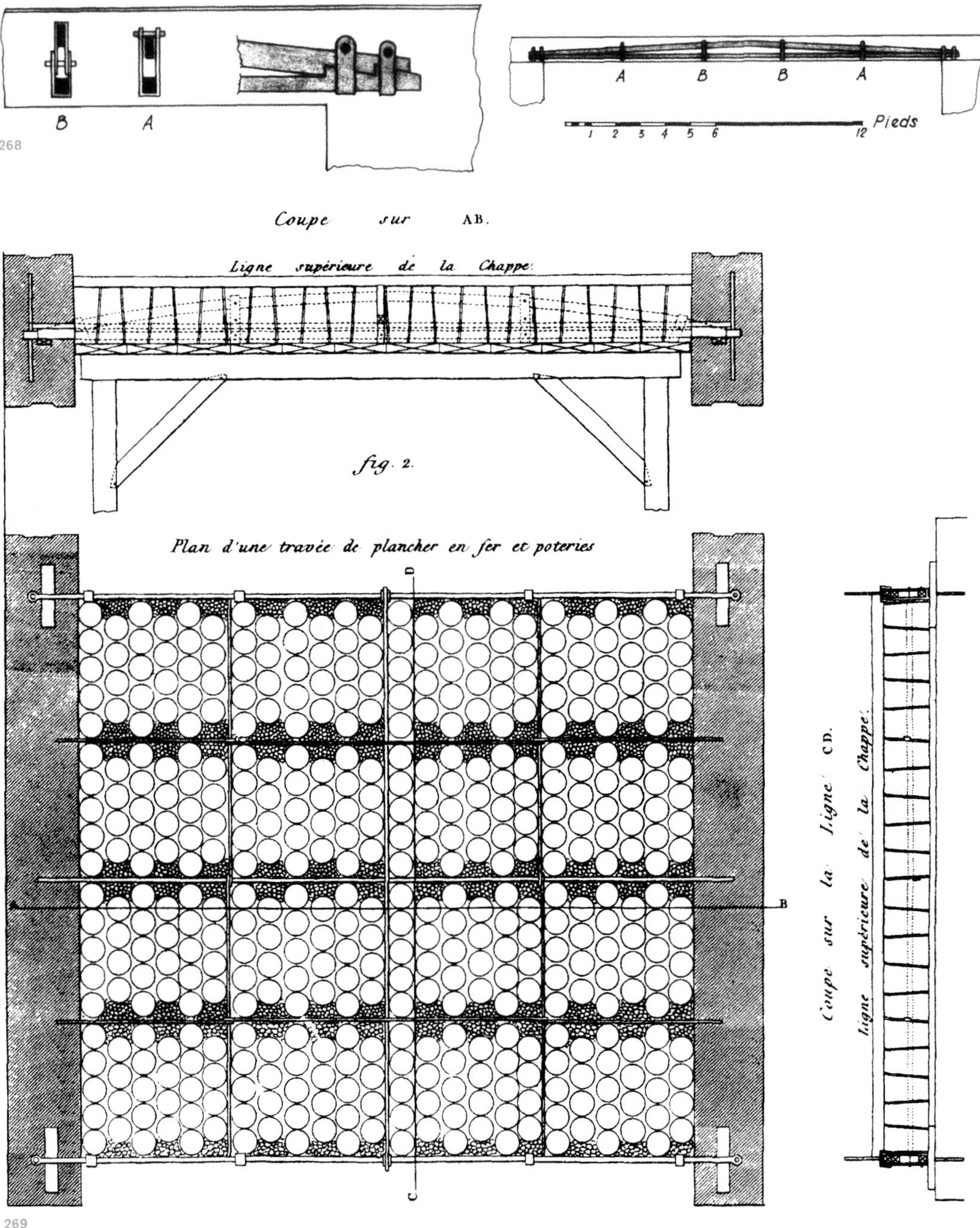

268 Fireproof flooring system devised by Parisian architect Ango, comprising wrought iron girders embedded in plaster of Paris, 1782. 269 Fireproof flooring system known as *poteries et fer*, devised by Eustache Saint-Fart, c. 1785. Hollow clay pots span wrought iron girders.

INTERIEUR DE LA NOUVELLE SALLE DE COMEDIE FRANÇAISE DE L'ANCIEN PROJET.

270

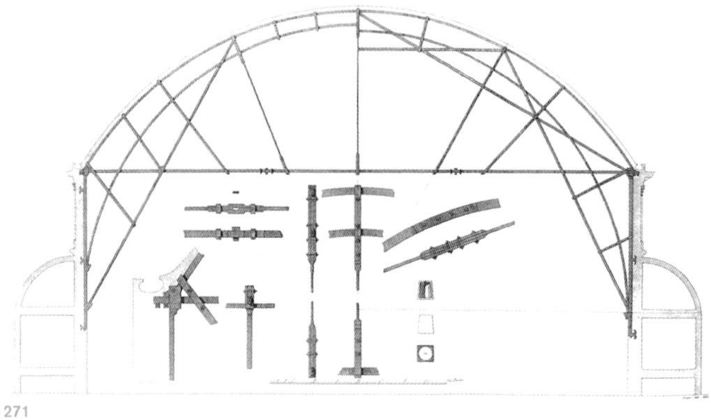

271

272

270 Théâtre de l'Odéon (home of the Comédie-Française), Paris, 1779–82. Architects: Marie-Joseph Peyre and Charles de Wailly. Cutaway section. 271 Théâtre du Palais Royale (renamed Théâtre Français), Paris, 1786–90. Architect: Victor Louis. The wrought iron roof had a floor of *poteries et fer* to ensure a fully fireproof roof structure. Illustration, showing two versions of the truss, in *Traité théorique et pratique de l'art de bâtir*, by Jean-Baptiste Rondelet, c. 1802–17. 272 Hartley fire plate, patented in England by David Hartley, 1773. Panels were made from 0.4 mm-thick wrought iron sheets. 273 (Overleaf) Theatre Royal, Drury Lane, London, 1794. Architect: Henry Holland. Illustration by Augustus Charles Pugin and Thomas Rowlandson, from Rudolph Ackermann's *The Microcosm of London*, London, 1808–10.

around a single power source. It was more economical, in terms of both money and space, to build a single large waterwheel to drive fifty machines than one small wheel for each. It was also sensible to stack the machines in multistory buildings to reduce the distance between a central power source and the equipment it had to drive. The internal columns, beams, and floors in Lombe's mill were all made of timber, and would have resembled the construction of warehouses in the later eighteenth century, some of which have survived to this day.

Conventional building construction would not suit the requirements of a large mill. Masonry construction was expensive; timber-frame buildings were too insubstantial to support the weight of the machinery, and to withstand the prolonged dynamic loads imposed by the drive shafts that distributed power from the waterwheel to the machines on every floor. The construction system devised to meet these new requirements consisted of perimeter walls made of stone or brick, according to local materials and building practice, with timber floor beams and posts or columns. Between the masonry walls the beams were supported by one or two intermediate columns, depending on the size of the machinery and width of the building; each span between wall and column, or column and column, was modest—no more than 3 or 4 meters. Although in some ways this resembled the construction of medieval castles and Tudor mansions, it was different in one important respect. The mills were formed as a series of identical, repeated units, or, as we call them now, bays, each one window wide, on several floors. At the dawn of industrialization, even the buildings themselves were being conceived as an assembly of nearly identical manufactured units.

The silk-spinning process required that the air temperature not fall too low, because if it did the silk fibers would be prone to breaking and the machinery would have to be halted. Generally, a minimum temperature of 16°C (60°F) was recommended (this is still the legal minimum temperature in the workplace in Britain). In his patent application, Thomas Lombe described this requirement:

> *Fine silk is strengthened and preserved from breaking in the working by a furnace in which the hott air is conveyed... by cavityes and pipes [and] it is hoped by the means of the invention for warming the air we shall be able to work this fine Organzine silk in England at all seasons of the yeare, at least as well as it is done in Bolognia, Piedmont or any other hot country.*[7]

The Italian Works was heated by warm air produced by a large furnace, probably at the southwest corner of the building. In the diary the journalist and novelist Daniel Defoe kept of his tour of England (published in 1748), he noted that "One fire-engine... conveys warm air to every individual part of the machine, and the whole work is governed by one regulator. The house which contains this engine is of a vast bulk, and five or six storeys high." A local man who had served his apprenticeship in the mill described the furnace rather less favorably as "a common stove, which warmed one corner of that large building and left the others to starve: but the defect is now supplied [that is, remedied] by fireplaces."[8] Such fireplaces may have been a means to drive the circulation of hot air from the stove more effectively.

At Lombe's silk mill, the waterwheel drove a dozen cylindrical throwing machines that were some 4 meters in diameter and 2 stories (6 meters) high and rotated on a vertical axis. Above this were three floors of smaller winding machines. The ground-floor arrangement was not typical of mills built later, when machinery was smaller and could fit on one floor. Indeed, it is not clear how the columns at the Lombe brothers' Italian Works were arranged. Timber columns 6 meters tall would have needed some lateral restraint at midheight, yet the first floor was not a substantial structure, since it was perforated by the throwing machines and served only to provide operational access to the upper parts of the machinery. It is possible that only a shaft penetrated the floor, providing direct drive from the throwing machine on the ground floor to another directly above.

The structure of mill buildings and the many warehouses built in the same manner is very ingenious in another way. Without buttresses, a masonry wall 30 276 meters long and 5 stories high would be blown over by the wind, and although there are columns and beams, there is no rigid connection between them and so no "frame action" to provide stability. In these buildings, wind loads impinging on their long face are conveyed horizontally through the floor structure to the walls at each end, where they are carried downward to the

273

274

foundations. Despite the ingenuity of this idea, we have no written record of anyone having been conscious of how wind loads were being carried in this mill, or any of the thousands of similar buildings constructed during the following century and a half.

Several other silk mills sprang up in the four decades following Lombe's mill, yet the silk trade never really boomed; it was a luxury market at a time when most people wore wool or, as trade across the Atlantic grew, cotton garments. The textile boom of the late eighteenth century was based on providing cheaper clothes for the mass market, first at home, then abroad. Many mechanical engineers, including the young Richard Arkwright (1732–92), saw the improvements that had transformed silk making—the machinery, the source of power, and the buildings themselves—and set about developing machinery and buildings that would similarly mechanize the production of wool and cotton textiles. The scientist and poet Erasmus Darwin (1731–1802), grandfather of Charles Darwin, wrote a description of Arkwright's machines in the lines devoted to *Gossypia*, the cotton plant, in his long poem "The Botanic Garden," published in 1789:

So now, where Derwent guides his dusky floods
Through vaulted mountains, and a night of woods,
The Nymph, Gossypia, treads the velvet sod,
And warms with rosy smiles the watery God;
His ponderous oars to slender spindles turns,
And pours o'er massy wheels his foamy urns;
With playful charms her hoary lover wins,
And wields his trident,—while the Monarch spins.
—First with nice eye emerging Naiads cull
From leathery pods the vegetable wool;
With wiry teeth revolving cards release
The tangled knots, and smooth the ravell'd fleece;
Next moves the iron-hand with fingers fine,
Combs the wide card, and forms the eternal line;
Slow, with soft lips, the whirling Can acquires
The tender skeins, and wraps in rising spires;
With quicken'd pace successive rollers move,
And these retain, and those extend the rove;
Then fly the spoles, the rapid axles glow;—
And slowly circumvolves the labouring wheel below.[9]

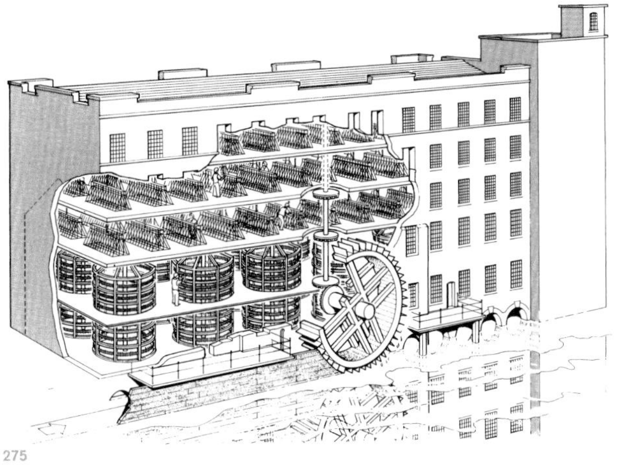
275

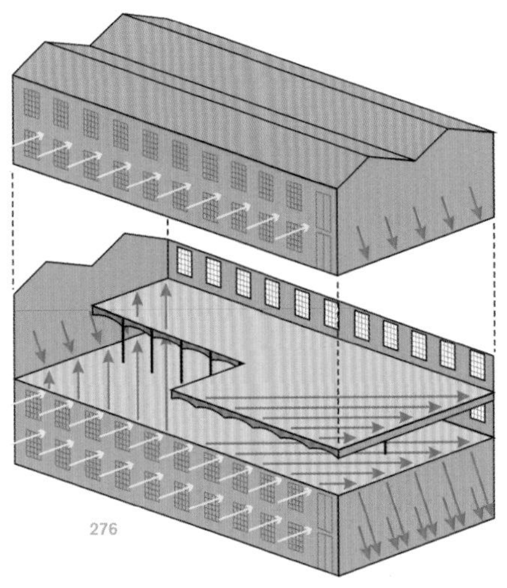
276

277

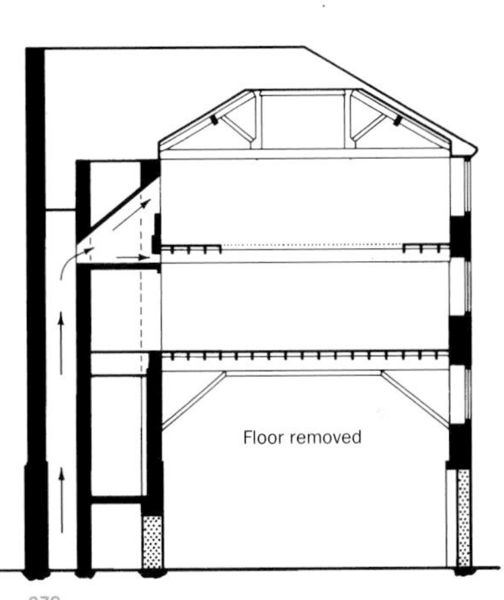

278

274 Thomas Lombe's silk mill, Derby, England, 1721. Engraving by J. Nixon. 275 Thomas Lombe's silk mill. Reconstruction drawing of the water-powered spinning machinery. 276 Diagram showing the paths by which wind loads are conducted through a typical mill. External masonry walls and internal columns support the floor. 277 Richard Arkwright's second (lower) mill in Cromford, England, 1777. Watercolor by Zachariah Boreman, 1787. 278 Richard Arkwright's second (lower) mill. Cross section showing the vent flue to the heating stove that conducted warm air to the upper two stories.

The twenty-six-year-old Arkwright patented his new machine for spinning cotton in 1769, and his search for financial help to develop it was finally rewarded when he was introduced to Jedediah Strutt (1726–97). Strutt had served an apprenticeship with a wheelwright near Derby and by his late twenties had become involved with the textile industry. He inherited a farm from his uncle, and this endowment enabled him to exploit a machine for knitting hosiery he patented in 1759. By the late 1760s his silk stocking business was highly successful, and he owned a silk factory in Derby. Strutt was impressed with Arkwright's machinery and, in return for an investment of £500, formed a partnership with him. Arkwright converted his workshop premises in Nottingham to enable production using machinery driven by horsepower. Even before it was complete, however, Strutt realized that the process had to be run on a larger scale and needed water power.

For the construction of the world's first successful water-powered cotton spinning mill in 1771, the Strutt/Arkwright partnership leased a site at Cromford near an existing flour mill on the Derwent River, which flowed south through Cromford, Belper, Milford, and Darley Abbey into Derby. Although this large, slow, steady river was ideal for driving waterwheels, it did not power the Cromford mill, which instead drew its water from Bonsall Brook, a small tributary. One reason may have been Strutt and Arkwright's failure to gain the rights to Derwent's water, which already powered a number of corn and paper mills. There was also, however, a good technical reason for this choice: the brook carried water drained from the lead mines above Cromford; hence its temperature and flow rate were almost constant, ensuring a reliable source of power even in freezing temperatures and periods of low rainfall.

The mill building itself resembled Lombe's silk mill at Derby, only fifteen miles away, in that it had five stories and internal timber columns and a timber floor and roof structure. As built, it was 28 meters long and consisted of eleven identical bays. It was a little less than 8 meters wide, somewhat narrower than Lombe's mill because the
277 machinery was smaller. The arrangements for heating the first Cromford mill remain unknown, but the second mill that Strutt and Arkwright built at Cromford used a stove in an adjoining building to produce warm air. This was conducted in a flue next to the staircase and the "privies" (toilets). At each floor the air was ducted above
the privy ceiling to vents just below level of the ceilings of 278
the working floors.

Strutt and Arkwright soon extended their first mill and built more, including several on the Cromford site and another, the Haarlem Mill, at nearby Wirksworth. However, both Bonsall Brook and the stream that supplied water to the Haarlem Mill were soon overextended, and Arkwright had the idea of recycling the water by back-pumping it from the tailrace to the mill reservoir using a reciprocating steam engine. In 1777 at his Cromford mill Arkwright installed a pumping engine made by Boulton and Watt, the Birmingham manufacturer of steam engines. At about the same time, for his Haarlem mill, he used a local firm that built pumping engines for dewatering the lead mines. In 1781 at the firm's Manchester mill, Arkwright made the first attempt to replace the waterwheel with a reciprocating steam engine to provide the rotary power needed to drive the spinning machines directly. However, the mechanical drive mechanism performed poorly and the attempt was unsuccessful; he reverted to using the engine to back-pump water to drive the waterwheel, as he had done at his Haarlem and Cromford mills. The first successful use of a reciprocating steam engine to drive spinning machinery was in 1785, at a cotton mill in Papplewick about 15 miles east of Cromford.

Arkwright and Strutt dissolved their partnership in 1781, and Arkwright settled in Cromford, building his grand Masson Mill on the River Derwent itself in 1783. Strutt developed his cotton-spinning business as a family concern, with his three sons taking increasing roles in running the firm. He had built his first mill in 1778 in Belper, a town on the Derwent a few miles to the south that had been a center for the nail-making industry for more than four hundred years. He built a second mill in 1785 in nearby Milford and several dozen more south along the Derwent valley to Derby. As we shall see later, several of these, from 1793, were among the first buildings in the world to use cast iron in their construction.

The machinery, waterwheels, and buildings that made up a mill were extremely expensive, but the rapid increase in number of such manufacturing facilities toward the end of the eighteenth century in this particular region, as well as throughout Britain and farther afield, reflects their great commercial success. So, too, did the growth of industrial espionage. Arkwright had taken out his first of many patents in 1769, and already in 1774 an act of Parliament had prohibited the export of the "tools or utensils" of the cotton and linen industries. Nevertheless, in 1784 Johann Gottfried Brügelmann began production of cotton in Germany using Arkwright's system in the development he called Cromford Mill, at Ratingen, near Düsseldorf. Arkwright machines were in use in France by 1785, in Bohemia possibly as early as 1780 and definitely from 1796, and, through the endeavors of Samuel Slater, an émigré mechanic from the Derwent Valley, at his mill in Pawtucket, Rhode Island, in New England. Soon throughout the world, Enlightenment would be overtaken by enrichment as the motivating force of the new age—the industrial age.

Fireproof Construction in Mills

The development of fireproof construction in Britain had its greatest impact not in the theatrical world or in domestic buildings but in the highly commercial textile industry. The financial impact of fires led to the widespread use of cast iron in building construction, but also drove the search for how to incorporate as little iron as possible in the interest of keeping costs down. This economic exigency quickly encouraged engineers to find ways of using this material to the limit of its structural performance according to the mathematical and scientific ideas that had been developed, in abstract form, during the Age of Reason.

The standard form of construction for these multistory buildings in the 1780s consisted of timber floors and beams spanning masonry walls, with one or two timber
279, 280 columns propping the beams at 3- to 4-meter intervals. By the 1780s it was evident that the new building form developed for mills and warehouses was extremely vulnerable to fire. Fires in mills were common and threatened not only the workers, but the expensive materials, the machinery, and the building itself. Flammable materials such as cotton fiber or flour dust, combined with the vapor of oils used to lubricate the machinery, the naked flames used for lighting, and the occasional sparks from the metal machines, created an explosive—and lethal—environment. In addition, the use of internal timber columns to support all the floors introduced a new problem that was absent in buildings with interior load-bearing masonry walls. If one or two columns and the area of floor they supported were to catch fire and collapse, not only could the fire spread freely, but the collapse would bring down adjacent sections of floor and columns above, below, and to the side. This could lead to the progressive collapse of a whole building—a mechanism now known as disproportionate collapse because of the relation between the magnitude of the initial cause and its consequences. Such was the fate in March 1791 of the magnificent Albion flour mill in London. Designed by 282, 283
Samuel Wyatt between 1783 and 1784, it was the state of the art in mill construction. The mills were powered by a Boulton and Watt steam engine; boats were unloaded at a dock inside the building, and wagons, too, were loaded under cover. Five stories were erected over the 6.7-meter-wide dock, supported by a timber transfer structure, with a light well that brought daylight to the in- 281
terior. The building rested upon the soft alluvium of the Thames River, calling for ingenious measures to reduce settlement and differential settlements of parts of the structure. The maximum load on the underlying alluvium was reduced by excavating a volume of earth that was half the weight of the building. The building itself was constructed on a huge raft foundation covering an area 49 meters by 37 meters, composed of seven inverted barrel vaults. This foundation was a descendant of the inverted arches used by Robert Hooke and Christopher Wren, mentioned in Alberti's book of 1485 and probably dating back to Roman times. When a small fire broke out in the building (arson was suspected but not proven), it soon consumed some of the columns; the floors these columns supported collapsed, bringing down the remaining floors and allowing the fire to spread through the building and destroy almost its entire contents of grain and flour. Neither the fire brigade at street level nor the fire floats on the river Thames could save the interior of the building. Only the west and north walls survived, along with the steam engines that were housed in rooms separated by a thick party wall.

The site of the building, in the center of London, brought the dangers of factory fires to the attention of the press and the public. No less significant was the great financial loss: as the frequency and cost of such fires increased, so too did the insurance premiums that owners had to pay—a sure stimulus for technical innovation. The use of cast iron and bricks in the fire-resistant construction methods that were quickly developed after the fire at Albion Mill would come to have a greater effect on the design and construction of buildings than at any time since the late medieval period.

Cast iron was, effectively, an entirely new construction material, the first one since the Romans introduced concrete on a wide scale. There were no precedents, no standard designs, no design rules. Most significant was the manner in which cast iron components were made. When making a column or a beam of stone or timber, the materials are cut down to size from a mountain or a tree, and there comes a point when it is increasingly risky and unnecessarily time-consuming to reduce its size further to reach the minimum possible dimensions. Cast iron, on the other hand, is effectively made up to size, and from early on, the high cost of the material encouraged the designer to use as little as possible. This had been true of wrought iron, too, but the manufacturing and forging processes limited the size of wrought iron components to bars no greater than about 50 millimeters across. The weight of a structure had, of course, also been a consideration for long-span bridges and roofs, but here the main concern was how best to arrange and connect a large number of small elements to work as an ensemble. With cast iron the need to create a minimum-weight structure was encountered every time it was used, no matter how large or small the component. Beginning in the eighteenth century, this became the key principle of structural engineering and remains the basis of most engineering design today, which seeks optimal and minimum-energy solutions.

In the 1780s, the cast iron industry was concentrated in very few areas of England—most of them in the English Midlands—and it is no coincidence that this was where the material was first used for both bridges and buildings. William Strutt (1756–1830) of Derby was instrumental in introducing cast iron into buildings. The eldest son of Jedediah Strutt, he began working in his father's mills at age fourteen. Of the three Strutt brothers who took over the family firm in the 1770s, William was the engineer, assuming responsibility for the machinery and buildings. Through his friendship with Erasmus Darwin he knew many prominent industrialists and scientists, including members of the Birmingham Lunar Society such as the Birmingham entrepreneur and industrialist Matthew Boulton (1728–1809); the Scottish engineer James Watt (1736–1819), who played a prominent role in the development of the steam engine and founded the world-famous firm of Boulton and Watt in 1773; the chemist and discoverer of oxygen, Joseph Priestley (1733–1804); and a manufacturer in the pottery industry, Josiah Wedgwood (1730–95). With Darwin, Strutt was a founder of the Derby Philosophical Society in 1783, and worked with his brother Joseph in setting up the Derby Mechanics' Institute in 1825. When he was elected a Fellow of the Royal Society in 1817, one of his nominators was the French-born engineer Marc Brunel (1769–1849), father of the more famous Isambard. He also later came to know and be related by marriage to Charles Fox, who would play a key role in constructing the Crystal Palace in London in 1850–51 (see chapter 6, pp. 354–59).

William Strutt was progressive and put into practice many of the radical ideas of his friend and younger contemporary Robert Owen (1771–1858), the Welsh educational and social reformer, who became widely known for the model community he strove to create in the first two decades of the nineteenth century at the cotton mills owned by his father-in-law at New Lanark in Scotland. During the same two decades at Belper and Milford, Strutt designed, financed, and constructed housing for the mill workforce, and helped finance several schools and chapels. He also promoted friendly societies—mutual insurance groups—and savings banks. Although this was still the age of child labor, Strutt insisted that mill machinery be designed to make it as convenient and safe as possible for twelve- or thirteen-year-olds to operate. The long, narrow room in the roof space of Strutt's North Mill at Belper served as a schoolroom for children of the firm's employees. In his hometown of Derby, he actively promoted better street paving and the development of gas streetlighting. His reputation spread throughout Britain, and the Derby Infirmary he designed (1805–10) became a showplace visited by medical authorities from both home and abroad. Apart from his role in introducing cast iron into building construction, he also developed new means of heating and ventilation for the buildings, and contributed to developing the tension waterwheel in which iron rods replaced timber spokes, an ancestor of the modern bicycle wheel.

279

280

The Strutt family textile business had lost its Nottingham mill in a disastrous fire in 1781 and, in 1788, another at Darley Abbey, just north of Derby in the Derwent Valley. News of the total destruction of London's Albion Mill in March 1791 spread throughout the country, and in the following twelve months, five more mills within 80 kilometers of Derby were destroyed by fire. This was just when William Strutt was planning a new mill at Derby. Deciding to take precautionary action, he devised the world's first successful "fireproof" floor construction. Strutt's design consisted of a series of brick arches carried by timber beams that were, in turn, supported on solid cast iron columns. These jack arches—"jack" indicates the diminutive size compared to a bridge arch, a small span and only one brick thick—spanned either 8 or 9 feet, depending on their location in the building. The arches and the upper parts of the timber beams were covered with sand, and the floor paved with brick tiles. The jack arches sprang from timber skewbacks—timber shaped to provide a support for the arch—which were covered with iron sheet, similar to the fire plates David Hartley had patented in 1773 and demonstrated publicly in 1792. The exposed lower surface of the timber beams themselves was covered with a 35 millimeter coating of plaster to protect it from fire. The timber beams were continuous from wall to wall, a distance of 27 feet, and supported at their third points by cruciform columns of cast iron. The load from the beams is conveyed to the column head via a cast iron "crush box" to prevent the beam from being damaged. Perpendicular to the line of the beams, wrought iron tie rods were fastened to the crush boxes. These have three functions: they stabilize the structure during construction, carry the outward thrust of the arches after their completion, and, most importantly, ensure that each bay is self-supporting, should an adjacent bay be removed, therefore helping to prevent a catastrophic progressive collapse like the one that had occurred at the Albion Mill.

William Strutt used this system for his six-story mill at Derby and a four-story warehouse at Milford, both com- 284, 285
pleted in 1793, and, in 1795, at the firm's new six-story West Mill at Belper, a few miles north of Milford. Only the Milford building, which was later converted for use as a mill, survives. At Derby the floor-to-floor heights were 3.12 meters and 3.23 meters for the first two stories,

279 No.1 Warehouse at West India Docks, London, 1800–02. Architect: George Gwilt; engineers: William Jessop and John Rennie. The masonry wall construction differs little from that used in Thomas Lombe's silk mill at Derby in 1721.
280 No.1 Warehouse. Interior.

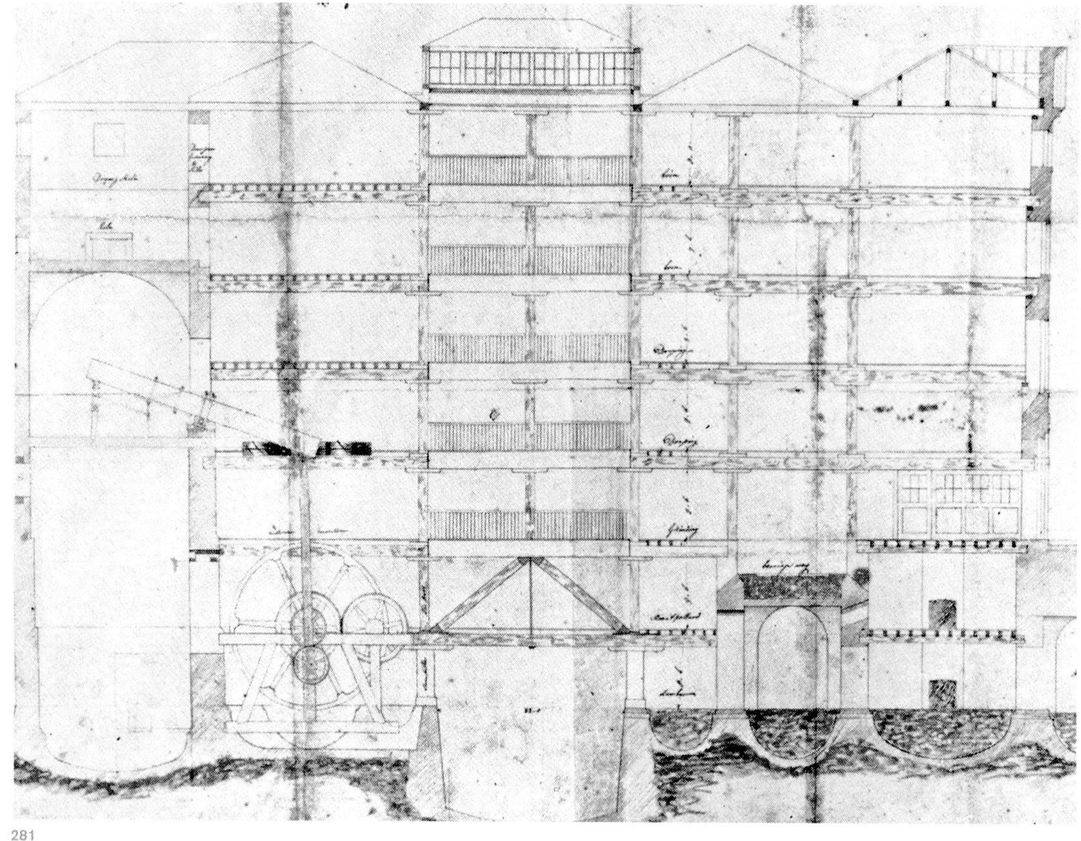

281

282

283

281 Albion Flour Mill, London, 1783–86. Designer: Samuel Wyatt. Section showing internal timber columns. The steam engine (left) and the inverted arches created a raft-like foundation suitable for building in the soft alluvial ground. 282 Albion Flour Mill. 283 Albion Flour Mill consumed by fire in 1791. Illustration by Augustus Charles Pugin and Thomas Rowlandson, from Rudolph Ackermann's *The Microcosm of London*, London, 1808–10.

and 3 meters in the upper stories. The columns, however, were a constant 2.49 meters tall throughout; the different story heights were achieved by varying the rise of the jack arches. The columns diminished in size as the building rose in height and as the total load they needed to carry was reduced. The brick walls also diminished in thickness, from 610 millimeters to 330 millimeters in the top story, with the consequence that the internal width of the top story was 480 millimeters greater than at ground level.

In the ceilings of the top stories of these buildings, Strutt introduced another new idea into mill construction – the use of hollow ceramic pots, about 7 inches tall and 3 inches in diameter (175 by 75 millimeters), to make a lightweight jack arch floor for a small room in the roof space that would also protect the timber roof truss from a fire below. News of this system had spread from Paris, where Saint-Fart had patented his system of poteries et fer in the mid-1780s and Victor Louis had used it in the ceiling of his Théâtre Français, completed in 1790. Strutt realized the structural benefits as well as fireproof qualities of such a lightweight method of construction. In fact, Strutt's friend Matthew Boulton had come across the hollow-pot construction independently in Paris as well, and wrote of them to Strutt in May 1793:

> *I understand that you have some thought of adopting the invention of forming Arches by means of hollow pots & thereby saveing the use of Timber in making Floors, & guarding against Fire. Allow me to say that I have seen at Paris floors so constructed, and likewise at Mr George Saunders' in Oxford St., London, who is an eminent architect... I have therefore no doubt but it might be applyd also with great success and security to a Cotton mill.*[10]

The new fireproof construction was not cheap; it was about 25 percent more expensive than the equivalent building in timber. However, the profitability of the cotton industry was not to be underestimated. In 1789 the Strutt business valued its investments in the mills at Belper and Milford at £26,000 and £11,000, respectively; the firm also claimed a return of £36,000 per annum.

Strutt's buildings were innovative in other respects. The machinery at the Derby mill was driven by a Boulton and Watt steam-powered, sun and planet beam engine—one of the first occasions when steam was used to power factory machinery rather than to pump water, or as a winding engine in mines. The power for the West Mill at Belper, on the other hand, was provided by two huge waterwheels, one 12 meters long and nearly 6 meters in diameter, and a second, added a couple of years later, that was 15 meters long and a little under 4 meters in diameter. The Milford warehouse incorporated some ventilation, and the Belper West Mill was heated inside, especially in a room to dry the cotton and thus reduce its tendency to break in the spinning machines. The Belper mill also incorporated an internal hoist in a shaft parallel to the stairwell.

Strutt's use of cast iron columns and his fireproof jack arch floors still relied on timber beams. The next important step toward replacing timber with cast iron was taken by Charles Bage (1751–1822), about whom a former business partner observed that he "was possessed of talent and understanding but he was not a man of business."[11] While his involvement with building engineering was short, however, it was of enormous significance. He was not only the first to use cast iron beams in a building, but the first to use a modest understanding of engineering science to help calculate and justify the sizes of both cast iron columns (in 1796–97 at Castle Foregate Mill in Shrewsbury, western England) and cast iron beams (in 1803 at Leeds).

Bage was born in Darley Abbey in the Derwent valley, which by the late eighteenth century had become the heart of the cotton-spinning industry. For several generations his family had run a paper mill there, and had close links with the Strutt family. In 1766 Charles' father sold his paper mill to raise money to open an iron works in the village of Wychnor, fifteen miles southwest of Derby, in partnership with Erasmus Darwin, among others, but it was not a success. Charles had thus been exposed to the iron industry during his teenage years, but chose not follow in his father's enterprise. He set up his own business as a wine merchant at age twenty-nine and settled in the town of Shrewsbury, where he became a prominent public figure, eventually serving as mayor in 1807. Shrewsbury was near the heart of the English iron industry centered on Coalbrookdale, where the Iron Bridge had been constructed in 1779. Bage knew many of the people who were prominent in using this new structural material, including the engineer Thomas Telford

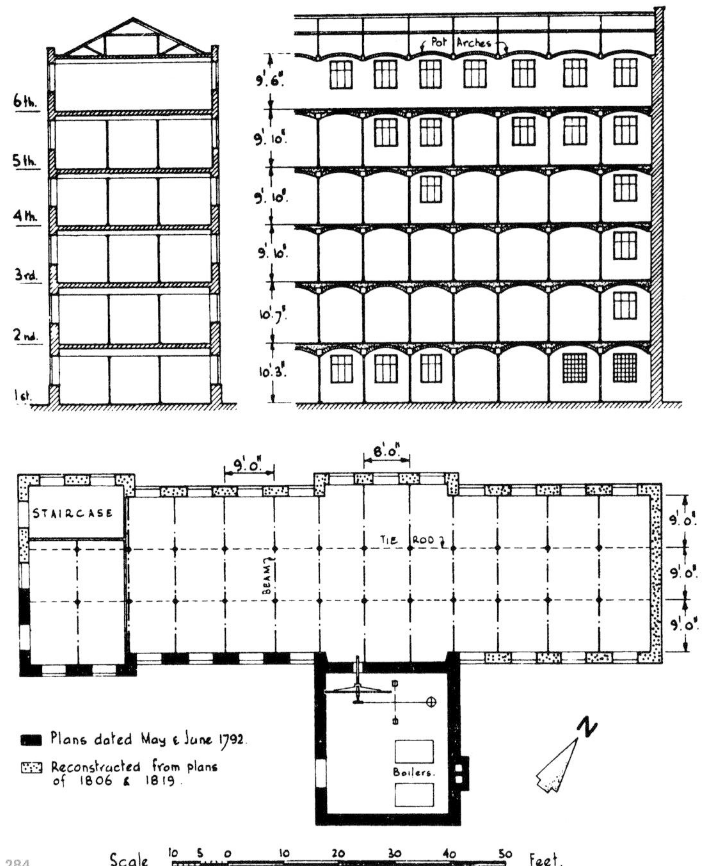
Pot Arches
6th.
5th.
4th.
3rd.
2nd.
1st.
9' 6"
9' 10"
9' 10"
9' 10"
10' 7"
10' 3"
9' 0"
8' 0"
STAIRCASE
TIE ROD
BEAM
9' 0"
9' 0"
9' 0"
Plans dated May & June 1792.
Reconstructed from plans of 1806 & 1819.
Boilers.
N
Scale 10 5 0 10 20 30 40 50 Feet.

284

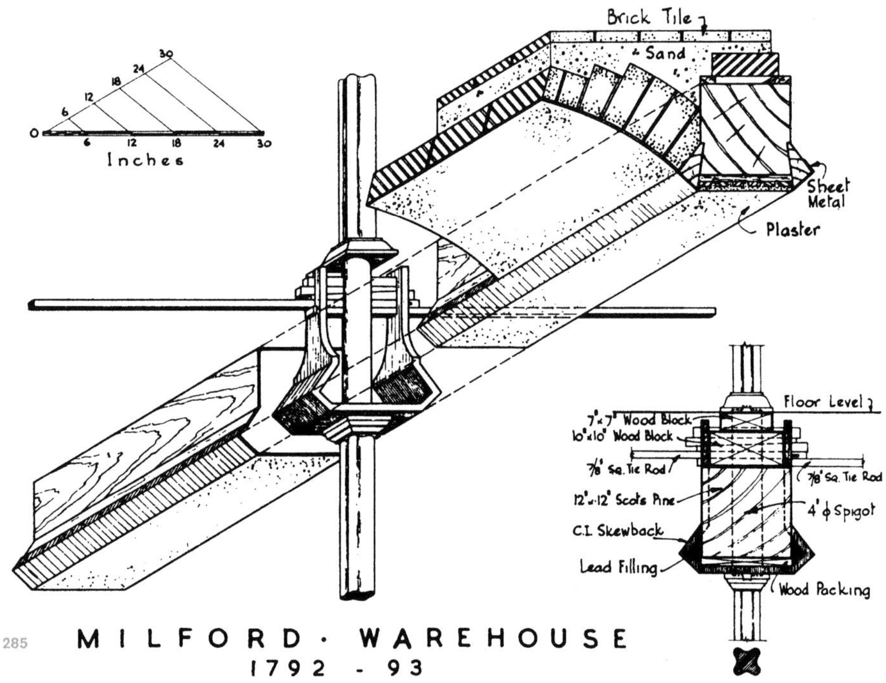
Brick Tile
Sand
Sheet Metal
Plaster
0 6 12 18 24 30
Inches
Floor Level
7"×7" Wood Block
10"×10" Wood Block
7/8" Sq. Tie Rod
7/8" Sq. Tie Rod
12"×12" Scots Pine
4' ϕ Spigot
C.I. Skewback
Lead Filling
Wood Packing
MILFORD · WAREHOUSE
1792 - 93

285

(1757–1834), who built a number of cast iron arch bridges and served as the first president of the Institution of Civil Engineers. Bage also knew the eminent iron founder William Hazeldine (1763–1840), whose Shrewsbury works supplied most of the iron Telford used and cast the columns and beams for Bage's mill.

Bage's involvement with mills and his contribution to building engineering came about through his association with Thomas and Benjamin Benyon, prominent wool merchants in Shrewsbury who had formed a business partnership with John Marshall, owner of a flax-spinning business in Leeds. In early 1796 the firm's steam-powered mill in Leeds was destroyed by what the *Leeds Intelligencer* reported as "the most dreadful fire we ever remember to have happened in this county." When the Benyons decided to expand the business in its home town, Bage offered his advice about using cast iron to construct a fireproof building. Bage gave up his wine business later that year and went into partnership with the Benyons and Marshall. He took responsibility for designing the mill, drawing on his father's experience of iron-making, as well as information about the fireproof mill at Derby from his acquaintance William Strutt and, no doubt, the 39-year-old Thomas Telford, who had been living in Shrewsbury since 1787. In March 1795 Telford had recommended to the Shrewsbury Canal Company that they build his cast iron aqueduct at Longdon-on-Tern a few miles east of Shrewesbury. Apart from the Castle Foregate Mill, Bage designed only two others for the partnership in between 1802 and 1804, and his involvement with weaving factories lingered as a rather unsuccessful commercial interest.

Castle Foregate Mill, which survives in a good state of repair, is a five-story building that originally housed machinery for spinning and weaving flax. For its internal structure Bage used cast iron columns to support cast iron beams that, in turn, supported floors of jack arch
287, 288 construction like those used by William Strutt. The
289 columns are noticeably thicker at mid-height than at the
ends. This shape arises from the logic of using material only where it is needed to give the maximum resistance to failure by buckling; the tendency of a column to bend when it fails by buckling is greatest at mid-height and diminishes toward the ends.[12] Bage used simple buckling theory to calculate the strength of the column as about 78 tons—approximately 2.5 times the load it would actually carry in the building. This figure is little different from the results we would obtain today. Here, in the last decade of the eighteenth century, we find cast iron columns being designed for the first time in history, in a rational and scientific way, to generate a minimum-weight structure.

The cast iron beams in Bage's mill were the first of their kind. Unlike the custom that prevailed in nearly all subsequent mills, the cast iron beams do not span from wall to column or column to column. Each beam in the first four stories was fabricated in two halves and bolted, and is continuous across the width of the building. It is supported at each end in the wall and by three columns equally spaced between the walls, making four spans in all. The beams are thus subject to sagging bending moments between the columns and hogging bending moments where they rest on the columns. In the top story, the intermediate props are absent, as there are no floor loads above. The 5.8-meter beams support jack arches that form a fireproof ceiling and support the tiled roof that rests directly on the arches.

From a letter that Bage wrote to Strutt in 1796, we know that Bage calculated the load each beam would need to carry—the dead weight of the beam, the floor and jack arch, plus an imposed load of about $5kN/m^2$ (100 lb/ft^2)—as about 8 tons. It is more than likely that he load-tested a beam to ensure that it would carry this load with some margin of safety. As far as is known, on this occasion Bage did not try to calculate the strength of the beams, and precise dimensions of their elevation are not known. In the one area of floor exposed during a recent investigation of the building, it can be seen that the beam is 175 millimeters deep at the wall end, 275 millimeters deep at mid-span, and 250 millimeters deep where it passes over the intermediate prop. It is thus clear that Bage had a good understanding of the magnitude of the bending moments. In this respect, he was not a pioneer. Galileo had provided, in 1638, the theoretical argument

284 Cotton mill, Derby, England, 1792–93. Engineer: William Strutt. Plan and sections. 285 Warehouse, Milford, England, 1792–93. Engineer: William Strutt. Details of fireproof floor construction.

for why a beam should be deeper at mid-span, and when passing over a support, and in the mid-seventeenth century, Leonhard Euler and others had provided full mathematical reasoning. In the less academic world of railway engineering, the English engineer William Jessop (1745–1814) had patented the "fish-belly" cast iron rail in 1789, which also had a symmetrical cross section in the form of an I. Jessop chose the geometry of his rail based on practical experience rather than on scientific
290 testing and theoretical justification. Indeed, his choice of a symmetrical I-section was not the best for cast iron; being weaker in tension than compression, the lower cast iron flange should have had an area about six times the upper flange. This error of understanding was corrected in the 1830s (see chapter 6). Bage would return to the design of beams in his next mill at Leeds.

The second iron-framed fireproof building was a seven-story mill in Salford (near Manchester) built by Boulton
291 and Watt between 1799 and 1801. They had come to know Bage's building when they installed their steam engine there, and they copied many of his ideas. There were some significant improvements, though. The first was an increase in the span of each bay, resulting in three bays of 3.9 meters instead of four spans of 2.9 meters. As at Castle Foregate Mill, the beams at Salford were continuous over the columns, and their depth reflected the degree of bending to which they were subjected. As in Bage's mill, there was no rigid frame action from floor to floor, as the columns simply rested one upon another. At the design stage the section of the beams incorporated a skewback, similar to Bage's, from which the arches would spring. These were eliminated when the beams came to be manufactured in favor of an inverted-T section. A further refinement was that the tie rods linking parallel pairs of beams were raised and fully embedded within the brick jack arch, giving a cleaner profile to the ceiling and protecting the tie rods from damage in a fire.

The most significant development at Salford was the creation of a hollow, circular column. This was technically more difficult that the solid cruciform section used by Strutt and Bage, requiring a clay core that ran the length of the column and was knocked out after casting. The benefits were twofold. First, the tubular section required 30 percent less material to achieve the same resistance to buckling (that is, second moment of area) as the solid cruciform section. The hollow columns also served as pipes through which steam was circulated to heat the workspace. This was the first major use of steam for heating a building, and was repeated in many mills. In his well-known book *The Principles of Warming and Ventilating* (1824), the engineer Thomas Tredgold (1788–1829) summarized the benefits of steam or, indeed, any other heating in mills:

> *Until the machinery acquires a certain degree of warmth, the spinners find it nearly impossible to keep their work in order; and this is most felt on Monday mornings, when everything has become cold and adhesive, through being a longer time at rest. It is an evil, because, in addition to producing bad work, it too frequently occasions the children employed to be treated with unmerited severity; than which nothing has a greater effect in debasing the sense of justice and honesty in a young mind.*[13]

In addition to making steam engines, the firm of Boulton and Watt was also a pioneer in providing gas lighting for buildings. William Murdock (1754–1839), the company's chief engine erector in Cornwall, had made an experimental gas plant in 1792 for lighting his house in Redruth. When he returned to the firm's Soho foundry in Birmingham as manager in 1798, he installed a gas-making plant large enough to light the works. Before this time, various scientists in Belgium and France had created continuous flames by burning the gas released when coal was heated, but their lights were little more than scientific curiosities. Murdock turned the process into a commercial opportunity. In March 1802 he put on a remarkable display of this new technology when the peace treaty of Amiens was celebrated with a spectacle that excited much publicity and admiration. As reported in a local newspaper at the time:

> *A magnificent star composed of multicoloured lights decorated the top of the building while an image of a young girl welcoming the return of peace was silhouetted against the fully illuminated central window in the façade. The entire building was illuminated by 2600 coloured lights which rose in the form of a giant cross of St George carrying the word "peace," above which was a royal crown adorned with a star of extraordinary brilliance.*[14]

In 1805 Boulton and Watt installed a gas lighting system in their own 1801 fireproof mill at Salford. It consisted of

COPYING

The copying of engineers' and architects' drawings at this time had to be done by hand. The usual method was to place the original on top of the copy sheet and prick through it using a pin to create a series of points that could be joined using a rule or a drawing compass.

In 1780 James Watt patented what was probably the earliest form of machine for copying. It resembled a small printing press, and he called it a press-copier, which he made and marketed through his own firm, James Watt & Co. The process required the use of ink mixed with gum arabic, applied when writing a document or making a drawing to be copied. A sheet of damp tissue paper was then pressed against the manuscript and some of the ink was absorbed, creating a mirror image of the original on the tissue paper. The tissue copy could then be read through the thin paper. His machine was highly successful and was soon made in a portable version. Watt's invention lost its monopoly of the market for copying letters and business documents following the development of carbon paper in 1806 by an Italian engineer, Pellegrino Turri, who also made the first working typewriter.

The copying of large engineers' and architects' drawings continued to be made using the pin-pricking method until the middle of the nineteenth century.

286

286 Portable copying apparatus designed by James Watt, Jr., c. 1800. The aparatus used a copying process patented by James Watt in 1780.

287

288

six retorts, each of which produced enough gas for about 150 lights. They also began installing gas lighting in other factories, and one of their very first contracts, in June 1806, was for William Strutt's mill at Derby.

As the partnership between Marshall and the Benyons was approaching its end, the Benyons decided to construct two new mills, one at Meadow Lane in Leeds, the other in Shrewsbury, and Bage was responsible for their design. By now, Bage's ideas had moved on. It is believed that he used, for the first time, a cast iron roof truss. In a letter to William Strutt, Bage described his tests of two such trusses of 38-foot span (the span of the Meadow Lane mill). Drawings of his second Shrewsbury mill, made seven years after its completion when gas lighting was installed, show such a truss. Despite the success of the cast iron beams in his first Shrewsbury mill, certain questions about their design must have remained unresolved in Bage's mind. At Meadow Lane, Bage used simply supported beams spanning from column to column, rather than the continuous beams he had used at Shrewsbury.

With hindsight, we can suggest that Bage's unease was probably due to the fact that he had not been able to apply to the beams the same rational and quantitative thinking that he had to the columns. From correspondence Bage sent to William Strutt in August 1803, it is clear that he had been giving the matter considerable thought. Most likely he learned about the strength of brittle beams from the *Carpenters' New Guide*, written in 1792 by Peter Nicholson (the author of many technical books on building, with whom Telford was acquainted), where these scientists' ideas were first published in English. Like them, Bage argues that the strength of a rectangular beam is proportional to its breadth, and inversely to the square of its depth. Bage went on, however, to address the question of the strength of an inverted T-section—a form that had previously never been considered theoretically. He did so by calculating the relative strength of such a beam, compared to a simpler beam whose strength he had found by testing. This method avoided the need for absolute values of the tensile, compressive, or shear strengths of cast iron. As he said in a letter to William Strutt in August 1803 (in words that clearly come from the pen of an engineer, not a mathematician or scientist):

> *From these comparative strengths, and from the knowledge that the Cast iron Bar 1 inch square and three feet long will sustain 8 cwt. [hundredweight] laid on the middle, the weight to break a beam of any other size or length can be calculated. NB Though I have broken a bar of the above dimensions which sustained above 8 cwt. I always calculate as if it sustained only 6 cwt.*[15]

Simply using proportionality to compare relative strengths was not new—the Romans had done so for their catapults, Rodrigo Gil de Hontañón had followed "the rule of three" to scale abutment dimensions, and, by the 1790s, the proportionality of the strength of a timber beam to its width and, inversely, to the square of its depth was well known. Bage, however, combined an understanding of the mechanics involved and the properties of the material being used with the translation from one structural form (a rectangular beam) to another (the inverted T). In this way he was able to deal with a genuinely new design problem.

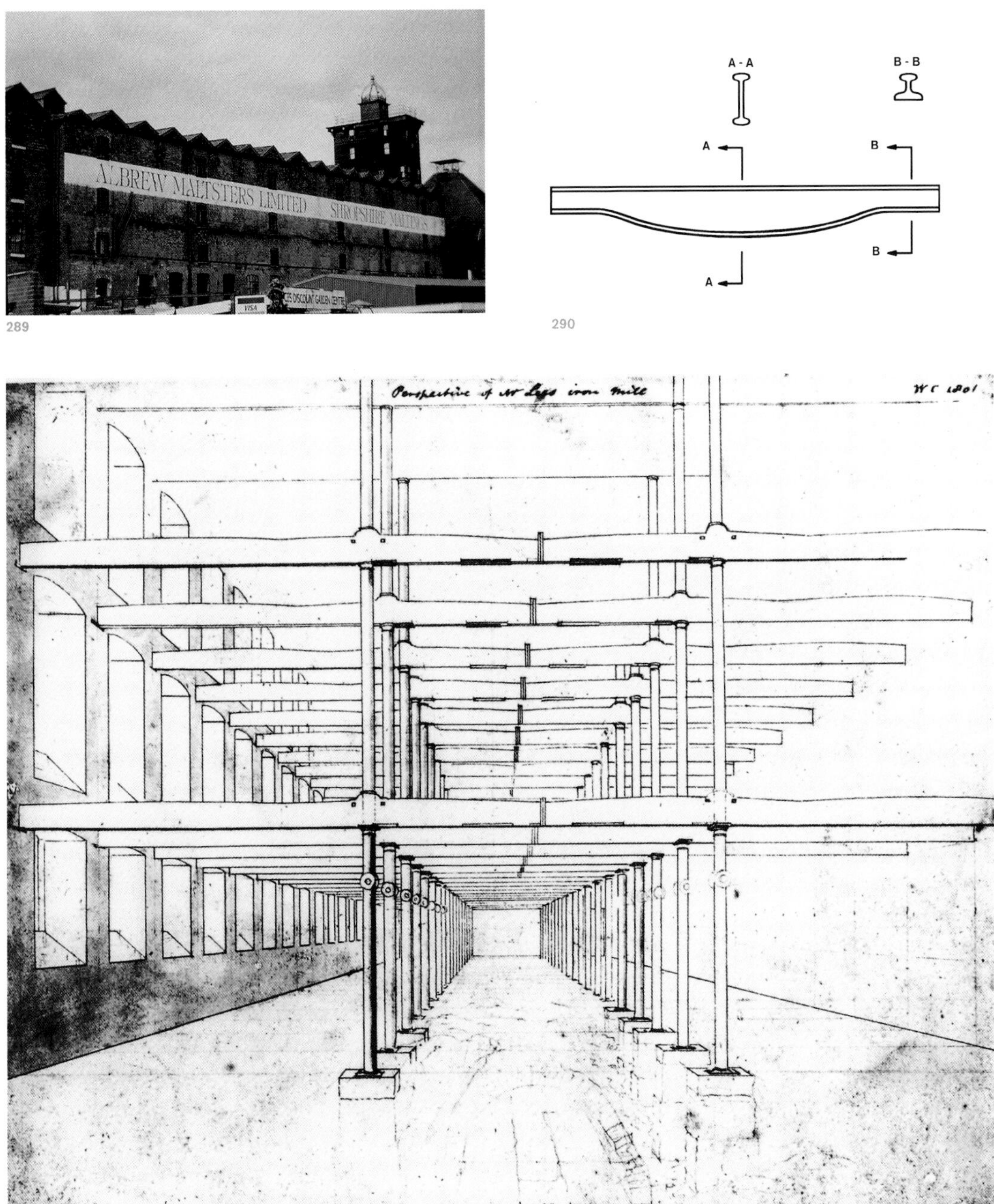

289

290

291

287 Castle Foregate Mill, Shrewsbury, England, 1796–97. Original cast iron beam, exposed after removal of an elevator fitted in the twentieth century. 288 Castle Foregate Mill. View of typical floor, showing cast iron columns with cruciform section, and brick jack arches. 289 Castle Foregate Mill. The earliest known fireproof building with cast iron columns and beams, with brick jack arch floors. 290 Cast iron fish-belly rail made by William Jessop, 1789. The shape, in elevation, reflects the bending moments carried by the rail. 291 Drawing of a factory in Salford, England, 1801, with cast iron columns and beams made by Boulton and Watt. Drawing shows the factory under construction, prior to building the jack arch floors.

From the first equation, and the results of the test Bage conducted, the value of k can be found by calculation to be 29 for his sample of cast iron. We know the dimensions of the beam Bage used at Meadow Lane from one of Telford's notebooks, which records the results of a test Bage undertook to check his calculated results: a span of 9 feet, a depth of 11.5 inches, and a flange 3 inches wide and 1.5 inches thick. Using these dimensions gives the beam a capacity of 13 tons at the center of the span. The beam Bage tested broke under a load of 14 tons. For a uniformly distributed load, his design method predicted failure at 26 tons, and this was precisely the load that caused collapse in his test. As Bage said, he took a cautious view of the strength of cast iron. From the test results he had obtained in 1795, he knew the strength varied from batch to batch, and hence he calculated using the figure of 6 hundredweight rather than the 8 hundredweight his test gave. This was equivalent to reducing the predicted strength of the beam from 26 tons, for a uniformly distributed load, to about 20 tons. The load each beam actually carried would have been similar to what Bage calculated at Castle Foregate—about 8 tons. It would appear, therefore, that Bage was designing his floor structure using a "safety factor" of about 2.5.

Although such calculations are commonplace today, the historical significance of Bage's engineering design methodology can hardly be overstated. Not only did he calculate the dimensions of the structural element to resist the expected loads while taking account of the material properties, he also intelligently simplified the mathematical model of the structure, in a conservative way, by ignoring the contribution of the web of the beam to its strength. Furthermore, in changing to a beam simply supported between two columns from a continuous beam supported by three columns (the science and mathematics of continuous beams was still several decades away), Bage was choosing a structural form that he was able to design. Put another way, he was designing a structure that mirrored the mathematical model he had conceived and was thus endeavoring to control the way the structure would behave.

Bage's designs for Meadow Lane were complete by the end of 1802. In January 1803 Strutt's original North Mill at Belper (1786) was totally destroyed by fire, and the waterwheel and spinning machinery were also lost. Worse still, because of the high insurance premiums, no part of the property was insured. Strutt invited Bage to visit him in Derby in March 1803, after which Bage wrote to him: "If on a balance of advantage and disadvantage you should at length prefer Iron beams, I should be glad to submit my reasoning on the strength and shape of them to your examination." Strutt's reply is lost, but on 29 August, Bage wrote: "My conscience has long upbraided me for having delayed to send you some theorems for ascertaining the strength of cast iron beams, but with the care of building two Mills... I really find but little time."[16] Strutt was persuaded by Bage's reasoning and used iron throughout, including for the roof truss.

The new North Mill came into operation late in 1804 and soon became widely known. It was featured as the exemplar building to illustrate the article on the manufacture of cotton in Abraham Rees's *Cyclopaedia* of 1819. It represents the culmination of ten years of rapid develop- 292, 293
ment in building engineering. The North Mill is full of 295, 296
engineering subtleties, such as the ingenious way the beams are located on the column heads. The beams end with a half cup that fits around the column spigot and is seated in a recess in the column capital; adjacent beams are linked with a wrought iron ring. Such a system was very quick to erect, yet provided sufficient integrity to the whole structure that would prevent the possibility of a progressive collapse should one beam fail. This was a matter that Bage and Strutt had recognized as important when they met in March 1803. Another example of Strutt's ingenuity is the way he integrated the large waterwheel into the building itself. Above the wheel, which was 5.5 meters in diameter and 7 meters long, he built two stone tied arches spanning 7 meters, upon which he constructed six stories of jack arch floors.[17] To reduce the weight the arches had to carry, the jack arches of the fifty-four bays above are constructed using hollow pots in place of brick. Strutt also paid great attention to detail; for instance, the wrought iron tie rods linking the cast iron beams are fully embedded within the brick of the jack arch, and the lower surface of the flange of the beams is chamfered to pick up the curve of the brick jack arch. The result is an elegant, uncluttered, undulating ceiling.

The building was innovative in other ways as well. The stairwell is fully enclosed to provide a separated fire es-

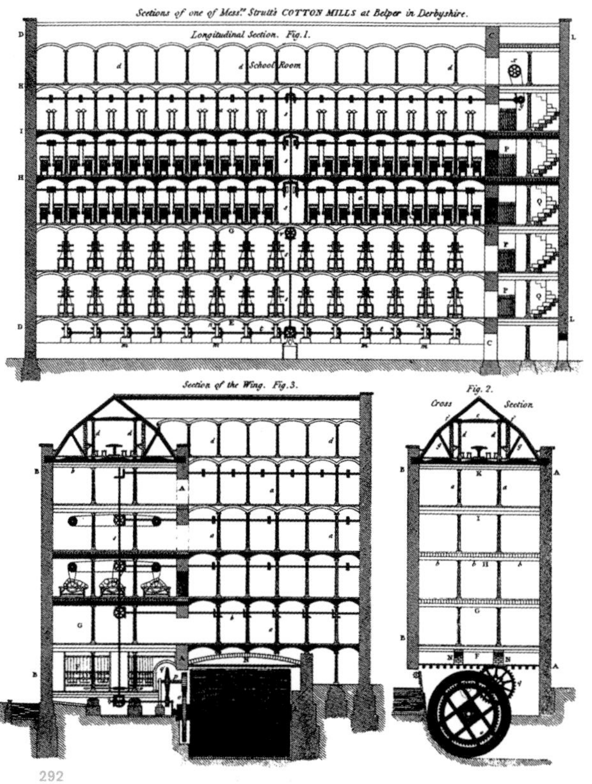

292

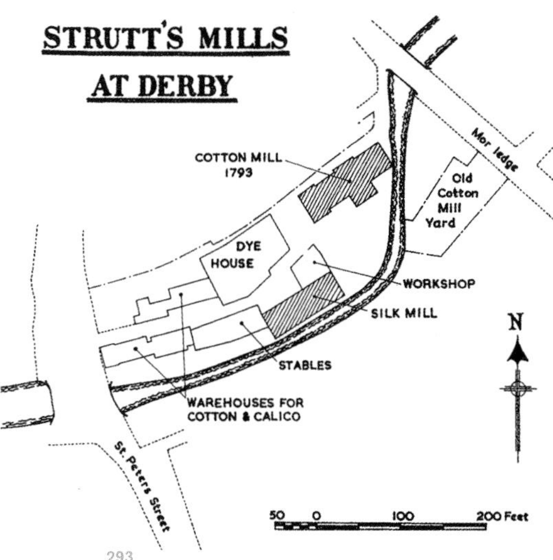

293

cape, and also contains a hoist. The mill was heated using Strutt's own hot air system, and gas lighting was introduced after a few years. This building justly deserves the description by A.W. Skempton, a modern authority on structural history, as "the most perfect of all the early iron-framed buildings."[18]

By around 1805, following the first decade of fireproof mills, a number of important changes in building construction had been made: cast iron had replaced timber for columns, beams, floors, and roof structures; a number of different beam sections had been tried, all with the aim of reducing the amount of iron needed; and cast iron beams were made to span from column to column, rather than connected to form continuous beams spanning over several columns. These developments in the 297
use of cast iron would set the pattern for the construction of industrial buildings for most of the nineteenth century. From the 1840s, they also served as the springboard from which wrought iron gradually replaced cast iron, first for the construction of beams, then columns, leading to the replacement of load-bearing masonry walls by columns to create the first fully framed iron buildings in the 1850s.

292 North Mill, Belper, near Derby, England, 1803–1804. Engineer: William Strutt. Sections showing location of waterwheel and mill machinery. 293 North Mill, Belper. Map showing location with respect to the Derwent River and the mill race providing water to drive the waterwheel.

Science, Comfort, and Well-Being

Although structural engineering was the first to benefit from a scientific understanding of the task at hand, physicists, chemists, and medical researchers were at work during the Age of Reason exploring matters affecting the comfort and well-being of people who used buildings. The science of modern heating, ventilation, and air-conditioning comprises a number of strands: the physical properties of the atmosphere, the constituents of air, the means by which heat is transferred from one place or body to another, and conversion of heat energy into mechanical work, and vice versa.

Galileo was the first person, in around 1592, to construct a device based upon the expansion of a liquid to indicate the intensity of heat, or what would later be known as temperature. His "thermoscope," as this instrument was called, allowed comparison of conditions at different times and places, although, because it was open to the atmosphere, its readings varied with atmospheric pressure and the weather. The sealed thermometer was used beginning around 1650; the first reliable sealed thermometers, filled with mercury or alcohol, were developed by the German physicist Daniel Gabriel Fahrenheit (1686–1736) in about 1715. However, it was not until the 1760s that Joseph Black (1728–99) precisely differentiated temperature (as a measure of the degree or intensity of heat measured in degrees) from the quantity of heat or heat capacity (today measured in Joules). Black also conceived the idea of the "latent heat" released when a gas condenses into liquid form with no change in temperature.

At this time heat was believed to be an invisible, weightless substance, called caloric, which objects were thought to possess in larger or smaller quantities and that passed in and out of them as they were heated or cooled. While this was a useful model, it had its limitations, primarily the apparently limitless quantities of caloric that could be generated by an object continually subjected to friction. This phenomenon is familiar to anyone who works with tools to cut or drill wood or metal; cutting edges quickly get hot and need cooling with water if the job is a long one. Benjamin Thompson (1753–1814), an American émigré serving in the Bavarian army, observed this in his duties while supervising the boring of brass cannon in Munich. He found it implausible that there should be an infinite supply of caloric, and considered the possibility that the heat was generated by the effort put into turning the cannon as it was bored. Thompson, or Count von Rumford, as he was known after he was awarded the honorific "Count of the Holy Roman Empire" in 1793 for his military service, conducted an experiment to measure the work needed to raise the temperature of the cannon by a certain amount. He repeated the experiment with the cannon underwater and continued until the water in the tank was actually boiling, a result that astonished the onlookers. He concluded that, rather than being a substance, heat must be some sort of motion that could be increased or excited by mechanical means such as friction. It would be another fifty years before the English physicist James Prescott Joule (1818–89) would conduct more careful experiments to establish the mechanical equivalent of heat.

Thompson undertook many more scientific studies related to heat. He was able to improve the Bavarian army's dress after establishing that heat is lost from the body mainly by convection and that the insulating qualities of clothing arise from the air trapped by its fibers. He also conducted experiments to improve the domestic fireplace, which was notorious for emitting its smoke into the room rather than up the chimney in cold weather. By streamlining the passage leading from the fire into the chimney, he allowed the hot gases to flow more easily and faster, enabling the air in the chimney to heat up more quickly and create the draw necessary for such a fire to work efficiently. Thompson was also one of several people in the late eighteenth century who experimented with heating rooms and greenhouses using steam fed 298 through pipes.

Another fundamental property of air was the pressure exerted by the atmosphere. One of Galileo's students, Evangelista Torricelli (1608–47), devised the mercury barometer that measures atmospheric pressure as the height of mercury in a glass tube that balances the pressure exerted by the atmosphere (usually about 760 millimeters). In 1659, Robert Boyle, a colleague of both Wren and Hooke, made his studies of "the spring of the air and its effects," and established that the pressure and volume of a gas are inversely proportional, the relationship known as Boyle's law. Boyle also established that sound travels as pressure waves in the air and,

ENGINEERING CALCULATIONS

Before the electronic hand calculator appeared in the early 1970s, the slide rule was the engineer's standard tool for making calculations. It had been developed soon after the invention of logarithms in 1614, and by the end of the seventeenth century was widely used by all those who needed to make calculations—scientists, mathematicians, artillery engineers, navigators, and ship designers. At this time, however, engineering was not a particularly quantitative activity; when it was, an engineer would consult a mathematician. This situation changed during the eighteenth century, by the end of which calculations were very much part of daily life and mathematics an important component of the engineer's education. It is not clear how the slide rule entered the engineer's life, but James Watt (1736–1819) played a part, in Britain at least. So crucial did he regard the slide rule to his work designing and making steam engines that, in 1775, he began manufacturing and selling them. For some years afterward they were often known in England as Soho scales, named after the district of Birmingham where Watt had his engineering works (see illustration below). They were made of boxwood and sometimes had other, nonlogarithmic scales that could perform dedicated and frequently used calculations, such as finding the area of a circle from its diameter, or the weight of a piece of timber knowing its dimensions. Useful numerical data were often engraved on the rear face of the rule. At this time slide rules seldom had a movable cursor, which became common only in the 1860s (see chapter 7, pp. 370–71).

DESCRIPTION OF THE SOHO SLIDING RULE. The rule itself is made of hard box-wood, $10\frac{1}{2}$ inches long, $\frac{8}{10}$ broad, and about $\frac{2}{10}$ thick. A groove is formed along the middle of one side of it; and a slider of the same wood, $\frac{3}{10}$ wide by $\frac{1}{10}$ thick, is fitted into the groove, so as to slide freely endways, backwards or forwards therein.

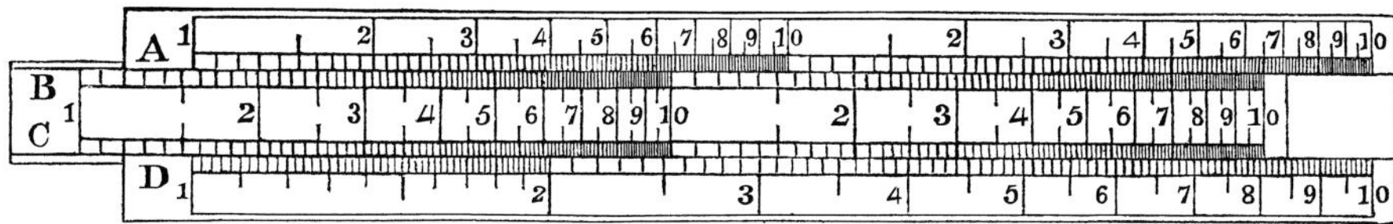

294

294 Description and drawing of the Soho sliding scale, an early slide rule manufactured and sold by James Watt beginning in the late eighteenth century. From "A Treatise on the Steam Engine," by John Farey, 1827.

hence, cannot travel through a vacuum. More than a century later, in 1787, the French chemist and physicist Jacques Charles (1746–1823) established further that, at constant pressure, the volume of a gas varies linearly with temperature; this is the relationship we now know as Charles' law.

The phenomena by which heat can be transferred—through a solid body by conduction, in the movement of a gas or liquid by convection, and directly through the air by radiation—were well known in a qualitative way. The quantification of the processes of conduction and convection was, however, complex, and became a practical proposition for engineers only in the early nineteenth century, especially following the publication of the classic work on the subject, *Théorie analytique de la chaleur* (Analytical Theory of Heat) (Paris, 1822), by Baron Jean Baptiste Joseph Fourier (1768–1830). Until that time, calculations of heat transfer were based on practical observations about the quantities of fuel needed to heat buildings. Calculating heat transfer by radiation was possible only from the late nineteenth century.

Our bodies are sensitive to temperature, which we feel in two ways: by the skin's physical contact with the air or a liquid or solid, and by radiation. Furthermore, our sensation of warmth and comfort is influenced by the humidity of the air, which determines the degree to which moisture (perspiration) evaporates from our skin; the more humid the atmosphere, the less perspiration evaporates and the warmer we feel. The presence of water vapor in the atmosphere, and the conditions under which this water vapor condenses to form water, were first elaborated by the physician and science writer William Charles Wells (1757–1817) in his book *An Essay on Dew, and Several Appearances Connected with It*, published in 1814 in London.

Fresh, Foul, and Miasmic Air

In parallel with establishing the physical properties of the atmosphere was the growing understanding of the importance of the constituents of the air to life and good health: the necessity for oxygen and the consequences of too much carbon dioxide. Robert Hooke established in the 1670s that the constituent of air essential for respiration was the same as that needed for burning. Joseph Black isolated carbon dioxide from air in the 1750s and identified it as the gas exhaled in animal respiration and one of the products of combustion. Two decades later, Joseph Priestley established that mice died when breathing carbon dioxide, and that both the breathability of air and its capacity to support combustion were improved by the presence of plants growing in the chamber of air being studied. Priestley and the eminent French chemist Antoine-Laurent Lavoisier (1743–94) both finally succeeded in isolating oxygen in the 1770s. The rapid growth of the industrial and commercial cities of England in mid-eighteenth century brought with it terrible consequences for the population; one of the most devastating was disease on a massive scale. The population increase had not been matched by a corresponding improvement in the provision of clean water or sanitary treatment of human and animal waste, and the fetid urban environment of the late eighteenth century is hardly imaginable today. Even more terrifying for most people at the time was that they did not know how disease originated, or how it was transferred from one person to another in the regular epidemics of typhoid, dysentery, and cholera.

Beginning in the 1750s, doctors, scientists, philosophers, and social reformers throughout Europe were starting to pay serious attention to health matters and the nature and causes of disease. Typical of ideas at the time was the miasmic theory, which proposed that disease was caused, or at least exacerbated, by a poisonous vapor that emanated from sources of corruption such as rotting meat or the bodies of sick animals and people. It was well known that disease spread freely in the confined quarters of ships, army barracks, prisons, and, ironically, hospitals. It was also believed that some diseases were airborne, and that cross-infection could be reduced by extracting infected or miasmic air from buildings where it was known to exist, especially in hospitals and prisons. While the benefits of isolating institutionalized people were understood, isolation was not always possible due to the function of a given building or the technical difficulty of heating and ventilating many individual small rooms.

In 1752, the scientist and curate of Teddington in southwest London, the Reverend Stephen Hales (1677–1761), a Fellow of the Royal Society, achieved an important breakthrough in persuading the authorities at Newgate Prison in London to create ventilation holes in

295

296

Tie rod
9' Arch span
brick arch
Inches
12" x 12" Scots Pine
(a) MILFORD
1792-93
STRUTT
Plaster
9' beam span
Column Axis

10'.6" arch span
(b) SHREWSBURY
1796-97
BAGE
11"
9'.6" beam span
5"

9' arch span
(c) SALFORD
1799-1801
BOULTON & WATT
13"
14' beam span
3½"

CAST IRON BEAMS

10' arch span
W.I. ring
(d) LEEDS
1802-03
BAGE
12"
9' beam span
3"

W.I. ring
7' arch span
(e) BELPER
1803-04
STRUTT
10"
9' beam span
3"

297

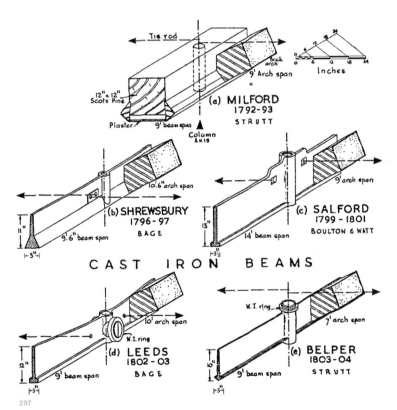

295 North Mill, Belper. Exterior. 296 North Mill, Belper. Interior view of fifth floor. 297 Drawings showing the evolution of fireproof construction of mills and warehouses in England, 1792–1804.

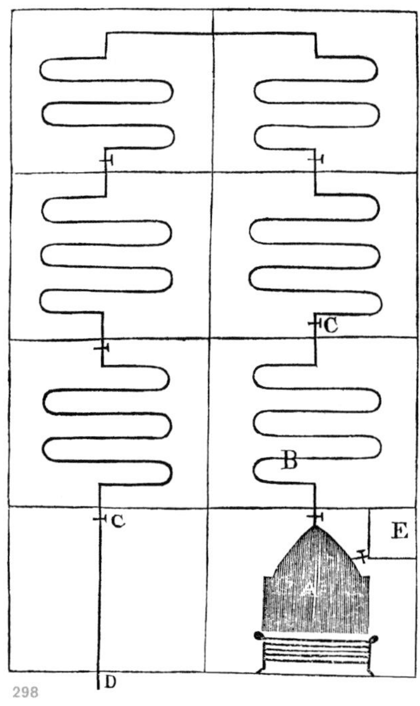

298

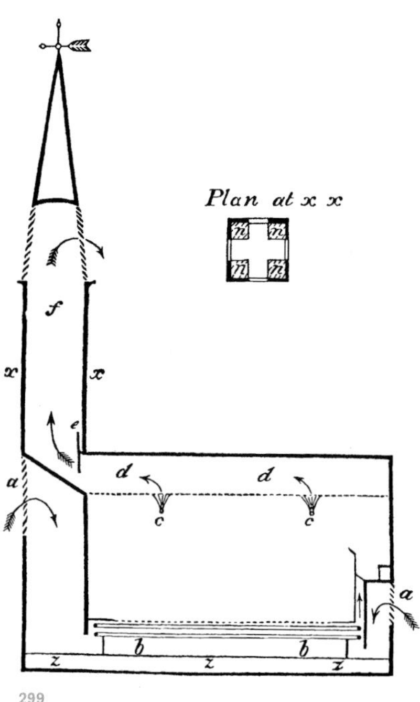

299

PLYMOUTH
VUE SUD-OUEST.
N. Thomas Direx.
1. 2. 3. 4. 5. 6. 7. 8. 9. 10. Quartiers séparés. 11. Quartier de la petite Verole. 12. Chambres des Gardes Malades. 13. Cuisine et Refectoire
14 Chambre des provisions. 15. Chapelle. 16. Loges des Domestiques et des Portiers. 17. Concierges et Offices
On a suprimé l'Elevation des quartiers 9. et 10.

300

298 Diagram of a steam heating system proposed by William Cook, England, 1745. Steam was conducted to every room of a house before being vented to atmosphere. 299 Natural ventilation system for a church, from *Practical Treatise on the Warming and Ventilation of Buildings*, by Charles Richardson, London, 1837. 300 Naval Hospital at Stonehouse, Plymouth, England, 1758–62. Its use of naturally ventilated island wards reduced cross-infection.

the cell walls and install a massive fan to feed fresh air into the rooms and force the stale air out. Sickness and mortality rates fell immediately. The lessons from Newgate spread quickly among military physicians and social reformers alike, such as John Howard, who visited hundreds of prisons throughout Europe. By the 1770s there was a scientific basis for supporting the common sense observation that fresh air was more pleasant, and that "foul" air, rich in carbon dioxide, water vapor, and the odors of burning candles or oil lamps, was less pleasant and even detrimental to human well-being. This decade also saw the proliferation of several types of buildings in which many people congregated: theaters, mills, infirmaries, prisons, and buildings for commerce, such as banks. All these buildings needed heat, light, and ventilation on a scale that could not be met using domestic installations. They called for more effective ventilation systems than was provided by simply opening windows. Taking inspiration from the newly developing factory system in the English Midlands, hospital designers began to think of their buildings as "curing machines." They began to approach their design in a more rational and scientific way, to achieve good ventilation and heating, both through attention to the layout of the internal spaces and the provision of the means for distributing heat and fresh air. A physician at Lyon Hospital in France, for example, had demonstrated that foul air from rotting meat fell to the floor of hospital wards, and he argued for the extraction of air at low level. Two methods of ventilation were possible—natural and forced.

Natural Ventilation

Natural ventilation could be achieved using the wind and the naturally occurring pressure differences between
299 the inside and outside of a building, or the convection currents arising from air warmed by human body heat within a building.

One of the first hospitals to embrace the latest thinking on disease, infection, and the benefits of ventilation was
300 the naval hospital at Stonehouse in Plymouth, England, built in 1758–62. It comprised a number of buildings, each containing several small wards separated by internal walls, to segregate different diseases. The wards had windows on both sides to ensure that foul air was continuously removed by cross-ventilation. These and other innovative ideas were publicized by John Aikin (1747–1822) in his book *Thoughts on Hospitals*, published in 1771. News of the quality of Stonehouse hospital spread abroad and, in 1787, it was one of fifty-two English hospitals visited by a party from the French Académie des sciences. The visit formed part of the work of a Royal Commission set up to design a new municipal hospital for Paris. Under the leadership of Jacques René Tenon, and with Charles Augustin Coulomb as one of its members, the party singled out Stonehouse hospital for special mention in its report of the visit: "in not one of the hospitals of France and England, we would say in the whole of Europe, except Plymouth hospital, are the individual buildings destined to receive patients as well ventilated and as completely isolated."[19] Tenon advocated a similar approach to designing hospitals in Paris in his *Mémoires sur les hôpitaux de Paris (Recollections of the Hospitals in Paris)*, written in the following year. Nevertheless, despite the book's subsequent fame as a source of guidance on hospital design, very few of its recommendations were implemented in Paris until well into the nineteenth century.

The success of Stonehouse Naval Hospital led to the adoption of these new designs in many new naval and military hospitals in England, especially in the 1790s during the Napoleonic wars. New naval hospitals built at Portsmouth in Hampshire and Deal in Kent had narrow wards with windows on opposite walls to facilitate cross-ventilation.

Forced Ventilation

The use of fire as the motive power to drive forced ventilation had been understood since the beginning of the eighteenth century. In addition to fire, the dozens of candles in candelabras used to light large rooms such as theater auditoria or meeting rooms would also heat the air and set up air movement. A duct above the candelabra led into a vent which might also have had a cowl to provide some suction by the wind outside. John Theophilus Desaguliers had used his understanding of forced convection to try to improve ventilation in the House of Commons, with some success (see chapter 4, pp. 215–16). Sir Humphrey Davy would use the same method in an attempt to improve ventilation in the House of Lords in 1811, again with some success. Despite the sound principle, however, and the limited success of the attempts at the Houses of Parliament, the driving power of forced convection is very low, and does not easily work effectively. Even today it requires careful design and construction to function well.

The designers of buildings that accommodated large numbers of people soon realized that it would be easier to create the necessary movement of air using a mechanical fan powered by a steam engine. Mechanical ventilation using fans had first been employed as a matter of necessity in the sixteenth century in lead, iron, and tin mines in Germany (see chapter 3, fig. 134); these early examples were powered by hand or by waterwheels. Desaguliers's attempts to improve the natural ventilation of the House of Commons in 1723 produced favorable but limited results. He returned to the problem during the years 1734 to 1736, when he installed a hand-powered, crank-driven centrifugal fan, 7 feet in diameter and made of wood, made to the same design as one he had devised
302 a decade earlier to ventilate lead mines. In his description of the trials of the installation, Desaguliers coined the word "ventilator," not for the machine but for the man whose job it was to turn the fan when the House of
303 Commons chamber was in use. In 1791, the heating and ventilating system was improved by moving the ventilator to the center of the ceiling and introducing a stove beneath the floor to heat air that entered the chamber through a grating in the floor.

Good ventilation was an important issue in ships, too, where disease was common and living conditions very cramped. Nor was the air quality below decks enhanced by the livestock kept there to provide mariners with fresh meat. A series of experiments was undertaken in the early 1740s to introduce fire-driven ventilation into the British navy's ships, whose increasing size and need to undertake longer journeys had made living conditions even worse than before. However, the inherent danger of open fires on the lower decks of ships proved an insurmountable problem, and interest turned toward mechanical ventilation. Stephen Hales, who had a long interest in improving public health, developed the idea of using large
301 wooden bellows to pump air through ventilation ducts. He undertook the first tests of his ventilator in 1741 near his home in Teddington in a granary, not with public health in mind, but to circulate the air and prevent the grain from becoming damp and rotting. Hales followed this with successful trials of his ventilator in both ships and buildings as a means of helping prevent the spread of disease. In his book *A Description of Ventilators* (1743) he likened a ship to an enormous whale, and his ventilators to the animal's lungs—a metaphor for ventilation that survived long after Hales's death. The timing could not have been better for Hales. A number of terrible outbreaks of disease in the 1740s had raised health to the top of the agenda in Parliament, and the *Gentleman's Magazine* reported the success of Hales's ventilators in Newgate Prison in London with enthusiasm. They captured the public imagination, not least because they offered a solution to the terrible conditions prevailing in ships (naval and slave ships alike), prisons and hospitals. His ventilators proved highly successful, and during the 1740s were installed throughout the British navy and over a dozen prisons and hospitals in Britain. In 1758, Hales reported in the second edition of his book (*A Treatise on Ventilators*) that they were also installed as far afield as Naples, Saxony, Silesia, St. Petersburg, and Lapland. Hales's book became widely known and did much to accelerate the installation of artificial ventilation throughout Europe.

There was just one minor inconvenience with Hales's ventilators—they were human powered, and the operators had to be recruited from among the inmates of the establishments in which they were installed. It is a testimony to both the perceived and the real benefits of mechanical ventilation that there were apparently few complaints from mariners, prisoners, or hospital patients about this addition to their daily routine. Nevertheless, the manpower needed to achieve adequate ventilation of buildings was considerable, and in most types of building, a relative luxury; for example, a century later in the 1840s, two men were required to provide fresh-air ventilation to Queen Victoria's box at the opera. Where a source of water power was readily available, such as in the early textile mills where ventilation was introduced, this was used—not for health reasons but to extract the dust-laden air and reduce the risk of fire. In other buildings, however, finding a suitable source of power was a major problem; both falling weights and spring-powered clockwork mechanisms were tried, but with little success. Generally speaking, mechanical ventilation was used only sporadically until the mid-nineteenth century, when small steam engines provided a practical means of driving the ventilation machinery.

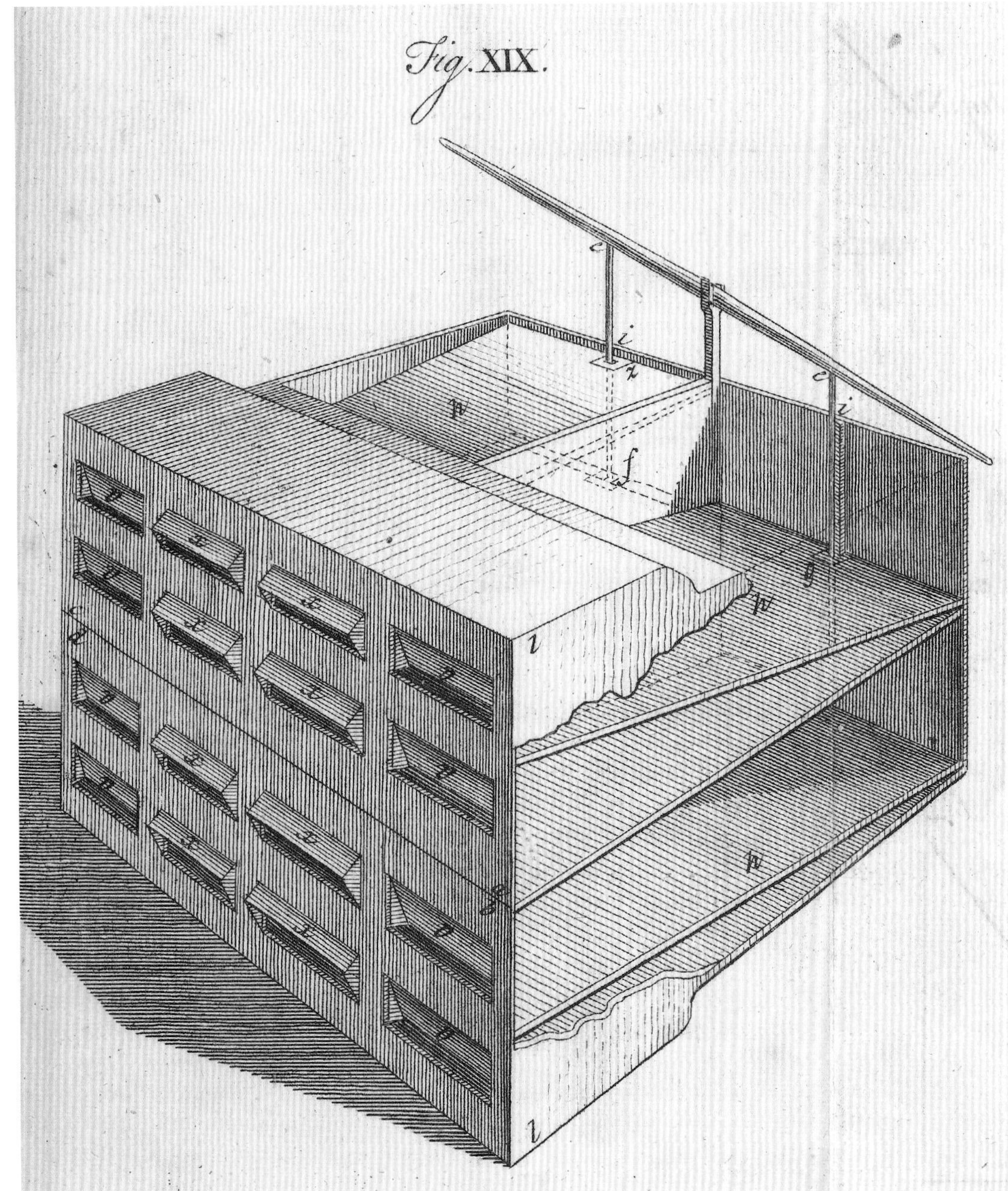

301

301 Stephen Hales, illustration of ventilation bellows, from *A Treatise on Ventilators*, 1758.

Architectural Acoustics

The main acoustical issue that concerned building designers of the seventeenth and eighteenth centuries, as in the ancient world described by Vitruvius, was the intelligibility of speech, especially in the debating chambers of politicians, and in the growing number of theaters. The Enlightenment also witnessed the growing popularity (at least in elite circles) of chamber music, largely encouraged by the invention and technical enhancement of musical instruments such as the harpsichord and fortepiano. These improved instruments used ingenious mechanisms and large sounding boards to produce plucked and percussive notes with unprecedented speed and at much greater volumes than those of earlier instruments such as the lute, harp, and clavichord. When played in a room with a very live or reverberant acoustic, the individual musical notes from the instruments merged with one another and became indistinguishable. This effectively defeated the objectives of the instrument makers and musicians to show off their virtuosity and technical skill.

It was already well understood that the size of a room and the reflectivity of the walls, floor, and ceiling affected the intelligibility of speech and music, and that two different factors were at work. One was the diminishing loudness or intensity of the sound, both with distance and according to the amount of sound absorbed by the room's surfaces and contents. The second was the increasing confusion of sounds caused by reflections from the room's surfaces.

This understanding led building designers to follow a number of pragmatic rules that helped them achieve acceptable room acoustics. The designer could choose between three different types of surfaces: stone or plaster would enhance reflections; woven fabric, such as tapestries and curtains, would absorb sound; and timber paneling was intermediate between the two. Based on the acoustic performance of existing rooms, a designer could choose what he hoped would be a suitable combination of the three surface types. The other design factors were the distance between the listener and the speaker or musical instrument, and the directness of the sound path. Theater designers tried to ensure that the entire audience could see the actors, not only for theatrical effect, but also so that at least some of the sound could travel directly to the listener without reflections off walls or ceiling. This was also especially important for high frequency tones, which diminish in intensity after reflection more than do low frequencies. It was generally agreed that an actor speaking in a normal voice could be understood clearly up to a distance of about 18 meters, and with difficulty up to about 25 meters. The result of applying these basic rules was the development of the familiar raked seating and tiers of balconies in theaters and dedicated concert halls.

The need for good acoustics was, however, not the only influence on theater design. There was a tension between, on the one hand, ensuring that the actors were understood, and on the other, the patron's desire to increase audience size and the income from ticket sales. Many theaters in the late eighteenth century were built with distances between actor and listener of more than 30 meters, which forced actors to change their style of delivery. They learned the skill of talking in increasingly louder tones while seeming to speak in a normal voice; a good actor could even fill an auditorium with what sounded like a whisper.

Designers of theaters intended for performances of both music and the spoken word faced a further, insuperable challenge, because the acoustic characteristics needed for good intelligibility of speech make music sound very dry and unpleasant. A hall well suited to music, on the other hand, rendered the spoken word almost incomprehensible to audience members occupying all but the seats nearest the stage. The most practical solution to this dilemma was to have different buildings dedicated to each form of entertainment. Theater, however, often relied on music to enhance the drama, and in most large venues orchestra pits were incorporated between the front seats and the stage. The acoustics of such theaters were inevitably a matter of compromise, usually favoring the intelligibility of the spoken word.

Design rules for theater acoustics were not very reliable in the eighteenth century, and many sonic disasters resulted. In his autobiography of 1740, the actor and playwright Colley Cibber wrote of the Queen's Theatre in the Haymarket, London, designed by the eminent architect and playwright Sir John Vanbrugh (1664–1726) and built in 1704–1705, that all its architectural elegance was of no avail:

> *...when scarce one word in ten could be distinctly heard... The extraordinary and superfluous space occasioned such an undulation from the voice of every actor that generally what they said sounded like the gabbling of so many people in the lofty aisles in a cathedral... [and] the articulate[d] sounds of a speaking voice were drowned by the hollow reverberations of one word upon another.*[20]

Throughout Europe the second half of the eighteenth century saw a boom in theater building in the major cities, and designers generally learned from the acoustic mishaps of the early part of the 1700s. By the late eighteenth century it was common practice to use the ceiling or soffit above the front of the stage as a "sounding board" (actually a reflector), and the ceiling over the orchestra pit to "throw the voice forward" from the stage to the back of the stalls and to the galleries.

The English architect George Saunders (c. 1762–1839) was the author of the earliest design guide for theaters: *A Treatise on Theatres*, published in London in 1790. In his opening chapters he paid a great deal of attention to "phonics" (that is, acoustics), criticizing, for example, theaters that had deep boxes and galleries, as their low height "obstruct[ed] the sound...[and] the little that enters is presently attracted and absorbed by the persons, clothes, etc. of the spectators in the foremost rows." Saunders conducted many experiments on the effect of the shape of theater auditoriums on intelligibility, comparing the results to those obtained in the open air, and concluded that the oval or horseshoe forms were best, but that these did not allow good views of the stage. He concluded that the semicircular form was best, "with its centre seventeen feet (five metres) in front of the speaker," and that the diameter of the circle should be no greater than 60 feet (18 meters). Saunders was also aware that the voice did not carry well above an angle of 45 degrees to the horizontal, and thus the height of the auditorium should be no greater than three quarters of the diameter of the circle. Concerning materials, he wrote:

> *Wood is sonorous, conductive and produces a pleasing tone, and is therefore the very best material for lining a theater; for not absorbing so much as some, and not conducting so much as others, this medium renders it peculiarly suitable to rooms for musical purposes; the little resonance it occasions being rather agreeable than injurious.*[21]

Saunders used his understanding of acoustics to produce designs for both what he called an "Ideal Theatre" and a similar opera house that also incorporated the latest ideas on protection against fire, including staircases constructed entirely of stone and enclosed by walls.

Saunders's experiments—and the practical guidance for designers he deduced from them—were repeated by the architect W.S. Inman, who wrote one of the first books to include general guidance on acoustics for building designers, *Principles of Ventilation, Warming and the Transmission of Sound*, published in London in 1836. He maintained, for example, that the hearer should never be more than 22 meters from the speaker, the ceiling should be used to convey sound to the upper seats of the auditorium, the circular plan is best, and the entire audience should have sight of the stage. Inman also repeated the advice of the German physicist Ernst Chladni (1756–1827), who had studied how musical instruments create their characteristic sounds. His experiments led him to explore both the vibration of sheets of wood and metal and how such vibrations were conveyed through the air to the listener's ear. He published the results of his investigations on the subject first in *Entdeckungen über die Theorie des Klanges* (Discoveries Concerning the Theory of Sound) in Leipzig in 1787, and then, in 1802, in *Die Akustik*, the first comprehensive textbook on acoustics, which was translated into French in 1809. Chladni's book included some useful instruction on designing auditoriums that drew both on his own scientific work and the practical experience of both Saunders and Johann Gottlieb Rhode (1762–1827), author of *Theorie der Verbreitung des Schalles für Baukünstler* (Theory of the Propagation of Sound for Building Designers), a small guide published in Berlin in 1800. Writing in 1836, Inman summarized Chladni's recommendations thus:

> *Rooms will be favourable to the transmission of sound:*
>
> 1. *When arranged to facilitate its natural progress;*
> 2. *When its intensity is augmented by resonance or simultaneous reflection, so that the reaction is undistinguishable from the primitive sound;*
> 3. *When not too lofty or too vaulted;*
> 4. *When there is not a too extensive surface for the sound to strike against at once;*
> 5. *When the seats are successively elevated.*
>
> *He [Chladni] observes that:*

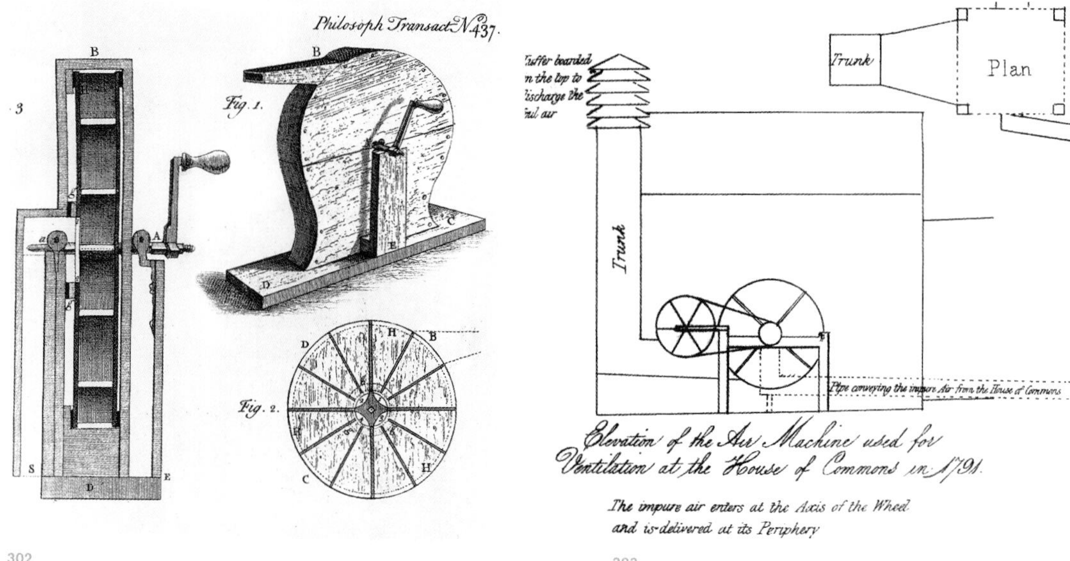

when the enclosed space does not exceed 65 feet, any form may be adopted for a room;
that elliptical, circular, and semi-circular plans produce prolonged reverberations;
parabolic plans and ceilings are the best for distinct hearing.[22]

Chladni recommended that for concert rooms, square and polygonal plans should have pyramidal ceilings, and circular plans domed ones, and that the orchestra be placed on high, in the center, to produce the best effect and avoid echo.

In *Die Akustik*, Chladni illustrates one intriguing design for a theater in which the walls are made of panels that can be rotated on their vertical axes to change their angle and, hence, the direction of reflected sound, and also to allow some sound to penetrate into the cavity behind, thus reducing the intensity of reflections; he does not say if the theater was built. Saunders's and Chladni's design rules were widely quoted and used for well over half a century, and were not really superseded until the early twentieth century, when the American physicist Wallace Sabine first measured and quantified the reflectivity and absorption capacity of different materials and surfaces and used these results to predict the reverberation time of a lecture theater or concert hall (see chapter 7, pp. 414–16).

The second half of the eighteenth century saw the appearance of a number of new building types: warehouses and factories, theaters and opera houses, hospitals and prisons. In each case the design and construction of early examples of these types followed traditional building precedent, little different from that used for large residential structures. As designers began to analyze the particular requirements of each type of building, however, so their layout, detailed design, structural systems, and construction methods evolved to suit more precisely the function of each building.

302 John Theophilus Desaguliers, hand-powered forced ventilation system, from *A Course of Experimental Philosophy*, London, 1734. 303 House of Commons, London, diagram showing the improved ventilation system installed in 1791, from *A Popular Treatise of the Warming and Ventilation of Buildings*, by Charles Richardson, London, 1837.

chapter 6

The Harmony of Theory and Practice 1800–1860

People and Events

1762–1836 Jean-Frédéric, Marquis de Chabannes

1764–1849 Johann Eytelwein

1766–1843 Charles Baird

1774–1828 Charles Sylvester

1776–1846 Matthew Clark

1785–1836 Claude Louis Marie Henri Navier

1788–1825 Thomas Tredgold

1789–1861 Eaton Hodgkinson

1789–1874 William Fairbairn

1796–1832 Nicolas Léonard Sadi Carnot

1803–59 Robert Stephenson

1804–54 August Borsig

1805–63 David Boswell Reid

1800–74 James Bogardus

1806–84 Daniel Badger

1807–86 Godfrey Greene

1810–74 Charles Fox

1813–59 Jean Barthélemy Camille Polonceau

1814–79 Eugène Emmanuel Viollet-le-Duc

1814–87 Joseph Louis Lambot

1818–89 James Prescott Joule

1819–1902 William B. Wilkinson

1820–72 William Rankine

1821–81 Karl Culmann

1822–88 Rudolf Clausius

1823–94 Johann Schwedler

1824–1907 William Thomson (Lord Kelvin)

Materials and Technology

1805 Gas lighting in mills

From c. 1820 Forced ventilation in large buildings

1820s Idea of thermo-dynamic cycle established by Sadi Carnot

1824 Portland cement patented by Joseph Aspdin

Knowledge and Learning

From c. 1800 Publication of books for practicing engineers and books on building services engineering

1800–55 Polytechnic schools founded throughout German-speaking Europe

1801 Johann Eytelwein, *Handbuch der Mechanik fester Körper und Hydraulik* (textbook)

1802 United States Military Academy, West Point, New York, founded

1802 Ernst Chladni, *Die Akustik* (first comprehensive acoustics textbook)

1818 Institution of Civil Engineers founded in Britain

1818 Thomas Tredgold, *Principles of Warming and Ventilating*

1820s First mechanics institutes founded in Britain

Design Methods

From 1820s Mathematical models of elastic behavior of structures (stress and strain) by Navier and others

1820s Amount of annual energy (coal) needed to heat a building first calculated by Tredgold

Design Tools: Drawing and Calculation

From c. 1800 Modern conventions for drawings of buildings

c. 1803 Use of proportionality by Charles Bage to calculate relative strengths

Buildings

1803–1804 North Mill, Belper, England

1806–10 Derbyshire General Infirmary, Derby, England

1808–13 Halle au blé, Paris, France

1817 Moscow Manege, Moscow, Russia

1827–30 Syon House, West London, England

1800 | 1805 | 1810 | 1815 | 1820 | 1825

1827–1909 Robert Henry Bow

1831–1906 Amedée Mannheim

1830s First passenger trains

1840s First artificially cooled buildings

1830s Development of the I-beam

1840s Caloric theory of heat finally superseded by energy theory

1830s Work on acoustics of new House of Commons by Reid

1840s Growth of ice harvesting industry

1850s First uses of reinforced concrete by Wilkinson and Lambot

1840s First rolled wrought iron sections

1850s Key components in place for development of skeleton frame structures

1840s Fireproof cast iron construction in U.S.

1844 Fireproof flooring patented by Henry Hawes Fox

1856 Bessemer steel making process developed

1836 Pin-jointed iron truss by R. Wiegmann and Polonceau

From 1857 Rolled steel rails

1837 Steam-powered riveting developed by Fairbairn

From 1840s Energy theory of heat

1856 William Rankine, "Harmony of Theory and Practice"

1829 École centrale des arts et manufactures, Paris, France, founded

1850s "Method of sections" developed by Johann Schwedler

1835 Rensselaer School in Troy, New York starts awarding degrees in civil engineering

1850s First and second laws of thermodynamics by Thomson and Clausius

1830s Model studies by Fairbairn and Hodgkinson to develop effective cast iron I-beam

1840s Model studies by Stephenson, Fairbairn, and Hodgkinson for Britannia Bridge, Menai Strait, Wales

From 1840s Use of statically determinate structures

From 1840s Forces in iron roof calculated using statics

Late 1850s Use of "factor of safety" by William Rankine to take account of imperfections of mathematical models

1840s Use of charts for multiplication and division

1855 Polar planimeter developed for measuring areas on drawings

1827 First mention of the slide rule in an engineering book (*A Treatise on the Steam Engine* by John Farey)

1850s–1860s Early work on graphical statics by Karl Culmann

1830s Graphical presentation of data by Léon Lalanne and Charles Joseph Minard

1850s Blueprint reproduction from original paper drawing

1850s Gelatin reproduction from original paper drawing

1851 Slide rule with cursor developed by Amédée Mannheim

From c. 1825 Glass and iron palm houses

1840–52 New House of Commons, London, England

1856–63 U.S. Capitol, Washington, DC

1828–30 Sayn foundry, Germany

1840s Long-span iron roofs for ship slips

From 1850s Era of long-span iron roofs for railway stations

1828–32 Aleksandrinskij Theater, Saint Petersburg, Russia

1835–39 Dome of Saint Isaac's Cathedral, Saint Petersburg, Russia

1850–51 Crystal Palace, London, England

1838 Euston Station, London, England

1846–50 Britannia Bridge, Menai Strait, Wales

1854–57 Les Halles, Paris, France

1834 Orrell's Mill, Stockport, England

1841–54 St. George's Hall, Liverpool, England

1858–60 Boat Store, Sheerness, England

The Harmony of Theory and Practice 1800–1860

Britain benefited enormously from the political and military events on the European continent during the late eighteenth and early nineteenth centuries. The mid-eighteenth century had seen France turn an age of enlightenment into an age of indulgence, and by the late 1780s war and the extravagance of the French ruling classes had all but bankrupted the country. The era of political upheaval that followed—from the French Revolution in 1789 to the rise of Napoleon and his eventual defeat in 1815—spanned a period of only some twenty-five years. Unlike his predecessors in imperial Rome, the Middle Ages, and Renaissance Italy, therefore, Napoleon left virtually no legacy of civil or miliatry construction.

This very period, between about 1790 and 1820, was precisely when various technical and economic developments of the previous century came together with dramatic effect. Like the Italians before them, the English learned how to make the capitalist system work. The weaving industry was the key to success; an increasing market of buyers of clothes meant more mills, and more workers who became richer and could buy more clothes. More mills, in turn, meant more machinery, more factories, more goods, and more infrastructure. The surplus production generated by this economic activity meant more available for export, which in turn fueled the slave trade. Ships exporting manufactured goods from England to Spain and the west coast of Africa then carried slaves to the plantations across the Atlantic, returning home laden with cotton for the mills of Lancashire.

By the end of the eighteenth century, enormous quantities of goods were being produced both for home consumption and for export. The increasing affluence that resulted led to private wealth and more opulent houses in town and country, as well as the beginning of public wealth and opportunities for towns to compete with one another by demonstrating their grandeur in built form.

In the nineteenth century, the most dramatic change was brought about by the development of the railways from the late 1820s. By the 1870s nearly every town in Britain, and by the 1890s in the rest of Europe, had been transformed—some would say destroyed—by railway stations and the lines that fed them. The railways soon came to serve not only to transport goods and people between major towns but also to reduce journey times. From the late 1850s on, the modern city was beginning to form in Europe—custom-made office buildings were being constructed, the age of the commuter was beginning, and transport had opened up the commercial potential for places of mass entertainment, from large exhibitions, museums, and botanic gardens to theaters and concert halls.

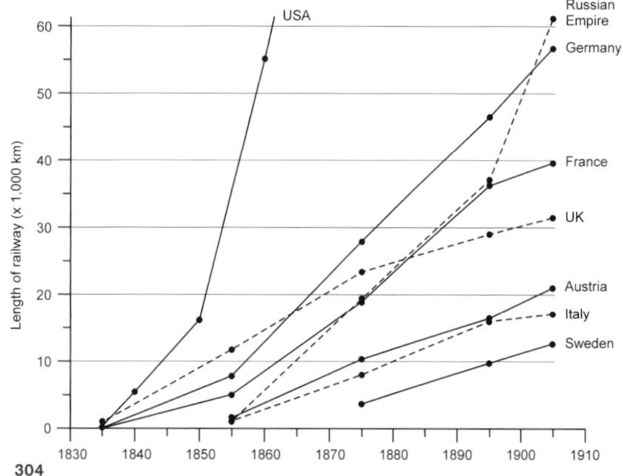

304

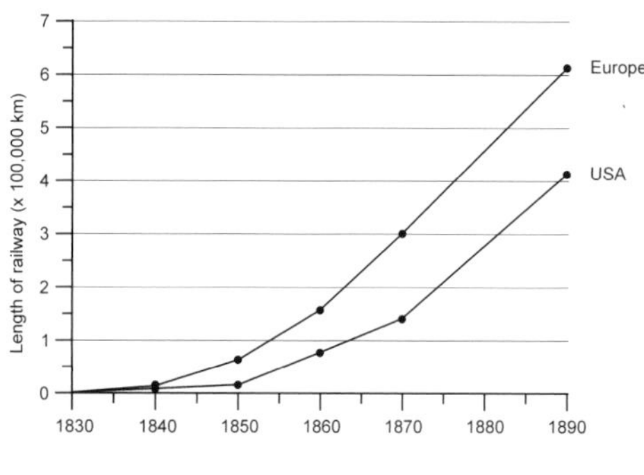

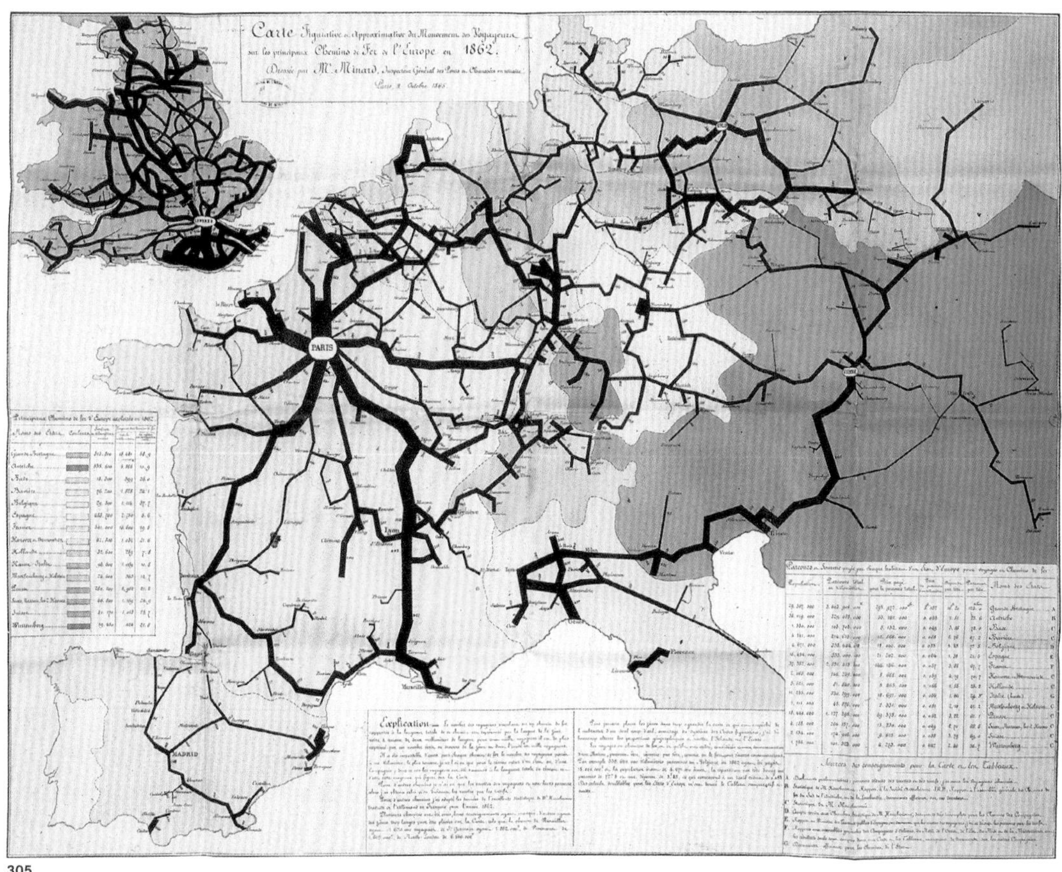

305

304 Charts comparing the growth of railways in Europe (left) and in Europe and the United States (right) during the nineteenth century. Growth parallels the increasing use of wrought iron and, from the 1880s, steel in construction. 305 French map of the European rail network in 1862. The expanding network helped bring the use of iron to areas remote from large iron works.

The economic benefits of the improved transport infrastructure became apparent in every sector of the manu-
305 facturing industry, both in the supply of raw materials and the distribution of the finished goods. The transportation business was a major product in itself, and the majority of the engineers whose names fill the pages of engineering history at this time were involved with transport: roads, canals, bridges, railways, docks and harbors, and, of course, the railway engines and ships that used these networks. During this period, building engineering benefited greatly from the boom in mechanical and civil engineering. There were indirect benefits, too. As civil and mechanical engineering contractors travelled the country, so they brought to the building site experience gained on much larger contracts such as canals, maritime ports, naval dockyards, roads, railways and tunnels. This included both technical improvements in new construction plant and processes and equally important project management skills such as contractual arrangements and financial management.

There were numerous improvements in the engineering infrastructure, such as the availability of skilled workers, engineering education, and books on engineering. The personal interactions between engineers were also important. The Lunar Society in Birmingham, the Derby Philosophical Society, the Society of Civil Engineers in London, and the Philosophical Society of Edinburgh—to mention just four examples—all counted among their members prominent and learned figures from nearly every engineering and scientific community. They were valuable and fertile places for the exchange of ideas and experience in the days before instant telecommunication.

While the influences of civil and mechanical engineering on building construction were important, they were utterly dominated by the far-reaching changes wrought by the development of iron as a construction material. In the last twenty years of the eighteenth century, wrought iron was predominant in France, cast iron in Britain. By the 1840s, cast iron and wrought iron were equally available throughout Europe and used freely according to their suitability for the job at hand, as befitted their very different engineering properties (see Appendix 2). While iron was embraced by engineers mainly for its strength and versatility, however, its rapid adoption in late eighteenth and early nineteenth-century building was due primarily to one characteristic: its resistance to fire. An additional benefit was its immunity to dry rot, which damaged so many timber buildings. The Paris wheat market, 306
the Halle au blé, was a noteworthy example. The original structure (1763–67) was covered in 1783 with a timber dome spanning 39 meters and built using de l'Orme's method (see chapter 4). It burned down in 1803, and
was replaced in 1808–13 with the first wide-span 307
iron roof, designed by François-Joseph Bélanger (1745–1818). Immediately following the fire, it was decided that a stone dome should be built, and only due to Bélanger's persistence was this decision overturned. The main ribs were of cast iron, the hoops of wrought iron. The roof weighed 220 tons and was covered with copper sheeting weighing 29 tons. When the wheat market was refurbished in the 1880s as the Bourse de Commmerce, the copper sheet was replaced by glass.

The fire resistance of iron was also of particular value
for the construction of industrial premises such as 308, 309
foundries and workshops, where furnaces and forges 310
were an operational requirement. Churches and cathedrals, too, could be threatened by fire; their soaring roofs were constructed of timber, and susceptible to lightning strikes. In 1836, three centuries after a lightning strike burned its north spire, the roof of the cathe- 311
dral at Chartres, France, was destroyed by fire, and replaced—following a competition—by a pointed arch in
cast iron, with tie rods of wrought iron. At the abbey of 312
Saint-Denis, France, where fire also destroyed the roof, its replacement (1843–45) was entirely constructed of wrought iron.

Initially iron was used as a direct substitute for timber, but at a price. It could be justified only when the benefits of using iron outweighed its high cost, which fell, gradually at first and then more rapidly, as the iron industry developed to meet the increasing demands of the civil and mechanical engineering industries. The technological research and development by iron manufacturers led to improvements in the quality of iron and new means of shaping, machining, and assembling it, as well as new processes for manufacturing it in larger quantities. Once iron was taken up in buildings for its fire-resisting qualities, its great strength and versatility were quickly discovered and exploited, especially for roof structures of unprecedented lightness and architectural complexity.

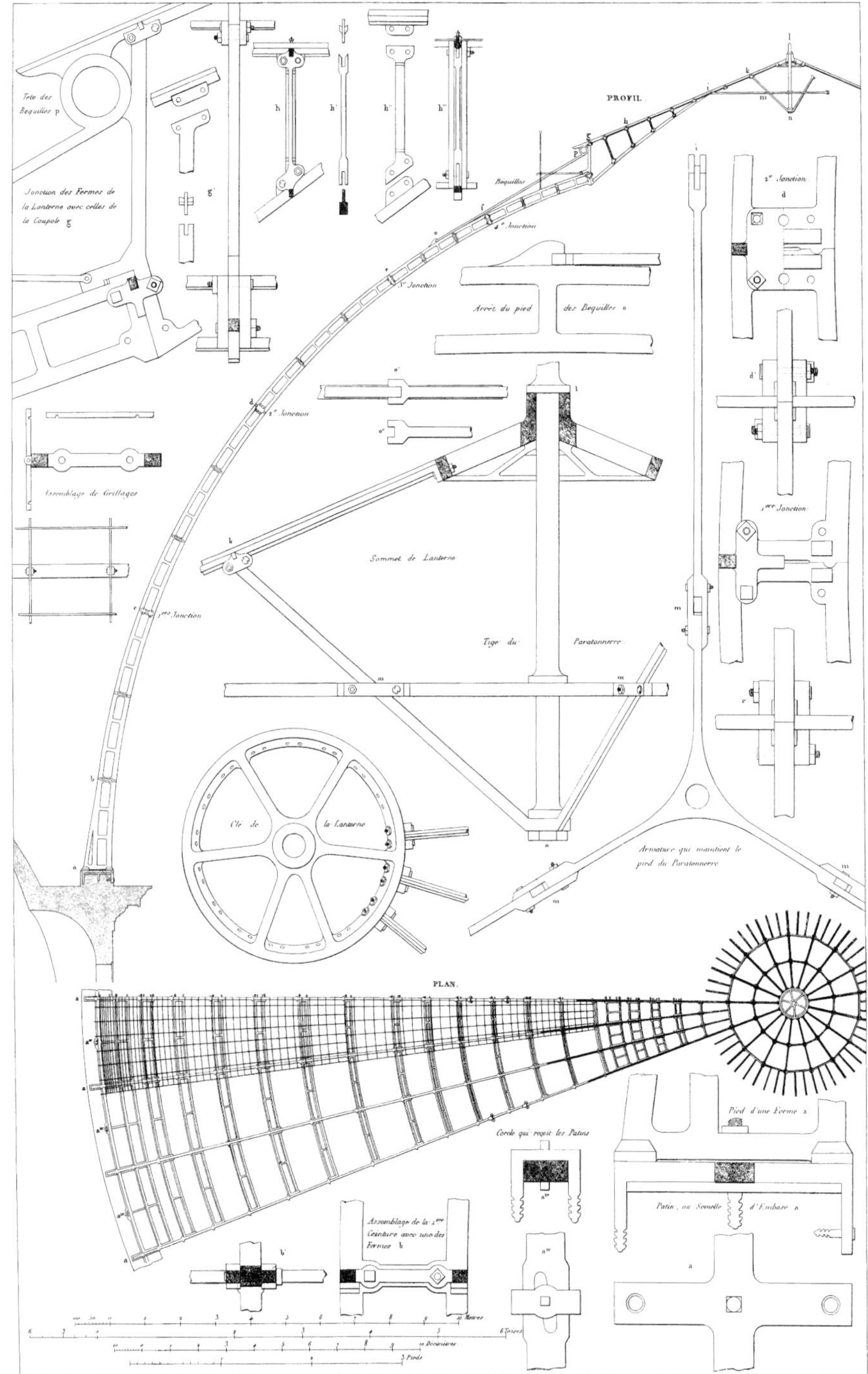

306

306 Halle au blé, Paris, 1808–13. Engineer: François Brunet; architect: François-Joseph Bélanger. Illustrations of iron work used in building dome. 307 Halle au blé, 1887. Exterior during refurbishment. The former wheat market became the Bourse de Commerce (completed 1889).

307

When originally designed in 1818, the dome of the new
313 Cathedral of Saint Isaac in Saint Petersburg, Russia, was
planned to be of masonry, copying Christopher Wren's
dome at Saint Paul's Cathedral (see chapter 4). During
nearly fifteen years of delays before the start of construction, ideas changed, largely influenced by the many British
manufacturing firms that had become established in Saint
Petersburg in the 1780s and 1790s, and the many French
architects and engineers who had been attracted to Saint
Petersburg following the French Revolution in 1789. The
iron manufacturing industry in that city was developed
largely by two Scottish engineers: Charles Baird
(1766–1843), who, from the early 1800s, owned and ran
the largest private foundry in Saint Petersburg, and
Matthew Clark (1776–1846), who worked for the Saint
Petersburg State Ironworks from 1801. By 1835, masonry was felt to be inappropriate for a new building, and
315 an iron structure was proposed to form the dome. The iron
structure also proved to be cheaper than a masonry
dome, and the other roofs of the cathedral were also built
of iron for its fireproof qualities. The architect, Auguste Ricard Montferrand (1786–1858), was a French émigré, and the ironwork was produced at Charles Baird's foundry, where his nephew, William Handyside (1793–1850), was chief engineer at the time. Montferrand was guided by Handyside on the design and erection of the ironwork; the design calculations were done by the Russian engineer P.K. Lomonovsky. The dome was widely acclaimed as one of the greatest examples of structural ironwork in buildings, and for this reason was later chosen as the prototype for the dome of the United States Capitol, built in Washington from 1856 to 1863.

The manufacturing process for iron, particularly cast iron, conferred a further benefit. Casting was ideal for producing large numbers of identical components, which encouraged designers to standardize wherever possible and reduce the number of different components. The components were also interchangeable, and the columns and beams could be assembled very easily, making it possible to construct buildings with unprecedented speed. An almost incidental advantage of using iron components in

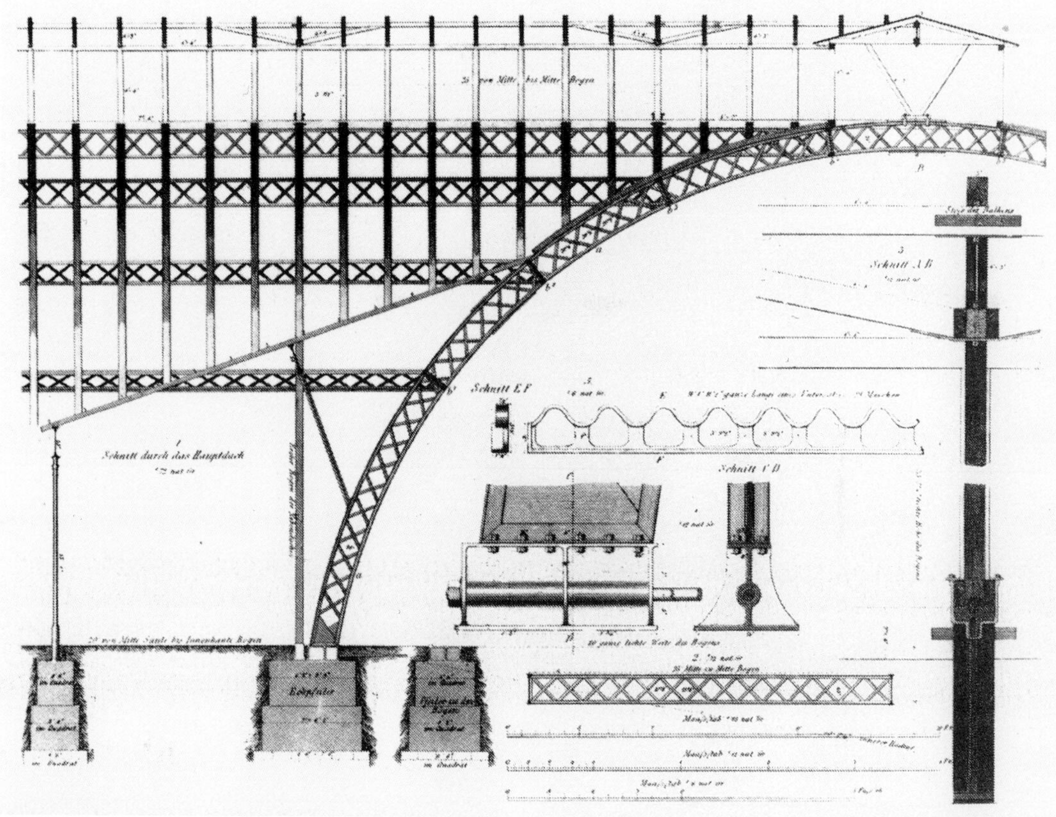

308

309

310

308 Section drawing of a lattice arch used in a German ironworks, c. 1860. 309 Iron foundry at Sayn, Germany, 1828–30. Architect: Karl Ludwig Althans. Interior. 310 Iron foundry at Sayn. 311 Chartres Cathedral, Chartres, France, 1194–1260. Cast iron roof erected in 1837 to replace original timber roof. 312 Abbey of Saint-Denis, near Paris, begun c. 1137. Wrought iron roof erected in 1843–45 to replace original timber roof.

311

312

313

314

buildings was their transportability—the ease with which the pieces could be moved from the foundries and forges to the site. From the 1830s there grew a healthy export trade in iron components for use in construction—columns, beams, and roof trusses—and even in whole buildings. The Scottish engineer William Fairbairn
314 (1789–1874) was one of the pioneers in this field, as he had already established an export trade in machine tools, waterwheels, and industrial machinery. His contract to set up a carpet factory in Turkey in the late 1830s included not only the spinning and weaving machinery but the building itself. Fairbairn also provided other buildings that served to sustain the industrial community created by the new factory, including a flour mill. The British and French were especially active in the export of buildings because of the established trade links with their colonies, which lacked indigenous iron industries.

Education and the Engineering Profession

Perhaps the most influential engineering exports from France, Britain, and Germany during the late eighteenth and early nineteenth centuries, however, were people, knowledge, and expertise. The professionalization of engineering had generated an infrastructure of scientific knowledge that was both transportable and easy to teach to others in a relatively short time. By the end of the eighteenth century people were taking a rational and experimental approach to every aspect of what we now call the engineering design of buildings—structural systems and materials, soils and foundations, heating, ventilation, fire protection, and acoustics. Strength of materials and structural engineering had already become quantitative disciplines. With the introduction of cast iron, the modern role of the structural engineer had become defined; it was the person who would be able to calculate the minimum amount of material necessary to do the job required of it, and to do so with an acceptable degree of confidence to ensure a satisfactory level of safety.

Since 1747, when the École des ponts et chaussées was established, the professional status of the civil engineer in France had been closely linked to the theoretical engineering knowledge that was deemed essential for its good practice. Many of the lecturers had written books based on the courses they taught, and became well known both in continental Europe and in Britain. In 1794–95 a new era of engineering schools was begun with the opening in Paris of the École centrale des travaux publics (the Central School of Public Works). The new school was a child of both the French Enlightenment and the French Revolution of 1789. The engineer Gaspard Monge, formerly a teacher at the military school

313 Saint Isaac's Cathedral, Saint Petersburg, Russia, 1818–58. Iron dome designed and built 1835–39. Engineer: Charles Baird; architect: Auguste-Ricard Montferrand. Illustration of interior of the iron domed roof. 314 Prefabricated, cast iron factory building by William Fairbairn, 1839–40. 315 Saint Isaac's Cathedral. Section of dome.

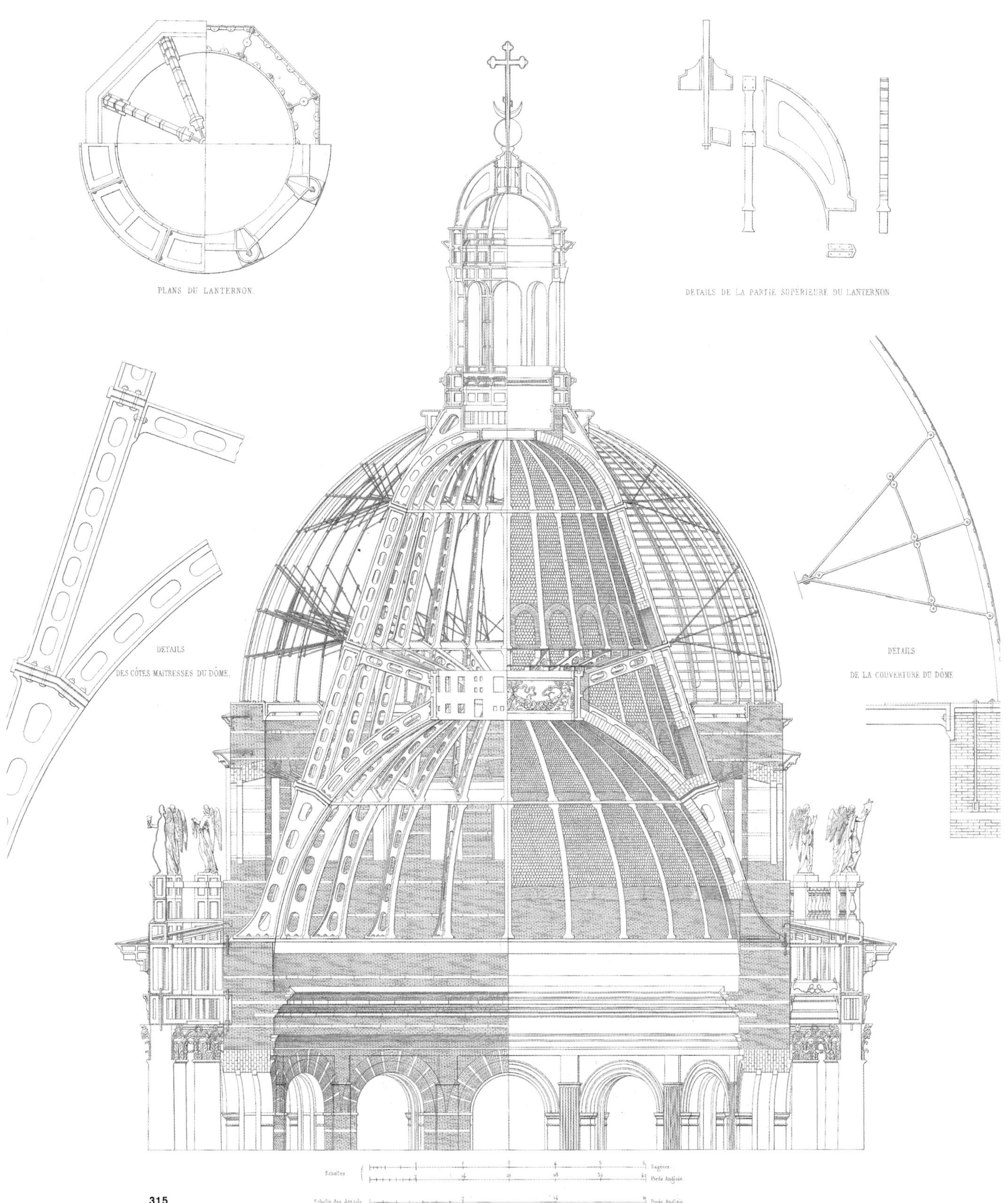
PLANS DU LANTERNON.
DETAILS DE LA PARTIE SUPERIEURE DU LANTERNON.
DETAILS
DES CÔTES MAITRESSES DU DÔME.
DÉTAILS
DE LA COUVERTURE DU DÔME.
Echelles
Sagènes.
Pieds Anglais.
Echelle des détails
Pieds Anglais.

at Mézières, found himself in the new French government and was able to persuade his colleagues to agree to set up the new school. There were three principal driving forces. First was the realization that France was rapidly falling behind Britain in its manufacturing industries, and it was decided that this relative decline could be reversed only by better technical education, building upon France's success with the École des ponts et chaussées. Second, a new kind of technical education was needed, not only to embody the intellectual and philosophical ideals of the new scientific culture (represented, for example, by the Académie Française), but to embrace a form of "encouragement pedagogy," which, in the words of Monge, required teachers to "fire the students' ambitions and learning motivations and ensure they never ceased striving to have their work achieve the greatest possible perfection."[1] The third goal of the new school was to bridge the gap between theory and practice, partly to help break down the social barriers between the intellectual elite and those working in industry, and partly to ensure that industrial technology would benefit from the many scientific advances of the previous decades. One example of this was the replacement of much of the mathematics that permeated the entire curriculum at the École des ponts et chaussées by the study of chemistry and the properties of materials such as iron, timber, glass, and concrete. While preparing the curriculum for the new school, it became clear that a new word was needed to describe this new type of knowledge and new approach to education. The word "polytechnic" was coined, and during its first year the name was changed to the École polytechnique.

The idea of polytechnical education, dedicated to the harmony of theory and practice, spread through continental Europe with remarkable speed. Seven polytechnic schools were formed in Germany in the next thirty years—in Berlin, the Bauakademie in 1799 and the Gewerbeschule in 1821, in Karlsruhe (1825), Munich (1827), Dresden (1828), Stuttgart (1829), Hanover (1831), and Darmstadt (1836); more were founded in the following decades. In Austria schools were formed in Prague (1806), Vienna (1815), Cracow (1833), Brno (1849), and Lemberg (1844). In Switzerland the polytechnic schools in Zurich and Lausanne were formed in 1855; Italy and other countries in continental Europe soon followed. Meanwhile in Paris, the original École polytechnique was much oversubscribed, and the École centrale des arts et manufactures was formed in 1829, with its emphasis on a more practical approach to engineering. Schools were also established in other major cities in France.

The importance and influence of the polytechnic movement on both civil and building engineering cannot be understated. Not only did these institutions train engineers, but the teachers also published books based both on their lectures and the theoretical studies and practical research they undertook.

In Germany, the leading figure was Johann Eytelwein (1764–1849), who, after military training, worked in Berlin's state building department. In 1797 he co-authored the very first technical periodical devoted to building engineering, produced by his employer, entitled *Sammlung nützlicher Aufsätze und Nachrichten, die Baukunst betreffend, für angehende Baumeister und Freunde der Architektur* (Collection of Useful Essays and Information Related to Building for Practicing Builders and Friends of Architecture). In 1799 Eytelwein was one of the founders of the Bauakademie, Germany's first building academy, and he wrote two widely used textbooks: *Handbuch der Mechanik fester Körper und Hydraulik* (Handbook of the Mechanics of Solid Bodies and Hydraulics) and *Handbuch der Statik fester Körper* 317 (Handbook of the Statics of Solid Bodies) published, respectively, in 1801 and 1808. These were the first engineering textbooks to appear written in a form that would be familiar to us today, concentrating heavily on mathematics and engineering science rather than on practical guidance for engineers and builders. They were conceived as integral to the new type of education for engineers who would not learn their profession as part of a military training.

Eytelwein's equivalent in the French language was Claude Louis Marie Henri Navier (1785–1836), a teacher at the École des ponts et chaussées in Paris who published his lecture notes first in 1820 and in several later, expanded editions. As polytechnic education expanded in Europe, so the numbers of teachers grew. During the nineteenth century many dozens of engineers published many hundreds of engineering textbooks, mainly in French and German, and later in Italian.

DRAWING

Before the development of specialized drawing papers in the late eighteenth century, building designers used high-quality writing papers for their work. Images were composed of inked lines and modest ink and watercolor washes. The first papers intended specifically for high-quality drawings were developed by James Whatman (1702–59) in the 1750s at his Turkey Mill near Maidstone, in England. His wove paper, made by hand from rags, was much smoother than ordinary papers. Sized with gelatin and cream-colored, it was also strong and highly durable. After the process was partially mechanized around 1800 by his son, Whatman paper was exported throughout the world and was widely used until the 1870s into the 1940s, in fact, by some architects, for presentations or competitions.

Machine-made drawing paper, often referred to as cartridge paper (from its original use for making cartridges) or German drawing paper, was available by the roll from early in the 1800s. It was of an inferior grade, cream or buff in color, and was generally used for sketches as well as for working drawings to be used on site. Before drawing ink became available in bottles in the 1830s, draftsmen had to make their own ink. This was made from an ink stick, composed of lampblack—a very fine carbon pigment—and a gelatin binder. Steel pen nibs became available in the early 1800s, and had to be kept sharp to ensure a clean line. Sometimes they might be too sharp and damage the paper, as did the practice of erasing ink lines by scraping the paper with a penknife.

Copying drawings at this time had to be done by hand, using one of four methods. Most commonly, the original was placed on top and pricked through using a pin to create a series of points that could be joined up using a ruler or drawing compass. Drawings could also be traced. Tracing paper, made by impregnating ordinary paper with oil or resin to render it translucent, had been known for centuries, and by the early 1800s was available ready-made from stationers and artists' suppliers. An image could also be created by using carbon paper or rubbing the underside of the lines of a drawing with pencil, then tracing the drawing using an agate stylus to imprint the lines on the copy paper beneath. Finally, the pantograph—invented c. 1630 by Christoph Scheiner (c. 1573–1650)—could be used not only to copy an image, but to reduce or enlarge it.

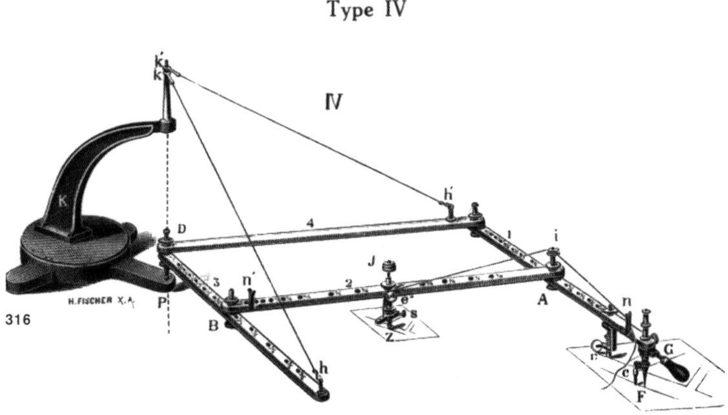

316 Pantograph manufactured by the Zurich firm of Gottlieb Coradi, early twentieth century. The pantograph was invented c. 1630 and widely used throughout the nineteenth century to make copies of drawings, either at full size or scaled up or down.

The first similar books in English were those written by W. J. M. Rankine in the 1850s and 1860s, including his *Manual of Applied Mechanics*.

It was not long before foreign-language textbooks reached the United States, frequently introduced there engineers who had emigrated from Europe to America, sometimes translating these works into English. A small but significant number of American engineers and architects crossed the Atlantic the other way to study in the European polytechnics, and they were often able to take their experience back with them. Thus the European polytechnics served as models that several American schools emulated. The first school of applied sciences in America, the Military Academy at West Point in New York, had been founded in 1802. After it was instituted as a school of engineering in 1818, it was remodeled on the École polytechnique by its director, Sylvanus Thayer. One of its graduates, D. H. Mahan (1802–71), spent four years in France studying its engineering works and public institutions in the late 1820s. In 1827 he translated into English (as *An Elementary Course of Civil Engineering*) one of the leading French textbooks on civil engineering and construction, *Programme ou résumé des leçons d'un cours de constructions, avec des applications tirées principalement de l'Art de l'Ingénieur des Ponts et Chaussées*, by J. M. Sganzin (1750–1837). These were notes of Sganzin's course at the École des ponts et chaussées, and served as a model for the courses that Mahan delivered when he returned to the U.S. and began lecturing at West Point. Rensselaer School in Troy, New York, was founded in 1824, initially focusing on agricultural studies. Beginning in 1827, surveying and several scientific and engineering courses were introduced, and its first civil engineering degrees were awarded in 1835. The school was reorganized again in 1850 based on the European polytechnical education methods and, in 1861, was renamed Rensselaer Polytechnic Institute.

In Britain things were different. Britain had dominated the seas for more than a century, and its naval forces maintained military superiority to protect the trade routes upon which the country depended. Since the 1750s its industrial might had been unchallenged, and there was no perceived need to change the education and training methods that had apparently served the country so well.

Until dedicated engineering courses were set up at some of the Britain's universities in the 1850s, four systems or education routes were in operation. The intellectual elite studied mathematics or natural philosophy, as the sciences were then called, at universities that were the equal of any in the world. The universities' traditional role was to turn out young people destined for careers as diplomats, lawyers, and academics, not engineers, though some did "stray" into the construction, railway, and manufacturing industries. Applied mathematics and sciences started to creep into curricula in the 1790s, particularly in Scotland. At Edinburgh University, the lectures on applied mathematics by John Robison (1739–1805) became well known, both through his books and his considerable entries on engineering themes in the historic third edition of the *Encyclopaedia Britannica* (1788–97). Half a century later, Glasgow was the first university to provide a course on civil engineering, and its first professor was William Rankine, discussed later in this chapter.

There were also several military academies, the most famous of which was the Royal Military Academy at Woolwich, in east London, established in 1741. It numbered among its teachers some of the foremost academics of the day, including the mathematicians Charles Hutton (1737–1823) and Peter Barlow (1776–1862), whose books were well used in the building industry, and Michael Faraday (1791–1867), who was a professor of chemistry between 1830 and 1851. The education and the engineering research at Woolwich were of the best caliber, but did not directly serve the needs of industry or civil and building engineering.

At the shop-floor level, so to speak, there was a highly effective apprenticeship system, which trained young men in the practical skills of manufacturing just as it had trained masons and carpenters for centuries. This included not only factory-based skills but, especially with the building of canals and railways, all their site-based manufacturing and construction activities.

The fourth and uniquely British educational route for engineers comprised the "mechanics institutes." In 1796, John Anderson (1726–96), a professor of natural philosophy at the University of Glasgow, founded a college dedicated to providing lectures on the sciences for

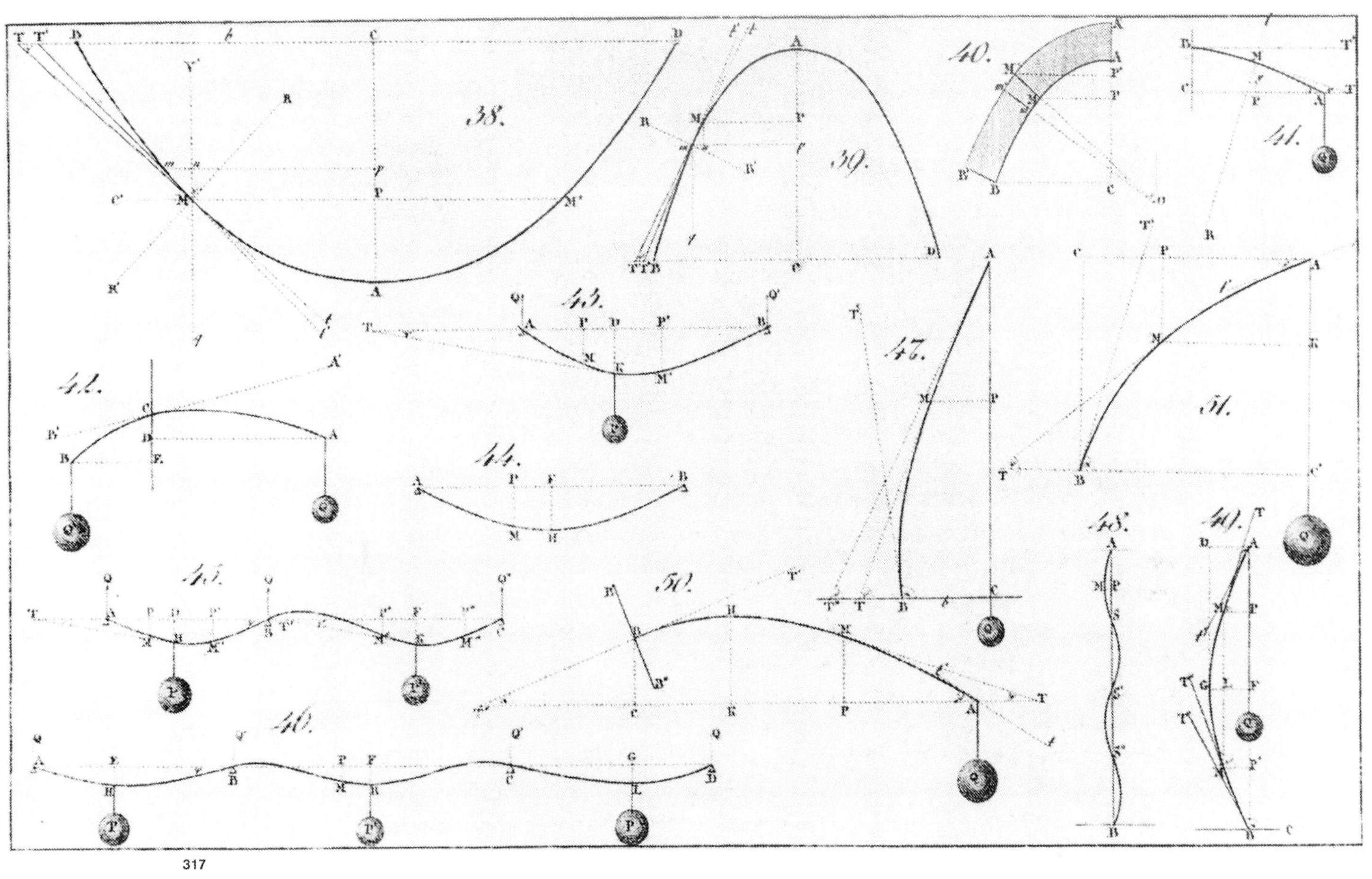

317

317 Plate from *Handbuch der Statik fester Körper*, by Johann Albert Eytelwein. Berlin, 1808.

"working men," "artisans," and others who could not attend the university. The first lecturer, Thomas Garnett (1766–1802), was succeeded in 1799 by George Birkbeck (1776–1841), a popular lecturer who added the subjects of applied science and "the mechanical arts." In 1821, the first mechanics' institute—the Edinburgh School of Arts—was established, offering a broad mix of classes and including laboratory apparatus for experiments and a library. Word of the institute spread south and some wanted a similar establishment to offer every subject in the name of social and political emancipation, but the time was not yet right for this. The London Mechanics' Institute was formed, on 11 November 1823, at a public meeting held at the Crown and Anchor Tavern on the Strand. Some two thousand people attended to hear about the proposal to offer engineering education from George Birkbeck, who became one of its most popular lecturers. The idea was clearly the right one at the right time, for by 1826 there were a hundred mechanics' institutes across the country, three hundred by 1841, and more than five hundred by 1850—one in nearly every town and in many villages. Some lasted only a few years but a good number were active into the twentieth century, and a few closed their doors only in the 1960s. Several of the mechanics' institutes proved very successful indeed, and survive in the modern university system. The London Mechanics' Institute, for example, gradually broadened its range of subjects, and in 1907, its name was changed to Birkbeck College, which, as part of today's University of London, still specializes in courses aimed at those returning as "mature students" after a period of time working. The Manchester Mechanics' Institute, founded in 1824 by William Fairbairn and others, later became UMIST, the University of Manchester Institute of Science and Technology. Fairbairn's collaboration in the 1830s with Eaton Hodgkinson (1789–1861), one of the institute's lecturers, would have far-reaching effects on building design, with their development of the I-section iron beam and, in the 1840s, their experimentation to develop the design of tubular-girder bridges. Part-time engineering study in the evenings became more formalized in the late nineteenth century as more mechanics' institutes became British versions of the polytechnic, offering vocational courses and remaining the normal route to professional qualification in the building industry until after World War II.

One significant consequence of this popular, part-time approach to engineering education was the unique role of the professional engineering and architectural institutions in Britain. Continental institutions and associations were formed to act as a forum for the concerns of professionals. The British institutions for civil engineers (formed in 1818), architects (1834), mechanical engineers (1847), electrical engineers (1871), building services engineers (1897), and structural engineers (1922) all played and still play a vital role in establishing the minimum standards of education that someone must reach in order to become professional in each field.

The creation of educational establishments for the engineering professions led, both in Britain and in continental Europe, to an increase in research more directly focused on the needs of engineering than the wider-ranging concerns of researchers in physics, chemistry, and mathematics. The polytechnics, military academies, and, later, some of the mechanics' institutes formed communities of people who had some time free to pursue their research interests. Over the decades many have criticized (and still do) the remoteness of much of this type of research from the real needs of engineers. Viewed in the long term, however, there is no question that engineering has benefited immeasurably. The first half of the nineteenth century was perhaps the most significant period of engineering history, for it was during that time that building engineers first learned how to use the abstract models of the world produced by mathematicians and other scientists. Two examples stand out and serve to illustrate the process: the development of the "rational" beam and the statically determinate truss.

The "More Rational" Beam

As we saw in the case of their early mills, William Strutt and Charles Bage designed both columns and beams to reflect precisely their structural duty and to use as little material as possible (see chapter 5). This approach was maintained for the following two decades or so. By the late 1820s larger machinery in the mills was pushing the need for longer spans between columns. By this time, too, the engineering science underlying the design of machines made from iron was developing. The numbers of mills being built was also growing, and it became clear to one engineer—William Fairbairn—that there might be significant economies to be made by studying more carefully

PRACTICAL ENGINEERING GUIDANCE

The thirst for engineering knowledge in Britain was marked not only by the popularity of the mechanics' institutes, but also by the appearance of books intended for practicing engineers who would have been unable to understand the learned textbooks that the continental polytechnic teachers were producing. The most common word found in the titles of such books was "practical," for their main aim was to bridge the gap between the academic and highly mathematical treatment of mechanics and the needs and abilities of engineers. This tradition of engineering guidance survived into the twentieth century both in Britain and America. Although some of these books were translated into French, German, Italian, and Spanish, this type of guide was never taken up by indigenous authors on the continent of Europe. Three of the most popular books were written by Thomas Tredgold (1788–1829), and their full titles alone convey the nature of their content:

- *Elementary Principles of Carpentry; a treatise on the pressure and equilibrium of beams and timber frames; the resistance of timber; and the construction of floors, roofs, centres, bridges, etc. With practical rules and examples. To which is added an essay on the nature and properties of timber, including the methods of seasoning, and the causes and prevention of decay, with descriptions of the kinds of wood used in building. Also numerous tables of the scantlings of timber for different purposes, the specific gravities of materials, etc.* This book made its first appearance in 1820 was followed by nearly three dozen editions, the later ones being improved, enlarged, revised, and edited by other authors, right up to 1946.

- *A Practical Essay on the Strength of Cast Iron; intended for the assistance of engineers, iron masters, architects, millwrights, founders, smiths, and others engaged in the construction of machines, buildings, etc. Containing practical rules, tables, and examples; also an account of some new experiments, with an extensive table of the properties of materials.* The first edition of 1822 was followed by four others, the last of which was published in 1861, after which time the use of cast iron developed no further.

- *Principles of Warming and Ventilating public buildings, dwelling-houses, manufactories, hospitals, hothouses, conservatories, etc.; and of constructing fire-places, boilers, steam apparatus, grates, and drying rooms; with illustrations experimental, scientific and practical. To which are added, observations on the nature of heat; and various tables useful in the application of heat.* The first edition was published in 1824 and soon translated into German and French. The third and final English edition was published in 1836.

Another popular book was *Mathematics for Practical Men*, written by Olinthus Gilbert Gregory (1774–1841), for thirty years a professor of mathematics at the Royal Military Academy at Woolwich, England; it contained many useful formulas and calculation methods for civil and mechanical engineers.

Similar practical guides began to appear in other countries within a couple of decades. In Germany, for instance, Julius Ludwig Weisbach (1806–71) published in the 1840s several collections of tables, formulas, and rules of arithmetic, geometry, and mechanics for engineers.

the shape and the dimensions of cast iron beams that would make most efficient use of the iron. Fairbairn was well placed both to undertake and to benefit from such a study, since he ran probably the largest ironworks in the world, in Manchester. He was not a scientifically trained man, and enlisted the help of his colleague Eaton Hodgkinson to plan a series of experiments to establish, once and for all, the ultimate, entirely rational cross section and elevation for a cast iron beam.

Hodgkinson had approached the problem from the other end, so to speak. His search, as a mathematician, was
318 for a "better" mathematical model for a beam subjected to bending caused by a transverse load. In this case, "better" meant one that would explain and hence allow prediction of the degree of deflection that beam would suffer under load. It would likewise have to predict the load at which fracture would occur and enable these predictions for any cross section of beam. Finally, the model should involve only the physical dimensions of the beam, the magnitude of the load, and measurable, general physical properties of the material—the properties of stiffness and ultimate tensile strength; most importantly, the model should require no empirical constants. The requirements of this "better" model seem obvious to us today, but had tested the greatest minds of two centuries, including Galileo, Robert Hooke, Edme Mariotte, Antoine Parent, Leonhard Euler, Charles Augustin de Coulomb, Thomas Young (1773–1829), Eytelwein, and Navier, to name just a few. Each had dealt successfully with some of the issues, but their work was constrained by, for instance, looking at fracture but not bending up to fracture (or vice versa); using beams of only rectangular section; assuming that beams of equal area of cross section could be interchanged; or failing to realize that small samples of a material would be highly susceptible to internal flaws. Most elusive of all was the location of what we now call the neutral axis—the position in the beam that is neither stretched nor compressed during bending. Hodgkinson was the first to show conclusively that it lies at the centroid of the section. Thus he was able to justify the most economical arrangement of material as an inverted T, with two flanges—the lower one to carry tension under normal loading, and the upper one to carry compression and to prevent the top edge of the web from buckling under compression. The areas of the two flanges should be in inverse proportion to the strength of cast iron in compression and tension—a ratio of about 1:6. Yet even Hodgkinson, who was building on the achievements of many earlier mathematicians and scientists, did not finish the job: he did not manage to eliminate the need for an empirical constant. The effects of shear stresses in beams, and the buckling of the web and compression flange under compressive loads, have continued to exercise scientists up to the present day.

Hodgkinson's work, however, did enable Fairbairn to make beams using 20 to 30 percent less iron, and that was the main concern of the building engineer. The results of this collaborative research work were first used in 1834 at Orrell's Mill in Stockport, England. It is a beam 319, 320
with an asymmetrical I-section, larger at the bottom because of cast iron's low strength in tension, and deepest and thickest at mid-span, tapering in both elevation and plan toward the supports in response to the bending moments to which the beam is subjected. For the first time this reflected the need for the top flange of a beam to resist buckling. (This type of failure is today called "lateral torsional buckling." The effect of the flange is similar to the stiffening effect of a fold in a sheet of paper, parallel to an edge.)

In fact, while economy of such beams and the contrast with sections of beams in earlier mills are striking, this 321
scientific investigation did little more than confirm much of what was already well known by engineers. I-section beams were already being used in many contexts—machine tools, steam engines, shipbuilding, the young railway industry, and bridge construction. The great value of Hodgkinson and Fairbairn's work was that it provided the engineering rationale that underpinned both the old, approximate design methods and new, more precise ones. People could now use the design methods with more confidence and, hence, more nearly approach the limit of what was possible and achieve the minimum weight of a beam of a certain length to carry a certain load.

The Pin-Jointed Statically Determinate Truss

The advantage of a pin-jointed truss to a structural engineer is that all the forces in the members of the truss are pure tension or compression, and can be calculated using statics alone. For this reason such a truss is called "statically determinate." It is made of a series of triangles, and so no member is redundant: cutting any one

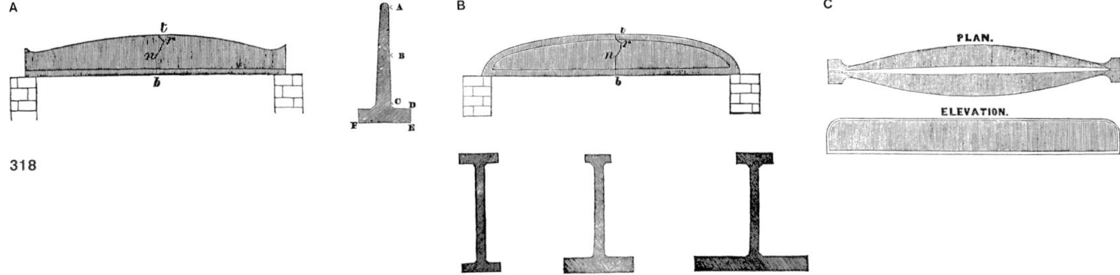

would cause the structure to collapse. The greatest advantage, though, is that because of how it is constructed, with the members able to rotate relative to each other at the joints, it is not possible for any bending to be introduced into the members. The truss is deliberately built to correspond as nearly as possible to the mathematical models used to analyze its structural behavior. Thus, the forces in the struts and ties of the real truss correspond very well with those predicted by calculation. The structural engineer is taking control of the situation, so to speak. Contrast this with the task set for a structural engineer presented with a roof structure that has been built by someone with little knowledge of the mathematical models. Today structural engineers, with the aid of computers, can go a long way to achieving this latter goal, but this was not the case in 1800. To put the statically determinate roof truss in context, it is worth looking first at what was being built without the benefit of this approach to structural design.

322 Most of the features of traditional timber roof structures make them virtually impossible to model accurately even today. Each structural member was usually loaded in both bending and compression or tension, and it would have been virtually impossible to ascertain the amount of bending. All the joints were rigid or, more usually, partially rigid to an unknown degree. To overcome the difficulty of making timber joints that carry tension, iron straps were often used to strengthen them, introducing further uncertainty as to the proportions of loads shared among different components.

When a truss of exceptional size was needed, a mathematician would be called in, and no doubt made a good job of calculating those few quantities that were possible to calculate, such as the overall loads acting on the structure, its weight, and hence the forces that the principal members would need to carry. In a large timber structure, such as the roof of the Moscow Manege (1817), many 323
slender lengths of timber had to be joined to act as one, using iron bolts and straps, which made an accurate analysis of forces and stresses impossible. While the elegance of its design leaves no doubt that this roof was the product of the mind of a rational, highly-trained engineer rather than a local carpenter, even this enormous truss was largely the product of experience and empirical design rules.

The situation was the same with the earliest roof trusses made in wrought iron. The roof over the Théâtre Française in Paris (1786) was not statically determinate, and displays what we would now consider an idiosyncratic arrangement of members (see chapter 5, p. 255). Although it worked, it was certainly not as economical as what engineers could have achieved in the 1830s. It is unlikely that royal patronage did much to encourage the economical use of construction materials. The Aleksandrinskij Theater in Saint Petersburg was also 324

318 Illustrations of Eaton Hodgkinson's beam theory, early 1800s. (A) Inverted-T section commonly used from 1790s; (B) I-section beam found to be the most efficient; (C) Flange widened at the center to increase resistance to lateral buckling.

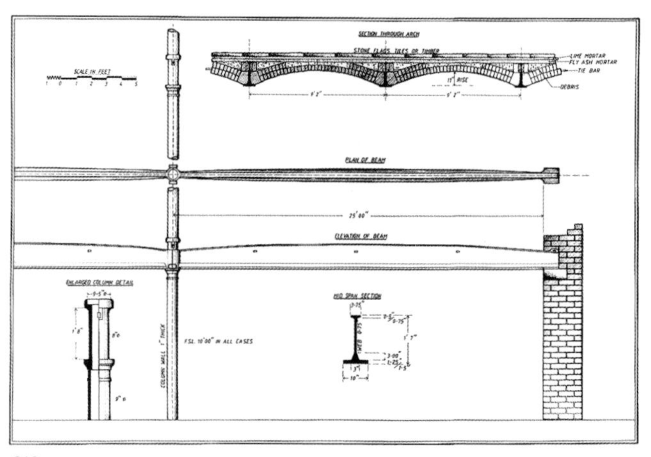

319

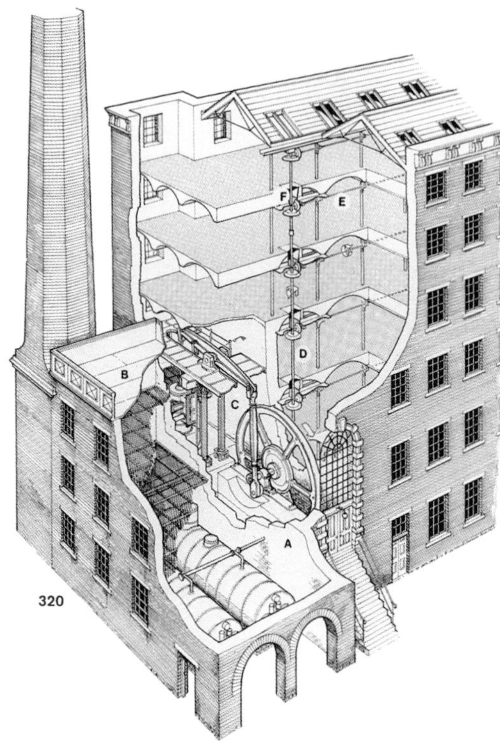

320

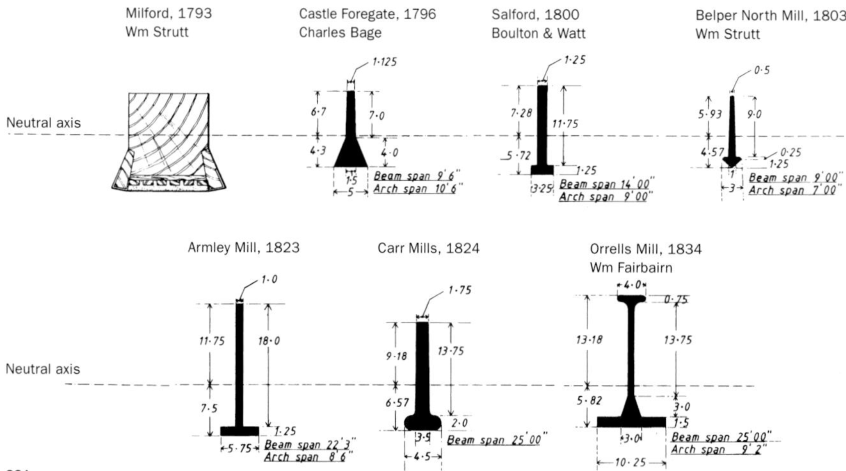

321

319 Cast iron beam used in Orrell's Mill, Stockport, near Manchester, England, 1834. Engineer: William Fairbairn. **320** Cutaway isometric showing a typical arrangement of a plant and machinery in a multistory factory similar in construction to Orrell's Mill, c.1850. **321** Illustration of the development of beam cross sections used in multistory factories, 1793–1834. **322** A timber roof of traditional construction, southern France, c. 1850. This example differs little from those familiar to Vitruvius in Roman times. **323** Moscow Manege, 1817. Engineer: Augustin Bétancourt. Timber roof truss with wrought iron reinforcements spanning 50 meters over the arena.

322

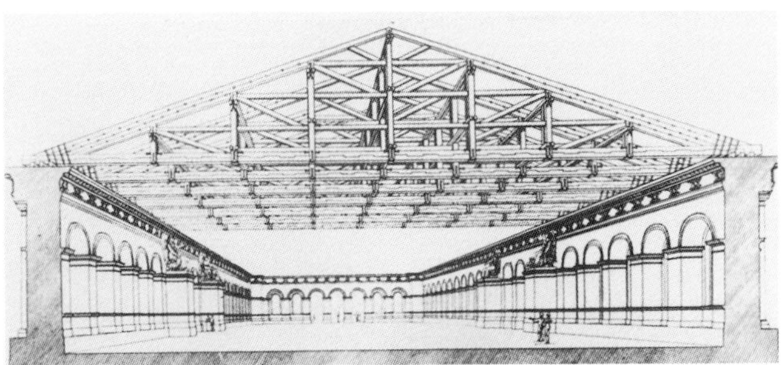
323

built under royal patronage, but in its late 1820s design, the iron is clearly being used more rationally. It was designed by the émigré Scottish engineer Matthew Clark, working with architect Carlo Rossi (1775–1849). The pitched roof over the entire theater is supported by a cast
325 and wrought iron lattice arch spanning 29.2 meters. Beneath this arch, a similar, three-ribbed wrought iron arch spanning 21 meters supports the ceiling of the auditorium below and the floor of the scenery workshop above. The roof of the scenery workshop is supported by a well-triangulated wrought iron truss spanning 22 meters. Above the fly gallery in the backstage area a relatively small triangulated iron truss, spanning about 10.5 meters, is supported by a series of massive cast-propped cantilevers.

It is likely that the first fully triangulated roof trusses were built for reasons of constructional convenience rather than because the forces involved could be calculated. There are constructional advantages in making a roof truss as a kit of parts assembled using wedges, pins, or bolts at each end of each member. The earliest was probably the roof over the foundry at Boulton and Watt's Soho
327 foundry in Manchester, England, designed by William Murdock and completed in 1810. Other examples soon
326 followed, for example, at the Beehive Mill in Manchester.

During the 1820s and 1830s a number of engineers in Germany, France, Russia, and Britain were all approaching the same goal: to make structures using the minimum quantity of iron. They sought to do this by conceiving structures that allowed the forces and stresses to be calculated, which was best done by designing the structures to resemble the mathematical models they would use to make the calculations.

Probably the most elegant form of the triangulated roof truss was that devised at the same time (1836) by a
German, R. Wiegmann, and a Frenchman, Jean 328
Barthélemy Camille Polonceau (1813–59). There was much argument at the time about who got there first, and the evidence favored Wiegmann, but he built none or only a few. Polonceau, on the other hand, built several hundred, of which many survive today. One of its earliest uses was by Matthew Clark at the Winter Palace (now the Hermitage) in Saint Petersburg, Russia.

The triangulated truss at Euston Station in London (1838) 329
was probably the first to be made entirely of wrought iron. It was designed by Charles Fox (1810–74), who later worked for Fox Henderson on covered ship slips and the
Crystal Palace. Compression members were rolled to 330
form an L-shaped cross section.

As spans increased, other arrangements of triangulation
were used, and different designs and contractors no 331
doubt favored their own versions. The principle of statical determinacy was the same, though, and has dominated the construction of all such structures to this day. Surprisingly, it took more than a decade for a straightforward design procedure to be developed for statically determinate trusses. Since about 1800 it had been common to consider the forces acting on the joints at the apex and the supports of a roof truss. From the earliest

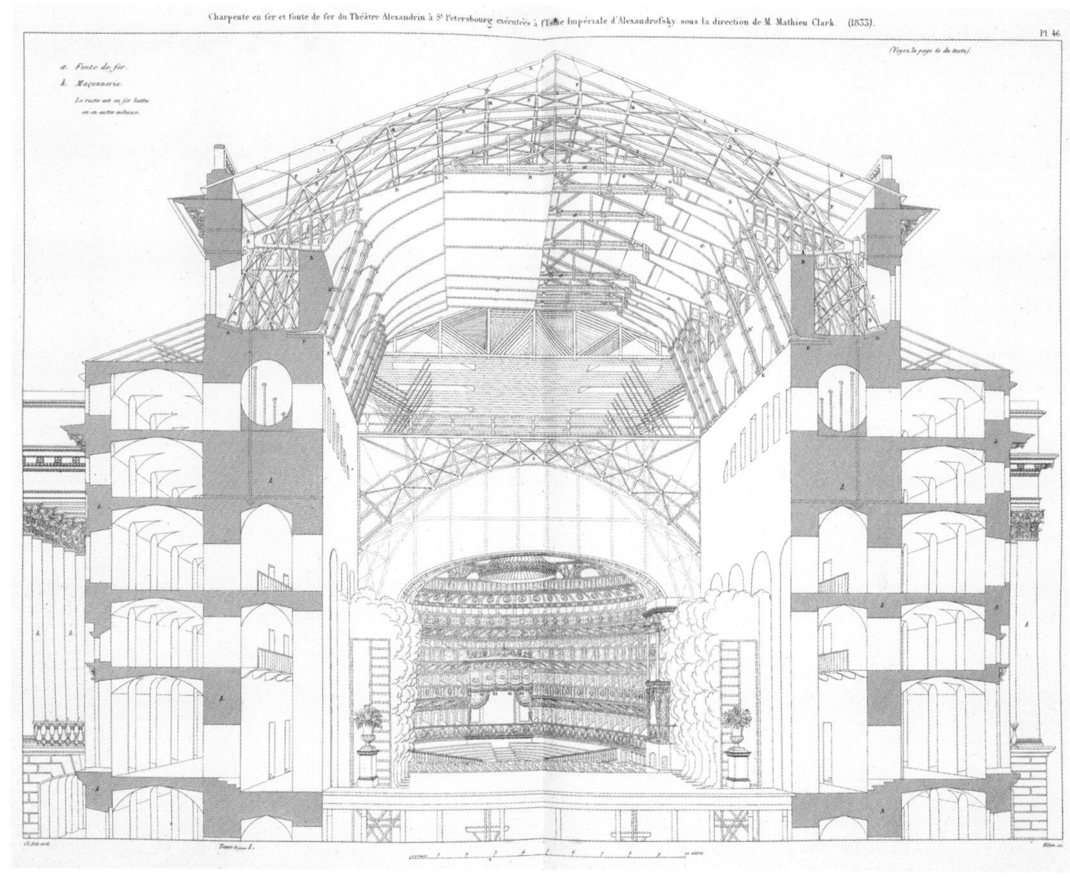
Charpente en fer et fonte de fer du Théâtre Alexandrin à St Petersbourg exécutées à l'Usine Impériale d'Alexandrofsky sous la direction de M. Mathieu Clark. (1833).
Pl. 46.
a. Fonte de fer.
k. Maçonnerie.

324

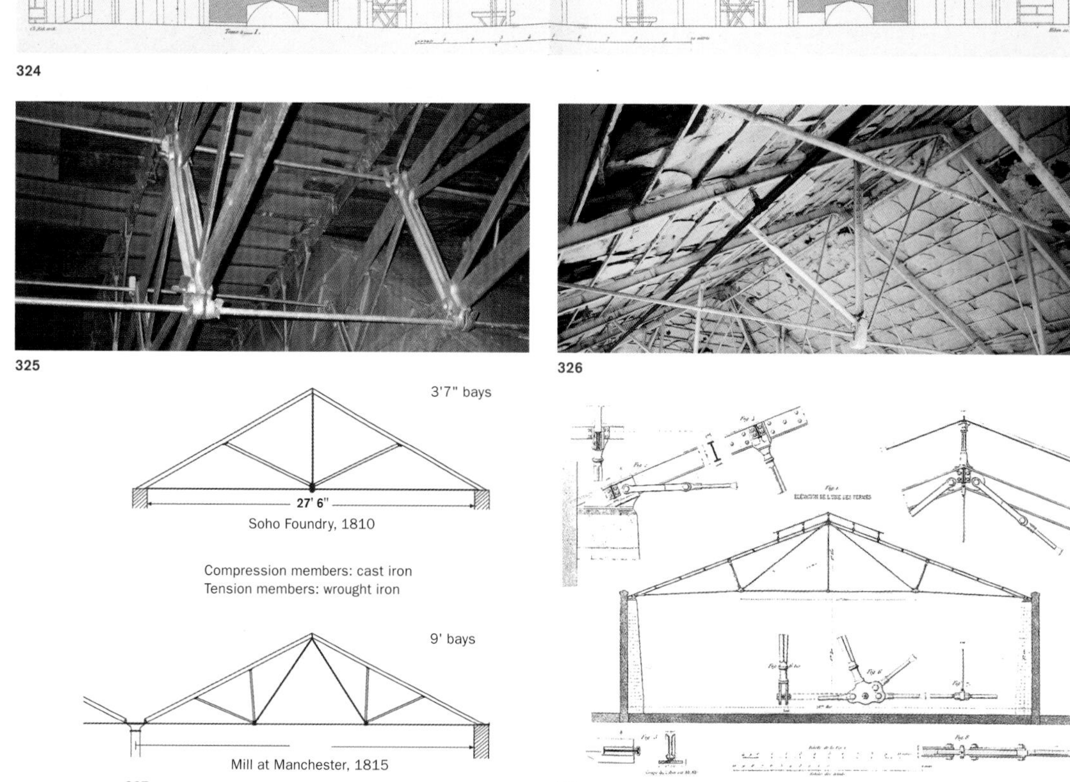
3'7" bays
27' 6"
Soho Foundry, 1810
Compression members: cast iron
Tension members: wrought iron
9' bays
Mill at Manchester, 1815

325

326

327

328

329

324 Aleksandrinskij Theater, Saint Petersburg, Russia, 1828–32. Engineer: Matthew Clark. Cutaway section showing cast and wrought iron roof structures. 325 Aleksandrinskij Theater. Detail of roof arch. 326 Beehive Mill, Manchester, England, 1824. Roof truss of cast and wrought iron. 327 Early roof trusses of cast and wrought iron in England, 1810 and 1815. 328 Roof truss of cast and wrought iron designed by French engineer Jean Barthélemy Camille Polonceau, c. 1836. 329 Nineteenth-century print of Euston Station, London, 1838.

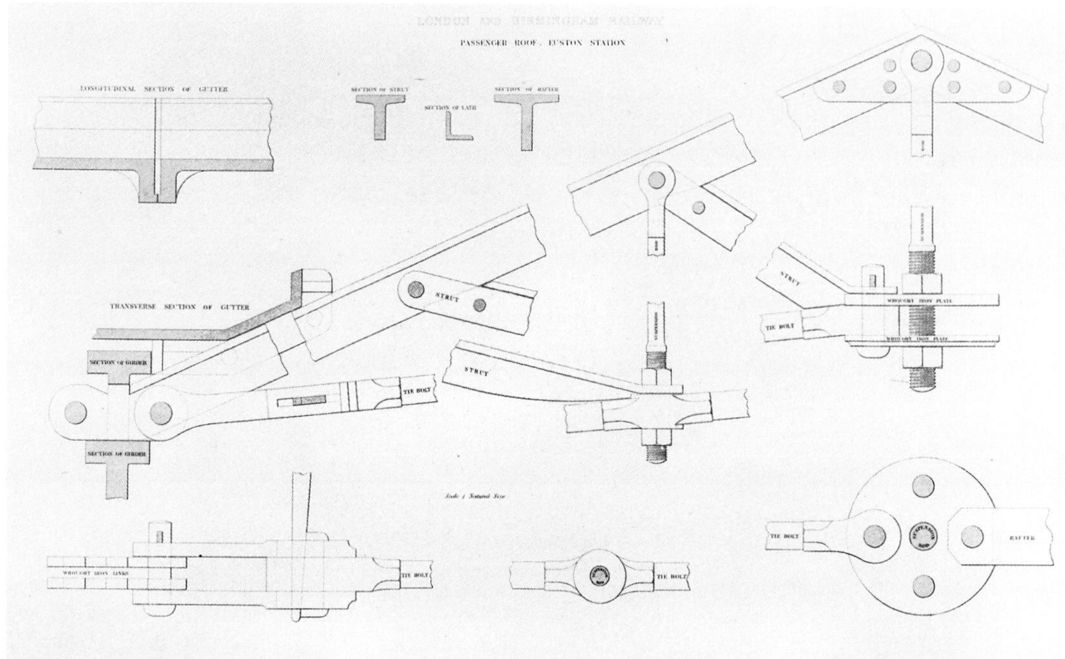

330

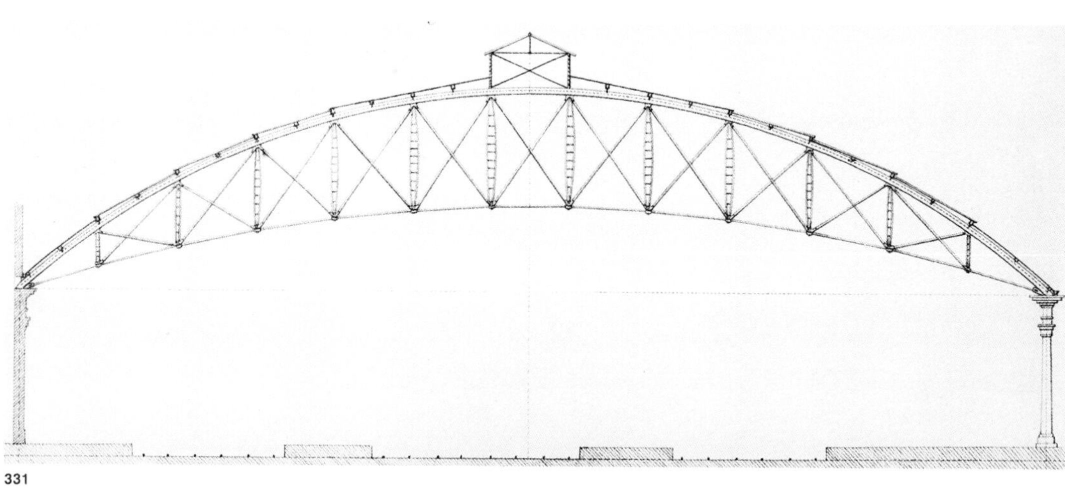

331

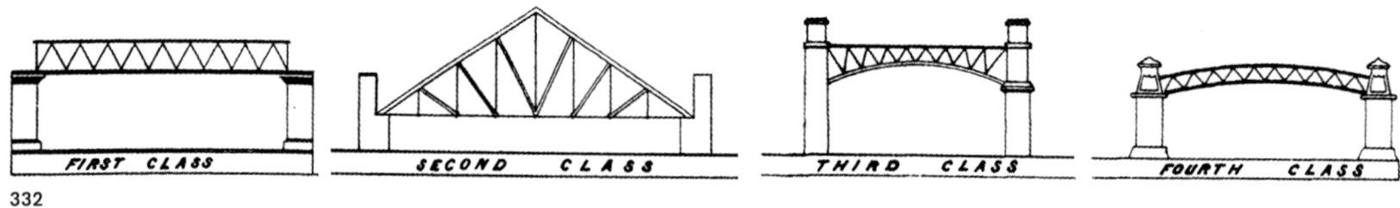

332

330 Original drawings of triangulated roof truss, Euston Station, London, 1833. Engineer: Charles Fox. 331 Birmingham New Street Station, Birmingham, England, 1854. Detail of large span roof truss. 332 Classification of bracing structures by Robert Bow, 1851.

days of truss bridges for railways in the 1840s, bridge engineers had designed their structures as if they were beams, with many large holes. Only in the 1840s did the Russian engineer D. J. Jourawski (1821–91) and the Venetian-born Austrian engineer Karl Ghega (1802–60) devise their methods for calculating directly the forces in the bars of a truss girder. Once developed for railway bridges, it was a simple matter to use the same methods for roof trusses. Very soon the German engineer Karl Culmann (1821–81) developed the method of "graphical statics" that would bring the design of even complex trusses within the reach of engineers with limited numerical skills (see chapter 7).

Once the concept of a statically determinate truss had been grasped, attention became focused on two issues that have run through structural engineering ever since: the categorization of structures into different types, and the relationship between forces (or stresses or deflections) calculated using mathematical models and those that are found in actual structures.

Robert Henry Bow (1827–1909) was one of the first engineers to class structures according to how they might be analyzed. He considered what we call trusses under a more general heading in his *Treatise on Bracing* (1851),
332 grouping structures in four categories:

1. *Two parallel beams with bracing between them, with the whole acting as a girder;*
2. *As 1, with two beams that are not parallel, and that meet at the supports;*
3. *A single arch, with triangulated bracing;*
4. *Two parallel or nearly parallel flexible arches, with bracing between them, the whole acting as a deep, rigid arch.*

Bow was only twenty-three when he first developed these ideas and wrote about iron roofs in a number of articles in the technical press. It is interesting that his thought process at this time did not lead him toward the Polonceau form of roof truss. His career took him into the design of bridges before he returned to roof structures after more than a decade (see chapter 7, p. 373).

Bow wrote lucidly about the second issue of concern to the structural engineer. "Such are the deductions in theory," he wrote, "but to ensure these we must have a structure far more perfectly framed than is practicable," and went on to consider "what the shortcomings of practice may entail."[2] However, neither Bow nor Johann Willhelm Schwedler (1823–94) and Culmann, who also wrote on analyzing the forces in trusses, considered how to deal with the relationship between the "deductions in theory" and the "shortcomings of practice." This would be articulated first by William John Macquorn Rankine (1820–72) a few years later.

Rankine and the "Harmony of Theory and Practice"

By the 1840s nearly every aspect of building design and construction had experienced the transition from craft to engineering. This reflected similar changes in civil and mechanical engineering, and can be summarized by the four characteristics that differentiate craft from engineering:

1. *the use of calculations to establish suitable sizes of components;*
2. *the use of scientific knowledge and understanding to inform decisions and to generate or raise confidence in a certain design proposal before it is built;*
3. *the ability to deal with power, forces, and temperatures whose magnitude far in excess of what a human can experience directly;*
4. *the ability to learn (certain) engineering knowledge from books and in the classroom, rather than by direct personal experience.*

The title of this chapter is taken from the inaugural lecture given by William Rankine when taking his chair as Regius Professor of Civil Engineering at the University of Glasgow in 1856. In his "Introductory Lecture on the Harmony of Theory and Practice in Mechanics," Rankine articulated, clearly, the philosophical basis by which an engineer could make use of the idealized mathematics that had been developed since Simon Stevin and Robert Hooke's day, but that had remained largely unexploited during the Enlightenment. It is one of the most significant papers in the history of engineering, for it described for the first time the process we now know and recognize as engineering design. Yet, although he wrote on the subject many times in papers and textbooks, he never used the word "design." For Rankine it remained a "third" or "intermediate kind of knowledge":

Mechanical knowledge may obviously be distinguished into three kinds: purely scientific knowledge, purely practical knowledge, and that intermediate kind of knowledge which relates to the application of scientific principles to practical purposes, and which arises from understanding the harmony of theory and practice.[3]

Rankine began his working life constructing railways after completing his studies at Edinburgh University, where he specialized in natural philosophy. He gained his early experience superintending a railway project his father was working on, and in 1838, at the age of eighteen, went to Ireland to work on the Dublin and Drogheda railway, where he undertook surveys and bridge construction. Among his earliest published papers, written in 1843, was one of the first on fatigue fracture of railway axles. From the evidence observed in broken axles, he noted the likely origin of fatigue cracks and recommended the avoidance of tight radii when turning axles on lathes. By 1848 Rankine had expanded his interests to include thermodynamics and molecular physics, and at the age of just thirty-three, he was elected a fellow of the Royal Society, followed, two years later, by his professorship at the University of Glasgow, where he remained until the end of his life.

As an academic Rankine made significant contributions to many fields of engineering science, including the buckling of struts, theory of elasticity, and hydrodynamics. His work in soil mechanics was probably the most important of the nineteenth century. For example, his analysis of the active and passive failure of loose earth led him to devise an entirely new approach to designing retaining walls, and revolutionized the design of embankments and earth dams. Rankine was one of the fathers of engineering thermodynamics, being one of the first scientists to propose what later came to be known as the First and Second Laws of Thermodynamics. He was also the first person to use the term energy, as we use the word today (replacing words such as work, force, and power, and similar concepts in other languages), embracing all its different manifestations as, for example, potential energy, including elastic and pressure energy, kinetic energy, and heat.

Rankine's greatest legacy was his textbooks on applied mechanics and civil engineering. These were the first comprehensive works in the English language, written initially to serve the needs of his own courses at the university. Almost single-handedly, he established the model that dominated British engineering education for more than a century. He was meticulous in his definitions of fundamental concepts such as stress, strain, and stability, and carefully built his arguments on these definitions, with the same rigor developed for geometry by Euclid. From such general theories he then turned to particular cases. While intellectually elegant, this approach, in the hands of lesser men, has often left British engineering students with a rather detached relationship with engineering reality and precedent.

Rankine's idea of the "intermediate kind of knowledge" quickly became embodied in his many textbooks and was no longer made explicit. Whereas the first edition of his *Manual of Applied Mechanics*, published in 1858, had contained the full text of his inaugural lecture, it did not appear in later editions or in his *Manual of Civil Engineering* (1861), which remained the classic textbook on the subject in Britain for many decades. Rankine did not manage to persuade the rest of the British academic world of the need to transcend the old dichotomy of theory and practice, and the nature of university education for engineers in Britain has been characterized by the concentration on theory ever since. In this sense, Rankine belonged firmly to the Continental "polytechnic" school of thought.

The activity we now know as engineering design has seldom been better described than by Rankine at the opening of the newly formed Mechanical Science section of the British Association for the Advancement of Science in 1855:

The study of scientific principles with a view to their practical application is a distinct art, requiring methods of its own . . . This kind of knowledge (intermediate between purely scientific and purely practical) . . . enables its possessor to plan a structure or machine for a given purpose without the necessity of copying some existing example—to compute the theoretical limit of strength and stability of a structure, or the efficiency of a machine of a particular kind—to ascertain by how far an actual structure or machine fails to attain that limit, and to discover the cause and the remedy of such shortcoming—to determine to what extent, in laying down principles for practical use, it is

> *advantageous, for the sake of simplicity, to deviate from the exactness required by pure science; and to judge how far an existing practical rule is founded on reason, how far on mere custom, and how far on error.*[4]

Perhaps the most significant idea he used was that of the limit toward which an engineer might strive. This same idea pervades nearly all modern engineering design and, indeed, it seems to have existed even in a thirteenth-century textbook that describes the "duty" of practical geometry as "giving measurements or limits which the work should not surpass" (see chapter 2, p. 79). Rankine's contribution was not that he invented new ways of engineering design. Rather, he devised a new way of looking at what engineers were already doing that would allow them to break through what was effectively an invisible barrier—the gap between "theory" and "practice" that led practical engineers to dismiss as useless the theoretical world of the mathematician and scientist. He achieved this by rethinking the concept of the "factor of safety" that had been used from the earliest days of designing structures, especially bridges, where it was considered to be the excess of a bridge's "actual" strength above the largest load it might ever need to carry. Bridges were often tested for loads larger than they would have to carry in common use. The factor of safety thus genuinely represented a degree of safety, though it did not embody any explanation of why such "safety" might be needed. Rankine redefined the idea of the "factor of safety" to embody the degree of approximation inherent in a mathematical model of a structure. This provided the philosophical basis by which design engineers could make use of both scientific knowledge and empirical knowledge.

The first design rules for beams that came into use in the second half of the eighteenth century always contained a multiplying factor or "empirical constant," which depended upon the material used and had to be determined by experiment. In the early nineteenth century the design rules became more general in their application by incorporating measured values for the strength or stiffness of the materials. The empirical constant, which still had to be determined experimentally, was now rather vaguely seen as catering to any unexplained differences between the mathematical predictions of structural behavior and the results found in tests of actual structures. The underlying implication was almost that, where differences were observed, a real structure was not behaving as it ought to behave.

Rankine approached the use of structural mechanics from the point of view of a design engineer. He effectively combined the idea of the empirical constant with the idea of the factor of safety. Put in modern language, he realized that the engineering "theory" was a mathematical model of a real engineering system, and was the means by which the appropriate scientific principles could be brought into consideration. It should not be expected that the model would accurately represent every aspect of a real-world structure, made of real-world materials and subject to real-world loads. Rankine now used the "factor of safety" to express the difference between the strength or stability of a structure, as calculated using mathematical models, and the closeness to that value that it would be sensible or safe to approach. The factor of safety was thus a measure of how approximate, imprecise, or uncertain the various mathematical models were. To this day engineers still talk, only slightly tongue-in-cheek, of the "factor of ignorance." Rankine also realized that there was an important difference between the degree of approximation or uncertainty when testing a beam or strut, for example, in the idealized conditions of a laboratory compared to its behavior in service in a real structure.

Rankine was describing a fundamental change in the way engineers undertook design, which took place gradually during the first half of the nineteenth century and was largely complete by the time Rankine delivered his inaugural lecture. Most engineers did not notice the change; yet in a remarkably short time the benefits of combining the scientists' theories and the results of large-scale experiments and tests became apparent. They were nowhere better seen than in the massive wrought iron tubular railway bridges over the River Conwy and the Menai Straits in North Wales. The engineering scientist Eaton Hodgkinson and iron manufacturer William Fairbairn collaborated on their cross section and overall design. When work began on the bridges in 1845, the largest iron-girder railway bridge had a span of about 27 meters. The main girder of the Menai Straits bridge had a span more than five times longer. The design and construction of this bridge is perhaps the greatest structural engineering achievement in history and influenced the design and construction of all subsequent structures; it demonstrated what was possible when, in Rankine's words, "scientific knowledge and empirical knowledge are united."

Engineering the Internal Building Environment

Once the link had been established experimentally in the 1770s between disease and air quality, the benefits of ventilating buildings became accepted, and ventilation soon followed strength of materials in becoming a quantitative discipline. Already by the 1810s the quantity of fresh air per hour that a person needs had been established, and design calculations quickly followed that would estimate the total quantity of fresh air that would have to be introduced into a building occupied by many people, such as a prison or hospital, to maintain satisfactory air quality. The demand could then be matched to the means of supply, both the capacity of ventilation fans and the size of ducts needed to introduce fresh air into rooms and to exhaust "foul air" from them. Although it was not yet possible to make quantitative measurements of other aspects of the environmental performance of buildings, such as humidity, acoustics, and lighting intensity, building designers were already formulating and using rational guidance of a qualitative nature.

Heating and Ventilating

The heating of buildings by passing steam through pipes and radiant panels began on a wide scale in the first decade of the nineteenth century. Two of the earliest ex-
334 amples date to 1799, one by Neil Snodgrass in a silk mill in northern Scotland and the other in Boulton and Watt's Salford factory. At the Salford factory, and a few years
333 later at Armley Mill in Leeds, the steam was conveyed to the upper floors through their hollow, cast iron columns.

The heating of mills by means of hot air dates back to Lombe's mill of 1720; there, air heated by a boiler was fed into the mill through ducts. Richard Arkwright, too, used warm air heating in the 1770s. However, it was William Strutt (see chapter 5) and one of his engineers, Charles Sylvester (1774–1828), who elevated the use of warm air heating to the status of what we would now call a building system. Strutt had installed his first warm-air system in his Derby mill in 1792–93 with the young Sylvester's help, and they used it in a number of Strutt's other mills during the 1790s. In that year Strutt had developed the warm air stove and the general arrangement of flues for the purpose of warming and ventilating buildings. His early stoves consisted of a fire chamber, made of iron and known as the "cockle," in which coal was burnt. Surrounding the cockle was a vaulted air chamber made of brick, which served to convey the heat from the burning coal to the air without allowing the air to be mixed
with the products of combustion. This so-called Belper 335
stove was later refined by embedding iron pipes in the brickwork to improve the efficiency of the heat transfer. Strutt and Sylvester's most celebrated building, however,
would be the new Derbyshire General Infirmary, con- 336
structed between 1806 and 1810.

The physician Erasmus Darwin had moved to Derby in 1781 and founded a dispensary that he hoped would be the "foundation stone for a future infirmary." Darwin had been a member of the Lunar Society in Birmingham and was, with William Strutt, a founder of the Derby Philosophical Society in 1783. Health, disease, and hospitals were a constant topic of debate; finally, around 1800, when Derby was the only major town in the area without a hospital, a number of men, including Strutt, formed a committee to design a new infirmary. The result would be the world's most sophisticated hospital, incorporating not only the best of established thinking, but many technical innovations also.The three-story building
consisted of rooms around a central atrium, which con- 338
tained the main staircase and was roofed by an iron and glass dome 7 meters in diameter. Parts of the building used Strutt's fireproof construction, with cast iron columns and beams and hollow-pot jack arch floors. Even the window frames were of iron; it was perhaps no coincidence that two members of the original design committee were partners at Ridings Ironworks, one of the largest ironworks in the county of Derbyshire.

At the Derby infirmary the Strutt-Sylvester heating and ventilation system was developed to allow the circulation of warm air in winter and cool air in summer. The airflow
was encouraged or driven using "turncaps"—cowls that 337
turned to face into the wind on the inlet side of the heat exchanger, and away from the wind on the outlet side.The air was taken in through an underground duct 70 meters long and 1.2 meters wide, so that the roughly constant temperature of the ground cooled the air in summer and warmed it a little in winter. Warm air from the stoves was

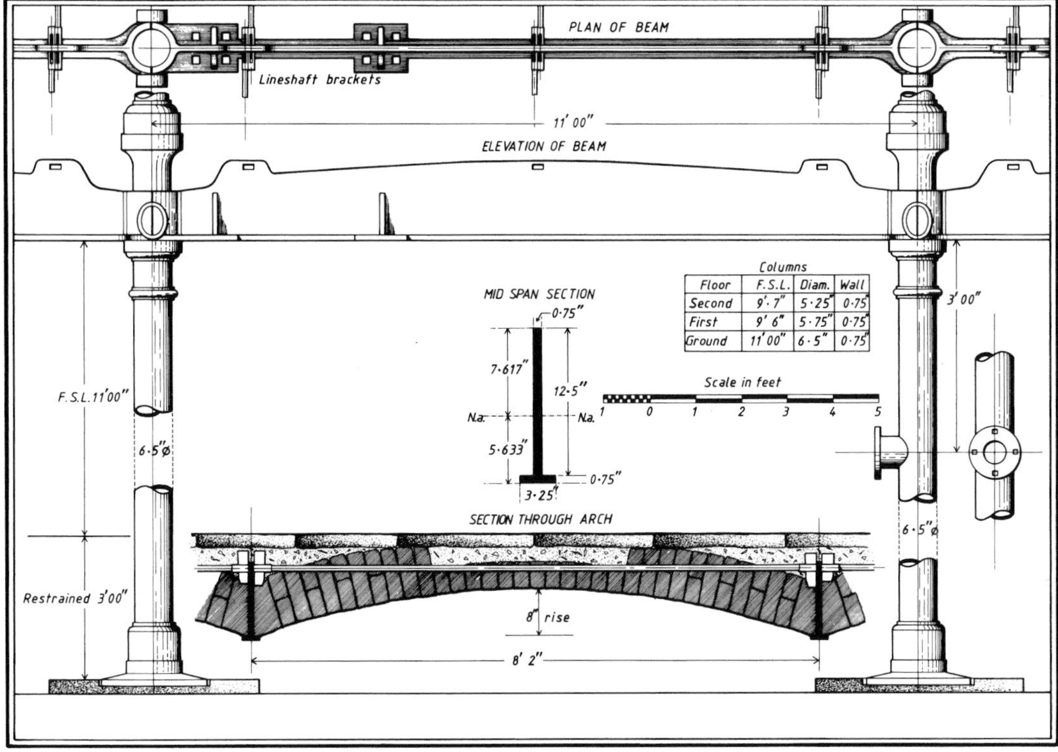

333

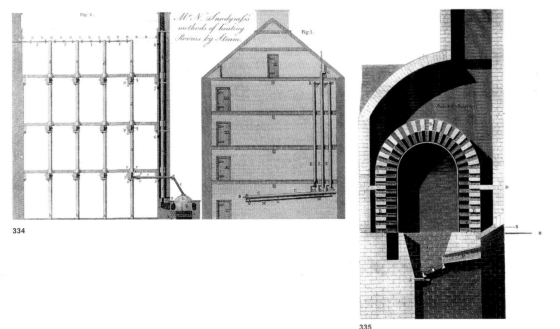

334

335

333 Detail of tubular cast iron columns used to disperse steam heat at Armley Mill, Leeds, England, 1803. 334 Silk mill near Dornoch, Scotland, 1799. Engineer: Neil Snodgrass. Illustration of heating system. 335 The "Belper stove," or cockle furnace, developed by William Strutt and Charles Sylvester, c. 1803. From Charles Sylvester, *The Philosophy of Domestic Economy*, Nottingham, 1819.

supplied to the rooms on all three floors, and also to the drying room adjacent to the laundry. Foul air from the wards was exhausted via the turncap on the roof. Water for the baths in the basement of the building was heated by steam, and the laundry was equipped with a washing machine designed by Strutt and driven by a steam engine. Wet linen from the laundry was moved into the drying room on clotheshorses that ran on rails. Strutt also devised toilets that were flushed automatically and were simultaneously fed with fresh air when the user opened the door. The wards were equipped with an adjustable sick bed that enabled nurses to manoeuvre patients easily. For this, Strutt adapted and improved the one devised by Joseph Bramah (1748–1814), the eminent English mechanical engineer who designed and made the first hydraulic press, a wood-planing machine, a machine for numbering bank notes as they were printed, and an impregnable lock for doors and safes. Even the kitchens did not escape Strutt's attentions, being equipped with a meat roaster and steamers of his own designs. Altogether the building was a technical marvel; as one visitor wrote, "Steam, gas, hot air, philosophy, and mechanics are all brought to bear on these premises and on every branch of domestic economy."[5]

Generally speaking, the building functioned very well. Other new devices and facilities such as foot warmers and steam baths continued to be installed after the hospital opened in various attempts to attract the fee-paying public to partake of new treatments. Nevertheless, there were some problems. In 1831 Charles Sylvester's son John was called in to deal with complaints from the patients that the dryness of the air gave "an unpleasant sensation," which he resolved by fitting an opening skylight in the roof to improve the airflow. The infirmary soon became well known and served as a model for many similar institutions, notably the Pauper Lunatic Asylum at Wakefield (1816–18) and a new fever house at Leicester Infirmary (1818–20). It became the object of interest to many dignitaries from throughout Britain and continental Europe, including Nicholas, the future tsar of Russia, Leopold, the future king of Belgium, and, most notably in building history, Karl Friedrich Schinkel (1781–1841), who visited England in 1826 specifically to learn about fireproof construction in iron. Gradually over later decades, however, the technical sophistication of the infirmary became its gradual undoing as things began to break down and require costly maintenance and repair. It was finally replaced in 1894.

Strutt never publicized his contribution to devising the infirmary, but did campaign widely to interest others in adopting the ideas. Strutt was elected a fellow of the Royal Society in 1817, partly in recognition of his "great improvements in the construction of stoves, and in the economical generation and distribution of heat which have of late years been so extensively and so usefully introduced in the warming and ventilation of hospitals and public buildings."[6] Sylvester eventually left Strutt's firm and set up a business installing the Strutt-Sylvester warm air heating system in many types of buildings throughout the country. He published his account of the Derbyshire Infirmary in *The Philosophy of Domestic Economy, as exemplified in the mode of warming, ventilating, washing, drying and cooking, and in various arrangements* (1819), which was consulted widely and translated into several languages. Charles Bulfinch (1763–1844), architect of the Massachusetts General Hospital in Boston, owned and annotated a copy of Sylvester's book.

As a consultant, Sylvester designed heating and ventilation systems for a number of hospitals, including Guy's Hospital in London; Sir Joseph Paxton's Victoria Regia House, built in 1850 at Chatsworth to display a lily native to South America being cultivated in England at the time; and for the pioneering Arctic discovery ships. Sylvester was succeeded by his son, John, who completed work on Guy's Hospital in London. Another pioneer in the field of heating was the French engineer Jean-Frédéric, Marquis de Chabannes (1762–1836), who achieved the first large-scale and successful use of heat-driven ventilation at Covent Garden Theater in London, c. 1815. Three stacks 339
exhausted air to the atmosphere through large turncaps similar to those devised by Strutt and Sylvester. Each was driven by a different source of heat. The air in the

336 Derbyshire General Infirmary, Derby, England, 1806–10. Engineers: William Strutt (structure) and Charles Sylvester (heating and ventilation). 337 Derbyshire Infirmary. Detail of turncap at roof level. 338 Derbyshire Infirmary. Plan showing staircase in the central glazed atrium. Air was removed at the atrium roof level through the turncap.

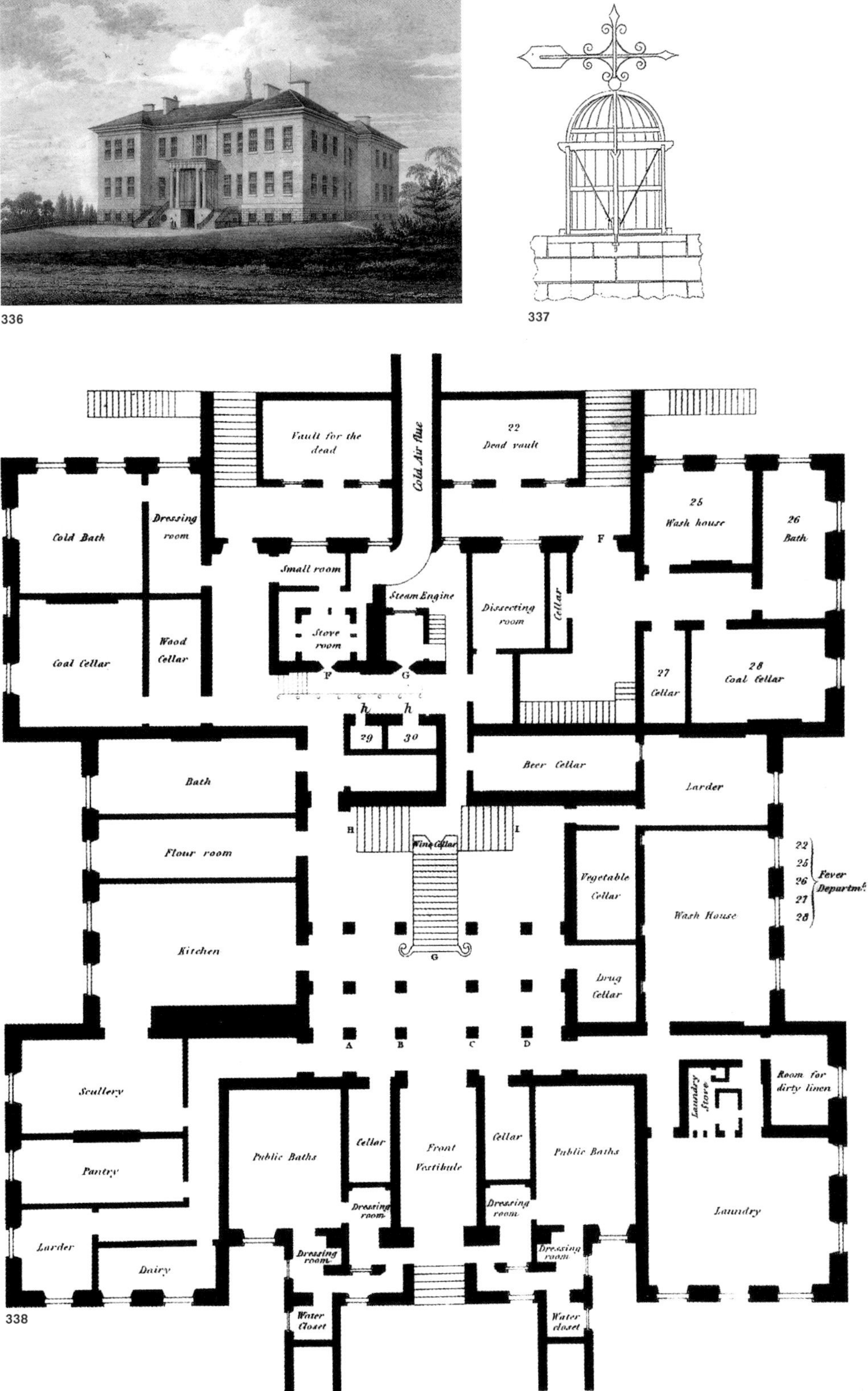
Vault for the dead
Cold Air flue
22
Dead vault
Cold Bath
Dressing room
25
Wash house
26
Bath
Small room
Steam Engine
Dissecting room
Cellar
Stove room
Coal Cellar
Wood Cellar
27
Cellar
28
Coal Cellar
29
30
Bath
Beer Cellar
Larder
Flour room
Wine Cellar
Vegetable Cellar
Wash House
22
25
26
27
28
Fever Departmt.
Kitchen
Drug Cellar
Scullery
Room for dirty linen
Laundry Stove
Cellar
Front Vestibule
Cellar
Public Baths
Public Baths
Pantry
Dressing room
Dressing room
Laundry
Larder
Dairy
Dressing room
Dressing room
Water Closet
Water closet

336

337

338

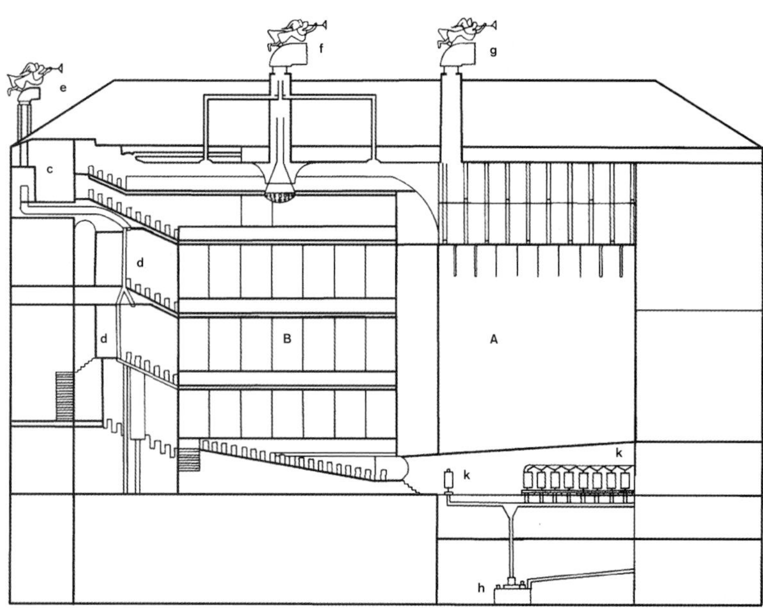

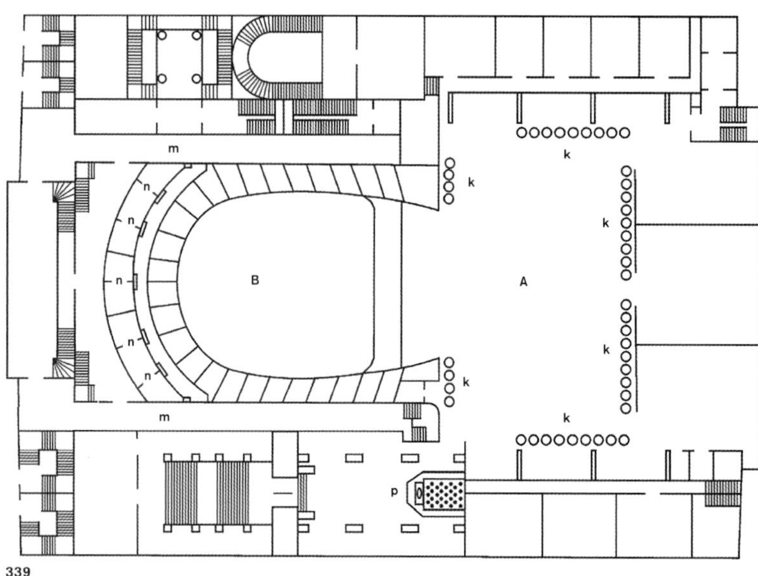

339

339 Covent Garden Theater, London, c. 1817. Heating and ventilation engineer: Jean Frédéric, Marquis de Chabannes. Section (top) showing ventilation ducts at rear of the raked seating (d) leading to the "ventilating fireplace" (c); from there to a turncap at roof level (e); gas lit chandelier driving air up to a turncap at roof level (f); steam-heated cylinders at the sides of the stage (k) that cause air to rise to the vent and turncap at roof level (g). Plan (bottom) showing ducts (n) conveying fresh air into the auditorium (B), and wooden ducts (m) conveying fresh air to the upper tiers of raked seating. In cold weather the large patent *calorifere fumivore* furnace (p) maintained the entrance hall off Bow Street at a temperature of 55–60°F (13–16°C).

stage and backstage areas was heated by both the lights and a substantial boiler feeding steam to iron radiators. Air in the top of the auditorium was heated by the gaslit candelabra directly below the exhaust stack, an idea that became widely used. Air from the tiered seating and boxes was heated by fireplaces specifically installed as part of the ventilation system. Chabannes designed and installed a similar system in the House of Commons in London from 1816 to 1818, where he used only iron cylinders heated by steam to circulate the air.

Although by this time the pioneering phase was over and both warm air and steam heating were widely accepted, little had been written on the scientific principles that underlay the art of heating and ventilation. The first author to approach the subject in a scientific manner was Thomas Tredgold (1788–1825), who had already gained considerable fame as the author of books on timber and cast iron construction. In his book *Principles of Warming and Ventilating* (1824), Tredgold dispelled the current belief that the quantity of heat needed was directly proportional to the volume of the space being heated. He offered a more rational design method based on the fact that heat loss from the room was the most important factor, and this depended on the area of glazing, the ratio of the surface area of the room to its volume, and the temperature difference between the outside air and the temperature desired inside. He checked these principles using simple experiments on the cooling of hot water cylinders, using his modest knowledge of physics most effectively. On the ventilation of buildings, he advocated the importance of seeking and removing the causes of foul air. He also based the amount of ventilation needed on the physiological needs of people, estimating these as a quarter of a cubic foot per minute to provide sufficient oxygen and three cubic feet per minute to remove the water vapor exhaled. To this he added a quantity of air needed to sustain the burning of candles for lighting, giving a total requirement of about four cubic feet per minute per person (114 liters per minute). Based on this human need for fresh air, Tredgold then expressed the requirement in terms of the number of air changes in a room per hour that would be needed to satisfy the needs of its occupants.

Turning to the question of how this air would be supplied, he observed that it must enter the room by infiltration through the gaps around windows and doors. To calculate quantity of this air, he proposed multiplying the total length of such gaps in a room by the airflow rate through a unit length of gap. In fact, Tredgold himself used a simpler method, assuming that all doors and windows allowed the same air infiltration rate of 310 liters per minute. Both of his design methods for ensuring that rooms were adequately ventilated were widely used during the following half century.

Tredgold also devised a scientific method for calculating the hourly quantity of coal needed to heat a room or a building using steam. First he measured the rate at which hot water in vessels of glass and cast iron cooled, depending on the surface area of the vessels and the temperature difference between the water and the air in the room. He used the results to calculate the volume of air that would be cooled by one degree Fahrenheit in one minute, by each square foot of glass in the windows—a volume of 1.5 cubic feet (43 liters) per minute (a value he later revised to 1.279 cubic feet). Multiplying this by the total area of glass gave him the equivalent volume of air that needed to be heated. To this he added the volume of air infiltrating into the room (310 liters per minute for each door and window), giving the total volume of air that had to be warmed by the steam heating from the outside air temperature to the desired indoor temperature. Tredgold next used the same approach to calculate the surface area of cast iron steam pipes needed to heat this quantity of air, and the hourly quantity of fuel needed to produce the steam from cold water. Finally, from this result, he calculated the annual quantity of fuel needed to keep a room constantly at a temperature of 13°C (rather lower than we would like today) for the 220 days a year when heating was needed in London, assuming an average outdoor temperature of 5°C. He also estimated the reduction in this quantity, taking into account the intermittent heating of rooms, and the time needed to preheat a building prior to its use, although he was optimistic in assuming this period would be a mere 24 minutes for a church with a volume of 2800 cubic meters. Tredgold used a similar approach to ensure that adequate ventilation was provided to glass houses to prevent their overheating in summer.

As the steam heating of buildings spread in the 1830s and 1840s, so the simple science-based design

BUILDING TYPE	INSIDE TEMPERATURE (DEGREES FAHRENHEIT) (60°F = 15.5°C)	HEATING SURFACE (FEET LENGTH OF 4-INCH PIPE, PER 1000 CUBIC FEET OF BUILDING)
CHURCH	55	5
LARGE PUBLIC ROOMS	55	5
DWELLING ROOMS	65	10
DWELLING ROOMS	70	12-14
HALLS, SHOPS, RAILWAY WAITING ROOMS	55-60	7-8
FACTORIES AND WORKROOMS	50-55	5-6
GREENHOUSES	55	35
GRAPERIES	65-70	45
PINERIES AND HOT HOUSES	80	55

340

methods were used more widely. To reduce the quantity of calculations required of an engineer, and to ensure the information was made available to engineers with little scientific education, the areas of heating surface required were often presented in the form of simple design tables. One, from the book *A Practical Treatise on Warming Buildings by Hot Water* by the engineer Charles Hood (1805–89), published in 1837, was calculated using Tredgold's design method, and was possibly
340 the first table giving engineers the surface area of steam-heated pipe needed to achieve various target design temperatures.

At this time design engineers still assumed that heat losses through walls, floors, and roofs were negligible, although the transfer of heat by both radiation and conduction had been known to physicists since the late eighteenth century. The first person to apply these ideas to the calculation of heat losses from a room or building, and hence to the design of heating systems, was the French physicist Eugène Péclet (1793-1857). He elaborated his revolutionary approach in his pioneering book *Traité de la Chaleur et de ses applications aux Arts et aux Manufactures* (Treatise on Heat and its Application to Arts and Manufacturing) (1828) which, through several editions, translations and derivative books, influenced design practice in France and Germany during the following half century. Despite the efforts of some English authors, notably the engineers Charles Hood and Thomas Box (c. 1825–c. 1880). Péclet's approach was not generally adopted in Britain or the U.S. until the twentieth century.

In order to calculate the pressure difference required across the ends of a chimney or a pipe carrying steam or gas to ensure delivery of the gases at the desired rate, Tredgold used the laws of basic fluid dynamics, developed in the mid-eighteenth century by the Swiss physicist Daniel Bernoulli (1700–82), among others. This design rule gave the required pressure difference as proportional to the square of the desired discharge rate. While this was a significant departure from earlier design rules for flow in pipes, which had been entirely empirical, his rule took no account of the resistance to flow in the pipe and he thus (incorrectly) assumed flow rates were independent of the length of the pipe. Tredgold was not aware of the recent research undertaken in France in the 1770s by the civil engineer Antoine de Chézy (1718–98), and in the 1780s by the civil engineer Gaspard Riche, Baron de Prony (1755–1839), who had established the resistance to flow in pipes caused by the viscosity of the fluid and, hence, the increase in resistance with the length of the pipe. Tredgold's oversight was addressed by Charles Hood, who used Prony's results in his book. Nevertheless, neither Chézy nor Prony had considered the roughness of the interior surface of the pipe, which

340 Table showing the surface area of steam-heated pipe required to achieve specific inside temperatures for various types of buildings, adapted from Charles Hood, *A Practical Treatise on Warming Buildings by Hot Water*, 1837.

leads to significant errors in predicting flow rates, especially for small-diameter pipes. Many design engineers thus preferred using simple empirical design rules until the late nineteenth century, when the effects of pipe friction were first established scientifically.

Tredgold's book was highly successful and served the needs of practicing engineers well. It was translated into French and German, ran to three editions in English and was still being recommended as essential reading in the 1880s. Most subsequent writers on heating and ventilation based their approach on Tredgold's, and he was credited as being the first author who, for the first time, brought together engineering, the needs of human physiology, and the idea of human comfort. We know of just one building with which his name can be linked. He designed the heating system for the conservatory at Syon
341 House, Isleworth, in West London, designed by the architect Charles Fowler (1792–1867). Despite his lack of experience with large-scale projects, however, Tredgold became widely respected in engineering circles. In 1821 he was elected a member of the Institution of Civil Engineers, and, in 1824, an honorary member. Sadly, Tredgold's work as an author was not lucrative, and at his death his wife and family were left nearly destitute. The Institution of Civil Engineers was moved to help them by buying one of Tredgold's books for the highly inflated price of £40; Thomas Telford was one of several eminent engineers who appealed for donations to a fund to ameliorate the family's situation.

With hindsight it is perhaps curious that neither Chabannes nor Tredgold described examples of hot water central heating systems, although the third edition of Tredgold's book (1836) included an appendix describing and illustrating such systems at the orangery of Windsor Palace and at Westminster Hospital. A disadvantage of the normal low-pressure hot water systems was that the pipes had to be quite large. Jacob Perkins, an American engineer working in London, overcame this inconvenience in the early 1830s by developing a high-pressure system that used much smaller pipes, easier to handle and conceal. One of the first buildings in which this sys-
342, 343 tem was installed was the Register Office in Edinburgh in 1832. By 1837, when the architect Charles Richardson (1806–71), pupil and amanuensis of Sir John Soane (1753–1837), illustrated the Edinburgh building in his book *A Popular Treatise on the Warming and Ventilation of Buildings*, he reported that high-pressure hot-water heating systems were in widespread use, though this claim might have been made with publicity in mind.

Despite the failure of John Theophilus Desaguliers's fire-driven ventilation at the House of Commons in 1734, the principle was sound. There was another opportunity to make a ventilation system work in the English Parliament after the House of Commons burned down in 1834. While the new House of Commons was being designed and built, the Members of Parliament were situated temporarily in the old House of Lords, refitted with a sophisticated heating and ventilating system designed by the Scottish
chemist and engineer David Boswell Reid (1805–63). 344, 345
This system would be the most elaborate ever installed and was an attempt to provide full control of the air entering the Members' Chamber. A room was provided "for moistening, drying, cooling, and producing other alterations in the air, besides those effected by the hot-water [heating] apparatus."[7] In warm weather the air was cooled by large blocks of ice placed in the air duct. Reid's system included various other means of treating the air drawn into the building for ventilation. Soot and other particles in the air were removed by filtration; the air was 346
cleaned by washing with both water and lime water (calcium hydroxide solution); acids in the air were neutralised using ammonia solution; the air was disinfected using chlorine. Although he did not use the phrase, this was full air-conditioning.

The spent air from the room was extracted through panels in a glass ceiling. As well as providing the openings needed for air extraction, the ceiling served as an acoustic reflector to improve intelligibility in the chamber. It also allowed daylight from the high-level clerestory windows to enter the chamber, and provided a void in which
gaslights could burn without the combustion products en- 347
tering the room beneath. The used air and combustion products were drawn out of this void by the forced draft created in the huge chimney adjacent to the building.

Reid was also responsible for the first large-scale use of
mechanical ventilation in St. George's Hall in Liverpool, 348, 349
designed and constructed between 1841 and 1854. The ventilation system was driven by four fans, each 3 meters in diameter, driven by a single steam engine

341

341 Conservatory at Syon House, Isleworth, West London, 1827–30. Engineers: Charles Fowler (structure) and Thomas Tredgold (heating and ventilation); architect: Charles Fowler. 342 Register Office, Edinburgh, Scotland, 1832. Heating engineer: Jacob Perkins. Cutaway section showing high-pressure hot water system. From Charles Richardson, *A Popular Treatise on the Warming and Ventilation of Buildings*, London, 1837. 343 Register Office, Edinburgh. Illustration of the distribution of high-pressure hot water. From Charles Richardson, *A Popular Treatise on the Warming and Ventilation of Buildings*.

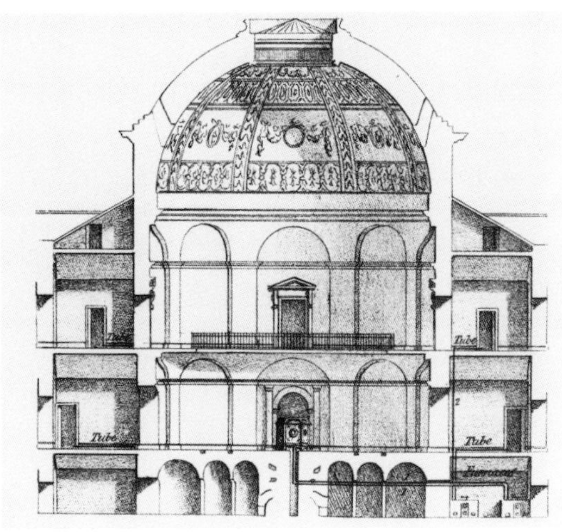

342

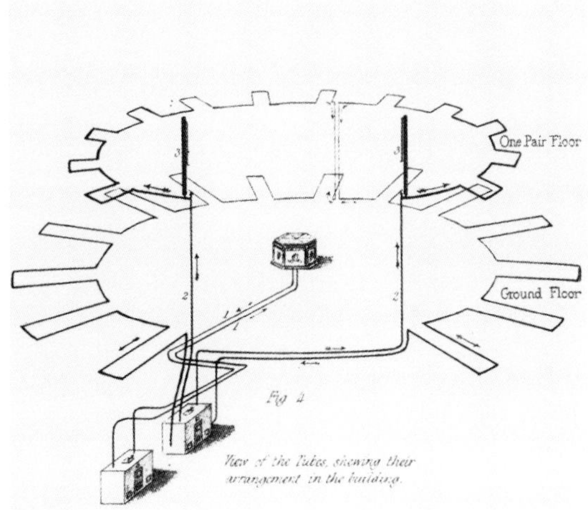

343

(which also drove the bellows for the great concert organ). The system provided 7 to 10 cubic feet of air per person per minute and could be adjusted to suit the number of people using the building, from 100 up to 5,000—a peak capacity of 50,000 cubic feet per minute. After filtering, warming, or cooling, as necessary, and humidifying using steam when necessary, the air was pumped into a large plenum (reservoir) beneath the main hall and entered the room through thousands of holes in the wall near floor level. The whole system had to be run by numerous operatives who could control airflows in ducts by adjusting a multitude of canvas flaps. As well as various thermometers and other indicators, the air speed in ducts was monitored, as Reid explained, by "threads of a known length and thickness, varying from a single fibre of silk, two or three feet long, to thick thread in use at the principal ventilation shafts. At either end of the ceiling at the principal escape of vitiated air from the Great Hall, bright coloured cylinders are suspended from short threads, and their inclination or movements may be recognised by the naked eye or with the assistance of a small telescope."[8] Although the thermal inertia of the building meant it was never possible to moderate the conditions in all the rooms as precisely as the sophisticated controls might have implied, the complex system worked successfully for nearly 130 years, and was considered many years ahead of its time.

Although few buildings were able to afford the sophistication of the systems at the temporary House of
Commons or St. George's Hall, the principles Reid had
demonstrated quickly spread worldwide. By the 1850s it
was common for prisons and hospitals especially to in- 351
corporate well-designed ventilation systems, often including warm-air heating. The skylines of nineteenth
century cities became dotted with evidence of the new
ventilation technology. 350

Across the Atlantic, an early ingenious approach to warm
air was heating used on a modest scale in the U.S.
Custom House at Wheeling, West Virginia. Designed in 352
1856 and completed in 1859, this was an early American
example of using wrought iron beams in building construction, some of which were rolled I-sections and oth- 353
ers built as hollow box girders. Background heating was
provided to each room by feeding warm air through the
hollow cast iron columns and wrought iron girders. Each
room also had a conventional fire.

EARLY BOOKS ON BUILDING SERVICES ENGINEERING

The ventilation of buildings had become a pressing issue during the 1760s and 1770s following several terrible outbreaks of disease in ships, prisons, and hospitals, and from this time a growing number of such establishments were fitted with means of ventilating and heating them. However, until nearly 1810 there had been just one book published on the subject—*A Treatise on Ventilators*, by Stephen Hales (1758). Following the descriptive books by Chabannes and Sylvester, Tredgold published the first book that addressed the engineering issues involved, including calculations, for example, of the total quantity of air needed to provide satisfactory ventilation in a hospital or prison. There soon followed a spate of books aimed at the building design professions, giving examples of heating and ventilating systems that had been successful installed. Nevertheless, until the 1860s, only the books by Tredgold, Péclet, Hood, and Box contained useful design methods based on a scientific approach. The rest were merely descriptive and illustrative. In this respect, building services was several decades behind structural engineering.

The following list illustrates the sudden profusion of these books in the first half of the nineteenth century.

1807 Robertson Buchanan, *An Essay on the Warming of Mills and Other Buildings* by Steam (Glasgow)

1818 Jean-Frédéric, Marquis de Chabannes, *On Conducting Air by Forced Ventilation* (London)

1819 Charles Sylvester, *The Philosophy of Domestic Economy: as exemplified in the mode of warming, ventilating, washing, drying and cooking …* (Nottingham)

1824 Thomas Tredgold, *Principles of Warming and Ventilating* (London)

1828 Eugène Péclet, *Traité de la chaleur, et de ses applications aux arts et aux manufactures* (Paris)

1836 W.S. Inman, *Principles of Ventilation, Warming and Transmission of Sound* (London)

1837 Charles Hood, *A Practical Treatise on Warming Buildings by Hot Water, and an Inquiry into the Laws of Radiant and Conducted Heat. To which are added remarks on Ventilation* (London)

1837 Charles Richardson, *A Popular Treatise on the Warming and Ventilation of Buildings* (London)

1844 David Boswell Reid, *Illustrations of the Theory and Practice of Ventilation; with remarks on warming, lighting and the communication of sound* (London)

1845 Walter Bernan (pseudonym of Robert Meikleham), *On the History and Art of Warming and Ventilating Rooms and Buildings* (London)

1846 Morrill Wyman, *A Practical Treatise on Ventilation* (Boston)

1850 Charles Tomlinson, *A Rudimentary Treatise on Warming and Ventilation* (London)

By 1860 there was thus a wealth of books, mainly in English or translated from English, on the heating and ventilating of large nondomestic buildings. Examples included hospitals, prisons, theaters, several gentlemen's clubs (especially the Reform Club), and a number of public buildings, including the Houses of Parliament and the British Museum in London, and St. George's Hall in Liverpool. A growing number of books in French and German appeared from the 1830s, though the German books had little influence in other countries because of the language barrier. Their main influence was in the United States, where large numbers of German-speaking immigrants lived.

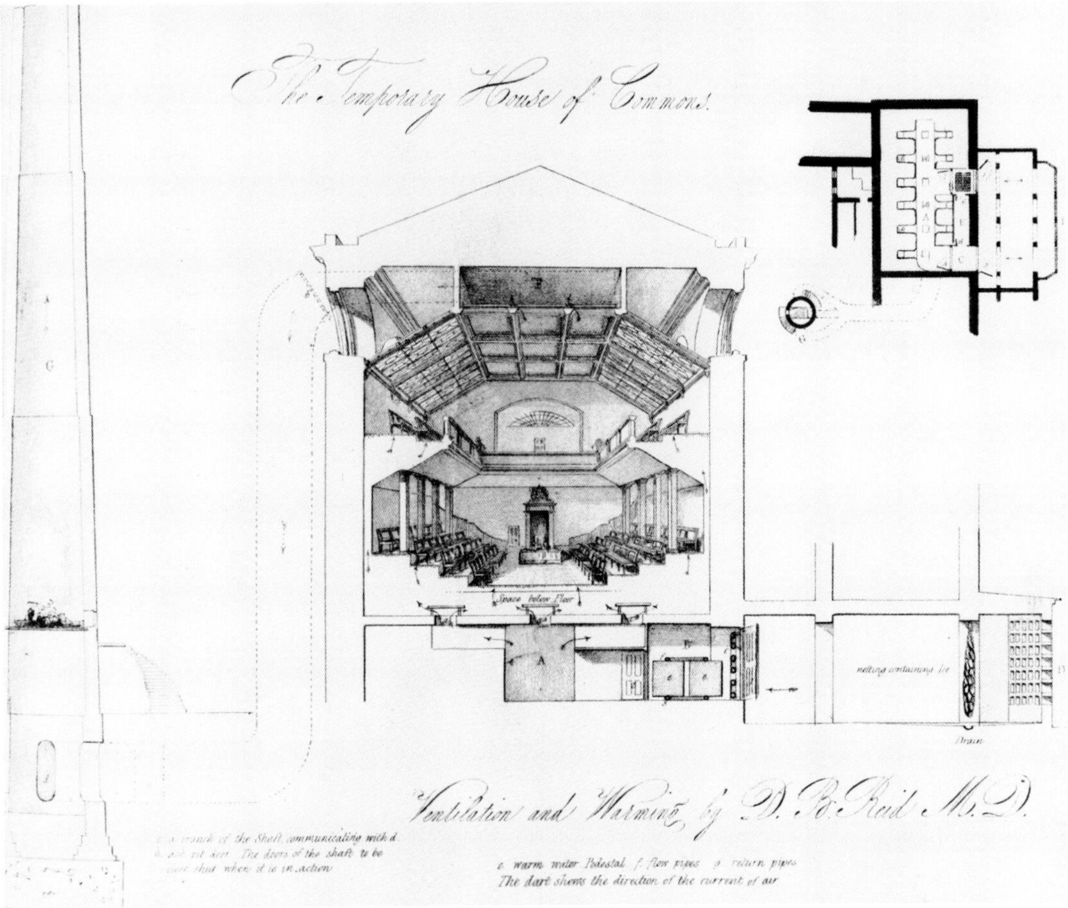

344

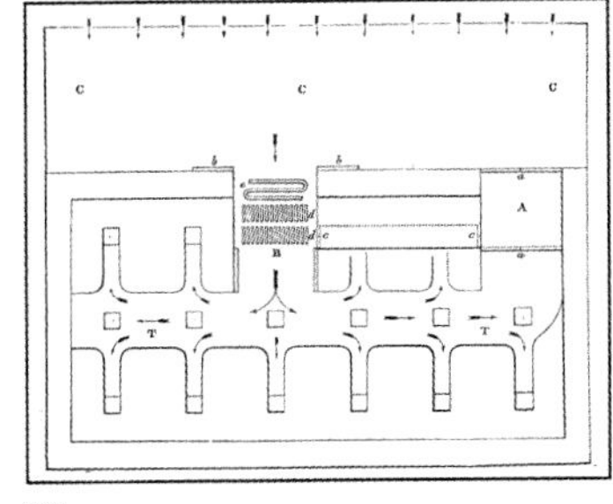

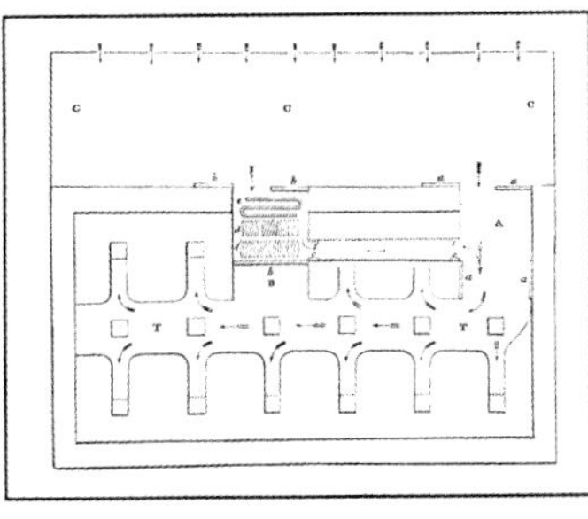

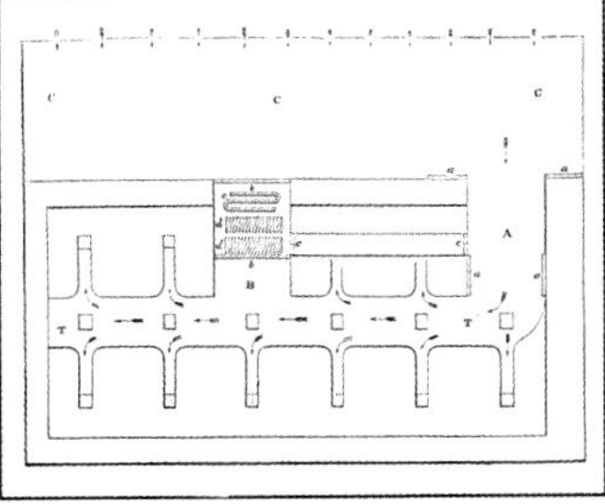

345

344 Temporary House of Commons (formerly the House of Lords), London, 1836. Heating and ventilation engineer: David Boswell Reid. Cross section of refitted building. 345 Temporary House of Commons. Illustrations demonstrating three modes of operation: heating only, mixed air heating and ventilating, and ventilation only.

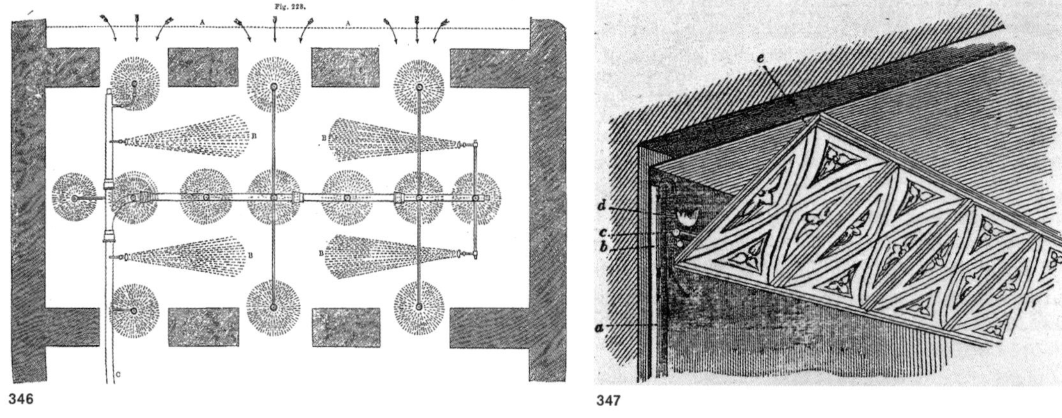

346

347

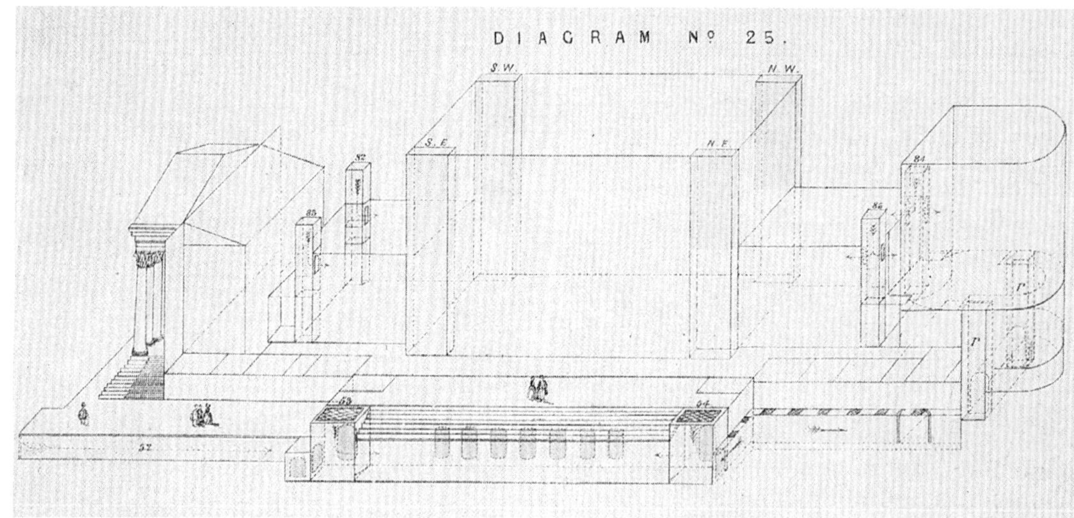

348

346 Temporary House of Commons (formerly the House of Lords), London, 1836. Heating and ventilation engineer: David Boswell Reid. Water sprays used to filter the air. 347 Temporary House of Commons. Illustration of gas lighting behind glass panels that formed the ducts conveying exhaust from the building. 348 St. George's Hall. Liverpool, England, 1854. Engineer: David Boswell Reid. Diagram of primary ventilation ducts. 349 St. George's Hall. Section illustrating ventilation system.

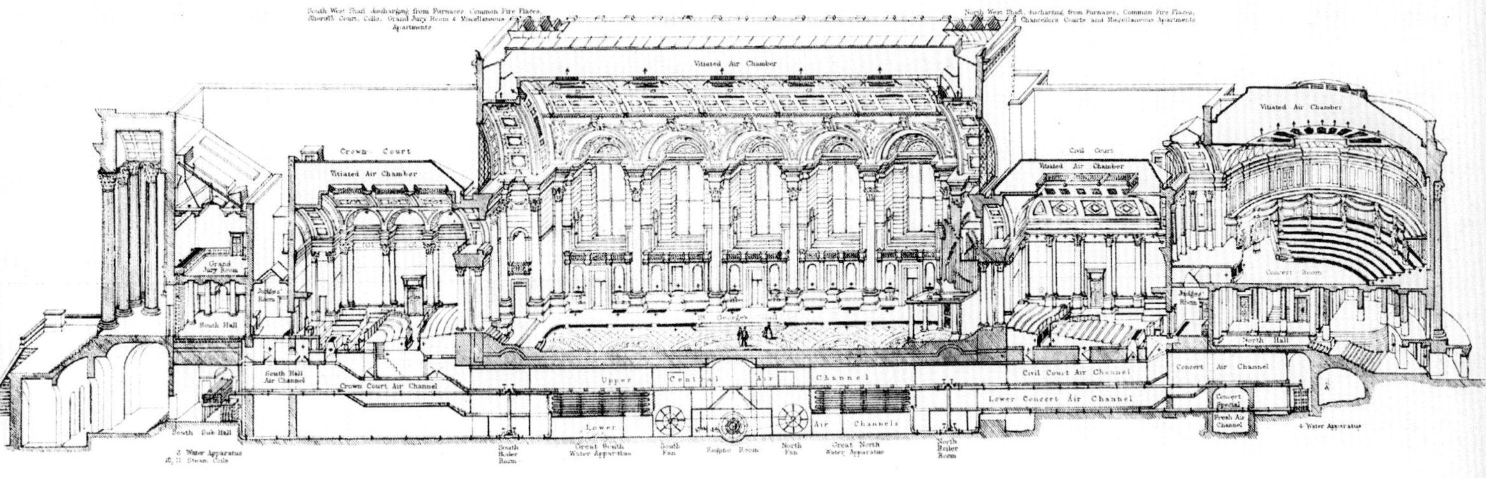

Comfort Cooling

Traditional and vernacular methods of cooling buildings dating from ancient times depended on evaporation. Warm air blown over water is cooled; heat energy is removed from the air as it is needed to turn the water into vapor by the process of evaporation. The process is more effective if the water is sprayed in a fountain, which provides a greater surface area for evaporation, or if the air passes through brick or a cloth kept constantly wet by soaking up water by capillary action. Indeed, hanging a wet sheet in front of an open window is still an effective means of cooling a room in a warm climate should all else fail. While this principle is still the basis of the cooling process, the technology and engineering science underlying modern air-conditioning took many decades to develop.

The heating and ventilating of buildings was well established by the middle of the nineteenth century, but effective cooling systems did not become common until the end of the century. Before that time there was no practical means of cooling the air sufficiently prior to circulating it around the building, nor was it possible to use fires and chimneys to drive such forced ventilation. Although fans driven by small steam engines were available for pumping air around buildings since the 1840s, efficient refrigeration machinery was developed only in the 1860s.

The main demand for cooling was to preserve food and to provide chilled drinks and ice cream. Well-off families in eighteenth- and nineteenth-century Europe would probably have had an icehouse on the grounds of their estates, but this was not an option for most families. The growing demand for ice in cities in the nineteenth century was met by ice harvesting. In Europe, Norwegian traders developed a large export industry for ice, which they had in limitless supplies. Ships laden only with ice served all the major ports of continental Europe and Britain, and the ice was dispatched inland by road and rail. In the United States, a similar trade was established in Boston during the first decade of the nineteenth century. The efforts of the Boston shipping merchant and entrepreneur Frederic Tudor (1783–1864) led to an export industry that served not only the ports of the southern U.S. but also Cuba and other Caribbean islands, every major port in Central and South America, and, by the 1840s, China, the Philippines, India, and Australia as well. With exports

350

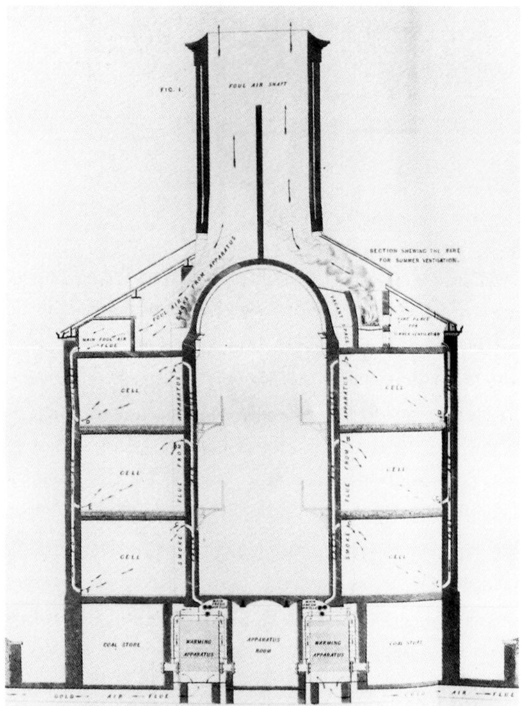

351

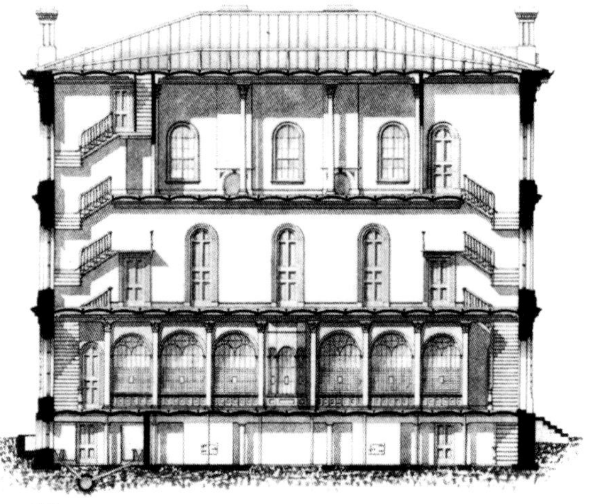

352

350 Study of the ventilation towers, columns, and spires of London's skyline. William Lionel Wyllie, c. 1900.

351 Pentonville Prison, London, 1841–42. Section illustrating warm-air heating and fire-assisted ventilation and extraction.

352 Custom House, Wheeling, West Virginia, United States, 1856–59. Fireproof construction with hollow cast iron columns and wrought iron beams conveyed warm air to heat each room. 353 Custom House, Wheeling. Detail of beam-column connection. 354 Illustration of the ice harvest in Pittsburgh, Pennsylvania, United States, 1877.

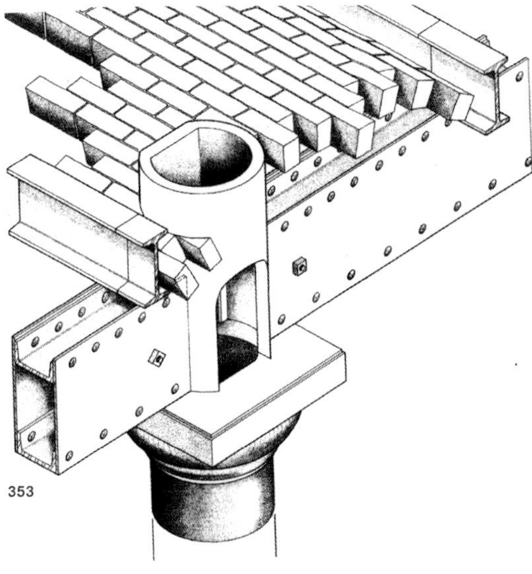

353

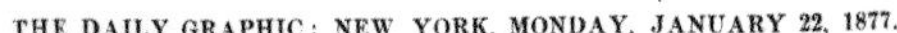

THE DAILY GRAPHIC: NEW YORK, MONDAY, JANUARY 22, 1877.

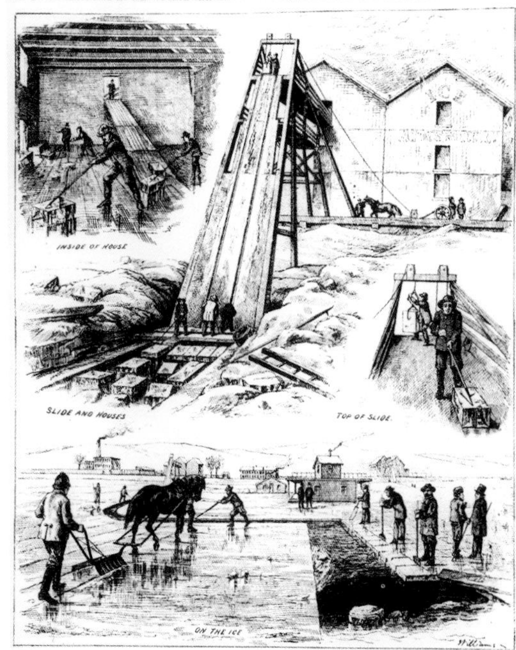

354

from Boston around 1850 reaching some 70,000 tons a year, Tudor was justifiably hailed the "Ice King of the World." By this time demand in Europe from the fishing industry and the rapidly growing brewing industry was outstripping supply, and, beginning in the 1840s, a transatlantic ice trade started to grow; soon ships were arriving almost daily in Liverpool and Bristol. In the 1860s, at the peak of the ice industry's prosperity, over 200,000 tons of "natural ice" were being exported world-
354 wide from the U.S., and well over ten thousand people were employed harvesting, transporting, storing, and shipping ice throughout America and abroad. The industry declined with the development, in the 1870s, of refrigeration plants that could manufacture "artificial ice" locally. Nevertheless, the trade in natural ice, which was marketed as superior in quality to artificial ice, survived into the twentieth century.

"Artificial Cold" and Refrigeration

Scientists during the late eighteenth century had studied the cooling that arose from allowing a gas to expand and that arose when a liquid evaporated. The Scottish physicist William Cullen (1710–90) had published a paper in 1756 entitled "Of the Cold Produced by Evaporating Fluids." However, it was an American steam engine mechanic, Oliver Evans (1755–1819), who first had the idea—which he described in a book on the steam engine in 1805—of turning the cooling from expansion into a repeatable or continuous cycle. He described, in essence, the process of refrigeration as the cycle employed in a steam engine working in reverse: Mechanical energy is used to compress a gas, sometimes into liquid form, which is then conveyed to another place, where it is allowed to expand and, in doing so, absorb heat from its new surroundings as it evaporates. Evans proposed ether as the refrigerant. Richard Trevithick (1771–1833), a Cornish maker of steam engines, also wrote on the subject in 1828 in "The Production of Artificial Cold."

It was neither Evans nor Trevithick, however, who took the idea further, but a colleague of Evans's, Jacob Perkins (1766–1849). Perkins was drawn to England by the British government's offer of a prize to print banknotes that could not be forged. He failed to win the prize, though late in life he did print the world's first postage stamp in England, the Penny Black, in 1840. In England Perkins worked mainly on improvements to steam engines and boilers, and this seems to have led him to patent a closed-cycle vapor-compression refrigerating system in 1834. Perkins used caoutchoucine, an organic solvent similar to ether that was used in the rubber industry, as his refrigerant. His prototype did manufacture a little ice, but was not turned to practical use. For the following three decades, many engineers and scientists in England, France, Germany, Australia, and the U.S. all developed machines for making ice and chilling food, but all with only modest success.

As with the steam engine, however, improving the effectiveness and efficiency of the refrigeration process quickly reached the limit of what was possible without using the fundamental concepts of thermodynamics.

The Development of Thermodynamics

The French scientist Nicolas Léonard Sadi Carnot (1796–1832) established the fundamental idea of the thermodynamic cycle in his paper, "Réflexions sur la puissance motrice du feu et sur les machines propres à développer cette puissance" ("Reflections on the motive power of heat and on the machines suitable for developing this power"), written in 1819 but not accepted for publication by the Académie Française until 1824. Carnot gained entry to the École polytechnique at the age of sixteen and during his short life spent time in the army, in industry, and following his theoretical studies. After learning about the design of steam engines, he noted that, despite the progress made since Thomas Newcomen's first endeavors,

> *. . . their theory is very little understood, and attempts to improve them are still directed almost by chance. The question has often been raised whether the motive power of heat is unbounded, whether the possible improvements in steam-engines have an assignable limit—a limit which the nature of things will not allow to be passed by any means whatever; or whether, on the contrary, these improvements may be carried on indefinitely.*[9]

With the insight of the scientist, he concluded that "if the art of producing motive power from heat were to be developed to the stature of a science, the whole phenomenon must be studied from the most general point of view, without reference to any particular engine, machine, or operating fluid."[10] Carnot established the concept of the heat engine as a continuously operating cycle in which work is produced by receiving heat at a high temperature and rejecting it at a low temperature. He established that the work produced was limited by the temperature difference between the heat supplied and that rejected. Finally, he also established that such a cyclic process was reversible—work could be used to cause heat to flow from a low temperature to a higher temperature, the basis of both refrigeration and the heat pump.

Carnot's seminal work was not well received, and lay virtually unknown for a quarter of a century. Only a few copies of his memoir were printed, and most were lost. Indeed, when a second edition was published, in 1872, there was great difficulty in finding a single original copy. This obscurity was in part because he had aligned himself with those who still adhered to the caloric theory of heat rather than the new idea that heat was a measure of the motion (now called kinetic energy) of atoms and molecules. It provides a profound insight on progress in science that ideas as timeless as those developed by Carnot could arise from what was later abandoned as a "false" theory of heat.

Carnot's work was rediscovered by the British physicist William Thomson, later Lord Kelvin (1824–1907), who used Carnot's ideas in a paper published in 1849 to calculate the limit to the output of some steam engines, finding that they were delivering less than 60 percent of the maximum work they could produce. Such calculations demonstrated both that improvements could be made and how someone could set about achieving the improvements. Like Carnot, Thomson still based his arguments on the caloric theory of heat, though he was already beginning to change his ideas since hearing of the work by James Prescott Joule, who had, in the early 1840s, conducted experiments to establish the "mechanical equivalent of heat" when mechanical energy was converted into heat energy. By 1850 Thomson had come to adopt the energy theory of heat and revise his understanding of the performance of steam engines, but was beaten into print on the subject by the German physicist Rudolf Clausius (1822–88), who had just been appointed professor of physics at the Royal Artillery and Engineering School in

Berlin. Over the next decade Thomson and Clausius established the science of thermodynamics as we now recognize it, and its two basic laws: the First Law, which states that heat and work are equivalent, and the Second Law, which states that heat cannot, of itself, pass from one body to a hotter body.

This fundamental work on steam engines also provided the basis of the heat pump, one version of which is the refrigerator, as a heat engine working in reverse. Mechanical work could be used to pump heat from a low temperature to a higher temperature. Thomson realized the practical benefits of such a machine and, in 1852, wrote a paper entitled “On the Economy of the Heating or Cooling of Buildings by Means of Currents of Air.” In his paper he described the theoretical basis of designs for both the heat pump as a means of heating air and the refrigerator. Although he seems not to have attempted to build such machines, he established the scientific basis on which such machines could be built or, more importantly, perhaps, since a few working refrigerators had already been built, how their performance could be improved using a rational approach rather than the random experimentation typical of enthusiastic inventors. The first experimental refrigeration machines using the vapor-compression cycle for making ice and chilling food were developed in the 1840s in France by Louis Tellier (1828–1913) and in the U.S. by John Gorrie (1803–55), a doctor working in Florida who sought an alternative to the ice imported by sea that he used to cool the air in his malaria hospital. Tellier went on to manufacture his refrigeration machines successfully in the 1860s, while Gorrie failed to find financial support for his invention, probably in view of the flourishing trade in natural ice. Another Frenchman, Ferdinand Carré (1824–1900), successfully developed and manufactured an alternative refrigeration method based on the vapor-absorption cycle, which avoided the need for a mechanical compressor and so required less energy to run.

Environmental Control: Glasshouses (Greenhouses)

The purpose of these early developments in controlling the internal environment was, of course, to improve the level of comfort for a building's human occupants. Humans, of course, are able to adapt to their surroundings by donning or removing clothing—something that is not the case for plants. It is not surprising, then, that the first means of controlling the internal environment of buildings should have been developed first for the various types of buildings—generically known as glasshouses (or greenhouses)—built to create artificial climates for plants. In the eighteenth and early nineteenth centuries, there were two reasons for wanting to create an artificial climate. First, the increasing commercialization of agricultural production in the seventeenth century led the Dutch and Germans, especially, to seek to lengthen the short growing season in northern Europe. Second, the growing numbers of explorer-botanists needed places to cultivate the specimens they had brought back from their trips to ever-more distant destinations. A growing fascination with exotic plants spread from the upper classes to the public at large and, from the 1830s, glasshouses began to be built in botanic gardens throughout northern Europe.

As we saw in the previous chapter, such buildings were developed on a small scale during the eighteenth century, but between about 1820 and 1850 they reached the height of fashion, as manifested by their increasingly large size. Beginning in the seventeenth century, steam from boilers had been used to create the desired humidity. However, it was soon realized that the need for this kind of heating would be reduced if the maximum use could be made of the sun's light and heat. Designers thus began to consider the facade of the building—the interface between outside and inside—as a part of the system needed to control the internal environment. A rational approach was fundamental to making the facade work. It had to admit light, heat, and water vapor at some times, and prevent heat and water vapor from escaping at other times. Most importantly, it had to perform in different ways in specific situations, and this performance had to be closely regulated. The facade also had to function as a structure, which involved somehow holding in place the large spans of glass required to create the necessary degree of transparency; the facade also had to carry the loads due to wind and snow.

The early examples had been rather mundane conventional buildings with large planar windows. Sometimes the windows were set at an angle to the vertical to try to ensure the sun's rays would strike the glass at a nearly-perpendicular angle, which at the time was believed to be

GRAPHICAL STORAGE AND RETRIEVAL OF DATA AND INFORMATION

Although the repetitive numerical calculations involved in engineering design have always been tedious, it was only in the mid-nineteenth century that the use of graphs was developed to reduce the tedium, to increase the accessibility of data, and to help perform calculations. A graph is, effectively, a means of storing a large amount of numerical data and of enabling its easy retrieval—the pre-computer-age equivalent of today's hard disk. But it is more than this. A large table of values of different variables can contain the same information, but in a far less accessible form and requiring calculations to interpolate between numerical values. Because it is visual, a graph is much quicker to read and easier to interpolate. Also, because a graph is a continuous line, it more usefully models the behavior of real-world phenomena. For example, a graph drawn of load against the deflection for a cast iron beam not only records a number of experimental measurements (say, for every 100 Newtons up to 1 Kilonewton), it also allows someone to predict, as it were, the outcome of an experiment that was not undertaken (say, the deflection due to a load of 355 Newtons).

Such a graph, however, is useful only for a beam with certain dimensions made of one material. With some imagination, the behaviour of beams of different dimensions and materials can be represented on the same sheet of graph paper. Graphs such as these—or charts, as they were often called—were the basis of nearly all engineering design methods (not only in building engineering) for more than a century between about 1860 and 1980, when computers began to arrive on engineers' desks. The groundwork for this revolution in design methods was developed in the mid-nineteenth century.

The means of generating a graphical representation of a multivariable relationship was developed by the French geographer Philippe Buache (1700–73). In 1737, he first represented the depth of the sea on a navigator's chart of the English Channel by plotting lines of equal depth, or isobaths as they are now known. He soon used the same idea to plot the heights of land in the form of contours. Over a century later, in 1843, another Frenchman, Léon Lalanne (1811–92), developed this idea for use by engineers in his seminal paper "Mémoire sur les tables graphiques et sur la géométrie anamorphique appliquées à diverses questions qui se rattachent à l'art de l'ingénieur" ("Memoir on graphical tables and anamorphic geometry applied to various problems of concern in the art of the engineer"). The first example he used was effectively a three-dimensional graph representing the ambient temperature in the town of Halle, Germany, at every hour of the day and during each month of the year—a masterpiece of condensing a great deal of information onto a very small area of paper.

Lalanne developed many other means of representing and storing data graphically and facilitating its easy retrieval. Of particular interest to the building designer was the wind rose, still widely used by engineers today. He employed a polar diagram for the first time to show the frequency of winds at a certain place coming from different directions. Lalanne was also the first to plot data on log-log graphical scales, allowing a very large range of values to be displayed. Yet another method of storing and representing data, resembling today's histograms and bar charts, was developed by Charles Joseph Minard (1781–1870) in the early 1840s.

355 Contour chart devised by Léon Lalanne in 1845, showing ambient temperature at every hour of the day throughout the year. 356–357 Wind roses devised by Lalanne, c. 1843, showing the proportion of time that winds blow from each direction. 358 Chart devised by Lalanne, c. 1845, with two logarithmic scales enabling rapid multiplication of two numbers.

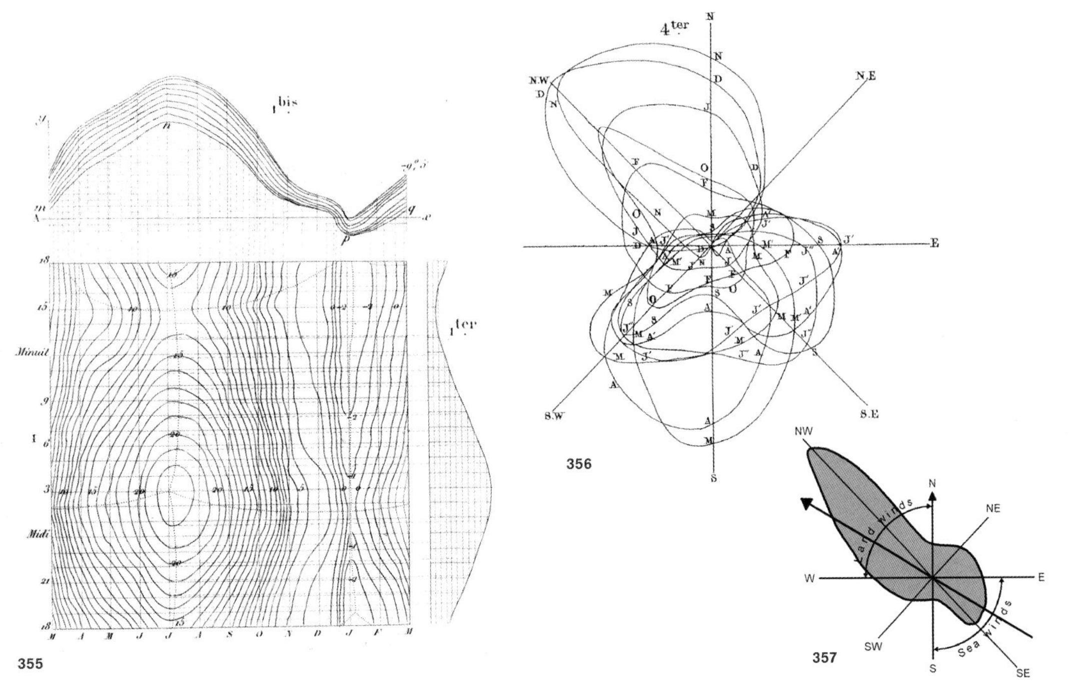

355

356

357

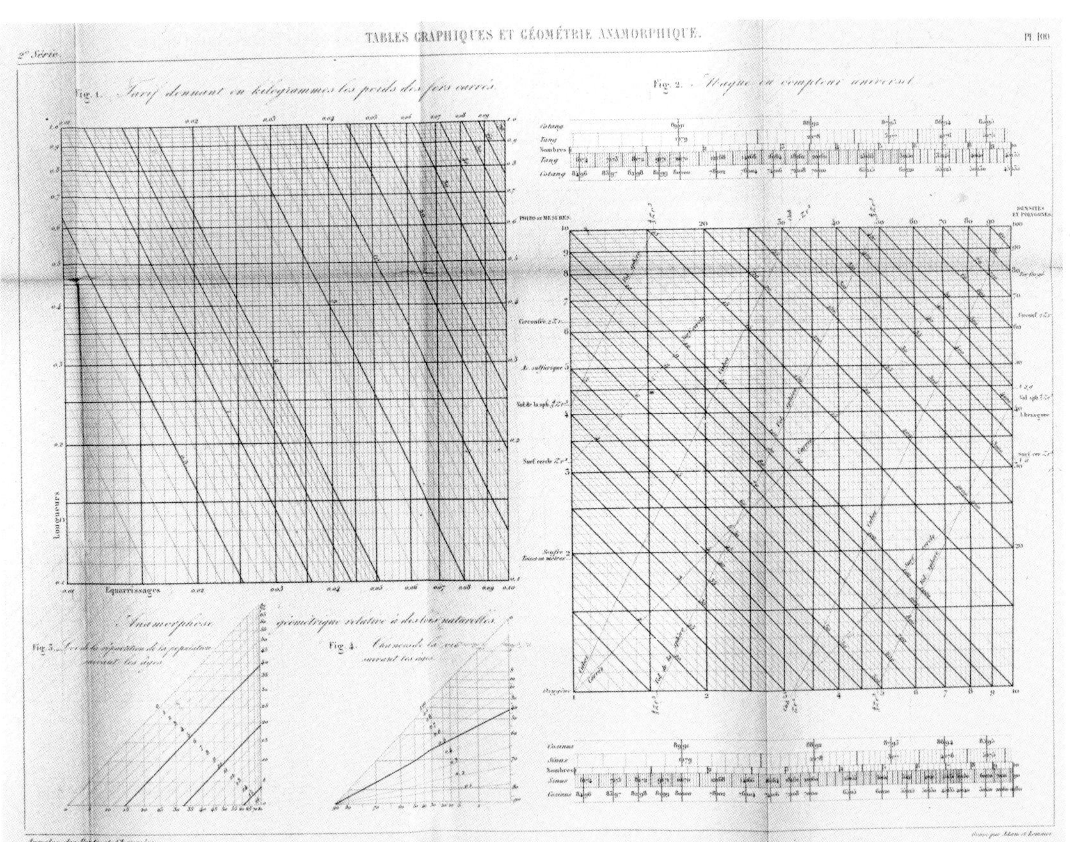

358

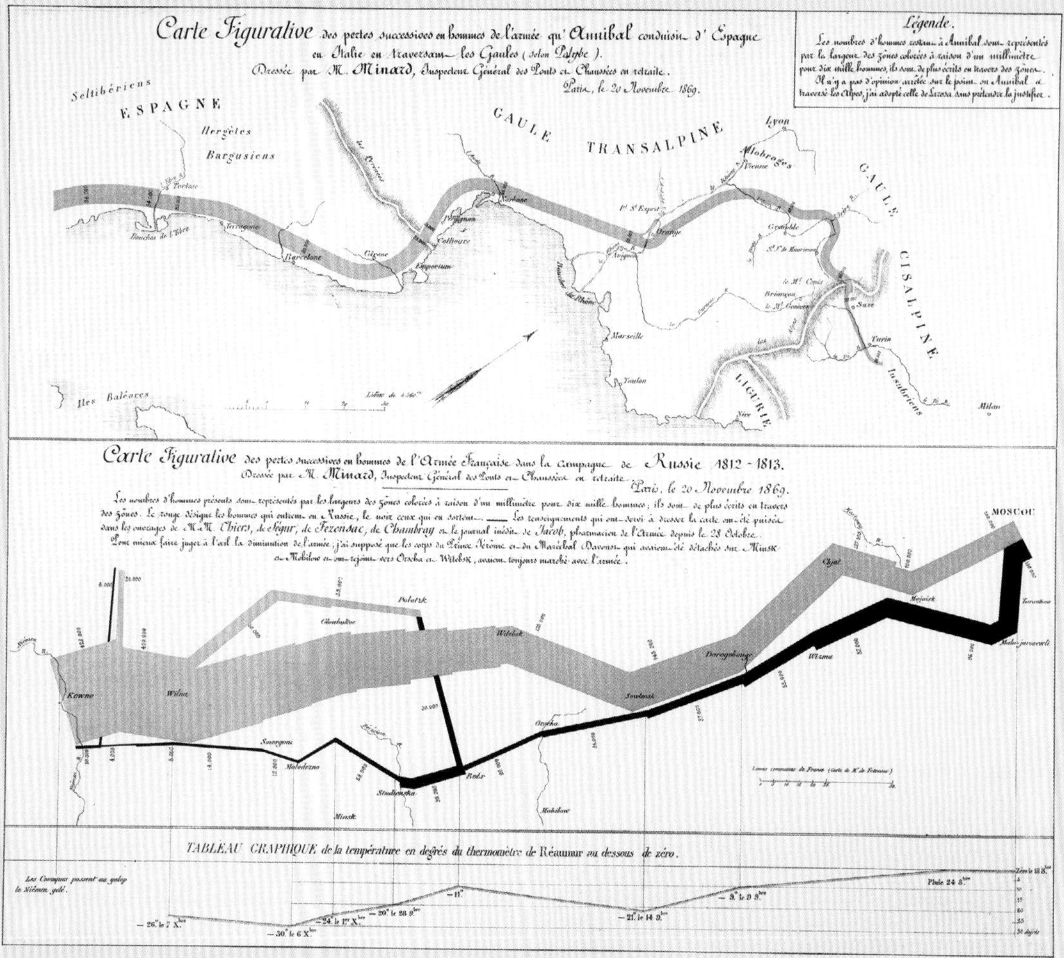

359 Information graphs by Charles Minard, summarizing large quantities of data in a single image, 1861. Top: *Carte figurative* representing troop losses in Hannibal's army as it crossed the Alps during the Second Punic War. Bottom: *Tableau-graphique* presenting variables in Napoleon's Russian campaign of 1812–13.

essential to ensure the best penetration of light. But the sun moves across the sky, and the angle at which its rays strike a window change constantly. To ensure that some part of the glazed envelope of a glasshouse is always perpendicular to the sun's rays, throughout the day and the year, its surface needs to be singly- or, preferably, doubly-curved. The solution to this requirement was due largely to the botanist John Loudon (1783–1843), who devel-
362 oped a wrought iron glazing bar that could be rolled to the desired section and bent along its length to achieve the desired curvature. Loudon's main argument in favor of iron glazing bars was that they cut out less light than those made of timber. (Reducing visual obstruction had been Christopher Wren's main reason for using iron columns in the House of Commons in 1693, and why they were introduced to support the balconies in Drury Lane Theatre in 1794.) When the glass panes were inserted into the iron skeleton, the result was a shell structure of iron and glass achieved through the composite action of the two materials. The best of the buildings that used his and many similar systems, such as the Palm House at
360 Bicton Gardens, East Devon (begun c. 1825 / 1844–45) and Syon House (see pp. 325, 326), are as breathtaking today as when they were new.

Loudon was by no means the only person interested in controlling the climate in hothouses, but he is best known to us through the various books he wrote, such as *A Short Treatise on Several Improvements Recently Made in Hot-Houses* (1805), *Remarks on the Construction of Hot-Houses* (1817), and the *Encyclopaedia of Gardening* (1822). These were full of many remarkable ideas, most of which had been executed and some that were merely dreams. Loudon was the first to realize that plants needed both ventilation—that is, changes of air in the hothouse—and movement of the air within, especially in winter when the building was sealed. As he observed in his 1805 treatise:

> *In hothouses, nature has been imitated more or less perfectly in most things. Heat is produced from the furnaces and flues. Light is admitted through the glass; rain is supplied from the syringe or watering-pot; dew is rarefied by pouring water upon the flues or by steam apparatus and fresh air is admitted at pleasure. There is still something missing. What makes up the want of those refreshing and genial breezes, which fan and invigorate the real nature?*[11]

To meet this need he devised many machines, including fans powered by falling weights, clockwork drive, or wind power. Another inventor proposed a reservoir of air in chambers adjacent to the hothouse that would be heated by the sun during the day and could be gently pumped into the hothouse at night using a fan. Others proposed and tried out various systems of heat exchange, such as drawing air past metal pipes that, during winter, were heated by hot water or steam. Perhaps the most sophisticated system was that devised and installed in several buildings by James Kewley. Loudon was impressed and wrote about it enthusiastically, christening it the "au- 361
tomaton gardener." By coupling this thermostatic device to a hopper-fed steam boiler and various types of ventilator and shading devices, the internal climate could be controlled "without the labour of man."

The ingenuity of designers in any age should never be underestimated. Just as Boulton and Watt had developed hollow cast iron columns to carry steam to heat their Salford Mill, so similar castings were used in several hot-houses, notably at Wollaton and Chatsworth, to conduct 363
rainwater from the roof down into an underground drainage system for collection in cisterns.

From the 1830s on, the sophistication of the heating and ventilation systems allowed glasshouses to be built on an ever-larger scale. Although well known as visual icons, glasshouses such as the Great Conservatory at Chatsworth, near Derby, England (1836–40), and the 364
Palm House at Kew Gardens, West London (1844–48), 365
were most remarkable for their precise control of internal climatic conditions.

Architectural Acoustics

Buildings in which large numbers of people congregated needed not just proper heating and ventilation, but proper acoustics as well. This was especially true of the lecture theaters in the new polytechnic colleges, as well as the chambers in which politicians and legislators congregated. The job of ensuring good acoustics naturally fell to the designers of the heating and ventilation systems, since they all relied on the common medium of the air. It was also often the case that acoustic performance could be adversely affected by noise borne into the room from outside through the ducts providing fresh air.

360

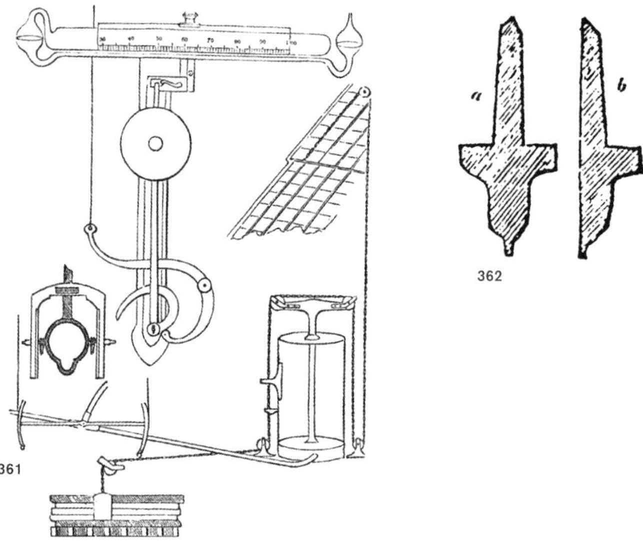

361

362

360 Palm House, Bicton Gardens, East Devon, England, begun c. 1825 / 1844–45 (completion date disputed). 361 The "Automaton Gardener," an early climate-control device, patented by James Kewley, 1816. 362 Wrought iron glazing bar devised by John Loudon, c. 1816, that paved the way for the great glass houses of the 1820s and later. 363 Engraving of the Camelia House, Wollaton Hall, Nottingham, England, 1823. Architect: Sir Jeffry Wyatville.

363

The destruction by fire in 1834 of the House of Commons in London provided an ideal opportunity for the acoustics of building interiors to be given special attention—a good room acoustic was the main requirement for the Members of Parliament to have their voices (and opinions) heard loud and clear. A comprehensive study of the subject was commissioned by Members of Parliament, reviewing both contemporary experience and published guidance, especially concerning theater design. The work of George Saunders and Ernst Chladni, and even the acoustic science and building designs from ancient Greece, as described in Vitruvius, were analyzed. The most notable proposal for a system of acoustics was made by David Boswell Reid.

At the outset, Reid first established the causes of the audibility problems in the House of Commons by interviewing members and by direct observation in the chamber itself. He identified "six principal causes of the defective communication of sound." The ceiling was too high, which meant the voice had a large volume to fill, a particular problem when a speaker was competing with a general background hum of conversation. The soft fabrics covering the walls of the chamber provided insufficient reflection of incident sounds; the noise entering the chamber through the windows, especially when these were opened for ventilation, was "extreme." Not only was there noise from the adjacent chamber, the House of Lords, but also "the noise of coaches, cabs and omnibuses, of the letter-carrier's bell and every other noise produced in the Old Palace Yard."[12] Reid found that the floor covering in the chamber produced a considerable noise when members walked upon it, and there was also disturbing noise produced by the opening and closing of the door to the room. Finally, he believed that the rising current of warm (and less dense) air in the center of the chamber refracted the sound passing from one side of the room to the other, just as a glass prism refracts light. In fact, while theoretically possible, it is unlikely that Reid would have been able to observe such an effect; more likely, the variable intelligibility depending on the listener's position in the room was due to the presence or absence of reflections from walls and ceiling.

Based on his observations and explanations, Reid incorporated a number of features in the new House of

Commons chamber built in the late 1830s. The ceiling was lowered, and panels of wood and glass were incorporated in the upper parts of the room to reflect sound downward and toward the center of the room. Both the floor and ceiling were made porous to allow fresh air in and foul air to be extracted, and these surfaces also reduced the proportion of sound reflected that had previously led to the "offensive reverberation" and lessened intelligibility. The new heating system meant the air temperature was the same throughout the chamber, and this prevented the refraction of sound. The floor of the chamber was covered with a "soft, thick, porous and elastic hair-cloth carpet,"[13] which prevented noise caused by people walking and also absorbed unwanted reflections in the room. Finally, the new and highly effective heating and ventilation system meant that it was no longer necessary to open windows, and thus disturbance from noises outside the chamber was avoided.

After his work on the new House of Commons, Reid went on to collect information and conduct many experiments on the acoustics of rooms. He reported his results and guidance for designers in his pioneering book, *Illustrations of the Theory and Practice of Ventilation; with remarks on warming, lighting and the communication of sound*, published in 1844. He noted particularly the importance of reverberation time and its effect on the intelligibility of speech. He measured an eight-second reverberation time inside an iron boiler and mentioned several large rooms he had visited where a sound remained audible for between eight and ten seconds; he had even heard of a room in a palace in Saint Petersburg where the noise made by stamping a foot was audible for a period of twelve seconds.

Reid realized that the key to intelligibility of speech depended on the ratio of the volume of direct and reflected sound reaching the listener. This was well exemplified by the benefit that the presence of an audience would bring to a room by reducing reflected sounds, both by absorption of sound by their clothing and by preventing sound being reflected from a hard floor. He was also aware that a speaker could be disturbed by loud reverberations of his or her voice from the rear wall of a room.

Reid mentioned many examples of how the acoustics of rooms had been improved by applying the rationale he described to reduce disturbing reverberation. In one large lecture room the plaster ceiling was removed, leaving the bare beams and laths. In other cases drapery, curtains, carpets, sofas, and soft furniture were used to absorb sound. Reid also carried out numerous experiments on the focusing effect of arched or domed ceilings, especially in Paris at the Halle au blé and in the many rooms of the Louvre Palace. In one room in Paris he found that the reflection from such a ceiling had been so strong as to prevent its being used; the problem was remedied by suspending a silk balloon in the center of the ceiling.

Reid's qualitative understanding of acoustics was little different from that of twentieth-century acousticians. He was prevented from taking acoustics into the realm of quantitative engineering only by the lack of equipment to measure sound intensities and to analyze sound of different frequencies. This step awaited the invention, in the late nineteenth century, of the microphone, which converted sound waves into a varying electric current, and in the early twentieth century the means of measuring, first, relative, and later, absolute sound intensities.

Fireproof Construction

Although fireproof construction, as we have seen, was developed in France for use in theaters, its use there spread only slowly; few theaters or other large buildings were constructed during Napoleon's reign, and power and iron were too expensive for use in small buildings. The widespread growth of fireproof construction methods occurred in Britain, where many thousands of multistory fireproof mills and warehouses were constructed during the first half of the nineteenth century. Most of these were built using the system devised by Strutt and Bage in
the 1790s—columns and beams of cast iron with a brick 367
jack arch floor (see chapter 5). The first fireproof roofs in mills were constructed in the 1810s, and soon became standard practice. Although most of these roofs were trusses made of cast and wrought iron, sometimes the entire top floor was spanned by a cast iron arch to create
a column-free area that could house larger machinery. 366

364 The Great Conservatory, Chastworth, near Derby, England, 1836–40. Designer: Joseph Paxton. 365 Palm House, Kew Gardens, West London, 1844–48. Engineer and contractor: Richard Turner; architect: Decimus Burton.

364

365

Among the many nearly identical buildings of this type, however, were examples of other interesting structural
368 ideas. The Beehive Mill in Manchester, erected in 1824, used an alternative system that is a direct ancestor of twentieth-century construction practice in frame buildings. The floor structure uses a hierarchy of primary cast iron beams supporting a series of secondary beams at right angles and, similarly, a series of tertiary beams. Thus, the area of floor that needs to be supported is reduced to about 600 millimeters square—a size that could be spanned by a single stone flag. This avoided much of the weight inherent in a jack arch floor structure, reducing the depth of the floor and, hence, the height of the building. It also allowed the bay size to increase beyond the 2- to 3-meter limit associated with jack arches. The increased distance between columns in the middle of the building allowed larger machines to be accommodated and greater flexibility in locating them.

Mills built before 1820 were generally three or four bays wide, constructed with cast iron beams between about 2.5 and 4 meters long. The width of multistory mills was limited to about 16 meters by the need to provide adequate daylighting across the whole floor area. Beginning in the early 1820s the development of larger textile machines required mills with larger, column-free spaces, and mill designers moved to a two-bay layout, with beams of about 8 meters supported by a single, central line of columns. This was not an upper limit for cast iron beams, however. Much larger beams could be produced where there was good reason. At London's British Museum, cast iron beams 12.5 meters long, made by John Urpeth Rastrick (1780–1856), were used to create an enormous
369, 370 column-free space in the King's Library, designed by the architect Robert Smirke (1780–1867).

Smirke's interest in using new construction techniques was not confined to using iron. He was one of the first architects to use concrete in buildings in post-Roman times. John Smeaton had published the results of his studies of natural hydraulic cements in 1791, and in 1796, the Reverend James Parker patented his "Roman cement," the first artificial hydraulic cement made using certain fired rocks rather than pozzolana from the volcanic regions of Italy. In the 1810s several French engineers, notably Louis Vicat (1786–1861), discovered how to make artificial hydraulic lime cement that would fully harden under water. Smirke used hydraulic lime concrete to repair the failing foundations of several buildings in London from 1817, notably the Custom House in 1825 on the banks of the river Thames, as well as several new buildings. In 1824 Joseph Aspdin (1788–1855) patented his "Portland cement," named after the well-known stone quarried in Portland in southwest England. However, it was probably not until the 1840s that furnaces reached the high temperatures (1300°C) needed to manufacture what we call Portland cement today. This was achieved at about the same time by Aspdin's factory in Wakefield in Yorkshire in northern England, and the firm of John Bazley White & Sons, a prominent cement manufacturer in the county of Kent in southern England.

The use of concrete in the construction of foundations and docks spread very rapidly in the 1820s, and by the 1830s it was being used for walls and floors of houses in both England and France. The first in England was probably a house in Swanscombe, Kent, built by John Bazley White & Sons in 1835 as a means of showing off the versatility of the firm's product. This and other houses built at about the same time captured the imagination of a number of architects, one of whom, the twenty-year-old George Godwin (1815–88), later became editor of the most influential building periodical in nineteenth-century Britain, *The Builder*. He wrote the "Prize essay upon the nature and properties of concrete, and its application to construction up to the present period," which was published as the very first paper in the transactions of the newly formed Institute of British Architects.

In 1844 Henry Hawes Fox (1788–1851) patented a flooring system that depended on concrete rather than brick for its fireproof qualities. It consisted of mass concrete placed on timber laths spanning the flanges of cast iron, inverted-T beams set about 450 millimeters apart. Developed and marketed jointly with James Barrett, this system became known as "Fox and Barrett flooring" and was widely used until the 1890s (after 1852 the cast iron beams were replaced by wrought iron I-section girders). From the 1840s various other engineers began to experiment with combining concrete and iron in fireproof flooring systems, notably William Fairbairn who, in 1845, developed a jack arch floor system for fireproof mills con-

366

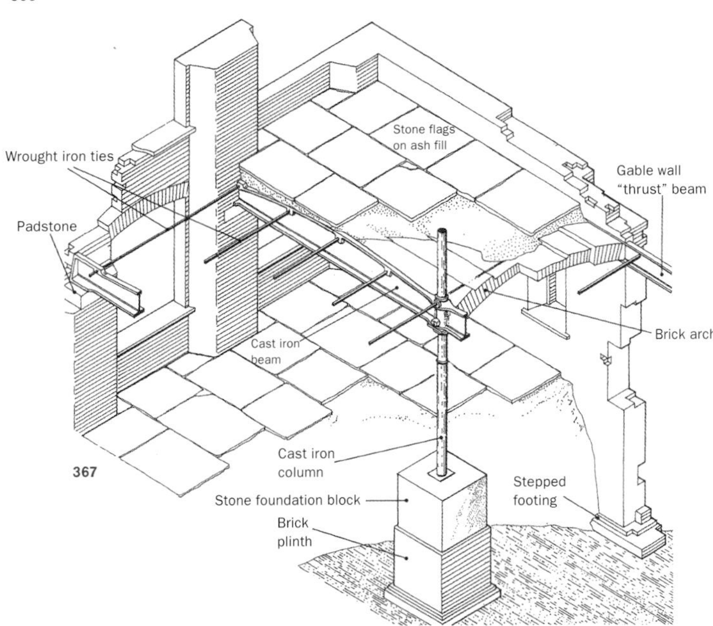

367

366 Illustration of a cotton mill with a full-span cast iron arch roof and a water- or steam-powered, "fully automatic, self-acting mule" on the top floor. From Edmund Baines, *History of the Cotton Manufacture in Great Britain*, 1835.
367 Diagram of the Strutt and Bage system used in the construction of the Havelock Cotton Mill, Manchester, England, 1845.

368

371 sisting of a concrete arch spanning two cast iron girders tied together with wrought iron rods.

Increasingly used because of its fireproof properties, concrete was also attracting the attention of landscape architects such as John Loudon, who proposed in his 1833 *Encyclopaedia of Cottage, Farmhouse and Villa Architecture and Furniture* that flat roofs might be constructed of a latticework of iron tie-rods, thickly embedded in cement, and cased with flat tiles. This idea resembles the poteries et fer system used in France in the 1780s, though with concrete in place of plaster. In 1844, a Frenchman, Joseph Louis Lambot (1814–87), patented a method of forming objects by applying cement to a framework or woven mesh of thin iron rods, 2mm to 3.5mm in diameter, making a total thickness of 30–40mm. He saw such a method of construction as ideal when "absolute impermeability" was needed.[14]

The earliest patent that clearly anticipated modern reinforced concrete is that of an English builder, William B. Wilkinson (1819–1902), in 1854. Wilkinson was a maker of ornamental plaster and "artificial stone" (concrete) products in Newcastle upon Tyne, in northeast
372 England. In his patent for "Improvements in the Construction of Fireproof Dwellings, Warehouses and other Buildings, parts of the same," he illustrated the use of iron cables salvaged from winding engines in collieries, or "iron in other forms of tension" such as strips of hoop iron. Wilkinson's firm placed advertisements such as the following in the public and trade press to the end of the nineteenth century: "W. B. Wilkinson Est. 1841. Concrete workers. Designers and constructors of concrete staircases and fireproof floors of all descriptions, with as little iron as possible, and that wholly in tension, thereby preventing waste."[15] Only one example of Wilkinson's system has been found: a cottage in Newcastle, recognized and documented only at the time of its demolition in 1952.

During the following half century hundreds of patents were granted in Germany, France, and Britain for a host of fireproof flooring systems using in situ concrete or precast concrete elements spanning between parallel girders of cast or, later, wrought iron. Such systems generally incorporated a wrought iron rod or strip stretching between the iron girders, as in jack arch construction. With time, some of these systems do start to suggest that their designers intended the iron strip linking the girders, and embedded in concrete or within hollow precast concrete or clay pots forming the voussoirs of a flat arch, to carry tension force arising from bending of the floor span. However, it would be of little consequence to pursue this argument to any conclusion; the string of patents for fireproof flooring systems simply ran in parallel with the second strand of the story.

369

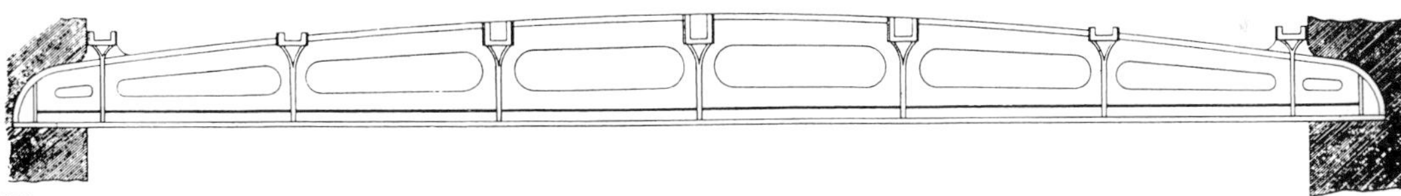

370

368 Beehive Mill, Manchester, England, 1824. The floor structure consists of primary, secondary and tertiary beams of cast iron, supporting square stone flags. 369 The King's Library, British Museum, London, 1823–27. Engineer: John Urpeth Rastrick; architect: Robert Smirke. 370 The King's Library, British Museum. Detail of cast iron beam. Each spanning 12.5 meters, these were the longest cast iron beams of their day, made lighter by large cut-outs in the web.

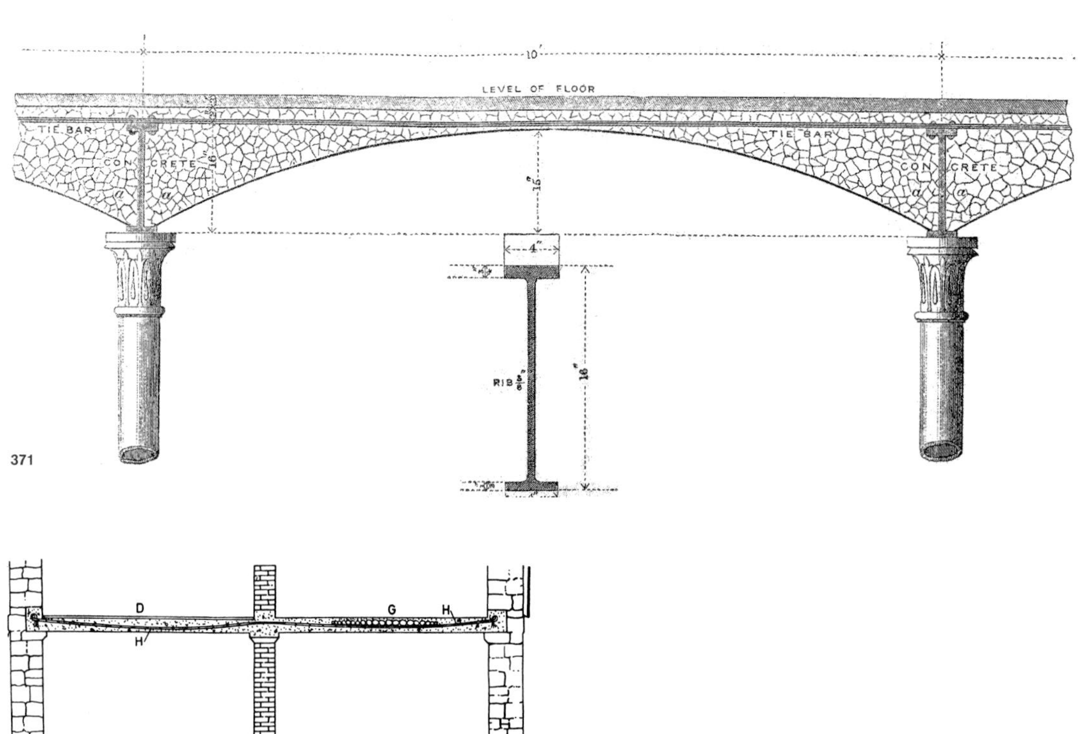

371

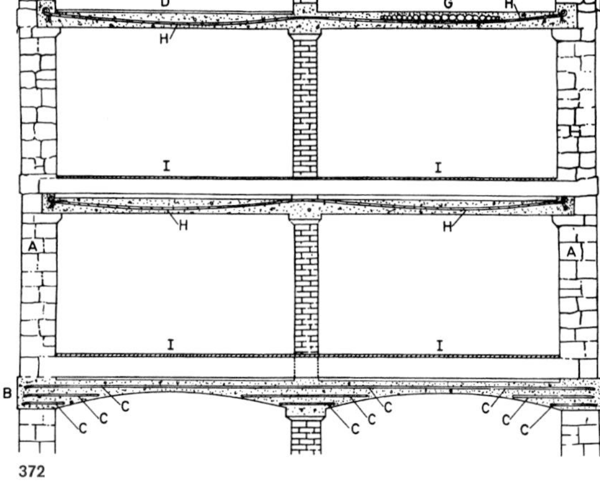
372

The common thread running through the fireproof flooring systems was that the main purpose of the concrete was to provide protection against fire to the iron girders.

Fireproof Construction in the United States

As in Britain in the 1780s, the first use of a cast iron column in a U.S. building was to support a balcony, both to reduce the obstruction of the view compared to a timber column, and to prevent collapse in the event of a fire. William Strickland (1788–1854) used cast iron columns to support the two tiers of balconies in his Chestnut Street Theater in Philadelphia, completed in 1822. He had trained as an engineer and architect, and designed a number of canals, railways, and dams, as well as a great many Greek Revival buildings in Philadelphia. Although he used iron columns again in 1833, to support a first-floor balcony in his United States Naval Asylum in Philadelphia, these isolated examples did not mark the widespread adoption of iron as a fireproof construction material.

371 Detail of a concrete jack arch floor in an eight-story factory, c.1845. Engineer: William Fairbairn. Iron rods stabilized the top flange of the beams. At center span, the concrete was just 75 mm thick and was reinforced by the iron rods.
372 Drawing from patent by William B. Wilkinson for "Improvements in the Construction of Fireproof Dwellings, Warehouses and other Buildings," 1854.

In Britain, the use of cast iron spread rapidly beginning in the 1790s because the owners of mills and warehouses wanted to prevent fires from breaking out and to ensure that a fire did not damage the structure and lead to the collapse of the entire building. In the U.S. the concerns about fire were different. The worst danger in 1830s New York, for example, was perceived not to be damage from a fire inside the building but rather from fire in adjacent buildings, much as had been experienced in the great fires in Europe's cities from medieval times up to the eighteenth century. Devastating fires in New York City spread rapidly through the tightly packed streets in 1835 and again in 1845, destroying more than a thousand buildings, many of which were of timber. A cast iron facade helped protect both the building and its contents, especially when iron roller blinds were also fitted to protect the glass windows, both from fire and thieves. This was the dream combination that the iron founder Daniel Badger (1806–84) began producing around 1843 in Boston and, from 1846, in New York at what he later
373 called his Architectural Iron Works. With his wonderfully illustrated catalogs proclaiming every possible advantage for his facade system and for iron in general, Badger's business grew rapidly during the next twenty years.

Apart from fire resistance, facades made from cast iron offered the client a wide range of architectural treatments and styles without the need for highly skilled masons; Badger generally favored the Venetian style. Only the facades facing the street would be of iron; the other walls, of brick, provided lateral stability for the buildings as they had done in the very first mill buildings. The internal structure of his early buildings consisted of cast iron columns with beams and floors of timber; the fully fireproof structural frame was still a little way off. The scale of Badger's building structures, up to six stories, meant that they did not require engineering calculations of any complexity. The iron columns and beams of timber and, later, of wrought iron, were standard products whose load-bearing capacity was well known. The other advantage of using cast iron was the ease with which the identical components could be manufactured and transported to the site, and the speed with which the buildings could be assembled.

One of Badger's most elegant buildings was the
374 Haughwout & Co. department store, completed in 1857. The department store was still a comparatively new idea, and owners were competing intensely for customers' attention. Not only did the Haughwout store have a striking cast iron facade, it was also the first public building in
which an Otis passenger elevator was installed. 375

James Bogardus (1800–74) was another engineer who saw the potential in using cast iron in buildings. He was apprenticed to a watchmaker from the age of fourteen, and built a reputation as a mechanical inventor. In 1828 he won a prize for a clock he had made and exhibited at the first inventors' fair organized by the American Institute of the City of New York with the specific aim of stimulating local industry to compete with and replace goods imported from Britain. Bogardus traveled to Europe in 1836, visiting many industrial works, including the cotton mills of England, where he saw the use of cast and wrought iron in building. He would also have seen, or at least heard about, William Fairbairn's iron flour mill that was made for export to Turkey. After returning to New York, Bogardus set up a machine shop to manufacture a sugar mill he had patented, and when he needed larger premises, he decided to build them using fireproof construction and located them less than 50 yards from
Badger's ironworks. The factory, completed in 1849, had 376
internal columns of cast iron and a cast iron facade on the two sides of the building facing the street. The beams and floor, however, were made of timber and not fireproof at all.

Completion of his own building was delayed by contracts he had obtained to make cast iron facades for two new shopfronts. Bogardus provided the wooden patterns for making the castings and supervised their erection. Despite the fireproof qualities of these facades, people at the time were rather more impressed by the speed with which they were erected (the street front of the five-story Milhau pharmacy (1848) was erected in just three days) and their striking appearance (the proportion of the facade occupied by windows was very large in comparison to buildings with masonry walls).

In his 1850 patent for the "Construction of the frame, roof and floor of iron buildings," Bogardus went on to advocate buildings made entirely of iron. This was the system he used to construct the building for the Harper & 377, 378
Brothers Printing House, completed in 1854. As well as

373

374

the facade and columns of cast iron, even the floor was made of cast iron plates with tongue-and-groove joints. The ingenious primary girders had a cast iron web and integral wrought iron tie rod, similar to one patented in Britain in 1848 by John Gardner, an iron founder. The most noteworthy feature of the building was that it was
379 the first in the U.S. to use rolled wrought iron girders.
These were made by the Trenton Iron Company, which had recently succeeded in making rolling wrought iron rail sections in the form of an inverted T. The girders Bogardus used were of similar form, 175mm deep. However, this all-iron building system must have proved very costly, for in most of the buildings he went on to construct, he used iron only for the facades and columns.

Development of the Skeleton Frame

By the 1830s the use of cast iron internally for columns and beams in mills and warehouses was well established. So too was the use of wrought iron for roof trusses. All these buildings, however, had external walls of masonry—and with good reason. The masonry walls provided good protection from the weather, were fireproof, and provided the building with stability against overturning. The skeleton frame has no masonry wall, and the structure needs a means for carrying wind loads and providing stability against overturning. This is provided by one of three means—the use of rigid connections between columns and beams, filling in the void bounded by columns and beam with a shear panel, or the use of bracing, either diagonal cross-bracing or, more recently, K-bracing. All these solutions had long been used in the iron frame's ancestor, the timber frame. Perhaps the first iron building 380, 381
that used rigid connections between column and beam
to provide stability was Hungerford Fish Market, 382
London (1831–33), designed by Charles Fowler, one of the first architects to exploit the sculptural qualities of cast iron. This was little more than a roof covering the market stalls, and, being open-sided, lacked the walls that would usually provide stability for a building. This

373 Architectural Iron Works, New York, 1865. Engineer: Daniel Badger. Lithograph by Sarony, Major & Knapp.
374 Haughwout & Co. department store, New York, 1857. Engineer: Daniel Badger. 375 Haughwout & Co. department store. Ground-floor Otis elevator door. 376 James Bogardus factory, New York, 1849. Street facades were of cast iron.
377 Harper & Brothers' Printing House, New York, 1854. Engineer: James Bogardus. 378 Harper & Brothers' Printing House. Workroom. 379 Harper & Brothers' Printing House. Detail of floor structure.

375

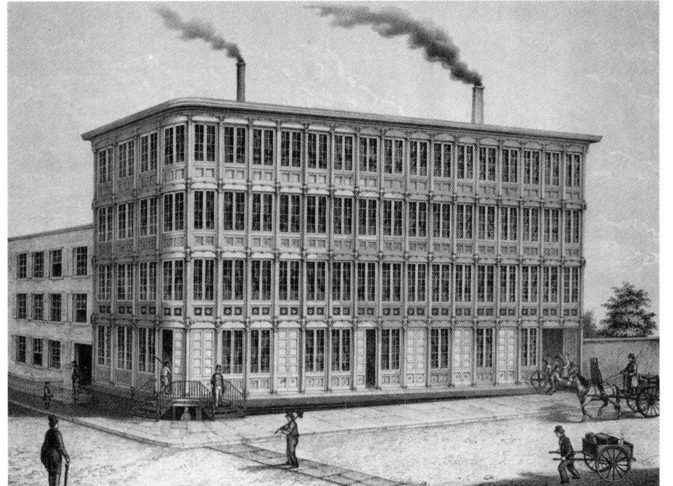

376

377

378

379

380

381

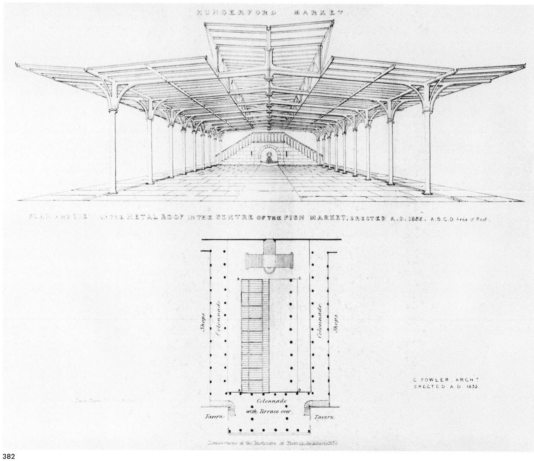

382

380 Timber frame construction with brick-infilled panels, Colmar, France, late eighteenth century. 381 Mast houses and mold loft, Chatham Historic Dockyard, Kent, England, 1753–58. Timber frame construction. 382 Hungerford Fish Market, London, 1831–33. Architect and engineer: Charles Fowler. View of cast iron roof structure (top) and plan (bottom).

383

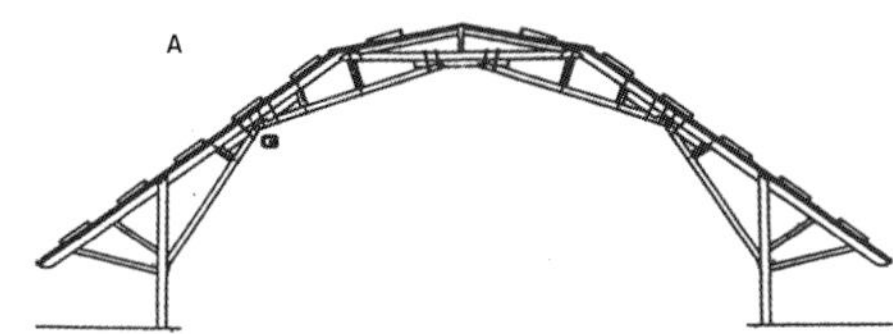

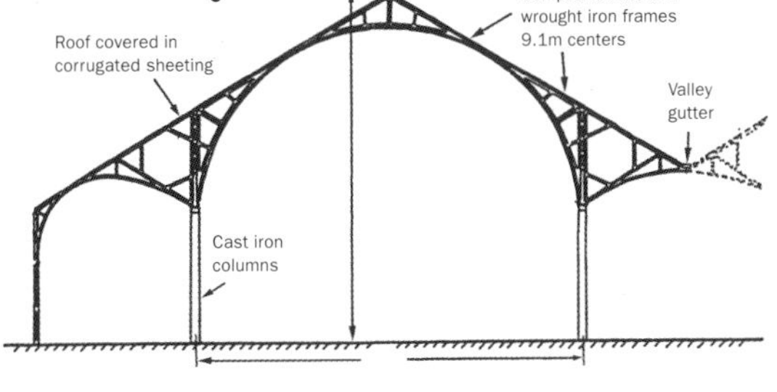

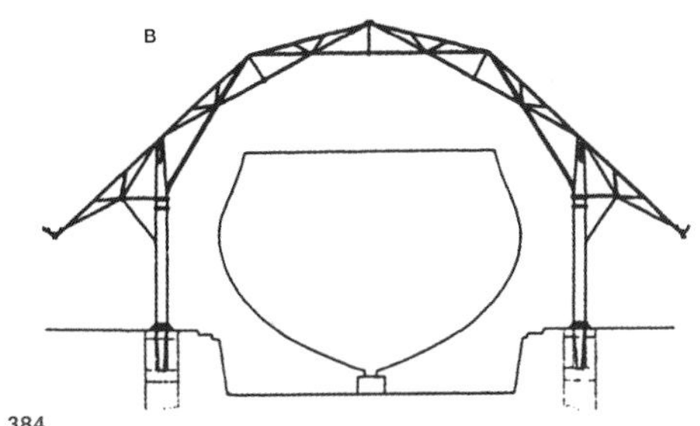

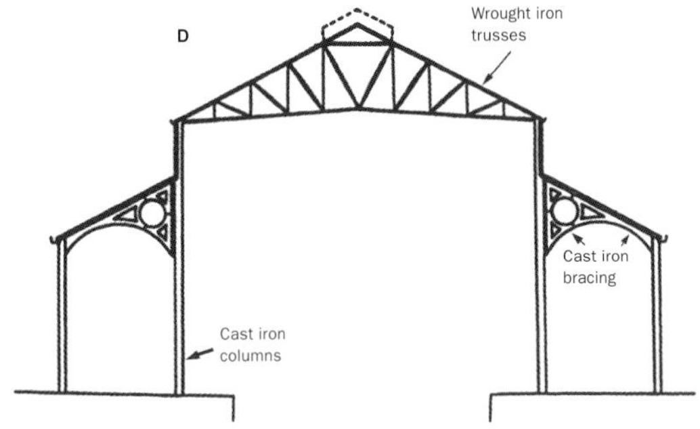

384

form became the pattern for many thousands of canopies over the platforms of small railway stations during the following decades.

The designers of a new type of structure developed during the early nineteenth century were also faced with a lack of walls to provide stability. This was the covered
383 slip, a roof over the slipway where ships were built or brought into dry dock for repair. Robert Seppings (1767–1840) devised a new type of long-span timber roof in around 1814 that was adopted by the British navy, and a score or so were built over docks during the new quarter century. They spanned up to 30 meters, and allowed the shipwrights to work under cover while gaining free access to the ships from every side.

383 Covered slip No. 3, Chatham Historic Dockyard, Kent, England, 1836–38. View from modern mezzanine, four meters above ground level. Span c. 25 meters; height c. 20 meters. 384 Sections of slip roofs in English naval dockyards, c. 1814–45. (A) Timber slip roof, c.1814–40, with spans up to 30 meters; (B) Iron slip roof, 1845, span 24.5 meters; (C) Iron slip roof, 1846–47, span 26 meters; (D) Iron slip roof, 1847, span 25.6 meters.

By the 1840s it was apparent that some of these timber roofs were suffering badly from rot and would have to be replaced. In a new wave of construction at Britain's five
384 main naval shipyards, sixteen new iron roofs were built. The first four, designed by Charles Fox, were versions in cast and wrought iron of Seppings' timber roofs, and built by his firm Fox Henderson. Like their timber ancestors, the buildings relied for their lateral stability on the rigid fixing of the columns in the ground. Eleven more roofs
385, 386 were built to a different design by George Baker (c. 1810–60). They are rather more elegant than those by Fox, with arches spanning 26 meters, made of both cast and wrought iron elements, supporting the roof of corrugated iron sheeting. In the history of structural engineering they are notable for two reasons. First, they are the first buildings to use columns with an H cross section, which is so familiar today; formerly, iron columns were all cruciform or circular in section. The H-section uses the least material to provide the necessary strength and stiffness, and reflects the same logic that had led Fairbairn and Hodgkinson to develop the I-section beam in the 1830s. The columns are made of cast iron and taper slightly from bottom to top, reflecting the bending moment they must carry. Second, Baker's design includes a small side span that adds to the lateral stability of the building by forming a frame with rigid connections between the bays. This was a step beyond Fowler's Hungerford Fish Market. Baker would also have been aware of the new fire station constructed in Portsmouth Dockyard in 1844, which derives its stability entirely from the rigid connections between the members. When Charles Fox came to design his final slip roof at Woolwich, he too conceived a structure that derived its stability from frame action, made possible by the rigid connection between columns and the side span.

A further crucial ingredient in the development of the skeleton iron frame was the progress in wrought iron technology from the 1820s to the 1840s. During this period the growth of the railways made increasing demands on the size, length, and quality of various rolled-iron sections, for rails and to make the many structures that rail-
387 ways needed. In 1847 a French structural engineer, Ferdinand Zorès, persuaded the owner of a rolling mill to produce the first I-section wrought iron beam for use in building construction; he used the beams, 125mm deep by 50mm wide, as floor joists.

Meanwhile, from the early 1800s, there had developed in several industries, especially boilermaking, the practice of joining iron plates and bars using rivets. When iron-hulled ships began to appear in the late 1830s, the hulls were stiffened by riveting rolled wrought iron ribs to the thin iron plates, and complex ribs were made by riveting together two or three sections. The technique of creating complex structural forms using a variety of simple iron sections, made monolithic by riveting them together, was quickly applied to all types of iron structures, notably bridge structures and large beams and columns in buildings. In 1838 the Scottish engineer Matthew Clark used riveted iron plates and angles to make beams with an elliptical section spanning up to 15 meters to support fireproof ceilings during the rebuilding of the Winter Palace in Saint Petersburg. In the early 1840s, several British engineers, including Robert Stephenson and William Fairbairn, joined lengths of plate and L-sections using rivets to make larger, built-up structural sections of wrought iron. Working mainly on boilers 388
and iron ships, Fairbairn's firm became the world's leading iron contractor, developing the technical skills of rolling, cutting, drilling, shaping and riveting the thick wrought iron plates. In around 1837, stimulated initially by a strike among the skilled men who did the riveting in his factory, the manager of Fairbairn's boiler works devised a steam-powered riveting machine. Similar pneumatic and hydraulic machines were developed in 1865 and 1871, respectively. Hydraulic-powered machines were also made for punching holes for rivets, rather than drilling them.

The experience gained in constructing the iron slip roofs would prove extremely valuable when the firm Fox Henderson won the contract to build the Crystal Palace 389
in London's Hyde Park. The idea of using a structure of cast iron and wrought iron was that of Joseph Paxton (1801–65), the manager of the Duke of Devonshire's Chatsworth estate in Derbyshire, just a few miles north of the many mills built by William Strutt and others. Iron and glass structures for botanic gardens were all the rage in the 1830s and 1840s, and Paxton had helped design one of the largest, known as the Great Conservatory, in Chatsworth, near Derby (see pp. 341, 343). He used many of the ideas he had put into practice for this and other glass houses when developing his remarkable scheme for the exhibition building with the

385

386

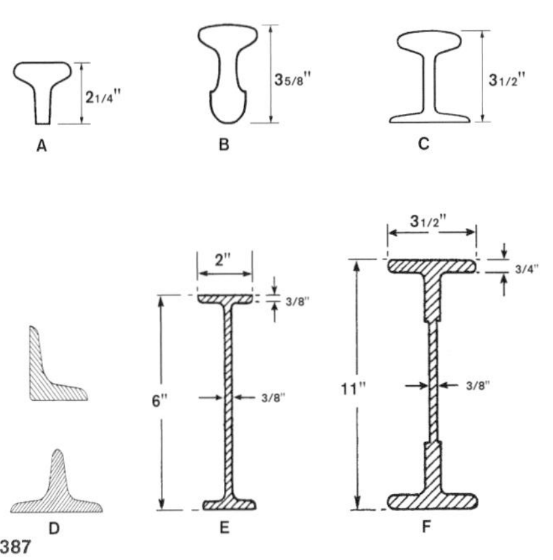

387

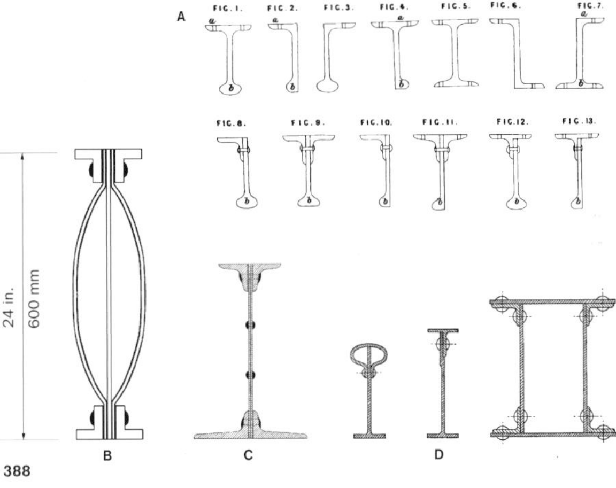

388

385 Covered slip No. 4, Chatham Historic Dockyard, Kent, England, 1847–48. Iron slip roof by George Baker & Son, span 26 meters. Detail of wrought iron roof structure supported on H-section cast iron columns. 386 Covered slip No. 4, Chatham Historic Dockyard. Exterior. 387 Rolled wrought iron sections, 1820–47 (to scale). (A) Birkenshaw rail, 1820; (B) Clarence rail, 1830; (C) Stevens rail, 1830; (D) angle and T-shaped structural sections; (E) and (F) I-section structural beams by Ferdinand Zorès, 1847. 388 Built-up wrought iron sections, 1832–44 (to scale). (A) Simple and built-up stiffening ribs used in ship construction, patented by James Kennedy and Thomas Vernon, 1844; (B) Beam, Winter Palace (now Hermitage Museum), Saint Petersburg, Russia, 1838. Engineer: Matthew Clark; (C) Asymmetric I-section, 1832. Engineer: William Fairbairn; (D) I- and tubular sections, 1840s. Engineer: William Fairbairn. 389 (Overleaf) Crystal Palace, Hyde Park, London, 1850–51. Engineers: William Barlow (competition entry) and Charles Fox (final design); architect: Joseph Paxton.

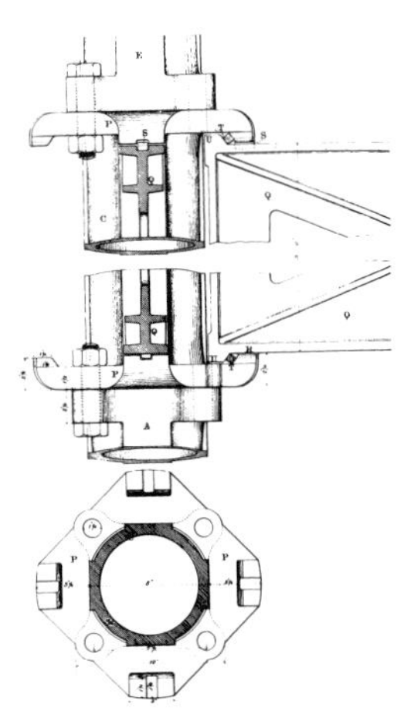

390

391

392

390 Crystal Palace, Hyde Park, London, 1850–51. Engineers: William Barlow (competition entry) and Charles Fox (final design); architect: Joseph Paxton. Detail of column-girder connection, fixed using cast iron/oak wedges. 391 Crystal Palace. Interior, showing cross-bracing in the main frame and vault. 392 Crystal Palace. During construction, the frame derived its stability from rigid connections (portal action).

young engineer William Barlow (see chapter 7) and his friend Robert Stephenson.

Like many remarkable buildings, the Crystal Palace is remarkable not for a single innovation, but for bringing together a certain set of ideas that precisely suit the particular circumstances. As Henry Cole said in his memoirs:

> *the one object with which the world first became acquainted for the first time . . . was the building itself which Paxton suggested. The Exhibition has taught the world how to roof in great spaces; how to build with iron and glass in a way never done before . . . Nothing very novel in iron columns resting on concrete foundations; nothing novel in Paxton gutters, which half a dozen persons claim to have invented, but something very novel in covering twenty acres with glass as an exhibiting room.*[16]

The engineering design of the building is pervaded by ingenious devices that were not only innovations in structural engineering, but also enabled the building to be constructed very economically and in incredibly quick time—from first arriving on site on 30 July 1850, the entire building, covering 70,000 square meters of Hyde Park, was constructed in just twenty seven weeks. The main features of the design were these:

- *the rigorous use of a modular approach (based on 8 feet) to developing both plan and elevation*
- *the use of rigid connections between columns and*
390 *girders to provide stability using frame action*
- *the use of wedges to fit girders and columns, rather than bolts or rivets*
392 • *the inherent stability of the frame during construction, which removed the need for scaffolding*
- *the use of a frame system that could be extended in two directions (iron frames generally could be extended in one direction only)*
- *the use of the transept as a means of providing lateral stability to the "nave"*
391 • *the highly visible use of diagonal bracing (now called cross-bracing) to provide additional stability*
393 • *the two-way spanning sub-structure of the gallery floor to distribute loads equally*
- *the pre-assembly and rapid erection, without scaffold-* 395
ing, of the vaulted transept
- *the use of horizontal bracing in the "lead flat" portion*
of the roof to create clear load paths for carrying the 394
thrust of the timber arches and wind loads to the ground
- *the provision of horizontal cross-bracing to carry wind loads from the glazed facades to the main frame and, via the vertical bracing, to the ground*
- *the use of cast iron to provide identical batches of components quickly and cheaply*
- *the widespread use of mass or at least batch production which, among other benefits, meant the workforce did not have to keep learning new construction details and methods*
- *the widespread use of small, lightweight components (1 ton max) that could be easily manoeuvred by people using simple cranes*
- *the use of a slatted floor at ground level to facilitate cleaning (although sweeping machines were available, it was found that "the dresses of the female portion of the visitors performed this office in a very satisfactory manner")*

The fame of the Crystal Palace spread worldwide almost instantaneously, helped very much by the reports of its design and construction in the *Illustrated London News*—one of the first newspapers to feature engraved illustrations. Subsequent international exhibitions in France, Germany and the U.S. all strove to match the achievements of Paxton and Fox and Henderson and many succeeded. To this day, similar exhibitions (or "expositions") are seen as an opportunity to show off innovative architecture and building engineering at their best.

The next steps in the development of the skeleton frame were an altogether much quieter affair. A new slip roof
was required at Chatham Dockyard, and its design was 396, 398
entrusted to Godfrey Greene (1807–86), the Admiralty's newly appointed Director of Engineering and Architectural Works—a grand title for a team of just four staff, the chief assistant William Scamp, and three draughtsmen. Greene based his design for the new slip roof, which spans 25 meters, on the earlier ones, especially that of Fox Henderson, and added a number of ideas that were

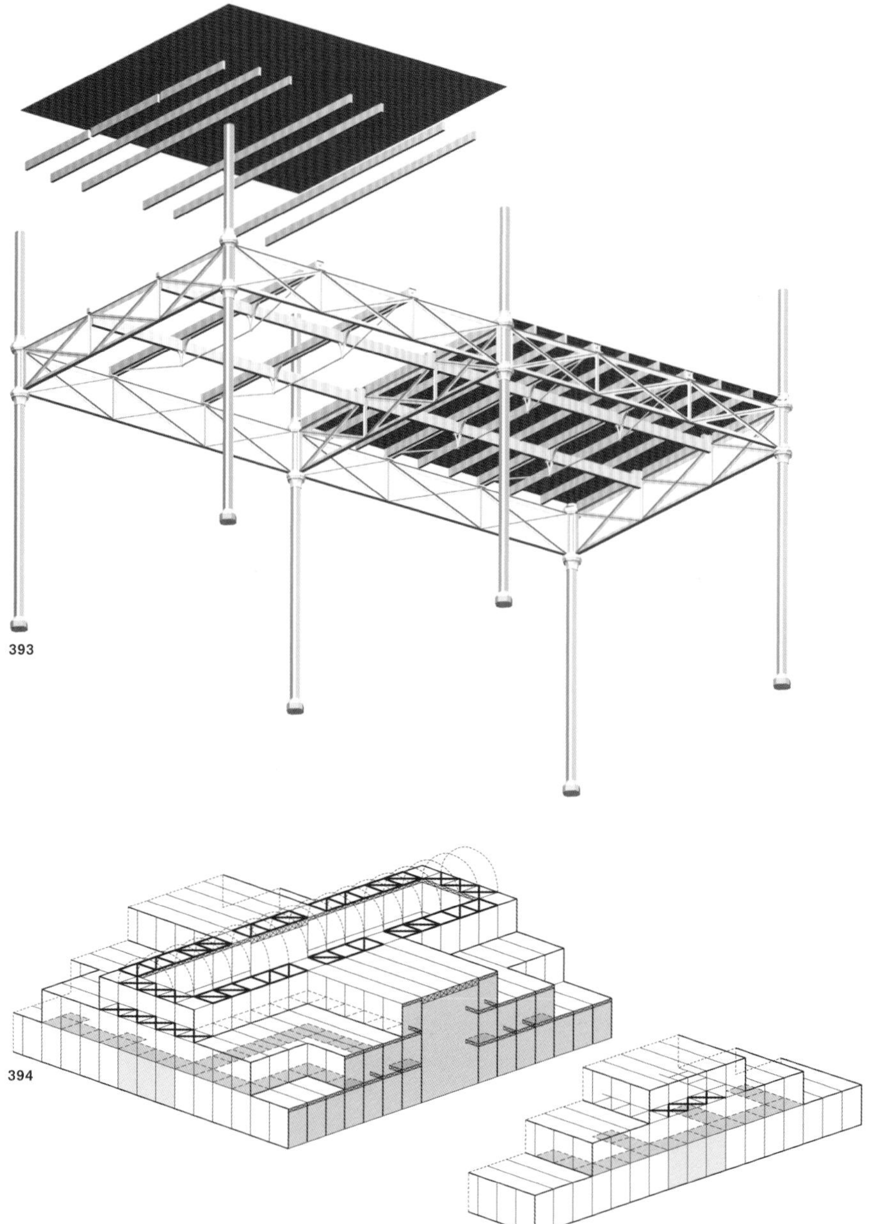

393 Crystal Palace, Hyde Park, London, 1850–51. Engineers: William Barlow (competition entry) and Charles Fox (final design); architect: Joseph Paxton. Exploded diagram showing two-way spanning, trussed beams supporting the gallery floors. 394 Crystal Palace. Diagram of horizontal cross-bracing carrying wind loads in the facades at the end of the nave and transept (right); horizontal, diagonal bracing in the "lead flats" at either side of the transept, carrying the lateral thrust of the vault and wind loads (left). 395 Crystal Palace. Illustration of construction: raising one bay of the timber vault into place. 396 Covered slip No. 7, Chatham Historic Dockyard. Section. 397 Boat Store, Sheerness, East London, England, 1858–60. Engineer: Godfrey Greene. The iron-framed structure is braced by portal action and clad with corrugated iron. 398 Covered slip No. 7, Chatham Historic Dockyard, Kent, England, 1853–55. Engineer: Godfrey Greene. Detail of wrought iron portal frame. 399 Boat Store, Sheerness. Plan and section. 400 Boat Store, Sheerness. Detail of connection between cast iron column, cast iron beam, and built-up wrought iron beam.

395

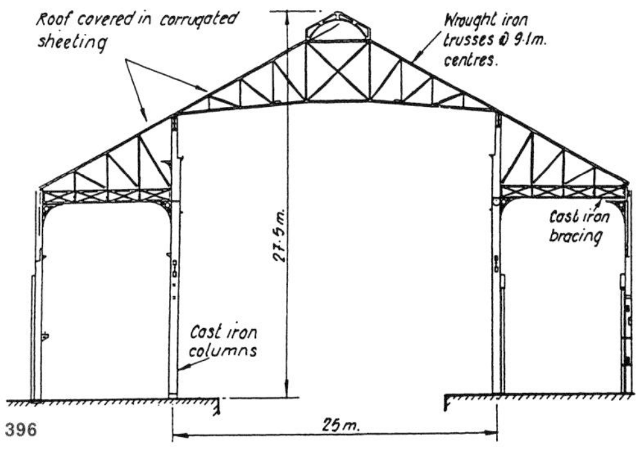

396

397

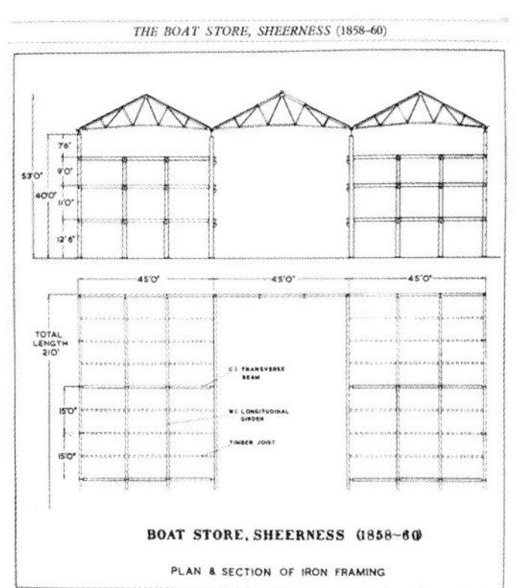

399

398

400

401

402

403

401 Illustration of cast iron bell tower for fire alarm, New York, 1851. Engineer: James Bogardus. Tower rose 30 meters; rigid connections provided stability. 402 Cast iron McCullough shot tower, New York, 1855. Engineer: James Bogardus. Tower rose 53 meters; rigid connections provided stability. 403 Water tower and chimney under construction at Sydenham, South London, 1853–54. Engineer: Isambard Brunel. 404 (Overleaf) Water tower and chimney at Sydenham.

clearly inspired by the Crystal Palace. Most remarkable is the lightweight appearance and feel of the building and a concern for economy and elegance.

The elegance of Greene's slip roof at Chatham would be
surpassed by his later building—the boat store at
397 Sheerness, a dockyard on the river Thames to the East of
London, designed in 1858 and completed by 1860.This
building is the earliest to capture all the various elements
of the modern structural frame. It is a modest four-story
399 building consisting of three upper floors on which light
boats such as dinghies and cutters were stored. The
boats were raised using a travelling crane in the central
bay, an arrangement that resembled the many iron fabrication shops that were being constructed by this time throughout Britain, Germany, France, and the U.S. The historical significance of this building is now well-recognized, though properly celebrated only since the building was "discovered" by engineering historians almost exactly a century after its construction.

1 *It was the first building whose lateral stability was provided entirely by rigid connections between beams and columns, without the use of brackets or curved girders as had been used in the Hungerford Fish*
400 *Market and early slip roofs.*

2 *It was the first to use symmetrical I-section girders; unlike beams loaded only by gravity (always in one direction), the floor beams at Sheerness had to withstand bending in either sense according to the direction of the wind loads they had to carry. It was one of the first to use I-section columns, predated only by Baker's slip roofs.*

3 *The corner columns were square, to accommodate the corrugated iron cladding in orthogonal directions and hollow, to carry rainwater from the roof.*

Most remarkable of all, though, is the sheer simplicity, functionality, and elegance of the building and all its details, quite uncharacteristic of its day and matched only by architects of genius in the twentieth century.

It is difficult to assess the influence of Greene's slip roof and the boat store. Being Admiralty buildings, they were effectively military secrets; on the other hand, word would have spread among the iron contractors if there had been any benefits to them. There were no obvious copies, and the real question is perhaps "Why bother?". They were so perfectly adapted to their function that copying them for a different application would have required significant adaptation. Single-story iron fabrication shops were developing in their own way to suit their purpose, as were railway stations. For multistory buildings of six or eight stories, iron beams and columns were being widely used by this time, and these would all have needed external walls. If you are building a masonry wall to hold the windows and keep the heat in, why not use it to carry the floor beams too? Adding columns in the external wall would have been an unnecessary expense.

The development of the skeleton frame was finally spurred on by the increased height of buildings in Chicago and New York in the late 1860s and 1870s. Above ten stories, the thickness of a load-bearing masonry wall became so great that it occupied a significant area of the lower floors and basements—floor space that could not be rented out, or that was needed for the growing quantities of machinery to pump air around the ventilation systems or to generate electricity. Nevertheless, James Bogardus built two structures in New York in the 1850s that, with hindsight, do point to a recognition of
the opportunities of rigidly jointed beams and columns. In
August 1851 he completed a six-story tower for a large 401
fire alarm bell with columns and beams of cast iron, connected by rigid joints. A few years later, Bogardus used
the same basic system for a shot tower erected just a few 402
hundred meters from his own New York factory. It was essentially the bell tower with the rectangular panels filled in with brick, in the manner of timber-frame construction in medieval Europe. Small windows were provided to light the spiral iron staircase. It is unlikely that structural calculations were undertaken or necessary for the towers, either for gravity or wind loads. Isambard Kingdom Brunel
(1806–59) had used the same idea in 1853–54 for two
water towers and chimneys at Sydenham in South 403, 404
London, where the Crystal Palace, removed in 1852 from its original site in Hyde Park, was rebuilt. Each tower had twelve stories reaching a height of 284 feet (86.6m).

By the late 1850s, then, the key ingredients had been developed that would be exploited with great speed by property developers who saw the commercial potential for high-rise building in New York and Chicago in the late 1860s and 1870s, when the economic climate was right.

OTEL.
GEORGES
HOVIS

chapter 7

The Birth of the Modern Building 1860–1920

People and Events

1810–79 William Froude
1823–94 Johann Schwedler
1832–1907 William LeBaron Jenney
1832–1923 Gustave Eiffel
1842–65 Rafael Guastavino
1842–1921 François Hennebique
1844–1900 Dankmar Adler
1844–1917 Ernest Ransome
1847–1914 Hermann Rietschel
1849–1924 Matthias Koenen
1850–91 John Wellborn Root
1850–1913 John "Earthquake" Milne
1851–1917 Gustav Wayss
1852–1926 Antonio Gaudí
1853–1939 Vladimir Shukov
1854–1924 August Föppl
1856–1924 Louis Sullivan
1859–1909 Alfred Wolff
1860–1948 D'Arcy Wentworth Thompson
1862–1938 Maurice d'Ocagne
1863–1935 Richard Mollier
1865–1928 Paul Cottancin
1868–1919 Wallace Sabine
1870–1919 Edwin O. Sachs
1872–1940 Robert Maillart
1874–1954 Auguste Perret
1876–1950 Willis Haviland Carrier
1879–1962 Eugène Freyssinet

1861–65 American Civil War
1871 Chicago fire

Materials and Technology

1860s–1870s Fireproof construction improvements in U.S., including use of iron load-bearing columns
1860s Rolled steel rails
1865 Pneumatic riveting developed
1861 First all-iron warship, HMS *Warrior*
1870s Hydraulic power used for various applications
1871 Hydraulic riveting developed
1880s Iron- and steel-frame construction of high-rise buildings
1880s Timbrel vaults for fireproof construction by Guastavino
1880s Statically determinate 3-D frames by August Föppl

Knowledge and Learning

1862 William Rankine, *Manual of Civil Engineering* (classic British textbook)
1864–66 Karl Culmann, *Die Graphische Statik* (analysis of graphical methods of problem-solving in statics)
1880s Writings on new American approach to building by John Wellborn Root

Design Methods

1871 Models and nondimensional parameters for ship hull design by William Froude
1871 First wind tunnel designed by Frank Wenham
1877–80 Measurement of loads caused by earthquakes, John Milne
Late 1880s Model studies of grid shell barrel vault by August Föppl

Design Tools: Drawing and Calculation

1860s Use of bending moment and shear force diagrams by Karl Culmann
1860s Graphical statics for statically indeterminate structures
1864 Reciprocal diagrams developed for graphical statics by James Clerk Maxwell
1870s "Hectograph" developed to copy drawings
1880s Nomograms devised for bespoke calculations by Maurice d'Ocagne
c. 1880 Fuller cylindrical slide rule gives 4 or 5 figure accuracy

Buildings

1863 Dome of New Synagogue, Berlin, Germany
1868–70 Equitable Life Assurance Society building, New York, USA
1869–71 Le Bon Marché store, Paris, France
1872 Menier Chocolate Factory, near Paris, France
c. 1873 Coal and Iron Exchange, New York, USA
1873–76 William Ward house, Port Chester, New York, USA
1878–79 First Leiter Building, Chicago, USA
1880–84 Statue of Liberty, New York, USA
1881–82 Montauk Building, Chicago, USA
1883–85 Home Insurance Building, Chicago, USA

1860 1865 1870 1875 1880 1885

1887–1953 Franz Dischinger

1914–18 World War I

c. 1900 Electric motors replace steam and hydraulic power

1889 First use of wind bracing in tall buildings

c. 1900 First use of air-conditioning in large buildings

1890s First reinforced concrete frame buildings

c. 1900 First flat slab floors

1890s Work on fire safety improvement in Britain by Edwin O. Sachs

1892 Reinforced concrete system patented by Hennebique

c. 1910 First ribbed thin concrete shells

1887 Testing Station for Heating and Ventilation Equipment founded by Rietschel in Charlottenburg, Berlin

1917 D'Arcy Wentworth Thompson, *On Growth and Form* (classic study of biological form)

1908 Concrete Institute founded in Britain

1890s–1920s Many university-based research institutes founded

1908 "Flat slab" construction developed by Robert Maillart

1904–08 Boundary layer discovered and first closed-loop wind tunnel developed by Ludwig Prandtl

1890s Form-finding of masonry structures using hanging models by Antonio Gaudí

1900–10 Standard design codes for steel and concrete adopted in most countries

1907 First calculation of portal frame resistance to wind loads

c. 1910 Analysis of different safety factors for dead and live loads by Robert Maillart

1912 Scale models used to test room acoustics (photographing sound waves) by Wallace Sabine

1890s Diazo/ozalid reproduction of drawings on tracing paper

c. 1890 Mollier diagram developed to chart thermodynamic properties

1908 First psychrometric chart published by Willis Carrier

1890–93 GUM Department Store, Moscow, Russia

1894–1904 Saint Jean de Montmartre, Paris, France

1907–09 Metropolitan Life Tower, New York

1908–11 Royal Liver Building, Liverpool, England

1886–89 Tacoma Building, Chicago, USA

1896 Exhibition buildings, Novgorod, Russia

1887–89 Galérie des Machines, Paris, France

1901–03 Stock Exchange building, New York, USA

1887–89 Auditorium Building, Chicago, USA

1902–03 Ingalls Building, Cincinnati, Ohio, USA

1911–12 Fagus Factory, near Hildesheim, Germany

1888–89 Tower Building, New York, USA

1898–99 GUM Department Store, Moscow, Russia

1911–13 Jahrhunderthalle, Breslau, Poland

1889 Eiffel Tower, Paris, France

1911–13 Théâtre des Champs-Élysées, Paris, France

1890 1895 1900 1905 1910 1915 1920

The Birth of the Modern Building 1860–1920

Engineering Calculations

By the 1860s engineers were making calculations for nearly every aspect of building design: foundations, columns, beams, floor structures, roof trusses, and heating and ventilation systems. They were also calculating construction costs based on estimates of quantities of materials, the manpower and construction plant required, and the duration of building activities. The range of engineers' scientific knowledge and calculation skills was wide. The best were able to deal with new engineering challenges, calculating from first principles the forces and deflections in a large railway station roof, for example, or the size of steam engine needed to drive the ventilation system in a large public building. These state-of-the-art calculations, however, were beyond the ability of most engineers, and in fact, most building design did not demand them. When a problem arose that was beyond the scientific or mathematical skills of an engineer, he could consult one of the growing number of textbooks or engineers' pocket guides or, if necessary, a specialist working in a polytechnic, research institute, or university.

The actual calculations that might be undertaken for a certain design problem would reflect both the level of education of the individual engineer and the general level of engineering knowledge at the time and in the country concerned. During the nineteenth century the scientific and mathematical skills of "average" engineers were highest in France and German-speaking countries, while other European countries and the United States lagged well behind. The calculations required in Germany in 1860 for a large roof structure, for example, would have been more sophisticated than those required in Britain or the U.S.

The art in engineering design calculations lay, and still lies, in the ability to make simplifications and approximations that reduce the difficulty and time needed to carry out the calculations to a realistic level, while still adequately representing the engineering behavior of the materials and structures being considered. For example, designing a basic iron-frame building in the 1860s was relatively straightforward. The loads on each column and beam were easy to estimate, and the structural properties of the iron and the columns and beams themselves were well understood, as a result both of practical testing and of the application of equations describing bending behavior (beams) and buckling behavior (columns). The beams and columns themselves were fabricated from rolled flat plates and angle sections, united by rivets. These were simple, small-scale structures compared with the railway bridges for which this technology had been developed. It was thus quite adequate to assume that the composite elements behaved as if they formed a solid section. The calculations made by engineers in the field were not as sophisticated or as accurate as those that could be carried out by a research scientist, but they did not need to be. They were satisfactory for the purpose at hand.

Of equal importance to the nature of engineering calculations were the means for undertaking them. Engineering design calculations have three basic components. First, there are arithmetic processes, such as multiplication. Then there are the formulae or algorithms that define the relationships among the various parameters, such as the formula for calculating the bending moment in a beam or the quantity of air pumped through a duct. Finally, there are empirical data such as the strength of iron or density of air. During the mid-nineteenth century, significant advances were made in each of these areas.

Arithmetic calculations were generally done by hand with the use of tables of squares, cubes, and higher powers; square, cube, and higher roots; and trigonometric functions. Logarithms were used for all complex multiplication and division calculations. In general, nineteenth-century engineers had far better arithmetic skills than today's engineers. In the absence of electronic calculators, people could perform complex calculations easily and knew a host of arithmetic tricks and shortcuts to get answers quickly. Few engineers today, for example, could calculate the square or cube root of a number to ten or twelve significant figures.

During the early nineteenth century slide rules—which had been available since the mid-seventeenth century—were used by some engineers for multiplication and division calculations, but were not yet widespread. The process of lining up the scales on a slide rule and reading the answer to a calculation had to be done very carefully, since it was usually the case that the numbers to be manipulated did not fall on the scale where lines were engraved. To overcome this difficulty, some slide rules were fitted with a movable, transparent cursor on which was scribed a hairline that could be used to temporarily mark what would otherwise have been an invisible point on the scale. Owners of slide rules without cursors could, if necessary, lightly mark lines on the rule with a pencil. The breakthrough that led to the slide rule becoming an engineer's indispensable tool came in 1851, when Amedée Mannheim (1831–1906) was still a student at the École d'application in Metz, France. Mannheim found that adding a movable cursor to the slide rule speeded up its use and improved the accuracy of calculations. These benefits were noticed by his teachers, and higher authorities were informed. Very soon use of the slide rule was introduced into every engineering curriculum in France. Mannheim also organized the different scales on the rule in a way that better suited the needs of engineers, and he gave them the labels that soon became standard the world over: A and B were for squares and square roots; scales C and D, for multiplication and division. Scales of trigonometric functions—sine, cosine, and tangent—also soon became standard. Expert users could carry out common calculations at about the same speed as a person using a modern electronic calculator. For his act of genius as a student, as anyone who has used a slide rule would attest, Mannheim deserves the engineer's equivalent of beatification.

The accuracy of slide rule calculations was limited by the
length of the rule: The standard 250-mm rule gave an accuracy of about 1 percent, which was adequate for most
engineering calculations. When greater accuracy was required, longer rules could be used, but they were impractical. One answer to the problem of length was developed
in 1878 by George Fuller, Professor of Engineering at
Queen's College, Belfast. By taking a line and wrapping it
around a cylinder, a long scale could be made very com- 405
pact. The scale of his cylindrical slide rule was 7,250 divisions over a length of 12.5 meters—50 times longer
than the standard rule—and users could achieve correspondingly more precise accuracy. Circular slide rules, 406
which had an endless scale and were relatively easy to
carry around, were also widely used.

Mannheim's generic slide rule was only one of many types in use. Early on, engineers realized that *any* scale could be inscribed on a slide rule. Thus common calculations such as deriving the area of a circle from its diameter or the weight of a beam from its dimensions could be performed simply by reading from one scale to another. The scale was, in effect, a means of representing scientific knowledge, such as a specific formula, or empirical data, such as the density of timber. Specialized slide rules with scales for many different engineering design calculations were made throughout the nineteenth and early twentieth centuries. Two hundred and twenty patents for such devices were granted in the United States between 1851 and 1964.

Although less well known than the slide rule, the polar planimeter was another early calculating tool of ines-

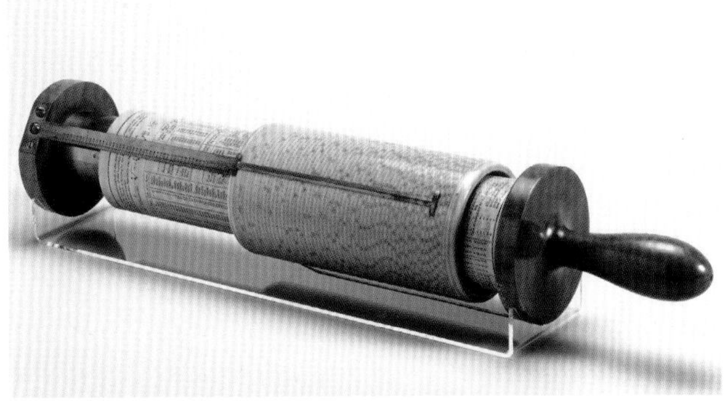
405

406

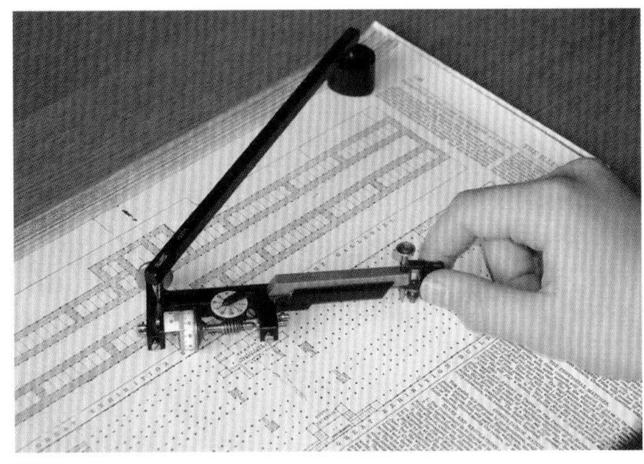
407

408

timable value. This miraculous device, which mechanically performed the mathematical operation of integration, was developed in 1855 by the Swiss mathematician Jacob Amsler (1823–1912). It was of such immediate practical value that he gave up his academic career to manufacture and sell his planimeters; Amsler's firm sold over 50,000 planimeters during his lifetime. The planimeter was operated by moving the end of one of its arms over the perimeter of a figure of any shape. As the wheel at the other end slid over the paper, it was turned,
407, 408 partly by rolling and partly by sliding. After the closed loop had been traced, the reading on the dial gave the area of the enclosed figure. The instrument was easy to use and gave results to an accuracy of one percent, quite adequate for most engineering needs.

By 1800 it was well known that the combined effects of several forces on an object could be calculated graphically using the triangle of forces or parallelogram of forces method. At that time, however, there were very few engineering design problems that could be solved by these techniques. This situation changed in the 1840s, when graphical statics was first used to determine the forces in the members of statically determinate bridge and roof trusses (see chapter 6, pp. 308–15). By the 1860s the use of graphical statics was being developed

405 A Fuller cylindrical slide rule, Belfast, Northern Ireland, c. 1880. Unwrapped, the scale would be 12.5 meters long.
406 A circular slide rule, c. 1900. 407 A polar planimeter, similar to that devised by Jacob Amsler in 1855, for measuring areas. 408 A polar planimeter. Close-up of the scale and wheel that turns and slides to different degrees.

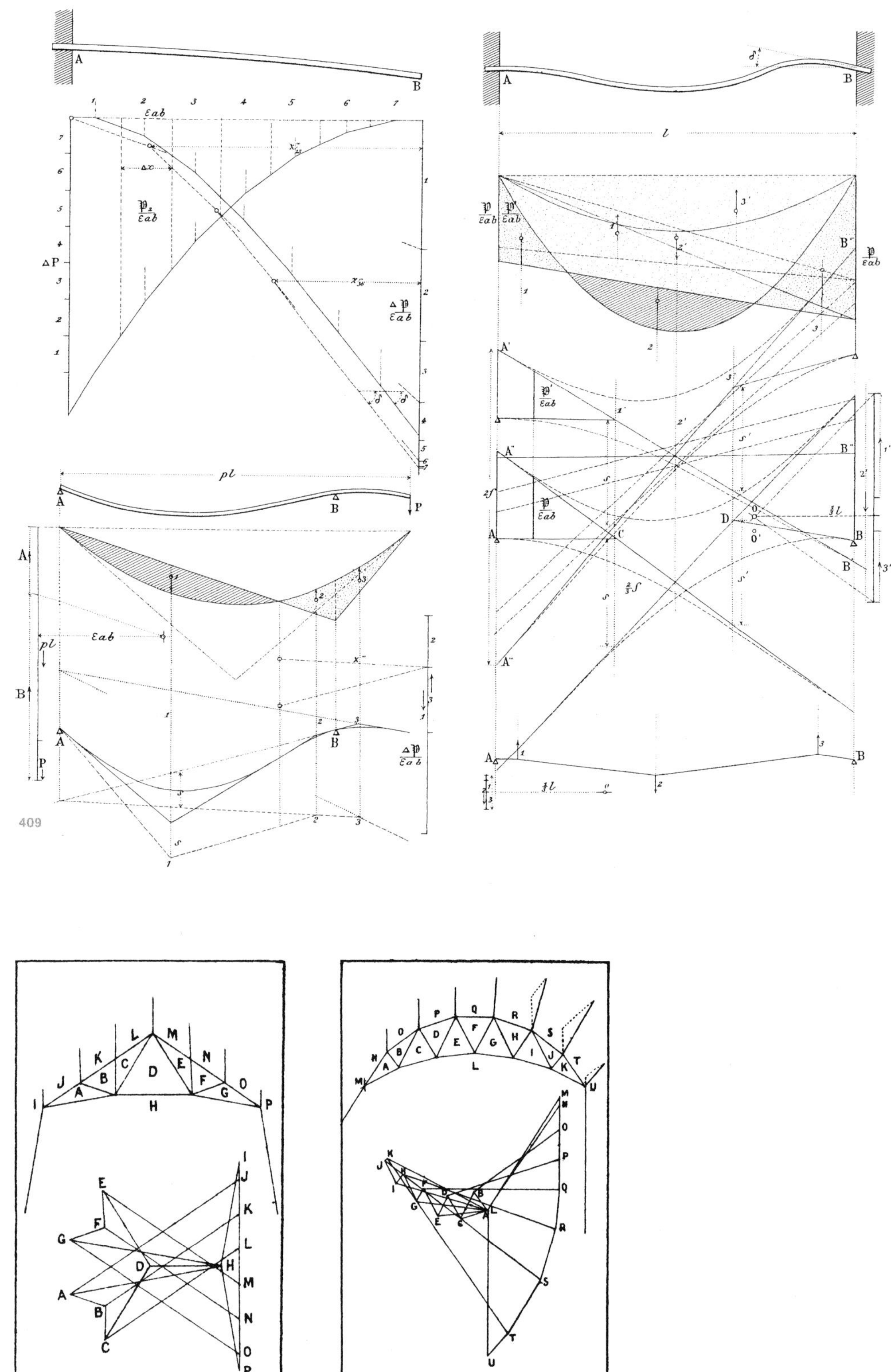

409

410

on many fronts. One limitation of the earlier methods was that structures were analyzed by considering one joint at a time. As the forces at each end of a member of a truss are equal and opposite, it is possible to combine the separate equilibrium diagrams for each joint into a single diagram for the whole truss, with the same number of lines as there are members in the structure representing forces. This goal was achieved in 1864 by the Scottish physicist James Clerk Maxwell (1831–79), who devised these so-called "reciprocal diagrams." Unfortunately, they proved too challenging for less mathematically gifted engineers, and their widespread adoption awaited the efforts of engineer Robert Henry Bow (1827–1909), who devised the method of notation which bears his name and which makes the creation of a reciprocal diagram a straightforward matter indeed. Bow's notation, as well as a host of practical examples illustrating its use in analyzing roof trusses, were published in his 1873 book *The Economics of Construction in Relation to*
410 *Framed Structures*. In this and an earlier book, *A Treatise on Bracing with its Application to Bridges* (see chapter 6, p. 315), and the many articles he wrote in the *Civil Engineer and Architect's Journal* during the 1850s and 1860s, Bow articulated a clear philosophy for the structures he designed. He devised a rigorous taxonomy of structural types that provided a rational means for comparing their advantages and disadvantages, both in structural terms (his first book) and in terms of the economical use of materials (his second). The intellectual economy of his whole approach to the subject matched the elegance of his application of Maxwell's reciprocal diagrams, and was far superior to the overcomplex and turgid approaches of many of his contemporaries. It was this clarity that explains the popularity of his method, at least in Britain, over the following century. Not only was it elegant and simple, it also provided a visual representation of the statics of a structure, enabling engineers to form a picture of how a structure was working. This visual component, which was not a characteristic of algebraic analysis, led to Bow's method still being taught in some engineering courses as late as the 1970s as a way to foster structural understanding in the minds of young engineers-to-be.

While the basic methods of graphical statics for simple bridge and roof trusses were becoming ubiquitous in Britain, it was in continental Europe that the subject was being developed to a high degree of sophistication. Many engineers contributed to this development, but the prime mover and dominant influence was the German engineer Karl Culmann (1821–81). He disseminated his ideas both through lectures at the Swiss Federal Polytechnic in Zurich in the 1850s and 1860s and in his book *Die Graphische Statik (Graphical Statics)*, published in two parts in 1864 and 1866. He was, of course, not starting from scratch, but building upon previous work by many scientists, mathematicians, and engineers. Culmann's books methodically analyzed the graphical methods that could be used to solve numerous problems in statics, including suspension bridges, retaining walls, simple and long-span beams, arches, trusses, and many others. Culmann was the first to make regular use of bending moment and shear force diagrams that so vividly show how
a beam is working as a structure. Much of his work dealt 409
with statically indeterminate structures, in which the distribution of loads is affected by the stiffness of the materials and structural members. Many of Culmann's students also left their own mark on the subject, notably Maurice Koechlin (1856–1946), who worked for Gustave Eiffel and in 1879 became the firm's chief analyst and designer (see p. 382).

It would be difficult to overestimate the impact of graphical statics on the world of structural engineering; it was certainly no less significant than the impact of the computer in the late twentieth century. Central to Culmann's philosophy was the importance of making visible in the method of calculation or analysis the workings of the inherently invisible stresses and forces inside structures. This point was remarkably illustrated one day in 1866, when Culmann had been working on the analysis of a
wrought iron crane made by William Fairbairn. He hap- 411
pened to drop in on a colleague from the anatomy department who had just cut through the head of a human femur bone. To his surprise and delight, Culmann observed in the structure of the bone the same pattern of principal
stresses that he had been calculating in the crane. Here 412

409 Graphical representation of bending moment and shear forces in beams. 410 Figures from *The Economics of Construction* by Robert Bow, Edinburgh, 1873. The lower figures are "reciprocal diagrams" of the loaded truss in the upper figures, showing the forces in the structure. Figure at left includes horizontal forces representing wind loading.

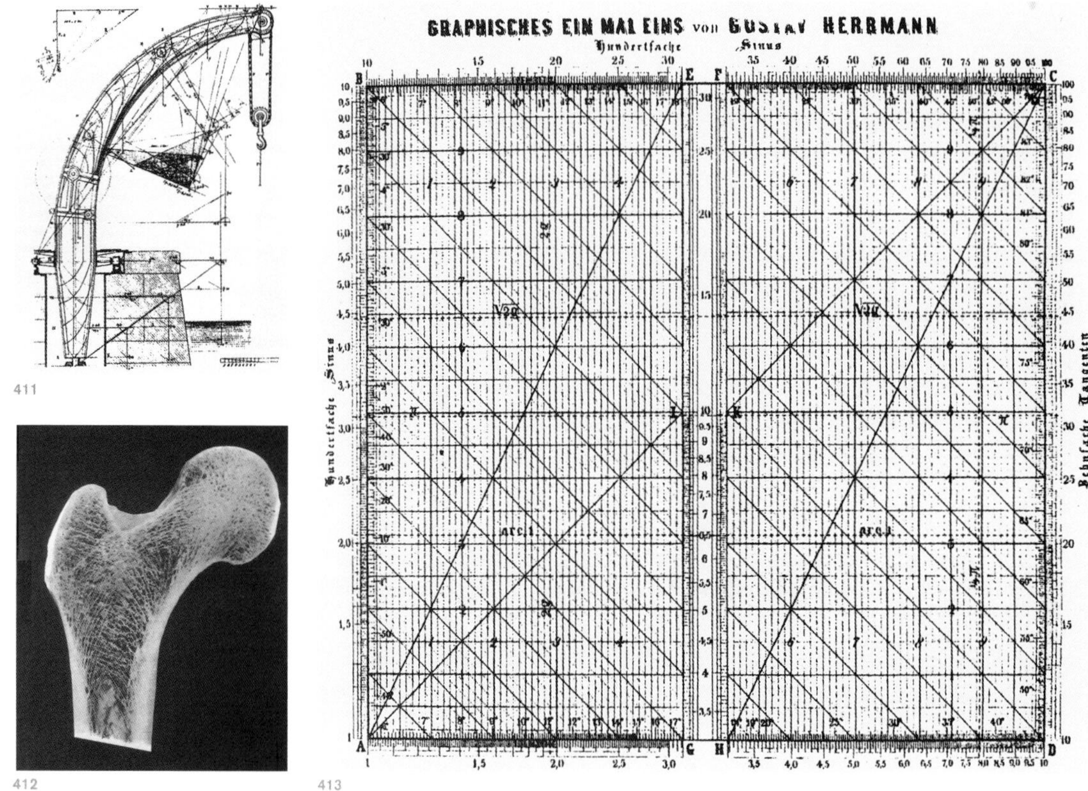

411

412

413

was nature making visible how one material—human bone—carried the stresses arising from the loads it had to bear.

The use of graphical methods to represent engineering knowledge and data also grew in the middle of the nineteenth century. From the eighteenth century on, information such as the "scantlings" (dimensions) of floor beams, columns, or components of roof trusses had been collected and presented in books as tables of numbers. These could be tedious to use and were often copied incorrectly. After the 1840s information began to be stored in the form of graphs, which were a quick way of retrieving data and allowed easy interpolation. The Frenchman Léon Lalanne, who had devised three-dimensional graphs using the same method as used on maps to show contour heights (see chapter 6, pp. 336–37), continued developing means of helping engineers in their calculations for the rest of his life. In the 1870s the German engineer Gustav Herrmann (1836–1907) took up the same challenge in his book *Das graphische Einmaleins oder die Rechentafel, ein Ersatz für den Rechenschieber* (Graphical Multiplication or Calculation 413
Tables: A Substitute for the Slide Rule). One of the most familiar multivariable graphs dating from that era still in use today is the Mollier or psychrometric chart developed for air-conditioning calculations.

An even more ingenious and sophisticated graphical means of calculating was developed by the French mathematician Maurice d'Ocagne (1862–1938) in the 1880s, a technique he called "nomography." Its purpose was to solve all equations of a given type by means of one diagram. In principle, a nomogram enables any number of variables to be handled, and the sequential mode of their operation resembles the sequential operations that form the basis of a computer program. A nomogram consists of a number of scales drawn parallel on the page at

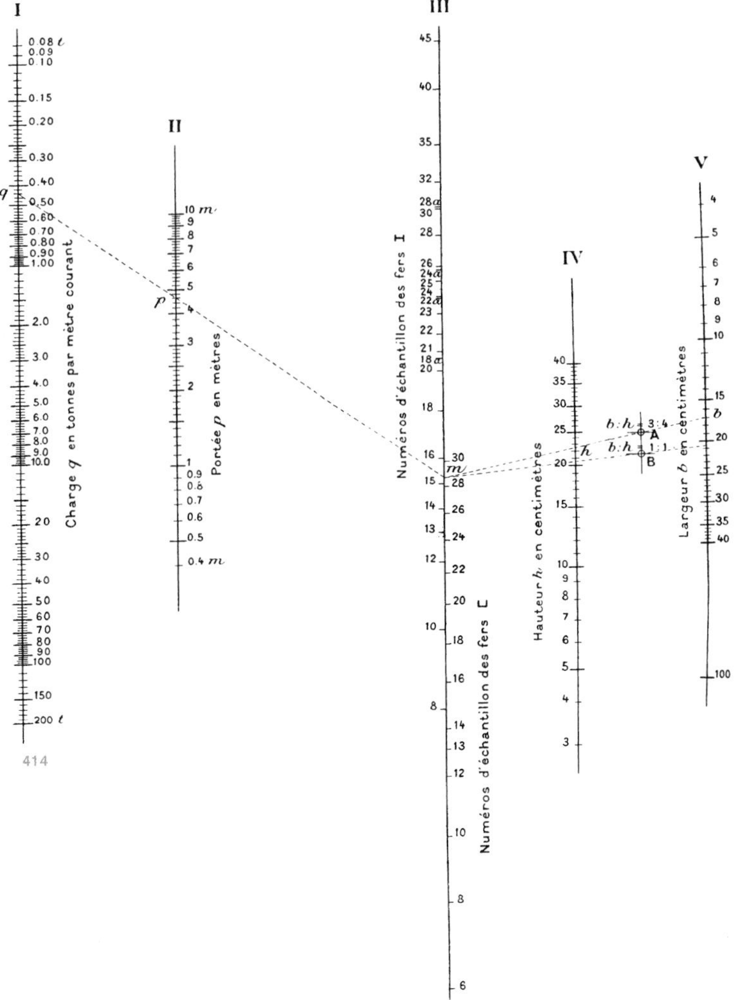

414

carefully calculated distances. Each "input" has a separate scale. By drawing lines between the values on the input scales, a point is created on the "output" scale that is the solution to the equation. Like the scales on a calculation-specific slide rule, a nomogram encapsulates what, for many engineers, would otherwise have required knowledge of complex engineering science; it can also incorporate empirical data such as the properties of materials. In the early days of reinforced concrete, nomograms were ideal as a means of enabling engineers to design
414 simple structures using the new material. Nomograms formed an important part of design methods in many branches of building engineering well into the 1980s.

The Rapid Spread of Iron and Steel Frame Construction

The middle of the nineteenth century witnessed yet another cycle of industrial growth as manufacturing industries in Europe and the United States accelerated production to meet the increasing demand for goods both at home and abroad. Civil and building engineers saw a corresponding increase in opportunities as they provided

411 Karl Culmann, graphical analysis of bending moments and lines of principal stress in a wrought iron crane.
412 Section of a human femur with bone structure reflecting the lines of principal stress. 413 Gustav Herrmann, chart showing graphical multiplication and division as a substitute for a slide rule. 414 A nomogram by Maurice d'Ocagne, 1899.

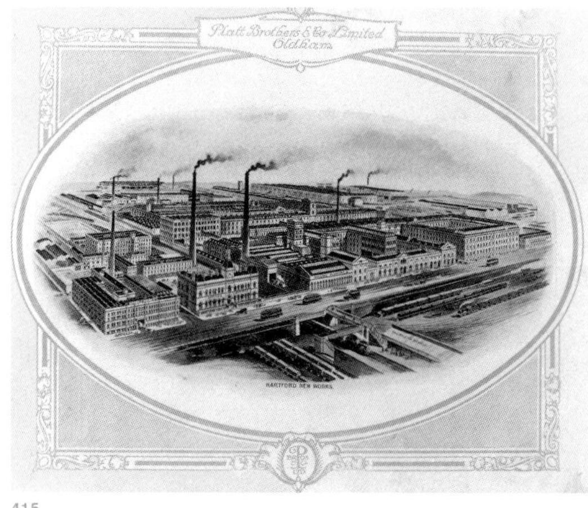

415

416

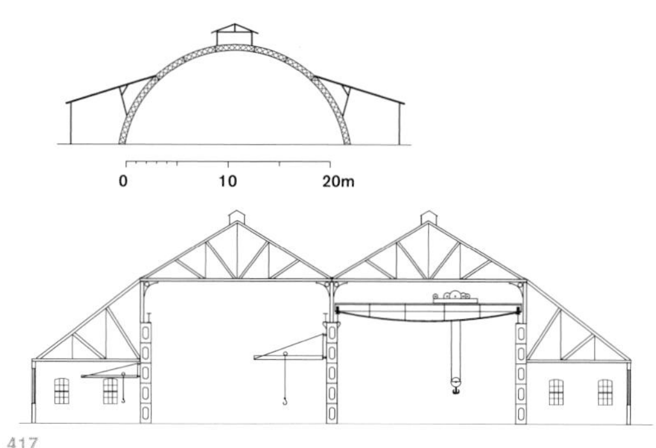

417

the infrastructure to transport these goods: railways, bridges, tunnels, harbors, and dock facilities, as well as their associated buildings—railway stations and warehouses at transport interchanges. The spinning and weaving industries continued to grow rapidly in Britain as the textile trade spread worldwide, and many hundreds of mills were constructed to the well-established pattern using cast iron columns and beams, and masonry jack arches and external walls. Mill owners proudly displayed their vast factory complexes in advertisements and vied with one another to make their buildings look the most
415, 416 modern and impressive.

Alongside the construction of multistory mills were a growing number of engineering works producing iron machinery of every kind—not only for the textile mills but for shipyards, steam engines, railroad engines and cars, and hundreds of types of machine tools. All these industries were housed in large single-story buildings that were, above all, functional and economical and, from the 1850s on, made mainly of wrought and cast iron rather than masonry and timber.

The typical works or fabricating shops had three bays—two single-height areas on either side of a central double-height space that contained one or more large gantry cranes for handling the heavy raw materials and finished
artifacts. The main structure consisted of cast iron or 417
wrought iron columns, wrought iron beams or trussed girders, and a roof of wrought iron trusses supporting a covering of corrugated iron and including, perhaps, roof lights to illuminate the working areas beneath. In the early nineteenth century, the walls were often still made of brick or stone, but in the second half of the century, these too would be replaced by iron columns supporting a curtain wall of corrugated iron. In many ways these

415 Aerial view of the Platt Brothers Hartford New Works, Oldham, England, c. 1900. 416 Roy Mill, Oldham, England, 1906. 417 Cross section of a typical engineering works from the late nineteenth century. 418 The single engineering drawing for the construction of an engineering works, c. 1890.

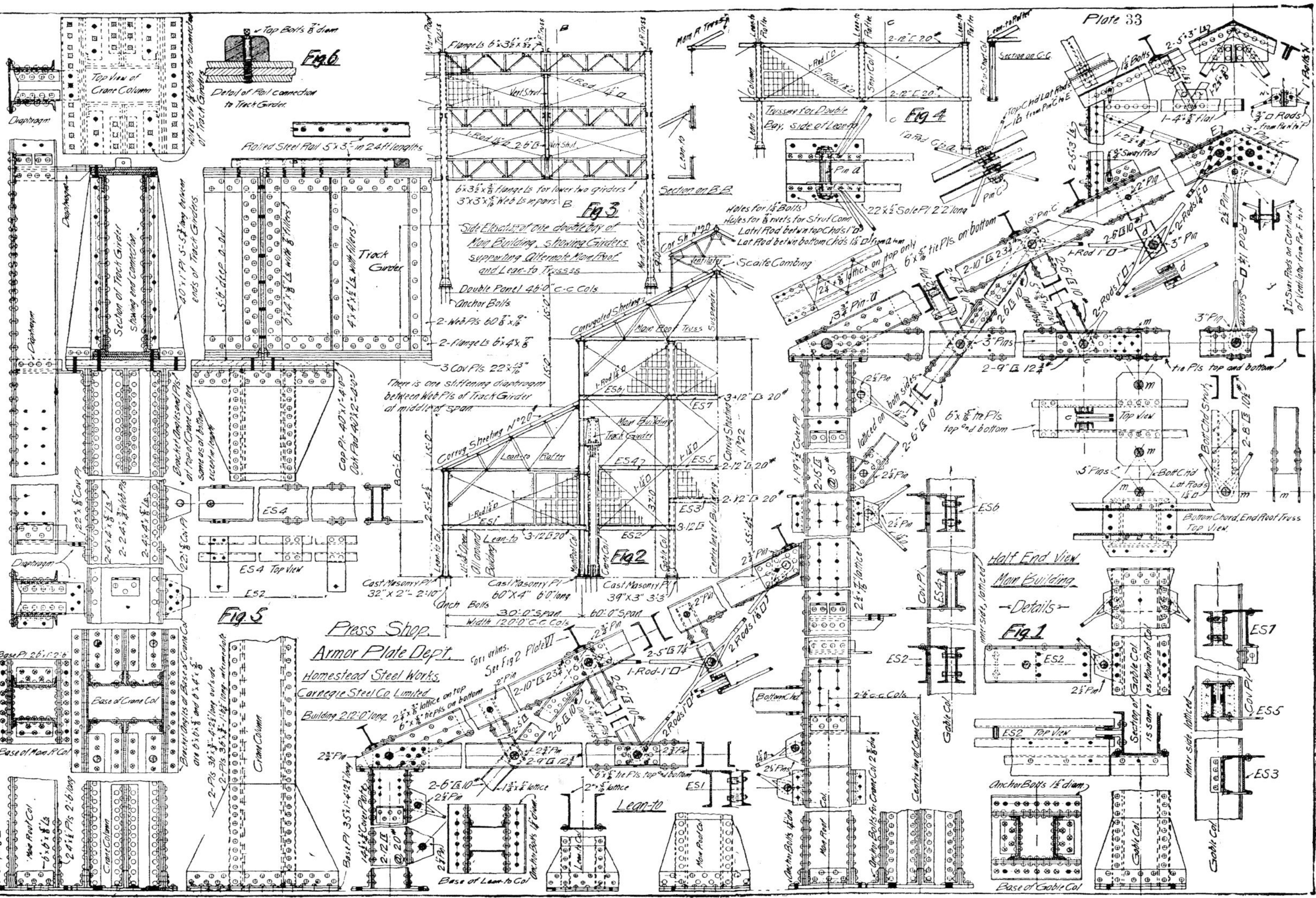
Plate 33
Fig 1
Fig 2
Fig 3
Fig 4
Fig 5
Fig 6
Half End View
Main Building
Details
Press Shop
Armor Plate Dept
Homestead Steel Works
Carnegie Steel Co Limited
Section on B.B
Section on C.C
Lean-to
Base of Gable Col
Base of Lean-to Col
Base of Crane Col
Crane Column

419

were descendants of the rudimentary structures built to cover dockyard slips and the minimalist construction used for the boat store at Sheerness, in England (see chapter 6, pp. 360–63).

Between the 1830s and the 1880s, tens of thousands of engineering workshops and factories were constructed of wrought iron in every industrial country of the world. Although of little architectural merit, they provided the opportunity to develop the skills needed to make wrought iron structures. Once these skills were mastered for the construction of small buildings, they could be applied to larger and larger structures. In the 1850s the only iron sections available were flat, angle, or T-sections. Larger box girders or I-beams were made by riveting together
418 several of these simple sections. These formed the basic vocabulary for the first large buildings constructed using wrought iron frames.

By the 1860s the world's railways and steamships were transporting growing numbers of people and goods, and this had a considerable effect on the ease and rapidity with which ideas spread from one country to another. New ideas and achievements in civil and building engineering spread throughout Europe, America, and major cities in the rest of the world in a matter of weeks, through either personal experience or contact with the growing number of technical books and periodicals that were being produced from the 1840s on. No longer was it ignorance of technical ideas that inhibited new developments; it was more likely the lack of engineers with the practical experience to use these ideas and the inherent conservatism of politicians, public servants, and those with money to invest in new commercial ventures of any kind.

No building type contributed more to spreading an awareness of iron construction than the railway station. 419, 422
Railway stations were highly visible, and their often massive scale was inherently impressive, both to the public at large and to travelers who could take their impressions of these imposing structures—regarded by many architectural historians as the cathedrals of the nineteenth century—back to their home towns. The firm of McKim, Mead and White, architects of the New York terminus of

419 St. Pancras railway station, London, 1865–68. Engineers: William Barlow and Rowland Ordish. 422 (Overleaf) Railway station interior, Frankfurt, Germany, c. 1860.

ENGINEERING DRAWINGS

By the 1860s, machine-made detail paper—commonly light buff in color—was available in large sizes from a roll. It included hemp or other fibers to enhance its strength, making it especially suitable for working or "shop" drawings. Paper premounted on muslin and often bound along the edges with fabric or tape, was also available. Finished drawings could be made on inexpensive tracing paper, and copied using the new "cyanotype" process.

The cyanotype or "blueprint" photographic process was first introduced by the astronomer John Herschel in 1842, although not commonly used by architects and engineers until the late 1850s. The copy paper was impregnated with a mixture of ferric ammonium citrate and potassium ferricyanide, and placed under the original. When exposed to bright light, the two chemicals reacted and turned blue; the paper shielded by the ink or pencil lines of the drawing remained white.

Early blueprints were rather laborious to make. The sensitized paper, with the translucent original on top of it, was placed in a glass-fronted printing frame that was then placed in the sun. After the paper had been adequately exposed, it was removed from the frame, thoroughly washed, and hung up to dry. In the 1860s, linen cloth made from flax became a more durable alternative to tracing paper, but fell out of favor by the 1930s because of its cost. The copying process was mechanized around 1900 using artificial ultraviolet and a rotating drum that transported the original and copy paper.

In the early 1870s, the "hectograph" (from hekaton, the Greek word for one hundred) was developed as a way of copying drawings. Descended from James Watt's copying process, it was much improved by the use of special pencils or ink that contained water-soluble aniline dyes, usually purple or bright blue. A drawing was pressed against a damp gelatin pad or "graph," which absorbed the dyes. After the original was removed, sheets of blank paper were pressed against the image on the graph; up to fifty prints could be produced before the ink was exhausted. Although the process was initially used mainly for copying correspondence or specifications, by 1900 aniline-dye inks and pencils were being sold in many colors so that colored drawings could be copied.

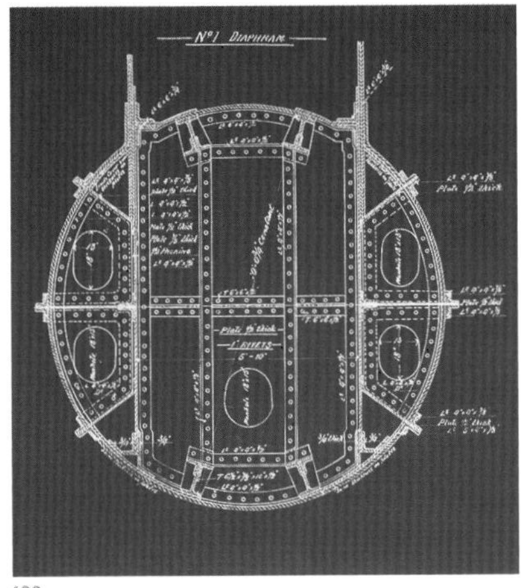

420

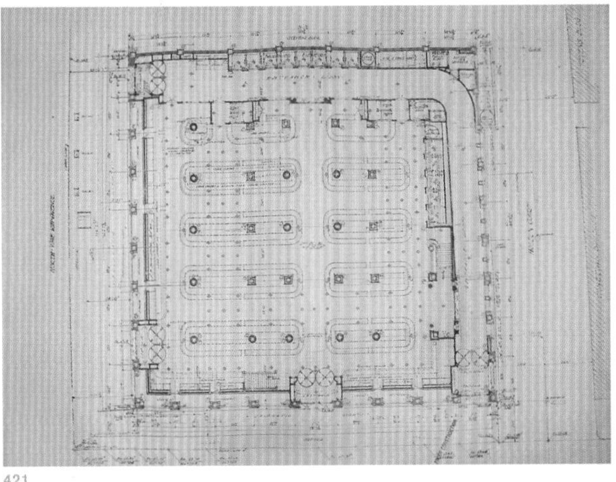

421

420 A cyanotype or "blueprint" copy of an engineering drawing, c. 1880. 421 A color hectograph by Daniel H. Burnham and Company, 1913.

the Pennsylvania State Railway completed in 1910, drew on an even earlier age than that of the great cathedrals in modelling its form on the vast tepidarium at the baths of the Emperor Caracalla in ancient Rome.

Following the precedent set by the Crystal Palace, a growing number of national and international exhibitions provided opportunities for showcasing the iron frame. One of these, the main building for the Paris exhibition of 1867, was the first major contract for Eiffel et Cie, the firm founded by Gustave Eiffel (1832–1923). His firm designed and built numerous types of iron structures, including many small buildings, hundreds of railway bridges, and the iron structures of two of the world's best-known monuments—the Statue of Liberty in New York (1880–84) and the Eiffel Tower, built for the Paris exhibition of 1889 celebrating the centenary of the French Revolution. Maurice Koechlin proposed the first design for the Eiffel Tower, with its famous tapered silhouette, a form that most efficiently withstands wind loads. He wrote his own book on graphical statics in 1889 to coincide with the opening of the tower, and was responsible for the design of many of Eiffel's huge iron-lattice railway bridges. Railway stations, exhibition buildings, and the ubiquitous market building were all well suited to iron construction because they were single-story buildings
423 that required no fireproofing.

In nineteenth-century France the regulations governing the fireproofing of iron buildings were less stringent than in other countries, and architects and engineers exploited the opportunities this offered. In 1870 Paris acquired the first of its *grands magasins*, or department stores, Le Bon Marché, which featured exposed iron on an impressive scale. It was the work of architect Louis-Charles Boileau (1837–1914) and engineer Armand Moisant (1838–1906), whose newly formed iron and steel fabrication firm Moisant-Laurent-Savey would soon
424, 425 grow to be one of the largest in Europe. At about the
426 same time that Moisant was designing Le Bon Marché, he was collaborating with the architect Jules Saulnier (1817–81) on designs for a new mill and factory building at the Menier Chocolate Factory (1872) outside Paris. They devised a unique and remarkable frame comprising a wrought iron lattice that stretched the full length and height of each wall and was infilled with brickwork. The internal columns of the building were of cast iron. 427

By the early 1870s, wrought iron frame construction had become an acceptable choice for virtually any type of building—banks, libraries, art galleries, and even churches. Riveted wrought iron girders in the ceilings and roofs of buildings became almost as familiar to the public as traditional masonry construction.

Steel became cheaper to manufacture, and its quality improved, following the development of two new methods for making it—the Bessemer process, developed in Britain in 1856, and the Siemens-Martin process, developed in Germany in 1863–64. Both processes enabled steel to be made in larger quantities; in addition, the all-important carbon content of the steel could be controlled much more precisely. Steel first began to replace wrought iron in the railway industry—the rolled-steel rails were laid at Derby in England in 1857 and in the United States in 1865—and later for high-pressure boilers for steam engines, then finally, from the early 1870s on, in the building industry. (For further details on iron and steel manufacture, see Appendix 2.)

Steel did not quickly replace wrought iron in building construction. It corroded more quickly than iron when exposed to water, and even more rapidly when exposed to salt water. Steel to be used in those environments required good corrosion protection, which was expensive. Wrought iron was more resistant to corrosion, and generally preferred until the late 1880s for ships and large outdoor structures such as bridges. Only in the 1870s were steel girders first used inside buildings, where they were protected from the weather. As with wrought iron, smaller spans were fabricated from rolled I-section joists, and larger girders were fabricated by riveting several smaller sections into a box section. The first use of steel for a large building, albeit a temporary one, was for the Galérie

423 Les Halles market, Paris, 1853–57. Architect: Victor Baltard. 424 Le Bon Marché department store, Paris, 1869–71. Engineer: Armand Moisant; architect: Louis-Charles Boileau. Wrought iron frame. 425 Le Bon Marché. Interior. 426 The workshop of engineering firm Moisant-Laurent-Savey, Paris, c. 1880. 427 Menier Chocolate Factory, Noisiel, France, 1872. Engineer: Armand Moisant; architect: Jules Saulnier. Wrought iron frame.

423

424

425

426

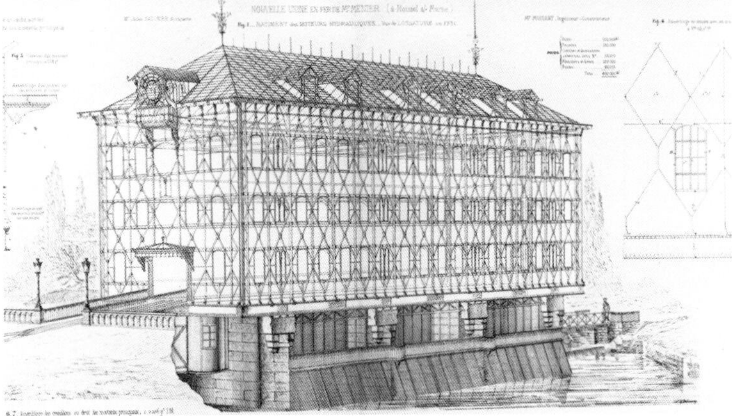

427

428

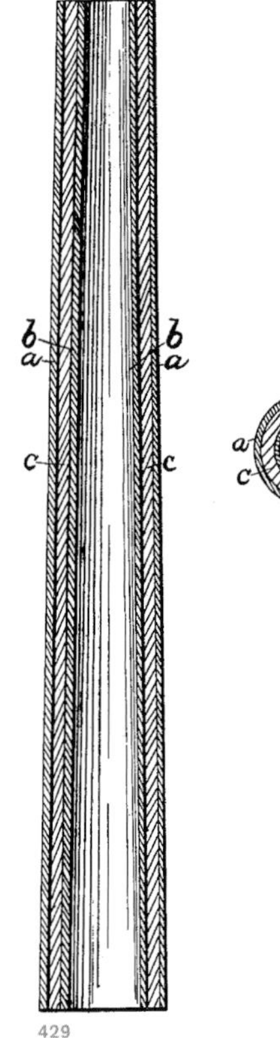

429

430

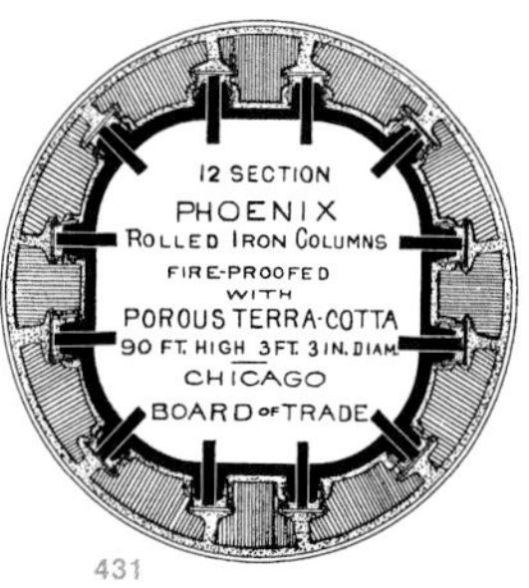

431

428 Galérie des Machines, Exposition Universale, Paris, 1887–89. Engineer: Victor Contamin; architect: Ferdinand Dutert. 429 Drawing from the patent by John Cornell for a fire-resistant cast-column, 1860. 430 Galérie des Machines. Interior showing three-pin arch. 431 The wrought iron Phoenix column, patented 1862. 432 Various methods of fireproof construction, c. 1890.

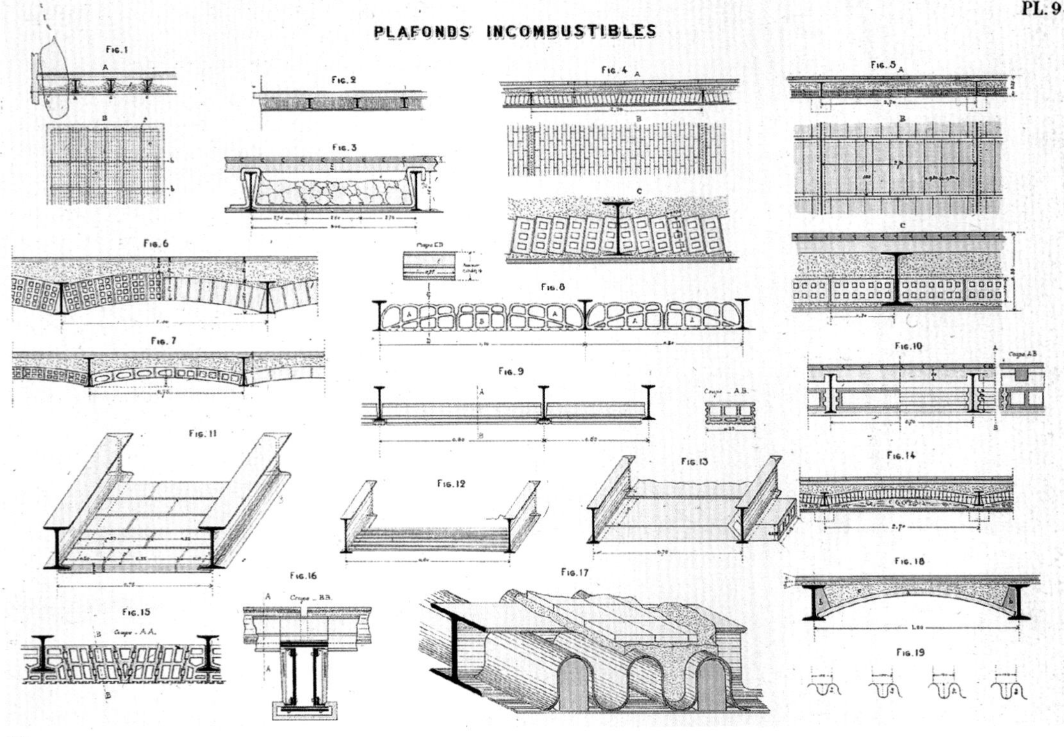

432

des Machines at the 1889 Exposition Universale in Paris; there, it stood alongside the Eiffel Tower, which was
428, 430 made of wrought iron. The Galérie des Machines was also among the first to use a three-pin arch, a device developed for bridges that renders the structure statically determinate and, hence, allows forces and bending moments to be predicted with greater accuracy.

Fireproof Construction

Despite the replacement of timber construction by various forms of so-called "fireproof construction" during the 1840s and 1850s, fire remained a major cause of death and of damage to buildings in the late nineteenth century. As construction boomed in large cities in Europe and America, the numbers of patented fireproofing systems for buildings proliferated. The importance of ensuring that columns did not fail in a fire was well recognized, and many types of fireproof columns were also patented. In 1860 John Cornell patented the idea of making columns using two concentric cast iron tubes and filling
429 the space between with fire-resistant clay. Probably the best known and most commercially successful column, though not inherently a fireproof one, was the Phoenix column, patented in 1862 by Samuel Reeves of the Phoenix Iron company. It was originally used as a way of making large compression members for iron bridges by riveting together four, eight, or more segments along their longitudinal flanges. The use of Phoenix columns spread into iron-frame buildings in the 1870s, and fire protection was afforded by terra-cotta tiles held in place by wrought iron bands. 431

The number of fireproof flooring systems continued to grow, partly because contractors often developed their own systems simply to avoid having to pay to use someone else's. As many hundreds of patents were filed in every country, the essential differences between the various systems became less and less significant. 432
Ultimately they all served to reduce the spread of fire from floor to floor and protected the iron beams from heat using concrete or tiles, often incorporating an air gap to achieve improved insulation. Among the many systems

433

434

devised were the antecedents of modern reinforced concrete, a composite material in which the steel and concrete perform distinct roles, carrying, respectively, tension and compression forces.

One system of fireproof construction used around this time, especially in New York, was extremely versatile, and, adapted from its vernacular European origins, produced a number of remarkable vaults, domes, and staircases that seem to stand as if supported by invisible wires. Known in Spain as *bóvedas tabicadas* (timbrel vaults) or *bóvedas catalanas* (Catalan vaults), they consist of tiles, around 300 x 150 mm, that are erected to form a vault or a dome without the use of centering during construction. The idea was brought to the United States in the 1880s by the Catalan architect Rafael
433, 434 Guastavino (1842–1908). Timbrel vaults had been used since the middle ages in many countries that bordered the Mediterranean Sea, and it is possible that this type of vault construction was known in Roman times, for there are similarities with tile vaults described by Vitruvius.

The shape of the finished vault is first defined in space using a method suited to its size and geometry—a template made of wood, an iron rod bent to the desired shape, or even a taut string, as used by bricklayers. The vault is then built up from the sides as a single layer of tiles, by sticking new tiles in place along the edges of the tiles already in position. This gravity defying trick is achieved by using a fast-setting gypsum cement that hardens in ten to twenty seconds. Once in place, the single-thickness vault, which might span from 2 to 3 meters up to 15 meters, serves as the support for two further layers of tiles bonded with a conventional high-strength and slower-setting cement mortar. Guastavino's commercial genius was to adapt the timbrel vault from its vernacular origins for use in high-rise iron and steel frame buildings. Not only did he use it for its structural

433 Timbrel vault, Municipal Building, New York, c. 1907–14. Engineer: Guastavino Fireproof Construction Company; architects: McKim, Mead & White. 434 Timbrel staircase in Southern Tower, St. Paul's Chapel, Columbia University, New York, 1904–07. Engineers: Guastavino Fireproof Construction Company; consulting engineer: Nelson Goodyear; architect: Howells and Stokes.

advantages, but also marketed it successfully as a fireproof form of construction and exploited its architectural qualities as well.

With so many patentees claiming to have invented fireproof materials and construction methods, the authorities in several countries, including Germany and Austria from the mid-1880s on and the United States starting in about 1890, began undertaking fire tests to investigate the claims. Tests were also developed by other interested parties, including insurance companies, the manufacturers of fire protection equipment such as sprinklers, and the manufacturers of electrical equipment, which was so often the cause of fires in the early days of electricity. Trade associations and professional institutions were founded in most countries to serve the interests of the various stakeholders and to encourage better knowledge and understanding of fires and how to limit their damage. In the United States, the Associated Factory Mutual Insurance Companies carried out tests in Boston, beginning in 1890, on fire protection devices. The New York Building department began testing the fire resistance of fireproof floors in 1896, the same year that the National Fire Protection Association was formed. By 1903 Underwriters Laboratories, one of many commercial testing facilities, was testing construction systems, building materials, electrical products, and fire protection equipment. Engineers employed by Underwriters Laboratories also set up what was probably the first course in fire engineering—at Chicago's Armour Institute of Technology, now the Illinois Institute of Technology.

In Britain the efforts of one man, Edwin O. Sachs (1870–1919), were especially significant. Born in London of German parents, Sachs trained as an architect in Berlin and developed an interest, indeed a passion, for the improvement of fire safety in buildings. While in Berlin, and later in Vienna and Paris, he worked in the fire brigade to gain firsthand experience of the subject, and claimed to have attended over three thousand fires. When he returned to London, Sachs wrote a monumental book, *Modern Opera Houses and Theatres* (1896–98).[1] As an architect he worked on the improvement of both Drury Lane Theatre (1898) and the Royal Opera House (1899–1901) in Covent Garden, London. At a time when theater fires were still common, he was ideally placed to understand the issues involved. He founded the British Fire Prevention Committee (BFPC) in 1897, which commissioned fire tests on construction elements and materials; he also established Europe's first fire-testing laboratory, in the garden of a house in London.

In 1903 Sachs and the BFPC organized the First International Fire Prevention Congress, where delegates heard reports from many countries, including an account of the fire-testing procedures developed by the Royal Technical Research Laboratory in Charlottenberg, Berlin. The congress adopted the BFPC's proposed Universal Standards of Fire Resistance, which distinguished between temporary, partial, and full protection: resistance against a fierce fire for at least 15, 90, and 150 minutes, respectively. Delegates at the congress also agreed to outlaw the use of the term "fireproof," recommending instead the term "fire-resisting." As the BFPC's aim was to encourage the prevention of fire by all possible means, it is not surprising that Sachs should have been an early advocate of concrete construction. In 1906 he established, published, edited, and even, for a while, funded the journal *Concrete and Constructional Engineering*, which for sixty years covered developments and new construction in concrete. Sachs was also a major force behind the founding of the Concrete Institute in 1908; in 1923 the Concrete Institute became the Institution of Structural Engineers.

Building Higher . . . and Higher

The development of what we now call the "structural frame," which is the basis of all modern multistory buildings, reached its final stages in the early 1880s in New York and Chicago after a decade of intense construction. The circumstances that led to this period of remarkable innovation by both architects and engineers were rooted in the economic climates of the two cities. In New York the local economy revived rapidly after the enforced restraint during the Civil War (1861–65), and there was soon a demand for buildings of every type, but especially new commercial and office buildings. In Chicago, although the economic revival was slower, the demand for new buildings became a matter of urgency after the terrible fire that swept through the central part of the city in 1871, destroying 18,000 buildings and leaving over 100,000 people homeless.

In the 1860s buildings were generally constructed in American cities as they were in Europe. Small buildings were made of masonry, with timber joists and floors; larger ones had load-bearing exterior masonry walls and interior columns of cast iron. The beams were of timber or cast iron, supporting masonry jack arches or timber floors. The huge demand for new building following both the Civil War and the Chicago fire, however, created enormous pressure to build more cheaply and more rapidly than traditional masonry construction allowed. This coincided with the pressure to generate higher financial returns on the capital investment in building, which meant improving the net-to-gross ratio (i.e., increasing the usable floor area for a given building footprint). This was achieved both by reducing the proportion of the building plan taken up by load-bearing masonry walls and, in those days before electric lighting, by increasing the depth to which daylight penetrated inside the building. The latter was done by using light wells, increasing story heights, and increasing the amount of glazing in the external envelope.

The Chicago fire renewed the drive to develop more effective fireproof construction. The load-bearing cast iron facades first made popular by Badger and Bogardus in the early 1850s showed the way forward. Although these had been built mainly to prevent the spread of fire from building to building, they had other advantages. They could be erected quickly, and, because iron is stronger than masonry, larger windows could penetrate the facade. Cast iron was expensive, however, and facades not on public display were still of masonry construction. Even buildings with cast iron facades generally still had timber floor beams and floors. During the late 1860s and the 1870s building designers, driven by developers keen to maximize the returns on their investment, began to address all the disadvantages of the traditional construction methods.

One of the first buildings to benefit from a reappraisal of these methods was the Equitable Life Assurance building
435, 436 in New York, designed in 1867 and completed in 1870. After the scheme for the building had been chosen, the young project architect, George B. Post (1837–1913), who had trained as a civil engineer, set about redesigning the internal structure of the building following precepts more typical of multistory mill buildings than of architect-designed buildings in New York. His redesign was said to have halved the cost of the internal structure. Wherever possible, internal masonry walls were replaced by iron columns on a regular grid. The columns for the lower three stories were cast iron, of hollow, circular cross section; those for the upper four stories were of riveted, wrought iron H-section. The roof structure was also of wrought iron. The floors were constructed using wrought iron I-section beams and brick jack arches. Neither the iron columns nor the exposed lower flanges of the beams were protected against fire, however, and the Equitable building was damaged beyond use in a fire in 1912. The building also incorporated passenger lifts and featured an innovative ventilation system; rather than using fans powered by steam engines, which was usual at the time, the air was driven by passing it through a series of heated shafts that set up convection currents. Although the engineer who devised the ventilation system gained a great deal of publicity from its use in this building, Post doubted whether it had removed any foul air at all.

In one of his later buildings, the New York Produce 437, 438
Exchange (1881–84), George Post created an even more radical structural solution. The upper four stories of the ten-story building were supported by a massive transfer structure, creating a large column-free area for the first-story double-height trading floor. Wrought iron girders spanned 11 meters between the external masonry wall and the huge internal cast iron columns. The central area of the trading floor was lit by daylight through an iron and glass roof spanning more than 16 meters. Although radical in those respects, however, the Produce Exchange was conservative in a significant way: Its outer walls were of load-bearing masonry.

The inefficiency resulting from the large amount of floor area occupied by load-bearing masonry columns and walls was overcome in three steps. The first was to carry the internal floor loads on iron columns of a much smaller cross section, as demonstrated in a building typical of its time, the Coal and Iron Exchange in New York, designed
by Richard M. Hunt (1828–95) and completed around 439
1873. The large size of the masonry walls and columns can be seen in the basement and first few stories. In the fourth floor and above, some of the internal masonry columns are replaced by iron columns of much smaller sections. Another notable feature of this building is the use of inverted arches in the foundations to distribute

435

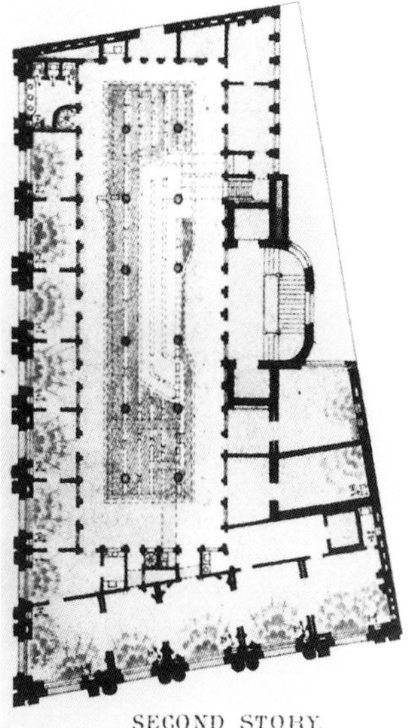

436

437

438

435 Equitable Life Assurance Society building, New York, 1868–70. Architect and engineer: George B. Post. 436 Equitable Life Assurance Society building. Plan of second floor. 437 Produce Exchange, New York, 1881–84. Architect and engineer: George B. Post. 438 Produce Exchange, New York. Building under construction.

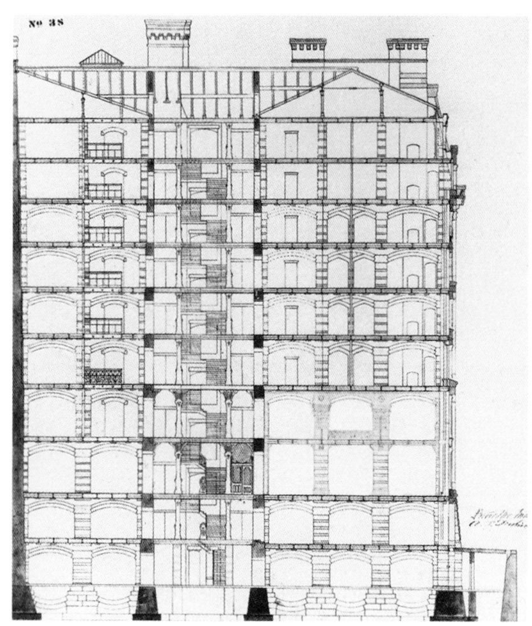

439

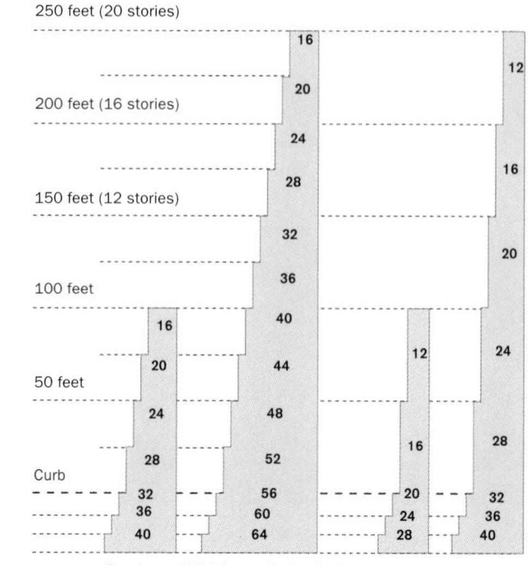

440

441

442

439 Coal and Iron Exchange, New York, c. 1873. Architect: Richard M. Hunt. Section showing thick load-bearing masonry walls and piers, and inverted arches in the foundations. 440 Diagram showing thickness of load-bearing walls (left) and curtain walls (right) required in the 1892 New York Building Code. 441 First Leiter Building, Chicago, 1878–79. Engineer and architect: William LeBaron Jenney. 442 Home Insurance Building, Chicago, 1883–85. Engineer and architect: William LeBaron Jenney.

the loads over a larger area of soil—a technique that, in turn, increased the height to which buildings could be constructed. In 1871, when this building was being designed, ten stories was unusually tall for a building in New York. The Coal and Iron Exchange building may have been the first in the U.S. to use inverted arches.

The second step toward replacing masonry construction was taken by William LeBaron Jenney (1832–1907) in
441 the First Leiter Building in Chicago (1878–79). He was the first engineer in the U.S. to place iron columns just inside the facade to carry the floor beams. While this followed the precedent set in many industrial workshops and, indeed, in the Crystal Palace, as discussed in the previous chapter, Jenney was the first to apply the idea to mainstream commercial office building. Since the masonry facade now had to carry only its own weight, it could be thinner, creating additional useful floor area in
440 the lower stories. This type of construction came later to be known as "cage construction," or the "cage frame."

Jenney had studied at the Lawrence Scientific School for about two years before enrolling in 1853 as an engineering student at the École Centrale des Arts et Manufactures in Paris, from which he graduated in 1856. After ten years as an engineer in the Union army, Major Jenney arrived in Chicago in 1867 and established his consulting office in the following year. Jenney's firm became a favorite of aspiring architects, including Louis Sullivan (1856–1924), William Holabird (1854–1923), and Daniel Burnham (1846–1912). His first major work was the seven-story Portland Building (1872) in Chicago, which had masonry walls and beams and internal columns of cast iron. His Lakeside Building (1873) also had masonry walls and internal columns of cast iron.

We can only assume that Jenney decided to use columns in the external facade as an extension of their use to replace internal walls. Daniel Badger, James Bogardus, and others had used cast iron in facades, though not as discrete columns. Bogardus had used an iron frame for his fire alarm and shot towers in the early 1850s, and one of Bogardus's engineers, George H. Johnson, worked in Chicago during the 1870s. Jenney would certainly have known London's Crystal Palace, and, while studying in France, he would have seen many buildings with wrought iron frames, including horticultural glass houses, railway stations, market buildings, and, more significantly perhaps, the warehouse at St. Ouen docks in Paris (1865). Finally, there was the wrought iron frame of Saulnier's chocolate factory on the outskirts of Paris, completed in 1872. Whatever Jenney's inspiration, his use of columns behind the external facade of the First Leiter Building had a dramatic effect on the architecture of Chicago. Suddenly here was an office building with almost an entire wall of glass windows. At the same time, the area of the ground plan occupied by masonry was reduced significantly. Building authorities were concerned about the use of both masonry and iron in the external facade because of the different degrees to which each material expands and contracts. In a fire, the inner iron structure might expand, pushing out the external shell, which could cause problems as the two elements moved relative to one another. Although this never became an issue with the Leiter Building, which was only seven stories high, Jenney did address the problem when designing the ten-
story Home Insurance Building, also in Chicago. 442

The Home Insurance Building, completed in 1885, was a landmark in the history of building construction. In it, Jenney took the third and final step in reducing the floor area occupied by masonry: Each story of the masonry facade was supported by beams at the floor level of that story. The maximum height of masonry was thus reduced to single-story height. Not only did this design, later called "skeleton-frame construction," greatly increase the usable floor space, it also avoided the problem of the different rates of expansion of iron and masonry. The building authorities, however, refused to allow Jenney to use iron columns in the party wall for fear of disturbing the neighboring building.

Another breakthrough was Jenney's use of rolled steel I-beams, manufactured by Carnegie Steel through the Bessemer process, instead of wrought iron above the sixth floor. This marked the first time in the U.S. building industry that permission was given to use Bessemer steel in building construction. The Home Insurance Building's iron-and-steel-frame structure weighed one-third that of an all masonry structure in a similarly designed building. This resulted in a huge saving in the cost of materials compared to traditional masonry construction. In addition, the foundations could be smaller, creating highly valuable basement space for the building services plant. Finally, Jenney's use of the skeleton frame meant that buildings could now be taller.

The introduction of the iron frame was accompanied by many developments that quickly came to characterize forms of building design and construction that are familiar to us today. One of the first tasks for the structural engineer was to calculate the loads carried by each column in the building, at each level—a calculation usually referred to as the "load takedown." The cumulative load at the foot of the columns gave the loads that each footing or foundation would have to carry, and the calculation
443 was entered on the "column sheet."

Now that the envelope of the building was non-load-bearing, entirely new methods had to be devised for supporting the windows and other elements of the facade. Because developers still wanted these buildings to have the appearance of masonry, the design of the facade involved much intricate detailing, in striking contrast to the
444, 446 simplicity of the structural frame. Using iron framing rather than load-bearing partition walls to support the floors also led to simplified building plans and a rationalized approach to the distribution of services throughout the building. The stairs, elevators, and risers that carried the services vertically through the building were clustered together to simplify construction and rationalize the layout of offices. The horizontal distribution of electricity and gas for lighting, and air for ventilation, was usually located above the ceilings in corridors that required less
445, 447 headroom than the offices themselves.

The foundations for tall buildings was an issue of particular significance in Chicago: beneath the city was a layer of highly compressible clay, 15 meters deep, that severely limited the loads that could be placed on conventional masonry foundations. As the eminent geotechnics scientist Ralph Peck wrote:

> *The history of building foundations in Chicago between the year of the great fire and 1915 epitomizes the development of foundation engineering throughout the world. Within less than half a century, and within the confines of the small area known as the Loop, the art of constructing building foundations grew to maturity by a process of trial, error and correction. Seldom in any field of engineering has so much experience been concentrated in so little time and space.*[2]

The engineer who took the first step in this crucial branch of building engineering was John Wellborn Root (1850–91), better known perhaps as one half of the firm Burnham and Root. Born in Lumpkin, Georgia, Root was sent to Liverpool, England, at the age of fourteen when his home town was occupied during the Civil War; in England his studies included both music and architecture. He returned after two years and studied civil engineering at New York University, graduating in 1869 at the age of nineteen. Root met Daniel Burnham during his first job as a draftsman, and they formed their partnership in 1873. The two complemented one another well: Burnham was the organizer and the businessman—the "impresario," as Frank Lloyd Wright called him—and Root was the technician and designer, who, despite a reputation for laziness and distraction from his active musical and theatrical life, did manage to get the work done on time.

Root recognized the importance of technical and engineering issues to the design of the increasingly large buildings of 1880s Chicago. With his engineer's mindset, he did much to formalize and articulate the highly organized approach that the new types of building demanded. This, he felt, characterized a uniquely American approach to architecture and building, an approach that was then establishing itself as distinct from the European tradition. He summarized the technical process of design as a nine-part set of goals:

1. *The design should provide the largest floor area and most spacious building consistent with financial success;*
2. *The floor plan must provide maximum daylight for rooms; an L-shaped plan would usually achieve this;*
3. *Lifts should be located centrally, either side of an entrance hall;*
4. *The building services—heating and ventilation equipment, electrical equipment and distribution, gas or electric lighting—should be located to allow easy use, maintenance and alteration;*
5. *The height of each story should be standardized at the optimum—10 feet 6 inches (3.2 meters);*
6. *Walls should contain as many openings as are consistent with their structural function;*
7. *The structural steel frame and fireproofing of the columns and beams should reflect not only the loads they need to carry, but also the soil conditions beneath;*

—	—	Sec.	4-	Sec.	9-12-21 10-19-22 11-20-23
			Lbs.		Lbs.
Attic	Roof		10,500		10,230
	Column and casing		1,500		..
	Tanks		..		
	Elevators . . .	183	18,000	186	
	Total . . .		30,000		10,230
18	Floor		11,780		17,670
	Column and casing		2,440		..
	Cornice, &c. . .		78,750		30,000
	Tanks	124	..		1,700
	Total . . .		122,970		59,600
17	Floor		15,500		23,250
	Column and casing		2,440		8,230
	Spandrel . . .		21,580		13,050
	Total . . .		162,490		104,130
	Floor		15,500		23,250
2	Spandrel-mullion .		9,950		12,240
	Total . . .		711,090		694,530
1	Floor		14,260		21,390
	Column and casing		2,840		12,000
	Spandrel-mullion .		19,600	136	8,820
	Total . . .		747,790		736,740
Basement	Floor		16,120		24,180
	Column . . .		2,000		10,200
	Sidewalk . . .		..		10,660
	Party wall . . .	124	26,780		
	Total . . .		792,690		781,780
Footing	Live load (deduct)		34,100		51,150
	Footing . . .		758,590		730,630

443

444

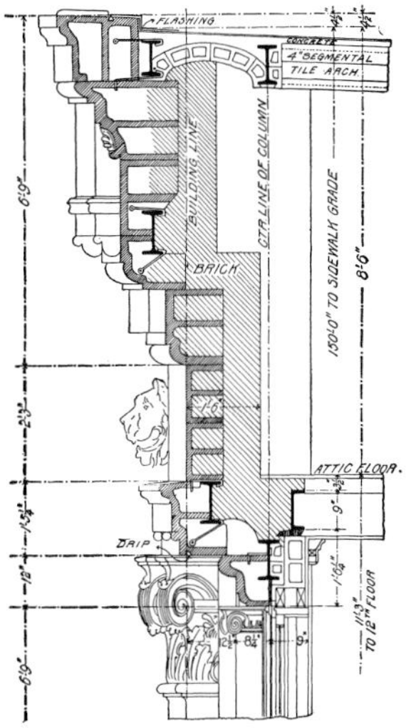

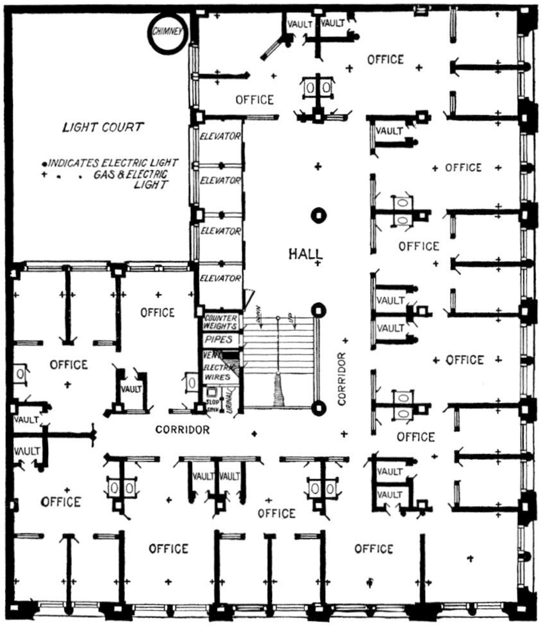

445

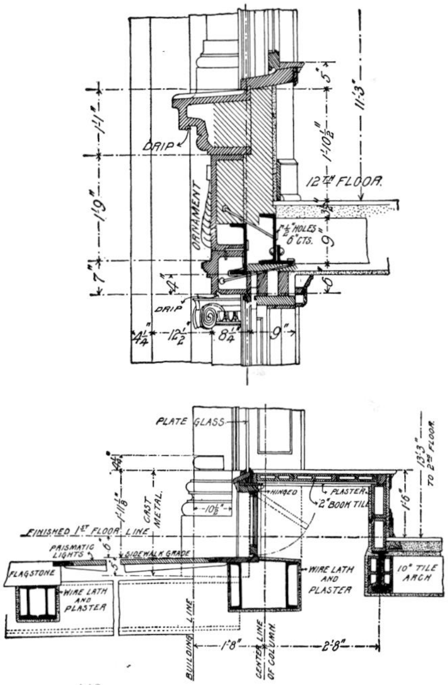

446

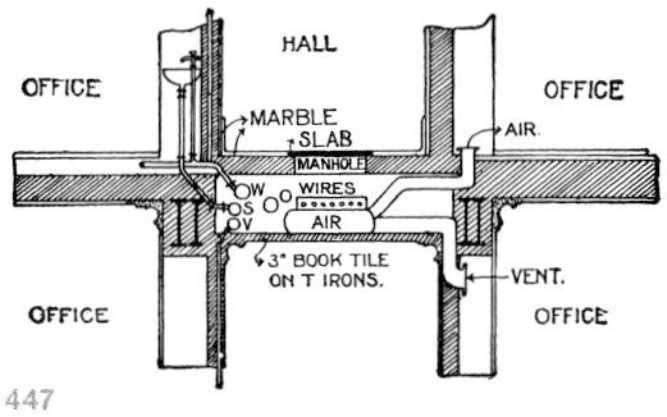

447

443 "Column sheet" for Fisher Building, Chicago, 1894–96. Architect: Charles Atwood. 444 Fort Dearborn Building, Chicago, 1893–95. Engineer and architect: Jenney & Mundie. 445 Fort Dearborn Building. Plan of typical office floor. 446 Fort Dearborn Building. Details of masonry facade fixed to the steel frame. 447 Fort Dearborn Building. Section showing services in ceiling void above corridor.

8 *In Chicago's notorious wet and sandy soil, foundations for walls or columns should be built on a grillage of steel rails embedded in concrete;*

9 *Construction of building should progress with equal speed over the whole area of foundations to avoid unequal settlement.*[3]

The idea that engineering goals should be central to the design process is now commonplace, but Root was the first to so clearly articulate that principle. Root was not saying that the architect had no role; he recognized that these matters would be entirely invisible to the public and even to the users of the buildings. Rather, the role of the architect would be different, and the architect had to respect the essential requirements of large, tall, steel-framed buildings. This, he felt, established a "new" architecture:

> *[B]earing in mind that our building is a business building, we must fully realise what this means. Bearing also in mind . . . that dust and soot are the main ingredients of our native air, we must realise what this means. Both point the same way. Every material used to enclose the structure we have rise must be, first, of the most enduring kind and, second, it must be wrought into the simplest forms.*
>
> *These buildings, standing in the midst of hurrying, busy thousands of men, may not appeal to them through more subtle means of architectural expression. . . . In them should be carried out the ideas of modern life—simplicity, stability, breadth, dignity. To lavish upon them profusion of delicate ornament is worse than useless, for this would better be preserved for the place and hour of contemplation and repose. Rather should they by their mass and proportion convey in some large elemental sense an idea of the great, stable, conserving forces of modern civilisation.*
>
> *One result of methods such as I have indicated will be the resolution of our architectural designs into their essential elements. So vital has the underlying of these buildings become, that it must dictate absolutely the general departure of external forms; and so imperative are all the commercial and constructive demands, that all architectural detail employed in expressing them must become modified by them.*[4]

The Montauk Building (1881–82) in Chicago was the first of Burnham and Root's many commercial buildings designed and constructed following the new approach that Root had articulated. Financial, functional, and technical requirements were studied with equal intensity and embraced in the design to ensure that the building would be successful. Such a utilitarian approach to building design, and the role of building engineering, had of course been applied to earlier commercial buildings such as mills and warehouses, but never before had the engineer's central role and the need for engineers to embrace non-technical (financial and functional) issues been so strongly emphasized.

It should not be imagined, however, that Root's approach was of his own invention; it was developed in response to the rapidly growing market for speculative office buildings by property developers. By good fortune the client's initial instruction to Burnham and Root for the Montauk Building has survived. The developer, Peter Brooks, was a shipping entrepreneur from Boston seeking a profitable investment in Chicago's booming economy. The letter shows how quickly the property developer learned how to exploit the business potential in the new "skyscraper," as well as how little commercial briefs have changed since that time:

> *Enclosed are rough plans but sufficient to express my idea of the ground floor of a building for the lot on Monroe Street. The architect can improve on them or submit better, giving also an idea of cost. Let his preliminary plans be on a small scale and not expensive.*
>
> *I prefer to have a plain structure of face brick, eight storeys and also a basement. With flat roof to be as massive as the architect chooses and well braced with iron rods if needed. The building throughout is to be for use and not for ornament. Its beauty will be in its all-adaptation to its use.*
>
> *Windows as well as doors should be all worked in brick with as little stone and terra cotta to be introduced as possible consistent with not absolute plainness. No projections on the front (which catch dirt). The brick arch over the main entrance might be carried in several feet over the vestibule and inside steps to show in face brick and to convey the idea of strength. Indeed all the entries might be of face brick with red or black mortar (if as cheap as plaster) which would convey the idea of "fireproof" to the whole structure—a valuable idea in a building of eight storeys. The first floor entry ought to be of tile. For all the other entries there is no better and cheaper flooring probably than good face brick.*
>
> *Have a fire escape and a standpipe on the outside at*

448

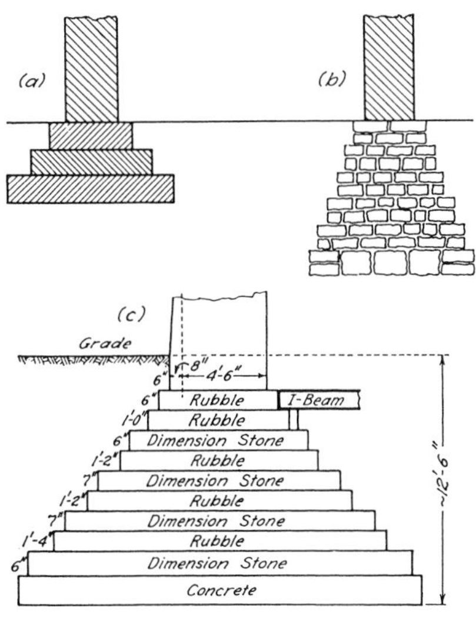

449

the southeast corner. Let the plastering in the rooms be directly on the interior brick walls wherever practical. The outer walls may require an intermediate air space between the footing and the walls and therefore furring off. Have a picture moulding all around the walls near the ceilings for picture hooks to avoid defacing with nails. At each floor let the space between the furring and the outer walls where the floor rafters rest be carefully filled with mortar and be made air tight to cut off the draft. This is important in case of fire. In case of a serious fire the draft up the elevator shaft would be violent and dangerous. There is space enough to have a brick wall on the east side of the shaft as well as on all the others if the architect thinks advisable; if simply a fire network, light would be obtained from it in the shaft, but if of brick there should be windows along the outer walls of the shaft for light. These would be inaccessible and hard to keep clean and repaired. Windows may possibly be introduced in the upper storeys on the west but must not be depended upon permanently for the adjoining building may be razed and a new one erected. Let the elevator car be as light as possible, with a seat that can be removed.

There should be fireplaces in each room for ventilation as well as heat, but if the Holley System [for hot air control] is introduced, giving ventilation, no doubt many fireplaces and chimneys can be dispensed with.

The less plumbing the less trouble. It should be concentrated as much as possible, all pipes to show and be accessible, including gas pipes. It might also be advisable to put in wire for future electric lights. It is not uncommon to do it in Boston now.[5]

448 Montauk Building, Chicago, 1881–82. Engineer: John Wellborn Root; architect: Daniel Burnham. 449 Foundation types for Chicago buildings before 1883. (a) Typical footing of "dimension stone"—rectangular blocks of hard limestone, with concrete mortar. (b) Rubble stone pier. (c) Section of a pier of Jenney's Home Insurance Building (1883–85).

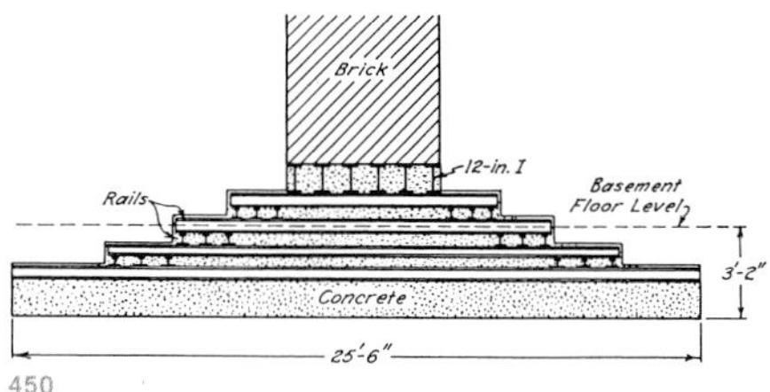

450

Burnham and Root's design was more elaborate than Brooks had indicated in his letter, and he remonstrated, insisting that unnecessary extravagances be removed. The client did approve of two features of the design. Locating all the building services into a single riser meant that more of the floor space was available for letting to tenants. Also, by lowering the ground floor below street level and squeezing each story to the minimum possible height, ten stories were provided, rather than the proposed eight; this meant, of course, more lettable floor area. The latter approach did backfire, however, because the basement headroom was too low for the elevator machinery and boilers, which had to be accommodated in an annex at the rear of the main building; further, the elevators started at the first-floor level, forcing users to climb a flight of stairs to reach them.

The structure of the building was of "fireproof" construction, consisting of hollow cast iron columns and wrought iron floor beams, both protected from fire by an envelope of ceramic tiles. The floors spanning the wrought iron beams were flat arches made from hollow ceramic blocks, or voussoirs. The internal partition walls of brick proved to be the building's undoing. They could not be easily moved or adapted to create different arrangements of rooms and corridors, and this inflexibility led to the building's premature replacement in 1902.

The Montauk Building's greatest innovation was its foundations. As buildings increased in height and weight, their loads needed to be spread over a greater area of the comparably weak soil underlying Chicago; this was accomplished by increasing the area of the foundations. In the Loop district of central Chicago, the ground consists of a number of layers. The top few meters are of sandy silt covered with a variety of fill materials imported during the development of the first settlements in Chicago. These layers are augmented by considerable quantities of rubble that remained after the fire of 1871. Beneath these are a layer of clay, which is hard and stiff enough to build upon as long as the loads are spread sufficiently to prevent a column or wall from penetrating this crust, which covers a very soft clay beneath.

Traditional footings for walls and columns, in Chicago and elsewhere, were of rubble, and typically deeper than they were wide. The depth could be reduced by making the 449
footings of dressed stone. However, in a ten-story building such as the Home Insurance Building, the footings needed to be over 4 meters square and nearly 3 meters deep—the full height of the basement. They weighed as much as an entire story of the building, and occupied much valuable space in the basement. In the case of the Montauk Building, it was found that the traditional footings would seriously obstruct not only the basement but the ground floor. The client insisted that additional room must be made to house the dynamos for generating electricity in the building. Root's response was to propose buying secondhand steel rails and laying them as a grillage to spread the loads over a large area without the need for massive stone footings. To prevent the steel from rusting, the bottom layer of rails was placed on a bed of concrete; the upper layers were encased in con- 450
crete. This solution proved to be both highly effective and very cheap, but Root initially saw it as a one-off solution, applicable only to the Montauk Building. Burnham and Root's next tall building had traditional masonry footings, and once again the lack of space in the basement made installing the plant and machinery very difficult. Only then did Root realize that the steel-rail and concrete grillage

450 Montauk Building, Chicago, 1881–82. Engineer: John Wellborn Root; architect: Daniel Burnham. Foundation. First use of a steel rail grillage and concrete footing, devised by Root.

could be of more general use. This idea alone enabled high-rise buildings to progress beyond the limit of about ten stories, and by 1892 heights had reached twice that number. The idea was taken up by Adler & Sullivan, Jenney, and Holabird & Roche, the firm of William Holabird and Martin Roche (1853–1927). In their Tacoma Building, Holabird and Roche further refined this idea by replacing the secondhand rails with I-beams of new steel. Steel grillage foundations became the preferred solution for all tall buildings in the Loop district of Chicago until the introduction of deep-pile foundations and caissons, after about 1890, and reinforced concrete foundations, after about 1905.

The thirteen-story Tacoma Building, designed in 1886 and completed in 1889, was interesting for a number of other reasons. The structural frame was the first to be assembled on site using rivets rather than bolts. It was also one of the first to incorporate an internal shear wall as the means of carrying wind loads down through the building to the foundations. Two parallel internal brick walls, supplemented by diagonal cross bracing, extended from the roof down to the foundations. Also, for the first time in a large building, all the toilet facilities were concentrated in a small area of each floor to reduce the quantity of piping needed and to enable it all to be conducted within a single shaft, or "services core," as it would now be called.

In 1894 Holabird and Roche found themselves working for the same developer who had commissioned the Montauk Building with Burnham and Root a decade earlier. Part of Brooks's briefing to the designers contained the following guidance, which indicates how his thinking, and indeed the thinking about commercial buildings as a whole, had moved on in ten years:

1 *The office building that gives up the most for light and air is the best investment;*

2 *second-class space costs as much to build as first-class space. Therefore, build no second-class space;*

3 *the parts every person entering sees must make the lasting impression, entrance, first storey lobby, elevator cabs, elevator service, public corridors, toilet rooms must be very good;*

4 *generally, office space should be about 24 feet from good light;*

5 *operating expenses must be constantly born in mind. Use proper materials and details to simplify the work;*

6 *carefully consider and provide for changes in location of corridor doors, toilet partitions, light, plumbing and telephones;*

7 *arrange typical layout for intensive use. A large number of small tenants is more desirable than large space for large tenants because:*
a higher rate per square foot can be added for small tenants
they do not move in a body and leave the building with a large vacant space when hard times hit
they do not swamp your elevators by coming and going by the clock;

8 *upkeep of an office building is most important. Janitor service must be of high quality, elevator operators of good personality, management progressive.*

With the exception of the advice about elevator operators, these guidelines are still applicable today.[6]

As more and more large buildings were constructed during the 1870s, a new attitude to building design developed. Individual designers as well as architecture and engineering firms gained the confidence, step by step, to take on increasingly complex challenges. This was no better illustrated than in the Auditorium Building designed by Adler & Sullivan at the end of the 1880s. The complexity of the building structure and the building services, not to mention the highly loaded foundations, would have made the project almost inconceivable only a few years earlier. That it was undertaken and completed is a measure of the degree to which engineering design and construction skills had progressed over the preceding decade. The firm that undertook this remarkable project was one of the most influential in American architectural history.

By the 1880s, most Chicago architectural firms had at least one partner with an engineering background. In Adler & Sullivan, formed in 1881, that partner was Dankmar Adler (1844–1900). Adler was born in Germany and emigrated to Detroit at the age of ten. His apprenticeship as a draftsman in an architect's offices was cut short by the Civil War: Adler enlisted in the Union army in 1862, where he trained as an engineer. On leaving the army in 1866 he began work in an architectural practice in Chicago. During the next decade he formed two partnerships with architects before establishing his own firm in 1878. His first independent commission was the Central Music Hall, completed in 1879. Constructed using masonry walls, with internal columns of cast iron and beams and floor girders of wrought iron, the Central Music Hall was not especially advanced for its time. It was noteworthy, however, for the complex arrangement of interior spaces within the unique, multifunctional building comprising seventy offices and half a dozen shops that surrounded the music theater itself. Devising a suitable structural system called for great imagination to ensure a safe and effective load-carrying path down to the foundations through a minimum number of columns and masonry walls.

The Central Music Hall became especially famous for its excellent acoustics, and established Adler as a leading acoustics engineer of his day. His skill in this field was not based on a knowledge of the science of acoustics, which had not yet begun to influence the design of buildings, but rather on his observations of other auditoriums, combined with some good engineering common sense. The seating curved gently upward away from the stage, ensuring good sight lines as well as an uninterrupted path for the direct sound. The curved ceiling served to focus much of the indirect sound toward the audience. The plane ceiling was also broken by steel roof trusses over the auditorium, which were boxed in and plaster-coated as a means of fire protection; these projected down, creating baffles that broke up the indirect sound and prolonged its reverberation. It was the multidisciplinary experience Adler gained on this project that put him in a position to take on the Auditorium Building.

In 1879 Adler's firm recruited the twenty-three-year-old Louis Sullivan, who had trained as a draftsman in Jenney's office and studied at the École des Beaux-Arts in Paris. (Sullivan stayed there for only a year, finding it too academic and sterile, and lacking in practical construction detail.) Sullivan must have shown his talents quickly, for he was made a partner in 1880, and in 1881 the practice was renamed Adler & Sullivan.

Together Adler and Sullivan would go on to design over a hundred major buildings in Chicago. Early in their collaboration the firm was commissioned to design what would become known as the Auditorium Building (1887–89), giving them the opportunity to develop many of the ideas that Adler had realized in the Central Music Hall. This 451, 452
enormous structure, which occupied an entire block, 453, 454
comprised a 4,200-seat theater, a 10-story commercial office block, a 10-story hotel, and a tower with some 15 stories of high-rent office space. Planning the structure for the range of different spaces and load factors to be incorporated in this building was a major challenge. The great elliptical vault over the theater auditorium, for example, spanned 35.7 meters, and the six transverse trusses, each carrying about 110 tons, resembled railway bridges rather than building components. Predicting the deflection of the various structural elements stretched the analytical tools and calculation methods of the time to the limit. Much of the column and beam structure could be treated as statically determinate, and was thus relatively easy to design. However, the differential settling of the different sections of the building would be expected to introduce secondary stresses in structural members that might initially have been statically determinate. The vault would also have involved some static indeterminacy, and many large approximations would have had to be made to enable loads and deflections to be calculated. The sensitivity of the behavior of the actual structure to the size of these approximations must have been a constant source of anxiety, and such a structure would be a major challenge even today.

Above the elliptical vault of the Auditorium Building theater, hidden from the audience, was only a void, which contained some of the building services and the roof structure. In a later, similar project, the Schiller Building (1891–92), Adler went on to demonstrate his mastery of structural complexity by constructing ten stories of offices above the large theater auditorium, using huge transfer structures to support the columns in the office complex. To support a large load-bearing brick wall above the stage area, Adler used two pairs of enormous columns in voids on either side of the stage area to carry the weight of the wall down through eight stories to their own foundations; each column was a staggering 28 meters long.

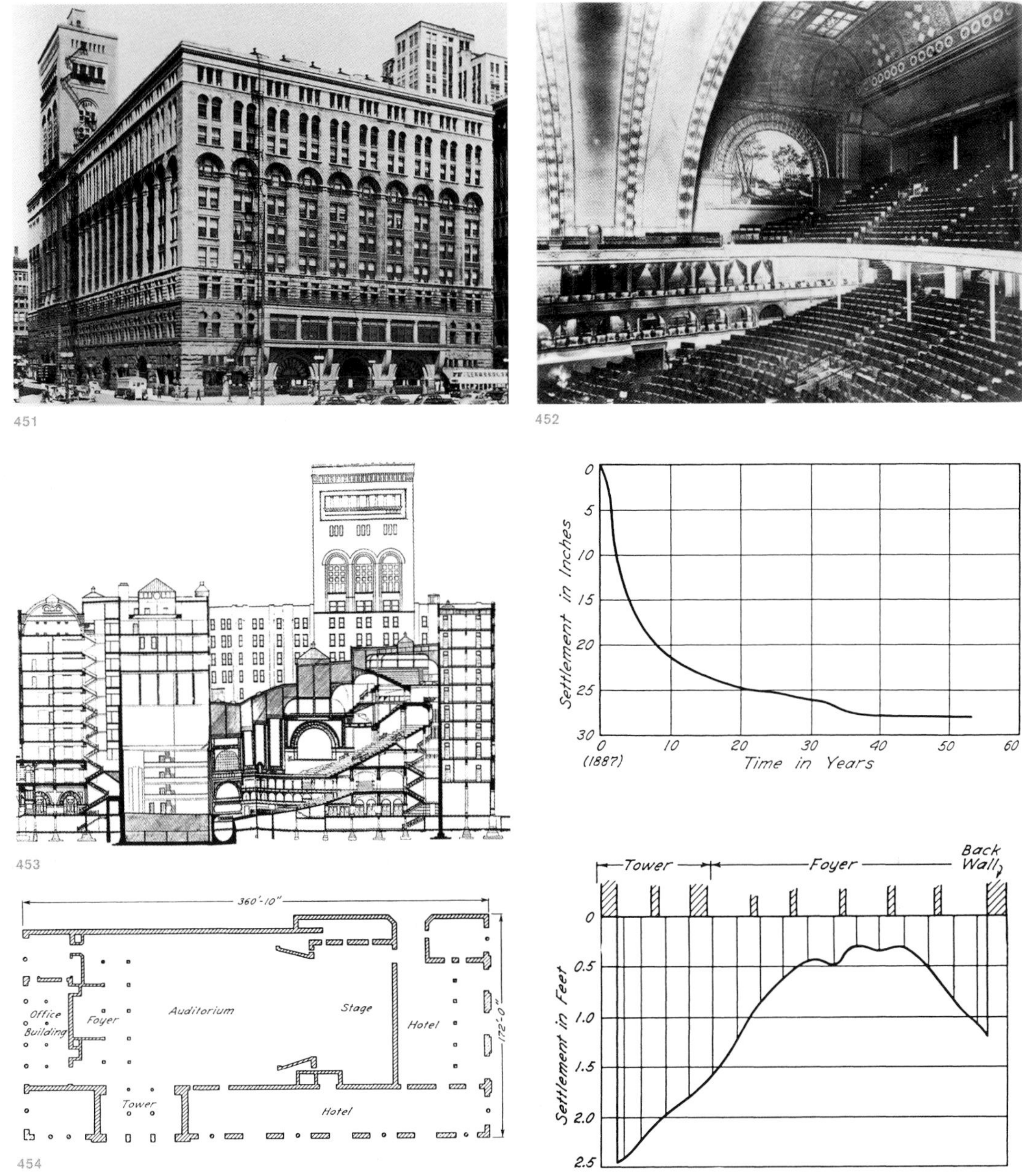

451 Auditorium Building, Chicago, 1887–89. Engineer: Dankmar Adler; architect: Louis Sullivan. 452 Auditorium Building. Interior of the auditorium. 453 Auditorium Building. Section. 454 Auditorium Building. Plan. 455 Graphs showing (top) settlement of foundations beneath the Auditorium Building tower, 1889–1940, and (bottom) differential settlement of foundations beneath the tower and foyer.

The foundations of the Auditorium Building presented particularly severe problems because of the large area of the site, the wide variation of the loads carried on each foundation, and the use of both discrete footings and continuous foundations beneath the load-bearing masonry walls that surrounded the theater auditorium. There was serious danger that the different foundations would settle at significantly different rates, which could lead to cracking of both nonstructural elements, such as windows and plastered partition walls, and the load-bearing masonry walls. At that time the prediction of foundation settlement was based on rather crude tests of the soil properties, and the effect of water on the behavior of soils under loads was not at all well understood. Beneath the theater and the 10-story parts of the building, Adler designed the structure and foundations to exert a uniform pressure on the soil of 4,000 pounds per square foot (190 kN/m^2); he predicted that this would result in a total settlement of the building under full load of 450 mm. Beneath the 19-story tower, however, he was not able to reduce the load on the soil to less than about 4,500 pounds per square foot (215 kN/m^2). To minimize the differential settlement between the tower and the rest of the building, he used a form of prestressing. Prior to the start of construction he loaded the soil where the tower would stand with kentledge of brick and pig iron equal to the weight of the building, to induce the predicted maximum settlement. Then, as construction proceeded, the kentledge was removed at the same rate as the weight of the building grew. To accommodate the inevitable difference in settlement that would likely occur, the water and waste pipes were fitted with flexible lead pipe connections.

Despite the care Adler took, there was indeed significant differential settlement across the site, and movement of the building was monitored carefully. Although no serious problems arose, by the 1940s, when it had reached its final equilibrium state, the settlement of the hotel foyer
455 floor varied from about 75 mm to nearly 750 mm in different areas.

The next quantum jump in the height of tall buildings in Chicago was made possible by the use of deep piles. These were driven by steam hammer through both the thin crust of clay near ground level and the layer of soft clay beneath until they reached harder clay, at a depth of 15 to 20 meters, that was able to bear the weight of the taller buildings. The first major building that rested entirely on piled foundations was Grand Central Station in Chicago, completed in 1890.

Wind Bracing

By the late 1880s buildings of twelve stories were common in both New York City and Chicago, and some were a few stories higher. Their external walls were still generally of load-bearing masonry, while the internal load-bearing structures comprised columns of cast or wrought iron and beams of wrought iron. Some of the internal walls might also be of load-bearing masonry, and there would be non-load-bearing internal partition walls of brick or concrete block. In essence, this was the same structural system used in the earliest five- or six-story mills and warehouses in eighteenth-century England. Wind loads impinging on the external masonry walls were conveyed horizontally through the floor structures to the end walls, where they could be carried down to the foundations. The external walls acted as shear walls. The sheer weight of the masonry and upper stories also served to prestress the walls in compression, which added to their stability, just as it had in medieval cathedrals. Two further characteristics of buildings in New York and Chicago were significant: Their location in city streets afforded some protection from extreme winds, and the heights of the buildings were not large compared to their widths—they were rarely taller than twice their width. All these factors together led engineers at the time to continue assuming that wind loads required no special consideration.

In the late 1880s a number of developments altered this picture as the introduction of the cage frame reduced the size and weight of the external masonry walls. Although the cage frame enabled the construction of taller buildings, it also separated the external wall from the main building structure, making it less practical to use external walls as shear walls. Additional dedicated structural elements would be needed. On the other hand, the columns of the cage frame were made of wrought iron, which meant they were able to carry bending loads imposed at rigid joints. This had not been possible with cast iron columns, which were designed to carry only compressive loads and to which girders or floor beams were seldom joined by a rigid connection. The cage frame, and the skeleton frame that followed it, allowed

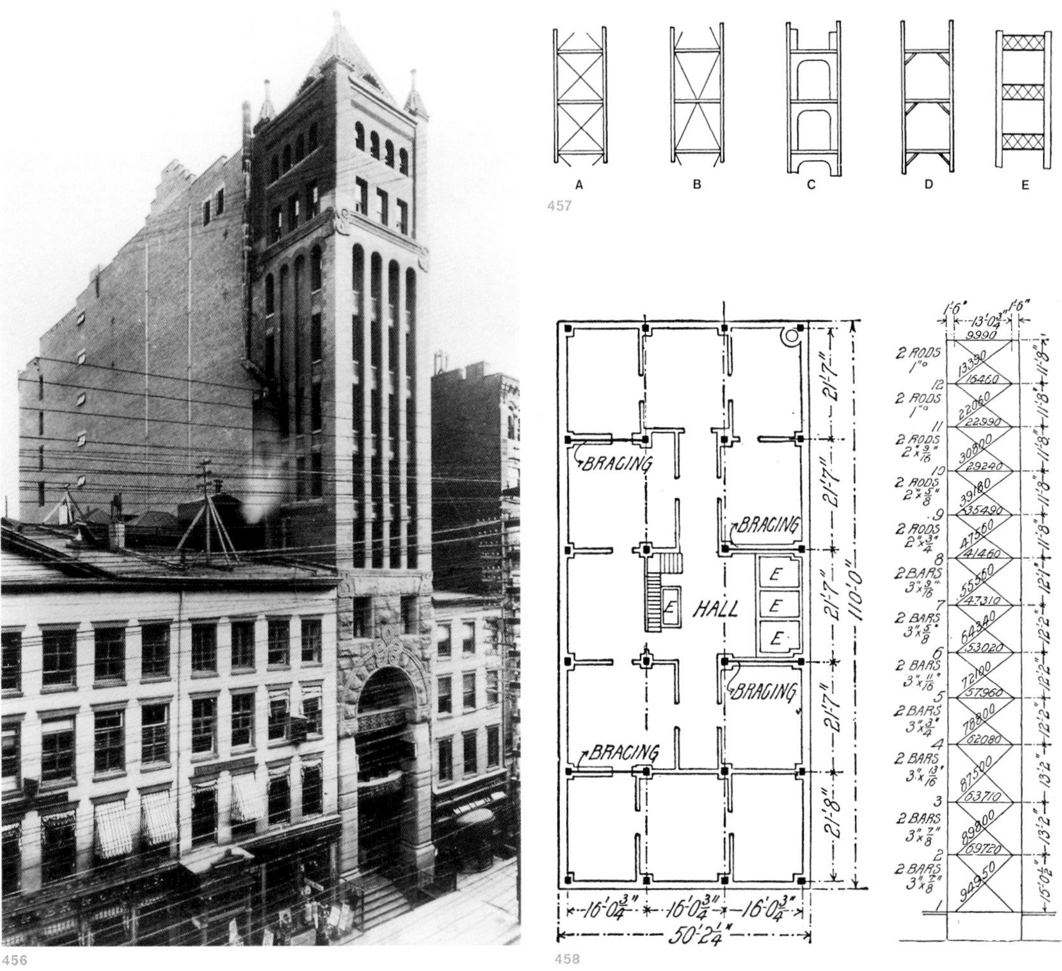

456 Tower Building, New York, 1888–89. Engineer: William Harvey Birkmire; architect: Bradford Lee Gilbert.
457 Techniques of wind bracing used in steel frame buildings in the U.S. from the 1890s: (A) and (B) cross bracing; (C), (D) and (E) frame or Vierendeel bracing. 458 Venetian Building, Chicago, 1890–92. Engineer: Corydon T. Purdy. Floor plan and section showing wind bracing.

459

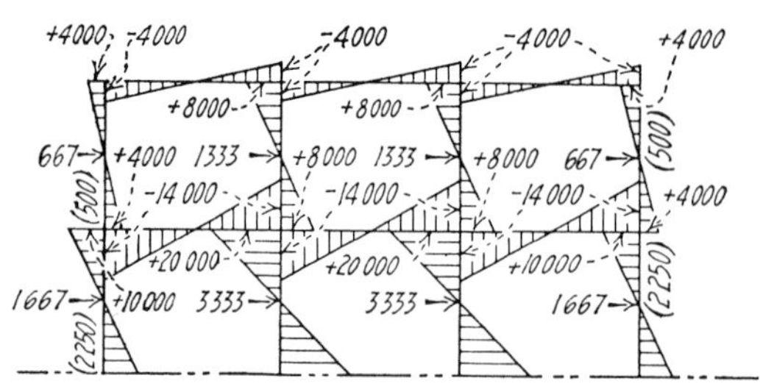

BENDING MOMENT DIAGRAMS FOR 6TH FLOOR AND ROOF

460

-88000 indicates bending moment in ft. lb.

(6000) indicates direct stress in lb.

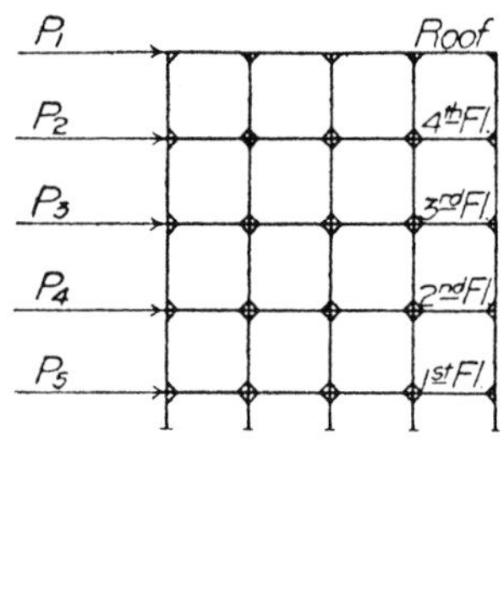

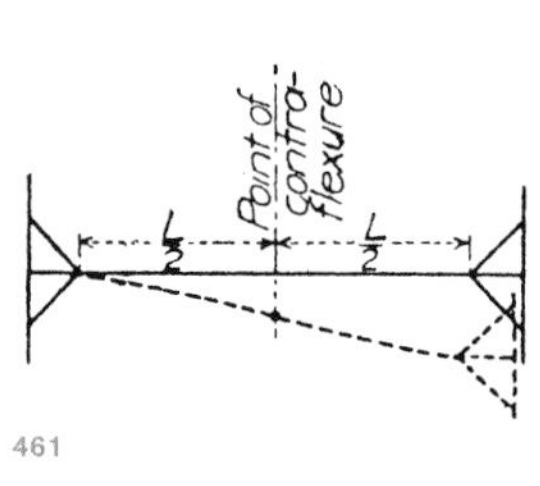

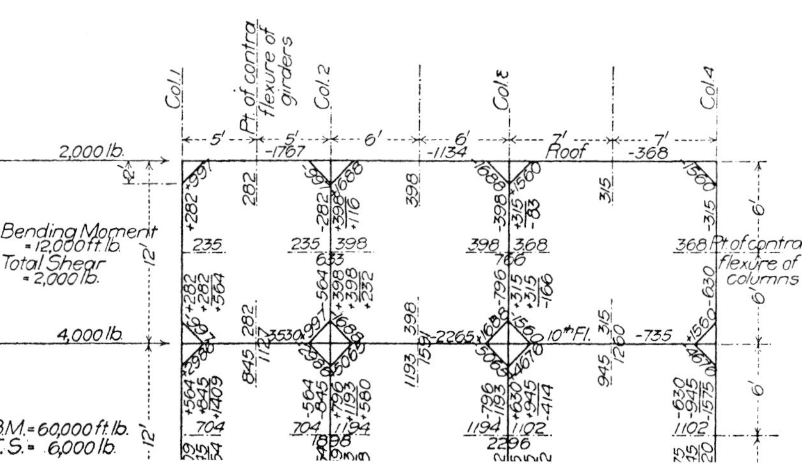

461

for the first time the structure of a tall building to be braced by using the rigidity of the connections between columns and beams. Such "frame" or "portal" action was not a new idea; it had been used in several British dockyard buildings, London's Crystal Palace, the boat store in Sheerness, England, and the warehouse at St. Ouen near Paris. But none of these were typical city buildings. The wrought iron cage frame also made it easier to incorporate diagonal bracing as an alternative, lightweight means of conducting the wind loads down to the foundations, as had been done at the Crystal Palace and Saulnier's Menier Chocolate Factory near Paris. Within a period of about two decades, from the late 1880s to around 1910, wind bracing was incorporated
457 into all new iron- and steel-framed tall buildings. Two forms of bracing were used, sometimes in combination—cross bracing, in which the wind loads are carried in tensile rods, and portal framing, in which the wind loads are conveyed down to the foundations by the rigid connections between beams and columns.

The earliest example of a tall building incorporating structural elements to carry wind loads was probably the
456 Tower Building in New York, completed in 1889. The very narrow footprint of the building and its exposed location on Broadway, in Lower Manhattan, were undoubtedly why engineer William Harvey Birkmire (1860–1924) felt that such elements were necessary. The inspiration for the diagonal bracing was the Warren truss, used widely in railway bridges, turned on end. When designing the wind bracing, Birkmire assumed that the building worked as a cantilever and was subject to loads caused by a wind of 70 miles per hour, the same wind factor used by engineers in designing bridges. However, as some engineers pointed out at the time, this structure, with single, alternating diagonals, was not ideal for wind bracing since the diagonals were far too slender to carry any compression loads. Thus, no matter what the direction of the wind, only half the diagonals, on alternate floors, would carry loads. The wind load path was not continuous from top to bottom of the building, a cardinal sin to structural engineers. That the building nevertheless stood for many years was no doubt due to the stability provided by the external and internal masonry walls and by the weight of the structure itself.

Soon many buildings incorporated cross bracing, and an important decision was where to locate it in the building plan. The most obvious location was in the walls around the stairs or elevator shafts, but often additional bracing was required elsewhere. The problem with cross bracing was that it restricted access through the building. Installing the bracing across two bays or two stories helped make space for doorways, as did reducing the proportion of the bay that the bracing spanned, as in the Venetian Building in Chicago (1890–92). 458

More rational wind bracing systems were first used in two sixteen-story buildings in Chicago designed during 1889—the Monadnock Building and the Manhattan Building, one using portal-frame bracing, the other diagonal cross bracing. Even though the Monadnock Building had a load-bearing masonry structure (the last of its kind in Chicago), its extreme height and slenderness led engineer John Wellborn Root to introduce a wind bracing 459
structure. The portal framing consisted of girders 325 mm deep riveted to the wrought iron columns. The structural calculations for portal bracing are more complex and less reliable than the calculations for diagonal bracing, since the former is not statically determinate. Indeed, satisfactory analytical methods to help designers of statically indeterminate frame structures—for example, the slope-deflection method—were developed only during the first decade of the twentieth century.

The wind bracing structure for the Manhattan Building (1889–91), designed by the engineer Louis E. Ritter, comprised both portal-frame bracing and crossed diagonal wrought iron rods fitted with turnbuckles. This light pre-tensioning ensured that the frame would carry tension loads, in even the lightest winds. Despite the expense incurred by using additional steel, many engineers employed portal bracing to create a fluid passageway throughout an entire building floor. Engineer Corydon T.

459 Monadnock Building, Chicago, 1889–91. Engineer: John Wellborn Root; architect: Burnham and Root. 460 Bending moment diagrams indicating how the steel frame carries wind loads by bending, used from c. 1913. 461 Diagrams showing calculation of bending moments in the members of a steel frame subject to wind loads, made possible by identifying the point of contraflexure at which the bending is zero, 1908.

THE EVOLUTION OF PROVIDING STABILITY TO THE STRUCTURAL FRAME 1790s-1910s

COLUMNS	BEAMS	BEAM / COLUMN CONNECTION	STABILITY / WIND BRACING	APPROXIMATE DATES / FIGURE NUMBERS
Single-story-height. Column rests on beam; no connection between columns.	Continuous timber beam spanning over 1–3 columns. Beam rests on column head / spreader.	Mechanical location only. Not rigid. Risk of column crushing the beam.	Loads conveyed in floor to perimeter masonry walls that provide overall lateral stability.	Up to c. 1810
Single-story height. Column rests on top of column beneath. Mechanical location; no rigid connection between columns.	Cast iron beam spanning more than one bay (rare). Beam rests on ledge on column head.	Mechanical location only. Not rigid.	As above	1795–1800
As above	Cast-iron beam spanning one bay. Beams rest on ledges either side of column head.	Mechanical location only. Not rigid.	As above	1790s–1860s Most U.K. textile mills
Wrought iron or (later) steel. 1- or 2-story-height units; made into continuous column with riveted splice joints in the plane of floor beams.	Wrought iron or steel.	Rivets locate beam on flange riveted to column. Negligible rigidity.	As above. Partition walls infilling some bays (bracing effect not calculated).	1870s
As above, with splice joints 0.3-0.6 meters above the plane of floor beams.	As above	As above. Easier to construct, because column splice above beam connections. Negligible rigidity.	As above	1880s
As above. In steel from 1880s. Individual lengths of column, usually 2-story. Alternate columns spliced on alternate floors.	As above. In steel from 1880s.	As above. Negligible rigidity.	As above, but deliberately to carry wind loads in taller buildings (10+ stories). Contribution not calculated.	1880s–c.1910
As above	As above	More substantial riveted connections. Some rigidity. Rigidity assumed to contribute to frame action; contribution not calculated.	As above	1880s
As above	As above	Built as a frame with fully rigid connections. Still calculated as continuous columns with single-span (pin-jointed) beams.	Cross-bracing (sway-bracing) in taller buildings. Capacity of cross bracing calculated.	From late 1880s
As above	As above	As above	Frame / portal action in taller buildings. Capacity of portal action estimated.	From mid 1890s
As above. Splices located near midstory height, where bending near zero.	As above	As above. Calculated as frame with fully rigid column-beam connections with pin joints at mid-height of columns and midspan of beams.	Cross bracing or portal bracing or both. Structural action calculated.	From 1910s

Purdy made striking use of this technology in the seventeen-story Old Colony Building in Chicago (1894).

In 1907, A.C. Wilson, a structural engineer from California, published a paper in *The Engineering Record* that presented a mechanism for accurately estimating portal action in steel-frame buildings. Wilson explained that when a frame is deflected by wind, each end of a beam and column is bent in opposite directions, while
461 the mid-point remains stable. As there is no curvature at the midway juncture, the beam could theoretically be replaced by a pin-joint or hinge (the pin-joint transfers only sheer or axial forces). This insight generated an entirely new mathematical model of a multi-bay frame structure. Rather than conceiving a steel frame as a series of beams and columns rigidly connected from end to end, the new statically determinate framework emerged as a series of cross-shaped members, rigid at the central axis, but pin-jointed at the four ends. This breakthrough enabled engineers to analyze the behavior of a multi-story/multi-bay portal-braced steel frame structure
460 under wind loading.

The Metropolitan Life Insurance Company Tower in New York (1907–09)—briefly the tallest building in the world at fifty floors—was one of the first buildings to integrate
462, 463 this new understanding of portal bracing. Up to the twelfth floor, the wind bracing consisted of deep girders with riveted connections to the columns; above the twelfth floor, where bending was less acute, bracing was provided by lightweight gusset plates and knee braces.

Engineering the Internal Environment

As people's expectations of comfort inside buildings grew during the nineteenth century, new means were devised for controlling the internal environment. The form these improvements took depended both on the type of building and its occupants and on the local climate. At the domestic level, in northern Europe, the primary need was for heating. Although standard fires and chimneys were still being installed in the late twentieth century, many experiments with alternative methods were successful. A luxurious house built near London in 1869 combined two of the very latest ideas: not only was it made entirely of concrete, it was also, as reported in *The Builder*, "heated by air, warmed by contact with earthenware, conducted mainly through flues formed in the body of the concrete walls and admitted by sliding valvular gratings in the skirtings of several rooms. Ventilation is provided for in every room by distinct flues, formed in the concrete, and entered by apertures near the ceiling."[7] 466

As discussed in the previous chapter, the heating and ventilation of large public buildings was well established by the 1850s, and the sizes of plant and equipment needed to provide them were calculated in rational if not fully scientific ways. In France and Germany, heating needs were calculated using heat-loss calculations, as they are today. In 1861 Eugène Péclet calculated the heat loss through double-glazed windows, which were widely used in the colder regions of continental Europe, and demonstrated that an air gap of greater than 20 millimeters did little to further reduce thermal transmittance. In Britain and the United States, Thomas Tredgold's method, based on air infiltration and the cooling effect of windows, continued to be used until the end of the nineteenth century (see chapter 6). A change was needed, in the United States at least, as the height of buildings began to increase significantly in the 1890s. In tall buildings the change of air pressure between the bottom and top of the building could not be ignored, and by around 1900, it was known that wind speeds could vary significantly with height; both of these factors affected air infiltration rates. Faced with such complications, many designers in the early twentieth century felt that precise air infiltration rates were unverifiable and simply assumed a constant infiltration rate, typically of two air changes in a room per hour. The British physicist Napier Shaw (1854–1945), the father of modern meteorology, made the first attempt to model the airflow throughout a building. He used the analogy of electricity flowing through an electric circuit, impeded by a number of resistances. This insight was well ahead of its time, however, and was largely ignored until the 1960s, when computers began to be used for the mathematical modeling of engineering systems.

During the mid- and late nineteenth century, buildings continued to rely on evaporative cooling: Air was passed through a water spray or, where it was available, over blocks of ice. A great step forward began in the 1870s with the development of refrigeration machines that

462

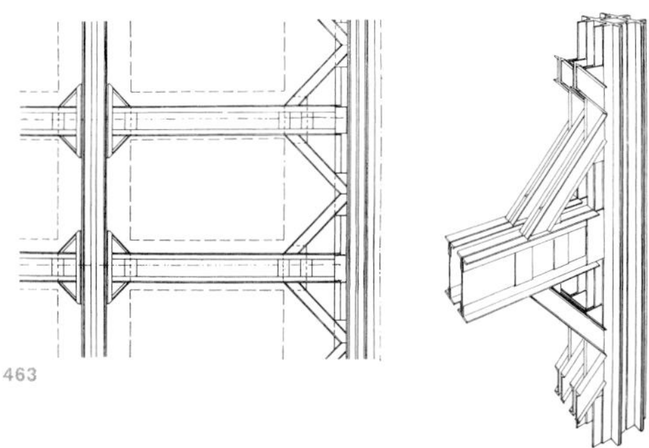

463

462 Metropolitan Life Tower, New York, 1907–09. Structural engineer: Purdy and Henderson; architect: Pierre LeBrun. 463 Metropolitan Life Tower. Knee bracing used to create rigid connections for carrying wind loads. 464 Werkbund exhibition pavilion, Cologne, Germany, 1914. Architects: Walter Gropius and Adolf Meyer. 465 Fagus shoe last factory, near Hildesheim, Germany, 1911–12. Architects: Walter Gropius and Adolf Meyer.

THE GLASS FACADE

The use of iron and steel in the external skin of buildings provided the opportunity to introduce larger windows and greater proportions of glazing in facades. Nevertheless, before toughened glass was available, safety issues prevented the use of large areas of glazing high above city streets. It was not long after the introduction of the skeleton frame, however, before architects began dreaming of the fully-glazed facade with no vertical load-bearing structure at all. The idea had been pioneered in the early nineteenth century in many glass and iron greenhouses in botanic gardens, exhibition buildings, and glazed roof structures, but even in these facades, the glazing was interrupted by supporting structural elements. Once the skeleton frame had been developed, so the external facade could be supported floor-by-floor. There was also the important matter of architectural style. The relatively conservative architects who designed hotels and office buildings for commercial clients, unwilling to take unnecessary risks, were not inclined to propose designs that deviated far from the appearance of conventional construction. It was the revolutionary architects of the Bauhaus movement in Germany who first conceived of full-story-height glazed facades, notably Walter Gropius and Adolf Meyer.

464

465

could manufacture "artificial" ice wherever it was needed (so-called to distinguish it from natural ice, which was harvested in North America and Norway and exported all over the world for cooling purposes).

The first successful refrigeration machines were developed by Carl von Linde (1842–1934), Professor of Mechanical Engineering at the Polytechnic School in Munich. He published his paper "The extraction of heat at low temperatures by mechanical means" in 1870, and followed it with "Improved ice and refrigerating machines" a year later. Within a few years his ideas had been noticed by the German and Austrian brewing firms, which were seeking ways to continue production of beer through the warm summer months. Linde was funded to develop new machinery based on his theoretical work, and he produced his first successful machine using methyl ether as the refrigerant in 1874. It was twice as efficient as other machines currently in use. In 1877 he constructed an even more efficient machine, with ammonia as the refrigerant, and it was installed in the Dreher Brewery in Trieste (now in Italy), where it continued in service for over a century. Linde began commercial production of his machines in 1879, and through export, and sale of manufacturing rights, they were soon being used to produce artificial ice throughout the world.

The availability of a constant supply of ice in any city meant that buildings in that city could now be designed to take advantage of cooling by ice, and the idea of "comfort cooling" began to take hold. In 1873 the French engineer A. Jouglet wrote perhaps the first treatise on comfort cooling, in which he described a number of methods of cooling air in ventilation systems. These included the use of ground pipes, as Charles Sylvester and William Strutt had used at Derbyshire General Infirmary in 1810 (see chapter 6, pp. 318–20); cooling by the evaporation of water; cooling by ice; the compression and reexpansion of
467 air; and the use of refrigeration machines.

The cooling of buildings by ice grew during the 1880s. Blocks of ice were placed on wooden racks so that incoming air passed over the ice as it was drawn into the ventilation ducts that supplied air to the building's interior. Such systems were able to chill air to perhaps 10 degrees Celsius below the outside air temperature, and their cooling capacity was quantified by specifying the quantity, in tons, of ice that had to be delivered to the building each day. In 1880, the Madison Square Theater in New York used 4 tons of ice each evening. The same system was used by the pioneering American heating and ventilation engineer Alfred Wolff (1859–1909) to cool the air for the
two auditoriums in Carnegie Hall, New York, in 1893. 468

The effectiveness of interior cooling systems was improved dramatically when refrigeration equipment was installed in the building itself. Designing such equipment demanded a scientific approach. Just as von Linde had applied the science of thermodynamics to devising an effective refrigeration system, so Hermann Rietschel (1847–1914) first applied thermodynamics principles to the heating and ventilation of buildings. Rietschel was the world's first Professor for Ventilation and Heating Engineering at the Royal Technical School at Charlottenburg in Berlin. In 1887 he founded his Prüfstelle für Heizungs- und Lüftungseinrichtungen (Testing Station for Heating and Ventilation Equipment), known today as the Hermann-Rietschel-Institut for
Heating and Ventilation Technology. In 1893 he published 470
his *Leitfaden zum Berechnung und Entwerfen von Lüftungs- und Heizungs-Anlagen* (Manual for the Calculation and Design of Ventilating and Heating Installations), which was quickly circulated around the world, which has gone through many editions in German, and is still in print today.

The pioneering European methods of comfort-cooling buildings quickly became known in the United States, both through dissemination of the printed manuals and, more directly, through contact with European engineers who immigrated to the U.S. as well as Americans who visited Europe and saw the systems in use. Alfred Wolff, who had designed the heating and ventilation system for Carnegie Hall, was among the first to adopt the scientific approach to design as elaborated in Rietschel's manual. He designed systems for the Cornell Medical College in Ithaca, New York, in 1899 and the Hanover National Bank in New York in 1903. His most impressive achievement, however, was the cooling system he designed in
1901 for the New York Stock Exchange, which comprised 469
what is today called a combined heat and power system of cogeneration. This was the first system that also controlled the humidity of the air in the ventilation system. Writing to the architect of the building, Wolff said that on

466

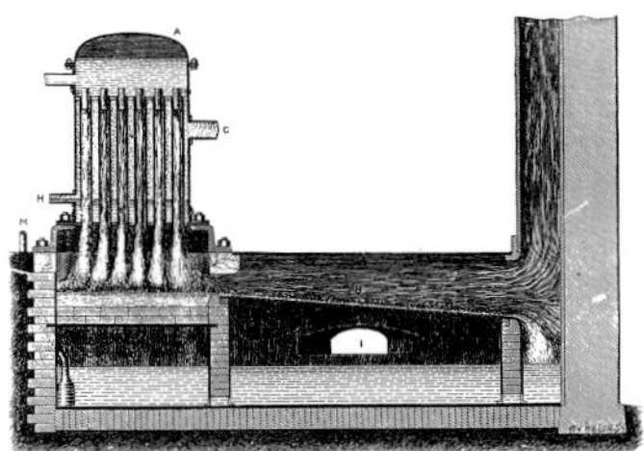
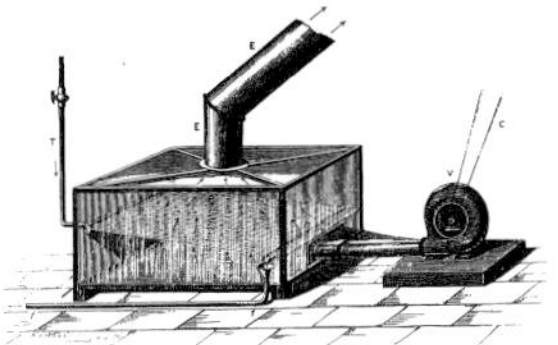
467

a day when the external temperature and humidity were 85°F and 85 percent, respectively, his system would reduce them to about 75°F and 55 percent, respectively.[8] Wolff felt that the reduction in humidity was of greater benefit to the users of the room than the reduction in temperature. The system he designed, which was the forerunner of modern air-conditioning, was intended to provide a specific performance in terms of temperature, humidity, and ventilation, and incorporated a control system to ensure those goals were achieved. Three 150-ton ammonia-absorption chillers were powered by the exhaust steam from the steam engines that drove the building's electrical generators. The waste water from the condensers (today called gray water) was recycled, stored in tanks on the roof, and used to flush the toilets. The system operated successfully for twenty years. However, Alfred Wolff was a consulting engineer and hence did only the work he was commissioned to do; his groundbreaking achievement at the New York Stock Exchange did little to change the attitudes of architects and building owners toward the idea of comfort cooling.

As with many developments in building engineering, the earliest applications of air-conditioning were in a commercial or industrial context, where the financial benefits of the new technology were most obvious and the return on investment sufficiently quick. The use of humidity control and air-conditioning systems in public buildings began slowly. One of the first uses was in a theater in Cologne, Germany, which opened in 1903. A brine-to-air heat exchanger using an ammonia-based refrigeration system cooled and dehumidified the incoming air in summer. The air was fed into the theater at ceiling level and removed through multiple openings in the floor. By the end of the decade a number of theaters in the United States had also installed humidity and temperature control. They were not, however, always successful because the temperature of the water in the air washer was often not adjusted in response to changes in the temperature and relative humidity of the ambient air.

The ability to predict the changes in heating levels and the quantity of water to be added or removed to achieve a desired air temperature and humidity required a good understanding of thermodynamics, which few engineers at the time had. The humidity of air cannot be measured directly. It has to be calculated from the temperatures recorded by two thermometers; one of these is

466 Fenlands Villa, Chertsey, England, 1869. A concrete house heated by warm air distributed through ducts cast into the walls. 467 Evaporative air cooler and air washer, 1873.

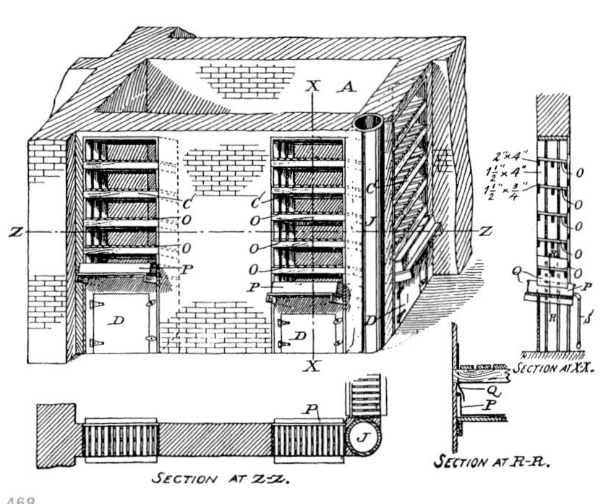

468

469

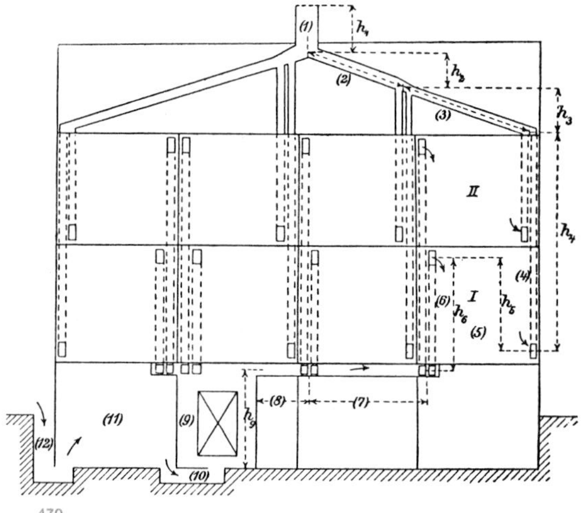

470

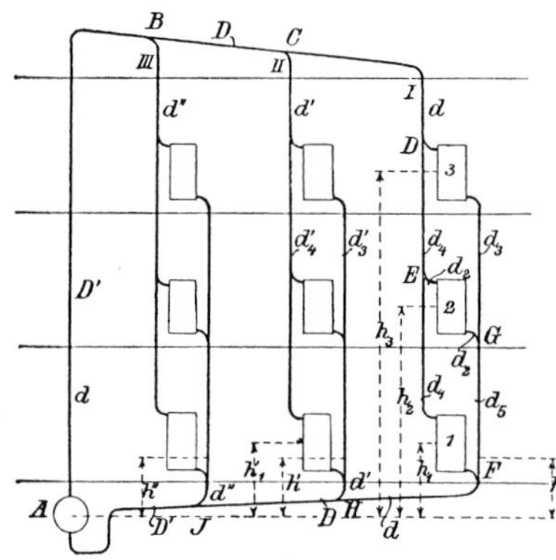

468 Ice racks in the air intake used for summer cooling at Carnegie Hall, New York, 1893. Heating and ventilation engineer: Alfred Wolff. 469 Cooling system for the New York Stock Exchange, New York, 1901–03. Heating and ventilation engineer: Alfred Wolff. 470 Diagrams illustrating the calculation of ventilation and heating systems by Hermann Rietschel, 1893.

uncovered (dry), and the other is covered with wet cloth and so is cooled as the water evaporates. A practical design method was first devised by Richard Mollier (1863–1935), an applied physicist who worked on the thermodynamics of heat and refrigeration engines in Munich, Göttingen, and finally at the University of Dresden in Germany. Mollier's most notable achievement, in the early 1890s, was inventing the theoretical concept of "Wärmeinhalt" (heat content or enthalpy) as a measure of the total energy contained in a thermodynamic fluid—for example, the steam in a steam engine, gases in an internal combustion engine, or the refrigerant in a refrigerator or chiller. In the field of thermodynamics this was as significant as the invention of the concepts of temperature, heat capacity, and latent heat had been in the seventeenth century. Using the general concept of enthalpy, Mollier was able to calculate all the properties of fluids as they passed through any thermodynamic process—heating or cooling, compression or expansion, humidification or dehumidification. In about 1892 he began using equations governing the properties of water vapor in air to create diagrams or charts that showed, graphically, the relationships among temperature, pressure, and enthalpy in different thermodynamic systems. In 1894 he produced charts for carbon dioxide as a refrigerant, and, in 1904, a complete set of diagrams for all the most common materials. Mollier diagrams were quickly adopted by engineers the world over.

For the particular case of air-conditioning, a Mollier diagram allowed the designer to trace the thermodynamic path followed by air that is humidified and heated or cooled as it passes through a conditioning system and delivered at the desired temperature and humidity. The diagram on p. 413 shows the relationships between dry-bulb temperature, wet-bulb air temperature, and relative humidity, and the heat content, or enthalpy, of the air-wa-
471 ter vapor mixture. In the English-speaking world most engineers now use an alternative way of presenting the same data, the "psychrometric chart," devised by the American engineer Willis Haviland Carrier (1876–1950) (see p. 412). First published in 1908, it usually omits enthalpy, and is plotted with the axes of the graph inverted
472 (as compared to the Mollier diagram). The Mollier diagram and psychrometric chart revolutionized the process for designing air humidifiers; a hundred years later they are still used by heating and ventilation engineers, not least, perhaps, because they give the engineer such a clear visual picture of what is going on in the humidifier. In recognition of Mollier's contribution to the field, the 1923 World Thermodynamics Congress in Los Angeles, California, agreed that all such diagrams should be called Mollier diagrams or charts.

The final ingredient that would lead to the successful air-conditioning of buildings was the reliable control of humidity, first achieved by Stuart Cramer (1867–1940), a textile engineer from North Carolina. From the earliest days of the textile industry it was well known that it is important to prevent cotton fibers from becoming too dry, since both the strength and brittleness of fibers are very sensitive to humidity. (This was why the cotton-spinning industry had developed in the damp climate to the west of the English Pennines a century earlier.) In the 1880s it was common practice in North Carolina to spray water, atomized by compressed air to form a mist, into textile factories. This method had two major disadvantages: It was difficult to regulate the humidity precisely and the water caused the machinery to rust quickly. Cramer devised a system utilizing a hygrometer, which measured the humidity level in the air, and a plant, which was located in a room outside the factory, for adding moisture to the air. His humidifiers were first successfully used in 1904–1905, and Cramer founded a firm that manufactured and installed humidifying equipment both in textile mills and in other buildings.

It was Cramer who coined the term "air-conditioning" in 1906, both in a patent application and in a paper, "Recent Developments in Air Conditioning," delivered to the convention of the American Cotton Manufacturers Association. The term first appeared in a textbook, *Air-Conditioning: Being a short treatise on the humidification, ventilation, cooling, and the hygiene of textile factories—especially with relation to those in the U.S.A.* by G. B. Wilson, in 1908, by which time it had already established its full modern meaning:

to maintain a suitable degree of humidity in all seasons and in all parts of a building;

to free the air from excessive humidity during certain seasons;

to supply a constant and adequate supply of ventilation;

to efficiently wash and free the air from all micro-organisms, effluvia, dust, soot and other foreign bodies;

to efficiently cool the air of the rooms during certain seasons;
to either heat the rooms in winter or help to heat them;
to combine all the above desiderata in an apparatus that will not be commercially prohibitive in first cost or cost of maintenance.[9]

Although many engineers contributed to the development of viable air-conditioning systems, the man sometimes known as the father of air-conditioning is Willis Haviland Carrier. Carrier's advances in the field and his subsequent fame were due both to his commercial savvy and to his engineering and scientific knowledge. After graduating from Cornell University, Carrier went to work for the Buffalo Forge Company, a firm that made and installed hot-blast heating equipment. In 1902 Carrier, who had by then established his own research facility, was asked by a printing and publishing company to solve a major problem: Lack of humidity control, which was producing disastrous effects on its color printing projects. Carrier first chose to dehumidify the air by means of refrigerated pipe coils, but the installation did not achieve its aim, mainly because it had not been integrated with the Buffalo Forge heating system. After this failed experiment Carrier came to the same conclusion as Rietschel had nearly a decade earlier: The air should be chilled using a spray of cold water in an air washer so that the air leaving it would then be fully saturated. The saturated air from the washer or "chiller" would then be mixed with the room air. The desired relative humidity and temperature in the room was achieved by adjusting the temperature and the quantity of saturated air leaving the chiller, according to the measured temperature and relative humidity of the untreated air.

In 1905 Carrier was given permission to set up a division of Buffalo Forge to design, make, and install air washers. A colleague told him of the benefits that humidity and temperature control would bring to the textile industry, and he immediately saw the commercial potential. He published an article on humidity control in *Textile World* in 1906 without, so the story goes, ever having visited a textile mill. He used his first few commissions as real-world experiments, meticulously monitoring the performance of both plant and changes in temperature and humidity levels in the building. Using these empirical data, he was quickly able to improve the performance of his systems. The Carrier Air-Conditioning Company of America was established as a subsidiary of the Buffalo Forge Company in 1907. Carrier went on to target many other industries for which humidity was a critical issue, including bread making, printing, and cigarette manufacture. The air-conditioning of nonindustrial buildings, such as movie theaters and some hotels, did not really take off until the early 1920s.

Architectural Acoustics

The late nineteenth century saw the construction of many new concert halls to meet the public's growing demand for concerts featuring symphony orchestras. These halls differed markedly from the three traditional venues for musical performance: churches, private salons where chamber music was played, and theaters and opera houses. The size and construction material of churches were guaranteed to give them long reverberation times (up to six or seven seconds), which limited the types of music that could be played successfully. Multiple reflections from the hard surfaces of walls and floor forced composers and musicians to avoid rapid rhythms, and staccato or percussive sounds, which would degenerate into harmonic and rhythmic confusion as new notes interfered with the reflections of earlier ones. Chamber music, which usually featured fewer than a score of musicians, developed and thrived during the eighteenth and early nineteenth centuries in the houses of the rich and was seldom intended for large audiences. The small sizes of the rooms and the plastered interiors gave a much shorter reverberation time (perhaps three or four seconds), and a lively room acoustic that well suited the Baroque and early classical music of Handel and Haydn. Such rooms were ideal for relatively quiet instruments such as the violin family, the woodwinds, and early keyboard instruments such as the harpsichord.

Theaters and opera houses, on the other hand, were dedicated mainly to the human voice. Their design was driven by the need to ensure intelligibility and to avoid the need for actors to have to speak unduly loudly. The maximum distance between the speaker or singer and the listener had to be no more than about 20 meters, and the interior of the auditorium was covered in fabric and soft furnishings that ensured a low reverberation time (between two and three seconds). The symphony orchestra, by contrast, playing the music of Beethoven or Mahler, could be very loud indeed, and the promoters of public symphony

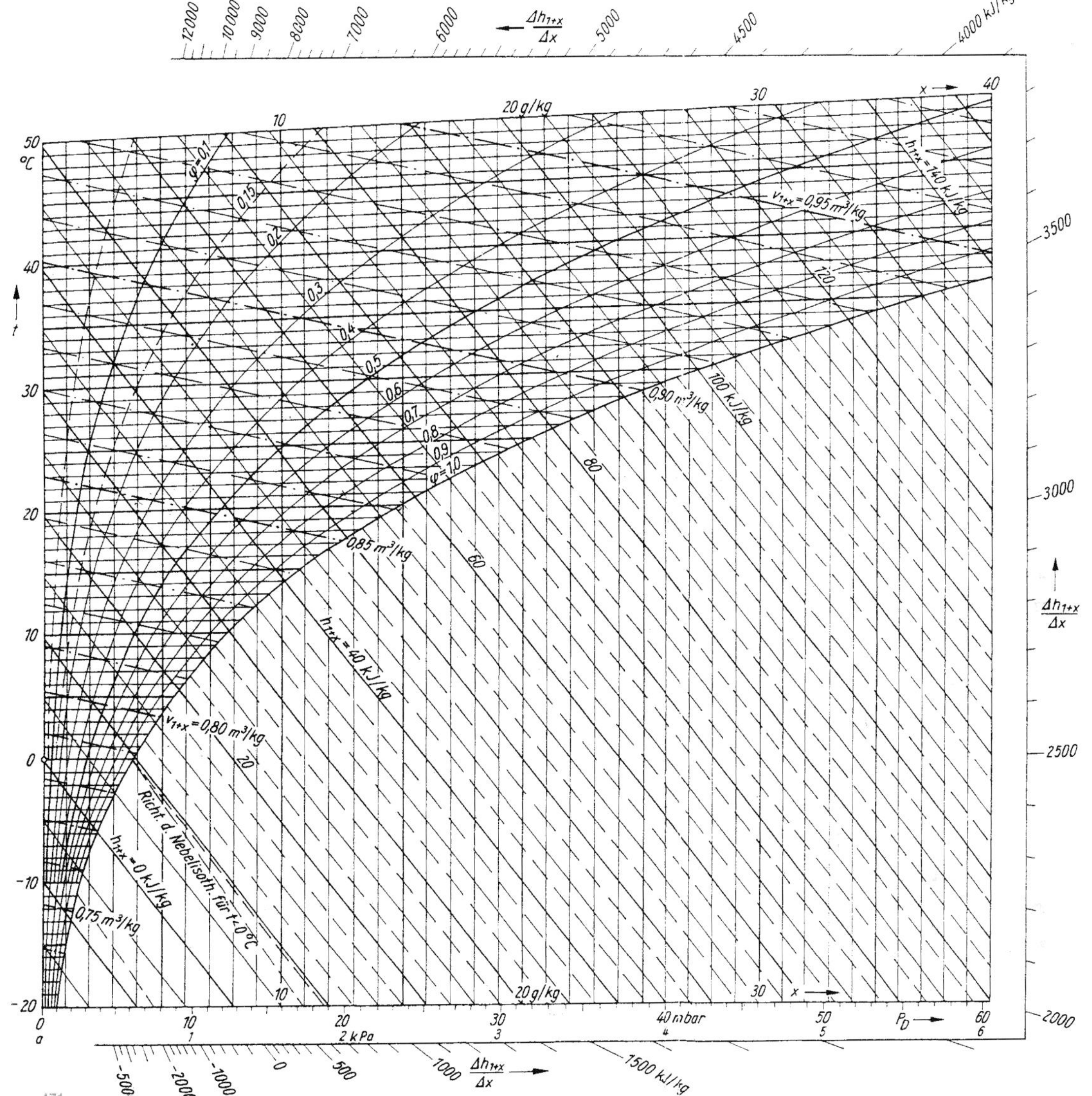

471 A Mollier diagram tracing the thermodynamic path followed by humidified and heated or cooled air. Devised by Richard Mollier in the early 1890s.

FORMULA
FOR
FINDING THE AMOUNT OF MOISTURE IN ONE POUND OF AIR HAVING A KNOWN WET BULB DEPRESSION.

T_D = DRY BULB TEMPERATURE.
T_A = ACTUAL WET BULB TEMPERATURE.
T_O = OBSERVED " " " .

$$T_A = (T_D - 1.02(T_D - T_O))$$

N_A = GRAINS OF MOISTURE IN ONE POUND OF AIR OF 100% HUMIDITY AT A TEMPERATURE T_A.
N_D = GRAINS OF MOISTURE IN ONE POUND OF AIR WITH A DRY BULB TEMPERATURE T_D AND A WET BULB TEMPERATURE T_O.

$N_D = N_A - X.$

$$N_A = \frac{E \times 7000 \times .623}{30 - E}$$

E = VAPOR TENSION CORRESPONDING TO A TEMPERATURE T_A.

$$\lambda = \frac{7000 \times .238 (T_D - T_A) + .48 N_A (T_D - T_A)}{(1114 - .695 T_A) + .48 (T_D - T_A)}$$

CONSTANTS
7000 GRAINS PER POUND. .238 SPECIFIC HEAT OF AIR.
.48 SPECIFIC HEAT OF WATER VAPOR.
1114 − .695 T_A = LATENT HEAT OF WATER VAPOR.
.623 = SPECIFIC WEIGHT OF WATER VAPOR.

472

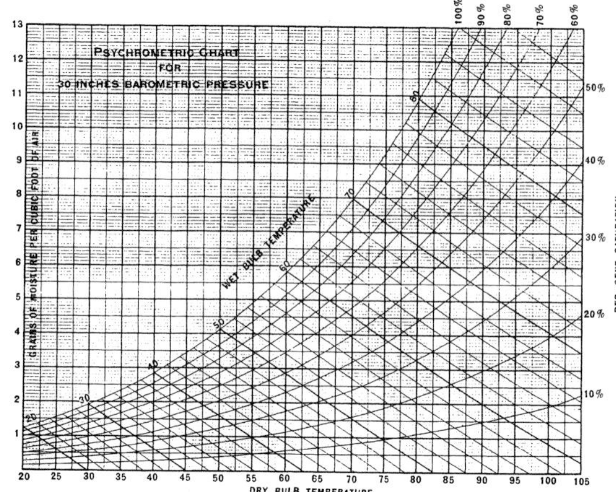

concerts wanted to seat as many listeners as possible. Both features called for much larger halls. The large assembly rooms in town and city halls often served, and still do serve, as acceptable music venues, although their multipurpose function often meant they were seldom ideally suited to any one type of music. The acoustical design of such halls was entirely empirical, and was based on the observed characteristics of previous halls that had proved successful. A number of halls earned widespread acclaim among musicians and concertgoers—for example, Vienna's Grosser Musikvereinssaal (1870), the Leipzig Gewandhaus (1885), and the Concertgebouw in Amsterdam (1888). Yet, until relatively recently, when a new hall was designed there was little agreement as to precisely which features of these "excellent" halls should be copied. Acoustical disasters were not uncommon. A famous example was London's Royal Albert Hall, opened in 1871, whose prominent echo gained it the unfortunate reputation for giving audiences "good value for their money" as they heard every concert twice (see chapter 9, p. 592).

The man who became known as the father of architectural acoustics was Wallace Clement Sabine (1868–1919). Sabine, a physics lecturer in the department of natural philosophy at Harvard University in Cambridge, Massachusetts, was approached in 1895 to advise on how to improve the poor acoustics of a new lecture theater in the University's Fogg Art Museum. The theater had been designed to emulate a classical Greek theater and followed the same principles of acoustical design that Vitruvius had articulated in 25 B.C. (see chapter 1, pp. 33–34). Such principles were intended for open-air theaters, however, and did not take into account sound reflected from walls or a roof. In an enclosed room, such reflected sounds also reach the listener's ear, and, since many sounds arrive at different times, the result is acoustical confusion, with direct sound from a speaker competing with reflections of earlier sounds.

Sabine realized, as had many before him, that this was how intelligibility was lost. Being a physicist, however, his approach was to conduct experiments to measure how the loudness of the reflections was influenced by the reflecting surfaces in the lecture theater. His aim was to discover the relationship between the dimensions of the room and the rate at which a sound becomes quieter and, eventually, inaudible. This "rate of decay" is the reverberation time, and is defined as the time for a sound to decay to one millionth of its original loudness.

Sabine had to work at night to ensure that all extraneous

472 The psychrometric chart. First published anonymously without explanations by Willis Carrier in 1908, and with explanations in 1911.

sounds were eliminated. He used a single organ pipe with a frequency of 512 Hertz (an octave above middle C). In 1895 there were no microphones or any other audio-electronic devices, and the judgment as to when a sound was inaudible had to be made by the experimenter. An electric chronograph recorded the times to one-hundredth of a second. By covering more and more of the auditorium's wooden seats with soft cushions, Sabine showed that the reverberation time was inversely proportional to the number of seats covered with cushions. He repeated the experiments in eleven other rooms in the university, with volumes ranging from a lecture theater of 9300 cubic meters down to an office of just 35 cubic meters. Extrapolating from the results, he derived an equation, for which his name is well known, that expresses the relationship between the reverberation time of a hall, its volume, and the absorptivity of the surfaces of the room. He used this as an objective means of comparing different auditoriums and, in particular, of comparing the proposed design for the new Boston Music Hall with the Leipzig Gewandhaus, on which its overall shape was based, and the old Boston Music Hall. He was able to specify, for the first time, the precise degree of sound absorption in the interior of the new hall needed to achieve the same reverberation time as the Leipzig Gewandhaus, whose seating capacity it exceeded by 70 percent, and whose volume it exceeded by 40 percent. Sabine's predictions were accurate, and the acoustics of the new hall were widely praised. He had fulfilled the goals he had set himself of overcoming the "unwarranted mysticism," as he called it, that then surrounded the subject of architectural acoustics and, most significantly, of undertaking "the calculation of reverberation in advance of construction."[10]

Acoustical problems were common with all types of rooms, and people had tried all sorts of curious measures to rectify them, usually without success. Sabine noted the persistent use of one traditional remedy despite the fact that it was wholly ineffective. This involved stretching a grid of steel wires in the top of a church, theater, or courtroom that suffered too much reverberation, in the mistaken belief that the wires would resonate and absorb sound. In New York and Boston he had seen theaters and churches with just four or five wires stretched across the room, while in other auditoriums several miles
473 of wire had been used, all without the slightest effect.

News of Sabine's success in rectifying the acoustical problems at his university spread, and he was approached by the owners of many types of rooms seeking advice on how to improve their acoustics. As part of his diagnosis, he would sometimes plot a contour map showing the distribution of the sound intensity. This 474
helped him identify the source of the worst sound reflections from the walls and ceiling; he could then reduce them by using sound-absorbing panels or adding decorations that would break up strong reflections from large plane surfaces.

Sabine also turned his attention to the design of new theaters, with the goal of creating a near-uniform acoustical experience for every member of an audience. Around 1912 he devised an experimental technique to help him better understand the behavior of sound waves in a theater auditorium. He made scale models, about 1:200, of a number of vertical and horizontal sections of the auditorium. By making a sharp noise he created a single sound wave that spread from the stage into the auditorium area of the model; he then photographed the model using a single electrical spark to illuminate it for an instant. After passing through the model, the light fell onto a photographic plate. As Sabine described this technique, at that time called the "Toeppler-Boys-Foley method" and now generically called "schlieren photography": "the light is refracted by the sound waves, which thus act practically as their own lens in producing the photograph."[11] By taking many similar photographs at different intervals after the initial sound, the shadows cast by the sound waves enabled Sabine to trace the increasing number of reflections and the gradual spread of the sound through the entire auditorium. Sabine first used 475
this technique to analyze the acoustics of the recently completed New Theater in New York; he then studied the proposed auditorium design for the Scollay Square Theater in Boston, and suggested how its acoustics could be improved by changing the form of the auditorium ceiling and the front face of the balcony.

Although the study of scale models had long been used in studying the behavior of building structures, Sabine's work was probably only the second example of using scale models to study the performance of full-size buildings, and it marked the beginning of a new phase in the development of building science and engineering. During the twentieth century the study of scale models would be used to gain a better understanding of all aspects of building performance, including air flow and ventilation, the effects of wind on buildings, the spread of smoke and fire, the relative contributions of daylight and artificial light, and the effects of a building's shading on adjacent buildings.

The Distribution of Power to Buildings

In the nineteenth century, individual steam engines generally powered the various types of equipment installed in buildings to provide heating, refrigeration, ventilation, and lighting, and to drive elevators. As the century progressed, several other means were developed to distribute power and energy to large numbers of buildings via a distribution network.

In some cities, private companies provided a supply of hot water for heating to avoid the need for each building to have its own boiler and pump. In 1879, for example, the Steam Heating and Power Company of New York began installing what became known as a "district heating scheme;" at the same time, Thomas Edison's electricity company was erecting wooden poles around the city to carry cables that would distribute electricity around the city. The German engineer Hermann Rietschel designed a districted heating scheme for the city of Dresden in the 1880s, and referred in his books to several coal-fired power stations in the 1910s that provided waste heat to district heating schemes. In 1911 in Manchester, England, the company running electric trams sold waste steam from its electricity generating station to heat nearby warehouses and other buildings. In many British cities at this time, some electricity was generated by using the heat from burning refuse in incinerators. Since thermal energy can be in the form of either heat or cold, an alternative approach was taken to distributing energy in a number of U.S. cities in the 1890s, including New York, Boston, Los Angeles, and Kansas City. Using a central refrigeration plant and a network of pipes carrying liquid refrigerants under the streets, "coolth" (a word dating from 1547), rather than heat, was distributed to buildings for cooling or cold-storage purposes.

From the 1870s on, hydraulic power distribution networks were installed in many cities, using pipes of cast iron to carry water at a high pressure (700 to 800 pounds per square inch). The Hydraulic Engineering Company, of Chester, England, for example, launched hydraulic power enterprises in Hull, Liverpool, Birmingham, Manchester, Glasgow, Melbourne, Sydney, Antwerp, and Buenos Aires. The London Hydraulic Power Company served the whole of central London, reaching a peak of 186 miles of pipes driving some 8,000 machines in about 1930. Hydraulic motors were about half the size of electric motors that delivered equivalent power, and they could also be used in damp locations, where electric motors would need careful protection. Industrial applications included railway turntables, cranes, dock gates, and the rising bascules of London's Tower Bridge. The most common application in buildings such as hotels and offices was the elevator, but other uses in London included revolving stages and safety curtains in theaters. A hydraulic motor was used to raise the organ in the Odeon Cinema in Leicester Square. At the Savoy Hotel in London, even the 476
vacuum cleaners were driven by hydraulic power. The London Hydraulic Power Company finally switched off power in 1977.

The principal impact on the building designer of the need to incorporate energy-using building services was the twofold task of providing space for the plants as well as access routes for the necessary ducts, pipes, wires, and 477, 478
so on. In the Cornelius Vanderbilt II house in New York, c. 1892, air for both heating and ventilation was distributed thorugh 97 risers (ducts) that provided a heated surface area of around 2000 square meters (nearly twenty thousand square feet). The air was driven by convection, with assistance from fans when necessary. These generally had to be hidden from view, and there were also obvious benefits to be gained from reducing the length of the distribution paths, where possible, to minimize the dissipation of energy. Commercial office buildings were the first to have comprehensive services installed, and people soon started demanding similar levels of service and comfort in their homes. Hot and cold running water, as well as hot-water or circulating steam heating in every room, soon became standard in both hotels and apartment blocks. The Palmer House in New York boasted in 1875 that it was the first apartment building to have electric lighting and telephones in every room. The introduction of air ducts for ventilation and heating soon forced building designers to change their approach to design. Since the heating and ventilation systems were integral

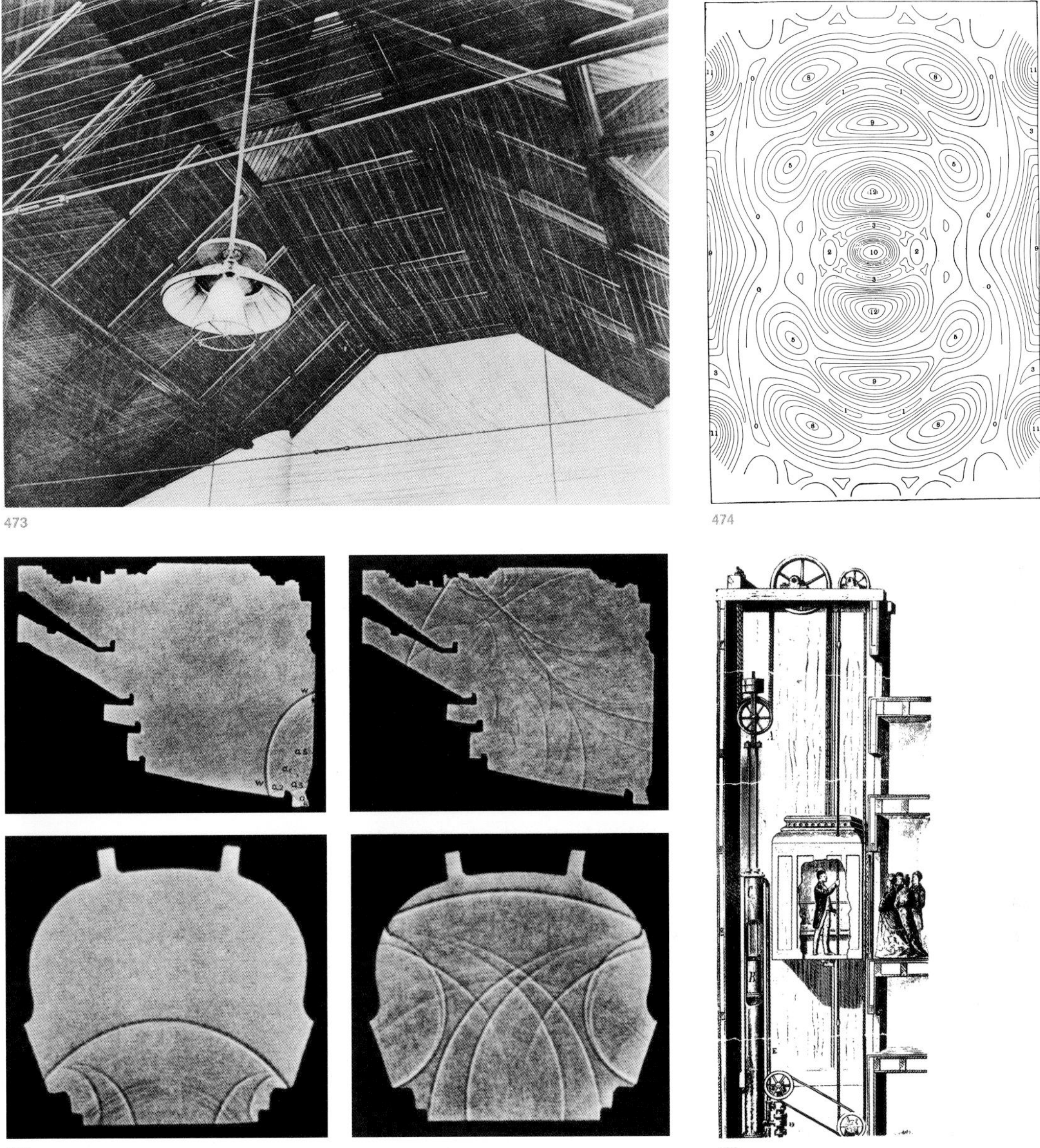

473

474

475

476

473 An early attempt to solve acoustical problems in a church in San Jose, California, c. 1910. Nearly 2 kilometers of steel wire were fixed near the ceiling in the mistaken belief that the wire would absorb sound. 474 Wallace Clement Sabine, contour map plotted to show the variation of sound intensity in a room, c. 1915. 475 Wallace Clement Sabine, photographs of model tests (taken c. 1920) to study the spread of sound waves in the auditorium of the New Theater, New York (c. 1911). 476 Engraving of an Otis roped hydraulic powered lift, c. 1870.

to the structure and fabric of the building, they had to be designed in close collaboration with the architect and structural engineer.

For some buildings the change to mechanical ventilation required a total reassessment of the entire layout. In the late nineteenth century, for example, hospitals were usually naturally ventilated. The wards had windows along each side to allow cross-ventilation and reduce the risk of airborne infections spreading between wards. The Royal Victoria Hospital in Belfast, completed in 1903,
479, 480 was one of the first to have mechanized or "forced" ven-
481, 482 tilation. To reduce the length of the ducts for air supply and foul air exhaust, all the wards were built parallel and contiguous. Air was supplied at one end of the wards through ducts running between adjacent wards at a high level, and removed at floor level into ducts leading to ventilating turrets at the other end. The air supply could be obtained either directly from the atmosphere or through a screen of wet ropes that cooled and humidified the air in warm weather.

The Reinforced Concrete Frame

The use of reinforced concrete to form the columns, beams, and floor structures of the structural frame of a building began in the 1880s. From the 1750s, when the benefits of hydraulic cement were studied and publicized by John Smeaton, "mass concrete" (concrete without reinforcement) was widely used in building foundations as a replacement for timber or stone. From the 1830s, experimental houses were constructed using mass concrete in many European countries and in the United States. In fact, the very first paper presented at the newly formed Royal Institute of British Architects in 1836 was devoted to the nature and properties of concrete and its application to construction up to that time. During the following four decades, many patents were granted for fireproof flooring systems that consisted of various forms of iron rods or strips embedded in concrete or encased by precast concrete blocks; the purpose of the iron, however, was often ambiguous—it served partly to carry forces and partly to act as a frame to hold the concrete in place until construction was complete. W. B. Wilkinson (1819–1902) had patented his fireproof flooring system using iron cables in 1854, and advertisements described his firm as designers and constructors of concrete staircases and fireproof floors of all descriptions, with as little iron as possible, and that wholly in tension, thereby preventing waste.

In 1867 a French gardener by the name of Joseph Monier (1823–1906) obtained a patent for a system similar to that of Joseph-Louis Lambot for making pots for ornamental flowers and shrubs and various waterproof vessels and pipes. Like the systems developed by Lambot and by François Coignet, the iron rods in his ciment armé were used to provide an armature for the concrete. However, Monier soon realized the potential for his idea in the building industry and obtained several more patents in the 483
1870s and 1880s, including one in 1886 for a system of cement and iron construction for permanent or movable houses that would be hygienic and economical. Initially, there was no evidence that his designs included placement of the iron where it could carry the tensile stresses that would develop in the structures. Instead, he concentrated on exploiting the waterproof qualities of ciment armé, building a large number of reservoirs for storing water on farms, some with a capacity as large as 50 cubic meters. Monier continued to promote his iron and concrete system for house construction, but few were built. 485
In the early 1870s Monier began experimenting with different arrangements of the iron reinforcement, and soon found the benefits of using the iron to carry tensile forces. His patent of 1878 shows this idea developed to its full maturity, and the now familiar arrangement of reinforcing bars to carry tension and shear forces is clear to see. The American mechanical engineer William E. Ward (1821–1900), who ran a factory making bolts and screws, designed and built for himself a large fireproof
concrete house in Port Chester, New York (1873–76). As 484
he wrote in a paper in 1883, "All the beams floors and roofs were exclusively made of beton, re-enforced [sic] with light iron beams and rods."[12] The reason for placing the iron beam so near the bottom of the mold was to utilize its tensile quality for resisting the strain below the neutral axis, the beton above this line was relied on for resisting compression. Ward also recognized the importance of the bond between the iron and concrete, both to ensure composite action of the two materials and for controlling the shrinkage of the concrete.

Until the mid-1880s, however, all the examples of reinforced concrete had been isolated experiments by individuals without the commercial backing of a contractor

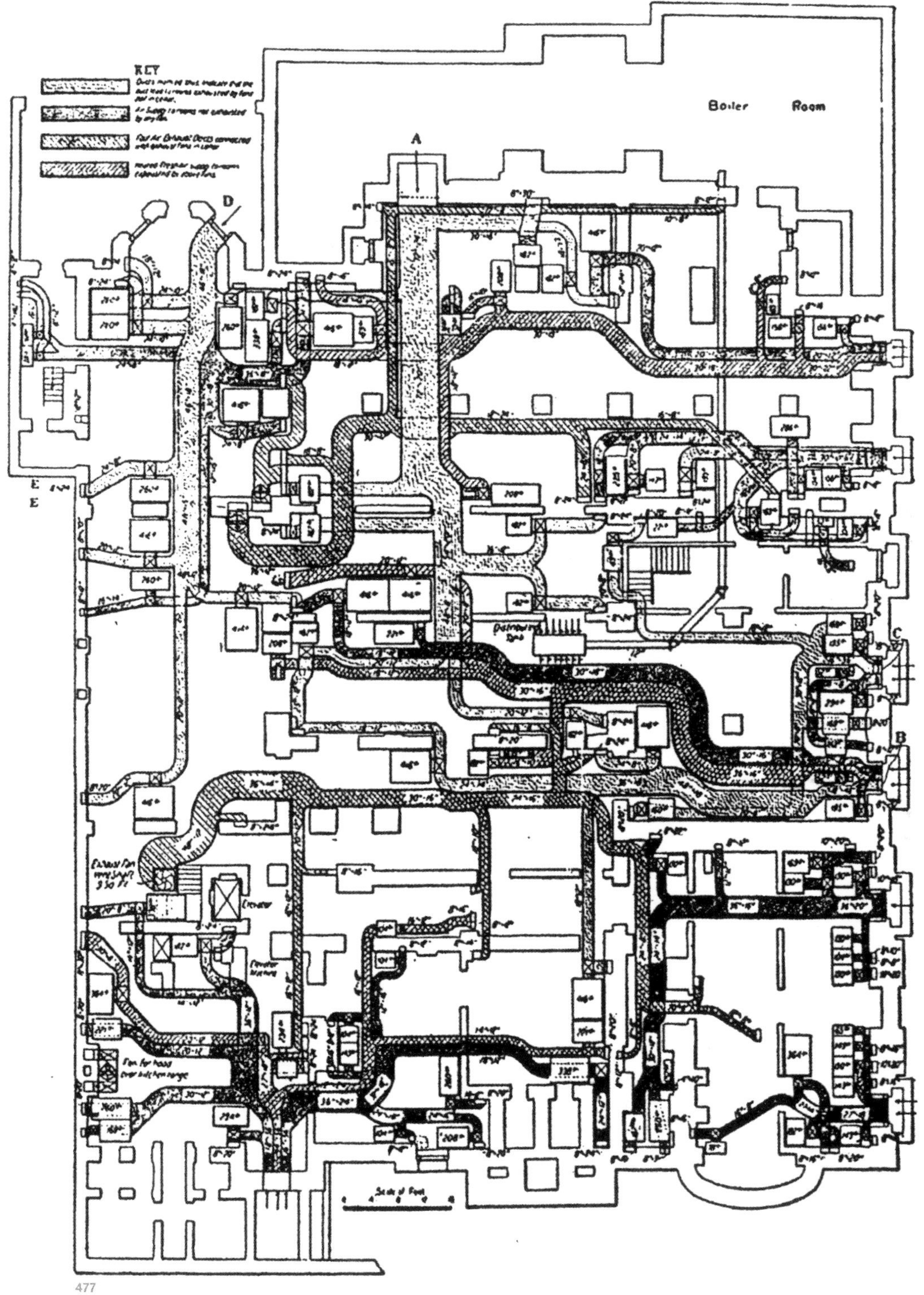

477 Basement layout of heating and ventilation system in Cornelius Vanderbilt II House, New York, c. 1892. Engineer: Alfred Wolff.

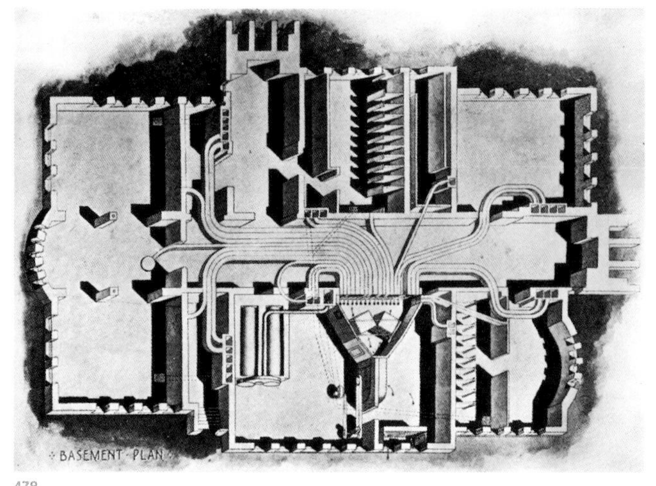

478

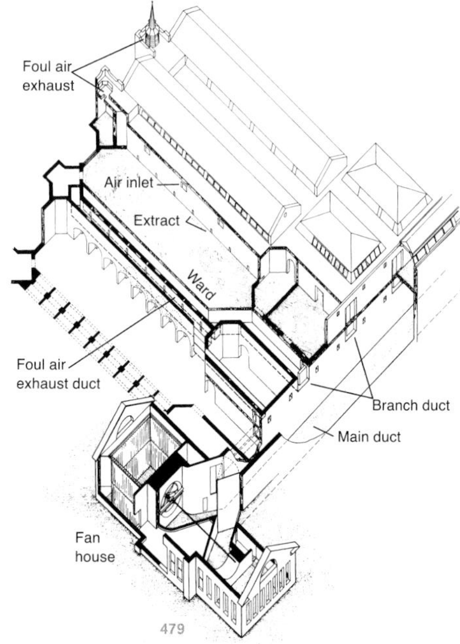

479

480

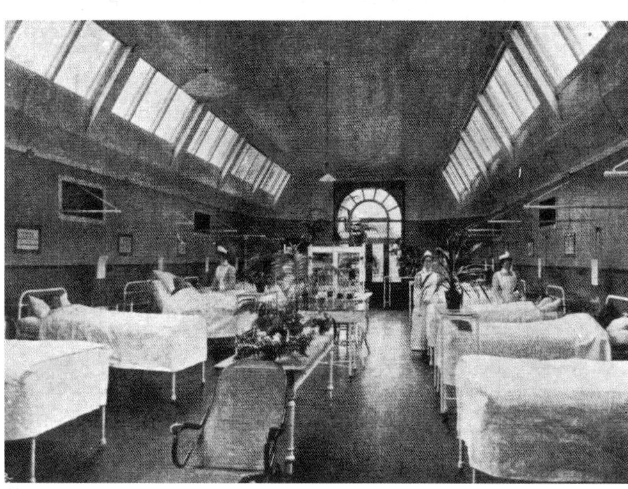

481

482

478 Basement plan of a school in Menominee, Michigan, showing boiler, fan, heating chamber, ducting, and risers. From Sturtevant company catalogue, 1906. 479 Royal Victoria Hospital. Cutaway isometric of the ventilation system. 480 Royal Victoria Hospital, Belfast, Ireland, 1903. Heating and ventilation engineer: Henry Lea. Ventilation turrets dominate the architecture. 481 Royal Victoria Hospital. Interior of a ward. 482 Royal Victoria Hospital. Fan driving air into the ventilation system.

that would ensure their widespread adoption. During the 1880s and 1890s, two contractors changed this situation and became largely responsible for the growth of reinforced concrete construction in Europe. One was the German firm founded by Gustav Wayss (1851–1917), which later became Wayss and Freytag; in 1885 this firm bought the rights to exploit Monier's system, patented in 1878. The other was the French firm founded by François Hennebique (1842–1921). Both firms conceived the idea of the complete reinforced concrete frame, making not only the floors from reinforced concrete, but also the piles, foundations, floor beams, floor slabs, columns, walls, facade, and roof structure. Crucial to the success of these two firms, however, was not that they were the first, or that their systems were the best, but that they benefited from the commercial acumen of their proprietors, and devoted great attention to the design of the structural elements and to the quality of the ingredients used to make the reinforced concrete. Both firms also undertook rigorous programs of experimentation, both independently and in collaboration with university research teams, to improve the quality and consistency of their products. This scientific approach helped accelerate the growth and spread of reinforced concrete construction in both civil engineering and building construction in the 1880s and 1890s, as can be judged by the numbers of papers written on the subject in technical journals.

The book on the Monier System published by Wayss in 1887 contained the method devised by his colleague Matthias Koenen (1849–1924) for designing reinforced concrete beams in which the steel and concrete were assumed to carry entirely the tensile and compressive stresses, respectively. This method was soon adopted by most engineers, though it needed to be developed to take into account the many variations in reinforcing systems. A generalized approach, suitable for a code of practice that could be used for any system, was developed by a number of French engineers in the 1890s. This method recognized the need to take into account the relative stiffnesses of the two constituent materials when calculating strains, and hence in proportioning the concrete and its reinforcement so that both would be of adequate strength. Otherwise there would be an inappropriate distribution of the loads between the steel and concrete and, eventually, cracking of the concrete. Known as the "elastic modular ratio method," it formed 486, 487
the basis of all design codes into the second half of the 488
twentieth century.

Hennebique patented his famous system in 1892. One of 489
the first large buildings constructed with this system was a factory at Tourcoing in France in 1895, after which the firm grew rapidly. The strength and durability of concrete depend very much on the precise mix and cleanliness of the ingredients of concrete, and Hennebique's firm was well known for stringent quality control of the concrete-making process and the production of detailed drawings of the reinforcement to ensure its correct placement. 490
When the Hennebique firm sold licences to use its system, employees of the licensee firm were rigorously trained by the Hennebique company, and had to gain experience using it under supervision before using it independently. In 1897, when the first large Hennebique building was built in Britain, all the steel, sand, and aggregate, properly cleaned, was imported to South Wales from France; only the water was local. By 1899 three thousand and sixty one projects using the Hennebique system had been built worldwide, a figure that had grown to nearly twenty thousand in 1909, by which time the company had sixty-two offices around the globe.

During the 1890s more and more firms devised and patented their own systems of reinforcing concrete with steel, each hoping to increase their profits by selling licences to use the systems. In such a climate it was commercial success rather than engineering issues that drove the adoption or nonadoption of the different systems throughout the world. In the United States, the early exploitation of reinforced concrete in the 1880s and 1890s was due almost entirely to Ernest Ransome (1844–1917), who had emigrated from England to the United States in 1869 to exploit his father's patent for "concrete stone." In the mid-1880s Ransome, like Monier and Hennebique, developed his own system, which employed twisted square bars of wrought iron for making beams and floor structures of "re-enforced" concrete. He first used his system for an entire building in a factory for the United Shoe Machinery Corporation in
1903–06. As in Hennebique's Tourcoing factory of 1895, 491
the facade consisted of huge areas of glass between the slender columns that provided excellent daylighting inside the building.

483

484

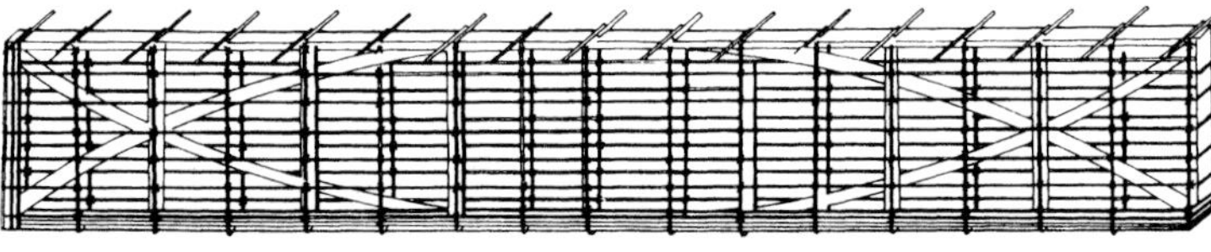
485

By 1902, four firms dominated the U.S. market in reinforced concrete construction. One of them, the Ferro-Concrete Construction Company of Cincinnati, Ohio, designed and built what can truly be called the first reinforced concrete skyscraper, the Ingalls Building in Cincinnati (1902–1903). At sixteen stories and 65 meters high, though just half the height of the tallest steel-
492, 493 framed building at the time, it was the world's tallest
494, 495 reinforced concrete building. As is typical of building height records, it did not hold this title for long, and in 1909 the Hennebique company was soon proud to feature in its publicity the Royal Liver Building in Liverpool (1908–11) as the tallest concrete building in the world. Its crowning Liver bird statue stands 94 meters above
496, 497 street level. The emergence of reinforced concrete raised a number of issues for contractors and design engineers. Reinforced concrete was a new material, and involved a new method of construction; uniquely, the material was manufactured at the construction site itself. The regulatory authorities had to consider both the safety of the proposed design for a structure and the quality of the material used; the latter meant regulation of the ingredients and their quantities, as well as how the reinforcement was positioned in the structural element. This task was further complicated by the fact that each contractor had its own system of reinforcement and method of calculation. There was also great apprehension about the fact that reinforced concrete relied on two constituent materials, steel and concrete, working together. Yet there was no universal agreement on how the loads would be shared between the steel and concrete, or the effectiveness of the different methods of bonding the steel in the concrete to prevent it from slipping.

Two other areas of concern were the effects of temperature and fire safety issues. The key factor that inhibited the introduction of steel frames in the facades of buildings in Britain was the difference between the rates of

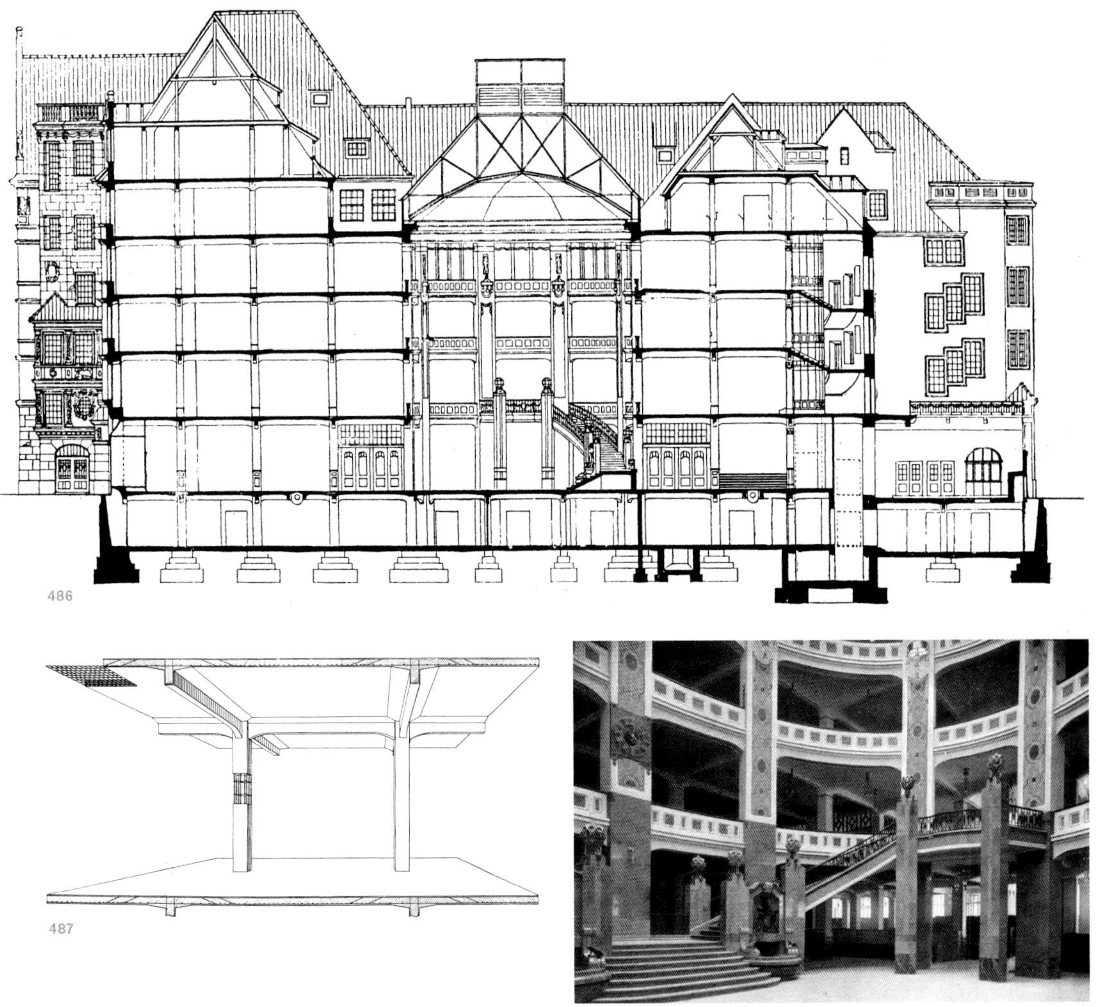

486

487

488

483 Pre-construction model for a house made of concrete and iron bars, built by Joseph Monier at rue de la Pompe, Paris, c. 1886. 484 Ward House, Port Chester, New York, 1873–76. Designer and mechanical engineer: William Ward. 485 Diagram from patent for a reinforced concrete beam by Joseph Monier, 1878. 486 Tietz store, Munich, Germany, 1905. Longitudinal section. Architect and general contractor: Heilmann and Littmann; concrete contractor: Eisenbeton company. 487 Tietz store. Drawing showing reinforced concrete construction. 488 Tietz store. Central hall.

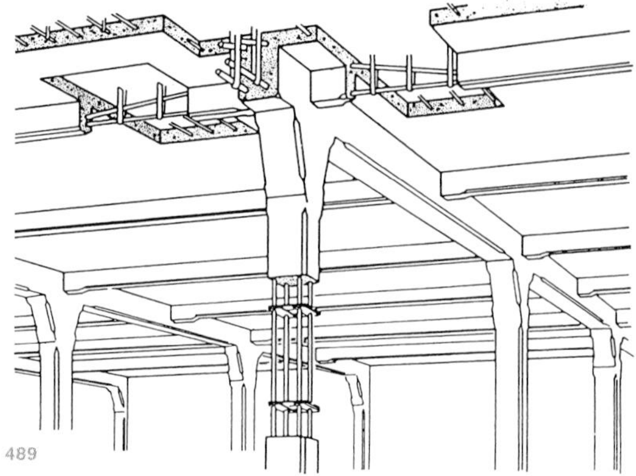
489

thermal expansion of steel and masonry; as temperatures rise or fall, the relative movement of these materials may cause the masonry to crack. If this were to happen with the reinforcement in concrete, the result would be the total disintegration of the beam or column. Fortunately, the rates of expansion of steel and concrete are very similar. Finally, there was the question of fire safety. Although everyone agreed that reinforced concrete performed better than exposed steel in a fire, the question was, how much better?

Getting the new material accepted by the regulatory authorities in all countries was not a straightforward matter. During the 1890s engineers had to rely on their own skills to persuade local officials to accept the new material. In order to inspire adequate confidence, it was common practice to conduct full-scale tests of parts of a structure. Since the best design methods based on engineering science, such as those developed by Koenen, were unfamiliar to many engineers, firms in the U.S. and Britain often resorted to tables and charts of span-to-depth ratios for the basic elements of a frame building: columns and beams. Such pragmatism, however, could only be short-lived. It was vital that well-founded and general design methods be established as the key step on the road to getting the new material accepted by the authorities and by relevant institutions. The issues raised by reinforced concrete forced changes on the professions and on the infrastructure of the construction industries in every country. In Britain, for example, the importance of these issues led directly to the founding of a new professional engineering institution.

The Royal Institute of British Architects (RIBA) had set up a Committee on Reinforced Concrete in 1905. One of its principal aims was to end the monopoly held by the proprietary concrete systems so that any competent person could use his engineering knowledge to design structures using reinforced concrete. Its report in 1907 contained much useful design guidance for both architects and engineers, despite the fact that the Institution of Civil Engineers had boycotted the committee. The Concrete Institute was formed in Britain in 1908 to address various issues relating to the new material and their implications for the work of architects and engineers. By good fortune Sir Henry Tanner, the chief architect of the Government's Office of Public Works, was a concrete aficionado. Not only did Tanner wield significant influence as chair of RIBA's Reinforced Concrete Committee, he was also able to insist that the new General Post Office for the City of London (1907–09) be built using the Hennebique ferro-concrete system by the firm of Louis Gustave Mouchel. (Government buildings were exempt from local construction regulations.) This building proved a milestone on the way to getting reinforced concrete widely accepted in London. A second committee, this time with the support of professional civil engineers, made further recommendations in 1911,

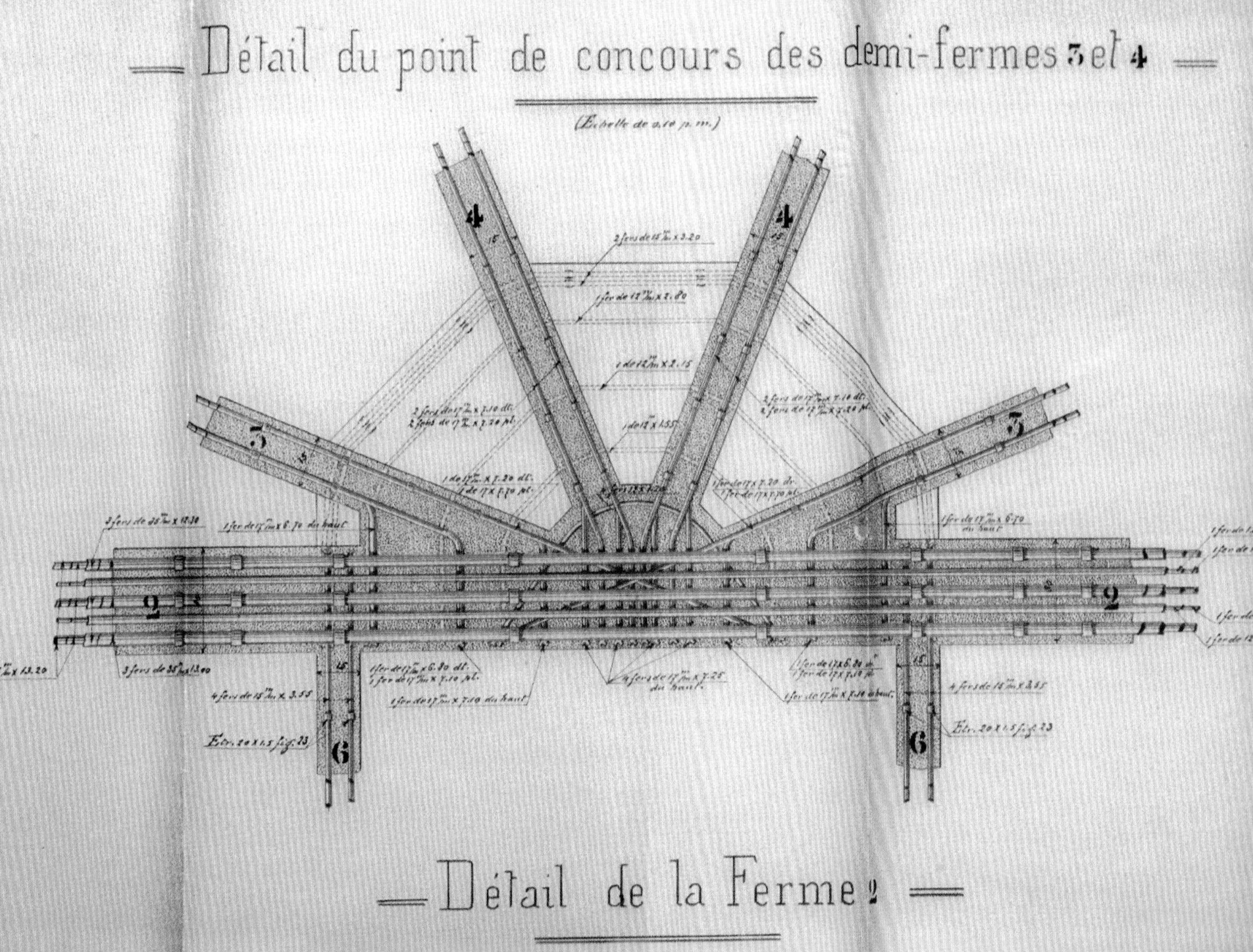

490

489 François Hennebique, diagram from patent for reinforcement system for concrete frame construction, 1892.

490 Drawing of reinforcement in a Hennebique building, c. 1910.

491

492

493

494

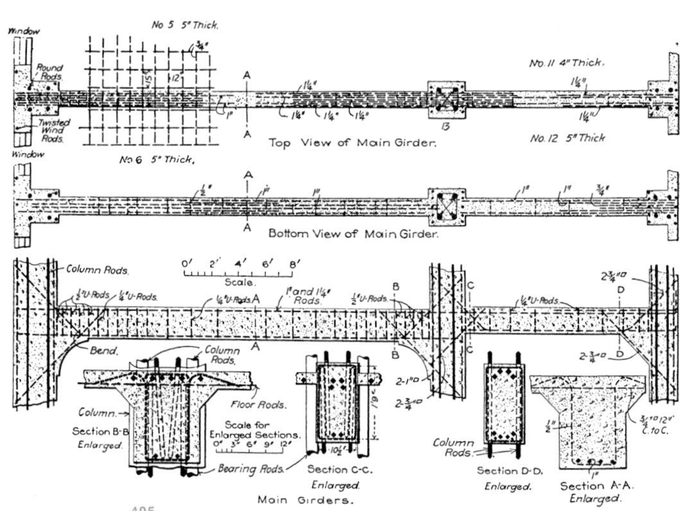

495

496

497

and a standard method of notation was adopted for concrete design calculations to enable easier comparison of designs done by different firms for their own reinforcing systems. In 1912 the Concrete Institute changed its name to "The Concrete Institute, an Institution of Structural Engineers, Architects, etc.," and in 1922 adopted its present name, the Institution of Structural Engineers. In 1915 a set of standardized generic reinforced concrete regulations was finally adopted by the London County Council, and their adoption led to the end of the restrictive practices of the specialist concrete firms; after 1915 no more patents were granted for new systems of reinforcing concrete.

Some architects were quick to see the design opportunities that reinforced concrete offered: one of the most striking was the ability to create curved structural members. One of the first nonindustrial buildings of note, made entirely from reinforced concrete, was the church of Saint Jean de Montmartre, Paris, from 1894 to 1904. This collaboration between the French architect Anatole de Baudot (1834–1915) and the structural engineer Paul Cottancin (1865–1928) offered ample opportunity to use the new material to echo the curved forms of masonry ribs and vaults. Cottancin's system of reinforcing 498, 499
concrete used a woven mesh of steel wires, usually about 4 mm in diameter and about 100 mm apart, rather than individual reinforcing bars. In many of his buildings, including Saint Jean de Montmartre and the Sidwell Street Methodist Church (1902–1905) in Exeter, England, Cottancin used both own system for reinforced concrete and his related system for reinforced brickwork. The bricks, he argued, carried compression stresses in the same way that the concrete did. The ten principal columns at Saint Jean de Montmartre, each about 25 mm high, are of reinforced brickwork; each brickwork

491 United Shoe Machinery Corporation building under construction, Beverly, Massachusetts, 1903–06. Concrete contractor: Ernest Ransome. 492 Ingalls Building, Cincinnati, Ohio, 1902–03. Concrete contractor: Ferro-Concrete Construction Company. Interior with exposed reinforced concrete. 493 Ingalls Building. Reinforced concrete floor. 494 Ingalls Building. Exterior. 495 Ingalls Building. Drawing of steel reinforcement system. 496 Royal Liver Building, Liverpool, England, 1908–11. Architect: Walter Aubrey Thomas. 497 Royal Liver Building under construction.

course comprises six perforated bricks with reinforcement passing through the perforations, and the central 500 core is filled with concrete. The roof of the crypt, at 10 meters, forms the floor of the main church, and at this point the square columns twist through 45 degrees in plan, enabling the columns to branch further up to create the cross-ribs that form the vaulted ceiling of the church. The steel reinforcement follows this twist.

The Belgian-born architect Auguste Perret (1874–1954), who would become the best-known architect to work in concrete in the 1920s, began working with the Hennebique firm to develop new building forms, including those for factories, a garage, and a showroom for auto- 501, 502 mobiles. Among the examples of Perret's early work of which the Hennebique company was especially proud was the new Théâtre des Champs-Élysées (1911–13), cited as a demonstration of how the firm's framing system created a fully integrated monolithic, sculptured structure, in contrast to the discrete beams and columns 503, 504 of a steel-frame building.

After the early prominence of French engineers in developing the use of reinforced concrete during the 1890s, the lead was soon taken by engineers from German-speaking countries. In the first decade of the new century they successfully experimented with virtually every form of reinforced concrete construction; the main exception was the thin concrete shell, which they developed in the 1920s. The main reason for the remarkable progress of these engineers was simple: They realized that the successful design of concrete structures demanded a thorough understanding of the theoretical basis of structural analysis—much better than what was being learned by young engineers in any other country. The investment, so to speak, in developing structural theory during the second half of the nineteenth century finally paid off handsomely. Structural analysis had been unnecessarily complex for many of the structures being designed in iron and steel during this period, and for this reason had not been widely taught in France, Britain, or the United States. For understanding and designing concrete structures, however, it was essential.

One company—the firm of Dyckerhoff and Widmann—was central to progress in this area. It had begun making concrete pipes, tanks, and other products in 1869, and began using reinforced concrete only in 1903, when Dyckerhoff finally became convinced that the corrosion of steel reinforcement could be satisfactorily prevented. Within a very short time the firm produced some of the most remarkable structures of the day. Most of the firm's early works were ribbed roof structures, with lighter-weight panel elements spanning between ribs—not unlike the basis of the medieval cathedral. Only six years after Dyckerhoff and Widmann began using reinforced concrete, the firm had designed and constructed the enormous entrance hall for the railway station at Leipzig. 505 At 265 meters long and 35 meters wide, this building is reminiscent of a cathedral or one of the grand Roman baths, both for its scale and its sense of drama. One side of the transverse hall is formed from six reinforced concrete arches, each spanning some 45 meters, which open onto the station platforms.

Many dozens of buildings of similar scale were built in German-speaking countries during the period, including factories, museums, and crematoriums. Smaller gems include the platform canopy, 8.4 meters wide, at Sonneberg Station in Thüringen from 1910, and an elegant factory roof in Nürnberg, from 1918, spanning over 506, 507
25 meters. 508

Although the thin, doubly-curved concrete shell was not fully developed until the 1920s, there were many earlier examples of thin concrete vaults used to span between ribs. The central ellipsoidal dome at the Ludwig-Maximilian University in Munich, completed in 1909, sprang from arch ribs spanning 16.75 and 13 meters. The shell itself was just 80 millimeters thick at the crown, increasing to 100 millimeters at the lowest points. 509, 510

One of the very first substantial concrete shells without ribs was a crematorium roof built by Wayss and Freitag in Dresden in 1911. The designers did not proceed without qualms, given that it was an untried form of structure. Built from a robust support at one end with a semi-ellipsoid at the other, the roof spans some 14 meters and is nearly 14 meters long. The shell has a horizontal ring beam, more than a meter wide that carries the outward thrust of the vault, and the shell is rather on the thick side compared to other shells built later—from 150 mm at the crown, it thickens to 200 mm at the side. In France, the 511, 512
engineer Eugène Freyssinet (1879–1962) was also ex-

498

499

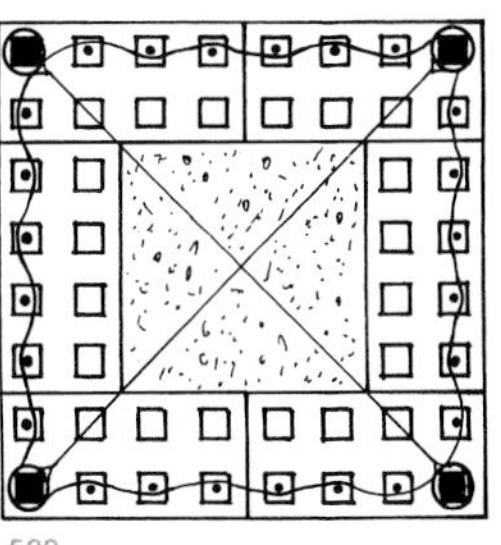
500

501

502

498 Saint Jean de Montmartre, Paris, 1894–1904. Engineer: Paul Cottancin; architect: Anatole de Baudot. Interior. 499 Saint Jean de Montmartre. Detail of ribs in vaulted roof. 500 Saint Jean de Montmartre. Detail of column of reinforced brickwork and a concrete core. 501 Garage at 51 rue de Ponthieu, Paris, 1905. Architect: Auguste Perret; contractor: the Hennebique company. 502 Garage at 51 rue de Ponthieu. Interior.

503

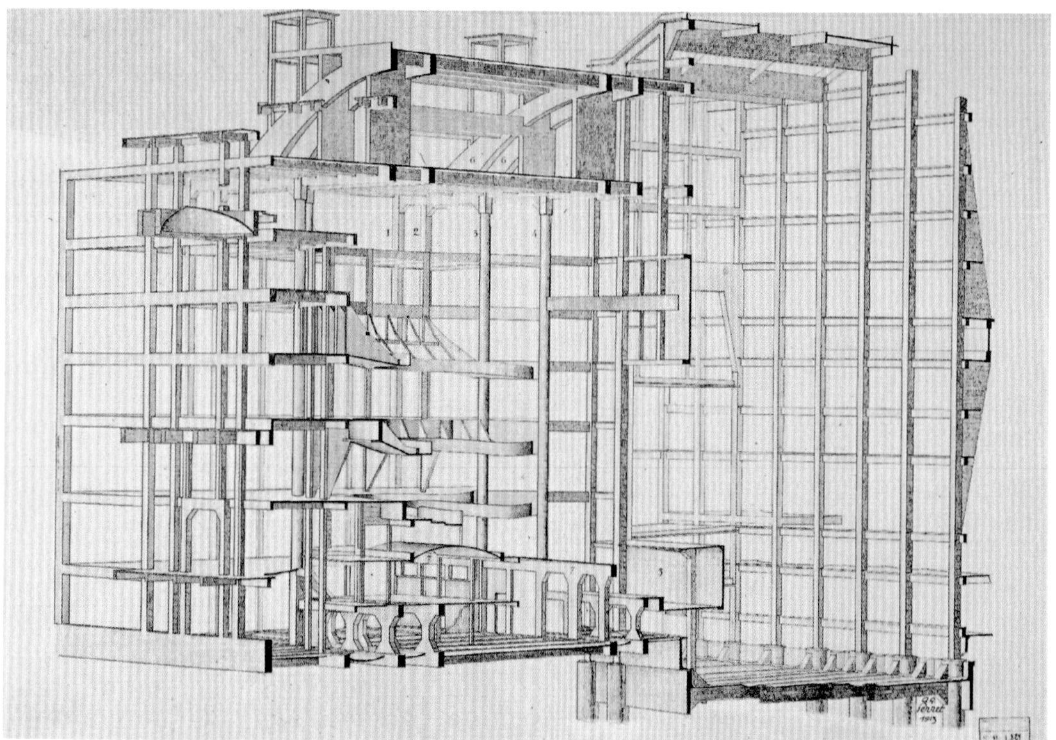

504

503 Théâtre des Champs-Élysées, Paris, 1911–13. Architect: Auguste Perret; contractor: the Hennebique company. Interior of foyer. 504 Théâtre des Champs-Élysées. Drawing by Perret showing the monolithic concrete frame.

perimenting with concrete shells. One of his first was a roof over a glass factory at Montluçon in central France, built in 1915.

The most remarkable building from this period is the Jahrhunderthalle in Breslau, in modern Poland. To form the dome, thirty-two primary ribs spring from a ring beam supported by four arches each 20 meters high and spanning 41 meters. Writing in 1928, the structural engineer Franz Dischinger (1887–1953) said of this building, "With its 65-meter ribbed dome, it is not only the widest-spanning concrete roof in the world, but also the most remarkable and statically-interesting work in
513, 514 reinforced concrete."[13] Coming from the man who devel-
515, 516 oped the thin concrete shell in the 1920s, this was
517 indeed a tribute.

The other major innovation in the use of reinforced concrete during this period was as a thin, structural sheet. Although the curved rib was ideally suited for concrete, similar structural elements had been possible in cast iron (Ironbridge, Saint Isaac's Cathedral), wrought iron (Halle au blé, many glass houses), riveted wrought iron girders (Borsig's factory and many railway stations), and laminated timber (de L'Orme's domes, the Crystal Palace). A flat or curved sheet of material with the capacity to carry large loads in the plane of the sheet, however, was unknown at the scale needed for building construction.

One of the first engineers to exploit reinforced concrete in the form of a thin, flat sheet was the Swiss engineer Robert Maillart (1872–1940). In 1898–99 he designed the Stauffacher Bridge in Zurich as a three-pin arch using two curved slabs of unreinforced concrete, each about 25 meters long and 20 meters wide and varying in thickness from 720 mm at the supports to 940 mm at the quarter span to 780 mm at the crown of the bridge. Though made of concrete, this three-pin arch is structurally similar to a masonry arch, carrying its loads in compression and with little capacity to resist bending. The deck of the bridge, on the other hand, is a flat slab of reinforced concrete about 200 mm thick, and it has the capacity to resist bending and to distribute loads to the vertical cross-walls on which it rests. Learning from his work on this bridge, Maillart realized that greater economy would be possible if the arch and the deck both worked to carry bending loads, and his next bridge—at Zuoz, near St. Moritz in southeast Switzerland—incorporated this principle. Spanning nearly 50 meters, again as 518, 519
a three-pin arch, it took the form of a box girder of reinforced concrete in which the maximum thickness of concrete was just 200 mm. The bridge was built for about half the cost per square meter of road deck as the Stauffacher Bridge.

Maillart began to see how reinforced concrete could be molded to create structures that derived their strength as much from their form as from the strength of the material itself. While this principle had long been known—in early cast iron beams, for example, and in the shape of arch bridges—it ran counter to contemporary thinking about reinforced concrete. In 1904 Maillart delivered a paper reviewing the use of reinforced concrete in structures not related to bridges, and mentioning, among others, concrete pipes and chimneys. In 1907 he had the opportunity to build and test to destruction a section of concrete pipe buried underground. He realized that the nonuniformity of the pressures from the soil would subject the pipe to bending, and that no matter how thick a section he used, the inevitable settling of the soil would cause cracks to develop that would allow water to penetrate and corrode the reinforcement. Instead of proposing to make the pipe as thick as possible to resist bending, he advanced the counterintuitive idea of making it thin enough to bend easily, without cracking, in response to the loads and the settling. The tests he carried out confirmed that this innovative approach would work, and led him to experiment with other uses of thin sections of reinforced concrete, in particular, the so-called "flat slab." A flat slab is a thin slab of uniform thickness, with no down-standing ribs or beams. He began testing models of flat slabs in 1908, and was granted a Swiss
patent for them the following year. Maillart first used his 520, 521
flat slab construction in 1910 in the Giesshübelstrasse 522
warehouse in Zurich, and within a few years he had built other industrial buildings as far afield as Saint Petersburg, Riga, and Barcelona.

As is often the case with new ideas, Maillart was not the only person who was experimenting with flat-slab floors. From around 1900, several American builders had patented reinforcing systems for flat-slab floors, the best known of whom was American railway bridge engineer

505

506

505 Railway station, Leipzig, Germany, 1907–15. Structural engineer: Louis Eilers; concrete contractors: Dyckerhoff and Widmann; architects: William Lossow and Max Hans Kühne. 506 Sonneberg railway station, Thüringen, Germany, 1910. Designed and constructed by Dyckerhoff and Widmann.

507

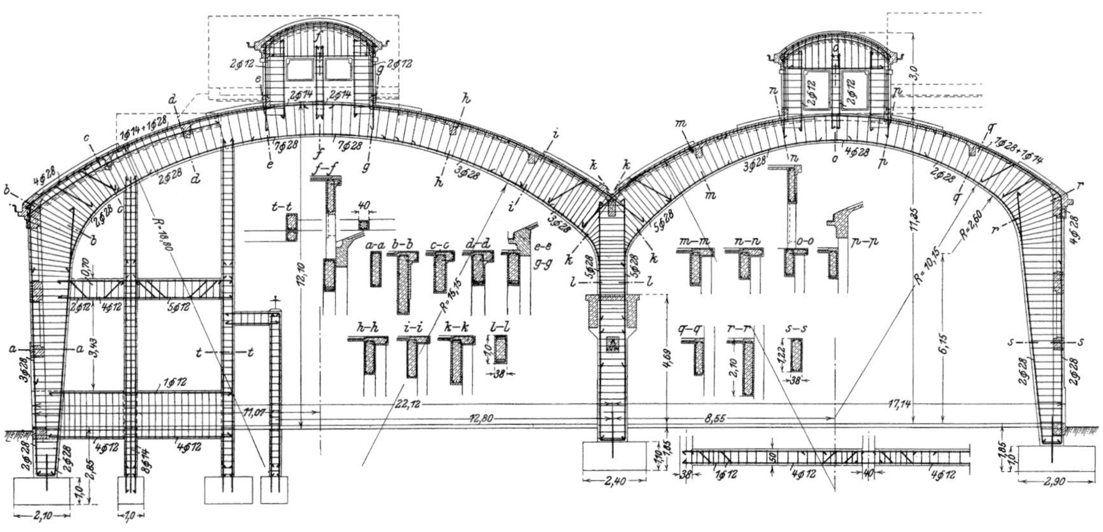

508

507 Factory building, Nürnberg, Germany, 1918. Designed and constructed by Dyckerhoff and Widmann. Interior.

508 Factory building, Nürnberg. Section.

509

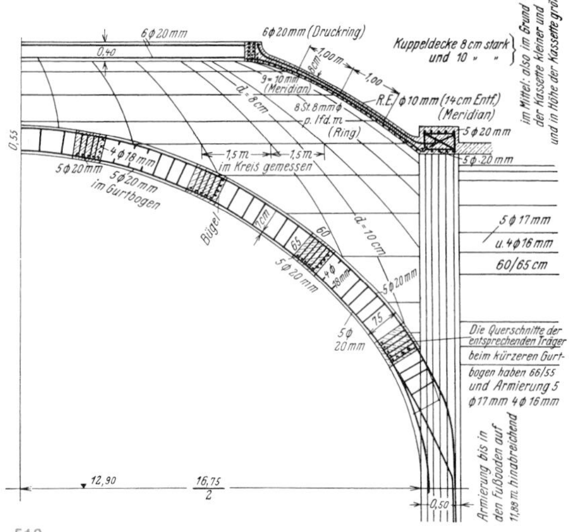

510

511

509 Ludwig-Maximilian University, Munich, Germany, 1908–09. Engineer: Leonhard Moll. Interior. 510 Ludwig-Maximilian University. Section. 511 Krematorium, Dresden, Germany, 1911. Engineering design and construction: Wayss and Freitag; architect: Fritz Schumacher. Under construction. 512 Krematorium, Dresden. Plan and section. 513 Jahrhunderthalle, Breslau, Poland, 1911–13. Structural engineers and construction: Dykerhoff and Widmann; architect: Max Berg. 514 Jahrhunderthalle. Interior. 515 Jahrhunderthalle. Aerial photograph, 1912.

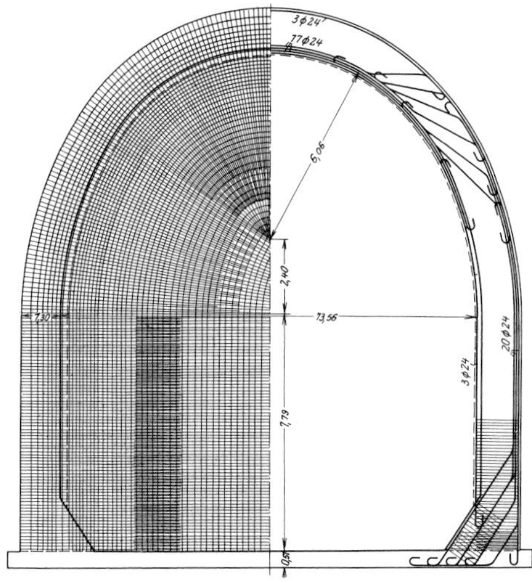
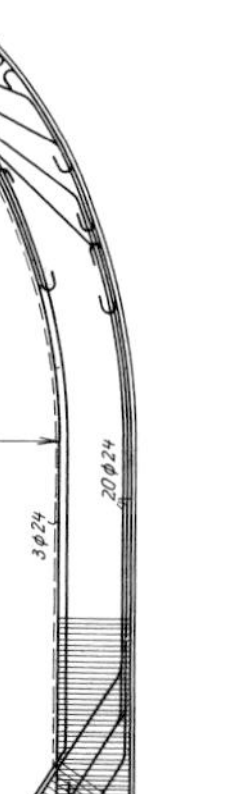
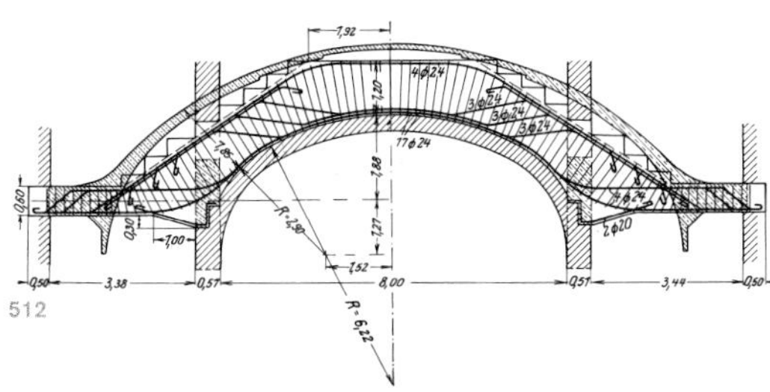

512

513

514

515

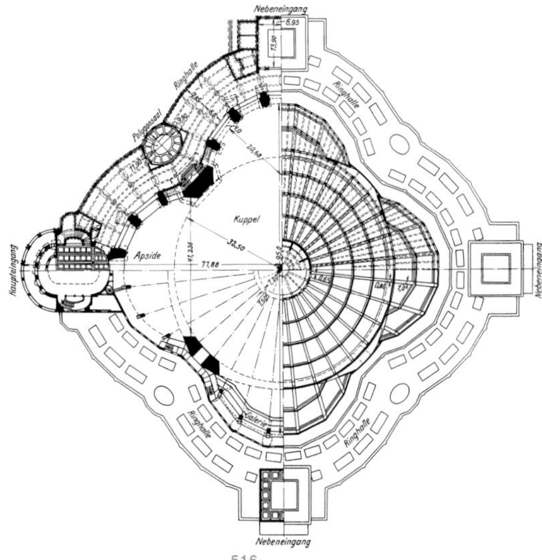

516

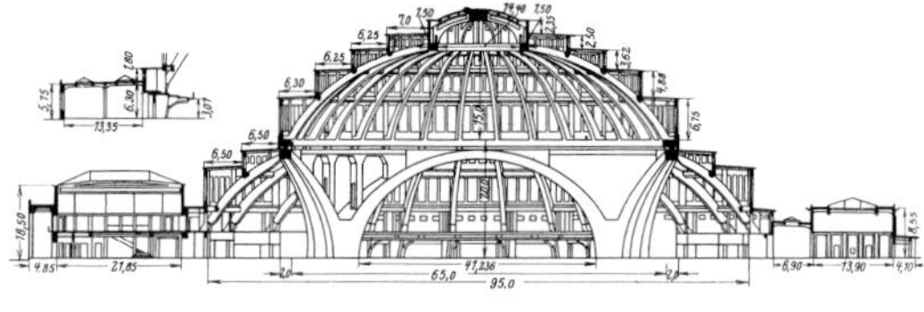

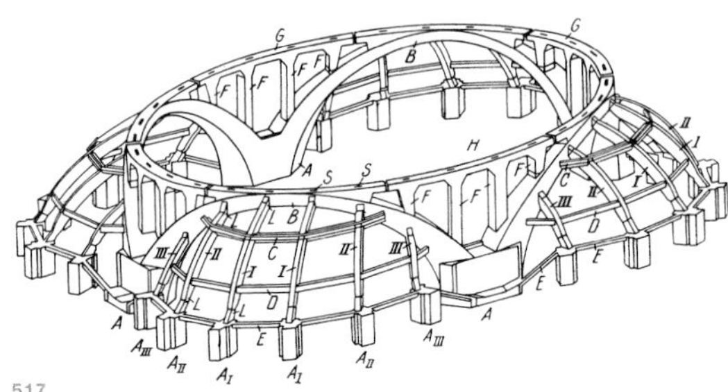
517

turned builder, Claude ("CAP") Turner (1869–1955), who openly challenged the conservatism of building engineers. He constructed his first building with flat-slab floors in 1906–1907, but his system was strongly criticized by the established building industry because he was not able to provide satisfactory calculations that demonstrated the strength of his floor system. Nevertheless, he went on to build over a thousand buildings using this system, and was granted a patent in 1911 in which he coined the phrase "mushroom slab," later widely used as a generic name for flat-slab construction. Between 1907 and the outbreak of World War I, the Russian engineer Artur Ferdinandovitch Loleit (1868–1933) also designed a number of buildings using elegant flat-slab floors just 180mm thick, spanning 4.8 meters between circular columns 300 mm in diameter. In a single-story section of a textile factory at Bogorodsk-Glukhovskoe near Moscow, designed by Loleit in 1907 with the architect Alexandr Kusnetsov, a large circular portion of the ceiling slab was replaced by a glazed skylight.

Maillart had learned through experiment that the behavior of reinforced concrete could not be likened to the behavior of homogeneous materials such as steel. In a 1909 paper entitled "The safety of reinforced concrete structures," he observed that "reinforced concrete, in spite of being composed of well-known materials, can be seen as a new material because its properties are not merely the sum of those constituent materials; rather it has new material properties." In the paper, he went on to criticize contemporary design codes that did not acknowledge the unique character of reinforced concrete. Concerning flat slabs, he had this to say: "Beam theory is completely invalid for the analysis of slab structures. No previously known material can be used to build such structures on a large scale because stone has too low a tensile strength and steel or timber can be used only in the direction of rolling or the grain, respectively." He summarized what he had learned from his experiments as follows:

1 *Theoretical methods used for other materials are worthless for calculating the safety of reinforced concrete structures.*

2 *A calculation method for flat-slab structures has still to be created through experiment in order to make a rational use of materials possible.*

3 *In the calculations for reinforced concrete structures, in view of the variety of external forces, there are so many different possibilities that it is not sensible to establish strict design codes. On the contrary, a certain freedom for the designers must be maintained.*

4 *Designers should be urged to sharpen their practical experience through load tests in which they establish the*

518

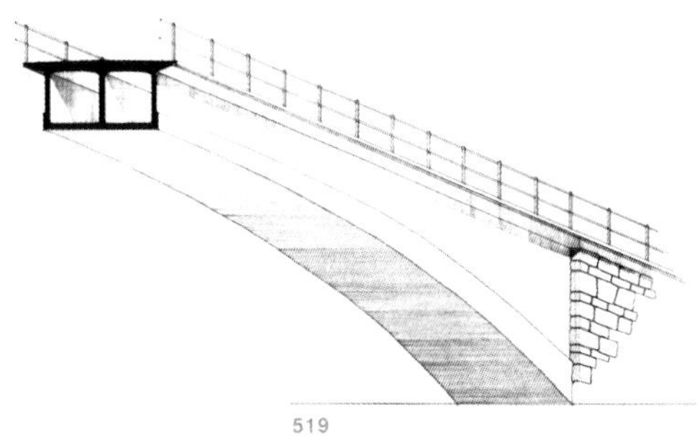
519

520

521

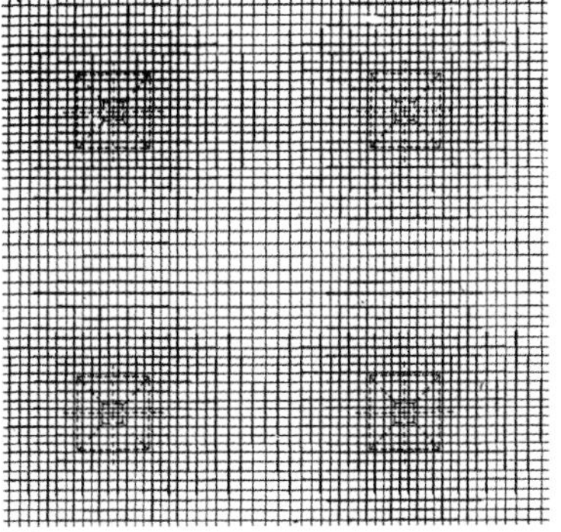
522

516 Jahrhunderthalle, Breslau, Poland, 1911–13. Plan and section. 517 Jahrhunderthalle. Cutaway isometric showing the rib structure. 518 Bridge at Zuoz, Engadin, Switzerland, 1901. Engineer: Robert Maillart. 519 Bridge at Zuoz. Drawing showing the use of thin concrete sheets (slabs) carrying axial and shear loads. 520 Grain warehouse, Altdorf, Switzerland, 1910. Engineer: Robert Maillart. Flat slab floors and mushroom-head columns whose diameter reflects the loads they carry. 521 Load test by Robert Maillart of a flat slab of reinforced concrete, Zurich, Switzerland, 1908. 522 Two-way reinforcement used by Maillart in his flat slabs.

deflections of the structure and thus learn the extent to which the initial design assumptions for their calculations prove to be correct.

5 *The safety of reinforced construction can be satisfactorily guaranteed by modern methods and experience, and criticisms of it have been shown to be invalid.*[14]

In developing the method for designing his flat slab, Maillart took a new and radical approach to assessing their capacity and addressing their safety—or, rather, how factors of safety should be used in the design of his floors. Current practice in Switzerland was to design floors to carry three times the sum of the "live" (imposed) loads and the "dead" loads, or self-weight. Maillart argued that this unfairly penalized a slab that was inherently heavy, such as his flat slab. He argued that a flat slab designed in this way would actually be able to support a much greater total load than a floor of lighter-weight construction. Furthermore, he argued, since the magnitude of the dead load is much less likely to vary from the estimated value, it should be subject to a smaller multiplying safety factor. Maillart's approach to estimating the safety of a structure was thus to link the size of the safety factor by which to multiply the load to the degree of uncertainty as to the estimate of the load—the less certainty, the greater the multiplying safety factor. This revolutionary approach to structural design was finally adopted in codes of design practice throughout the world only in the 1950s.

Maillart's work is especially important because it pointed the way to so much that came to characterize structural engineering in the twentieth century. When cast iron had was introduced in the 1790s, engineers quickly realized the importance of being able to use the minimum amount of material in a beam or a column (see chapter 5). The design methods and the understanding of structural behavior that developed were applicable only to elements made of a single piece of materials. During the mid-nineteenth century, graphical statics had enabled engineers to design minimum-weight structures made of numerous discrete elements, such as roof trusses. Reinforced concrete, however, comprises two materials that work both separately and together. The behavior of reinforced concrete depends crucially on where the reinforcement is placed—ideally, only where it is needed. To establish where it is needed, however—"to make a rational use of the materials," as Maillart put it—required a much deeper understanding of the stresses inside each structural element than was possible using the engineering science from the nineteenth century that was available at the time.

In devising a rational design for his flat slabs, Maillart had realized the need to look at the total picture of structural behavior. He had to consider three mathematical models: the model for the loads acting on the structure, including the built-in safety factors; the model of the structure; and the model of the material. The structure and the material were new, and so the mathematical models pertaining to them could only be used with confidence after experiments to test their validity and reliability. There had, of course, been experimental testing of materials (e.g., iron) and whole structures (e.g., bridges) throughout the nineteenth century. However, the complexity of reinforced concrete as a material, and the variety of structural forms that it could be used to make, provided a crucial stimulus to the art and science of experimentation in structural engineering. This, in turn, led to advances in the sciences of structural behaviour and materials, and in the use of this new understanding as a basis for design methods that could be used for new types of structure that had no historical precedent.

Structural Forms Enter the Third Dimension

Until the end of the nineteenth century virtually all iron structures—both large, complex roof structures and the many variations on the orthogonal structural frame—had been strictly two-dimensional. That is, the forces, stresses, and bending moments were calculated by considering structural actions in a flat plane. Structures were used to create three-dimensional forms by simply repeating a series of two-dimensional elements such as frames (beams and columns), arches, or trusses, either parallel or at right angles to one another. Apart from the cost benefits of such repetitive methods of construction, the main reason for continuing to think in two dimensions was to keep the design calculations as simple and reliable as possible. During the 1850s and 1860s two alternative methods had been developed for analyzing the forces in two-dimensional statically determinate frameworks. Karl Culmann had shown engineers how to use graphical methods to analyze trusses and bending moments in beams (see pp. 373–74). Johann

Schwedler (1823–94), primarily a bridge engineer, had devised his "method of sections," in which a statically determinate truss is analyzed by imagining that various members are cut to divide the remaining structure into sections held in equilibrium by the forces in the cut members. The elegance of this method, first published in 1851 and still widely used today, lies in its appeal to the engineer's imagination in linking the way the structure works with both its geometric form and the magnitude of the forces. Of course, both Culmann's graphical methods and Schwedler's numerical methods are equally applicable to truly three-dimensional structures, but the complexities of three-dimensional geometry and trigonometry would put off all but the most talented of mathematicians.

The dome was the single exception to the general use of two-dimensional structures. With antecedents in masonry dating back to Roman times and timber in the Renaissance structures of Philibert de l'Orme, the dome was a powerful architectonic symbol. Little surprise, then, that engineers should want to build domes of iron too. The first was the Halle au blé in Paris (1808–13), which was constructed to replace the 38-meter-diameter timber dome (1783) that had been destroyed by fire. The iron structure consisted of fifty-one radial ribs that echoed the former timber structure, made from curved timber planks in the manner of de l'Orme. From the 1820s onward, a number of glass houses were constructed using curved ribs to create domes or semi-domes, and in 1839 the 24-meter-diameter dome of Saint Isaac's Cathedral in Saint Petersburg was completed. This dome, which used curved radial ribs of both cast and wrought iron, was the latest in a series of similar timber and iron domes built in Saint Petersburg starting in the early 1800s.

When, in about 1862, Schwedler turned his thoughts to designing the iron structure for a dome at a new synagogue in Berlin, he, too, conceived of a ribbed dome that was given its stability using highly efficient diagonal
523, 525 cross bracing. Calculating the forces and bending such a highly statically indeterminate structure was too challenging even for Schwedler, and he turned his attention to devising a structure for a dome that was statically deter-
524 minate. He used this fully triangulated structural idea for the roofs of a number of gasholders.

The Schwedler dome inspired another German engineer, August Föppl (1854–1924), Professor at the University of Leipzig, to explore rigorously the field of three-dimensional structures, or "space trusses" (Fachwerk im Raume), as he called them. Although Föppl was above all 526
an engineering mathematician and scientist, and one of the most influential of his time (one of his textbooks sold over 100,000 copies), he was also concerned with the practical application of his structural ideas. He made and tested many models, and in 1891 used a space truss for the roof over a market hall in Leipzig. Föppl's investiga- 527
tions went beyond fully braced space trusses; he studied the possibility of using bars to form what we would now call a grid shell, for example, in the form of a barrel vault. This was braced in the plane of the shell, and relied on rigid joints to maintain the form of the shell. To establish the degree to which the behavior of the entire shell was influenced by the rigidity of the joints, he built and tested a large model. Although no roofs of this type seem to have been built at the time, Föppl's work proved invaluable to Walter Bauersfeld and his colleagues at Zeiss when they were developing the geodesic dome for the planetarium at Jena in the late 1910s, and to Bauersfeld, Franz Dischinger, and Ulrich Finsterwalder, who constructed the first barrel shells of reinforced concrete in the 1920s (see chapter 8, pp. 480–88).

Independently of Föppl, a Russian engineer, Vladimir Shukhov (1853–1939), who was also exploring the third dimension in structures, created a barrel vault to form a steel and glass arcade in Moscow's first department store, GUM (1890–93). By using steel wires to stabilize 528
and stiffen each rib to carry wind or snow loads, Shukhov was able to reduce the size of the ribs to be almost invisible. The ingenious use of tension and compression elements was a radical departure from conventional trusses, and the *Gum* arcade was an early example of what would become a standard technique for creating lightweight structures in the late twentieth century.

Shukhov went on to design four remarkable pavilions for the All-Russian Arts and Industry Exhibition in Novgorod 529, 530
in 1896. The roofs were formed of a tensile membrane of interwoven strips of steel, riveted at their intersections. There were four pavilions in all: two rectangular ones, each 70 m long and 30 m wide with a central row of steel columns; the circular Pavilion for Engineering and

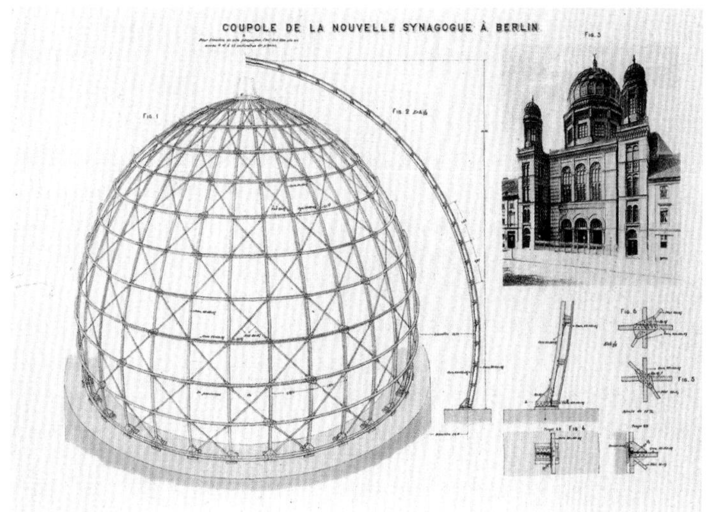

523

524

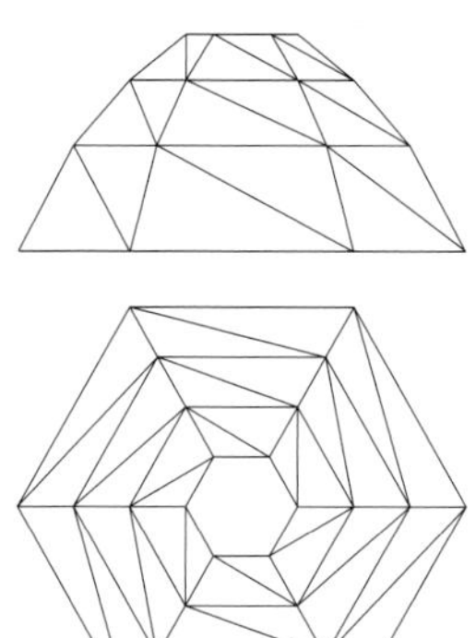

525

Building Construction, 68 m in diameter; and the largest, oval in plan, 98 m long by 51 m wide, with just two supporting columns. These unprecedented structural forms would not be seen again until the 1950s, when lightweight polyester membranes were used by Frei Otto.

Shukhov's use of interlaced strips of steel to create a tensile membrane made it theoretically possible to create a lattice dome using interlaced angle sections. Although no such dome is known, he used the idea to create several dozen structures—water towers, radio masts and pylons—of breathtaking delicacy. Each of the towers comprised a number of hyperboloids of diminishing size; the tallest, at a height of 150 meters, was a radio mast built in Moscow in 1920–22. Shukhov continued to refine the design of his towers. The most elegant and delicate ones—though, at only 120 meters in height, not the tallest—were the pylons carrying electrical cables over the river Oka in northern Russia, designed when he was 531, 534
over seventy years old.

A wonderful example of how designers' exploration into the third dimension came to influence even the most traditional methods of building in masonry is provided by the work of the Catalan architect Antonio Gaudí (1852–1926). He devised his own method for creating masonry compression structures by extending into three dimensions Robert Hooke's axiom stating that the form of a stable arch is that of an inverted hanging chain (see chapter 4, p. 209). To establish the form for the vault of

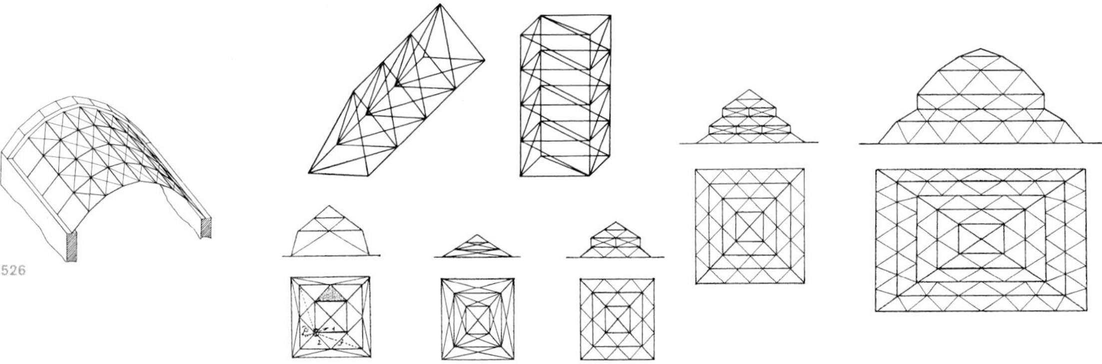

526

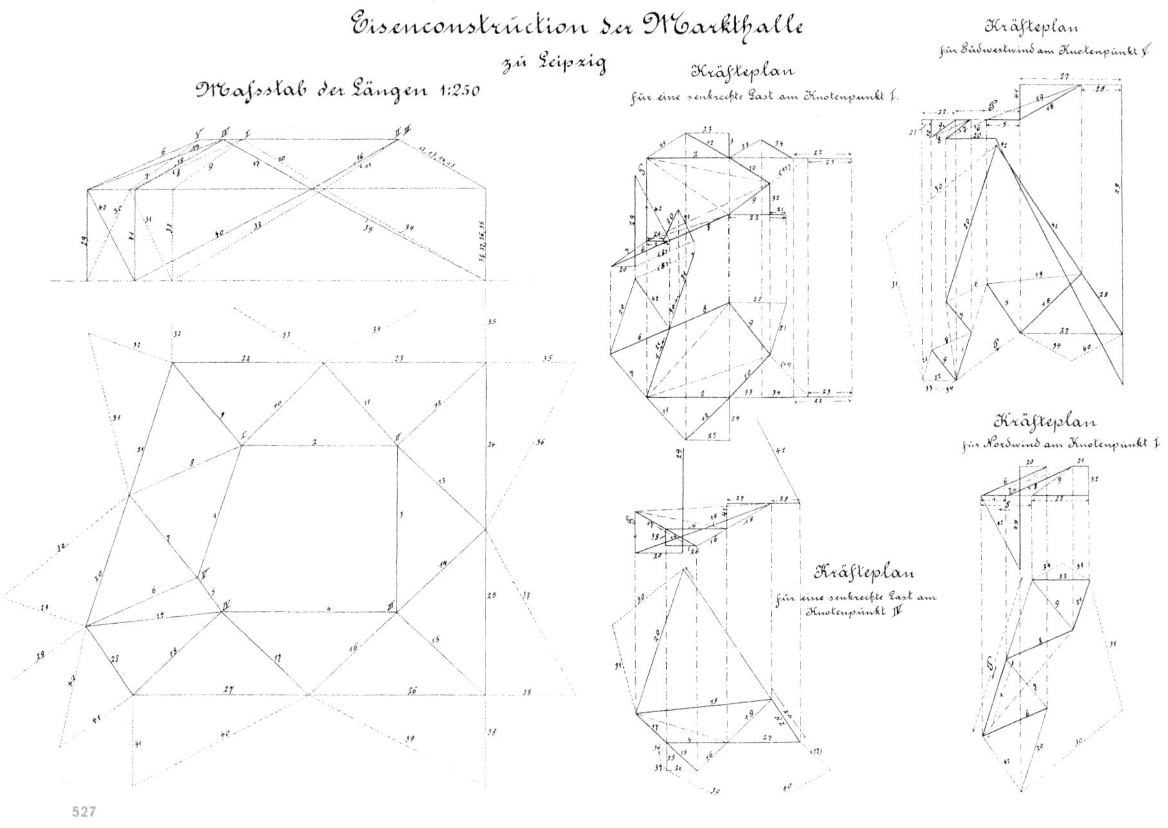

527

523 Dome of the New Synagogue, Berlin, 1863. Engineer: Johnann Schwedler. 524 Dome of the New Synagogue. Detail. 525 Diagram of three-dimensional, triangulated, statically determinate framework devised by Johann Schewedler, c. 1864, sometimes called a "Schwedler dome." 526 Barrel vault formed by a lattice framework by August Föppl, c. 1890. The diagonal wires can carry no compression forces; therefore, the structure can be treated as statically determinate.
527 Market hall, Leipzig, Germany, 1890. Engineer: August Föppl. The diagrams (right) show the graphical calculation of the forces in the statically determinate structure.

528

529

a chapel, Gaudí created a three-dimensional model using wires and bags of sand to represent the weight of the masonry elements and canvas to visualize the vaults. When inverted, this would give a stable arrangement of ma-
532 sonry columns and vaults. Only the crypt of this chapel was built, and the Sagrada Familia Cathedral in Barcelona, whose vault he designed in the same manner, is still under construction 120 years after the corner-
533 stone was laid. The use of models for structural form finding, especially for three-dimensional structures, would be taken up by Frei Otto in his Institute for Lightweight Structures in Stuttgart in the 1960s and 1970s (see chapter 9, pp. 552–54), as well as by the Swiss engineer Heinz Isler, who today uses similar methods to generate the forms of his elegant concrete-shell roofs.

These various ventures into the third dimension were indicative of a more fundamental change in perception—the birth of the abstract idea of structure. Louis Sullivan alluded to such a notion in 1896 in his paper "The tall office building artistically considered," where he coined his famous phrase "form ever follows function":

> *Whether it be the sweeping eagle in his flight or the open apple-blossom, the toiling work-horse, the blithe swan, the branching oak, the winding stream at its base, the drifting clouds, over all the coursing sun, form ever follows function, and this is the law. Where function does not change form does not change.*[15]

The idea that structural form in nature was literally a reflection of mathematical and scientific laws began to be developed in the early years of the twentieth century by D'Arcy Wentworth Thompson (1860–1948). Thompson was, in equal measure, a Greek scholar, a biologist, and a mathematician. He was one of the first to reflect on the idea of structure in an abstract way, both in a geometric sense and in terms of the idea of a "minimum weight structure" as an ultimate goal that both natural and designed structures could approach. Thompson gained his knowledge of classics from his father, a university professor of Greek, and this enabled him to study, at first hand, the works of the Greek mathematicians and biologists. After studying natural sciences and zoology at Cambridge University, he was invited to become Professor of Biology at Dundee University in Scotland at the age of twenty-four. He became professor of Natural History at St. Andrews University in 1917, a post he held until he died at the age of eighty-eight—by which time he had held a university chair for a record sixty-four years, a record not likely to be surpassed. Thompson was the first person to rigorously apply mathematics and basic laws of physics to the natural world; for instance, he observed that the forms of many living things can be described mathematically, most famously the logarithmic spiral of the nautilus 535
shell. Thompson also looked at how natural forms are built up from the regular repetition of single units—snowflakes, for example, and the hexagonal cells of a honeycomb.

Of particular interest to Thompson was the work of Ernst Haeckel (1834–1919), a professor of botany in the University at Jena who had meticulously catalogued many thousands of similar organic structures. Among the many astonishing forms drawn by Haeckel were certain sponges called "radiolaria," which are of particular interest to structural engineers because they so clearly resemble many modern lattice structures. In 1887 Haeckel 537
published a monograph on these organisms, illustrated by 140 remarkable color plates which became widely known well beyond the field of botany. The radiolarian *Aulonia hexagona* particularly fascinated Thompson because it appears to be constructed entirely of hexagons. In fact, it is not. Indeed, the Swiss mathematician Leonhard Euler had established in the eighteenth century an important mathematical (topological) truth—namely, that no volume can be enclosed by a series of hexagons, whether regular or irregular. This truth frustrated Thompson in his search for mathematical algorithms for generating the geometry of natural structures, but it proved very useful to the designers of the first geodesic dome for the planetarium at the Zeiss factory in Jena in the early 1920s.

Thompson was the first to look carefully at how animals and plants work as load-carrying structures, anticipating the modern science of biomechanics. He noted a chance

528 GUM department store, Moscow, Russia, 1890–93. Engineer: Vladimir Shukov. Interior view of glazed vault over central arcade. 529 Rectangular pavilion at the All-Russia Arts and Industry Exhibition, Novgorod, Russia, 1896. Engineer: Vladimir Shukov.

530 531 532 533

530 Oval pavilion at the All-Russia Arts and Industry Exhibition, Novgorod, Russia, 1896. Engineer: Vladimir Shukov. 531 Pylons, River Oka, Russia, 1927–29. Engineer: Vladimir Shukov. 532 Hanging model of the Colonia Guell Chapel, Barcelona, 1889–1908. Architect: Antonio Gaudí. 533 Plaster model of the proposed vault of the cathedral of the Sagrada Familia, Barcelona, 1883–present. Architect: Antonio Gaudí. 534 Pylons at the River Oka.

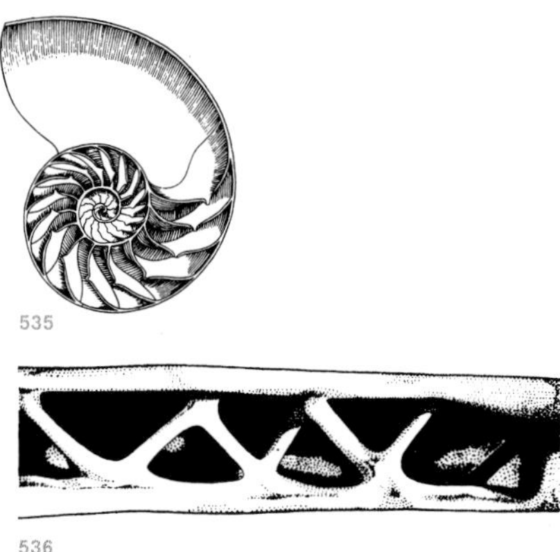

535

536

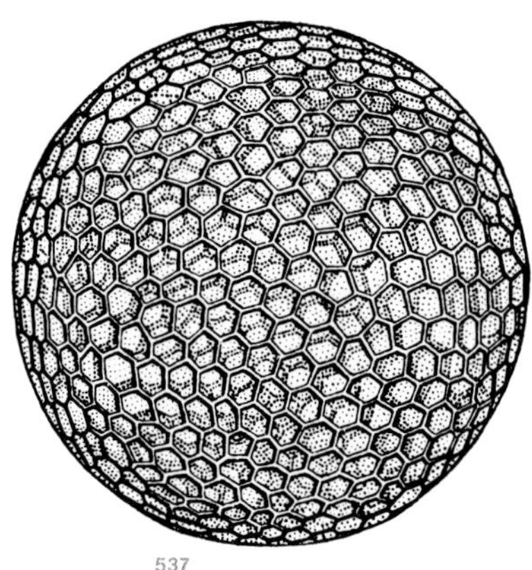

537

discovery, in 1866, by Karl Culmann, who, in analyzing the principal stresses in one of William Fairbairn's iron cranes, recorded that the crane resembles the structure of the bone that forms the similarly shaped head of the human femur (see pp. 373–74). He also noted that the internal structure of the wing bone of a vulture was, ef-
536 fectively, a fully triangulated Warren truss.

From the structural engineer's point of view, Thompson's most interesting ideas relate to the importance of the scale of structures, an observation Galileo had also made some 300 years earlier. It is a fundamental truth about the world that, as size increases, different parameters increase at different rates. Area, for example, increases as the square of the increase in linear dimension, mass as the cube; other quantities, such as stiffness or bending moments, vary in more complex ways. He summarized this phenomenon as the "principle of similitude," and related it to a passage in *Gulliver's Travels* (1726) describing Gulliver's visit to Lilliput, where "His Majesty's Ministers, finding that Gulliver's stature exceeded theirs in the proportion of twelve to one, concluded from the similarity of their bodies that his must contain 1,728 [123] of theirs, and must needs be rationed [with wine] accordingly."[16] Thompson's ideas led directly to the structural engineer's concept of "specific stiffness" as a means of comparing the structural effectiveness of different materials. Although timber and steel have very different stiffnesses and densities, their specific stiffness—the amount of stiffness you get per kilogram of material—is virtually identical. It is because glass and carbon fiber composite materials have specific stiffnesses 10-15 times greater than steel and timber that they are used for many applications where great stiffness and low weight are needed together—carbon fibers in aircraft structures, tennis rackets and fishing rods; glass fibers in aircraft and yachts; lightweight partitions and external cladding in buildings.

Thompson's highly influential book *On Growth and Form*, published in 1917 and reprinted in an enlarged edition in 1942, has been available since 1961 in an abridged version. It quickly became essential reading for all biologists, and any engineer concerned with the design of minimum-weight structures. Nevertheless, despite near-universal recognition of the importance of Thompson's work for both biologists and many design engineers, his considerable influence has been almost at a subliminal level—"intangible and indirect," as the eminent mathematician Peter Medawar put it.[17] Thompson's ideas were also reflections of the time he conceived them; others, too, were having similar thoughts, especially relating to three-dimensional structures and to the significance of scale. Understanding the effect of scale, not only on the behavior of structures but on many physical phenomena, would help engineers, through the sophisticated use of scale model testing, gain the confidence to build many of the remarkable structures that would be constructed during the remainder of the twentieth century.

535 Section through a nautilus shell. 536 Internal structure of the metacarpal bone of a vulture's wing. 537 The radiolarian *Aulonia hexagona*—nature's prototype for the geodesic dome.

chapter 8
Architectural Engineering
1920–1960

People and Events

1861–1919 Henry Gantt

1879–1962 Eugène Freyssinet

1879–1959 Walter Bauersfeld

1880–1968 Arturo Danusso

1883–1963 Karl von Terzaghi

1885–1959 Hardy Cross

1886–1969 Ludwig Mies van der Rohe

1887–1965 Le Corbusier

1887–1953 Franz Dischinger

1890–1969 Owen Williams

1891–1979 Gio Ponti

1891–1979 Pier Luigi Nervi

1893–1963 A. A. Griffith

1895–1983 R. Buckminster Fuller

1895–1988 Ove Arup

1897–1976 Lydik Jacobsen

1897–1988 Ulrich Finsterwalder

1899–1961 Eduardo Torroja

1899–1990 Fred Severud

1900–55 Bernard Lafaille

1901–85 John Baker

1901–84 Jean Prouvé

1903–98 Alfred Pugsley

1929–1930s The Great Depression

Materials and Technology

1910s–1920s Scientific management and Gantt charts

1920s Understanding of brittle fracture

1920s Concept of "effective stress" in soils

From c. 1925 Welding of structural steel

1930s Understanding of ductile behavior of metals

1930s–1950s Understanding of plastic behavior of steel structures

Knowledge and Learning

1919 Newcomen Society for the history of engineering and technology formed (UK)

1921 Building Research Station (UK) opened

1930 First congress of International Association of Bridge and Structural Engineering (IABSE)

1930s First learned societies for history of engineering and technology

Design Methods

1920s Model tests used by Dischinger for design of concrete shells

1923 Zeiss-Dywidag system patented

1927 Boundary layer wind tunnel testing of wind loads on buildings

1930s Model tests of wide-span concrete roof structure by Eduardo Torroja and Pier Luigi Nervi

1930 Wind-tunnel testing of model of Empire State Building

1930 Model tests of soil loaded in a centrifuge conducted by Karl Terzhagi

1930s Scale model tests for room acoustics (using microphones)

1930s Acoustic and electrical resistance strain gauge developed

1930–31 Model testing of dynamic building response to earthquakes

1931 Heliodon devised to demonstrate effects of sunlight

Design Tools: Drawing and Calculation

c. 1920 Relaxation method of calculation developed for airship structures

1920s Spirit duplication / Hectograph method of copying drawings

1922 "Comfort zone" chart developed

c. 1920–1970s Four-function electro-mechanical calculators

From 1920s Ray tracing used to help design concert hall acoustics

mid-1930s Moment distribution method introduced by Hardy Cross

Buildings

1921–23 Concrete shell airship hangars at Orly, France

1922 Church of Le Notre Dame, Le Raincy, France

1923 Prototype Zeiss dome, Jena, Germany

1924 "Gesolei" exhibition buildings, Dusseldorf, Germany

1924–25 Bauhaus building, Dessau, Germany

1924–25 Schröder House, Utrecht, Netherlands

1927 Salle Pleyel, Paris, France

1928–29 Leipzig market hall, Leipzig, Germany

1930–32 Boots factory "Wets" Building, Beeston, England

1935 Frontón Recoletos, Madrid, Spain

1931 Empire State Building, New York, USA

1936 Aircraft hangar, Orvieto, Italy

1936 Simpsons, Picadilly, London, UK

1933 First hyperbolic paraboloid shell

1937–39 Maison du peuple, Clichy, France

1920 | 1925 | 1930 | 1935

1902–59 Felix Samuely

1902–89 Nicolas Esquillan

1903–79 Hubert Rüsch

1903–88 Max Mengeringhausen

1909–2002 John Blume

1910–97 Felix Candela

b. 1925 Frei Otto

1939–45 World War II

1950s Major structural use of aluminum

1940s Glued, laminated timber ("Glulam") developed

1952 Plastic design of steel frames

mid-1940s Ferro-cement developed by Nervi

1952 Use of glass for structural elements

1945 Development of glass-reinforced polymers

1939 First edition of *Principles of Modern Building* by the Department of Scientific and Industrial Research (UK)

1958 First issue of *Technology and Culture* published by the Society for the History of Technology (USA)

1930s–1940s MERO system developed by Max Mengeringhausen

1950s Photoelastic stress analysis of models

Mid-1950s Scale models used in acoustic design

1950 Curta Calculator II, 10-figure hand-held mechanical calculator

From mid-1950s Mainframe computers used for structural analysis

1949–54 Hunstanton School, Hunstanton, England

1951 Skylon, Festival of Britain, London (prestressed cable structure)

1952 Raleigh Livestock Arena, Raleigh, North Carolina (cable net roof)

1952 Lever House, New York, USA

1953 Schwartzwaldhalle, Karlsruhe, Germany (prestressed concrete roof)

1955 Music pavilion, Kassel, Germany (doubly-curved membrane)

1956–58 CNIT Building, Paris, France

1955–57 Inland Steel Building, Chicago, USA

1958 Pirelli Tower, Milan, Italy

Architectural Engineering 1920–1960

The advances in high-rise building during the 1880s and 1890s in the United States were made possible by certain developers recognizing that their real estate dreams would be realized not by architects working alone, but by architects working in collaboration with engineers. Compared to the traditional, European Beaux Arts idea of the architect's role, this generally meant the architect had a smaller part to play. Indeed, it was difficult for architects to find ways of expressing their individuality in multistory iron- or steel-frame commercial office buildings or hotels. In the extreme, the role of the architect could be little more than providing a decorative facade and lavish interiors in the foyer and other public areas.

Engineers were prominent in many of the early building design firms in the United States. In New York, George B. Post had trained as a civil engineer before turning to building design, and in Chicago William Le Baron Jenney was an engineer who employed both architects and engineers in his firm. Other practices soon learned the benefits of collaboration between architect and engineer, and several of the most successful had one or more partners who had trained as an engineer—Adler of Adler & Sullivan, Root of Burnham & Root, and both partners of Holabird and Roche. It was these firms' engineering innovations that were so attractive to developers in helping reduce the cost and increase the speed of constructing steel-frame buildings in the United States. And it was as a direct result of this close collaboration with engineers that a few architects of genius would, indeed, find ways to forge their identity on steel-frame buildings—for example, Louis Sullivan's Guaranty Building in Buffalo, New York (1895), and in New York City, Cass Gilbert's Woolworth Building (1913), William Van Allen's Chrysler Building (1930), and Mies van der Rohe's Seagram Building (1958). In Europe, the first building that truly celebrated steel in its architecture—the Centre Pompidou in Paris, designed by architects Renzo Piano and Richard Rogers in collaboration with the engineering firm of Ove Arup—was not completed until 1977.

Two remarkable features of steel-frame construction were how quickly the height of buildings grew and how quickly the technology spread through North America and to many large cities of South America, South Africa, Australia, and the Far East. By the second decade of the twentieth century. twenty-story steel-frame buildings with heating and mechanical ventilation had become part of everyday construction practice. Built in 1931, the Empire State Building, with its 102 stories, would remain the world's tallest building for nearly four decades. How was 538, 540 it that such progress could be achieved in such a short span of time? Surprisingly, perhaps, the answer has little

538

SCHENECTADY WORKS MACHINE

PART		FRAMES									
PUR ORD; SKETCH; PAT. OR CARD DR. No.											
OPERATION		REC'D		PLANED		SLOTTED		DRILLED		ASSEM'D	
TO BE BEGUN											
TO BE FINISHED											
NUMBER WANTED		15		15		15		15		15	
NUMBER FINISHED		DAILY	TOTAL	DAILY	TOTAL	DAILY	TOTAL	DAILY	TOTAL	DAILY	TOTA
1903 JAN	20	2	2	2	2						
	21	2	4								
	22			2	4						
	23	1	5								
	24	2	7	1	5	3	3				
	26	4	11	2	7	1	4				
	27										
	28	1	12	2	9	3	7	2	2		
	29	2	14	1	10	1	8	1	3		
	30	1	15	1	11	2	10	1	4		
	31			3	14	1	11	1	5		
FEB	2					1	12	1	6	2	2
	3			1	15	1	13	3	9	1	3
	4							2	11	2	5
	5							2	13	1	6
	6					2	15			2	8
	7							2	15	1	9
	9									2	11
	10									1	12
	11									1	13
	12									1	14
	13									1	15
	14										
	16										
	17										
	18										
	19										
	20										
	21										
	23										
	24										
	25										
	26										

RECORD AS ACTUAL

FIG. 290.

539

540

538 Empire State Building, New York, 1931. Chief engineer: Andrew J. Eken of Starret Bros. and Eken Inc. Structural engineer: H. G. Balcom and Associates; architect: Shreve, Lamb and Harmon. Under construction in July 1930. 539 Chart by Henry Gantt, first developed c.1918, to help plan the effective allocation of manufacturing operations to the various machines in a workshop. 540 Empire State Building.

to do with building engineering. A seemingly offhand but extraordinary statement by the American building historian Carl Condit highlights a remarkable feature of engineering in general:

> *For all its height, the design of the steel framing [for the Empire State building] was a straightforward job of determining the sizes of members adequate to meet buckling and wind loads. . . .* [1]

Following certain breakthroughs, enormous progress can be made in a relatively short time simply by exploiting the new opportunities. Neither the Empire State Building nor dozens of other buildings constructed in the first half of the twentieth century were particularly innovative. They were designed and built largely using construction techniques, design methods, and engineering science that had been established by the 1870s. Most of the developments during the following sixty years or so were in the field of what would be called, in manufacturing industries, "production engineering"—improving the quality of the materials used, the methods for their manufacture and assembly, and, not least, managing the whole process.

American engineer Frederick Taylor (1856–1915) published his paper "The Principles of Scientific Management" in 1911 while working for the Bethlehem Steel company on the construction of warships for the U.S. government. His rational analysis of the activities needed to complete manufacturing tasks revolutionized the process of organizing production. Taylor's principles were rapidly adopted in many countries, in part because of the rush to manufacture armaments during World War I. They were championed in the construction industry by the building contractor Frank Gilbreth (1868–1924), who, to some extent, gave them a bad name through the overenthusiastic use of stopwatches to time the activities of construction site workers down to the last second. By the mid-1920s American trade unions had already ensured that such extremes were on the decline.

One of the most useful tools to come out of these early
539 days of modern management was the "Gantt Chart." Henry Gantt (1861–1919) was a mechanical engineer and management consultant who had worked for many years under Frederick Taylor in the American defense industry. Gantt charts, which were first used at the end of World War I, served as visual tools for comparing the targeted and the actual progress of projects. After the war, the charts were soon adopted to help the organization and management of any large project, and were used with particular success in the construction of many dams in the United States during the 1920s.

Applying such tools in the management of large construction projects enabled both the construction time and the cost of such projects to be dramatically reduced. This, in turn, enabled real estate developers to propose ever larger buildings in the secure expectation of higher profits. The construction statistics for many of the 1930s skyscrapers in America are truly astonishing. The steel frame of the Empire State Building was built at an average speed of four and a half stories per week, for a total of just 410 days for the entire building.

Taller buildings were, however, made possible not only by the application of principles of scientific management, but also as the result of a breakthrough in the understanding of the behavior of soil under load. Taller buildings were heavier and needed more substantial foundations. Engineering scientists began studying soil as a material, in the same way they studied the behavior of iron or timber. During the early decades of the twentieth century a wider transformation was underway that touched the theoretical and experimental study of all materials. Following the progress made in physics in understanding the atomic structure of matter, scientists studying all types of material began asking a more fundamental question: Why did soil (and other materials) have the strength and stiffness that it did? Seeking and finding explanations for the properties of materials became a new discipline known as "materials science," and led to a revolution in the design and manufacture or construction of all man-made artifacts.

Materials Science, Soil Mechanics

The load-bearing capacity of soils is, both metaphorically and literally, the foundation of all building. The science of soil mechanics had first been developed in the eighteenth century, especially by Charles Augustin de Coulomb, and continued in the nineteenth century, especially by William Rankine. Their main concern had been the stability of retaining walls and the faces or slopes of soil newly created or exposed when excavating the ground to build foundations for buildings and bridge piers, digging cuttings, and building embankments for fortifications, dams, canals, and railways. This work, however, had relatively little impact on the design of actual building foundations, which, even into the twentieth century, had not changed significantly since Roman and medieval times.

Foundations were of two types: a footing made of timber, stone, concrete, or steel and concrete that distributed the load over a sufficiently large area; or, in soft soils, a series of piles driven so deeply that they either rested on rock beneath the soil or were prevented from sinking by
541, 542 friction between the pile and the soil. The design proce-
543 dures for both these types were empirical, and took little account of any scientific material properties of the soil. "According to some of the best authorities," said the sixteenth edition of Rankine's classic *Manual of Civil Engineering* (1887), "the test of a pile's having been sufficiently driven is that it shall not be driven more than *one-fifth* of an inch by *thirty blows* of a ram weighing 800 pounds and falling 5 feet at each blow" (italics in the original).[2] The same textbook advised that footings on firm ground, including sand, gravel, and hard clay, should be made large enough to ensure that the pressure on the earth was between 2,500 and 3,500 pounds per square foot (125–175 kN/m^2). Footings on soft earth should be built on sand or concrete to a depth that took account of the angle of repose of the earth, which reflected the ability of the soil to resist shear forces. This was a minor adaptation of the well-established design procedures for earth embankments.

The main preoccupation of foundation engineers was not to avoid settlement, since this was considered inevitable, but to ensure that each separate foundation settled at the same rate and, eventually, by the same amount. This was an intelligent aim and could theoretically be achieved by adjusting the area of each footing in proportion to the load it must carry, thus creating the same pressure on the soil everywhere beneath the building. However, this aim depended on the soil having identical properties across the entire building footprint, an ideal situation that is seldom found in practice. Measurements taken in 1892 on a number of buildings in Chicago, including the Auditorium Building, showed that differential settlements of up to 450 mm were not uncommon.

Karl Terzaghi (1883–1963) was the engineering giant who found the solution to this problem. Born in Prague, he studied mechanical engineering at the Technische Hochschule in Graz, Austria, before joining the army. During this time he spent two years in Saint Petersburg designing reinforced concrete structures; he went on to write his doctoral thesis on reinforced concrete. In 1914 he began a two-year visit to the United States, where he worked on the design and construction of a number of large dams, and it was during this time that he began to turn his professional attention to his childhood passion for geology. Terzaghi was struck by the fact that he was not able to account for the behavior of engineering structures and their foundations in terms of the geology of the soils themselves. Thus he began developing the principle that would guide his work on soil mechanics for the next forty years: The key to understanding the behavior of soil is the careful and meticulous observation of its behavior, both in the field and in laboratory experiments. On his return to Austria in 1916 the Austrian government asked him to accept a teaching post at the Imperial School of Engineers in Constantinople (now Istanbul). During his nine years in that post he undertook the theoretical and experimental work that established soil mechanics as a truly scientific discipline and culminated, in 1925, with the publication of *Erdbaumechanik auf bodenphysikalischer Grundlage* (The Mechanics of Earth Construction Based on the Physical Properties of Soil). This book laid the foundations for the modern subjects of soil mechanics and geotechnical engineering. After 1925 he spent four years at the Massachusetts Institute of Technology in Cambridge, Massachusetts, where he introduced and developed the science of soil mechanics. In 1929 he returned to Austria as a professor at the Technical University of Vienna, which soon became the world center for engineers interested in geotechnical engineering. In 1936 the International Society of Soil Mechanics and Foundation Engineering was founded, and Terzaghi was elected as its first president, a position he held for more than two decades, until the age of seventy-four.

Terzaghi's insight was, in hindsight, simple: He recognized the vital role played by the water content of soil in the soil's ability to carry loads. Yet this insight brought about a revolution in understanding the behavior of soil. When water fills the voids between soil particles, the total stress at any point comprises two components: the pressure in the water, that is, the "pore-water pressure," and the stresses in the matrix of particles, the "effective stress." The presence of water reduces the forces between individual soil particles and, hence, reduces the force needed to cause the particles to shear past one another. Expressed in the language of Coulomb's concept of internal friction (see chapter 6, p. 244), this means that the presence of water in soil reduces the internal friction and, hence, its shear strength and its ability to carry loads. While this conclusion was the most radical and far-reaching consequence of Terzaghi's work, his observational approach to the behavior of soils was hardly less significant.

For virtually the first time in any building engineering discipline, an experimental approach to the subject was established that put it on a par with the great scientific work of German and British physicists and chemists of the late nineteenth century, in whose tradition Terzaghi had been steeped as a young engineer. He was driven by the goal of devising a set of material properties that would explain the curious, and often apparently inexplicable, behavior of soils when subject to loads. He felt it should be possible to predict the behavior of soils as reliably as that of other materials. Thus in addition to inventing the concept of effective stress, he devised or formalized all the tests that are today undertaken in site investigations to establish the properties of a soil that allow its load-bearing behavior to be predicted with confidence. Because the presence or absence of water is so important, many of these tests relate to the propensity of a soil to allow water to flow through it, that is, its permeability, and the factors that might affect permeability. These include the degree of "consolidation" of the soil—the amount by which the sizes of voids between soil particles have been reduced, for example, by the action of water when the soil was formed, or increased, as a result of disruption by landslides, earthquakes, or excavations. He thus demonstrated the need to place great emphasis on the history of a soil, both over geological time and in its more recent past.

To model the movement of water underground, Terzaghi promoted the use of "flow nets," which had been devised in about 1900 by an Austrian hydraulic engineer, Philipp Forchheimer (1852–1933) to visualize in two and three dimensions how water flows through soils. Through the graphical construction of an orthogonal grid of flow lines and lines of equal pore-water pressure, it is possible to calculate the pressure gradient in the soil and, hence, the rate at which water flows through soil. Thus any potential adverse consequences of water flowing beneath buildings or dams can be predicted, and suitable means devised for controlling the water flow and avoiding the 544
problems. Terzaghi was always conscious of the risk to a project, and hence to the client's purse, that resulted from the incomplete knowledge of the nature of the soils beneath a construction site. Such a lack of knowledge always compromises the engineer's ability to determine an economical and safe design solution before construction has started. In order to avoid the overdesign of structures in the ground, Terzaghi insisted on a thorough site investigation and soil analysis before construction began, and continuous observation of the behavior of the soil as construction progressed, to enable the designs to be modified to reflect the true soil conditions as they were revealed. Thus he was able to save the client money if the initial assumptions about the soil proved to be too conservative, and to avoid disaster if the assumptions were found to have overestimated strength or stiffness of the soil.

Terzaghi's worldwide fame was a result of the rigor, thoroughness, and reliability of his approach, which began with understanding the geology of a site, followed by analysis of geotechnical conditions, structural considerations, and, often, hydrological issues. His advice was sought on every type of construction work. The technical reports he wrote for his clients were highly regarded both for their quality and their forthright nature, and for many decades they served as models for other geotechnical engineers.

Aircraft Design and Structural Engineering

During the early decades of the twentieth century, structural engineering benefited considerably from research undertaken in the aircraft industry, especially the search for lightweight structures for airships and planes. Much of this research involved the study of metals and how it might be possible to improve their strength-to-weight ratio. This, in turn, was made possible by a number of recent developments in physics. In about 1910 the properties of materials were at the forefront of research in physics. In about 1910 the German physicist Max von

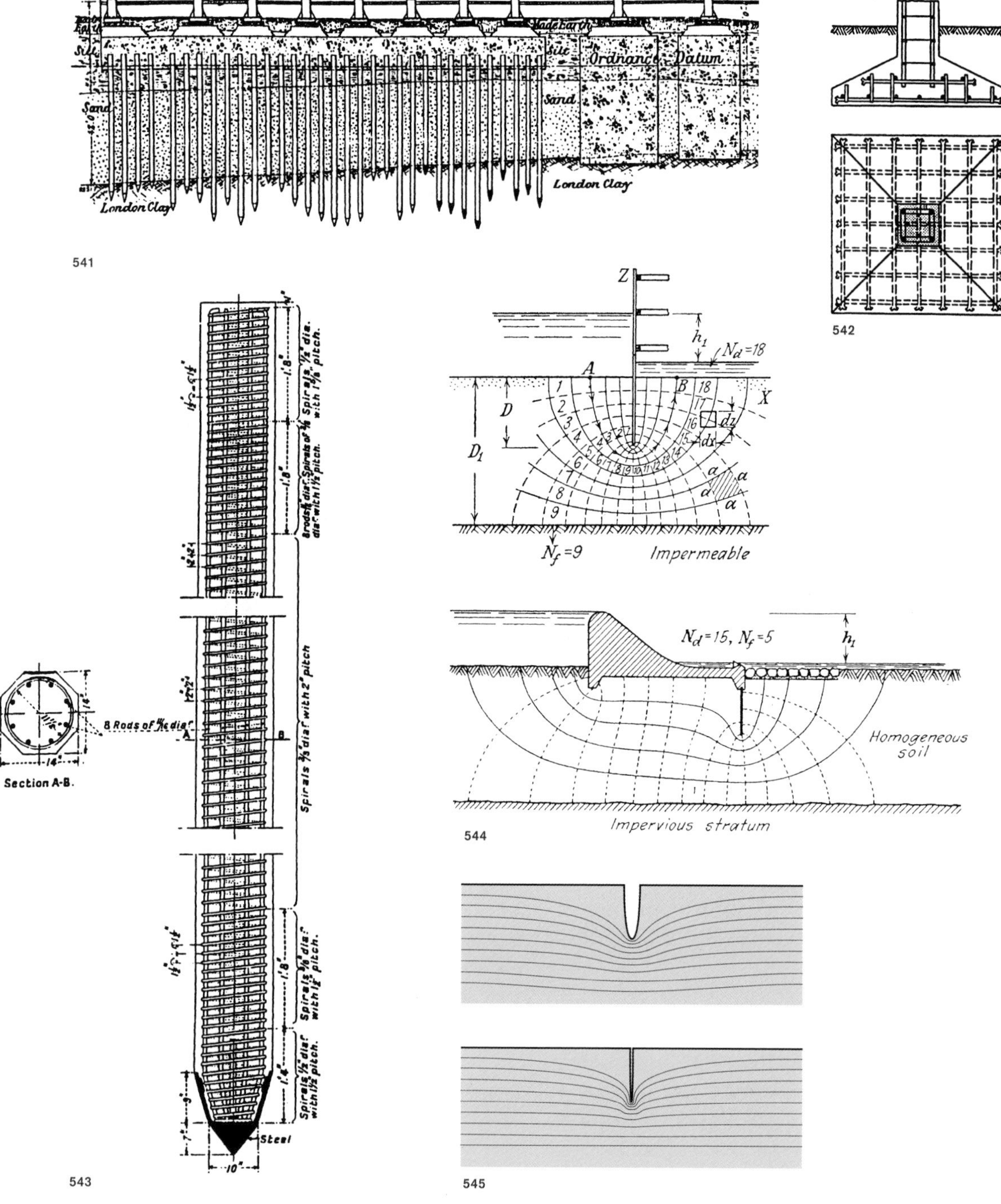

541 Victoria Station, London, 1900. Timber piles used for extension works. 542 Victoria Station. Mass concrete foundations used for extension works. 543 Early twentieth-century foundations. (left) Typical Hennebique pad foundation, c. 1907; (right) pile made using the Considère system, c. 1908. 544 Flow net showing flow of water in soil beneath a sheet pile (top) and a dam (bottom). 545 Lines of stress cracks with different root radii; the smaller radius causes greater stress concentration.

Laue (1879–1960) had discovered that X-rays (identified by Wilhelm Röntgen in 1895) are diffracted (scattered) by the atoms of a crystal in ways that depend on the structure of the crystal. A few years later, the British scientist William Henry Bragg (1862–1942) and his son William Lawrence used the knowledge of X-ray diffraction to deduce the precise nature of crystal structures, and developed the technique known as "X-ray crystallography." Laue and both Braggs were awarded Nobel Prizes for their work, which, for the first time, enabled scientists to look at the properties of materials at the atomic scale. A host of scientists worldwide was soon engaged in exploring the chemical and physical consequences of the new theories and discoveries about the structure of matter. One line of inquiry was of particular concern to all design engineers: analysis of the physical properties of matter—including strength, stiffness, hardness, brittleness, ductility, metal fatigue, and creep—in terms of atomic structure. It proved to be an arduous task, one that was completed only in the second half of the twentieth century, but its significance cannot be overstated. Today the explanation of materials properties in terms of atomic structure forms the core of university courses in nearly every engineering discipline.

Two scientists whose contribution was of particular significance for structural engineering were Alan Arnold Griffith (1893–1963), a materials scientist at the Royal Aircraft Establishment (RAE) at Farnborough in England, and Geoffrey Ingram Taylor (1886–1975), a scientist who worked for much of his life at Cambridge University in England.

The Work of A. A. Griffith and G. I. Taylor

Much of the research on the strength of materials undertaken after World War I at the RAE was done on "ordinary" materials such as metals and timber. However, these are complex, nonhomogeneous materials. A. A. Griffith decided to use glass as a "model" material—a material on which to conduct experiments and obtain results that might then be applied to the "real" materials such as timber and metals. The idea of using small-scale model tests was familiar to aeronautical engineers for aerodynamic tests in wind tunnels. Using thin fibers of glass, Griffith noted three curious and unexplained facts. First, the tensile strength of a single fiber of glass was about one hundred times less than the theoretical strength calculated using the known strength of bonds between individual atoms or molecules. Second, for very fine thicknesses, below a tenth of a millimeter or so, the strength of the fibers increased markedly as the diameter decreased. Finally, the strength of thin fibers decreased with the age of the fiber. The explanation for these phenomena led to perhaps the most profound change of the twentieth century in our understanding of fracture and the strength of materials.

For some decades it had been recognized that stresses in materials under load are raised around holes or at the end of cracks in the material. Such areas are called "stress concentrations." In 1913 C.E. Inglis, an engineering 545 professor at Cambridge University, had demonstrated that the stress concentration factor increases significantly as the radius of curvature of the hole, or crack tip, decreases. A practical consequence of this phenomenon is that the strength of a structure is effectively reduced if cracks causing high stress concentrations are present. Griffith extended the work of Inglis by considering not only the elastic energy stored in a strained material, but also the energy needed to create new surfaces in a crack. He showed that if less strain energy is released from an extension to a crack than would be required to create the new surfaces, then the crack does not grow or spread. However, if the strain energy released is greater than needed to form new surfaces, then the crack does grow and spread—not just gradually, but even explosively. Since this explanation does not involve the radius of the crack tip, it directly relates the stress that a material can bear to the length (actually the square root of the length) of the longest crack in the material, and also to two material properties—the "modulus of elasticity" and the "free surface energy." Thus, for a given stress, a material will fracture if the longest crack is equal to or greater than a critical crack length, now universally known as the "Griffith crack length."

This understanding of the conditions necessary for a crack to propagate enabled Griffith to explain the curious results of his tests on glass fibers. When the fibers are freshly drawn, their surfaces are undamaged and there are no cracks that could begin to propagate. Older fibers invariably become scratched, and these scratches act as microscopic cracks. If the energy balance at the tip of such a microcrack is such that the microcrack length exceeds the Griffith crack length, then the crack will propagate and the fiber will fracture.

"Griffith crack theory," as it is known, quickly became invaluable to forensic engineers seeking the causes of engineering disasters later in the twentieth century, many of which were found to involve the brittle fracture of metals. Furthermore, these metals are often ductile at normal temperatures and become brittle at low temperatures (typically below about –10°C). The most famous of these forensic inquiries concerned the world's first jet-powered airliner, the Comet, which suffered a series of unexplained crashes in the early 1950s, apparently arising from midair explosions. It was finally determined that the stresses in the aircraft's fuselage were such that the diagonals of the near-rectangular windows were fractionally short of the Griffith crack length. Also, the fuselage material, an aluminum alloy, was ductile at ordinary temperatures and brittle at the air temperature at the cruising altitude. When fatigue cracks just a few millimeters long formed at the corners of some of the windows, as tends to occur in all materials subject to repeated changes of stress, the aperture increased to the critical Griffith crack length. The conditions were then such that the crack propagated with the explosive speed and violence of a balloon bursting. (This analogy is apt. Griffith's theory explains why a small hole in a partially inflated balloon merely causes it to deflate, while a hole of the same size in a fully inflated and highly stressed balloon causes it to burst.) Since that time, aircraft windows have been made significantly smaller than the Griffith crack length. They are also more oval-shaped to reduce the level of stress concentration where a fatigue crack would tend to form.

The implications of Griffith's work for engineers have been enormous. Perhaps most significant has been the development of a whole family of new materials known as fiber-reinforced composite materials, or "composites." These use very high-strength fibers of glass, carbon, aramids, and other materials embedded in a matrix usually made of a polymer resin. The hulls of most small boats are today made of fiberglass, and tennis rackets are often made from carbon-fiber composites. Composites are used in the building industry, too, in the construction of cladding panels, for example.

The most significant impact of Griffith's work for building engineers was that it alerted them to the potential dangers of any stress concentration that might become the starting point for a fatigue crack and might eventually lengthen to the critical Griffith crack length, resulting in disastrous brittle fracture. This new insight into the behavior of materials led, in the 1920s, to the reassessment of the detailed design of all steel structures. This reassessment focused on all holes cut in steel, especially the bolted connections between columns and beams in steel-frame buildings, which required large numbers of holes set close together.

The 1920s also saw the introduction of both gas and electric arc welding as a means of joining steel members. At first, welding seemed an ideal way to create a fully rigid connection between steel members while avoiding the large numbers of holes that created stress concentrations. Welding, however, brought its own difficulties. One was that the heating process often changed the crystalline structure of steel from one that allowed ductile deformation to one that is very brittle. In addition, the welding process could artificially introduce discontinuities inside the steel, and these could behave exactly like cracks at sites of stress concentrations and ideal starting points for Griffith cracks.

These difficulties led to important research programs in Germany and the United States, where electric arc welding was actively developed in the 1920s in both the shipbuilding and building industries. Not only was it necessary to improve the welding process to eliminate cracks, it was also necessary to develop methods of nondestructive testing to verify both that welded connections penetrated the steel sections fully, providing a full-strength connection, and that there were no discontinuities or cracks that might be the starting points for brittle fracture.

One of the first welded steel structures used in a building was a 12-meter roof truss erected at the factory of the Electric Welding Company of America, in Brooklyn, New York, in 1920. Welding was also used to fix to the steel columns the large brackets that supported the rails of an overhead traveling crane in the factory. All the welded connections were fully load-tested to prove their strength. For several years the use of electric arc welding

546

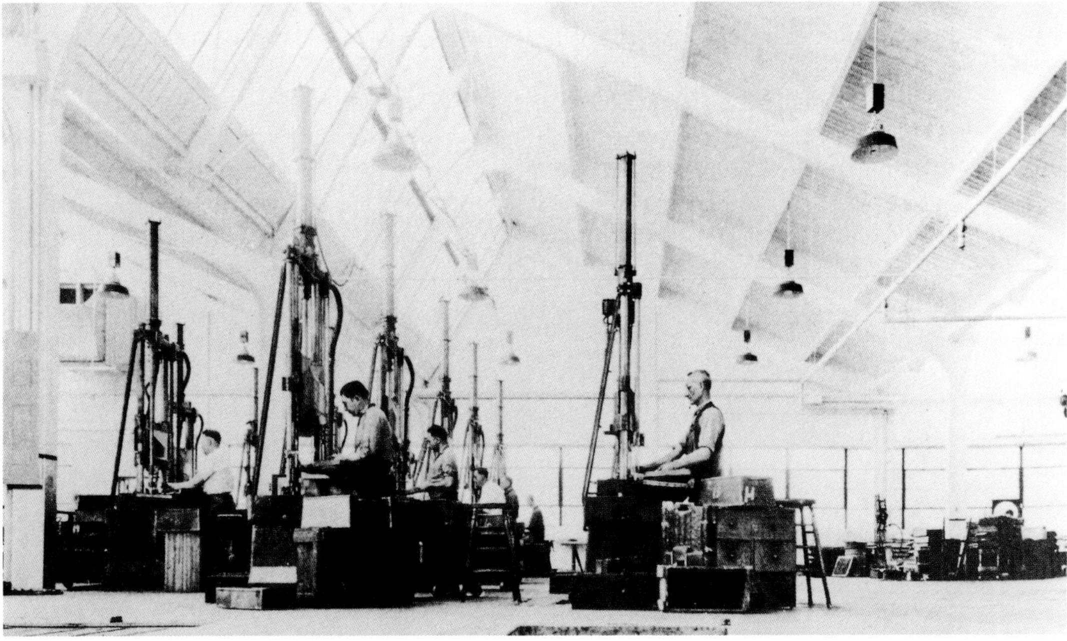

547

546 Westinghouse Electric and Manufacturing Company building, Sharon, Pennsylvania, 1926. 547 International Silver Company factory, Meriden, Connecticut, 1937. Exposed welded steel frame.

grew and spread, but only as a substitute for some of the riveted connections; it did not result in changes to the overall design of the structures. Only in 1926 was the first fully welded frame structure constructed: a five-story building at the Westinghouse Electric and Manufacturing
546 Company in Sharon, Pennsylvania. In this building the beams and columns, themselves built up from flat plates by welding, were welded to form a continuous, homogeneous frame. The structure achieved the necessary rigidity to resist gravity and wind loads using about 12 percent less steel than a conventional riveted frame—790 rather than 900 tons. Before the building was erected, full-size prototypes of the key connection were built and tested to destruction to verify their stiffness and strength. Over the next four years the Westinghouse company constructed twenty-four welded frame buildings including, in 1930, the eleven-story Central Engineering Laboratory Building at its Pittsburgh factory. In 1931 the tallest welded frame of the time—the nineteen-story Dallas Power and Light Building—was completed. During the 1930s welded steel frames were widely used for industrial buildings, primarily because they required less steel, but designers soon learned that welded connections brought to steel structures an elegance that could never be achieved with
547 riveted or bolted connections.

Despite the understanding of brittle fracture developed in the 1920s and 1930s, many structural failures were ultimately attributed to the formation of Griffith cracks because it can be very difficult to detect them or prevent them from forming, due to metal fatigue. In recent years an understanding of Griffith crack theory has been particularly valuable to engineers seeking to work confi-
548 dently with brittle materials such as glass and to refurbish and reuse nineteenth-century buildings with beams and columns of cast iron. The use of highly stressed tensile membranes such as those pioneered by Frei Otto in the mid-1950s (see p. 506 and chapter 9) has also benefited from Griffith's insight. Understanding the mechanism by which a hole or tear might propagate in such highly stressed membranes has enabled design engineers to keep stresses below the critical level and avoid potentially catastrophic consequences.

While designing aircraft and propellers during the World War I, Griffith had worked closely with the British physicist and engineer G. I. Taylor. Taylor, like Griffith, was concerned with why different materials had the strength they did. Taylor's particular interest was to explain why it becomes progressively more difficult for metals to "yield" as they are bent back and forth. This phenomenon, which can be observed by bending a steel paper clip, is known as "work hardening." Indeed, how is it that a crystalline material deforms in a ductile or plastic way at all? The explanation Taylor proposed in 1934 was that the ductile behavior of metals is caused by imperfections, which he called "dislocations," in an otherwise regular crystal
structure. These dislocations could move relatively freely 549
by the minor rearrangement of bonds between atoms, without the bonds having to be broken.

Taken together, the work of Griffith and Taylor, and of D'Arcy Thompson (see chapter 7, pp. 443, 446), transformed engineers' understanding of the strength of materials and made it possible to raise the art of structural design to an altogether higher scientific plane. In the case of buildings, however, this new knowledge was not always applied. Aircraft and aircraft engines had always been designed to the limit of a material's strength, but building components were and are designed to such limits only when weight is especially important, for example, in a long-span roof. Taylor's work did, however, have an immediate impact on the design of structural steelwork through the work of John Baker and the Steel Structures Research Committee in the 1930s (see pp. 470, 472).

Minimum-Weight Structures

As we saw in chapter 5, the conscious search for a minimum-weight structure began in the 1790s with the need to minimize the quantity of iron used to make cast iron beams and columns. In the 1830s, Eaton Hodgkinson and William Fairbairn established the most economical form for a beam, and a decade later conducted experiments to establish the best structure for tubular girders. After the middle of the nineteenth century the quest for minimum-weight structures was taken up by the designers of long-span roof structures. To this end design engineers devised the "pin-jointed" truss, which enabled them to control the way the structure worked: The pin joints prevent the transfer of bending moments from one member to the next, and thus ensure that all the members carry only tension or compression forces and no bending moments. Such structures are easily amenable

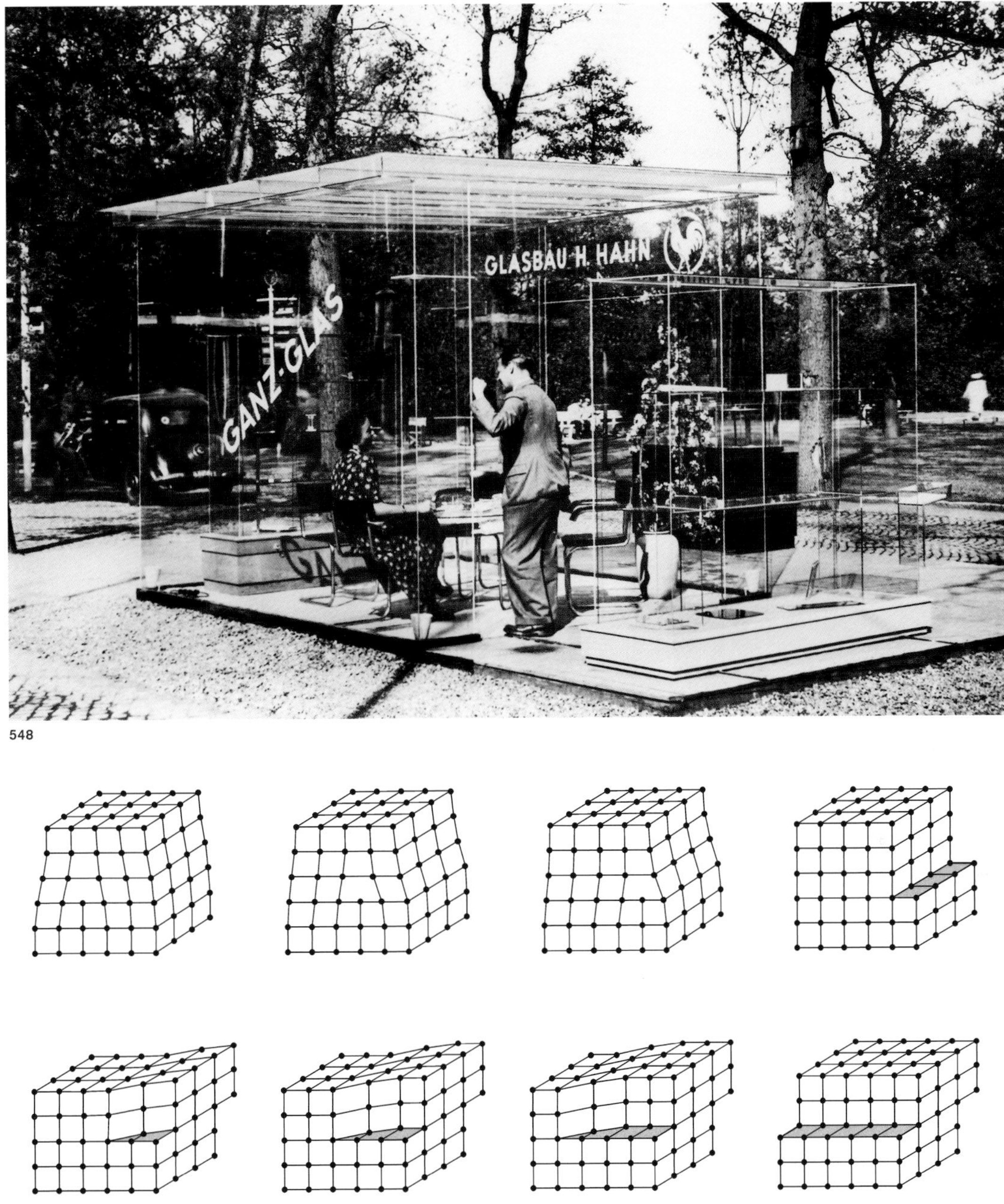

548 Exhibition Pavilion for the firm Glasbau Hahn, Frankfurt am Main, c. 1952. One of the first buildings to use glass as a structural material for beams and columns. 549 Diagrams showing how edge (top) and screw (bottom) dislocations can move through a crystal structure, allowing plastic deformation of an apparently rigid and brittle material.

550

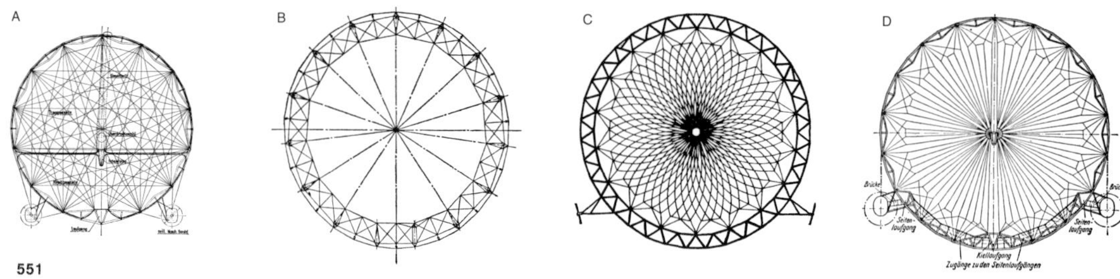

551

550 The rigid airship Schütte-Lanz 1 under construction in Germany, 1911. The helical girders were of timber.

551 A selection of the many methods used to create the rigid transverse frames and bulkheads for rigid airships. (A) Graf Zeppelin (German, 1928); (B) R101 (English, 1930) (C) Macon (USA, 1933) (D) Hindenburg (German, 1935).

to precise determination of forces and deflections using either analytical or graphical techniques.

In the twentieth century, engineering design benefited considerably from the development, during World War I, of two entirely new types of structure that made severe demands on structural engineers: the rigid airship and the airplane. The rigid airship was developed first in Germany in 1900. The British were quick to follow the German lead, and the 1920s saw a race between engineers in the two countries to design larger and larger
550 machines. Not only did these structures have to be sufficiently strong and stiff to withstand loads that were still poorly understood, they also had to be sufficiently light to fly.

The structure of airships generally consisted of a series of disks, made rigid like a bicycle wheel using wires that
551 could be tightened to prestress the compression elements. Parallel disks were linked by perpendicular longitudinal members, and the whole frame was made sufficiently rigid using additional wires to provide tensile cross bracing. Such a structure was far from statically determinate, and calculating the forces that the struts and wire ties needed to carry presented structural engineers with an enormous challenge. In order to reach the necessary strength-to-weight efficiency, airships and airplanes had to be designed much more precisely than buildings. Aircraft designers could not make the crude approximations made by building engineers to simplify their design calculations, nor could they give reassurance to the results of such approximations by using safety factors of three or four. Aircraft designed like this would be too heavy to fly. There was also the matter of size and complexity: Although it was not difficult to set up the many equations that defined the state of equilibrium in the frame of an airship, there were so many that it was impossible to solve them all in the pre-computer age.

Research on how best to design such structures was carried out in many establishments throughout the world, but it was work done at the RAE in England that would later have the most direct influence on the design of structures in the building industry. In the late 1910s and early 1920s the engineer Richard Southwell (1888–1970) developed what later became known as the "relaxation method" for analyzing the forces and deformations in braced frameworks such as airships and airplanes. This iterative method for finding a set of solutions to the large number of equations involved was not mathematically exact, but it was accurate enough for practical purposes. First, a simple analysis was used to calculate a set of approximate forces in all the struts and ties in the frame. This set of data was then used as the input for a new calculation, which reduced the inconsistencies within the first set of data and generated a second set that was closer to the "true" solution. This, in turn, was used as the input for yet another set of calculations, and so on, each successive calculation cycle being closer to the true solution. Finally, the changes from one calculation to the next were judged to be insignificant, typically after six or seven cycles. Nevertheless, the process was a lengthy one. Novelist Neville Shute, a designer of airship frames in the 1920s, describes in his autobiography *Slide Rule* the elation he and his colleagues felt when reaching the end of such a process, often after two weeks or more.

While relaxation methods were more sophisticated than the building industry needed at the time, their development was significant for two reasons. First, they were ideally suited for use in computer programs developed during the 1950s and 1960s to analyze frameworks and tensile cable-net and membrane structures. Most importantly, however, relaxation methods provided, in the 1920s, the ability to check the accuracy of more approximate methods. This had previously been impossible, and engineers using approximate methods of analysis were usually in the dark as to just how "approximate" they really were.

The ability to make more accurate calculations, and to compare these both with the results of experiments and with approximate calculations, was especially useful for research in structural engineering. In particular, it enabled engineers to undertake a more careful study of the safety of structures and thus to address safety issues when designing structures. In the 1850s Rankine had shown engineers how to use the factor of safety to make allowance for the inevitable inaccuracies that result from using simple mathematical models of materials, loads, and structures to predict the actual behavior of built structures. In the 1910s the Swiss engineer Robert Maillart (1872–1940) argued that, since the self-weight of a structure is more reliably known than the live loads that acted on a structure, the former should be subject to a lower factor of safety (see chapter 7, pp. 431, 436–38). A number of engineers working at the RAE in the 1920s and 1930s, notably Alfred Pugsley (1903–98), began to take this approach further, making an assessment of the different contributions to the overall safety of a structure and the degree of uncertainty in each of the mathematical models used to build the full model of an entire structural system. They also looked carefully at the consequences of the failure of individual members; some, for example, might cause a catastrophic failure, whereas others might have a less important effect on an aircraft's performance and so could be designed with a lower margin of safety. By this means designers were able to reduce significantly the weight of materials used in airframe structures. After World War II, Pugsley brought his expertise directly into the building industry when he became Professor of Civil Engineering at the University of Bristol in England. The approach he and his colleagues had developed in the 1930s became the basis of modern reliability analysis using what are now called "partial safety factors," not only in the structural design of aircraft and buildings but also in the design of bridges, ships, cars, and other structures.

The Design of Building Structures

In the nineteenth century iron- and steel-frame construction had been innovative, requiring an understanding of the most sophisticated engineering science of the day. By the early twentieth century it had become mainstream, and by 1930, the job of the structural engineers designing the Empire State Building had become a straightforward task of determining the sizes of members (see pp. 451–52).

The ability to transform the "innovative" into the "straightforward" was testimony to the ingenious design methods that structural engineers developed. The behavior of building materials—steel, concrete, and brickwork—and, especially, the soil beneath a building is far from straightforward. The way they behave when acting together is even more complex. The actual loads that will impinge on buildings are highly variable and seldom known with certainty. Despite the power and speed of today's computers, calculating precisely the "actual" stresses and deflections even in a modest steel or concrete-frame building would be far too complex, and far too time-consuming, to be carried out by most structural engineers. The point is that the highest precision is not necessary: The art of structural engineering design lies in being only as precise as is necessary: it is the art of approximation and the intelligent use of Rankine's great invention, the factor of safety. The design procedures developed for frame buildings as tall as the Empire State are testimony to the fact that a little science can go a long way. The next major impact on the design of frame buildings by advances in engineering science did not occur until the 1970s and 1980s. Only with the aid of computers could the complexities of the buckling and torsional behavior of structural elements and of the dynamic loads from wind, earthquakes, and fire be satisfactorily modeled.

Although design methods for both steel- and concrete-frame structures were already widely understood and in use by about 1910, they were mainly to be found in textbooks. New methods proliferated rapidly, and practicing engineers often had to choose between alternative methods and approaches without sufficient understanding to establish which was the best to use. Most countries soon recognized that there was a need to standardize design procedures for both steel-frame and reinforced concrete structures. Three types of information were collected into national standards:

- *Properties of materials, including the quality of their manufacture*
- *The various loads that building structures should be designed to carry*
- *Codes of design practice that provided suitable methods for designing the various structural elements of buildings—columns, beams, floors and shear walls—and the connections between them.*

The information in each of these areas could be combined to create a mathematical model of the behavior of an entire structure and ensure that the proposed design fell within acceptable limits. Generally speaking, the most important limits were in two areas: serviceability, especially a maximum deflection for beams and floors, and strength, for example, a maximum or "permissible" level of stress derived by calculation. The overall stability of structures—their ability to resist horizontal (wind) loads—was often presumed to be satisfactory without doing any specific calculations, just as it was in the 1880s before tall buildings were provided with wind bracing.

It was widely agreed that the aim of standardizing design practices was a sensible one, but it was soon found not to be so straightforward. The minimum requirement was, of course, that acceptable safety standards be met. Different people had different opinions as to the best or most suitable ways of meeting that requirement. The consensus as to what was considered acceptable by the scientific and design communities—the “engineering climatology” as Alfred Pugsley called it—varied with both time and place. Thus, what might have been acceptable as a design method in 1900 might not be acceptable in 1930 or 1960, both because of the experience and understanding gained in the intervening period and because of society’s changing expectations.

In Britain, for example, the London County Council published its Reinforced Concrete Regulations in 1915, followed in 1933 by a “Code of Practice for the Use of Reinforced Concrete in Buildings” drafted by a subcommittee of the Building Research Board of the Department of Scientific and Industrial Research, the Reinforced Concrete Structures Committee. A different code was issued in 1939 by the Building Industries National Council, but once World War II began, this was rarely used. Both of these codes, as their predecessors at the turn of the century had been, were “permissible stress” codes. The first British Standard code of practice for the design of reinforced concrete, CP 114, which dealt essentially with in situ concrete work, appeared in 1948. It largely followed the prewar codes, but incorporated guidance on the ratio of water to cement and on the minimum cover to be provided to reinforcement where conditions were corrosive. It encouraged, but did not require, inspections every three to five years to identify cracking and corrosion of reinforcement, which was, by then, recognized as a problem. Codes of practice for prestressed concrete (CP 115) and for precast concrete (CP 116) followed in 1959 and 1965 respectively. The code-updating process has continued to the present day: CP110 was issued in 1972, BS8110 in 1985, and the European design code EC2 in the mid-1990s. Although each was intended to be an improvement over its predecessor, the new codes have not always been perceived as improvements, especially by busy practicing engineers, who routinely observe that using the previous codes very seldom led to failures or collapses. This sequence of events has been replicated for other construction materials and in other countries.

A key function of the codes of practice was to assist regulatory authorities in assessing the safety of proposed structures. However, in discharging this function, they had to err on the side of caution; the result was that they often found themselves at odds with engineers in the field, as the following two examples illustrate.

In 1904, the Ritz Hotel in London’s Piccadilly became 552
the first building in London for which a fully steel-framed structure was proposed. However, the Swedish engineer Sven Bylander (1876–1943), who worked for an American contractor, was prevented from using a steel frame of the type already common in the United States because it was not permitted by the London building regulations. These required a building to have external masonry walls that carried the loads from each floor to the foundations; internal columns were permitted only to carry floor beams. Bylander’s compromise, made simply to comply with the regulations, was to construct the steel frame he wanted, stopping just a meter or so short of the external wall. Short beams spanned the remaining distance to the substantial external masonry wall, which had very little load from the floors to carry. By the time Bylander started to design his next building, the Selfridges Department Store on Oxford Street, London, the regulations had been changed to allow columns in the external wall, as is immediately apparent in the building elevation. 553

In 1935–36, London’s Piccadilly was the location of another conflict between building designers and the regulatory authorities. A new shop was being designed for Simpsons clothing store by architect Joseph Emberton 554
(1889–1956) working with engineer Felix Samuely (1902–59). They wanted a dramatic, entirely column-free elevation at street level. Samuely proposed a steel Vierendeel frame at the first-floor level spanning the full width of 24.4 meters, which would carry the loads from all the upper-story columns to the columns at either side of the shop front. However, this did not comply with reg- 555
ulations that required floor loads to be conveyed by the

552

553

554

552 Ritz Hotel, Piccadilly, London, 1904–06. Engineer: Sven Bylander. Under construction. 553 Selfridges Department Store, Oxford Street, London, 1906–09. Engineer: Sven Bylander. 554 Simpsons Store, Piccadilly, London, 1936. Engineer: Felix Samuely; architect: Joseph Emberton. 555 Simpsons Store. Steel frame structure as designed by Felix Samuely (left); as modified to meet London Building Regulations (right).

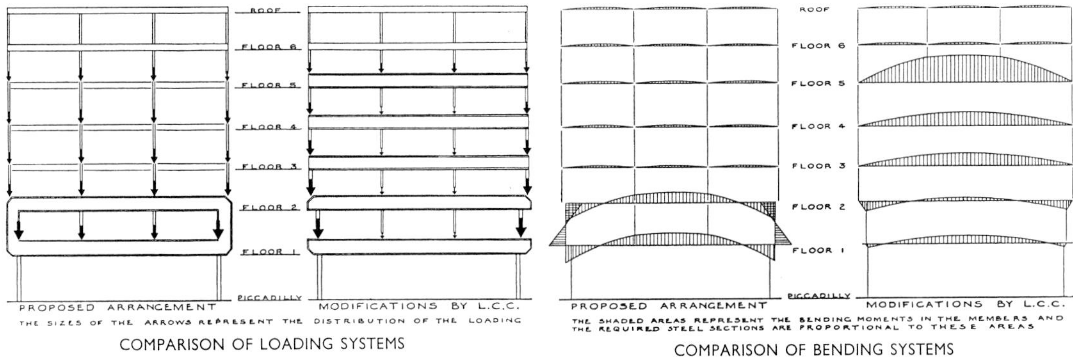

555

most direct route to the nearest column resting on a foundation: they could not be carried downward a few floors, and then sideways through a transfer girder to a column on a foundation. Samuely and the architects argued their case against the London County Council until the last possible moment, but they lost. Full-width transfer girders had to be introduced at every story, at
556 considerable unnecessary cost and weight.

The Vierendeel girder was fabricated by welding to achieve the necessary strength at the connection between the vertical and horizontal portions of the girder. This was the first substantial use of welding on a building project in England—a technology that Samuely had brought from his previous work in Germany and Russia, where welding had been developed in the shipbuilding industry during the early 1920s. To satisfy the authorities, the welded frame had to be cut in situ to form two large independent beams at first- and second-floor levels. Even after this surgery their size was impressive, more in keeping with the scale of bridge engineering than the scale of building structures. The coda to this story is that Samuely's battle, like Bylander's before him, did force a rethinking of the regulations, and they were subsequently changed to allow any arrangement of columns and beams as long as their safety could be documented.

As design codes for the structures of buildings were articulated, there followed the inevitable establishment of committees that reviewed codes' content to ensure that they incorporated the latest needs and developments in the industry. Three groups of interested parties were (and are) generally represented on these committees: materials producers, practicing designers, and the engineering research community. Typically, when such committees met to discuss changes to the codes, the engineering scientists felt it was most important to include the latest engineering research. Practicing engineers, on the other hand, were usually in favor of simpler, quicker—and, above all, safer—design methods, even if they were, strictly speaking, less accurate. Even as late as the 1920s the design of structural frames was undertaken as a series of independent columns and beams. It was widely perceived that this was both unrealistic and unduly pessimistic, and that it led to more steel being used than was actually necessary. In practice, however, there was no alternative. A frame structure that relies on the rigidity of the connections between beams and columns cannot be determined by statics alone because it is statically indeterminate. In principle, this problem had been solved in the 1850s by the French engineer Émile Clapeyron (1799–1864), who devised what was called the "theorem of three moments," which enabled engineers to calculate the unknown bending moments. However, this required solving as many simultaneous equations as there were unknowns—an impractical method for a whole building.

In the 1910s the German engineer Axel Bendixen reformulated Clapeyron's method in terms of the rotation of the ends of each structural member of a frame. Bendixen's "slope-deflection method" was widely used for simple structures, but it still required solving the same number of equations as there were unknown

556

UNSYMMETRICAL BENT As a Continuous Girder Corrected for Sidelurch

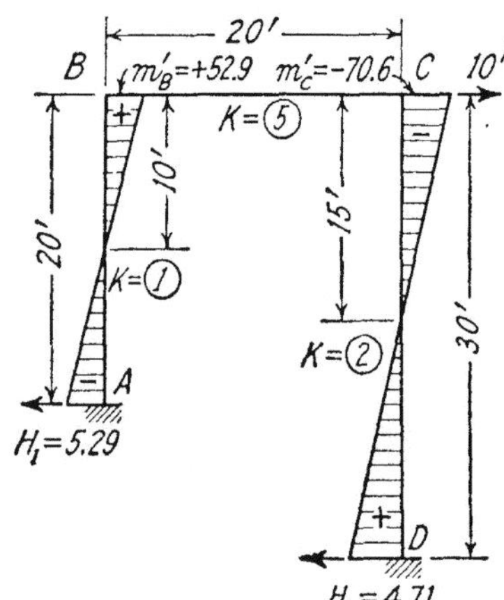

Assuming the girder rigid the column shears will be proportional to the values of $\frac{K}{L^2}$*; that is, to* $\frac{1}{4}$ *and* $\frac{2}{9}$ $\quad \frac{1}{4}+\frac{2}{9}=\frac{17}{36}$

$$H_1=\frac{9}{17}\times 10.0=5.29 \qquad m'_B=5.29\times 10=+52.9$$

$$H_2 \qquad =4.71 \qquad m'_C=4.71\times 15=-70.6$$

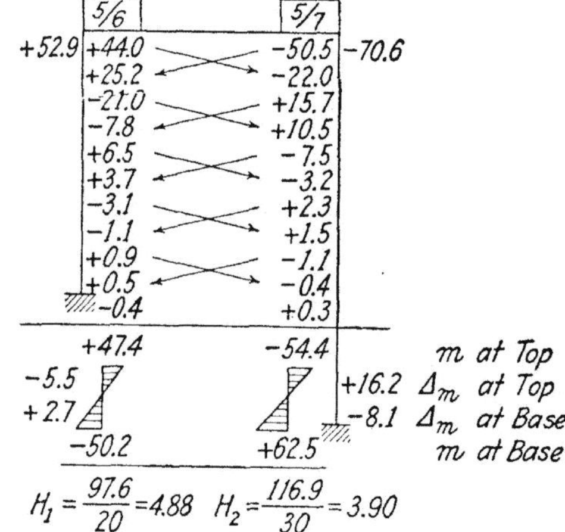

$$H_1=\frac{97.6}{20}=4.88 \quad H_2=\frac{116.9}{30}=3.90$$

Since these moments correspond to a total shear of 8.78, the moments for a shear of 10.0 will be $\frac{10}{8.78}$ *of these values:-*

$$M_A=-57.0^{k'}$$
$$M_B=+54.0$$
$$M_C=-61.8$$
$$M_D=+71.3$$

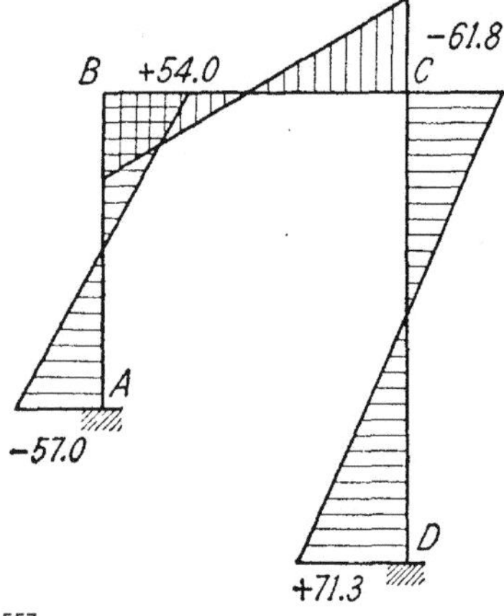

557

556 Simpsons Store, Picadilly, London, 1936. Engineer: Felix Samuely; architect: Joseph Emberton. Building under construction, with huge welded steel girders, as modified to London building regulations. 557 Description of the moment distribution method, developed by Hardy Cross, c. 1930.

bending moments, and calculating the sizes of individual structural members of a multistory building would involve many hundreds of such equations. In the days of manual calculation, this was either unrealistic or, for engineers with limited mathematical skills, simply impossible. During the early 1930s two engineers found different ways out of this dilemma: Hardy Cross (1885–1959) in the United States, and John Fleetwood Baker, later Lord Baker (1901–85), in England.

As Southwell had done, Hardy Cross devised an iterative means of solving an almost unlimited number of equations. It was a brilliant and elegant simplification of the calculation procedures that had to be undertaken to analyze the bending moments in rigid-jointed frame buildings. In a world that seemed ever more complex to most engineers, it came as a ray of sunlight. Hardy Cross's "moment distribution method" brought the design of rigid frames within reach of the engineer with ordinary calcula-
557 tion skills, armed only with a slide rule. It was conceived in terms of the bending moments carried in the members—an approach more in keeping with the way engineers think about how frames actually work than Bendixen's method, which considered the angles of rotation at the ends of individual members. The moment distribution method required, first, imagining all the connections fixed and carrying out the relatively simple calculations to find the moments at the ends of each member. Then each connection would, in the mind of the engineer, be "released," and any out-of-balance moments distributed among the other members meeting at the connection, in proportion to the stiffness of the members. Repeating this process just four or five times generated successive approximations that rapidly converged on the equilibrium solution. Cross's method was also just as easy to use for the calculation of forces and bending moments resulting from wind loads as for those resulting from gravity loads—a significant benefit for the designers of high-rise buildings.

An important consequence of using Cross's moment distribution method was that it required engineers to draw bending moment diagrams for the frames they were designing. Not only did this help them visualize how the structure was carrying the loads, it also drew attention to the many places where there was no bending moment in the structural members—at or near the center of every column and beam. This meant that an alternative mathematical model could be imagined which considered the frame as made up not from a series of beams and columns, but from a number of cross-shaped elements connected at pin joints. This model of the frame was very much easier to calculate, and has become the standard way of thinking about how such frame structures can be analyzed. Most importantly, the act of drawing the bending moment diagram forced the engineer to think about how the structure was actually working. From the bending moment diagram, it was but a small step to sketching the shear force diagram and the deflected shape of the beams and columns.

The moment distribution method was quickly adopted by design engineers throughout the world because of the ease with which it could provide answers that were accurate enough, even for large and complex structures. It also became popular with university lecturers, for at the same time that it generated numerical results, it helped instill into students an understanding of how the structure was working. In this respect the moment distribution method stands alongside the methods of graphical statics that revolutionized structural design in the latter half of the nineteenth century and remained current for nearly a century. Both are still regularly taught today by those who seek to develop in students a deep feeling for structural behavior.

The Plastic Behavior of Steel

At the same time that Hardy Cross's method was making the structural engineer's work in analyzing and designing steel structures easier, some fundamental doubts were beginning to appear as to the validity of treating steel as an ideal elastic material. In addition, it began to be recognized that designing a steel-frame building as a series of independent columns and beams was both unrealistic and pessimistic. In the 1920s it was common practice to design steel members so that the stress never exceeded the so-called "elastic limit," with a certain margin of safety. However, there were a number of well-known facts about the use of steel in real structures that contradicted this ideal picture of steel. It was known that rolled-steel components used in building structures already contained significant internal stresses resulting from the manufacturing and assembly processes, and that these "residual stresses" could be almost as high as the elastic limit for steel. It was also well known that parts of a steel structure, for instance the area around the rivet holes in connections, could and did deform permanently, or plastically, without serious cause for concern. Many designers of steel structures were also aware that some of the basic assumptions they made in their design calculations were unnecessarily conservative or simply unrealistic. For example, steel has a considerable reserve of strength beyond the so-called point of "failure" that is usually defined as a certain, safe (but rather arbitrary) proportion of its ultimate strength or its yield strength (the limit of its elasticity). There was also the matter of differential settlements between the various foundations supporting the columns of a building. Such movements are inevitable in all buildings, and yet they were ignored when designing steel frames. Had they been taken into account, the calculations would have shown that many of the columns and beams would "fail," in the sense that the elastic stresses would exceed the maximum values laid down in the design codes.

These observations about the behavior of actual steel structures led to two conclusions: Steel structures were usually overdesigned, and significant savings could be achieved through a more efficient use of steel; and, more fundamentally, the whole basis of elastic design methods for steel was irrational and needed to be reassessed. In 1929 the British Steelwork Association set up the Steel Structures Research Committee, under the chairmanship of John Baker (1901–85), to review the situation and make recommendations for new design procedures.

The work of the Steel Structures Research Committee was initially directed at investigating just how far the usual assumptions upon which steel frame design was based deviated from the actual conditions found in simple frames. A thorough program of testing model and full-scale structures using various techniques of stress analysis, including the newly developed vibrating-wire and electrical-resistance strain gauges (see pp. 475–76), demonstrated that the deviations were often considerable. A second stage of the committee's work was directed toward developing new design procedures. Although the new procedures would still consider only the elastic behavior of the steel, they would be based upon more rational assumptions, with the goal of achieving an improved correspondence between predicted and actual forces and stresses in structures.

A series of service trials of the new design procedures was carried out in the mid-1930s, and it was generally agreed that they did, indeed, achieve their intended aim. However, despite requiring the design engineer to use more complex engineering science and mathematics, the new procedures did not produce steel structures that were either significantly safer or cheaper, nor did they address the apparently safe plastic behavior of steel above its yield point or the remaining doubts about elastic design methods in general. Simplified versions of the new procedures were developed, but these, too, were finally rejected by the profession.

Baker and his research engineers became increasingly concerned at this outcome. Despite their best efforts, they had failed to resolve the serious doubts about the validity of elastic design methods. Indeed, it seemed that they were incapable of further development or improvement to regain the confidence of engineers that is fundamental to all structural design methods. A state of crisis had been reached.

A breakthrough became possible only with the realization that the problems with the existing elastic design procedures could be addressed only by means of a radically different approach. The key to the solution came in the form of a new idea of what constituted failure. The idea that a failure was the point at which a certain limiting stress was reached (the limit of elasticity) was replaced by the notion that the limit should be the collapse of the structure. A certain amount of plastic deformation could therefore be tolerated as long as sufficient parts of the structure remained below their yield point, thus preventing the structure as a whole from becoming a "mechanism," defined as a structure lacking sufficient bracing or rigid joints to prevent its collapse. This realization forced a total reexamination of structural design procedures. No longer was the level of stress in every part of the structure of prime interest; the main concern became the

558 Hunstanton School, Norfolk, England, 1949–54. Engineer: Ron Jenkins of Ove Arup & Partners; architects: Alison and Peter Smithson. 559 Morrison air raid shelter developed by John Baker, 1937–38.

558

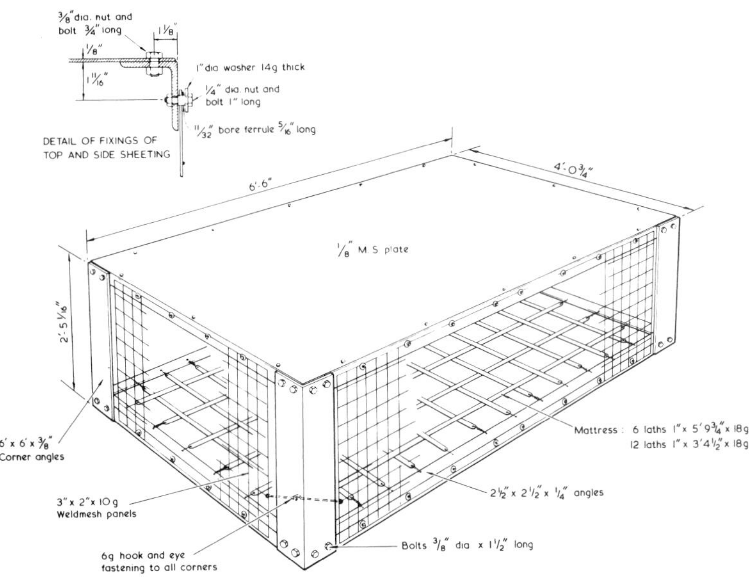

3/8" dia. nut and bolt 3/4" long
1 1/8"
1/8"
1" dia washer 14g thick
1 11/16"
1/4" dia. nut and bolt 1" long
11/32" bore ferrule 5/16" long
DETAIL OF FIXINGS OF TOP AND SIDE SHEETING
6'-6"
4'-0 3/4"
1/8" M S plate
2'-5 1/16"
6' x 6' x 3/8" Corner angles
3" x 2" x 10 g Weldmesh panels
6g hook and eye fastening to all corners
Mattress: 6 laths 1" x 5'9 3/4" x 18g
12 laths 1" x 3'4 1/2" x 18g
2 1/2" x 2 1/2" x 1/4" angles
Bolts 3/8" dia x 1 1/2" long

559 MORRISON SHELTER: FINAL DESIGN

location and relative magnitude of local maximum bending moments as the applied loads were all increased, in proportion, up to the point at which sufficient plastic hinges had formed to transform the structure into a mechanism that might collapse. The safety of the structure under working loads could be achieved by ensuring that the applied loads were less than the collapse load by a margin which came to be known as the "load factor."

The new approach required new theoretical concepts, such as "plastic hinge," "full plastic moment," "shape factor," and "incremental collapse," as well as new definitions of old concepts, such as "failure" and "collapse." The new plastic design procedures, as they came to be known, were not readily accepted by many members of the established community of designers. Indeed, even half a century after this design revolution, they are still not universally accepted.

The first structure that Baker designed using his plastic design methods, immediately before the outbreak of World War II, was a lightweight bomb shelter for use by
559 the civilian population. Named the "Morrison Shelter" after the then Home Secretary Herbert Morrison, it made full use of the ability of steel to absorb huge amounts of energy when deforming plastically beyond its elastic limit. Its light steel frame was designed to absorb the impact energy of falling masonry by deforming plastically without total collapse. Tens of thousands of the shelters were made, and many thousands of deaths and severe injuries were prevented. The same principle is at work today in the thousands of miles of crash barriers alongside our highways. It is also the principle underlying the construction of many buildings designed to withstand earthquakes without collapse. In such buildings, the plastic hinges in steel members are the means by which the energy of the earthquake is absorbed.

As with many developments in building engineering, the consequences of the plastic design revolution are virtually invisible to those outside the engineer's world. A number of test buildings were constructed, including one at the Cambridge University Engineering Department, where John Baker was a professor in the 1950s, but the first architectural use of plastic design methods was for a modest steel structure at Hunstanton School in
558 Norfolk, England (1949–54). For certain classes of building structures, for example, single-story steel-frame warehouses and industrial units, plastic design procedures are now widely used. They are much simpler to use than elastic procedures, and can lead to substantial economies of material—one of Baker's original goals. However, there has been less impact on the design of larger steel-frame buildings, where the sizes of steel beams and columns are governed not by the need to prevent collapse but by the need to limit elastic deflections that lead, if too large, to the cracking of the windows and plaster finishes inside buildings. Nevertheless, the most recent design codes for both steel and reinforced concrete buildings and bridges allow the use of plastic design procedures.

Experimental Engineering Science

Not only did the growth of experimental physics in the late nineteenth century lead to results that had a direct impact on building engineering, for example, in the work of Griffith and Taylor, it also led to the widespread growth of experimentation as a means of solving practical engineering problems. The idea of experimentation was certainly not new, but it wasn't until the late nineteenth and early twentieth centuries that the benefits of setting up teams of research scientists to deal with a subject systematically were recognized. Many universities that had previously concentrated on theoretical studies augmented by a few experiments began to refocus their efforts on experimental work. Some government agencies, like the Federal Materials Testing Station in Switzerland, founded in 1880, and the National Physical Laboratory in Britain, which opened in 1902, were set up specifically to undertake research into materials science and provide authoritative data about materials.

By the early 1920s the benefits to be gained from an experimental approach to research were becoming clear in many fields of building engineering. A growing number of research facilities and institutes were established that carried out studies in the increasing range of fields in science and engineering that had an impact on building design and construction. Many of these were established in universities; others were independent, such as the Hermann-Rietschel-Institut for Heating and Ventilation Technology established in Berlin in 1887 (see chapter 7, p. 408). In the 1890s, testing stations were set up in a number of countries in continental Europe and the United

States to study the performance of construction materials in fires. In 1920 a national Building Research Station was established in Britain to study all subjects related to construction. The Earthquake Research Institute was established at the University of Tokyo in 1924. Individuals not affiliated with a university or research organization were also able to use experiments and careful measurements to make their impact on building engineering.

A particular benefit of the various research institutes was that they provided links to research in fields of inquiry outside but related to the building industry such as geology, materials science, and mechanical and electrical engineering. At the beginning of the twentieth century, one of the most fruitful areas of research, one that would have important impacts on the design of buildings, was the relatively new field of aerodynamics.

Wind is of particular concern, of course, in the design of tall buildings. The first wind tunnel had been built in 1871 by Frank H. Wenham (1824–1908), a member of the Aeronautical Society of Great Britain, to measure lift forces on aerofoils. Gustave Eiffel built a wind tunnel in 1912, and in 1916 Ludwig Prandtl (1875–1953) designed and built the first closed-circuit wind tunnel, at the University of Göttingen in Germany, which was the prototype for all modern tunnels. Prandtl discovered that the air in contact with a surface is stationary, and its speed increases to the ambient wind speed across a thin layer of air he called the "boundary layer." He found that the thickness of the boundary layer was highly sensitive to surface roughness. This was especially significant for building engineers, as buildings are all located in the boundary layer and themselves contribute to the roughness of the earth's surface.

In 1927 Otto Flachsbart (1898–1957), one of Prandtl's co-workers, undertook the first wind tunnel experiments on buildings, to study the effect of the thickness of the
560 boundary layer on wind pressures on buildings. He measured air pressures on the walls and roofs of various types of buildings, including small apartment blocks, and compared the results for buildings standing in isolation with those for groups of buildings in close proximity. He also used experimental equipment in which water was used to
561 simulate the flow of air. The movement of the water was made visible by sprinkling aluminum powder on the water surface and recording the test on film. For the case of a large aircraft hangar which had one side open to the wind, these tests revealed the creation of a large vortex that created unexpected positive pressures on the lee side of the building.

One of the earliest uses of a wind tunnel to measure
wind pressures on tall buildings was for the Empire 562
State Building in the early 1930s. The air pressure was measured at various places around the circumference of the model building and at several different heights. This enabled the designers to estimate the wind loads on the entire building and on individual windows. On the lee side of a tall building, for example, the air pressure is significantly lower than it is inside the building, thus tending to suck the windows out. At this time only static loads were investigated. The role of vortices in causing periodic loads on structures was first recognized during the investigation of the spectacular collapse of the mile-long Tacoma Narrows Bridge in Washington State in 1940. Wind tunnel tests revealed how vortices first built up on one side of the bridge deck and were then shed into the lee of the structure. The next vortex then built up on the other side of the deck, and so on. The vortices thus exerted alternating loads on the bridge deck that set it in oscillating motion. The role of vortices in causing periodic loads on tall buildings became significant when engineers began designing very slender towers in the late 1950s.

Experimental Stress Analysis

Underlying the design procedures for all load-bearing elements of buildings is the idea that the stress in the material should be less than a certain prescribed level. The design engineer thus needs to know the magnitude of stresses inside the materials of which the structural elements are made. This approach had been used throughout the nineteenth century by the designers of many types of structure that carry loads—bridges, locomotives, ships, high-pressure boilers, machine tools, and many more. Unfortunately, it is not possible to measure internal stresses directly. It is, however, possible to measure the loads applied to a structure and the particular load that causes it to collapse. It is also possible to measure the deflection of various parts of a structure, or the change in length of one of its members, and the degree to which the surface of a structural component has

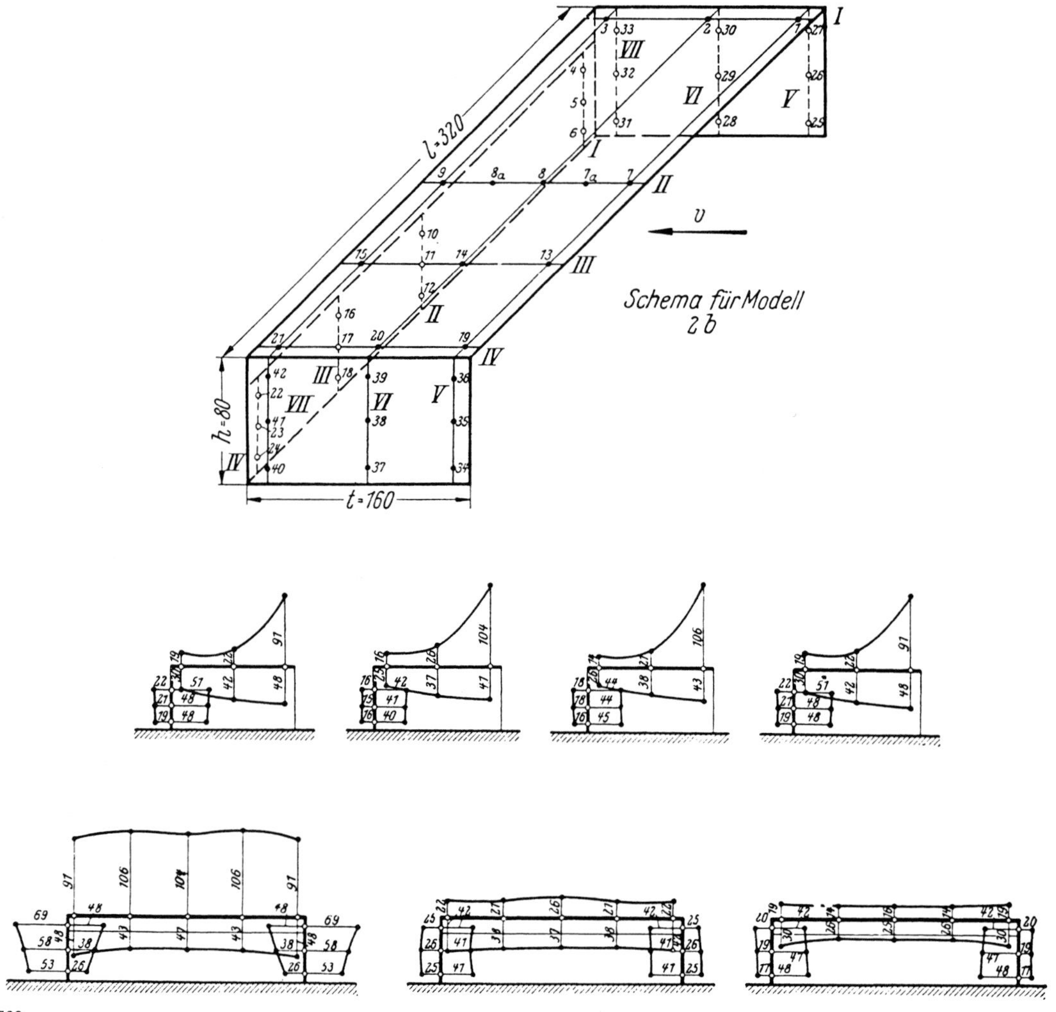

560

560 Diagram showing the results of Otto Flachsbart's wind tunnel tests on a model of an aircraft hangar, Göttingen, Germany, 1927. 561 Otto Flachsbart's wind tunnel tests. Selected frames from film recording the movement of water (representing air) flowing past a model of the aircraft hangar. 562 Wind tunnel model of the Empire State Building, New York, used to measure wind pressures on the facade, c. 1931.

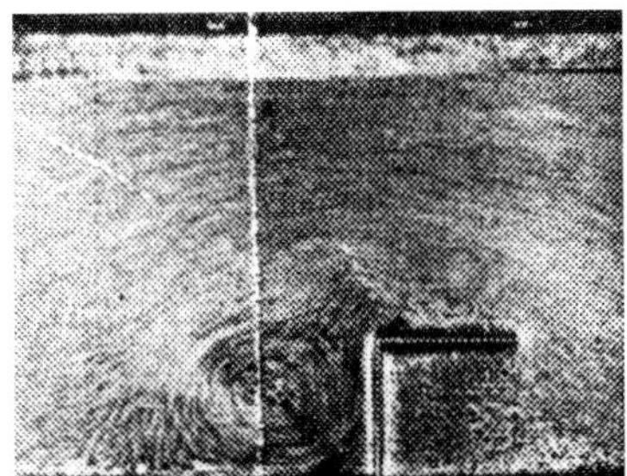
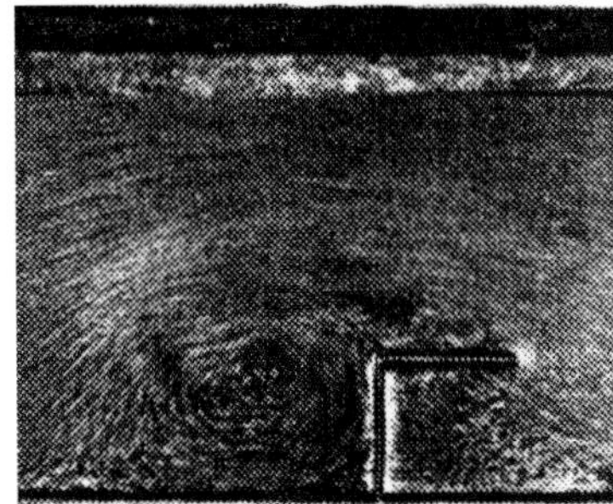

561

562

been strained in tension or compression. It is then necessary to construct mathematical models of the structure and the materials, based on the appropriate engineering science, in order to establish the relationship between the measurable external variables and the internal stresses. Following the lead taken in experimental physics during the late nineteenth century, engineering scientists gradually began to appreciate the benefits that could accrue from a rigorous and methodical approach to their subject. By the early twentieth century the study of the microbehavior of materials under load was flourishing, and it soon became known as "experimental stress analysis." During the next half century experimental stress analysis followed two distinct lines of development. One was based on the strain gauge, the other on photoelastic stress analysis.

The Strain Gauge

For simple tension and compression elements, the internal stress is calculated as the force in the element divided by the area of cross section. The stresses inside elements subject to bending are calculated from measurements of the load, the deflection and the geometry of the cross section. This allows the second moment of area, I, to be calculated, and the internal stress calculated, using the elastic theories of bending that were developed during the eighteenth and nineteenth centuries.

The main limitation of these approaches was that they focused on the overall behavior of a structure rather than the behavior of the material itself. In the early nineteenth century, scientists began measuring the strain (deformation) on the surface of a piece of material under load.

They did this by measuring the change in the distance between two gauge marks on the surface when a load was applied to the structure. Once the stiffness of the material (Young's modulus) was known, the surface stress could be calculated. However, the process was extremely tedious. It required the use of a traveling microscope to obtain results that were sufficiently accurate, and so was of no use for components with inaccessible surfaces or those subject to dynamic loads.

All this changed in the 1930s with the invention of the strain gauge. The first and still most widely used strain gauge is the electrical resistance strain gauge, the design of which is based upon the fact that the cross section of an electrical conductor is reduced when stretched and this, in turn, increases its electrical resistance. Electrical resistance strain gauges were first used by the American engineer Charles Kearns in the early 1930s for studying the stresses in aircraft propellers. He ground flat a conventional carbon-composite electrical resistor and mounted it onto an insulating strip which he cemented to the blade. He made the electrical connection to the stationary measuring equipment by means of brushes and rings similar to those used in electric motors. In the late 1930s Arthur Ruge and Edward Simmons in the United States both used arrays of fine wires to achieve the same effect. In 1952 the English engineer Peter Jackson, working with Saunders-Roe, an aircraft manufacturer on the Isle of Wight in Britain, used a technology that had been developed for producing printed circuit boards to make foil strain gauges that were much smaller, easier to mount, and more reliable than wire strain gauges. Foil gauges still form the basis of experimental stress analysis, both singly and in the form of a rosette with three gauges at 120 degrees to enable the
563 principal stress directions to be established. Although strain gauges were developed in the aircraft industry, their use for measuring stresses in both full-size and model structures and components quickly spread to all other industries.

Another strain gauge technology, developed by the Maihak company in Germany in 1936, was based on the well-known relation between the pitch at which a string vibrates and the tension in the string. A wire, perhaps 200 to 400 mm long, is fixed at both ends, and its pitch measured electronically as its length, and hence its tension, changes due to relative movement of the two ends. 564
Vibrating-wire strain gauges, which are bulkier than electrical resistance strain gauges, are used mainly for studying larger building elements and the geotechnical investigation of rock movements in building foundations, which need to be monitored over long periods of time. Two problems with all strain gauges are their instability over time and their sensitivity to temperature changes. For the most careful measurements, therefore, an electrical thermometer is essential, and the gauges need to be constantly recalibrated to compensate for creep in the mounting of the gauge on the component being tested.

Since their invention, strain gauges have been the essential tool of all research into structural behavior, and their impact on structural engineering has been enormous. They have enabled countless design procedures and mathematical models to be tested for their accuracy and reliability in predicting structural behavior and, hence, improved. Today, the readings from strain gauges are fed directly into computers, and stress levels and patterns can be calculated and displayed in real time if desired.

Photoelasticity, Photoelastic Stress Analysis

Photoelastic stress analysis, like strain gauge technology, was first developed in the aerospace industry. Because of its relatively high cost, it has been used in the construction industry mainly for large structures such as bridges and dams and only occasionally in building engineering. However, it has had an enormous impact on the understanding of stress and strain inside materials under load, and thus warrants mention here. An optical technique that uses models made of a transparent material, photoelastic stress analysis allows engineers to see directly what is going on inside a component under load. Although the stresses themselves are not made visible, the technique allows the visualization and measurement of the next best thing—the magnitude of the difference between two orthogonal stresses at any point. A relatively simple process allows calculation of the stresses themselves.

Photoelastic stress analysis depends upon the property of certain transparent materials to affect polarized light as it passes through the material, and in proportion to the stresses inside it. This phenomenon, called "birefringence," or "double refraction," was first observed in

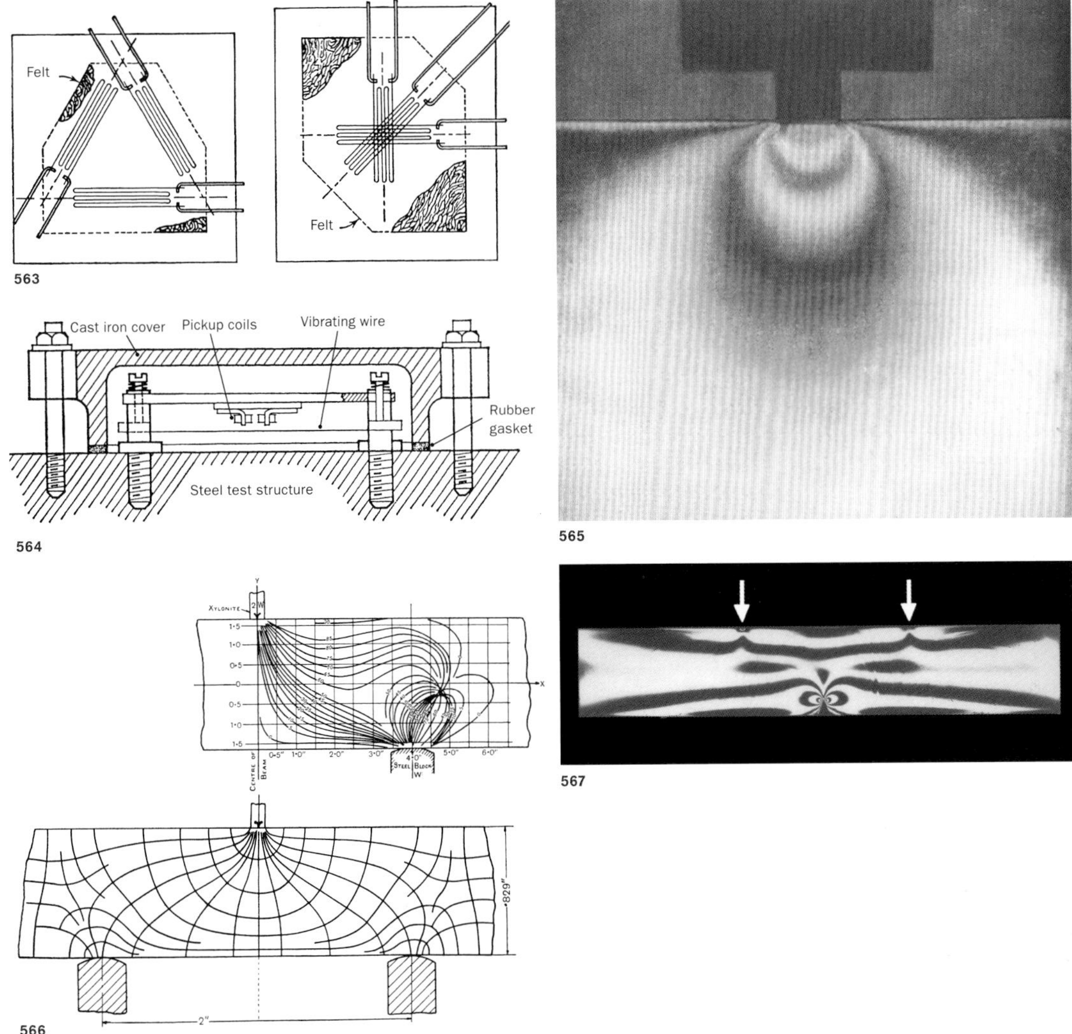

563 Diagrams of electrical resistance strain gauge rosettes that measure the strain on the surface of a test piece in three directions. 564 Acoustic or vibrating wire strain gauge. Typically 100–150 mm long. 565 Photograph of photoelastic model. The model shows the distribution of stresses caused by a load on a surface. 566 Generation of the lines of principal stress in a model subject to bending. First the lines of equal inclination of the stress directions are plotted (top), then the lines of principal stress. The lines showing tension (bottom of the beam) show the ideal position for steel reinforcement in a reinforced concrete beam. 567 Photoelastic model showing a model under bending load, and stress concentration at the root of a crack.

glass in 1815 by the Scottish physicist David Brewster (1781–1868), and given comprehensive theoretical treatment by the German scientist Franz Neumann (1798–1895). Using this analysis, internal stresses can be computed from the observed degree to which the plane of polarization of the light is rotated. In fact, the degree of rotation depends not upon the magnitude of the stress, but upon the difference between the magnitudes of the "principal stresses," and this enables the precise direction of the internal stresses to be computed.[3]

The early development of the technique of photoelastic stress analysis was undertaken in the 1910s at University College, London, using test models made of glass. Although glass is widely available, it is not highly birefringent; it is also difficult to cut to shape, and is vulnerable to fracture. Photoelastic stress analysis became more accessible with the development of transparent epoxy resins, such as Araldite, in the 1940s. The technique reached its peak in the 1960s in the aerospace industry, for example, at Rolls-Royce in England, where two- and three-dimensional models of aero-engine components were analyzed in order to find ways of reducing stress concentrations, which are usually the points at which potentially catastrophic fatigue cracks originate.

Even dynamic stresses can be established by loading a model in an oven and cooling it while still under load, literally freezing the stresses into the Araldite. Thin slices are then cut from the model for analysis. The model is then viewed in a polariscope to reveal the varying degree of rotation of the incident polarized light as a pattern of
565 highly colorful interference fringes. For quantitative work, monochromatic light (usually sodium) is used to produce sharper fringes and measure the magnitude of the inter-
567 nal stresses to an accuracy of a few percentage points. The same fringes can be used in qualitative analysis to establish the directions of the internal principal stresses (tension and compression) and to generate a diagram that shows the flow of forces through an object or, as it is
566 usually called, the "load path."

Photoelastic models provided a direct visual representation of the internal effects of external loads on a structure. This unique ability ensured their continued survival as a teaching tool long after the quantitative use of photoelastic stress analysis in research laboratories was replaced by computer models. Photoelastic stress analysis can be used to great benefit, for example, in developing an understanding of reinforced concrete by indicating where steel reinforcing bars in a beam should be best located, since they should, ideally, follow the lines of the tension stresses inside the beam.

Experimental Analysis Using Scale Models

Photoelastic stress analysis is a sophisticated example of using a test model to simulate, in an experimental laboratory, the behavior of an actual, full-size structure. The making and testing of model structures is as old as building itself. The earliest models would have been used to establish the stability of a structure such as an arch—its very ability to work as a structure—or the load that can be carried by an individual beam or an assembly of structural elements making up a bridge or a roof truss, for example. The technique only really becomes useful in structural engineering, however, when the results of testing a scale model of a structure can be used to predict accurately the behavior of a geometrically similar structure built at a larger scale.

As we know from observing Roman arches and medieval cathedrals, the stability of masonry structures is independent of their scale. If a model arch, flying buttress, or dome is made to stand, then a similar structure, with all dimensions increased proportionately, will also stand. The stability of a masonry structure depends only on its geometry (the plan, section and sizes of its components); it is virtually independent of the strength, stiffness, or density of the masonry. The designers of masonry buildings could, therefore, scale up the results obtained from a model building in direct (linear) proportion, and design a satisfactory full-size building. This process cannot be used for structural components that are subject to bending or that may fail due to buckling, since these phenomena do not vary linearly with scale. The fact that no engineering science is needed to use scale models for the design of masonry structures helps explain why masonry structures developed to such a high degree of sophistication so early in building history. Scale models could not be used to help design bending structures, for example, until the engineering science necessary to scale up the results of model tests for such structures was developed in the mid-eighteenth century.

The shape of simple tensile structures is also independent of size; for example, the form of a hanging chain of weights depends only on the relative sizes of the weights, not their absolute weights. This fact was known to Robert Hooke in the 1670s. Hooke also knew that the results obtained using a hanging (tensile) model could be used (inverted) to establish the form of compression structures such as arches. As we saw in chapter 4, this technique was used by engineers in 1742 to analyze the stability of the dome of Saint Peter's Basilica in Rome. In the 1840s, models of suspension bridges were built and tested to establish how they would deflect as a load passed over them. In the 1890s Antonio Gaudí scaled up the geometrical forms established using three-dimensional hanging models to design the forms of many masonry vaults in his buildings (see chapter 7, pp. 441, 443). If the self-weight of the structure is ignored, the axial forces in the members of a triangulated, statically determinate, pin-jointed truss are also independent of scale. From the 1850s on, models of such truss bridges were sometimes tested to compare the forces in each member with the values calculated using mathematical models.

The situation is very different, however, for a structural element subject to bending or loaded in compression to the point at which it may fail by buckling. The strength and the stiffness of a beam depend on the properties of the material; the self-weight increases with the cube of the increase in scale; and, if self-weight is ignored, the stiffness of the structure increases with the cube of the scale and its strength with the square of the scale. Reaching this understanding of the effect of scale had been the goal of scientists since they first began to look at structural behavior, from Galileo and Hooke. However, it was only with the work of Eaton Hodgkinson and William Fairbairn, who found the most effective shape for a cast iron beam around 1830, and the most efficient cross section for the tubular wrought iron girders of the railway bridges over the River Conwy and the Menai Strait in North Wales in the mid-1840s, that the scale effects in bending structures were fully understood. The case of a beam loaded in bending, however, is much simpler than the case of a thin reinforced concrete shell curved in one or two dimensions. An analysis of the structural behavior of such a shell requires consideration of overall bending, the tension and compression in the plane of the shell, and the effects of local strengthening needed at the points of support and stiffening of the unsupported edges. The task of trying to create a scale model using real reinforced concrete, with its sand, aggregate, and hundreds of steel bars of different sizes, shapes, and degrees of restraint within the concrete, was also tricky. With so many variables to consider, it must have seemed most unlikely, in the early days of designing shells, that designers would be able to predict with confidence the behavior of a concrete shell spanning 50 meters or more from tests on a model just a meter or two across. Yet, by the 1950s, this seemingly impossible goal had, indeed, been achieved, though it had not been reached in a single step.

The significant breakthrough came from the application of an idea developed for an entirely different engineering problem—the search for the most efficient shape for a ship's hull. This became an issue for ship designers in the 1860s, when steam engines were first used to power ships. In order to determine the size of engine that a new ship would require, before the ship was built, it was necessary to know the resistance the ship would encounter when moving through water. Initially, it was assumed that the resistance comes only from friction between the hull of the ship and the water. Calculations based on this assumption, however, were found to be seriously wrong. At first it had been thought that testing a model of a ship's hull might enable the resistance of the full-size ship to be determined. The results of such tests by the British Admiralty, however, proved to be "embarrassing and expensive mistakes," as one official report concluded.[4]

In the 1850s, the designers of the largest steamship built to date, the *Great Eastern* (launched in 1859), were faced with similar problems of scale. This ship was to be the largest the world had ever seen: At over 200 meters long and 26 meters wide, she would be nearly twice as long and have five times the displacement of the next largest ship. In around 1853, William Froude (1810–79), an engineer working for Brunel's Great Western Railway company constructing the line from London to the west of England, joined Brunel and John Scott Russell on the design team for the *Great Eastern*. Froude, who had studied mathematics and physics at Oxford University, worked on two vital issues for the new ship—how it would roll in high seas, and how much power and fuel would be needed to take her across the Atlantic. His analysis of the rolling of ships was so successful that it was still in use in the second half of the twentieth century. His work on the resistance of a ship's hull to moving through the sea soon led him to the conclusion that friction is not the only cause; he realized that the surface wave created by a ship also impedes its movement. This insight led him to believe, contrary to prevailing opinion, that models of ships' hulls might indeed be used to predict the resistance to movement of full-size ships. In 1867 Froude tested models of two different hull shapes in three sizes—3, 6, and 12 feet long—and found that they generated similar wave patterns when towed at speeds proportional to the square of the length of the models. He concluded that the wave resistance of the model and a full-size ship would be proportional if the ratio $V/\sqrt{(g\ D)}$ for the model and prototype had the same value. This ratio, known as the "Froude number," is dimensionless, which means, effectively, that it is independent of the scale of the model.[5]

Froude's model tests were conducted in the open water of the river Dart in South Devon, hardly ideal for precise measurements. Nevertheless, their success persuaded the British Admiralty to grant Froude £2000 to build the world's first towing tank near his home in Torquay, where, in 1871, he conducted model tests that influenced the design of the HMS *Greyhound*. The sea trials a year later showed that Froude's design method was a complete success.

Froude's work formed the basis for one of the most powerful tools available to the engineer. As long as a designer could find a suitable dimensionless constant, it was possible to use a scale model to simulate the behavior of a full-size prototype. Froude's method was used to great effect in wind tunnels in the early years of the twentieth century, and for many other engineering problems involving fluid flow.

The development of experimental engineering science in general, and the use of scale models in particular, transformed nearly every aspect of building engineering design during the first half of the twentieth century. In addition to predicting the static and dynamic behavior of structures, scale-model tests have played a major part in the development of design methods for acoustics, the flow of air and smoke inside buildings, both at normal temperatures and at elevated temperatures in a fire, the interaction between foundations and soils, earthquake engineering, the effects of wind on buildings, and many more.

Indeed, in the early days of any new branch of building engineering, full-size and scale-model tests are still the only means by which mathematical models can be tested and the accuracy of their predictions established prior to their use in engineering design.

The Development of Concrete Shells

In building engineering, the first widespread application of nondimensional constants to model testing was in the development of thin, curved concrete shells in the 1920s and 1930s. These structures, more than any other, would exploit the three essential attributes of reinforced concrete that set it apart form all other construction materials—it can be made into a thin, load-bearing sheet of unconstrained or theoretically unlimited extent; it can be formed into any three-dimensional shape; and, by judicious placement of the reinforcement, it can be made as strong and stiff as necessary for a particular application. No such material had previously been known. Here was a concept that had a unique appeal to engineers, who had always had the intellectual ideal of creating structures that used material only where it was absolutely necessary, and in minimum quantities. A designer of a reinforced concrete structure was, effectively, designing the properties of the material itself.

Since curved concrete shells were ideally suited to form the roofs of buildings, their design also necessarily inspired the search for ways to maximize the span of roofs while minimizing their thickness. Maximizing the efficiency with which materials are used was virtually the same goal that had been achieved in the evolution of structural forms in the plant and animal kingdom that had been identified by D'Arcy Thompson. In principle, thin shells of reinforced concrete could emulate the shell of an egg, a flower petal, a seashell, or the exoskeleton of a crab. Crucially, seeking such a goal would also appeal to inquiring minds in ways that steel- and concrete-frame structures did not. It would demand an unprecedented understanding of both the behavior of structures and the properties of materials—an understanding that Karl Terzaghi had brought to the analysis of soils and A. A. Griffith had brought to the

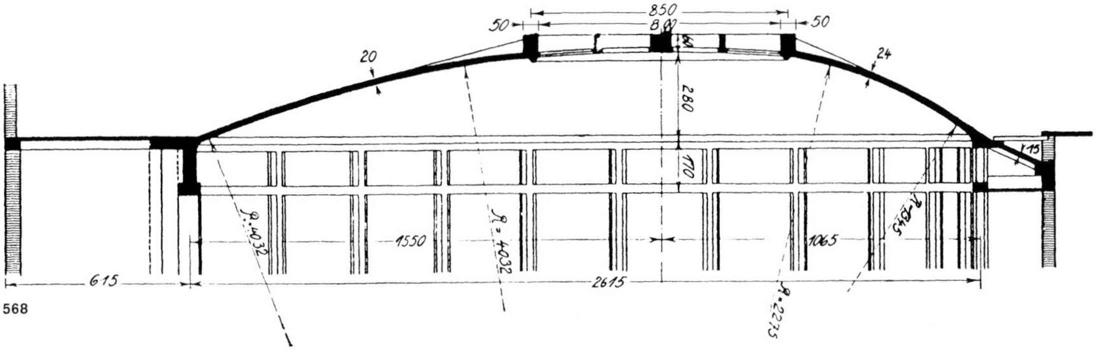

568

fracture of materials. It would require the development of new mathematical models for structures and materials, and this, in turn, required experimentation to establish the accuracy and effectiveness of those mathematical models.

In 1920, however, it was far from clear how the goals of maximum efficiency might be achieved. Few concrete contractors had the necessary knowledge of theoretical engineering science; universities and other research institutes, where the theoretical understanding was to be found, were not equipped to test concrete structures, and building and testing a full-size roof structure would have been as costly as it was impractical. Nevertheless, some firms and individuals continued to make progress as they used their experience to develop more effective design and calculation methods. The contracting firm of Dyckerhoff & Widmann (see chapter 7) was not the only company building concrete shells, but from the first decade of the century on, it had gradually developed its expertise in designing and building some of the largest and most complex shell roofs then extant, using ribs to provide adequate stiffness for the thin shells when necessary. By measuring the behavior of the shells it constructed, the firm developed more accurate and reliable design methods and was able to build bolder and bolder roofs. The roof of the Union Theater in Saarbrücken, Germany, for example, completed in 1923, spanned 26.15 by 23.5 meters, with a rise of just 2.8 meters—
568 an unprecedented span-to-rise ratio of 8.4 to 1. The structural engineer for the dome, Professor Georg Rüth (1880–1945) of the Technical University at Dresden, remarked that since it was not possible at that time to make precise calculations for such a structure, the bending moments in the asymmetric and highly stressed shell had to be calculated using a series of iterative calculations to match the outward deformation of the shell and the resistance of the tension ring.[6] At the center of the span, where the compressive forces were highest, ten thin ribs were added to the top of the shell to prevent buckling.

In the early 1920s, the development of thin concrete shells benefited the fortuitous collaboration of certain individuals and firms who had been brought together by the need to build a planetarium in Jena, Germany. One firm was Dyckerhoff & Widmann; the other was Zeiss, which made scientific optical equipment and had a strong tradition of basing its product development on scientific research. The chief design engineer at Zeiss, Walter Bauersfeld (1879–1959), was a mechanical engineer who had developed several of the optical projection devices for which Zeiss was well known. In 1919 Bauersfeld had a practical problem to solve: He wanted to design a new type of planetarium, in which the stars and planets would be projected onto the interior surface of a perfectly hemispherical dome from an array of projectors that could move to simulate the rotation of the earth. For nearly five years Bauersfeld and his team worked on the twin problems of creating the projection system and the hemispherical screen. His first task was to find a plane-faced polyhedron that approximated the shape of a hemisphere to create a screen for each projector. The dome had to be very light, as it was to be constructed on the roof of one of the buildings at the Zeiss works. He set about devising a workable structure without any of the traditions and preconceptions of the building industry, approaching it as an inventor and research engineer, from first principles.

Devising a regular grid of triangles to form a hemisphere was not, however, straightforward. By good fortune Bauersfeld knew Ernst Haeckel, the professor of botany at the University at Jena who, in 1887, had published remarkable illustrations of many microorganisms. Among these was the radiolarian *Aulonia hexagona*, the structure of which was a nearly perfect sphere made from hexagons and pentagons (see chapter 7, p. 443). Bauersfeld found that he could create a regular version of such a structure from an icosahedron with the vertices cut to form twelve pentagons and twenty hexagons of nearly equal area. This form not only provided the basis for the screens, but also defined the arrangement of bars needed to construct a framework that could support the screens. Each pentagon and hexagon was triangulated to give them the necessary rigidity and, in essence, came to resemble the triangulated domes that Johann Schwedler had developed in the 1860s and August Föppl had developed in the 1890s, both of whose work Bauersfeld had encountered during his engineering studies. The skeleton of the prototype 16-meter-diameter dome comprised 3,480 steel rods each about 600 mm long, and each manufactured to an accuracy of less than one-hundredth of a millimeter—a degree of precision more characteristic of an optical instrument than a conventional roof structure. The elegant simplicity of the final solution—which was, in essence, the first geodesic dome—gives little indication of the extreme rigor with which Bauersfeld had tackled the challenge. To form the surface on which to project the images of the stars,
569, 570 Bauersfeld had first considered using gypsum, but this proved difficult to waterproof. Only after the skeleton had been constructed did he seek advice about how he might best use concrete as a more water-resistant alternative to gypsum. He made contact with the engineer Franz Dischinger (1887–1953), who had worked on a number of buildings at the Zeiss factory. The solution he proposed was to use the newly developed Torkret process (named after the company that developed it), in which the concrete was sprayed onto a mesh of wire and supported from beneath by a lightweight movable timber form. The thickness of concrete was chosen to achieve 571
the same span-to-thickness ratio as an eggshell, about 1:130. The combination of the framework and concrete covering was patented in 1923 as the Zeiss-Dywidag system, taking letters from the firm Dyckerhoff & Widmann AG, for whom Dischinger worked. In 1924 Bauersfeld and Dischinger designed and built a shell roof over a workshop, using the Zeiss-Dywidag system, for another firm in Jena; this one spanned 40 meters and had a thickness of just 60 mm. Their third collaboration on a 572
major structure was another planetarium at the Zeiss works, spanning 25 meters.

From his first project with Zeiss, Dischinger had recognized the potential of this new structural form in the building industry; however, he also realized there would be limited opportunities to use the circular plan. His first thought was to build on an elliptical base, creating a roof with double curvature. The calculations of the forces in the shell would be extremely complex, and the regular geometry of the geodesic Zeiss framework could not be used. This led him to recognize the benefits of a cylindrical shell, curved in only one direction and able to span as a long, curved beam in the other direction. Both the formwork and the calculations would be simpler, and the shell could be adapted to a rectangular building plan. Bauersfeld and Dischinger constructed their first cylindrical barrel vault over a workshop at the Zeiss works in Jena in 1924; they were assisted in the analysis of this shell by the young engineer Ulrich Finsterwalder (1897–1988), who had joined Dyckerhoff & Widmann a year earlier. During the following decade Dischinger and Finsterwalder, joined in 1926 by Hubert Rüsch (1903–79), went on to develop methods for designing all the main forms of shell—shells with single and double curvature built on circular, rectangular, and polygonal plans.

The process developed by Dischinger was essentially that of the research scientist, for none of these early shells had a useful precedent. First, a theoretical analysis was made considering only forces in the plane of the shell (membrane theory), combined with simple bending theory. To this was added an analysis to ensure that the compressive forces would not cause the thin shell to buckle. However, this was hardly a comprehensive model of the system, and the next stage was to build and test a

569

570

571

568 (page 481) Union Theater, Saarbrücken, Germany, 1922–23. Engineer: Dyckerhoff and Widmann. Elevation.
569 Zeiss dome under construction, Zeiss glass works, Jena, Germany, 1923. Engineers: Walter Bauersfeld and Franz Dischinger. 570 Completed Zeiss dome. 571 A geodesic structure under construction using the Zeiss-Dywidag system, Jena, Germany, 1924. Engineers: Walter Bauersfeld and Franz Dischinger. Torkret (gunite) is sprayed over moveable formwork.

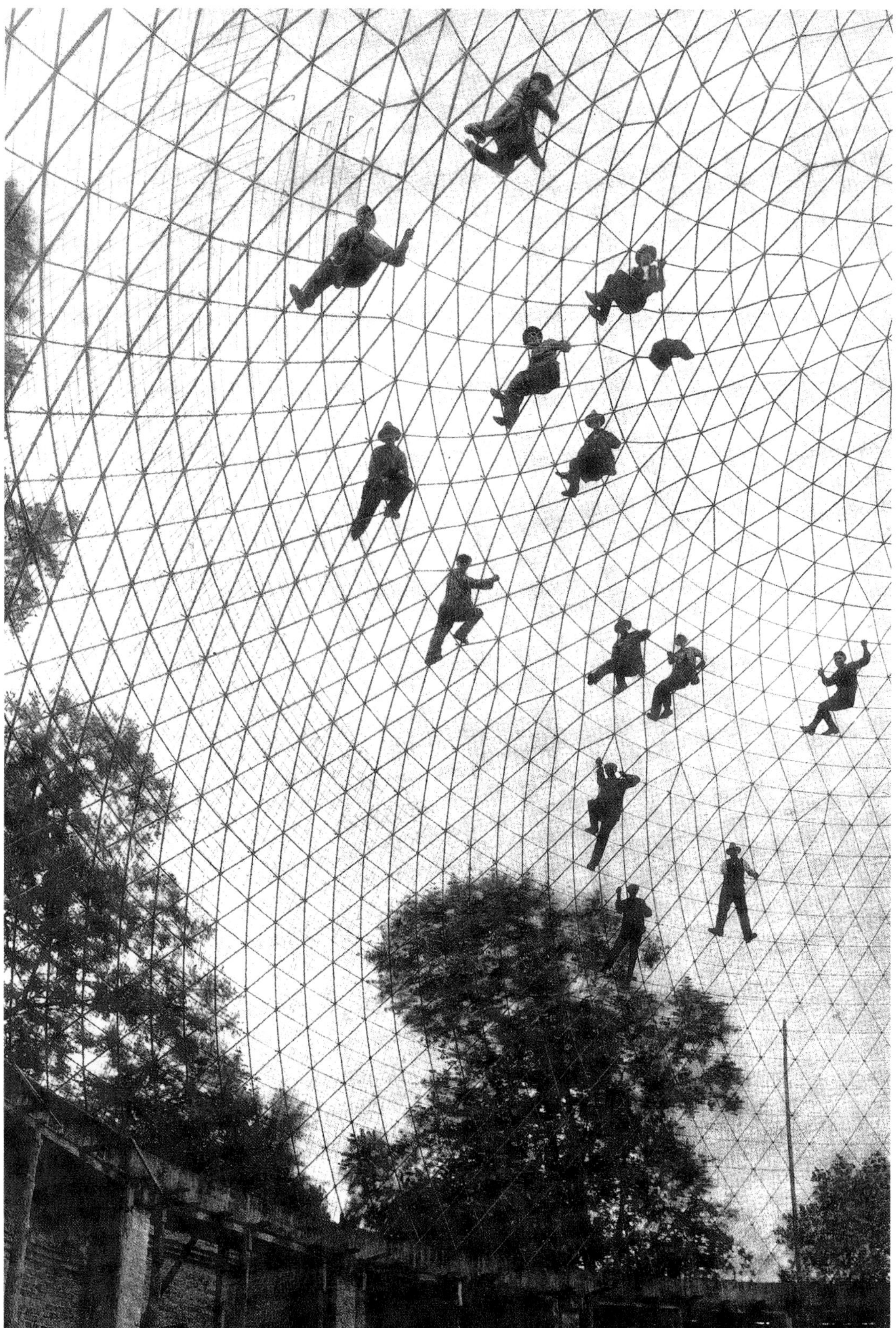

model of the shell. Not only the structure, but also the material and the loads had to be modeled at a reduced scale. The various parameters, including load, bending moment, and stiffness, varied differently with the scale factor, some linearly and others with the square or the cube of the scale. To deal with this complexity, Dischinger and Finsterwalder were able to benefit from Froude's use of nondimensional ratios to ensure that the scale factors were appropriate for representing the specific behaviors of the full-scale system being studied—the overall stress distribution or the buckling of the shell, for example. From careful measurements of the displacement of points on the surface of the model of the shell, and the displacement at its edges, the designers were able to establish the forces in the shell and the degree of bending it would be subject to across its span. By this means they were able to reconcile the various calculated values of stress and deflection derived from the different mathematical models; they could then make minor changes to the predicted values, and the results formed the basis for specifying the thickness of the concrete and the size and disposition of the steel reinforcement. Finally, prototype sections of some of the shells were made to ensure that the predictions of the structure's behavior made from mathematical models and small-scale models were
573 borne out at full size. Following this process it was possible to reduce the thickness of the shell to the absolute minimum. And the thickness (or, rather, thinness) of the shells was astonishing: A shell roof spanning several tens of meters could be just a few tens of millimeters thick. The economy in the use of materials that this made possible was truly remarkable: For example, the dome of St. Peter's Basilica in Rome weighs about 10,000 tons, and the ribbed arch roof of the Breslau Jahrhunderthalle weighs some 6,340 tons; the roof of the market hall at Leipzig, which covers a larger area than both, has a reinforced concrete shell that is only 100 mm thick and weighs just 2,160 tons.

In 1924 Dischinger and Finsterwalder designed their first major cylindrical shell roof for "Gesolei"—the "Gesundheit, Sozialefürsorge und Leibesübungen" (Health, Social Welfare and Physical Exercise) exhibition
574 buildings in Dusseldorf in 1925. A year later they designed a circular shell roof for a factory that manufactured electrical machinery. Supported on columns at the corners of an octagon, the shell, which was a portion of a sphere, was 40 mm thick, spanned 26 meters, and had a rise of just 3.3 meters. The following three years saw the first use of Zeiss-Dywidag shells in public buildings—several spectacular market halls at Frankfurt,
Leipzig, Budapest, and Basel. The twin octagonal domes 575, 577
of the market at Leipzig were 65m in diameter at the base of the 100mm-thick shell, with a clear span of about 80m at ground level. To raise his confidence in understanding how the full-size structure would perform, as well as undertaking a mathematical analysis of the behavior of the structure, Dischinger also built a 1:60 scale model of the dome and measured its deformation under a variety of loads. Dischinger's theoretical studies of polygonal shell vaults, and the experience he gained designing and constructing the Zeiss-Dywidag roofs at the Leipzig and Basel markets, formed the basis of his doctoral thesis, and he was awarded his doctorate in 1929. Following this he developed a means for calculating doubly curved shells on a rectangular base. An early prototype using this form of structure was a modestly sized roof at a factory in Wiesbaden built in 1931. The roof was built on a 7.3-by-7.3-meter square plan, and the shell was just 15 mm thick at the crown. In 1930 Finsterwalder was awarded a doctorate for his work on the theory of cylindrical shells using the Zeiss-Dywidag system as exemplified in the market hall at Budapest. During the 1930s the firm of Dyckerhoff & Widmann was responsible for the construction of shell roofs all over the world, not only from its own offices—Hubert Rüsch ran the firm's headquarters in Buenos Aires from 1931 to 1934—but also selling licenses to use the Dywidag system to firms in other countries. For example, the Austrian engineer Anton Tedesko worked for two years with Dyckerhoff & Widmann in Germany before being asked to establish the firm's presence in the United States through collaboration with the Chicago firm of Roberts and Schaefer. The first Dywidag shells in the United States were the Hayden Planetarium in New York, completed in 1935, and an exhibition building at the Chicago World's Fair of 1933. Most spectacular, perhaps, was the ice rink built for the Hershey Chocolate

572 A dome under construction using the Zeiss-Dywidag system, Jena, Germany, 1924. Engineers: Walter Bauersfeld and Franz Dischinger.

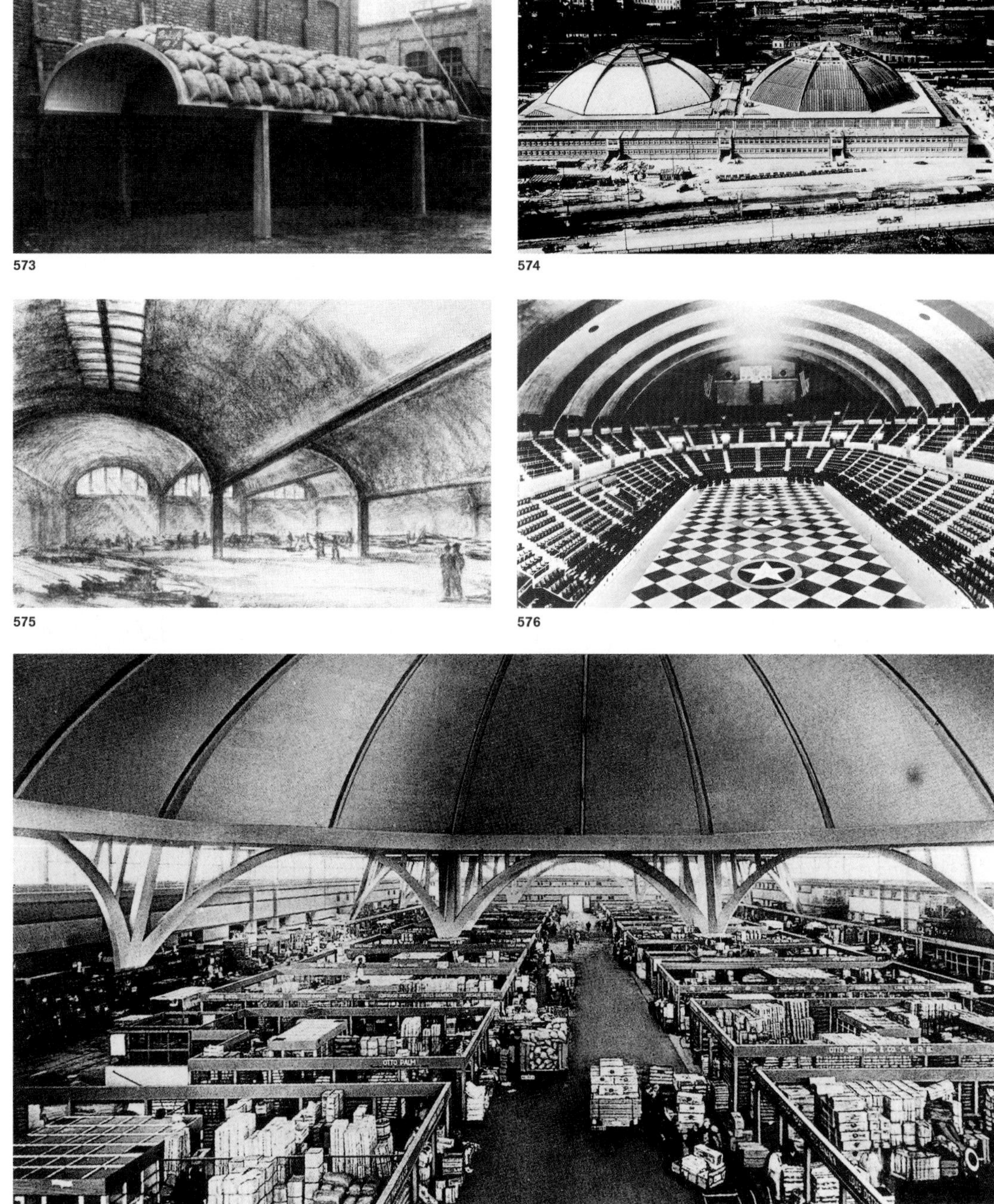

573 574 575 576 577

573 Load testing a prototype barrel vault prior to erection of the Gesolei (Gesundheit, Sozialefürsorge und Leibesübungen) exhibition building, Dusseldorf, 1925. Engineer: Franz Dischinger. 574 Gesolei exhibition building, Dusseldorf, 1925. 575 Market hall, Leipzig, Germany, 1928–29. Rendering of interior. Engineers: Franz Dischinger and Hubert Rüsch; architect: Hubert Ritter. 576 Hershey ice rink, Hershey, Pennsylvania, 1936. Engineer: Anton Tedesko. 577 Market hall, Leipzig. Interior.

578

579

578 Schwarzwaldhalle, Karlsruhe, Germany, 1953. Engineer: Ulrich Finsterwalder. 579 Schwartzwaldhalle.

Company in Hershey, Pennsylvania, in 1936, which cov-
576 ered an area 73 meters by 104 meters.

Dyckerhoff & Widmann pioneered nearly every application of shell roofs, offering building designers unprecedented column-free spaces beneath the roofs of market buildings, exhibition halls, aircraft hangars, bus depots, railway stations, railway platforms, sports halls, and, most numerous of all, factory buildings. One of the largest of the factory roofs was built for Ferdinand Porsche's Volkswagen works in Wolfsburg, Germany, which covered 166,000 square meters.

In addition to their work on shells, Dischinger, Finsterwalder, and Hubert Rüsch were also pioneers in prestressed concrete bridge construction in the late 1930s and 1940s. In 1953 Ulrich Finsterwalder designed one of the first prestressed concrete roofs for the Schwarzwaldhalle, in Karlsruhe, Germany, an auditorium with seating for 4,500 spectators and a stage that could accommodate 1,500 performers. It had a suspended saddle-shaped roof that spanned 73.5 by
578, 579 48.6 meters.

The contributions made by Dischinger, Finsterwalder, and Rüsch to the art of designing reinforced concrete structures can hardly be overestimated. These engineers developed an extraordinary understanding of material and its performance through a combination of increasingly complex theoretical analyses of shells and careful observations of the behavior of real structures, both scale models and at full size. A series of seminal publications describing the methods they had developed for designing concrete shells was distributed throughout the world, and their work was also embraced by designers who wanted to use reinforced concrete for applications other than shell roofs. Dischinger and Rüsch's influence continued through their educational and research work as professors of concrete construction at the Technische Hochschule in Berlin, from 1933, and the Technische Hochschule in Munich, from 1948, respectively.

By the late 1920s reinforced concrete was no longer just a material that provided a fireproof alternative to the steel frame. It allowed the construction of an entirely new family of structural forms whose visual and architectural impact could not be ignored. Nevertheless, concrete shells were seldom adopted and exploited by architects. The reasons for this are complex, but a major factor was probably the considerable technical expertise needed to design them. Other reasons may be that their scale is too large, and that they tend to have little impact on the elevation of a building. Another may be that the concrete shell is opaque; architects in the nineteenth century embraced transparent iron and glass roofs with enthusiasm, and in the 1980s and 1990s much use has been made of translucent, tensile, membrane structures. What seems to have been the architect's loss, however, was the engineer's gain. Concrete shells—both in their simplest form and when used in combination with stiffening ribs and other structural elements, whether cast in situ or constructed from precast units or exploiting the advantages of prestressing—have inspired what was surely the most creative period in the history of structural engineering since the late Middle Ages, the era of the great cathedrals.

During the years between about 1930 and the 1960s, a dozen or so structural engineers became known well beyond the world of engineering for their mastery of reinforced concrete and brickwork and the extraordinary architectural forms they created: Pier Luigi Nervi (1891–1979), Eduardo Torroja (1899–1961), Felix Candela (1910–97), Eladio Dieste (1917–2000), Riccardo Morandi (1902–89), Anton Tedesko (1903–94), Eugène Freyssinet (1879–1962), Oscar Faber (1886–1956), Owen Williams (1890-1969), Ove Arup (1895–1988), Bernard Lafaille (1900–55), Nicolas Esquillan (1902–89), René Sarger (1917–88), and Heinz Isler (b. 1926). Although all these engineers collaborated with architects, they also worked independently, virtually creating their own architectural vocabulary, a phenomenon unheard of at any other time in the history of building engineering. They were able to build upon the work of Dischinger and Finsterwalder through the technical papers and textbooks those men had written, and, most importantly, through adopting and developing the experimental approach that Dischinger had pioneered. The use of both model testing and prototype testing, together with the increasingly sophisticated techniques of experimental stress analysis as part of the design process, allowed innovative structural engineers to take their designs beyond the range of familiar experience with confidence.

DRAWINGS AND COPYING

From the 1920s on, the reproduction of drawings by the blueprint process began to be replaced by the diazo, or dyeline. Developed in the 1890s, the diazo method was also a photographic process but produced a positive copy, rather than a negative, of an original on translucent paper or linen. Depending on which chemicals were used to impregnate the copy paper, the lines produced were magenta, blue, black, or brown. The Diazotypes or Ozalids, the two best-known trade names, were much quicker to produce than blueprints and did not require a washing bath. A further advantage over blueprints was that diazo copies could be made of lines drawn with pencil, which allowed draftsmen to correct their drawings more easily since pencil is erasable but ink must be scraped off the paper. There were also some disadvantages. The diazo developing process involved the use of ammonia, which lingered on the copies for some time and created an unpleasant atmosphere in the print rooms of drawing offices. Also, the copies remained sensitive to light, which meant they had to be stored either in plan chests or rolled up. The use of tracing cloth declined in the 1930s because of its high cost, but tracing paper remained in use until the 1950s, when polyester films such as Mylar were introduced.

580

581

580 Engineering design office of R. Travers Morgan & Partners, London, c. 1968. 581 Detail of engineering drawing on woven linen cloth, c. 1930.

582

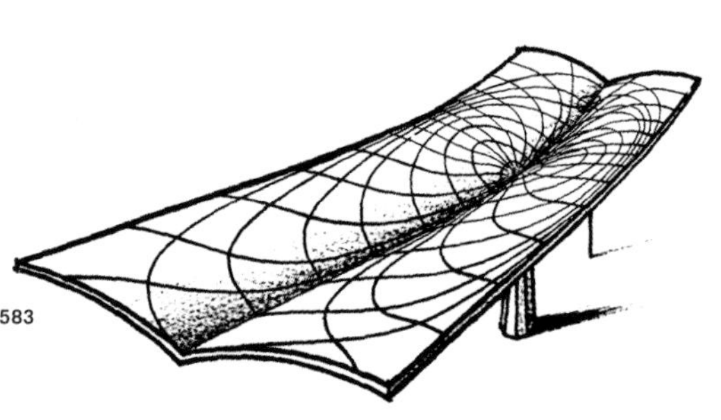

583

584

585

The Spanish engineer Eduardo Torroja, who began using concrete shells in the mid-1930s, created some of the most innovative structures of their kind. For the canopy at the Madrid hippodrome (1935), for example, he used a concrete shell resembling a gently curved and folded
582 sheet of paper. The canopy cantilevers 13 meters over the seating, and yet is just 50 mm thick. To help establish where best to place the tensile steel reinforcement, Torroja augmented his general understanding of structural behavior by studying the behavior of a simple model made of thin card, to sketch the approximate pat-
583 tern of the internal stresses. This gave him a basis for calculating the thickness and spacing of the steel rein-
584 forcing bars. To verify Torroja's understanding of this unprecedented structural form, and the reliability of the design calculations, the contractor built and tested a
585 prototype unit. The test also served as a trial of the reusable formwork devised for the construction of the canopy. Undertaken at a time when steel was in short supply, the contractor broke up the prototype shell after the test and reused the reinforcement to make one unit of the final roof.

Possibly the boldest structure Torroja designed was the roof over the Frontón Recoletos sports hall in Madrid (1935). He proposed a cylindrical shell in two lobes spanning 32 meters wide by 55 meters long, with a concrete shell that was 80 mm thick everywhere but at the inter-
586 section of the two lobes, where it was 150 mm. As with the Hippodrome roof, Torroja first had to understand in qualitative terms how the structure worked. A simple model made of card, fixed to model end walls made of wood, confirmed the overall stiffness of the curved form and the need to provide firm support to the longitudinal edges of the curved shells, especially where the two lobes intersected. Because the necessary calculations for this asymmetrical structure form were so complex, the mathematical model had to be greatly simplified. This made the calculations of stresses and deflections particularly uncertain, especially in the perforated parts of the shell containing the windows. To inspire sufficient confidence in his innovative design Torroja built and tested a
587 1:25 scale model. He measured deflections under dead load and simulated wind and snow load, and compared the results with those predicted by calculation. They were found to be close enough to convince Torroja that his understanding of the behavior of the structure was sufficient to go ahead and build it. When the roof was complete, he measured its actual deformations and compared them with the predictions made from calculations, from the model tests, and found they agreed to within
100 mm. Not only did this give Torroja final confirmation 591
of the soundness of his design for this roof, it also raised his confidence, and that of all other engineers engaged in similar projects, in the power of his design procedure using model tests combined with relatively simple mathematical calculations.

At the Pont de Suert church (1952) in the Spanish Pyrenees, Torroja devised an innovative way of making a complex, curved structural shell that could be built without using the timber formwork that was then standard practice when making shells of reinforced concrete. He combined the traditional technique of the Catalan brick vault (see chapter 7, p. 386) with steel reinforcement to form the five pairs of shells that make up the nave. The shells, each comprising three layers of hollow brick tiles 30 mm thick, were built without formwork, using guides to define the curved shape of the vault and quick-setting
mortar for the inner layer. The steel reinforcement was 589, 590
laid on the outer surface and covered by the outer layer of cement mortar facing. As a vault is not a funicular shape in cross section (as masonry vaults must be), it needs to resist some bending. The curved profile of the lobes enables the thin shell, just 200 mm thick, to resist this
bending, just as a seashell does. 588

Like Torroja, the Italian engineer Pier Luigi Nervi was a pioneer in the use of scale models during the development of many of his structures, both to develop a better understanding of how they worked and to predict the deformations that the full-size structure would experience under load. Over many years Nervi collaborated with Professor Arturo Danusso (1880–1968) at the Polytechnic Institute of Milan, who developed many techniques for building and loading scale models of structures and measuring

582 Hippodrome, Madrid, 1935. Engineer: Eduardo Torroja. 583 Hippodrome, Madrid. Diagram of the principal stresses in the canopy. 584 Hippodrome, Madrid. Prototype of the canopy, showing tensile steel reinforcement. 585 Testing the Hippodrome canopy prototype with sandbags.

586

deflections and strains. Nervi frequently required model tests to complement theoretical calculations simply because he so often designed structures that were breaking new ground. One example was an aircraft hangar he designed and built for the Italian Air Force in 1936. It covered an area 111.5 by 44.8 meters, and one of the long sides had to provide access through doors that were 50
592 meters wide. Despite its apparent complexity, Nervi's design was selected because it was the cheapest. (It was probably the cheapest because Nervi was a contractor as well as a designer, and conceived all his remarkable structures with their method of construction foremost in his mind.) Model tests were essential for such an innovative structural form, one whose asymmetry and high degree of statical indeterminancy meant that considerable simplifications and approximations had to be made to yield a practical mathematical model. The model tests 593a–c
confirmed Nervi's prediction that the many structural el-

586 Frontón Recoletos sports hall, Madrid, 1935. Engineer: Eduardo Torroja. 587 Frontón Recoletos. Model, 1935. 588 Pont de Suert church, Lleida, Spain, 1952. Engineer: Eduardo Torroja. Plaster model of one bay of the nave. 589 Pont de Suert church. Nave, constructed of steel-reinforced brickwork. 590 Pont de Suert church. Cross section of reinforced brickwork shell. 591 Frontón Recoletos. Illustration showing comparative deformations of the roof, 1935.

587

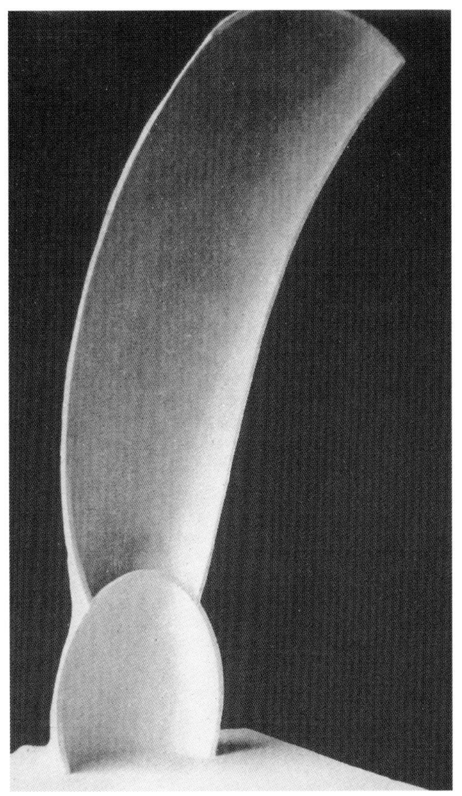
588

589

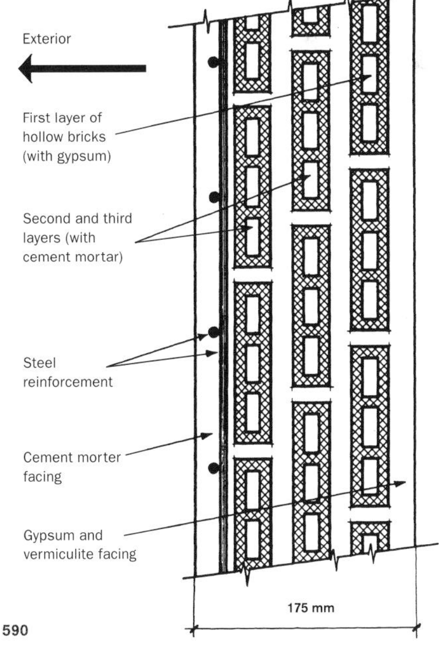
Exterior
First layer of hollow bricks (with gypsum)
Second and third layers (with cement mortar)
Steel reinforcement
Cement morter facing
Gypsum and vermiculite facing
175 mm
590

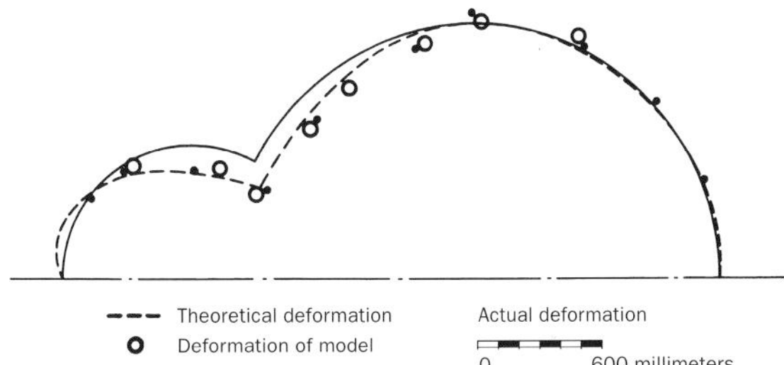
Theoretical deformation
Deformation of model
Actual deformation
Actual deformation
0
600 millimeters
591

592

ements would work much better in combination than he was able to justify using the highly simplified theoretical calculations. They also demonstrated that the dimensions he had chosen in the preliminary design would largely be satisfactory, and only a few of the diagonal ribs of the lamella roof had to be increased in thickness. Measurements of the deformation of the actual structure taken during and after construction showed that the results of the model tests had been sufficiently accurate. They also enabled Nervi to monitor the plastic and viscous deformations of the structures caused by the tendency of concrete to continue to deform under prolonged loading. Further deformation ceased after about five years. Toward the end of his life, Nervi still considered the technical studies he undertook for this hangar among the most complex of his career.

Probably Nervi's greatest innovation was a new material he called "ferro-cemento," which was concrete made using fine aggregate (sand) reinforced with a mesh of wire just one or two millimeters in diameter. He used this material to make very thin precast elements that could be assembled on formwork and stitched together using conventional steel reinforcement and concrete placed in situ. This was the innovation of a practical builder, and he used many versions of this technique to create some of the most remarkable and beautiful structures ever built. One of these was the large sports palace built for the Rome Olympics in 1960. The corru- 594
gated dome, which spans just over 100 meters, is made from V-shaped ferro-cement units around 1 meter deep and 4.5 meters long, with walls just 25 mm thick. 596

592 Aircraft hangar, Orvieto, Italy, 1936. Engineer: Pier Luigi Nervi. 593a–c Aircraft hangar, Orvieto. Model used to measure deformations and calculate stresses in the grid shell. Combinations of gravity and wind loads were applied using weights, and deformations measured using clock gauges.

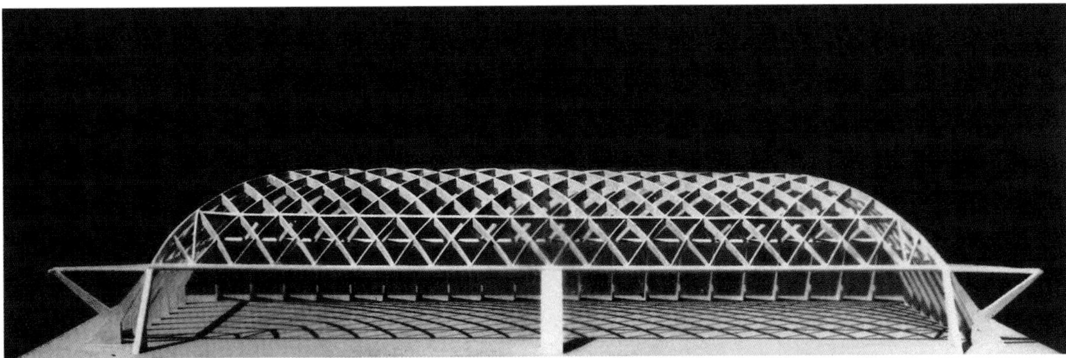
593a

593b

593c

Eugène Freyssinet was one of several French engineers who began experimenting with using concrete in the form of a thin sheet, for example, for the airship hangars at Orly (1921–23), which were some 200 meters long and 60 meters high, spanning over 85
595 meters. The deeply corrugated reinforced-concrete arches, acting structurally as a folded plate, were just 90 millimeters thick. Sadly, they did not survive American bombs in 1944.

The French engineer Bernard Lafaille built many types of concrete shell in the 1920s before beginning to experiment, in about 1933, with a new structural form for shell structures, the hyperbolic paraboloid. This family of anticlastic curved surfaces can be generated by moving a straight line through space, and is unique in the history of structures as being the only form that was identified using mathematics and engineering science before it had been conceived and constructed by an engineer. It has the practical advantage that the formwork needed to create the curved shape in concrete can be 597, 598
built using straight and flat timber planks. 599, 600

Hyperbolic paraboloids caught the imagination of many architects in the 1940s and 1950s, both because of their form and because they provided large column-free spaces needing only a few supports around the perimeter. The acknowledged master of the form was the Spanish engineer Felix Candela, who constructed many hundreds of buildings with roofs made using hyperbolic paraboloids of reinforced concrete, mainly in his adopted home, Mexico. Some were used for mundane industrial buildings, but many others were used in churches of considerable architectural merit, and their appearance was always striking. Candela's tour
de force was his restaurant Los Manantiales at 601
Xochimilco near Mexico City (1958), constructed using his own versionof ferro-cement. It spans 42.5 meters and yet is just 42 millimeters thick, except at the free edges which are slightly thicker. Its form is generated

594

595

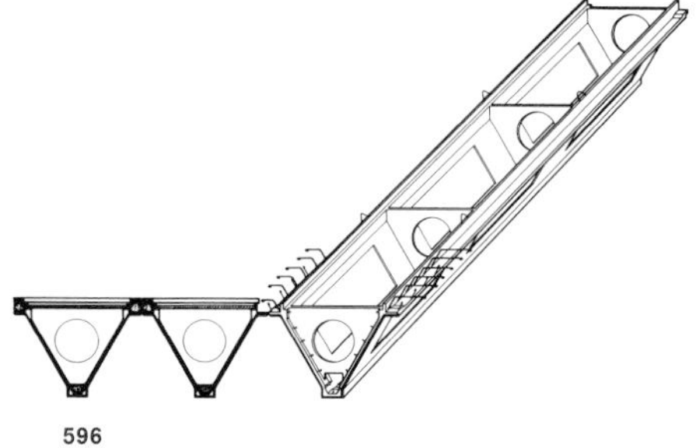

596

594 Palazzo dello Sport, Rome, 1960. Engineer: Pier Luigi Nervi. 595 Airship hangars, Orly, France, 1921–23. Engineer: Eugène Freyssinet. 596 Palazzo dello Sport. Diagram of typical precast unit made from ferro-cement. 597 First experimental hyperbolic paraboloid shell built by Bernard Lafaille, 1935. 598 Hyperbolic paraboloid shell roof covering storage sheds at Alfa-Romeo works, Milan, 1937. Engineer: Giorgio Baroni. 599 Sketches of proposed applications of hyperbolic paraboloid shells by François Aimand, c. 1934. 600 Diagram of the first experimental hyperbolic paraboloid shell built by Bernard Lafaille, 1935. 601 Iglesia de San José Obrero, Monterrey, Mexico, 1959. Engineer: Felix Candela.

597

598

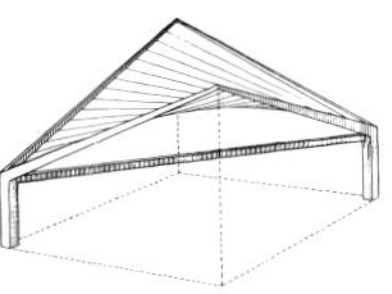

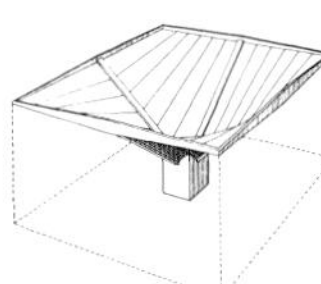

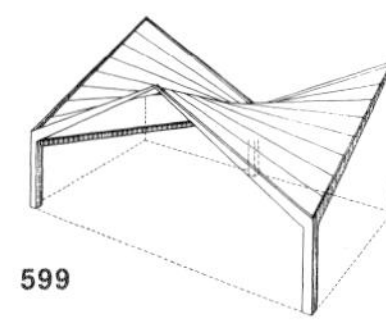

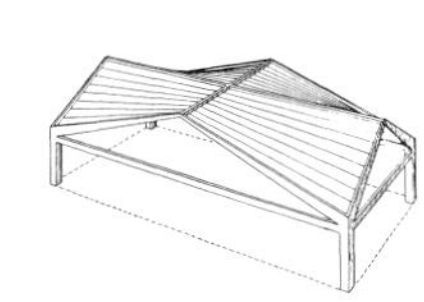

599

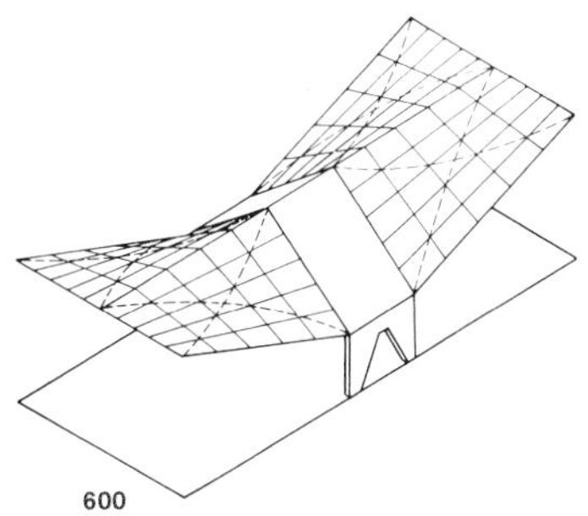

600

601

602

603

602, 603 by four intersecting hyperbolic paraboloids.

The Uruguayan engineer Eladio Dieste also built many shell structures in the 1940s and 1950s, mainly using reinforced brickwork rather than reinforced concrete. This has the advantage that the external finish was less monotonous, and does not require the expensive form-
604 work needed to make concrete shells. The largest concrete shell roof ever constructed is the double-skinned shell of the Centre des Nouvelles Industries et Technologies (CNIT) exhibition hall, built in Paris between 1956 and 1958. The span between the corners of its triangular plan is 208 meters. The enormous span was made possible by the ingenious design of the French engineer Nicolas Esquillan, who devised a lightweight scheme using two shells about 3 meters apart and only 65 mm thick. These are joined by a series of diaphragm walls, creating what is effectively a series of thin-walled tubes. The top and bottom surfaces of the tubes are curved, resembling a straw or the fibers in a tree trunk, to increase the capacity of the walls to carry compression
605, 606 forces without buckling.

By the 1950s, in addition to their use for large and spectacular roofs, concrete shells were being used throughout the world, for many tens of thousands of roofs of moderate span, in buildings such as markets, school halls, factories, sports and exhibition halls, railway and bus stations, gas stations, garages, and warehouses. Having once required the efforts of the world's foremost engineers, concrete shells had become mainstream building products supplied off the shelf, so to speak, by specialist contractors.

The Dynamic Behavior of Buildings

The idea that buildings could be designed and constructed to resist damage by severe earthquakes developed in Japan and the West Coast of the United States during the 1920s. The key issue was understanding exactly what forces a building had to resist. This question was first studied in depth in Japan in the 1880s, not by the Japanese, but by three British engineering scientists who had taken jobs at the Imperial College of Engineering in Tokyo. The leader of this team was John Milne (1850–1913), later known as "the father of seismology" and "Earthquake Milne." Milne arrived in Tokyo in 1875 to teach mechanics, and gradually became interested in the nature of earthquakes. Following an earthquake in 1880 he invited two other British scientists to join him, and together they developed various ways of measuring and recording the actual movements that make up an earthquake. What they discovered over the next two years was contrary to then-current theories: An earthquake was not a single big bang whose effects then died down, nor was it a regular periodic movement. Rather, the motions were of long duration and irregular in frequency, and occurred in all three dimensions. After his two colleagues returned to Britain, Milne stayed in Japan and studied the movements of several two-story buildings during earth tremors. He found that timber buildings moved more than those built of brick, and that the movements on the second floor were greater than those on the first (ground) floor. He also found that a building built on what was locally considered to be "soft ground" moved more than a similar one built on "hard ground."

In 1880 Milne founded the Seismological Institute of Japan, and Fusakichi Omori (1868–1923) became its director. In the 1890s Milne and Omori conducted the first "shaking table" experiments to simulate the movement of an earthquake on model buildings. The table, restrained by springs and mounted on wheels to allow it to move horizontally, was pulled sideways by ropes and suddenly released to simulate the movements of an earthquake. Omori went on to study the behavior of brick columns in earthquakes. Apart from Omori little local interest in seismology developed, and by 1892 the Seismological Institute had ceased to exist. Milne returned to Britain in 1895 after his laboratory was destroyed by fire, and set up the Shide Seismological Observatory on the Isle of Wight. For nearly twenty years the Shide Observatory was, effectively, the world headquarters for earthquake seismology.

Worldwide interest in earthquakes was revived after the great earthquake in San Francisco, California of 1906, and in that year F. J. Rogers, a Stanford University physics professor, built what he called a "shaking machine," driven by an electric motor and crank, to study the effect of simulated earthquake movements on soil. In 1915

602 Los Manantiales Restaurant, Xochimilco, Mexico, 1958. Engineer: Felix Candela. 603 Los Manantiales Restaurant.

604

605

606

604 Chiesa parrocchiale, Atlántida, Uruguay, 1955–60. Architect and engineer: Eladio Dieste. 605 Centre des Nouvelles industries et technologies (CNIT), Paris, 1956–58. Engineer: Nicolas Esquillan. Under construction. 606 CNIT.

Riki Sano (1880–1956), a practicing engineer who was also a professor at the University of Tokyo, wrote the first textbook on the subject, *Earthquake Resistant Building*. More elaborate shaking tables were constructed in Tokyo's Earthquake Research Institute, founded in 1924, and at the California Institute of Technology (Caltech) in Pasadena after the 1925 Santa Barbara earthquake. The first systematic research into earthquake-resistant timber housing began in 1929, both at the Tokyo Earthquake Research Institute and by Professor Lydik Jacobsen (1897–1976), the director of the Vibration Laboratory at Stanford. Rather than assuming a building to be a static structure subject to a dynamic load, Jacobsen recognized the need to consider also the dynamic response of the building. In 1930–31 he and his research students undertook the first shaking-table tests on a model of a proposed multistory building—the Olympic Club in San Francisco. This work used a monolithic model to study the different modes of vibration of the building, and highlighted the need to make a more sophisticated model, one that would take into account the independent movement of each story of a proposed building. Jacobsen's work inspired the next generation of research students, including John Blume (1909–2002), who devised and built a 1:40 scale model of the pro-
607 posed fifteen-story Alexander Building in San Francisco in 1932–33. The model was a masterpiece of mechanical engineering design, and allowed each story to move in five independent ways: two horizontal, one vertical, and two rotational about horizontal axes. A mass of aluminum and steel plates and tubes, steel springs, and steel ball bearings allowed each floor to roll. Movements were displayed by pointers at every story. The analysis undertaken by Blume and other research students demonstrated how modes of vibration could be calculated from construction drawings of a building. It showed the effect of floors and nonstructural elements such as partition walls on the stiffness of a building, and the damping effect they contributed. It also demonstrated that buildings deflect more markedly by bending as a cantilever fixed in the ground than by the horizontal shear between one story and the next. This work by Blume and his researchers finally raised the understanding of the effects of earthquakes on high-rise buildings to a level that allowed structural engineers to consider loads due to earthquakes when designing their buildings, so providing structures that would safely resist these loads. Blume continued working in the field of earthquake engineering as a consulting engineer in private practice. In 1964 he returned to Stanford to continue his research after a gap of over thirty years, and earned his Ph.D. degree in 1967 at the age of fifty-nine. A few years later Stanford responded to his suggestion for establishing a dedicated research center, and, when it opened in 1974, the university honored its former student by naming it the John A. Blume Earthquake Engineering Center.

In 1956 Pier Luigi Nervi and the Italian architect Gio Ponti (1891–1979) faced the challenge of designing a thirty-two-story building in reinforced concrete for the Pirelli Company in Milan. High-rise steel-frame buildings were standard products in the 1950s, especially in the United States, but concrete-frame buildings were not. Concrete has the advantage that it does not vibrate as readily as steel, and oscillations induced by wind die down more rapidly. This was an important design consideration for the 33-story, 127-meter high Pirelli Tower, which was, at the time, the only high-rise building in Milan. The building 608
is about 70 by 18 meters in plan, and has four main columns and four secondary columns, which are combined with the stairwell and shear walls at each end of the building. From ground level, the cross section of the columns diminishes as the load they have to support reduces. Slender floor beams span up to 20 meters between the columns and are cast integrally to create a rigid frame that provides resistance to wind loads. Nervi used 609, 610
his experience of model testing during the previous 611
twenty years to augment and confirm his design calculations for wind loads. In addition to measuring static 612
deflections, he studied the response of the building to dynamic loads to ensure that there was no possibility of the wind causing potentially disastrous vibrations near the building's natural frequencies. A 12-meter-tall model at a scale of 1:10 was built and tested at the Experimental Institute of Bergamo using materials that modeled the strength and vibration characteristics of concrete. Wire strain gauges provided electrical signals that could be displayed on the screen of an oscilloscope to identify the various natural vibration frequencies of the structure and to study how the vibrations decayed.

Structures in the Third Dimension, Spatial Structures

The German mathematician August Möbius (1790–1868) had shown in his *Lehrbuch der Statik* (Textbook of

607

608

Statics) (1837) that, for a two-dimensional framework to be fully triangulated and statically determinate, there is a simple relationship between the number of nodes (n) and the number of bars (k) working in either tension or compression, namely, $k = (2n - 3)$. He also showed that for a three-dimensional framework, the relationship is $k = (3n - 6)$. Unfortunately, his work remained unknown to structural engineers, and both of these simple relationships were rediscovered independently by engineers later in the century: the rule for two dimensions by Otto Mohr in 1874 and the rule for three dimensions by August Föppl in 1892. Meanwhile, two-dimensional trusses were already being widely used for roof structures in the 1860s, and Johann Schwedler had designed many domes using a triangulated, statically determinate framework, also in the 1860s (see chapter 7, p. 439). In the first decades of the twentieth century, three-dimensional statically determinate and statically indeterminate frameworks were widely used in the young airship and aircraft industries, where minimum weight was the overriding design constraint. In buildings, however, the only significant uses of a three-dimensional framework during this time were the geodesic domes and barrel vaults devised by Bauersfeld and Dischinger for their

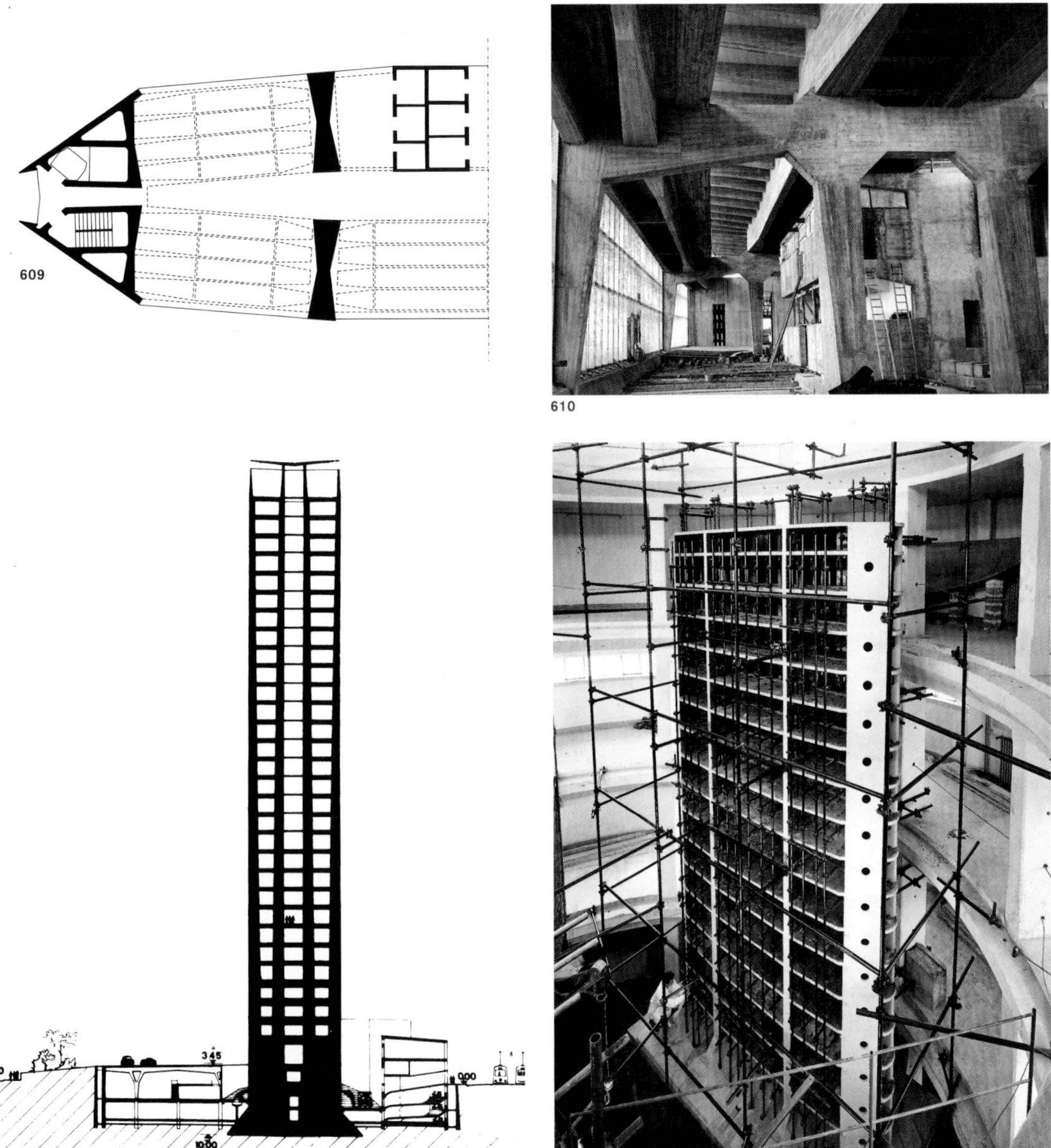
609
610
611
612

607 Scale model (1:40) of the Alexander Building in San Francisco, California, used to measure dynamic deformations induced by earthquakes, 1932–33. 608 Pirelli Tower, Milan, 1958. Engineer: Pier Luigi Nervi; architect: Gio Ponti. 609 Pirelli Tower. Plan showing large cross section of main columns near the foot of the tower. 610 Pirelli Tower. Interior. 611 Pirelli Tower. Section. 612 Pirelli Tower. Scale model (1:10) to assess dynamic behavior arising from wind loads.

613

614

615

616

613 Max Mengeringhausen displaying nodes of his MERO system. 614 Railway Station, Adamstown, Dublin, Ireland, 2006. Engineering design and construction of roof by MERO (UK); architect: Building Design Partnership. 615 Union Tank Car Company, near Baton Rouge, Louisiana, 1958. Engineer: R. Buckminster Fuller. Geodesic dome spanning 118 meters. 616 MERO system. Detail of steel node connecting multiple members of framework.

planetariums and many Zeiss-Dywidag shell roofs, where the framework was embedded in concrete, thus effectively becoming part of the reinforcement.

The potential of three-dimensional frameworks to span and enclose large spaces remained unexplored until the 1930s, when the German engineer Max
613 Mengeringhausen (1903–88) began developing ways of assembling buildings quickly using a standard kit of parts, a method that was already common for mass production of cars and other items. His investigations into the many ways in which identical shapes can be stacked or arranged took him into three-dimensional geometry, crystallography, and the study of organic forms through the work of D'Arcy Thompson. For the assembly of frameworks, he quickly realized that the key to a construction system lay in the method of connecting the bars. The elegant solution he eventually devised, like most good engineering, seems incredibly simple and obvious. The steel node has threaded holes that allow up to eighteen members from different direc-
616 tions to be connected at a single point. The bars were made in a series of standard lengths to create various types of framework, in different cross sections, to accommodate the forces they needed to carry. Mengeringhausen used his MERO system for various temporary structures during the 1940s before using it as a lightweight roofing system in the 1950s, including
614 as a support for roofs of glass or transparent plastics. The large numbers of members and nodes made the full structural analysis of such space trusses rather tedious, and engineers usually managed by using simplified calculations. The simple and repetitive geometry, however, made such structures ideal material for the engineers who were writing the first computer programs for structural analysis in the late 1950s.

Like Mengeringhausen, the American inventor Richard Buckminster Fuller (1895–1983) saw the potential of three-dimensional frameworks made of standard parts as the key to rapid construction. Structurally, the geodesic dome patented by Fuller in 1954 was no different from that developed in 1920 by Bauersfeld for his planetarium. Fuller, however, saw its potential as a lightweight roof structure that could be transported easily and assembled rapidly. The key difference lay in the building envelope: By the 1950s a variety of lightweight cladding systems were available in aluminum or plastic; these had not been available in 1920. By the mid-1980s more than 300,000 geodesic domes had been built in sizes ranging from a few meters in diameter to over 100 meters. 615

Prestressing

The idea underlying prestressed structures is very old. Masonry structures derive their stability from the weight bearing down on the lower parts of the building, and medieval cathedral builders often added pinnacles to buttresses to increase their stability. Outside the building industry many structures, from ancient sailing ships to umbrellas and bicycle wheels, derive much of their stiffness from prestressing using ropes or other tensile materials. Prestressed concrete began to be used for bridges in the 1930s. The appeal of prestressing to the structural engineer is that it effectively enables a cable to be loaded in compression and, hence, allows the designer to avoid bulky struts. One of the most elegant examples of prestressing was the Skylon, built in 1951 for the Festival of
Britain in London. The Skylon was a 76-meter tall column 617, 618
made from aluminum, suspended 12 meters above the ground by just three cables at the base and stabilized by three more cables at its midpoint. These supports were barely visible, even when seen close-up, and the column appeared to float above the ground.

In 1952, the roof of the new Raleigh Livestock Arena in North Carolina (now known as the Dorton Arena) became the first substantial prestressed cable-net structure
ever built. The Norwegian-born engineer Fred Severud 619, 620
(1899–1990)—later known for his work on the Ingalls Hockey Rink at Yale University and the Gateway Arch in St. Louis (see pages 520–21)—was called in to complete the structure that had been designed by Polish architect Matthew Nowicki (1910–50). Killed in a plane crash in Egypt, Nowicki did not live to see his unique design come to fruition. The doubly curved arena roof consisted of two virtually orthogonal sets of steel cables stretched between inclined concrete arches, and it was clad with steel sheeting. The shape of this roof was simple enough, and the steel cables were few and regular enough for the roof to be calculated as an elastic prestressed structure. Such a calculation procedure was already familiar to engineers with experience designing prestressed concrete structures. The Raleigh Arena proved to be a tremendous inspiration to many architects, including Eero Saarinen

617

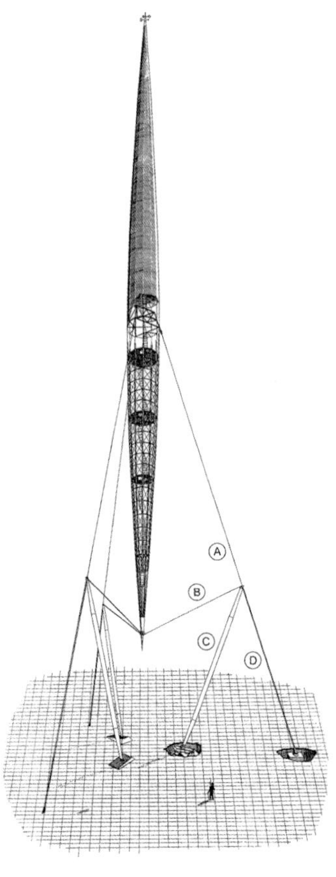

618

and Kenzo Tange, who wanted to exploit the architectural possibilities of tensile structures. What they were able to design conceptually, however, was severely limited by the very restricted range of simple geometrical shapes for which engineers were then able to undertake calculations: The calculations could only be done for surfaces that could be uniquely described using mathematical equations. And from a practical point of view, in the days of hand and slide rule calculations, there was a low limit to the number of simultaneous equations that could be solved. The large structures of the 1950s and early 1960s thus still belonged within the tradition of freely hanging structures, for which engineers were able to make the necessary calculations.

In 1951 Fred Severud's design office in New York was working on the plans for the Raleigh Stadium when they were visited by a German student of architecture, Frei Otto (b. 1925). He, too, was impressed by the possibilities that doubly curved prestressed surfaces would seem to offer architects. Returning to Stuttgart in Germany, he began making models with a variety of materials—string, chains, nets, soap bubbles, and elastic sheets—to generate a range of curved shapes

617 The Skylon at the Festival of Britain, London, 1951. Engineer: Felix Samuely; architects: Philip Powell and Hidalgo Moya. 618 The Skylon. Approximate prestressing forces: (A) 50 tons (tension); (B) 100 tons (t); (C) 150 tons (compression); (D) 150 tons (t). 619 Raleigh Livestock Arena (now Dorton Arena), Raleigh, North Carolina, 1952. Engineer: Fred Severud; architect: Matthew Nowicki. 620 Raleigh Livestock Arena.

619

620

and surfaces. Working with the long-established maker of circus tents, Strohmeyer, Otto soon devised his first full size doubly curved prestressed tensile structure in 1955, a modest canopy under which musicians could
621 perform outdoors. It spanned 18 meters across the diagonals, which was twice the maximum span found in Strohmeyer's traditional circus tents.

The fact that the form was simple and the span relatively small, by today's standards, is deceptive. This was not merely a sheet stretched between a couple of tent poles. It was a fully engineered roof structure. The stress in the fabric was 1.6 tons per meter width, and Strohmeyer had to weave custom-made fabric from high-quality cotton that was equally strong and stiff in both directions, unlike normal tent fabrics. Steel cables 16 mm in diameter were sewn into the edges of the membrane, and their length and the precise shape of the curved boundaries of the fabric were established from tests on scale models. The cutting pattern for the individual strips of fabric also had to be carefully shaped and measured using physical models.

New Structural Materials

New structural materials do not come along very often: cast iron in the 1790s, reinforced concrete in the 1890s. The decade immediately after World War II saw the arrival of two more, both of which owe their development to the wartime aircraft industries: glued, laminated timber (Glulam), and aluminum.

The high specific strength and stiffness of timber has always made it especially suitable for large-span roofs. In the United States and Canada there was a long tradition of building timber-truss railway bridges, partly because timber was so readily available and also because it was easy to transport over long distances to locations with no locally grown timber. For the same reasons, and because the skills needed to erect timber structures were readily available, American engineers used timber for many large roofs in the 1930s, 1940s, and 1950s when engineers in Europe were more inclined to use reinforced concrete or steel.

The high specific stiffness and strength of wood seemed to make it an ideal material for aircraft, but in an age when adhesives were weak and water-soluble, this advantage was offset by the weight of nails or screws needed to assemble the wooden components. Suitable adhesives were developed in the 1940s for the manufacture of plywood and other built-up wooden elements used in aircraft—for example, the laminates that formed the monocoque plywood fuselage of World War II's Mosquito aircraft. The research to create a strong and waterproof adhesive led to the development of epoxy resin glues, and these opened up an entirely new range of timber products for use in the building industry, including both structural materials, such as Glulam, laminated veneer lumber (LVL), and plywood, and nonstructural products, such as chipboard and fiberboard. This benefited the building industry after the war, especially in the United

States and Canada, where timber was plentiful and steel
623, 625 in short supply.

Aluminum was also in abundance immediately after World War II, when it was no longer needed for building aircraft. The Dome of Discovery built for the Festival of Britain in 1951 was probably the largest aluminum structure ever constructed; aluminum was chosen not only for its lightness but also because it captured the spirit of the postwar years, which inspired many new im-
622, 624 ages, ideas, and designs. A particular advantage of aluminum is that, unlike any other material, it can be easily manufactured in many shapes using three different processes—rolling, casting, and extrusion. This appealed to the sculptor, architect, and engineer Jean Prouvé (1901–84), and he exploited the characteristics of all three processes when he designed, in 1954, the pavilion for an exhibition in Paris celebrating the centen-
626 nial of the discovery of aluminum.

It is worth noting how easily these new materials were incorporated into the structural engineer's repertoire. By the 1950s engineers had learned to analyze materials from the point of view of scientists rather than craftsmen. Engineers now knew that materials had a series of unique generic properties, such as strength, stiffness, ductility, hardness, creep, fatigue behavior, and so on. Knowing these properties meant that it was relatively easy for engineers to incorporate a new material in their designs—a far cry from the early days of cast iron or reinforced concrete, the use of which had required that hands-on experience be built up over many years.

Toward "Total Design"

In the summer of 1969 the engineer Ove Arup (1895–1988), who was then seventy-four years old, responded to a request by the partners of the firm he had founded in 1946 by writing a paper outlining the aims of the firm (reprinted in Appendix 1). There has seldom, if ever, been a better summary of what modern building engineering is. Central to the firm's aims was what Arup called "total design" or, in later papers, "total architecture"; the term echoed the title of Walter Gropius's 1956 book *The Scope of Total Architecture*. To Arup it meant that "all relevant design decisions have been considered together and have been integrated into a whole by a well-organized team empowered to fix priorities."[7]

In one sense, "total design" represents the culmination of Arup's own experience and career—from his first work designing buildings with architects in the 1930s, to founding his consulting engineering practice Ove Arup and Partners in 1946, and, finally in 1963, the formation of the daughter firm Arup Associates, with design teams comprising engineers of different disciplines and architects delivering a fully integrated building design. In another sense, it was the conclusion of a much longer story, indeed, arguably, the history of building design itself. After the sixteenth century, as more and more design issues became too technical for generalists to master, the field of building design as a whole splintered into various specialties. "Total design" represented a return to the ideal of a process whereby many different specialties could be considered together when designing a building—not by a single individual, but by a team.

Collaboration between architect, engineer, and builder was not a new idea. Since the early nineteenth century growing numbers of architects and engineers had worked together to create designs that were, so to speak, greater than the sum of their individual parts: Saint George's Hall in Liverpool and London's Crystal Palace were two prominent examples. And the high-rise buildings in late nineteenth-century America were made possible only by an unprecedented degree of collaboration between engineer, architect, and building contractor. But the total design concept—the conscious aim to achieve better design by forming an integrated team of designers—took the idea of collaboration to a new level. It had its philosophical origins in the Deutsche Werkbund and the Bauhaus group of designers in Germany in the 1910s.

Throughout the nineteenth century, architects still clung to traditional construction materials despite the fact that buildings in iron and steel were being erected all around them. As building materials, iron and steel presented two problems that limited architects' opportunities to express themselves in the ways they had been used to with masonry. First of all, they were inherently skeletal materials. In a multistory building they provided a frame on which to hang the elements that gave body and solid form to a building—the floors, facade and windows, roof, air-conditioning, and elevators. Secondly, iron and steel in multistory buildings were subject to stringent fireproofing requirements. Thus architects had little opportunity,

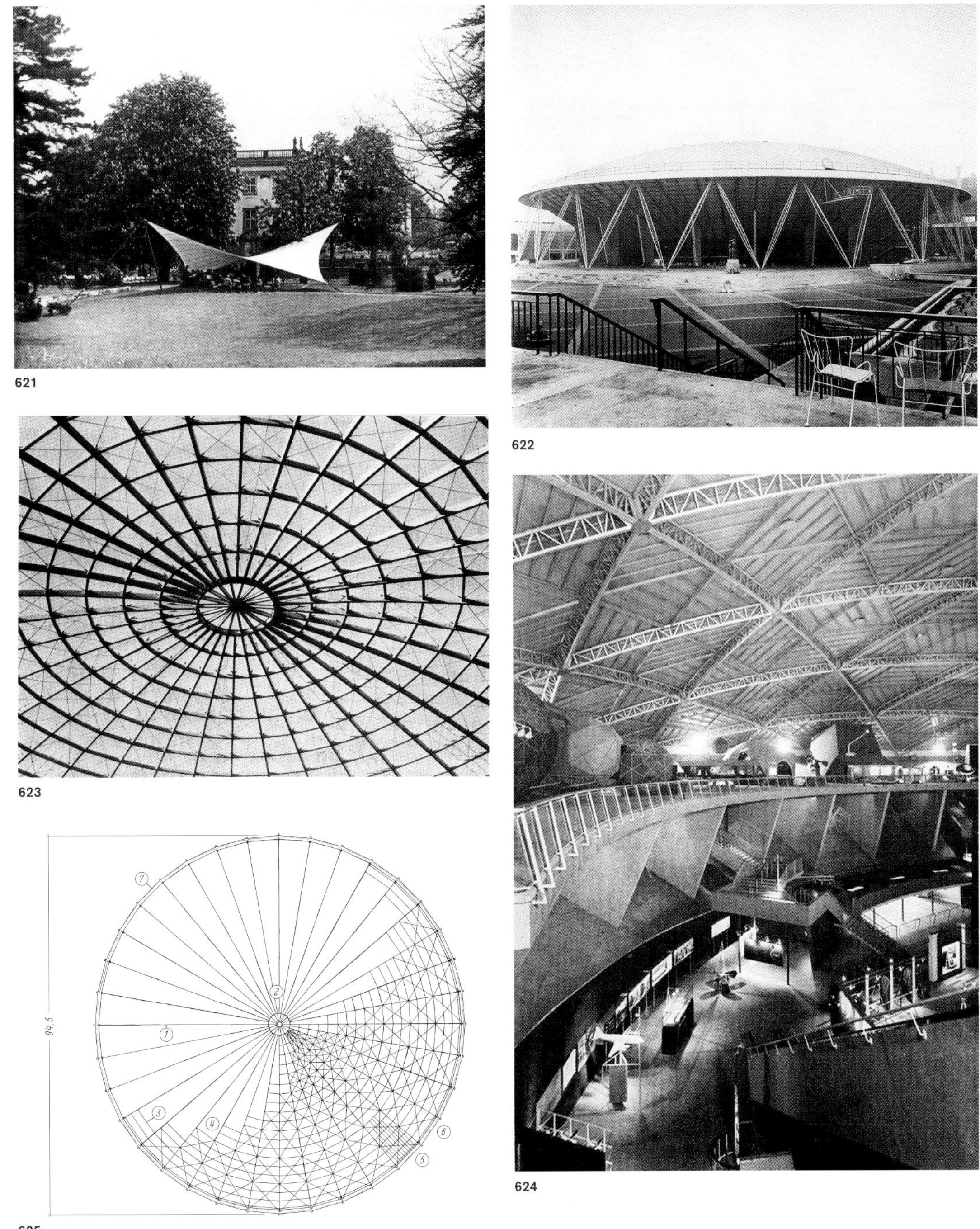

621 Music pavilion, Kassel, Germany, 1955. Designed by Frei Otto; constructed by tentmaker Peter Strohmeyer. 622 Dome of Discovery at the Festival of Britain, London, 1951. Engineer: Freeman Fox and Partners; architect: Ralph Tubbs. 623 Glue-laminated timber dome at Field House (Brick Breeden Fieldhouse), Montana State College, Bozeman, Montana, 1956. Structure: Timber Structures, Inc. Diameter: 94.5 meters; rise: 15.2 meters. 624 Dome of Discovery. Interior, showing the triangulated lattice roof trusses. 625 Field House dome. Key: (1) Radial ribs of laminated timber; (2) Compression ring; (3) Beams of laminated timber; (4) Steel cross-bracing; (5) Timber rafters; (6) and (7) Tension ring.

626

in most buildings, to put iron and steel on show. The exceptions—where designers could express the nature, or "soul," of iron or steel in their architecture—were mainly single-story buildings, which were not subject to the codes that regulated fire protection for taller buildings. They included thousands of manufacturing works and hundreds of market halls, as well as railway stations, exhibition buildings, and glass houses in botanical gardens.

In the United States, from the 1880s on, commercial pressures to increase net usable floor areas had favored steel-frame buildings. These required increased input from engineers in designing the foundations, structure, and building services; the architect's role was correspondingly diminished. In Europe, however, such a diminution of the architect's role did not appeal to the architectural establishment, which had developed over many centuries during which masonry was the dominant construction medium. European architects hung on to tradition, as if blind to the world growing about them. They faced a crisis of identity. Without the sculptural opportunities that masonry offered, and with so much of the design of steel-frame buildings in the hands of engineers, what role was there for architects? Their dilemma was how to maintain their Beaux Arts heritage while embracing the new methods of construction. In Britain, where architects hung on to tradition especially grimly, the situation was reflected in the architectural press. In 1896 a new weekly periodical—*The Builders' Journal and Architectural Record*—was launched, and its pages were full of articles on traditional architecture in masonry and timber. The Arts and Crafts Movement was in full swing; the domestic buildings of Charles Voysey (1857–1941) represented the pinnacle of architectural merit. For four years the only mention of steel or reinforced concrete in the journal's pages was in a few advertisements.

Finally, in 1900, *The Builders' Journal and Architectural Record* published its first article on steel-frame buildings. It was written by a Mr. Homan of Homan and Rogers, Engineers, whose advertisements had appeared regularly in the journal offering "Homan's fireproof floors" and "constructional steel and ironwork, roofs, piers, bridges, joists and girders and concrete fireproof floors (used in nearly 2000 buildings)" and, after 1897, "constructional steel skeleton buildings (American System)." Two years later there appeared a

626 Pavillon du centenaire de l'aluminium, Paris, 1954. Architect: Jean Prouvé.

lengthy report on ferro-concrete that discussed the Hennebique system as used in Britain by the Mouchel company. In 1904 the new monthly Fire Supplement to the journal strongly advocated an engineering approach to building design. In 1904 and 1905 the journal reported at length on the construction of the Ritz Hotel, the first major steel building in London, built by American contractors with German steel. By this time, however, Britain was some twenty years behind the United States and at least a decade behind France and Germany in their use of steel-frame construction. Finally, in May of 1906, the journal changed its name to *The Builders' Journal and Architectural Engineer*, and a new monthly supplement, Concrete and Steel Supplement, proclaimed:

> *[W]ith the advent of [the steel-frame and reinforced concrete] the architect is gradually finding that a far greater amount of engineering knowledge is required of him than was previously the case. Some architects overcome this by employing engineering assistants or by having consultative advice on the engineering aspect of the problems put before them. But, no matter what assistance be obtained, he would be a poor architect who did not carefully study and thoroughly inform himself of the primary principles of the construction and calculation that are involved.*[8]

During the next few years the various titles of the journal continued to reflect the architects' search for a new identity. In 1910 it was renamed *The Architects' and Builders' Journal*. In 1919 it became *The Architects' Journal*, subtitled "For architects, surveyors, builders and civil engineers," and a year later it became *The Architects' Journal and Architectural Engineer*. Only in 1926 was the name shortened to *The Architects' Journal*, the name it retains today.

While engineers' increased contribution to building design was as inevitable in Europe as it had been in 1890s America, the outcome was different. Generally speaking, architects in Europe managed to retain their leading role in building design, and there developed two common types of building construction. Where steel-frame construction did become well established, especially in Germany and Britain, it comprised a structural frame hidden by a substantial facade of masonry with a traditional appearance. The alternative was to adopt reinforced concrete as the material of construction.

Architectural Concrete

Reinforced concrete construction had developed in the late nineteenth and early twentieth centuries in response to two goals: to establish more effective fireproof construction methods, and to find cheaper alternatives to the expensive steel frame. These goals were especially important for industrial buildings, such as warehouses and factories, and for commercial office buildings. The catalogues of firms such as Hennebique and Wayss and Freytag were full of such buildings, which were, fundamentally, almost identical to their steel-frame equivalents: columns were located on a regular grid, between which spanned beams that supported the floors. Architects' roles in designing such concrete-frame buildings were similar to the roles they played in designing steel-frame buildings.

Gradually, after about 1910, a number of pioneering architects began to realize that reinforced concrete offered new sculptural opportunities that arose from the very nature of the material and its method of manufacture. It takes the shape of the mold into which the liquid concrete is poured, and so, to a large extent, the structural engineer is able to introduce steel reinforcement to provide the necessary internal strength without necessarily affecting the outer form. Reinforced concrete thus offers architects three entirely new opportunities that structural steel does not. It can generate solid, three-dimensional forms. It can easily form curved lines and surfaces. It can be used to create thin "sheets" of structure with the ability to carry loads; thus it can be used to make load-bearing walls, floors that can cantilever out beyond their supports, and, most spectacularly, concrete-shell roofs. Together these formed the basis of a new architecture, one not limited to elements in one dimension, as with a steel column or beam, but that can work in two dimensions, as with a slab, and in three dimensions, as with a solid sculptural form or a curved shell such as a vault, dome, or doubly curved hyperbolic paraboloid. These opportunities led to achievements that would match and even surpass the achievements in masonry construction in the temples of ancient Greece, the baths of Imperial Rome, the cathedrals of medieval Europe, and the great domes of the Renaissance.

The architect Le Corbusier (Charles Edouard Jeanneret) (1887–1965) conceived his "Dom-ino" skeleton in 1914. 629

627

628

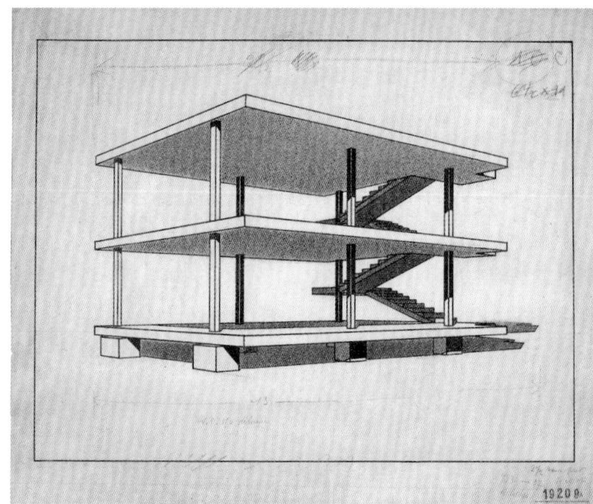
629

627 Unidentified reinforced concrete factory, Paris, 1906. Engineer: François Hennebique. 628 (top and bottom) Grain silos, from Le Corbusier, *Vers une architecture*, 1923. 629 Le Corbusier, Maison Dom-Ino, 1914.

Here, for the first time and with characteristic economy, was the architectural expression of the flat slab, albeit supported by architecturally superfluous columns.

By the early 1920s Le Corbusier had begun to realize some of his dreams for the new material, and he celebrated them in his book *Vers une Architecture* (Towards a New Architecture), first published in Paris in 1923 and available in English in 1927 in a translation, by Frederick Etchells, of the thirteenth French edition. Uncharacteristically among the writings of architects, it was a paean to engineers and builder: he eulogized the "engineer's aesthetic" and the need to create the "mass-production spirit" of conceiving, constructing, and living in mass-produced houses. His inspiration was the engineering of cars, ocean liners, and aircraft. While he extolled the merits of the buildings of ancient Greece and Rome, and the Renaissance, he also rejoiced in the modern factory buildings
627 that were being built by the hundreds throughout Europe.

Le Corbusier shunned the architect's traditional preoccupation with style—"what a feather is on a woman's head . . . sometimes pretty, though not always, and never anything more." Architecture, he said, has "graver ends," and set down "three reminders to architects" that their art is manifested in mass and surface which, in turn, are generated from the plan. To illustrate this point, he uses not medieval churches or Renaissance palaces, but photographs of eight massive reinforced concrete grain silos from the wheat-growing areas of Canada and the United States—"the magnificent FIRST-FRUITS of the new age,"
628 as he described them.[9]

After about 1918 Le Corbusier's cause was bolstered by the fact that most countries had ceased to grant patents for supposedly new means of reinforcing concrete with steel. Reinforced concrete had finally become a generic construction material like masonry, steel, or timber. The way was now open for architects to work directly with engineers independently of the contractors who had owned the patent rights to the reinforcing systems. Initially, the new material was exploited by architects on a rather modest scale—often, literally, at the domestic scale, as the more adventurous private clients patronized the revolutionary thinkers. There can be no more durable image of the flat slab than the Schroeder House by Gerrit Rietveld
630 (1888–1964), built in Utrecht in 1924–25.

As architects became more familiar with the new material, they realized they could only use it with confidence through collaboration with engineers and contractors. Throughout the 1920s architects gradually began to tackle larger projects in concrete; buildings with a new and distinct appearance began to emerge, especially in
continental Europe. These were a far cry from the indus- 631, 632
trial, engineer-led buildings of the 1910s. 633, 634

Reinforced concrete offered the unique opportunity for the architect and engineer to develop jointly the form of the building elements—the mass and the surface, in Le Corbusier's terms; indeed, this was almost a requirement. An architect had to listen to the engineer's advice, at least about what was possible and what not. A receptive architect could also listen to an engineer's proposals about what the most rational forms might be both for structural elements and the entire structures. Here was the same engineer's aesthetic that Le Corbusier had recognized in the design of aircraft, ships, and cars. In fact, had he looked closely at the individual components of these machines, he could have found even more inspiration in their scientifically crafted shapes and ingenious methods of assembly.

Among the first designers to articulate the rational approach to the detail of building structures was the Welshman Owen Williams, one of very few building designers who excelled as both a structural engineer and an architect. In a number of outstanding buildings in the 1920s and 1930s, he consciously used the structural and sculptural characteristics of concrete to express the
structural function or duty of building elements. This had 635, 636
long been the unconscious outcome of engineers striving to achieve minimum weights for structures such as bridges, the cast iron beams and columns of early nineteenth-century mills, and the many types of roofs of large buildings. The idea had been captured by Louis Sullivan in 1896 when he observed that it is a law of the natural world that "form ever follows function"; in about 1918, the Bauhaus group of designers adopted this as their guiding principle. When expressing structural function in reinforced concrete, however, there was a certain deception at work, since the outward appearance of reinforced concrete gives no indication of where the reinforcement is located, or how much is used. More recently, when structural expression again became fashionable in the

630

631

632

633

630 Schroeder House, Utrecht, 1924–25. Architect: Gerrit Rietveld. 631 Notre Dame, Le Raincy, France, 1922. Architect: Auguste Perret. 632 Bauhaus building, Dessau, Germany, 1926. Architect: Walter Gropius. 633 Schocken store, Stuttgart, Germany, 1926. Architect: Erich Mendelsohn. 634 Notre Dame, Le Raincy.

634

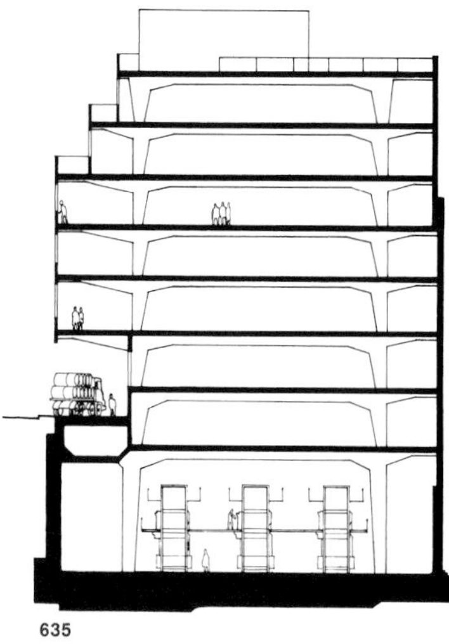

635

636

1980s, the idea that structural function should be expressed in architectural form was nicely captured in the term "archi-structure," a word coined by Derek Sugden, an engineer with Arups for nearly forty years and a founding member of Arup Associates.

During the 1950s, the Italian engineer Pier Luigi Nervi also delighted in expressing the structural function of many elements of his buildings through their forms, although in many instances the forms are not as
637, 638 strictly necessary as might appear—classic examples of
639 archi-structure.

Design for Construction

The final aspect of building construction included in Arup's total design ideal was consideration, at the design stage, of how the actual construction of the building should be facilitated. Such an idea was familiar to industries where mass production was well established, such as machine tool works in the nineteenth century and Henry Ford's automobile factories in the twentieth, but it was not common in the building trades. The very procurement process for buildings, enshrined in codes of professional practice, mitigated against it. This required architects to complete a design and then submit the design to a number of contractors. By this means, it was presumed that the client would be able to get the cheapest, or best-value, building. This process did not seem to allow the possibility of an architect designing a building that was inherently expensive though inappropriate choice of materials, selection of structurally inefficient spans between columns, or poor or nonexistent integration of building services. The Crystal Palace was an early, rare exception, with the engineer William Barlow involved at the very start of the design, which demonstrated how effective a closely-integrated design and construction team could be (see chapter 6, pp. 355–59). The designers and builders of American high-rise buildings achieved similar efficiencies when driven by strong commercial pressures from developers.

Le Corbusier was perhaps the first architect to embrace the manufacturing process in his philosophy of building. He was prophetic not only in his articulation of the

635 Daily Express Building, London, 1930–32. Engineer: Owen Williams; architects: Ellis and Clarke with Owen Williams. Section showing columns in the rigid portal frame. 636 Boots factory "Wets" building, Beeston, England, 1930–32. Engineer and architect: Owen Williams. 637 Palace of Labor, Turin, Italy, 1960–61. Engineer: Pier Luigi Nervi. 638 Palace of Labor. Plan of floor slab. 639 Palace of Labor. Drawing for the reinforcement of floor slab.

637

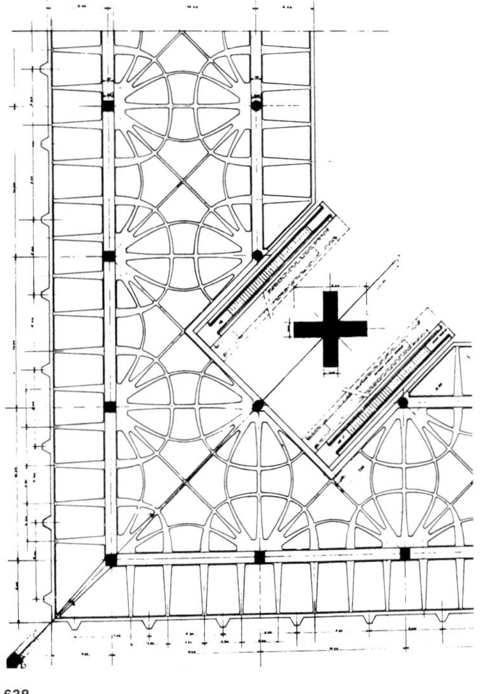

638

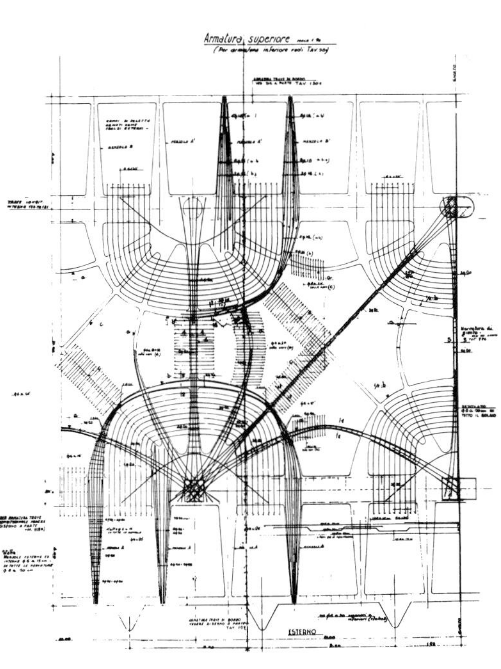

639

building as a machine, like a car or airplane, but in his understanding of the significance of the manufacturing methods that had developed in the automobile industry. Indeed, Le Corbusier was inspired as much by the methods of mass production as by the idea of reinforced concrete as a material. One of his earliest proposals for residential buildings was that they should be built not of steel-reinforced concrete, but cement reinforced with asbestos fibers, which had been developed recently as a cheap roofing material and as a way to provide fireproofing for structural steelwork. He saw the use of asbestos-reinforced cement as the most suitable means of
640 providing mass-produced buildings.

While Le Corbusier had the vision to see the potential benefits for architecture in considering construction issues at the design stage of buildings, he was not a contractor. Ove Arup was. He worked for the Danish contracting firm Christiani & Nielsen, which was expanding its activities in Britain, and later as chief engineer with another Danish contractor, Kier. Arup saw how his knowledge of construction could help architects, for example, by adapting for use in buildings many techniques of concrete construction that had been developed in civil engineering and industrial construction projects, such as docks, warehouses, and grain silos. One example, which today seems rather obvious, was to speed up concrete construction by choosing shapes and profiles that could be cast using simple formwork, erected and dismantled quickly, and reused many times. Arup realized his dream of bring his engineering expertise to benefit the design of buildings from their very conception to their completion in the work he undertook with the Russian architect Berthold Lubetkin (1901–90) and Tecton, the architectural practice he formed in 1932. Arup and Tecton collaborated first on a number of buildings at the London Zoo, then, in 1935, on the first of two Highpoint apartment buildings in north London, now
641 considered an icon of engineer-architect collaboration. The simple lines and forms of the building were a striking contrast to many concrete buildings, which seemed to emulate masonry in their use of intricate detail. Like other innovative engineers before and since, Arup came up against the building regulations at Highpoint. In accordance with the current regulations Lubetkin had proposed a standard concrete frame building. Not only did this form of construction limit the flexibility of internal layouts, it also often led to cracks in concrete or plaster finishes as the heavily loaded columns compressed and moved relative to the unloaded wall panels. Arup suggested replacing the columns by thin load-bearing reinforced-concrete walls, which would place fewer constraints on the layout of the interior and would avoid the problem of cracking, as well as being more economical 642
to build. At the time, however, the London County Council building regulations, which were often used beyond London's boundaries, did not permit internal walls to be load-bearing. Permission to build was granted only because the building lay a few hundred meters outside the London County Council boundary, and the local district surveyor was able to take an independent view. Nevertheless, Arup was forced to compromise by adding some additional and wholly unnecessary reinforcement in order to get his idea accepted.

Immediately after World War II, Arup set up the consulting engineering firm that today still bears his name. Free now from the constraints of working for a firm of contractors, Arup was able to begin developing his vision of total design, in which architects and engineers collaborate on equal terms in developing building designs from the concept stage through to the completion of detailed design. His firm soon attracted the attention of more and more architects who wanted to work together to create 643, 644
buildings that combined engineering prowess with 645, 646
architectural flair. 647a–d

Engineering the Internal Environment

The growing influence of engineers on the design of buildings was not limited to the structure of buildings. In the United States during the 1920s, for example, air-conditioning was becoming a standard feature of factories, hotels, theaters, and especially cinemas. Three main factors contributed to this growth. The first was demand. For hotels and places of entertainment, air-conditioning became an essential feature to attract customers.

640 Maison Monol, France, 1919. Architect: Le Corbusier. 641 Highpoint I, North London, 1935. Engineer: Ove Arup; architects: Berthold Lubetkin and Tecton. 642 Highpoint I. (left) Floor plan of standard concrete frame solution originally proposed; (right) Arup's plan for using load-bearing concrete walls.

640

641

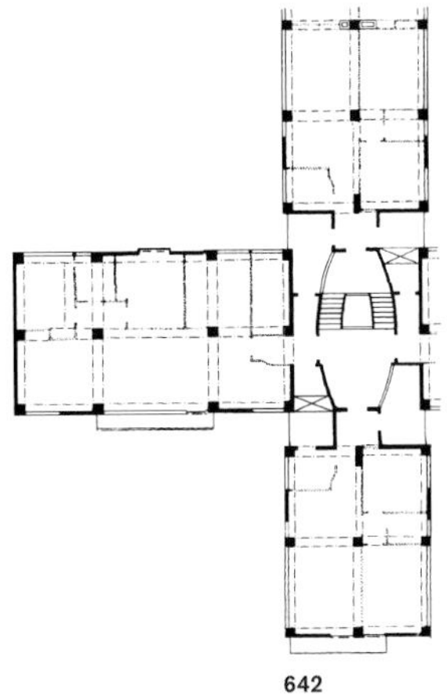
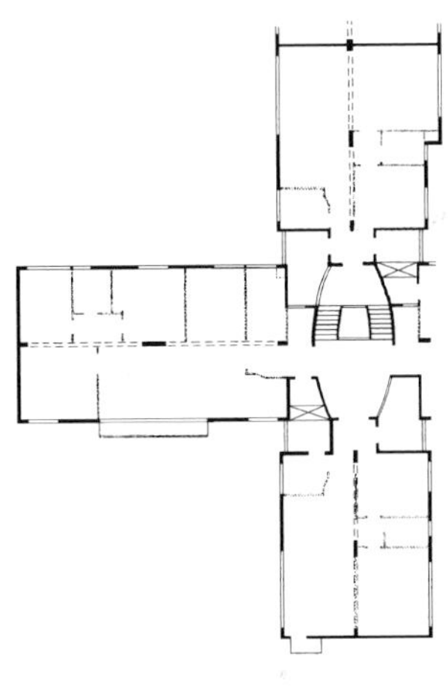
642

643

644

643 Brynmawr Rubber Factory, South Wales, 1946–51. Engineer: Ove Arup & Partners; architect: Architects Co-Partnership.

644 Coventry Cathedral, Coventry, England, 1958–62. Engineer: Ove Arup & Partners; architect: Sir Basil Spence.

645

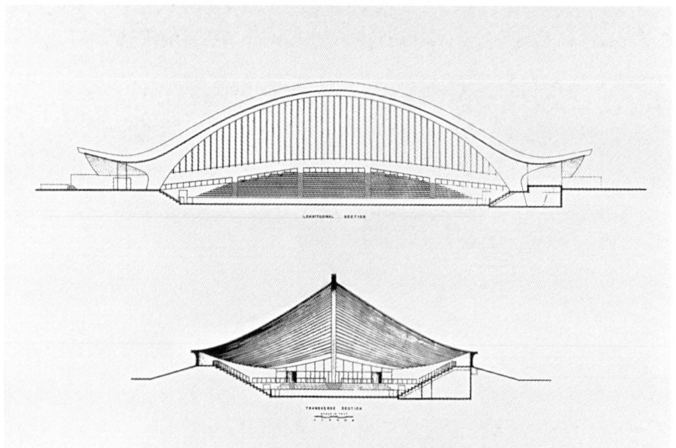

646

645 David S. Ingalls Hockey Rink, Yale University, New Haven, Connecticut, 1956–59. Engineer: Fred Severud; architect: Eero Saarinen. 646 Ingalls Hockey Rink. Sections. 647a–d, St. Louis Gateway Arch (Jefferson National Expansion Memorial), St. Louis, Missouri, 1947–65. Engineer: Fred Severud; architect: Eero Saarinen. Completed arch and construction details.

647a

647b

647c

647d

Indeed, one factor in the growth of the film industry was the fact that movie theaters offered a pleasant way of escaping the unbearable heat and humidity in many American cities.

Second, the entrepreneurial efforts of a number of men, most notably Willis Carrier (see chapter 7, p. 411–12), ensured that the performance of air-conditioning equipment continued to improve to meet the growing demand. The capacity of early air-conditioning systems had been limited by the slow speed of reciprocating compressors, which were usually still powered by reciprocating steam engines. Manufacturers of refrigeration plants for the cold storage industries, especially in France, Germany, and Switzerland, had continued to develop their products, improving their effectiveness, making them smaller, and increasing their capacity. This was achieved by three means: by devising the mechanical means for accomplishing new thermodynamic cycles in the refrigeration process (the unique combination of compression, expansion, heating, and cooling to which the refrigerant is subjected); by experimenting with different refrigerants, of which many hundreds were tried, and by developing various types of rotary compressors to replace the slow, limited-capacity reciprocating machines. New refrigerants and compressors had to be developed together, since the geometry of the blades in the compressor depended on the density of the refrigerant and the speed of the motor. In addition, the various refrigerants, many of which were unpleasant, toxic, or corrosive chemicals, had to have new types of seal developed to contain the vapor, and suitable lubricants found that did not react with them. One means of avoiding some of these difficulties was the further refinement of an absorption refrigeration process which had been devised in France by Carré and Tellier in about 1860 and which avoided the need for a compressor. The key feature of the thermodynamic cycle of an absorption chiller is that the energy that drives the system is heat—a counterintuitive notion that has puzzled many an owner of a gas-powered domestic refrigerator using what became known as the “Electrolux cycle” after the firm that first developed it.

Carrier’s prominent place in the air-conditioning industry between 1910 and the 1930s was ensured by his diligent search for ways to adapt the various new technical developments in the refrigeration industry, mainly in Europe, for use in air-conditioning systems. The improvements in refrigeration technology took place at the same time that the steam engine was being replaced by the electric motor as the power source for both compressors and fans. This resulted in a huge increase in the capacity of air-conditioning systems—enough to service the very largest cinemas on the hottest and most humid days. A major problem in such large buildings, however, was controlling the temperature and humidity sufficiently precisely and rapidly. The engineer Leo Lewis of the Carrier Corporation devised an innovative way of achieving the desired control. His technique was not entirely new, but, as is often the case in engineering innovation, was a combination of several ideas that had previously been used separately. In his system, three different streams of air were used. One stream was passed through the conditioning plant; another comprised some of the air that had been extracted from the auditorium and recirculated; the third was unconditioned fresh air. The resulting pre-mixed air stream was introduced into the auditorium at ceiling level. Lewis’s innovation in 1922 at Grauman’s Metropolitan Theater in Los Angeles was to use the recirculated, partially conditioned, and downward supply together in one building. It set new standards of comfort 648, 649
for theaters and cinemas.

Finally, air-conditioning was more readily introduced into buildings as the number of engineers and architects who were familiar with its requirements grew. Clearly, a large air-conditioning system could not be installed as an afterthought. Yet inexperienced contractors might well not have been prepared to, or in fact invited to, work closely with the design team for a new hotel or theater. The situation was similar to what had occurred in 1870s Chicago and New York when it was becoming clear that structural engineers had to be involved early in the design process of large iron-framed buildings. One consequence was the emergence of guidance provided by air-conditioning contractors eager to influence both clients and design teams and to sell the equipment they supplied. Another was the 650
gradual emergence during the 1920s of consulting engineers who specialized in the design and specification of ventilation and air-conditioning systems. These specialists were engaged by the client and/or design team to provide advice specific to the needs of a particular building, and were independent of contractors whose advice might not have been impartial since their profit was made from installing the equipment they supplied.

Although the spread of air-conditioning appears, in retrospect, to have been a smoothly progressing technical triumph, the road was not always obstacle-free. From the very beginning there had been dissenting views, especially on medical grounds, concerning both the benefits of air-conditioning and the quantity of fresh or conditioned air that each person needed. During the first two decades of the twentieth century a debate had raged as to the nature of “right air” that should be provided for children in schools, in particular how much fresh air each child needed for good health. Since the 1890s, a figure of 0.85 cubic meters per minute (30 cubic feet per minute, cfm) per person had been promoted by ventilation engineers, with the backing of doctors. Such a quantity could only be provided using mechanical ventilation, and equipment suppliers were quick to attack proposals to allow a reduced quantity of 0.28 cubic meters per minute per person (10 cfm), which could be achieved by opening windows and providing natural ventilation. Further confusion arose when airborne dust and humid-

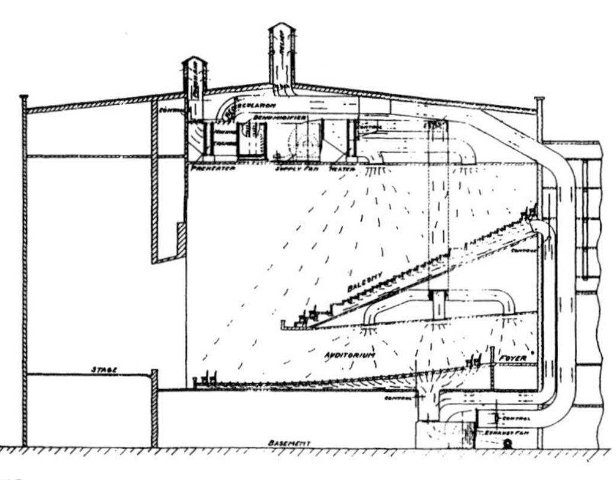

648

649

Don'ts For Theatre Ventilation

1. Don't use the mushroom system of supply for cold air.
2. Don't pass all air through the cooler.
3. Don't omit complete mechanical exhaust with refrigerating systems.
4. Don't omit automatic temperature control with refrigerating systems.
5. Don't supply cold air at low points and expect to pull it up with the exhaust.
6. Don't supply warm air at high points and expect to pull it down with exhaust.
7. Don't expect to pull air any place. You can push, but you cannot pull.
8. Don't conceive of a theatre as a tight box. It never is.
9. Don't introduce air into a theatre auditorium from the rear unless you know exactly where it is going and can accurately control its temperature and velocity.
10. Don't expect a thermostat on the main floor to maintain conditions of comfort in the balcony, or vice-versa.
11. Don't supply air to the main floor and balcony, or to the main floor and dressing rooms with the same fan.
12. Don't expect air currents to follow trained arrows on the plans, unless you are sure the arrows are thoroughly and properly trained.
13. Don't expect a Rolls-Royce ventilating system at the cost of a Ford.

650

651

648 Grauman's Metropolitan Theater, Los Angeles, 1922. Cross section showing the mixing of recirculated, fresh, and conditioned air. 649 Rivoli Theater, New York, opening day, May 1925. The Rivoli was one of the first air-conditioned theaters in the United States. A sign at rear advertises "cooled by refrigeration." 650 Design rules for theater ventilation, published in *Heating and Ventilation* magazine, March 1925. 651 Cover illustration of *The Aerologist* magazine, December 1931, representing the dilemmas facing American air-conditioning engineers.

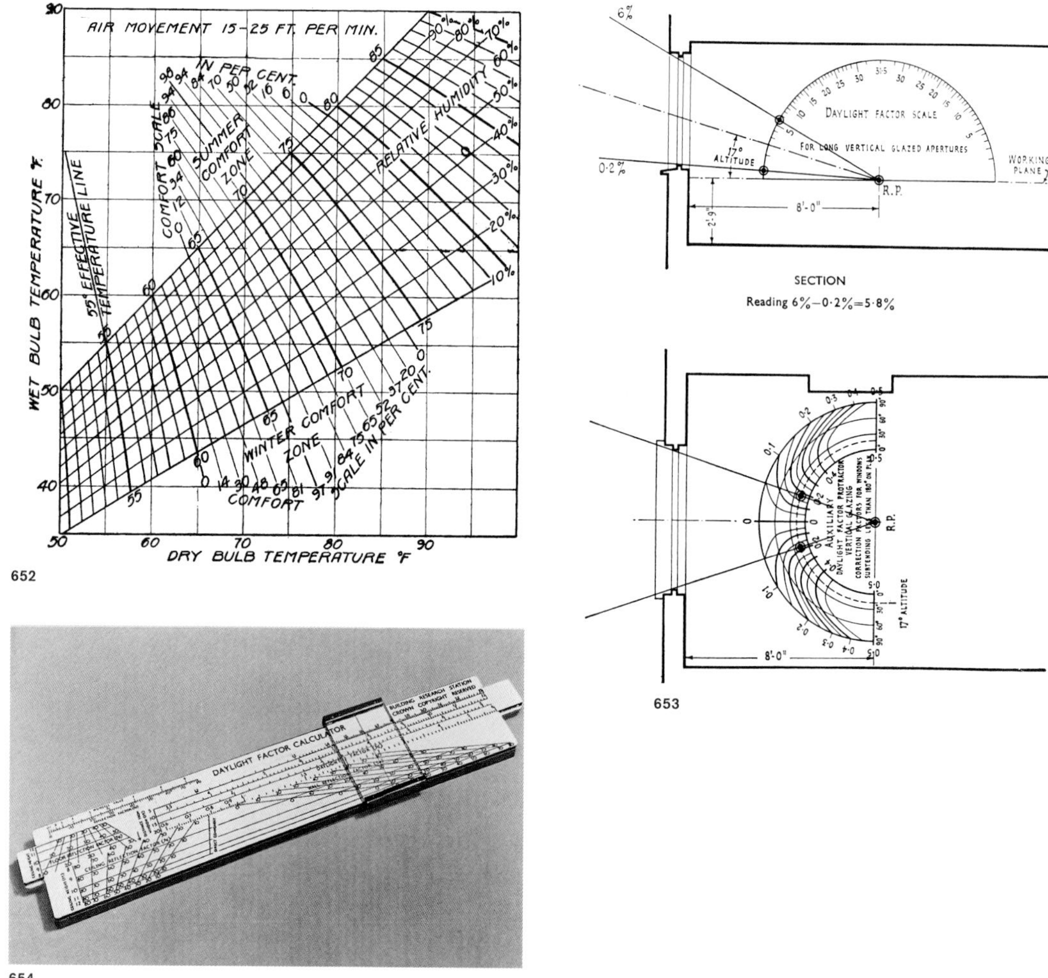

652

653

654

652 The Comfort Zone Chart, published by the American Society of Heating and Ventilation Engineers, 1922.
653 Sky factor protractors, devised by the Building Research Station, England. 654 Daylight factor slide rule, devised by the Building Research Station, England.

ity were brought into the debate. Matters were resolved in 1922, temporarily at least, when the American Society of Heating & Ventilation Engineers (ASH&VE) published the results of research it had undertaken to establish a scientific definition of comfort in terms of wet- and dry-bulb air temperatures. The results were plotted as a
652 "comfort zone" on the psychrometric chart that Carrier had published in 1908 (see chapter 7, p. 411). This not only provided the means for specifying the cooling level that an air-conditioning engineer should strive to achieve, it also served to suggest that the engineers' arguments had a firmer scientific basis than the arguments put forward by advocates of natural ventilation. Research continued throughout the 1920s at the ASH&VE laboratories to establish the ranges of temperature and humidity that different people judged to be "more" or "less" comfortable.

Although it was recognized that an air-conditioning system could deliver a controlled internal atmosphere, there was disagreement about which environment to create. Should an engineer seek to reproduce the atmosphere of the seaside beach or the mountain resort? It was widely believed that the action of waves on a beach creates ozone, and that this is what makes the sea air so healthy and invigorating. By the end of the 1920s the members of ASH&VE had voted to ban the term "fresh air" from their literature, since it was seen as favoring the idea of natural ventilation; the term "outside air" was to be used instead. Matters were further confused by some unscrupulous contractors who installed ventilation systems that provided chilled air with no humidity control, claiming that it was full air-conditioning. To compensate for the lack of humidity control, air speeds were increased to raise the wind chill factor, resulting in complaints from members of cinema audiences who suffered stiff necks and chilled feet. The front cover of the air-conditioning periodical *The Aerologist* in December 1931 caught the mood of the various arguments that were raging concerning the choice between air-conditioning and natural ventilation and the various ways of achieving them—a debate
651 that continues to the present day.

Despite the controversies, air-conditioning, or "man-made weather" as many called it, did maintain a foothold, and continued to spread throughout the country. During the 1910s and 1920s it was widely installed in factories. Cinemas, theaters, some hotels, and prestige buildings for large corporations followed in the 1920s and 1930s. In the early 1930s, a number of firms began breaking into the domestic market with small standalone room air-conditioners—the predecessors of the now-ubiquitous window air units—that provided an easy way to retrofit air-conditioning in a building without a central system. For commercial landlords the window unit system meant that each tenant renting office space could provide air-conditioning, but at its own expense. Air-conditioning became a standard feature of commercial offices in the United States only during the building boom that followed World War II. A similar pattern occurred in each major city: Once the proportion of office buildings with air-conditioning reached about 20 percent, the rest had to follow quickly to prevent their tenants from moving to better premises. New York and Philadelphia reached this point in 1953, after which virtually all new office buildings were designed and built with air-conditioning.

From today's standpoint, when energy is a global concern in terms of both its financial and environmental costs, it seems astonishing that, before the 1960s, so little effort was devoted to reducing the energy used to run buildings. The exception was the exploitation of the heat pump. This device, first conceived by the British physicist William Thomson (later Lord Kelvin) in the 1850s, is essentially a reversible refrigeration plant: It takes heat from a low-temperature source such as a river and pumps it into the building at a high temperature. In summer it takes heat from a building's interior and delivers it into the relatively low-temperature water in the river. The benefit to the building owner is that the energy needed to pump this heat is less than half the quantity of heat energy delivered to or removed from the building—a rare example of a device that effectively operates at more than 100 percent efficiency. Possibly the first working heat-pump installation was by Thomas Graeme Nelson Haldane (1899–1981), a consulting engineer who was to become president of the British Institution of Electrical Engineers in 1948. In 1928, Haldane used an experimental machine to heat his Scottish home and London office. By the 1930s it was reported that over fifty domestic heat pumps were in operation in the United States. In 1931 the Southern California Edison company installed an 800-horsepower vapor-compression refrigeration system in its Los Angeles office that also worked as a heat pump in the winter. In Switzerland in the 1940s, heat pumps were used for a number of district heating schemes, and Zurich Town Hall was the first major building to use a heat pump to combine winter heating with summer cooling. A similar system was installed in London's Royal Festival Hall in 1951, taking heat from the river Thames in winter and using the river as the heat sink for summer cooling. Despite their highly efficient technical performance, heat pumps never became popular, partly because they were difficult to maintain but mostly because of their additional capital cost and the low price of fuel.

Lighting

The quality of the internal air in buildings was the object of considerable attention during the interwar period in the United States, and occasionally in other countries, both because air quality had a direct, perceivable influence on people's comfort and because the growing heating and ventilating industry had an enormous financial interest in providing temperature-controlled building environments. Developments in two other engineering fields concerned with the internal environment—lighting and acoustics—did not proceed with the same intensity because the need was less acute and there was less money to made by contractors.

The design of windows to provide adequate inside daylighting had been an empirical process until the end of the nineteenth century, partly because there was no convenient means of measuring lighting intensity and also because there were no agreed-upon data on how much light people needed. This situation changed around the turn of the century, when scientists in Germany, Austria, Britain, and the United States began to suspect that there was a link between vision problems in schoolchildren and lighting levels. By 1920 many countries had set minimum lighting levels for different types of room that had to be achieved using either daylight or artificial light. The "daylight factor" had been defined in 1896 by the British electrical engineer Alexander Trotter (1857–1947) as a means of assessing what proportion of the maximum available daylight reached the interior of a room. Calculating this required complex three-dimensional geometry and the analysis of light reflected off walls and ceilings, and these were not easily done. To help designers, scientists at the Building Research
Station in England developed custom-made protractors 654
and nomograms that provided the means to estimate daylight factors on the basis of architects' drawings.
They also produced a dedicated slide rule. 653

The effects of direct sunlight on a building—both the shadows cast by adjacent buildings and the sun's energy entering a window—are as important as the level of daylight inside a room. To assess the effect of direct sunlight falling on a building and entering a room through the windows, the Building Research Station developed a simple and ingenious device called a "heliodon." This modeled the shadows cast by the sun at any time of day, and could be set up to investigate a building at any position on the earth's surface. It enabled designers to see the full range of shading conditions that a building would experience, and quickly to establish the periods of the day when shadows might be a nuisance—calculations in three-dimensional geometry that would otherwise have been far too tedious to undertake in the precomputer age.

The Building Envelope

The growing awareness of the importance of providing good daylight inside buildings also had its effect on the construction of buildings. Concrete, being opaque, did not endear itself to many architects. This limitation was overcome by the development in Germany in 1908 of a means of embedding glass blocks into a reinforced concrete slab or shell roof to make what became known as "glass concrete." Under various trade names, it became popular for a while during the 1930s. Glass technology improved markedly in the early twentieth century, resulting in improved quality, larger sizes, and lower prices. The glass-making process of J. H. Lubbers, which was developed in about 1905 in the United States, made it possible to manufacture single sheets of glass up to 8 by 1.6 meters. At about the same time the Belgian engineer Émile Fourcault (1862–1919) successfully developed a continuous process for making drawn glass on an industrial scale. A band or ribbon of glass was lifted from a vat of molten glass; once solidified, the band could be cut into individual panes without pausing the drawing process. The modern float-glass process, which revolutionized glass-making by further increasing the size and quality of glass and reducing its cost, was developed by the English firm Pilkington during the 1950s.

655

655 Boots factory "Wets" building, Beeston, England, 1930–32. Engineer and architect: Owen Williams. Glass-concrete roof.

656

Cost and quality were not the only factors that revolutionized the use of glass. Normal sheet glass from the factory is relatively weak and brittle. To reduce its susceptibility to breakage, glass used in large building facades is either laminated or toughened, or both. The first laminated "safety glass," consisting of a film of transparent Celluloid sandwiched between two sheets of glass, was developed for use in automobile windshields in 1910 by the French chemist Édouard Benedictus, and was soon being used in buildings. Multiple-sheet laminated glass screens were first produced in the 1930s, and the laminating material polyvinyl butyral (PVB), which is still used today, was developed in 1940. Toughened glass was developed around 1930 for automobile windshields by the French firm Saint-Gobain, and it was quickly being used in windows and building facades. This glass is prestressed by quickly cooling the outer surface of hot glass sheets using air jets. As the entire glass section cools, the outer surface is drawn into compression by the inner core acting in tension, which helps prevent the spread of micro-cracks in the surface of the glass. In the mid-1950s the German firm Glasbau Hahn developed glass cement, which enables glass elements to be bonded to form larger structural units such as beams or fins for stiffening large sheets of plate glass. All these developments encouraged engineers and architects to make building envelopes ever more transparent. One of the earliest examples of an all-glass facade in Britain was Owen Williams's building for the Boots company in Nottingham (1930–32). 655

The means used to support the glass in a transparent building facade is as important as the glass itself. The specialist discipline now known as "facade engineering" began to develop in the 1930s at a time when many architects, engineers, and builders, for different reasons, were striving to streamline building manufacturing processes. For some architects, the very process of prefabrication and off-site production was an aesthetic in itself, very much in the spirit of Le Corbusier's idea of the building as a machine. The French designer Jean Prouvé was particularly influential. He had trained as an apprentice in the art of metalworking, and throughout his life as a designer retained a passionate concern for how things were made as well as how they appeared. He began his work in buildings designing and making architectural ironwork for staircases, doors, elevators, lights, and a host of other interior fittings. He later turned his attention to windows and the building envelope, using his knowledge of metalworking to devise systems of

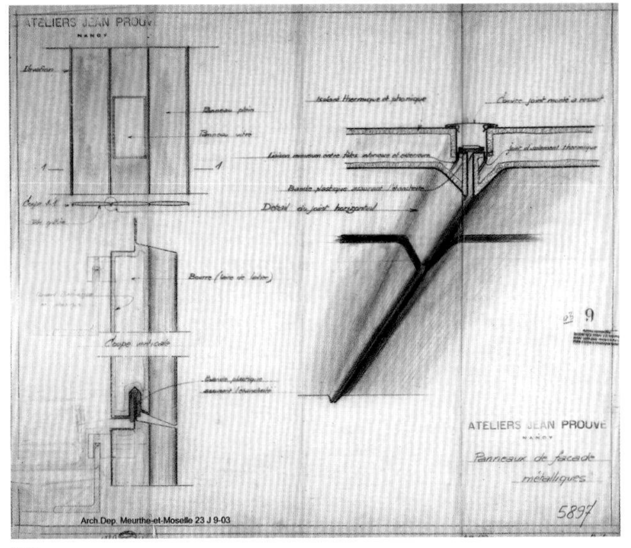

657

658

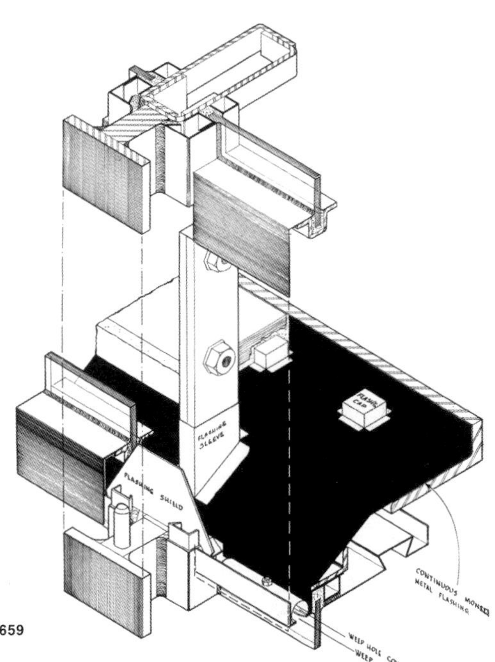

659

660

656 Maison du peuple, Clichy, France, 1937–39. Glazed facade by Jean Prouvé. 657 Maison du peuple. Detail of mullions for the facade. 658 Lever House, New York, 1952. Structural engineer: Weiskopf and Pickworth; architect: Skidmore, Owings & Merrill; designer: Gordon Bunshaft. 659 Lever House. Diagram showing juncture of the horizontal mullion and vertical rail that guides the window cleaning gondola. 660 Apartments, Square Mozart, Paris, 1953. Aluminium facade by Jean Prouvé.

mullions and glazing bars for supporting glass that were
656, 657 both easy to manufacture and to install in buildings. Since the early 1950s, both steel and aluminum have been used in curtain walling systems, which have developed along two lines: The "strong-back system" consists of rigid panels that are suspended directly from the building frame; in the "stick system," a secondary structure is constructed in situ to receive the glazing. One of the first large buildings to use the latter type of curtain wall was
658, 659 Lever House in New York.

660 Like many designers after World War II, Jean Prouvé was keen on exploiting certain specific characteristics of aluminum—its lightness, its resistance to corrosion, and its ability to be pressed into panels, cast into complex three-dimensional shapes, and extruded to form an infinite variety of complex cross sections. It was this ability of aluminum to form extruded sections that made it so suit-
661 able for window mullions and facade systems.

Acoustics

Today we think of double glazing as a means of providing effective thermal insulation; indeed, this was its purpose when the Romans used it in a some public baths and private palaces in the first century. The first use of sealed double-glazing, however, was in the 1930s in a number of nondomestic buildings, including hotels, apartment blocks, and commercial offices, where it was used as a means of providing acoustic insulation against the growing noise from traffic on city streets. Indeed, at this time, the science of building acoustics consisted largely of seeking ways of solving the problem of noise transmission between rooms. Although this was simply a nuisance for people in apartments and hotel rooms, it was essential to eliminate such noise when designing the growing number of sound studios for radio stations and recording studios. Especially challenging was the need to achieve acoustical separation of the control cubicle of a studio while maintaining visual contact between the music or program producer and the performers.

When designing recording studios, auditoriums, and concert halls in the 1920s and 1930s, the reverberation time could be predicted using Sabine's method, but otherwise the acoustics was addressed largely as an empirical process. Good common sense guidance had been available in the books of David Boswell Reid, W. S. Inman, and others since the 1830s. This had served designers moderately well, and was usually adequate as long as concert halls were built in traditional ways. In the 1920s, however, architects began experimenting with new shapes of auditoriums to which the familiar acoustics design rules did not apply. It became necessary to think about the acoustics of such spaces from first principles, considering the different paths by which sound might reach the listener in the auditorium and the correct balance between direct sound and sound reflected off the walls or ceiling. The French acoustician Gustave Lyon (1857–1936) was one of the pioneers of
this approach, which he used at the Salle Pleyel in Paris, 662
completed in 1927.

It was well known that sound travels in straight lines and is reflected like light from hard surfaces, and that this phenomenon can lead to a nonuniform distribution of sound throughout an auditorium. Some designers
went to great trouble to try to predict sound paths using 663, 664
what we now call "ray tracing." Before the advent of computers this meant laboriously drawing lines and adjusting the position and curvature of the walls and ceiling to achieve a number of suitable sound paths, in this way avoiding a nonuniform sound field. When designing the Salle Henry-le-Boeuf in Brussels in 1928, the architect Victor Horta took a great interest in its acoustics, including the use of ray tracing as a design tool. Despite his client's wishes, Horta (1861–1947) refused to consult Gustave Lyon, then considered to be the leader of the French school of acoustical design, because he considered that Lyon's purely scientific approach paid insufficient attention to how music actually sounded in concert halls. In making his design decisions on the hall's volume and shape and the form of the ceiling, Horta visited a great many halls in Europe and the United States; he also used ray tracing. In the early 1930s some German acousticians used rays of light in three-dimensional models of theaters to study the path taken by sound waves, but such models were of no help in considering different sound frequencies,

661 Republic National Bank, Dallas, Texas, 1955. Architects: Wallace Harrison and Max Abramovitz. Full-story pressed aluminum panels form the facade of the thirty-six-story building.

661

662

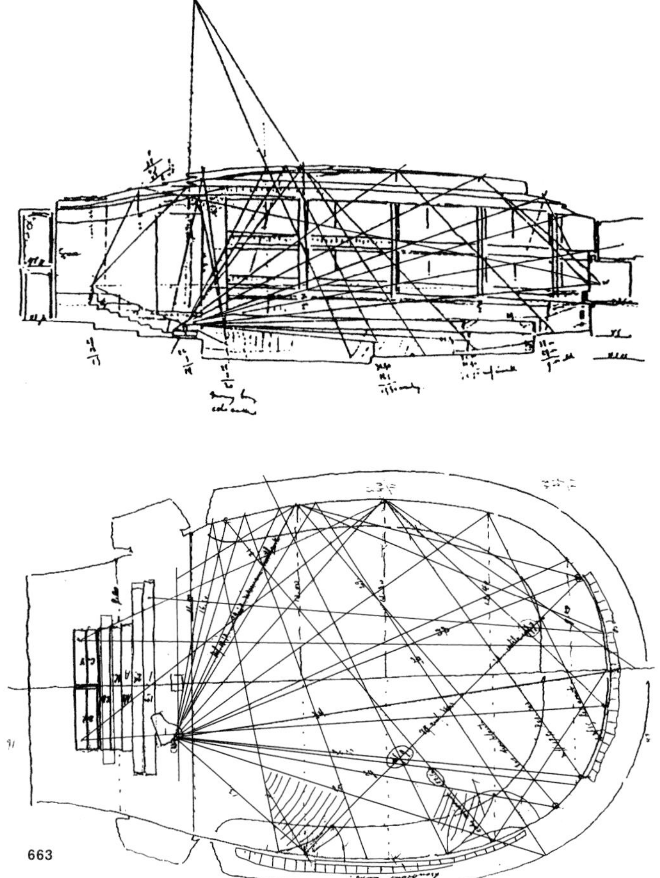

663

664

665

reverberation times, or the different times a sound takes to reach a listener by different sound paths.

Scale models were first used to analyze the acoustical performance of auditoriums by the German physicist Friedrich Spandöck in the early 1930s. Using simple dimensional analysis to find suitable dimensionless constants, he showed that the acoustical behavior of a room varies inversely with the model scale; for a one-fifth scale model, for example, the sound frequencies used for testing need to be five times higher than normal frequencies. He also recognized the need to ensure that the temperature, pressure, and density of the air in the model room were identical to the air in a real room, since these all affect the speed at which different frequencies of sound travel. Spandöck's first concern was to demonstrate that tests on a model were indeed a reliable way to represent the acoustical behavior of a full-size room. He then studied the effect on both the decay of sound and its distribution throughout an auditorium of raked seating (which improved the acoustics) and a semicircular wall behind the stage (which made the acoustics worse). Using a microphone, he displayed the decay of sound in the model auditorium on the screen of an oscilloscope, and recorded the results photographically. In the late 1930s similar studies were undertaken in a number of other university physics departments demonstrating the possibility of using models during the design of an auditorium.

The science of acoustics received an unexpected boost during World War II, when sound was the primary means for locating the sites of enemy guns and, before the development of radar, for detecting the approach of enemy aircraft. Because sound is transmitted for longer distances in water than in air, underwater microphones were used to detect the engines of ships and submarines. Most sophisticated of all was the development of sonar, an underwater version of radar that detects and locates underwater objects such as mines and vessels by means of sound-wave reflection, and can also be used to build up a three-dimensional map of the seafloor. After the war, many of the experts on underwater sound waves became consultants advising building designers on acoustics. Wartime developments in the science of acoustics did not, however, transform building design overnight. When the Royal Festival Hall was being designed in 1949–50, the primary consultant on acoustics based his advice on over thirty years of experience in building design and discussions with musicians, conductors, music critics, music lovers, and others with

662 Salle Pleyel, Paris, 1927. Acoustic design by Gustave Lyon. Section. 663 Salle Henry-le-Boeuf. Palais des Beaux-Arts, Brussels, 1929. Architect and acoustic design: Victor Horta. Manual ray tracing. 664 Salle Henry-le-Boeuf. 665 Royal Festival Hall, London, 1949–51. Acoustic consultant: Philip Hope Bagenal; architect: Leslie Martin for the London County Council Architects.

practical experience rather than on the latest developments in the science of acoustics. Some thirty years after Sabine's work, the only measurable and (relatively) predictable design parameter was the reverberation time. Yet consultants differed in their recommendations for the most desirable reverberation—time value for the Festival Hall: One said 2.2 seconds and another said 1.7 seconds, a very large difference. Designers settled on 1.7 seconds, but, as it turned out, the reverberation time of the finished hall was just 1.5 seconds, which most people agreed was too short. Acoustics was still far from being a precise science, and assessment was subjective; some musicians and conductors liked the acoustics
665 of the hall, others did not. In its early days a great many studies were undertaken to search for ways of lengthening reverberation time, but with little success. Following further studies in the early 1960s when the hall was being refurbished (it was said that the Royal Festival Hall was the "most studied" hall in the history of acoustics), a number of microphones and loudspeakers were installed to provide "assisted resonance." This increased the reverberation time to the desired value of 1.7 seconds, and the acoustics of the refurbished hall met with widespread acclaim. Nevertheless, taste in the world of music changes. After many discussions and a number of trials, it was finally agreed, in 1995, to stop using assisted resonance, yet the acoustics of the hall are still widely regarded as excellent.

The period between about 1920 and 1960 saw the building industry in every major country transformed. The experimental sciences had had an impact on most aspects of building design, and by the 1950s most buildings were being designed and built much as they are today. When deemed necessary, engineering calculations could be made for the structure and foundations, thermal performance, ventilation, acoustics, lighting design, and fire safety. Only the balance between empirical and scientific design calculations has changed since then. New construction materials such as aluminum could be integrated into building design almost immediately because their engineering properties and behavior were fully understood down to the atomic level—a far cry from the early days of cast iron and reinforced concrete. It was easy to recognize when a building design lay outside the normal range of experience that could be handled by standard design procedures. In such cases, model tests could be carried out to raise a designer's level of confidence sufficiently to allow the proposed design to be built.

In 1959 the Building Research Station in Britain published a new edition of *The Principles of Modern Building*. First published in 1939, this book had become a classic of its kind, seeking to encourage building designers to base all their thinking about buildings on scientific principles, as was already standard practice in, for example, the design of aircraft or long-span bridges. Nevertheless, even in 1959 the design of many aspects of buildings still involved empirical design rules which lacked an underlying basis of engineering science or in which the underlying science was not apparent. The book encouraged the use of basic physics and engineering science to achieve water-tight buildings, to design thermal and acoustical insulation, to achieve adequate levels of illumination from daylight and artificial light, to avoid condensation problems by controlling the change of temperature and humidity across the building envelope, and so on. The design issues were the same as they had been throughout history, and, surprisingly perhaps, much of the current design guidance was little different from what had existed a hundred or more years earlier.

Of particular interest is what the book did not cover. There was little space devoted to building services, or the principles underlying the provision of comfort. There was no mention of energy. A section headed "The economics of heat insulation" began: "In some heated buildings the heat input may be restricted by the capacity of the heating plant or by the willingness of the owner or occupier to supply heat. Under such conditions, improved insulation may contribute partly to reducing fuel consumption, and partly to providing a higher internal temperature; its value must take both into account."[10] There was no mention of how to design the acoustics of a room in a building, although there was a section on how to reduce problems of noise transmission by means of sound insulation. In these branches of building engineering, designers still tended to rely on post-construction remedies rather than design a building with the aid of engineering science to avoid the problems in the first place. Fire protection fared rather better, and there was a section on designing buildings to reduce the spread of fire. There was, however, no mention of the term "fire engineering"; this did not appear until the 1980s.

chapter 9
The Computer Age and the Greening of Construction
1960–present

People and Events

1909–82 Vilhelm Jordan
1917–88 René Sarger
b. 1921 Jørn Utzon
b. 1926 Olek Zienkiewicz
b. 1926 William LeMessurier
b. 1926 Heinz Isler
b. 1928 Leslie Robertson
1929–82 Fazlur Khan
1935–89 David Geiger
1935–92 Peter Rice
1951–2003 Tony Fitzpatrick
1969 First manned lunar landing (Apollo 11)
1973–74 "Energy crisis" caused by dramatic rise in oil prices

Materials and Technology

1958 Program Evaluation and Review Technique (PERT) developed
From 1960s Fiber-reinforced composite materials used in buildings
From 1960s Polymers (plastics) become widely used in buildings
Mid-1970s High-strength polymer membranes
Mid-1970s Teflon-coated glass-fiber membranes

Knowledge and Learning

From 1960s Growth of international conferences for sharing engineering knowledge
1969 Ove Arup articulates his ideas of "Total Design" and "Total Architecture"
1976 *History of Technology* first published in the UK

Design Methods

1960s Form-finding for tensile structures using physical models
1960s Boundary layer wind tunnel testing of buildings grows
1960s Acoustic scale model testing of Sydney Opera House, Sydney, Australia
1960s Hanging fabric models used to design concrete shells (Heinz Isler)
1964 First large boundary layer wind tunnel (Ontario, Canada)
From c. 1972 Energy use of buildings considered
From c. 1974 Fire engineering approach to design of structures

Design Tools: Drawing and Calculation

From 1960s Finite element method of stress analysis developed by Olek Zienkiewicz
c. 1960 Wet photocopier developed
1965 Dry photocopier developed
1970 Computer-generated drawings
1972 First hand-held, scientific electronic calculator (HP-35)

Buildings

1960 Palazzo dello Sport, Rome, Italy
1960 Palace of Labor, Turin, Italy
1960–73 Sydney Opera House, Sydney, Australia
1964 Houston Astrodome, Houston, Texas, USA
1964 DeWitt–Chestnut Apartments, Chicago, USA
1965–70 German Pavilion at Expo '67, Montreal, Canada
1970 John Hancock Center, Chicago, USA
1971–77 Centre Pompidou, Paris, France
1972 World Trade Center, New York, USA
1972 Munich Olympic Stadium, Munich, Germany
1973 Sears Tower, Chicago, USA ("bundled tubes")
1975 Exhibition building for Garden Festival, Mannheim, Germany

1960 | 1965 | 1970 | 1975

From early 1980s Legislation dealing with environmental issues and their impact on construction

1985 British Antarctic Survey discovers hole in ozone layer over the Antarctic

1985 "Cable-dome" tensegrity structure (David Geiger)

Late 1970s "Expert systems" developed to assist knowledge management

1977 Tuned mass dampers used to combat sway of tall buildings

1990 ETFE clear film for air-inflated cushions becomes available

1980s Knowledge-based "expert systems" developed for storing engineering design knowledge

1985 *Construction History* first published by the Construction History Society, UK

2003 First International Congress on Construction History, Madrid, Spain

From c. 1985 Environmental impact of buildings considered

From c. 1986 Form-finding using computer models

1990s Computer visualization of lighting (using ray tracing)

1980s Saline water visualization of turbulent air flow inside buildings

1990s Computational Fluid Dynamics (CFD) models of air flow and flame

1990s Computers used for form-finding for membrane structures

Mid-1970s Desktop personal computing

Late 1970s Electrostatic/laser printing and photocopying

c. 1990 Computational Fluid Dynamics (CFD)

c. 1975 Interactive drawing via visual display unit (VDU)

1979 VisiCalc: First computer spreadsheet program

c. 1980 3-D modeling on computer

1977 Citicorp Center, New York, USA

1984 World Memorial Hall, Kobe City, Japan (Pantadome system)

1990 Science and Technology Museum, La Villette, Paris, France

1990–97 Peninsula, Terminal 2F, Charles de Gaulle airport, Paris, France

1986 Seoul Olympics gymnastics stadium, Seoul, South Korea

1988 Bank of China Tower, Hong Kong

1988–92 Pavilion of the Future, Expo '92, Seville, Spain

1991–93 Eastgate building, Harare, Zimbabwe

1999 Millennium Dome, London, UK

1992 Century Tower, Tokyo, Japan

1992 Izumo Dome, Izumo, Japan

1980 1985 1990 1995 2000

The Computer Age and the Greening of Construction 1960–present

The engineering design and manufacture of a great many articles of daily use changed remarkably in the latter part of the twentieth century, primarily due to the development of new materials, especially plastics, and advances in solid-state electronics—first the transistor, then the integrated circuit and microchip. Home appliances, cars, toys, boats, and aircraft all look very different from how they looked in the 1960s, and they often work quite differently as well. The same cannot be said of most buildings, which work in more or less the same way as they did at mid-century, and with most of the same materials. The obvious differences are architectural and stylistic, not technological. Generally speaking, for example, modern buildings make more effective use of resources; they are more economical in their use of materials and more efficient in their use of energy for heating and cooling. Thus, the main difference between a building today and one from around 1960 is entirely invisible in the finished artifact. It lies in the degree and the accuracy to which the engineering performance of the building was predicted at the design stage, then delivered in the completed building. This progress can be attributed almost entirely to two things: the integration of scale models in the design process, and the development of computers. Together these have enabled building engineers to create mathematical models of different parts of buildings and of their engineering systems. Thus it has become possible to model the performance of buildings—not only their structural performance, but also their thermal, lighting, air quality, acoustic, and fire safety performance.

The impact of computers on design in building engineering has been especially great because each new building is effectively a prototype—there is just one chance to get things right. In these circumstances the most sensible approach is to rely heavily on precedent, in other words to do more or less what you did last time. This contrasts with mass-produced products, such as cars, machinery, or electronic equipment, for which many prototypes are made and tested, often to destruction. Each prototype incorporates the lessons learned from the previous one, and the performance is gradually improved before a final design is reached, then manufactured in large numbers. In buildings, the development of the most economical form for a cast iron beam in the early nineteenth century was a rare example of this approach to product development. Otherwise, the only opportunity to investigate and improve several prototypes was by using scale models, and even this was constrained by the considerable expense of such model testing. Computers have enabled engineers to work with mathematical models and to study many alternative designs, though expense is still a constraint, as complex computer models can take many weeks or months to develop.

Structural considerations have had the most prominent impact on the appearance of buildings in the last half century, largely as a result of the use of computers to model structural behavior. Just as structural engineers pioneered the use of scale models, so were they the first of the disciplines of building engineering to integrate

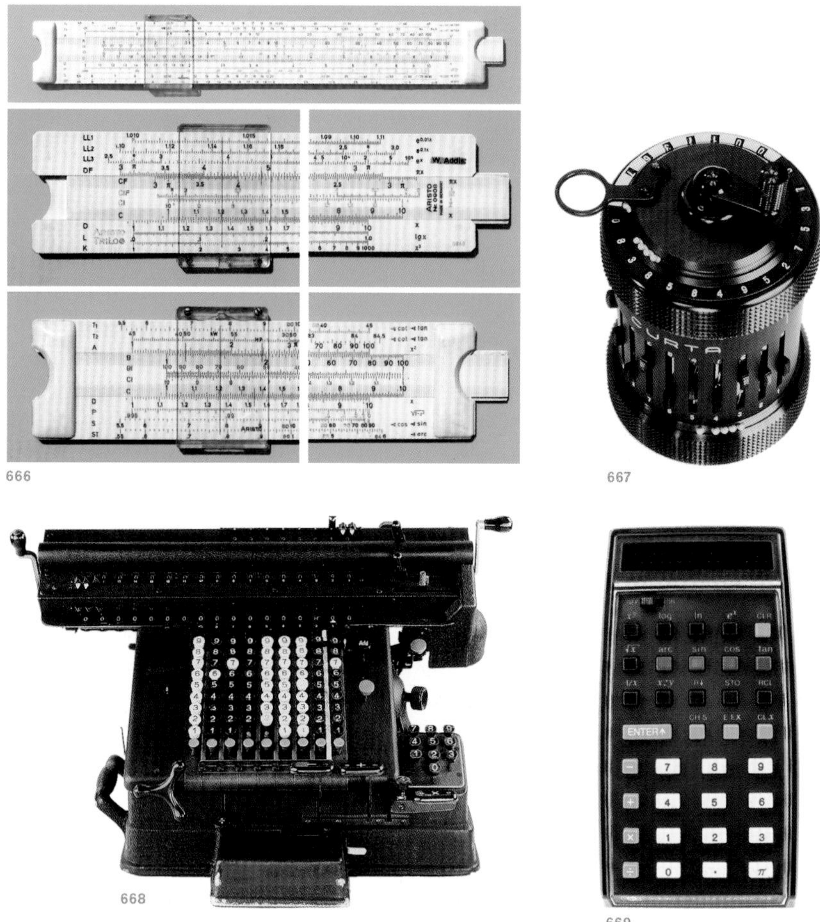

666

667

668

669

computers into their work. Buildings such as the Sydney Opera House in Australia (1957–73), the timber gridshell exhibition building for the Mannheim Garden Festival in Germany (1975), and tensile membrane roofs such as the one at Denver International Airport in Colorado (1994) would have been impossible to design and build without the use of computer models.

During the last half century, technological progress in building construction—developing and using new materials, new methods of manufacture and production engineering, and new methods of analysis and calculation—has continued to benefit from developments in other industries, mainly the automotive, aerospace, and petroleum industries. For example, fiber-reinforced plastics developed in the aerospace industry are now used in thousands of building products, and high-strength glass developed for car windshields led directly to improved glass for use in the building envelope. Less visible has been the development of the "systems approach" to engineering, developed in the military and aerospace industries, which focuses on

666 Aristo Trilog slide rule, c. 1965, including log-log scales. 667 Curta Calculator II, Germany, 1950. Mechanical calculator invented by Curt Herzstark. 668 Mercedes-Euklid electromechanical adding machine. Germany, 1940. 669 HP-35 calculator, 1972. Designed and manufactured by Hewlett-Packard.

the performance of whole systems rather than individual components. Most significant, though, has been the development of the computer, in the military and aerospace industries.

The Impact of Computers on Building Engineering

The first programmable electronic computer, the "Colossus," was developed in Britain during World War II for use at the British intelligence center at Bletchley Park, near London, to help break the codes used by the Germans for transmitting radio messages. The Colossus was designed and built in 1943 by a team led by Tommy Flowers (1905–98), an electronics engineer who worked for the British Post Office. It was the realization of the idea developed some six years earlier by Alan Turing (1912–54), one of the thousand or so code breakers at Bletchley Park, that data could be manipulated by providing a sequence of operational instructions, what we now know as a computer program. The machine's memory and processor had over 1,500 thermionic valves, and the data and the program were fed into the machine via paper tape with holes punched in binary code. The first machine was operational by January 1944, and ten more were soon in use. Though limited to reading just 5,000 characters a second, the Colossus could perform up to a hundred statistical calculations simultaneously and solve each coded message in just a few hours, a process that would have taken many weeks of work by a team of people.

Beginning with their first use by structural engineers in the late 1950s, electronic computers transformed the work of the building design engineers in three main areas: performing calculations, producing drawings, and using a mathematical model to predict behavior. Initially, it was thought that the computer's main advantages were accuracy and speed of calculation, but it soon became clear that its ability to carry out the same calculation again and again with new input data—the process of iteration—was even more important.

Calculation

Until the early 1970s the engineer's most frequently used calculating device was still the slide rule. Although many engineers used circular slide rules, and some favored cylindrical slide rules that provided four-figure accuracy, most designers used a standard 250-mm
Aristo or Faber-Castell rule. This provided accuracy to 666
three significant figures, which was adequate for the vast majority of building engineering calculations. Engineers made do with this degree of accuracy either because they felt that greater accuracy was unnecessary or because it would have been too time consuming and costly to achieve.

Cylindrical slide rules, equivalent to a linear rule about 12 meters long, could give an additional accuracy, to four or five significant figures. When even greater accuracy was
needed, mechanical calculators—such as the Curta 667
Calculator, which could give ten-figure accuracy—were used. Mechanical adding machines powered by an electric motor we also used, but they could perform only addition, subtraction, multiplication, and division. When 668
calculations involving logarithms, square and cube roots, and all the trigonometric functions had to be done to an accuracy greater than the three significant figures provided by the 250mm (ten inch) slide rule, printed tables of the functions were still used. These gave up to ten-figure accuracy.

The very first electronic desk calculators began to appear on engineers' desks in 1970 and 1971, but they were very expensive (over $1,000), and performed only arithmetic calculations. Slide rules and mechanical calculators remained in common use until 1972, when the price of electronic calculators fell to a price that engineers could afford. The first hand-held calculator able to handle scientific functions such as logarithms and trigonometric functions to ten-figure accuracy was the
Hewlett-Packard HP-35, which appeared in 1972 at the 669
"affordable" price of $495—equivalent to about $5,000 in today's dollars. It was advertised as "a fast, extremely accurate electronic slide rule." The HP-35 and its family of descendants were notable for using "reverse-Polish logic," which requires the operating function (+, -, x, or ÷,) to be entered after the two numbers being operated upon; they thus had no need of the = sign. By modern standards, the HP-35 was incredibly slow. Performing even simple calculations, such as sin 30° or 3^5, could take as long as a second or two. Other models soon appeared, and by 1975 the cost of basic scientific calculators had fallen to one tenth of the original model. Almost overnight the slide rule became obsolete for most engineering calculations.

The earliest computer programs written to solve problems in building engineering were developed in the late 1950s—mainly by university-based researchers who had access to mainframe computers—to calculate the forces, stresses, bending moments, and deflections in structures. At the same time, engineers wrote many rather less sophisticated, but nonetheless useful, programs to solve simple calculations that had to be undertaken regularly, for example, the properties of structural sections: area, center of gravity, and second moment of area (I-value). Such programs enabled engineers to solve a problem once and use the solution to generate answers any number of times, according to the specific data for a given case. In this respect the computer was performing a process identical to that of the nomogram developed at the beginning of the twentieth century (see chapter 7, p. 374). The computer's potential was, however, much greater.

The computer's capacity to perform rapid repetitive calculations makes it suitable for two different types of solution. The first is solving large numbers of equations simultaneously—particularly suitable for the calculation of forces and deflections in pin-jointed plane trusses. The second is iteration, which allows complex mathematical functions to be computed using a series of calculations that approach the correct answer ever more closely. This is in fact how computers calculate trigonometric functions as they are needed. The sine and cosine function can be expressed as an infinite arithmetic series, but this cannot be calculated exactly. By computing a sufficient number of terms in the series, however, a value such as that of sin 30° can be calculated with sufficient accuracy—say to ten significant figures. When handling more complex functions that represent the behavior of structures, such as the deflection of beams and columns in a frame building, the trick, so to speak, is to use a method of structural analysis that quickly converges on the precise answer. Rapid convergence had been the particular elegance of the moment distribution method developed by Hardy Cross in the 1930s (see chapter 8, p. 469), and Cross's method was easily adapted for computers.

Using these two main approaches to computation, quite complex bridge structures could already be analyzed by the late 1950s, including beams of variable section and concrete slab bridge decks. The use of computers by design engineers, however, was impractical at that time. Computers were too expensive to be included in most project budgets, and even if project engineers had access to computers, they lacked the skills to program them and the time to learn to use them. The means of making the new technology available to practicing engineers differed little from those used in the seventeenth century following the invention of logarithms. Those who had the necessary computer skills prepared tables that could be used by practicing engineers, who in turn generated design tables with data needed to solve specific design tasks.

This stage in the development of computers, in fact, passed rather more quickly than had been expected. Large computer firms developed mainframe computers to suit the needs of military and aerospace engineers, and programming languages were developed that could be used by the design engineers themselves, who then no longer needed the complex binary code that drove the computer applications. By the early 1960s most aerospace engineers were familiar with mainframe computers and had learned to write computer programs using one of two programming languages: FORTRAN (derived from IBM's Mathematical FORmula TRANslating System) or ALGOL (ALGOrithmic Language). At this time computer programs and data were written out by hand, and given to copyists who typed them using a machine that stored the code on rolls of perforated paper tape or punched cards, 670
one line of program or data per card. After they had been checked for typing errors, the punched cards were fed into the computer. This was done on a schedule that suited the computer manager, not the design engineer. The engineer might thus have to wait more than a day to see the results of the computation. The output of computer program was available in alpha-numerical form only (no diagrams at all), printed in lines up to 132 characters long onto perhaps many hundreds of sheets of fan-fold paper. It could be a tedious and error-prone process; a single missed comma or period would cause an entire program to fail and the unlucky engineer might be delivered a single sheet informing him that the program had "failed to compile," or perhaps many hundreds of sheets of gibberish or blank paper generated when a subroutine had not received the instruction to stop a repeated calculation.

The process accelerated in the late 1960s when it became possible for engineers to type their programs directly into computer, via a keyboard terminal. The key strokes were printed at the terminal as they were entered, and the whole program could also be printed at the terminal to allow checking for errors before the program was run. The engineer would then instruct the computer to run the program, and it would join a queue. The results were delivered to his desk several hours later, or the following day.

Until the early 1960s computer programs were written to solve specific problems, and large structural engineering practices built up suites of programs for the design of common elements, such as columns, beams, and slabs made from reinforced concrete. These programs were proprietary, and not made available to other engineering practices. The goal of many university-based research teams, however, was to develop general structural analysis programs that would be available to all. One of the earliest, written to run on IBM mainframe computers, was STRUDL (STRUctured Design Language), developed at the Massachusetts Institute of Technology in 1965 and 1966. From the late 1960s on, the number of programs in structural analysis has proliferated—and their sophistication has steadily increased—as structural engineers all over the world have worked to capture a share of the growing and lucrative software market.

Nevertheless, the slow turnaround time involved in using mainframe computers meant that even well into the 1970s engineers continued to use calculation tools from the precomputer age for simple and repetitive design calculations—for example, a slide rule to calculate the size
671 of the steel bars in reinforced concrete—and a nomogram to represent daylight factors.

Direct programming and interaction between engineer and computer via visual display units became common in the mid-1970s. VisiCalc, the first commercial spreadsheet program, was developed for the Apple computer in 1979; this brought the ability to do repetitive calculations, such as those involved in accounting and other types of financial analysis, within the reach of a new generation of computer users who did not need to know how to write computer programs. Spreadsheet programs allowed users to change data quickly and easily and see, the consequences of the changes on-screen. For several reasons, however, most engineers were slow to use spreadsheet programs on personal computers. Engineers were able to program large computers themselves to perform simple or unique calculations, and they generally used bespoke, technical software written to undertake specific calculations such as forces in frameworks or flow rates of air in air-conditioning systems. In addition, engineers generally used IBM personal computers rather than computers made by Apple, which pioneered the visual approach to calculation; finally, the early spreadsheet programs were aimed mainly at the financial user (arithmetic functions only) and supported few scientific features. Engineers began to learn and exploit the power of spreadsheets from the late 1980s when they began to use desktop or personal computers.

In order to achieve the three-figure accuracy of slide rules, engineers had to make many approximations and simplifications concerning the behavior of actual buildings. Indeed, the very art of engineering analysis had been to reduce highly complex engineering systems to a series of simplified systems that could be analyzed without materially affecting the accuracy of the predicted engineering behavior. Although computers did not remove the need for approximation, they certainly enabled more complex calculations to be undertaken. In the field of structural engineering, for example, it became possible to analyze complex statically indeterminate structures, which required the solution of many simultaneous equations, instead of having to approximate such structures to a series of simple, statically determinate ones. The sheer speed of computer calculation meant that it was now possible to analyze the same problem many times, making minor changes—for instance, changes to the dimensions of the components of a large roof structure—to see what effect the changes had on the results. It thus
became possible to approach optimal solutions, such as 672
designing a structure with minimum weight or cost, by calculating and comparing many alternatives.

Iterative computational methods form the basis of the "finite element method," which was developed during the 1960s and which is now, in effect, a universal computing tool applicable to any branch of engineering. It can be illustrated using the example of heat flow through the fabric of a building. First, the building component, no matter what its geometry, is divided into a large number of discrete elements of finite size; this distinguishes the finite

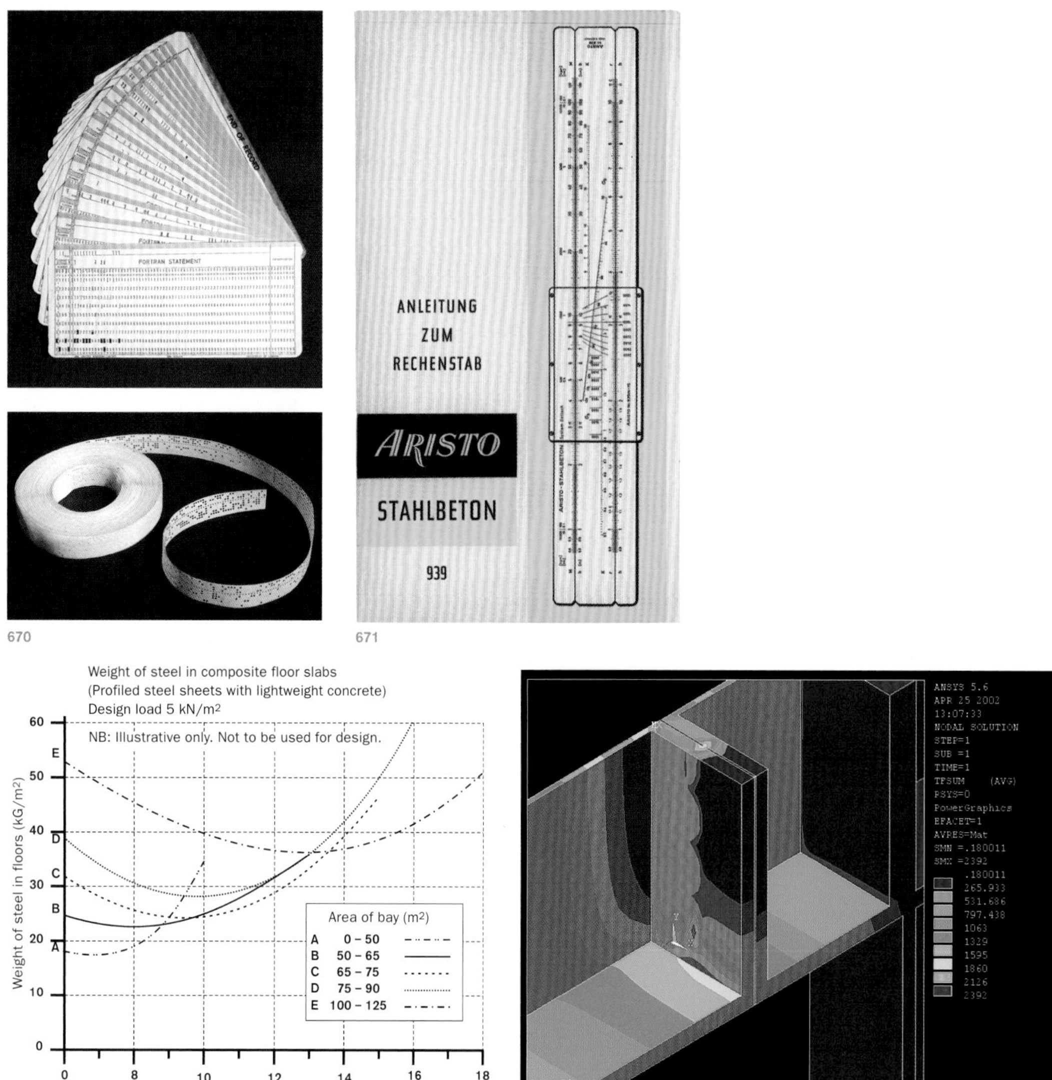

672

673

670 Punched cards (top) and data tape (bottom) used for computer data storage, 1960s. 671 Aristo slide rule 939, Aristo, Germany, c. 1970, designed for calculating dimensions of steel reinforcement bars in concrete. 672 Graph showing variation of weight of floor structure with span of beams and type of floor, 1970s. This is typical of many charts indicating where a minimum or optimum solution lies. 673 A computer screen showing the result of using a finite element model to analyze heat flow through a building facade, 2002. Different temperatures are represented by different colors.

element method from differential and integral calculus, in which materials are considered as a continuum represented by elements of infinitesimal size. Each element is of similar geometry, such as a triangle, and the smaller the element, or finer the mesh or grid, the more precise the final answer. The heat flow across a single element can easily be analyzed because it depends only on the thermal resistance of the material and the temperature differences between the different boundaries of the element. The result of the heat flow calculation across one element can then be fed in as the input to the heat flow calculations for the neighboring elements. After millions of similar calculations have been carried out, the computer can finally calculate the temperatures of every point (i.e., at the boundary of each finite element) within the building component and, hence, calculate the total heat flow through the component. Such a method would clearly not be possible without the use of a computer.

The English engineer Olek Zienkiewicz (b. 1921) is widely regarded as the "father of the finite element method," devoting his entire academic career at the University of Swansea in Wales to the study of the flow of stresses through materials. In the early 1960s, he developed the underlying mathematics to a point where it could be used to calculate the stresses inside a body of material such
673 as a dam or a pressure vessel. Finite element analysis was soon used in the aerospace industry in the design of highly stressed components such as turbine blades, where it replaced the use of photoelastic stress analysis for this purpose. Finite element analysis was first used in the building industry around 1970 for the calculation of internal stresses. Since that time, Zienkiewicz and many others have extended the method to analyze stresses in three dimensions, and have applied it to many other phenomena, including the flow of water through soils, air movement inside buildings, the pressures due to wind impinging upon buildings, and the flow of smoke and hot gases in a fire. Engineers now have the ability to undertake calculations of almost unimaginable complexity and difficulty in any field of building engineering. Theoretically, this means that engineers can now model and predict any engineering aspect of a building's behavior. In practice, there are many limitations: all computer models are only as good as the assumptions used when they are created, and these assumptions are as open to engineering judgment as they were before the computer age. Most experienced engineers still consider the results of computer analysis as a good guide to future events in the real world, but, like weather forecasting, not to be relied upon absolutely.

From Computer-Aided Drawing to Modeling in Three Dimensions

When the use of computers to produce drawings began in the 1960s in the aerospace and other military industries, the process involved typing in, on a keyboard, the individual points in two-dimensional space using x-y coordinates. The output from the computer was sent direct to a pen plotter. As the drawing software was developed to incorporate more power to calculate, so it could perform such classic drafting tasks as finding the line of intersection between two surfaces—for example, a sphere and a cylinder. It could also calculate results of direct use to the engineer, such as calculating the position of the center of gravity of an object, or the second moment of area of a structural component.

During the 1970s the term used to describe the use of computers to produce drawings changed from "computer-aided drawing" or "drafting" to "computer-aided design," all generally abbreviated to CAD. By the end of the decade it had become possible to put information into the computer in real time, using a pointing device such as a "light pen" rather than a keyboard, with the output displayed simultaneously on a visual display unit (VDU). As with spreadsheet programs, by providing immediate feedback from their actions, the use of the VDU with CAD software allowed users to perform the all-important "what-if?" activity that is so fundamental to the design process.

When graphical software moved from two dimensions to three in the late 1980s, a striking change of perception occurred. No longer was the process called drawing or drafting, or even design: It had become "modeling." The analogy was clear—the operator was building, in the computer, a three-dimensional replica, or model, of an object in the real world.

At about the same time, scientists and engineers were also starting to use the word "model" to describe what they were creating when they programmed their computers. No longer were they writing a program to calculate something; they were creating a model—a mathematical or computer model—of some aspect of the real world; and a key aspect of such models is often its geometrical form. As engineering software has developed, so too have the links between the geometric computer models of a building and the models representing different aspects of its engineering behavior. Thus, the computer screen can now display an image of, for example, the structure of a building, to each element of which is "attached" (in the computer's memory) its structural and material properties. The image on the screen is no longer merely an image—it effectively has physical properties, just as a physical model does.

It is now possible to apply a load to a model structure in the virtual world, then have the structural response to the load calculated and displayed on-screen. An engineer can also carry out any number of what-if? questions to investigate the consequences of changing different parameters of the model, thus building up an understanding of the "behavior" of the computer model, as if it were a physical model. Indeed, so rapid are today's computers that they can produce and display many images of successive responses to input data, creating the illusion of movement in real time. While such sequences may give the appearance of film animation, they are not mere animations; they display the engineering behavior of a working model in the virtual world, representing engineering behavior in the real world. Such sequences are particularly spectacular when showing the dynamic response of a tall building subject to loads from wind or an earthquake, or the spread of hot gases in a fire.

The Systems Approach to Engineering

During the second half of the twentieth century, there was a shift in how engineers thought about the artifacts they were designing. Rather than considering the design of individual components, engineers began to think in terms of the performance of the components and, more generally, how the components formed part of a larger system. This came to be known as the "systems approach" to engineering.

The idea of engineering systems had its origins in military projects, especially air defense, in Britain in the late 1930s and in both Britain and the United States during and after World War II. At the time, the term "system" was already used in the aerospace and automotive industries to describe the various functioning elements of airplanes or automobiles and their engines—the fuel system, braking system, cooling system, lubrication system, and so on. In the 1960s the National Aeronautics and Space Administration (NASA) Systems Engineering Handbook defined "system" as "a set of interrelated components which interact with one another in an organized fashion toward a common purpose."

In highly complex projects involving many engineers, there was a tendency for each engineer to focus too closely on his or her own task, at the expense of keeping in mind how that component would function as part of the project as a whole. The systems approach to engineering helped both project managers and engineers to change this narrow approach. For NASA and many other organizations undertaking large and complex projects, systems engineering serves to keep the big picture in mind while not overlooking the fine detail; it maintains a disciplined focus on the end product, its enabling products, its internal and external operational environment (in other words, a system view), and a consistent vision of a client's expectations independent of daily project demands (the system's purpose).

In the building industry, use of the word "system" be- 674
came common at about the same time as the first use of computer models, and the two have come to be closely linked. A building's systems are, in effect, those aspects of the building's performance being represented or modeled in a computer. The structural system of a building, then, as represented by the computer model, may be subdivided into the vertical load-bearing system, the horizontal load-bearing system, the wind bracing system, and so on.

An engineering model of a building system has several components:

- *A model of the geometry of the building and the building elements;*
- *A mathematical representation of the engineering science that describes how the system behaves: the deflection of a beam under load, the passage of heat, light, water vapor, or sound through a building facade, and so on;*
- *The engineering properties of the building elements: such as the stiffness or thermal conductivity of the*

materials, the acoustical reflectivity and absorptivity of a ceiling or a member of the audience in a concert hall, and the capacity and efficiency of a water pump;

- *The inputs to the system: a load on the structure, the heating effects of people, computers, or solar gain, a fire with a certain intensity, the energy powering an elevator motor, and so on;*
- *Finally, the output, or response, of the system—its "behavior."*

It would be fair to say that the building industry has not yet fully embraced the philosophy of the systems approach to engineering. Over the last two decades, however, the phrase "building system" has become part of most engineers' vocabulary, and the more progressive firms are focusing more and more on their clients' overall needs. The next few decades will no doubt see the systems approach being adopted more widely in building projects, especially large and complex ones.

Another manifestation of the systems view in engineering has been the modeling of a building project as a sequence of activities required to complete the project:
675 what we now know as project planning. This had its origins in the Gantt chart (see chapter 8, pp. 452–53), which served the construction industry well after its introduction by the Bethlehem Steel works for use in building ships for the U.S. Navy at the end of World War I. The Gantt chart, however, displays only the duration and sequence of work activities; it does not show the logical connections between dependent activities. The "program evaluation and review technique" (PERT), which was developed as a computer tool in 1958 by the U.S. Navy to help manage its Polaris submarine program, shows the links between dependent activities. By this means it is possible to identify a chain of dependent activities that has no spare time, or "float." Any delays or overruns in this chain will thus result in an overrun in the entire project. Such a sequence of activities is usually called a "critical path," from which came the name of one variant of PERT, the "critical path method" (CPM). Critical path methods are well-suited to running on a computer, and by the late 1960s they were widely used to help manage large building construction projects.

New Materials

During the second half of the twentieth century the development of a large number of new materials—notably the many hundreds of polymers, or plastics, as they are commonly called—had a major impact on building engineering. Plastics are ubiquitous in buildings—in electrical sockets, switches and insulation; window frames; clear polycarbonate (as a substitute for glass); pipes for gas and hot and cold water, sewage and rain water, as well as a host of small fixtures, fittings, and surface finishes.

Like most advances in technology, plastics and other new materials were first developed in the aerospace and military industries, and introduced into building construction by what is sometimes called a process of "technology transfer." In fact, there is no deliberate process called technology transfer; the migration of ideas and technologies from one industry to another generally occurs though normal commercial and human activities. Once organizations have completed research for military projects, they then look for opportunities to sell their products and skills in new markets. The building industry has also been the direct beneficiary of the regular downturns in the aerospace and military industries when highly-skilled engineers are laid off and seek employment elsewhere. This phenomenon is not a new one. Vitruvius, for example, moved into the construction industry after retiring from the army, and many military engineers in the Renaissance worked on civil projects during periods of peace.

Although the many new materials developed in recent decades have had a great impact on buildings and their components, in most cases the day-to-day work of building design engineers has not been fundamentally changed. First, new materials seldom have a fundamental effect on how a building system performs. Second, even when a new material does have characteristics that affect the performance of a building system (a very high strength-to-weight ratio, for example, or a high capacity to absorb vibrations, such as those from passing rail traffic), it is now a straightforward task for engineers to develop suitable models for its behavior that enable them to use it in their designs. A good example is the use of high-strength polymers such as Kevlar instead of steel. Kevlar is as strong as steel, and just one third of its density. It is also an electrical insulator, and it was this property that led to its being used for the upper

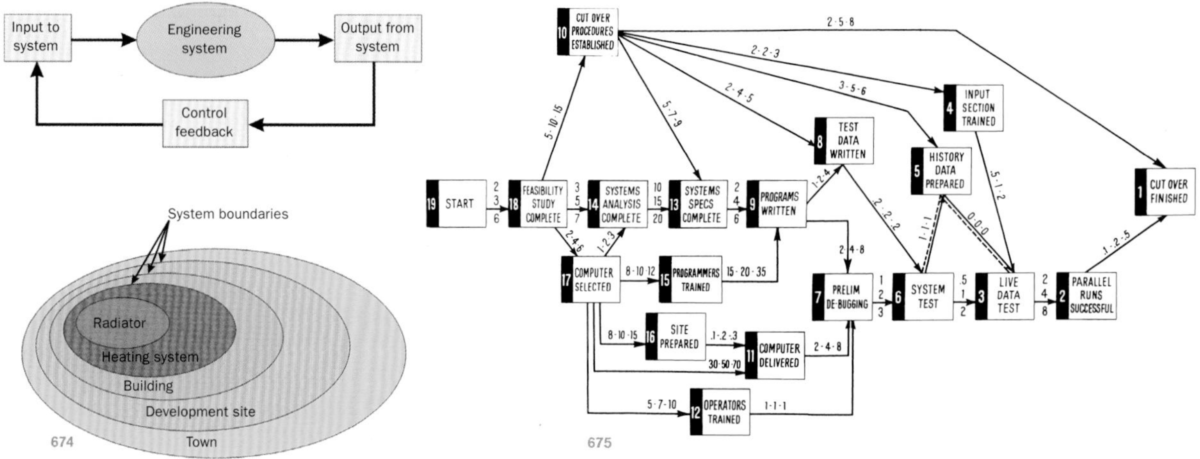

three cables supporting the floors of the Collserola
676 Communications Tower in Barcelona (1992), designed by Norman Foster and Partners, with Ove Arup & Partners as engineers. Kevlar was used in preference to steel to prevent lightning strikes from being conducted to the rooms containing the communications equipment. When using a material that is already in use in another industry, the building engineer can also turn to firms that have had experience with it and have learned its characteristics and limitations—both durability and sensitivity to temperature, humidity, and ultraviolet light, as was the case with Kevlar in the Collserola tower. It is usually up to the suppliers of new materials to provide full data about their performance and to demonstrate their suitability for use in buildings. The main barriers to the introduction of new materials have little to do with their engineering performance, but rather are three factors: the lack of hard evidence about the durability of new materials over time, and hence the period of warranty that can be assured; and the general resistance to new materials and methods by an industry used to certain ways of building.

One class of new materials that has made a particularly noticeable impact on building engineering is fiber-reinforced composites—high-strength fibers, usually of glass, carbon, or aramid (a high-strength polymer), that are embedded in a low-strength matrix, usually a polymer. Fiber-reinforced composites are typically of low density, and high strength and stiffness, and can be molded to suit the particular needs of different components. They were first developed in the late 1940s for aerospace applications, and began to be used for civil applications during the 1960s. Products made with these composites have included hulls for yachts and dinghies, the fuselages and wings of gliders, and tennis rackets and fishing rods.

Actually, it could be argued that the building industry had developed composites much earlier, in the form of reinforced concrete, in which reinforcing steel is the "fiber" and cement is the matrix. An even better case can be made for asbestos cement—cement reinforced with fine fibers of asbestos, which was developed in the early 1900s and widely used for making panel products.[1] Glass fibers were found to be a suitable replacement for asbestos, and glass-fiber reinforced cement 677
was used quite widely, especially during the 1960s and 1970s, for the manufacture of architectural cladding panels for buildings.

674 Diagram illustrating example of an engineering system of the 1960s. 675 A typical project planning chart showing links between activities, 1960s. 676 Collserola Communications Tower, Barcelona, 1992. Engineer: Ove Arup & Partners; architect: Norman Foster and Partners. Kevlar tendons support the equipment floors. 677 Credit Lyonnais bank, London, 1965. Engineer: Ove Arup & Partners. Glass-reinforced cement panels in the facade.

676

677

Apart from polymers, another class of new materials that have had a significant impact on the building industry is that of adhesives. The first synthetic waterproof adhesives were created during World War II. Since then, many new high-strength adhesives have been developed that can bond nearly any two materials to one another—including the highly loaded metal components used in both the aircraft and automobile industries. At present, the use of structural adhesives in buildings is still rare. One application is the strengthening of old structural timber or reinforced concrete elements by bonding strips of steel or carbon fiber to their surfaces.

Structural adhesives were used for the granite structure
678 of the Pavilion of the Future at Expo '92 in Seville, Spain.
Each voussoir of the arch, and the similar elements in the
679 columns, is made from a number of granite struts and
end plates that were bonded using an epoxy resin adhesive stronger than the granite itself. The granite elements were cut to the required degree of accuracy with a laser, and located precisely during the gluing process using stainless steel pins.

The most dramatic example of the use of new materials by structural engineers has involved a range of materials that can be used to form tensile membranes. These include fabrics woven from polyester or Teflon-coated glass fibers that have been used since the mid-1970s to create canopies and roofs with an astonishing variety of complex geometric forms (see, for example, pp. 580–83). More recently, ethylene tetrafluoroethylene (ETFE)—a chemical relative of the "nonstick" materials polytetrafluoroethylene (PTFE) and Teflon—has become available as a transparent or translucent film from which can be
made air-inflated cushions with extremely good thermal 680
insulation properties.

The Use of Physical Models in Building Design

The growing power and sophistication of techniques of analysis and design methods in the early and mid-twentieth century led to rapid progress in building engineering. This generally came about in one of two ways. Sometimes a steady stream of research and applications of new ideas in buildings gradually built up understanding and expertise of a generic kind that was later

678

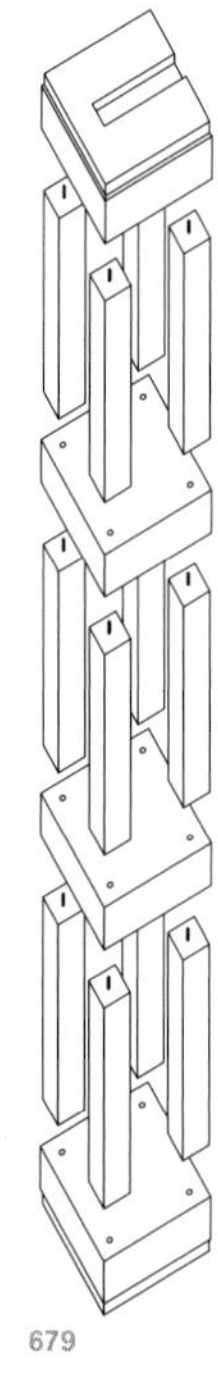
679

680

678 Pavilion of the Future, Expo '92, Seville, Spain, 1988–92. Engineer: Ove Arup & Partners; architects: MBM in association with Jaime Freixa. Granite structure. 679 Pavilion of the Future. Diagram showing granite components assembled by bonding with epoxy resin. 680 Hampshire Tennis and Health Centre, Eastleigh, near Southampton, England, 1994. Engineer: Buro Happold; architect: Euan Borland and Associates. Air-inflated ETFE foil cushions form the roof.

applied to new design challenges—for example, the development of tension structures and fire engineering, which are discussed later in the chapter. Sometimes, however, design engineers working on a particular project realize that current design procedures and engineering science are inadequate to generate sufficient confidence in a proposed design scheme to begin construction. Such situations have often stimulated specific experimental studies or research, usually involving physical models, to augment the existing engineering science. The aim of such research is not to generate new, universally applicable design methods, but to gain sufficient understanding of a particular situation to assist designers in solving a specific problem.

From the 1920s on, the techniques of scale model testing were developed in a wide range of research organizations, including universities, especially in the fields of aerodynamics and structural behavior. By the 1950s, model testing was an established method throughout the engineering research community, and it became increasingly available for building design engineers as the need arose, usually when a building design problem lay outside normal experience. There is no better example than
686, 681 the Sydney Opera House, begun in the late 1950s, to illustrate how physical scale models, in conjunction with theoretical analysis, can be used to deal with unprecedented engineering challenges.

The Danish architect Jørn Utzon (b. 1918) had conceived of a number of curved, triangular, thin concrete shells resembling the sails of a boat in Sydney Harbor and rising to a height of some 70 meters. Not only were they very large, but they were not like any previous form of concrete shell roof, being predominantly vertical in orientation and appearing to be supported mainly on just one corner. Because the shells were vertical, the wind loads were as significant as the gravity loads, and the space they enclosed created a very unusual shape for the auditoriums within.

These design challenges were not overcome easily or
682 quickly. Many different forms for the roof were studied over a period of five years. It was essential to find a way of creating the illusion of a thin shell, yet providing it with enough stiffness to resist the gravity and wind loads, and the appearance of standing on one corner. It also had to be possible to build. For the first time ever, many of the geometrical and structural design calculations for a major building were performed using a computer. A 1:60 scale model of an early version of the structure was tested at Southampton University in England to establish the bending moments and forces in the shell. They were 683
found to be much higher than had been anticipated, and it became clear that a thin shell as originally proposed by Utzon would not be possible. Two alternatives were considered: a steel frame covered with a concrete skin, and a concrete shell stiffened with corrugations. The latter was finally selected.

In conjunction with the structural model testing, another model of the building form was tested in a wind tunnel to establish the wind loads on the shell—both the positive pressures on the windward side of the building and the negative pressures, or suction, on the leeward side. Rotating the model allowed the experimenters to compare pressures created by wind coming from different directions. The 1:100 scale model of solid wood had a series of small tubes embedded in its surface leading from the points at which the air pressure was to be measured to manometers outside the wind tunnel. The suction pressures at some locations on the leeward side were found to be over three times the pressures on the windward side, and this information proved valuable in designing the fixings for the precast concrete "tiles" covering the surface of the roof. Another wind tunnel test involved 684
fixing telltales to the model to identify the points at which the airflow separated from the surface and might generate vortices or turbulent airflow.

At the same time that the external shell structures were being designed, the various auditoriums in the Opera House were also being designed. And, just as the design of shells represented a departure from familiar structural precedents, so too did the proposals for the large and small halls. Many designs were proposed, some reflecting the shape of the external shells, others not. The Danish acoustician Vilhelm Jordan (1909–82), a pioneer in the use of scale models in acoustic design, was appointed to advise on how to achieve satisfactory acoustics for the many different proposed uses, including concerts, opera, and oration. Since these different uses required different acoustical characteristics, one early plan was to provide a large movable ceiling that

681

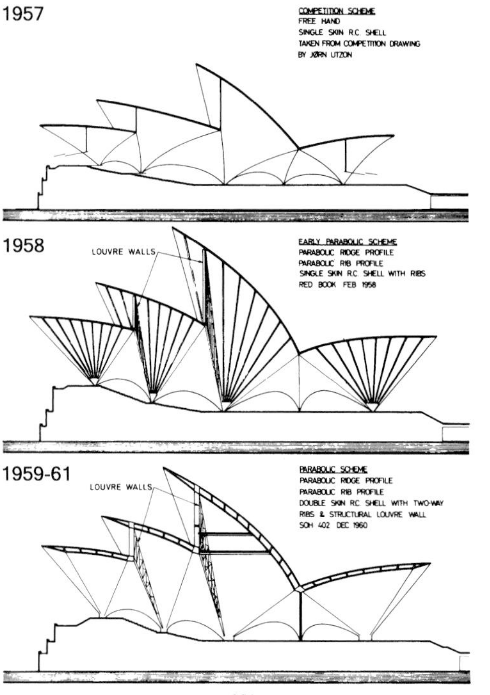
1957
COMPETITION SCHEME
FREE HAND
SINGLE SKIN R.C. SHELL
TAKEN FROM COMPETITION DRAWING
BY JØRN UTZON
1958
LOUVRE WALLS
EARLY PARABOLIC SCHEME
PARABOLIC RIDGE PROFILE
PARABOLIC RIB PROFILE
SINGLE SKIN R.C. SHELL WITH RIBS
RED BOOK FEB 1958
1959-61
LOUVRE WALLS
PARABOLIC SCHEME
PARABOLIC RIDGE PROFILE
PARABOLIC RIB PROFILE
DOUBLE SKIN R.C. SHELL WITH TWO-WAY
RIBS & STRUCTURAL LOUVRE WALL
SOH 402 DEC 1960

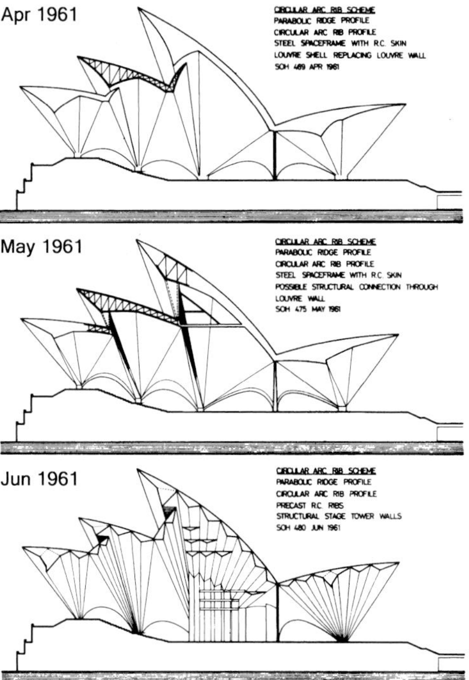
Apr 1961
CIRCULAR ARC RIB SCHEME
PARABOLIC RIDGE PROFILE
CIRCULAR ARC RIB PROFILE
STEEL SPACEFRAME WITH R.C. SKIN
LOUVRE SHELL REPLACING LOUVRE WALL
SOH 489 APR 1961
May 1961
CIRCULAR ARC RIB SCHEME
PARABOLIC RIDGE PROFILE
CIRCULAR ARC RIB PROFILE
STEEL SPACEFRAME WITH R.C. SKIN
POSSIBLE STRUCTURAL CONNECTION THROUGH
LOUVRE WALL
SOH 475 MAY 1961
Jun 1961
CIRCULAR ARC RIB SCHEME
PARABOLIC RIDGE PROFILE
CIRCULAR ARC RIB PROFILE
PRECAST R.C. RIBS
STRUCTURAL STAGE TOWER WALLS
SOH 480 JUN 1961

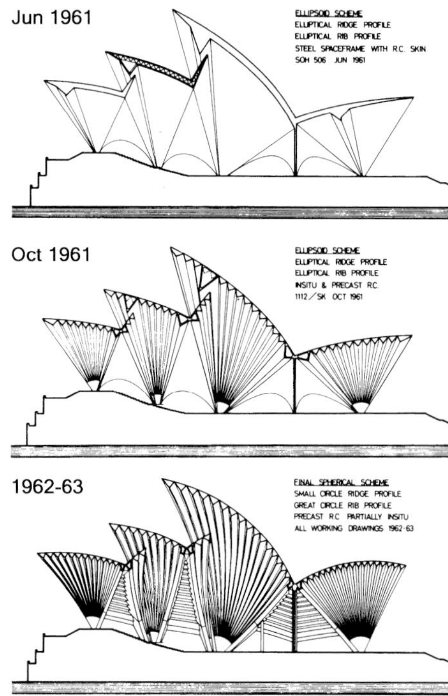
Jun 1961
ELLIPSOID SCHEME
ELLIPTICAL RIDGE PROFILE
ELLIPTICAL RIB PROFILE
STEEL SPACEFRAME WITH R.C. SKIN
SOH 506 JUN 1961
Oct 1961
ELLIPSOID SCHEME
ELLIPTICAL RIDGE PROFILE
ELLIPTICAL RIB PROFILE
INSITU & PRECAST R.C.
1112/SK OCT 1961
1962-63
FINAL SPHERICAL SCHEME
SMALL CIRCLE RIDGE PROFILE
GREAT CIRCLE RIB PROFILE
PRECAST R.C. PARTIALLY INSITU
ALL WORKING DRAWINGS 1962-63

682

683

684

685

686

could be adjusted to create different reverberation times. So radical were the proposals for the auditoriums, and so different from established forms, that Jordan advised it would be necessary to carry out tests of acoustics using scale models. Over five or six years, during which Utzon resigned and new architects were appointed, models of several different proposals for the two auditoriums were made at a scale of 1:10. Made of wood, they included
685 models of the audience members, with neoprene bodies and cardboard heads. The various model tests soon established that the curved form of the roof vaults was unsuitable for distributing the reflected sound to all parts of the two main auditoriums, and additional internal walls would have to be built. They also established that it would not be possible to create a room-acoustic that could serve the original idea of two multipurpose auditoriums; the compromise was made to design the two auditoriums to suit different purposes.

The model tests demonstrated the benefits of introducing flat side walls to the auditoriums to provide lateral reflections and reflective interiors to the boxes. It also showed that the original ceiling of the larger auditorium, consisting of large catenaries hung longitudinally from

681, 686 Sydney Opera House, 1957–73. Engineer: Ove Arup & Partners; architect: Jørn Utzon. Exterior and auditorium. 682 Sydney Opera House. Nine of many forms proposed for the main roof structure. 683, 684 Sydney Opera House. Scale model and wind tunnel model. 685 Sydney Opera House. Acoustician Vilhelm Jordan inside a scale model.

the external shell, left the orchestra seating suffering from a deficiency of early reflected sound, so that the musicians would have had difficulty in hearing what they were playing or singing. Adding suspended reflectors over the stage did not substantially change this situation, and it was decided to reduce the distance between the side walls and raise the auditorium ceiling by several meters. Many different shapes and positions of reflectors suspended above the orchestra were studied throughout design development; the final arrangement incorporated small toroidal discs (slightly convex on the underside) suspended from the ceiling by adjustable cables.

The acoustics of the finished auditoriums were finally assessed in a number of test performances with real orchestras and audiences. Microphones and tape recorders were used to record the decay of sound, both after firing a gun on stage (with a blank cartridge), and after getting the conductor to halt the orchestra abruptly while playing Beethoven at full power. The results of these tests were used to recalibrate the model tests and to identify a number of adjustments that could be made to the various movable reflectors to achieve the best acoustic results.

Jordan's work on the Sydney Opera House was a milestone in the development of the acoustical design of building and of the science of acoustics. His goal was to seek suitable criteria or parameters that could be used to define the acoustics of an auditorium. Since Wallace Sabine's work in the 1910s, it had become accepted that the key parameter—indeed, the only one—was the reverberation time. Increasingly, however, auditorium designers and musicians were beginning to realize that reverberation time was not the only factor that made some halls good for concerts and others bad. Other parameters needed to be identified, and ways to measure them had to be devised. Musicians and audiences use terms such as "warmth," "intimacy," "resonance," and "fullness of tone," and the challenge for acousticians is to establish what physical characteristics might influence such criteria. One criterion for speech, proposed in 1953, was named Deutlichkeit ("intelligibility"), which translated into the vocabulary of acoustics as "definition."[2] This was the proportion of the total sound energy that reached the listener within the first 50 milliseconds. For music, a criterion suggested by Jordan was "rise time"—the time it takes for the sound intensity to reach half its steady-state value. Another was "steepness"—the rate at which the energy arrives to the listener. Jordan also established that the people on stage need to hear sounds before the audience does in order to keep accurate musical time. To capture this property of an auditorium, Jordan proposed the "inversion index"—the ratio of the rise time measured in the auditorium to the rise time measured on the stage. Another parameter Jordan proposed was the "early decay time," or the rate at which the sound intensity decays during the first few milliseconds, rather than later, when the sound has reached every part of the auditorium. The measurement of such factors became possible only with the development of electronic equipment and tape recorders that were first developed in the 1950s.

In the 1960s, other researchers proposed such curiously named criteria such as "hall-mass," "point of gravity time," and "index of room impression." As is the case today, different acousticians preferred their own approaches to defining acoustic performance and how to design auditoriums to create the right conditions for different uses. In the end, acoustical quality is judged by humans rather than measuring instruments, meaning that some subjectivity remains inevitable.

Form-Finding Models

At around the same time that models were being used so effectively to help meet the design challengees of the Sydney Opera House, the German architect Frei Otto (b. 1925) was developing their use as an integral part of the process of designing cable-net or membrane structures. Unlike traditional circus tents, this entirely new type of tensile structure is doubly curved and highly prestressed to prevent the membrane or steel cables from deflecting excessively under snow or wind load, and from vibrating or flapping in a wind.

The challenge facing the designers of tensile structures arises because the forces, stresses, and deflections can only be calculated if the geometry of the structure is known and can be expressed by mathematical equations. However, the geometric form of tensile structures is determined by the magnitude of the forces in the cables, the stresses in the membrane, the stiffnesses of the cables and membranes of which the structures are made,

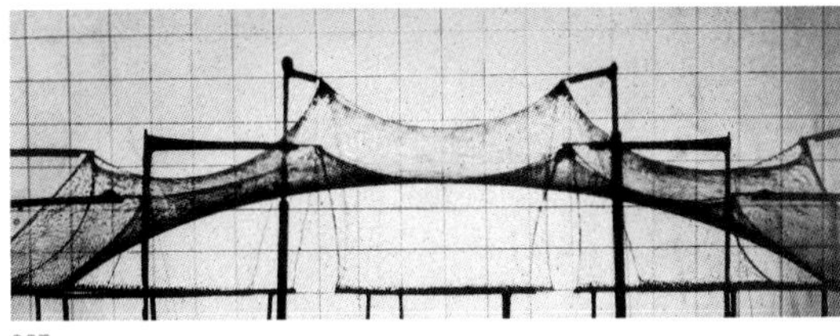
687

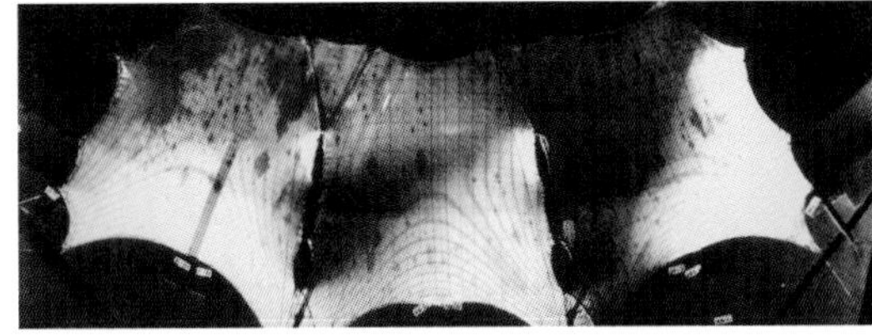
688

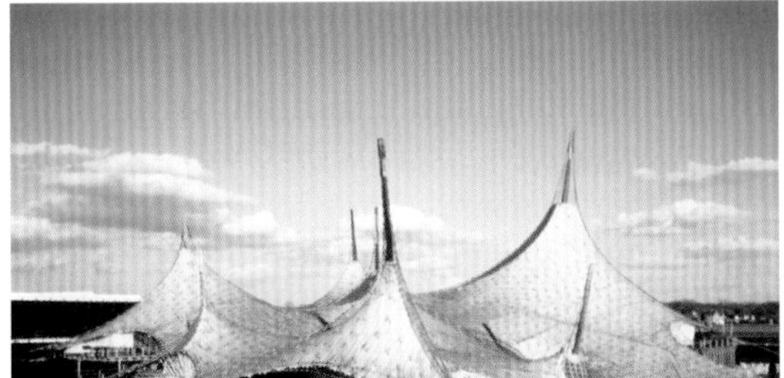
689

690

and the way the doubly-curved membrane is fabricated by sewing together flat panels of material. Together, these constraints led both to surfaces that could not be defined by mathematical equations, and to a vicious circle between forces and geometry that could only be solved by a very large number of complex, iterative calculations—far too complex for the computers available in the 1960s and 1970s.

Otto's resolution of this impasse was to use models, for which he developed an entirely new design and manufacturing process. He was thus able to generate forms that were, quite literally, inconceivable in mathematical terms. During the following thirty years or so Otto continued to develop his form-finding methods using models, both for membranes and cable-net roofs. The main challenge he faced was the need to develop a technique of making and testing models that would be appropriate representations of the materials to be used in a full-size structure. The tests had to generate precise data about the form, stresses, and forces in full-size structures that gave sufficient confidence to the contractors' engineers to build them. He achieved this by conducting tests with three types of material: a variety of inelastic chains, nets, and fabrics from which to make models whose geometry was governed only by statical considerations; various elastic sheets; and the purely plastic material that forms a soap film (the surface stress in a bubble is independent of its size). No single one of these model materials was found to be an adequate representation of materials in full-size structures, and so models of all three types often had to used.

The soap film models presented the greatest technical 687
challenge. No one had ever made bubbles up to a meter across that would last long enough to be studied and measured. Fresh soap solution had to be fed continuously into the bubble film itself to compensate for the evaporation losses. A second challenge involved devising ways of surveying the dimensions and form of the models precisely enough that, after scaling up the measurements by perhaps a hundred times, they would be

687 A soap film model, about 1 meter across, used to establish the natural form of a membrane structure. 688 Olympic Stadium, Munich, Germany, 1972. Engineer: Leonhardt, Andrä and Partners; architect: Günther Behnisch with Frei Otto (architect of canopy). Fabric model used to find the form. 689 German Pavilion at Expo '67, Montreal, Quebec, 1965–67. Architects: Frei Otto and Rolf Gutbrod. 690 Olympic Stadium, Munich.

sufficiently accurate to satisfy the requirements of the fabric and cable manufacturers. A number of different techniques were developed. Models made from chains and nets were not too difficult, and could be surveyed
688 using a theodolite. For fabrics and elastic sheets, a regular grid was drawn on the surface to provide a series of points whose position could be surveyed. Soap bubbles presented the greatest difficulty. Their profile could be measured by projecting a shadow of the bubble onto a screen on which a grid had been drawn. To reveal the form of the bubble in plan view, a grid of parallel lines was projected onto the surface of the bubble from the side, and photographed from above. The form of the bubble was thus revealed just as contour lines reveal hilly terrain on a map. Finally, it was necessary to establish the best cutting patterns for the individual pieces of material that would need to be sewn together to make the membrane in the full-size structure. For this process, it was sometimes found to be easier to make a solid plaster cast of the forms created with models made from fabric or elastic sheet than to use the flexible models themselves.

In one sense the forms developed for tensile structures using models were accepted as reliable simply because the model structure had been shown to work—the geometry of the shape is governed by the statics and elasticity of the materials of which the model is made and is independent of scale. The forces in the model generated the final form just as they would in the full-size prototype. There remained, however, the not inconsiderable problem of scaling the anticipated loads and elastic properties of the materials between the model structure and the full-size version, and vice versa. The reliability of this process had to be established by making and testing a number of trial structures, spanning only a few meters, before using the process to scale up the design to the scale of the full-size structure. Throughout Otto's career, as part of the work of his Institute of Lightweight Structures at Stuttgart University, he used the data he gathered when designing every structure he built to improve the reliability of the design procedures for new structures.

Otto's designs progressed rapidly from spans of a few meters to the 40-meter cable-net roof of the German
689 Pavilion at Expo '67 in Montreal and the 135-metre cable-
690 net roof over the stadium at the 1972 Munich Olympics.
The complex forms of these roofs were developed by using results obtained from the initial mathematical analysis to make the first physical model, and using the results for the physical model in more accurate mathematical calculations, then repeating this cycle several times. Using the interchange of data between physical and mathematical models, Otto had created a new class of structures that had become possible only by developing an entirely new type of design procedure which overcame the limitations inherent in previous, wholly analytical design methods. They could, quite literally, not have been designed a decade earlier.

Frei Otto's model studies were not restricted to tensile structures. He and his research teams looked at every possible form of structure. His particular fascination, however, was with forms generated in nature, whether bubbles or the branches of trees or flowers or animal bones and skeletons. The natural world was an inspiration for Otto, as well as a source of fundamental truths. He was able to exploit one of these fundamental truths in devising a building to house a garden festival in
Mannheim in 1975. He drew on the principle first noted 691
by Robert Hooke in the 1650s: the equilibrium shape of an arch formed by a number of stones is the same, but inverted, as the equilibrium shape taken up by the same
masses suspended as a hanging chain. In the 1890s, 692
Antonio Gaudí too had used this principle, in three dimensions rather than two, to generate a form for the nave of his Sagrada Familia Cathedral in Barcelona. Otto and his team used several crude hanging chain models to establish an approximate form for the building before making the final model, at 1:100 scale, which was then used to generate the precise geometry for the timber grid shell. There was, however, a complication with a compression structure that tensile structures do not suffer—possible collapse by buckling, either of individual timber elements or of the grid shell as a whole, especially where it had little two-dimensional curvature. The huge span of the building (about 80 by 60 meters) and the extreme delicacy of the timber sections (a single orthogonal grid of laths of western hemlock, just 50 mm square, at 300 mm centers) meant that either mode of structural failure was entirely possible. To ensure that neither would occur, a computer analysis of the structure was undertaken by the engineers at Arup's firm. The computer model of the roof was simplified by assuming the laths were spaced at 900mm centers (rather than 300mm, as

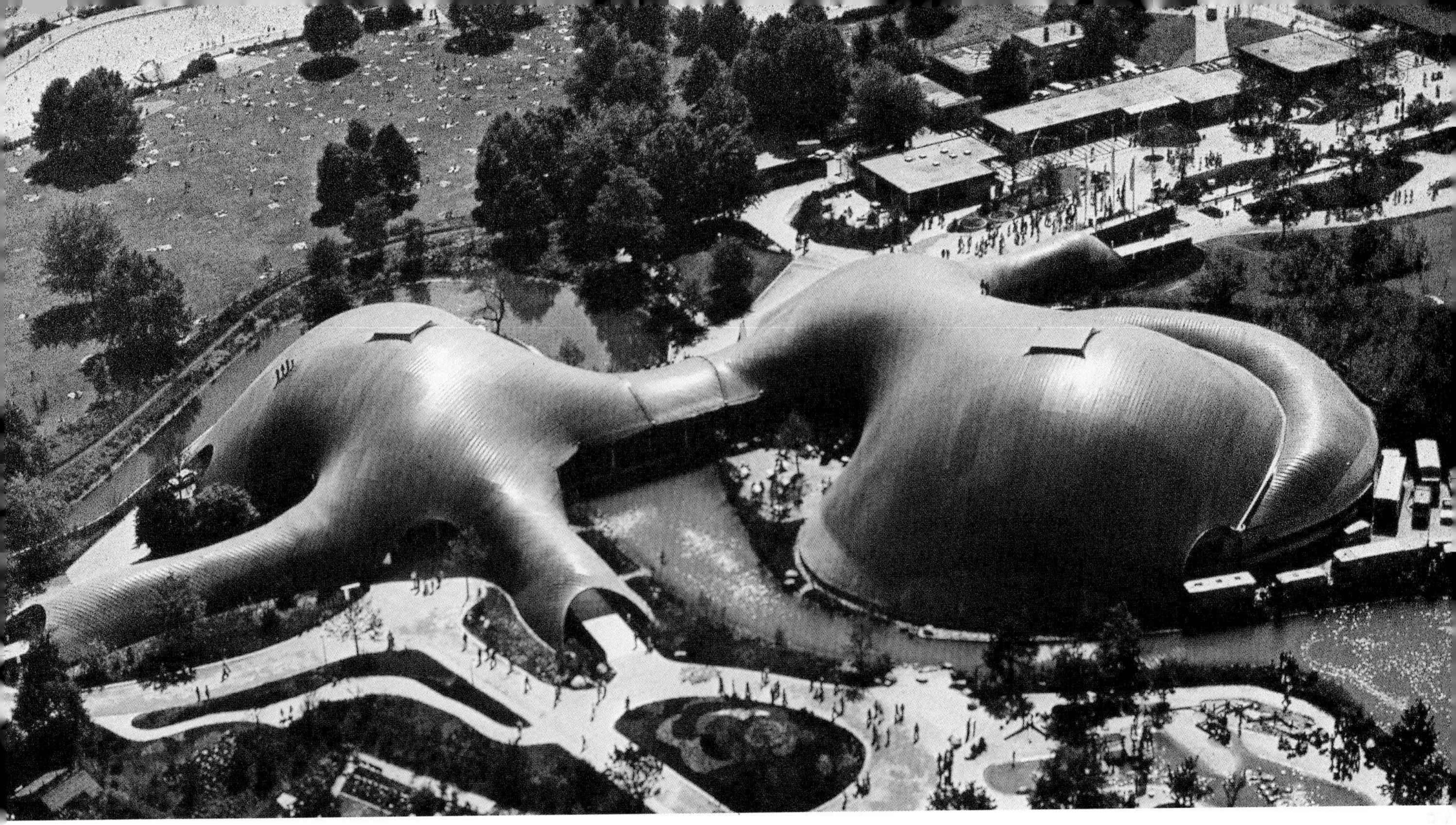

691

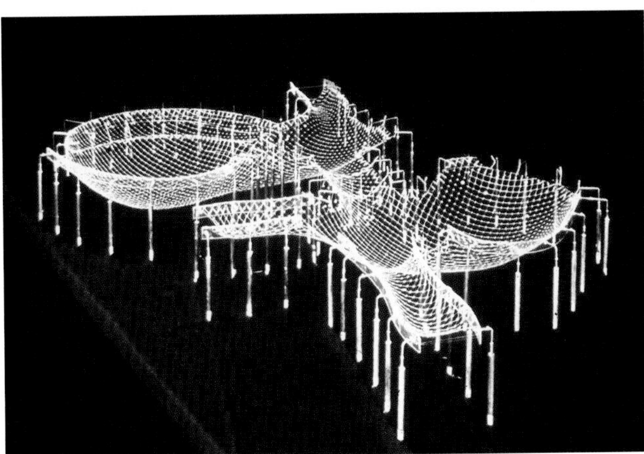

692

691 Exhibition building for the Garden Festival, Mannheim, Germany, 1975. Engineers: Ove Arup & Partners with Frei Otto; architect: Carlfried Mutschler and Partners. 692 Garden Festival building. Hanging chain model used to find the form for the timber grid shell.

693

694

695

696

693 Exhibition building for the Garden Festival, Mannheim, Germany, 1975. Engineers: Ove Arup & Partners with Frei Otto; architect: Carlfried Mutschler and Partners. Interior of main hall. 694 Standard sections of timber formwork used to make a concrete shell. Engineer: Heinz Isler, Switzerland, c. 1975. 695 Form-finding for a concrete shell vault using a hanging membrane. Engineer: Heinz Isler, Switzerland, c. 1975. 696 Garden Festival building, Mannheim, Germany, 1975. Detail showing laths of western hemlock and structure for controlling forces in the free edge. 697 Concrete shell roof of a garden center near Paris, France. Engineer, Heinz Isler, c. 1985.

697

built), thus reducing by nine the number of nodes that had to be calculated. The analysis revealed the likelihood that the shell would indeed buckle in some places, and it was decided to increase its resistance to buckling by using two orthogonal grids of laths. Despite the thicker grid shell, the building is surely one of the boldest structures ever constructed and, though originally in-
693, 696 tended as a temporary building, is still in use.

The Swiss engineer Heinz Isler (b. 1926) has also used the geometric similarity between hanging structures and dome or shell structures. For many years after the heyday of concrete shells in the 1950s, he has continued to produce concrete shell roofs using an elegant design procedure similar to that used by Otto at Mannheim. He first establishes a suitable plan for the roof, then uses a hanging fabric model to generate the statically-correct geometry, which he then measures and scales up to generate the dimensions of the finished shell of reinforced concrete. To ensure that the model retains its geometry while being measured, the fabric is soaked in a liquid plaster, which hardens. Another technique Isler has used
is to hang wet fabric outdoors and allow it to freeze 695
overnight. There is, of course, more to it than that. Calculations are also necessary to ensure the shell will not buckle. In addition, Isler and his contractor have devised an economical method of construction that uses a 694, 697
formwork system to support the dome, while it is cast, that can be dismantled and reused again and again for shells of different shapes and sizes.

By the early 1980s, the speed of computers had increased sufficiently for complex iterative calculations to become feasible. This opened up a new way to design the shapes of tensile membrane structures. The designer first inputs the approximate surface geometry of a membrane, its support conditions, and the elastic properties of the membrane material. The computer then analyzes the structure and finds the equilibrium form, if there is one, for the given input conditions. If this form is not what the designer wanted, the input conditions can be altered and the new equilibrium shape calculated. This highly interactive approach to form-finding effectively gives the designer the feeling of experimenting with a physical model

698

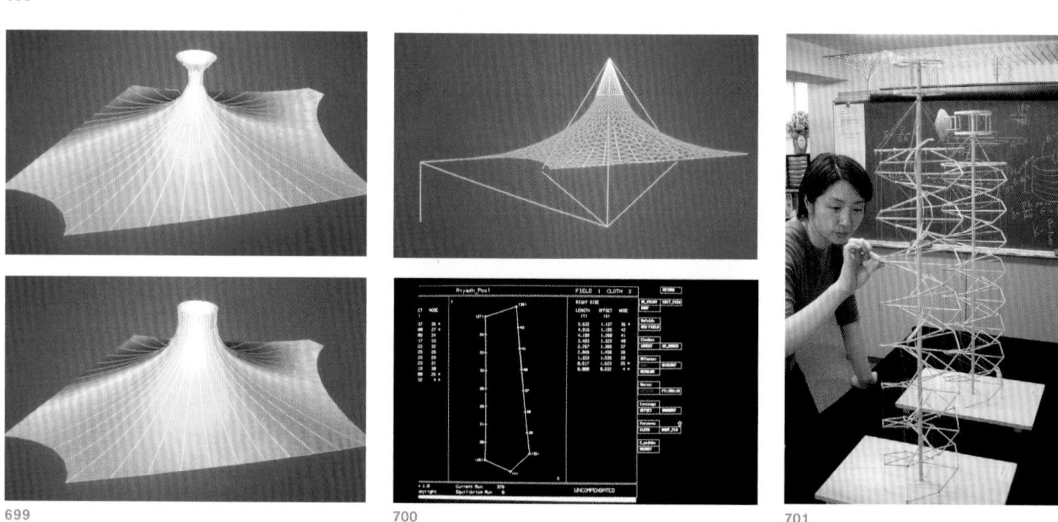

699 700 701

698 Don Valley Stadium, Sheffield, England, 1990. Engineer: Anthony Hunt Associates; membrane form finding: Mike Barnes; architect: Sheffield Design and Build Services. 699 Don Valley Stadium. Computer-generated form-finding model: (top) unsuitable form with radius of upper aperture too small; (bottom) suitable form. 700 Don Valley Stadium. Computer-generated cutting pattern: (top) for the whole membrane; (bottom) for a single panel of the membrane fabric. 701 Genome Tower, Hyogo, Japan, 2001. Engineer: Mamoru Kawaguchi. 1:25 scale model used to establish the least visually intrusive way of stiffening of the tower's double-helix structure.

in the real world. Not only do such programs find the equilibrium form, they can compute the stresses in the membrane. This allows identification of areas that are overstressed, understressed, or unstressed in one direction, leading the membrane to wrinkle. Finally, the computer is able to calculate the most suitable cutting patterns that the membrane manufacturer needs to build up the curved surfaces from a series of flat pieces of fabric, and to calculate precisely the lengths of the steel ca-
698, 699 bles used to reinforce the edges of the membrane. With
700 the ability to see the results immediately on a computer screen, the interactive design process has finally come to mirror the method devised by Otto using physical models.

Despite the sophistication of engineering analysis using computer models today, physical models are still widely used when buildings are designed. The Japanese engineer Mamoru Kawaguchi (b. 1932) is one of many designers of innovative structures who regularly uses models. After proposing a double helix of tubular steel for the design of the Genome Tower in Hyogo, Japan
701 (2001), he and his colleagues built several scale models to assess, by feel, the least visually intrusive way to provide the strength and stiffness needed to resist winds and earthquake loads. Once a suitable arrangement had been chosen, the sizes and structural behavior were confirmed using a computer model. Kawaguchi used models to great advantage in developing and perfecting his
702, 703 Pantadome system, a method of constructing wide-span
704 roofs by building them at ground level and raising them by jacking up the central portion. The models help ensure that structural stability is maintained throughout the erection process and that the structure can withstand the forces created during the lifting process; they also confirm that every part of the hinged mechanism can move freely, without interference from other parts of the structure.

Physical scale models are also used to help understand the flow of air in and around buildings. They can serve a number of purposes: to make airflow visible, to make quantitative measurements of air pressure and speed, to model turbulent flow that cannot be reliably modeled using computers, and to calibrate computer simulation models by providing a "reality check" on the output of computer software. Scale models can also still provide a cheaper alternative to conducting full-size tests. In the case of the spread of smoke and fire throughout a building, they can replace tests that would be unpleasant or even dangerous to conduct at full scale. By using suitable nondimensional constants it is possible to establish the appropriate size of scaled-down fire to use, and to scale up the test results to full scale to predict, for example the time that would be available to evacuate a building should a fire break out, and the different speeds that hot gases spread depending on the location of the fire.

The natural ventilation of buildings has been a subject of growing interest during the late twentieth century, and model tests can be used to study the slow speed airflow that is driven by warm (low density) air rising in the atriums of buildings, usually in a highly turbulent way. Since it is difficult to track the movement of air, the use of an analog model is particularly useful. The warm and cool air can be modeled by, respectively, saline water and pure water, which have different densities. The saline water is dyed to make it visible, and the whole test conducted upside down so that the high-density saline water falls through the pure water in the same way that the warm air rises through cooler air. Apart from making the process visible, measurements of the flow rates can be scaled up
using nondimensional constants to predict the ventilation 705
rates that would be achieved in the full-size building.

The effects of wind on buildings can be particularly significant, and scale models can be used to study many effects that cannot be studied in full-scale tests. For example, during the design of the tensile membrane roof for the new Jeppesen Terminal at Denver International Airport, Colorado, in 1992, it was necessary to study how snow might collect in the valleys of the roof. As snow would be difficult to handle in a laboratory, an analog model was used in which the air was replaced by water
and the snow by grains of sand. In other building projects, 706
similar tests have been carried out using sawdust in a wind tunnel.

Wind tunnel testing has progressed considerably since the early 1960s, when only the wind pressures on the building were studied (for example, in the design of the Sydney Opera House). These earlier studies ignored two important issues: the variation of wind speed with height above the ground, and the effects of a building on the wind conditions around the base of the building and in its

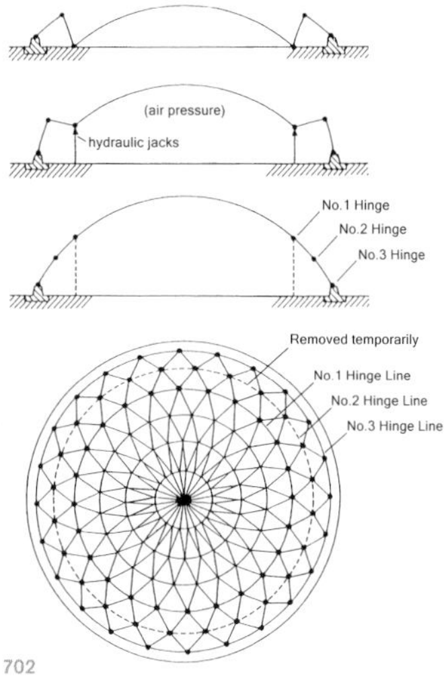

(air pressure)
hydraulic jacks
No.1 Hinge
No.2 Hinge
No.3 Hinge
Removed temporarily
No.1 Hinge Line
No.2 Hinge Line
No.3 Hinge Line

702

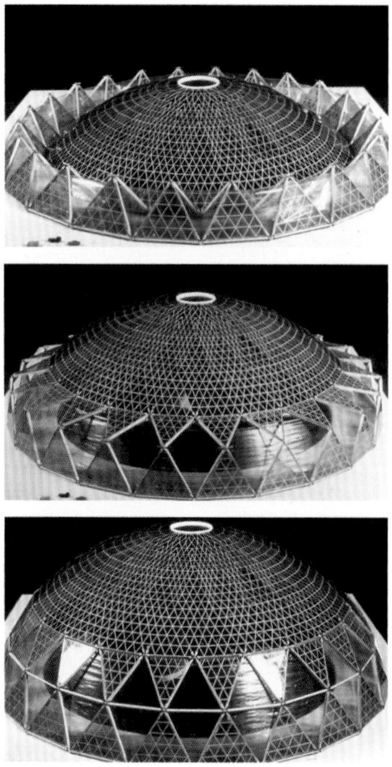

703

704

nearby vicinity, where pedestrians would be affected. Since the mid-1960s the designers of large or tall buildings have been able to get useful data from what are known as "boundary layer wind tunnels," the first and
707 best known of which was set up in 1965 in London, Ontario, Canada, by the Englishman Alan G. Davenport (b. 1932). In these wind tunnels, the variation of wind speed in the boundary layer is addressed, and buildings are studied in the context of adjacent buildings and geographical features such as hills and valleys. Many effects of wind on structures, and of buildings on their local microclimate, can now be studied, both qualitatively and quantitatively: the force of the wind; the pressures on the building envelope, which can be negative and cause windows to be sucked out of their supporting frames; the tendency for vortices to be shed from the edges of buildings, which can cause the building to sway; the discomfort to pedestrians at ground level caused by downdrafts from tall buildings; the effect of nearby hills, cliffs, or valleys on winds that impinge on buildings; and the acceleration of wind speeds as air squeezes through narrow gaps between adjacent buildings.

The field of architectural acoustics is another area in which model testing is still an essential part of the process of designing large theaters and concert halls. Techniques have come a long way since the pioneering work of Vilhelm Jordan and others in the 1940s and 1950s. Ultra small microphones, little larger than a pin head, are now available and can be used to study the

705

706

707

708

sound conditions in a 1:10 scale model seat-by-seat
708 through an entire auditorium. The scale effects of acoustic models mean that the frequencies of the sound in a 1:10 scale model must be ten times higher than in the full-size auditorium. This was impossible to capture with the sound recording equipment available in the 1960s; today it can be recorded and stored in digital form, and can be analyzed in minute detail using a computer. Using nondimensional constants to analyze the model test results, quantitative predictions of the reverberation times of an auditorium can be made for different sound frequencies, as well as the many other quantitative measures of the acoustic performance of auditoriums. The acoustic disasters that were not uncommon in the nineteenth and early twentieth centuries are unlikely to be repeated today. It is also somehow comforting to know that, despite the sophistication of today's computerized measuring techniques, simple technologies still have a place. The quickest way to measure the all-important volume of a model auditorium, for example, is to fill it with small polystyrene balls, decant them into a rectangular wooden box, and then measure their volume.

Finally, it should not be imagined that full-size testing has been entirely replaced by the testing of scale models. All models involve approximations and simplifications, and there are many occasions when engineers want the assurance that comes only through testing the real thing, so to speak. In 2004, an earthquake research laboratory in Japan constructed a shaking table capable of testing a full-size seven-story building. The 20- by 15-meter platform can be moved by up to a meter in any direction to simulate the movement of the ground in a major earthquake. During the late 1990s the Building Research

702 Diagram of Mamoru Kawaguchi's Pantadome system. 703 1:100 scale model used to test the Pantadome system. 704 World Memorial Hall, Kobe City, Japan, 1984. 120 meters by 70 meters. Engineer (Pantadome system): Mamoru Kawaguchi; architect: Syowa Sekkei. Erection of the dome. 705 Model test used to simulate the flow of warm air through the atrium of a building. 706 Jeppesen Airport, Denver, Colorado, 1994. Engineer: Horst Berger. Model used to simulate build-up of snow on the roof. 707 Boundary Layer Wind Tunnel, University of Western Ontario, London, Canada. 708 Bridgewater Hall, Manchester, England, 1996. Acoustic engineer: Ove Arup & Partners. Acoustic scale model.

709

710

709 Establishment in England constructed a new test facility
710 for studying the effects of real fires in real buildings. Tests were undertaken on steel-frame and concrete-frame buildings seven stories high. Full-scale tests were also undertaken during the development of a cast steel
711, 712 connector used in the large and complex roof truss in a new factory for the l'Oréal cosmetics company near Paris. The roof had to span up to 60 meters to create an entirely column-free space, and its weight was reduced to a minimum by interweaving different structural systems to carry the gravity loads and the uplift loads due to the wind. The resulting structure was highly complex. Each of the hundred and fifty or so connectors, or nodes, in the truss would be subject to different loading conditions according to its position in the structure, the number of links to adjacent nodes (up to twelve), and the magnitude of the positive and negative wind pressures. It was decided to use a single basic design for all the nodes, and considerable effort went into designing the 850-millimeter long steel casting to ensure it would be able to perform its many different duties satisfactorily. The design engineer and the contractor felt that a computer model alone would not provide them with the confidence they needed, given the complex geometry of the node and the interaction between the cast steel node and the mild steel inserts to which some structural members were attached. A test rig was built to simulate the different loading conditions, and a trial casting was manufactured. Strain gauges were used to measure the surface strains in the steel and confirm that the theoretical calculations were reliable. Following the tests, several minor adjustments were made to the geometry of the node, enabling
the thickness of the hollow casting, and hence its weight 713
and cost, to be reduced.

Innovations in Structural Engineering since the 1950s

The last half century has seen some incredible achievements in structural engineering, and many of these were the products of great imagination and innovation. They need to be seen, however, in the context of what is considered not to be innovative. By the late 1950s there had developed a well-defined demarcation in building design methods between those used for mainstream or "standard" buildings, so to speak, and those that were

711

712

713

709 A test facility built in a disused airship hangar at Cardington, England, for studying the effects of fire on full-size buildings, 1990s. 710 Fire test facility, Cardington. Post-fire test photograph. 711 L'Oréal factory, near Paris, 1992. Engineer: Ove Arup & Partners; architect: Valode et Pistres et Associées. Roof truss spanning around 60 meters, with steel nodes connecting up to twelve ties or struts. 712 L'Oréal factory. 713 L'Oréal factory. One of the hollow cast steel nodes awaiting finishing.

somehow unusual or especially innovative. For the former—which included some of the tallest skyscrapers in the United States—standard design methods had become well established. During the first decade or two of the twentieth century, most countries developed their own codes of design practice for conventional buildings made of steel or reinforced concrete. Utilizing the collective experience of designers, the engineering research community, materials manufacturers, and building contractors, they contained a combination of the latest engineering science and empirical constants and factors of safety used to modify idealized formulas when calculating, for example, the buckling strength of a column. While not prescribing exactly how to calculate various stresses and bending moments (this would be covered in textbooks on structural analysis), they gave guidance based on the results of authoritative testing and other information not easy to derive from the first principles of engineering science. They specified, for example, the height of a building above which wind loads should be taken into account; the thickness of concrete cover needed to protect reinforcement from corrosion and fire; and the best configuration of bolts for achieving the required strength and stiffness in a bolted steelwork connection.

Design codes for nonstructural aspects of building design, such as heating, air-conditioning, acoustics, and lighting, were also developed, although these were generally less prescriptive because the consequences of a failure were seldom a threat to people's health or life. Building designers were advised to achieve certain levels of performance that were agreed to be satisfactory in different areas—room temperature, humidity, reverberation time, lighting level, and so on. Issues of safety regarding electricity, gas, and appliances were and are generally dealt with by contractors rather than building designers.

In many ways, modern design codes of practice are the descendants of the Code of Hammurabi (see chapter 1, pp. 13–14), the design procedures described by Vitruvius, and those used by the designers of medieval cathedrals. From a historical point of view, such design codes serve as an indicator of the maturity or sophistication of a society or even of an entire civilization. They reflect important cultural factors, such as what a society and its engineers—at a given time, in a given place—consider to be "satisfactory performance." They also reflect what is considered a satisfactory degree of confidence in a proposed design and the means by which this confidence is created by the design engineer, as well as the level of engineering education and experience assumed that the users of the design code will have. Being produced by leading members of each profession and given a government's stamp of authority, design codes represent a distillation of engineers' collective experience in a certain field. They are intended to ensure that, by using them, any competent engineer will be able to arrive at a satisfactory design and to achieve the level of confidence in a proposed design that society considers acceptable.

In parallel with the development of design codes and regulations over the last century, there have also appeared countless textbooks in every major language encapsulating the engineering knowledge needed to develop design codes. By the 1960s many thousands of universities were producing well-trained graduates in every building engineering discipline. The engineering design of standard buildings could now be undertaken by any competent firm of engineers, in nearly every country in the world.

It is a remarkable reflection of the cumulative nature of engineering experience, and the ease with which so much engineering knowledge is now communicated and learned, that so many extraordinary structures built during the last fifty years were considered standard, or mainstream. Yet to say that a building is "mainstream" does not mean that it is simply a copy of an earlier building. Such was the power of engineers' design methods, and the level of understanding of the behavior of buildings, that a considerable degree of innovation could be introduced without any significant increase in the risk of failure. Even buildings as remarkable as the John Hancock Center and the Sears Tower in Chicago, and the Houston Astrodome, which had no precedents, were designed, more or less, as mainstream buildings. The designers used well-understood engineering science and the design tools available at the time. In cases in which an issue was identified that needed some additional confirmation—such as the stiffness of the roof of the Houston Astrodome—a model test was undertaken. Generally, however, the engineering principles involved were all tried and tested. And yet the resulting buildings—and many thousands of others that could have been cited as examples—appear

714

to be very different from their predecessors and peers, both in overall design scheme and in detail.

What, then, is the nature of the engineering innovation in so-called "mainstream buildings"? Generally, it consists in achieving the same overall results as those achieved in the past, but using less materials, or achieving greater size and complexity at minimal extra cost. The creativity and innovation involved in obtaining such results lie in combining "old" ideas in a new way—just as Haydn's creativity lay in the novel way he arranged and combined known musical notes using the same instruments that were available to every other composer of his day. Such creativity is often of the type that, with hindsight, appears only too obvious. This is the point of the story of Brunelleschi and the egg, recounted in the introduction to this book.

Fire Engineering

Some engineering innovation may not be visible to the naked eye or form the basis of an architectural style, but may nevertheless have a profound effect on building design. One such strand of development in building engineering during the last half century has been the way buildings are designed to resist fire, and the outcome has been the creation of a new engineering discipline—fire, or fire safety, engineering.

By the end of the nineteenth century it was realized that merely replacing timber in buildings by iron or steel did not achieve the goal of fireproof construction. Iron and steel are both weakened to the point of becoming structurally inadequate when heated above about 550C. Such temperatures are reached quickly in most fires, and it was realized that the only safe solution is to ensure that

714 Edith Farnsworth House, Plano, Illinois, 1946–51. Architect: Ludwig Mies van der Rohe.

the metal is protected from the source of heat. Columns were often encased by ceramic tiles, brick, or blockwork. From the early 1900s they could also be encased with plaster applied to sheets of "expanded metal" that provide an excellent key for the plaster. Beams made of steel were usually encased partially or wholly in concrete or were protected by the hollow pre-cast concrete elements of the floor structure.

During the interwar period, fireboard products such as plasterboard began to replace the wet-trade construction, but these introduced a new problem. Boxing in the columns and beams created air gaps between the fire protection and the steel that could allow hot gases to flow through the building and contribute to the spread of fire. This problem was the principal motivation behind the development of spray-on fireproofing products in the mid-1950s, and this in turn led to an important innovation in floor construction. For the first time it was possible to apply fire protection to floors by using profiled steel decking with a concrete topping. Corrugated steel sheeting and concrete were first used in floors in the United States in about 1890, but the thin layer of concrete acted only as a hard-wearing surface and vibration damper. Such flooring elements were not allowed in high-rise buildings because of their vulnerability in a fire. When metal decking floors were introduced in the United States in the mid-1950s, after the development of spray-on fire protection, the concrete layer was made thick enough to act compositely with the steel decking. Although it had long been realized that steel and concrete in floor structures could provide composite action, only in the 1950s were engineers allowed to rely on it in their design calculations. This resulted in a considerable savings in both weight and money, even with the cost of fire spray included.

The problem with all these methods of fire protection was that the steel had to be hidden from view. Two solutions emerged. The first relied on the application of intumescent, or fire-retardant, paint, which was developed during the 1970s. In a fire, intumescent paints blister and bake hard, entrapping air bubbles to form an insulating layer that reduces the rate at which the structural steelwork heats up. Fire-retardant coatings are used only on large structural members (not metal decking) because they rely for their effectiveness on the large metal section to conduct the heat away. They can also, of course, be applied to the metal structure of existing buildings, and this has proved very useful to those engaged in conserving exposed cast and wrought iron in old buildings. However, intumescent coatings are a relatively expensive solution.

The other solution—a more radical one—was originally driven by the desire of a few bold architects, Mies van der Rohe in particular, to show off structural steelwork in their architecture. The solution, put simply, was to design the structural elements to continue to function safely in a fire. Changing the views of the regulatory authorities, however, took some thirty years.

The scientific study of fires and their consequences had begun around the turn of the century, when experimenters began testing various materials and structural forms in controlled fires. By the 1930s most countries had established fire research institutes. Such experimentation helped establish the temperatures experienced in real fires, and the time it takes for different structural elements to heat up. The result, by the early 1950s, was that regulatory agencies began to require that different building elements be given a "fire rating"—a time for which the element must survive a hypothetical "standard fire," typically between half an hour and two hours. Fire ratings were empirical figures, based on conservative estimates, and they depended on where the element was in the building, the building's size, and its likely occupancy.

This approach, however, based on a notional time to evacuate buildings, seemed to fly in the face of common sense in some cases, such as for buildings that could be evacuated in just a few minutes, or for cases when structural steel was on the outside of a building and would never be subject to the full effects of a fire inside the building. This was the argument put forward by Mies van der Rohe when designing his Farnsworth House in the 714
mid-1940s by reducing rooms to their essence—a series of steel-framed boxes. Although the house probably did not violate building regulations, he anticipated objection to the use of exposed steel and put forward an argument to justify why fire protection would not be needed: it was effectively outside the building, and would be adequately protected from an internal fire by the external wall. He advanced the same argument a few years later when designing Crown Hall, at the Illinois Institute of Technology, 715
Chicago, and managed to convince the regulatory

715

715 S. R. Crown Hall, Illinois Institute of Technology, Chicago, 1950–56. Architect: Ludwig Mies van der Rohe.

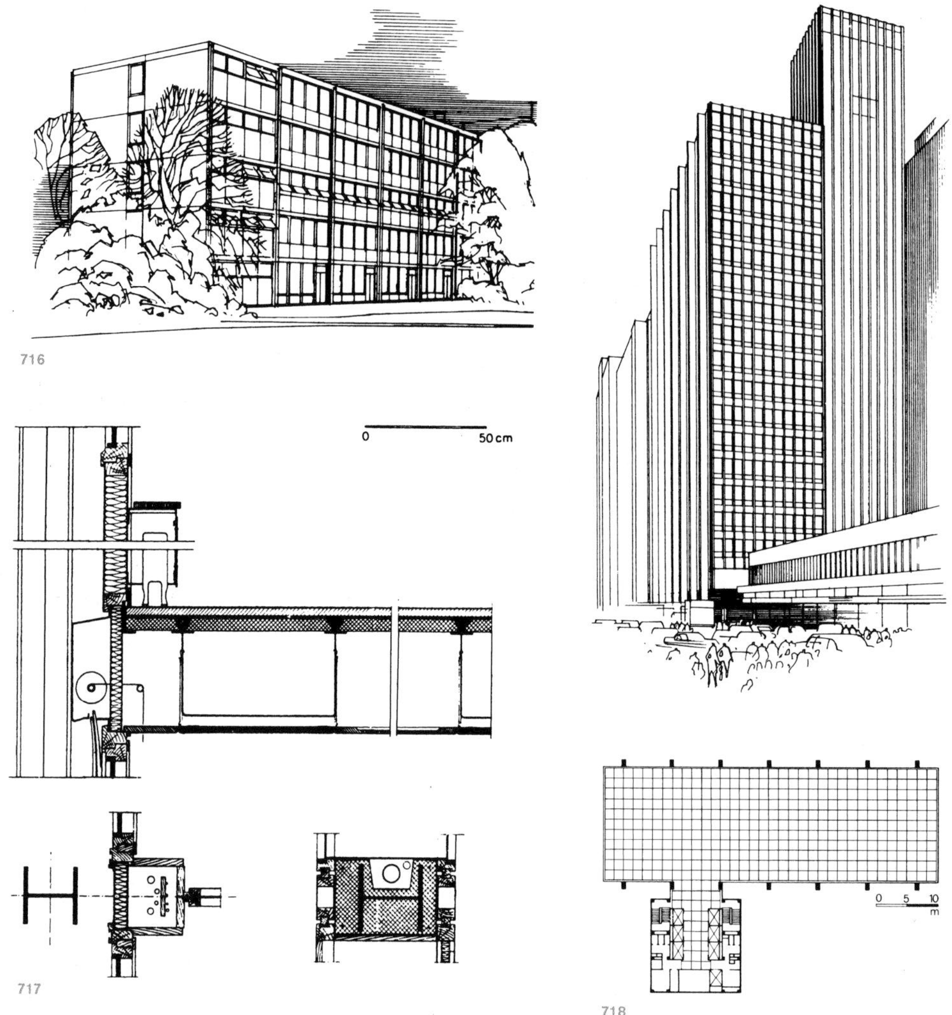

authorities of the robustness of his argument. A precedent had been set, although initially the approach was accepted for only a limited range of building types.

One of the earliest multistory buildings with exposed columns of steel without fire protection was a five-story administrative building designed and built by the German
716 engineering firm MAN for its own use. The external
717 columns were 150 mm clear of the facade, through which the floor beams passed. Permission to construct the building was granted only after exhaustive testing to verify the predicted performance in a fire.

At about the same time, the Chicago-based firm Skidmore, Owings & Merrill (SOM) was designing a nineteen-story building for Inland Steel. This building, which 718
opened in 1957, firmly established the use of steel without fire protection, and became an icon in the history of

716 Office building for MAN, Gustavsburg, Germany, 1955. Engineer: MAN. 717 Office building for MAN. Drawings of the exposed steel columns with no fire protection. 718 Inland Steel building, Chicago, Illinois, 1955–57. Engineer and architect: Skidmore, Owings & Merrill. Exposed steel structure. 719 John Deere building, Moline, Illinois, 1962–64. Architect: Eero Saarinen.

719

fire engineering. It was also constructed almost entirely using welded connections rather than rivets or bolts. In the Inland Steel Building, like the MAN Building, the columns are located outside the glass curtain walls, creating a 23.5 meter-deep column-free interior space.

The use of exposed steelwork and the fire engineering approach to design was further advanced by the development of corrosion-resistant steels. The problem with putting structural steelwork on view was that this also exposed the steel to the elements. From a financial point of view, the money saved by not having to protect the steel against fire now had to be spent on protecting it against corrosion. The steel industry responded by developing corrosion-resistant steels. Probably the best known of these is COR-TEN, which was developed in the United States. Containing about 2 percent copper and chromium, COR-TEN is much cheaper than stainless steel and, over time, forms a protective layer of oxides that is an attractive purple-brown. The first major structure to use COR-TEN was a nineteen-story building
719 for the John Deere company, designed by Eero Saarinen in 1956 and completed in 1964, three years after the architect's death.

Despite their architectural impact, the growing number of buildings featuring exposed steel did little to foster new, more rational methods of designing buildings to resist fires. The first step in this direction was made in the 1950s, when the concept of a "fire load"—analogous to the concept of a statical load on a structure—was conceived. A building can be considered to respond to a fire load in much the same way as a structure responds to gravity or wind load. A fire load is quantified as the combustion energy, measured in MegaJoules (or British Thermal Units) per unit floor area. For convenience, this is often converted to the weight of timber, in kilograms, equivalent to the total combustion energy of the materials in a room. The way the combustible material burned was expressed as a graph relating temperature and time, which was used to define the form of a "standard fire." Subsequent calculations involved analyzing the consequences of a given amount of combustion energy released into a room, which first heats the air and then the

720

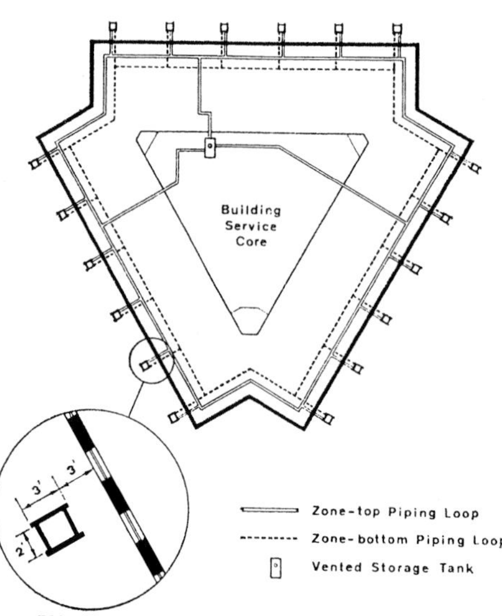

721

fabric and structure of the room. In fact, this design approach was no less revolutionary than the first use of forces and stresses in structural design methods at the end of the eighteenth century.

Looking at the consequences of a fire in this manner allowed engineers to see the fire protection of a structure as a cooling problem, just as the designers of automobile engines had to devise ways of cooling engines' cylinder blocks. Indeed, the idea of circulating water through steel columns to cool them was first patented in 1884, and the idea was thoroughly investigated by research engineers in Germany, Britain, and the United States in the early 1960s. The first major building constructed with this form of fire protection was the sixty-four-story
720, 721 Pittsburgh headquarters of the U.S. Steel Corporation, completed in 1971. The eighteen external columns are made from COR-TEN plate steel up to 100 mm thick, forming 600-mm square hollow sections. Each column is 256 meters tall and contains about 92,000 liters of water and antifreeze.

This same idea was used by Ove Arup for the Centre
722 Georges Pompidou in Paris (1971–77). The circular stain-
723 less steel columns are filled with water. In the event of a
724 fire, water flows around a circuit, driven by convection, and removes heat from the steel exposed to the hot gases. The pipe for keeping the water and antifreeze at the correct level is visible at the top of each column.

At the Royal Exchange Theatre in Manchester, Arup engi- 725
neers were able to achieve what had hitherto been considered an impossible dream—the use of steel to provide the entire load-bearing structure of a building with no fire protection at all. The unusual nature of the project—a small theater built inside a large Victorian corn exchange—meant there were compelling grounds for preferring steel. The main reason was the need to minimize the weight of the structure that had to be supported on the foundations of the existing building. It was also felt that the intumescent paints then available (the mid-1970s) would not provide adequate fire protection for the slender steel members. Faced with these constraints, the engineers went back to first principles and carefully built up a rational approach exploring all the plausible consequences of a fire, not just for the structure, but also for the theater audience and those occupying the older building that contained the theater. Four arguments were put forward to the local regulatory authorities:

- *by providing many exits, the audience could vacate both the theater and the Exchange building quickly enough to avoid danger;*
- *even if a fire continued after evacuation, the collapse of the theatre structure would not significantly affect*

722

720 United States Steel Corporation building, Pittsburgh, Pennsylvania, 1971. Engineer: Leslie E. Robertson Associates; architect: Harrison Abramovitz & Abbe. 721 United States Steel Corporation building. Plan showing hollow steel columns, 0.9 meters outside the building facade, filled with water to provide fire protection. 722 Centre Georges Pompidou, Paris, 1971–77. Engineer: Ove Arup & Partners; architects: Richard Rogers and Renzo Piano.

723

724

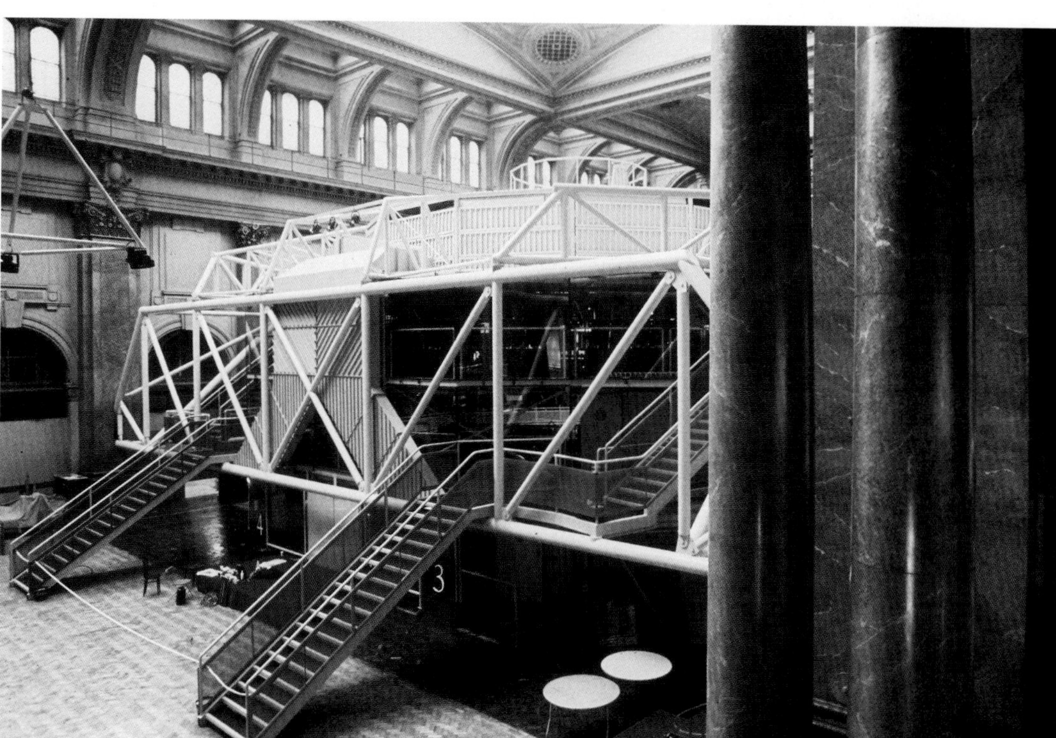
725

723 Centre Georges Pompidou, Paris, 1971–77. Engineer: Ove Arup & Partners; architects: Richard Rogers and Renzo Piano. Detail of main columns filled with water for fire protection. 724 Centre Georges Pompidou. Detail of supply pipe for topping up water in the columns. 725 Royal Exchange Theatre, Manchester, 1976. Engineer: Ove Arup & Partners; architect: Levitt Bernstein. 726 DeWitt-Chestnut Apartments, Chicago, 1965. Engineer: Fazlur Rahman Khan/Skidmore, Owings & Merrill; architect: Myron Goldsmith/Skidmore, Owings & Merrill. 727 John Hancock Center, Chicago, 1970. Engineer: Fazlur Rahman Khan/Skidmore, Owings & Merrill; architect: Bruce Graham/Skidmore, Owings & Merrill.

726

727

- *either the fire fighters or the Exchange building;*
- *the standard fire profile defined in the current British Standard for fire protection of buildings was unrealistically severe and pessimistic (recent tests have shown that the temperatures defined in the "British Standard fire" can be achieved only if fuel is continuously added to the fire);*
- *the likelihood of a fire beginning and spreading was reduced by selecting only non-combustible or low flammability materials for the theater's interior.*[3]

The local regulatory authorities agreed, and sanctioned the use of structural steel without fire protection and without undertaking any tests except the usual trial evacuations of a theater audience.

Within a few years this approach to designing building to resist fires was being widely used, mainly because of the huge savings it offered to building clients, and it soon became known as fire engineering, or fire safety engineering. As the power of computers grew during the 1980s, the qualitative logio of fire engineering concepts was augmented by increasingly sophisticated analytical calculations of building performance in fires. The ability to make reliable calculations of temperatures throughout a building's structural steel during the entire duration of a fire was a major step forward. Using such calculations, it could be demonstrated that at no time would the strength of the steel fall below that required to support the structural loads, which, after the evacuation of the building, would not include the weight of the occupants. Although now obvious, this latter assumption had not been permitted a decade or so earlier, and it has enabled some architects to exploit the use of exposed steel both externally and internally.

High-Rise Construction

The 1960s saw a renewed interest in constructing tall buildings, an interest that has continued to the present day. This was largely a result of the efforts and ingenuity of one man—the Bengal-born engineer Fazlur Rahman Khan (1929–82). Khan, together with his colleagues at SOM, challenged the conventional approach to providing wind bracing in high-rise buildings by rigidly connecting all columns and beams to create a stiff structural frame, a method that had become so costly that the construction of very tall buildings was not economically viable. Khan's stroke of genius was to look at a tall building as a single structural entity, rather than many hundreds of elements working together, each playing a separate role. He realized the implications of looking at the facade of a building as a structural "skin." This approach was similar to that

728

729

taken by the designers of aircraft. It had also become
fashionable in car design in the 1960s with the development of monocoque construction, in which the chassis of
a car was replaced by using the car body as a structural
shell. In buildings this idea became known as the "framed
tube" concept, and it was first used by Khan in the forty-
726 three-story DeWitt–Chestnut Apartments in Chicago in
727 1964. In the 100-story 344-meter John Hancock Center,
Khan developed his idea of making the envelope of the
building a structural element by incorporating cross bracing on a massive scale to carry the wind loads. Each
braced section spans the full width of the building and extends over eighteen stories rather than floor by floor and
bay by bay. The result was a saving of some $15 million.
Another of Khan's innovations was the "tube within a
tube," which enabled the necessary stiffness for a tall
building to be achieved with great economy of steel. In
1971-73 Khan extended his concepts of structural skin,
and the macroscopic view of a structure of tall towers, by
conceiving the idea of "bundled tubes" for the Sears 728
Tower in Chicago. At 109 stories and 443 meters, the
Sears Tower was, for twenty years, the tallest building in
the world. All nine of the independent tubes, with walls of
steel columns and beams, rise to the forty-ninth story;
seven continue up to the sixty-fifth story, five to the
eighty-ninth story, and only two to the very top. The economy that this structural scheme achieved is remarkable.
The Sears Tower is 62 meters taller than the Empire

728 Sears Tower, Chicago, 1973. Engineer: Fazlur Rahman Khan/Skidmore, Owings & Merrill; architect: Bruce Graham/Skidmore, Owings & Merrill. 729 Bank of China Tower, Hong Kong, 1988. Engineer: Leslie E. Robertson Associates; architect: I.M. Pei. 730 Citicorp Center, New York, 1977. Engineer: William LeMessurier; architect: Hugh Stubbins and Associates. 731 Diagrams of methods of bracing tall buildings in earthquake zones. 732 Century Tower, Tokyo, 1992. Engineer: Ove Arup & Partners; architect: Norman Foster and Partners.

730

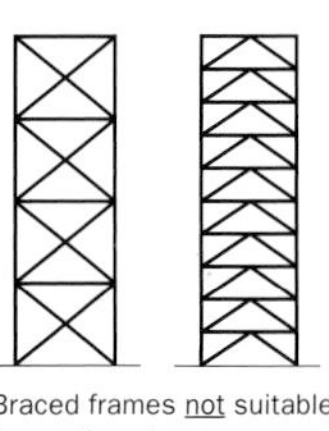

Braced frames not suitable for earthquake zones

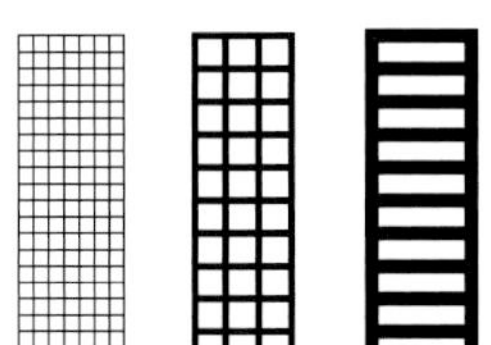

Vierendeel frames suitable for earthquake zones

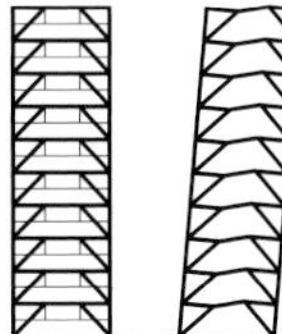

Plastic deformation of eccentrically-braced frame in earthquake

731

732

State Building, but uses only 223,000 tons of steel, nearly 40 percent less than the 365,000 tons used by the Empire State Building.

Like Fazlur Khan, the engineer Leslie Robertson (b. 1928) took a macroscopic view when devising the wind-bracing structure for Pei Cobb Freed & Partners's 369-
729 meter Bank of China Tower in Hong Kong, completed in 1989. The bracing in the external skin is fully triangulated in both elevation and plan, and great economy of materials was achieved despite that fact that the building was designed to withstand both typhoons and earthquakes. The result is widely held to be the most elegant of all the modern skyscrapers.

Tall buildings need to be very stiff for two reasons. One is to minimize the overall deflection, which can cause windows to crack. The other is to ensure that winds do not cause the building to sway in a manner that causes discomfort to the occupants. Wind-tunnel tests can be used to establish the manner in which a tower will shed vortices and, hence, the frequency and magnitude of the periodic forces that might excite oscillations. The structural engineer then needs to ensure that the natural frequency of vibration of the proposed tower is not in the region of these forces. However, increasing the stiffness of a tower to change its natural frequency requires a lot of steel-and a lot of money. An alternative solution is to introduce a passive device that dampens oscillations if they begin to build up. A "tuned mass damper," as it is called, incorporates a large mass that can move freely but is constrained by springs and devices similar to the shock absorbers in an automobile's suspension system. In this way the vibration energy is absorbed and oscillations are not able to build up.

When structural engineer William LeMessurier (b. 1926)
proposed a lightweight steel frame for a new Citicorp 730
Center to be built in New York, he knew that wind-induced oscillations would need to be considered. He

733

734

commissioned wind tunnel tests at the Boundary Layer Wind Tunnel Laboratory at the University of Western Ontario in Canada, and the model tests revealed that the natural frequency of the proposed frame was indeed near that of the vortex-induced wind loads. The laboratory's director, Alan Davenport, recommended a tuned mass damper as the means of reducing the amplitude of oscillations. The damper designed by LeMessurier uses a 400-ton block of concrete resting on a thin film of oil.[4]

In earthquake-prone regions such as California and Japan, the key aim of designers seeking the most economical structure is to ensure that the building will not collapse during a severe earthquake, but without designing to eliminate all permanent deformation. A diagonally braced frame cannot be used because when such frames are loaded to failure, the only possible failure mechanisms are catastrophic: fracture in tension, buckling of elements in compression, or shearing of welds and bolts. To resist an earthquake, a tall building must be designed to deform in a noncatastrophic way, and this is usually achieved by exploiting the capacity of steel to undergo some plastic deformation. The accepted solution is to use rigid Vierendeel frames, in which the plastic deformation of the connections absorbs the kinetic energy of the earthquake; an example is the Morrison air raid shelter, constructed in 1938 (see chapter 8, pp. 471–72). The disadvantage of these frames is that the columns and beams must either be very numerous or very large. Either
731 alternative means that buildings cannot have either large open floor plans or large windows. A solution devised in California in the 1980s was to use an "eccentrically braced frame," in which the plastic deformation is taken by short beams rather than connections; however, this does not allow an appreciable increase in open floor plans or window size. For the Century Tower in Tokyo, 732
Arup engineer Tony Fitzpatrick (1951–2003) devised an eccentrically braced frame on a massive scale—two stories high and the full width of the building. The result was a twenty-story building with unprecedentedly large windows and open internal spaces.

Long-Span Roofs

Sometimes the sheer scale of a building using familiar materials is impressive. The steel lattice dome of the Houston Astrodome, completed in 1965, spans 196 me- 733, 734
ters and covers an area of 3 hectares. This unprecedented span led the engineers to do structural tests on a 1:100 scale model to confirm their structural calculations, and a model of similar size was tested in the wind tunnel of the McDonnell Aircraft Company in St. Louis to establish the loads that a hurricane with continuous wind speeds of 215 km per hour would exert on the building. The roof was designed to admit about 50 percent daylight to enable grass to grow on the baseball field, but this was not a success, and artificial turf was laid after one season.

For the widest spans, tensile structures have proved to be the most versatile and economic, and no structural form has better illustrated the fruitfulness of close collaboration between engineer and architect. The pioneering structures by Frei Otto and the many engineers with whom he collaborated have inspired many engineers and architects to devise their own imaginative and visually striking tensile structures.

735

736

733 Houston Astrodome, Houston, Texas, 1964. Engineer: Walter P. Moore Engineers and Consultants with Roof Structures, Inc.; architects: Hermon Lloyd & W.B. Morgan and Wilson, Morris, Crain & Anderson. Building under construction. 734 Houston Astrodome. Interior. 735 American Pavilion at Expo '70, Osaka, Japan. Engineer: David Geiger; architect: Davis, Brody & Associates. 736 American Pavilion at Expo '70. Air-inflated interior.

737

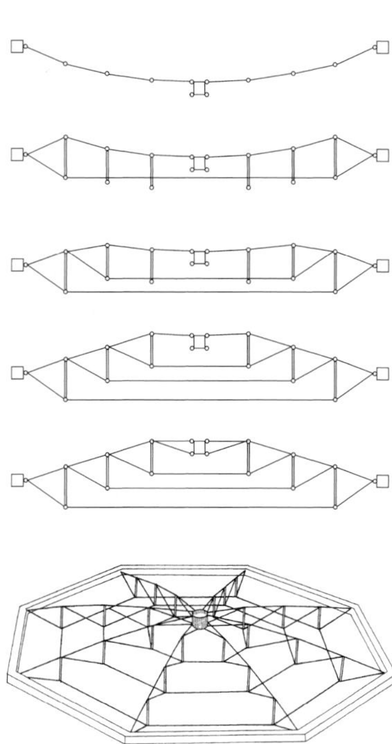

738

737 Seoul Olympics gymnastics venue, Seoul, Korea, 1986. Engineer: David Geiger. Dome under construction. 738 Seoul Olympics gymnastics venue. Diagrams illustrating erection sequence of the Geiger tension dome. 739 Jeppesen Terminal, Denver International Airport, Denver, Colorado, 1994. Engineers: Severud Associates with Horst Berger Associates (membrane structures); architect: Fentress Bradburn Architects Ltd. 740 Jeppesen Terminal. Interior. 741a–c Izumo Dome, Izumo, Japan, 1992. Engineer: Kajima Design with Masao Saitoh; architect: Kajima Design. (a) Preparing to erect dome of the scale model; (b) load testing the model when fully erect; (c) roof panels ready for erection.

739

740

741a

741b

741c

Following the precedent set by the Crystal Palace in 1851, international exhibitions have become a regular theatre where designers have experimented with new
735 ideas. At Expo '70 in Osaka, Japan, for example, architects Davis, Brody & Associates and the American engineer David Geiger (1935–89) demonstrated the first large-scale membrane roof supported by air pressure from beneath. The membrane, spanning 142 x 83 me-
736 ters, was restrained from excessive ballooning by a mesh of steel cables.

Large sports arenas, too, have provided designers with yet more opportunities for showing off the engineer's ingenuity and creativity. David Geiger's gymnastic hall,
737 120 meters in diameter, built for the Seoul Olympics in 1988, seems to defy common sense—it is a dome with hardly any sign of compression members. Geiger's
738 so-called "cable-dome," devised around 1985, is one of the few practical structures that has exploited Buckminster Fuller's idea of "tensegrity." Such structures work by employing what are, effectively, discontinuous compression members; several short compression members working together with cables in tension, not unlike the structure of the human spine. The elegance of tensegrity structures lies in the compression members being kept very short and, hence, able to resist buckling without being unduly bulky—"small islands [of compression] in a sea of tension,"as Fuller poetically described tensegrity. A particularly ingenious feature of the cable dome is that it can be erected without special lifting gear by tightening the circumferential cables one at a time, working out from the center. The membrane covering the cable dome is not part of its structural system.

In their early days, highly-stressed membrane structures were used mainly as canopies to protect the public from sun or rain. They were often temporary and had at least one side open. Since the mid-1980s, a number of designers have used them for the permanent enclosure of large spaces, such as the atriums of buildings. This always poses the problem of how to provide a flexible seal between the rigid frame of the building's facade and the
more flexible membrane roof. At the Jeppesen Terminal 739, 740
of Denver International Airport in Colorado, the German engineer Horst Berger (b. 1928), who studied with Frei

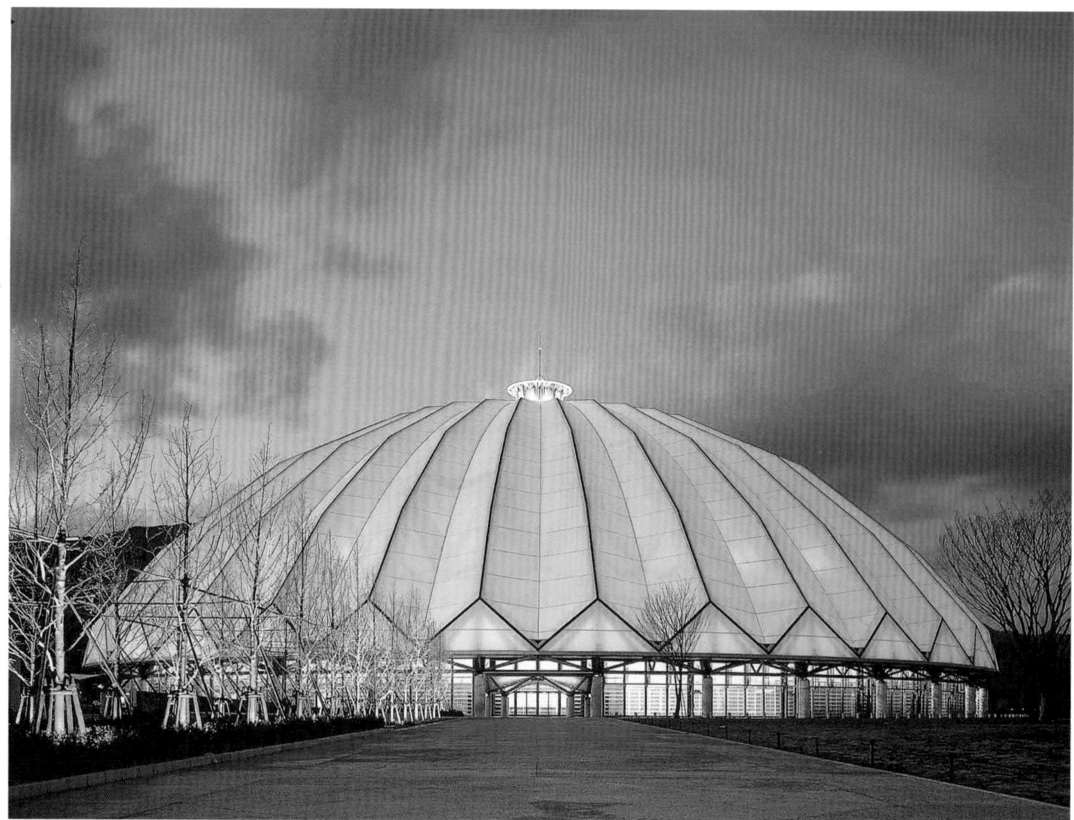

742

743

742 Izumo Dome, Izumo, Japan, 1992. Engineer: Kajima Design with Masao Saitoh; architect: Kajima Design. 743 Izumo Dome. Interior. 744 Millennium Dome, London, 1999. Engineers: Buro Happold with Birdair Inc. (membrane structure); architect: Richard Rogers and Partners. Teflon-coated, woven glass-fiber fabric being fitted to the cable grid. 745 Millennium Dome. 746 Science and Technology Museum, La Villette, Paris, 1990. Engineer: RFR Associates. Details of the "spider" structure to which the glass panels are fixed. 747 La Villette. Detail of the cable structure that carries wind loads on the facade. 748 Foreign Office building, Berlin, Germany, 1999. Engineer: Schlaich Bergermann and Partner. Detail of the connection between glazing and supporting cables.

744

745

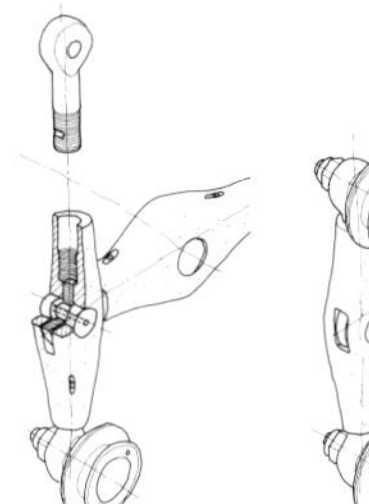
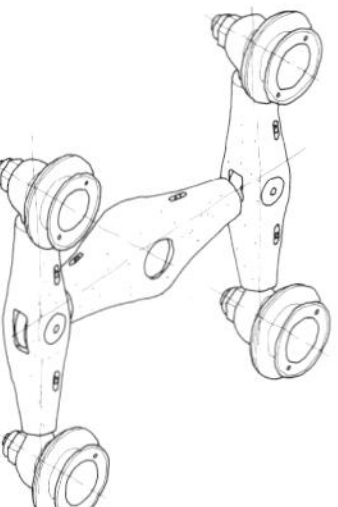
746

747

748

749

Otto and is one of the masters of tensile structures, used air-inflated membrane tubes up to a meter in diameter to seal the gap whose size varies along the length of the interface.

742, 743 The form of the Izumo Dome in Japan, completed in
1992, was inspired by traditional Japanese paper and
wood umbrellas and lampshades made of folded paper.
The dome is 140 meters in diameter, and it was decided
741a–c to build a 1:20 scale model to test both the innovative
method of erection and the stiffness of the extremely
lightweight structure under asymmetric loads. The
scaled load was applied using a 7-ton weight of water.
The glulam ribs were laid radially on the ground, and alternating panels were fully stiffened using cables, struts, and the membrane itself. The dome was erected by raising the central node to its final height of 49 meters.

744, 745 For sheer size. London's Millennium Dome (1999), with a diameter of 320 meters, is unrivalled. The membrane panels are stretched between a cable grid suspended from twelve 100-meter tall struts.

Structural Glazing

For many years architects have dreamed of "invisible
walls," and this dream has been made reality through a
combination of advances in glass technology and the
work of design engineers. The work of two engineers, the
Irish-born Peter Rice (1935–92), and Jörg Schlaich (b.
1934), from Germany, has been especially important in
achieving this goal. Rice created a 32 x 32-meter glass
747 facade at La Villette in Paris in 1981, which set a precedent for all subsequent glazed walls. He realized that there are two key factors to keep in mind when using glass—which is rather weak in tension and very brittle—to carry significant loads. The first is to ensure that the loads are precisely predictable and, especially, that no bending is applied to the panes. The second is that any shock loads, such as bird impact or the sudden redistribution of loads caused by one pane shattering, must be sufficiently dampened to prevent a domino effect, in which a failure in one pane causes adjacent panes to fracture. At the top of each 4x4 panel, the panes are suspended from sprung supports to prevent sudden loads from being transmitted to the glass. The four-pronged
connector supporting the corners of each pane, known
as a "spider," contains a ball joint and rubber gasket to 746
ensure no bending or shock loads are transferred to the glass. Both positive and negative wind loads are carried by horizontal cable trusses.

For the facade of the Foreign Office building in Berlin 748
(1999), Schlaich took a different approach. Each pane of glass is fixed to an orthogonal grid of cables and carries only its own weight. Rather than providing additional structural elements to carry the wind loads, the facade is allowed to move under the action of wind. When wind impinges on the facade, the cables resist the load, much like the strings of a tennis racket resist the impact of a ball. To resist a strong wind, the center of a glass wall has to have the ability to deflect by some 800 mm. Such a deflection in a glazed wall sounds alarming, but such alarm can induce us to revisit our preconceived notions about the nature of glass, and to adjust them to reflect the engineer's ingenuity in overcoming the limitations inherent in the characteristics of glass. By taking an original and radical approach to the problem, Schlaich designed a window that is 24 meters wide and 20 meters high, with a supporting structure that is no more visually
intrusive than the joints between panes of glass. When
providing a roof to cover the courtyard at the Museum of 749
the History of Hamburg, Schlaich reduced the visual impact of the structure to the absolute minimum by creating a shell roof using short steel struts stabilized in the plane of the shell by diagonal cables. The form of the shell is maintained by three sets of radial ties. To ensure the shell's stability under both statical and dynamic loads, every aspect of the geometry of the roof had to be calculated with great precision, as did the forces in the cables and ties. Similarly, the precisely calculated geometry and forces had to be faithfully reproduced in reality when the roof was constructed. Only by using the sophisticated three-dimensional structural analysis software that became available in the late 1980s could such a structure have been built.

The Virtual Building

The final step in the development of building engineering design methods brings us to the twenty-first century. During the forty years or so of designing buildings

749 Museum of the History of Hamburg, Germany, 1989. Engineer: Schlaich Bergermann and Partner; architect: Volkwin Marg.

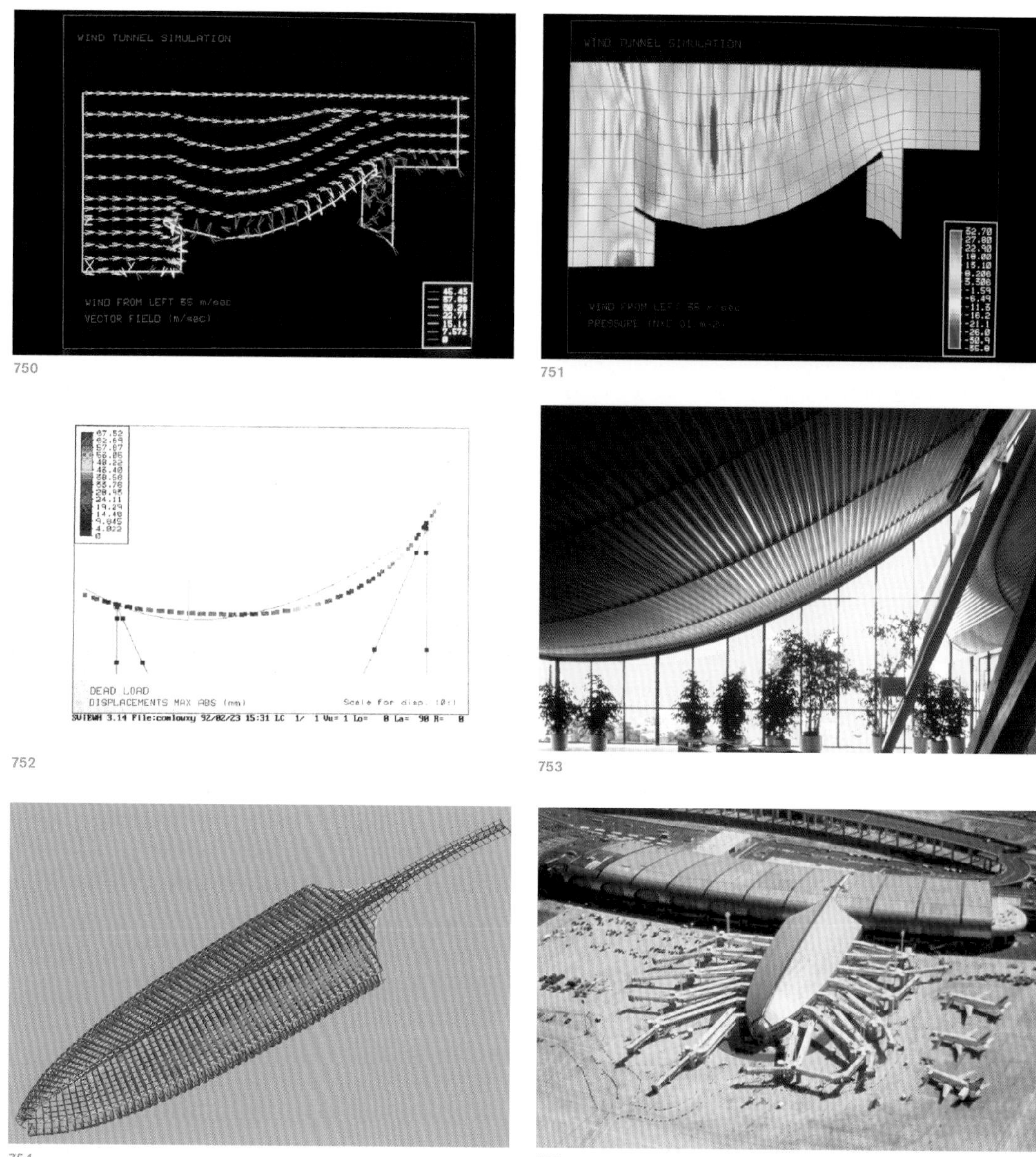

750 Office building at the Lowara factory, Vicenza, Italy, 1984–85. Engineer: Favero–Milan; architect: Renzo Piano. Computer model of air flow. 751 Lowara factory office building. Computer model of air pressures. 752 Lowara factory office building. Computer model of deflected shape of the roof. 753 Lowara factory office building. Interior. 754 Peninsula, Terminal 2F, Charles de Gaulle Airport, Roissy, France (Paris), 1990–97. Engineer: RFR; architect: Paul Andreu. Computer model showing stresses in the roof structure. 755 Peninsula, Charles de Gaulle Airport.

using computers, not only have the power and speed of computers increased, the accuracy and reliability of the mathematical models that the computers use have also been improved. This has been achieved by constantly investigating discrepancies between the results that computers generate and measurements of the real-world behavior of both scale models and actual buildings; when satisfactory explanations have been found for the discrepancies, the computer model can be modified to provide a better representation of the real world. Today it is also possible to model every aspect of the engineering performance of a building—its thermal behavior throughout the year, illumination by both natural and artificial light, the spread of fire, dynamic behavior under wind or earthquake loads, and much more besides. The aggregate of these different models means it is now possible to simulate the entire engineering behavior of a virtual building.

One important consequence of using computer models has been to provide the opportunity to evaluate more options during the design stages of projects. Whereas fifty years ago, the process of optimizing an engineering solution would have involved looking at just a few different options, engineers can now consider literally thousands of alternatives. Thus, for example, it is possible to establish the best shape for a roof in order to minimize the bending moments in the beams caused by wind loading, and hence to minimize their size and weight. Using a computer to simulate the wind flow over the building, the virtual model test can be run many times, altering the shape of the roof by tiny increments each time. This approach was used by the engineers who designed the "simple," lightweight, hanging roof conceived for new offices of the
753 Lowara company in Vicenza, Italy. With many different wind and snow loads to consider, it was far from simple to arrive at the optimum hanging shape and reduce the thickness of the structural elements to give the required
750, 751 feeling of lightness and elegance. A computer simulation of wind flow generated data for the distribution of air pressure, and this in turn was applied to the model of the structure to calculate the bending moments and the de-
752 flected shape. In 1984, when the building was designed, this iterative process of optimization was relatively new and took several weeks to carry out. Today, such procedures are commonplace and can be completed much more rapidly.

Another important benefit of using computer models in the design process is the sheer complexity of engineering
problems that can be tackled. The new Peninsula at 755
France's Charles de Gaulle Airport, for example, is 200 meters long and 50 meters wide, yet it has no expansion joints to accommodate movement due to temperature changes. Instead, the entire roof is fixed only at the terminal end of the building, and all fifty ribs supporting the building envelope are articulated at their lower support. To analyze the stresses and movements of this huge structure, a 10,000-element computer model was built.
The output was presented visually, with color coding indi- 754
cating the magnitude of the stresses. Not only did the visual output allow engineers to see the results of the stress calculations, it proved extremely useful when discussing the development of the design with the client and architect. The graphic images of the many alternatives demonstrated the architectural benefits of certain changes to the structure much more dramatically than simply presenting the numerical output of engineers' calculations could have.

The development of extremely powerful computers in the 1990s has brought "computational fluid dynamics" (CFD), developed initially for weather forecasting and the design of aeroengines, within the reach of building design engineers. This technique is a development of the finite element method that models the state of statical stress in thousands of adjacent elements. In CFD, the dynamic and thermal properties of adjacent elements are modeled and, when the behavior of many thousands of elements is aggregated, the result is a model of the flow of a liquid or gas. This enables design engineers to predict the temperatures of structural members during a fire, and
even to represent the turbulent flow of hot gases in a fire. 756a–b

Computers have even been used to simulate the behavior of people when moving in a building such as a large railway station or in the more chaotic situation of escaping from a building on fire—a technique that owes its inspiration more to the world of video games than to
conventional engineering science. Each "person" in the 757
model is assigned characteristics across a range that is typical of human beings: more or less physically fit, more or less rational in choosing their path, more or less determined, and so on. Thus engineers are now able to predict with some accuracy the conditions that lead to

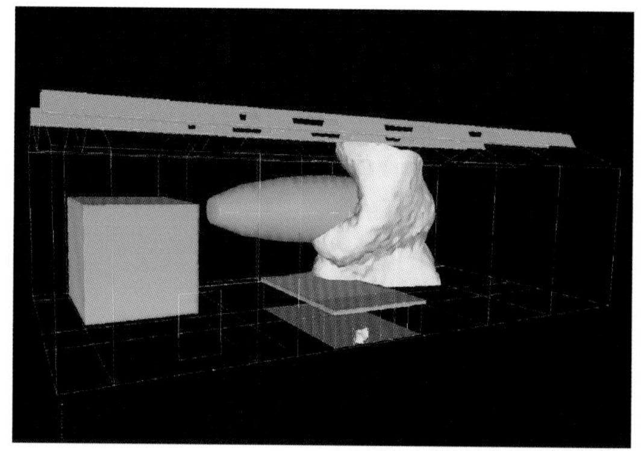
756a

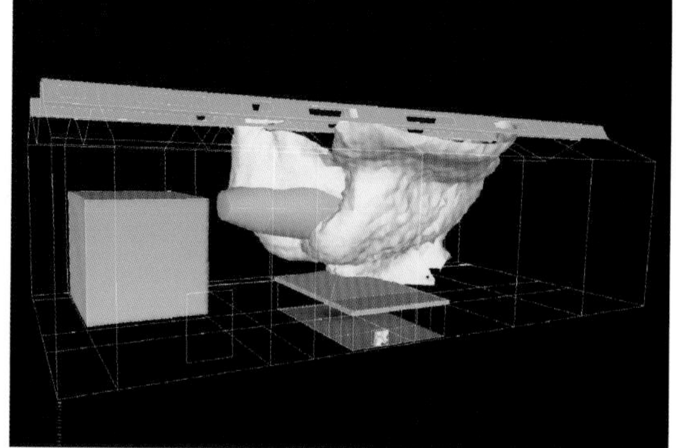
756b

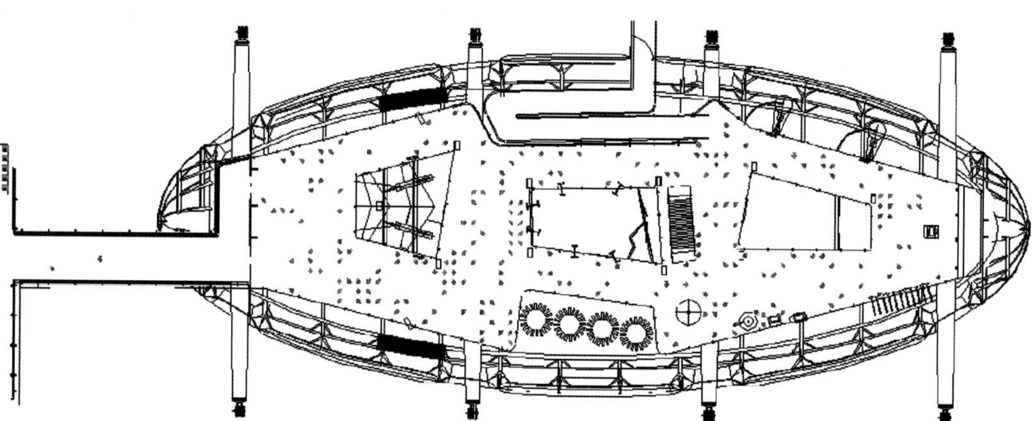
757

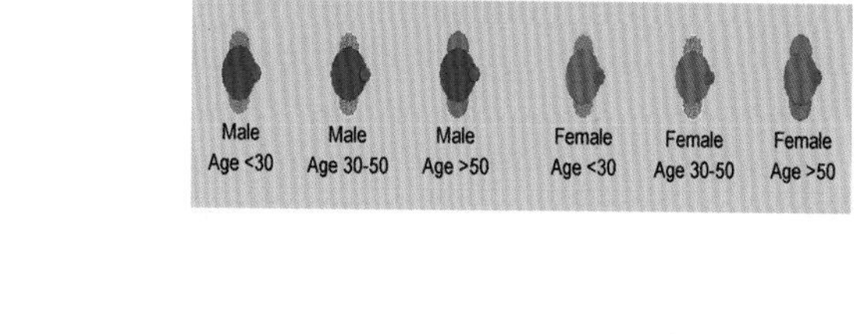

758

congestion in a busy space, or the time it would take to evacuate a building.

The full range of engineering design techniques made possible using computer models of buildings and their engineering systems is beyond the scope of this book. Suffice it to say that the visualization of engineering behavior has transformed the work of the engineer. Engineers can now design their buildings interactively, with computer images providing almost instant feedback on the consequences of a change to the design. Today's visual methods have much in common with the what-if? simplicity of the pencil and sketchpad in the hands of a designer exploring how something will look, or how components will fit together—the method first devised by Renaissance engineers, especially Brunelleschi and Leonardo. Now, however, the "sketch" is both a visual representation and a fully working computer model of the engineering behavior of the real thing.

Forensic Engineering

It is easy to overstate the practical benefits that may arise from studying the history of building engineering, especially the idea that we might be able to avoid future engineering failures by studying past engineering failures. Failures can arise for many reasons, some foreseeable, others not, and nearly all failures occur in a set of contextual circumstances that will never recur. Nevertheless, it is now accepted practice that engineering failures are investigated to establish their cause and, whenever possible, to identify suitable remedies. Sometimes such investigations may be needed to resolve claims for compensation. Indeed, engineers now use the phrase "forensic engineering" to describe the process of establishing causes of engineering failures especially, but not only when there is a possibility of prosecution in law.

There is no doubt that the studies of many engineering failures have deepened our fundamental understanding of materials, or led to new approaches to engineering design. For example, the search for the cause of the Comet air disasters in the 1950s established the potentially disastrous consequences of small fatigue cracks (see chapter 8, pp. 457–58). Sometimes forensic inquiries find that human error or misunderstanding was the cause. A large part of engineering design involves imagining how something might fail and then—by design—ensuring this failure cannot occur. Yet it is impossible for designers to anticipate every possible type of failure; engineers are subject to human nature, and as Henry Petroski observed in the title of one of his books, to engineer is human.[5] The job of investigative engineering is to establish what to do next time, with the benefit of hindsight.

A recent example of a change to the engineering context after a flaw in a building structure went unrecognized was the dramatic collapse of a corner of a new block of flats, Ronan Point, in East London in 1968. The twenty-three- 758
story building was made using a new method of constructing tall buildings in which precast concrete wall panels were stacked rather like a house of cards; each wall panel rested on the one below, and was tied in to the reinforced concrete core of the building. The engineering design calculations had been undertaken according to the current design codes and, indeed, in its original state, as built, the building was both stable and safe. What the designers had not considered was what might happen if one of the wall panels were removed. This is just what occurred when a faulty gas boiler led to a small explosion in a kitchen on the eighteenth floor; this blew out one of the wall panels, leaving the ones above it without support; these then fell, bringing down the rooms beneath. The lesson learned was to ensure that wall panels in such buildings should be more firmly anchored to the floors and, hence, to the core of the building. This requirement was incorporated into the next edition of the design codes. Despite the dramatic collapse, the designers were not prosecuted; they had followed accepted practice and used the appropriate design code. It was accepted as unreasonable to expect an engineer to predict a possible failure that had not previously occurred and had never been considered.

The collapses of the two towers of the World Trade 759
Center in New York in 2001, following the impact of fully

756a–b Two frames from a sequence of computer-generated images showing the spread of hot gases in a fire.
757 Single frame from a computer model of people escaping from a building in a fire. 758 Ronan Point apartment building, East London, England, 1968. A corner of the building collapsed after a gas explosion in 1968.

759

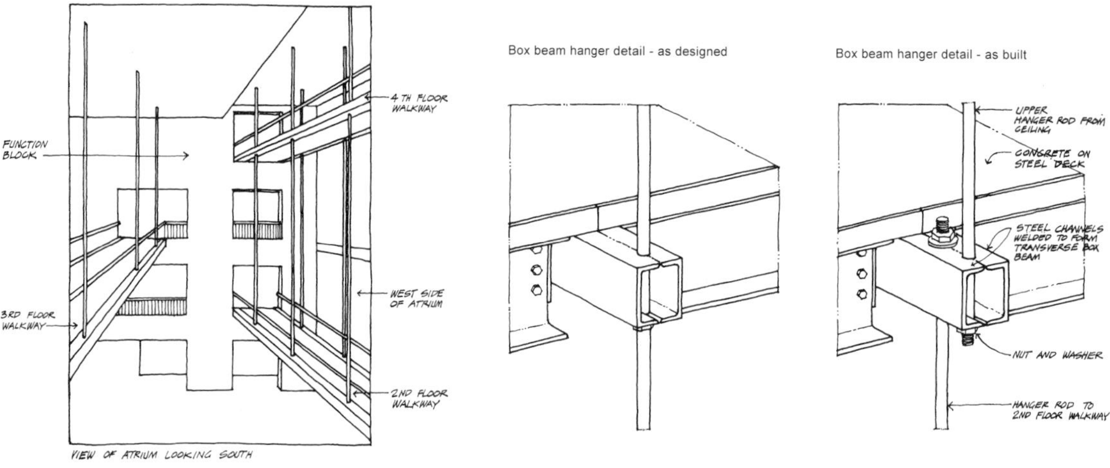

760

759 World Trade Center, New York, 1972. Structural engineer: Leslie E. Robertson and Associates; architect: Minoru Yamasaki. 760 Hyatt Regency Hotel, Kansas City, Missouri, 1980. Diagrams of connection details for an atrium walkway that collapsed in 1981 in one of the worst engineering disasters in United States history. Left: General construction of atrium; center: detail of connection as designed; right: detail of connection as constructed.

laden passenger aircraft, were subject to detailed forensic investigation, not to identify the cause, which was obvious, but to establish the precise process and sequence of events which led to the collapses. The buildings were constructed in 1972 as square tubes with walls made of a lattice of steel columns and beams that carried a substantial proportion of the building's weight. These load-bearing walls were braced at every story by the floor beams that connected the facade to the central core of the building in which were the staircases, elevators, and services risers. The engineering investigation established that the impact had removed a substantial number of the steel columns in the facade of the building, though not enough to cause collapse. The collapse was the direct result of the fire that soon raged inside the building. In the immediate vicinity of the impact, a significant amount of the fireboard that provided the floor beams with their fire protection had been dislodged. Some of these beams soon heated up to the point where they collapsed and pulled away from their end supports. They then fell on the floors beneath and some of these beams also soon collapsed. This left a number of the steel columns in the facade unbraced by floor beams for up to four stories. These columns buckled, and the load they had carried was diverted to other columns, which themselves became loaded in excess of their design load; they too collapsed by buckling and a chain reaction followed.

While the towers had not been designed to withstand the impact they suffered, the possibility of aircraft impact had been considered. The Empire State Building had successfully withstood the impact of a small aircraft in the 1940s. The impact by a large passenger aircraft had also been considered, but only in structural terms; as the forensic study established, the towers survived this aspect of the impact. What had not been considered was the incendiary effects of an aircraft fully laden with fuel. With hindsight, it can perhaps be suggested that the fire protection of the beams could have been more robust. The great tragedy of the collapses, however, was the loss of life, and perhaps the most important lesson that will be applied to future tall buildings is the need to provide better-protected means of escape for the occupants, and more effective ways of keeping these means of escape free from smoke in the event of a fire.

Many building failures—whether catastrophic collapses or less dramatic failures, such as water penetration through a building's envelope—have not been the result of mistakes by building designers. They have, rather, been the result of poor construction practices or the redesign of details by building contractors who have modified original designs hoping to save money by using less material or making something easier to build. Although redesign is common practice, and often does save money, it may, usually through a misunderstanding of the original designer's intentions, lead to failure. This was the case when the raised arm of the Statue of Liberty collapsed during construction. The contractor had modified Gustave Eiffel's original design to make it easier to construct but, in doing so, committed the structural sin of failing to ensure that the structure was fully braced by triangulation. At one crucial connection the structural members did not meet at a single point, and the out-of-balance forces caused bending in a member not designed to carry bending loads, leading to the inevitable collapse.

A contractor's redesign of a crucial connection was also found to be the cause of one of the worst collapses in the late twentieth century—that of a suspended walkway in the Kansas City Hyatt Regency Hotel in Kansas City,
Missouri, in 1981, which killed 114 people. Two walk- 760
ways, at the second- and fourth-story levels, were suspended from a truss at roof level. The original design of the hanger showed both walkways suspended by a single continuous steel bar. However, the designer's proposed method for attaching the fourth-story walkway to the hanger was impractical. The contractor suggested an alternative solution that, at first glance, appeared satisfactory, and was approved by the structural engineer. In fact, as is apparent from a second glance, the modification was structurally unsound. In the original design, the box beam supporting the fourth-story walkway had to carry the weight of only that walkway. In the modified design, the beam also had to carry the weight of the second-story walkway below. Not surprisingly, now overloaded by a factor of two, the nut on the end of the upper hanger pulled through the box beam. In this case, following the forensic inquiry, two key staff in the firm of structural engineers that had designed the walkway, and approved the modification, had their license to practice revoked on the grounds that they should have been able to predict the consequences of the change.

Of course, not all building design failures lead to collapse. Many "failures," for example, air-conditioning systems that do not deliver the required levels of temperature and humidity, can be corrected as soon as they are discovered. Others, however, may not be so easy to correct. Until relatively recently it was not uncommon for concert and theater auditoriums to be revealed as acoustic disasters when built, simply because the understanding of acoustics was inadequate at the time they were designed. There is no better example than London's
761 Royal Albert Hall, which opened in 1871. The elliptical auditorium is 70 meters long, 61 meters wide, and 43 meters high, giving it about twice the volume of most halls regularly used for concerts. The huge ellipsoidal roof acted as an effective reflector and the audience of up to 7,000 people heard a loud reflection of every sound a fraction of a second after the original sound. Of the opening ceremony it was remarked that the Prince of Wales' address was "distinctly heard in duplicate." It was sometimes quipped that concerts at the Albert Hall were particularly good value because the audience heard each piece of music twice. Tests undertaken in the 1960s revealed that this reflection was about a quarter of a second later than the original sound, and, in some seats, the reflected sound was 20 percent louder than the original. Attempts to remedy the problem began in the 1880s, when a fabric valerium of about 1500 m^2 was hung from the roof. This did little to prevent the offending reflections, however, and it was removed in 1949, along with about a thousand kilograms of dust that had collected on the fabric. The valerium was replaced by a series of curved reflectors comprising felt sandwiched between two aluminum sheets. However, this solution attenuated only the high frequency reflections; bass notes continued to echo as loudly as before. The echo was finally removed in 1969 after a careful investigation established the causes of the problem and indicated a suitable remedy. One hundred and nine fiberglass reflectors shaped like flying saucers, with a total area of over 1000 m^2, were hung from the roof. The reflectors serve both to reduce the proportion of sound reaching the inner surface of the dome, and to diffuse the reflected component of the sound throughout the auditorium. A reflecting canopy was also added above the orchestra to project sound more effectively to the seats farthest from the stage. The Albert Hall saga illustrates the relatively late development of the science of acoustics compared, say, with advances in structural engineering. The ultimate success of the remedial action, however, is also testament to the ability of today's building engineers to master every aspect of building performance, even the invisible and highly subjective world of acoustics.

There has perhaps been no better known engineering failure than the leaning tower of Pisa. Soon after construc- 762
tion began in 1173 it began to lean and, despite some minor corrections in the masonry to curve the tower toward the vertical, deformation of the soft clay beneath continued and the tower was inclining by about 4.5° to the south by the time it was completed. Over the next 500 years many dozens of commissions were set up to establish the cause of the leaning, and to propose possible remedies—sixteen in the twentieth century alone. The degree of tilting continued to increase gradually, and by 1900 had reached over 5°. Five separate attempts in the twentieth century to halt the tilting in fact led to sudden small increases. In 1990 it was found that the rate at which the inclination of the tower was increasing was accelerating and, when another masonry tower in Italy collapsed spontaneously, it was decided to close Pisa's tower to the public. It had finally reached the point when a remedy had to be found, both to prevent an imminent collapse, and to safeguard the tower into the future. Professor John Burland (b. 1936), of Imperial College London, was one member of the commission set up to undertake this work. After exhaustive study of the data about the tower's history and its continuing movement caused by changes in the groundwater level, solar heating on the south side, and strong winds, he made proposals for a two-stage remedy that were accepted. The 763
immediate danger of collapse was reduced by placing 600 tons of lead weights at the foot of the tower on the north side; this was increased to 900 tons in 1995 to further reduce the danger.

Burland's computer model of the tower's foundations and the soil beneath indicated that the tower had been on the verge of collapse when it was closed. He established that stability in the long term could only be assured, at a sufficiently low level of risk, by reducing the inclination of the tower by half of one percent—equivalent to reducing the overhang of the seventh level parapet from about 4.5 meters to around 4 meters. This would be achieved by removing soil from beneath the

761

762

Drilling rig

~26 m

220 mm dia. casing

22°

180 mm dia. extraction drill

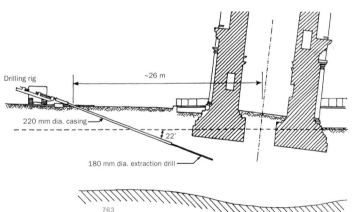

763

761 Royal Albert Hall, London, England, 1871. Acoustic diffusing discs installed 1969. 762 "Leaning Tower" of Pisa, Italy, c. 1370. 763 "Leaning Tower." Diagram showing how soil was removed from beneath the tower to reduce its inclination and halt its gradual tilting in the early 1990s.

764

765

foundations of the north side of the tower using an array of 41 extraction augers, 180 millimeters in diameter, spaced at half meter intervals. A trial of the method in early 1999 successfully reduced the inclination by 30 millimeters, and extraction of the full amount of soil proceeded at a rate of about 20 liters a day during most of the year 2000. The lead counterweights were gradually removed as the tower was straightened. During the process, the verticality in the east-west direction was monitored continuously, and was carefully controlled by altering the relative proportions of soil excavated by the 41 drills. The delicacy of this balancing operation was extremely high, not only because of the consequences of a mistake—as Burland described it, the instability of a heavy tower on soft soil was similar to that of a tower of wooden blocks built on a soft-pile carpet—except that the tower at Pisa weighed 14,500 tons. The tower is now open to the public again.

The Widening Scope of Building Engineering

Despite the considerable technical advances during the first two-thirds of the twentieth century, the scope of building engineering design had remained essentially unchanged. The issues addressed in engineering textbooks, technical periodicals, and trade publications in architecture and building construction in 1900 differed little from those addressed in the late 1960s. Around that time two major new issues began to emerge that altered the social, economic, and political context in which building engineers operate, and have since come to affect the nature of their work. These were the gradual realization that the demolition of old buildings to make way for the new often had a detrimental effect on the heritage of towns and cities, and a growing concern for the environmental impact caused by the construction and operation of buildings.

Restoration and Rehabilitation of Existing Buildings

The mid-1960s saw the beginning of a change in attitude toward old, and even not-so-old, buildings. Various architects, members of the public, and, later, some politicians, began to decry the worldwide dash to build more and more new buildings in our cities, which seemed to be having an adverse effect on the cities' appearance and character. In particular, it was noticed that a growing number of wonderful buildings were being demolished and replaced by buildings of little or no architectural merit. During the 1960s, where this trend was most apparent, England and the United States led the way. There were many examples, but a few became notorious: the 1837 Euston Station in London, and the heroic arch that stood in front of it, were demolished in 1962; the magnificent New York terminus of the Pennsylvania Railroad, demolished in 1963; 764, 765 large numbers of exquisite Georgian buildings in Bath in the West of England, demolished during the mid-1960s. Nearly every major British city lost a host of nineteenth-century commercial and industrial buildings to the developers' new world vision. Meanwhile, outside the cities, hundreds of England's large country houses and stately homes were also being lost, although this was as much due to neglect and government imposition of punitive death duties as to the wrecker's ball.

The reaction to this destruction was a growing concern for the part of our national heritage that is represented by the built environment. The consequence, for many engineers and architects, has been a need to devise ways of conserving, rehabilitating, and reusing old buildings, if at all possible. Planning legislation now generally makes it much more difficult for owners to demolish or even to alter the appearance of buildings judged to be of cultural, architectural, or historical merit or significance. This had long been the case for important buildings dating from the eighteenth century and earlier, such as cathedrals and palaces of the nobility. Now the same criteria are applied to nearly all building types. A typical example is architect Rafael Moneo's conversion of Madrid's Atocha Railway Station into a shopping center and public garden, completed in 1992.

Engineers, however, had not all been innocent bstanders to the destruction of old buildings. Many structures were demolished on the evidence of engineers who asserted that they were unsafe or would be too costly to rehabilitate. In practice, this often meant that the engineers appointed to undertake such assessments were unable or unwilling to refurbish the buildings; they might not be familiar with materials such as cast or wrought iron, or with

764 Pennsylvania Station, New York, 1903–10 (demolished 1963). Architect: McKim, Mead and White. Waiting room, based on tepidarium of the Baths of Caracalla, Rome. 765 Pennsylvania Station. Station concourse, based on the Roman cross vault.

766

767

construction methods used in past centuries. If appointed, they were also likely to earn more money designing a replacement building in steel or reinforced concrete. Fortunately, the last three decades have seen a growing number of old buildings being saved and brought back into use for an entirely different purpose—for example, warehouses, churches, offices, and railway stations turned into apartments, offices, university buildings, theaters, museums, or craft workshops.

When an old building is refurbished, the building services are generally replaced, partly because of the difficultly of reconditioning heating, ventilation, and electrical equipment in situ and getting it warrantied, and partly because of the difficulty of adapting existing equipment to a new building function and new internal arrangements in the building. The fabric and the structure of a building, on the other hand, can usually be reused. This needs careful consideration, and structural engineers have had to develop new skills to assess the stability of existing buildings and the load-carrying capacity of floors, walls, and columns. They have had to develop forensic skills to assess and explain any minor damage they might find, as well as to establish both how the original designer might have intended the structure to work and, as far as possible, how the structure is actually working. It is also important to realize the dangers inherent in trying to apply modern codes of design practice to old buildings. For example, if assumptions made about the hidden structure of a building are too conservative, it is common to find that the floors "will not carry" the loads that they have been carrying for many decades, and that the building "should" already have collapsed. Engineers lacking experience of old buildings are likely to condemn a building on such "evidence." Wiser engineers will believe their eyes. Starting from the fact that the building is obviously still standing, they will look again at the assumptions made; if, as is usually the case, the assumptions are found to have been inaccurate or too pessimistic, they can be refined accordingly.

The case of a cotton mill built in Huddersfield, England, in 1865 illustrates these points. The building has cast iron columns and beams spanning between load-bearing masonry walls. The first assessment, based on conservative assumptions about the structure and the properties of the materials, showed the floor could not carry modern
floor loads by a margin of about 40 percent. The building 766
was saved from demolition by taking a more enlightened approach to understanding the structure and how it was working. First, small samples of the cast iron beams were tested. It was found that the iron was around 10 percent stronger in tension than had first been assumed. Accurate measurements were made of the dimensions of the brick jack arches and cast iron beams to calculate their strength more precisely. The new mathematical model of the structure established that the floors could be made to carry the required loads by using lightweight concrete on top of the jack arches, and by casting this concrete around the cast iron beams to create a floor

766 Canalside West, restored mill in Huddersfield, England, constructed 1865. Original jack arch floor. 767 Canalside West. Exterior after renovation in 1996; building houses the computing and engineering department at the University of Huddersfield.

structure in which the original beams and new concrete work together compositely. The painted soffits of the brick jack-arches were cleaned and left exposed in the refurbished building that now serves as the University of
767 Huddersfield's computing and engineering department.

Careful study of old buildings is essential during rehabilitation in order to understand their designers' intentions, and it frequently turns up highly ingenious engineering. Examples of such ingenuity are the so-called "cantilevered" stone staircases found in many buildings throughout Europe from Palladio's time until the nineteenth century (see chapter 3, pp. 150, 152). Some intelligent thinking, and the building of a wooden model of such a staircase, revealed that the stone treads actually carry their loads by working in torsion, not bending, and the wall serves only to prevent them from rotating. Thus it was possible to explain how these delicate sections are able to carry the loads of several people, not only on the stairs themselves, but also at the intermediate landings. Occasionally, seeming to defy gravity, they can even pass across a window opening; this magic is achieved by replacing the missing section wall by an iron bar. The understanding gained from studies of these early cantilever stairs enabled the design engineers of a new building for St John's College at Oxford University in 1994 to mimic the idea in a modern setting and create a dramatic result.

The Greening of Construction

In the 1960s a growing number of scientists had begun to study the natural environment and became increasingly concerned about the adverse impact of many twentieth-century manufacturing processes and farming methods that were polluting both the atmosphere and water in rivers and lakes, as well as damaging wildlife habitats and the ecosystem in general. They also began to be concerned at the increasing rate at which natural resources were being consumed. Two texts were especially influential in awakening interest in environmental issues. In 1962, Rachel Carson's *Silent Spring* warned that the use of certain pesticides and removal of countryside hedgerows had caused the deaths of many birds and other wildlife, and that the consequences would become even more severe unless such practices were changed. In 1972 *The Ecologist* published "A Blueprint for Survival," which argued that western economies were rapidly consuming many finite resources such as fuels, minerals, and tropical hardwoods, which, if the trends continued, would be depleted perhaps in only a few decades. While the dates when these resources run out have since been revised as more sources have been discovered, their eventual depletion has simply been postponed, not prevented.

In 1973–74 the so-called "energy crisis"—when the cost of oil virtually tripled within a year or so—put pressure on building designers to reduce the amount of energy that buildings use. In the 1990s scientists identified the phenomenon of global warming, and attributed it mainly to the production of large quantities of greenhouse gases, such as carbon dioxide, which prevent heat escaping from the earth. It was also discovered that certain chemicals used in many industries, such as chlorofluorocarbons (CFCs), have been depleting the ozone layer of the atmosphere, which filters out a large proportion of harmful ultraviolet radiation from the sun. The discovery, by scientists of the British Antarctic Survey in 1985, of a large hole in the ozone layer over the Antarctic accelerated agreement of the Montreal Protocol in 1987 which has led to phasing out the use of ozone-depleting substances both in buildings and all other manufactured products.

Gradually, over recent decades, environmental legislation in some countries has done much to reduce human impact on the environment. In most countries, for example—since the early 1980s for civil engineering projects, and since the late 1990s for large building projects—it has been a requirement that environmental impact assessments be undertaken to establish the nature and extent of impacts, both during the construction phase and the subsequent life of a building, and to identify the mitigation measures proposed. This has had a direct impact on the work of engineers who were not previously required to address such issues.

In some ways, the building industry has been very quick to respond to these new mandates. When required by law, manufacturers of many materials and products used in construction have been quick to find or develop alternatives to, for example, ozone-depleting materials used in refrigeration equipment or for fire protection. Where there have not been direct impacts on human health,

768

however, changing the materials used in construction has been slower and less significant. For example, although timber has a lower environmental impact than plastics, steel, aluminum, and concrete, the opportunities for using timber to replace these materials is very limited. Likewise, while there are many potential opportunities to use reclaimed components and recycled materials in place of new ones, examples of their use are rare and on a small scale. There are still considerable nontechnical (mainly economic) barriers to realizing these opportunities on a large scale, and patience will be a virtue in effecting widespread change to the materials used to construct the built environment. To date, the most significant change in the use of materials has been the growing reuse of entire (existing) buildings, as discussed above.

The one area of building design in which there has been significant change is in improving the energy efficiency of buildings; this is partly because energy use is easy to measure and because the reductions bring immediate cash benefits to building owners. Buildings specifically designed to use less energy were first considered in the 1960s but, because the cost of energy was then low in relation to other costs, these designs were rather ahead of their time and attracted relatively little interest. Indeed, in the 1960s it was not uncommon for many of the services in a building to be designed and provided by the very people who made their money by selling and installing energy-consuming equipment, such as heating and air-conditioning systems, and it is hardly surprising that they did not recommend natural ventilation methods that did not need such equipment. Of course, at that time it was also still very rare for building services engineers to become involved in the early stages of designing a building, when such strategic decisions are usually made.

One of the first attempts to involve services engineers in early-stage design decisions was initiated by Arup Associates in London. This multidisciplinary building design firm had been set up by Ove Arup to realize his aspi-

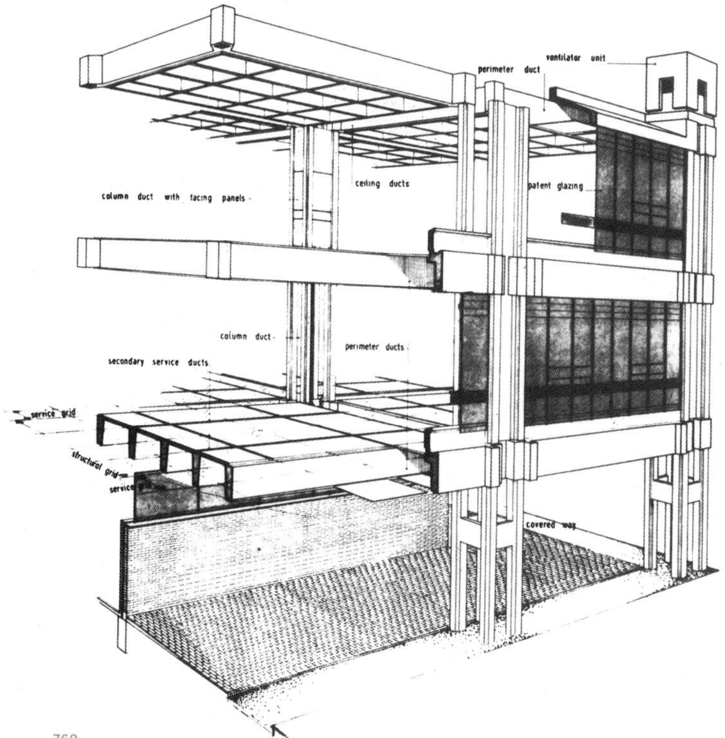

769

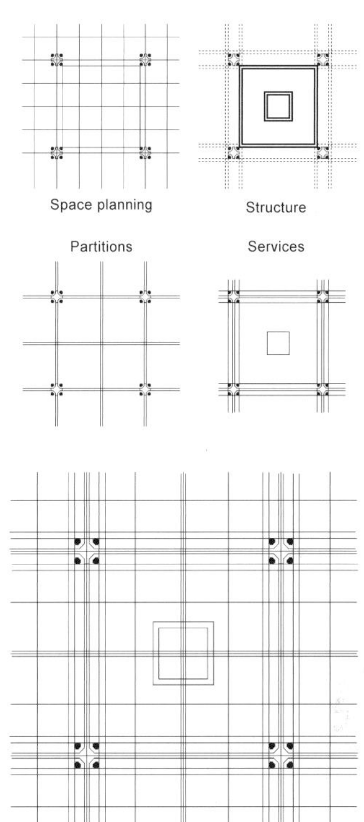

770

ration for "total architecture." The firm began in the 1960s with a number of laboratory buildings, notably the
768 Mining and Metallurgy Building at Birmingham University, and was followed by a number of commercial office buildings. The result was a series of highly acclaimed buildings that incorporated more and more sophisticated ways
769 of integrating all the engineering aspects of buildings to create a unified whole. Arup Associates' technique for structuring the different zones within the building layout
770 became known as the "tartan grid" because of its resemblance to that plaid pattern.

At the height of the oil crisis in 1973, Arup Associates' disciplined approach to integrating the various engineering systems led them to develop a radically different approach to reducing the energy needed to run buildings. In a sense, they returned to an old idea: taking advantage of the intrinsic thermal capacity of the materials in a building to store thermal energy (heat) either as warmth in cold weather or as coolth in hot weather. Thick mud or masonry walls had long been used in vernacular architecture to this end. For large, modern office buildings, the high thermal capacity of reinforced concrete made it the obvious choice. Concrete also has the capacity to carry large structural loads, and it can be easily manufactured in complex solid forms: thus it can be sculpted to create the interpenetrating voids of the tartan grid through which the services pass horizontally through floor structures and vertically through risers.

Arup Associates designed their pioneering building for the
Central Electricity Generating Board in Bristol, England, in 771
1973. In summer, cool night air passes through ducts in the concrete structure and cools it down; this thermal en-

768 Mining and Metallurgy Building, University of Birmngham, England, 1964–66. Engineer and architect: Arup Associates.
769 Mining and Metallurgy Building. Cutaway isometric showing integrated zones for structure and building services.
770 The "tartan grid" developed by Arup Associates to facilitate a structured approach to integrated design.

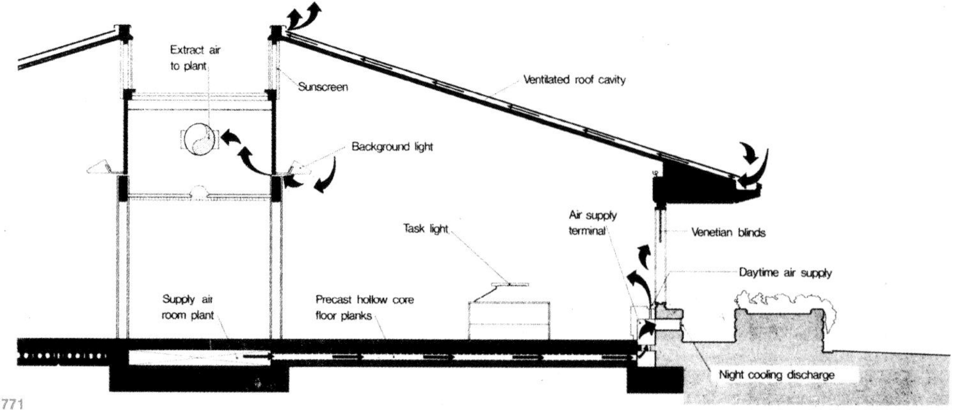

771

772

773

774

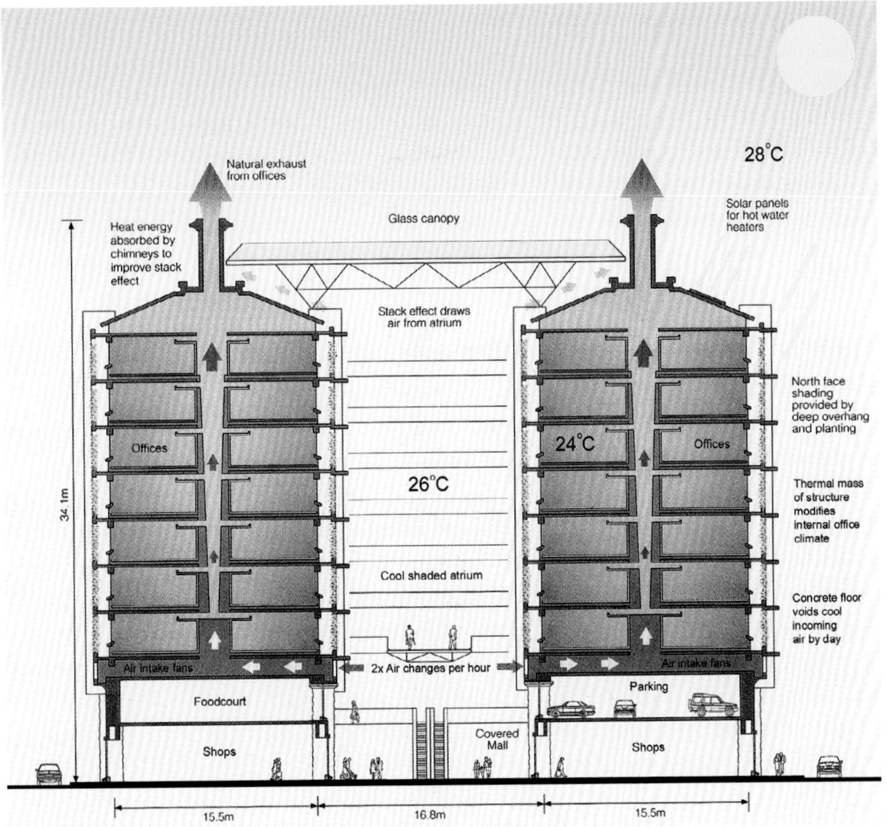

775

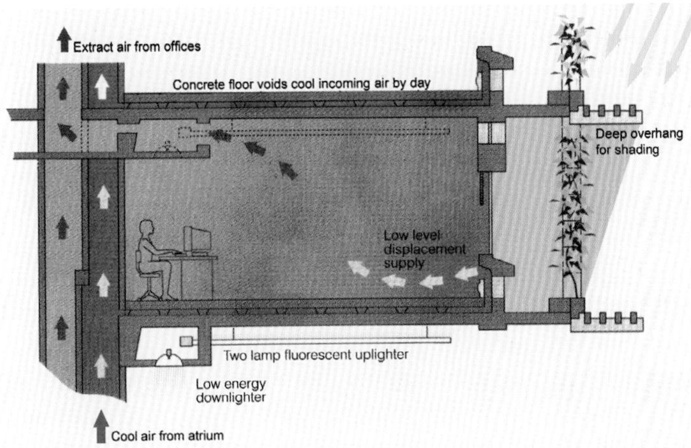

776

771 Central Electricity Generating Board headquarters building, Bristol, England, 1973–78. Engineer and architect: Arup Associates. Diagram of energy system. 772 Eastgate building, Harare, Zimbabwe, 1991–96. Engineer: Ove Arup & Partners; architect: Pearce Partnership. Atrium. 773 Eastgate building. 774 Beddington Zero Energy Development (BedZED), London, 1999–2000. Engineer: Ove Arup & Partners; architect: Bill Dunster. Large rotating cowls at roof level promote air flow through the building. 775 Eastgate building. Diagram showing cooling in summer by 4 degrees Centigrade using natural ventilation. 776 Eastgate building. Diagram showing natural ventilation strategy for each office floor.

ergy is stored as coolth. During the warmer daytime, the coolth is released from the concrete, and cools the room interiors, thus reducing the need for mechanical cooling systems and saving the energy needed to drive them. In winter, during the day, waste thermal energy generated by lights and computer equipment heats the internal air, which is passed through the concrete structure and warms it. This thermal energy is stored as warmth in the concrete overnight and released the next day, heating the air in the room spaces and reducing the demand for electric or gas fuelled heating.

Since the mid-1970s, designing for energy efficiency has favored the use of reinforced concrete and masonry, which combine the necessary thermal capacity with architectural aesthetic. This mirrors the way architects and engineers since the 1930s have used materials—especially reinforced concrete and steel—to express how the structure of a building functions. This becomes a significant matter when architects (especially) are committed to delivering environmentally responsible buildings when it can be important to ensure that such buildings somehow look energy efficient or "green." During the 1990s and early 2000s the number of such striking and different appearance has been steadily increasing. The appearance of a naturally ventilated commercial and retail
772, 773 development in Harare, Zimbabwe, is dominated by the exposed concrete, tessellated to increase the effective surface area and, hence, the efficiency of heat exchange
775, 776 between the air and concrete fabric of the building. The energy consumed by buildings can be considerably reduced in many climates by using natural ventilation as an alternative to mechanical ventilation. A number of architects have made a strong feature of large rotating cowls
774 that can be turned by the wind to achieve the maximum flow of air through a building. It is interesting to note that when this same idea was used by William Strutt and Charles Sylvester at the Derbyshire General Infirmary in 1806–10 (see chapter 6, pp. 318, 320–21), the rotating cowls were kept well out of sight.

The last half century or so has seen a growing number of architects who collaborate closely with engineers to help realize their dreams and, often, to give their buildings an appearance that somehow emphasizes the idea of new or "high" technology. This may mean simply exposing the technology underlying the building services and structure, as Richard Rogers and Renzo Piano did at the Centre Georges Pompidou in Paris (see pp. 572–73). Alternatively, it may involve using exotic materials, traditionally unfamiliar in the building industry, as the Canadian-born architect Frank Gehry (b. 1929) did at the Guggenheim Museum of Art in Bilbao by cladding the 777
building in titanium, a material used mainly in the aerospace industry. Several properties of titanium make it suitable for use as a cladding material: its density is about half that of steel, and it is virtually inert, which means that, unlike normal steel or aluminum, it does not corrode. Titanium can also be treated by an electrochemical process called "anodizing," which can give the surface any one of a range of different colors.

Although most good buildings arise from an effective collaboration between engineer and architect, a few people have been equally talented as both engineer and architect—for example, Owen Williams, Eladio Dieste, and Pier Luigi Nervi in the mid-twentieth century (see chapter 8), and Santiago Calatrava (b. 1951) in our own time. Calatrava's statical understanding of both the stability of structures and the flow of forces and stresses through structural components has enabled him to achieve a remarkable sense of balance and poise in his structures, 778
as well as a visual expression of the structural duty of the individual elements, both in their relative disposition and their form and cross-section.

Many architects now use the sculptural qualities of structure to striking effect. For example, at the Tokyo International Forum (1996), architect Rafael Viñoly 779
(b. 1944) wanted to create a huge glazed atrium some 225 meters long by 30 meters wide. The Japanese engineers, Sasaki Planning Laboratory, devised a structure supported on just two columns, one at either end, to carry the atrium roof as well as a 60-meter-high curtain wall made of laminated glass. The very transparency of building facades often lends them to the expression of a certain structural philosophy—for example, the organic use of tendon-like ties in the glass wall at La Villette by Peter Rice, and the glazed roof covering a street at the Hamburg Museum in Germany (1989) by the engineer Jörg Schlaich, or the gravity-defying inclined glazed roof over the reading room of the Seattle Central Library in 780, 781
Seattle, Washington (2004), by the Dutch architect Rem Koolhaas (b. 1944). Not only must this facade withstand

777

778

777 Guggenheim Museum of Art, Bilbao, Spain, 1997. Structural Engineer: Skidmore, Owings & Merrill; architect: Frank O. Gehry & Associates. 778 Lyon-Satolas Airport Railway Station, Lyon, France, 1994. Engineer and architect: Santiago Calatrava.

780

781

779 (opposite page) Tokyo International Forum, Tokyo, 1996. Architect: Rafael Viñoly. 780 Seattle Central Library, Seattle, Washington, 2004. Architect: Rem Koolhaas/Office for Metropolitan Architecture (OMA). 781 Seattle Central Library. Detail.

782

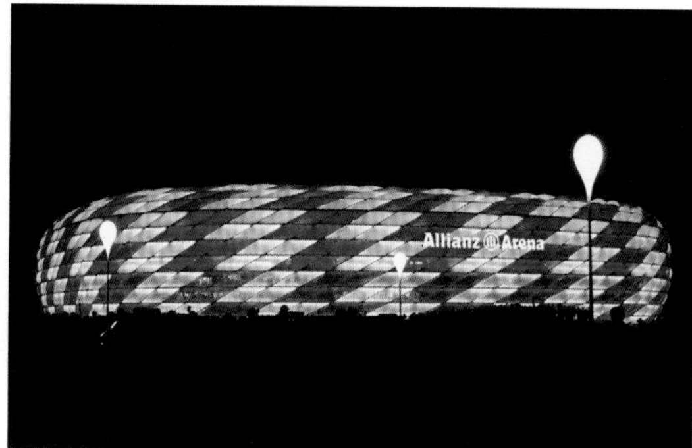

783

loads arising from high winds and earthquakes, it also forms an integral part of the strategy for controlling the internal environment, which has resulted in energy savings of more than 30 percent.

At the Allianz Arena in Munich, by Swiss architects Herzog & de Meuron (2005), the facade is formed from
782, 783 2,874 air-inflated ETFE cushions that not only create a re-
784 markable appearance for a sports stadium but also change color according to circumstances. Each of the translucent cushions can be lit from within—independently to indicate which team is playing (red for FC Bayern München, blue for TSV 1860 München, and white for the German national team), or in combination, for dramatic visual effect.

As is increasingly common today, architects can face particularly difficult problems when they are asked to design buildings for locations and climates with which they are unfamiliar. The Italian architect Renzo Piano (b. 1937) was faced with this challenge for the Tjibaou Cultural
785, 786 Center in Nouméa, New Caledonia, an island in the southwest Pacific (1998). By collecting weather data for an entire year, the engineers, Arup Associates, were able to advise on the best materials to ensure durability and low maintenance in this remote tropical location, and to provide a comfortable environment for users. Depending on the strength and direction of the wind, a number of louvres and windows can be opened or closed in different combinations to achieve a comfortable indoor climate using natural ventilation, with no need for mechanical ventilation or air-conditioning. The theoretical model of the various ventilation modes was analyzed by testing a 1:50-scale model in the boundary layer wind tunnel in Nantes, France. The predictions of the air velocity inside the building data derived from the wind tunnel test were then combined with the humidity and temperature data to calculate the "comfort index" for each hour of the day during the critical periods of the year. These results, in turn, enabled the engineeres to establish the precise settings for the various louvres necessary to achieve the optimum indoor climate.

In the future, as architects, developers, politicians, and society in general demand buildings with increasingly challenging performance requirements, the contributions of building engineers will become even more influential. Buildings will need to incorporate, as a matter of course, many "green" design features such as the generation of energy from solar, wind, and geothermal sources, and systems for recycling water. Also, as the practice of sending waste to landfill sites becomes less politically acceptable and more expensive, so building designers will need to strive to achieve the goal of "zero-waste construction." Thus it will become necessary to take a whole-life view of designing and constructing buildings; for example, buildings will need to be constructed in ways that allow for easy dismantling so that components and materials can be reused or recycled. Engineers and architects will, of necessity, collaborate ever more closely in devising new building forms and methods of construction to meet these new challenges.

782 Allianz Arena, Munich, Germany, 2005. Engineer: Ove Arup & Partners. Architect: Herzog & de Meuron. 783 Allianz Arena. 784 Allianz Arena. Exterior detail.

785

786

785 Tjibaou Cultural Center in Nouméa, New Caledonia, 1998. Engineer: Ove Arup & Partners; architect: Renzo Piano. 786 Tjibaou Cultural Center in Nouméa. Detail.

afterword: Toward a history and philosophy of building engineering

To some extent the ideas of history and progress are two sides of the same coin—one looking back, the other forward. The history reviewed in this book allows us to see the progress achieved over the past three thousand years in the various strands of engineering: the development of an understanding of materials and manufacturing, of better design methods, and of improved ways of conveying designs and performing mathematical calculations. A more detailed look at the nature of this progress is beyond this book, but therein lies the real philosophy of engineering, analogous to the philosophy of science that seeks to explain scientific progress. Further reading on these matters is given in the endnotes.

Today, the scope of building engineering is defined by the various professional disciplines that are involved in building design. As each new discipline is born, it develops its own set of characteristics that distinguish it from other disciplines:

- the establishment of a new professional institution
- published authoritative design guides
- textbooks on the relevant aspects of engineering science
- polytechnic or university courses with standard curricula
- techniques of experimental engineering science
- custom-designed computer software.

The last item on this list is becoming increasingly important in the demarcation of disciplines, for it establishes bodies of professional knowledge not available to those outside the discipline. Specialist software enables each engineer to model that aspect of a building and its systems that concerns him or her; today, this means being able to model virtually every aspect of a building's performance—acoustics; thermal and structural performance; air flow, both in normal circumstances and in a fire; and so on.

Developing design rules and procedures is an activity common to all the disciplines of building engineering today. As we have seen throughout this book, some are highly empirical—rules of thumb, as they are often called—while others are based entirely on a considerable body of scientific knowledge. Design rules in all branches of building engineering tend to begin as empirical rules and gradually become more scientific in nature.

- *Empirical (experience-based) design rules* encapsulate collective experience, allowing users to interpolate within the usual range of experience and, to a limited extent, extrapolate beyond it. Empirical rules are not based on a scientific understanding or explanation of phenomena, but they work.

- *Grounded design rules* are also based on experience, but they incorporate some scientific understanding and explanation. They incorporate empirical constants when necessary. Such rules generate what nineteenth-century engineers called relative properties or values.

- *Scientific design rules* are based on a full scientific understanding and explanation of the relevant phenomena. Generally, they do not require the use of empirical constants to take account of unexplained phenomena. Nineteenth- century engineers referred to the output of such rules as absolute properties or values. Most modern design rules are of this type.

As each building engineering discipline develops, it passes through three further stages that augment the use of design rules:

1. Specifying engineering performance in quantitative terms When a phenomenon can be expressed in quantitative terms, and sufficient data have been collected about the behavior of actual buildings, it becomes possible to specify the level of performance that a component or engineering system in a new building should achieve—for example, what strength of iron or steel is required to make a roof structure; what reverberation time, measured in seconds, should be achieved; what temperature or level of humidity in a room is required; and so on.

2. Understanding the scaling factors in physical models Unless the effect of scale in a given engineering phenomenon can be determined, the phenomenon cannot be said to be fully understood. The designers of masonry structures were, in a sense, fortunate in that the stability of such structures is independent of scale: If a model vault stands, then so, too, will a faithful reproduction, scaled up linearly to full size. This linear relationship does not hold for other structural forms, such as beams and shell structures, or for fluid flow, acoustics, or the thermal behavior of buildings. These phenomena are governed by scientific relationships that involve quadratic, cubic, reciprocal, and other non-linear relationships. The effect of scaling factors on these various phenomena could only be understood when the underlying science had been developed. This occurred at different times, between the seventeenth century and the present day, for each of the many engineering disciplines.

3. Using the factor of safety, and other empirical constants Even when design rules are thoroughly based on scientific understanding, quantitative specifications, and an understanding of scaling factors, it is still usually necessary to incorporate an empirical factor that takes into account the many approximations inherent in the process of creating a mathematical model. By this means, engineers have been able to use mathematical models that they know to be inaccurate; the empirical factor is, effectively, a measure of the inaccuracy or degree of approximation. Even today, such factors are often referred to colloquially as "factors of ignorance." In structural engineering this has become known as the "factor of safety" since William Rankine first developed the idea in the 1850s. Other fields of engineering design employ their own similar empirical factors.

The latter part of the twentieth century has seen almost incredible engineering progress in every industry, yet the public awareness and recognition of these achievements is now very different from those of one or two generations ago. Before World War II it was widely perceived that engineering works—especially in civil, building, and electrical engineering—were truly heroic. Many books carried lofty titles such as *The Wonder Book of Engineering Wonders*.

By the 1990s, engineers had become victims of their own successes. They could take man to the moon and fly passengers in the Concorde at supersonic speeds. They could develop materials with hitherto unimaginable strength, stiffness, and other properties. Through the Internet they provided people with unprecedented access to information, and they made technological luxuries such as cars and home entertainment available at prices that most people, at least in the Western world, could afford. Today it is almost expected that engineers can do anything, and with the computer, they can do it in almost no time at all. Far from making the engineer's life more relaxed, progress has made it more hectic than ever.

The future of the building engineering professions will be less about the technical issues in the engineering disciplines—these are now taken for granted. It will be more about developing robust reasons for employing building engineers. If employing an engineer does not add value to a project, why should a client employ one?

The climate in building engineering is changing. In the past, being an engineer was perceived as mainly being about having technical know-how. In the future it will be more about using this know-how to serve the needs of clients and society:

- Devising buildings that work for the client and occupier
- Creating value for the client
- Exploring the unknown, managing risk, and delivering confidence
- Reducing the impact of buildings on the environment
- Realizing the dreams of clients, architects, and society.

Today, a more efficiently engineered building must become more perfectly designed for one function, like an automobile or an airplane. Once such objects have served their function, they are scrapped and the materials recycled. Yet most building owners do not want to treat buildings like cars; they still want to keep them for a long time. They want buildings to be designed so that they can be adapted for new patterns of use, or even for entirely new functions. It is likely, then, that two different types of buildings will emerge that will make very different demands of building engineers. One type will be like the automobile: highly engineered, lightweight, mass-produced, cheap, and unable to be adapted for other uses. The other, designed to be capable of adaptation for unimagined, even unimaginable uses, will—like the castles, cathedrals, civic buildings, and skyscrapers of eras past—be built to last, creating in their turn a living legacy for engineers of the future.

glossary

ARCH – A structural element, usually spanning between two walls or piers, in which individual stones or **VOUSSOIRS**, or a continuous member of steel or reinforced concrete, act mainly in compression. A stable arch can take many forms – semicircular, pointed, ellipsoidal, and even flat.

BARREL VAULT – A masonry or concrete vault of semi-circular cross section along its length.

BEAM – A structural element spanning between two supports that carries loads by acting in **BENDING**. Most commonly used in floor structures.

BENDING – The structural action that tends to bend a straight member such as a floor beam. The ability to resist deflection arises from internal compressive and tensile forces within the beam.

BENDING MOMENT – A measure of the amount of bending to which a structural member is subjected.

BRACED FRAMEWORK – A structure that derives its stability from ensuring all the members enclose a triangular void (**TRIANGULATED**) rather than a polygon with four or more sides. Often this is achieved by one or two braces formed by the diagonals of a rectangle. The connections in a braced framework need not be rigid; indeed, they are often constructed with pin joints and generally analyzed assuming pin-jointed connections even when they are not literally made thus. Braced frameworks are usually designed to be **STATICALLY DETERMINATE**, by having no **REDUNDANT MEMBERS**.

BRACING – The means by which a structure is made stable and prevented from being a mechanism. The bracing of a structural frame is also the means by which it carries lateral loads due to wind or earthquakes to the foundations. This can be achieved by cross bracing, in which one or both diagonals of a rectangle area are inserted, or by knee-bracing, in which the connections are stiffened and strengthened by knees (in timber frames) or gusset plates (in steel frames).

BRITTLE BEHAVIOR OF MATERIALS – The propensity of a material to break or fracture with little or no plastic deformation. Typical of glass, stone, concrete, and cast iron.

BUCKLING – The failure of a structural element under the action of a compressive force or compressive stresses that cause it suddenly to lose its stability and bend perpendicular to the line of action of the force – e.g., buckling of a **COLUMN** or **STRUT**, or a thin plate in an iron or steel **GIRDER**, or a thin reinforced-concrete **SHELL STRUCTURE**.

BUTTRESS – A structural element used to carry horizontal forces (wind and the lateral thrusts of arches, vaults, and domes) from the upper levels of a building to the foundations. They are usually external to the building. A flying buttress carries such forces over a void beneath.

CAGE CONSTRUCTION – The form of construction comprising a steel frame structure that supports the floor loads, behind a masonry facade that is self-supporting, but which does not carry any loads from the floor. First used by William Jenney for the First Leiter Building, Chicago, in the mid-1870s. The stability of the frame is provided by bracing or rigid joints. (**FRAME** or **SKELETON CONSTRUCTION**)

CANTILEVER – A structural element that acts in **BENDING**, while supported only at one end. It can be considered, effectively, as half a beam. It was famously illustrated by Galileo in his treatment of bending.

CATENARY – The name of the mathematical shape taken up by a uniform cable or chain loaded only by its own self-weight.

CENTERING – The temporary support, traditionally of timber, built to carry the stones or **VOUSSOIRS** of a masonry **ARCH** or **VAULT** during construction. It is removed once the structure is complete and becomes self-supporting.

COLUMN – A vertical compression member made of stone, timber, iron, steel, or reinforced concrete, supporting other load-bearing members above (compare **STRUT**).

COMPRESSION – The **STRAIN** that results from the action of forces tending to reduce the length of a structural component; opposite of **TENSION**.

COOLTH – Heat energy at a temperature lower than ambient air temperature.

CREEP – The propensity of some materials, such as timber and concrete, to continue deforming or deflecting long after the application of a load.

CURTAIN WALL – (medieval) The outer wall that enclosed the main buildings of a castle; (modern) a non-load bearing building facade attached to a structural frame of steel or reinforced concrete.

DEAD LOAD – The load that a structure must support due to the self-weight of the structure and other permanent features such as floors (compare **LIVE LOAD**).

EFFECTIVE STRESS – A measure of the proportion of stress in a soil that is carried by the solid material; the remainder is carried by the water in the pores within the soil (and called "pore-water pressure"). Conceived by Karl Terzaghi.

ELASTIC BEHAVIOR OF MATERIALS – The capacity of a material to deflect when loaded and return to its original shape when unloaded again. In most materials the degree of deflection is directly proportional to the load (see **HOOKE'S LAW** / Mariotte's Law).

EQUILIBRIUM (or **STATICAL EQUILIBRIUM**) – The stable state of a structure, or any part of a structure, in which the forces or stresses are in balance, and at rest (static).

EXTRADOS – The outer or upper surface of a masonry **VOUSSOIR, ARCH,** or **VAULT** (opp. **INTRADOS**).

FACTOR OF SAFETY – The theoretical or actual additional capacity of a structure in excess of the loads that it is expected to support. In design calculations it is used to allow for the uncertainty that arises from the inevitable approximations in mathematical models of real loads, materials, and structures.

FAILURE – Any behavior of an engineering system that means it does not perform the duty for which it was designed. Often used of materials and structures – for example, when a **BEAM** deflects beyond acceptable limits or **FRACTURES**, or when a **COLUMN** or **SHELL STRUCTURE BUCKLES** under compressive loads.

FATIGUE – The fracture of a material caused by the repeated application of loads to a structure, e.g., vibrations from a steam engine or electric motor on its metal supports. **FAILURE** will occur, eventually, even when the magnitude of the loads leads to stresses well below the statical stress that would cause **FRACTURE**.

FLANGE – The (usually) horizontal upper and lower portions of an **I-BEAM**, whose main function is to carry compressive or tensile stresses. The two flanges are joined to, and usually perpendicular to, the **WEB**.

FRACTURE – The failure mechanism for a material or structure in which two or more new surfaces are created. Usually associated with **BRITTLE BEHAVIOR**. The "energy of fracture" or "fracture energy" is the energy needed to create the new surfaces.

FRAME ACTION – The means of providing a structural frame or **PORTAL FRAME** with stability by the use of rigid connections. Also called **PORTAL ACTION** and **VIERENDEEL ACTION**. Contrast with a **BRACED FRAMEWORK**.

FRAME CONSTRUCTION – The structure of a building comprising posts (of timeber) or columns (of steel or reinforced concrete) and beams, whose stability is provided by bracing rigid joints (i.e. without the use of load-bearing masonry walls as shear walls). (compare **CAGE CONSTRUCTION**).

FUNICULAR – The shape taken up by a cable, chain, or other tensile structure under any combination of loads, including self-weight.

GIRDER – Almost a synonym for **BEAM**, though often implying it is large, made of iron or steel, and has been made by riveting or welding together a number of smaller structural elements.

GLULAM – A trade name, now in common use, for glued, laminated timber.

GRIDSHELL – A two- or three-dimensional shell structure made from a lattice of intersecting members of timber, steel, or reinforced concrete.

GROINED VAULT – The vault formed without the use of masonry ribs by two pointed or **BARREL VAULTS** crossing, usually at right angles.

HUMIDITY – The amount of water vapour in the air. Measured either in grams per cubic meter or as **RELATIVE HUMIDITY**.

HYPERBOLIC PARABOLOID – A doubly-curved, anticlastic surface that can be generated by two straight lines moving through space. A hyperbolic paraboloid shell structure carries uniform loads only in the plane of the shell, as shear stresses; the shell is not subject to **BENDING**.

I-BEAM – The most common form of rolled steel **BEAM**. The I-shape is a highly efficient way of using the material to provide a cross-section with a high **STIFFNESS** or **SECOND MOMENT OF AREA**. It comprises two **FLANGES** joined by a **WEB**. When this same form is used in a **COLUMN**, it is usually called an "H-section."

INTRADOS – The inner or lower surface of a masonry **VOUSSOIR, ARCH,** or **VAULT** (opp. **EXTRADOS**).

ISOSTATIC LINES – Contours of equal compressive or tensile stresses (called "principal stresses") within a material.

JACK ARCH – A small masonry arch, usually with a tie rod to balance the outward thrust of the arch, used widely in the nineteenth century for fireproof floor construction. "Jack" means "small."

LIVE LOAD or **IMPOSED LOAD** – The load that a structure must support in addition to its own self-weight and that varies with time, for example, loads arising from people, furniture, snow, wind, temperatures, or earthquakes.

LOAD – The action of forces upon a structure. More particularly defined by an explanatory prefix, such as gravity load, **DEAD LOAD**, **LIVE LOAD**, **IMPOSED LOAD**, wind load, snow load, etc.

MEMBER – A component of a structural framework, especially a **TRUSS**.

NEUTRAL AXIS – The imaginary plane through a **BEAM** that remains unextended when a beam is subject to **BENDING** action. On one side of the neutral axis of a bent beam, material carries compressive stresses; on the other it carries tensile stresses. First conceived as the "axe d'équilibre" (axis of equilibrium) by Edme Mariotte in the 1680s. The term "neutral axis" was first used by Thomas Tredgold in 1820.

NEWTON – The standard measure of force, named in honor of the physicist Isaac Newton.

NOMOGRAM / NOMOGRAPH – A gra-phical method of calculation, using several parallel logarithmic scales, that allows rapid evaluation of formulae used by design engineers. Devised by Maurice d'Ocagne in the 1890s.

OVERTURNING MOMENT – The degree to which a vertical structure, such as a wall or tower, is caused to overturn due to the action of horizontal forces, especially wind loads or the lateral thrust of an arch, vault, or dome.

PIN JOINT – A connection between two or more **MEMBERS** of a **TRUSS** or framework that consists of a single rivet or bolt, or, is assumed to be so when forces in the structure are calculated using statics. At such a connection, the members are free to rotate and so no **BENDING** can be conveyed between members. As opposed to a **RIGID JOINT**

PLASTIC BEHAVIOUR OF MATERIALS – The permanent deformation of a material (usually metals, especially steel) when it is loaded beyond its yield point. When thus loaded, a beam or frame will form one or more plastic hinges, with constant resistance to rotation, that can continue to give stability to a structure. This action is now the main means for preventing the collapse of steel structures subject to earthquake loads.

PORTAL ACTION / FRAME ACTION – The structural action by which a structure achieves its rigidity by means of rigid joints rather than **TRIANGULATED BRACING**. As in **PORTAL FRAME** or **VIERENDEEL** frame.

PORTAL FRAME – A structure that achieves its rigidity by **PORTAL ACTION**. Portal frame structures are **STATICALLY INDETERMINATE**.

PRE-STRESSED STRUCTURE – A structure whose constituent elements are already carrying forces, or are in a state of stress before the application of the main load the structure is intended to carry. In a pre-stressed concrete floor beam, for example, the steel reinforcement is stretched into a state of tension, balanced by the concrete that is forced into compression, before the beam carries the load on the floor.

REDUNDANT MEMBER – A component of a structure that could be removed without causing collapse. A structure with redundant members is **STATICALLY INDETERMINATE** and cannot be analyzed by considering only the equilibrium of applied forces; it is necessary also to consider the elasticity of the structural members themselves.

RELATIVE HUMIDITY – The ratio, expressed as a percentage, of the weight of water vapour in a sample of air to the maximum weight that would be found in "saturated air" (at the same temperature and pressure).

RIGID JOINT – A connection between two or more **MEMBERS** of a **TRUSS** or framework that prevents the members rotating relative to one another. At such a connection, **BENDING** is conveyed between members. As opposed to a **PIN JOINT**.

SCANTLINGS – The sizes of timber elements in a roof or bridge structure, e.g., 6 inches by 8 inches.

SECOND MOMENT OF AREA – A measure of the **STIFFNESS** of a structural section that derives from its geometric shape, and is independent of the material used. Sometimes called "section stiffness" or "moment of inertia."

SHEAR – A structural action that tends to cause sliding or racking, e.g., causing layers of soil to slide over one another, or a rectangular frame to deform into a parallelogram. A "shear wall" is a structural element, of masonry or reinforced concrete, that prevents a structural frame deforming in this way, for example, due to the action of wind loads.

SHELL STRUCTURE – A two- or three-dimensional structure, usually of reinforced concrete, in which the thickness is very much less than the span of the structure, typically 1 to 200 or 300. In an egg shell the ratio is about 1 to 100.

SKELETON CONSTRUCTION – The form of frame construction, comprising a structural frame or "skeleton frame," usually of steel or reinforced concrete columns and beams, that both carries the floor loads and supports the facade of the building. Stability is provided by bracing or rigid joints. (Compare **CAGE CONSTRUCTION**)

SOFFIT – The underside of an **ARCH**, **VAULT**, **BEAM,** or floor slab, usually one made of concrete cast in situ.

SPECIFIC STIFFNESS / STRENGTH – The stiffness or strength of a materical or structure divided by its wight; i.e. a measure of the stiffness or strength per kilogram of material or structure.

SPRINGING – The lowest point of an arch or vault, usually the top of a column or wall.

STABILITY – The fundamental requirement of any structure – the ability to carry the vertical and horizontal loads applied without continuing to move or deform, and to remain in a state of equilibrium.

STATICALLY DETERMINATE STRUCTURE – A structure whose internal forces and forces acting on supports depend only on the arrangement of structural elements (e.g., **STRUTS** and **TIES**), and can be calculated using only statics. These forces are not dependent on the materials of which the structure is made. Compare **STATICALLY INDETERMINATE STRUCTURE**.

STATICALLY INDETERMINATE STRUCTURE – A structure whose internal forces depend both on the arrangement of structural elements (such as **BEAMS**, **STRUTS,** and **TIES**) and the elastic properties of the materials of which the elements are made. Forces cannot be calculated using only statics. Compare **STATICALLY DETERMINATE STRUCTURE**.

STIFFNESS – A measure of the ability of a material or structure to resist deformation when subject to load. The ratio of load to deflection, or of stress to strain. The material property is known as **YOUNG'S MODULUS** after the Scottish scientist Thomas Young, who described it in 1807, although it was already well understood by others, including Leonhard Euler, half a century earlier.

STRAIN – The dimensionless ratio of the extension of a material to its original dimensions. Often expressed as a percentage. Compare **STIFFNESS**.

STRENGTH – The **LOAD** that a material or structure carries at **FAILURE**. Different measures of strength indicate the particular manner in which the failure occurs – fracture, yield, tensile, compressive, shear, fatigue, creep, etc.

STRESS – The local intensity of the internal force carried by a material, measured as force per unit area (e.g., **NEWTONS** per square millimeter).

STRUT – A member of a truss structure that carries compressive forces; can be at any angle to the vertical (compare **COLUMN**).

SURFACE ENERGY – The energy stored in the surface of a material such as a soap bubble; a measure of the energy needed to create a surface, for example in forming a crack.

TENSION – The **STRAIN** that results from the action of forces tending to increase the length of a structural component; opposite of **COMPRESSION**.

THERMAL CAPACITY – The quantity of heat that a material can absorb or store.

THERMODYNAMIC CYCLE – A sequence of changes to the temperature, pressure, and volume of gasses in a heat engine such as a refrigerator or internal combustion engine.

THRUST – A compressive force or stress in a structure, usually applied to masonry structures. The "line of thrust" is an imaginary line that indicates the flow of compressive forces and stresses through a structure, especially through the **VAULTS**, **BUTTRESSES**, **COLUMNS,** and walls of a medieval cathedral.

TIE – A member of a **TRUSS** structure, carrying tensile forces. Also, a tensile member used to carry the outward forces that arise in an **ARCH** – hence, a "tied arch."

TRABEATED CONSTRUCTION – Construction method comprising columns and beams, usually of stone, to form a building structure.

TRIANGULATE – To create a structure whose members form a series of triangles. Triangulated structures are **STATICALLY DETERMINATE**.

TRUSS – Nowadays a structure, usually supporting a roof or a floor, made from discrete elements intended to carry either compressive or tensile forces (but little or no **BENDING**). Also, traditionally, the name of any timber or iron structure supporting a roof, whose various members are subject to bending as well as carrying either compressive or tensile forces.

VAULT – A two- or three-dimensional curved masonry structure whose stones are loaded in **COMPRESSION**. A Roman or barrel vault was typically semicircular, made of brick or concrete, and of constant section along its length. In medieval cathedrals, vaults were made of stone and usually pointed, with ribs at the lines of intersection of two vaults. In a "fan vault," ribs were absent, and the vault resembled a modern shell structure.

VIERENDEEL ACTION – A structure, or Vierendeel girder, that achieves its rigidity by virtue of rigid joints or **PORTAL / FRAME ACTION**. Named after the Belgian engineer Arthur Vierendeel (1852–1940), who exploited, but did not invent, this structural form for steel railway bridges in the 1890s.

VOUSSOIR – A stone, usually wedge-shaped, used to form a masonry **ARCH**.

WEB – The (usually) vertical portion of an **I-BEAM**, whose main function is to convey stresses between the upper and lower **FLANGES**.

YIELD POINT – The transition point, when a material is subject to increasing load, between **ELASTIC BEHAVIOR** and **PLASTIC BEHAVIOR**. When loaded beyond its yield point, a metal does not return to its original dimensions.

YOUNG'S MODULUS – see **STIFFNESS**.

Units

Dealing with engineering in different centuries and in many countries, it has been necessary to compromise. The metric system has been used as far as possible, with some exceptions. Feet and inches have occasionally been retained when it would be too awkward to use meters or millimeters. Ton is used rather than tonne, for reasons of familiarity. Approximate conversion factors for the most common units are as follows:

LENGTH
1 meter (m) = 1000 millimeters (mm) = 39.37 inches (in) = 3.28 feet (ft)
1 kilometer (km) = 1000 m = 3209 ft = 1094 yards = 0.621 miles

WEIGHT
1 kilogram (kg) = 2.205 pounds
1 tonne = 1000 kg = 0.98 tons (UK) = 1.10 tons (US)

FORCE
1 Newton = 0.98 kg force = 0.2248 pounds force
1 kiloNewton (kN) = 1000 Newtons

FLOOR LOADING
1 kN/m^2 = 20.8 lb/ft^2

STRESS
1 N/mm^2 = 145 pounds per square inch (lb/in^2 or psi)

TEMPERATURE
1 Celsius degree = 1.8 Fahrenheit degrees
0°C = 32°F; 20°C = 68°F; 30°C = 86°F; 100°C = 212°F

appendix 1: "Aims and Means," by Ove Arup

In 1969, at the age of 74, Ove Arup responded, in print, to his colleagues' request to summarize the ethos of the firm he had created 33 years before. It was published in the firm's Newsletter (Number 37, November 1969). It is the best articulation I know of what building engineering is today, and merits reprinting in its entirety. This article was the precursor to Arup's "Key Speech" (9 July 1970), which can be read in the book Arups on Engineering (see the Bibliography for details), or on the company's Web site, www.arup.com.

I have been asked by my partners to prepare a statement on the aims of the Arup Organisation—what it's all about, what we stand for.

This is not easy. An enumeration of lofty aims will sound obvious, banal and smug, like the platitudes of a political party speech. We must go further and dig deeper to put across what I suggest we feel we stand for, although it has never been put down in black and white.

To aim high is not to boast, to show how virtuous we are. But we must aim if we are not to miss the target altogether. And we, the partners, must agree on what we want to aim at, as I think we do, and we must try to get support of all our members for these aims if we are to have any hope of achieving them. We say in effect—These are the things which we think we should try and do. If you agree, help us to do them, if you don't agree, let us have your option—and if we then still can't reconcile our aims, you should consider whether you would not be better off in another organization.

To aim is one thing, achievement is another. Between them lies a struggle, against external odds, against internal shortcomings. We need to keep our aims in sight to help us in this struggle, to measure the gap between aim and achievement, to fix priorities, to identify odds and shortcomings.

In the following, the term 'firm' or 'organisation' means the same thing, means 'us' in fact.

Our aims as an organisation are naturally coloured by the fact that we are a collection of engineers, architects, scientists, administrators, economists, etc, earning our living as a firm by offering our services as designers of what we inelegantly, but comprehensively, may call 'static hardware'.

They are equally coloured by the fact that this is a firm which originated in Great Britain, using English as its main means of communication and basing its values on what is hoped to be the best in Western European Culture—a humanism which should be able to embrace all humanity if not all ideologies or narrow nationalisms.

When trying to state the aims of an organisation like ours we must distinguish between these aims and the private aims of the individual members. The latter may vary widely, and could even be antagonistic to the collective aims, in which case it would properly be best to terminate the membership. But the basis of any organisation based on voluntary membership must of course be that the collective aims do not run counter to the private aims, that they do in fact form part of, and support, the private interests. Otherwise the organisation would soon wither away. This applies especially to an organisation like ours whose assets consist of the contributions the individual members can make, and which must be freely and eagerly made to be of any value.

It would also be useful to distinguish between aims and means, in order to establish priorities. This is far from easy, for one desirable state of affairs which can rightly be classified as an aim in itself may at the same time be a means to another aim, or may clash with another aim. Besides, means tend, in the heat of the battle, to become aims in themselves.

Individual Needs
What does the individual member want from the firm?

1. Money—and rather more than less.
2. Interesting work.
3. To gain experience.
4. To use and develop his potential.
5. To have or gain a position of responsibility with power to take decisions.
6. Possibilities of advancement in all these respects.
7. Security of employment.
8. Opportunities to travel.
9. Opportunity for attending conferences or courses of instruction.
10. To work in a friendly atmosphere.
11. To work in pleasant surroundings.
12. To feel that his/her work is worth doing.
13. To work in a firm respected inside and outside his or her profession.

This list could be varied, of course, but is a reasonable sample of what most people would like to get from their job, if possible. It is a mixture of aims and means, and the list could perhaps be reduced to four basic items:

1. Money.
2. Interesting and satisfying work.
3. Pleasant atmosphere and surroundings.
4. The moral satisfaction and prestige attached to doing useful and good work.

These individual aims are reasonable enough, and apply to any firm. They are therefore too general to be of much use, except in that they represent the expectations of our members which we must try to meet as far as possible if the firm is to succeed as we want it to succeed. That they are difficult to satisfy in toto is obvious, and the greatest and most fundamental difficulty is perhaps the fact that the interests of the individual members tend to clash. How can we make five people happy if they all want the same job? Who is going to do the dull work? etc. The policy of the firm must take account of this difficulty, but the aims—or what I may perhaps, reluctantly, call the philosophy of the firm must be more specific and must relate to the nature of our work, and the role we think our firm could, and should play in society.

1 We are designers. The design—what I have called the 'Total Design'—determines what is being built. This again determines the environment in which we will have to live, and which will profoundly influence our lives. Not only visually, but functionally and spiritually, it affects our health and happiness—everything. In short, our work is important for our society. So it should be taken seriously. We have an obligation to be useful members of society.

2 As designers, we have an obligation towards our clients. And we are in a position of trust. We could easily cheat the client by doing indifferent work—it would be easier, we could earn more, and he would probably not know the difference between what he gets and what he might have got. We must endeavour to justify that trust. And this is part of a general obligation to act honourably in all dealings with the outside world.

3 We also have an obligation towards our professional institutions, not in a narrow, parochial way, but to assist in the process of transformation which is necessary to make them serviceable in the new epoch of industrialisation. It means taking part in the discussions going on, helping to break down barriers, co-operating with universities, research establishments and government agencies to further efficiency of building and the power of the designer to co-ordinate all design decisions.

4 We have an obligation to our members as human beings. We have seen that to satisfy their aspirations as far as possible is a necessary condition for the firm to flourish; the firm depends on them—it is them. But there is more in it than that. By creating a model fraternity, so to speak, we make a contribution to what is almost the central problem of our time: how to overcome the social friction and strife which threatens to overwhelm mankind. We could become a small scale experiment in how to live and work happily together. This would also have a profound influence on the quality of our work.

These are broad aims, still too general, one could say, partly obvious because understood without being stated and partly irrelevant. But they outline the area inside which our work must be done. Many would, I suppose, pay lip-service to the same ideals: what matters is what we can and are prepared to do about it.

We must now proceed to a closed definition of these aims, under the general headings of:

A QUALITY OF WORK.
B QUALITY OF BEHAVIOUR.
C IMPROVING PROFESSIONAL EFFICIENCY.
D LEARNING TO WORK HAPPILY TOGETHER.

and we will try to deal with aims first, bearing in mind that aims are not enough, are in fact 'Easy to draw, but difficult to get', as the pavement artist of old used to scribble under a drawing of a cottage loaf. Afterwards we must then investigate whether these aims are capable of achievement, whether they can be reconciled with each other and with the private aims of our member, what steps must be taken to achieve them, and whether we are prepared to make the sacrifices entailed.

A QUALITY OF WORK. The relentless pursuit of quality, of excellence even, in design. The creation of total architecture, with all that implies.

This is the primary aim of our organisation. And it may be out of place here to enumerate some of the benefits, or secondary aims, which would result if we were able to reach this goal in a larger number of cases. We would have a large number of satisfied clients, giving us more work , the reputation of the firm would grow, we would be able to get more interesting work, thus we would attract good collaborators, who would help to keep up the standard, it would be a boost to morale, etc. All this is obvious. Eventually we might even derive a financial benefit from such a course—but whether it would outweigh the extra cost is doubtful. But there is more in it than that. Quite apart from all the glamour and excitement, there is a satisfaction in doing any work well, no matter how seemingly trivial, if it is work which is necessary foundation for the more spectacular achievement. Doing your work well, you gain self-respect, and gradually, the respect of others. To spell out in more detail what we mean by quality or excellence could be a very big job and I don't think it is necessary. But perhaps I should say a few words about why I bring in this business of 'total architecture'.

A house, a bridge, anything we build, consists of many parts. But it's the house we are interested in, not the parts, but the totality of the part. But even that is not quite right, because the house is something more than the totality of parts, it is the embodiment of somebody's idea of a house, a dream come true. When man built with his own hands, guided by his own vision of what was to be, the result was a direct, if imperfect, expression of his aspiration, a synthesis of ends and means, of the desirable and the possible, of dream and action. As such it was a form of art—it was primitive architecture.

When his imagination was widened by artistic exploration, by study of space through solid geometry, and when the possible was extended by a better understanding of materials and physical laws, by the invention of better ways of building, by specialisation and co-ordination of effort and the handing down of experience through generations, the result could still be architecture, as long as this synthesis was achieved, as long as the vision and the extended possibilities were united by a master-mind or by a tradition embodying human aspirations and experience. It was when this synthesis was lost, when the activity of building was split between a number of separate professions and businesses, when it was not any more a way to satisfy human aspirations for a better life, but a way to make money for various sectarian interests—it was then, and to that extent, that building came to lose its humanity and even to be a menace to man.

I claim no historical accuracy for this outburst. It is a clumsy was of expressing some elusive fact which nevertheless is important, and important to us. Any building or structure for which we are reasonable should have this quality, character, unity, call it what you like. This is what some people mean by architecture. Not the architecture which is only sculpture or aesthetic self-expression, but one which serves a worthwhile human aspiration in an honest and straightforward and practical way, but can rise to great art where this is required. We know that this can only be achieved by an integration, a synthesis of all different elements, the skills, know-how and resources which are needed to create the whole thing, and that to excel in this undertaking requires a mental effort, a relentless passion for perfection. What I want to stress is that we must always be aware of the fact that the part must fit into the design of the whole, and that the whole must relate to the other larger units. We must not wear blinkers; a wider outlook may affect basic assumptions. This is not to make a nuisance of ourselves, but in pursuit of our fundamental aim of being as useful to society as possible. In any work we undertake we must try, to the best of our ability, by diplomacy, by persuasion and by, if necessary, privately and gratuitously overstepping our brief to counteract the sometimes absurd effects of multiple design responsibility, so that the claims both of architecture, structure and efficient construction (cost) are met. We must think of it as total architecture. In cases where we are the principal designers for a well-defined scheme, as civil engineers or architects, it is mainly up to us to achieve this, but where we are only part-designers, engineers for the structure only, working with outside architects, we must do all we can to help these architects to produce total architecture. Where there are other separate designers involved, this becomes more difficult and it would therefore be highly desirable to develop one or several services divisions, so that we can offer the architects advice on any technical aspects of the building.

We will also, as architects, be more and more concerned with advice on briefing, because the right decision on what to build is usually much more important than how we build it, and it affects our work profoundly. We must take a critical look at the brief, and that means in many cases relating our work to its wider framework. Planning deals with this—sooner or later we may have to expand in this direction as well in the interest of unity—in the meantime we must be aware of this wider framework—just as our engineers must be aware of the architectural framework, our service divisions must be aware, and interested in, the work they are helping us with—in short: away with the blinkers! The quality of our work will be enhanced thereby. To achieve full control of the design and method of construction it might also be desirable in certain cases to take over the role of the general contractor, organising the work of the specialist sub-contractors.

B QUALITY OF BEHAVIOUR. There is not much to be said about our relationship with clients, except that it is our job to look after their true interests, and, where necessary, to guide with regard to their brief in cases where they don't quite know what they want or what they could get. We should do this even if we thereby reduce our fees or incur extra expense, within reason at least. Of course, there are cases where we may have to defend our interests, but we should do it openly. Where we don't approve of the client's intention, where they are to some extent anti-social or unprofessional in our opinion, we should probably not undertake the job. We should keep clear of bribery and corruption. It is difficult to formulate rules about what we can consider honourable dealing—except to say that it is better to keep away from anything that would tarnish our reputation if it were known, or which we later would be ashamed of. That we should honour our obligations is obvious—and therefore we should avoid promises which we cannot keep, like giving firm commitments on time and cost before we know the relevant facts.

C IMPROVING PROFESSIONAL EFFICIENCY. We are professional people, i.e. we have received a useful education and are expected to use our knowledge in the service of the community. The public must however take our 'expertness' on trust—and we must see to it that their trust is justified. That, shortly, explains the need for professional standards and professional rules of conduct. We should therefore be sure that we have the necessary qualifications and where we feel that our knowledge is inadequate in a particular field, we should add to our strength in that direction or advise the client to call in other experts or suggest that he should go to other consultants. And we should collaborate with our professional bodies, universities, colleges, etc.

D LEARNING TO WORK HAPPILY TOGETHER. We have obligations to all our members, and most to those who have thrown in their lot with us and intend to stay. But how much we will be able to do in the direction of schooling, welfare, insurance for sickness and old age, etc., and how much we will be able to satisfy their professional ambitions, is another matter. This can perhaps be left to the general discussion of the possibility of fulfilling all these aims.

Looking at these aims purely as aims, they do not contradict each other. To be in the forefront of our profession, doing interesting and socially important work, and therefore being honoured and looked up to and asked for advice all over the world—and known for our human and friendly outlook, etc.—that is all very marvellous. But is there any chance at all of reaching this state of bliss?

appendix 2: Iron and its Alloys

The history and use of iron plays an important role in the development of structural engineering for two reasons. Its high strength enables it to perform duties that other materials cannot, and hence allows new types of structure to be built. Even masonry buildings such as the Parthenon and medieval cathedrals rely on iron, even if only to tie together the large blocks of stone. The second reason is that iron has always been expensive and the need for economy drove engineers to minimize the quantity of metal used. This was especially important when cast iron was first used for columns and beams in "fireproof" buildings in the 1790s, and again when wrought iron was used to make bridges carry the unprecedented loads of railway locomotives from the 1840s. These two periods both led to rapid developments in the use of structural theory. The use of different alloys of iron is dependent on their material properties, which in turn depend on the percentage of carbon in the alloy, as was first established in the 1760s by the Swedish metallurgist T.O Bergman (1735–84).

	WROUGHT IRON	MILD STEEL	GREY CAST IRON	MALLEABLE CAST IRON
% carbon	0.02 – 0.1	0.1 – 1.0	2.5 – 4.0	2.5 – 4.0
tensile strength N/mm²	280–370	350–700	120	400
comp. strength N/mm²	240–310	350–700	600–800	400
stiffness (Young's modulus) kN/mm²	155–220	210	85–90	200
structure	fibrous	amorphous	crystalline	amorphous
fracture	ductile	ductile	brittle	ductile
castability		good	very good	very good
corrosion resistance	good	poor	very good	poor
weldability	possible	very good	difficult	possible

appendix 3: Concrete and Reinforced Concrete

The word "concrete" has become a precise term only in the last two centuries. Previously it was used to describe many mixtures of ingredients that shared the characteristic of undergoing a chemical reaction when mixed with water and forming a hard, durable material. We now describe concrete as having a binder or chemically-active ingredient – gypsum or lime cement – which binds a number of filler or passive ingredients called aggregates, usually sand and gravel. Gypsum and limestone are naturally occurring rocks made chemically active by heating to around 900°C, which removes the water molecules that are chemically bound into the rock. They are then ground to a powder which is called quicklime or cement. When used, the cement is mixed or "slaked" with water, starting a chemical reaction in which water and carbon dioxide in the air recombine to form a solid mass. After an initially rapid chemical reaction which generates a lot of heat, pure lime hardens by reaction with atmospheric carbon dioxide to form calcium carbonate. This is a slow process, and cannot occur under water. Hence such lime is called "non-hydraulic."

The main differences between plaster, mortar and concrete are the quantity and size of the aggregate that is added to the cement/water mixture to achieve a suitable consistency and bulk. Gypsum cements become hard particularly quickly, which makes them suitable for plastering walls and ceilings. Mortars made with lime cement and sand aggregate cure far more slowly. They are used to bed bricks and stones in walls and masonry vaults and domes. When used in bulk, for instance in foundations, concrete is made with both sand or other fine aggregate, and aggregates of larger sizes, nowadays typically gravels up to about 20mm diameter. In earlier times, larger stones and a wider variety of sizes were used, and pieces of broken brick and rubble were often included, according to what materials were available.

The chemical properties of cements, and hence the precise nature of the chemical reactions that occur when mortar or concrete is made, vary considerably with the chemical composition of the rocks, the proportions of water and cement, and the degree of exposure to the atmosphere. These all affect the mechanical properties, especially the strength of the mortar or concrete. For this reason, selecting the right *mix design* is a crucial aspect of making concrete.

The idea of using a material with good tensile properties to strengthen or reinforce a material weak in tension, such as concrete, is very old indeed. Straw was used to reinforce mud bricks from before the dawn of recorded history, and was the first fibre-reinforced or *composite* material. For centuries, plaster for normal use has been reinforced with horsehair, and, when used for making mouldings, has been reinforced using small strips of cloth. There is evidence from eighteenth-century France that mass concrete used in foundations was reinforced with tree roots and other strong plant fibres. This idea was probably used much earlier. For any such composite action to be achieved, it is essential that the fibres bond to the filler material – mud grips the straw in ancient bricks, cement bonds chemically to the steel reinforcement in modern reinforced concrete. The effectiveness of the composite action is improved if the bond is strengthened or improved to prevent pull-out (e.g., ribs or profiling on steel reinforcement).

	Antiquity	1400
Non Building Use of Wrought Iron	**From c.1500 B.C.** Various implements and hand tools; swords, etc. **100 B.C.** Iron tires for wooden wheels; nails; straps to protect wooden doors; bars over windows for security; locks **c. A.D. 400** Iron pillar of Delhi, India, originally located elsewhere and moved to the Qutb complex at Mehrauli; 7.2 m tall, 0.41 m in diameter, and weighing 6 tons. Originally supported a statue.	**c.1350** Cannon weighing 600 kg made from parallel iron bars and iron hoops **1500** Leonardo describes measurement of tensile strength of iron wire **1586** Iron straps weighing 13 tons are used in moving the Vatican Obelisk, Rome
Wrought Iron in Building	**c. 400 B.C.** Dovetails and cramps for linking stone blocks (e.g., the Parthenon, Athens), particularly to prevent dislodging in earthquakes **c. 280 B.C.** Iron framework supporting bronze exterior of Colossus of Rhodes **c. 25 B.C.** Iron rods as support/form for tile vaults in baths described by Vitruvius, *De Architectura* **c. A.D. 72–80** Over 300 tons of iron used in the Flavian Amphitheater (Colosseum), Rome **211–16** Over 100 tons of iron used for cramps and ties in the Baths of Caracalla **530 ff.** Iron ties for masonry arches—e.g., Saint Sophia, Constantinople **c. 670** Great Mosque, Qairawan, Tunisia **c. 786–805** Iron chain used to carry outward thrust in masonry dome of the Palatine Chapel, Aachen, Germany **1000 ff.** Iron widely used in cathedrals (cramps; support for stained glass windows) **c. 1170** Iron ties in vault of cathedral, Soissons, France **1246–8** Multiple ties in main arches and apse of Sainte-Chapelle, Paris **1306** Use of 25m iron ties in timber arch roof of Palazzo della Ragione, Padua—an idea brought to Italy from India	**1400 ff.** Regular use of wrought iron in tied arches; growing use of iron window frames **1550s** Iron chains in dome of St Peter's Cathedral, Rome **1600 ff.** Use of iron ties and straps in timber roof trusses in Italy **c.1670** Extensive use of iron to reinforce masonry in the new façade of the Louvre Palace, Paris (Claude Perrault) **c.1680** Hangers to support bookcases, Trinity College Library, Cambridge (Sir Christopher Wren) **c.1690** Hangers to support mezzanine floor, Hampton Court Palace, London (Wren) **1692** Iron columns in new balcony in Houses of Parliament, London (Wren) **1744** Iron chains added to reinforce dome of St Peter's Basilica, Rome
Non Building Use of Cast Iron	**Pre-500 B.C.** Jewelry created when cast iron was made by accident in smelting furnace	**1360s** Cast iron cannon in Germany, gradually spreading to northeastern France and northern Italy; also cannon balls **1638** Cooking vessels, fire grates
Cast Iron in Buidling	**c. 300** Cast bronze used for solid and hollow columns made using same techniques as cast iron in 1790s	**1638** Beam in Coalbrookdale iron furnace **1682** Water pipes at Versailles Palace, France **1710** Railings around St Paul's Cathedral, London (Wren)
Non Building Use of Steel	**500 B.C.** Swords **A.D. 100** Wootz steel (also called Damascus steel) imported to Rome from south India; made the best weapons **12th c.** Steel helmets **1370s** Steel crossbows	**1670s** Steel springs for vehicle suspension **1722** First scientific treatise on the chemistry of iron and steel: *L'art de convertir le fer forgé en acier et l'art d'adoucir le fer fondu* [The Art of Converting Forged Iron into Steel and the Art of Rendering Cast Iron Ductile], by French physicist René Antoine Ferchault de Réaumur (1683–1757)
Steel in Building		

1750	1820	1860
1740s Christopher Polhem rolls iron bars in Sweden **1768–72** Comte de Buffon builds Grande Forge, Burgundy, France **From 1750s** Riveted wrought iron boilers for steam engines **1783–4** Henry Cort puddles wrought iron and rolls iron bars, England **1788** Timber beams of steam engines strengthened by iron trussing rods by James Watt **1803** Pont des arts, Paris	**c.1820** First iron ship hulls **1826** Menai Suspension Bridge by Thomas Telford with iron chains **1820–30** Rolled iron rails (Birkenshaw, 1820; Clarence, 1830; Stevens, 1830) **1830s** All-iron waterwheels for mills, 6.5m diameter by 8m long **1840s** Iron rods for tension members of truss railway bridges (Howe truss, 1840; Pratt truss, 1844) **1843** SS *Great Britain*, by I.K. Brunel, almost 100 m long **1845–50** Conwy and Britannia tubular girder bridges by Stephenson and Fairbairn **1852–59** Royal Albert Bridge, Saltash, by Brunel	**1887–9** Eiffel Tower, Paris Exhibition
1752 Wrought iron beams supporting hood over kitchen hearth near Lisbon **1770–2** Iron "reinforced" masonry in Panthéon, Paris, by Jacques-Germain Soufflot **1773** David Hartley's iron "fire plates" patented **1781** Iron roof truss at Louvre Palace, designed by Soufflot, completed **1780s** Iron floor beams by Ango, Paris **1780s** "Poteries et fer" fireproof floors developed **1790** Iron roof truss with 28m span, Théâtre Français, Paris, by Victor Louis **1797** Iron safety curtain added at Theatre Royal, Drury Lane, London (opened 1794) **1808–13** Halle au blé (wheat exchange) in Paris	**1820s** Trussing rods used to strengthen timber beams **1834** Corrugated iron roofing and cladding **1838** All-wrought iron roof truss, using rolled sections, at Euston Station, London **1838** 12m lenticular beam of riveted iron plate, St Petersburg **1840s** Wrought iron roofs common in factories, railway stations, and theaters **1841** Built-up I-section beam, Robert Stephenson **1844** James Kennedy and Thomas Vernon patent riveted ribs for stiffening ship hulls **1848–49** First rolled I-beam, Zorès, France **1850–51** Built-up girders, trussed girders and iron ties in Crystal Palace, Hyde Parkl, London **From 1850s** Widespread use of built-up wrought iron beams	**1870s** Multi-story frame buildings in Europe and U.S. **1872** Wrought iron frame at Menier Chocolate Factory, Noisiel, France
1750s Smeaton uses cast iron for wearing parts of mills **1779** Iron Bridge at Coalbrookdale in English West Midlands **1785** First all-cast iron flour mill machinery **1789** "Fish-belly" rail patented by William Jessop **1795** Structure of aqueducts at Longdon-on-Tern, Shropshire, England (1795–6) and Pontcysyllte, North Wales (1795–1805), both by Thomas Telford	**1820–40** Voussoir arch road bridges by Telford (1800 ff.) much copied by others **1847** Collapse of Dee railway bridge (28 m cast iron beam with wrought iron truss rods)	
1752 Columns and beams supporting hood over kitchen hearth near Lisbon **1768–72** Beams in St Petersburg **From 1770s** Columns in several churches in England **1792–3** Columns in Derby mill by William Strutt **1796–7** Beams and columns in Castle Foregate mill, Shrewsbury by Charles Bage	**c.1820** Cast iron and glass conservatory at Bicton, England **1831–3** Single-story rigid iron frame at Hungerford Fish Market, London **1834** Rational I-section for beam at Orrell's Mill (Fairbairn and Hodgkinson) **1835–9** Ribs for dome of St Isaac's Cathedral in St Petersburg **1844** First all-iron, rigid-framed building (fire station, Portsmouth Dockyard, England) **1845** Progressive collapse of Oldham Mill due to brittle fracture of cast iron beam **1846** First H-section column by George Baker **1846** Facades in New York by Daniel Badger	**1900** Occasional use of circular solid and hollow-section columns
1751 Wootz steel first made in Europe for clock springs near Sheffield, England **1760s** Swedish metallurgist T.O. Bergman (1735–84) first recognizes the importance of carbon content in determining the properties of iron alloys	**1850s** "Air-boiling" process developed in Britain by Henry Bessemer (1813–98)—to make better steel for cannon—and in the U.S. by William Kelly (1811–88)	**1860s** "Open hearth" (Siemens-Martin) process developed in Germany **1867–74** Tubular, stainless steel arch, Eads Bridge, Mississippi River at St Louis, Mo. **1870–93** Suspension cables of Brooklyn Bridge, New York **1883–90** Forth Rail Bridge, west of Edinburgh **1920s–1930s** High-strength steel—e.g., Chromador
		1885 Era of steel-frame buildings begins with Home Insurance Building, Chicago **1889** First major building in steel, Galérie des machines, Paris **1920s–1930s** Welded steel structures—e.g., Simpsons Store, Piccadilly, London (1936) **1940s–1950s** Use of exposed structural steel in single-story buildings by Mies van der Rohe **1949–54** Plastic design of steel frames—e.g., Hunstanton School, England **1955** Exposed structural steel in multi-story building: MAN office, Germany **1962–4** Weathering steels such as COR-TEN used for exposed structural members in John Deere Building, Illinois **1971** Fire protection by water-cooling in U.S. Steel building, Pittsburgh **1971–7** Cast steel used in Centre Pompidou, Paris

	Antiquity	1500
Use of Mass Concrete	**c. 100 B.C.** Hydraulic cements using volcanic ash from Pozzuoli, Italy and other places **c. 50 B.C.–A.D. 400** Widespread use for foundations, walls, floors, balconies, vaults, and domes **c. 72–80** Flavian Amphitheater (Colosseum), Rome **c. 118–26** Pantheon, constructed using five different densities of concrete	**1600s** Hydraulic cements made with trass from the Rhine valley, used in Holland for harbours and foundations of bridges and waterside buildings **1780s** Concrete fill between iron beams in France **1790s** Concrete used as fill in jack arch construction, Britain **1845** Jack arches made entirely of concrete by William Fairbairn **1830s–1870s** Many thousands of all-concrete buildings (mainly houses) built in France and Britain
Use of Reinforced Concrete		**1833** Landscape architect John Loudon suggests embedding iron rods in concrete to form it into complex, free-standing shapes **1844** Joseph Louis Lambot patents the use of iron rods with concrete to make waterproof vases and tanks **1848** Reinforced concrete boat by Lambot **1854** W.B. Wilkinson patent for reinforced concrete floors **1855** François Coignet makes various building elements using concrete and iron frame, which also add strength **1862** Coignet builds house of reinforced concrete **c. 1865** Date of only known Wilkinson building (demolished 1952), Newcastle, England **1870s** Precast reinforced concrete panels on timber studding covering walls of concrete, brick, or blockwork made by W.H. Lascelles, London **1873–6** William E. Ward builds entire house of reinforced concrete in Port Chester, N.Y. **1877** Thaddeus Hyatt (1816–1901), an American living in London, patents and tests several fireproof flooring systems containing iron and concrete. Some were used in buildings, but not widely **1878** Joseph Monier patent for beams
Concrete Technology	**Ancient** Wooden formwork used as mold for bricks and mud construction (pisé) **200 B.C.** Use of mortar in timber formwork **100 B.C.** Lining of timber formwork with brick pieces to create cheap walls mainly of concrete with the appearance of brick **Roman** Use of tufa and volcanic ash to make lightweight concrete for vaults and domes **Roman** Concrete delivered to in situ location in baskets—10–20 kg per person. The Baths of Caracalla (A.D. 211–16) used well over a million tons of concrete.	**1750s** John Smeaton undertakes scientific testing of hydraulic concrete mixes to establish best performance for use in his Eddystone Lighthouse. **1830s** Precast concrete blocks **1840s** Timber formwork for walls that could be reused without full disassembly **1840s** Continuous concrete manufacture and placement

1860s–1890s

Many examples of large unreinforced concrete spans in Britain. Examples include:

- Six-story (18.3 m) concrete walls in a warehouse
- Flat slab spanning 8 x 6 meters, 175mm thick
- Arched slab 15 x 3.5 meters, 275mm down to 75mm thick, carrying "an immense weight of machinery and men" in a warehouse
- 1.22m balcony supported on cantilevers, cast in situ, tapering from 280mm to 75mm. Twelve days after casting, the balcony was successfully tested by three men running along it.

1883 Use of tinted mass concrete and various surface finishes to mimic dressed and rough-faced natural stone (e.g., Anerley Swedenborgian church in Surrey, South London); earlier examples may exist

1880s François Hennebique develops reinforced concrete system (patented 1892)

1885 Gustav Wayss buys the rights to develop and exploit the Monier system. The book *Das System Monier* was published in 1887.

1884 Ernest Ransome patents ribbed and twisted reinforcing bars to ensure better grip between bar and concrete

1889 Ransome uses ribbed slabs and coffered ("waffle") slabs

1890s Use of expanded metal (slashed metal) for reinforcement

1894–1904 Church of Saint Jean de Montmatre using system of Paul Cottacin

1895 Hennebique's factory at Tourcoing, France

1897 Weaver's Flour Mill, Swansea, South Wales, built by Hennebique (demolished 1984)

1900–10 Ribbed shells developed by Dyckerhoff & Widmann

1902 Flat slab patented by Orlando Norcross, Boston

1902 Reinforcing system invented by Julius Kahn, whose firm became the Trussed Concrete Steel Company, later known as Truscon

1902–3 Sixteen-story Ingalls Building, Cincinatti, built using Ransome system

1906 Flat slab used by C.A.P. Turner in U.S. (patented 1908)

1908 Flat slab tested, then patented (1909), by Robert Maillart, Switzerland

1910 Flat slab tested in U.S. by Arthur R. Lord

1910 Doubly-curved shell without ribs

1910–15 Unit system for precast concrete elements developed by J. E. Conzelman of St. Louis

1923 Zeiss-Dywidag system for concrete shells (Zeiss company with Dyckerhoff & Widmann) patented

1926–34 Church of Saint Christophe-de-Javel, Paris, by Charles-Henri Besnard (prefabricated reinforced concrete)

1928 Eugène Freyssinet patents prestressing system for concrete

1939 Ferro-cement proposed by Pier Luigi Nervi, but first used in 1945 for a 165-ton yacht with a hull thickness of 35mm. First used in building in 1946.

From 1940s Gradual development of higher and higher strength concretes

1868 Steam-powered concrete mixers

1870s Larger precast concrete elements

1870s Climbing formwork for walls that could be repositioned without dismantling and reassembly

1875 Precast concrete panels strengthened by iron bars made by W.H. Lascelles

1900 Permanent metal shuttering

1905 Reusable, "universal" metal shuttering

1905 Cranes with 360° delivery arc

1910 Slip forming—formwork movable without dismantling, advanced in discrete "jumps" and not continuous

1910 Use of hoists and chutes to deliver concrete throughout a construction site

1911 "Unit system" developed by Ransome for constructing entire buildings from precast components

1911 "Tilt-up" construction used for four-story building at Rogers Park, Illinois

1917 Mechanical compaction (vibration) of concrete shown to produce concrete with higher density and strength by removing entrapped air (Freyssinet)

1918 Duff Abrams publishes his definitive reports on mix design

1920 Placement of concrete by spraying onto mesh formwork/reinforcement (Torkret in Germany; Shotcrete in U.S.; Gunite in Britain)

1925 Large batching and mixing plants

1927 Pumping of concrete

1920s Delivery of ready-mixed concrete by motorized vehicle

1940s Continuous slip forming (grain silos)

1880

1920

endnotes

chapter 1

1 Throughout this book, the term "ton" is understood to be equivalent to a U.S. ton, an English ton, and a European tonne.

2 Horace L. Jones, trans., *The Geography of Strabo*, 8 vols., Loeb Classical Library (London: Heinemann; Cambridge, Mass.: Harvard University Press, 1930; rpt., 1966), Vol. 7, p. 199.

3 The book, entitled *De septem orbis spectaculis*, has been attributed to Philon of Byzantium. An edition with notes was published by the Greek scholar Leo Allatius (Rome, 1640).

4 The area around Rome suffered a similar fate in the first century B.C. See p. 44.

5 Aristotle, *The Politics*, Book 7, Part XI, trans. Benjamin Jowett. See The Internet Classics Archive, <http://classics.mit.edu/index.html>

6 Bernadotte Perrin, trans., *Plutarch's Lives*, Loeb Classical Library (London: Butterworth–Heinemann; and Cambridge, MA: Harvard University Press, 1917; rpt. 1971), Vol. 5 (Marcellus XV), p. 473.

7 Ibid., p. 475.

8 Ibid., p. 479.

9 Philon of Byzantium, *Mechanics*. See the Web site of the School of Mathematics and Statistics, St. Andrews University, Scotland, <http://www-history.mcs.st-andrews.ac.uk/> [hereinafter referred to as the "MacTutor History of Mathematics Web site"]. The biography of Philon can be viewed at < http://www-history.mcs.st-andrews.ac.uk/Biographies/Philon.html>.

10 Heron's dates are still the subject of speculation. Until recently he was widely believed to have lived around 300-250 B.C. in the early days of the University of Alexandria. Now he is thought to have lived in the first century A.D., which would explain why Vitruvius does not mention him.

11 Pappus of Alexandria. *Mathematical Collection*, Book VIII. See the MacTutor History of Mathematics Web site, < http://www-history.mcs.st-andrews.ac.uk/Biographies/Pappus.html>.

12 Suetonius, "Life of Augustus," section 28.

13 Vitruvius, *De Architectura* [hereinafter referred to as "Vitruvius"], Book I, Chapter 1, section 1. Translation by the author.

14 Vitruvius, original Latin text of Book I, Chapter 1, section 1.

15 Vitruvius, Book IV, Chapter 3, section 3.

16 Vitruvius, Book I, Chapter 6, section 4.

17 Vitruvius, Book V, Chapter 3, section 1.

18 Vitruvius, Book V, Chapter 4, section 1.

19 Vitruvius, Book V, Chapter 5, section 7.

20 Vitruvius, Book V, Chapter 2, section 2.

21 Vitruvius, Book V, Chapter 10, section 2.

22 Vitruvius, Book V, Chapter 10, section 3.

23 *Scriptores Historiae Augustae*, "The Life of Antoninus Caracalla," section 9(v).

chapter 2

1 Procopius, *De Aedificiis* [hereinafter referred to as "Procopius"], Book I, Chapter 1, 27, 29–35, 50–53. Procopius was mistaken about how the lead was used. A sheet of lead was laid on the surface of a stone before the stone above it was placed. Acting as a plastic mortar, the lead would be squeezed wherever the dressing of the bearing surface had left material proud of the generally flat face. This formed a good, thin compression joint, and ensured that loads were carried by the whole cross section of the stones.

2 Procopius, Book I, Chapter 1, 23–24.

3 The use of pozzolana and similar agents for making hydraulic cement was preserved only in the regions where these materials occurred naturally (especially near Naples and in the Rhine Valley). Hydraulic cement was completely lost elsewhere in Europe from the sixth century until the mid-eighteenth century, when the Englishman John Smeaton—father of the British Institution of Civil Engineers—"discovered" them on a visit to the Netherlands. More accurately, he was the first person to establish the most effective mix design for hydraulic cement for his Eddystone Lighthouse near Plymouth, and to publish the results. A more thorough discussion of Smeaton appears in Chapter 5. For more information on hydraulic cement, see Appendix 3.

4 O. G. von Simson, *The Gothic Cathedral* (New York: Pantheon, 1956).

5 S.K. Victor, "Practical Geometry in the High Middle Ages: An Edition of the '*Artis cuiuslibet consummatio*' [The complete collection of every art]," *Memoirs of the American Philosophical Society* 134 (1979).

6 Ibid.

7 Simson, The Gothic Cathedral.

8 See the biography of Bacon on the MacTutor History of Mathematics Web site at <http://www-history.mcs.st-andrews.ac.uk/Biographies/Bacon.html>.

9 Ibid.

10 H. Colvin, J.M. Crook, K. Downes, and J. Newman, *The History of the King's Works* (London: HMSO, 1976), Vol. 1, p. 398.

11 Theodore Bowie, ed., *The Sketchbook of Villard de Honnecourt* (Bloomington, Ind.: Indiana University Press, 1959).

12 L.R. Shelby, *Gothic Design Techniques: The Fifteenth-Century Design Booklets of Mathes Roriczer and Hanns Schmuttermayer* (Carbondale, Ill.: Southern Illinois University Press, 1977).

13 The transactions of these Expertises were fully recorded and published in eight volumes in 1877–85. Their engineering significance is discussed in some detail in J.S. Ackerman, " '*Ars sine scientia nihil est*': Gothic Theory of Architecture at the Cathedral of Milan," *Art Bulletin* 31 (1949): 84111; Paul Frankl, *The Gothic: Literary Sources and Interpretations Through Eight Centuries* (Princeton, N.J.: Princeton University Press, 1960); and Jacques Heyman, *Arches, Vaults, and Buttresses: Masonry Structures and their Engineering* (Aldershot, England: Ashgate; Brookfield, Vt.: Variorum, 1996).

14 See Frankl, *The Gothic*, as well as Jacques Heyman, "Beauvais Cathedral," *Transactions of the Newcomen Society* 40 (1967-68) 15–36.

chapter 3

1 Giorgio Vasari, *The Lives of the Artists* (Harmondsworth, England: Penguin Classics, 1987), Vol. 1, p. 157.

2 Ibid., p. 213.

3 Leon Battista Alberti, *The Ten Books of Architecture*, trans. James Leoni, 1755 (rpt. New York: Dover Publications, 1986), Book III, Chapter 13. Editions of Alberti published after 1550 were all illustrated, and distorted the actual content in proportion to the growing love affair with everything classical. Leoni's 1755 edition, for example, has sixty-seven plates, of which about half depict buildings or details in the classical styles. The four orders Alberti mentions differ from those in Vitruvius. While Vitruvius had also named four styles or orders, the three Greek styles and the Tuscan style that had developed in Italy, he did not mention the Composite style—a mixture of Ionic and Corinthian that was developed after his time. Palladio was the first author to refer to the *five* classical orders, as they became known.

4 See L.R. Shelby and R. Mark, "Late Gothic Structural Design in the 'Instructions' of Lorenz Lechler (1516)," *Architectura* (Journal of the History of Architecture, Munich) 9 (1979), 113–31.

5 William Barclay Parsons, *Engineers and Engineering in the Renaissance*, 2nd ed. (Cambridge, Mass.: MIT Press, 1967), p. 16.

6 Ibid., p. 17.

7 Ibid., p. 21.

8 Ibid., p. 22.

9 Ibid., p. 72.

10 See the BBC's "Science & Nature" Web site, <http://www.bbc.co.uk/science/leonardo/>.

11 Santiago Huerta, Arcos, *bóvedas y cupolas: Geometria y equlibrio en el cálculo traditional e estructuras de fábrica* (Madrid: Instituto Juan de Herrera, 2004), Chapter 7. Translated by the author. The text, as it appears in the original, published in 1868, is as follows (accents differ from those in modern Spanish): Probado hé muchas veces a sacar razon del estribo que habrá menester una cualquiera forma y nunca hallo regla que me sea suficiente, y tambien lo he probado entre los arquitectos españoles y extranjeros, y ninguno paresce alcanzar verificada regla, mas de su solo albedrío; y preguntando por qué sabrémos ser aquello bastante estribo, se responde porque lo há menester, mas no por qué razon. Unos le dan el 1/4 y otros, por ciertas líneas ortogonales lo hacen y se osan encomendar á ello, teniéndolo por firme.

12 Ibid.

13 See the biography of Napier on the MacTutor History of Mathematics Web site at <http://www-history.mcs.st-andrews.ac.uk/Biographies/Napier.html>.

chapter 4

1 Just as the Renaissance produced almost a surfeit of painters, sculptors, and architects, so the Enlightenment produced more than its fair share of thinkers and masters of the intellectual arts. *Mathematics and science*: Boyle, Galileo, Hooke, Huygens, Lavoisier, Newton, Pascal; *Philosophy*: Berkeley, Descartes, Hume, Locke, Spinoza; *Encyclopedias*: Chambers, Diderot, d'Alembert; Music: Albinoni, Bach, Corelli, Couperin, Handel, Haydn, Mozart, Purcell, Rameau, Scaralatti, Telemann, Vivaldi; Literature: Dryden, Milton, Molière, Pope, Racine, Swift.

2 Galileo Galilei, *Dialogues Concerning Two New Sciences* (1638), trans. H. Crew and A. de Salvio (New York: Macmillan, 1914; rpt. New York: Dover Publications, 1954), p. 109.

3 Descriptions of Galileo's deductions are the author's own.

4 Jonathan Swift, *Gulliver's Travels* (Harmondsworth, England: Penguin Classics, 1967), pp. 223–24.

5 Gauthey (1732–1806) was a bridge engineer and the uncle of Navier. who edited his book on bridges; Lambardie (1747–97) succeeded Jean-Rodolphe Perronet as the director of the École des ponts et chaussées; Girard (1765–1836) published, in 1798, the first book on the strength of materials, *Traité analytique de la résistance des solides*.

6 See James Elmes, *Memoirs of the Life and Works of Sir Christopher Wren* (London, 1823), p. 128.

7 Ibid., p. 129.

8 H. Colvin, J.M. Crook, K. Downes, and J. Newman, *The History of the King's Works* (London: HMSO, 1976), Vol. 5, p. 404.

9 In Wren's notes for a book on building, mentioning the use of iron hoops in Saint Peter's dome, he includes the following interesting sentence: "Iron, at all adventures, is a good caution but the architect should so poise his work, as if it were not necessary." See Elmes, p. 130.

10 Jacques Heyman, *Coulomb's Memoir on Statics: An Essay in the History of Civil Engineering* (Cambridge: Cambridge University Press, 1972), p. 125.

11 Theosophilus Desaguliers. *A Course of Experimental Philosophy* (London, 1744), pp. 560–61.

12 *L'Architecture hydraulique* was published in two parts, each consisting of two volumes. Publication dates are as follows: Part I: Vol. 1, 1737; Vol. 2, 1739; Part II: Vol. 1, 1750; Vol. 2, 1753.

chapter 5

1 A.W. Skempton, ed., *John Smeaton, FRS* (London: Thomas Telford, 1981).

2 Ibid., p. 217.

3 Ibid., p. 219.

4 Ibid., p. 99.

5 A.W. Skempton and H. R. Johnson, "The First Iron Frames," *Architectural Review* 131 (March 1952), 175–86, fn 24. Reprinted in R. J. M. Sutherland, ed. *Structural Iron, 1750–1850*, Studies in the History of Civil Engineering 9 (Aldershot, England: Ashgate, 1997).

6 See Charles Louis Augusts Eck, *Traité de construction en poteries et fer* (Paris: J.C. Blosse, 1836–41), Volume 1 and 2.

7 Anthony Calladine, "Lombe's Mill: An Exercise in Reconstruction," *Industrial Archaeology Review* 16, no. 1 (Autumn 1993), p. 94. The "fine Organzine silk" referred to in Lombe's patent is the thread used in weaving, and was made in three stages. First, the raw silk was spun to create a single fiber, then two silk fibers were spun together ("doubled") to form the silk yarn; finally, a number of strands of yarn were twisted together, according to the thickness and strength required, to form Organzine silk. It was this last stage that the Italian weavers had perfected, and was the secret behind their high-quality fabrics.

8 Daniel Defoe, *Tour thro' the Whole Island of Great Britain* (1724-27), 3 vols. The local man was William Hutton (1723–1815), who "was offered employment at a silk-mill in Derby in 1730 [i.e., at the age of six or seven] and served seven hard years of apprenticeship, rising at five every morning." See his *History of Derby*, 2nd ed. (London: Nichols, Son, and Bentley, 1817), p. 169. A biography of Hutton can be found on the Web site of Literary Heritage–West Midlands, <http://www3.shropshire-cc.gov.uk/huttonw.htm>.

9 Erasmus Darwin, *The Loves of the Plants*, Canto II, in *The Botanic Garden* (Lichfield, England, 1789), Vol. 2. (Published privately and anonymously.)

10 H. R. Johnson and A. W. Skempton, "William Strutt's Cotton Mills, 1793–1812," *Transactions of the Newcomen Society* 30 (1955–57), 179–205.

11 John Marshall, one of the partners in the Castle Foregate Mill, as quoted in the *Autobiography of J Marshall of Leeds* (typescript presented by Mrs. Hilary Marshall to the Shropshire Archives, 2000). Ibid. See also "Charles Bage: Business and Local Affairs," on the Revolutionary Players Web site, <http://www.revolutionaryplayers.org.uk/home.stm>.

12 While it is tempting to draw a parallel between the shape of Bage's columns and the entasis of ancient Greek stone columns, there is no evidence that Greek builders shaped their columns in this way based on structural logic. Entasis did not achieve any savings of material, and, indeed, a reduction in the cross section of a column at its ends would result in less stability in an earthquake. Entasis in Greek buildings was used entirely for aesthetic reasons.

13 Thomas Tredgold, *Principles of warming and ventilating public buildings, dwelling houses, manufactories, hospitals, hot-houses, conservatories, &c.; and of constructing fire-places, boilers, steam apparatus, grates, and drying rooms; with illustrations experimental, scientific, and practical ...* (London: J. Taylor, 1824).

14 Quoted in N.S. Billington and B.M. Roberts, *Building Services Engineering: A Review of its Development* (Oxford: Pergamon Press, 1982), p. 414.

15 Quoted in A. W. Skempton, "The Origin of Iron Beams," *Actes du VIIIe Congrès International d'histoire des sciences*, Florence, Italy (3–9 September 1956), pp. 1029–39. Reprinted in William Addis, *Structural and Civil Engineering Design*. Studies in the History of Civil Engineering 12 (Aldershot, England: Ashgate [Variorum], 1999), p. 215.

16 Addis, *Structural and Civil Engineering Design*, p. 214.

17 In John Farey's 1812 drawing of the North Mill (fig. 292), the dimensions of the arches are not quite accurate. They actually span three bays, not four, and are not as shallow as in the illustration. Farey (1766–1826) was a mechanical engineer who, with his son John Farey, Jr., supplied illustrations for such reference works as Abraham Rees's *Rees' Cyclopaedia* (1802–20) and Olinthus Gregory's *A Treatise of Mechanics* (1815). The drawing was used to illustrate Farey's article on the manufacture of cotton in *Cyclopaedia*.

18 Skempton and Johnson, "The First Iron Frames," p. 186.

19 Jacques René Tenon, *Journal d'observations sur les principaux hôpitaux et sur quelques prisons d'Angleterre* [Journal of Observations on the Principal Hospitals, and Some Prisons, in England] (1787). Reprinted in 1992 by the Association des publications de la Faculté des lettres et sciences humaines de Clermont–Ferrand. See Chapter 8 in Christine Stevenson, *Medicine and Magnificence: British Hospital and Asylum Architecture, 1660–1815* (New Haven, Ct.: Yale University Press, 2000).

20 Robert W. Lowe, ed., *An Apology for the Life of Mr. Colley Cibber*, 2 vols. (London: J. C. Nimmo, 1889), Vol. 1, pp. 321–22. In *Architecture in Britain*, 1530–1830, 7th ed., rev. and enl. (London: Penguin Books, 1983), p. 273, John Summerson calls the Queen's Theatre "a project which failed acoustically as well as financially."

21 George Saunders, *A Treatise on Theatres* (1790). Also summarized in W.S. Inman, *Principles of Ventilation, Warming and the Transmission of Sound* (London, 1836), pp. 18–19.

22 Inman, p. 21.

chapter 6

1 P. J. Booker, "Gaspard Monge (1746–1818) and his Effect on Engineering Drawing," *Transactions of the Newcomen Society* 34 (1962–63), p. 24.

2 Robert Henry Bow, *A Treatise on Bracing* (Edinburgh, 1851), p. 29.

3 William J. M. Rankine, *Introductory Lecture on the Harmony of Theory and Practice on Mechanics* (London and Glasgow: Griffin, 1856). See also William Addis, *Structural Engineering: The Nature of Theory and Design* (Chichester, England: Ellis Horwood, 1990), p. 34.

4 William J. M. Rankine, "Opening Remarks on the Objects of the [Mechanical Science] Section." *Report of the British Association for the Advancement of Science*, Vol. 25 (1855), pp. 201–202. See also Addis, *Structural Engineering*, p. 35.

5 Harriet Richardson. *English Hospitals 1660–1948: A Survey of Their Architecture and Design* (London: English Heritage (Royal Commission on the Historical Monuments of England), 1998), Chapter 10.

6 R. S. Fitton and A. P. Wadsworth, *The Strutts and the Arkwrights, 1758–1830: A Study of the Early Factory System* (Manchester: Manchester University Press, 1958).

7 David Boswell Reid, *Illustrations of the theory and practice of ventilation, with remarks on warming, exclusive lighting and the communication of sound* (London, 1844).

8 Ibid.

9 Sadi Carnot, *Reflections on the Motive Power of Heat, and on Machines Fitted to Develop This Power*, trans. R.H. Thurston (New York: American Society of Mechanical Engineers, 1943). As quoted in John F. Sandfort, *Heat Engines* (London: Heinemann, 1964), pp. 64–65.

10 Sandfort, *Heat Engines*, pp. 61–62.

11 John Loudon, *A Short Treatise on Several Improvements Recently Made in Hot-Houses* (London, 1805). As quoted in John Hix, *The Glasshouse* (London: Phaidon Press, 1996).

12 Reid, *Illustrations of the theory and practice of ventilation*, p. 315.

13 Ibid., p. 317.

14 The phrase "absolute impermeability" is my translation of *Imperméabilite absolue*, which appeared in a French advertisement linked to the exhibition of Lambot's reinforced concrete boat at the Exposition Universelle in Paris in 1855. See Jean-Louis Bosc et al., *Joseph Monier et la naissance du ciment armé* (Paris: Éditions du Linteau, 2001).

15 J. M. Brown. "W. B. Wilkinson (1819–1902) and his Place in the History of Reinforced Concrete." *Transactions of the Newcomen Society* 39 (1966), 129–42.

16 John McKean, *Crystal Palace: Joseph Paxton and Charles Fox* (London: Phaidon, 1994). Cole's figure of 20 acres includes the exhibition space on the first-floor galleries. The ground floor covered about 17 acres.

chapter 7

1 Edwin O. Sachs and Ernest A. E. Woodrow, *Modern Opera Houses and Theaters* (London: B. T. Batsford, Ltd., 1896–98). To complete this three-volume opus, Sachs traveled far afield, including to Russia and Egypt.

2 Ralph B. Peck, *History of Building Foundations in Chicago*, Engineering Experiment Station, Bulletin Series, No. 373 (Urbana, Ill.: University of Illinois Press, 1948), p. 9. Reprinted in Addis, *Structural and Civil Engineering Design*.

3 Author's paraphrasing of Root's ideas, as summarized in Carl W. Condit, *The Chicago School of Architecture: A History of Commercial and Public Building in the Chicago Area, 1875–1925* (Chicago: University of Chicago Press, 1964), pp. 48–49. It is not clear what the "iron rods" referenced in paragraph two might have been; it is unlikely they were wind-bracing. More likely, the rods were embedded in the concrete flat roof to tie together the tops of columns and internal walls in a manner similar to the tie rods used in the fireproof floors of mills from the late eighteenth century.

4 Condit, *The Chicago School of Architecture*, p. 49.

5 Ibid., pp. 52–53.

6 Ibid., p. 120.

7 *The Builder* (London), 12 February 1870, p. 125.

8 Barry Donaldson and Bernard Nagengast, *Heat and Cold: Mastering the Great Indoors. A Selective History of Heating, Ventilation, Air-Conditioning and Refrigeration from the Ancients to the 1930s* (Atlanta: American Society of Heating, Refrigerating and Air-Conditioning Engineers, 1994), p. 275.

9 As quoted in Donaldson and Nagengast, *Heat and Cold*, p. 286.

10 Wallace C. Sabine. *Collected Papers on Acoustics* (Cambridge, Mass.: Harvard University Press, 1922; rpt. New York: Dover Publications, 1964), p. 67.

11 Sabine, *Collected Papers*, p. 180. The *schlieren* method, from the German "to streak," makes visible the streaking or irregularities in glass by revealing how they refract light, rather as air above the surface of hot desert sand or a road appears to shimmer.

12 William E. Ward, "Béton in Combination with Iron as a Building Material," *Transactions of the American Society of Mechanical Engineers* 4 (1883), pp. 388–89.

13 Translated from the German by the author. As quoted in H. J. Kraus and Franz Dischinger. *Dachbauten: Kragdächer, Schalen und Rippenkuppeln*, 4th ed. (Berlin: Ernst und Sohn, 1928), p. 373.

14 Translated from the German by the author. From Max Bill, *Robert Maillart: Bridges and Constructions*, 1st ed. (Zurich: Verlag für Architektur, 1949), p. 168.

15 Louis H. Sullivan, "The Tall Office Building Artistically Considered," *Lippincott's Magazine*, March 1896. It is a little disappointing to find that, in fact, Sullivan was speaking metaphorically, using the rhetoric as a justification for his division of tall buildings into three zones: "Does this not readily, clearly, and conclusively show that the lower one or two stories will take on a special character suited to the special needs, that the tiers of typical offices, having the same unchanging function, shall continue in the same unchanging form, and that as to the attic, specific and conclusive as it is in its very nature, its function shall equally be so in force, in significance, in continuity, in conclusiveness of outward expression? From this results, naturally, spontaneously, unwittingly, a three-part division, not from any theory, symbol or fancied logic."

16 Jonathan Swift, *Gulliver's Travels*, Chapter 1, "Voyage to Lilliput."

17 D'Arcy Wentworth Thompson, *On Growth and Form*, abridged edition, ed. John Tyler Bonner (Cambridge: Cambridge University Press, 1961), p. xiv.

chapter 8

1 Carl W. Condit, *American Building Art: The Twentieth Century* (New York: Oxford University Press, 1961), p. 18.

2 William J. M. Rankine, *A Manual of Civil Engineering*, 16th ed. (London: Charles Griffen, 1887), p. 603.

3 The degree of rotation depends on the differences between the stresses in the three principal directions, that is ($\hat{U}_1 - \hat{U}_2$), ($\hat{U}_1 - \hat{U}_3$) and ($\hat{U}_2 - \hat{U}_3$). If a two-dimensional test piece is used, one principal stress is zero and the magnitude and direction of the remaining two principal stresses can be established. The only point at which the photoelastic fringes give a direct indication of stress is at the model boundary, where a second principal stress (perpendicular to the surface) is necessarily also zero.

4 This quotation from the report appears in several biographies of William Froude. For one example, see Derek K. Brown and Andrew Lambert, "William Froude," *Oxford Dictionary of National Biography* (Oxford, UK: Oxford University Press, 2004).

5 For more information on dimensionless constants, see Henry J. Cowan, J. S. Gero, G. D. Ding, and R. W. Muncey, *Models in Architecture* (New York: Elsevier Publishing, 1968), and Heinz Hossdorf, *Model Analysis of Structures* (New York: Van Nostrand, 1974).

6 Kraus and Dischinger, *Dachbauten*, p. 300.

7 See "The Key Speech," by Ove Arup, delivered on 9 July 1970 at Winchester, England. It can be found on the Arup Web site, <www.arup.com>, and is reprinted in David Dunster, ed. *Arup on Engineering* (Berlin: Ove Arup & Partners and Ernst und Sohn, n.d. [c. 1996]). See also similar explanations in "Ways and Means" by Ove Arup, reprinted in Appendix 1 of this book.

8 *Builders' Journal and Architectural Engineer* (May 1906), *Concrete and Steel Supplement*, Vol. 23, No. 589.

9 Le Corbusier, *Towards a New Architecture*, trans. Frederick Etchells (London: Architectural Press, 1927).

10 F. M. Lea, ed., *The Principles of Modern Building*, 3rd ed., Vol. 1 (London: HMSO, 1959), p. 39.

chapter 9

1 "Asbestos" is a generic term for some half-dozen different naturally occurring metallic silicates. The crystals are easily crushed to form short, high tensile strength fibers that are extremely fine—typically about 30 nanometers in diameter. Their fire-resistant properties have been known since antiquity; indeed, the term "asbestos" is derived from the Greek word for "indestructible." The fibers were mixed with clay to strengthen pottery, and the Romans wove asbestos fibers to form wicks for oil lamps and heat-resistant cloth.

2 R. Thiele, "Richtungsverteilung und Zeitfolge der Schallrückwürfe in Räumen," *Acustica* Vol. 3 (1953), p. 291. See also W.L. Jordan, *Acoustical Design of Concert Halls and Theatres* (London: Applied Science Publishers, 1980).

3 *Arup Journal*, Vol. 11, No. 4, (1976), pp. 18–23.

4 The Citicorp Center occasioned a genuine scare several years after it was completed, when it was discovered that some of the steel connections were not strong enough to withstand the very highest wind loads that the building might suffer during its life. At considerable expense, many connections were strengthened without disrupting the building's occupants.

bibliography

Where there are two or more entries by the same author, entries are listed in chronological order (earliest to latest). Entries edited by that author (if any) are listed next, followed by entries co-written or co-edited by that author.

ABRAMS, Duff. “Design of Concrete Mixtures.” *Bulletin 1*, Structural Materials Research Laboratory, Lewis Institute, Chicago, 1918.

ACHE, Jean-Baptiste. *Éléments d'une histoire de l'art de bâtir*. Paris: Éditions du Moniteur des travaux publics, 1970.

ACKERMAN, J. S. “ *'Ars sine scientia nihil est'*: Gothic Theory of Architecture at the Cathedral of Milan.” *Art Bulletin* 31 (1949): 84–111.

ACKERMANN, Kurt. *Building for Industry*. London: Watermark, 1991.

ACKERMANN, M. E. *Cool Comfort: America's Romance with Air-Conditioning*. Washington, DC: Smithsonian Institution Press, 2002.

ACLAND, James H. *Medieval Structure: The Gothic Vault*. Toronto: University of Toronto Press, 1972.

ADAM, Jean-Pierre. *Roman Building: Materials and Techniques*. London: Batsford, 1994.

ADDIS, William. *Structural Engineering: The Nature of Theory and Design*. Chichester, England: Ellis Horwood, 1990.

ADDIS, William. *The Art of the Structural Engineer*. London: Artemis, 1994.

ADDIS, William. “Free Will and Determinism in the Conception of Structures.” *Journal of the International Association for Shell and Spatial Structures* 38, no. 2 (1997): 83–89. Also in **HANGLIETER** 1996.

ADDIS, William. *Structural and Civil Engineering Design*. Studies in the History of Civil Engineering 12. Aldershot, England: Ashgate (Variorum), 1999.

ADDIS, William. *Creativity and Innovation: The Structural Engineer's Contribution to Design*. Oxford: Architectural Press, 2001.

ADDIS, William. Entries on *Christopher Wren* (pp. 799–802) and *Robert Hooke* (pp. 334–37) in **SKEMPTON** 2002.

ADDIS, William. “A History of Using Models to Inform the Design and Construction of Structures.” In **HUERTA** 2005, pp. 9–44.

AGRICOLA, Georgius (Georg **BAUER**). *De re Metallica*. Basel, 1556. English translation by Herbert C. and Lou H. Hoover. London: Mining Magazine, 1912; rpt. New York: Dover Publications, 1950.

AIA (Association for Industrial Archaeology). Issues of *Industrial Archaeology Review* dedicated to textile mills: 10, no. 2 (Spring 1988) and 16, no. 1 (Autumn 1993). Royal Commission on the Historical Monuments of England and Association for Industrial Archaeology.

ALBERTI, Leon Battista. *De re Aedificatoria*. Florence, 1485. Translated by James Leoni (1755) as *The Ten Books of Architecture*; rpt. New York: Dover Publications, 1986.

ALI, Mir. *Art of the Skyscraper: The Genius of Fazlur Khan*. New York: Rizzoli, 2001.

ANDERSON, James C. *Roman Architecture and Society*. Baltimore and London: Johns Hopkins University Press, 1997.

ANDERSON, Stanford, ed. *Eladio Dieste: Innovation in Structural Art*. New York: Princeton Architectural Press, 2004.

ASPRAY, William, ed. *Computing Before Computers*. Ames, Iowa: Iowa State University Press, 1990. Available online at http://ed-thelen.org/comp-hist/CBC.html.

BACH, Klaus, Berthold **BURKHARDT**, and Frei **OTTO**. *Seifenblasen / Forming Bubbles*. IL18. Stuttgart: Institut für leichte Flächentragwerke, University of Stuttgart, 1988.

BALDI, Bernardino. *In Mechanica Aristotelis Problematica Exercitationes*. Mainz, 1621.

BANHAM, Reyner. *The Architecture of the Well-Tempered Environment*. London: Architectural Press, 1969.

BANHAM, Reyner. *A Concrete Atlantis*. London: MIT Press, 1986.

BANNISTER, Turpin C. “The First Iron-Framed Buildings.” *Architectural Review* 107 (April 1950): 231–46.

BANNISTER, Turpin C. “Bogardus Revisited. Part I: The Iron Fronts.” *Journal of the Society of Architectural Historians* 15, no. 4 (1956): 12–22. (Reprinted in **THORNE** 2000.)

BANNISTER, Turpin C. “Bogardus Revisited. Part II: The Iron Towers.” *Journal of the Society of Architectural Historians* 16, no. 1 (1957): 11–19. (Reprinted in **THORNE** 2000.)

BAUERSFELD, Walter. “Projection Planetarium and Shell Construction.” *Proceedings of the Institution of Mechanical Engineers*, 1957. (Reprinted in **JOEDICKE** 1963.)

BAYNES, Ken, and Francis **PUGH**. *The Art of the Engineer*. Woodstock, N.Y.: Overlook Press, 1981.

BEAMON, Sylvia P., and Susan **ROAF**. *The Ice-Houses of Britain*. London: Routledge, 1990.

BECCHI, Antonio. *Q. XVI: Leonardo, Galileo e il caso Baldi*. Venezia: Saggi Marsilio, 2004.

BECCHI, Antonio, and Federico **FOCE**. *Degli archi e delle volte: arte del costruire tra meccanica e stereotomia*. Venezia: Saggi Marsilio, 2002.

BECCHI, Antonio, Massimo **CORRADI**, Federico **FOCE**, and Orieta **PEDEMONTE**, eds. *Towards a History of Construction: Dedicated to Edoardo Benvenuto*. Basel: Birkhäuser, 2002.

BECCHI, Antonio, Massimo **CORRADI**, Federico **FOCE**, and Orieta **PEDEMONTE**, eds. *Essays on the History of Mechanics; In Memory of Clifford Ambrose Truesdell and Edoardo Benvenuto*. Basel: Birkhäuser, 2003.

BECCHI, Antonio, Massimo **CORRADI**, Federico **FOCE**, and Orieta **PEDEMONTE**, eds. *Construction History: Research Perspectives in Europe*. Genova: Instituto Edoardo Benvenuto / Kim Williams Books, 2004.

BEGGS, G. E. “The Accurate Mechanical Solution of Statically Indeterminate Structures by the Use of Paper Models and Special Gauges.” *Journal of the American Concrete Institute* 8 (1922): 58–78.

BÉLIDOR, Bernard Forest de. *La Science des ingénieurs dans la conduite des travaux de fortification et d'architecture civile*. Paris, 1729.

BÉLIDOR, Bernard Forest de. *L'Architecture hydraulique*. 4 vols. Paris: 1737–53.

BELOFSKY, Harold. “Engineering Drawing: A Universal Language in Two Dialects.” *Technology and Culture* 32, no. 1 (1991): 23–46.

BENVENUTO, Edoardo. *An Introduction to the History of Structural Mechanics*. 2 vols. New York and Berlin: Springer-Verlag, 1991.

BERGER, Horst. *Light Structures, Structures of Light: The Art and Engineering of Tensile Architecture*. Basel: Birkhäuser, 1996.

BERGERON, Louis, and Maria Teresa **MAIULLARI-PONTOIS**. *Industry, Architecture and Engineering: American Ingenuity 1750–1950*. New York: Harry N. Abrams, 2000.

BEYER, Robert T. *Sounds of Our Times: Two Hundred Years of Acoustics*. New York: Springer-Verlag, 1999.

BILL, Max. *Robert Maillart: Bridges and Constructions*. Zurich: Verlag für Architektur, 1949; 3rd ed. London: Pall Mall Press, 1969.

BILLINGTON, David P. *Robert Maillart's Bridges: The Art of Engineering*. Princeton, N.J.: Princeton University Press, 1979.

BILLINGTON, David P. *The Tower and the Bridge: The New Art of Structural Engineering*. Princeton, N.J.: Princeton University Press, 1985.

BILLINGTON, N.S., and B.M. **ROBERTS**. *Building Services Engineering: A Review of its Development*. Oxford: Pergamon Press, 1982.

BINDING, Günther. *Baubetrieb im Mittelalter*. Darmstadt: Wissenschaftliche Gesellschaft, 1993.

BINDING, Günther, and Norbert **NUßBAUM**. *Der mittelalterliche Baubetrieb nördlich der Alpen in zeitgenössischen Darstellungen*. Darmstadt: Wissenschaftliche Buchgesellschaft, 1978.

BJERRUM, L., et al., eds. *From Theory to Practice in Soil Mechanics: Selections from the Writings of Karl Terzaghi*. London: John Wiley and Sons, 1960.

BLANCHARD, Anne. *Vauban*. Paris: Fayard, 1996.

BLOCKLEY, D.I. *The Nature of Structural Design and Safety*. Chichester, England: Ellis Horwood, 1980.

BLOCKLEY, D.I., and J.R. **HENDERSON**. “Structural Failures and the Growth of Engineering Knowledge.” *Proceedings of the Institution of Civil Engineers (PICE)*, Part 1, 68 (1980): 719–28. Discussion reported in *PICE*, Part 1, 70 (1981), 567–79. (Reprinted in **ADDIS** 1999.)

BOOKER, P.J. *A History of Engineering Drawing*. London: Northgate Publishing, 1979.

BOOTH, L.G. “Thomas Tredgold (1788–1829): Some Aspects of his Work. Part 1: His Life.” *Transactions of the Newcomen Society* 51 (1979–80): 57–64.

BOSC, Jean-Louis, et al. *Joseph Monier et la naissance du ciment armé*. Paris: Éditions du Linteau, 2001.

BOW, Robert Henry. *A Treatise on Bracing*. Edinburgh, 1851.

BOW, Robert Henry. *The Economics of Construction in Relation to Framed Structures*. London: Spon, 1873.

BOWIE, Theodore, ed. *The Sketchbook of Villard de Honnecourt*. Bloomington: Indiana University Press, 1959.

BOWLEY, Marian. *The British Building Industry: Four Studies in Response and Resistance to Change*. Cambridge: Cambridge University Press, 1966.

BRODIE, Allan, et al. *English Prisons: An Architectural History*. London: English Heritage, 2002.

BROWN, André. *Peter Rice*. London: Thomas Telford, 2001.

BROWN, J.M. “W. B. Wilkinson (1819–1902) and his Place in the History of Reinforced Concrete.” *Transactions of the Newcomen Society* 39 (1966): 129–42. (Reprinted in **NEWBY** 2001.)

BRUEGMANN, Robert. “Central Heating and Forced Ventilation: Origins and Effects on Architectural Design.” *Journal of the Society of Architectural Historians* 37, no. 3 (1978): 143–60.

BUCCARO, Alfredo, and Salvatore d'**AGOSTINO**. *Dalla Scuola di applicazione alla Facoltà di ingegneria: la cultura napolitana nell'evoluzione della scienza e della didattica del costruire*. Napoli: Hevelius Edizioni, 2003.

BUCCARO, Alfredo, and Fausto de **MATTIA**, eds. *Scienziata, artisti: formazione e ruolo degli ingegnieri nelle fonti dell'Archivio di Stato e della Facoltà di Ingegneria di Napoli*. Napoli: Electa Napoli, 2003.

BUCHANAN, R.A. *The Engineers: A History of the Engineering Profession in Britain, 1750–1914*. London: Jessica Kingsley, 1989.

BUILDING ARTS FORUM (New York). *Bridging the Gap: Rethinking the Relationship of Architect and Engineer*. New York: Van Nostrand Reinhold, 1991.

BUTTI, Ken, and John **PERLIN**. *A Golden Thread: 2500 Years of Solar Architecture and Technology*. London: Marion Boyars, 1980.

BUTTON, David, and Brian **PYE**, eds. *Glass in Building*. Oxford: Butterworth Architecture (with Pilkington Glass Ltd.), 1993.

BYLANDER, Sven. “Steelwork in Building: Thirty Years' Progress.” *The Structural Engineer* 15 (1937): 2–25, 128–32. (Reprinted in **THORNE** 2000.)

CAJORI, Florian. *A History of the Logarithmic Slide Rule and Allied Instruments*. New York: Tapley, 1909.

CAJORI, Florian. *A History of Mathematical Notations*. 2 vols. Lasalle, Ill.: Open Court Publication Co., 1928–29; rpt. New York: Dover Publications, 1993.

CALLADINE, Anthony. “Lombe's Mill: An Exercise in Reconstruction.” *Industrial Archaeology Review* 16, no. 1 (Autumn 1993): 82–99.

CAMPBELL, James, and Will **PRYCE**. *Brick: A World History*. London: Thames and Hudson, 2003.

CAMPIOLI, Mario E. “Building the Capitol.” In **PETERSON** 1976.

CASCIATO, MARISTELLA, et al., eds. *150 anni di costruzione edile in Italia*. Roma: Edilstampa, 1992.

CHABANNES, Jean Baptiste Marie Frédéric, Marquis de. *On conducting air by forced ventilation and regulating the temperature in dwellings*. London, 1818.

CHANNELL, David F. “A Unitary Technology: The Engineering Science of W.J.M. Rankine.” Ph.D. dissertation, Case Western Reserve University, 1975.

CHARLTON, T.M. *A History of Theory of Structures in the Nineteenth Century*. Cambridge: Cambridge University Press, 1982.

CHILTON, John. *Heinz Isler*. London Thomas Telford, 2000.

CHOISY, Auguste. *L'Art de bâtir chez les Romains*. Paris: Ducher et Cie, 1873.

CHOISY, Auguste. *L'Art de bâtir chez les Byzantins*. Paris: Librairie de la Société anonyme des publications périodiques, 1883.

CHOISY, Auguste. *Histoire de l'architecture*. Paris: Éditions Vincent, Freal et Cie, 1899; rpt. Paris: SERG, 1976.

CHOISY, Auguste. *L'Art de bâtir chez les Égyptiens*. Paris: Librairie George Baranger Fils, 1904.

CHOISY, Auguste. Vitruve. Paris: Imprimerie-Librairie Lahure, 1909.

CHRIMES, M.M. "Concrete Foundations and Substructures: A Historical Review." *Proceedings of the Institution of Civil Engineers: Structures and Buildings* 116, nos. 3 & 4 (1996): 344–72. Revised version in **SUTHERLAND** 2001.

CIRIA (Construction Industry Research and Information Association). *Structural Renovation of Traditional Buildings*. Report 111. Rev. ed. London: Construction Industry Research and Information Association, 1994.

COENEN, Ulrich. *Die spätgotischen Werkmeisterbücher in Deutschland: Untersuchung und Edition der Lehrschriften für Entwurf und Ausführung von Sakralbauten*. Beiträge zur Kunstwissenschaft 25. München: Scaneg, 1990.

COKER, E.G., and L.N.G. **FILON**. *A Treatise on Photo-elasticity*. 2nd ed. Cambridge: Cambridge University Press, 1957.

COLLINS, A.R., ed. *Structural Engineering: Two Centuries of British Achievement*. Chislehurst, England: Tarot Print, for the Institution of Structural Engineers, 1983.

COLLINS, Peter. *Concrete: The Vision of a New Architecture*. London: Faber and Faber, 1959.

CONDIT, Carl W. *American Building Art: The Nineteenth Century*. New York: Oxford University Press, 1960.

CONDIT, Carl W. *American Building Art: The Twentieth Century*. New York: Oxford University Press, 1961.

CONDIT, Carl W. *The Chicago School of Architecture: A History of Commercial and Public Building in the Chicago Area, 1875–1925*. Chicago: University of Chicago Press, 1964.

CONDIT, Carl W. *American Building*. Chicago: University of Chicago Press, 1968.

CONDIT, Carl W. *Chicago, 1930–70: Building, Planning, and Urban Technology*. Chicago: University of Chicago Press, 1974.

CONRAD, Dietrich. *Kirchenbau im Mittelalter: Bauplanung und Bauausführung*. Leipzig: Edition Leipzig, 1990.

COOPER, Gail. *Air-conditioning America: Engineers and the Controlled Environment, 1900–1960*. Baltimore: Johns Hopkins University Press, 1998.

COTTAM, David. *Sir Owen Williams, 1890–1969*. London: Architectural Association, 1986.

COULTON, J.J. *Ancient Greek Architects at Work: Problems of Structure and Design*. Ithaca, N.Y.: Cornell University Press, 1977.

COURTENAY, Lynn T., ed. *The Engineering of Medieval Cathedrals*. Studies in the History of Civil Engineering 1. Aldershot, England: Ashgate, 1997.

COWAN, Henry J. "A History of Masonry and Concrete Domes in Building Construction." *Building and Environment* 12 (1977): 1–24.

COWAN, Henry J. *An Historical Outline of Architectural Science*. 2nd ed. London: Applied Science, 1977.

COWAN, Henry J. *The Master Builders*. New York: Wiley, 1977.

COWAN, Henry J. *Science and Building*. New York: Wiley, 1978.

COWAN, Henry J., J. S. **GERO**, G. D. **DING**, and R. W. **MUNCEY**. *Models in Architecture*. New York: Elsevier Publishing Co., 1968.

CROSS, Hardy. *Engineers and Ivory Towers*. New York and London: McGraw-Hill, 1952.

CULMANN, Karl. *Die graphische Statik*. Zürich: Meyer & Zeller, 1866.

D'OCAGNE, Maurice. *Traité de nomographie*. Paris: Gauthier-Villars, 1899.

DAVEY, Norman. *A History of Building Materials*. London: Phoenix House, 1961.

DE CAMP, L. Sprague. *The Ancient Engineers*. London: Souvenir Press, 1963.

DE COURCY, John W. "The Emergence of Reinforced Concrete: 1750–1910." *The Structural Engineer* 65A, no. 9 (1987): 315–22. (Reprinted in **NEWBY** 2001.)

DELAINE, Janet. *The Baths of Caracalla: A Study in the Design, Construction, and Economics of Large-Scale Building Projects in Imperial Rome*. Portsmouth, R.I.: Journal of Roman Archaeology, Supplementary Series No. 25, 1997.

DELLA TORRE, S., ed. *Immagini, materiali, testimonianze per la storia dell'edilizia nel comasco e nel lecchese, 1850–1950*. Como: Nodo Libri, 1994.

DENNIS, Bernard G., et al. *American Civil Engineering History: The Pioneering Years*. New York: American Society of Civil Engineers (ASCE), 2003.

DESIDERI, Paolo, et al., eds. *Pier Luigi Nervi*. Bologna: Zanichelli, 1979.

DESWARTE-ROSA, Sylvie, and Bertrand **LEMOINE**. *L'Architecture et les ingénieurs: Deux siècles de construction*. Paris: Éditions du Moniteur / Centre Georges Pompidou, 1980.

DIAMANT, R.M.E. *Industrialised Building - 50 International Methods*. London: Iliffe Books, 1964; *Industrialised Building (Second Series) - 50 International Methods*. London: Iliffe Books, 1965; *Industrialised Building (Third Series) - 70 International Methods*. London: Iliffe Books, 1968.

DONALDSON, Barry, and Bernard **NAGENGAST**. *Heat and Cold: Mastering the Great Indoors. A Selective History of Heating, Ventilation, Air-Conditioning and Refrigeration from the Ancients to the 1930s*. Atlanta: American Society of Heating, Refrigerating and Air-Conditioning Engineers, 1994.

DUFTON, A.F., and H.E. **BECKETT**. "The Orientation of Buildings." *Journal of the Royal Institute of British Architects* (16 May 1931): 509–10.

DUNKELD, M., et al., eds. *Proceedings of the Second International Congress on Construction History* (Cambridge University). 3 vols. Ascot, England: Construction History Society, 2006.

DUNSTER, David, ed. *Arups on Engineering*. Berlin: Ove Arup & Partners and Ernst und Sohn, n.d. (c.1996).

DURM, Josef. *Die Baustile: Historische und Technische Entwicklung des Handbuches der Architektur Zweiter Teil. 1. Band: Die Baukunst der Griechen*. Darmstadt: Verlag von Arnold Bergsträsser, 1892.

DURM, Josef. *Die Baustile: Historische und Technische Entwicklung des Handbuches der Architektur Zweiter Teil. 2. Band: Die Baukunst der Etrusker; Die Baukunst der Römer Zweite Auflage*. Stuttgart: Alfred Kroner, 1905.

DURM, Josef. *Die Baukunst der Renaissance in Italien*. Leipzig: J.M. Gebhardt, 1914.

ELLIOTT, Cecil D. *Technics and Architecture: The Development of Materials and Systems for Buildings*. Cambridge, Mass.: MIT Press, 1992.

EMMERSON, George S. *Engineering Education: A Social History*. Newton Abbot, England: David & Charles, 1973.

ERLANDE-BRANDENBURG, Alain. *The Cathedral Builders of the Middle Ages*. London: Thames and Hudson, 1995.

EYTELWEIN, J.A. *Handbuch der Mechanik fester Körper und der Hydraulik*. Berlin: Lagarde, 1801.

FABER, Colin. *Candela, the Shell Builder*. New York: Reinhold, 1963.

FAIRBAIRN, William. *On the Application of Cast and Wrought Iron to Building Purposes*. London, 1854.

FALCONER, Keith A. "Fireproof Mills – The Widening Perspectives." *Industrial Archaeology Review* 16, no. 1 (Autumn 1993): 11–26.

FEDEROV, Sergei. "Matthew Clark and the Origins of Russian Structural Engineering 1810–40s: An Introductory Biography." *Construction History* 8 (1992): 69–88. (Reprinted in **SUTHERLAND** 1997.)

FEDEROV, Sergei. *Der Badische Ingenieur Wilhelm von Traitteur als Architeckt russischer Eisenkonstruktionen*. Karlesruhe: Institut für Baugeschichte der Universität Karlesruhe, 1992.

FEDEROV, Sergei. "Early Iron-Domed Roofs in Russian Church Architecture: 1800–1840." *Construction History* 12 (1996): 41–66.

FEDEROV, Sergei G. "Construction History in the Soviet Union – Russia 1930–2005. Emergence, Development and Disappearance of a Technical Discipline." In **DUNKELD** et al. 2006, pp. 1093–1112.

FERGUSON, Eugene S. "An Historical Sketch of Central Heating 1800–1860." In **PETERSON** 1976.

FERGUSON, Eugene S. *Engineering and the Mind's Eye*. Cambridge, Mass.: MIT Press, 1992.

FITCHEN, John. *The Construction of Gothic Cathedrals*. Oxford: Clarendon Press, 1961.

FITCHEN, John. *Building Construction before Mechanization*. Cambridge, Mass.: MIT Press, 1986.

FITTON, R.S., and A.P. **WADSWORTH**. *The Strutts and the Arkwrights, 1758–1830: A Study of the Early Factory System*. Manchester: Manchester University Press, 1958.

FITZGERALD, Ron. "The Development of the Cast Iron Frame in Textile Mills to 1850." *Industrial Archaeology Review* 10, no. 2 (Spring 1988): 127–45. (Reprinted in **SUTHERLAND** 1997.)

FLACHSBART, Otto. "Beitrag zur Frage der Berücksichtigen des Windes im Bauwesen." *11 Jahrbuch der Deutschen Gesellschaft für Bauingenieurwesen*. Berlin: Vereins Deutscher Ingenieure (VDI), 1928, pp. 160–69.

FLETCHER, Banister. *A History of Architecture*. 20th ed. London: Architectural Press, 1996.

FÖPPL, August. *Das Fachwerk im Raume*. Leipzig: Teubner, 1892.

FORSTER, Brian. "Cable and Membrane Roofs – A Historical Survey." *Structural Engineering Review* 6, nos. 3–4 (1994): 145–74. (Double issue devoted to tension structures.)

FRANCESCO DI GIORGIO MARTINI. Treatise on civil and military engineering and architecture. Manuscript, Urbino, Italy, 1470s. Published as *Trattato dell' Architettura civile e militare*. Turin, 1841.

FRANKL, Paul. *The Gothic: Literary Sources and Interpretations Through Eight Centuries*. Princeton, N.J.: Princeton University Press, 1960.

FREITAG, Joseph K. *The Fireproofing of Steel Buildings*. New York: John Wiley & Sons, 1899.

FREITAG, Joseph K. *Architectural Engineering*. 2nd ed. New York: John Wiley & Sons, 1909.

FRÉZIER, Amédée-François. *La théorie et la pratique de la coupe de pierres et des bois, pour la construction des voûtes et autres parties des bâtiments civils et militaires; ou, Traité de stéréotomie à l'usage de l'architecture*. Strasbourg/Paris: Charles-Antoine Jombert, 1737–39.

FRIEDMAN, Donald. *Historical Building Construction: Design, Materials and Technology*. New York and London: W.W. Norton, 1995.

GALILEI, Galileo. *Discorsi e Dimonstrazioni matematiche, intorno a due nuove scienze attenenti alla mecanica e i movimenti locali*. Leida, 1638. English translation [*Dialogues Concerning Two New Sciences*] by H. Crew and A. de Salvio. New York: Macmillan, 1914; rpt. New York: Dover Publications, 1954.

GIEDION, Sigfried. *Space, Time, and Architecture: The Growth of a New Tradition*. 3rd ed. Oxford: Oxford University Press, 1954.

GILES, Colum, and Ian H. **GOODALL**. *Yorkshire Textile Mills: The Buildings of the Yorkshire Textile Industry, 1770–1930*. London: HMSO (Royal Commission on the Historical Monuments of England), 1992.

GILLE, Bertrand. *The Renaissance Engineers*. London: Lund Humphries, 1966.

GILLMOOR, C. S. *Coulomb and the Evolution of Physics and Engineering in Eighteenth-Century France*. Princeton, N.J.: Princeton University Press, 1971.

GIMPEL, Jean. *The Cathedral Builders*. Salisbury, England: Michael Russell, 1983.

GOODMAN, Richard E. *Karl Terzaghi: The Engineer as Artist*. Reston, Va.: American Society of Civil Engineers (ASCE), 1999.

GORDON, J. E. *The New Science of Strong Materials: or, Why You Don't Fall Through the Floor*. Harmondsworth, England: Penguin Books, 1968.

GORDON, J. E. *Structures: or, Why Things Don't Fall Down*.

Harmondsworth, England: Penguin Books, 1978.
GRAEFE, Rainer. "Hängedächer des 19. Jahrhunderts." In **GRAEFE**, 1989, pp. 168–87.
GRAEFE, Rainer. *Vladimir G. Suchov, 1853–1939: Die Kunst der sparsamen Konstruktion*. Stuttgart: Gappoev & Pertschi, 1990.
GRAEFE, Rainer, ed. *Zur Geschichte des Konstruierens*. Stuttgart: Deutsche Verlags-Anstalt, 1989.
GRAYSON, Lawrence P. *The Making of an Engineer: An Illustrated History of Engineering Education in the United States and Canada*. New York: Wiley, 1993.
GROTE, Jupp, and Bernard **MARREY**. *Freyssinet, la précontrainte et l'Europe, 1930–1945*. [In French, German, and English.] Paris: Éditions du Linteau, 2000.
GUENZI, Carlo, ed. *L' Arte di Edificare: Manuali in Italia, 1750–1950*. Milano: Be-Ma Editrice, 1992.
GUILLERME, André. "From Lime to Cement: The Industrial Revolution in French Civil Engineering (1770–1850)." *History and Technology* 3 (1986): 25–85.
GUILLERME, André. *Bâtir la ville. Révolutions industrielles dans les matériaux de construction: France - Grande-Bretagne (1760–1840)*. Seysell, France: Éditions du Champ Vallon, 1995.
HÄGERMANN, Gustav, Günter **HUBERTI**, and Hans **MÖLL**, eds. *Vom Caementum zum Spannbeton; Beitrage zur Geschichte des Betons*. 3 vols. Wiesbaden: Bauverlag, 1962–65.
HAGN, H. *Schutz von Eisenkonstruktionen gegen Feuer.* Berlin: Springer, 1904.
HALES, Stephen. *A Treatise on Ventilators*. London, 1758.
HAMILTON, S. B. "The Place of Sir Christopher Wren in the History of Structural Engineering." *Transactions of the Newcomen Society* 14 (1933–34): 27–42. (Reprinted in **ADDIS** 1999.)
HAMILTON, S.B. "The Development of Structural Theory." *Proceedings of the Institution of Civil Engineers* 1 (1952): 374–419.
HAMILTON, S.B. *A Note on the History of Reinforced Concrete in Buildings. National Building Studies Special Report No. 24*. London: HMSO, 1956.
HAMILTON, S.B. *A Short History of the Structural Fire Protection of Buildings. National Building Studies Special Report No. 27*. London: HMSO, 1958.
HANGLEITER, Ulrich, ed. *Conceptual Design of Structures*. Proceedings of the International Symposium at the University of Stuttgart, IASS (International Association of Shell and Spatial Structures), Stuttgart, October 1996.
HAPPOLD, E., I. **LIDDELL**, and M. **DICKSON**. "Design Towards Convergence: A Discussion." *Architectural Design* 46, no. 7 (1976): 430–35.
HART, F., W. **HENN**, and H. **SONNTAG**. *Multi-Storey Buildings in Steel.* Ed. G. Bernard Godfrey. 2nd ed. London: Collins, 1985.
HART, Franz. *Kunst und technik der Wölbung*. München: Callwey, 1965.
HARTIG, Willfred, and Günter **GÜNSCHEL**. *Grosse Konstrukteure. 1. Freyssinet, Maillart, Dischinger, Finsterwalder*. Berlin: Ullstein, 1966.
HARVEY, J.H. *The Mediaeval Architect.* London: Wayland, 1972.
HARVEY, J.H. *Mediaeval Craftsmen.* London: Batsford, 1975.
HAWKES, Dean. "A History of Models of the Environment in Buildings." *Land-use and built-form studies, Working Paper No. 34*. Cambridge: University of Cambridge School of Architecture, 1970.
HAY, G.D., and G.P. **STELL**. *Monuments of Industry: An Illustrated Historical Record*. Royal Commission on the Ancient and Historical Monuments of Scotland, 1986.
HEILMEYER, W.-D. "Apollodorus von Damascus, der Architekt des Pantheons." *Jahrbuch des Deutschen Archäologischen Instituts* 90 (1975): 317–47.
HESS, Friedrich. *Konstruktion und form im Bauen*. Stuttgart: Julius Hoffmann, 1943.
HEWES, Lawrence, and Herbert L. **SEWARD**. *The Design of Diagrams for Engineering Formulas and the Theory of Nomography.* London: McGraw-Hill, 1923.
HEYMAN, Jacques. *Coulomb's Memoir on Statics: An Essay in the History of Civil Engineering.* Cambridge: Cambridge University Press, 1972.
HEYMAN, Jacques. *The Stone Skeleton: Structural Engineering of Masonry Architecture*. Cambridge: Cambridge University Press, 1995.
HEYMAN, Jacques. *Arches, Vaults, and Buttresses: Masonry Structures and their Engineering.* Aldershot, England: Ashgate; Brookfield, Vt.: Variorum, 1996.
HEYMAN, Jacques. *Structural Analysis: An Historical Approach.* Cambridge: Cambridge University Press, 1998.
HIGGS, Malcolm. "Felix James Samuely." *Architectural Association Journal* 76, no. 843 (June 1960): 2–31.
HIX, John. *The Glasshouse*. London: Phaidon Press, 1996.
HODGKINSON, Eaton. "Theoretical and Experimental Researches to ascertain the Strength and Best Form of Iron Beams." *Memoirs of the Literary and Philosophical Society of Manchester*, 2nd ser., Vol. 5 (1831): 407–544.
HOLGATE, Alan. *The Art of Structural Engineering: The Work of Jörg Schlaich and his Team*. Stuttgart: Axel Menges, 1997.
HOSSDORF, Heinz. *Model Analysis of Structures*. New York: Van Nostrand, 1974.
HOSSDORF, Heinz. *Das Erlebnis Ingenieur zu sein*. Basel: Birkhäuser, 2003.
HUERTA, Santiago. *Las bóvedas de Guastavino en América*. Madrid: Instituto Juan de Herrera, 2001.
HUERTA, Santiago. *Arcos, bóvedas y cupolas: Geometria y equlibrio en el cálculo traditional e estructuras de fábrica*. Madrid: Instituto Juan de Herrera, 2004.
HUERTA, Santiago, ed. *Actas del Primer Congreso Nacional de Historia de construcción*. Madrid: Instituto Juan de Herrera, 1996.
HUERTA, Santiago, ed. *Actas del Secundo Congreso Nacional de Historia de construcción*. Madrid: Instituto Juan de Herrera, 1998.
HUERTA, Santiago, ed. *Actas del Tercer Congreso Nacional de Historia de construcción*. Madrid: Instituto Juan de Herrera, 2000.
HUERTA, Santiago, ed. *Proceedings of the First International Congress on Construction History.* Madrid, 2003.
HUERTA, Santiago, ed. *Actas del Cuarto Congreso Nacional de Historia de construcción*. Madrid: Instituto Juan de Herrera, 2005.
HUERTA, Santiago, ed. *Essays in the History of the Theory of Structures*. Madrid: Instituto Juan de Herrera, 2005.
ICE (Institution of Civil Engineers). *Ove Arup (1895–1988)*. London: Institution of Civil Engineers, 1995.
INGLIS, Margaret. *Willis Haviland Carrier, Father of Air-conditioning*. Garden City, N.Y.: Country Life Press, 1952.
INMAN, W.S. *Principles of Ventilation, Warming and the Transmission of Sound*. London, 1836.
IORI, Tullia. *Il cemento armato in Italia: dalle origine alla seconda guerra mondiale*. Roma: Edilstampa, 2001.
JAMES, John. *Chartres: The Masons who Built a Legend*. London: Routledge & Kegan Paul, 1982.
JARDINE, Lisa. *The Curious Life of Robert Hooke, the Man who Measured London*. London: HarperCollins, 2003.
JESBERG, Paulgerd. *Die Geschichte der Ingenieurbaukunst*. Stuttgart: Deutsche Verlags-Anstalt, 1996.
JOEDICKE, Jürgen. *Shell Architecture*. London: Alec Tiranti, 1963.
JORDAN, Vilhelm Lassen. *Acoustical Design of Concert Halls and Theatres*. London: Applied Science Publishers, 1980.
KAWAGUCHI, M. "Physical Models as Powerful Weapons in Structural Design." See **MOTRO** 2004.
KELLER, Alex. *A Theatre of Machines*. London: Chapman & Hall, 1964.
KERISEL, Jean. *Down to Earth: Foundations Past and Present - The Invisible Art of the Builder*. Rotterdam: A.A. Balkema, 1987.
KERISEL, Jean. "History of Retaining Wall Design." Proceedings of the conference *Retaining Structures*, organized by the Institution of Civil Engineers, held at Robinson College, Cambridge, England, 20–23 July 1992. Ed. C.R.I. Clayton. London: Institution of Civil Engineers, 1993. (Reprinted in **ADDIS** 1999.)
KERR, J. "A Short History of Investigations on the Natural Lighting of Schools." *The Illuminating Engineer* 7, no. 1 (January 1913): 27–30.
KING, Ross. *Brunelleschi's Dome*. London: Chatto & Windus, 2000.
KIPLING, Rudyard. "The Ship that Found Herself." In *The Day's Work*. London: Macmillan, 1908.
KIRIKOV, B. *History of Earthquake Resistant Construction from Antiquity to our Times.* Madrid: Instituto de Ciencias de la Construcción Eduardo Torroja, 1992.
KRAUS, H.J., and Franz **DISCHINGER**. *Dachbauten: Kragdächer, Schalen und Rippenkuppeln*. 4th ed. Berlin: Ernst und Sohn, 1928. (Vol. 6 of *Handbuch für Eisenbetonbau*. Ed. Fritz von Emperger.)
KURRER, Karl-Eugen. *Geschichte der Baustatik*. Berlin: Ernst und Sohn, 2002.
KYESER, **K**onrad. *Bellifortis*. Manuscript, Southern Germany, c. 1405. Facsimile ed. Dusseldorf: VDI Verlag, 1967.
LALANNE, **LÉON**. "Mémoire sur les tables graphiques et sur la géométrie anamorphique appliquées à diverses questions qui se rattachent à l'art de l'ingénieur." *Annales des Ponts et Chaussées*, 2nd ser., Vol. 11 (1846): 1–69.
LANDAU, S. B., and Carl W. **CONDIT**. *Rise of the New York Skyscraper, 1865–1913*. New Haven, Ct.: Yale University Press, 1996.
LANDELS, J.G. *Engineering in the Ancient World (History and Politics)*. Rev. ed. London: Constable, 2000.
LAWRENCE, J.C. "Steel Frame Architecture versus the London Building Regulations: Selfridges, the Ritz and American Technology." *Construction History* 6 (1990): 23–46. (Reprinted in **THORNE** 2000.)
LE CORBUSIER. *Vers une architecture*. Paris: Éditions Crès, 1923. English translation [*Towards a New Architecture*] by Frederick Etchells. London: Architectural Press, 1927.
LEA, F.M. *Science and Building: A History of the Building Research Station*. London: HMSO (Building Research Station), 1971.
LEA, F.M., ed. *The Principles of Modern Building*. 3rd ed. 2 vols. London: HMSO (Building Research Station), 1959 and 1961.
LEACROFT, Richard and Helen. *Theatre and Playhouse: An Illustrated Survey of Theatre Building from Ancient Greece to the Present Day*. London: Methuen, 1984.
LEMOINE, Bertrand. *L'Architecture du fer*. Seysell, France: Éditions du Champ Vallon, 1986.
LEMOINE, Bertrand. *Gustave Eiffel*. Paris: Fernand Hazan, 1986.
LEMOINE, Bertrand, and Marc **MIMRAM**. *Paris d'ingénieurs*. Paris: Éditions du Pavillon de l'Arsenal and Picard Éditeur, 1995.
LEON, C. "Apollodorus von Damascus und die Trajanische Architektur." Dissertation, Innsbruck University, 1961.
LEONHARDT, Fritz. *Der Bauingenieur und seine Aufgaben*. Stuttgart: Deutsche Verlags-Anstalt, 1981.
LEVI, Franco. *Cinquant' anni dopo il cemento armato dai primordi alla maturita*. Torino: Testo & Immagine, 2002.
LEVY, Matthys, and Mario **SALVADORI**. *Why Buildings Fall Down: How Structures Fail*. New York: W.W. Norton, 1992.
LIPKA, Joseph. *Graphical and Mechanical Computation.* New York: Wiley, 1918.
LORENZ, Werner. "Classicism and High Technology – The Berlin Neues Museum." *Construction History* 15 (1999): 39–55.
MACAULAY, David. *Cathedral: The Story of its Construction*. London: Collins, 1974.
MACDONALD, Angus. *Anthony Hunt*. London Thomas Telford, 2000.
MACDONALD, William L. *The Architecture of the Roman Empire*. New Haven, Ct., and London: Yale University Press, 1982.
MAINSTONE, Rowland J. "Structural theory and design before 1742." *Architectural Review* 143 (1968): 303–10. (Reprinted in **MAINSTONE** 1999.)
MAINSTONE, Rowland J. "Brunelleschi's Dome of Santa Maria del Fiore and Some Related Structures." *Transactions of the Newcomen Society* 42 (1969–70): 107–26. (Reprinted in **COURTENAY** 1997 and **MAINSTONE** 1999.)

MAINSTONE, Rowland J. *Hagia Sophia*. London: Thames and Hudson, 1988.
MAINSTONE, Rowland J. "Stability Concepts from Renaissance to Today." In *StableUnstable? Structural Consolidation of Ancient Buildings*. Ed. R.M. Lemaire and K. van Balen. Leuven: Leuven University Press / Centre for the Conservation of Historic Towns and Buildings, 1988, pp. 65–78. (Reprinted in **ADDIS** 1999.)
MAINSTONE, Rowland J. *Developments in Structural Form*. 2nd ed. Oxford: Architectural Press, 1998.
MAINSTONE, Rowland J. *Structure in Architecture: History, Design and Innovation*. Aldershot, England: Ashgate, 1999.
MARK, Robert, ed. *Architectural Technology up to the Scientific Revolution: The Art and Structure of Large-Scale Buildings*. New Liberal Arts Series. Cambridge, Mass.: MIT Press, 1994.
MARREY, Bernard. *Le fer à Paris*. Paris: Picard Éditeur & Pavillon de l'Arsenal, 1989.
MARSDEN, E.W. *Greek and Roman Artillery: Historical Development*. Oxford: Clarendon Press, 1969.
MARSDEN, E.W. *Greek and Roman Artillery: Technical Treatises*. Oxford: Clarendon Press, 1971.
MAURER, Bertram. *Karl Culmann und die graphische Statik*. Stuttgart: Verlag für Geschichte der Naturwissenschaft und der Technik, 1998.
MCGIVERN, J.G. *First Hundred years of Engineering Education in the United States (1807–1907)*. Spokane, Wash.: Gonzaga University Press, 1960.
MCNEIL, Ian. *Hydraulic Power*. London: Longman, 1972.
MEHRTENS, G.C. *Vorlesungen über Ingenieurwissenschaften*. 6 vols. Leipzig, 1903–23.
MESQUI, Jean. *Les châteaux forts: de la guerre á la paix*. Paris: Gallimard, 1995.
MISLIN, Miron. *Geschichte der Baukonstruktion und Bautechnik.* Band 1: *Antike bis Renaissance*. 2.Auflage. Dussedorf: Werner Verlag, 1997.
MISLIN, Miron. *Industriearchitecktur in Berlin*. Berlin: Ernst Wasmuth Verlag, 2002.
MONGE, Gaspard. *Géometrie descriptive*. Paris, 1799.
MORDAUNT-CROOK, J. "Sir Robert Smirke: A Pioneer of Concrete Construction." *Transactions of the Newcomen Society* 38 (1965): 5–20. (Reprinted in **NEWBY** 2001.)
MOTRO, R., ed. *Shell and Spatial Structures: From Models to Realization*. International Symposium, International Association for Shell and Spatial Structures. Montpellier, France: University of Montpellier, 20–24 September 2004 (published on CD only).
MUJICA, Francisco. *The History of the Skyscraper*. New York: Archaeology and Architecture Press, 1930.
MÜLLER, Werner. *Grundlagen gotischer Bautechnik*. München: Deutscher Kunstverlag, 1990.
NAVIER, C. L. M. H. *Leçons données à l'École royale des Ponts et Chaussées, sur l'application de la mechanique*. Paris, 1820. (Later versions and editions in 1826, 1833, 1864.)
NEDOLUHA, Alois. *Kulturgeschichte des technischen Zeichnens*. Vienna: Springer-Verlag, 1960.
NERDINGER, Winifred, ed. *Frei Otto: Complete Works*. Basel: Birkhäuser, 2005.
NERVI, Pier Luigi. *Scienza o arte del construire?* Rome: Edizione della Bussola, 1945.
NERVI, Pier Luigi. *Construire correttamente*. Milan: Edizioni Hoepli, 1954.
NERVI, Pier Luigi. *Structures*. New York: F.W. Dodge Corp., 1956.
NERVI, Pier Luigi. *Aesthetics and Technology in Building*. Cambridge, Mass.: Harvard University Press, 1966.
NEWBY, Frank, ed. *Early Reinforced Concrete*. Studies in the History of Civil Engineering 11. Aldershot, England: Ashgate, 2001.
NEWLON, Howard, ed. *A Selection of Historic American Papers on Concrete,1876–1926.* Detroit: American Concrete Institute, 1976.
NISBET, James. *Fair and Reasonable: Building Contracts from 1550 - A Synopsis*. London: Stoke Publications, 1993.
NISBET, James. *A Proper Price: Quantity Surveying in London, 1650–1940*. London: Stoke Publications, 1997.
O'DEA, W.T. *A Short History of Lighting*. London: HMSO, 1958.
OTTO, Frei. *Tensile Structures*. 2 vols. Cambridge, Mass.: MIT Press, 1973.
PACEY, Arnold. *The Maze of Ingenuity*. London: Allen Lane, 1974; 2nd ed., Cambridge, Mass.: MIT Press, 1992.
PARSONS, W.B. *Engineers and Engineering in the Renaissance*. Baltimore: Williams & Wilkins, 1939; 2nd ed., Cambridge, Mass.: MIT Press, 1967.
PASQUALE, Salvatore di. *L'arte del costruire: tra conoscenza e scienza*. Venezia: Marsilio, 1996.
PASQUALE, Salvatore di. *Brunellleschi: La constructione della cupola di Santa Maria del Fiore*. Venezia: Marsilio, 2002.
PECK, R. B. *History of Building Foundations in Chicago*. University of Illinois, Engineering Experiment Station, Bulletin Series 373, 1948. (Reprinted in **ADDIS** 1999.)
PEDRESCHI, Remo. *Eladio Dieste*. London Thomas Telford, 2001.
PETER, John. *Aluminum in Modern Architecture.* Vol. 1: *Buildings*. Louisville, Ky.: Reynolds Metals Company / New York: Reinhold Publishing Company, 1956. (For Vol. 2, see **WEIDLINGER** 1956.)
PETERS, Tom. *Time is Money: Die Entwicklung des modernen Bauwesens*. Stuttgart: Julius Hoffmann, 1981.
PETERS, Tom. *Building the Nineteenth Century*. Cambridge, Mass.: MIT Press, 1996.
PETERSON, Charles E., ed. *Building Early America*. Radnor, Pa.: Chilton Book Co., 1976.
PETROSKI, Henry. *To Engineer is Human: The Role of Failure in Successful Design*. London: Macmillan, 1985.
PFAMMATTER, Ulrich. *The Making of the Modern Architect and Engineer: The Origins and Development of a Scientifically Oriented Education*. Basel: Birkhäuser, 1992.
PICON, Antoine. *Architectes et ingénieurs au siècle des lumières*. Marseilles: Éditions parenthèses, 1988.
PICON, Antoine. *L'invention de l'ingénieur moderne: l'École des Ponts et Chaussées, 1747–1851*. Paris: Presses de l'École nationale des ponts et chaussées, 1992.
PICON, Antoine, ed. *L'Art de l'ingénieur: constructeur, entrepreneur, inventeur*. Paris: Éditions du Centre Pompidou, 1997.
PICON, Antoine, and Michel **YVON**. *L'ingénieur artiste : Dessins anciens de l'École des ponts et chaussées*. Paris: Presses de l'École nationale des ponts et chaussées, 1989.
POLE, William. *The Life of Sir William Fairbairn*. London: Longmans, 1877; rpt. Newton Abbot, England: David & Charles, 1970.
POWELL, Christopher. *The British Building Industry since 1800: An Economic History*. 2nd ed. London: Spon, 1996.
PUGSLEY, A. G. "The History of Structural Testing." *The Structural Engineer* 22, no. 12 (December 1944): 492–505.
RADELET-DE GRAVE, Patricia, and Edoardo **BENVENUTO**, eds. *Entre Mécanique et Architecture – Between Mechanics and Architecture*. Basel: Birkhäuser, 1995.
RANDALL, Frank A. *The History of the Development of Building Construction in Chicago*. Urbana, Ill.: University of Illinois Press, 1949; 2nd ed., 1999.
RANKINE, W. J. M. *Introductory Lecture on the Harmony of Theory and Practice in Mechanics*. London and Glasgow: Griffin, 1856. (Included in **RANKINE** 1858.)
RANKINE, W. J. M. *A Manual of Applied Mechanics*. London and Glasgow: Griffin, 1858.
REID, David Boswell. *Illustrations of the theory and practice of ventilation, with remarks on warming, exclusive lighting and the communication of sound*. London, 1844.
RICE, Peter. *An Engineer Imagines*. London: Artemis, 1994.
RICE, Peter, and Hugh **DUTTON**. *Le verre structurel*. Paris: Éditions du Moniteur, 1990. 2nd ed. (in English): *Structural Glass*. London: Spon, 1995.
RICHARDSON, Harriet, ed. *English Hospitals 1660–1948: A Survey of Their Architecture and Design*. London: English Heritage (Royal Commission on the Historical Monuments of England), 1998.
RICKEN, Herbert. *Der Bauingenieur: Geschichte eines Berufes*. Berlin: Verlag für Bauwesen, 1994.
RIETSCHEL, Hermann. *Leitfaden zum Berechnen und Entwerfen von Lüftungs- und Heizungsanlagen*. Berlin, 1893. English translation by Karl Brabbée. New York: McGraw-Hill, 1927.
ROBBIN, Tony. *Engineering a New Architecture*. New Haven, Ct.: Yale University Press, 1996.
ROLAND, Conrad. *Frei Otto – Spannweiten: Ideen und Versuche zum Leichtbau*. Berlin: Verlag Ullstein, 1965.
RONDELET, J. *Traité théorique et pratique de l'art de bâtir*. 5 vols. Paris, 1812–17. Supplement by G. A. Blouet, 1847.
ROSE, W. N. *Line Charts for Engineers*. 8th ed. London: Chapman & Hall, 1947.
ROSENBERG, N., and W.G. **VICENTI**. *The Britannia Bridge: The Generation and Diffusion of Technical Knowledge*. Cambridge, Mass.: MIT Press, 1978.
RUSSELL, Loris S. "Early Nineteenth-Century Lighting." In **PETERSON** 1976.
RUZICKA, Stanislav. "The Provision of Adequate Daylight Illumination in Schoolrooms." *The Illuminating Engineer* 1 (1908): 539–43.
SAALMAN, Howard. *Filippo Brunelleschi: The Cupola of Santa Maria del Fiore*. London: Zwemmer, 1980.
SABBAGH, Karl. *Skyscraper: The Making of a Building*. London: Macmillan, with Channel Four Television, 1990.
SABINE, Wallace C. *Collected Papers on Acoustics*. Cambridge, Mass.: Harvard University Press, 1922; rpt. New York: Dover Publications, 1964.
SAITOH, M. " '0 to 1' – From Imagination to Creation." See **MOTRO** 2004.
SALVADORI, Mario. *Why Buildings Stand Up: The Strength of Architecture*. New York: W.W. Norton, 1990.
SANABRIA, S.L. "The Mechanisation of Design in the 16th Century: The Structural Formulae of Rodrigo Gil de Hontañón." *Journal of the Society of Architectural Historians* 41 (1982): 281–93. (Reprinted in **ADDIS** 1999.)
SCHULZE, K.W. *Der Stahlskelettbau: Geschäfts- und Hochhäuser*. Stuttgart: Zaugg, 1928.
SHANKLAND, E.C. "Steel Skeleton Construction in Chicago." *Minutes of the Proceedings of the Institution of Civil Engineers* 128 (1897): 1–22. Rpt. in *Thames Tunnel to Channel Tunnel: 150 Years of Civil Engineering*. Ed. Will Howie and Mike Chrimes. London: Thomas Telford, 1987, pp. 151–78.
SHELBY, L.R. "The Geometrical Knowledge of the Mediaeval Master Masons." *Speculum* 47 (1972): 395–421. (Reprinted in **COURTENAY** 1997.)
SHELBY, L.R. *Gothic Design Techniques: The Fifteenth-Century Design Booklets of Mathes Roriczer and Hanns Schmuttermayer*. Carbondale, Ill: Southern Illinois University Press, 1977.
SHELBY, L.R., and R. **MARK**. "Late Gothic Structural Design in the 'Instructions' of Lorenz Lechler (1516)." *Architectura* (Journal of the History of Architecture, Munich) 9 (1979): 113–31. (Reprinted in **COURTENAY** 1997.)
SIMONNET, Cyrille. "The Origins of Reinforced Concrete." *Rassegna* 49, no. 1 (March 1992): 6–14. (Reprinted in **NEWBY** 2001.)
SIMSON, O. G. von. *The Gothic Cathedral*. New York: Pantheon, 1956.
SKEMPTON, A.W. "The Origin of Iron Beams." *Actes du VIIIe Congrès International d'histoire des sciences*. Florence: 3–9 September 1956, pp. 1029–39. (Reprinted in **ADDIS 1999**.)
SKEMPTON, A.W. "Evolution of the Steel Frame Building." *Guilds Engineer* 10 (1959): 37–51.
SKEMPTON, A.W. "The Boat Store, Sheerness (1858–60) and its Place in Structural History." *Transactions of the Newcomen Society* 32 (1959–60): 57–78. (Reprinted in **THORNE 2000**.)
SKEMPTON, A.W. "Landmarks in Early Soil Mechanics." *Proceedings of 7th European Conference on Soil Mechanics and Foundation Engineering, Brighton*, 1979, pp. 1–26.
SKEMPTON, A.W. *Civil Engineers and Engineering in Britain, 1600–1830*. Aldershot, England: Ashgate/Variorum, 1996.
SKEMPTON, A.W., ed. *John Smeaton, FRS*. London: Thomas Telford, 1981.

SKEMPTON, A.W., ed. *Biographical Dictionary of Civil Engineers in Great Britain and Ireland. Vol. 1: 1500–1830*. London: Institution of Civil Engineers / Thomas Telford, 2002.

SKEMPTON, A.W., and H.R. **JOHNSON**. "The First Iron Frames." *Architectural Review* 131 (March 1952): 175–86. (Reprinted in **SUTHERLAND** 1997.)

SMILES, Samuel. *Lives of the Engineers*. 5 vols. London: John Murray, 1874–1900 (many editions of each volume).

SMITH, Denis, ed. *Water-Supply and Public Health Engineering*. Studies in the History of Civil Engineering 5. Aldershot, England: Ashgate, 1999.

SMITH, Norman. "Cathedral Studies: Engineering or History?" *Transactions of the Newcomen Society* 73 (2001–2002): 95–137.

SMITH, Stanley. "The Design of Structural Ironwork 1850–1890: Education, Theory and Practice." *Construction History* 8 (1992): 89–108. (Reprinted in **ADDIS** 1999.)

SPANDÖCK, Friedrich. "Akustische Modelversuche." *Annalen der Physik* 20 (1934): 345–60.

SPECHT, Manfred, ed. *Spannweite der Gedanken: Zur 100. Wiederkehr des Geburtstages von Franz Dischinger*. Berlin: Springer-Verlag, 1987.

STANLEY, C. C. *Highlights in the History of Concrete*. Wexham Springs, England: Cement & Concrete Association, 1979.

STEINER, Frances H. *French Iron Architecture*. Ann Arbor, Mich.: UMI Research Press, 1978.

STEVENSON, Christine. *Medicine and Magnificence: British Hospital and Asylum Architecture, 1660–1815*. New Haven, Ct.: Yale University Press, 2000.

STEVIN, Simon. *De Beghinselen der Weeghconst*. Leiden: Françoys van Raphelinghen, 1586.

STIGLAT, Klaus. *Bauingenieure und ihr Werk*. Berlin: Ernst und Sohn, 2004.

STRAUB, Hans. *A History of Civil Engineering*. English translation by E. Rockwell. London: Leonard Hill, 1952.

STRAUB, Hans. *Die Geschichte der Bauingenieurkunst*. 4th ed. Basel: Birkhäuser, 1992.

STRIKE, James. *Construction into Design: The Influence of New Methods of Construction on Architectural Design, 1690–1990*. Oxford: Butterworth-Heinemann, 1991.

STURROCK, Neil, and Peter **LAWSON-SMITH**. "The Grandfather of Air-Conditioning: The Work and Influence of David Boswell Reid, Physician, Chemist, Engineer (1805–63)." In **DUNKELD** et al., 2006, pp. 2981–98.

SULZER, Peter. *Jean Prouvé: Oeuvre complet*. Vol. 1: 1917–1933; Vol. 2: 1934–1944; Vol. 3: 1944–1954. Basel: Birkhaüser, 1999, 2000, and 2002.

SUTHERLAND, R.J.M. "Pioneer British Contributions to Structural Iron and Concrete: 1770–1855." In **PETERSON** 1976.

SUTHERLAND, R.J.M. "Shipbuilding and the Long-Span Roof." *Transactions of the Newcomen Society* 60 (1988–89): 107–26. (Reprinted in **SUTHERLAND** 1997.)

SUTHERLAND, R.J.M. "The Age of Cast Iron, 1780–1850: Who Sized the Beams?" Contained in Essays to accompany an exhibition at the RIBA Heinz Gallery (ed. Robert Thorne). London: RIBA, June 1990, pp. 24–33. (Reprinted in **SUTHERLAND** 1997.)

SUTHERLAND, R.J.M., ed. *Structural Iron, 1750–1850*. Studies in the History of Civil Engineering 9. Aldershot, England: Ashgate, 1997.

SUTHERLAND, R.J.M., et al., eds. *Historic Concrete*. London: Thomas Telford, 2001. (A revised and expanded version of *Proceedings of the Institution of Civil Engineers: Structures and Buildings* 116, nos. 3 and 4 (1996): 255–480.)

SYLVESTER, Charles. *Philosophy of Domestic Economy as exemplified in the mode of warming, ventilating, washing, drying and cooking ... adopted in the Derbyshire General Infirmary, etc*. Nottingham and London, 1819.

TANN, Jennifer. *The Development of the Factory*. London: Cornmarket, 1970.

TAYLOR, Jeremy. *The Architect and the Pavilion Hospital: Dialogue and Design Creativity in England, 1850–1914*. Leicester: Leicester University Press, 1977.

TAYLOR, Jeremy. *Hospital and Asylum Architecture in England, 1840–1914*. London: Mansell, 1991.

TAYLOR, Rabun. *Roman Builders*. Cambridge: Cambridge University Press, 2003.

THOMPSON, Emily. " 'Mysteries of the Acoustic': Architectural Acoustics in America, 1800–1932." Ph.D. dissertation. Princeton University, 1992.

THOMPSON, Emily. *The Soundscape of Modernity: Architectural Acoustics and the Culture of Listening in America, 1900–1933*. Cambridge, Mass.: MIT Press, 2002.

THORNE, Robert, ed. *Structural Iron and Steel, 1850–1900*. Studies in the History of Civil Engineering 10. Aldershot: Ashgate, 2000.

TIMOSHENKO, Stephen P. *History of Strength of Materials*. New York: McGraw-Hill, 1953. Rpt. New York: Dover Publications, 1983.

TODHUNTER, Isaac, and Karl **PEARSON**. *A History of the Theory of Elasticity and Strength of Materials: From Galilei to the Present Time*. Cambridge: Cambridge University Press, 1886–93.

TORROJA, Eduardo. *The Structures of Eduardo Torroja*. New York: F.W. Dodge Corp., 1958.

TORROJA, Eduardo. *The Philosophy of Structures*. Berkeley: University of California Press, 1967.

TREDGOLD, Thomas. *Principles of Warming and Ventilating Public Buildings, Dwelling Houses, Manufactories, Hospitals, Hot Houses, conservatories, etc*. London, 1824.

TROTTER, Alexander. *The Elements of Illuminating Engineering*. London: Pitman, 1921.

TRUESDELL, Clifford A. *Essays in the History of Mechanics*. Berlin and New York: Springer-Verlag, 1968.

TRUESDELL, Clifford A. "The Mechanics of Leonardo da Vinci." In **TRUESDELL** 1968.

TRUÑÓ, Ángel. *Construccion de bóvedas tabicadas*. Madrid: Instituto Juan de Herrera, 2004.

VASARI, Giorgio. *The Lives of the Artists*. Florence, 1550. English translation by George Bull. Harmondsworth, England: Penguin, 1987.

VICENTI, W.G. *What Engineers Know and How They Know It*. Baltimore: Johns Hopkins University Press, 1990.

VICTOR, S.K. "Practical Geometry in the High Middle Ages: An Edition of the '*Artis cuiuslibet consummatio*' [The complete collection of every art]." *Memoirs of the American Philosophical Society* 134 (1979).

VILLARD DE HONNECOURT. *The Lodge Book of Villard de Honnecourt*. Manuscript, Northern France, c. 1175–1240. For modern ed., see **BOWIE** 1959.

VITRUVIUS POLLIO, Marcus. *De Architectura*. Rome, c. 25 BC. English translation [*Vitruvius: The Ten Books on Architecture*] by Morris Hicky Morgan. Cambridge, Mass.: Cambridge University Press, 1914; rpt. New York: Dover Publications, 1960.

WARD-PERKINS, J.B. *Roman Imperial Architecture*. Harmondsworth, England: Penguin, 1981.

WEIDLINGER, Paul. *Aluminum in Modern Architecture*. Vol. 2: *Engineering Design and Details*. Louisville, Ky.: Reynolds Metals Company / New York: Reinhold Publishing Company, 1956. (For Vol. 1, see **PETER** 1956.)

WERMIEL, Sara. "The Development of Fireproof Construction in Great Britain and the United States in the Nineteenth Century." *Construction History* 9 (1993): 3–26. (Reprinted in **THORNE** 2000.)

WERMIEL, Sara. *The Fireproof Building: Technology and Public Safety in the Nineteenth-Century American City*. Baltimore: Johns Hopkins University Press, 2000.

WERNER, Ernst. *Technisierung des Bauens: Geschichtlichte Grundlagen moderner Bautechnik*. Düsseldorf: Werner Verlag, 1980.

WERNER, Frank, and Joachim **SEIDEL**. *Der Eisenbau: Vom Werdegang einer Bauweise*. Berlin: Verlag für Bauwesen, 1992

WHEELER, Mortimer. *Roman Art and Architecture*. London: Thames and Hudson, 1964.

WHITE, K.D. *Greek and Roman Technology*. London: Thames and Hudson, 1984.

WHITE, Lynn. *Medieval Technology and Social Change*. Oxford: Oxford University Press, 1962.

WILLIS, Carol, ed. *Building the Empire State*. New York: W.W. Norton, 1998.

WILLIS, R. "On the Construction of the Vaults of the Middle Ages." *Transactions of the Royal Institute of British Architects* 1, Part II (1842): 1–69.

WILMORE, David, ed. *Edwin O. Sachs: Architect, Stagehand, Engineer and Fireman*. Summerbridge, North Yorkshire, England: Theatresearch, 1998.

WILSON-JONES, Mark. *Principles of Roman Architecture*. New Haven, Ct.: Yale University Press, 2000.

WISELY, W.H. *The American Civil Engineer 1852–1974. The History, Traditions and Development of the American Society of Civil Engineers, founded 1852*. New York: American Society of Civil Engineers, 1974.

WITTEK, Karl H. *Die Entwicklung des Stahlhochbaus, von den Angangen (1800) bis zum Dreigelenkbogen (1870)*. Düsseldorf: Verlag des Vereins Deutscher Ingenieure, 1964.

WYMAN, Morrill. *A Practical Treatise on Ventilation*. London: Chapman Bros., 1846.

YEOMANS, David. "Designing the Beam: From Rules of Thumb to Calculations." *Journal of the Institute of Wood Science* 11, no. 1, issue 61 (1987): 43–49. (Reprinted in **ADDIS** 1999.)

YEOMANS, David. *The Trussed Roof: Its History and Development*. Aldershot, England: Ashgate/Scolar Press, 1992.

YEOMANS, David. *Construction since 1900: Materials*. London: Batsford, 1997.

YEOMANS, David. "The Pre-History of the Curtain Wall." *Construction History* 14 (1998): 59–82.

YEOMANS, David, ed. *The Development of Timber as a Structural Material*. Studies in the History of Civil Engineering 8. Aldershot, England: Ashgate, 1999.

YEOMANS, David, and David **COTTAM**. *Owen Williams*. London Thomas Telford, 2001.

ZONCA, Vittorio. *Novo Teatro di Machine et Edificii*. Padua, 1607.

further reading

As well as directing the reader to further reading material on each of the periods covered by the chapters of the book, these endnotes provide an opportunity to draw out a number of themes that run through the history of building engineering. These include, in particular, the histories of individual ***engineering disciplines***, of ***construction materials*** and certain ***building types***, as well as the ***development of the professions*** and ***education of engineers***, ***national histories***, and ***biographies*** of a number of the more eminent engineers who have contributed to the history of our subject.

The history of building engineering sits within the wider fields of the history of technology, the history of science, and the history of civil engineering, and the classic books in these fields not only provide an overview of our subject, but help set it in the wider context. The best overview of ***civil engineering*** history in English, which also deals extensively with buildings, is still the translation of the book written by the Swiss engineer Hans Straub in the 1940s (**STRAUB** 1952), a book that has now reached its fourth edition in German (**STRAUB** 1992). Civil engineering, of course, embraces many disciplines, several of which touch on the construction and engineering of buildings, and each of these has its own literature. The recent twelve-volume series *Studies in Civil Engineering History* deals with all aspects of the subject, including bridges, ports and harbours, dams, canals, railways, and land drainage, as well as subjects closer to the engineering of buildings, including water supply and public health engineering (**SMITH** 1999), timber (**YEOMANS** 1999), iron (**SUTHERLAND** 1997 and **THORNE** 1999), concrete (**NEWBY** 2001), and design in civil and structural engineering (**ADDIS** 1999). Generally, however, civil engineering history, like military history, tends to be rather nationalistic, focusing on a particular country's achievements, for example **WISELY** (1974), **SKEMPTON** (1996), and **DENNIS** (2003).

The history of buildings is dominated by books on the history of architecture, though these seldom address the question of how they were constructed or designed from the engineering point of view. Nevertheless, alongside histories of technology, science, and civil engineering, histories of architecture provide a further context within which developments in building engineering can be set. Not least, they provide a helpful catalogue of what was being built in different countries, and when the buildings were constructed. Of particular use are classic general works such as **CHOISY** (1899) and the many editions of Sir Banister Fletcher's *A History of Architecture* (**FLETCHER** 1996).

There are very few equivalent books devoted to the full range of building engineering disciplines over the last three thousand years or so – indeed, perhaps only the two volumes by **COWAN**, *The Master Builders* (1977) and *Science and Building* (1978). A second contender (**ELLIOTT** 1992) deals predominantly with recent times, since the eighteenth century, and covers only developments in Britain and the U.S.

Engineering Disciplines

Structural Engineering

The history of structural engineering has received more attention than other building engineering disciplines, both because it can be traced so far back into history and, significantly, because the science and mathematics of mechanics and forces were developed earlier than other sciences related to building. **COWAN** (1977 and 1978, as cited above), **MAINSTONE** (1998 and 1999), **GRAEFE** (1989), and **JESBERG** (1996) have all dealt with the entire history of structural engineering, from around 1000 BC to the last century. The pre-scientific era has been well-treated by **MARK** (1994) and **MISLIN** (1997), and the last three centuries have been covered by **WERNER** (1980), **BILLINGTON** (1985), **RICKEN** (1994), and **PICON** (1997). Developments by individual nations have been portrayed by many authors, for example, France (**DESWARTE-ROSA & LEMOINE** 1980 and **LEMOINE & MIMRAM** 1995), Britain (**COLLINS** 1983), Italy (**GUENZI** 1992, **BUCCARO & AGOSTINO** 2003, and **BUCCARO & MATTIA** 2003), and the U.S. (**CONDIT** 1960, 1961 *et al.*). Among many teachers of structural engineering who have used historical examples to illustrate structural principles, Professor Mario Salvadori is perhaps the best known (**SALVADORI** 1990 and **LEVY & SALVADORI** 1992).

The process of designing building structures dates back to ancient times, long before modern mathematics and engineering sciences were first developed in the seventeenth and eighteenth centuries. Today's scientific design methods were preceded by a host of design rules whose origins have been traced in **MAINSTONE** (1968, 1988, and 1999) and **ADDIS** (1990 and 1999). Particular attention has been given to the design of the masonry structure of medieval cathedrals by **ACKERMAN** (1949), **SHELBY** (1977), **SHELBY & MARK** (1979), **SANABRIA** (1982), and **HUERTA** (2004). The development of design methods for the beams and columns in timber and iron, which form the basic elements of modern frame structures, has been addressed by **YEOMANS** (1987), **SKEMPTON** (1956), **SUTHERLAND** (1990), and **SMITH** (1992).

Since the first use of mathematics and science, or "theory" as it is often called, to help design buildings, there have been regular discussions of the relationship between such theory and the practice of building. This debate began in medieval times (**VICTOR** 1979, **ADDIS** 1990) and was largely resolved by **RANKINE** (1856), though the theme has been regularly revisited since that time, notably by **CROSS** (1952).

The greatest breakthrough in the development of structural design methods since the use of mathematics and science has been the use of ***scale models*** to predict the behavior of full-size buildings. While this technique has its origins in medieval and even ancient times, its power has been fully exploited only since the 1930s (**TORROJA** 1958, **NERVI** 1956, **COWAN** *et al.* 1968, **HOSSDORF** 1974).

The nature of structural engineering design in recent times has become the frequent object of discussion, and notable contributions have been made by **HAPPOLD** *et al.* (1976) and **PETROSKI** (1985). A recent conference was the first to be devoted to *the conceptual design of structures* (**HANGLEITER** 1996), and many publications use case studies as exemplars of good engineering design (e.g., **SALVADORI** 1990, **ADDIS** 1994, and **ADDIS** 2001).

The history of ***structural engineering science*** goes back to the earliest days of applying mathematics and science to solving practical engineering problems. The earliest surviving exposition of the classic questions in mechanics was by Aristotle in around 350 BC. His thirty-five questions were considered by many medieval philosophers, but the earliest evidence of genuine progress in answering them is found first in Leonardo's copious notes (**TRUESDELL** 1968b, **MISLIN** 1997, **BECCHI** 2004). Of greatest significance in the development of the modern science of strength of materials was Aristotle's Question 16, which asked why it is easier to break a long beam (or rod) than a short one of the same cross section. This was the question that both **BALDI** (1621) and **GALILEO** (1638) went much further toward answering than Leonardo (**BECCHI** 2004). The strength and elasticity of beams has preoccupied structural scientists ever since, and the definitive authority on this development is still **TODHUNTER & PEARSON** (1886–93). **HEYMAN** (1972) has given a condensed summary of the story, and the key contribution made by Coulomb in his 1773 *Essai*. Of great practical significance was the work undertaken by William Fairbairn and Eaton Hodgkinson in the 1830s in developing the most economical cross section for iron beams (**HODGKINSON** 1831).

The introduction of statics and the science of strength of materials into the world of the design engineer during the last three centuries has been thoroughly covered by many authors from many points of view. Comprehensive reviews have been written by **TIMOSHENKO** (1953), **HEYMAN** (1998), **BENVENUTO** (1991), and **KURRER** (2002). Good summaries of the key developments in structural theory are given by **HAMILTON** (1952), **MAINSTONE** (1968 and 1988), **COWAN** (1977 and 1978), and **CHARLTON** (1982). This early work led in the early nineteenth century to the use of graphical methods to calculate forces in structures and, eventually, to the groundbreaking books by **BOW** (1851 and 1873) and **CULMANN** (1866) (see **MAURER**, 1998). The last few decades have seen the appearance of a growing number of specialist studies into the application of mechanics and statics to the design of buildings and structural elements (**TRUESDELL** 1968a, **HEYMAN** 1998, **RADELET-DE GRAVE & BENVENUTO** 1995, **PASQUALE** 1996, **MAINSTONE** 1999, **HUERTA** 2003, and **BECCHI** *et al.* 2003).

The first engineering textbooks that included engineering science as we would recognize it were those of **BÉLIDOR** (1729 and 1737-53). The first devoted to structural science and the strength of materials were by **EYTELWEIN** (1801) and **NAVIER** (1820).

All large ***masonry structures*** built before the eighteenth century have inspired scholars to use their modern knowledge of structures to understand how these buildings work and, often, to consider how they might have been constructed. Such individual studies have led to a number of works that deal with the engineering of masonry structures: **HEYMAN** (1995 and 1996), **BECCHI** (2002), **HUERTA** (2004), and **COWAN**, "A History of Masonry and Concrete Domes" (1977).

The development of the ***structural frame*** in the late eighteenth and early nineteenth century replaced masonry as the principal means of providing the structure of certain buildings. The use of timber beams (**YEOMANS** 1987) paved the way for making beams of cast iron (**SKEMPTON** 1956, **SUTHERLAND** 1990) and structural frames comprising cast and later wrought iron and steel (**SKEMPTON & JOHNSON** 1952, **SKEMPTON** 1959, **SKEMPTON** 1959–60, and **WITTEK** 1964). Later developments of the frame are covered in the development of high-rise buildings, below.

The development of ***roof trusses***, from their early days made of timber to their construction from wrought iron to cover engineering works, docks, railway stations, and exhibition halls during the nineteenth century, is covered by many authors, including **YEOMANS** (1992), **WITTEK** (1964), **LEMOINE** (1986), **SUTHERLAND** (1988–89 and 1997), **THORNE** (2000), and **MISLIN** (2002).

In the twentieth century, the ***concrete shell*** provided a spectacular alternative to the roof truss, and its early development in Germany, especially the Zeiss-Dywidag shell, is chronicled in **KRAUS & DISCHINGER** (1928), **BAUERSFELD** (1957), and **JOEDICKE** (1963). As the shell spread to other countries, its progress is best shown through the works of the three acknowledged masters of the art: **TORROJA** (1958 and 1967), **NERVI** (1956 and 1966), and Candela (**FABER** 1963). This heroic era of concrete shells is celebrated by many authors, including **COWAN** (1977, as cited above), **BILLINGTON** (1985), and **SALVADORI** (1990).

An interesting hybrid between masonry vault and concrete shell is the ***timbrel vault*** or *bóveda tabicada* made of tiles and used for centuries in a number of places on the Mediterranean coasts of Spain, France, and Italy (**TRUÑÓ** 2004). Also known as the Catalan vault, it was exported to the U.S. in the late nineteenth century by Rafael Guastavino, and used widely in New York as a form of fireproof floor construction (**HUERTA** 2003).

The use of ***tensile structures*** to form long-span roofs or canopies began in the nineteenth century (**GRAEFE**, "Hängedächer des 19. Jahrhunderts," 1989). The Russian engineer Vladimir Shukhov created several spectacular exhibition halls using woven strips of steel in the 1890s (**GRAEFE** 1990). In the 1950s the German architect Frei Otto experimented with tensile roofs made with membranes and cables (**ROLAND** 1965, **OTTO** 1973), and both **FORSTER**

(1994) and **BERGER** (1996) have charted the development of this type of structure during the late twentieth century.

Fire Engineering
Throughout history, an important influence on the construction of buildings has been the need to prevent them and their contents – both goods and people – from being damaged by fire. Today this aspect of building design is called ***fire engineering***, a term that dates only from the 1970s. A full history of fire protection and so-called "fireproof construction" has yet to be written. A short review of these subjects, from the early days of theaters and multistory buildings in the mid-eighteenth century, has been written by **HAMILTON** (1958). Fireproof construction began in earnest with the introduction of wrought and cast iron into building construction in the late eighteenth century (**SKEMPTON & JOHNSON** 1952, **FALCONER** 1993), a story which Sara Wermiel has taken into the nineteenth century, especially in Britain and the U.S. (**WERMIEL** 1993 and 2000). The contribution of Edwin O. Sachs, who organized the world's first International Fire Congress in London in 1903, is told in **WILMORE** (1998). For a detailed understanding of the situation in the late nineteenth century, it is best to look at contemporary books such as **HAGN** (1904) and **FREITAG** (1899).

Foundations, Soil Mechanics, and Earthquake Engineering
All buildings and bridges require firm ***foundations***, and practical methods for their construction were devised long before there was any useful understanding of the science underlying the curious and often capricious behaviour of the sand, soil, and earth upon which foundations were constructed. The Roman engineer **VITRUVIUS** devoted several pages to his manual on building to the construction of foundations for temples (Book 3, Chapter 4) and retaining walls (Book 6, Chapter 8). **ALBERTI**, too, addresses the subjects on several occasions in his book on construction (1485). There is nothing like a public inquiry for revealing the current state of knowledge about an engineering subject, and we are fortunate that the building of the new Rialto Bridge in Venice in the late 1580s was the subject of such an inquiry. The various and vivid arguments about the best construction for the foundations of the bridge were recorded *verbatim* and have been expertly summarized by **PARSONS** (1939).

Comprehensive histories of foundations and retaining wall design and construction have been written by **KERISEL** (1987 and 1993), while the use of concrete in foundations has been traced by **CHRIMES** (1996). Modern methods of constructing foundations were developed in Chicago in the late nineteenth century as engineers strove to support taller and taller buildings on the weak soil beneath the city. This dramatic period of progress has been told by **PECK** (1948).

Our success in building foundations today, and since the early twentieth century, depends entirely on our understanding of the properties of soils, the science known as ***soil mechanics***. This subject was first developed in France in the eighteenth century and by the Scottish engineer Rankine in the mid-nineteenth century. This period of history is covered by **HEYMAN** (1972) and **SKEMPTON** (1979). The breakthrough that transformed soil mechanics in the early twentieth century was due entirely to one man – the Czech engineer Karl Terzaghi. His experimental approach to studying the behavior of soils, both in the laboratory and in the field, enabled him to understand how the presence of water affected the strength of soils (**BJERRUM** *et al.* 1960, **GOODMAN** 1999).

While the design of ***earthquake-resistant structures*** goes back to ancient times (**KIRIKOV** 1992), their quantitative design using estimates of the loads that act upon buildings in an earthquake began only in the late nineteenth century. The twentieth-century history can be gleaned from the website of the Consortium of Universities for Research in Earthquake Engineering (http://www.curee.org). The contributions made by Lydik Jacobsen and his pupil John Blume are given on the Web site of the John A. Blume Earthquake Engineering Center (http://blume.stanford.edu).

Building Services Engineering
As well as ***heating and ventilation***, the discipline now known as "building services engineering" embraces the supply of water, drainage, gas, electricity, and telecommunications services, as well as the provision of air-conditioning, suitable natural and artificial lighting, and a desirable acoustic performance of interior spaces. Such a range virtually defies comprehensive treatment, though one book has made an excellent attempt (**BILLINGTON & ROBERTS** 1982). The early development of central heating and forced ventilation in the late eighteenth and early nineteenth centuries has been reviewed by **BRUEGMANN** (1978), and the story is continued into the early twentieth century, especially in the U.S., by **ELLIOTT** (1992) and **DONALDSON & NAGENGAST** (1994). Developments in heating in the first half of the nineteenth century have been covered by **FERGUSON** (1976).

BANHAM (1969) has written about the sometimes conflicting demands of achieving a good internal environment and creating good architecture. Before electricity, ***hydraulic power*** was used to drive various pieces of building equipment, especially elevators, and a history of this interesting technology, which survived in London into the 1970s, has been written by **MCNEIL** (1972). The recent interest in generating energy for use in buildings from renewable sources might suggest it is a new idea; but not so. **BUTTI & PERLIN** (1980) tell the story of using solar energy from its earliest use in ancient Greece.

The provision of natural ***daylight*** inside a building became of great concern in the nineteenth century for two reasons. As new and taller buildings were built ever closer in cities, it became important to establish whether a new building infringed the right to daylight of occupiers of an existing, adjacent building. Objective methods had to be devised for assessing the quality and quantity of daylight inside rooms (**HAWKES** 1970). The second stimulus was the growing belief, from the 1860s, that poor lighting would permanently affect the eyesight of schoolchildren, and several scientists proposed assessing the intensity of light relative to normal daylight (**KERR** 1913, **BILLINGTON & ROBERTS** 1982). Before the development of electrical instruments to measure absolute light intensity, measurements in actual rooms and in scale-model rooms were made using "relative photometry" (**RUZICKA** 1908, **TROTTER** 1921). Various attempts were made in the early 1900s to predict the movement of shadows throughout the day, in different seasons and at different latitudes. **DUFTON & BECKETT** (1931) devised their "heliodon" to solve these calculations using a light source to simulate the sun's movement relative to a model building. ***Artificial lighting*** using coal gas began around 1800 (**RUSSELL** 1976, **BILLINGTON & ROBERTS** 1982), though, for the first few decades, gas lights were used as much to provide the motive power for forced ventilation as for providing light (**BRUEGMANN** 1978).

Refrigeration and ***air-conditioning*** were first successfully accomplished in Europe in the mid-nineteenth century, but their widespread use – including precise humidity control, first in industrial, then in commercial and domestic buildings – was a wholly American story that has been well told by **COOPER** (1998) and **ACKERMANN** (2002). The so-called father of air-conditioning, though not its inventor or first American practitioner, was Willis Carrier, whose biography was compiled by one of his firm's employees (and one of the few women to feature in this book), Margaret **INGLIS** (1952). The grandfather of air-conditioning, David Boswell Reid, has been celebrated for the first time in a recent paper (**STURROCK & LAWSON-SMITH** 2006). The pre-history of domestic refrigeration – the icehouse – is thoroughly covered in **BEAMON & ROAF** (1990).

The ***acoustics*** of both open-air theaters and enclosed spaces was a subject of great interest to the scientists of ancient Greece (c. 500 BC), and some of their ideas on the science of harmonics and theater design are presented by the Roman engineer **VITRUVIUS** (Book 5, Chapters 2–8). Several nineteenth-century books on ventilation and heating also addressed room acoustics and how best to achieve suitable results, though they admitted it was not a precise or predictable art (e.g., **INMAN** 1836, **REID** 1844). In America and Europe alike, acoustics remained a mystery to building designers through most of the nineteenth century (**THOMPSON** 1992). The father of the modern science of acoustics was the Scottish physicist Lord Rayleigh (John William Strutt), though he did not concern himself with building design (**BEYER** 1999). The first acoustician to apply a scientific approach to assessing the acoustic qualities of lecture rooms, concert halls, and churches was Wallace **SABINE**, who described his experiments in a series of ground-breaking papers (**SABINE** 1922). His ideas were soon being applied by building designers (**BEYER** 1999, **THOMPSON** 1992 and 2002). The acoustic design of concert halls lost much of its unpredictability only with the introduction of model testing to study the otherwise incalculable behavior of sound waves inside complex shapes. This approach was first studied in the 1930s (**SPANDÖCK** 1934) and developed to an (almost) exact science in the 1950s, especially by the Danish acoustician Vilhelm Jordan, whose most well-known commission was the Sydney Opera House (**JORDAN** 1980).

The specialist design of the building envelope has only recently acquired the name of ***facade engineering***, and dates from the introduction of curtain walling systems in the 1930s, although some would argue that the Crystal Palace (1851), the Sheerness Boat store (1858), and the many steel-framed buildings in New York and Chicago from the 1890s deserve credit as early "facades" (**FREITAG** 1909). **YEOMANS** (1998) and **BANHAM** (1969) have looked at these early days, and **SULZER** (1999) has made a detailed study of the work of Jean Prouvé, who developed curtain walls in France in the 1930s. The intricacies of the modern, fully-glazed facade are best studied in **RICE & DUTTON** (1990), who describe how they developed one of the first such facades at La Villette in Paris.

Construction Materials
The history of ***construction materials*** is often addressed alongside studies of the craft skills involved in building, such as **DAVEY** (1961), **ADAM** (1994), **FITCHEN** (1986), **HARVEY** (1975), and **GUILLERME** (1995). Engineering in today's construction industry tends to be divided according to material simply because there exist different design codes of practice for timber, steel, masonry, and concrete. General histories of recent times tend to follow the same demarcation (e.g., **ELLIOTT** 1992, **YEOMANS** 1997). The revolution in ***materials science*** in the early twentieth century, which led to an understanding of *why* materials are as strong (or weak) as they are, has been well told by **GORDON** (1968).

Measuring the structural properties of materials progressed in the seventeenth and eighteenth centuries alongside the development of the theoretical concepts of stress, strain, strength, and stiffness (**TIMOSHENKO**, 1953). This early work grew into the larger activity known as ***structural testing***, which has been so important in enabling designers to specify material properties and hence make assessments and predictions of ***structural safety*** (**PUGSLEY** 1944, **BLOCKLEY** 1980).

The history of building materials is also dealt with in a wide range of publications dealing with the repair and refurbishment of old buildings – part of the growing heritage industry. Such works are generally outside the scope of this review.

Masonry construction is covered in the general works mentioned above, in the section on structural elements and in the notes below dealing with the construction of medieval cathedrals. **CAMPBELL & PRYCE** (2003) have written a history of using ***brick*** in construction. ***Timber*** engineering is dealt with in many books on vernacular building, as well as a few that focus on engineering (e.g., **YEOMANS** 1992 and 1999). The use of ***glass*** in buildings from the eighteenth century is covered in **ELLIOTT** (1992), and many early iron and glass buildings are featured in **HIX** (1996). The modern, highly-engineered use of glass is described in **RICE & DUTTON** (1990), and several case studies of such buildings are given in **HOLGATE** (1997) and **ADDIS** (2001). After World War II, when it was produced in large quantities for aircraft, ***aluminum*** had a short-lived period of popularity as a structural material in building construction, as well as in building facades, a use which continues today. Shortly before the downturn in its use, America's largest producer of aluminium, Reynolds Metals, published two fine books on its use in construction (**PETER** 1956 and **WEIDLINGER** 1956).

The use of ***wrought iron*** from ancient times in the form of tie-bars and cramps is covered in general works on construction materials mentioned above. Its use for compression elements in bridge construction was taken up from the 1790s by Thomas Telford. Telford and others used wrought iron chains for suspension bridges from the early 1800s. The heyday of wrought iron arrived with the coming of the railways in the 1820s, and soon railway stations and bridges of ever-increasing spans were needed. Most spectacular of all was the Britannia railway bridge (1846–50) over the Menai Straits in North Wales (**ROSENBERG & VICENTI** 1978). Wrought iron became widely used for building from the mid-nineteenth century (**STEINER** 1978, **LEMOINE** 1986, **SUTHERLAND** 1997, **THORNE** 2000).

The use of cast iron in buildings is covered under the sections on structural engineering (above) and industrial and high-rise buildings (below). William Fairbairn was one of the most prominent iron masters in Britain, and wrote the first manual on using both cast and wrought iron in buildings (**FAIRBAIRN** 1854, **POLE** 1877). A number of key papers on the use of iron are collected in **SUTHERLAND** (1997) and **THORNE** (2000). The historical introduction to **HART, HENN & SONNTAG** (1985) provides a good review of the evolution of steel-framed buildings, and complements a number of similar reviews (**SKEMPTON** 1959, **STEINER** 1978, **LEMOINE** 1986, **MARREY** 1989, and **WITTEK** 1964). **BANNISTER** 1956 and 1957, as well as **WERNER & SEIDEL** (1992), look at the early use of iron in the U.S. Finally, the structural engineers **SHANKLAND** (1897) and **BYLANDER** (1937) describe their own experience on many large steel-framed buildings.

Concrete

The making and use of ***Roman concrete*** is discussed by **VITRUVIUS** and reviewed by many modern writers, including **DAVEY** (1961), **ADAM** (1994), **DELAINE** (1997), and **TAYLOR** (2003).

Mass concrete was in use for foundations, in both bridges and buildings, from the late eighteenth century (**MORDAUNT-CROOK** 1965, **GUILLERME** 1986 and 1995, **CHRIMES** 1996). By the 1860s, many hundreds of houses had been built entirely of mass concrete, with no reinforcement (**STANLEY** 1979).

The development of ***reinforced concrete*** and its engineering use are covered by **DE COURCY (1987)**, **HUBERTI** (in **HÄGERMANN, HUBERTI & MÖLL** 1962–65), **NEWBY (2001)** and **SUTHERLAND** (2001), as well as the general books on materials mentioned above. For the impact of reinforced concrete on architecture, see **LE CORBUSIER** (1923), **COLLINS** (1959), **COTTAM** (1986), and **BANHAM** (1986). More than is the case for other materials, the history of reinforced concrete consists of a number of national stories which need to be read in parallel, so to speak. Some examples include the following:

France - **GUILLERME** 1986, **SIMONNET** 1992, **BOSC** *et al.* 2001, **GROTE & MARREY 2000**

Germany - **HÄGERMANN, HUBERTI & MÖLL** 1962–65, **KRAUS & DISCHINGER** 1928

U.K. - **HAMILTON** 1956, **BROWN** 1966

U.S. – **CONDIT** 1960 and 1961, **NEWLON** 1976

SWITZERLAND - **BILLINGTON** 1979

Italy – **NERVI** 1945 and 1956, **IORI** 2001, **LEVI** 2002

Spain - **TORROJA** 1958 and 1967

Building Types

The construction of ***cathedrals*** and large churches has probably attracted more interest than any other type of building built before 1900. Of the many works mentioned above under structural engineering, and below under the different eras covered by individual chapters, the following provide a good cross-section: **HART** 1965, **ACLAND** 1972, **BINDING & NUßBAUM** 1978, **COENEN** 1990, **CONRAD** 1990, **BINDING** 1993, **HEYMAN** (1996), **ERLANDE-BRANDENBURG** (1995), **COURTENAY** (1997), **SMITH** (2001-2002), and **HUERTA** (2004).

The construction of ***fortifications and castles*** is also covered by a large bibliography through all periods of history (e.g., **MESQUI** 1995). As might be expected in military history, books often treat their subject along nationalistic lines. Several of the earliest works on engineering dealt with the design of fortifications (**KYESER** c. 1405, **FRANCESCO DI GIORGIO** 1470s, **PARSONS** 1939, **GILLE** 1966). Biographies of famous military engineers or architects such as Leonardo, various members of the Sangallo family, and Michelangelo discuss the design of fortifications they designed. The French engineer Vauban has justly received considerable attention from historians of fortifications (**BLANCHARD** 1996).

Although they seldom get favorable treatment in histories of architecture, ***industrial buildings*** contributed more to progress in structural engineering in the nineteenth century than any other building type. The pioneering work, especially in cast iron, occurred in Britain between about 1770 and 1860. The story is told in **BANNISTER** (1950), **FITZGERALD** (1988), **SUTHERLAND** (1988–89), **SKEMPTON & JOHNSON** (1952), **SKEMPTON** (1956 and 1959–60), **GILES & GOODALL** (1992), and **HAY & STELL** (1986). More general studies of the development of factories and engineering works are found in **TANN** (1970), **ACKERMANN** (1991), and **MISLIN** (2002).

The modern ***high-rise building*** owes its success to the use of riveted wrought-iron construction, which was developed not only in engineering works but in other buildings that demanded wide spans, especially railway stations, theaters, exhibition buildings, and department stores (**WITTEK** 1964, **LEMOINE** 1986a, and **SCHULZE** 1928). The story of high-rise building from around 1870 is largely an American one. The first half century is covered by **CONDIT** (1964), **LANDAU & CONDIT** (1996), **SHANKLAND** (1897), **MUJICA** (1930), **BYLANDER** (1937) and **LAWRENCE** (1990). A fascinating first-hand report of constructing the Empire State Building is reprinted in facsimile in **WILLIS** (1998), and an equally vivid, blow-by-blow account of designing and constructing the Worldwide Plaza in New York in the 1980s is given in **SABBAGH** (1990). Developments in Chicago since the 1930s are given by **CONDIT** (1974). The nature of the creative genius that lies behind the best skyscrapers is provided by the biography of their greatest exponent, Fazlur Khan (**ALI** 2001).

The development of both ventilation and central heating for buildings was largely a consequence of constructing the first buildings to house large numbers of the public, namely ***prisons*** (**BRODIE** 2002 and **BRUEGMANN** 1978), ***hospitals*** (**TAYLOR** 1977, **RICHARDSON** 1998, and **STEVENSON** 2000), and ***theaters*** (**LEACROFT** 1984). Theaters also played important part in the development of modern fire engineering (**WILMORE** 1998) and, together with concert halls, the development of acoustic engineering (**JORDAN** 1980).

The Nature of Engineering

Throughout the nineteenth century, most people were constantly aware of the impact that civil, building, mechanical, and electrical engineering had on their lives. The latest achievements in these fields were subjects of popular interest, both in the press and in books, in the way that the latest digital cameras and mobile phones are today. People regularly attended evening lectures on engineering subjects, not only to become more highly qualified, but simply out of interest. The English writer Rudyard Kipling wrote several stories that touched on engineering matters, including one in which he personified the iron plates and rivets of a ship, and the pistons and the steam in its engines, by way of conveying to his readers how they all contributed to a safe journey across the Atlantic (**KIPLING** 1908).

Today the engineer's work, especially that of the building and civil engineer, tends to be taken for granted, and building engineers have seldom made the effort to describe for others the nature of what they do. **LEONHARDT** (1981) has written a rare overview of the nature of civil and building engineers' work, and, more recently, the firm of consulting engineers founded by Ove Arup has published an excellent overview of its activities to help raise understanding of what its engineers do (**DUNSTER** c. 1996). There is no better summary of the scope of modern engineering of the built environment. The present book can be considered as the story of how mankind got to the state summarized in Arup's book.

Writing mainly about the aircraft industry, but equally relevant to buildings, **VICENTI** has written on "*What engineers know and how they know it*" (1990). The best insights into the nature of structural engineering design come from the pens of those few engineers who have written about their own work – for example, **NERVI** (1956), **TORROJA** (1967), **RICE** (1994), and **HOSSDORF** (2003).

The nature of engineering is also reflected in the birth of the modern professional engineering institutions that were created in nearly every country to define and protect the professional status of engineers, and to ensure their distinctness from one another and, especially, from the profession of architect (**PICON** 1988 and 1992, **BUCHANAN** 1989, and **RICKEN** 1994). The education of engineers has played an essential role in establishing and maintaining the highest qualities in the profession (**MCGIVERN** 1960, **EMMERSON** 1973, **PFAMMATTER** 1992, **GRAYSON** 1993, **BUCCARO & AGOSTINO** 2003, **BUCCARO & MATTIA** 2003).

Like the mason's hammer and chisel and carpenter's saw and plane, design engineers have needed their own "tools of the trade" – drawing and calculating. The Renaissance engineers Brunelleschi, Francesco di Giorgio, and especially Leonardo illustrate the earliest days of using drawings as a means of visualizing, developing, and communicating engineering designs (**GILLE** 1966). Formal engineering drawings were developed in France in the eighteenth century to show not only the size and appearance of the finished artifact, but often also its method of construction (**PICON & YVON** 1989). The technique of orthographic projection for representing three-dimensional space on paper (e.g., today's third-angle projection) was developed by Gaspard **MONGE** (1799). The broader history of the development of engineering drawing is told by **NEDOLUHA** (1960), **BAYNES & PUGH** (1981), **BELOFSKY** (1991), **BOOKER** (1979), and **FERGUSON** (1992).

The most important development in understanding the engineering behavior of buildings and in designing unprecedented buildings has been the use of ***scale models*** to predict the behaviour of full-size buildings. While this technique has its origins in ancient and medieval times, its use grew in the mid-eighteenth century when engineers began to make use of science to enhance their understanding of problems (e.g., **SKEMPTON** 1981, **ROSENBERG & VICENTI** 1978). The full power of scale model testing was exploited first in the late nineteenth and early twentieth centuries in the fields of hydraulics and aerodynamics before being applied in civil and building engineering, for structures (**BEGGS** 1922, **TORROJA** 1958, **NERVI** 1956, **COKER & FILON** 1957, **COWAN** *et al.* 1968, **OTTO** 1973, **HOSSDORF** 1974, **BACH** *et al.* 1988, **CHILTON** 2000, **KAWAGUCHI** 2004, **SAITOH** 2004, **MOTRO** 2004, **ADDIS** 2005), wind loading (**FLACHSBART** 1928), lighting (**RUZICKA** 1908, **KERR** 1913, **HAWKES** 1970), and acoustics (**SPANDÖCK** 1934, **JORDAN** 1980).

General histories of mathematics tell how man's ability to make ***calculations*** developed using geometry, numbers, trigonometry, algebra, logarithms, and calculus (e.g., **CAJORI** 1928–29, **ASPRAY** 1990). The use of geometry in cathedral design is discussed by **SHELBY** (1972) And **VICTOR** (1979). Before the age of electronic calculators and computers, engineers used three devices for calculating – graphical charts, slide rules, and mechanical calculators. Many enthusiastic collectors of the latter two maintain interesting Web sites. The history of the slide rule is told in a classic work by **CAJORI** (1909), now available in facsimile form on the Web. Graphical calculation methods, including nomography, were developed in France, especially by **LALANNE** (1846) and **D'OCAGNE** (1899). They have not attracted the enthusiasm of collectors, but, as they were still in regular use into the 1960s, they can be studied in any of the hundreds of books on such techniques written for professional engineers (e.g., **LIPKA** 1918, **HEWES & SEWARD** 1923, and **ROSE** 1947).

The work of the design engineer involves both art and science, and requires intimate collaboration with many other professions, especially architects, builders, contract lawyers, and those concerned with finance and profit. The work of each profession has significant impacts on the work of the others, and many writers have addressed these issues (e.g., **GIEDION** 1954, **BOWLEY** 1966, **STRIKE** 1991, **PETERS** 1981 and 1996, **NISBET** 1993 and 1997, and **POWELL** 1996).

A number of authors have addressed the ***philosophy of engineering design***, and the process by which engineering design progresses (**PACEY** 1974, **ROSENBERG & VICENTI** 1978, **BLOCKLEY** 1980, **BLOCKLEY & HENDERSON** 1980, **PETERS** 1981 and 1996, and **ADDIS** 1990 and 1999).

National Histories

History is often a highly nationalistic activity, though this is probably less pronounced in engineering history than in economic, social, political, and military history. Many writers have a tendency to concentrate on those aspects of engineering history that have featured most prominently in their own country's development. This may, of course, simply reflect an author's linguistic skills and the stock of even the best libraries in all countries. The following are some examples of books providing particular insight into the history of building engineering in individual countries: France – **ACHE** (1970), **STEINER** (1978), **PICON** (1992); Germany – **MISLIN** (2002); Italy – **GUENZI** (1981), **CASCIATO** (1992), **DELLA TORRE** (1994); Russia – many books referred to in **FEDEROV** (2006); U.K. – **COLLINS** (1983); U.S. – **CONDIT** (1960, 1961, and 1968), **PETERSON** (1976), **GRAYSON** (1993), **BERGERON** *et al.* (2000).

Biographies

There are relatively few engineers and engineering scientists whose work related to buildings has attracted the attention of biographers. Before the twentieth century, engineers and scientists from many disciplines contributed to building design, and their biographies are often to be found in other disciplines. From ancient times until the eighteenth century, most engineers were, for at least part of their career, military engineers concerned equally with fortifications, weapons, earthworks, and hydraulic engineering; they generally devoted their energies to civil construction only in times of peace (**VASARI** 1550, **GILLE** 1966, **PARSONS** 1939, **HARVEY** 1972). Since the eighteenth century, many engineers engaged on buildings were also civil or mechanical engineers, making their biographies easier to find (e.g., **SMILES** 1874–1900 and **SKEMPTON** 2002). A few modern collections of building engineers' biographies have been published (e.g., **HARTIG** 1966, **STIGLAT** 2004). Several of the books dealing with the history of building science and engineering also contain short biographies of the key individuals (e.g., **TIMOSHENKO** 1953, **DONALDSON & NAGENGAST** 1994, and **KURRER** 2002). Biographies of many engineers and engineering scientists (from about 800 BC), reporting their mathematical achievements, can be found on the excellent MacTutor Web site, run by the School of Mathematics and Statistics at the University of St. Andrews in Scotland (http://www.history.mcs.st-andrews.ac.uk/history/).

The following list indicates sources of biographical material about some of the most eminent building design engineers and some engineering scientists.

Apollodorus of Damascus – **LEON** 1961; **HEILMEYER** 1975; **MACDONALD** 1982; **ANDERSON** 1997

Ove Arup – ICE 1995

Bernardino Baldi – **BECCHI** 2004

James Bogardus – **BANNISTER** 1956 and 1957

Filippo Brunelleschi – **VASARI** 1550; **PASQUALE** 2002; **KING** 2000

Felix Candela – **FABER** 1963

Willis Carrier – **INGLIS** 1952

Matthew Clark – **FEDEROV** 1992

Charles Augustin Coulomb – **GILLMOOR** 1971; **HEYMAN** 1972

Karl Culmann – **MAURER** 1998

Eladio Dieste – **PEDRESCHI** 2001, **ANDERSON** 2004

Franz Dischinger – **HARTIG & GÜNSCHEL** 1966, **SPECHT** 1987

Gustave Eiffel – **LEMOINE** 1986

William Fairbairn – **POLE** 1877

Ulrich Finsterwalder – **HARTIG & GÜNSCHEL** 1966

Francesco di Giorgio – **GILLE** 1966

Robert Hooke – **JARDINE** 2003; **ADDIS** 2002

Anthony Hunt – **MACDONALD** 2000

Heinz Isler – **CHILTON** 2000

Fazlur Khan – **ALI** 2001

Leonardo da Vinci – **PARSONS** 1939; **TRUESDELL** 1968; **GILLE** 1966; **MISLIN** 1997

Robert Maillart – **BILL** 1949, **HARTIG & GÜNSCHEL** 1966, **BILLINGTON** 1979

Pier Luigi Nervi – **NERVI** 1956; **DESIDERI** *et al.* 1979

Frei Otto – **ROLAND** 1965, **NERDINGER** 2005

Jean Prouvé – **SULZER** 1999, 2000, 2002

W.J.M. Rankine – **CHANNELL** 1975

David Boswell Reid – **STURROCK & LAWSON-SMITH** 2006

Peter Rice – **RICE** 1994, **BROWN** 2001

Edwin O. Sachs – **WILMORE** 1998

Felix Samuely – **HIGGS** 1960

Jörg Schlaich – **HOLGATE** 1997

Vladimir Shukhov – **GRAEFE** 1990

John Smeaton – **SKEMPTON** 1981

William Strutt – **FITTON & WADSWORTH** 1958

Karl Terzaghi – **BJERRUM** *et al.*1960; **GOODMAN** 1999

Eduardo Torroja – **TORROJA** 1958

Wilhelm von Traitteur – **FEDEROV** 1992

Thomas Tredgold – **BOOTH** 1979–80

Sébastien Le Prestre Vauban – **BLANCHARD** 1996

Owen Williams – **COTTAM** 1986, **YEOMANS & COTTAM** 2001

Christopher Wren – **HAMILTON** 1933–34; **ADDIS** 2002

Notes by Historical Period

Ancient Times (Chapter 1 – Before A.D. 500)

A number of works on military engineering have survived from Greco-Roman times, notably Heron and Philon (**MARSDEN** 1971) and **VITRUVIUS** (c. 25 BC), which are often informative and tantalizing in equal measure because of what they do not contain. Of the many dozens of works on building engineering and architecture we know were written in ancient times, the only one that survives is that of Vitruvius. He provides us with invaluable insight not only into the Roman building and engineering practices of his own day, but the work of Greek builders, architects, and scientists from four or five centuries earlier. However, translations of his Latin text into modern languages have been done mainly by non-engineers, whose lack of engineering understanding is often a source of confusion (rare exceptions are the translations into French by the engineer Jean Rondelet in 1812–17, and architect Auguste Choisy (**CHOISY** 1909). There are many glimpses of the activity of the Roman construction industry in the writings of Roman historians, especially the elder and younger Pliny. There are many good general studies of Greek and Roman science and technology (e.g., **WHITE** 1984), though these do not usually deal well with engineering and the issues that faced engineering designers. For this, the best sources are histories written by engineers (**DE CAMP** 1963, **STRAUB** 1952) or by historians who have made studies of engineering (**MARSDEN** 1969 and 1971, **LANDELS** 2000).

Although now superseded by more recent scholarship, the classic nineteenth-century studies of building in ancient times by Choisy and Durm are still valuable sources of information and ideas (**CHOISY** 1873, 1883, and 1904; **DURM** 1892 and 1905). The best general study of the problems facing the designer of buildings in Classical Greek times is **COULTON** (1977), and there are many detailed studies of the design and construction of prominent buildings such as the Parthenon. The Roman building industry is well described in **ADAM** (1994) and **TAYLOR** (2003), and many books on Roman architecture deal with issues facing building designers, whether we think of them as engineers or architects (e.g., **ANDERSON** 1997, **MACDONALD** 1982, **WARD-PERKINS** 1981, **WHEELER** 1964 and **WILSON-JONES** 2000). Particularly rewarding is Janet DeLaine's study of the Baths of the Emperor Caracalla (**DELAINE** 1997), which explores nearly every aspect of the construction of this remarkable building. Although there are studies of the work of Trajan's chief engineer Apollodorus of Damascus (**LEON** 1961, **HEILMEYER** 1975, **MACDONALD** 1982, and **ANDERSON** 1997), we still await a large-scale study of his enormous contribution to structural engineering history.

The Medieval Period (Chapter 2 – 500–1400)

From the early medieval period, the church of Hagia Sophia in Constantinople (mid-sixth century) has been the object of much attention (e.g., **MAINSTONE** 1988). The period between about 500 and 1000 is still often referred to as the "dark ages," as if nothing of interest happened between the decline of the Roman empire and "Gothic" cathedrals. In fact, a great deal was happening, and the misnomer is gradually being eroded by good studies of technological and engineering progress, both in general works (e.g., **SINGER** 1954–58) and specialist studies such as the seminal work by Lynn **WHITE** (1962). From this period, the architectural and engineering significance of the cathedral at Aachen (early ninth century) has attracted the attention of many authors (e.g., **MISLIN** 1997).

Although no written equivalent of Vitruvius' book is known from the medieval period, a great many illustrations from around 1100 onwards have survived. These include illustrations in manuscripts and a number of designs for fortifications, castles, and cathedrals. The skills used in constructing magnificent masonry cathedrals were generally developed first for the construction of fortifications and castles. Throughout this period (and arguably, throughout history), large-scale civic and religious construction took place only when construction engineers were not occupied on military projects (**MESQUI** 1995).

Medieval cathedrals have probably received more attention than any other type of building (for discussion of this phenomenon, see **SMITH** 2001–2002). The one relatively complete sketchbook that has survived from this period – that of Villard de Honnecourt, dating from around 1200 – is now available in facsimile version on the Web, and has been the object of much analysis and comment (**BOWIE** 1959). In the late medieval period (overlapping with the Renaissance), there appeared the first manuals on geometry and its use by masons in designing cathedrals (**ACKERMAN** 1949, **SHELBY** 1972 and 1977, **VICTOR** 1979, **SHELBY & MARK** 1979, **SANABRIA** 1982, and **HUERTA** 2004).

The classic studies of cathedrals dealing with general design and construction issues are **SIMSON** (1956), **FRANKL** (1960), **HARVEY** (1972 and 1975), and **JAMES** (1982). These are complemented by many excellent books, ranging from those intended for children (e.g., **MACAULAY** 1974) and general interest readers (e.g., **ERLANDE-BRANDENBURG** 1995, **GIMPEL** 1983) to mainstream works of scholarship (e.g., **WILLIS** 1842, **FITCHEN** 1961 and 1986, **BINDING & NUßBAUM** 1978, **COENEN** 1990, **CONRAD** 1990, **BINDING** 1993, and **COURTENAY** 1997). Studies generally approach the subject in two ways – studies by modern engineers of how cathedrals work as engineering structures, and historical studies of contemporary ideas about their design and construction (**SMITH** 2001–2002). Most general histories of building and engineering provide a good overview of the structural engineering of cathedrals (e.g., **STRAUB** 1952, **COWAN** 1977, **MARK** 1994, **JESBERG** 1996, and **MISLIN** 1997). Comprehensive analytical studies have been undertaken by **HART** (1965), **ACLAND** (1972), **HEYMAN** (1995 and 1996), and **HUERTA** (2004). Structural design methods for masonry structures have also been discussed by **ADDIS** (1990 and 1999) and **MAINSTONE** (1968, 1988, and 1999).

The Renaissance (Chapter 3 – 1400–1630)

It is during the Renaissance that we find the first modern manuals on engineering matters – mainly military engineering and, until the birth of movable type printing in the 1450s, in manuscript form only. Two of the earliest were Konrad **KYESER** (c. 1405) and **FRANCESCO DI GIORGIO MARTINI** (1470s). Many pages of Leonardo's copious notebooks (1470s–1520s) have been published in facsimile versions, especially his mechanical inventions. The earliest printed works showing a large number of military and non-military devices are **AGRICOLA** (1556) and **ZONCA** (1607). These and other works have been well covered by **KELLER** (1964) and **GILLE** (1966).

From the early fifteenth century, copies of a few drawings by the Florentine engineer and architect Filippo Brunelleschi have survived, and from the year 1485 we have the book on building by the Florentine gentleman architect **ALBERTI**. We are indebted to **VASARI** (1550) for biographies of these men and many other Renaissance engineers, architects, and artists, though their engineering work – especially their military engineering and architecture – is seldom mentioned either by Vasari or most modern biographers of these "Renaissance men."

For a thorough overview of Renaissance engineers and engineering, much of which concerns buildings and civil engineering projects, there is no better work than that of the engineer William Barclay **PARSONS** (1939). **DURM** (1914) gives a thorough review of the practical art of building in the Renaissance.

One building achievement from the Renaissance overshadows all others – the dome of Florence Cathedral, designed and engineered by Brunelleschi in the early 1400s. Its remarkable design, and the vivid story of its construction, is told in all general histories of building engineering, and in more detail by **MAINSTONE** (1969–70), **SAALMAN** (1980), **KING** (2000), and **PASQUALE** (2002). Several authors have compared Brunelleschi's dome with the equally large dome of Saint Peter's Basilica in Rome (built 1588–1626), designed and constructed by a number of architects and engineers, but in essence by Michelangelo, Della Porta and Domenico Fontana; see **DURM** (1914), **COWAN**, "A History of Masonry and Concrete Domes" (1977), and **MAINSTONE** (1999).

In Leonardo's notebooks we find the earliest sketches that indicate a theoretical and generalized understanding of many ideas we now call mechanics or statics. These are covered in some detail by **PARSONS** (1939), **MISLIN** (1997), and **TRUESDELL** (1968). Nevertheless, there is still no comprehensive work collecting together all his sketches and notes concerning civil and building engineering. The pioneering work on the theory of structural behaviour by Bernadino **BALDI** in the late sixteenth century, published posthumously in 1621, is assessed by **BECCHI** (2004). **TIMOSHENKO** (1953) and **STRAUB** (1952) have discussed the contribution of the other early pioneer of statics, Simon Stevin.

In parallel with the very earliest developments in statics, building designers were developing further the design methods that had been established in the late medieval era (**SHELBY** 1972, **SHELBY & MARK** 1979, **SANABRIA** 1982, **MAINSTONE** 1968, **BECCHI & FOCE** 2002, and **HUERTA** 2004).

The 17th and 18th Centuries (Chapter 4 – 1630–1750; Chapter 5 – 1750–1800)

The seventeenth and eighteenth centuries saw the scientific revolution, which gave birth to the modern concept of *force* in astronomy and mechanics and paved the way for the modern sciences of statics and strength of materials (**GALILEO** 1638, **STRAUB** 1952, **TIMOSHENKO** 1953, **TRUESDELL** 1968, **KURRER** 2002, **BECCHI** 2004, **HUERTA** 2004). This work was developed by a great many French scientists, including, especially, Coulomb (**GILLMOOR** 1971, **HEYMAN** 1972).

The two building designers who first exploited their understanding of mechanics and statics were Christopher Wren and Robert Hooke, who, as leading scientists themselves, were well placed to do so (**HAMILTON** 1933–34, **TIMOSHENKO** 1953, **JARDINE** 2003, **ADDIS** 2002).

The eighteenth century also saw the birth of modern chemistry, thermodynamics, and human biology, which quickly came to influence building design by identifying the importance of ventilation in preventing the creation and spread of "foul" and "miasmic" air leading to discomfort and the spread of diseases in hospitals, prisons, theaters, and other public buildings (**BRUEGMANN** 1978, **BILLINGTON & ROBERTS** 1982, **TAYLOR** 1977, **RICHARDSON** 1998, **STEVENSON** 2000, and **BRODIE** 2002,)

The eighteenth century saw the birth of the profession of civil engineering (including much that we now call building engineering), not only in the work of individual engineers such as John Smeaton (**SKEMPTON** 1981), but also the creation of the first polytechnic colleges devoted to non-military engineering in France and the German-speaking countries of continental Europe (**PICON** 1988 and 1992, **PFAMMATTER** 1992, **KURRER** 2002), as well as the first moves toward the formation of the professional engineering institutions (**BUCHANAN** 1989).

As the demand for what were later called civil, mechanical, and structural engineers grew, so began the appearance of the first textbooks summarizing the knowledge that such engineers needed to know, and the engineering science that provided the intellectual foundation of the new art of engineering (e.g., **BÉLIDOR** 1729 and 1737–53).

Meanwhile, building construction was beginning to change. New types of buildings such as theaters (**LEACROFT** 1984) and factories (**TANN** 1970, **FITZGERALD** 1988, **CALLADINE** 1993, **MISLIN** 2002) began to appear, and the new construction material – cast iron – made its impact on buildings (**BANNISTER** 1950, **SKEMPTON & JOHNSON** 1952, **FITZGERALD** 1988, and **SUTHERLAND** 1997).

The 19th Century (Chapter 6 – 1800–1860; Chapter 7 – 1860–1920)

During the first half of the nineteenth century, engineers in every field of civil and building engineering learned and consolidated how to make effective use of mathematics and various branches of science. They learned how to reduce the quantities of materials they needed, while also increasing the confidence with which they could predict the behavior and performance of their structures and buildings before construction began. Following the pattern set by Bélidor's first scientific textbooks on engineering (**BÉLIDOR** 1729 and 1737–53), a number of lecturers at the first continental European engineering polytechnics began publishing books of their own lecture courses, most notably **EYTELWEIN** (1801) in Berlin and **MONGE** (1799), **RONDELET** (1812–17), and **NAVIER** (1820) in France. The theory of statically determinate structures (especially roof trusses), and the elastic behavior of structural elements, developed rapidly during this period (**TIMOSHENKO** 1953, **CHARLTON** 1982, **BENVENUTO** 1991, **KURRER** 2002), and, if anything, gave the impression to many engineers that the gap between "theory" and "practice" was widening, not narrowing. Rankine helped bridge this gap by redefining the use of the established "factor of safety" to serve as the means of reconciling precise mathematical predictions with the known variability in the properties and behavior of real materials and structures (**RANKINE** 1856 and 1858). This firmly established the role of the design engineer, intermediate between the scientist and the contractor.

As the behavior of fluids and heat became better understood, so the design of heating, ventilation, and water supply began to develop from purely empirical methods in 1800 to methods based on scientific understanding and experimentation by the 1850s (**FERGUSON** 1976, **BRUEGMANN** 1978, **BILLINGTON & ROBERTS** 1982, **DONALDSON & NAGENGAST** 1994). Gas lighting was introduced into factories from around 1800 (**BILLINGTON & ROBERTS** 1982, **RUSSELL** 1976), and for several decades was used equally as the motive power for forced ventilation (**BRUEGMANN** 1978). There still remains much to research in this rich field of building design history, and the earliest manuals on the subject are full of interest (e.g., **HALES** 1758, **CHABANNES** 1818, **SYLVESTER** 1819, **TREDGOLD** 1824, **INMAN** 1836, **REID** 1844, and **WYMAN** 1846).

The development of building structures during the first half of the nineteenth century consists largely of the growth and spread of cast and wrought iron as fireproof construction materials, especially in Britain (**SKEMPTON & JOHNSON 1952**, **FITZGERALD** 1988, **SUTHERLAND** 1997), France (**LEMOINE** 1986, **MARREY** 1989, **LEMOINE & MIMRAM** 1995), Russia (**FEDEROV** 1992, 1996, and 1997), and Germany (**MEHRTENS** 1903–23, **JESBERG** 1996, **LORENZ & ROHDE** 2001, **MISLIN** 2002). Iron began to be used in the U.S. in the 1850s for fireproof construction, both for building facades and load-bearing elements (**BANNISTER** 1956 and 1957, **CONDIT** 1960, **WERMIEL** 1993 and 2000, **PETERSON** 1976). One of the first spectacular structures in cast iron in the U.S. was the dome of the Capitol, built in the late 1850s in the manner of the iron dome of Saint Isaac's Cathedral in Saint Petersburg, Russia, constructed in the 1830s (**CAMPIOLI** 1976, **FEDEROV** 1996).

It should not be forgotten that during this period concrete was also being established as a construction material both for building foundations (**MORDAUNT-CROOK** 1965, **GUILLERME** 1986 and 1995, **CHRIMES** 1996) and for a great many houses built of mass concrete (**STANLEY** 1979). The first significant use of iron reinforcement in concrete was in the 1850s (**BROWN** 1966, **DE COURCY** 1987, **SIMONNET** 1992, **NEWBY** 2001).

The late nineteenth and early twentieth centuries saw the fully scientific approach spread to all aspects of building design. For structures, this meant the development of graphical statics (**CULMANN** 1866, **BOW** 1873, **MAURER** 1998), and the integration of elastic behavior into the statical treatment of structures to allow the design of statically indeterminate structures (**MEHRTENS** 190323, **TIMOSHENKO** 1953, **CHARLTON** 1982, **BENVENUTO** 1991, **KURRER** 2002). For the first time, engineers tackled the analysis of genuinely three-dimensional frameworks, shells and tensile structures (**FÖPPL** 1892, **KRAUS & DISCHINGER** 1928, **GRAEFE** 1990). For heating and ventilation, it meant the integration of thermodynamics into design methods (**RIETSCHEL** 1894, **BILLINGTON & ROBERTS** 1982). In the 1910s, Wallace Sabine introduced the idea of reverberation time into acoustic design (**SABINE** 1922).

Wrought iron quickly replaced cast iron for the construction of large buildings in the 1850s and 1860s (**LEMOINE** 1986, **MARREY** 1989, **THORNE** 2000), especially for utilitarian industrial buildings (**TANN** 1970, **MISLIN** 1997). Steel made its impact on building construction from the 1880s (**SKEMPTON** 1959, **WERNER** 1980), and its greatest impact was in the development of the high-rise commercial buildings in New York and Chicago (**CONDIT** 1964 et al., **LANDAU & CONDIT** 1996, **FRIEDMAN** 1995).

Although reinforced concrete made its first appearance in the 1850s, it had little impact on mainstream building construction until the 1890s, when it was taken up quickly in both Europe and America (**NEWBY** 2001, **SUTHERLAND** 2001; *France* - **SIMONNET** 1992; *Germany* - **HÄGERMANN, HUBERTI & MÖLL** 1962–65, **KRAUS & DISCHINGER** 1928; *U.K.* - **HAMILTON** 1956; *U.S.* – **CONDIT** 1961 and **NEWLON** 1976; *Italy* – **IORI** 2001, **LEVI** 2002; see also references for concrete, above).

The 20th Century (Chapter 8 – 1920–1960; Chapter 9 – 1960–Today)

The late nineteenth century had seen great progress in experimental physics and chemistry, leading, most importantly, to an understanding of the atomic structure of matter. This was of enormous significance for the construction industry, as it became possible to explain the mechanical properties of materials and to use the scientific experimental approach to improving these properties (**TIMOSHENKO** 1953, **GORDON** 1968). Few of the major developments in building construction in the twentieth century would have occurred without this better understanding of materials and the better and more reliable prediction of their structural properties (for example, soils - **BJERRUM** 1960, **GOODMAN** 1999; concrete - **ABRAMS** 1918; steel - **HART, HENN & SONNTAG** 1985; glass - **GORDON** 1968). No less significant was how the improved understanding of the properties of materials led to their more efficient and more imaginative use by building designers and contractors (**STRIKE** 1991, **RICE** 1994, **RICE & DUTTON** 1995, **ROBBIN** 1996, **YEOMANS** 1997).

The experimental methods developed by scientists in the nineteenth century were soon put to use by engineers to predict the behaviour of full-size structures and buildings using tests conducted on scale models. (See **COWAN** *et al.* 1968, and other references cited above under *The Nature of Engineering*.) This technique led to rapid progress in every field of building engineering, and was the essential forerunner of using computers, beginning in the late 1950s, to model the engineering behaviour of buildings.

The gradual introduction of scientific methods and experimental science into the construction industry can be traced through the many research institutes dedicated to building science and engineering that have been established in most countries, either in books (e.g., **LEA** 1959 and 1971) or, nowadays, through these institutes' Web sites.

The progress of building construction during the twentieth century can be traced along four relatively independent lines.

Reinforced concrete has been a favorite material among engineers and architects wanting to create new building forms, especially thin shells and highly sculptural forms reflecting the casting technique by which concrete structures are made (**LE CORBUSIER** 1923, **COLLINS** 1959, **BANHAM** 1986, **TORROJA** (various), **NERVI** (various), **KRAUS & DISCHINGER** 1928, **FABER** 1963, **DESIDERI** 1979, **CONDIT** 1961). The second main strand of development has been the continuing development of high-rise buildings (**MUJICA** 1930, **RANDALL** 1949, **CONDIT** 1960 et al., **HART, HENN & SONNTAG** 1985, **SABBAGH** 1990, **WILLIS** 1998, **ALI** 2001).

In parallel with relatively conventional building structures, the last century saw a growing interest in structures that shun the rectilinear and orthogonal constraints of framed structures, and clearly work in three dimensions. As well as many concrete shells, there has developed a large family of dramatic structures using tensile cables and membranes suspended from steel struts (**ROLAND** 1965, **OTTO** 1973, **GRAEFE** 1990, **FORSTER** 1994, **RICE** 1994, **ROBBIN** 1996, **BERGER** 1996, **HOLGATE** 1997, **NERDINGER** 2005).

The fourth main strand of development in the twentieth century was the engineering of the internal environment of buildings and the full control of humidity and temperature in buildings – what we now call air-conditioning. This was achieved by using thermodynamics in design calculations, and an experimental approach to testing and improving the effectiveness of installed systems. Many engineers succeeded in these aims (**COOPER** 1998, **ACKERMANN** 2002), but none was commercially more successful than Willis Carrier, who led the air-conditioning revolution in America. This spread from weaving and other factories in the early 1900s to theaters and cinemas in the 1920s and commercial offices in the 1930s (**INGLIS** 1952). The rest of the world followed around twenty years later (**BANHAM** 1969).

Other specialist fields of building engineering, such as fire, facade, earthquake, and acoustic engineering, are still too young to have had their histories charted. A few key works have been mentioned above under the discipline headings. Their development can be traced both in the literature written for professionals in their fields and through the professional and research institutes that have been established to promote the disciplines and to encourage research into their technical development.

The technical, professional literature of engineering disciplines is, however, rather unapproachable for the non-professional. A number of authors have written books specifically to convey the nature of the work of the modern engineer in the building industry, with both students and non-engineering professionals such as architects in mind (e.g., **DUNSTER** c. 1996; **ADDIS** 1994 and 2001). There has also been some good analysis of the work of the modern engineer in studies of how the industry has progressed (e.g., **BOWLEY** 1966) and, especially, the relationship between engineer and architect in design buildings (e.g., **GIEDION** 1954, **BUILDING ARTS FORUM** 1991, **RICE** 1994).

In Conclusion

Hitherto the history of building engineering has fallen between several stools – the histories of military and civil engineering, the history of science and technology, and the history of architecture. The large number of works in this bibliography that have been published in the last three or four years indicate that things are changing, and that a new discipline seems to be forming. In English it is generally called "*Construction History*." A periodical of that name has been published in Britain by the Construction History Society since 1985. In Spain, the first national congress on Construction History was held in 1996, and three others have followed (**HUERTA** 1996, 1998, 2000, 2005). The first international congress on Construction History was held at Madrid in 2003, and its proceedings ran to over 2100 pages (**HUERTA** 2003); the second was held at Cambridge, England, in 2006 (**DUNKELD** *et al.* 2006), and the third is planned for 2009 in Cottbus, Germany. Previously disparate individuals and specialist groups are beginning to learn of each others' existence, and publications such as **BECCHI** *et al.* (2002 and 2004) are facilitating this process.

index

Page numbers in **boldface** refer to illustrations.

G

H

I

J

T

U

V

W

X

Y

Z

illustration credits

chapter 1

1: Reproduced from R.H. Cunnington, *Stonehenge and its Date* (London: Methuen, 1935). **2**: BA, courtesy Duncan Birmingham and Laurence King Publishing **3**: BA **4**: The J. Paul Getty Museum, Los Angeles **5**: ICE, courtesy Miron Mislin **6**: ICE **7**: Digital Visualization by William Munns **8**: BA **9**: BA **10**: BA **11**: ICE **12**: BA **13**: BA **14**: BA **15**: BA **16**: BA **17**: Deutsches Museum, Munich **18**: ICE **19**: ICE, from Rabun Taylor, *Roman Builders* (Cambridge, UK, and New York: Cambridge University Press, 2003). Reprinted with the permission of Cambridge University Press. **20**: BA **21**: BA, reprinted with permission from Vitruvius, *Ten Books on Architecture* (New York: Dover, repr. 1960). **22**: ICE **23**: BA **24**: Alinari Archives, Florence **25**: BA **26**: Ediciones Dolmen **27**: BA **28**: ICE, reprinted with permission from A.M. Reggiani, *Anfiteatro Flavio: Immagine Testimonianze Spettacoli*, (Rome: Edizioni Quasar, 1988) (photo Soprintendenza Archeologica di Roma) **29**: Erich Lessing / Art Resource, NY **30**: BA **31**: BA **32**: Courtesy Mark Wilson-Jones **33**: BA **34**: ICE **35**: General Research Division, The New York Public Library, Astor, Lenox and Tilden Foundations **36**: General Research Division, The New York Public Library, Astor, Lenox and Tilden Foundations **37**: ICE **38**: Alinari / Art Resource, NY **39**: BA **40**: BA **41**: BA **42**: Fototeca Unione, American Academy in Rome **43**: BA **44**: courtesy Bill Jennings, www.pompeiitoday.com **45**: ICE **46**: ICE, from Rabun Taylor, *Roman Builders* (Cambridge, UK, and New York: Cambridge University Press, 2003). Reprinted with the permission of Cambridge University Press. **47**: ICE **48**: BA **49**: BA **50**: École Nationale Supérieure des Beaux-Arts, Paris **51**: Fototeca Unione, American Academy in Rome

chapter 2

52: Reprinted from J. B. Bullen, *Byzantium Rediscovered* (London: Phaidon Press, 2003), p. 29. **53**: Rowland J. Mainstone. Reproduced from *Hagia Sophia: Architecture, Structure and Liturgy of Justinian's Great Church*, by R. Mainstone (London: Thames and Hudson, 1988) **54**: Art & Architecture Collection, Miriam and Ira D. Wallach Division of Art, Prints, and Photographs, The New York Public Library, Astor, Lenox and Tilden Foundations. **55**: Vanni / Art Resource, NY **56**: © Angelo Hornak **57**: Courtesy Saskia Ltd., Ronald V. Wiedenhoeft **58**: ICE; RIBA Library Drawings Collection **59**: ICE; RIBA Library Drawings Collection **60**: © ND / Roger-Viollet **61**: ICE **62**: BA **63**: Foto Marburg / Art Resource, NY **64**: Stiftsbibliothek St. Gallen **65**: Bibliothèque nationale de France **66**: Hartill Art Associates **67**: BA; Reproduced from *The Castle Story*, by Sheila Sancha (London: Collins, 1991): 54. Drawing by Sheila Sancha. **68**: BA; Reproduced from *The Castle Story*, by Sheila Sancha (London: Collins, 1991). Drawing by Sheila Sancha **69**: BA **70**: Terry Ball / Cadw. Crown Copyright **71**: John Crook **72**: The Cathedral Library, Durham Cathedral **73**: Hartill Art Associates **74**: Courtesy of Archivision **75**: Angelo Hornak **76**: Hartill Art Associates **77**: Angelo Hornak **78**: Bibliothèque nationale de France **79**: ICE **80**: ICE **81**: Rouen, musée des Beaux-Arts, © Musées de la Ville de Rouen **82**: BA **83**: BA **84**: BA; Reproduced from *Der Münsterbaumeister Mattäus Ensinger*, by L. Mojon (Bern: Benteli Verlag, 1967) **85**: Courtesy Saskia, Ltd., Ronald V. Wiedenhoeft **86**: BA; © 1977 by Southern Illinois University Press **87**: BA; © 1977 by Southern Illinois University Press **88**: Biblioteque Royale Albert I, Brussels **89**: ÖNB/Vienna, Picture Archive, Cod. 2549, fol. 164r **90**: Monum **91**: ICE; Reproduced from *The Cathedral Builders of the Middle Ages* by Alain Erlande-Brandenburg (London: Thames & Hudston/New Horizons, 1995): 116 **92**: BA **93**: Leemage **94**: BA; Reproduced from *Light, Wind, Structure: The Mystery of the Master Buildings*, by Robert Mark (Cambridge: The MIT Press, 1990) **95**: BA; RIBA Library Drawings Collection **96**: BA **97**: BA **98**: John Crook **99**: Courtesy Saskia, Ltd., Ronald V. Wiedenhoeft **100**: BA **101**: BA; Reproduced from *Light, Wind, Structure: The Mystery of the Master Buildings*, by Robert Mark (Cambridge: The MIT Press, 1990) **102**: Hartill Art Associates **103**: BA; Courtesy Duncan Birmingham and Laurence King Publishing **104**: John Crook **105**: BA **106**: © Angelo Hornak Photograph Library, London **107**: John Crook **108**: ICE **109**: BA; Reproduced with permission from Thames & Hudson Ltd. **110**: John Crook **111**: BA **112**: BA **113**: Royal Georgraphic Society **114**: ICE **115**: BA **116**: Trinity College **117**: National Trust

chapter 3

118: ICE **119**: ICE **120**: Scala/Art Resource, NY **121**: ICE **122**: ICE; Reproduced from *Filippo Brunelleschi: The cupola of Santa Maria del Fiore*, by Howard Saalman (London: Zwemmer, 1980): 49 **123**: ICE; Reproduced from *Die Geschichte der Bauingenieurkunst*, by Paulgerd Jesberg (Stuttgart: Deutsche Verlags-Anstalt, 1996): 48 **124**: ICE **125**: ICE **126**: Courtesy Saskia Ltd., Ronald V. Wiedenhoeft. **127**: Phaidon Archive; A.H.V Grandjean de Montigny, *Architecture toscane ou palais, maisons et autres edifices de la Toscane* **128**: from Piero Sanpaolesi *Brunelleschi*, Edizioni per il club del libro, Milano, 1962. New York Public Library **129**: BA; Reproduced from *The Architecture of the Italian Renaissance*, by Peter Murray, 2nd ed. (London: Thames and Hudson, 1986): 48 **130**: ICE **131**: The Royal Collection © 2005, Her Majesty Queen Elizabeth II **132**: ICE **133**: Goettingen State and University Library, 2° Cod. Ms. Philos. 63 Cim. Fol. 114v **134**: ICE **135**: ICE **136**: ICE **137**: ICE **138**: Angelo Hornak **139**: Angelo Hornak **140**: © Copyright The Trustees of The British Museum **141**: © Copyright The Trustees of The British Museum **142**: By concession of the Ministero per i Beni e le Attività Culturali della Repubblica Italiana/Biblioteca Nazionale Centrale di Firenze, shelfmark: II.I.141, f. 58r **143**: Scala/Art Resource, NY **144**: BA **145**: ICE **146**: ICE **147**: ICE **148**: V&A Images/Victoria and Albert Museum **149**: Biblioteca Nacional de España. Madrid **150**: ICE **151**: © British Library Board. All Rights Reserved. Shelfmark: Arundel 263 **152**: BA **153**: From *Engineers and Engineering in the Renaissance*, by Barclay Parsons (Cambridge: MIT Press, 1968; reprint of the 1939 original): 71 **154**: BA **155**: By permission of the Syndics of Cambridge University Library **156**: ICE **157**: BA **158**: BA **159a**: BA **159b**: BA **160**: ICE; From *Geschichte der Baukonstruktion und Bautechnik, Vol. I*, by Miron Mislin (Dusseldorf: Werner Verlag, 1997): 281 **161**: Biblioteca Nacional de España, Madrid **162**: BA **163**: ICE **164**: ICE **165**: BA **166**: Courtesy Saskia Ltd., Ronald V. Wiedenhoeft. **167**: BA **168**: BA **169**: BA **170**: Jeroen van Duivenbode, Veldhoven, the Netherlands **171**: Bibliothèque nationale de France **172**: Vanni / Art Resource, NY **173**: Marquess of Salisbury's Estates/Hatfield House **174**: BA **175**: BA **176**: ©NTPL/Roy Twigge **177**: Courtesy of Methuen Publishing Ltd, London, drawings by Richard and Helen Leacroft **178**: Courtesy of Methuen Publishing Ltd, London, drawings by Richard and Helen Leacroft **179**: Courtesy of Methuen Publishing Ltd, London, drawings by Richard and Helen Leacroft **180**: Jim Steinhart of TravelPhotoBase.com **181**: © iStockphoto.com / Marc Vermeirsch **182**: BA **183**: The Pepys Library, Magdalene College, Cambridge **184**: ICE **185**: ICE **186**: ICE **187**: BA **188**: ICE **189**: By permission of the Syndics of Cambridge University Library **190**: BA **191**: BA **192**: Science Museum/SSPL **193**: Science Museum/SSPL **194**: Science Museum/SSPL

chapter 4

195: Nederlands Scheepvaartmuseum Amsterdam **196**: Nederlands Scheepvaartmuseum Amsterdam **197**: Science Museum/Science & Society Picture Library **198**: Courtesy Association "Les Amis de la Maison Vauban" **199**: ICE **200**: Franck Lechenet **201**: ICE **202**: ICE **203**: Courtesy Ecole nationale des ponts et chaussées **204**: Erich Lessing / Art Resource, NY **205**: Hartill Art Associates **206** ICE **207**: From the Castle Howard Collection **208a, b, c**: BA **209**: BA **210**: ICE **211a, b, c**: ICE **212**: ICE **213**: BA; reproduced from *Timber in Construction*, ed. By John Sunley and Barbara Bedding (London: TRADA, 1985): 77 **214**: BA; reproduced from *Timber in Construction*, ed. By John Sunley and Barbara Bedding (London: TRADA, 1985): 76 **215**: Master and Fellows of Trinity College Cambridge **226**: BA; Reproduced from *Hampton Court: a Social and Architectural History* (London: Yale University Press, 2003): 69. Drawing by Daphne Ford. **217**: BA **218**: RIBA Library Photographs Collection **219**: ICE **220**: by permission of the Syndics of Cambridge University Library **221**ICE **222**: The British Museum Images **223**: V&A Images / Victoria and Albert Museum **224**: ICE **225**: RIBA Library Drawings Collection **226**: BA **227**: BA **228**: BA **229**: BA **230**: BA **231**: ICE **232**: BA **233**: BA **234**: BA **235**: BA **236**: ICE **237**: ICE **238**: BA **239**: BA **240**: BA; Reproduced from *Ice Houses of Britain*, by Sylvia P. Beamon and Susan Roaf (London: Routledge, 1990): 74. Drawings by Tim Buxbaum. **241a, b**: ICE **242**: Megan **243**/4.59: Megan **244**: Megan **245**: Megan **246**: Megan **247**: ICE **248**: BA **249**: Megan **250**: ICE

chapter 5

251: ICE **252**: ICE **253**: Smeatons Tower ©tonyhowell.co.uk **254**: ©The Trustees of the National Museums of Scotland **255**: ICE **256**: BA **257**: BA **258**: BA **259**: BA **260**: ICE **261**: © National Museum of Photography, Film & Television / Science & Society Picture Library **262**: BA **263**: BA **264**: ICE **265**: ICE **266**: © Historic Royal Palaces; photograph: Robin Forster. **267**: ICE **268**: BA **269**: BA **270**: Musee de la Ville de Paris, Musee Carnavalet, Paris, France / Archives Charmet / The Bridgeman Art Library **271**: BA **272**: BA **273**: V&A Images / Victoria and Albert Museum **274**: © Derby Museum and Art Gallery **275**: © English Heritage **276**: BA **277**: © Derbyshire Archeology Society **278**: © English Heritage **279**: BA **280**: BA **281**: ICE **282**: ICE **283**: ICE **284**: BA **285**: BA **286**: © Science Museum / Science & Society Picture Library **287**: BA **288**: BA **289**: BA **290**: BA **291**: ICE **292**: BA **293**: ICE **294**: BA **295**: BA **296**: BA **297**: ICE **298**: BA **299**: BA **300**: © The Wellcome Trust Medical Photographic Library / J. Howard **301**: © The Wellcome Trust Medical Photographic Library **302**: © The Royal Society **303**: ICE

chapter 6

304: BA **305**: ICE **306**: BA **307**: ICE **308**: ICE **309**: ICE **310**: BA **311**: BA **312**: BA **313**: ICE **314**: BA **315**: Courtesy St. Isaac's Cathedral State Museum **316**: BA **317**: ICE **318**: BA **319**: ICE **320**: BA; © English Heritage **321**: BA **322**: BA **323**: ICE **324**: BA **325**: BA **326**: BA **327**: BA **328**: ICE **329**: ICE **330**: ICE **331**: ICE **332**: BA **333**: BA **334**: ICE **335**: © Wellcome Trust Medical Photographic Library, London **336**: © Wellcome Trust Medical Photographic Library, London **337**: © Wellcome Trust Medical Photographic Library, London **338**: BA **339**: BA **340**: BA **341**: BA **342**: ICE **343**: ICE **344**: ICE **345**: ICE **346**: Reproduced from the Journal of the Society of Architectural Historians, June 1986. **347**: Reproduced from the Journal of the Society of Architectural Historians, June 1986. **348**: ICE **349**: ICE **350**: © National Maritime Museum, London **351**: Reproduced from the Journal of the Society of Architectural Historians, June 1986. **352**: ICE **353**: BA; Courtesy Dr. Emory L. Kemp **354**: Library of Congress **355**: ICE **356**: BA **357**: BA **358**: ICE **359**: © La Bibliothèque de l'Ecole Nationale des Ponts Chaussèes **360**: Courtesy Bicton Gardens Archive **361**: BA **362**: ICE; Courtesy R.J.M. Sutherland **363**: ICE **364**: ICE; Courtesy R.J.M. Sutherland **365**: BA **366**: ICE **367**: BA **368**: ICE **369**: © The British Museum **370**: ICE **371**: ICE **372**: BA **373**: Library of Congress **374**: ICE **375**: Library of Congress **376**: © Museum of the City of New York, Gift of Mrs. Elon Huntington Hooker **377**: ICE **378**: ICE **379**: ICE **380**: BA **381**: BA **382**: ICE **383**: BA **384**: BA **385**: BA **386**: BA **387**: BA **388**: BA **389**: ICE **390**: BA **391**: ICE **392**: ICE **393**: BA **394**: BA **395**: ICE **396**: BA **397**: BA **398**: ICE; Courtesy R.J.M. Sutherland **399**: BA **400**: BA **401**: ICE **402**: ICE **403**: ICE **404**: ICE

chapter 7

405: © Science Museum / Science & Society Picture Library **406**: © Whipple Museum of the History of Science **407**: BA **408**: BA **409**: BA **410**: BA **411**: ICE **412**: BA; Courtesy Cambridge University Press **413**: ICE **414**: BA **415**: Reproduced with permission from Oldham Local Studies & Archives **416**: Reproduced with permission from Oldham Local Studies & Archives **417**: BA **418**: BA **419**: ICE **420**: Courtesy Architech Gallery, Chicago **421**: Courtesy Architech Gallery, Chicago **422**: ICE **423**: ICE **424**: ICE **425**: BA **426**: ICE **427**: ICE **428**: ICE **429**: BA **430**: ICE **431**: BA **432**: ICE **433**: © Guastavino / Collins Archive, Avery Architectural and Fine Arts Library, Columbia University **434**: © Guastavino / Collins Archive, Avery Architectural and Fine Arts Library, Columbia University **435**: ©AXA Financial, Inc. **436**: ICE **437**: ICE **438**: ICE **439**: ICE **440**: BA **441**: ICE **442**: Library of Congress **443**: BA; Reproduced from *Architectural Engineering*, by J.K. Freitag (New York: Wiley, 1909). **444**: BA; Wayne State University **445**: BA **446**: BA **447**: BA **448**: ICE **449**: BA **450**: BA **451**: ICE **452**: ICE **453**: ICE **454**: BA **455**: BA **456**: ICE **457**: BA **458**: BA **459**: ICE **460**: BA **461**: BA **462**: ICE **463**: BA; Reproduced from *Rise of the New York Skyscraper 1865–1913*, by Sarah Landau & Carl Condit (Yale University Press, 1996). Image © Yale University Press. **464**: ICE; © Bauhaus-Archiv, Berlin. **465**: ICE **466**: BA **467**: BA **468**: BA **469**: © American Society of Heating, Refrigerating and Air-Conditioning Engineers Inc. **470**: BA **471**: BA **472**: BA **473**: ICE **474**: ICE **475**: BA **476**: Courtesy Otis Elevator Company **477**: BA **478**: BA **479**: BA **480**: BA **481**: BA **482**: BA **483**: BA **484**: ICE **485**: BA **486**: BA **487**: BA **488**: BA **489**: BA **490**: BA **491**: Courtesy of the Beverly Historical Society & Museum, Beverly, MA **492**: © Cincinnati Historical Society Library **493**: © Cincinnati Historical Society Library **494**: © Cincinnati Historical Society Library **495**: BA **496**: BA **497**: ICE **498**: BA **499**: ICE **500**: BA **501**: ICE **502**: ICE **503**: ICE **504**: ICE **505**: ICE **506**: ICE **507**: ICE **508**: ICE **509**: ICE **510**: BA **511**: BA

512: BA **513**: BA **514**: ICE **515**: BA **516**: BA **517**: BA **518**: ICE **519**: BA; © Prof. David P. Billington **520**: BA **521**: BA; *Bridges and Constructions*, by Max Bill and Robert Maillart (New York: Frederick A. Praeger Publishers, 1969). **522**: BA; © Prof. David P. Billington **523**: BA **524**: BA **525**: BA **526**: BA **527**: BA **528**: BA **529**: BA **530**: BA **531**: BA **532**: © Taller de escultura, Luis Gueilbert, Colección A. Gaudí **533**: © Taller de escultura, Luis Gueilbert, Colección A. Gaudí **534**: BA **535**: BA **536**: BA **537**: BA

chapter 8

538: World-Telegram photo **539**: ICE **540**: courtesy Alan Batt / Battman Studios, NY **541**: BA **542**: BA **543**: BA **544**: BA; with permission from Margaret Terzaghi-Howe and Eric Terzaghi **545**: BA **546**: Mercer County Historical Society, PA **547**: ICE **548**: Courtesy of GLASBAU HAHN, Frankfurt am Main **549**: BA **550**: BA **551**: BA; Reproduced from *The Achievement of the Airship*, by Guy Hartcup (David & Charles PLC, 1975): 162 **552**: Courtesy The Ritz London **553**: The History of Advertising Trust Archive **554**: BA **555**: BA **556**: BA **557**: BA **558**: BA **559**: BA; Reproduced from *Enterprise versus bureaucracy: the development of structural air-raid precautions during the 2nd World War*, by Lord John Baker (Oxford: Pergamon Press, 1978): 45 **560**: BA **561**: BA **562**: ICE **563**: BA; Society for Experimental Mechanics, Inc. **564**: BA **565**: BA; Reproduced from *A Treatise on Photoelasticity*, by E. G. Coker and L. N. G. Filon (Cambridge: Cambridge University Press, 1931) **566**: BA **567**: BA **568**: BA; Verlag Ernst & Sohn, Berlin **569**: courtesy Carl Zeiss archives **570**: courtesy Carl Zeiss archives **571**: courtesy Carl Zeiss archives **572**: courtesy Carl Zeiss archives **573**: BA **574**: BA **575**: BA; Verlag Ernst & Sohn, Berlin **576**: courtesy Carl Zeiss archives **577**: BA; Collection Schalenbau-J. Joedicke, photo H. Walter **578**: BA; Reproduced from *Shell Architecture*, by Jurgen Joedicke (New York: Reinhold Publishing Corp., 1963): 288 **579**: BA; courtesy Dr. Ing. Hans-Ulrich Litzner **580**: BA **581**: BA **582**: Archivo Torroja, CEHOPU-CEDEX **583**: BA; Reproduced from *The Structures of Eduardo Torroja: An Autobiography of Engineering Accomplishment* (New York: F. W. Dodge Corporation, 1958): 12 **584**: Archivo Torroja, CEHOPU-CEDEX **585**: Archivo Torroja, CEHOPU-CEDEX **586**: Archivo Torroja, CEHOPU-CEDEX **587**: BA; Reproduced from *The Structures of Eduardo Torroja: An Autobiography of Engineering Accomplishment* (New York: F. W. Dodge Corporation, 1958): 12 **588**: Archivo Torroja, CEHOPU-CEDEX **589**: Archivo Torroja, CEHOPU-CEDEX **590**: Archivo Torroja, CEHOPU-CEDEX **591**: BA **592**: Centro Studi e Archivio della Comunicazione dell'Università degli Studi di Parma **593a, b, c**: Centro Studi e Archivio della Comunicazione dell'Università degli Studi di Parma **594**: © International Olympic Committee **595**: ICE; courtesy of the British Cement Association **596**: BA; Reproduced from *Aesthetics and Technology in Building*, by Pier Luigi Nervi (Cambridge: Harvard University Press, 1965): 168 **597**: BA **598**: BA **599**: BA **600**: BA **601**: BA **602**: ICE **603**: BA **604**: © Alejandro Leveratto, courtesy Mondadori Electa S.p.a. **605**: BA; Reprinted from *Developments In Structural Form*, Rowland Mainstone, Oxford: Architectural Press (1998), with permission from Elsevier **606**: Nicolas Janberg (www.structurae.de) **607**: BA **608**: Gio Ponti Archives – Milano **609**: BA; Reproduced from *Aesthetics and Technology in Building*, by Pier Luigi Nervi (Cambridge: Harvard University Press, 1966): 168 **610**: Gio Ponti Archives – Milano **611**: Gio Ponti Archives – Milano **612**: Gio Ponti Archives – Milano **613**: courtesy MERO **614**: courtesy MERO **615**: Courtesy Union Tank Car Company, archive photo **616**: courtesy MERO **617**: RIBA Library Photographs Collection **618**: BA **619**: North Carolina Department of Agriculture & Consumer Services **620**: North Carolina Department of Agriculture & Consumer Services **621**: BA; Reproduced from *Frei Otto – Spannweiten*, by Conrad Roland (Berlin: Verlag Ullstein GmbH, 1965): 19 **622**: courtesy Alcoa **623**: BA/ Reproduced from *Shell Architecture*, by Jurgen Joedicke (New York: Reinhold Publishing Corp., 1963): 123 **624**: BA/ Reproduced from *Shell Architecture*, by Jurgen Joedicke (New York: Reinhold Publishing Corp., 1963): 124 **625**: courtesy Alcoa **626**: Photographe Philippe Jacob **627**: BA **628**: © 2006 Artists Rights Society (ARS), New York / ADAGP, Paris / FLC 629: FLC / ARS **629**: © FLC/ARS **630**: Collectie Centraal Museum, Utrecht **631**: Photo Jean BERNARD © **632**: © Bauhaus Dessau Foundation **633**: bpk Berlin **634**: © Martin Charles **635**: BA; Reproduced from *Owen Williams*, by David Cottam (London: Architectural Association, 1986): 20, drawing by Stephen Rosenberg **636**: © Martin Charles **637**: ICE; Reproduced from *Aesthetics and Technology in Building*, by Pier Luigi Nervi (Cambridge: Harvard University Press, 1965): 80 **638**: ICE; Reproduced from *Aesthetics and Technology in Building*, by Pier Luigi Nervi (Cambridge: Harvard University Press, 1965): 81 **639**: ICE; Reproduced from *Aesthetics and Technology in Building*, by Pier Luigi Nervi (Cambridge: Harvard University Press, 1965): 81 **640**: © FLC/ARS **641**: BA **642**: BA **643**: BA **644**: BA **645**: © Balthazar Korab Ltd. **646**: © Cranbrook Archives **647a**: © Balthazar Korab Ltd. **647b**: National Park Service, Jefferson National Expansion Memorial **647c**: National Park Service, Jefferson National Expansion Memorial **647d**: National Park Service, Jefferson National Expansion Memorial **648**: BA; © American Society of Heating, Refrigerating and Air-Conditioning Engineers, Inc **649**: Courtesy Carrier Corporation **650**: BA; © American Society of Heating, Refrigerating and Air-Conditioning Engineers, Inc **651**: BA **652**: © American Society of Heating, Refrigerating and Air-Conditioning Engineers, Inc **653**: ICE; Reproduced from *Principles of Modern Buildings, Vol. I*, Department of Scientific and Industrial Research, Building Research Station London, H.M.S.O., 1959: 70 **654**: ICE; Reproduced from *Principles of Modern Buildings, Vol. I*, Department of Scientific and Industrial Research, Building Research Station London, H.M.S.O., 1959: 60 **655**: © Martin Charles **656**: ICE **657**: courtesy Archiv Meurthe-et-Moselle, fonds Jean Prouvé **658**: © J. Paul Getty Trust **659**: courtesy of Skidmore, Owings & Merrill LLP (SOM) **660**: courtesy Centre Georges Pompidou, Bibliotheque Kandinsky, fonds Jean Prouvé **661**: Avery Architectural and Fine Arts Library, Columbia University **662**: courtesy Archives of Pleyel **663**: BA; © 2006 – Victor Horta – SOFAM – Belgium **664**: Christine Bastin et Jacques Evrard, Bruxelles **665**: courtesy Trevor Cox and Bridget Shield

chapter 9

666: BA **667**: © Deutsches Museum **668**: © Deutsches Museum **669**: Courtesy Rick Furr **670**: © Science Museum / Science & Society Picture Library **671**: © Deutsches Museum **672**: BA **673**: BA **674**: BA **675**: ICE **676**: BA; Courtesy Ove Arup & Partners **677**: BA; Courtesy Ove Arup & Partners **678**: BA; Courtesy Ove Arup & Partners **679**: BA; Courtesy Ove Arup & Partners **680**: BA **681**: BA; Courtesy Ove Arup & Partners **682**: BA; Courtesy Ove Arup & Partners **683**: BA; Courtesy Jordan Akustik **684**: BA; Courtesy Jordan Akustik **685**: BA; Courtesy Jordan Akustik **686**: BA; Courtesy Ove Arup & Partners **687**: BA; Courtesy Institute of Lightweight Structures and Conceptual Design **688**: BA; Courtesy Institute of Lightweight Structures and Conceptual Design **689**: © Institute of Lightweight Structures and Conceptual Design **690**: © Institute of Lightweight Structures and Conceptual Design **691**: BA; Courtesy Ove Arup & Partners **692**: BA; Courtesy Ove Arup & Partners **693**: BA **694**: BA; Courtesy Heinz Isler **695**: BA; Courtesy Heinz Isler **696**: BA **697**: BA **698**: BA; Courtesy Anthony Hunt Associates **699**: BA; Courtesy Mike Barnes **700**: BA; Courtesy Mike Barnes **701**: BA; Courtesy Saitoh **702**: BA; Mamuro Kawaguchi **703**: BA; Mamuro Kawaguchi **704**: BA; Mamuro Kawaguchi **705**: BA **706**: BA **707**: BA; Courtesy Alan G. Davenport Wind Engineering Group **708**: BA; Courtesy Ove Arup & Partners **709**: BA; Courtesy British Steel **710**: BA; Courtesy British Steel **711**: BA; Courtesy Valode et Pistre et Assoccie's **712**: BA; Courtesy Valode et Pistre et Assoccie's **713**: BA; Courtesy Ove Arup & Partners, Mike Banfey **714**: Photograph by Jack E. Boucher, Library of Congress **715**: Courtesy Mies van der Rohe Society; photograph by Todd Eberle **716**: ICE **717**: ICE **718**: ICE **719**: © Balthazar Korab **720**: Courtesy United States Steel Corporation **721**: ICE **722**: Courtesy Renzo Piano Building Workshop **723**: BA **724**: BA **725**: BA; Courtesy Ove Arup & Partners **726**: Courtesy Skidmore, Owings & Merrill; photograph by Hedrich Blessing **727**: Courtesy Skidmore, Owings & Merrill; photograph by Timothy Hursley **728**: Courtesy Skidmore, Owings & Merrill; photograph by Timothy Hursley **729**: © Pei Cobb Freed / John Nye **730**: BA **731**: BA **732**: BA; Courtesy Ian Lambot **733**: BA **734**: Courtesy Walter P. Moore **735**: Courtesy of Davis Brody Bond, LLP; Photograph by Y, Ernest Sato **736**: Courtesy of Davis Brody Bond, LLP **737**: Courtesy Geiger Engineers **738**: Courtesy Geiger Engineers **739**: Courtesy Denver International Airport; photograph by Chris Carter **740**: Courtesy Denver International Airport; photograph by Chris Carter **741**: BA; Courtesy Saitoh **742**: BA; Courtesy Kajima Design **743**: BA; Courtesy Kajima Design **744**: Courtesy Buro Happold and Mandy Reynolds **745**: BA **746**: Courtesy RFR **747**: BA **748**: BA; Courtesy Schlaich Bergerman and Partner **749**: BA; Courtesy Schlaich Bergerman and Partner **750**: BA; Courtesy Studio d'Ingeneria: Favero-Milan **751**: BA; Courtesy Studio d'Ingeneria: Favero-Milan **752**: BA; Courtesy Studio d'Ingeneria: Favero-Milan **753**: BA; Courtesy Studio d'Ingeneria: Favero-Milan **754**: BA; Courtesy RFR **755**: BA; Courtesy RFR **756a**: Courtesy Burro Happold, FEDRA **756b**: Courtesy Burro Happold, FEDRA **757**: Courtesy Burro Happold, FEDRA **758**: Courtesy Burro Happold, FEDRA **759**: © Balthazar Korab **760**: BA **761**: Courtesy Architectural Association, © Richard Booth **762**: BA **763**: BA **764**: ICE **765**: ICE **766**: BA **767**: BA **768**: BA **769**: BA; Courtesy Ove Arup & Partners **770**: BA **771**: BA; Courtesy Ove Arup & Partners **772**: BA; Courtesy Ove Arup & Partners **773**: BA; Courtesy Ove Arup & Partners **774**: BA **775**: BA; Courtesy Ove Arup & Partners **776**: BA; Courtesy Ove Arup & Partners **777**: © James Cohrssen **778**: © Palladium Photodesign **779**: Courtesy Rafael Viñoly Architects **780**: © Phillipe Ruault **781**: © Phillipe Ruault **782**: Courtesy Ove Arup & Partners **783**: Courtesy Ove Arup & Partners **784**: Courtesy Ove Arup & Partners **785**: Courtesy Renzo Piano **786**: Courtesy Renzo Piano